trotman

Your one-st

over 7 s

Careers 2009

Careers 2009

This fifth edition published in 2008 by Trotman Education, an imprint of Crimson Publishing, Westminster House, Kew Road, Richmond, Surrey TW9 2ND

Editor of the first four editions: Jan Champney

Contributors: Julie Bhagat, Monica Brand, Helen Downie, Michele Gladden, Katherine Speed, Camilla Zajac

Case Studies: Dee Pilgrim

Design by Paul Canham

Qualifications and courses information provided by TIS

With special thanks to the students and staff of Lytchett Minster School, Dorset, for their valuable contribution to the production of this book, and in particular Christy Hehir, Alaina McNally and Samantha Atkins

British Library Cataloguing in Publication Data

A catalogue record for this book is available from the British Library

ISBN 978–1–906041–38–0

Typeset by RefineCatch Limited, Bungay, Suffolk

Printed and bound in Great Britain by Bell & Bain Ltd, Glasgow

Contents

Welcome to Careers 2009

The world of work is continually changing.

Finding all the information you need to help with your career choices can therefore be difficult – and when you find it, it is not always easy to understand.

We all have different values, interests and ambitions, so *Careers 2009* lists only those aspects we have been told people find most important when they start to research their future careers.

Although you can go straight to the pages on the jobs you're already interested in, to get the most from using Careers 2009 we suggest you first read the opening section, as this will explain more about the content and how to use the publication.

Within *Careers 2009* you will find brief but detailed entries on over 750 different jobs, each of which includes entry requirements, advantages and disadvantages, working conditions, the future outlook, a description of the type of person suited to the area of work and an earnings guide. In addition, there are over 30 case studies describing how the individual got to where they are today and their personal feelings about their job. A full list of these is given on pages viii–xiii.

The first edition of this book was developed in consultation with young people and professional advisers to ensure that it would meet the needs of end users. We are particularly grateful to the staff of Lytchett Minster School in Dorset for their help in developing the style and content of the first edition. This fifth edition has been revised and updated taking into account the feedback we received from readers on publication of the previous editions.

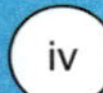

We are confident that *Careers 2009* offers a new approach, is interesting and is easy to use. More importantly, however, it will help you to find the answers to the questions you've told us matter to you:

- Which careers will suit me?
- What qualifications will I need?
- How much can I hope to earn?
- What's the future likely to hold?
- Will the studying be worthwhile?

Take a look at the sample page opposite to see how you can use this book to find out exactly what you need to know.

We hope you enjoy using Careers 2009 and wish you all the best with your future career choices.

Heading / job title

This refers to the title of the job you will find on the page. However, some jobs have specialist areas you can enter. If this applies to the jobs you're interested in you'll find details of these specialist areas throughout the entry.

What the work involves

These opening points will give you a quick flavour of what the job is like.

The type of person suited to this work

Within this category you will find lots of information to help you match your own strengths, weaknesses, likes and dislikes to the individual job.

Sadly, it is very common for someone to start a job not knowing everything they'll be expected to do. They may then be confronted with something they find either too hard or not enjoyable; this might mean leaving a job they studied a long time for. To make sure this doesn't happen to you, think carefully about the information provided here and whether it matches your skills, experience and personality.

Working conditions

Are you an outdoor person, or are you happiest indoors?

Have you any health issues that might affect you doing certain jobs or working in some environments?

Within this section you will get a feel for the types of places and the working conditions you can expect in the job area.

The future outlook

There are lots of external influences affecting how different jobs might change in the future. This section suggests what might happen in this job area due to things like the ongoing impact of information technology, reductions or increases in the labour force or the stability of national and international economies.

No one can predict the future with absolute certainty, but the information here will help you get a balanced idea of each job and its context so that you can decide if it's right for you.

An example job entry

Most of the job pages within Careers 2009 are laid out using the same style.

All use the same headings. On these pages you will find out what you can expect to find within each entry and what each of the headings contains.

Private Investigator

What the work involves:

- You'll be collecting information for a client by asking questions, researching, obtaining evidence and making sense of what you find out.
- Private Investigators (PIs) do a variety of different jobs such as surveillance, tracing people, serving legal documents or investigating road accidents, suspected fraud or employee backgrounds. Some PIs specialise in a particular area, for example insurance or domestic investigations.
- You'll probably take witness statements, attend court hearings and give evidence.

entry level

1-2

Qualifications and courses

- There are no formal entry qualifications for this work. However, many entrants have degrees or advanced level qualifications.
- You'll need a driving licence and most successful PIs work in a related job, such as the police, law, customs and excise or security work, first.
- Most of the training takes place on the job.
- A scheme is being introduced where a government licence issued by the Security Industry Authority (SIA) will be required to practise. Check with the SIA for the latest developments.
- Courses are available from a number of private companies and listed by the Association of British Investigators (ABI). Topics such as theft, court work, investigation and surveillance are offered. A City & Guilds Certificate in conflict management and communication skills is also available, offered through the National Investigations Group.

Security, Emergency and Armed Forces

CRCI : UK

CLCI : MAG

511

The type of person suited to this work

Much of the day-to-day work of this exciting-sounding job is actually routine, so you'll need to be the patient, persistent type and be happy with your own company. You may spend hours, sometimes days watching and waiting for something to happen.

You need to be interested in learning about the law. The evidence you collect needs to be admissible in a court of law so you will need to know your stuff.

Your communication skills also need to be good as you will have to write reports and take witness statements. You'll also need to calm down anxious or aggressive people when you serve legal papers or repossess their car to pay a debt.

Working conditions

Most of your working hours will be spent driving or walking around. You may be sat in your vehicle for hours or out in all weathers.

Hours are irregular and on some cases they could be long and include evening and weekend work.

You may be at risk of assault from aggressive individuals you are serving legal papers on.

The future outlook

The majority of the [illegible] UK private investigators are self-employed or work for an agency. There is work but also competition and many PIs do not stay in the business for long. With the introduction of licensing there may be more opportunities for those with licences. A lot of the work is for legal, insurance or financial companies.

Some PIs go on to specialise in areas such as commercial piracy or insurance fraud. A few set up their own agencies and others move into supervisory or security management work.

Other related opportunities

- Police p50[illegible]
- Customs and Excise Officer p497
- Store Detective p521
- Bailiff p332

Advantages/disadvantages

- Private investigators are usually self-employed and so need to [illegible] their own equipment such as a computer, car, and camcorder. Licences and training will also add to the expense.
- A lot of the work is routine, but PIs say that there's a lot of satisfaction when, after months of patient work, you manage to find the evidence your client needs.

Earnings guide

- Many PIs are self employed and pay rates vary depending on the job and the area you are working in. Rates are higher in the south-east of England.
- Starting salaries are around £15,000 per year.

Experienced investigators could earn up to £20,000.

Well-qualified specialists can get £60,000.

- If self-employed, you could expect to get £20,000–£25,000.
- Top salaries for a corporate investigator can be £70,000+

Further information

Skills for Security
Security House
Barbourne Road
Worcester
WR1 1RS
08450 750111
www.skillsforsecurity.org.uk

Security Industry Authority
PO Box 9
Newcastle upon Tyne
NE82 6Y[illegible]
0870 24[illegible] 0100
www.the-sia.org.uk

Association of British Investigators
27 Old Gloucester Street
London
WC1N 3XX
0871 474 0006
www.theabi.org.uk

Institute of Professional Investigators
83 Guildford Street
Chertsey
Surrey
KT16 9JL
0870 330 8622
www.ipi.org.uk

Careers | **2009**

Entry level

The entry level wheel shows you what level of qualifications you will normally need to enter this career. You will find more information about qualification entry levels on page vii.

Qualifications and courses

- We have only included the most common or the main qualification routes normally needed to enter each job.
- Through your own research you will probably come across alternative entry routes or qualifications.
- We strongly recommend checking these out before starting by getting advice from the organisations listed in the Further Information section. See page vi for more information about this section.
- If there are different requirements between England, Wales, Scotland and Northern Ireland, you will find these listed here too.

CRCI (Connexions Resource Centre Index)
CLCI (Careers Library Classification Index)

These codes show you where you will be able to find additional information about the job title within school, college, university or community-based careers information areas.

Earnings guide

For some people one of the most important things they'll consider before undertaking a new course, qualification or a career is 'how much can I expect to earn?'.

To help you, we have included:

- The most up-to-date information about pay scales
- Where possible, what you can expect at entry, intermediate and senior levels
- Any regional differences.

Other related opportunities

So that you can look at other jobs that are similar in style and skills to the one on each page, we have included a list of others with their page numbers that could also interest you. You might not have considered or heard of some of these before, so it will help you to broaden out your ideas further.

Further information

Listed here are the contact details of organisations, helplines, websites and other ways to help you continue your research into your chosen job areas.

The Sector Skills Council (SSC) for the occupational sector that each job belongs to will usually be listed.

Advantages/disadvantages

Every job is different and everybody has different expectations about what they want to achieve in their career. Important additional information is bullet-pointed here, on things like: entering the career area, the pay, conditions, training or competition and availability of posts.

Entry levels

Most courses include a combination of research, practical experience, learning of skills and theory. Some take much longer to complete than others and the qualifications needed to enter can be higher or lower depending on what you want to study. How can you begin to compare qualifications when they are so diverse?

Until fairly recently, trying to find out how different qualifications compared with each other in terms of difficulty or what each was roughly equivalent to led to a great deal of confusion. However, a few years ago representatives from education and occupational organisations worked together to agree a set of levels to help everyone compare one qualification with another. They considered factors like:

- The time taken to study
- The degree of difficulty
- The entry requirements.

As a result of this research, most qualifications have been given a 'level' so that they can easily be compared. These levels have been mapped against each other to form three different qualifications frameworks, each of which is briefly outlined below.

The National Qualifications Framework (NQF)

The NQF includes academic and vocational qualifications offered in England, Wales and Northern Ireland up to and including further education level. There are nine levels – from Entry Level up to Level 8.

The Framework for Higher Education Qualifications (FHEQ)

The FHEQ includes higher education qualifications from Certificates of Higher Education through to Doctoral degrees. It applies to qualifications offered in England, Wales and Northern Ireland and includes five levels, each indicated by a letter corresponding with the initial of the main qualification offered at that level.

The Scottish Credit and Qualifications Framework (SCQF)

The SCQF is a 12-level framework including vocational, occupational and academic qualifications offered in Scotland. It covers all levels including further and higher education, from Access through to Doctoral degrees.

Each framework is under continuous review, but information in this book was correct at the time of writing. For further details and the most up-to-date information, refer to the following websites:

- **NQF:**
  www.qca.org.uk/qualifications
  www.qca.org.uk/openquals
  www.accac.org.uk
  www.ccea.org.uk
- **FHEQ:**
  www.qaa.ac.uk/academicinfrastructure/fheq
- **SCQF:**
  www.scqf.org.uk

Careers 2008 levels

For the purposes of this book, the three frameworks outlined above have been simplified into our own, nine-level framework shown below, to which we will refer throughout the book.

In the table below, qualifications available in England, Wales, Northern Ireland and Scotland are in plain text. *Qualifications available in England, Wales and Northern Ireland are in italics.* **Qualifications available in Scotland are in bold.**

Careers 2009 Level	Rough equivalent framework level	General and academic qualifications	Vocational and occupational qualifications
8	NQF Level 8 FHEQ Level D SCQF Level 12	• Doctorate	• Specialist awards and diplomas from professional bodies
7	NQF Level 7 FHEQ Level M SCQF Level 11	• Master's degree • Postgraduate Diploma (PgDip) • Postgraduate Certificate (PgCert)	• NVQ/SVQ Level 5* • *Level 7 Diploma/Fellowship* • *Level 7 Advanced Professional Certificate*
6	NQF Level 6 FHEQ Level H SCQF Level 10	• Bachelor's degree with Honours • Graduate Diploma • Graduate Certificate	• *Level 6 Certificate/Diploma*
5	NQF Level 5 FHEQ Level I SCQF Levels 8 and 9	• Bachelor's degree • Diploma of Higher Education • *Diploma of Further Education* • *Foundation Degree* • *Higher National Diploma*	• NVQ/SVQ Level 4* • Higher National Certificate/Diploma • *Level 5 Certificate/Diploma*
4	NQF Level 4 FHEQ Level C SCQF Level 7	• Certificate of Higher Education • **Scottish Advanced Higher** • **Higher National Certificate**	• *Level 4 Certificate/Diploma*

3	NQF Level 3 SCQF Level 6	• *A level* • **Scottish Higher**	• NVQ/SVQ Level 3 • *A levels in applied subjects* • *Level 3 Certificate/Diploma* • *BTEC National Award/Certificate/Diploma* • *Advanced Apprenticeship (England)* • **Modern Apprenticeship (Scotland, Wales, Ireland)**
2	NQF Level 3 SCQF Level 5	• *GCSE grade A*–C* • **Intermediate 2** • **Credit Standard Grade**	• NVQ/SVQ Level 2 • *Level 2 Certificate/Diploma* • *BTEC First Certificate/Diploma* • *Apprenticeship* • **Skillseekers**
1	NQF Level 1 SCQF Level 4	• *GCSE grade D–G* • **Intermediate 1** • **General Standard Grade**	• NVQ/SVQ Level 1 • BTEC Introductory Certificate/Diploma • Level 1 Certificate
Entry Level	NQF Entry Level SCQF Access Levels 1–3	• Entry Level Certificate • **SQA Access 1, 2 and 3** • **Foundation Standard Grade**	

Notes
* NVQs, SVQs and a small number of related qualifications correspond with NQF Levels 4 and 5 following the original five-level NQF system. The NVQ/SVQ Level 4 corresponds roughly with NQF Levels 4–6 and the NVQ/SVQ Level 5 corresponds roughly with NQF Levels 7–8.

Warning!

The comparisons in the table above are very approximate and cannot accommodate the subtleties of the three different frameworks from which they are drawn. They should therefore be used only as a very rough guide to comparable qualifications, and readers should refer in detail to the relevant websites for more information.

Qualification level entry wheel

The qualification level entry wheel is designed to give you an at-a-glance idea of the qualifications you might need to enter a career. The numbers shown in the centre indicate the level of qualification you are most likely to need

- To enter the job *and*
- To enter the job and to train while working.

(See above for an explanation of the qualification levels used.) The information in the qualification level entry wheel does *not* represent the level at which you can simply train for a job. For example, you can normally enter retail/shop work at Level 1–2, so the entry level for a shop assistant would be shown as follows:

To be doctor you will need to gain qualifications at Level 4–8, shown as:

Immediately after the entry level symbol you will find detailed information about the qualifications and courses you will normally need to take for every specific job listed.

Occupational clusters

To help you find your way around **Careers 2009** you will see we have divided the main part of the publication into sections, each of which represents a different occupational cluster.

We have done this for three main reasons:

1. **If you know which jobs you want to research** you will be able to look at others including similar ideas, some of which you may not have heard of before.
2. **If you don't have any job ideas yet**, you can match your own skills and interests to the different cluster groups, which will help give you ideas.
3. **If you want to research jobs across several clusters**, you will be able to find your way around much more easily.

To start, look at the following list and think about which of the following aspects are important to you within your future career or job.

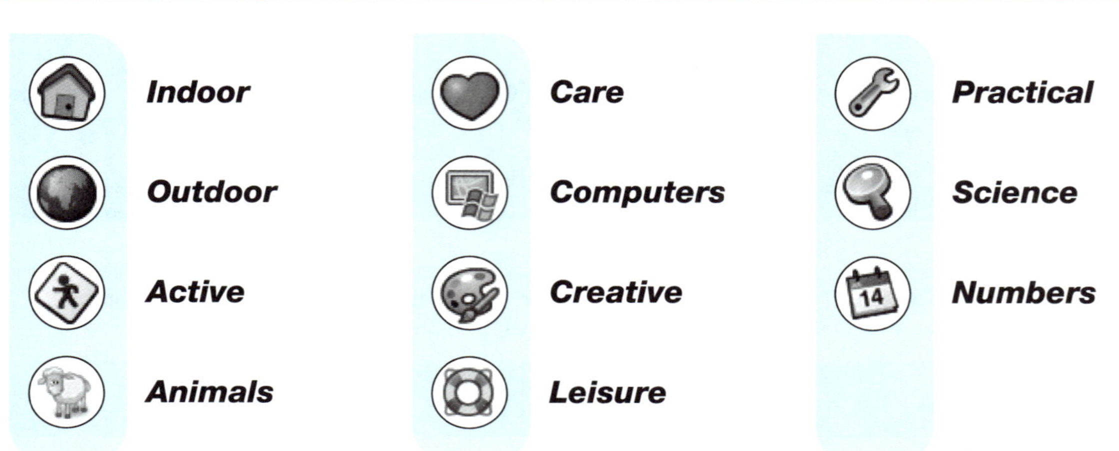

Now look at the following guide to see which cluster group most closely matches your interests, then look at the examples of the types of jobs. You can go straight to that section, where you will find jobs listed alphabetically. You'll also find case studies giving you an idea of what it's really like to work in the sectors.

Here is a quick guide to each of the occupational clusters within **Careers 2009**:

Administration, Business, Office and Financial Services

If you like using computers, want to understand more about how businesses work or enjoy numbers, the world of business and finance could be for you. The sort of careers in this cluster include:

- Accounting Technician – page 4
- Building Society Manager – page 9
- Secretary – page 28
- Switchboard Operator – page 32

Case studies in this occupational cluster:

- Human Resources/Personnel Officer – page 20

Building and Construction

Do you enjoy using your hands, using tools and designing or constructing new buildings? The construction industry includes jobs at all levels – check out some of these for ideas:

- Architect – page 36
- Bricklayer – page 39
- Carpet Fitter – page 42
- Plumber – page 65
- Town Planner – page 75

Case studies in this occupational cluster:

- Plumber – page 35
- Civil Engineer – page 47

Catering and Hospitality

  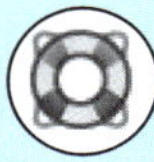 

Do you like meeting new people, enjoy preparing food and like keeping places clean and tidy? The catering and hospitality industry has lots of opportunities in these sorts of jobs:

- Bar Person – page 84
- Chef – page 87
- Hotel Manager – page 95
- Kitchen Porter – page 99

Case studies in this occupational cluster:

- Bar Manager/Owner – page 81
- Party Organiser – page 101

Computing and IT

Are computers or IT your thing? Some of the jobs in this cluster are so new they are still developing. Here are some ideas to start you thinking:

- Computer Games Designer – page 106
- IT Operator – page 113
- Multimedia Designer – page 115
- Software Developer – page 119
- Website Designer – page 122

Case studies in this occupational cluster:

- Computer Games Designer – page 103

Design, Arts, Media, Marketing, Advertising and Printing

Do you care about what things look like and enjoy designing, communicating or making things? This cluster includes all jobs with a creative aspect, such as:

- Artist – page 131
- Designer – page 136
- Marketing Manager – page 151
- Signwriter – page 165

Case studies in this occupational cluster:

- TV Researcher – page 123
- Fashion Designer – page 145

Education and Training

      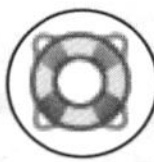   

Do you want to get involved within the world of teaching, learning or education? This section includes job ideas involving helping people of all ages.

- Play Worker – page 180
- Teacher – page 184
- Teaching/Classroom Assistant – page 187

Case studies in this occupational cluster:

- Crèche Manager – page 169
- Teaching Assistant – page 190

Engineering, Manufacturing and Production

Are you interested in how and why things work? Do you enjoy using your hands and working with tools or machinery? Engineering, manufacturing and production is a huge and varied section. Here are some of the careers included:

- Engineer – Craft – page 203
- Motor Vehicle Body Repairer – page 217
- Railway Fitter – page 223

Case studies in this occupational cluster:

- Gas Distribution Worker – page 191

Environment, Animals and Plants

If you care about the environment or the welfare of animals, or enjoy helping things to grow, this could be the cluster for you. Try some of these ideas:

- Animal Work – page 231
- Farm Work – page 241
- Forestry Worker – page 246
- Gamekeeper – page 248
- Veterinary Surgeon – page 262

Case studies in this occupational cluster:

- Gardener/Garden Designer – page 227
- Conservation Officer – page 230

Health and Medical

Do you want to help people to recover from illness by treating and caring for them? The healthcare cluster includes jobs you may not be aware of, so research your ideas carefully:

- Acupuncturist – page 271
- Dietitian – page 277
- Health Promotion Specialist – page 281
- Nurse – page 289
- Reflexologist – page 271

Case studies in this occupational cluster:

- Aromatherapist – page 265
- Nursing Assistant – page 291

Languages, Information and Culture

  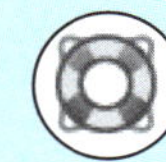

Do you enjoy history or researching information, or want a job that involves using another language? The information and culture section includes some unusual job ideas, for example:

Case studies in this occupational cluster:

Legal and Political Services

Are you interested in fairness and justice? Law and politics includes jobs that make sure everyone is given an equal voice. This cluster includes:

Case studies in this occupational cluster:

Leisure, Sport and Tourism

   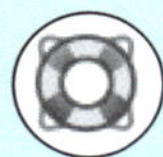 

Are you sporty or interested in aspects of the leisure and tourism industry?
The types of jobs included here are:

Case studies in this occupational cluster:

Performing Arts

   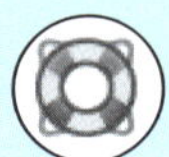

Do you want to appear on stage, singing, dancing or acting? Would you like to work behind the scenes supporting a production? This cluster includes:

Case studies in this occupational cluster:

Personal and Cleaning Services

Do you know you want to work with people but not exactly how? This broad cluster includes jobs that provide both personal services like hair or beauty treatment, and cleaning services. It includes jobs such as:

- Beauty Consultant – page 412
- Chimney Sweep – page 417
- Dry Cleaning Assistant – page 421
- Nail Technician – page 426
- Wigmaker – page 431

Case studies in this occupational cluster:

- Nail Technician – page 411
- Recycling Operative – page 432

Retail Sales and Customer Services

Do you enjoy meeting new people and helping them get what they need? The retail world includes lots of opportunities in areas such as:

- Antiques Dealer – page 434
- Customer Services Manager – page 442
- Shelf Filler – page 452
- Specialist Shop Assistant – page 455
- Trading Standards Officer – page 460

Case studies in this occupational cluster:

- Store Manager – page 433

Science, Mathematics and Statistics

If you enjoy using numbers or science to solve problems, the range of opportunities available to you includes all levels and will require careful research, for example:

- Astronomer – page 466
- Chemist – page 472
- Ecologist – page 478
- Geographer – page 480
- Laboratory Technician – page 481

Case studies in this occupational cluster:

- Laboratory Technician – page 465

Security, Emergency and Armed Forces

Do you want a job involving security, or helping or protecting people? This cluster includes many jobs that involve wearing a uniform, such as:

- Army Officer – page 492
- Firefighter – page 502
- Police Officer – page 506
- Store Detective – page 521
- Traffic Warden – page 504

Case studies in this occupational cluster:

- Prison Officer – page 491
- Customs and Excise Officer – page 522

Social Care and Counselling Services

   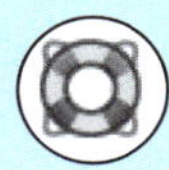 

Interested in helping people by talking, caring and improving their quality of life? Advice, psychology and counselling services are part of many jobs in social care, for example:

- Advice Centre Worker – page 524
- Childminder – page 528
- Education Welfare Officer – page 532
- Youth and Community Worker – page 551

Case studies in this occupational cluster:

- Youth Worker – page 523
- Counsellor – page 552

Transport and Logistics

    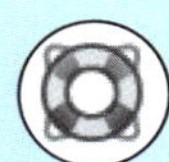  

Intrigued by how air, rail or road travel can help improve our lives? Lots of jobs include transport services or systems, such as:

- Air Cabin Crew – page 555
- Driver – page 563
- Rail Track Maintenance Worker – page 578
- Transport Manager – page 585
- Warehouse Manager – page 586

Case studies in this occupational cluster:

- Importer/Exporter – page 553
- Air Traffic Controller – page 561

With over 750 jobs in **Careers 2009**, not every one will be found in the examples above. You will also find some that could fit into a number of different sections. For example, there are lots of similarities between

- Health and Medical cluster and Social Care and Counselling Services cluster
- Design, Arts, Media, Marketing, Advertising and Printing cluster and Performing Arts cluster
- Computing and IT cluster and Science, Mathematics and Statistics cluster.

This means that if you like the idea of the jobs in the first cluster you will probably like some from the second one too.

If you are interested in one particular job, look it up in the Index that appears at the end of the book. To get an idea of all the different jobs you could enter with qualifications at a particular level, take a look at the Index of Levels on page 589.

Remember: before making your final decision try and keep your options open and research as many ideas as you can.

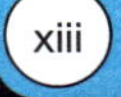

About the earnings guide

In our original research for this book, you said that the following were amongst the most important questions on pay:

- Will the final job and pay be worth all the studying?
- How much can I expect to earn when I am fully qualified?
- Will my earnings increase as I gain more experience?

In response, we've included information about the range and level of salaries you can expect. So you will find every job has an earnings guide covering the following levels:

- Entry/probationary
- Fully qualified with experience
- Senior/specialist level with several years' experience.

We recognise that figures on a page don't really illustrate everything you will need to consider, so here are some additional facts for you:

The Annual Survey of Hours and Earnings (ASHE) shows that the median gross annual pay for women in full-time employment increased by 2.8% in 2007 to £20,476. In the same year males in full-time employment earned a median gross annual salary of £26,297, up 2.7% on the previous year. Depending on your chosen area of work, some jobs pay more or less than this.

Try to use the 'earnings guide' information as just another factor when choosing your career idea, rather than letting it become the major one.

It's important to remember that the overall figure, or 'gross', is not the actual amount you will take home, as income tax, national insurance and probably pension and other personal contributions like union subscriptions will all be taken out first. You'll then get what is left – this is called the 'net'.

You need to think carefully about what you'll need to earn and whether your job idea will cover this immediately or in the longer term once you've done all your training.

Where you live can also affect how much you are likely to earn.

In 2007 average weekly earnings in London were £634.20. This is much higher than other regions, where they ranged from £388 in the north-east of England to £474 in the south-east. This is mainly due to the types of work available in the local and regional economies. In addition, London is the centre for jobs that traditionally pay some of the highest salaries (such as the financial, IT and legal sectors) – so it generally comes out on top.

However, what you earn doesn't always indicate how high your standard of living will be, as London is traditionally more expensive for buying things like houses and consumer items. This means that you will need the higher salaries to be able to afford to live there.

Remember: it is generally accepted that it can be cheaper to live in some areas where salaries are not as high, such as Wales or the north-east of England, as house and shopping prices here are lower, so things do balance out.

With the impact of things like the cost of higher education and the rising cost of living we recognise how important information about your potential earnings is to you. Whilst understanding the reasons for this, we also believe there are other important issues you need to consider, such as your suitability for the job, your educational background, and any health issues and interests you might have.

Where to go for help

Everyone needs advice and support, and when it's something as important as choosing your career, getting help is even more important. So where can you go and who out there is able to help?

Here is a brief explanation with some contact details of the main organisations available to you depending on where you are:

England

The Connexions Service

Designed to offer every young person the 'best start in life', the Connexions service is available across England for 13- to 19-year-olds and provides information, advice and guidance on all aspects that affect you. The range of issues covered

includes careers, education, training and all life issues such as health, leisure and housing information. The service is managed locally and you should contact your local partnership to see if you can make an appointment to speak to a Connexions Personal Adviser.
For more information:
www.connexions.gov.uk

Connexions Direct

Offering a telephone support service and detailed website, Connexions Direct can help you with information and advice on issues such as your career and learning options, money, health, housing, and relationships with family and friends. It can also let you know about activities you can get involved in.
You can contact Connexions Direct on:
Freephone: 080 800 13 2 19
Text phone: 08000 968 336
Text Message: 07766 4 13 2 19
www.connexions-direct.com

Northern Ireland

If you want advice from a careers adviser you can attend one of the 35 JobCentres and Jobs and Benefits Offices throughout Northern Ireland. Here you will get information on all aspects of work, education and employment issues. Careers Advisers visit schools regularly and you should speak to your careers teacher to arrange careers interview. If you have left school you should contact your local JobCentre to make an appointment to speak to a Careers Adviser. There are also 27 Careers Service Support Units spread throughout the region offering access to Careers Advisers and resources, and the Careers Service NI website is packed with information.
Tel: 028 9044 1781
www.careersserviceni.com

Scotland

Careers Scotland

Careers Scotland is available to both young people and adults looking for information about careers, education or employment options. If you want to meet a trained adviser you can either visit one of the 100 centres that are available across Scotland or visit the Careers Scotland website.
For more information contact:
Freephone 0845 8 502 502
Textphone: 0141 889 8581
Typetalk: 18001 0845 8502 502
www.careers-scotland.org.uk

Wales

Careers Wales

Offering help both to young people and to adults, Careers Wales provides advice on any issues you have related to careers, work, education or training.

Youth Gateway

In addition to the help and advice Careers Wales has available, they have now introduced Youth Gateway. This is designed specifically for you if you are aged 16–19 and looking for advice about training, employment and education. You will get help from Careers Advisers and Personal Advisers who are working together to make sure you get the help you need.
For further information on both Careers Wales and Youth Gateway see:
www.careerswales.com

Clic

Clic is an information and advice service for young people in Wales. It offers help and guidance on a range of issues – from education and employment to relationships, health and housing. For more information see: www.cliconline.co.uk

England, Wales and Northern Ireland

learndirect

If you need advice on any aspect of your careers, training or educational options try contacting Learndirect. Learndirect has trained advisers who can discuss your options over the phone or you can attend one of the many learndirect centres available throughout England, Wales and Northern Ireland. Their help is available to anyone of any age, although it is mainly aimed at adults.

If you want some more information or advice contact:
08000 150 450
www.learndirect.co.uk and www.learndirect-advice.co.uk

The remainder of Careers 2009 has been listed under 19 categories where you will find the details about each job. We hope you enjoy using the resource and, if you would like to give us any feedback to help us keep improving future editions, please let us know!

Careers 2009
Trotman Education, an imprint of Crimson Publishing
Westminster House
Kew Road
Richmond
Surrey TW9 2ND

WorldSkills

What is WorldSkills?

WorldSkills is the biggest skills competition in the world and it represents the ultimate in excellence in vocational training.

Every two years, hundreds of highly skilled young people from across the world come together to compete against each other and test their knowledge and ability in a wide variety of trades and specialisms.

Competitions take place in over 40 skill categories ranging from mechatronics and web design to floristry and jewellery, plumbing and bricklaying to hairdressing and confectionery.

Participants battle against the clock, and in front of a live audience, to tackle challenges that would be frequently found in the workplace.

Who can take part?

All competitors must be 22 years old or under and either a student, trainee or employee. Skills competitions are often held regionally, with the winners going through to national finals.

Over 60 regional events take place in the UK and medal ceremonies celebrate the success of competitors as well as the support of their tutors, colleges, training providers and employers.

Competitors at WorldSkills represent the very best of the best and are drawn from 49 countries in every corner of the globe – from Belgium and Ireland to Brazil and Venezuela, Tunisia and South Africa to Saudi Arabia and New Zealand.

Taking part in WorldSkills represents a unique and invaluable learning experience for all competitors. Many go on to excel in their chosen careers.

London 2011

The UK recently won the bid to host the 2011 WorldSkills in London.

City & Guilds was a member of the successful bid team and has confirmed its commitment to WorldSkills by pledging £1 million in sponsorship of the competition.

WorldSkills is the Olympics of the vocational qualifications world and London 2011 will allow the UK's elite young men and women to demonstrate their talents in front of an enthusiastic and supportive home crowd.

Medal winner

Gary Tuddenham is 22 years old and lives in Longtown, North Cumbria. He successfully completed an NVQ at Levels 2 and 3 in Fine Furniture Making at Carlisle and Kendal College and now works at Edward Barnsley Workshop. At WorldSkills 2007 Gary won a Gold Medal in the Cabinet Making competition.

"WorldSkills is vast, the sheer size of it is amazing and the standards are really high. You have to train and practice again and again. The more you practice the more your performance improves.

Once I calmed down I treated WorldSkills like every other competition I'd done. All the training I'd put in meant I was able to maintain good concentration throughout the competition. I made a silly mistake at one point, but by keeping calm and controlled I was able to see what I'd done and correct it – something perhaps I'd have missed if I hadn't been so prepared.

WorldSkills helps you develop personally and professionally. It has given me confidence and skills which I'd never have achieved without competing but I've still got a long way to go in my career and I'll continue to learn and grow at work. I want to be the best I can and maybe run my own business one day."

So what would Gary say to anyone thinking about taking part in WorldSkills?

"Get involved. It is the best thing you could ever, ever do."

WorldSkills 2007 Japan

In November 2007 the UK WorldSkills team travelled to Japan to compete in the gruelling four day event.

Watched by over 200,000 spectators the team competed hard in 21 different skill categories and won a fantastic four medals and nine medallions of excellence.

Managed by UK Skills, a not-for-profit organisation which champions skills and learning for work, the 22-strong team of highly talented young people were ranked 11th in the world overall and 4th in Europe. This improved the UK's position in the team league table by one place from 2005.

Government backing

"WorldSkills is about raising the status and the standards of vocational education. For our team to have achieved such great results in Japan 2007 proves we have skills in this country at world class levels. The team is helping to break down the snobbery around skills training – there is nothing second best about good skills-based careers. I hope that young people seeing what has been achieved in Japan will feel inspired to take up skills they can excel at professionally. I want many more to rise to the challenge themselves for the next competition in Canada in 2009 and again in 2011 when London will be hosting WorldSkills – and when we can show we can be the best!"

John Denham, Secretary of State

For more information about WorldSkills and the work of City & Guilds visit our website **www.cityandguilds.com/wordskills**

City & Guilds
1 Giltspur Street
London EC1A 9DD
Tel: 020 7294 2468

City & Guilds

City & Guilds is the UK's leading body dedicated to vocational learning. It offers over 500 qualifications in 28 different industry areas so that learners can gain the skills and knowledge they need to fulfil their career ambitions.

In operation for the last 130 years, 20 million people in the UK have City & Guilds qualifications and the organisation awards a further 1.5 million qualifications to learners every year.

City & Guilds qualifications are offered through 8500 centres in approximately 100 countries worldwide, so learners are never too far from a place where they can gain the skills they need.

City & Guilds qualifications are valued by employers because they are developed in conjunction with key industry bodies – so they are always relevant and up to date. Many leading businesses and organisations, such as Honda, Tesco and the London Underground, work with City & Guilds to train and develop their staff.

The Happiness Index

What is the Happiness Index?

The City & Guilds Happiness Index provides an annual snapshot of how happy and fulfilled British workers are in their jobs. In 2008, 2,000 people across 20 different professions were surveyed to measure how happy they were at work. The Index highlights the key contributors to happiness and how these factors change over time.

The Happiness Index 2008

The results of the 2008 survey reveal that financial rewards are not enough to guarantee job satisfaction. An overwhelming 95% of workers questioned agreed that having an interest in what you do for a living is the number one factor for ensuring on-the-job happiness. Happiness levels stay the same regardless of the size of workers' pay cheques.

The happiest workers are beauty therapists, with one in three of all those surveyed registering a happiness level of 10 out of 10.

Position	Profession	Position	Profession
1	Beauty Therapists	9	Engineers
2	Hairdressers	9	Architects
2	Armed Forces	13	Journalists
4	Catering / Chefs	13	Mechanics / Automotive
5	Retails Staff	13	Human Resources
6	Teachers	16	Call Centre
6	Marketing / PR	17	IT Specialists
6	Accountants	17	Nurses
9	Secretaries / Receptionists	17	Banker / Finance
9	Plumbers	17	Builders / Construction

The best and the worst

The UK's happiest worker profile

- Female
- Beauty Therapist
- Over 60 years old
- From north-east England

The UK's unhappiest worker profile

- Male
- Builder
- 40-49 years old
- From Northern Ireland

Loyalty and satisfaction

The 2008 Happiness Index provides a unique insight into why workers in the UK choose to stay with their employer:

57% remain with their current employer because they have a strong interest in what they do for a living

56% stay as a result of good relationships with work colleagues

48% appreciate the work / life balance they have achieved in their present job

Reasons to be cheerful

The Happiness Index reveals the essential keys to job satisfaction:

- Having a keen interest in what you do
- Undertaking hands-on / vocational work
- Feeling appreciated for what you do

A happy professional

Beauty Therapist Naomi Watts is set for a positive future career despite the fact that she has only been working in the beauty industry for a short time. Originally from Durham, 23-year-old Naomi relocated to East Bolton in order to study for a City & Guilds Levels 2 and 3 in Beauty Therapy, and since gaining her qualifications she has gone from strength to strength. She works as a Beauty Therapist at the popular Relax and Glow beauty clinic in Cleadon and has even won a Gold Award at the WorldSkills competition.

"I'm really happy in my job because I love meeting new people who come from all walks of life, which I get to do every day. I also get job satisfaction from the idea that what I do for a living makes a difference. I can help some people change their lives by building up their confidence and self-esteem, so I feel like I'm making a valuable contribution."

For more information on The Happiness Index and the work of City & Guilds visit our website www.cityandguilds.com/happiness

City & Guilds
1 Giltspur Street
London EC1A 9DD
Tel: 020 7294 2468

City & Guilds

City & Guilds is the UK's leading body dedicated to vocational learning. It offers over 500 qualifications in 28 different industry areas so that learners can gain the skills and knowledge they need to fulfil their career ambitions.

In operation for the last 130 years, 20 million people in the UK have City & Guilds qualifications and the organisation awards a further 1.5 million qualifications to learners every year.

City & Guilds qualifications are offered through 8500 centres in approximately 100 countries worldwide, so learners are never too far from a place where they can gain the skills they need.

City & Guilds qualifications are valued by employers because they are developed in conjunction with key industry bodies – so they are always relevant and up to date. Many leading businesses and organisations, such as Honda, Tesco and the London Underground, work with City & Guilds to train and develop their staff.

Diplomas

What are Diplomas?

Diplomas are a new type of qualification that aim to provide young people with a unique combination of academic and vocational skills. They have been developed to improve the employability of 14 to 19 year olds by:

- Providing training in the specific workplace skills that employers are looking for
- Focusing on key general skills such as numeracy, literacy, communication and IT
- Providing preparation for the world of work through relevant placements and team projects
- Delivering a new and different way of learning that offers a route into both higher education and employment

AQA and City & Guilds – working together

AQA – the UK's main provider of GCSEs and A levels – and City & Guilds – the UK's leading body dedicated to vocational learning – have joined together to develop and deliver the new range of Diplomas.

Their combination of experience and expertise in both academic and vocational qualifications guarantees that the Diplomas offer the very best in general education as well as specific workplace skills.

Together they are committed to delivering the highest quality qualifications and providing full support to ensure that Diplomas provide a successful route to both work and higher education.

Subjects available

Launched in September 2008 the first four Diplomas focus on:

- Construction and the built environment
- Creative and media
- Engineering
- Information Technology

Construction and the Built Environment

Exploring the fabric and significance of the built environment, this Diploma provides learners with the underpinning knowledge and basic skills needed in a wide range of industry areas. From architecture and surveying to painting and decorating, the Construction and the Built Environment Diploma provides an understanding of how this key sector works from the inside out.

Creative and Media

Focusing on knowledge, skills and creativity, this Diploma enables learners to experience the wide variety of career paths encompassed by the media and creative arts. From graphic design and advertising to creative writing and computer games, the Diploma allows learners to bring their ideas to life through making, doing and performing, whilst also encouraging critical thinking and good communication skills.

Engineering

Introducing learners to the fascinating world of engineering, this Diploma covers key principles and explores significant aspects of the role of an engineer including research, design, product development, manufacturing and production. It will captivate the imagination of all potential engineers and provide an understanding of how their future role could contribute positively to the world around them.

IT

Exploring the knowledge and abilities needed to succeed in the IT and Telecommunications sectors, this Diploma transforms technology-related education for young people. By allowing learners to experience key functions such as project management, IT support, website development and the design of new business solutions, the IT Diploma provides a realistic reflection of the blend of business, technical and interpersonal skills required by today's successful IT specialists.

Coming soon

From September 2009 Diplomas will be available in:

- Business, Administration and Finance
- Environmental and Land-based Studies
- Hair and Beauty Studies
- Hospitality

A range of benefits

As well as combining academic and vocational learning, Diplomas also help students to develop both general and specific knowledge and skills. Every Diploma includes:

- Functional skills – the practical skills in English, mathematics and ICT that have been identified as vital to enable young people to succeed
- Additional and specialised learning (ASL) – the opportunity for students to specialise in particular areas and take up complementary studies. This can include options such as languages, music or science which relate to individuals' needs, interests, hopes and ambition
- Projects–specific tasks which are designed to support each student's individual progression and development

For more information about Diplomas and the work of City & Guilds visit our website **www.diplomainfor.org**

City & Guilds
1 Giltspur Street
London EC1A 9DD
Tel: 020 7294 2468

City & Guilds

City & Guilds is the UK's leading body dedicated to vocational learning. It offers over 500 qualifications in 28 different industry areas so that learners can gain the skills and knowledge they need to fulfil their career ambitions.

In operation for the last 130 years, 20 million people in the UK have City & Guilds qualifications and the organisation awards a further 1.5 million qualifications to learners every year.

City & Guilds qualifications are offered through 8500 centres in approximately 100 countries worldwide, so learners are never too far from a place where they can gain the skills they need.

City & Guilds qualifications are valued by employers because they are developed in conjunction with key industry bodies – so they are always relevant and up to date. Many leading businesses and organisations, such as Honda, Tesco and the London Underground, work with City & Guilds to train and develop their staff.

If you like using computers, want to understand more about how businesses work or enjoy numbers, the world of business and finance could be for you.

The sort of careers in this cluster include:

- **Accounting Technician**
- **Building Society Manager**
- **Office Manager**
- **Secretary**
- **Switchboard Operator**

But what's it like working in this area?

Here's Kate Wilson's story:

Human Resources Officer

As Head of Management Development at Alliance and Leicester, Kate is responsible for everything from spotting graduate trainees with potential leadership skills to dealing with claims of bullying and harassment. She herself started out as a graduate trainee at the Nationwide Building Society before being seconded into what was then the Personnel Department. She moved across to Alliance and Leicester six years ago, first as Personnel Manager, and gained her current position two years ago.

WHAT THE JOB ENTAILS

'What I do now has a lot of responsibility and is quite specialised. One of my main jobs is Succession Planning – do we have the people with the ability to become managers in the future? I have to identify people who could be our potential senior managers. We also have a Women In Balance programme recognising there is a gender imbalance at the top of the business and addressing how we can encourage more women to go on to senior positions. For me one of the most important aspects of what I do is getting people to really understand the business side of things, and that it is people that make businesses successful.'

A BAD DAY IN THE OFFICE FOR KATE

'These are the days when you have to deal with sensitive issues such as bullying, harassment and redundancies. There are definitely some days when I know I have to take the tissues in with me because things like cost reduction, downsizing and change always make people fearful. My colleagues and I always try to make events of this kind as painless as possible, but at the end of the day you are saying "here is the bad news", so we try to handle it in a positive way.'

WHAT MAKES KATE GOOD AT HER JOB

'You need to be a good listener and have the ability to ask the right questions. I love the analysing process – not analysing the data from tests and exercises as such, but looking at what members of staff are doing when they meet you and do presentations. It is more about understanding what they are saying beneath their actual words.'

WHAT KATE PERSONALLY GETS OUT OF IT

'I like actually seeing people develop, seeing them deal with issues they haven't dealt with before and seeing them grow in confidence. I like helping people come to good decisions by giving them advice on how to achieve that. Human resources has also become increasingly involved in how you help people to cope with changes, how you inspire them and how you motivate them to develop. Because of that, I believe if you want to come into human resources you have to be interested in both business and people, because most businesses need people in order to succeed.'

Accountant

What the work involves

- Accountancy involves keeping and analysing financial records for companies or individuals, helping them to increase their profits.
- It includes advising on financial planning and development, tax returns and future costs and budgets.
- You will keep detailed accounts and internal audits and produce regular statements on whether the company's systems are efficient and cost effective.
- You can obtain qualifications from one of six different professional bodies.

There are three main areas of work:

Industrial and commercial

- Employed directly by a company, you will provide a range of services and could work for a small local company or a huge multinational.
- You will help to plan the company's development, predicting the costs, benefits and risks.

Private practice

- This involves working for a specialist accountancy firm that offers services to clients.
- Smaller practices usually work for small local businesses. However, accountancy firms can be huge and some companies provide services to multinational corporations.

Public sector

- Working for public bodies like the NHS, universities and local authorities you will offer advice on tax, financial problems, raising money, financial ICT systems and management consultancy.
- Your role will be to help them provide an efficient, quality service that is within the budgets set by the government.

The type of person suited to this work

As you will be making presentations and working with people at all levels, you will need excellent written and verbal communication skills. Much of your work will include confidential reports and financial information, so you will need to be honest and reliable. You will also need to be able to work under pressure and to deadlines and be prepared to study in your own time and to continue to keep up to date with new developments.

An ability with figures and an interest in how businesses work will be essential. You will also have to be able to research and understand complicated financial information, use your skills and knowledge to analyse it, think of solutions to problems and finally produce written reports showing your findings and conclusions.

Working conditions

You could be working in an organisation of any size and will generally be office based, spending a lot of time using ICT, sitting at a desk or meeting clients.

Depending on your role, you might have the opportunity to travel both in this country and abroad, in order to meet your clients. A driving licence could be useful and you might need to be prepared to spend time away from home, sometimes for fairly long periods.

Although you will normally work office hours from Monday to Friday, you may need to work extra hours at busy times, especially during February to March (the end of the financial year).

The future outlook

The growing importance of information technology is having a major impact on the accountancy sector. Access to faster communication systems means more major companies are becoming global, which in turn will have an impact on the numbers required within the accountancy sector. If accountancy is your chosen route, it is recommended you think very carefully about the area you would like to focus on at an early stage of your career.

In the long term you could choose to become self-employed, offering consultancy services to clients.

Industrial and commercial

There is a high demand for trainees and opportunities throughout the country but, as you would probably be working for a larger organisation, most jobs are in towns and cities. Once you are qualified and experienced you could move into highly paid senior management positions, or you could choose to move to a larger company for promotion.

Private practice

You could work for a small company, offering a personal service to local businesses and individuals or for a huge multinational firm. Job opportunities are good and there is a high demand for qualified people.

Public Sector

The public sector covers a wide range of services, including education, healthcare and social services. Government changes mean that budgets are increasingly held at local level, for example schools and hospitals now manage their own finances. This means that there are increasing opportunities across the country.

If you do well, you can move into high-level management jobs. Many people at the highest levels within the public sector started their careers within accountancy.

Qualifications and courses

- Most people start with a degree (usually 2.2 classification or higher). If your degree is in accounting or a related subject you may be exempt from certain papers for some of the professional qualifications.
- The minimum entry requirements for a degree are normally 2 A levels/3 H grades and 5 GCSEs/S grades (A–C/1–3), including maths and English, or equivalent; HNC/HND in accounting or a business-related subject followed by a top-up degree may be another route into the profession.
- It is possible for school leavers, with a minimum of 4 GCSEs/S grades, including English and maths, to follow a vocational training route. This is normally offered by the Association of Accounting Technicians (AAT) and The Chartered Institute of Management Accountants (CIMA), who offer the Technician route to qualification. There are varied exam requirements, depending on qualifications offered at entry.
- Accountants hold a qualification from a recognised accountancy body: Association of Chartered Certified Accountants (ACCA), Institute of Chartered Accountants in England and Wales (ICAEW), Institute of Chartered Accountants in Scotland (ICAS), Institute of Chartered Accountants in Ireland (ICAI), Association of International Accountants (AIA). The Chartered Institute of Management Accountants (CIMA) and the Institute of Financial Accountants (IFA) provide qualifications for management accountants and financial accountants working in industry, commerce or the public sector.

Public sector

- Accountants working in the public sector usually hold the Chartered Institute of Public Finance and Accountancy (CIPFA) qualification.

entry level

To both enter and train while working in this career, you will need qualifications at Level 3–8. Please refer to explanation on page vii.

Other related opportunities

- Accounting Technician p4
- Actuary p5
- Auditor p8
- Bank / Building Society p9
- Financial Adviser p18
- Insurance p21

Advantages/disadvantages

- If you work within the right organisation you can expect to earn extremely high salaries. To achieve this you will need to be very dedicated and able to cope with a lot of responsibility, stress and pressure.
- Accountancy is a very varied career and there are a lot of opportunities both in this country and abroad.
- You will be office based and usually need to be prepared to dress formally.
- You will need to be committed and determined to cope with the training, studying and taking exams whilst you work.

Earnings guide

- Successful accountants can earn very high salaries but a lot will depend on your level, experience and location. The highest salaries are within London and the south-east of England, the lowest are in Northern Ireland, Scotland and the north-east of England.

Private practice

- As a graduate starting training you can earn between £18,000 and £25,000 per year depending on where you work and your responsibilities.
- Recently qualified graduates earn between £27,000 and £43,500.
- When fully qualified, with several years' experience, and perhaps a specialist area of work, salaries can increase to £150,000+.

Public sector

- A trainee usually starts on £16,000–£25,000 per year. On completion of training you could earn between £25,000 and £50,000.
- Fully qualified senior managers can earn from £50,000–£120,000 per year, while directors could earn £250,000+.
- Your salary will depend on the type of organisation you work for, the qualification you have studied, and your location. ACCA qualified accountants typically earn more than those with CAT. Accountants working in London can expect to earn up to 20% more than in other areas.

Further information

Association of Chartered Certified Accountants
29 Lincoln's Inn Fields
London
WC2A 3EE
020 7059 5000
www.acca.co.uk
info@accaglobal.com

Institute of Chartered Accountants in England & Wales
Chartered Accountants Hall
PO Box 433
London
EC2P 2BJ
020 7920 8100
www.icaew.co.uk

Institute of Chartered Accountants of Scotland
CA House
21 Haymarket Yards
Edinburgh
EH12 5BH
0131 347 0100
www.icas.org.uk

Chartered Institute of Management Accountants
26 Chapter Street
London
SW1P 4NP
020 8849 2251
www.cimaglobal.com
cima.contact@cimaglobal.com

Association of International Accountants
Staithes 3
The Watermark
Metro Riverside
Newcastle upon Tyne
NE11 9SN
0191 493 0277
www.aia.org.uk
aia@aia.org.uk

Institute of Financial Accountants
Burford House
44 London Road
Sevenoaks
Kent
TN13 1AS
01732 458080
www.ifa.org.uk
mail@ifa.org.uk

Accounting Technician

What the work involves

- As an accounting technician you will work on a range of financial issues including company expenditure, tax returns, payroll and auditing. This will involve collecting and analysing information, keeping records and writing reports.
- In a large firm you will probably be part of a team, supporting qualified accountants.
- In a smaller company, you might cover a wider range of tasks and be responsible for most of the finances.
- Once you are qualified you could specialise, for example in insolvency or taxation.

The type of person suited to this work

You must be confident working with numbers and have good verbal and written communication skills, as you will have to explain complicated financial issues to clients in a clear and simple manner.

You should also be able to gather information, analyse and record it accurately, and be able to work under pressure and meet deadlines.

You will need an interest in all areas of business and finance and be prepared to study and pass exams. It is essential for accounting technicians to keep up to date with changes in the law so you will have to continue learning throughout your career.

Good ICT skills are important as there will be a lot of computer work.

Working conditions

You will be office-based doing most of your work on computer and will usually be expected to dress formally.

You could be in a small accountancy practice or a huge multinational company.

Your may work as part of a team and might be required to visit clients at their place of work, so a driving licence could be useful.

Most accountancy technicians work normal office hours, Monday to Friday with extra hours at busy times. It is possible to work part time or from home or be self-employed.

The future outlook

The finance industry employs a lot of people but only a small percentage of the work force holds higher qualifications so there is a skills shortage within the sector. Taking the highest level of qualification that you can will improve your future prospects.

Demand for staff is high as more organisations such as schools and hospitals are now managing their own budgets and many small or medium-sized companies now employ their own accounting technicians.

Prospects for promotion are good, and in smaller companies particularly, many accounting technicians are taking on more responsibility working at senior levels to improve company profits. You could go on to become self-employed or train as a chartered accountant.

entry level

2–3

To both enter and train while working in this career, you will need qualifications at Level 2–3. Please refer to explanation on page vii.

Qualifications and courses

- Most people enter and train in this career with qualifications at Level 2 or 3 but you could enter with Level 1.
- There are no minimum requirements, but you will usually require some GCSEs/S grades (A–C/1–3), including English and maths. Employers also welcome mature applicants.
- The Association of Accounting Technicians (AAT) and Association of Chartered Certified Accountants (ACCA) award Accounting Technician qualifications.
- AAT qualifications are at three levels: NVQ/SVQ Levels 2 (Foundation), 3 (Intermediate) and 4 (Technician), usually studied part time at college or work. Exemption from the Foundation Stage is possible with an A level or Scottish Higher in Accounting, or with 2 A levels/Scottish Highers, Applied A levels or National Certificate/Diploma in Business, or equivalent.
- The Certified Accountancy Technician (CAT) qualification, awarded by ACCA, is 1 year's practical experience with exams at three levels. With certain qualifications you may receive exemption from some papers.
- Both the AAT and CAT allow students to go on and qualify as Chartered Accountants. Students who complete the CAT can progress directly to ACCA Part 2. The AAT technician qualification provides exemption from the earlier stages of CIPFA, ICAEW, ICAS, CIMA and ACCA qualification schemes.
- Apprenticeships/Skillseekers may be available to those between 16 and 25.

CRCI:IA

CLCI:NAB

Other related opportunities

- Accountant p2
- Bank / Building Society p9
- Accounts Clerk p12
- Insurance p21

Advantages/disadvantages

- You could become self-employed, progress into senior management jobs or take further qualifications and train to be a fully qualified Chartered Accountant.
- Work can be pressured and you will need to meet regular deadlines.
- You will need to study and take exams whilst you are training.

Earnings guide

- As a trainee working and taking foundation level qualifications, you can earn £11,500–£18,000 per year.
- At Intermediate level earnings are £14,000–£18,000.
- Fully qualified you can earn £18,000–£25,000.
- You can earn up to £45,000 once you have gained experience and have progressed onto management level or if you are self-employed.

Further information

www.cityandguilds.com/myperfectjob

Association of Accounting Technicians
140 Aldersgate Street
London
EC1A 4HY
0845 863 0800
www.aat.org.uk
aat@aat.org.uk

Association of Chartered Certified Accountants
29 Lincoln's Inn Fields
London
WC2A 3EE
020 7059 5000
www.acca.co.uk
info@accaglobal.com

Institute of Chartered Accountants in Ireland
11 Donegall Square South
Belfast
BT1 5JE
028 9032 1600
www.icai.ie
ca@icai.ie

Actuary

What the work involves

- Actuaries calculate financial risk. Using statistics and knowledge of investments, law and business, they make financial predictions to help design products such as insurance and pensions.
- As an actuary you would help set insurance prices based on statistics, probability and risk. You would also use your knowledge and skills to help companies make long-term decisions on their investments, insurance and pension funds.
- You might work in insurance, life assurance, pensions, investments or for the government.

The type of person suited to this work

An ability with figures and enjoyment of solving complicated mathematical problems is essential. You should also be able to think clearly and logically, be able to analyse information and data and solve complex financial problems.

You will need to have excellent communication skills for working with other people and explaining complicated financial issues clearly and simply.

Actuaries must pay close attention to detail and you will be working to deadlines and keeping up to date with new developments such as the laws and regulations governing the industry.

You will be expected to dress formally and have excellent ICT skills.

Working conditions

Most of the work is office-based, working normal office hours, but you will also visit clients at their work at times to suit them. This will involve some evening and weekend work and travel, possibly staying away from home. A driving licence and transport could be required.

As a trainee you will have to study in your own time.

Once you are qualified you could work abroad and might be able to work part time.

The future outlook

Most actuaries work within life assurance companies and numbers in general insurance are increasing rapidly. Although the profession is growing, entry is competitive and you will probably need relevant work experience. Jobs are available throughout the country but most are in Edinburgh, London and the south-east.

As a fully qualified actuary you can work within a specialism or in consultancy, or you could travel as your qualifications will be welcomed all over the world. Within larger companies there are opportunities for promotion to very senior positions.

entry level

To both enter and train while working in this career, you will need qualifications at Level 3–8. Please refer to explanation on page vii.

Qualifications and courses

- Most people enter this career with a degree in maths or a related subject; some entrants have a postgraduate qualification in actuarial science.
- Actuaries are almost always graduates, with a professional qualification from the Institute of Actuaries (England and Wales) or the Faculty of Actuaries (Scotland).
- Normal entry requirements for a degree course are 2 A levels/3 H grades and 5 GCSEs/S grades (A–C/1–3), or equivalent. For a degree in maths, this will include an A level/H grade in a maths subject.
- You could become a trainee actuary after A levels or Scottish Highers. The minimum entry requirements are 2 A levels including a mathematical subject at grade B, or 3 Scottish Highers including maths at grade A.
- Trainees are employed by a firm of actuaries, training from 3 to 6 years. To become a Fellow of the Institute or the Faculty of Actuaries, you must be at least 23 years old, have 3 years' work experience, and pass the professional exams.
- Trainees with a degree or diploma in actuarial science/studies may get exemptions from some of the training. Other degrees may give exemption from certain exam papers.

Other related opportunities

- Accountant p2
- Bank / Building Society p9
- Company Secretary p11
- Financial Adviser p18
- Stockbroker p31

Advantages/disadvantages

- Training after university takes up to 6 years and involves studying whilst working full time.
- Actuaries are in demand, there are good promotion prospects and the pay is good.
- UK qualifications are recognised everywhere so you could work abroad.

Earnings guide

- As a graduate trainee you can expect a salary between £20,000 and £28,000 per year.
- Newly or part qualified staff can expect £40,000–£53,000.
- Senior staff can earn up to £75,000 and it is possible to earn over £100,000.
- Salaries vary based on location and specialism, and are expected to be higher in London and the south-east of England.

Further information

Institute of Actuaries
Staple Inn Hall
High Holborn
London
WC1V 7QJ
020 7632 2100
www.actuaries.org.uk
institute@actuaries.org.uk

Faculty of Actuaries
Maclurin House
18 Dublin Street
Edinburgh
EH1 3PP
0131 240 1300
www.actuaries.org.uk
faculty@actuaries.org.uk

Administrator

What the work involves

- Administrators deal with paperwork and use manual and ICT systems to keep organisations running smoothly and efficiently, keeping their records and information up to date and easy to find. They use office equipment like photocopiers and fax machines.
- Businesses and organisations of all different types and sizes need administrative staff. Here are some of the different types of work you could do.

General

- This involves dealing with the post and maintaining efficient filing and computer systems.
- You may take minutes of meetings and deal with customers and the public.
- You could work in a specialist department like accounts or sales.

Civil service

- The civil service works for the government, advising ministers and providing services to the public.
- Your role would be to help your department or agency to run efficiently.
- Your work could involve working with the public and dealing with high-level staff.

Health authority

- You will probably work in a hospital or doctors' surgery, keeping patient records, making appointments or working on reception.
- During your work you will do general clerical tasks, like keeping track of admissions and discharges and recording deaths.

Local government

- You could work in lots of different areas, such as leisure, environment or public health.
- A lot of your work could involve helping the public and supporting high-level staff.
- Your role will be to help your department to run efficiently.

The type of person suited to this work

You will need to be well organised and efficient, and enjoy keeping accurate records and files. You will need good written English and to be able to deal with people at all levels, and stay calm working with the public who may be anxious, upset or angry.

You will have to prioritise your own work, deal with several things at once, pay attention to detail and meet deadlines. You will need to be able to use your own initiative and enjoy working with people and as part of a team.

As you could be dealing with confidential information, you should be discreet and tactful.

Working conditions

Most of this type of work is office-based. The type of environment is often dependent on the size of the firm. The largest often have the best facilities, such as air-conditioning and canteens. However, if you work for a smaller company you could have more responsibility and variety.

Although a lot of your time will involve being seated at a desk using a computer, some of your work might also involve visiting other departments – taking post, files or boxes with you. You will use a range of office equipment, including photocopiers, fax machines and telephone systems. If you deliver or sort the post you could be on your feet for large parts of the day.

On a reception desk, you will be responsible for greeting visitors and showing them to their meeting room or contacting colleagues. You might have to deal with people who are rude or abusive if you work for a public service or local authority organisation.

You will probably work normal office hours and there are a lot of opportunities to work part time or on flexitime.

The future outlook

Around 13% of all jobs within the UK are in business administration, so there are a lot of jobs available, many of them at entry level. In most areas of the country the largest employers are local government, the civil service and the health service. These three services employ huge numbers of people, many of them in administrative jobs.

Many civil service jobs are based in London but there are opportunities across the UK, for example in Jobcentres or the Inland Revenue.

General

Administrative staff work in a huge variety of settings, from small local businesses to large organisations like insurance companies or industry. You can start work when you leave school and get qualifications through an Apprenticeship/Skillseekers or you could go to college first and take a full-time course in administration. As your skills and experience develop, you could take on more responsibility, perhaps supervising other staff or specialising in an area like accounts or human resources. The construction industry is having difficulty getting the right number of qualified administrative staff to enter the sector, making it an area worth considering if you are interested in this type of work.

Civil service

The civil service has an established training and development programme for staff and you can enter with GCSEs, A levels or a degree. You will learn on the job and through external courses and can get promotion if you do well. There are opportunities throughout the country.

Health authority

Hospitals are increasingly having to show that they are meeting government targets, so the administrative role is important and opportunities are increasing. You will get training and work experience and can move into a supervisor's job or more senior administrative positions.

Local Government

Around half of local government staff work in administrative jobs and there are opportunities all over the country. You will get in-house training and could take on more responsibility and get promoted to high-level posts. You could use your skills to move into a range of other areas.

Qualifications and courses

- You can enter and train in this career with qualifications at Level 1 or go in with higher qualifications.
- There are no minimum entry requirements for this work. Administrative staff are normally trained on the job, and progress with experience.
- School-leavers can go straight into this work, and may begin by working as an office junior. 4 or 5 GCSEs/S grades (A–C/1–3) are normally required, including English and maths. Equivalent qualifications such as an NVQ/SVQ Level 1 or 2 in administration are accepted. However, candidates are increasingly offering A level/H grade or degree-level qualifications before looking for work.
- Apprenticeships/Skillseekers may be available in administration/business administration.
- People who are already working in administrative roles may study part time towards an NVQ/SVQ or OCR Certificate or Diploma in administration. Further education colleges offer a wide range of relevant part-time courses, for example OCR/RSA and City & Guilds qualifications in word processing, spreadsheets, databases, audio typing, etc.
- To become a civil service adminstrator you will need 4 or 5 GCSE/S grades (A–C/1–3) including English and you may be asked to sit a test. All civil service jobs are open to British nationals and most are also open to Commonwealth and European citizens.
- To work as a health authority administrator you will need the above qualifications and you will be subjected to a criminal records bureau check.

entry level

To both enter and train while working in this career, you will need qualifications at Level 1–8. Please refer to explanation on page vii.

Other related opportunities

- Clerk p12
- Court Administrative Officer p335
- Arts Administrator p318
- Receptionist p25
- Personal Assistant p24
- Travel Agency Sales Consultant p385

Advantages/disadvantages

- There are plenty of job opportunities in a wide range of companies and environments – you could be sharing an office with one or two people in a small company, or working in a large open-plan office or a busy reception area.
- You don't always need many qualifications and there are opportunities to progress into higher level jobs.
- The work can be routine and repetitive when you start, with not much variation.

Earnings guide

- Salaries vary across the UK, but you will earn between 10% and 20% more in the south-east of England and London.

General

- As a starting salary outside London you can expect to earn £13,000–£18,000 per year within a private organisation – some may pay more.

Civil service

- In London the average starting salary is around £15,000–£17,000.
- With experience and promotion to junior manager level this could rise to £19,500.
- Middle managers can expect around £30,000+.

Health authority

- As a starting salary you could earn around £11,500–£13,000 per year.
- In a senior position you could expect £30,000.
- The NHS has grades for different jobs, so your salary will depend on your actual job.
- With experience and promotion you could earn £14,000–£17,000 per year.

Local authority

- Pay scales vary greatly between different authorities. As a guide, you can earn anything between £13,000–£25,000 according to your grade and level of responsibility.

Further information

Civil Service
Most recruitment is via individual departments and agencies
www.careers.civil-service.gov.uk
CivilServiceJobs@cabinet-office.x.gsi.gov.uk

Council for Administration
6 Graphite Square
Vauxhall Walk
London
SE11 5EE
020 7091 9620
www.cfa.uk.com
info@cfa.uk.com

London Chamber of Commerce and Industry
33 Queen Street
London
EC4R 1AP
020 7248 4444
www.londonchamber.co.uk
lc@londonchamber.co.uk

OCR
1 Hills Road
Cambridge
CB1 2EU
01223 553 998
www.ocr.org.uk
general.qualifications@ocr.org.uk

Scottish Qualifications Authority
The Optima Building
58 Robertson Street
Glasgow
G2 8DQ
0845 279 1000
www.sqa.org.uk
customer@sqa.org.uk

Pitman Training Group
Head Office UK
Sandown House
Sandbeck Way
Wetherby
West Yorkshire
LS22 7DN
0800 220454
www.pitman-training.com

Government Skills
Cabinet Office
Admiralty Arch
The Mall
London
SW1A 2WH
020 7276 1611
www.government-skills.gov.uk

www.cityandguilds.com/myperfectjob

CRCI:AB/AC | CLCI:AT/CAB/CAG

Auditor

What the work involves

- You will be a fully qualified accountant specialising in audit work, exploring all aspects of a business, talking to staff and ensuring that the paperwork and accounts give a true picture of the company's finances.
- Internal auditors work for a company preparing their accounts for external auditors to check.
- All businesses and government departments must be externally audited, by law. As an external auditor your work will include creating a detailed report, stating that the accounts are true and accurate and recommending possible improvements to the business.

entry level

To both enter and train while working in this career, you will need qualifications at Level 3–8. Please refer to explanation on page vii.

The type of person suited to this work

You must be happy working with numbers and interpreting statistics and be a thorough, methodical person who pays close attention to detail.

As you will be using your skills and experience to solve financial problems you will need to enjoy researching information and looking into all aspects of a business.

It is important that you have excellent communication skills so that you can present your findings clearly, both verbally and in writing. You should also be able to work effectively as part of a team and with the company you are auditing.

You should be well organised, able to work under pressure, meet deadlines and have excellent ICT skills.

Working conditions

Large companies have internal auditors who prepare their accounts for inspection. External auditors are based temporarily in the firms they are auditing, so they may have to travel and stay away from home. A driving licence and own transport can be useful.

You might have to visit a company's factories or warehouses to check their stock and equipment.

You will do normal office hours but will be working to deadlines and so may have to work evenings and weekends.

The future outlook

There is an increasing demand for qualified auditors. As an internal auditor you could work for a business or government department, or work for yourself, offering consultancy or advice and doing internal audits for companies.

External auditors are employed by accountancy firms or you might work for the National Audit Office (the Accounts Commission in Scotland), auditing central government departments, or the Audit Commission, working with public sector organisations such as local authorities or the NHS.

Qualifications and courses

- In order to become an auditor, you will need to obtain a professional accountancy qualification (see p3).
- Most entrants to this profession are graduates.
- Private accountancy firms audit companies in the private sector and some public sector organisations. A chartered accountancy qualification with CIPFA, ACCA, ICAEW, ICAS, ICAI or CIMA is required.
- Public sector auditing is usually carried out by national audit bodies such as the Audit Commission, the National Audit Office, Audit Scotland and the Northern Ireland Audit Office. A chartered accountancy qualification with CIPFA, ACCA, ICAEW, ICAS, ICAI or CIMA is required.
- The national audit bodies offer graduate training schemes, which allow graduates in any subject to train as auditors and gain a chartered accountancy qualification. The National Audit Office has a 3-year training programme, leading to qualification with the Institute of Chartered Accountants. Minimum entry requirements are a 2.1 Honours degree and 300 UCAS points at A level/H grade or equivalent.
- The Audit Commission offers a 4-year training programme including a professional qualification with CIPFA. Minimum entry requirements are a 2.2 Honours degree and 240 UCAS points at A level/H grade or equivalent.

Other related opportunities

- Accountant p2
- Actuary p5
- Bank / Building Society p9
- Company Secretary p11
- Financial Advisor p18
- Insurance p21
- Stockbroker p31

Advantages/disadvantages

- Accountancy training takes about 3 years after university and involves taking exams and studying, often in your own time.
- Pay is good and external auditors visit other companies and meet new people.
- There are opportunities for management and consultancy work.

Earnings guide

- As a graduate starting training you could earn £14,000–£25,000 per year.
- This could rise to £29,000–£45,000 a year when you are first qualified.
- A senior manager can earn up to £120,000.
- Salaries can be up to 20% higher in London.

Further information

Association of Chartered Certified Accountants
29 Lincoln's Inn Fields
London
WC2A 3EE
020 7396 5800
www.acca.co.uk
info@accaglobal.com

Institute of Chartered Accountants of Scotland
CA House
21 Haymarket Yards
Edinburgh
EH12 5BH
0131 347 0100
www.icas.org.uk
enquiries@icas.org.uk

Chartered Institute of Management Accountants
26 Chapter Street
London
SW1P 4NP
020 8849 2251
www.cimaglobal.com
cima.contact@cimaglobal.com

Institute of Internal Auditors – UK and Ireland Ltd
13 Abbeville Mews
88 Clapham Park Road
London
SW4 7BX
020 7498 0101
www.iia.org.uk
studentsupport@iia.org.uk

Bank / Building Society

What the work involves

Cashier/Customer Adviser

- You will be the first point of contact for the bank or building society, providing a service direct to customers.
- You may be working in a branch dealing with customers face to face, or you could be in a contact centre dealing with them over the phone or by email.
- You will be dealing with customers' accounts, paying in and withdrawing money using computerised systems and answering queries. You will be expected to sell the company's products and services so will need a good knowledge of what is available and may have to work to targets.

Manager

- As a manager you will be responsible for running one large branch or you could be in charge of several smaller branches.
- With responsibility for organising and motivating your staff, you will have to meet targets for selling the different products and services such as loans and mortgages.
- You will need to keep up to date with a range of financial products and market your services to individuals and businesses.
- Attending meetings and preparing reports on the work of the branch for both staff and head office will also be important tasks.

The type of person suited to this work

Assistant

You will need excellent customer service skills as you will be working with the public and gaining their trust in order to sell them a range of financial products. You should be confident working with figures and ICT and working to targets. As you are dealing with money, you should be trustworthy and able to work accurately, paying attention to detail.

Manager

As a manager, you will need to be able to motivate and lead a team, take responsibility and work with people at all levels. You should be able to negotiate with people and be able to solve problems and maximise profits. You will be expected to make decisions and cope with an industry which is changing and evolving rapidly.

Working conditions

In a branch you will probably work office hours and also cover weekends. You should be well presented and may wear a uniform.

In call centres you will probably work shifts, offering a 24 hour service.

As a manager you may be based in one branch or cover several in a region and may visit clients' businesses. You will be expected to dress formally. If you manage a call centre, you could be based out of town and required to work shifts.

The future outlook

Because there are so many different products available, as a bank or building society customer adviser you could specialise in a particular area such as mortgages and from there progress to trainee manager. You would have to meet your sales targets and probably get professional qualifications whilst you work, and could go on to manage your own branch.

As telephone and internet banking increases, local branches are closing so there are now fewer opportunities for dealing face to face with the public, but there is a shortage of applicants to work within regional call centres. This means that although the more traditional jobs have reduced, other newer ones are replacing them.

Although some banks have merged recently, there are still management jobs available although competition is stiff and managers, rather than being based in one branch, are more likely to be in charge of several within a region. You will probably have to move to gain promotion.

As a manager, you could go on to work in the company's head office and use your skills and experience to specialise in an area like training, human resources or marketing.

The UK, particularly London, is one of the leading financial centres in the world and the Bank of England plays a vital role in the country's economy, so there are opportunities for very high-level careers.

Banks and building societies operate across the world whilst investment and merchant banks offer services to national and international businesses, so there are opportunities to work abroad.

Qualifications and courses

Assistant

- To enter and train in this career you need a minimum of 4 GCSEs/S grades (A–C/1–3), including English and maths.
- You could start on an Apprenticeship/ Skillseekers. You would get NVQs/SVQs at Levels 2, 3 and 4 in Providing Financial Services (Banks and Building Societies). You could also take modules from the Institute of Financial Services (IFS) or the Chartered Institute of Bankers in Scotland (CIOBS). The IFS/CIOBS Associateship course would lead to promotion. In England and Wales this includes a BSc Honours degree awarded in partnership with the University of Manchester.

Manager

- You can enter this career with qualifications at Levels 2 or 3 but many people go in with a degree (normally second-class or higher) or equivalent qualification. If you start work with A levels/H grades or equivalent you would progress by taking professional qualifications. You would probably need IFS/CIOBS Associate qualifications or the IFS Diploma in Financial Services Management.
- From university, you will probably need a 2.2 or 2.1 Honours degree. A relevant subject, such as maths, business studies, economics or accountancy, is often preferred. Management training schemes for graduates usually take 18–24 months.
- You would work towards Associateship of the Chartered Institute of Bankers (CIB) including the BSc Honours degree from the University of Manchester or to Associateship of CIOBS. You may have to take extra qualifications to meet the Financial Services Authority (FSA) requirements.
- Also available are NVQs/SVQs at Levels 2, 3 and 4 in Providing Financial Services (Banks and Building Societies).

entry level

To both enter and train while working in this career, you will need qualifications at Level 2–3. Please refer to explanation on page vii.

Other related opportunities

Advantages/disadvantages

- There are lots of opportunities in this challenging, fast-moving industry which has changed dramatically in recent years with the huge growth in telephone and internet banking and organisations such as supermarkets offering banking services.
- You will need to meet challenging targets in an increasingly competitive market which can be affected by changes in the national and global economy.
- Within investment and merchant banking you can earn extremely high salaries.

Earnings guide

Assistant

- Customer Advisers starting out can expect to earn £11,500–£14,000 per year.
- As a senior cashier you can earn up to £25,000, depending on your role and where you work.
- You may get bonuses for meeting your targets and will probably get cheaper mortgages, pensions, loans and insurance.

Manager

- Bank managers on training schemes can get £20,000–£25,000.
- With experience and after qualifications this increases to £30,000–£43,000. Senior staff can earn salaries of £50,000–£100,000.
- Salaries vary and you may get bonuses for meeting targets. You will probably get cheaper mortgages, pensions, loans and insurance.
- Merchant and investment bankers can earn higher salaries.

Further information

City&Guilds

www.cityandguilds.com/myperfectjob

ifs School of Finance (previously the Chartered Institute of Bankers & Institute of Financial Services)
ifs House
4–9 Burgate Lane
Canterbury
Kent
CT1 2XJ
01227 762600
www.ifslearning.ac.uk
customerservice@ifslearning.ac.uk

Chartered Institute of Bankers in Scotland
Drumsheugh House
38b Drumsheugh Gardens
Edinburgh
EG3 7SW
0131 473 7777
www.ciobs.org.uk
info@ciobs.org.uk

British Bankers' Association
Pinners Hall
105–108 Old Broad Street
London
EC2N 1EX
020 7216 8900
www.bba.org.uk
publications@bba.org.uk

Building Societies Association
6th Floor, York House
23 Kingsway
London
WC2B 6UJ
020 7520 5900
www.bsa.org.uk

Bank of England
Threadneedle Street
London
EC2R 8AH
020 7601 4444
www.bankofengland.co.uk
enquiries@bankofengland.co.uk

Chartered / Company Secretary

What the work involves

- This is a high-level administrative and managerial job, very different from secretarial work.
- You will be in a very senior position advising executives and company directors on all areas of finance and company law.
- You will be responsible for the legal reports all companies are required to keep, making sure that they are accurate and comprehensive and reporting to Companies House and other institutions such as the Stock Exchange.
- You will be responsible for running board meetings and could be responsible for financial planning, accounts, wages, human resources and all administrative and ICT systems.

The type of person suited to this work

You will need excellent communication skills to be able to work with people at all levels, make important decisions and take responsibility. You should be interested in business and have a thorough knowledge of how your organisation works. You will need to understand complicated legal and financial issues and be able to use your knowledge to solve problems, maximise efficiency and advise directors and executives on ways of improving and developing the company.

You should be highly organised, able to deal efficiently with several tasks at once and pay close attention to detail. You will analyse figures and accounts and work to strict legal guidelines. You will be organising meetings and should be confident making presentations to high-level staff and customers.

Working conditions

Most of your work will be office-based, attending lots of meetings, including working at other sites and outside organisations which could involve some travel and possibly going abroad.

You will normally work office hours but will have a heavy workload and a lot of responsibility, so will require commitment and dedication to work overtime and meet deadlines.

To be successful, a high level of personal and professional integrity is important.

The future outlook

The Companies Act 2006 means that private companies are no longer legally required to have a Company or Chartered Secretary. Despite this change, businesses will still have to meet a range of legal requirements so most will continue to employ a Company Secretary.

An experienced Company Secretary will have opportunities to work in highly paid jobs in a range of organisations, and you could go on to specialise or could become a self-employed consultant.

entry level

To both enter and train while working in this career, you will need qualifications at Level 3–8. Please refer to explanation on page vii.

Qualifications and courses

- You will probably need a degree, Foundation degree, HNC/HND, or equivalent to enter and train in this career, but you may be able to start with lower-level qualifications.
- At least 1 A level/2 H grades or equivalent are required for entry on to HNC/HND course, whilst degree courses require 2 A levels/3 H grades and 5 GCSEs/S grades (A–C/1–3) or equivalent.
- You will probably need to become a member of the Institute of Chartered Secretaries and Administrators (ICAS), by taking their International Qualifying Scheme. This has four stages: Certificate in Business Practice, Diploma in Business Practice, and the Professional Programme Parts 1 and 2.
- There are no formal entry requirements for the ICAS Certificate; candidates can enter at the Diploma stage with a CertEd in a relevant subject, a non-relevant Foundation degree or HNC/D, or equivalent qualification; for direct entry to the Professional Programme Part 1, a degree, a relevant DipHE, Foundation degree or HNC/D, or equivalent is required; for Part 2, a relevant degree, Master's or equivalent qualification.
- To become an associate member (ACIS), you will need at least 3 years' work experience (6 if you have not got a degree).
- After at least 5 years (8 if you have not got a degree), and when you are working at a very senior level, you can become a Fellow of the Institute (FCIS).
- ICSA offer courses for extra qualifications, which can be done full or part time depending on your job and responsibilities.

Other related opportunities

- Accountant p2
- Bank / Building Society p9
- Barrister / Advocate p334
- Company Director p14
- Human Resources / Personnel Officer p20
- Auditor p8
- Stockbroker p31

Advantages/disadvantages

- This is a high-level career which is interesting, varied and challenging.
- You will use a wide range of skills and knowledge, prospects are good and earnings can be high.
- You will have to take a lot of responsibility and work long hours.
- You could have to prepare information for directors if the company is doing badly.

Earnings guide

- Graduates starting out can expect to earn anything between £21,000 and £27,000 per year.
- With some experience you can earn between £35,000 and £55,000.
- Very experienced secretaries can earn between £70,000 and £120,000.
- The highest earners can expect up to £205,500.

Further information

Institute of Chartered Secretaries and Administrators
16 Park Crescent
London
W1B 1AH
020 7580 4741
www.icsa.org.uk
info@icsa.co.uk

Council for Administration
18–20 Bromell's Road
Clapham Common
London
SW4 0BG
020 7627 9876
www.cfa.uk.com
info@cfa.uk.com

www.cityandguilds.com/myperfectjob

Clerk

What the work involves

- Clerks work for all types and sizes of organisations, dealing with paperwork and information to make sure the companies work efficiently.

General

- You will be responsible for organising efficient ways of keeping and recording information using both paper and ICT systems.
- Clerks use a range of equipment: photocopiers, email, fax machines and telephones; and also type letters and documents.
- You will probably do other administrative tasks, such as dealing with post and covering the reception or switchboard.

Payroll

- You will be working out wages including tax and National Insurance and will be responsible for making sure staff are paid the right amount.
- You might keep staff records and issue P45 forms to people who leave the company, and work out overtime and holiday, maternity or sick pay.
- Your job will also include other general administrative and clerical tasks, and will involve using a range of ICT packages.

Health Records

- You will work in a hospital or health centre and will be responsible for organising patient records, making sure that they are accurate and up to date.
- You may also book appointments and deal with test results and letters.

The type of person suited to this work

Clerical staff are vital to helping organisations run efficiently, they keep information systems up to date and well organised so that all staff can find what they need. To be a good clerk you will need a thorough knowledge of how your organisation works and should be organised and methodical and able to work accurately and to deadlines whilst paying attention to detail.

You will need good communication skills, written and verbal, and may work as part of a team so should be able to get on with others and be able to follow instructions. In smaller organisations you could be working alone so will need to be self motivated and able to use your initiative and prioritise your own work.

You may be dealing with the public either face to face or over the phone so should be able to remain polite and calm.

You should enjoy working with computers and other office equipment and be able to concentrate on work which could be quite repetitive.

Payroll
As a payroll clerk you will be working with figures so should be confident with numbers and able to keep accurate and detailed records.

Health Records
You will be dealing with confidential information and with patients who could be distressed or angry so will need to be discreet, calm and polite.

You will need to be well organised and efficient and enjoy using databases and other ICT packages.

Working conditions

Offices vary from huge, modern, open-plan buildings to small companies employing only a few staff.

You may work as part of a team or on your own and could be dealing with the public either face to face or over the telephone.

As a payroll clerk you will probably be part of a finance team and could have to work extra hours at busy times.

As a health records clerk you will be based in a hospital or health centre and may have to work shifts and bank holidays.

The future outlook

General

There has been a reduction in the number of clerical jobs available as more sophisticated ICT systems now do some clerical tasks more quickly and efficiently. However, because most organisations employ clerks there are still a lot of opportunities, especially for people with good ICT skills. There are opportunities in all areas of the country in every kind of organisation and business. As a clerk, you could work within local government, the civil service, health service, banks, factories or schools.

You can take a range of qualifications whilst you work and can progress to be a supervisor or office manager or become a personal assistant. A lot of jobs look for clerical experience so you could move into other areas like human resources or marketing.

Payroll

Many organisations employ payroll clerks or you could work for a specialist company, usually called a payroll bureau, which provides payroll services to companies which do not have their own payroll department.

With experience and by taking extra qualifications whilst you work, you can get promotion within payroll departments up to supervisor or manager.

Health Service

You will probably work for the NHS in a hospital or large medical practice but could also work for a private hospital or voluntary organisation. You can take professional qualifications and gain promotion.

Qualifications and courses

entry level

To both enter and train while working in this career, you will need qualifications at Level 2–8. Please refer to explanation on page vii.

- You can enter and train in this career with qualifications at Levels 2 or 3.

General

- There are no minimum requirements but you may need GCSEs/S grades at A–C/1–3 in English language and maths, or NVQs/SVQs in Administration at Levels 1 and 2. A BTEC First or National Diploma in Business may also be useful. There are suitable qualifications offered by Pitman, OCR or the London Chamber of Commerce and Industry Examinations Board that may be useful.
- On an Apprenticeship/Skillseekers you would get NVQs/SVQs at Levels 2, 3 and possibly 4.
- You may get day release or have to study in your own time at a local college to get qualifications in typing, word processing and ICT.
- NVQs/SVQs at Levels 3 and 4 could lead to supervisory or management jobs.

Payroll

- There are no minimum entry requirements but you may need GCSEs/S grades at A–C/1–3, in English language and maths, or NVQs/SVQs in Administration at Levels 1 and 2.
- On an Apprenticeship/Skillseekers you would get NVQs/SVQs at Levels 2, 3 and possibly 4.
- You could train on the job to get qualifications such as NVQs/SVQs in Payroll Administration at Levels 2 and 3 leading to Affiliate of the Association of Accounting Technicians (AAT).
- The Foundation in Payroll Administration from the Institute of Payroll and Pensions Management (IPPM) is equivalent to NVQ/SVQ Level 3.
- You could get higher qualifications from IPPM: Supervision and Team Leading Certificates in Payroll or Pensions or Diplomas in Local Government Pensions Management or Payroll Management.

Other related opportunities

- Accounting Technician p4
- Administrator p6
- Barrister's Clerk p333
- Personal Assistant p24
- Receptionist p25

Advantages/disadvantages

- Most businesses and organisations employ clerical staff so there are plenty of opportunities in all areas and you can choose to work in a large multinational company, a small local business or in local government or the health service.
- Office experience can help you get promotion or move into specialist areas like sales, marketing or human resources. Health records and payroll clerks can take professional qualifications.
- The work can be repetitive and you will probably be doing the same tasks each day.

Earnings guide

- Salaries vary depending on the company and are higher in the south-east of England.

General

- Starting salaries are around £13,000 per year, increasing to around £24,000 with experience. Senior staff can earn over £25,000.

Payroll

- Starting salaries are around £12,000–£14,000, going up to around £16,000 with experience.
- A senior payroll clerk could earn up to £25,000.

Health Records

- Starting salaries are around £11,500–£12,500 increasing to around £17,000 with experience, while senior staff can earn up to £25,000.

Further information

Pitman Training Group
Head Office UK
Sandown House, Sandbeck Way
Wetherby
West Yorkshire
LS22 7DN
01223 553 998
www.pitman-training.com

OCR
1 Hills Road
Cambridge
CB1 2EU
01223 553311
www.ocr.org.uk
general.qualifications@ocr.org.uk

London Chamber of Commerce and Industry
33 Queen Street
London
EC4R 1AP
020 7248 4444
www.londonchamber.co.uk
lc@londonchamber.co.uk

www.cityandguilds.com/myperfectjob

Company Director

What the work involves

- As company director you will have responsibility for every aspect of your business. You will need a thorough knowledge of its products and services and must ensure that it achieves its aims as efficiently as possible and continues to grow and develop.
- You might own the company or head a board of directors. In a large company you will probably lead a team of managers who specialise in specific areas such as sales, finance or product development but you will have overall responsibility.
- You will oversee all areas – staff, finances, products, services and future developments.
- Company directors have to lead and motivate staff and managers, helping them to develop their skills and use them in the best way to help the company succeed and grow.

The type of person suited to this work

You will need to be extremely focused, dedicated and tough, with clear aims and objectives and practical and efficient ideas for achieving them.

The ability to analyse problems, find solutions, make decisions and think through their long-term effects is vital. You will need excellent communication skills to motivate staff and help sell your ideas, products and services to your customers and investors.

You should be highly organised, motivated and prepared to work long hours, be able to prioritise and work to deadlines, supervise others, take advice and respond to changes and developments.

An excellent knowledge and understanding of your business and its markets will be necessary to make your company successful, and you will need to understand and apply financial information and be able to use ICT systems effectively.

Working conditions

You will probably be office-based but attend a lot of meetings with customers, potential customers, financial and legal advisers, managers and staff. You should be prepared to work long hours and to travel in this country and abroad.

Being a successful company director can be extremely demanding and stressful. Although you will probably be advised by a team of experienced and knowledgeable managers, you will make the final decision and must be prepared to take risks and accept consequences.

The future outlook

There is no set route to becoming a director. You might train in a profession such as engineering or catering and then progress into management and could end up running a company.

Alternatively, you could get business qualifications and work your way up in a career such as banking or manufacturing. Once you are at manager level, you can take professional courses to develop your skills and become a member of the Institute of Directors.

You could use your professional skills or an interest like adventure holidays to start up your own business or offer a consultancy service.

If you are successful, there is no limit to what you can achieve.

Qualifications and courses

- There is no set route to becoming a company director, but you will usually need to acquire experience at senior management level. Possible entry routes are listed below.
- You could enter the company at any level and with qualifications and work experience progress up to management-level jobs and then to director.
- You could start on a management trainee scheme after taking Level 3 qualifications, but probably after doing a degree. The degree could be in a specialist subject related to the company's business such as engineering, or you could do a business-related degree.
- On a management training scheme, you could learn general management skills or specialise in a particular field such as sales or marketing.
- You will do in-house training, learning about the company to develop your management skills.
- The Chartered Management Institute (CMI) and the Institute of Administrative Management (IAM) offer courses for the professional development of managers, or you may be able to take them through the lead body or professional institute related to your business.
- Once you have got management experience you could take a Master's degree in Business Administration (MBA).

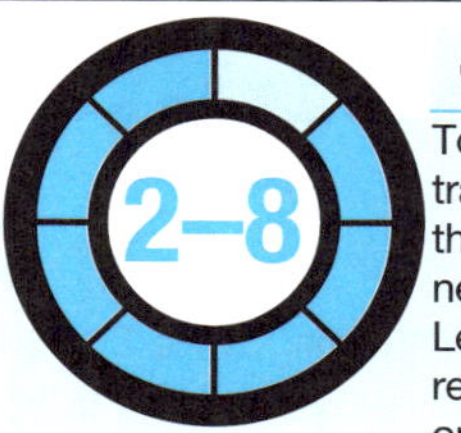

entry level

To both enter and train while working in this career, you will need qualifications at Level 2–8. Please refer to explanation on page vii.

- You may be able to do NVQs/SVQs in Management at Levels 3 and 4 either on a management training scheme or through an Apprenticeship/Skillseekers.
- Level 5 NVQs/SVQs are available in specialist areas including Operational Management.
- You could also study for a Foundation degree in Business Management/Development.

Other related opportunities

- Accountant p2
- Barrister / Advocate p334
- Chartered or Company Secretary p11
- Financial Adviser p18
- Management Consultant p349

Advantages/disadvantages

- You can get enormous rewards and satisfaction from seeing the company grow and succeed.
- You could start your own business based on a personal interest or skill.
- You will have huge responsibility and need to be dedicated, hard working and able to cope with failure as well as success.

Earnings guide

- Earnings for company directors will vary enormously depending on the size and success of the business.
- As a trainee manager you may start at around £20,000 a year.
- With a year or two of experience and qualifications this can rise to around £36,000+.
- Directors of large private companies can earn between £60,000 and £180,000 – more in London.
- The sky's the limit! As director of a large company, you could earn as much as £1,500,000 plus huge bonuses, or as the owner of your own company you could become extremely rich.

Further information

Chartered Management Institute
Management House
Cottingham Road
Corby
Northamptonshire
NN17 1TT
01536 204222
www.managers.org.uk
enquiries@managers.org.uk

Institute of Administrative Management
6 Graphite Square
Vauxhall Walk
London
SE11 5EE
020 7091 2600
www.instam.org
info@instam.org

Business Link
0845 600 9 006
www.businesslink.gov.uk

Institute of Directors
116 Pall Mall
London
SW1Y 5ED
020 7839 1233
www.iod.com

www.cityandguilds.com/myperfectjob

Consultant

What the work involves

- You will work with organisations and companies helping them to develop and improve their efficiency, services, products or staffing
- This might involve observing and evaluating working practices, researching information, training staff or developing new ways of operating.
- You will need extensive knowledge of the sector you are working within.
- Consultants can work for a private consultancy organisation, be members of a specialised team or be freelance/self-employed.

entry level

To both enter and train while working in this career, you will need qualifications at Level 4–8. Please refer to explanation on page vii.

The type of person suited to this work

You will need to be dynamic, confident and self motivated. You will need to be able to research information, talk to staff and develop a thorough knowledge of an organisation. You will need to be able to identify problems and devise creative solutions and possibly develop training programmes.

You will need excellent communication skills for writing reports, dealing with staff and presenting your findings.

You may have to review budgets and make savings and your decisions might result in redundancies or spending cuts so you will need to have good financial skills and be able to justify your decisions and cope with criticism.

Working conditions

You will spend a lot of time visiting the companies you are advising, so will probably have to travel and spend time away from home.

The work can be pressured and stressful as you will be working to deadlines and taking responsibility for high-level decisions which could have far-reaching consequences.

You could be self-employed, work for a private consultancy service or be part of a team of company improvement specialists.

The future outlook

The consultancy market in this country has grown to become the largest in Europe as many private and government organisations have reduced costs by cutting management staff and employing consultants for specific tasks. There are opportunities in all areas and types of organisation but competition is intense.

To succeed you will need to deliver an excellent service, build a reputation and be able to secure new contracts and work to deadlines.

Qualifications and courses

- Entry to this profession generally requires an Honours degree (minimum 2.1). Any subject is usually acceptable, but if you have a degree in business, management, maths, economics or a related area, this can be an advantage. Typical minimum entry requirements for a degree are 2 A levels/3 H grades and 5 GCSEs/S grades (A–C/1–3).
- A postgraduate qualification, such as an MBA (Master's of Business Administration), can be an advantage; entry usually requires a good first degree, and substantial work experience may also be required.
- Mature entry may also be possible through relevant work experience in management or a related area. Some entrants have an accountancy qualification with one of the main accountancy firms.
- Entrants usually receive training on the job, which may include the chance to study for an employer-sponsored MBA. The Institute of Management Consultancy (IMC) offers professional training courses, including a Diploma in Management Consultancy and the Certified Management Consultant (CMC) award. For the latter, candidates need to be Associate Members of the IMC with appropriate qualifications and at least 3 years' experience as a management consultant.

CRCI:AA

CLCI:COD

Other related opportunities

- Company Director p14
- Equal Opportunities / Equalities Officer p17
- Financial Adviser p18
- Human Resources / Personnel Officer p20
- Lecturer p178

Advantages/disadvantages

- This is a rewarding, varied and interesting career with lots of opportunities.
- You can earn a lot of money and may be able to travel.
- The work can be stressful and demanding.
- Hours can be long and unpredictable.

Earnings guide

- If you are freelance or self-employed you will probably be paid per day and your earnings will depend on your success.
- An experienced consultant could earn up to about £50,000.
- Senior consultants can earn over £50,000 and you may get commission and bonuses.

Further information

Chartered Management
Institute Management House
Cottingham Road
Corby
Northamptonshire
NN17 1TT
01536 204222
www.managers.org.uk
enquiries@managers.org.uk

Management Consultancies Association
Institute Management House
60 Trafalgar Square
London
WC2N 5DS
020 7321 3990
www.mca.org.uk

Equal Opportunities / Equalities Officer

What the work involves

- You will be promoting equality, ensuring businesses and public organisations do not discriminate on disability, race, gender, sexuality, age or religion.
- You will make sure that services such as education and health are accessible to everyone.
- You will promote positive images of all groups – including disabled people, men and women and those from different ethnic backgrounds.
- You will advise on how to attract job applicants from all sections of the local community and ensure the company is following all the relevant legislation.
- You will organise special projects and events aimed at different groups.

The type of person suited to this work

You should feel strongly about equal opportunities for all and be committed to working for change. You should be able to identify problems and find creative solutions. You will need to be sensitive and tactful and good at negotiating and arguing your case.

You will need excellent communication skills and should be confident in making presentations, advising management and delivering training.

You will need to be able to understand all the relevant equal opportunities laws and regulations and be able to apply them to all policies and procedures within the company, and offer advice on any new developments and how to implement them.

For some jobs you may need specialist skills like being able to speak an ethnic minority language.

Working conditions

Much of your time will be office-based doing normal office hours. However, you will probably do quite a bit of evening and weekend work too; organising special events and working with community groups.

You could be visiting businesses and organisations, so a driving licence may be useful.

The future outlook

Opportunities are increasing but competition is strong. Government departments, local authorities and large companies employ specialist equal opportunities advisers. In smaller companies the work is covered by the human resources department.

You could progress into management and will develop specialist knowledge and experience, so you could work for yourself offering a consultancy service to companies who want to ensure they are working within equal opportunities legislation.

Lots of public services are focusing upon delivering services to asylum seekers and immigrants. This means many organisations are employing officers to work specifically with these minority groups.

entry level

2–3

To both enter and train while working in this career, you will need qualifications at Level 2–3. Please refer to explanation on page vii.

Qualifications and courses

- It is possible to enter this career with qualifications at Levels 2 or 3, but most people have a degree, HND or equivalent, and you will need relevant experience. A background in community work may also be useful.
- There are no formal entry requirements but a professional qualification would be useful. The most likely route is through experience working in law, human resources, social work or teaching. Many equal opportunities advisers have degrees and are members of the Chartered Institute of Personnel and Development (CIPD).
- Degrees and HNDs in education, business administration and law are all relevant to this career.
- Relevant postgraduate courses include race relations or disability studies. For postgraduate studies, applicants must have a first degree.
- The CIPD offer short courses for further study, including Discrimination and the Law, and The Psychology of Diversity. These courses are open to people who are working in a relevant environment.
- A number of short courses are run by colleges and training centres. These include Equal Opportunities (Good Practice), Equal Opportunities (Legislation) and Ensuring Equal Opportunities in the Workplace.

Other related opportunities

- Advice Centre / Benefits Adviser p524
- Connexions Personal Adviser p539
- Human Resources / Personnel Officer p20
- Mobility Officer – Visually Impaired p537
- Training Officer p33

Advantages/disadvantages

- You will be working for a cause you feel passionately about and could be making a real difference to people.
- It can be a varied, interesting job.
- The work can be stressful – you will be dealing with sensitive issues and may be working with people who do not share your beliefs or want to change.

Earnings guide

- Starting salaries are around £18,000+ per year.
- With experience you can expect up to £26,000.
- Those in senior positions in large companies can earn over £50,000.

Further information

Equality & Human Rights Commission
Arndale House
Arndale Centre
Manchester
M4 3AQ
0161 829 8100
www.equalityhumanrights.com
info@equalityhumanrights.com
(Incorporates Equal Opportunities Commission, Commission for Racial Equality and Disability Rights Commission)

Equality Commission for Northern Ireland
Equality House
7–9 Shaftesbury Square
Belfast
BT2 7DP
028 9050 0600
www.equalityni.org
information@equalityni.org

Financial Adviser

What the work involves

- You will be advising clients on a wide range of financial issues including mortgages, pensions and investments.
- Tied advisers work for a financial institution, like a bank, advising clients on their services.
- Independent advisers sell products and services from a range of companies.
- You will need to be able to understand financial matters such as investments, insurance, mortgages and pensions.
- Your work will also involve finding out about your clients' finances and advising them on areas such as investing their savings, buying a house or planning for retirement.

The type of person suited to this work

You will need to enjoy working with figures and be confident with numbers. You will need to be able to analyse and understand complicated financial information and be able to explain things clearly and simply to your clients, helping them to choose the best product and plan for their future.

You will also need an understanding of the relevant laws and to keep up with changes in the industry.

You will need to be honest and reliable, with excellent communication skills and able to gain the trust of your clients and to sell your products. You will need good written English for writing reports.

You will also need to be self-motivated and organised with good ICT skills.

Working conditions

You will probably be office-based but might also work from home. You will work office hours but must be prepared to work longer at busy times.

Tied advisers usually work some Saturdays, and independent advisers may have to work evenings and weekends to suit their clients.

You will be expected to dress formally and to visit clients in their homes or offices so you will probably have to be able to drive and be prepared to stay away from home.

The future outlook

The financial sector is growing and becoming more complicated and as people change jobs more frequently, they increasingly have to organise their own pensions and finances. This means that demand for financial help and advice is increasing.

Financial advisers work in insurance, banks and other businesses and many are self-employed. Although jobs are available throughout the UK, many are based within the south-east of England and London as they are closest to the financial centre of the country.

Promotion prospects are good and you can take extra qualifications and move into management jobs. You could also specialise in a particular area, perhaps training others or marketing products.

entry level

3–8

To both enter and train while working in this career, you will need qualifications at Level 3–8. Please refer to explanation on page vii.

Qualifications and courses

- Entrants to this career have a range of qualifications. There are no specific entry routes, and requirements depend on the employer. 2 A levels/3 H grades and 5 GCSEs/S grades (A–C/1–3), including English and maths, or equivalent, are the normal minimum requirements sought by employers. Communication and personal skills are also essential.
- Trainee financial advisers may be graduates in business-related subjects. They may have undertaken work-related training at a college, or have completed an Apprenticeship/Skillseekers opportunity.
- Training is done on the job, with theoretical study undertaken part time or through distance or online learning. Training must be regulated by the FSA. Qualified financial advisers usually hold a Financial Planning Certificate (awarded by the Chartered Insurance Institute) or a Certificate for Financial Advisers (awarded by the Institute of Financial Services). In Scotland, the relevant qualifying body is the Chartered Institute of Bankers in Scotland (CIOBS). Advisors will normally take exams, awarded by one of these bodies, before being allowed to advise clients.
- The Chartered Insurance Institute, Chartered Institute of Bankers in Scotland and Institute of Financial Services also offer more specialised qualifications for financial advisers, for example the Certificate in Mortgage Advice and Practice.

CRCI:IF

CLCI:NAK

Other related opportunities

- Accountant p2
- Actuary p5
- Auditor p8
- Bank / Building Society p9
- Stockbroker p31

Advantages/disadvantages

- Pay and prospects are good, you can gain professional qualifications and become self-employed.
- The work is varied and you will be meeting new people.
- It is a highly responsible job and you will be under pressure to sell products and meet targets.
- You may work unsocial hours.

Earnings guide

- Salaries are often based on performance and meeting targets, so the rates vary between companies. Most financial consults work either on a fee or commission basis.
- Starting as a trainee you could earn £18,000–£25,000 per year.
- Salaries of £40,000–£50,000 are possible if you are experienced and meeting targets.
- For the most successful advisers, a salary of £80,000–£100,000+ is possible if they are experienced in performance records and hitting sales targets.

Further information

Financial Services Skills Council
51 Gresham Street
London
EC2V 7HQ
0845 257 3772
www.fssc.org.uk
info@fssc.org.uk

Personal Finance Society
42–48 High Road
South Woodford
London
E18 2JP
020 8530 0852
www.thepfs.org
customer.serv@thepfs.org

Chartered Insurance Institute
42–48 High Road
South Woodford
London
E18 2JP
020 8989 8464
www.cii.co.uk
customer.serv@cii.co.uk

ifs School of Finance (previously the Chartered Institute of Bankers & Institute of Financial Services)
ifs House
4–9 Burgate Lane
Canterbury
Kent
CT1 2XJ
01227 762600
www.ifslearning.ac.uk
customerservice@ifslearning.ac.uk

Health and Safety Adviser

What the work involves

- You will help maintain a safe workplace by developing and implementing health and safety policies and procedures.
- You will inspect premises and ways of working and ensure all relevant laws and regulations are followed.
- The work involves investigating and reporting on accidents and giving specialist advice and training to staff and managers on health and safety issues like fire regulations and dealing with dangerous chemicals.

entry level

2–8

To both enter and train while working in this career, you will need qualifications at Level 2–8. Please refer to explanation on page vii.

The type of person suited to this work

You should be interested in health and safety and be able to research a company thoroughly, understand the work and think of ways of improving and ensuring safety.

In industries like engineering you will need to understand technical processes and be able to explain your findings and recommendations simply and clearly, verbally and in writing.

You should be thorough, methodical and able to understand and apply relevant laws and regulations. Because you will be giving presentations and working with people, good communication skills are vital.

You will also need good ICT and administrative skills and need to be reasonably fit for working safely on large outdoor and industrial sites.

Working conditions

You will be office based but depending on where you work, may have to spend a lot of time visiting factories, oil rigs and building sites. This could mean having to wear protective clothing, working outdoors in all weathers and at heights or in hot, noisy conditions.

You will do normal office hours but many need to be on call at other times in case of emergencies.

The future outlook

Every year thousands of people are injured, and sometimes killed, while at work in the UK. To help reduce these figures, the government and European Union are producing more regulations and guidelines to help companies ensure a safe working environment for staff. This means that opportunities for health and safety advisers are increasing as employers need help implementing and monitoring new legislation.

Many health and safety advisers work in engineering, construction and manufacturing, there are also opportunities in other industries or large organisations like hotels, hospitals or government departments or with the Health and Safety Executive.

Qualifications and courses

- Entry to this career normally requires an industry-recognised qualification, which can be a degree, diploma, or equivalent professional qualification. It is possible to gain experience first or alongside taking qualifications, for example at an operational level, such as in a scientific or technical field.
- There is no specific entry route. Health and safety advisers are normally corporate members of the Institute of Occupational Safety and Health (IOSH).
- The main professional qualifications are the newly revised National Diploma awarded by the National Examining Board in Occupational Safety and Health (NEBOSH), and the NVQ/SVQ Level 4 in Occupational Health and Safety Practice. Candidates with the NEBOSH Diploma or NVQ/SVQ Level 4, and 3 years' relevant experience, are eligible for corporate membership of IOSH.
- Entry to the NEBOSH Diploma requires an approved qualification in health and safety accredited at Level 3 or above. Evidence of relevant work experience may also be needed.
- Some universities and colleges offer degrees, diplomas and postgraduate courses in occupational health and safety or health and safety management accredited by the Institute of Occupational Safety and Health. With an accredited degree and 3 years' relevant experience you could become a corporate member of IOSH.

CRCI:AA

CLCI:COT

Other related opportunities

- Environmental Health Practitioner / Officer p280
- Human Resources / Personnel Officer p20
- Road Safety Officer p583
- Trading Standards Officer p460

Advantages/disadvantages

- The work can be varied and you could be out and about visiting different sites and meeting people.
- You will be dealing with important issues that affect people's safety and well-being, so there is a lot of responsibility.
- You will help to save people's lives.

Earnings guide

- Salaries vary for this work, depending on the company you work for and your location.
- Starting salaries can range from £20,000 to £22,000 per year.
- With experience salaries can increase to around £27,000.
- You could earn over £40,000 per year, if you are experienced and working for a high-risk industry such as construction or an oil or gas company.

Further information

Institute of Occupational Safety & Health
The Grange
Highfield Drive
Wigston
Leicestershire
LE18 1NN
0116 257 3100
www.iosh.co.uk

Health & Safety Executive
Rose Court
2 Southwark Bridge
London
SE1 9HS
www.hse.gov.uk
hse.infoline@natbrit.com

British Safety Council
70 Chancellors Road
London
W6 9RS
020 8741 1231
www.britishsafetycouncil.co.uk
mail@britsafe.org

www.cityandguilds.com/myperfectjob

Human Resources / Personnel Officer

What the work involves

- Human resources officers are responsible for all aspects of their company's work force.
- You will be responsible for recruiting the right staff for jobs at all levels and helping them get the training and development that they and the company need.
- You will be involved with negotiations between staff and trade unions on issues such as pay and conditions. You will also be involved with discipline, complaints and redundancy.

The type of person suited to this work

You will work with people at all levels and will deal with personal information and with staff who could be angry or upset so will need excellent communication skills.

You should be interested in people and able to solve problems and help with negotiations between staff and managers over issues like pay and conditions.

You may be involved with disciplinary procedures and redundancies which can be very stressful and you will need to be tactful and diplomatic.

You will have to understand and implement employment legislation, may manage a budget and will also need to write clear and accurate reports and be organised and methodical and able to work under pressure.

Working conditions

Much of your work will be office-based, working normal office hours, 9–5.30, Monday to Friday, but you may need to work extra time at busy periods. You will visit the different locations and sites of your organisation so that people get to know and trust you, which could also involve being outdoors or in noisy, dirty places.

You will probably be working as part of a human resources team so you should enjoy working with others.

The future outlook

There are plenty of opportunities as all types of businesses employ HR staff but it's a popular, competitive career so work experience is vital. Many HR officers have a degree but you could work your way up from an administrative role.

You may get more responsibility in a small company but have better prospects in a larger one. You will need to take professional qualifications and could work abroad or become a self-employed consultant.

entry level

To both enter and train while working in this career, you will need qualifications at Level 3–8. Please refer to explanation on page vii.

Qualifications and courses

- There are no minimum entry requirements for this career, but most human resources officers have a degree or postgraduate qualification. Relevant subjects include business studies, human resource management, management, social administration and psychology.
- Employers are likely to ask school leavers for 5 GCSEs/S grades (A–C/1–3), including English and maths, and some A levels/H grades.
- Personnel assistants or administrators can take the Chartered Institute of Personnel and Development's Certificate in Personnel Practice (CPP) or Certificate in Recruitment and Selection (CRS), usually part time at college. The CIPD also offers NVQ/SVQ Level 3 in Personnel Support, a work-based equivalent to the CPP. Either route makes you eligible for Associate membership of the CIPD.
- With a degree or HND you train on the job, usually taking CIPD professional qualifications. Some degrees and postgraduate qualifications give exemptions from parts of the Professional Development Scheme (PDS). The PDS has four parts: Core Management, People Management and Development, Specialist and Generalist Personnel and Development, and Applied Personnel and Development. Part 1 leads to licentiate membership of the CIPD, and completion of all four leads to graduate membership. Graduates may also need to do the CPP. The CIPD offers NVQ/SVQ Levels 4 and 5 as a work-based alternative to the PDS.
- Some companies offer a graduate training scheme.

CRCI:AA

CLCI:CAS

Other related opportunities

- Careers Adviser p526
- Personal Adviser – Connexions p539
- Recruitment Agency Consultant p27
- Store Manager p459
- Training Officer p33

Advantages/disadvantages

- This is a rewarding career if you are interested in people and helping them to develop their skills.
- You can study for professional qualifications and gain promotion.
- You will be involved in solving disputes between staff and the organisation which can be stressful.
- You may have to sack staff or make them redundant.

Earnings guide

- Salaries start at around £22,000–£25,000 per year.
- Once qualified and with experience, around £40,000 is possible.
- Senior staff and HR Managers can earn over £55,000 a year.

Further information

www.cityandguilds.com/myperfectjob

Chartered Institute of Personnel and Development
CIPD House
151 The Broadway
London
SW19 1JQ
020 8612 6200
www.cipd.co.uk

ENTO
Kimberley House
47 Vaughan Way
Leicester
LE1 4SG
0116 251 7979
www.ento.co.uk
info@ento.co.uk

Insurance

What the work involves

- Insurance is used to protect companies and individuals against illness or death, or loss or damage to belongings.

Broker

- You will advise individuals and companies on the content and cover of insurance policies. You will find out what they need and research the best options to meet their needs. For large risks, you might use more than one company.
- You will be researching policies, negotiating deals, selling products and advising on claims.

Underwriter

- You will be assessing the size of risks to work out how much a policy should cost. The price should be high enough to cover any claims but low enough for customers to be able to afford to buy.
- For standard risks you will use standard rates. In complicated cases you will use your knowledge and skills to gauge the risks and costs involved to set a price.

Claims settler

- You will be dealing with the claims made on customers' insurance policies, checking the details and evidence of what has happened so that you can work out how much to pay.
- Part of your work will be arranging for money to be paid to customers and in more complicated cases, doing some of the research.

Loss adjuster

- You will work for insurance companies as an independent specialist, investigating and advising on large or complicated claims or where there is a dispute.
- During your work you will visit premises, check damage and inspect reports from specialists such as the fire service or police force.
- On completing your research, you will recommend the size of payments and offer advice to both sides.

The type of person suited to this work

All insurance work involves communicating and listening to people. Insurance claims are made following things like acts of burglary, fire or accidents, so you will have to listen and be sympathetic but fair to both the insurance company and the customers. This can be stressful work, you will have to analyse complicated information and work to targets.

Broker

To make sure you sell the correct policy you will need excellent verbal and written communication skills. You will need to obtain the right information, negotiate and sell policies and explain complicated financial issues clearly and simply. It is important that you are comfortable working with numbers, very honest and reliable.

Underwriter

This is a specialised job that requires an in-depth knowledge of risk. You will have to pay close attention to detail and be able to use your knowledge and experience to solve very complex problems and write accurate and detailed reports. You should be able to research information and use your knowledge to make predictions, think through situations logically and solve problems.

Claims settler

You will need ICT skills and to be able to work accurately and to deadlines. During your work you are likely to deal with people who are very distressed and angry, so this work can be stressful. You will need to have excellent communication skills, be patient, organised and able to explain complicated procedures simply and clearly.

Loss adjuster

Part of your job will be solving disputes between organisations and/or individuals. To do this job it is important that you can remain calm and focused, research the facts and make impartial decisions based on evidence. You will need excellent verbal and written communication skills and to be numerate, trustworthy and able to take responsibility and deal with a range of situations.

Qualifications and courses

entry level

To both enter and train while working in this career, you will need qualifications at Level 2–8. Please refer to explanation on page vii.

- You can enter and train in this profession with qualifications at Levels 2 or 3, or with a degree, HND or equivalent.

Broker

- There are no formal entry requirements, but many organisations prefer at least 2 A levels/3 H grades and 2 GCSEs/S grades (A–C/1–3) including English and maths. It is also possible to enter with work experience in an insurance-related environment. You could have problems with getting into this work if you have a criminal conviction, especially any connected to fraud.
- Many entrants are graduates. Useful subjects include accounting, finance, business, management, economics, maths, statistics and business with languages.
- The Chartered Insurance Institute (CII) and the British Insurance Brokers' Association (BIBA) run courses in insurance broking and other relevant subjects, some of which may be linked to qualifications at NVQ/SVQ Levels 2–3. Most new entrants to this career study for the CII examinations. The CII programme consists of a Foundation Award, Certificate, Diploma and Advanced Diploma in Insurance, leading to Associate membership (ACII). Entry is available at different levels: there are no formal entry requirements for the Foundation Award or the Certificate; entry to the Diploma is available with 4 GCSEs/S grades (A–C/1–3) or equivalent, to the Advanced Diploma with 3 A levels/H grades or equivalent. Relevant degrees can give part-exemption from the CII Associateship examinations. The CII's premier qualification, the Fellowship (FCII), is available to Associate members with at least 3 years' further work experience and appropriate training and qualifications.
- Additional qualifications are offered by the Institute of Financial Services (IFS). These include: Certificate of Regulated General Insurance; Certificate in Mortgage Advice and Practice; Certificate for Financial Advisers; Certificate in Financial Services Practice. These are particularly suitable for those working or seeking to work in financial planning.
- It is possible to enter as a trainee broker technician and progress to training as a broker; entry requirements are usually 4 GCSEs/S grades (A–C/1–3) or equivalent.

  Apprenticeships/Skillseekers in insurance may also be an entry route for candidates aged 16–24.
- Brokers wishing to work for Lloyd's must pass the Lloyd's Introductory Test within 15 months of starting work.

Underwriter

- There is no standard entry route into underwriting work. Many companies ask for 2 A levels/3 H grades and 2 GCSEs/S grades (A–C/1–3), including English and maths, but individual employers tend to set their own entry qualifications. Work experience in insurance can be an advantage. Entry may be through a company training scheme or via promotion from an administrative job within insurance.
- Many entrants are graduates (a 2.1 degree or higher is the norm). Useful subjects include insurance, finance, business studies, management, economics, law and maths.
- Apprenticeships/Skillseekers programmes may be available for candidates aged 16–24.
- Relevant professional qualifications and/or training programmes are offered by the Chartered Insurance Institute (CII), the Institute of Financial Services (IFS), and the British Insurance Brokers' Association (BIBA); see above.

Claims settler

- There are no formal entry requirements to train as an insurance claims settler. However, most companies require at least 4 GCSEs/S grades (A–C/1–3) including English and maths. A degree can be an advantage, but is not always necessary. Useful degree subjects include business, finance, insurance, economics, law or maths. Good ICT skills are a distinct advantage.
- Apprenticeships/Skillseekers may be available for candidates aged 16–24.
- Claims staff can study for the Associateship examination of the CII. Entry qualifications for the Chartered Insurance Institute (CII) Associateship exams may be waived for mature candidates
- An experienced claims manager is usually responsible for on-the-job training. Claims settlers need either the CII Certificate or CII Diploma in claims

Loss adjuster

- Most loss adjustors become Associate Members of the Chartered Institute of Loss Adjustors (CILA). To take the CILA exams, you need to be an ordinary member of the CILA, have at least two years' work experience in the office of a member company, and have a relevant professional qualification, such as the Associateship of the CII (see above) or the CII Diploma in Claims. To become an ordinary member of the CILA, you need to be over 18 years of age and working for an independent loss adjusting firm or company.
- Most new entrants have a professional qualification and work experience in a relevant area, such as risk management, law, insurance or accountancy.
- For those without a professional qualification, typical entry requirements to this career include 2 A levels/3 H grades and 2 GCSEs/S grades (A–C/1–3), including English and maths, or an HNC/HND or degree in such subjects as insurance, business studies, accounting or finance, law, maths or economics.
- Entrants without a professional qualification normally start work in a support role and study for the Certificate in Claims from the Claims Faculty of the CII (formerly offered by the Society of Claims Technicians). You can then progress to the Diploma in Claims.

Working conditions

Insurance jobs are office-based but some include local and international travel. You will be attending meetings and working at a computer using software to help you calculate policies, risk or the amounts due to customers.

During your work you will spend a lot of time on the telephone and, in some jobs, meeting members of the public. You may have to work shifts in order to offer a 24-hour service.

Broker/Claims settler

You could work in a high-street location, selling policies to members of the public, or work in an office where customers ring you for quotes or progress on their claims. You will spend a lot of time visiting customers and making contacts in order to gain new clients.

Underwriter/Loss adjuster

As well as having an office you will make site visits and meet customers at work or home, viewing the damage and estimating the value for insurance companies. You could specialise in one type of product, such as car insurance, or do general underwriting. You will do a lot of work over the phone and may also have to investigate dangerous or distressing situations.

The future outlook

The insurance sector within the UK is the largest in Europe and third largest worldwide. In 2003, there were 348,000 people working within the UK insurance sector of which over 70,000 were members of the Chartered Institute of Insurance making this the largest professional insurance body. Currently the insurance industry is undergoing a period of change. This is due to new regulations, which arrived in early 2005, increasing competition for customers. Some of this is due to the impact of the newer insurance sellers, including those online and supermarkets, which have entered the insurance market. The main advice for anyone wanting to join the insurance sector is to aim to stay up to date with regulations, undergo training throughout your career and remain flexible when choosing your future promotional options.

Broker

As a broker you could work anywhere in the country. Insurance companies vary from small and independent, to large multinationals with international offices. Recent arrivals within the insurance market have been the online companies and the supermarket chains which have made competition more intense. This has meant that insurance brokers have had to offer a wider range of services, but demand is still high for people with specialist knowledge

If you work in a small firm you will probably deal with all types of insurance but in larger companies you could specialise in one area such as house or car insurance.

Underwriter

You could work in a firm offering a wide range of cover or a specialist organisation. As your career develops you could progress into larger companies where there may be opportunities to work abroad. You could apply for promotion within your own company or apply to a different one to further your career. As you progress, you will attract the more difficult and complicated cases which will offer new challenges. Although you could work in general insurance, you might enter a highly specialised area such as equine or marine insurance.

Claims settler

There are insurance companies of different sizes all over the country and as insurance claims are increasing so are the job opportunities for claims staff. You could move into supervisory or management jobs, or, with experience and by taking professional qualifications, could move into other areas of insurance.

Loss adjuster

This is a very competitive area of work but opportunities are increasing, particularly for specialists. Most loss adjusters work for several insurance companies advising on claims so they can be processed quickly.

There are opportunities all over the UK and you could be able to work abroad. With experience you could become self-employed as a consultant or specialist, or move into other areas of insurance or even fraud investigation.

Other related opportunities

- Accountant p2
- Actuary p5
- Bank / Building Society p9
- Financial Adviser p18
- Solicitor / Notary Public p349

Advantages/disadvantages

- The insurance market is growing, resulting in plenty of opportunities. You could move into management jobs or specialise in something which particularly interests you, such as marine or aviation insurance.
- Lloyd's of London specialises in major risks and their underwriters can earn extremely high salaries.
- The work can involve a lot of responsibility and stress, dealing with huge sums of money and sometimes major disasters like plane crashes.
- Insurance is a major industry within the UK and is respected worldwide. This means international opportunities will be available if you want to work abroad.

Earnings guide

Broker

- £25,000 per year is an average wage for trainees. This could increase up to £50,000 with 3 to 5 years' experience.
- You could earn £80,000+ as a senior broker.
- £100,000+ is possible for those working in the City of London.

Underwriter

- £13,000–£28,000 per year is usual for trainees. With 3 to 5 years' experience this could rise to £28,000 or around £46,000 in London.
- You could earn £45,000–£95,000 as a senior underwriter.
- Lloyd's of London underwriters can earn £300,000+.

Claims settler

- Starting salaries for trainees are around £11,000–£16,000 per year. Graduate trainees could expect up to £19,000. This rises to £18,000–£24,000+ with experience.
- You could earn £30,000–£45,000+ as a manager.

Loss adjuster

- Starting salaries are around £17,000–£21,000 per year. This rises to £29,000–£35,000 with a few years experience.
- £40,000–£80,000 is possible as a senior loss adjuster, more if you work in London.

www.cityandguilds.com/myperfectjob

Further information

Chartered Insurance Institute
42–48 High Road
South Woodford
London
E18 2JP
020 8989 8464
www.cii.co.uk
customer.serv@cii.co.uk

British Insurance Brokers Association
14 Bevis Marks
London
EC3A 7NT
0901 814 0015
www.biba.org.uk
enquiries@biba.org.uk

LOSS ADJUSTER

Chartered Institute of Loss Adjusters
Warwick House
65/66 Queen Street
London
EC4R 1EB
020 7337 9960
www.cila.co.uk
info@cila.co.uk

Association of British Insurers
51 Gresham Street
London
EC2V 7HQ
020 7600 3333
www.abi.org.uk
info@abi.org.uk

Financial Services Skills Council
51 Gresham Street
London
EC2V 7HQ
0845 257 3772
www.fssc.org.uk
info@fssc.org.uk

Financial Services Authority
25 The North Colonnade
Canary Wharf
London
E14 5HS
020 7066 1000
www.fsa.gov.uk

UNDERWRITING

International Underwriting Association
London Underwriting Centre
3 Minster Court
Mincing Lane
London
EC3R 7DD
020 7617 4444
www.iua.co.uk
info@iua.co.uk

Personal Assistant

What the work involves

- Personal Assistants work directly with one or more senior managers, helping them to be as efficient and well organised as possible.
- You will arrange appointments, make travel arrangements and type letters and reports.
- It will be your job to organise efficient administrative systems both paper- and ICT-based.
- You will probably arrange meetings, organise refreshments and take minutes as well as answering phone calls, taking messages and greeting visitors.
- You may have to deal with budgets and could be supervising other clerical staff.

The type of person suited to this work

You should be efficient and well organised, be able to deal with several things at once and work to deadlines. You will have to follow instructions but also use your initiative and prioritise your own work. You will need a good knowledge of the company you work for and may have to deal with budgets. Excellent written and verbal communication skills are vital as you will be working with people at all levels and writing minutes and reports.

You may be dealing with confidential information so should be discreet and reliable. You will need excellent ICT skills and to be accurate and pay attention to detail.

Working conditions

You will work in an office, usually doing normal office hours but may have to work longer at times to meet deadlines. You may have to go to other premises for meetings and will be expect to dress fairly formally.

Personal assistants work in all types and sizes of organisations and companies. You could be working in a very small business or a large company with smart, modern offices, or anything in between.

The future outlook

There are opportunities throughout the UK.

Being a PA can be the first step in some very competitive careers such as the media, but these types of jobs will be popular.

With experience you could work for a more senior manager or move into another area of the company, such as marketing.

With language skills you could work abroad, or you could become self employed providing 'virtual' PA services using the internet.

entry level

1

To both enter and train while working in this career, you will need qualifications at Level 1. Please refer to explanation on page vii.

Qualifications and courses

- There is no set minimum qualification required although employers will look for a good general standard of education and some may expect a bachelor's degree or equivalent. Some GCSEs (A–C) may be advantageous, such as English, and having a business-related BTEC HND or degree could help you find a position with greater responsibilities.
- You may find it useful to have NVQ level 2 and/or 3 in Business and Administration, or a secretarial qualification from City & Guilds.
- Previous experience is vital and therefore you should be able to demonstrate that you have worked in other administrative or clerical based roles.
- You should be computer literate and able to use a variety of office computer software. Extra skills like shorthand, audio typing or a foreign language can also be useful for many jobs.

CRCI:AD

CLCI:CAT

Other related opportunities

- Administrator p6
- Customer Services p442
- Public Relations p161
- Receptionist p25
- Secretary p28

Advantages/disadvantages

- The job can be varied and interesting with a lot of responsibility
- Opportunites are good and the experience and skills you will develop could lead to other areas.
- The work can be routine.
- You will have to meet deadlines and the work can be pressured.

Earnings guide

- Salaries vary according to the size and type of company you work for and you will probably earn more in London and the south-east of England.
- A starting salary for a Personal Assistant is around £18,000 per year.
- With experience you could earn around £24,000 – £25,000 per year.
- A senior Personal Assistant with a lot of experience and responsibility, probably in a large company, could earn £30,000+ per year.

Further information

City & Guilds
1 Giltspur Street
London
EC1A 9DD
020 7294 2800
www.cityandguilds.co.uk

Council for Administration
6 Graphite Square
Vauxhall Walk
London
SE11 5EE
020 7091 9620
www.cfa.uk.com
info@cfa.uk.com

London Chamber of Commerce and Industry
33 Queen Street
London
EC4R 1AP
020 7248 4444
www.londonchamber.co.uk
lc@londonchamber.co.uk

Institute of Qualified Professional Secretaries
Suite 464
24–28 St Leonards Road
Windsor
Berkshire
SL4 3BB
0844 8000 182
www.iqps.org
office@iqps.org

Receptionist

What the work involves

General

- You will be the public face of your company, the first person visitors see.
- As well as greeting visitors and directing them to the right place or arranging for someone to meet them, you will also be answering the telephone and taking messages.
- You might take deliveries, organise tea and coffee for visitors and do general clerical tasks like typing letters and dealing with post.

Hotel

- Your job will be to greet guests, making them feel welcome and at ease, provide them with services during their stay and advise them on the local area.
- Receptionists take bookings and cancellations over the phone and email, giving visitors information about the hotel and its facilities.
- You will take payments, deal with cash, cheques, credit and debit cards.

Medical

- Working in a hospital or surgery you will book appointments for patients, either over the phone or face to face, and will organise the appointments diary, making sure that cancelled appointments are filled.
- You will greet patients when they arrive, direct them to the right place, take messages and answer queries.
- Your job will also include general administrative work, preparing patients' notes and files, dealing with post and typing letters.

The type of person suited to this work

You will create the first impression of your organisation, so it is vital that you should be friendly, welcoming, outgoing and well presented.

You will need to speak clearly and give information in a simple, straightforward way and should be outgoing and able to deal with people who could be angry, upset or frightened, or have very little English.

You will be very busy at times but will have to stay calm and polite even under pressure, making sure that each visitor gets the service they expect.

You should be well organised and efficient, making sure that callers get a prompt service. You should also be able to be discreet when dealing with sensitive or personal information.

You may have to handle cash or other forms of payment, so need to be comfortable dealing with figures.

Working conditions

General

Receptionists work in an office or reception area. You will spend a lot of your time on the telephone, may operate a switchboard and will use computers to find and input information. Reception areas are seen as the face of the organisation so they tend to be very inviting and well presented, but conditions will vary depending on the organisation and its premises.

You will need to dress smartly and may have to wear a uniform. You may work normal office hours but could have to work shifts; there are opportunities for part-time and temporary work.

Hotel

The reception is vital to a hotel as it aims to show the standard of the rest of the accommodation to new guests.

As hotels are open for guests 24/7 you will probably do shift work, including late nights, early mornings and weekend working. Depending on the size and age of the hotel, you may get extra benefits such as access to leisure facilities and meals. You will probably wear a uniform.

Medical

As a medical receptionist you would work in a hospital or GP's surgery dealing with patients who could be angry or upset so the work can be busy and stressful. You may work shifts to cover evenings and weekends and could work part-time. You should be smart and well presented and may have to wear a uniform.

The future outlook

General

Many different types of organisations employ receptionists, so there are varied opportunities in all areas of the country. There can be strong competition though, especially for the more glamorous jobs.

Large companies may have senior receptionists who have more responsibility but promotion might be limited in smaller organisations.

There is no set career structure, although you can gain qualifications whilst you work, and you may have to move into other areas of work to get promotion. Reception work can be a way of starting a career in a very competitive industry.

Hotel

Smaller hotels may not offer much opportunity for promotion, but in larger hotels and chains you could probably take qualifications whilst you work and move into more senior jobs. If you work for an international chain you may get the chance to work abroad.

The tourism industry is growing and there are hotels in all parts of the country so opportunities are good but competition will be strong for some jobs.

Medical

There are hospitals and doctors' surgeries all over the country so there are opportunities everywhere, mainly within the NHS, but entry can be competitive.

You can take specialist qualifications whilst you work and could go on to supervise others or move into other areas of work.

Qualifications and courses

- There are no minimum entry requirements, although employers are likely to ask for 5 GCSEs/S grades (A–C/1–3), including English and maths or NVQs/SVQs at Levels 1 or 2. Some office work experience and computer skills may also be required.
- Some further education and private colleges offer courses in reception work. Specialist training courses are available in, for example, medical or hotel reception work. Entry requirements will vary according to the institution.
- Apprenticeships/Skillseekers may be available for candidates aged 16–24.
- Further training is usually provided by the employer, and new entrants often work under the supervision of more experienced reception staff. Courses available include NVQs/SVQs in reception Levels 1–2, customer service Levels 2–4, or business and administration Levels 2–4. Again, courses in specialist areas of reception are available.

entry level

To both enter and train while working in this career, you will need qualifications at Level 2–3. Please refer to explanation on page vii.

Other related opportunities

- Administrator p6
- Clerk p12
- Sales Assistant p450
- Secretary p28
- Travel Agency Sales Consultant p385

Advantages/disadvantages

- This is a great job if you enjoy meeting people and providing a service.
- The work can be glamorous in a multinational or high-profile company.
- You could move into other office or customer service work.
- In a hotel you could be dealing with people tired and stressed from travelling.
- Medical receptionists deal with patients who can be ill, worried or angry.
- You may have to work shifts and will often work on your own.
- The public can be rude and demanding.

Earnings guide

General

- Salaries will depend on the size and type of organisation. Generally, you will earn more in London and the south-east of England, and for shift work.
- Salaries start at about £10,000–£12,000 per year.
- With experience this can rise to around £17,000. In a senior position you can expect £24,000+.

Hotel

- You may receive benefits such as meals accommodation and access to facilities. Salaries vary depending on your responsibility and the type and size of hotel.
- Salaries start at around £10,000 and can rise to around £26,000 with experience. In large hotels you can earn up to £30,000.

Medical

- Salaries start at around £12,000 a year, going up to about £15,500 with experience. Senior staff can earn £20,000+.

Further information

GENERAL

Council for Administration
6 Graphite Square
Vauxhall Walk
London
SE11 5EE
020 7091 9620
www.cfa.uk.com
info@cfa.uk.com

London Chamber of Commerce and Industry
33 Queen Street
London
EC4R 1AP
020 7248 4444
www.londonchamber.co.uk
lc@londonchamber.co.uk

OCR
1 Hills Road
Cambridge
CB1 2EU
01223 553 998
www.ocr.org.uk
general.qualifications@ocr.org.uk

Pitman Training Group
Head Office UK
Sandown House, Sandbeck Way
Wetherby
Yorkshire
LS22 7DN
0800 220454
www.pitman-training.com

Scottish Qualifications Authority
The Optima Building
58 Robertson Street
Glasgow
G2 8DQ
0845 279 1000
www.sqa.org.uk
customer@sqa.org.uk

HOTEL

Institute of Hospitality
Trinity Court
34 West Street
Sutton
Surrey
SM1 1SH
020 8661 4900
www.instituteofhospitality.org

Springboard UK
3 Denmark Street
London
WC2H 8LP
020 7497 8654
www.springboarduk.org.uk

Northern Ireland Tourist Board
St Anne's Court
59 North Street
Belfast
BT1 1NB
028 9023 1221
www.nitb.com

VisitScotland
Ocean Point One
94 Ocean Drive
Edinburgh
EH6 6JH
0131 472 2222
www.visitscotland.org

MEDICAL

Association of Medical Secretaries, Practice Managers, Administrators and Receptionists
Tavistock House North
Tavistock Square
London
WC1H 9LN
020 7387 6005
www.amspar.co.uk
info@amspart.com

NHS Careers
0845 60 60 655
www.nhscareers.nhs.uk

www.cityandguilds.com/myperfectjob

Recruitment Agency Consultant

What the work involves

- Working for an agency, you will help companies attract and recruit the right staff for permanent and temporary jobs. To do this effectively you will need to research the company and its staffing needs.
- Your work will include helping people find a job or temporary work to suit their skills and experience.
- You will assess people's skills to help them decide on the type of work they want, and may suggest further training, which could be available through your company.
- You will spend time making contacts with new companies to sell your agency's services.
- You will also advertise jobs, organise files and arrange appointments.

The type of person suited to this work

You will be selling your agency's services to companies and helping candidates present themselves well to employers so will need to be enthusiastic and well presented with excellent communication skills and sales ability.

You will probably be working on commission so should be able to keep to tight deadlines and remain calm under pressure.

You will need to be well organised and have administrative skills so that you can keep your files accurate and up to date, place job adverts, arrange interviews and appointments and follow them up.

You will need a sensitive, mature attitude to work with job seekers who are anxious about their prospects. A good telephone manner and ICT skills are also helpful.

Working conditions

You will probably work Monday to Friday but hours can be long as you may have to speak to clients outside working hours.

You will be based in an office or shop, usually in the centre of a town or city. You will be doing a lot of work over the phone and some agencies are internet based. You may need to visit employer premises, so could need a driving licence. You will probably work in a team and be expected to dress smartly.

The future outlook

Around 100,000 people work within the UK recruitment sector. Opportunities are good as increasingly people are changing jobs more frequently or working on a contract basis.

There are agencies across the UK and there are growing numbers of online recruitment agencies.

You could work for a specialist agency, for example supplying medical staff or legal staff but may need experience within that sector first. Some people work as 'head hunters', actively searching out people for specific high-level jobs such as company director.

If you get good results you could get promotion to management level and go on to start your own agency or you could go into a related area such as human resources.

entry level

2–8

To both enter and train while working in this career, you will need qualifications at Level 2–8. Please refer to explanation on page vii.

Qualifications and courses

- You can enter and train in this career with qualifications at Level 2 but people often have Level 3 or 4 qualifications.
- There are no specific entry requirements, and entrants come from various backgrounds such as sales, marketing or customer service.
- Entrants often have previous experience in personnel, sales or administration.
- Employers may recruit graduates from any subjects as trainee recruitment consultants.
- Administrators working in an agency may be promoted to consultant.
- Trainees receive training on the job, and may take courses accredited by the Recruitment and Employment Confederation (REC). The REC's Certificate in Recruitment Practice is designed for those new to the industry or who have no formal training or qualifications. It can be taken over 15 weeks by distance learning, or as a 3-day intensive course. The Diploma in Recruitment Practice is aimed at consultants with a year's experience, or those with A levels, a degree or equivalent. It can be taken by distance learning or through evening classes in London. The Diploma can serve as the first year of the degree in Business Practice at Middlesex University Business School. The REC qualifications are not a requirement, but are useful. Passing the Diploma makes you eligible for full membership of the REC.
- Some consultants take the Chartered Institute of Personnel and Development examinations, for example, the CIPD Certificate in Recruitment and Selection.

CRCI:AA

CLCI:KED

Other related opportunities

- Careers Adviser p526
- Human Resources / Personnel Officer p20
- Personal Adviser – Connexions p539

Advantages/disadvantages

- You will meet lots of different people at all levels and will get satisfaction from helping them find the right job or career, and businesses to find the right staff.
- Working on commission can be stressful and clients and businesses could be difficult or demanding.
- This is a very competitive career and your success will depend on your sales ability and communication skills.

Earnings guide

- Consultants often get commission and a small basic salary. They earn their commission when they successfully get new business or place staff, so salaries vary – but you will earn more in London and the south-east of England.
- Trainees start on between £14,000 and £20,000 per year.
- When you are qualified and have experience you can earn up to £25,000.
- It is possible for the most successful consultants to earn £50,000+.
- You could earn extra bonuses or commission.

Further information

www.cityandguilds.com/myperfectjob

Recruitment & Employment Confederation
15 Welbeck Street
London
W1G 9XT
020 7009 2100
www.rec.uk.com
info@rec.uk.com

Chartered Institute of Personnel and Development
CIPD House
151 The Broadway
London
SW19 1JQ
020 8612 6200
www.cipd.co.uk

ENTO
4th floor
Kimberley House
47 Vaughan Way
Leicester
LE1 4SG
0116 251 7979
www.ento.co.uk
info@ento.co.uk

Secretary

What the work involves

- Working for a senior executive you will support them in their day-to-day work.
- You will organise their diaries, arrange meetings, make travel arrangements, sort their post and type letters and reports.
- You will develop administrative systems (both paper- and ICT-based) to keep information organised and easily accessible.
- You will deal with staff and clients at all levels, taking phone calls, answering queries and providing information.
- You may write reports and produce agendas and minutes for meetings.

Bilingual

- Using your language skills you will translate and write letters, emails and reports.
- You will deal with staff and clients, using your foreign language both in person and on the phone and possibly interpreting for your manager in meetings.
- In addition, you will do other secretarial tasks such as making appointments, arranging meetings and trips, filing and typing.

Farm

- You will help to run the farm, particularly the financial side. You will be keeping accounts and records and be involved in estimating costs and financial planning and budgeting.
- On the financial side, you will also be researching and applying for any government grants or money and doing the staff payroll.
- It will be important that you keep up to date with relevant health and safety and environmental regulations and check that they are being followed. You will also do other clerical and administrative tasks.

Legal

- This role includes the full range of secretarial duties: you will arrange meetings and appointments, do the post and deal with clients over the phone and in person.
- Using ICT you will create and update legal documents, which need to be absolutely accurate, perhaps using dictated audio notes involving specialist legal language.

Medical

- You will work in a GP's surgery or hospital, giving administrative support to medical staff.
- Although it will not be the major part of your job, you might have contact with patients, booking appointments and working on reception.
- You will also organise patient notes making sure that all relevant documents are sent to the right place.

School

- Working on reception or in the school office you will greet visitors and take telephone calls.
- You will keep staff and pupil records up to date and do any paperwork needed by the teachers.
- In some schools you might also collect dinner money and money for school trips, and could be in charge of the sick room.

The type of person suited to this work

For all secretarial work you will need to be highly organised and efficient with excellent written and verbal communication skills. You should be confident dealing with people at all levels and may have to work with people who are ill, angry or upset.

You should have excellent keyboard skills, be able to use ICT packages and organise and maintain information systems. You will have to take responsibility, be flexible and use your initiative and should be able to work accurately under pressure, meet deadlines and handle confidential information.

As a bilingual secretary you will need excellent foreign language skills. Farm secretaries must be good with figures and interested in farming and the countryside.

Legal and medical secretaries need particularly good written English for dealing with technical language accurately.

Qualifications and courses

entry level

To both enter and train while working in this career, you will need qualifications at Level 2–8. Please refer to explanation on page vii.

- The basic requirements are GCSEs/S grades (A–C/1–3), usually including English and maths, and keyboard and word-processing skills. Other ICT skills and shorthand are useful.
- School-leavers can start as an office junior and progress to a secretarial job with further experience and training.
- Apprenticeships/Skillseekers may be available for candidates aged 16–24.
- With GCSEs or equivalent qualifications you can study at college towards a secretarial qualification. These include the Pitman Diploma and Advanced Diploma in Secretarial Studies, the OCR Higher Diploma in Administrative and Secretarial Procedures, and the LCCI Private Secretary's Diploma. NVQs/SVQs in administration are also available.
- With A levels or a degree/HND you could do secretarial training courses. Some colleges offer intensive business/secretarial skills courses aimed at graduates.

Bilingual

- Bilingual secretaries need secretarial skills and fluency in at least one foreign language. Entrants often have an A level/H grade or a degree in languages and GCSE/S grade (A–C/1–3) in English is usually required.
- Awarding bodies such as OCR, LCCI, Edexcel, City & Guilds and SQA offer qualifications and/or modules specifically for bilingual secretaries. These include word processing and audio typing in relevant languages.
- LCCIEB offers qualifications in French, German and Spanish for business at Levels 1, 2 and 3. Another relevant qualification is the European Computer Driving Licence (ECDL) awarded by the British Computer Society.

Farm

- Specialist training is required to become a farm secretary. The main qualifications are recognised by the Institute of Agricultural Secretaries and Administrators (IAgSA), and are offered at a number of agricultural colleges. The National Certificate takes one year, the National Diploma 2 years. Candidates for the Diploma need to be over 18 years of age with 4 GCSEs/S grades (A–C/1–3) or equivalent, including ability in English and maths. IAgSA also runs a continuing professional development programme.
- Other qualifications such as the BTEC First Diploma in Rural Business and Finance and the National Certificate in Rural Business Administration also include farm secretarial skills. An HND in Business Management in Rural and Land-based Industries is also available.
- It is possible for candidates with secretarial skills/qualifications and some knowledge of agriculture to become farm secretaries without specialist training.

Legal

- The Institute of Legal Executives provides training and qualifications for legal secretaries through its business division, ILEX Paralegal Programmes. The Legal Secretarial Certificate at Level 2 and Legal Secretarial Diploma at Level 3 can be studied in the workplace, by distance learning or by full- or part-time attendance at a college. There are no specific entry requirements; candidates should usually have GCSEs/S grades and/or work experience.
- Qualifications are also available through the Institute of Legal Secretaries and PAs. The Institute offers a diploma for new and experienced legal secretaries, and single-subject diplomas to enhance particular areas of knowledge.
- OCR qualifications and SQA National Certificate modules can be taken in legal text processing.
- People with general secretarial qualifications and/or experience may be able to move into the legal secretarial field.

Medical

- Most employers will look for GCSEs/S grades (A–C/1–3) including English, maths, plus good ICT skills.
- The main qualification for medical secretaries is the Advanced Diploma of the Association of Medical Secretaries, Practice Managers and Administrators (AMSPAR). Entry requirements are 4 GCSEs/S grades (A–C/1–3) or the AMSPAR Intermediate Diploma in Medical Reception. There are no formal requirements for the Intermediate Diploma. To gain the Advanced Diploma, you will also need to pass RSA/Pitman certificates in two of the following areas: medical shorthand, medical audio transcription, and medical word processing.

School

- There are no formal entry requirements but you will need a good standard of maths and English. You will need keyboard and word-processing skills and probably office experience. Other ICT skills and shorthand are also useful.

Working conditions

You will usually be office-based, doing normal office hours, probably as part of a team. Secretaries work in companies of all sizes from small businesses to large multinational corporations. You will use a computer, telephone, fax machine and other office equipment. You will spend a lot of your time sitting, but might have to escort guests around the organisation too.

Bilingual

Most of your work will take place during normal office hours within an office environment. Depending on the organisation that you work for, you will spend a lot of your time sitting at a desk reading and translating documents or talking to people on the phone from other countries. In addition, you might get the chance to travel and could be dealing with the public.

Farm

Farm secretaries are either based within one farm or work for a number of smaller farms providing a mobile service. You will be office-based and may work alone, and part-time work is available. If mobile, you will need a driving licence and access to your own transport.

Legal

You would spend most of your time at a desk, working at a computer doing normal office hours. Sometimes, you might visit other organisations, go to court to deliver documents, attend business meetings and possibly visit police stations. You might be expected to wear formal dress, such as a black suit, especially if you have to attend court.

Medical

You will work in a GP's surgery, hospital or other medical organisation at a desk where you will spend a lot of your time on the phone or computer. This can be busy and stressful and may involve shifts and part-time hours. You will probably also have contact with patients.

School

School offices are open to visitors and pupils and can be very busy. Lots of school secretaries work part time and do not work during all of the school holidays.

The future outlook

Secretaries work in all kinds of organisations so there are opportunities all over the country, but the most interesting and well-paid jobs are competitive. You can start as a junior secretary and build your career to work with high-flying executives.

Secretarial work can be the first step in a creative or professional career such as personnel or journalism.

Secretaries are increasingly working from home using the internet, as self-employed 'virtual secretaries'.

Bilingual

There is a shortage of bilingual secretaries so there are lots of opportunities particularly in cities and large towns. The most useful languages are European (including Welsh in Wales), Japanese and Chinese languages.

The work can be a route into translating or interpreting or a career like sales or human resources.

Farm

You might work for one farm or several smaller farms or for a Farm Secretarial Bureau offering services to several farms.

Changes in agriculture mean that more secretaries are needed to help keep farms up to date with new laws and financial regulations. Much of the work is part time.

You could become self-employed, providing a mobile service, or you could use your financial skills to take accountancy qualifications or move into administration or management within the agricultural industry.

Legal

There are opportunities throughout the country. You could work for a firm of solicitors or barristers, a court, or the legal department of large organisations such as banks, police forces or a local authority.

Prospects are good. You could become a senior secretary or office manager and take further qualifications such as a certificate or diploma in legal administration. You could then go on to train as a legal executive, progress to do law at university and become a barrister or solicitor.

Medical

You can work in the NHS or private sector, in GPs' surgeries, dentists or hospitals.

You can take professional qualifications to become a supervisor or practice manager.

School

There are job opportunities in all areas of the country, although jobs can be competitive. Much of the work is part time and there are not usually many opportunities for promotion but you could go on to become a teaching assistant.

Other related opportunities

- Accounting Technician p4
- Administrator p6
- Interpreter p322
- Legal Executive p342
- Receptionist p25
- Personal Assistant p24

Advantages/disadvantages

- There are lots of opportunities and the work can give you a good knowledge of a firm or department which you could use to get promotion.
- Secretarial work can be a way into competitive areas like magazines or jobs using languages, or give you an insight into a career like law.
- It can be a practical way of using your skills and interests, such as languages, the law, or an interest in the countryside or health issues.
- The work can be routine and you will often be in the background, organising other people's work.
- If you have family commitments there are part-time opportunities.

Earnings guide

- Salaries start at around £10,000–£12,000 per year.
- This can rise to £20,000. However, salaries can vary a lot with some top personal assistants earning £30,000+.

Bilingual

- Generally you will start around £16,000–£20,000, rising with experience to around £35,000. You could earn as much as £55,000 if working for a large corporate company and perhaps more in London.

Farm

- You could earn around £15,000 to start with. This could increase up to £25,000 with experience and responsibility. If you are self-employed your earnings will depend on the success of your business and the local demand for your services.

Legal

- Starting salaries for new recruits are £12,000–£15,000. This could rise to over £30,000 for those with lots of experience. You would earn more in central London and major cities.

Medical

- Many medical secretaries work for the NHS which has a set pay scale. Salaries are lower in some parts of the country but you can earn more in the private sector than in the NHS. You will probably start on around £11,500 and could earn up to £25,000 with experience.

School

- On average you could earn £10,000–£15,000 if you are working full time in a state school.
- This could rise to around £20,000+ if you are working in a large secondary school and have additional responsibility or staff to manage. Salaries in private schools vary a lot.

Further information

Council for Administration
6 Graphite Square
Vauxhall Walk
London
SE11 5EE
020 7091 9620
www.cfa.uk.com
info@cfa.uk.com

Institute of Qualified Professional Secretaries
Suite 464
24–28 St Leonards Road
Windsor
Berkshire
SL4 3BB
0844 8000 182
www.iqps.org
office@iqps.org

OCR
1 Hills Road
Cambridge
CB2 1PB
01223 553 998
www.ocr.org.uk
general.qualifications@ocr.org.uk

Pitman Training Group
Head Office UK
Sandown House, Sandbeck Way
Wetherby
Yorkshire
LS22 7DN
0800 220454
www.pitman-training.com

Scottish Qualifications Authority
The Optima Building
58 Robertson Street
Glasgow
G2 8DQ
0845 279 1000
www.sqa.org.uk
customer@sqa.org.uk

BILINGUAL

CILT – The National Centre for Languages
3rd Floor
111 Westminster Bridge Road
London
SE1 7HR
020 7379 5101
www.cilt.org.uk
info@cilt.org.uk

FARM

Institute of Agricultural Secretaries and Administrators Ltd (IAgSA)
Stoneleigh Park
Kenilworth
CV8 2LG
024 7669 6592
www.iagsa.co.uk
IAgSA@IAgSA.co.uk

LEGAL

Institute of Legal Executives (ILEX)
Kempston Manor
Kempston
Bedfordshire
MK42 7AB
01234 841000
www.ilex.org.uk
info@ilex.org.uk

MEDICAL

Association of Medical Secretaries, Practice Managers, Administrators and Receptionists
Tavistock House North
Tavistock Square
London
WC1H 9LN
020 7387 6005
www.amspar.co.uk
info@amspar.co.uk

Stockbroker

What the work involves

- Companies and the government raise money to fund their work by selling stocks and shares in their business; these are what stockbrokers trade in.
- Stockbrokers work for individuals or companies investing their clients' money to make them a profit by buying and selling stocks and shares.
- You will be advising your clients on investing their money, often dealing with huge amounts.
- You will have to keep up to date with economic trends and predict how a company's stocks and shares are likely to perform.

The type of person suited to this work

To succeed as a stockbroker you must be confident, determined competitive and outgoing.

You will have to predict trends in a constantly changing market and take risks with huge sums of money so must be decisive and able to work under pressure. You will need to be trustworthy and honest with a good reputation and excellent people skills.

You should be confident and accurate with figures and able to absorb and analyse a lot of detailed information in a short time and then make decisions.

You will need excellent ICT skills and will be expected to work long hours and to dress smartly.

Working conditions

You will be office-based, getting a lot of information from computers and doing much of your work by telephone. Hours are long: you will probably start early and finish late in order to trade on international markets working in different time zones. You will probably have to work over the weekend. Much of your day will be spent in a very busy, tense and pressurised environment.

The future outlook

You could be working for a stockbroking firm which specialises in this work or for other financial institutions such as banks or building societies. Your career will develop by taking on more responsibilities and more important clients.

Competition for jobs is intense so work experience is vital. Economic changes can happen fast so jobs are not always secure.

Most jobs are in London but there are opportunities in other large cities.

This is a high pressure job and many stockbrokers finish their careers in their 40s. You could move into other areas within finance or become self-employed as a consultant.

entry level

4–8

To both enter and train while working in this career, you will need qualifications at Level 4–8. Please refer to explanation on page vii.

Qualifications and courses

- You will normally need at least a 2.1 degree, particularly in such subjects as economics, business studies, maths, physics, accountancy or law. Increasingly, in a very competitive market, possession of a postgraduate qualification such as an MBA (Master of Business Administration) or MSc in subjects such as business or economics, together with another language, will prove very useful.
- Useful degree subjects include economics, law, business or accountancy. Typical entry requirements for a degree course are 2 A levels/3 H grades and 5 GCSEs/S grades (A–C/1–3) or equivalent; specific subjects may be required.
- Individuals with relevant experience may be able to move into stockbroking from an analyst, research or investment banking role and graduates are allowed to register for the Chartered Financial Analyst (CFA) Institute's exams before starting in stockbroking.
- New entrants must be registered by their employer as an 'authorised person' with the Financial Services Authority (FSA). To gain registration, you need to pass an FSA-approved examination, for example the Investment Management Certificate awarded by the UK Society of Investment Professionals, or the Securities and Investment Institute's Certificate in Investment Management.
- Many companies have their own, very detailed selection procedures, including psychometric and aptitude testing.

CRCI:IF

CLCI:NAL

Other related opportunities

- Accountant p2
- Bank / Building Society p9
- Economist p93
- Financial Adviser p18

Advantages/disadvantages

- The hours are long and the work is very pressurised and stressful.
- It is a very competitive job and you will need to be tough and determined to succeed and do well.
- The work can be exciting and rewarding and is extremely well paid.

Earnings guide

- You could earn £25,000–£35,000 a year when you first start work and training after university, with a fairly small number of clients.
- With experience you could earn between £45,000 and £80,000.
- After many years of experience and depending on location, some stockbrokers can earn over £150,000.
- Stockbrokers get bonuses on the trade they do and can earn extremely high salaries.

Further information

London Stock Exchange
10 Paternoster Square
London
EC4M 7LS
020 7797 1000
www.londonstockexchange.com

Securities and Investment Institute
8 Eastcheap
London
EC3M 1AE
020 7645 0600
www.sii.org.uk
info@sii.org.uk

Financial Services Authority
25 The North Colonnade
Canary Wharf
London
E14 5HS
020 7066 1000
www.fsa.gov.uk

Financial Service Skills Council
51 Gresham Street
London
EC2V 7HQ
0845 257 3771
www.fssc.org.uk
info@fssc.org.uk

Switchboard Operator / Telephonist

What the work involves

- Switchboard operators work at a switchboard, answering calls, connecting callers to the right person and advising them on which department or person they need to speak to.
- You would answer callers' questions about the company, take messages, test phone lines and report faults.
- Some use computer databases to find the numbers of internal staff and connect calls to them.
- You might do other reception duties like meeting and dealing with visitors, taking deliveries and other clerical work.

entry level

To both enter and train while working in this career, you will need qualifications at Level 1. Please refer to explanation on page vii.

Qualifications and courses

- There are no formal entry requirements for this work, but 5 good GCSEs/S grades (A–C/1–3), including English language and maths, are a distinct advantage. Basic computing skills or an ICT qualification are also useful.
- Apprenticeships/Skillseekers may be available in your area for candidates aged 16–24.
- Many colleges offer courses in customer service and call centre techniques at Levels 1–3.
- Mature entry is possible, and many employers regard maturity and experience as an asset in dealing with the public.
- Most training is done on the job. You may be able to work towards an NVQ/SVQ Level 3 in Operating and Maintaining the Performance of Telecommunications Equipment.

The type of person suited to this work

Switchboard operators need an excellent telephone manner so you should have good spoken English and be able to speak clearly. You will also need to have good hearing.

Because you will be dealing with the public, you will need good customer service skills, which means staying polite and calm even when you are busy and when dealing with rude or impatient callers.

You should be someone who enjoys working with people in a team and who can work quickly and accurately. You will also need to be able to take messages and remain calm even when you are busy.

Working conditions

Most of your work will be in an office or telephone room, probably with other people. You might be based at a reception desk.

Although you will probably do normal office hours, you may need to be at work to take calls before the company opens. Some switchboards provide a 24-hour service which means working shifts including nights and weekends.

You will probably wear a headset and use computer databases and automated switchboards.

The future outlook

Most large or medium-sized companies need people to answer their phones and provide a reception service, so job opportunities are good.

You could work in a call centre where opportunities have increased significantly in recent years. Recent changes in the telecommunications industry have meant more job opportunities as the number of companies providing these services has increased

You could become a senior telephonist receiving training in customer service skills and gaining administrative experience. You could then move into a wide range of jobs working in business administration in offices or with the public.

CRCI:AD

CLCI:CAT/OM

Other related opportunities

- Call Centre Operative p439
- Court Administrative Officer p335
- Receptionist p25
- Secretary p28

Advantages/disadvantages

- On a busy switchboard you will be working under pressure and could be working shifts.
- Dealing with the public means staying polite and calm no matter how they speak to you!
- You will gain valuable customer service and administration skills to help you progress.

Earnings guide

- As a trainee your starting salary is normally around £12,000 per year.
- With more experience this rises to £15,500+.
- Earnings could reach £17,000+ for a senior switchboard operator who has experience.
- Earnings could reach £21,000+ for a senior switchboard operator who has experience and more responsibility, perhaps supervising other staff.

Further information

Institute of Direct Marketing
1 Park Road
Teddington
Middlesex
TW11 0AR
020 8977 5705
www.theidm.com
enquiries@theidm.com

Institute of Customer Service
2 Castle Court
St Peter's Street
Colchester
Essex
CO1 1EW
01206 571716
www.instituteofcustomerservice.com
enquiries@icsmail.co.uk

e-skills UK
1 Castle Lane
London
SW1E 6DR
0207 963 8920
www.e-skills.com
info@e-skills.com

Training Officer

What the work involves

- You will be responsible for making sure your company's staff have the skills and knowledge they need to make the business as efficient as possible.
- You will look at job roles and assess staff training needs.
- Your role will be to provide training for all levels of staff from new recruits to experienced managers.
- Some of your work will involve looking at how to provide the best training at the lowest cost – from different options such as in-house, distance learning, ICT packages or college courses.
- You will also deliver training yourself or organise other trainers to do this. You will have to write reports and make presentations assessing the value of training.

entry level

To both enter and train while working in this career, you will need qualifications at Level 2–8. Please refer to explanation on page vii.

The type of person suited to this work

You should be interested in people and in helping them to develop and improve their skills. You will need to be able to pass on your knowledge and expertise in a lively, interesting way by designing imaginative and varied training that appeals to everyone.

Using excellent communication skills to motivate and encourage staff, you should be happy making presentations to groups and dealing with people at all levels.

You will need to be organised and able to plan ahead, meet deadlines and assess the effectiveness of training. To do this you will need excellent ICT skills and an understanding of costs and budgets.

Working conditions

You will usually do normal office hours but may have to work longer at busy times or attend residential, evening or weekend events.

You will be based in an office, probably working as part of a team, but will spend a lot of your time out and about – delivering training, finding training venues, going to meetings and visiting staff in their work places.

You will spend a lot of time in the office using a computer but will oversee and deliver training at a range of venues.

The future outlook

Training officers come from a variety of backgrounds as they often become experts in their own field before moving into training people within the industry, but it is possible to go straight in, possibly as a graduate trainee.

There are opportunities all over the country as all types of organisations have training officers. Developments in new technology and more on the job training have increased the need for staff training. More companies are using consultants to deliver training to their staff so opportunities to become a self-employed consultant are increasing. It is also possible to gain promotion or move into related areas such as personnel.

Qualifications and courses

- There are no formal requirements for entry into this profession, but some employers may require relevant vocational qualifications, such as an NVQ/SVQ Level 3 Training and Development. Relevant paid or voluntary work experience in areas such as teaching, youth work, leadership, personnel or management can also be useful.
- Training officers are often trained in-house but there are some relevant courses of study.
- Some employers require a degree or HND in a subject such as business studies, management, training or personnel.
- The Chartered Institute of Personnel and Development (CIPD) offers a range of relevant courses, including: the Certificate in Personnel Practice (CPP); Certificate in Training Practice (CTP); and a Professional Development Scheme. The latter consists of 4 modules, completion of which allows the candidate to become a graduate member of the CIPD.
- Other relevant NVQs/SVQs include Direct Training and Support at Level 3; Management and Development of Learning Provision, Training and Development (Learning Development) and Training and Development (Human Resource Development) at Level 4, and Training and Development Strategy at Level 5.
- Postgraduate qualifications in training and development are also available. Entry usually requires a degree, a relevant professional qualification, or equivalent work experience.

Other related opportunities

- Adult Education Organiser / Tutor p170
- Careers Adviser p526
- Human Resources / Personnel Officer p20
- Lecturer p178
- Personal Adviser – Connexions p539
- Teacher p184

Advantages/disadvantages

- The work can be very varied and you will have the satisfaction of passing on your expertise to help people learn and develop.
- You may need to work hard to motivate staff who are having to do training they are not interested in or do not feel they need.

Earnings guide

- Starting salaries are around £18,000 per year.
- As an experienced and qualified training officer you can earn £28,000+.
- This could rise to £60,000 a year in some companies for a training manager with responsibility for other staff.
- Salaries vary, depending on experience and the size of the company.

Further information

www.cityandguilds.com/myperfectjob

Chartered Institute of Personnel and Development
CIPD House
151 The Broadway
London
SW19 1JQ
020 8971 9000
www.cipd.co.uk

ENTO
4th floor
Kimberley House
47 Vaughan Way
Leicester
LE1 4SG
0116 251 7979
www.ento.co.uk
info@ento.co.uk

Lifelong Learning UK (LLUK)
0870 757 7890
www.lifelonglearninguk.org
enquiries@lluk.org

Do you enjoy using your hands, using tools and designing or constructing new buildings? The construction industry includes jobs at all levels – check out some of these for ideas:

- **Architect**
- **Bricklayer**
- **Carpet Fitter**
- **Plumber**
- **Town Planner**

But what's it like working in this area?

Here's Paul Tudor's story

Plumber

When 37-year-old Paul was still at school the careers advisor gave him some brochures on plumbing, and he was subsequently recruited by British Gas where he was trained on the job and at Medway College. He was an apprentice for three years before getting his ACS accreditation and his CORGI (Council for Registered Gas Installers) accreditation. He started out working on domestic appliances such as boilers. He then joined TRANSCO, the safety division of British Gas that deals with 24-hour emergency call-outs, and throughout his career he has attended many refresher courses and training courses to keep up with the latest health and safety standards. However, last year Paul decided to go freelance so he could spend more time with his family and he is currently working on a big project involving a converted block of flats in south London.

WHAT THE JOB ENTAILS

'At the flats I am installing all the boilers and doing all the plumbing including the showers, baths, sinks, toilets and absolutely all the pipework. It's a massive project and I like to do a nice neat job with no pipes showing. Doing pipework is really fiddly, so your concentration levels need to be high and mentally it is really hard work. For instance, at the bottom of a boiler you need to connect the gas pipe, a vent pipe, a hot water pipe, a cold water pipe and pipes to all the radiators and they all go in different directions, so it can get confusing and there's a lot of thinking involved.'

Paul likes the sense of satisfaction he gets when a job has gone well; he also likes the camaraderie within the building team including the plasterers and electricians. The biggest downside for him is that most of his life is spent on his knees and the older he gets the more he starts to feel it. However, financially plumbing can be a very rewarding occupation.

WHAT YOU NEED TO SUCCEED

'Being a gas plumber you need to be very safety-conscious and dextrous. In fact, gas plumbers probably have to be better trained than anybody else because they have to keep in touch with all the new technology. If you decide to become self-employed you will be relying on getting work through word of mouth, so you need to be polite, neat and tidy. I always give customers a card with my address and number on it so they know where to find me if there are any problems.'

Paul is enjoying being self-employed but would like to progress by taking on a big project and then employing other people to work alongside him, eventually owning his own business.

Architect

What the work involves

- Architects design new buildings and the spaces around them. They also design changes to existing buildings.
- Your work as an architect will include agreeing design briefs with clients, researching development sites, deciding which materials to use for particular buildings, drawing technical plans, testing new ideas, obtaining planning permission and inspecting building work while it is in progress.
- You could specialise in a particular field such as building heritage and conservation, sustainable and environmental design, or project management.

The type of person suited to this work

You should enjoy drawing as most schools of architecture will expect you to have a portfolio of drawings. You must be able to produce creative, detailed designs that meet the needs and wishes of your clients and other people in the community.

You will need excellent verbal communication skills for working with other professionals, such as surveyors, planners and builders, and for presenting your ideas to them and your clients. You also have to be organised and have good research and problem-solving skills.

As you will use computer-aided design (CAD) in your work, ICT skills are also useful.

Working conditions

Although architects are based in offices, you will go out to visit construction-sites and meet clients. You will need to pay attention to health and safety regulations when on-site and wear a hard hat and other protective clothing. A driving licence may be necessary.

You are likely to work regular office hours, although to meet deadlines you may have to do some work at weekends and during the evenings.

The future outlook

Generally, you would start work in a private architect's practice to gain wide experience of the work, but you may also work for other employers, such as local or central government, later on.

More than 30,000 architects work in the UK. Self-employment is common for qualified and experienced architects.

In the long term, your career will be dependent on your experience, ability and competence. If you decide to remain in private work you could progress to associate level and possibly become a partner. Some of the larger architectural practices win international contracts so you could work on projects abroad.

entry level

To both enter and train while working in this career, you will need qualifications at Level 4–8. Please refer to explanation on page vii.

Qualifications and courses

- Professional architects must have chartered membership of the Royal Institute of British Architects (RIBA) and registration with the Architects Registration Board (ARB). The main route to qualification is via a RIBA/ARB recognised degree.
- Entry requirements for an architecture degree are a minimum of 2 A levels or 1 A and 2 AS levels, which should be drawn from academic fields of study. In addition you must have passed at least 5 GCSEs which include English language, maths and a double award at science, or a separate science such as physics or chemistry. Equivalent qualifications such as a National Certificate/Diploma may be accepted. Most schools of architecture also ask to see a portfolio of freehand drawings and sketches. Candidates without the usual entry requirements may be able to take a foundation year at a school of architecture to prepare for entry.
- Training as an architect takes 7 years. Candidates undertake a 5-year degree programme, divided into three parts. Part 1 takes 3 years and Part 2 takes 2 years. A year is spent working in an architect's office after Part 1, and a further year after Part 2. Candidates then take the Part 3 examination in Professional Practice and Management, leading to chartered membership of RIBA.
- If you have passed Part 1, you may be able to join an architectural practice as a part-qualified architect and complete the training over a longer period by part-time study. Part-qualified architects can also work as architectural technicians.
- Some schools of architecture offer a part-time degree or diploma, which can be studied by people already working in an architect's office. Students must have 6 years' relevant experience and the qualifications required for entry to a degree.

CRCI:BA

CLCI:UB

Other related opportunities

- Architectural Technician / Technologist p38
- Cartographer p43
- Construction Manager p48
- Designer p136
- Landscaper/Landscape Architect p255
- Model Maker p155
- Technical Illustrator p166
- Town Planner p75

Advantages/disadvantages

- There may be problems to overcome when making design decisions. For example, there might be conflicting needs and views to deal with.
- There is personal satisfaction in dealing with these problems and creating designs for buildings that will influence the landscape for many years to come.

Earnings guide

- There are no set pay scales for this work but generally you can earn more if you work in the private sector rather than the public sector.
- On starting out, with RIBA part 3 qualifications, you could earn around £25,000 per year. Average salaries for experienced architects are from £30,000 – £40,000.
- Senior architects can earn more than £40,000. However, earnings vary depending on the type, size and location of the practice, the individual employer and changes in the economy. If self-employed, earnings will depend on the success and ability of the individual.

Further information

ConstructionSkills
Bircham Newton
King's Lynn
Norfolk
PE31 6RH
01485 577577
www.cskills.org
www.bconstructive.co.uk construction careers site

Royal Institute of British Architects
66 Portland Place
London
W1B 1AD
020 7580 5533
www.architecture.com

Architects Registration Board
8 Weymouth Street
London
W1W 5BU
020 7580 5861
www.arb.org.uk

Royal Incorporation of Architects in Scotland
15 Rutland Square,
Edinburgh
EH1 2BE
0131 229 7545
www.rias.org.uk

Architectural Technician / Technologist

What the work involves

- Architectural technicians/technologists work as specialists in the design and specification of projects alongside architects and other construction professionals
- You will translate design ideas into detailed technical drawings and plans for all members of the construction team to work from.
- You will also work out the materials needed for each project – by producing a detailed technical specification.
- As an architectural technologist, you will play a leading role in the construction team including developing project briefs, coordinating, negotiating contracts, providing guidance and possibly acting as project manager.

The type of person suited to this work

You need to be able to use drawing skills in your work, both hand and computer-aided design (CAD). You must also be able to develop a scientific and technological knowledge of building materials. You will need an ability to visualise in three dimensions and must understand the different processes and regulations involved in building design and planning.

You will need good verbal communication skills for working with other professionals, such as architects, surveyors and engineers.

Your organisational, management, research and problem-solving skills will need to be excellent. You will need to understand planning regulations and construction law, and be able to explain complex information to different people including colleagues and clients.

Working conditions

Architectural technologists and technicians are based in offices, but you may visit sites to inspect work in progress. You will need to be aware of health and safety regulations when on-site and will be expected to wear safety clothing. You may need a driving licence.

You are likely to work normal office hours, although you may have to work late and at weekends on some projects.

The future outlook

There are around 15,000 architectural technicians/technologists working in the UK, including 7,000 members of the Chartered Institute of Architectural Technologists (CIAT).There are opportunities throughout the UK. Most architectural technicians/ technologists start their careers working in private architectural practices or for local authorities.

An architectural technician may take further CIAT-accredited training to develop their skills and apply to work as an architectural technologist.

Architectural technologists, with CIAT qualifications and experience, may set up their own practice or work in a partnership with other architectural technologists or architects.

It is also possible to progress within private firms to more senior positions or move to other companies which attract larger and possibly international contracts. Work overseas is possible, as is consultancy or training work.

entry level

4–8

To both enter and train while working in this career, you will need qualifications at Level 4–8. Please refer to explanation on page vii.

Qualifications and courses

- Entrants to architectural technology normally start as trainees. In addition to practical training from the employer, trainees usually attend university or college on a day-release basis, working towards HNC Architectural Technology or Building Studies, or NVQ/SVQ Level 4 Architectural Technology.
- It is also possible to enter after a degree or HND. Candidates with an accredited degree in Architectural Technology or a related built environment subject, an HNC/ D in Architectural Technology or Building Studies or an NVQ/SVQ Level 4 are eligible for associate membership of the Chartered Institute of Architectural Technologists (CIAT).
- The degree route is recommended for those wanting to become architectural technologists, while the HNC/D route is recommended for architectural technicians.
- Once you have achieved a recognised qualification, either by work-based or full-time study, you can work towards technician membership and full membership of CIAT. Up to 3 years' further experience is required, during which candidates complete a Professional and Occupational Performance Record.
- For Apprenticeship training, the qualifications are normally 4 GCSEs/S grades (A–C/1–3) usually from subjects such as English, maths, science, design technology, engineering, applied ICT and art.

Other related opportunities

- Architect p36
- CAD Draughtsman / Woman p197
- Cartographer p43
- Construction Manager p48
- Designer p136
- Home Inspector / Energy Assessor p58
- Landscaper/Landscape Architect p255
- Model Maker p155
- Technical Illustrator p166
- Town Planner p75
- Town Planning Technician p76

Advantages/disadvantages

- There may be problems to solve at any time during the architectural process, for example problems with the supply of the right materials.
- It is rewarding to make your contribution to the design and construction of buildings that will influence the landscape for many years to come.

Earnings guide

- Technicians/technologists can expect a starting salary of £16,000–£18,500 per year.
- Experienced technicians/technologists earn on average £25,000 and project managers may earn £40,000+.
- Earnings vary widely depending on location and the individual employer.
- If you are self-employed you can set your own hourly rate and this is normally a higher rate than those employed by a company.

Further information

ConstructionSkills
Bircham Newton
King's Lynn
Norfolk
PE31 6RH
01485 577577
www.cskills.org
www.bconstructive.co.uk

Chartered Institute of Architectural Technologists
397 City Road
London
EC1V 1NH
020 7278 2206
www.ciat.org.uk

GRCI:BA

CLCI:UB

Bricklayer

What the work involves

- Bricklayers build and repair external and internal walls.
- As a bricklayer, you will use a range of materials including bricks, stones and mortar to build walls that often include ornamental and decorative effects.
- You will use specialist tools such as trowels to spread mortar and different types of hammers to cut and trim bricks and blocks.

entry level

To both enter and train while working in this career, you will need qualifications at Level 1–2. Please refer to explanation on page vii.

The type of person suited to this work

As the work requires you to move around a lot and lift materials, you must be physically fit. And you must not mind working at heights.

You need to be able to follow plans and work with accuracy and attention to detail, so that the walls you build are structurally perfect and create the right visual effect.

You also need to work in a team with other bricklayers and those in other construction trades and professions.

Working conditions

You will often be working outdoors in all weather conditions. This can mean being cold and wet in the winter and hot and dusty in the summer.

To keep yourself and others safe you will need to observe health and safety regulations, which will include wearing protective clothing.

You are likely to work a normal working week, although weekend work may also be available.

The future outlook

There are currently plenty of opportunities to enter bricklaying. About 30% of the construction workforce is due to retire within the next 10 years and there will be a continuing need to recruit more young people into the industry.

If you work for a major national construction company you may have to work away from home as most demand is currently within the south-east of England.

In the long term, you could progress to technical, supervisory and managerial roles. The construction industry has one of the highest percentages of self-employment of any occupational sector and bricklayers are no exception. Many have set up their own businesses, often working on smaller, more local contracts.

Qualifications and courses

- There are no specific entry qualifications for this career. You could start work after leaving school and train on the job or train through an Apprenticeship/Skillseekers.
- Apprenticeships/Skillseekers are open to those aged 16–24. Some GCSEs/S grades (A–E/1–5) are normally required, in subjects such as English, maths, science and technology. In England and Wales, a Construction Apprenticeship Scheme allows you to study for NVQ Level 3. Students at school can apply for a Construction Apprenticeship in January of Year 11.
- Vocational qualifications include: BTEC Introductory Certificate and Diploma in Construction; BTEC First Diploma in Construction; City & Guilds Certificate in Basic Skills (6081). Bricklayers who train on the job can work towards NVQs/SVQs in Trowel Occupations at Levels 1–3 specialising in Bricklaying.
- The Construction Industry Training Board (CITB) Construction Award in Bricklaying allows those who have difficulties in gaining work experience to train for an NVQ. You can apply straight to the CITB before or after finding employment or gaining a place on a training scheme.
- New Deal offers taster courses and placements with an employer for at least 26 weeks. It may be possible to stay on and study for NVQs/SVQs. To qualify you must be aged 16–24 and unemployed for more than 6 months, or 25 or over and unemployed for 2 years.

CRCI:BB

CLCI:UF

Other related opportunities

- Building Technician p40
- Carpenter p41
- Dry Stone Waller p50
- Labourer p60
- Road Worker p66
- Stonemason p69

Advantages/disadvantages

- The work can be physically demanding for some people.
- There are opportunities to be creative when producing decorative effects.
- Bricklayers are in demand particularly in the south-east of England.
- This is a great career if you like being outdoors, doing practical and creative work.

Earnings guide

- Once you have achieved NVQ/SVQ Level 2 qualifications you can expect to earn around £17,000 per year.
- £20,500 is the average for bricklayers trained to NVQ/SVQ level 3.
- Experienced and qualified bricklayers can earn £25,000+.
- Overtime is often available, and on some projects there are bonuses based on outputs, which can lead to higher earnings.

Further information

ConstructionSkills
Bircham Newton
King's Lynn
Norfolk
PE31 6RH
01485 577577
www.cskills.org
www.bconstructive.co.uk

City & Guilds

www.cityandguilds.com/myperfectjob

Building Technician

What the work involves

- Building technicians support the work of construction professionals including surveyors and construction managers.
- Your work will vary depending on your employer and each project, but might include planning work schedules, drawing up plans, estimating project costs, buying materials, checking that plans meet building regulations, measuring and preparing construction-sites, and supervising work on-site.

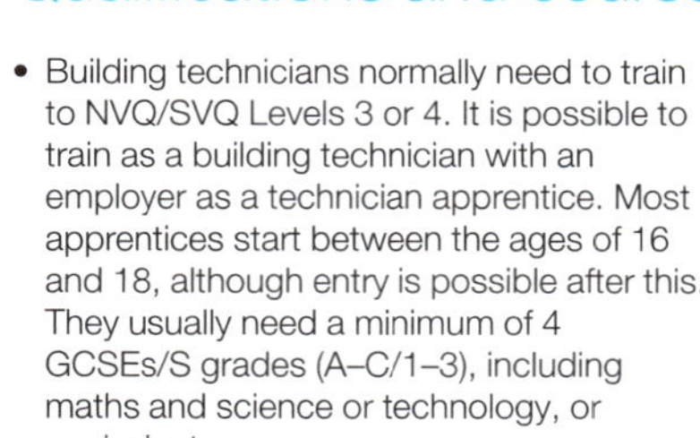

To both enter and train while working in this career, you will need qualifications at Level 3–8. Please refer to explanation on page vii.

The type of person suited to this work

You will have to be well-organised to make sure that each construction job is completed properly and on time. Mathematical and ICT skills are important for calculating costs, taking measurements and using computer-aided design.

You must be able to develop knowledge of the technical aspects of construction. You will also need strong communication skills for working with suppliers, site teams and other professionals such as surveyors, engineers and construction managers.

You will need to be able to do a number of tasks at the same time and remain calm!

Working conditions

You may work on construction-sites or in an office. Building technicians often divide their time between the two.

You must work safely on-site, by wearing a safety helmet, overalls and boots.

You are likely to work a normal working week, but you may also have to start early, finish late or work at weekends on occasion.

The future outlook

There are about 20,000 building technicians in the UK and currently a shortage of qualified applicants for the steady supply of vacancies..

Building technicians work for employers such as contractors, construction companies, property developers, surveyors' practices and in the public sector.

With experience and further qualifications, you may move up to a higher position such as building/construction manager.

You may also be able to work in countries other than the UK.

Qualifications and courses

- Building technicians normally need to train to NVQ/SVQ Levels 3 or 4. It is possible to train as a building technician with an employer as a technician apprentice. Most apprentices start between the ages of 16 and 18, although entry is possible after this. They usually need a minimum of 4 GCSEs/S grades (A–C/1–3), including maths and science or technology, or equivalent.
- HNDs in Building Studies or similar subjects can be studied over 2 years full time. Applicants should ideally have a science A level/H grade. Introductory courses to a career at technician level include BTEC National Certificate/Diploma or Scottish Group Award in Construction.
- It is possible to enter as a trainee and study part time for a National Certificate or HNC in Building Studies. Trainees may follow the site management education and training scheme, the first line supervisors scheme or NVQs/SVQs in Building Site Supervision/ Management.
- Many companies run training schemes, which often involve experience of different departments in the company, day-release study (for HNC and Chartered Institute of Building exams), time spent on building sites, in-house training courses, and the Construction Industry Training Board (CITB) Technician Training Scheme.
- It is possible to train in craft skills such as bricklaying, carpentry or plumbing through the Construction Apprenticeship Scheme, and work your way up by continuing to train to be a technician.

CRCI:BB

CLCI:UD

Other related opportunities

- Architectural Technician/Technologist p38
- Construction Manager p48
- Home Inspector / Energy Assessor p58
- Surveyor / Surveying Technician p70
- Technician (Construction) p72
- Town Planning Technician p76

Advantages/disadvantages

- It can be stressful having to work to deadlines.
- The work is interesting because you are likely to carry out many different tasks.
- You are an important part of the team that contributes to producing buildings of all kinds.

Earnings guide

- Starting out you can expect to earn around £14,500 per year.
- This can rise to £23,500 for building technicians with an increased level of experience.
- Up to £30,000 is possible for experienced senior building technicians.

Further information

ConstructionSkills
Bircham Newton
King's Lynn
Norfolk
PE31 6RH
01485 577577
www.cskills.net
www.bconstructive.co.uk

Chartered Institute of Building
Englemere
Kings Ride
Ascot
Berkshire
SL5 7TB
01344 630700
www.ciob.org.uk

Carpenter / Joiner

What the work involves

- Carpenters/Joiners make, put in place or repair the wooden parts of buildings.
- You may make and install floorboards, skirting boards, cupboards, partitions, windows and doors.
- You will work with different types of wood and use specialist hand tools such as hammers, chisels and planes, as well as power tools like jigsaws and sanders.

entry level

To both enter and train while working in this career, you will need qualifications at Level 1–2. Please refer to explanation on page vii.

Qualifications and courses

- You will normally need 3 to 5 GCSEs/S grades (A–E/1--5), preferably including English, maths, science and technology. Once employed, you can work towards NVQs/SVQs and City & Guilds qualifications, both on the job and at college.
- Apprenticeships/Skillseekers opportunities may be available for candidates aged 16–24, and normally take 3 years to complete.
- NVQs/SVQs are available in Wood Occupations, Levels 1, 2 and 3 and Wood Machining, Levels 2 and 3.
- City & Guilds certificates are available in Basic Carpentry and Joinery Skills (6111); Carpentry and Joinery (5859); Fine Woodwork (5770) and Machine Woodworking (5860).
- A Construction Award in Wood Occupations (Carpentry and Joinery Sitework) offered by the Construction Industry Training Board (CITB) allows those who have difficulties in gaining the work experience to train for an NVQ. You can apply straight to the CITB before or after finding employment or gaining a place on a training scheme.
- New Deal offers taster courses and placements with an employer for at least 26 weeks. It may be possible to stay on and study for NVQs/SVQs. To qualify you must be aged 16–24 and unemployed for more than 6 months, or 25 or over and unemployed for 2 years.
- Qualified carpenters can take more specialised courses in areas such as cabinet-making, roofing, French polishing or restoration.

The type of person suited to this work

Most importantly, you will need to have good practical skills and enjoy working with your hands and different tools.

You will be expected to follow plans and work carefully with attention to detail so that the structures you make fit into place correctly. As you will need to take measurements and calculate angles and dimensions, you will have to be good at maths and be accurate.

You will need to be physically fit, because you will have to move around and lift materials.

You must also be able to work in a team with other carpenters and those from the other construction trades and professions.

Working conditions

You may work in a workshop or on construction-sites, or divide your time between the two.

This can be heavy, dangerous and dusty work. You will need to keep to health and safety regulations, which may include wearing protective gear such as safety goggles and a mask. If you suffer from allergies, you could find this work difficult due to the dust.

You are likely to work a normal working week, although weekend work may also be required.

The future outlook

Across the UK, there are currently around 240,000 carpenters/joiners but employers are finding it difficult to recruit well-qualified and experienced carpenters. Many qualified carpenters are self-employed or work as sub-contractors

With experience, you could move into a related occupation like shopfitting, kitchen fitting or furniture-making, or you may progress to training, technical, supervisory and managerial levels Self-employment is also a possibility.

Other related opportunities

- Building Technician p40
- Fence Erector p53
- Glazier p55
- Labourer p60
- Locksmith p212
- Window Fitter p79

Advantages/disadvantages

- You may come across problems when carrying out your work and this can be challenging.
- You will develop a lot of new skills and knowledge.
- You can get a sense of achievement when you see your woodwork in place in a building.
- Carpentry can be dusty work, which can be difficult if you suffer from some allergies.

Earnings guide

- Salaries for trainees range between £12,500–£16,000 per year.
- Qualified carpenters can earn between £17,000–£25,000.
- Very experienced joiners could have an income of £25,000+.
- Overtime is often available, and on some projects there are bonuses based on outputs, which can lead to higher earnings.

Further information

Institute of Carpenters
3rd Floor D
Carpenters Hall
1 Throgmorton Avenue
London
ECZN 2BY

020 7256 1700
www.carpenters-institute.org

www.cityandguilds.com/myperfectjob

Carpet Fitter

What the work involves

- Carpet fitters lay new carpets in homes, shops and offices.
- After collecting the carpet, you would clear your work area, take down doors if needed, and remove any existing floor covering.
- You will then use various tools such as knives, staplers, trimmers and stretchers to cut the underlay and carpet to size, stretch and lay it flat, and fix the carpet into place.

entry level

To both enter and train while working in this career, you will need qualifications at Level 1–2. Please refer to explanation on page vii.

The type of person suited to this work

You must have good practical skills for working with tools and carpet materials, and be able to work out simple calculations, such as estimating the amount of carpet you might need for an area and measuring the carpets accurately.

As you will be working on your hands and knees and lifting heavy carpets you will need to be physically fit. Being able to work alone or with one other person all day will also be important. To keep your customers happy you should enjoy meeting and talking to all types of people. You will also have to be trustworthy as you could be working in peoples' homes, moving their possessions around.

Working conditions

You will work indoors in different locations every day, so a driving licence is often necessary.

You may work a normal working week from Monday to Friday, but you may also need to work outside of normal hours so that you can lay carpets without disrupting the work of shops and businesses, etc.

You will be on your hands and knees, often working in cramped conditions.

The future outlook

There are good prospects for finding work as a trainee carpet fitter because there is a shortage in many areas, and the industry needs more young people to take up the career.

Work is available with carpet retailers, flooring companies or flooring contractors throughout the UK.

With experience, you could set up on your own as a self-employed carpet fitter.

Qualifications and courses

- There are no formal entry requirements, but it is useful to have GCSEs/S grades (A–E/1–3) in maths, English, design and technology.
- Your training will mainly take place on the job with experienced carpet fitters. It is likely to take 2 years or more to become fully proficient.
- NVQs/SVQs in Floor Covering at Levels 1, 2 and 3 are available, which you can take while working.
- Your employer may also send you on short courses run by the Flooring Industry Training Association (FITA) to learn about all aspects of the work. Courses cover topics such as carpet types, floor presentation, cutting and seaming techniques, estimating and planning and health and safety.
- A driving licence is useful, and may be required for some jobs.
- Carpet fitters must have a good standard of physical fitness and normal colour vision.

CRCI:O

CLCI:OFZ

Other related opportunities

- Floor Layer p54
- Wall and Floor Tiler p77

Advantages/disadvantages

- Working on floors can make you dusty and dirty, and the work can be physically demanding especially on your knees and back.
- A well-laid carpet can transform a room. The ability to use your skills to do this can be very rewarding, especially when the job has been tricky, for example when working on an awkward staircase.

Earnings guide

- Starting as a trainee you could earn about £11,000–£12,500 per year.
- With experience you could earn £13,000–£21,000.
- Carpet fitters who manage others can earn up to £23,000.
- Earnings vary among employers and different parts of the country. Salaries in London are higher.

Further information

www.cityandguilds.com/myperfectjob

Flooring Industry Training Association
4c St Mary's Place
The Lace Market
Nottingham
NG1 1PH
0115 950 6836
www.fita.co.uk

Cartographer

What the work involves

- Cartography involves collecting, evaluating and displaying information gained from a variety of sources, including satellite technology, to create or update maps and navigation charts.
- This is achieved by using artistic, scientific, ICT and technological methods.
- You will often use sophisticated information technology for a range of tasks – from collecting to displaying the information.

The type of person suited to this work

You will need a sense of design, ICT, scientific and mathematical skills, and an interest in geography.

It can take months to produce one sheet of a map, so you need to be patient, dedicated and able to concentrate on one piece of work. You also need to work with accuracy and attention to detail so that the map provides the best possible information for the user.

Finally, you need to be willing to keep up with new techniques and experiment with new ways of producing maps. This means you will have to be happy to keep training and developing your skills throughout your career.

Working conditions

You are likely to work normal office hours at a workstation where you will have access to a computer.

Here, you will use graphics software and the different information collected by surveyors or other specialists to produce your maps. You may have some surveying duties.

The future outlook

Most work is available in government departments, such as Ordnance Survey, the Hydrographic Office and the Meteorological Office. You may also work for local authorities, universities, councils, commercial map publishers, oil companies and motoring organisations.

Entry to the work is competitive and you need to keep developing your skills once in the industry.

With experience, you may be able to find work as a freelance cartographer, provide consultancy services or work within higher education as a tutor.

If you are interested in working abroad, there are opportunities to work in cartography all over the world.

entry level

3–8

To both enter and train while working in this career, you will need qualifications at Level 3–8. Please refer to explanation on page vii.

Qualifications and courses

- The usual entry requirement for a cartographer is a relevant degree. Useful degree subjects include geography, geographical information systems, urban/land studies, surveying and mapping sciences. GCSE/S grade maths is generally needed for entry to these degrees, and an A level/H grade in science or maths may be required for some courses.
- It is useful to hold a postgraduate qualification in a relevant subject, for example cartography, geographical information systems or remote sensing. Also useful are art and design technology, maths and computing. Those with additional languages have greater opportunities to work overseas.
- Entrants receive on-the-job training in relevant software and techniques. Government departments that employ cartographers have their own training schemes. It is also possible to work towards an NVQ/SVQ Level 4 in Spatial Data Management.
- The minimum entry requirements for a cartographic technician are GCSEs/S grades (A–C/1–3), including maths, English and a science. In practice, most entrants have A levels/H grades, and some enter with a National Certificate/Diploma or HNC/D in a relevant area.
- It may be possible for people entering as school-leavers to study for a Certificate/Diploma or HNC/D by day-release, whilst training on the job.

Other related opportunities

- Architect p36
- Architectural Technician/Technologist p38
- Designer p136
- Earth Sciences p475
- Geographer p480
- Surveyor / Surveying Technician p70
- Town Planner p75
- Town Planning Technician p76

Advantages/disadvantages

- You can get great satisfaction from producing a map that looks good and is user-friendly. Potentially, a large number of people could use your maps.
- Sometimes, you may need to work late so that you can meet deadlines.
- The work is varied and combines a variety of subject areas, from design to geography to maths.

Earnings guide

- When starting out you can earn around £15,000–£18,000 per year.
- With three to five years' experience you can get £20,000–£25,000.
- It is possible for experienced or senior cartographers to earn up to £45,000.
- Earnings vary depending on the region, type of employer, your qualifications and experience.

Further information

British Cartographic Society
Wellington
Somerset
TA21 9AT
01823 665775.
www.cartography.org.uk

Cavity Wall Insulator

What the work involves

- Cavity wall insulators insulate the space between the walls of new and existing buildings.
- Your work will include checking that the building is suitable for insulation, drilling holes into the mortar between the bricks, injecting the insulating material into the holes, filling in the holes and checking that air vents are free from blockage.
- You will use a machine and hose to inject the insulation material into the holes and check that the cavity has been filled.

The type of person suited to this work

You will need practical skills to operate and maintain the drills and machines containing the insulation material. As you will climb ladders and carry tools and equipment you must be physically fit and feel comfortable working at heights.

Ability in maths is useful for calculating the quantities of materials you will need. English is helpful for following written instructions. You must have good communication skills and be able to get on well with people, including your customers.

Working conditions

You will work mainly outdoors, often on ladders or scaffolding. You will use a van to travel from job to job, so you may need a driving licence.

You need to work within health and safety regulations, which includes wearing a mask to prevent you from breathing in fibres, a helmet and ear protectors.

You are likely to work a normal working week, although you may also work at weekends.

The future outlook

According to the National Insulation Association, 9 million UK homes have uninsulated cavity walls. Awareness of the need to reduce fuel consumption and government grants to help with the costs has increased the demand for cavity wall insulators.

Companies, which are often small, employing fewer than ten people are located across the UK.

Many insulators choose to become self-employed once they have enough experience.

entry level

1

To both enter and train while working in this career, you will need qualifications at Level 1. Please refer to explanation on page vii.

Qualifications and courses

- There are no minimum entry requirements for this job although GCSEs/S grades (A–E/1–5) in English and maths are useful.
- Training follows British Board of Agreement (BBA) and British Standards Institution (BSI) regulations. It involves working with experienced cavity wall insulators as well as attending short classroom courses run by manufacturers and takes 3–6 months to become proficient.
- NVQs in Installing Insulation at Levels 1 and 2 and SVQ in Thermal Insulation Engineering at Level 2 are available, which you can take while you are working.
- Your employer may also send you on short courses to learn about different kinds of insulation material and safety awareness.
- A driving licence is an advantage.

CRCI:BB

CLCI:UF

Other related opportunities

- Bricklayer p39
- Glazier p55
- Labourer p60
- Painter and Decorator p63
- Roofer p67
- Scaffolder p68

Advantages/disadvantages

- Working at heights can be difficult for some people.
- It can be satisfying to know that you are making a positive contribution to the environment by helping to reduce the heat loss from buildings.

Earnings guide

- Earnings start at £12,000–£15,000 per year.
- £17,000–£20,500 is usual for fully trained cavity wall insulators.
- £21,000–£25,000+ is possible for senior experienced cavity wall technicians.
- Earnings vary depending on individual employers and location. Overtime is often available, which can lead to higher earnings. If you are self-employed you may charge a set rate per square meter.

Further information

www.cityandguilds.com/myperfectjob

National Insulation Association Limited
3 Vimy Court
Vimy Road
Leighton Buzzard
LU7 1FG
01525 383313
www.nationalinsulationassociation.org.uk

Ceiling Fixer

What the work involves

- As a ceiling fixer you will fit suspended ceilings into new and existing large commercial or public buildings.
- Your work will include fitting a ceiling grid in place and inserting tiles, by using tools such as metal cutters and screwdrivers.
- The ceiling is fitted to the concrete floor of the room above and may hide wiring and systems like air conditioning.

The type of person suited to this work

As most of your work will be done on ladders you will need to be comfortable working at heights. You will also need to be physically fit to do the necessary climbing, carrying and bending.

You will be expected to understand technical plans and be able to use basic maths skills to work out the amounts of materials needed. You will also have to manage your own time.

It will be important to get on with people as you will work alongside other ceiling fixers and those from other construction trades such as electricians, heating and ventilating fitters, painters and decorators.

Working conditions

You will work indoors in different kinds of buildings in a variety of locations so a driving licence may be useful.

You will need to take safety precautions for yourself and your colleagues and you will be expected to wear protective clothing such as a helmet. You will also have to work to strict procedures while setting up and taking down platforms, and whilst working.

You are likely to work a normal working week, although weekend work may also be available.

This could be dusty work, which might be difficult if you suffer from some allergies.

The future outlook

There is currently a shortage of qualified ceiling fixers in the construction industry.

Work is available with interiors companies and building contractors across the UK.

As well as ceiling fixing, you may work in other related trades such as partition fixing.

With experience, you may progress to a supervisory or managerial position, or perhaps run your own company. Most specialist interiors companies and contractors are owned or run by someone who started out as a tradesperson.

entry level

To both enter and train while working in this career, you will need qualifications at Level 1–2. Please refer to explanation on page vii.

Qualifications and courses

- No specific qualifications are required, although GCSEs/S grades or a BTEC Introductory Certificate/Diploma in Construction may be useful. Maths, design and technology, science and English are useful subjects.
- You will be trained on the job while working towards qualifications. This may also involve going to a college or training centre on day- or block-release.
- NVQs/SVQs in Interior Systems (Ceiling Fixing) at Levels 1, 2 and 3 are available.
- Apprenticeships/Skillseekers may be available to those aged 16–24.
- You can also train by doing a Construction Industry Training Board (CITB) Construction Apprenticeship Scheme in Ceiling Fixing.
- The Construction Industry Training Board (CITB) Construction Award in Interior Systems allows those who have difficulties in gaining the work experience to train for an NVQ. You can apply straight to the CITB before or after finding employment or gaining a place on a training scheme.

CRCI:BB

CLCI:UF

Other related opportunities

- Building Technician p40
- Glazier p55
- Labourer p60
- Painter and Decorator p63
- Plasterer p64
- Roofer p67
- Scaffolder p68

Advantages/disadvantages

- Working at heights may be demanding for some people.
- It is satisfying to see the transformation that takes place when you have worked on fitting a ceiling and hidden away unsightly features such as air conditioning.

Earnings guide

- When starting out as a newly qualified ceiling fixer you can expect to earn around £18,000 per year.
- For those with supervisory responsibility and lots of experience, £25,000–£40,000 is possible.
- Overtime is often available, and on some projects there are bonuses based on outputs, which can lead to higher earnings.

Further information

ConstructionSkills
Bircham Newton
King's Lynn
Norfolk
PE31 6RH
01485 577577
www.cskills.net
www.bconstructive.co.uk

www.cityandguilds.com/myperfectjob

Civil / Construction Engineer

What the work involves

- Engineers working in construction often specialise in different areas. Different jobs include:

Civil engineer (consulting)

- Designing and developing construction projects like roads, tunnels, bridges, railways, reservoirs, pipelines and major buildings.

Civil engineer (Contracting)

- Making a building project a reality, costing it up, bidding for the work and then managing its construction.

Structural engineer

- Ensuring that any structure or building will cope with the stresses it will face in its lifetime, by looking at the design, shape, and building materials used.

Building services engineer

- Designing systems that make buildings useable and comfortable. Systems include lighting, power, heating and ventilation, plumbing, lifts and escalators. include lighting, power, heating and ventilation, plumbing, lifts and escalators.

The type of person suited to this work

Regardless of the area you decide to work in, you will need to enjoy finding creative, but workable, solutions to problems

You will need to be happy and confident when using computers to produce designs and do research and costings. You will also have to be good at maths and science for making accurate calculations and understanding the different materials available to you. You will also have to be able to think three dimensionally, so that you can visualise and design different buildings and structures.

Written and verbal communication skills are important as you will have to write reports, explain your designs and supervise different construction staff. Your work will involve being a member of a team, so you will have to be able to communicate with people at all levels including other professionals and clients, explaining what you require so that everyone understands what you intend.

Of increasing importance is the need to be interested in protecting the environment, for example by using energy efficient building materials and systems.

Working conditions

Your work will involve both being indoors and on-site.

When you are in your office, you will be based at a workstation where you will use a computer with specialised software and possibly a drawing board. You will attend meetings and speak to clients on the phone or in person. The amount of time you spend in the office or on-site will depend on your employer and the type of job you do.

You may work a normal working week, but many engineers have to start work early, finish late or work at weekends to meet deadlines.

When you are working on-site you will need to stick to health and safety regulations and be aware of your own and colleagues' safety. You will have to wear safety clothing including a helmet. You could work in dangerous places including working up ladders or on scaffolding, or in difficult environments. You could be outdoors in all weather conditions.

It is likely that you will have to work away from home, including abroad. However, this will depend on the size of the company you work for, and the type of contracts they attract.

The future outlook

Around 100,000 professional civil engineers work in the UK for a range of employers including health trusts, local authorities, central government, energy suppliers including water, gas, nuclear and electricity companies, contractors, consultancies and transport networks

Due to the severe skills shortages in this sector there is a high demand for new entrants to civil, structural and building services engineering. For those with qualifications, work is available throughout the UK on a wide range of projects such as the building of new schools, hospitals and the upgrading of public transport networks. There is a particular shortage in the south and east of England with huge building projects underway such as the 2012 Olympics build and the Thames Gateway regeneration project.

Many UK civil engineering companies also operate globally, increasing the opportunities to work overseas. One large UK company manages projects in 39 countries. The range and size of opportunities open to you will depend on the size of the company you work for, and the types of contracts won.

With experience, you could progress into management or possibly associate/partnership positions within UK or international companies, management and chief engineer jobs in public services work, provide training or consultancy services or choose self-employment.

CRCI:BB

CLCI:UN/UJ

Other related opportunities

- Architect p36
- Building Technician p40
- Construction Manager p48
- Engineer: Professional p205
- Engineer: Technician p208
- Surveyor / Surveying Technician p70
- Technician (Construction) p75
- Town Planner p000

Advantages/disadvantages

- Sometimes the hours can be long and you may have to juggle a number of projects.
- You will play an important part in the design and construction of buildings and structures throughout the world. Seeing your ideas being built is satisfying.
- Having an engineering career and qualifications are keys to entering other non-engineering careers at senior levels.
- Construction is a growth area, and is expected to have staff and skills shortages for the foreseeable future.

Earnings guide

- The salary figures below apply to all the areas of engineering (civil, structural, municipal and building services).
- Starting salaries for new graduates are around £22,000–£23,000 per year.
- With five or more years experience you could earn between £35,000 and £50,000.
- Senior chartered engineers can earn more than £60,000.
- Earnings vary among regions and employers. Salaries are generally higher in London and other large cities.

Qualifications and courses

- Professional engineering (chartered or incorporated engineer) is usually a graduate profession, although there are opportunities to progress from craft or technical level in some branches of engineering.
- The main route to becoming an engineer is a degree in the relevant branch of engineering, or a closely related subject. The normal minimum entry requirements for an engineering degree are 3 A levels or 5 H grades including maths and a science, usually physics or chemistry. Equivalent qualifications such as BTEC/SQA National qualifications may be accepted.
- Candidates who do not have the relevant A levels or equivalent may gain entry to an engineering degree by taking a 1-year Foundation course. Foundation courses are offered by universities and are sometimes taught at local partner colleges.
- Professional engineers can be chartered or incorporated members of one of the engineering professional bodies, for example the Institution of Civil Engineers (ICE) or the Chartered Institution of Building Services Engineers (CIBSE). The professional bodies accredit BEng and MEng degrees. The usual requirement for chartered status is an accredited MEng degree, or equivalent. For incorporated status, a three-year accredited BEng or BSc degree or an HND or equivalent, plus an additional period of learning (matching section) is required.
- It is possible to enter engineering after taking GCSEs and progress to technician or professional level by studying part time for an HNC/D or NVQ/SVQ Levels 4 or 5.

entry level

To both enter and train while working in this career, you will need qualifications at Level 4–8. Please refer to explanation on page vii.

Further information

ConstructionSkills
Bircham Newton
King's Lynn
Norfolk
PE31 6RH
01485 577577
www.cskills.net
www.bconstructive.co.uk

CIVIL/MUNICIPAL
Institution of Civil Engineers
1 Great George Street
Westminster
London
SW1P 3AA
020 7222 7722
www.ice.org.uk

STRUCTURAL
Institution of Structural Engineers
11 Upper Belgrave Street
London
SW1X 8BH
020 7235 4535
www.istructe.org.uk

BUILDING SERVICES
Chartered Institution of Building Services Engineers
222 Balham High Road
Balham
London
SW12 9BS
020 8675 5211
www.cibse.org

Chartered Institute of Building
Englemere
Kings Ride
Ascot
Berkshire
SL5 7TB
01344 630700
www.ciob.org.uk

Association of Building Engineers
Lutyens House
Billing Brook Road
Weston Favell
Northampton
NN3 8NW
0845 126 1058
www.abe.org.uk

Here's Emma Young's story:

Civil Engineer

Having achieved good A levels in biology, maths, and chemistry, 22-year-old Emma decided she didn't want to go to university. She looked around for jobs that had work-based training and discovered there were a lot of vacancies in the engineering sector. She decided civil engineering involved the skills she enjoyed using, so she took a full-time HND Civil Engineering course and has now joined a company where she is reading towards a degree in Civil Engineering on a part-time basis. Her company has sponsored her membership of the Institution of Civil Engineers (ICE) and its professional development training towards a Chartership.

WHAT THE JOB ENTAILS

'I have to read and interpret technical drawings. This involves using technical and practical construction knowledge, as well as mathematical skills. I'm also actively involved in the quality assurance of the construction, be it a road, a bridge or a skyscraper, ensuring the correct methods are used, the work meets specifications, and that the structure is in the right place! I take a supervisory role in the works and often communicate instructions to the workforce and receive instructions from management. I play a supporting role to management, acting as their eyes and ears on-site.'

Emma always wanted a hands-on job, which is why she likes engineering so much. She likes coupling the technical side with the practical application. She likes to be physically as well as mentally active. One of the downsides of being on-site so much is that the weather can get very cold in winter; this has not put her off, though. She is hoping to complete her degree and then follow a career path into management, as she has the ambition needed, and her company actively encourages her to take on more responsibility.

WHAT YOU NEED TO SUCCEED

'The willingness to work. Sometimes it is hard juggling a full-time job and studying for a degree, so you need to be motivated. It would be easy for me to just stay at HND level, so you really do need to be ambitious. I urge anyone, who wants to do what I am doing, to get practical experience on-site. There are courses that can be done on a part-time basis and if you do choose to go the full-time course route, then get vacation work experience or take an industrial year placement. With a shortage of skills in the industry, loads of companies are now offering these opportunities, so use them to your advantage.'

Construction Manager

What the work involves

- Building/construction managers run construction-sites – new builds or maintenance projects.
- Your duties will include planning the build, preparing the site, arranging for the delivery and storage and checking the quality and costings of building materials and equipment, overseeing the construction project, making sure everyone is safe on-site, managing construction staff and solving problems when they arise.

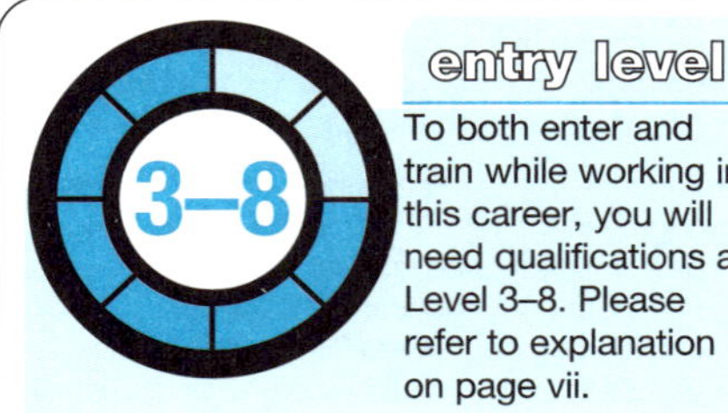

entry level

To both enter and train while working in this career, you will need qualifications at Level 3–8. Please refer to explanation on page vii.

The type of person suited to this work

You have to be able to plan ahead and have good management and problem-solving skills so that projects run smoothly. To ensure that projects run within financial forecasts, numeracy skills are important too.

You will use computer software packages to plan workflow, so ICT skills are useful.

You must be able to develop an in-depth knowledge and understanding of all aspects of the construction business.

So that you can supervise the site's workforce and consult with other professionals such as architects and engineers, excellent communication skills are vital

Working conditions

During construction, you will be based on a site and are likely to work from a portable office. You will also work outdoors in all weathers, for example when consulting with the workforce about a problem or making regular safety inspections.

You will need to keep yourself and your staff safe, which includes wearing a safety helmet, overalls and boots.

You may work a normal working week, but you may also have to start early, finish late or work at weekends on some projects. As some companies win contracts all over the UK, you may have to work away from home.

The future outlook

Across the UK construction industry, there is a shortage of qualified construction managers. There are opportunities across the UK on a wide range of projects including multi-million pound builds. Particular shortages exist in the South and South East of England.

Building/construction managers work for contractors, construction companies, project management companies, surveyors' practices and public services.

With experience, you may be promoted to work as a contract manager on bigger and more prestigious projects.

You may also be able to work on projects in other parts of the world.

Qualifications and courses

- Building/construction managers enter the profession with relevant educational qualifications and/or industrial experience.
- The normal entry qualification to be a construction manager is a degree, HND or Foundation degree. Relevant subjects include construction project management, building services and construction management. For entry to a degree, 5 GCSEs/S grades (A–C/1–3) and 2 A levels/3 H grades are normally required. Maths and/or a science may be required.
- It may be possible to work your way up from technician level. The NVQ/SVQ Level 3 Site Supervision and Level 4 Site Management are open to anyone with experience in building site supervision and management. Technicians can also study part time towards an HNC or degree.
- Recently qualified graduates are likely to continue training on programmes designed for professional and managerial staff. The Chartered Institute of Building (CIOB) runs a Professional Development Programme (PDP) leading to corporate membership of the Institute.

CRCI:BB | CLCI:UD

Other related opportunities

- Architectural Technician / Technologist p38
- Building Technician p40
- Civil / Construction Engineer p46
- Surveyor / Surveying Technician p70

Advantages/disadvantages

- It will be great to know that you can begin with an empty piece of land and leave a finished construction behind, a relatively short time later.
- When there is a tight deadline to meet and a problem arises, the work can be stressful – particularly as many projects are on large but tightly planned budgets.

Earnings guide

- Salaries for graduate trainees start from £16,000–£23,000 per year.
- This can quickly rise to £26,000–£37,000 for managers with experience.
- For managers running the largest projects £40,000+ is possible.
- Earnings vary depending on geographical location and your particular employer.

Further information

www.cityandguilds.com/myperfectjob

ConstructionSkills
Bircham Newton
King's Lynn
Norfolk
PE31 6RH
01485 577577
www.cskills.net
www.bconstructive.co.uk

Chartered Institute of Building
Englemere
Kings Ride
Ascot
Berkshire
SL5 7TB
01344 630700
www.ciob.org.uk

Construction Plant Operator

What the work involves

- Construction plant operators work on construction-sites. They operate and maintain the different forms of plant (machinery) used for tasks such as moving soil and building materials, flattening the earth and preparing concrete.
- The kinds of plant you may be trained to operate include bulldozers, excavators, diggers, cranes and fork-lift trucks.
- In larger organisations you may be required to specialise in operating one type of plant.

entry level

1–2

To both enter and train while working in this career, you will need qualifications at Level 1–2. Please refer to explanation on page vii.

The type of person suited to this work

As you will be handling sometimes large and complex machines you must have good practical skills. You will be working in various construction-sites dealing with lots of different terrain and working conditions. This means that being flexible and adaptable will be important requirements.

You have to be able to keep your concentration and communicate with your workmates so that you can operate the plant safely. You will be expected to work responsibly and make sure you and your colleagues are safe.

If you are working on certain types of plant, such as cranes, you need to be comfortable working at heights. It will also be helpful if you have some mechanical knowledge when working with plant in case problems occur.

Working conditions

You will work outdoors in all weathers and in a variety of construction-site locations. Expect to get hot, dusty and dirty in the summer and cold, muddy and wet in the winter.

You will have to stick to health and safety regulations, which will include wearing a protective helmet and boots.

You are likely to work a normal working week from Monday to Friday, but you may also work extra hours at weekends. Some construction firms operate longer hours during the summer months and shorter during the winter. You might have to travel away from home on some contracts.

The future outlook

There is a particular shortage of qualified crane and heavy plant operators, and a demand in general for construction plant operators. Work is available across the UK with plant hire companies and construction companies that specialise in plant operation. Many of the major contracts are in the south-east of England or in major cities.

With experience, you may progress to using a wider range of plant, and you may supervise or train plant operators or work as a safety inspector. You may also choose to specialise in operating one type of plant such as cranes or fork-lift trucks.

With experience and financial backing, it may be possible to start your own construction plant operation or hire business.

Qualifications and courses

- There are no set academic entry requirements, although GCSEs/S grades or equivalent in English, maths and science or technology are useful, along with equivalent vocational qualifications like the Edexcel (BTEC) Introductory Certificate or Diploma in Construction. A full driving licence is sometimes a requirement.
- The minimum age to operate plant is 18, but 17-year-olds may work under supervision while they are training.
- You will train and gain vocational qualifications while you work. You will be taught practical skills and may spend time off site at a college or training centre.
- It is also possible to take NVQs/SVQs at Levels 1 and 2 in Specialised Plant and Machinery Operations and Construction Plant and Equipment Supervision at Level 3.
- Apprenticeships/Skillseekers may be available to those aged 16–24.
- The main standard for plant operators is the Construction Plant Competence Scheme (CPCS) card, which is required to operate most categories of plant. It certifies the holder's operating skills and health and safety awareness. There are two routes to obtaining the full card. Plant operators aged over 21 with at least 3 years' experience can apply directly for the CPCS Operator Test. New entrants who have completed basic training and passed a health and safety test can obtain the 'red' CPCS card, and convert it to the full 'blue' card on completion of an NVQ/SVQ.

CRCI:BB

CLCI:UV

Other related opportunities

Advantages/disadvantages

- Working on construction-sites can be noisy, dusty and dirty although you will have safety gear such as ear protectors. Working at heights may be demanding for some people.
- It is a skilled and varied career where you are responsible for some awesome machinery. It can be satisfying to be able to control the machinery efficiently and safely.

Earnings guide

- Starting as a trainee you can expect to earn around £13,000 per year.
- This can rise to £15,000–£20,000 with qualifications and experience.
- Highly experienced staff can earn more than £25,000.
- Earnings vary depending on the type of plant you are operating. Operators of special types of crane may earn up to £40,000.
- Overtime is often available, and on some projects there are bonuses based on outputs, which can lead to higher earnings.

Further information

ConstructionSkills
Bircham Newton
King's Lynn
Norfolk
PE31 6RH

01485 577577
www.cskills.net
www.bconstructive.co.uk

www.cityandguilds.com/myperfectjob

Dry Stone Waller

What the work involves

- Dry stone walls are built as boundaries in rural landscapes, and sometimes in gardens and parks. Unlike other walls, they are built without the use of mortar or cement.
- You will build new walls and maintain and rebuild existing walls.
- Preparing foundations, setting up a frame and laying stones, as well as stripping out any existing wall or stones, will be part of the job.

entry level

To both enter and train while working in this career, you will need qualifications at Level 1–2. Please refer to explanation on page vii.

The type of person suited to this work

As the work requires you to move around and lift heavy stones, you must be physically fit and be able to handle the stones safely. Practical skills and a methodical approach to the work are necessary.

An eye for design is useful for creating decorative effects. You may also need to work in a team with other dry stone wallers. You will need to respect the plants, animals and insects that live within, on or around the walls and other parts of your working area so having an interest in conservation and the environment is useful.

Working conditions

Your work will be physically demanding and take place outdoors in most weather conditions. The work may also be dusty and dirty

You will need to pay attention to health and safety regulations, for example the wearing of protective gear such as boots, strong gloves and safety goggles.

Your working hours are likely to vary according to when the work is available. You may work at weekends.

The future outlook

There are around 600 dry stone wallers working in the UK and numbers are increasing. With a demand for walls on farms, and in parks and gardens, work is available in all rural areas of the UK for skilled dry stone wallers.

Employment is possible with organisations such as National Parks – although most experienced dry stone wallers are self-employed.

You can begin by working for an experienced dry stone waller and gain the necessary skills before working for yourself. Many experienced wallers travel around the UK to complete projects. A few wallers combine this work with traditional bricklaying work.

Qualifications and courses

- No specific qualifications are required. Many people enter the work after working on a farm and hearing about the work by word of mouth.
- You can train with an experienced dry stone waller or do a land-based training course that includes dry stone walling.
- Lantra Certificates at Levels 1 and 2 are available in Dry Stone Walling.
- The Dry Stone Walling Association of Great Britain (DSWA) runs a National Certification scheme at four levels – Initial, Intermediate, Advanced and Master Craftsman – which is open to anyone, including complete beginners.
- Lantra offer an Apprenticeship in Dry Stone Walling (England and Wales). Apprentices work towards NVQ Level 2 in Environmental Conservation, the Lantra Level 2 Certificate in Dry Stone Walling, and Key Skills in Communication and Application of Number. There are no formal entry requirements to an Apprenticeship; commitment to a career in dry stone walling is more important. The Apprenticeship normally takes 12 months.

CRCI:B

CLCI:UZ

Other related opportunities

- Bricklayer p39
- Labourer p60
- Stonemason p69
- Thatcher p74

Advantages/disadvantages

- The work can be physically demanding.
- It is rewarding to use craft skills to build dry stone walls that are not only functional, but also enhance the landscape and become part of our heritage.
- You also have the chance to be creative when producing decorative effects.

Earnings guide

- The normal starting point for new entrants is around £8,000 per year.
- For dry stone wallers with some experience £10,500–£14,500 is possible.
- For very skilled dry stone wallers up to £21,000 is likely.
- Earnings vary widely across the UK. The rates self-employed dry stone wallers can charge depend a lot on their expertise. They often charge by the metre, and in some areas the demand for this diminishing craft is quite high.

Further information

www.cityandguilds.com/myperfectjob

ConstructionSkills
Bircham Newton
King's Lynn
Norfolk
PE31 6RH
01485 577577
www.cskills.net
www.bconstructive.co.uk

Dry Stone Walling Association of Great Britain
Westmorland County Showground
Lane Farm
Crooklands
Milnthorpe
Cumbria
LA7 7NH
01539 567953
www.dswa.org.uk

Lantra (Sector Skills Council for the environmental and land-based industries)
Lantra House
Stoneleigh Park
Coventry
Warwickshire
CV8 2LG
0845 707 8007
www.lantra.co.uk

Electrician (Installation)

What the work involves

- Installation electricians install the wiring systems (including cables, switches and sockets) into new and existing buildings. This includes working on systems for equipment, lighting and power.
- You will follow diagrams and plans and install new systems. Once installed you will test them to make sure they are safe.
- You may work on quite complex wiring systems for security circuits and computer networks.

entry level

To both enter and train while working in this career, you will need qualifications at Level 1–2. Please refer to explanation on page vii.

The type of person suited to this work

You must have practical skills to be able to use tools such as pliers, screwdrivers and drills. You will also need to be physically fit as the work involves bending, stretching, kneeling and generally being active. It can also involve working at heights, so you must be comfortable with this. You will be expected to follow wiring diagrams and work to strict safety procedures. You must have normal colour vision.

You may have to work alone for some jobs; for others you may need to be able to work in a small team. Verbal communication skills are also important for talking to customers.

Working conditions

Electricians work in a variety of locations from people's homes to offices or building sites. You will almost certainly need a driving licence.

The work can be dusty and dirty.

You will need to keep to health and safety regulations, because working with electricity is dangerous otherwise.

You may work a normal working week from Monday to Friday, but some electricians work shifts or at weekends, and travel away from home could be required.

The future outlook

There is currently a shortage of trained electricians, so employment prospects for new trainees are good. There are opportunities throughout the UK and in particular the South and South East of England where there are large numbers of existing and planned construction projects.

Work is available in housing associations, general building companies and public services such as local authorities and health trusts. With further qualifications and experience, you can progress to approved grade, then technician grade. You may also hold supervisory or management positions and owning your own company is an option. There are also opportunities to work abroad.

Qualifications and courses

- Entry requirements for this sector include 4 GCSEs/S grades (A–C/1–3) including English, maths and science subjects. If candidates do not have these qualifications some employers may require the successful completion of an aptitude test.
- Most people enter the profession through an Apprenticeship/Skillseekers although those holding City & Guilds Electrical Installation (2360) may qualify. Applicants need to be aged 16–24.
- Those experienced in other relevant areas such as electronics may also qualify.
- Apprentices work towards three separate qualifications, which are the Certificate in Electrotechnical Technology (City & Guilds 2330) at Levels 2–3 and NVQ/SVQ Level 3 in Electrotechnical Services (assessed in the workplace).
- Other qualifications on offer include the City & Guilds Engineering Systems Maintenance (2140), the BTEC National Certificate in Engineering or the NVQ/SVQ Engineering Maintenance Level 3.

Other related opportunities

- Electricity Generation Worker p201
- Engineer: Craft p203
- Engineer: Technician p208
- Gas Distribution Worker p211
- Heating and Ventilating Engineer p56
- Motor Vehicle Work p217
- Railway Fitter / Electrician p223
- Technician (Construction) p72

Advantages/disadvantages

- Working in hot or cold (depending on the weather) and often cramped conditions, possibly underground, in roof spaces or at heights, can be difficult for some people.
- Seeing a job through from start to finish is satisfying. You are part of a vital service and it is particularly rewarding to be able to solve problems for people.

Earnings guide

- JIB (Joint Industry Board) for the Electrical Contracting Industry sets salary rates, and travel allowances for apprentices and qualified electricians.
- As an Apprentice you would start at £4.67 per hour rising to £9.66 per hour. Increases in pay are linked to training.
- As a general rule newly qualified electricians' salaries rise to £20,000–£25,000.
- Experienced electricians can earn £30,000 or more.
- If you do not have your own transport or if you work in one location only, the rates are a bit lower. Rates in London are higher and overtime is paid at a higher rate.

Further information

SummitSkills (Sector Skills Council for Building Services Engineering)
Vega House
Opal Drive
Fox Milne
Milton Keynes
MK15 0DF
08000 688336
www.summitskills.org.uk

Joint Industry Board for the Electrical Contracting Industry
Kingswood House
47–51 Sidcup Hill
Sidcup
Kent
DA14 6HP
020 8302 0031
www.jib.org.uk

www.cityandguilds.com/myperfectjob

Estate Agent

What the work involves

- An estate agent's job is to sell property for their clients, earning a fee for their work
- You will work for your client (the seller of the property) by marketing the property to potential buyers. This may involve finding suitable properties for people to view and showing them around properties.
- When a buyer is found, you will help the buyer and seller to agree a price for the property.

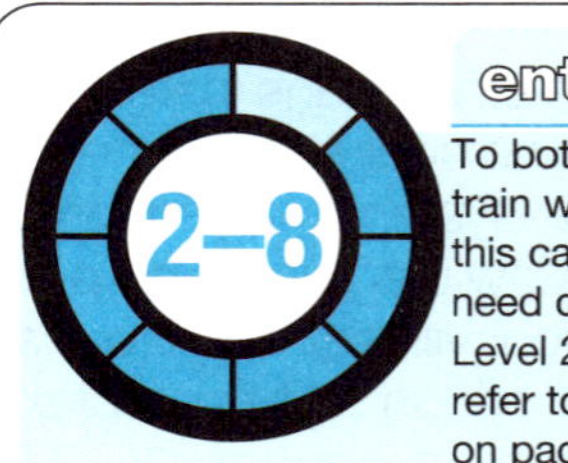

entry level

To both enter and train while working in this career, you will need qualifications at Level 2–8. Please refer to explanation on page vii.

The type of person suited to this work

You will need excellent listening and speaking skills so that you can recommend suitable properties to potential buyers. You also have to be good at negotiating so that you can help buyers and sellers to agree prices for properties.

You must be confident dealing with people and prepared to work hard to achieve sales.

As you will be dealing with figures when valuing properties or negotiating prices, you will need numeracy skills and an interest in keeping up to date with what is happening in the housing and property markets.

You will also have to dress smartly and be polite when meeting clients.

Working conditions

Some of your time will be spent in the branch office, and the rest of the time you will be visiting properties, so a driving licence is needed.

Estate agency branches are often modern and open-plan with up-to-date equipment. You will spend a lot of your time working at a computer and speaking to your customers on the phone. This can be very stressful work as you will have sales targets to reach and your earnings will depend on your selling ability.

You are likely to need to work at weekends and evenings (with some time off during the week instead).

The future outlook

Estate agents are located throughout the UK. At the moment, there are plenty of vacancies, but the situation can change depending on the property market – with fewer opportunities in a poor housing market.

If you do well and gain experience and qualifications, there are opportunities for promotion – especially in larger estate agencies. For example, you may move from trainee to negotiator, then to senior negotiator and on to branch manager.

Estate agencies vary from small, family-owned companies to large chains with a number of branches throughout the UK.

Qualifications and courses

- It is useful for entrants to have GCSEs/S grades (A–C/1–3). Most entrants have A levels/H grades or a degree. Relevant degree subjects include property management and real estate management.
- Training can be done on the job. It may involve studying for qualifications through the National Association of Estate Agents (NAEA). The NAEA offer Technical Awards in Sale of Residential Property and Residential Letting and Property Management aimed at new entrants. Diploma programmes in Residential Estate Agency, Residential Property Letting and Commercial Property Agency are intended for those with around 3 years' experience. Both the Technical Awards and the Diplomas may be studied by distance learning, or part-time at a college.
- TTC Training offers an Apprenticeship for young people, leading to NVQ Level 2 or 3 in the Sale of Residential Property. The Apprenticeship also includes The National Association of Estate Agents' (NAEA) Technical Award, and Apprentices gain student membership of the NAEA after three months.
- Qualifications are also offered by the Royal Institution of Chartered Surveyors (RICS). For estate agents who are interested in moving into surveying, the NAEA Diplomas can provide an entry routes to RICS general surveying courses.

Other related opportunities

- Car Salesperson p440
- Customer Services p442
- Home Inspector / Energy Assessor p58
- Land Valuer / Auctioneer p61
- Sales Assistant p450
- Surveyor / Surveying Technician p70

Advantages/disadvantages

- The work can be stressful if you are finding it hard to meet sales targets, especially if you are working on a commission-only basis in a slowing housing market.
- On the other hand, the financial rewards can be high if the property market is booming.

Earnings guide

- Earnings vary widely depending on region and may be affected by the number of sales you make. Bonuses and commission payments are often added to salaries. Some estate agents work for commission only.
- New entrants earn about £13,000 a year.
- This can rise to £20,000+ for experienced advisers, negotiators and managers. As a partner in a business you could earn around £35,000.
- Top earners such as area managers could earn up to £40,000.

Further information

www.cityandguilds.com/myperfectjob

Asset Skills (Sector Skills Council in property services, housing, cleaning services and facilities management)
2 The Courtyard
48 New North Road
Exeter
Devon
EX4 4EP
01392 423399
www.assetskills.org

National Association of Estate Agents
Arbon House
6 Tournament Court
Edgehill Drive
Warwick
CV34 6LG
01926 496800
www.naea.co.uk

Royal Institution of Chartered Surveyors
Surveyor Court
Westwood Way
Coventry
CV4 8JE
0870 333 1600
www.rics.org

Fence Erector

What the work involves

- Fence erectors put up many different kinds of fences in a wide range of locations. For example, they erect motorway barriers, perimeter fencing around prisons and safari parks, as well as fencing for gardens, farms and forests.
- Before putting up a fence, you will measure the area, work out how much fencing you need and prepare the ground.
- As a fence erector, you will work with a range of materials such as wire, wood, concrete or metal.

The type of person suited to this work

You will need to have good practical skills to work with a range of materials, tools and equipment. The job involves working to plans and taking measurements, so you must also be able to work accurately and have basic maths skills.

As you will be working with some heavy materials you will need to be physically fit.

The ability to work in a team with other fence erectors is important. You will also need to understand the use of all types of fencing and related construction materials, and be aware of the environment.

Working conditions

You will work mainly outdoors in a range of locations from people's gardens to construction-sites and motorways. You may need a driving licence and for some projects you will sometimes have to stay away from home.

You will need to work to health and safety regulations, for example the wearing of protective gear such as a safety helmet, gloves and boots.

You are likely to work a normal working week, although weekend work may also be available.

The future outlook

The fencing industry is made up of around 4,000 specialist fencing businesses employing about 25,000 fencing operatives. There are currently plenty of opportunities for skilled fence erectors and the range of work available is as varied as the types of fences needed!

Work is available with fencing companies of all sizes throughout the UK. You may work in the construction, landscape, environmental, forestry and agricultural industries. Some companies specialise in providing soundproofing, while others supply agricultural or roadside fencing.

You may progress to supervisory and managerial levels and, after you have gained enough experience, you could run your own business.

entry level

1–2

To both enter and train while working in this career, you will need qualifications at Level 1–2. Please refer to explanation on page vii.

Qualifications and courses

- No specific qualifications are required, although GCSEs/S grades (A–E/1–5), in English, maths and technology may be useful. New entrants need to do health and safety training before working on construction-sites.
- You will be trained mainly on the job, and you may also attend a college or training centre. You could work towards NVQs/SVQs in Fencing at Levels 2 and 3.
- Apprenticeships/Skillseekers are available for candidates aged 16–24.
- Lantra awards a card (required by many construction-sites) from a Fencing Industry Skills Scheme (FISS), which is run in partnership with the Construction Skills Certification Scheme (CSCS). The card is provided following attendance on approved health and safety training, passing a health and safety test, and enrolling on an NVQ/SVQ.

CRCI:BB | CLCI:UF

Other related opportunities

- Bricklayer p39
- Building Technician p40
- Carpenter / Joiner p41
- Dry Stone Waller p50
- Labourer p60

Advantages/disadvantages

- The work may be physically demanding for some people.
- Your fencing will help to protect people, buildings, animals and vehicles.
- You will develop a range of skills and knowledge on a variety of projects.
- You will be outside in all weathers.

Earnings guide

- Starting out as a trainee you could earn between £12,000 and £14,500 per year.
- Trained and experienced fence erectors could earn from £23,000 to £25,000.
- Up to £40,000 is possible for the highest earners, who may manage a team of workers.
- Overtime and bonuses based on outputs may be available, which can lead to higher earnings.

Further information

Lantra (Sector Skills Council for the environmental and land-based industries)
Lantra House
Stoneleigh Park
Coventry
Warwickshire
CV8 2LG
0845 707 80007
www.lantra.co.uk

Fencing Contractors Association
Warren Road
Trellech
Monmouthshire
NP25 4PQ
07000 560722
www.fencingcontractors.org

www.cityandguilds.com/myperfectjob

Floor Layer

What the work involves

- Floor layers fit many different types of flooring materials into buildings. For example, they may work with vinyl, wood, carpet tiles, rubber or plastic.
- You will decide on the best material to use for the particular type of floor. You will then use various tools to prepare the surface, cut the flooring material to size and lay the floor.

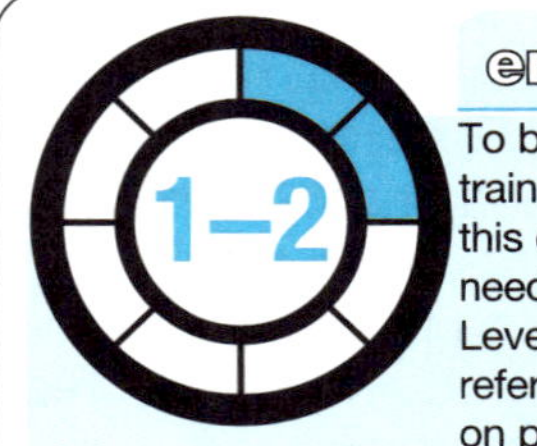

entry level

To both enter and train while working in this career, you will need qualifications at Level 1–2. Please refer to explanation on page vii.

The type of person suited to this work

To do this work you will need mathematical skills to calculate the exact amount of flooring material you will need for each job.

You will need to be physically fit for the lifting and carrying of materials, and a lot of your time will be spent working on your hands and knees.

You may work alone for some jobs, such as in people's homes, but you must also be able to work in a team with people in other construction trades and professions when you are working on larger jobs.

It will also be important that you can plan your workload and be happy meeting and talking to lots of different people.

Working conditions

Most of your work will be spent indoors in a variety of locations including people's homes, hospitals, offices and construction-sites – some of which will be dirty and dusty.

You may work a normal Monday to Friday week, but you may also need to work through the night on some contracts so that you can lay floors without disrupting the work of shops and businesses. You might have to spend time away from home on some contracts.

This is mobile work, so a driving licence is useful.

The future outlook

There are good prospects for finding work as a trainee floor layer, because there is a shortage of floor layers nationwide and the industry needs more young people to take up the career. There are currently about 44,000 people employed in the floor laying industry,

Regardless of your chosen flooring materials, work will be available with specialist flooring companies or contractors across the UK once you have qualified. You may choose to specialise in using one type of flooring material such as tiles or laminates.

With experience, you may progress to technical, supervisory or managerial posts in larger floor laying companies. Or you could set up on your own as a self-employed floor layer.

Qualifications and courses

- No specific qualifications are required, although GCSEs/S grades (A–E/1–5) or a Foundation GNVQ/GSVQ Level 1 in Construction and the Built Environment may be useful. Maths, design and technology, science and English are useful subjects.
- You will be trained on the job while working towards qualifications. This may also involve going to a college or training centre on day- or block-release.
- NVQs/SVQs in Floor Covering at Levels 1, 2 and 3 are available.
- Apprenticeships/Skillseekers may be available to those aged 16–24.
- You can also train by doing a Construction Industry Training Board (CITB) Construction Apprenticeship Scheme in Floor Laying.
- The Construction Industry Training Board (CITB) Construction Award in Floorcovering allows those who have difficulties in gaining the work experience to train for an NVQ. You can apply straight to the CITB before or after finding employment or gaining a place on a training scheme.

Other related opportunities

- Building Technician p40
- Carpenter / Joiner p41
- Carpet Fitter p42
- Labourer p60
- Wall and Floor Tiler p77

Advantages/disadvantages

- You will spend a lot of time travelling to and from jobs, and may need to spend time away from home on big flooring projects.
- An attractive and well-laid floor can transform a room. The ability to use your skills and a range of materials to create this effect can give you great job satisfaction.

Earnings guide

- Starting rate for trainees is around £12,500 per year.
- With experience and qualifications you can earn between £14,500 and £25,000.
- For highly skilled, experienced floor layers you could earn up to £30,000.
- Earnings vary among employers and different parts of the country. Salaries in London are higher. Many floor layers are self-employed and earnings will depend on the ability to win contracts.

Further information

www.cityandguilds.com/myperfectjob

ConstructionSkills
Bircham Newton
King's Lynn
Norfolk
PE31 6RH
01485 577577
www.cskills.net
www.bconstructive.co.uk

Tile Association
Forum Court
83 Copers Cope Road
Beckenham
Kent
BR3 1NR
020 8663 0946
www.tiles.org.uk

CRCI:BB | CLCI:UF

Glazier

What the work involves

- Glaziers use specialist cutting and fixing tools to cut glass to the correct size and fit it into place.
- You might fit glass into houses, shop fronts, office blocks or roofs.
- You might be working on new buildings or replacing existing or broken glass.
- You will use your knowledge to choose a suitable type of glass for each job.

entry level

1–2

To both enter and train while working in this career, you will need qualifications at Level 1–2. Please refer to explanation on page vii.

Qualifications and courses

- There are no set entry requirements, but you may need some GCSEs/S grades (A–C/1–3) or equivalent, vocational qualifications such as a BTEC Introductory Certificate/Diploma in Construction. Maths, English and technology subjects are useful for the parts of the job that involve measurements and calculations, and for theoretical training.
- You can train and gain vocational qualifications while you work. You will be taught practical skills and may spend time off-site at a college or training centre.
- You are likely to work towards NVQs/SVQs in glass-related subjects. These include Glazing Installation and Maintenance, Automotive Glazing, and Fenestration Installation and Surveying at both Levels 2 and 3.
- There is a 3-year Construction Apprenticeship Scheme (CAS) open to people aged 16–25. You will be registered by an employer and earn a wage at the same time as following a structured training programme.
- A scheme is promoted by Glass Training Limited (GTL) called 'Learning for All', whereby companies set up flexible learning programmes, known as 'learning pathways'. In the scheme, NVQs and SVQs can be delivered through distance-learning programmes.

The type of person suited to this work

You will be measuring and cutting glass accurately so that it fits perfectly into the frame. As you will be using different hand tools a practical ability will be necessary.

You will also need to be physically fit so that you can carry glass and be comfortable working at heights (sometimes extreme heights).

You may work alone for some jobs, such as in people's homes, but you must also be able to work and communicate with other glaziers, especially when working on large jobs with big, heavy panes of glass.

Working conditions

You will work indoors and outdoors in many different locations. A driving licence may be useful.

You will need to work safely and be aware of your own, the public's and your colleagues' safety when carrying, cutting and fixing glass.

You may work normal working hours during the week, but you may also need to work at weekends and during evenings, possibly offering emergency cover for households and businesses when replacing broken glass.

The future outlook

Work is available with glazing and construction companies throughout the UK and the demand for trained glaziers is high. The range of jobs in glazing work is also increasing to include specialist areas, for example automotive glass repair and replacement

After gaining sufficient experience, you may progress to technical or supervisory levels, or you could decide to start your own glazing business. The majority of glaziers are self-employed.

Other related opportunities

- Building Technician p40
- Carpenter / Joiner p41
- Ceiling Fixer p45
- Labourer p60
- Painter and Decorator p63
- Roofer p67
- Scaffolder p68
- Window Fitter p79

Advantages/disadvantages

- Working at extreme heights may be demanding for some.
- You will get to work in a variety of locations on a wide range of projects.
- Cutting tools and glass can be dangerous, so you will have to be aware of health and safety regulations.
- You could be called out at all hours for emergency jobs.

Earnings guide

- The Building and Allied Trades Joint Industrial Council (BATJIC) agrees minimum recommended wage rates annually.
- Newly qualified glaziers earn round £14,000.
- With experience, glaziers can expect to earn £23,000–£26,000.
- Those highly skilled, with experience and extra responsibilities, such as emergency call-outs, might achieve up to £40,000.

Further information

Proskills UK (Sector Skills Council for process and manufacturing industries)
Centurion Court
85b Milton Park
Abingdon
Oxfordshire
OX14 4RY
01235 833844
www.proskills.co.uk

ConstructionSkills
Bircham Newton
King's Lynn
Norfolk
PE31 6RH
01485 577577
www.cskills.net
www.bconstructive.co.uk

Glass Qualifications Authority
Provincial House
Solly Street
Sheffield
S1 4BA
0114 272 0033
www.glassqualificationsauthority.com

Glass and Glazing Federation
44–48 Borough High Street
London
SE1 1XB
0870 042 4255
www.ggf.co.uk

Heating and Ventilating Engineer

What the work involves

Heating and ventilating fitter

- Heating and ventilating fitters install equipment such as pipework and boilers for systems including central heating, hot and cold water services and gas supplies in industrial and commercial buildings.
- The systems you will work on are very large ,and your work will include cutting, bending and joining pipes that will need to withstand high pressures, so welding is an important part of the work.
- When you have installed a system, you will test it to make sure that everything is working as it should.

Gas fitter

- Your job will be to install, maintain, repair and test gas appliances such as fires, cookers and heating systems.
- Once installed you will test the appliances and give advice.
- You could work in private homes or on business premises.

The type of person suited to this work

Heating and ventilating fitter

You must be a practical person so that you can use the tools and equipment for the job. Understanding and following diagrams is an essential part of the work, so you need a logical, mechanically minded approach to your work. You will also need to be good at maths for making calculations.

It can be physically demanding work, as you will be bending, kneeling and working in tight spaces. You also need a head for heights and a safety-conscious attitude, because you will often be working from ladders and scaffolding.

Teamwork and communication skills are also important when you are installing large systems.

Gas fitter

You will need excellent practical skills and to enjoy using tools and making things work. Some work will involve finding faults – this area needs people who like investigating and working out why things go wrong.

Gas and gas appliances are potentially dangerous, so you should be very thorough and reliable. As you will be working in homes you should have good communication skills to advise customers.

Working conditions

A lot of your time will be spent indoors, but you will also need to work outdoors for part of the work. You may work on building sites, and in buildings such as factories, hospitals and schools. You will need to wear safety gear such as a helmet, goggles and gloves.

You may work a normal working week, but there may be times when you will work different hours, for example to avoid disruption to clients.

You might work weekends and evenings, especially if you provide emergency cover.

The future outlook

Heating and ventilating fitter

There are around 34,000 heating and ventilation fitters within the UK and the heating and ventilating industry has a workforce of about 50,000. There is currently an acute shortage of skilled heating and ventilating fitters.

Once you undertake training and are qualified, work will be available across the UK with specialist heating and ventilation companies, or organisations such as the NHS or local authorities. Many qualified fitters also become self-employed, joining up with other fitters to offer sub-contracting services.

There are good prospects for advancement to supervisory roles and it is possible for you to become a heating and ventilating technician. If you take additional qualifications and higher education, progression to professional engineering level is also possible. There are also opportunities to work overseas.

Gas fitter

There is a shortage of gas fitters. You can work for national or private companies or become self-employed. In larger companies you can progress up to supervisory posts or apply for training posts at local colleges or within private organisations.

CRCI:BB

CLCI:UJ

Qualifications and courses

entry level

To both enter and train while working in this career, you will need qualifications at Level 1–2. Please refer to explanation on page vii.

Heating and ventilating fitter

- Most employers train young entrants through Apprenticeships/Skillseekers. 4 GCSEs/S grades (A–C/1–3), including maths, English and science subject may be required for entry to these.
- Training for Apprentices/Skillseekers includes attending college on day- or block-release. You will work towards NVQ/SVQ Level 2 in Mechanical Engineering Services: Heating and Ventilation Installation, progressing to NVQ/SVQ Level 3. NVQs/SVQs cover industrial, commercial and domestic installation, and maintenance of components.
- The same NVQ qualifications are available to adults, but for entry to these you may be required to be in related work or have relevant experience.
- Other training includes: City & Guilds Certificate in Energy Efficiency for Domestic Heating (6084), for domestic fitters; and the Oil Firing Technical Association for the Petroleum Industry's (OFTEC) training scheme for those working with oil-fired equipment.

Gas service technician

- At least 4 GCSEs/S grades (A–C/1–3) including English, maths and sometimes science or technology subjects are normally required for entry to this career. Practical subjects such as metalwork and woodwork are useful.
- Apprenticeships/Skillseekers are available for people aged 16–24. Apprentices work towards NVQ/SVQ in Domestic Natural Gas Installation and Maintenance, awarded by City & Guilds. Gas service companies also run their own apprenticeship schemes.
- Trainees must gain registration with CORGI (Council of Registered Gas Installers). To become registered, trainees need to work towards the NVQ/SVQ in Domestic Natural Gas Installation and Maintenance at Level 2 or 3, or complete equivalent in-house training with a company. Technicians with qualifications or training other than the NVQ/SVQ must complete ACS (Accredited Certification Scheme) assessments.
- Gas service technicians have to demonstrate their gas safety competence on a 5-year cycle by successfully completing nationally agreed Accredited Certification Scheme (ACS) assessments.

Other related opportunities

- Civil / Construction Engineer p46
- Engineer: Craft p203
- Gas Distribution Worker p211
- Plumber p65
- Technician (Construction) p72
- Thermal Insulation Engineer p225

Advantages/disadvantages

- Working in cramped and awkward spaces can be uncomfortable.
- Transforming a building from an empty shell into a warm, comfortable environment can be rewarding.
- Career progression opportunities are excellent.
- There is demand across the country for work in this area.

Earnings guide

Heating and ventilating fitter

- The Heating and Ventilating Contractors' Association (HVCA) publishes recommended salary rates. Overtime is often available, which can lead to higher earnings.
- As a new fitter you could start at around £11,500 per year. As a qualified building services graduate you could earn £21,000–£25,000.
- With experience and additional responsibilities, you could earn £35,000–£50,000.

Gas fitter

- New apprentices earn around £13,000 per year which, after training, can rise to between £17,000 and £25,000.
- The most experienced can earn up to £33,000+. It is also possible to earn extra for overtime and shift work.

Further information

SummitSkills (Sector Skills Council for building services engineering)
Vega House
Opal Drive
Fox Milne
Milton Keynes
MK15 0DF
08000 688336
www.summitskills.org.uk

Building Engineering Services Training Ltd
The Mere, Second Floor
Milestone House, Upton Park
Slough
Berkshire
SL1 2DQ
01753 531188
www.best-ltd.co.uk

Heating and Ventilating Contractors' Association
Esca House
34 Palace Court
London
W2 4JG
020 7313 4900
www.hvca.org.uk

Building Engineering Services Training Ltd (Scotland)
Unit 4
Bush House
Penicuik
Midlothian
EH26 0BB
0131 445 5900
www.best-ltd.co.uk

GAS FITTER

Council for Registered Gas Installers (CORGI)
1 Elmwood
Chineham Park
Crockford Lane, Basingstoke
Hampshire
RG24 8WG
0800 915 0485
www.trustcorgi.com

www.cityandguilds.com/myperfectjob

CRCI:BB

CLCI:UJ

Home Inspector / Energy Assessor

What the work involves

- Home inspectors and energy assessors are qualified and accredited to inspect a property and produce a report called a Home Condition Report (HCR) and/or Energy Performance Certificate (EPC).
- As part of an energy assessment, you will survey the level of energy efficiency, grade the property's energy performance and suggest ways to cut fuel bills.
- As part of a home condition assessment you will inspect a property internally and externally giving each part of the property a condition rating.

The type of person suited to this work

Written and verbal communication skills are important, as you will be writing technical reports in plain English that are easy for buyers and sellers to understand.

You will need a logical and methodical approach and to be precise and accurate in your work. You also need to be able to use computers and be good at maths, for example when taking measurements.

Finally, you need an interest in and knowledge of buildings and building regulations, construction and energy efficiency.

Working conditions

Home inspectors/energy assessors spend some time indoors working in an office, writing reports, but most of their time is spent visiting properties in their local area carrying out inspections.

A driving licence may be necessary.

You may have to work early, late or at weekends to see clients when they are at home.

The future outlook

The jobs of home inspector and energy assessor were created as a result of government legislation that introduced additional requirements for people selling their property. Now fully implemented, this legislation requires all sellers to have a home information pack, which includes a mandatory energy performance certificate (EPC) and an optional Home Condition Report (HCR), before they market their property.

Demand is set to increase for energy assessors with additional requirements being introduced by the Government for private landlords to have an EPC before marketing their property for letting. New builds too now need EPCs.

Employers include property surveying companies, estate agents, construction companies and building service firms. It is difficult to predict long-term prospects in this new job – which will, like estate agency, be dependent on the state of the housing market.

entry level

2–8

To both enter and train while working in this career, you will need qualifications at Level 2–8. Please refer to explanation on page vii.

Qualifications and courses

- Although there are no set academic entry requirements, it is useful for entrants to have GCSEs/S grades (A–C/1–3). Many entrants have A levels/H grades, a degree or vocational qualifications. Relevant degree and vocational subjects include surveying, construction, property management and real estate management.
- To work as a Home Inspector you will have to pass the Level 4 Diploma in Home Inspection (DipHI) – awarded by the Awarding Body for the Built Environment (ABBE).
- To work as an Energy Assessor there are a range of qualifying Diplomas including the Level 3 Diploma in On Construction Energy Assessment (DipOCEA), Level 3 in Domestic Energy Assessment (DipDEA), Level 3 Diploma in Non Domestic Energy Assessment (DipNDEA) and the Level 4 Diploma in Non Domestic Energy Assessment.
- ABBE Diplomas are offered by Assessment Centres approved by the ABBE and can be prepared for by using an accredited provider (Listed on ABBE website). Accredited providers offer courses and training programmes to help you meet Diploma requirements.
- To work as an inspector/assessor you will also need to be a member of an approved accreditation scheme, have a Criminal Records Bureau check and take out personal indemnity insurance.

CRCI:BC

CLCI:UH

Other related opportunities

- Architectural Technician / Technologist p38
- Building Technician p40
- Estate Agent p52
- Surveyor / Surveying Technician p70
- Technician (Construction) p72
- Town Planning Technician p76

Advantages/disadvantages

- You may need to work anti-social hours, to visit working home-sellers who can only be at home for your inspection in the evening or at weekends.
- You won't be stuck in an office and you will meet a wide variety of people.

Earnings guide

- Starting salaries for newly qualified entrants are between £20,000 and £25,000 per year.
- Experienced inspectors can earn £30,000–£40,000.
- Earnings vary widely among regions and employers, and you may improve your salary by changing employer. Salaries are generally higher in London.
- A top salary of between £40,000 and £50,000 may be possible employer and your particular role and responsibilities.

Further information

www.cityandguilds.com/myperfectjob

Asset Skills (Sector Skills Council in property services, housing, cleaning services and facilities management)
2 The Courtyard
48 New North Road
Exeter
EX4 4EP
01392 423399
www.assetskills.org

Association of Home Information Pack Providers
55 The Ridgeway
Market Harborough
Leicestershire
LE16 7HG
0870 950 7739
www.hipassociation.co.uk

Awarding Body for the Built Environment (ABBE)
Room A045
Birmingham City University
Franchise Street
Perry Barr
Birmingham
B42 2SU
0121 331 5174
www.cihscotland.org

National Association of Registered Home Inspectors
1 Glenagles House
Vernon Gate
Derby
DE1 1UP
01332 225106
www.narhi.org

Housing Officer

What the work involves

- You will manage and maintain rented housing, usually for a housing association or local authority.
- Tasks include assessing housing needs in an area and making policies to provide for them, allocating housing to applicants, planning property maintenance and repair, setting rents, dealing with tenants who are behind with their rent, resolving neighbourhood disputes and answering tenants' enquiries.

entry level

To both enter and train while working in this career, you will need qualifications at Level 2–8. Please refer to explanation on page vii.

Qualifications and courses

- There are varying entry levels to this career. It is possible to enter with GCSEs/S grades (A–C/1–3) and study part time while working. Many people enter with an HNC, Foundation degree, degree or postgraduate qualification in housing studies.
- The National Certificate in Housing Studies is often taken before the HNC in Housing. Entrants must be at least 16, with 4 GCSEs/S grades (A–C/1–3) or equivalent.
- For entry to a Foundation degree in Housing Studies, at least 2 A levels/three H grades are required. Typical entry requirements are a Scottish Group Award (SGA), a BTEC/SQA national award, or an NVQ/SVQ Level 3.
- Housing Officers whose degrees do not include a work placement will be expected to gain appropriate industrial experience before they become a member of the Chartered Institute of Housing.
- The CIH also recognises relevant work experience as a route to Stages 1 and 2 of the Professional Qualification.

The type of person suited to this work

As most of your work will involve talking and listening to people, you will need excellent verbal communication skills. You should also be able to work with and relate to a variety of people, including other professionals and tenants.

Maths and numeracy skills are useful for dealing with rental payments, maintenance and repair costs, and budgets.

You will need to keep up to date with a range of housing and tenant welfare issues, and be flexible and able to solve problems as and when they arise.

You will also need to be able to work as part of a team as well as on your own.

Working conditions

Many housing officers are based in an office, but regularly travel to make property inspections, visit tenants or attend meetings. Not all of your tenants will be polite, so expect to deal with some who may be rude and angry.

Some of your work will involve visiting tenants and looking at damage or possibly collecting rents, so a driving licence is required for many posts.

Although you will normally work standard office hours, you could have to do some unsocial hours and weekend work too.

The future outlook

The employment situation is buoyant at the moment, as social housing is a growth area, with organisations taking on a number of new trainees as well as experienced staff. Work is available in towns and cities throughout the UK.

You can increase your chances of employment by doing work experience or voluntary work in housing first.

Most housing officers work for local authorities and housing associations, but you may also work for other employers such as voluntary organisations, property companies, private landlords and housing trusts. You may also be able to specialise in a particular area such as neighbourhood management or welfare benefits.

There are opportunities for promotion from housing officer to roles such as principal housing officer or housing manager.

Other related opportunities

- Advice Centre / Benefits Adviser p524
- Housing Manager p535
- Warden (Accommodation) p549
- Welfare Rights Officer / Worker p550

Advantages/disadvantages

- You may need to deal with difficult situations, for example cases of misuse of property or disputes between residents.
- The job can be personally rewarding because you are helping to provide people with a good place to live.

Earnings guide

- Starting out you can expect to earn £17,000–£20,000 per year. This can rise to £25,500–£27,000 for experienced housing officers.
- Up to £35,000 is usual for housing managers.
- More than £50,000 can be achieved in the most senior posts.
- Earnings vary widely depending on region, employer and your particular role and responsibilities.

Further information

www.cityandguilds.com/myperfectjob

Asset Skills (Sector Skills Council in property services, housing, cleaning services and facilities management)
2 The Courtyard
48 New North Road
Exeter
EX4 4EP
01392 423399
www.assetskills.org

Chartered Institute of Housing
Octavia House
Westwood Way
Coventry
CV4 8JP
02476 851700
www.cih.org

Employers in Voluntary Housing
Regent House
4th Floor
76 Renfield Street
Glasgow
EH12 5AA
0131 225 4544
www.cihscotland.org

Scottish Federation of Housing Associations
38 York Place
Edinburgh
EH1 3HU
0131 556 5777
www.sfha.co.uk

Labourer / Construction Operative

What the work involves

- Labourers/construction operatives support the work of other construction workers by doing various practical tasks.
- Your work might include tasks such as digging trenches, moving building materials and tools, putting up signs and safety barriers, mixing and laying cement or helping to lay drains.
- The work may also include operating different plant (construction equipment) such as cement mixers, and driving vehicles on the construction-site.

entry level

1

To both enter and train while working in this career, you will need qualifications at Level 1. Please refer to explanation on page vii.

The type of person suited to this work

As the work requires you to lift and carry heavy materials, and be on the move a lot, you must be physically fit. And you must not mind working at great heights or depths.

You need to be able to follow and carry out instructions, and work in a team with other labourers/construction operatives and construction tradespeople and professionals.

Your work will be extremely varied, so you need to be flexible and trustworthy.

Working conditions

You will be working outdoors in all weather conditions, as well as indoors. The work is often dusty and dirty and may be difficult for people suffering from certain allergies.

You will need to pay attention to both your own and colleagues' health and safety. You will be expected to follow the different procedures for each type of work you do, including the wearing of protective clothing.

You may work a normal working week, although evening and weekend work may also be available, and you may need to start early or finish late for some projects.

The future outlook

Building projects, new builds and renovations, can't happen without construction operatives so they are in strong demand when the construction industry is doing well.

You could work for small and large construction companies across the UK.

You may progress to specialist craft careers and supervisory roles. You could also become self-employed.

Qualifications and courses

- No specific qualifications are required to enter this work.
- Your training will be given mainly on the job by experienced labourers/construction operatives and tradespeople.
- There may be opportunities to work towards NVQs/SVQs at Levels 1 and 2 in Construction and Civil Engineering Services and in Specialised Plant and Machinery Services while you are working.
- City & Guilds also offers a certificate in Basic Construction Skills (6051).
- You can also train by doing a Construction Industry Training Board (CITB) Construction Apprenticeship Scheme.
- The Construction Industry Training Board (CITB) Construction Award in Construction Operations allows those who have difficulties in gaining the work experience to train for an NVQ. You can apply straight to the CITB before or after finding employment or gaining a place on a training scheme.

Other related opportunities

- Bricklayer p39
- Building Technician p40
- Carpenter / Joiner p41
- Construction Plant Operator p49
- Lift Truck Operator p568
- Lock Keeper p570
- Mastic Asphalter p62
- Plasterer p64
- Port Operative p575
- Road Worker p66
- Roofer p67
- Water Distribution / Sewerage Operative p78

Advantages/disadvantages

- The work can be physically demanding for some people.
- This job could be good for you if you enjoy doing something different every day and learning a wide range of skills.
- You have an important role to play on-site as without your help the tradespeople will not be able to do their work.

Earnings guide

- As a trainee starting out you can expect to earn around £9,000–£11,000 per year.
- As a skilled labourer/construction operative you could earn £16,000–£18,000.
- Overtime is often available, and on some projects there are bonuses based on outputs, which can lead to higher earnings.
- Skilled operatives may be able to earn more than £20,000 on some projects.

Further information

ConstructionSkills
Bircham Newton
King's Lynn
Norfolk
PE31 6RH
01485 577577
www.cskills.net
www.bconstructive.co.uk

www.cityandguilds.com/myperfectjob

Land Valuer / Auctioneer

What the work involves

- Land and property valuers are specialist surveyors who value and sell property, businesses and land. They help their companies make profits from the sales.
- Your job would include valuing and writing a report for use by your client for sale, loan or accounting purposes.
- You will also arrange, market and run live auctions.

entry level

To both enter and train while working in this career, you will need qualifications at Level 4–8. Please refer to explanation on page vii.

Qualifications and courses

- Land or property valuers and auctioneers must be qualified chartered surveyors, who are trained in auctioneering by experience on the job. Chartered surveyors are surveyors who have usually done a degree or postgraduate course that is recognised by the Royal Institution of Chartered Surveyors (RICS), followed by a period of structured practical learning known as the Assessment of Professional Competence.
- Auctioneers of other items do not need to be professionally qualified, although you can become a member of the National Association of Valuers and Auctioneers (NAVA) with relevant qualifications and experience.
- To qualify as a chartered surveyor specialising in plant and machinery, Units 5 and 6 of the Diploma in Valuation (Plant and Machinery) are required. There is a postgraduate conversion course. For details on the Diploma contact RICS.
- Degree courses are available in relevant subject areas such as Real Estate and Property Management.
- The Institute of Revenues, Rating and Valuation (IRRV) offers training covering valuation, legal and tax matters
- Details about the NVQ in Valuation at Level 4 can be obtained from The Awarding Body for the Built Environment (ABBE).

The type of person suited to this work

You will need good numeracy skills for valuing and dealing with bids. Communication skills, an ability to concentrate and a high degree of confidence are all important for conducting auctions. You will also need knowledge of the value of local land and properties so you can advise your clients accurately.

Although you will work in a team with other professionals you could also visit clients on an individual basis so you will need good project management skills.

You will have to have an expert knowledge of the particular markets that you are working in and be enthusiastic, with good selling skills.

Working conditions

You will normally work between 37–40 hours a week including evenings and weekends. Many auctions are run at weekends to encourage attendance.

You will spend some of your time outdoors, visiting properties and clients in all weathers. A driving licence is essential and you may have to travel substantial distances.

Your indoor work will involve using the computer and phone to do research, arrange meetings, prepare for sales and write reports. You will also liaise with colleagues to organise auctions.

The future outlook

Internet auctions are increasing in popularity for smaller value items but opportunities are stable with most valuers working for estate agents, surveyors and auction houses. With experience you could start your own company or progress to a senior position.

Some valuers also become consultants and work on a freelance basis.

The RICS qualification is recognised worldwide, so you may work anywhere in the world once you are fully qualified.

Other related opportunities

- Antiques Dealer p434
- Estate Agent p52
- Restorer / Conservation Officer p329
- Specialist Shop Assistant p455
- Surveyor / Surveying Technician p70

Advantages/disadvantages

- It can be frustrating when it is difficult to get bids for particular items.
- This can be a varied career as you are valuing and auctioning various items, and dealing with different people all the time.

Earnings guide

- Salaries vary depending on experience, size of the organisation and location. Some specialisms also attract higher salaries than others.
- While training you can expect around £20,000+ per year. With experience this rises to around £30,000.
- Average salary at senior level with 10–15 years experience is £40,000+, but will vary considerably with the area and type of work specialisms.
- Freelancers can charge according to their experience and contracts.

Further information

Asset Skills (Sector Skills Council in property services, housing, cleaning services and facilities management)
2 The Courtyard
48 New North Road
Exeter
Devon
EX4 4EP
01392 423399
www.assetskills.org

National Association of Valuers and Auctioneers
Arbon House
6 Tournament Court
Edgehill Drive
Warwick
CV34 6LG
01926 417 767
www.rics.org/careers

Royal Institution of Chartered Surveyors
Surveyor Court
Westwood Way
Coventry
CV4 8JE
0870 333 1600
www.rics.org/careers

Institute of Revenues, Rating and Valuation
41 Doughty Street
London
WC1N 2LF
020 7831 3505
www.irrv.org.uk

British Antique Dealers Association
20 Rutland Gate
London
SW7 1BD
020 7589 4128
www.bada.org

Mastic Asphalter

What the work involves

- You will work with material called mastic asphalt, a mixture of limestone and bitumen which turns liquid when heated.
- After spreading hot liquid mastic asphalt onto areas such as roofs or floors, it cools into a tough, waterproof surface.
- You will use various specialised tools and equipment in order to prepare surfaces and apply the mastic asphalt.

entry level

To both enter and train while working in this career, you will need qualifications at Level 1–2. Please refer to explanation on page vii.

The type of person suited to this work

You need to have good practical skills to be able to spread and form the mastic asphalt. Maths skills will be useful too, for calculating the right quantity of mastic asphalt.

It is important to be able to understand plans and instructions and work in a team with other mastic asphalters or people from other construction trades.

As it is an active job you must be physically fit, and you must be happy climbing and working at heights when working on roofs.

Working conditions

You will mainly work outdoors, although some of the work may be under cover.

You will need to stick to health and safety procedures, which include wearing protective gear such as a safety helmet, gloves and boots.

You are likely to work a normal working week, although you may have the opportunity to work at weekends as well.

The future outlook

There is good demand throughout the UK for mastic asphalters.

Most opportunities are with specialist mastic asphalt contractors. Self-employment is also common for skilled mastic asphalters.

Mastic asphalters can work their way up to become a supervisor or trainer in large companies, or set up their own contracting business

Qualifications and courses

- To train in this field, it is useful to have some GCSEs/S grades (A–E/1–5) in English, maths, design and technology, or vocational qualifications such as GCSE in Construction and the Built Environment, Scottish Progression Award/Skills for Work Award in Building Crafts, BTEC Introductory, First Diploma or Certificate in Construction, Foundation, Intermediate and Advanced level Construction Awards
- Most training is done on the job whilst attending college to obtain qualifications such as NVQs in Mastic Asphalting at Levels 2 and 3.
- Apprenticeships/Skillseekers may be available to those aged 16–24.
- You can also train by doing a Construction Industry Training Board (CITB) Construction Apprenticeship Scheme in Mastic Asphalting.
- The Construction Industry Training Board (CITB) Construction Award in Mastic Asphalting allows those who have difficulties in gaining the work experience to train for an NVQ. You can apply straight to the CITB before or after finding employment or gaining a place on a training scheme.
- Mastic asphalters employed on construction-sites require a Construction Skills Certification Scheme (CSCS) card. This demonstrates that the holder has health and safety training, as well as aiming for or competence in a particular occupation (usually requiring an appropriate NVQ/SVQ or equivalent).

CRCI:BB

CLCI:UF

Other related opportunities

- Building Technician p40
- Floor Layer p54
- Labourer p60
- Plasterer p64
- Road Worker p66
- Roofer p67
- Thatcher p74

Advantages/disadvantages

- Working at heights on roofs, or in cramped conditions when working in tanks or underground spaces, can be demanding for some people.
- You will develop a range of skills and work on a variety of surfaces including roofs, floors, bus stations, car parks and pathways.

Earnings guide

- £10,000 per year is average for a trainee starting in this work.
- With experience you could earn an average of £22,500.
- £31,000 or more is possible for the highest earners.
- Overtime is often available, and on some projects there are bonuses based on outputs, which can lead to higher earnings.

Further information

ConstructionSkills
Bircham Newton
King's Lynn
Norfolk PE31 6RH
01485 577577
www.cskills.net
www.bconstructive.co.uk

Mastic Asphalt Council
PO Box 77
Hastings
TN35 4WL
01424 814400
www.masticasphaltcouncil.co.uk

www.cityandguilds.com/myperfectjob

Painter and Decorator

What the work involves

- Painters and decorators paint and decorate the interior and exterior of people's homes and other new or old buildings. They also paint large structures such as bridges.
- Your work will include preparing surfaces by making sure they are clean and smooth, applying primers, undercoats and topcoats of paint, and putting up wall coverings such as wallpaper.
- You will use a range of tools including brushes, rollers and spraying equipment.

entry level

1–2

To both enter and train while working in this career, you will need qualifications at Level 1–2. Please refer to explanation on page vii.

The type of person suited to this work

You need to be good with your hands, and particularly skilful and careful when using fine decoration techniques. You will also need an eye for colour and design.

When working on their premises you must be able to get on with your customers. You may also need to work in a team with other painters and decorators, or with those from other construction trades and professions.

As you will need to climb ladders and carry tools and equipment you should be physically fit, and you should not mind working at heights.

You must be able to measure accurately so that you can work out how much paint and other material you will need. A creative ability and a high attention to detail could be useful.

Working conditions

Most of the work is indoors, but some is outdoors. You will regularly work up ladders or on scaffolding.

You need to work within health and safety regulations, which might include wearing a mask to prevent you from breathing in paint fumes.

You are likely to work a normal working week, although weekend work may also be available. You may need a driving licence.

The future outlook

There are good employment opportunities for painters and decorators in the UK at the moment.

You can work for painting and decorating companies or building contractors across the UK. Painting and decorating companies may offer a range of work or may specialise in work such as domestic, commercial, new build or industrial. A few large organisations who maintain a lot of property may also employ painters and decorators.

After you have gained enough experience, you could progress to a supervisory role or go into business for yourself.

Qualifications and courses

- To train as a painter and decorator, it is useful to have some GCSEs/S grades (A–E/1–5) in subjects such as maths, design and technology and English. You could also enter with a vocational qualification in a relevant area, such as a BTEC Introductory Certificate/Diploma in Construction.
- Construction Apprenticeships offer a structured training programme leading to NVQ/SVQ Level 3. Apprenticeships are validated by the Construction Industry Training Board (CITB) and last 3 years in England and Wales, and 4 years in Scotland.
- Most training is done on the job whilst attending college to obtain qualifications such as NVQs/SVQs in Painting and Decorating (Levels 2/3), CITB Intermediate/ Advanced Construction Award in Decorative Occupations (Painting and Decorating), or City & Guilds (6217–03) Level 1 Certificate in Basic Construction Skills (Painting and Decorating).
- The Construction Industry Training Board (CITB) Construction Award in Painting and Decorating allows those who have difficulties in gaining the work experience to train for an NVQ. You can apply straight to the CITB before or after finding employment or gaining a place on a training scheme.
- There are several new schemes whereby painters and decorators may apply for a card which proves their skills and qualifications. By 2010, this card will be a prerequisite for employees on construction-sites, although it is already required by many employers. All applicants need to have a relevant NVQ/SVQ qualification and to pass a health and safety test.

CRCI:BB | CLCI:UF

Other related opportunities

- Designer p136
- Labourer p60
- Plasterer p64
- Signwriter / Signmaker p165
- Wall and Floor Tiler p77

Advantages/disadvantages

- Working at extreme heights may be difficult for some people.
- It can be rewarding to see the improved look of a newly painted building or structure.
- There are opportunities to be artistic and use decorative effects.

Earnings guide

- New entrants/trainees can expect to earn between £13,500 and £15,000 per year.
- For trained painters and decorators £16,000–£20,000 is possible.
- Decorators with specialist skills and supervisory duties can earn £25,000 or more.
- Overtime is often available, and on some projects there are bonuses based on outputs, which can lead to higher earnings.

Further information

www.cityandguilds.com/myperfectjob

ConstructionSkills
Bircham Newton
King's Lynn
Norfolk
PE31 6RH
01485 577577
www.cskills.net
www.bconstructive.co.uk

Painting & Decorating Association
32 Coton Road
Nuneaton
Warwickshire
CV11 5TW
024 7635 377
www.paintingdecoratingassociation.co.uk

Plasterer

What the work involves

- There are three types of plastering that you could do: solid, fibrous or dry lining.
- Solid plastering involves the application of plaster or cement to internal and external walls, ceilings and floors.
- Fibrous plastering involves making ornamental plaster work, such as the kind you see on decorative ceilings. This includes short lengths of fibre to hold it together.
- Dry lining involves the use of plasterboard to construct walls or partitions and then skimming over the joins with plaster making them ready for decoration.

The type of person suited to this work

To be able to use your tools skilfully, you need to be good with your hands. An ability to use basic maths for calculating the amounts of materials you will need for a particular job is also helpful.

You will need to be able to work in a team with other plasterers, and with those in other construction trades and professions.

You should be physically fit, as the work is very active and can be tiring. It can also be dusty when working with the plaster powder; this may be difficult if you suffer from certain allergies. You will be climbing ladders and possibly scaffolding, so you must not mind working at heights.

An artistic ability is useful when working with fibrous plaster.

Working conditions

Solid/dry lining

Most of the work for solid plasterers and those doing dry lining work is indoors, although you may have to work outdoors if working on exteriors. You will work from ladders and scaffolding.

Fibrous

Most fibrous plasterers work in workshops, although you may also install your work on-site.

All plastering requires an understanding and appreciation of health and safety regulations, which includes wearing protective gear. You may work a normal working week, although you may need to start early or finish late, and weekend work may also be available.

The future outlook

Across the UK there is a shortage of qualified plasterers – and in particular dry lining specialists – who are needed to help finish off new builds getting them ready for decoration. Shortages exist especially in the south and south-east of England.

Once qualified, you will be able to work for plastering companies, building contractors and ornamental plaster work firms across the UK.

After you have gained sufficient experience, you could progress to technical, supervisory or managerial roles or become self-employed.

entry level

To both enter and train while working in this career, you will need qualifications at Level 1–2. Please refer to explanation on page vii.

Qualifications and courses

- There are no set entry requirements. To be eligible for an apprenticeship you will need some GCSEs/S grades in subjects, such as English, maths, design and technology.
- Construction Apprenticeships offer a structured training programme leading to NVQ/SVQ Level 3. Apprenticeships are validated by the Construction Industry Training Board (CITB) and last 3 years in England and Wales, and 4 years in Scotland.
- Most training is done on the job whilst attending college to obtain qualifications such as NVQs/SVQs in Plastering (Levels 1, 2 and 3), or City & Guilds certificates in Basic Construction Skills – Plastering (6217–04). NVQ Level 3 entitles you to craftsperson status. Construction Skills Certification Scheme (CSCS) cards are required by plasterers employed on construction-sites to demonstrate that they have health and safety training, are competent in their field or are working towards becoming so.
- The Construction Industry Training Board (CITB) Construction Award in Plastering allows those who have difficulties in gaining the work experience to train for an NVQ. You can apply straight to the CITB before or after finding employment or gaining a place on a training scheme.

CRCI:BB

CLCI:UF

Other related opportunities

Advantages/disadvantages

- Working at heights may be difficult for some people.
- You will be able to work in a variety of locations, especially as a solid plasterer.
- There are opportunities to be creative when producing fibrous plaster work.

Earnings guide

- As a trainee starting out in this work you could earn around £14,000 per year. With a Level 2 qualification this can rise to £16,000+.
- After qualifying to Level 3 you can expect to earn £18,000–£25,000.
- Experienced plasterers can earn up to £35,000 or more.
- Overtime is often available, and on some projects there are bonuses based on outputs, which can lead to higher earnings.

Further information

ConstructionSkills
Bircham Newton
King's Lynn
Norfolk
PE31 6RH
01485 577577
www.cskills.net
www.bconstructive.co.uk

Federation of Plastering and Drywall Contractors
1st Floor
8/9 Ludgate Square
London
EC4M 7AS
020 7634 9480
www.fpdc.org

www.cityandguilds.com/myperfectjob

Plumber

What the work involves

- Plumbers install, maintain and repair heating and water systems in various locations including people's homes and construction-sites.
- You will use a range of hand and power tools, such as wrenches, cutters and welding equipment, to cut, bend and join metal and plastic pipes.
- When you have completed a job, you will need to test the system to make sure that everything is working properly.

entry level

To both enter and train while working in this career, you will need qualifications at Level 1–2. Please refer to explanation on page vii.

The type of person suited to this work

You must have good practical skills to be able to use the various tools. You have to be able to work carefully, measuring accurately and following plans and instructions correctly so that systems work properly and safely. Problem-solving skills are important for finding faults.

You need to be physically fit for bending, kneeling and working in tight spaces. You may also need to be comfortable working at heights, for example when working on drainpipes.

You are likely to work alone for some jobs, for example when in people's homes, and you must be able to deal directly with customers. You also need to be able to work in a team when you are working on larger jobs.

Working conditions

You will work both indoors and outdoors, possibly within confined spaces and at heights. As you will travel to a variety of locations, a driving licence and own transport will be useful.

You may work a normal working week but, if your organisation offers a 24/7 call-out service, you may also need to work at weekends and be available all times of the day.

The future outlook

There are around 28,000 plumbers in the UK. Plumbers may be employed by plumbing or maintenance firms, or by building contractors but 80% of plumbers are self-employed.

Once qualified, work is available across the UK.

With additional training and CORGI registration, you could move into gas central heating installation and repair. You could also move into related career areas such as heating and ventilation, refrigeration or air conditioning.

With experience, you may progress to technical, supervisory, training or managerial positions or set up your own plumbing business.

Qualifications and courses

- To train as a plumber, either on the job or via an Apprenticeship/Skillseekers, you will normally need 3–4 GCSEs/S grades (A–C/1–3) preferably including English, maths, and science and technology. Equivalent vocational qualifications, such as an Intermediate 2 in Construction and the Built Environment, SGA Intermediate in Construction or BTEC First in Construction may also be accepted.
- Trainees can work towards a City & Guilds (6089) NVQ Level 2 and 3 in Mechanical Engineering Services: Plumbing (Domestic) to become a qualified plumber. Otherwise, City & Guilds (6129) Technical Certificates: Level 2 Basic Plumbing Studies and Level 3 Plumbing Studies are available.
- Entrants for apprenticeships or training schemes will need to pass a selection test and have their colour vision tested. Relevant work experience can be helpful.
- Most training is done on the job whilst attending college to obtain qualifications such as NVQ/SVQs in Plumbing (Levels 2 and 3). The British Plumbing Employers Council (BPEC) provides a range of assessments through its own training and assessment centres, covering domestic gas safety and appliances, oil-fired appliances and water regulations.
- CORGI registration and possession of a CORGI ID card is a legal requirement for anyone, including plumbers, installing or repairing gas fittings or appliances.

CRCI:BB

CLCI:UF

Other related opportunities

- Engineer: Craft p203
- Gas Distribution Worker p211
- Heating and Ventilating Engineer p56
- Technician (Construction) p72
- Thermal Insulation Engineer p225
- Water Distribution / Sewerage Operative p78

Advantages/disadvantages

- You could be called out at all times of night and day, to deal with plumbing emergencies, which can be difficult for those with family commitments.
- Being able to solve a difficult problem and make a customer happy can be very rewarding.

Earnings guide

- The Joint Industry Board for Plumbing Mechanical Engineering Services (JIBPMES) agrees wage rates. Overtime is often available, which can lead to higher earnings.
- You can start at around £6,000–£7,500 per year as a first-year apprentice.
- This can rise to £15,000–£17,000 in the final year of training. When qualified you could get £17,500–£21,000
- With experience you could expect anything between £22,000 and £30,000.
- Earnings for self-employed plumbers can be much higher. Top earners can get £35,000–£40,000 or more. Salaries are highest in London and the south-east of England.

Further information

www.cityandguilds.com/myperfectjob

SummitSkills (Sector Skills Council for building services engineering)
Vega House
Opal Drive
Fox Milne
Milton Keynes
MK15 0DF
08000 688336
www.summitskills.org.uk

BEST (Building Engineering Services Training Limited)
The Mere
Second Floor,
Milestone House
Upton Park
Slough
Berkshire
SL1 2DQ
0800 917 8419
www.best-ltd.co.uk

ConstructionSkills
Bircham Newton
King's Lynn
Norfolk
PE31 6RH
01485 577577
www.cskills.net
www.bconstructive.co.uk

Institute of Plumbing and Heating Engineering
64 Station Lane
Hornchurch
Essex
RM12 6NB
01708 472791
www.plumbers.org.uk

Road Worker

What the work involves

- Road workers' tasks include building new roads, re-routing or widening existing roads, and repairing potholes and cracks in roads.
- You will also have other duties such as putting up warning signs and barriers, controlling the movement of traffic near the work site, laying kerbstones and pavements, and gritting roads in the winter.
- You will use a range of building materials including concrete, tarmac and paving slabs, and you will use a range of tools and equipment in your work.

The type of person suited to this work

As the work requires you to move around a lot, lifting and carrying heavy materials, you must be physically fit.

You will be using tools such as picks and shovels, and operating equipment such as cement mixers, diggers and rolling machines, so practical ability is useful.

As much of your work will be as part of a team of road workers and supervisors, it is important that you can get along with colleagues as well as members of the public.

Working conditions

Most of the day, you will be working outdoors in all weather conditions. The work is usually dusty and dirty, and there may be fumes from materials such as tarmac.

You will need to be aware of the danger of traffic and health and safety for yourself and your colleagues. On-site, you will wear protective clothing such as a safety helmet, fluorescent jacket and boots.

You are likely to work a normal working week, although you may also work weekends and evenings to avoid disrupting traffic. On some large contracts that take months, such as the building of a new motorway, you could be expected to live on-site in a mobile home.

The future outlook

Road workers may work for local authorities or, as work is increasingly contracted out, for specialist road-building or civil engineering companies.

Work is available across the UK. Some work is short term or seasonal. You could become self-employed and work on contract basis.

As you develop and gain experience and qualifications, you may go on to lead a small team (gang) or become a supervisor. You may be able to work abroad for some companies.

entry level

1

To both enter and train while working in this career, you will need qualifications at Level 1. Please refer to explanation on page vii.

Qualifications and courses

- There are no formal entry requirements for this work, but GCSEs/S grades in maths, English and design and technology may be helpful. Personal skills and physical fitness are usually more important than qualifications.
- Your training will be given mainly on the job by experienced road workers. You may also go to college to gain qualifications.
- You may be able to work towards NVQs/SVQs in Construction and Civil Engineering Services' Highway Maintenance at Levels 1 and 2, Road Building at Level 2 and Winter Maintenance Operations at Level 2 while you are working.
- To become a qualified site operative, you need one of the following: a City & Guilds award in Streetworks, Excavation and Reinstatement; an SQA National Award in Excavation and Reinstatement; or a CABWI award in Street Works Excavation and Reinstatement.
- An Apprenticeship/Skillseekers may be available for people aged 16–24.
- If working with plant machinery, you will need to be 18 or over. A driving licence will also be required, and an LGV licence may be needed for some jobs.

CRCI:BB | CLCI:UN

Other related opportunities

- Bricklayer p39
- Dry Stone Waller p50
- Labourer p60
- Mastic Asphalter p62
- Water Distribution / Sewerage Operative p78

Advantages/disadvantages

- You will be outdoors doing physically demanding work in all weathers; hot in the summer and cold in the winter
- You will be helping to maintain and improve the safety of the roads in your local area, which can be personally rewarding.

Earnings guide

- Trainee road workers start at around £12,000 per year. With experience you could get £15,000–£17,000.
- The highest-earning road workers with a lot of experience and relevant qualifications can expect around £19,000+.
- If you have supervisory skills you could earn £22,000 or more.
- You can increase your earnings with overtime and shift work.

Further information

ConstructionSkills
Bircham Newton
King's Lynn
Norfolk
PE31 6RH
01485 577577
www.cskills.net
www.bconstructive.co.uk

CABWI Awarding Body
1 Queen Anne's Gate
London
SW1H 9BT
020 7957 4523
www.cabwi.co.uk

The Street Works Qualification Register (SWQR)
The Optima Building
58 Robertson Street
Glasgow
G2 8DQ
0845 270 2720
www.swqr.org.uk

www.cityandguilds.com/myperfectjob

Roofer

What the work involves

- Roofers remove old roofs and replace them, cover new roofs and repair existing ones.
- You will have a choice of roofing materials to work with. For example, you may work with tiles, slates, felt, mastic asphalt or sheet materials.
- You will use different specialised tools and equipment for each type of roofing material that you work with.

entry level

To both enter and train while working in this career, you will need qualifications at Level 1–2. Please refer to explanation on page vii.

The type of person suited to this work

You need to have good practical skills to be able to use the tools and equipment.

You must also be physically fit so that you can climb ladders and scaffolding, and carry roofing materials. You must be comfortable working at heights.

It is important to be able to understand plans and instructions. You also need to be able to work in a team with other roofers and those from other construction trades and professions.

Good verbal communication skills will help you to be able to talk to your colleagues and your customers. It will also be useful if you have a pride in your work and enjoy being outdoors.

Working conditions

You will be working outdoors on roofs in various locations from people's homes to historic cathedrals and construction-sites. The work can be dusty and dirty, and you will have to be outdoors in all weathers.

As you will be working up ladders, on scaffolding or on the roof itself, you will need to pay close attention to all health and safety procedures, which includes wearing protective gear such as a safety helmet and boots.

You are likely to work a normal working week, although extra work may also be available at weekends.

The future outlook

There is a good demand for qualified roofers across the UK at the moment.

Work is available within roofing companies, contractors, local authorities, roofing material suppliers and other public organisations. Self-employment is common.

You can decide to specialise in using one type of roofing material (such as slate) or you can train to become skilled in using several types.

You may work your way up to technical, supervisory and managerial levels. After you have gained enough experience, you could start your own roofing company.

Qualifications and courses

- To train as a roofer it is useful to have some GCSEs/S grades (A–E/1–5) or a vocational qualification. Maths, English, craft, design and technology are all relevant subjects.
- Construction Apprenticeships offer a structured training programme leading to NVQ/SVQ Level 3. Apprenticeships are validated by the Construction Industry Training Board (CITB) and last 3 years in England and Wales, and 4 years in Scotland.
- Most training is done on the job whilst attending college to obtain qualifications such as NVQs/SVQs in Roofing Occupations Level 1, Applied Waterproof Membranes Level 2, Mastic Asphalting Levels 2 and 3, Roof Sheeting and Cladding Levels 2 and 3, and Roof Slating and Tiling Levels 2 and 3. City & Guilds Certificates are also available.
- The Construction Industry Training Board (CITB) Construction Award in Roofing allows those who have difficulties in gaining the work experience to train for an NVQ. You can apply straight to the CITB before or after finding employment or gaining a place on a training scheme.
- Many employers on construction-sites require workers to have a Construction Skills Certification Scheme (CSCS) card. This demonstrates that the holder has health and safety training, as well as aiming for or competence in a particular occupation (usually requiring an appropriate NVQ/SVQ or the equivalent).

CRCI:BB | CLCI:UF

Other related opportunities

- Building Technician p40
- Carpenter / Joiner p41
- Labourer p60
- Mastic Asphalter p62
- Scaffolder p68
- Thatcher p74

Advantages/disadvantages

- Working at heights may be difficult for some people.
- It is satisfying to produce a lasting structure that is functional and looks good.
- You could get to work on some impressive projects such as fitting the roof on a new football stadium.
- You will gain an understanding of other construction work, such as joinery.

Earnings guide

- The Building and Allied Trades Joint Industrial Council (BATJIC) agrees minimum wage rates annually.
- Trainee salaries are about £12,500 per year. After NVQ/SVQ qualifications this rises to around £15,000.
- As a trained roofer with qualifications you can earn £16,500–£21,000.
- £26,000+ is possible for very experienced roofers.
- Overtime is often available, and on some projects there are bonuses based on outputs, which can lead to higher earnings.

Further information

www.cityandguilds.com/myperfectjob

ConstructionSkills
Bircham Newton
King's Lynn
Norfolk
PE31 6RH
01485 577577
www.cskills.net
www.bconstructive.co.uk

The Institute of Roofing
Roofing House
31 Worship Street
London
EC2A 2DX
020 7448 3194
www.instituteofroofing.co.uk

Scaffolder

What the work involves

- Scaffolders put up scaffolding so that new constructions, or the maintenance of existing buildings and structures such as bridges, can take place.
- You will put together metal tubes, fittings and wooden or metal platforms to create the scaffolding.
- You will use tools such as swivel spanners and spirit levels in your work.
- You may also put up spectator stands, stages and rigging for outdoor concerts and events.

entry level

To both enter and train while working in this career, you will need qualifications at Level 1–2. Please refer to explanation on page vii.

Qualifications and courses

- There are no set entry requirements to train as a scaffolder, but it may be useful to have some GCSEs/S grades (A–E/1–5) or a vocational qualification such as the BTEC Introductory Certificate or Diploma in Construction.
- Training is normally provided on the job with part-time attendance at college or training centres to get qualifications such as NVQs/SVQs or City & Guilds certificates.
- The Apprenticeship/Skillseekers scheme is a 2-year programme that combines learning on the job with 11 weeks spent on residential training at one of the National Construction College's sites. This leads to an NVQ/SVQ Accessing Operations and Rigging – Scaffolding Level 2 and the Construction Industry Scaffolders Record Scheme (CISRS) Basic Card.
- Trainees can, after at least 6 months' scaffolding experience, do the Scaffolding Basic Part 1 course, followed by Part 2, and then go on to the NVQ/SVQ Accessing Operations and Rigging – Scaffolding Level 2. The CISRS operates a card system for operatives, from labourer, trainee, basic/advanced scaffolder, aiming to ensure that they are properly trained and sufficiently experienced to work safely and correctly.
- The Construction Industry Training Board (CITB) Construction Award in Scaffolding allows those who have difficulties in gaining the work experience to train for an NVQ. You can apply straight to the CITB before or after finding employment or gaining a place on a training scheme.

The type of person suited to this work

Safety is the main priority in scaffolding. You need to make sure that it is safe for the people who will be working on it, passers-by, workmates and yourself. For this reason, you have to be able to keep your concentration, have good practical skills, be well organised and be able to follow instructions and take measurements accurately.

You must be physically fit so that you can lift and carry equipment up and down ladders and, of course, you must be happy working at heights.

You also need to be able to work as part of a team of scaffolders.

Working conditions

You will be working mainly outdoors in most weather conditions, often at great heights.

You will need to wear protective equipment such as a helmet, boots and a safety harness.

You may work a normal working week from Monday to Friday, although you may need to start work early or finish late. Extra hours at weekends may also be available.

The future outlook

There is a good demand for scaffolders across the UK and opportunities with specialist scaffolding firms and building contractors as well as oil and power companies.

You may progress from basic to advanced scaffolder, and then on to supervisory and managerial positions. Some experienced scaffolders set up their own businesses.

You may also work offshore or in other countries.

CRCI:BB

CLCI:UF

Other related opportunities

- Building Technician p40
- Labourer p60
- Roofer p67
- Stonemason p69

Advantages/disadvantages

- This can be physically challenging work and working at heights can be demanding for some people.
- You will get to work in a variety of locations and you have the chance to put up scaffolding for major sports and music events, or for film sets.

Earnings guide

- Starting as an apprentice or trainee you can expect to earn £12.500–£13,000 per year.
- With qualifications you could get £16,000–£23,500.
- Very experienced scaffolders can earn £25,000 or more.
- Overtime is often available, and on some projects there are bonuses based on outputs, which can lead to higher earnings.

Further information

ConstructionSkills
Bircham Newton
King's Lynn
Norfolk
PE31 6RH
01485 577577
www.cskills.net
www.bconstructive.co.uk

National Access and Scaffolding Confederation
Carthusian Court
12 Carthusian Street,
London
EC1M 6EZ
020 7397 8120
www.nasc.org.uk

www.cityandguilds.com/myperfectjob

Stonemason

What the work involves

- Stonemasons cut and shape stone and fix it to buildings. Some work on new buildings, but many work on restoring and repairing old ones.
- There are two types of stonemason. Banker masons cut, shape and carve the stone, while fixer masons assemble and fix the stones into place.
- You will use traditional hand tools, modern power tools and cutting machines.

entry level

To both enter and train while working in this career, you will need qualifications at Level 1–2. Please refer to explanation on page vii.

Qualifications and courses

- Training is normally provided on the job with part-time attendance at college or training centres to gain relevant NVQs/SVQs. Apprenticeships/Skillseekers may be available for those aged 16–24.
- NVQs/SVQs at Levels 2 and 3 are available in relevant subjects (e.g. Architectural Stonemasonry, Carving, Heritage Skills), as well as City & Guilds Certificates. There is also a City & Guilds Diploma in Advanced Stonemasonry, designed to provide traditional techniques to NVQ/SVQ Level 3 and the skills necessary to become self-employed stonemasons.
- The Construction Industry Training Board (CITB) Construction Award in Stonemasonry allows those who have difficulties in gaining work experience to train for an NVQ. You can apply straight to the CITB before or after finding employment or gaining a place on a training scheme.
- A new NVQ/SVQ Level 3 in Heritage Skills for craftspeople working in the heritage sector, or those wishing to transfer from mainstream construction, provides a qualification reflecting the required skills and knowledge for the protection of the historic built environment.
- Many employers on construction-sites require workers to have a Construction Skills Certification Scheme (CSCS) card. This demonstrates that the holder has health and safety training, as well as aiming for or competence in a particular occupation (usually requiring an appropriate NVQ/SVQ or the equivalent).

The type of person suited to this work

Banker mason

As a banker mason, you have to be good with your hands to cut, shape and carve stone accurately. You also need artistic skills for producing decorative finishes.

Fixer mason

You must be physically fit so that you can lift the stones, although you will use special equipment to lift heavy stones. And as a fixer mason, you must not mind working at heights.

It is also useful to be interested in architecture and history, as much of the work involves restoring old buildings. As this can be slow and laborious work you should have patience and pride in your work.

Working conditions

Banker masons mainly work in a workshop, while fixer masons work on-site, often at heights. Both types of mason work can be dusty and noisy and unsuitable for people who have dust allergies.

You will need to follow health and safety procedures, including wearing protective clothing such as a mask, a helmet and boots.

You are likely to work a normal working week, although extra work at weekends may also be available.

The future outlook

There is good demand for stonemasons in the UK.

You can choose to work for stonemasonry companies and larger building contractors. If you work for a small stonemasonry company you are likely to have to do both banking and fixing work

After training you can decide to specialise in new building or restoration work. You can also specialise as a memorial mason, making and carving gravestones.

After you have gained enough experience, you could start your own business. Most stonemasons tend to prefer to stick to their own craft rather than move into management roles.

You may also use your skills abroad.

Other related opportunities

- Bricklayer p39
- Building Technician p40
- Dry Stone Waller p50
- Labourer p60
- Roofer p67
- Scaffolder p68

Advantages/disadvantages

- Working at heights and the physical side of the work may be demanding for some people.
- You may have the opportunity to work on impressive restoration projects such as those on cathedrals.
- It can make you proud to produce work on a building that will be admired for many years.

Earnings guide

- As a new entrant you could earn between £8,000 and £13,500 per year
- When trained and with some experience you could get £17,000–£21,000.
- Senior and experienced stonemasons can achieve up to £30,000.
- Overtime is often available, and on some projects there are bonuses based on outputs, which can lead to higher earnings.

Further information

www.cityandguilds.com/myperfectjob

ConstructionSkills
Bircham Newton
King's Lynn
Norfolk
PE31 6RH
01485 577577
www.cskills.net
www.bconstructive.co.uk construction careers site

National Heritage Training Group
Carthusian Court
12 Carthusian Street
London
EC1M 6EZ
01159 217562
www.nhtg.org.uk

Stone Federation Great Britai
Channel Business Centre
Ingles Manor
Castle Hill Avenue
Folkestone
Kent T20 2RD
01303 856123
www.stone-federationgb.org.uk

Surveyor / Surveying Technician

What the work involves

- Surveyors measure, assess, value, manage and develop all types of land and the buildings on it. They usually specialise in a particular aspect of surveying.

Surveying Technician

- Technicians work alongside chartered and professional surveyors providing advice and technical support. They specialise in their employer's branch of surveying.

Chartered surveyor

- Chartered surveyors take a leading role in projects and may work in a number of different areas such as land, construction, environment and business.

Building control surveyor

- Building control surveyors make sure that buildings meet regulations in areas such as health and safety, energy conservation and access. As well as checking building plans, they also check the work in progress on construction-sites.

Commercial and residential property surveyor

- Commercial and residential property surveyors' tasks include valuing and surveying land and property to be sold, managing property and advising individuals and businesses on property investment.

Geomatics/land surveyor

- Geomatics/land surveyors collect and analyse information to map the land, and sea. They use satellite images as well as other surveys to record features such as contours, materials below the Earth's surface and man-made objects. The information is used to make maps and plan construction projects.

Insurance surveyor

- Insurance surveyors provide information to insurers on the risks of specific requests for insurance cover. They collect information about properties by visiting them and assessing their condition and location.

Quantity surveyor

- Quantity surveyors deal with the financial side of construction projects. Tasks include calculating costs, issuing contracts, keeping projects to time and within budget, and arranging payments for the work.

Rural practice surveyor

- Rural practice surveyors manage and develop the countryside, giving advice to rural landowners about how to develop and manage their assets such as land, buildings and livestock. They also value and auction rural property such as machinery and livestock.

The type of person suited to this work

All types of surveyors work in teams with people at all levels, including other professionals and clients. Much of the work involves explaining and talking to people, so written and verbal communication skills are important. You should enjoy writing reports, negotiating and making presentations.

You will need a logical, analytical and practical approach to work and the ability to coordinate projects. Team management and good organisational skills will be essential.

As much of the work involves computers and different electronic equipment, you will need to have good ICT skills. You should also be good at maths as you will need to work out the cost of a project, take measurements or value property.

You will also need an interest in buildings, construction, land and the environment, an awareness of the property market and an interest in commerce and the economy.

Qualifications and courses

- It is possible to enter this profession with a degree or diploma accredited by the Royal Institution of Chartered Surveyors (RICS), or to combine employment in a surveyors' practice with part-time study.
- You may study full time at university for a RICS-accredited degree in a relevant subject. For a degree course, the usual qualifications needed are 3 A levels/4 H grades or a relevant BTEC/SQA national award. To become a chartered member of RICS, you then need to complete the 2-year APC, consisting of structured practical training and experience.
- Candidates with a non-accredited degree, or a degree in a non-vocational subject (for example geography) can take a postgraduate conversion course, followed by the APC.
- You can undertake degree studies part time at a university or college whilst employed in surveying. The College of Estate Management offers RICS-accredited degrees and a Diploma in Surveying by distance learning.
- Qualified technical surveyors can undertake a bridging course to chartered level.
- Surveyors may also work towards the professional examinations of the Institute of Revenues, Rating and Valuation, the Association of Building Engineers, the Chartered Institute of Building (Faculty of Architecture and Surveying), the Chartered Institute of Housing, the Royal Town Planning Institute or the Institution of Civil Engineering Surveyors.

entry level

To both enter and train while working in this career, you will need qualifications at Level 4–8. Please refer to explanation on page vii.

- The Chartered Surveyors Training Trust offers work-based training for young people aged 16–24 in London and the south-east of England. Applicants must have a minimum of 4 GCSEs (A–C) or equivalent.

Working conditions

Most surveyors divide their time equally between being indoors working in an office, and being out of the office, visiting clients, carrying out surveys or visiting construction-sites.

When on-site you will need to stick to health and safety regulations and be prepared to get muddy, wet and cold. You will have to wear protective clothing, and a driving licence and own transport may be required.

The different locations that you will visit will depend on the type of surveying you do. For example, you could visit farms, value rural properties, support the building of roads in major cities or take ground samples from around the world.

Most of your work is likely to take place in normal office hours, although you may have to vary your hours to fit in with particular projects. This might include working early, late or at weekends.

The future outlook

At the moment there is a steady demand for new entrants to surveying, with shortages in some branches of surveying. You could work for a variety of employers including surveying practices, construction companies, local and central government departments, mortgage companies and property companies, both throughout the UK and internationally. Freelance and consultancy work are also a possibility.

Surveying Technician
There are opportunities to work in surveying practices supporting the work of chartered and professional surveyors. You can work towards becoming a chartered surveyor by gaining further experience and qualifications.

Chartered surveyor/Building control/ Commercial land residential property surveyor
The RICS qualification is recognised worldwide. However, your opportunities will depend on the state of the housing market. You could work in surveying companies, local government, banks, mortgage companies and other national organisations. There are also opportunities for progression to senior management positions or partnership in private practice.

Geomatics/land surveyor
On average over 40% of all geomatic surveyors work for companies that operate overseas contracts. Within the UK, organisations include surveying companies, the Royal Navy Ordnance Survey, central and local government.

Insurance surveyor
Insurance surveyors work for insurance companies, insurance brokers, specialist insurance surveying firms and risk management consultancies. With experience you can progress to senior surveyor or head of department. You might be able to become a partner in an insurance surveying firm or set up your own consultancy.

Quantity surveyor
Your opportunities are likely to be within local authority or government departments, private practices, building contractors, property companies or commercial organisations both in the UK and abroad.

Rural practice surveyor
There are around 4000 registered rural practice surveyors in the UK. Work is offered by rural landowners, local authorities, public authorities, lending institutions and insurance companies.

Other related opportunities

- Building Technician p40
- Civil / Construction Engineer p46
- Construction Manager p48
- Home Inspector / Energy Assessor p58
- Land Valuer / Auctioneer p61
- Town Planner p75

Advantages/disadvantages

- Sometimes, you may need to work extra hours so that you can meet deadlines.
- Surveying is a varied career and each day is different.
- You can play an important part in developing land, buildings and the environment throughout the world.
- There are a wide range of different areas of surveying to choose from.

Earnings guide

- Salaries for surveying technicians range from around £16,000 on entry to £30,000 when experienced.
- Average earnings for new graduates are between £20,000 and £23,000 per year.
- With qualifications and with a few years of experience, you can expect to earn £25,000–£40,500.
- £45,000+ is possible for senior/chartered status surveyors with 5 to 10 years' experience.
- Salaries are generally higher in London. If you choose self-employment, your earnings will depend on your ability to win contracts and your personal drive.

Further information

ConstructionSkills
Bircham Newton
King's Lynn
Norfolk
PE31 6RH
01485 577577
www.cskills.net
www.bconstructive.co.uk

Chartered Surveyors Training Trust
Downstream Building
1 London Bridge
London
SE1 9BG
020 7785 3850
www.cstt.org.uk

Royal Institution of Chartered Surveyors
Surveyor Court
Westwood Way
Coventry
CV4 8JE
0870 333 1600
www.rics.org/careers

Institute of Revenues, Rating and Valuation
41 Doughty Street
London
WC1N 2LF
020 7831 3505
www.irrv.org.uk

Chartered Institute of Building
Englemere
Kings Ride
Ascot
Berkshire
SL5 7TB
01344 630700
www.ciob.org.uk

Association of Building Engineers
Lutyens House
Billing Brook Road
Weston Favell
Northamptonshire
NN3 8NW
01604 404121
www.abe.org.uk

Institution of Civil Engineering Surveyors
Dominion House
Sibson Road
Sale
Cheshire
M33 7PP
0161 972 3100
www.ices.org.uk

Technician (Construction)

What the work involves

Civil engineering technician

- Civil engineering technicians support civil engineers in the design and construction of roads, tunnels, bridges, railways, reservoirs, pipelines and major buildings. Your tasks may include preparing design drawings and plans, surveying construction-sites and supervising work on-site.

Engineering construction technician

- Engineering construction technicians support engineers in the design and construction of complex buildings and structures, such as oil refineries, factories and chemical plants. Your tasks may include using computer-aided design (CAD) to produce detailed designs, buying equipment and materials for a project and making sure that work is completed to standard.

Heating/refrigeration/air conditioning technician

- Heating/refrigeration/air conditioning technicians support building services engineers in designing and installing systems in buildings such as offices, factories, hospitals, schools and sports centres. Your tasks may include producing the drawings that are used to install systems, estimating the quantities of materials needed, installing systems and handling technical problems that may arise during installation.

The type of person suited to this work

All technicians in the construction sector need to have an interest in maths, physics and practical skills. You also will need excellent verbal and written communication skills in order to work with your colleagues and clients, including suppliers, site teams and other professionals, such as civil engineers and building services engineers. You may also have to do presentations. You will work in a team so you should be able to work with others and on your own.

Civil engineering technician
You will use computers to do the design, calculations and testing of your projects. Some of your work will include making drawings, so you will have to be neat and accurate.

You will also have to be well organised and able to manage your own and others' work.

Engineering construction technician
You will have to be interested in developing knowledge of engineering and the technical aspects of the work. You may also need hands-on practical skills.

You will be expected to translate complex engineering terms to both colleagues and clients. You will also need good problem-solving skills and an awareness of health and safety.

Heating/refrigeration/air conditioning technician
You will interpret complex diagrams in order to fit heating, ventilation and pipe work. You should be able to solve problems and produce easy-to-understand solutions that meet the needs of your clients and their buildings. You will also need normal colour vision for this work, as you will be using and installing wiring.

Working conditions

Depending on the area you choose to specialise in, you may work in an office, on-site or a combination of the two. The amount of time you spend in the office or on-site will depend on your employer and the particular tasks that you do. You must work safely on-site, which may include wearing a safety helmet and boots.

You will probably work a normal working week, but you may also have to start early, finish late, or work at weekends on occasion.

Civil engineering technician

If you work for an organisation that provides emergency cover, you may have to provide call-out cover, probably on a rota basis. This could mean evening and weekend work. You may need a driving licence to get on-site. You could be out in all weathers and may work on ladders and scaffolding.

Engineering construction technician

You may do some of your work outdoors in all weathers. You could also undertake some work in laboratory conditions.

Heating/refrigeration/air conditioning technician

Due to the nature of the industry your work could take you to contracts around the country. This can be difficult if you have family commitments, as you could be away for days or weeks at a time.

The future outlook

At the moment, there are plenty of employment opportunities for all technicians. There is a particular shortage in the south and east of England.

Work is also available throughout the UK for a variety of employers, including construction companies, building services companies, contractors, consultancies, local authorities and utility companies.

Civil engineering technician

There are a wide range of opportunities for technicians in civil engineering. Examples include consulting, public sector work, power and distribution, transport, mining and overseas projects.

Engineering construction technician

The engineering construction industry within the UK is currently the largest in the EU. This means future opportunities are good. Of the organisations involved, over half operate abroad.

Some of the larger employers offer their technicians the chance to take degree level qualifications that lead to professional level in engineering.

Heating/refrigeration/air conditioning technician

Heating and ventilation is an area that is expanding at present, so many UK companies deliver their services abroad as well as in the UK. Opportunities both at home and overseas are currently excellent.

CRCI:BB

CLCI:UN/UJ

Qualifications and courses

- Technicians should hold at least a Level 3 qualification such as an NVQ/SVQ, BTEC National Certificate or Diploma, or equivalent City & Guilds Certificate. Full-time, part-time and work-based routes are available.
- You can gain the required qualifications through full-time study at college. For entry to a BTEC National Diploma or Certificate, four GCSEs/S grades (A–C/1–3) are usually required including English, maths and science. Alternative entry qualifications include Intermediate GNVQ or BTEC First Certificate/Diploma.
- You can undertake work-based training through an Advanced Apprenticeship/ Skillseekers. The normal entry requirements are 4 GCSEs/S grades (A–C/1–3). You can then work towards an NVQ/SVQ Level 3, and study part time at college for BTEC National and City & Guilds qualifications.
- Engineering technicians with a Level 3 or 4 qualification and 3 years' responsible work experience are eligible to become technician members of one of the engineering professional bodies. It is also possible to continue to HNC/D or degree-level study.

entry level

To both enter and train while working in this career, you will need qualifications at Level 2–3. Please refer to explanation on page vii.

Other related opportunities

- Architectural Technician / Technologist p38
- Building Technician p40
- Construction Manager p38
- Engineer: Technician p208
- Heating and Ventilating Engineer p56
- Home Inspector / Energy Assessor p58
- Surveyor / Surveying Technician p70
- Town Planning Technician p76

Advantages/disadvantages

- Sometimes you may have to work on a number of projects at once, and it can be stressful having to work to deadlines.
- The work is interesting because you are likely to carry out a variety of tasks.
- You are an important part of the team that contributes to producing buildings, structures and building services of all kinds throughout the world.
- There are opportunities to work and progress your career overseas.

Earnings guide

- The salary figures below apply to all the technician careers (civil engineering, engineering construction, heating, refrigeration and air conditioning).
- As a trainee you can earn around £14,000–£18,000 per year.
- Once qualified this rises to around £24,000.
- With experience you can expect to earn £25,000–£35,000.
- Earnings vary among regions and employers. Salaries are generally higher in London and other large cities.

Further information

SummitSkills (Sector Skills Council for building services engineering)
Vega House
Opal Drive
Fox Milne
Milton Keynes
MK15 0DF
08000 688336
www.summitskills.org.uk

ConstructionSkills
Bircham Newton
King's Lynn
Norfolk
PE31 6RH
01485 577577
www.cskills.net
www.bconstructive.co.uk

Building Engineering Services Training Ltd
The Mere, Second Floor
Milestone House, Upton Park
Slough
Berkshire
SL1 2DQ
01753 531188
www.best-ltd.co.uk

Heating and Ventilating Contractors' Association
Esca House
34 Palace Court
London
W2 4JG
020 7313 4900
www.hvca.org.uk

Engineering Construction Industry Training Board
Blue Court
Church Lane
Kings Langley
Hertfordshire
WD4 8JP
01923 260000
www.ecitb.org.uk

Institution of Civil Engineers
1 Great George Street
Westminster
London
SW1P 3AA
020 7222 7722
www.ice.org.uk

www.cityandguilds.com/myperfectjob

CRCI:BB

CLCI:UN/UJ

Thatcher

What the work involves

- Thatching is the covering of roofs with plant stems such as water reed, combed wheat reed and long straw.
- Your tasks will include removing old thatched roofs and replacing them, thatching new roofs and repairing or re-thatching existing thatched roofs.
- Your work will include using many different thatching tools, including mallets, hooks, needles, knives and shears to prepare, to cut and to fix the thatch.

The type of person suited to this work

You need to have good practical skills to be able to use the specialised tools and equipment, and to develop an expertise in the craft. You must also be physically fit so that you can climb ladders and scaffolding, carrying thatching materials. You will need to be comfortable working at heights.

It is important to be able to measure roofs accurately so you can work out the required amount of thatching material. Communication skills are necessary for talking to customers and planning officers. You will also need to be interested in learning a traditional rural craft.

Working conditions

You will work outdoors on roofs in rural locations in most weather conditions. The work can be dusty, which can be difficult if you suffer from certain allergies.

You will need to pay close attention to health and safety procedures when working on roofs.

Your working hours are likely to vary according to when the work is available. You may work at weekends and this can be seasonal work, meaning you will be busiest during the spring and summer months when the weather is best.

The future outlook

There are about 1000 thatchers in the UK and, as about a half of all thatched buildings are protected and need to be re-roofed every 15–20 years, there is a steady demand for thatching work. However, there is fierce competition for training vacancies and some thatchers have another job to supplement their income. Not all areas of the UK have thatched buildings – they are concentrated in the Midlands and south of England – so you may have to relocate to find work.

It can take a number of years to become highly skilled. Many thatchers become self-employed once they are fully trained.

It is possible to find work in Ireland and other countries with thatched buildings.

entry level

1–2

To both enter and train while working in this career, you will need qualifications at Level 1–2. Please refer to explanation on page vii.

Qualifications and courses

- There are no set entry requirements for this work. It may help to have GCSEs/S grades (A–E/1–5) in English, maths and ICT, which are useful for running small businesses.
- The Countryside Agency has a New Entrants' Training Scheme aimed at candidates aged 16–25 working in rural areas. Candidates must have worked in the industry for at least six months. The scheme takes 2 years and leads to NVQ/SVQ Level 2 in Thatching. An optional third year leading to NVQ/SVQ Level 3 is available, which places greater emphasis on the skills of thatching, covering the detailing and decorative effects.
- Candidates may be taken on as trainees by thatchers and receive training on the job.
- The Construction Industry Training Board (CITB) Construction Award in Thatching allows those who have difficulties in gaining the work experience to train for an NVQ. You can apply straight to the CITB before or after finding employment or gaining a place on a training scheme.
- The National Society of Master Thatchers offers seminars and short courses in areas such as health and safety for its members. Practising thatchers may join as trainee or full members.

Other related opportunities

- Dry Stone Waller p50
- Mastic Asphalter p62
- Roofer p67

Advantages/disadvantages

- Working at heights may be demanding for some people and potentially dangerous.
- It is rewarding to work in an ancient craft and create thatched roofs that are both functional and decorative.
- This may be difficult work if you suffer from certain allergies.
- You may need a second job to supplement your earnings from thatching.

Earnings guide

- Earnings vary from county to county and among different employers. These salaries are guidelines only.
- As a trainee you can earn between £14,000 and £15,000 per year.
- An experienced thatcher can earn £17,000–£23,000.
- £35,000 or more is possible for very experienced thatchers able to negotiate their own contracts.

Further information

www.cityandguilds.com/myperfectjob

Lantra (Sector Skills Council for the environmental and land-based industries)
Lantra House
Stoneleigh Park
Coventry
Warwickshire
CV8 2LG
0845 707 80007
www.lantra.co.uk

National Heritage Training Group
Carthusian Court
12 Carthusian Street
London
EC1M 6EZ
01159 217562
www.nhtg.org.uk

Thatching Advisory Services
The Old Stables
Redenham Park Farm
Redenham
Andover
Hampshire
SP11 9AQ
01264 773820
www.thatchingadvisoryservices.co.uk

Town Planner

What the work involves

- You will manage and develop urban or rural areas to best serve the population for now and in the future.
- You will need to analyse conflicting demands to decide on the best use of land. For example, you need to balance the demand for housing, employment, transport, environmental and conservation issues, and so on.
- You could specialise in different types of planning, such as historic buildings or environmental conservation.

entry level

To both enter and train while working in this career, you will need qualifications at Level 4–8. Please refer to explanation on page vii.

Qualifications and courses

- A qualification accredited by the Royal Town Planning Institute (RTPI) is necessary in order to become a town planner.
- You can take a full-time or sandwich degree, or a postgraduate qualification accredited by the RTPI. The normal minimum entry grades for a planning degree are 2 A levels/3 H grades.
- For entry to a postgraduate planning course, a degree in a related subject such as geography, architecture, geology or statistics is normally required. Postgraduate courses are available full time, part time or by distance learning.
- When you have completed an accredited qualification and gained 2 years' relevant planning experience (one of which must be completed after qualification), you can apply for full membership of the RTPI.
- You will also need to pass the Assessment of Professional Competence (APC) by following a professional development plan.

The type of person suited to this work

You will need an interest in improving the quality of people's lives and their environment. As you will be meeting other professionals and members of the public, being confident and having good verbal skills will be helpful. Having good writing skills for producing reports is also useful.

You will also need to be organised and have excellent research, problem-solving and analytical skills, so that you can find out the effects of the different proposals for land use and decide on the best options.

IT skills are also useful, as you may be using computer software such as computer-aided design (CAD) in your work. You should also be interested in the environment, maps and buildings.

Working conditions

Most town planners are based in offices but often go out on-site visits to view the areas of potential development or to attend meetings. A driving licence may be necessary.

You are likely to work regular office hours, although you may sometimes need to attend meetings in the evening. It is possible to work overseas and increasing numbers of planners are working on a job-share basis.

The future outlook

Town planning is a growing profession, with more than 20,000 UK planners, but there is still a demand for more qualified planners in the UK and overseas.

Most town planning work is with local authorities and planning consultancies, but opportunities also exist with central government, construction companies and environmental organisations.

With experience, you may be promoted to senior or chief town planner or move sideways into related careers such as recreation management, market research or property development.

Work is available in Europe, especially if you are able to speak another European language.

Other related opportunities

- Cartographer p43
- Geographer p480
- Housing Officer p59
- Landscape p255
- Surveyor / Surveying Technician p70
- Town Planning Technician p76

Advantages/disadvantages

- You may be frustrated by the need to compromise when making planning decisions because there is either a lack of money or there are many conflicting demands and views to deal with.
- However, there is personal satisfaction in dealing with these problems and helping to improve the environment in which people live and work.

Earnings guide

- Earnings vary depending on the region and type of employer.
- As a trainee you can expect to earn £14,000–£19,500 per year.
- Newly qualified town planners earn around £20,000–£27,000.
- With experience this can rise to £28,000–£45,000.
- Chief planning Officer/Directors earn an average of £64,000 and can earn up to £80,000.

Further information

Royal Town Planning Institute
41 Botolph Lane
London
EC3R 8DL
020 7929 9494
www.rtpi.org.uk

Royal Town Planning Institute in Scotland
57 Melville Street
Edinburgh
Scotland
EH3 7HL
0131 226 1959
www.scotland.rtpi.org.uk

Town Planning Technician

What the work involves

- You will support the work of town planners in developing urban or rural areas to best serve the population both now and in the future.
- Your tasks are likely to be varied and may include carrying out surveys, mapping, taking measurements, recording information, analysing and presenting information, and providing advice to people enquiring about planning permission.

entry level

To both enter and train while working in this career, you will need qualifications at Level 2–3. Please refer to explanation on page vii.

The type of person suited to this work

As you are likely to deal with members of the public, builders and developers, for example when considering planning applications, you will need good verbal communication skills. You will also need good written communication skills for writing reports.

To work effectively in a team with town planners and other colleagues you will also need to be well organised and able to manage your own and others' workload.

You might need to use computer software such as computer-aided design (CAD) to produce illustrations or maps, so ICT skills are useful. And you may need numeracy skills to analyse statistical information.

An interest in improving people's quality of life and environment is also useful.

Working conditions

Most town planning technicians are based in offices, but you may work out of the office, for example when conducting surveys in the street or when attending planning meetings. A driving licence is therefore useful.

You are likely to work normal office hours, although some meetings are held in the evenings.

The future outlook

Work is available throughout the UK to support the work of the growing profession of town planning. Most planners work for local authorities, but you could work for other employers such as central government departments, planning consultancies, developers, National Park authorities and environmental organisations.

With experience and further qualifications, you could move into related areas such as planning administration or enforcement and, as opportunities for promotion are limited, some technicians progress to become town planners (after taking additional degree level qualifications).

Qualifications and courses

- There are no set entry qualifications for this career, but at least 4 GCSEs/S grades (A–C/1–3), including English and maths, are normally required.
- Many entrants have A levels/H grades, other Level 3 qualifications such as a BTEC/SQA National in Construction, or a higher qualification such as an HND or Foundation degree.
- Relevant experience in areas such as surveying, computer-aided design, or administrative experience in a planning department, can be an advantage.
- Planning technicians are trained on the job and may also undertake part-time study. To achieve Technical Membership of the Royal Town Planning Institute (RTPI), you need a recognised qualification at Level 3 or higher and 2 years' work experience.
- Qualifications include NVQ/SVQ Level 3 in Town Planning Support and Level 4 in Town Planning, and HNC/D in planning.

CRCI:BC

CLCI:US

Other related opportunities

- CAD Draughtsman / Woman p197
- Cartographer p43
- Geographer p480
- Home Inspector / Energy Assessor p58
- Housing Officer p59
- Surveyor / Surveying Technician p70
- Town Planner p75

Advantages/disadvantages

- You may need to deal with people who are unhappy, for example when their application for planning permission has not been approved.
- It is rewarding to know that every day you are making a contribution towards improving the environment in which people live and work.

Earnings guide

- As a trainee you can expect to earn £13,000–£18,000 per year.
- With experience you could get £19,000–£25,000.
- Qualified technical planners with supervisory duties can earn £28,000.
- Earnings vary depending on region, type of employer, and your qualifications and experience.

Further information

www.cityandguilds.com/myperfectjob

Royal Town Planning Institute
41 Botolph Lane
London
EC3R 8DL
020 7929 9494
www.rtpi.org.uk

Royal Town Planning Institute in Scotland
57 Melville Street
Edinburgh
Scotland
EH3 7HL
0131 226 1959
www.scotland.rtpi.org.uk

Wall and Floor Tiler

What the work involves

- Wall and floor tilers fit tiles in various locations, from bathrooms and kitchens to hospitals and swimming pools.
- The tiles you work with may range from small mosaic tiles to large heavy-duty tiles.
- You will plan the work by making sure you have enough tiles of the right type. You will then use various tools to prepare the surface, cut tiles, apply adhesive, fix the tiles in the correct position and grout them.

The type of person suited to this work

You must be able to plan your work and use your mathematical skills to work out the number of tiles you will need for a particular job. You have to work carefully and accurately when cutting and placing tiles. It is important to match colours and patterns, so a flair for design is useful.

You need to be physically fit for carrying the materials, and for working on your hands and knees. You also need to be flexible to adapt to the range of working environments.

You may work alone for some jobs, such as in people's homes, but you must also be able to work in a team when you are working on larger jobs.

Working conditions

You will work mainly indoors in a variety of locations, including people's homes, offices, factories and construction-sites. A driving licence may be useful.

You may work a normal working week, but you may also need to work evenings or weekends so that you can tile walls and floors without disrupting businesses.

As you will use special cutting tools and adhesives, you will need to be aware of health and safety procedures.

The future outlook

Due to the increased demand across all of the construction industry there is currently a lot of work available for skilled tilers.

Work is available with specialist tiling companies and building contractors, or you may choose to become self-employed, providing services to individuals or sub-contracting to organisations.

It is possible to specialise in using one type of tiling, for example flooring tiles, mosaic work or bathrooms.

With experience, you may progress to technical, supervisory or managerial positions. Or you could go into business as a self-employed wall and floor tiler.

1–2 **entry level**

To both enter and train while working in this career, you will need qualifications at Level 1–2. Please refer to explanation on page vii.

Qualifications and courses

- No specific qualifications are required, although GCSEs/S grades (A–E/1–5) may be useful in subjects like maths, technology or English. Similar subjects may be needed to be eligible for an Apprenticeship or equivalent vocational qualifications like the Edexcel Introductory Certificate or Diploma in Construction.
- You will be trained on the job while working towards qualifications. This may also involve going to a college or training centre on day- or block-release.
- NVQs/SVQs in Wall and Floor Tiling at Levels 2 and 3 are available.
- Apprenticeships/Skillseekers may be available to those aged 16–24. In Scotland, applicants for a construction apprenticeship need to take a selection test.
- You can also train by doing a Construction Industry Training Board (CITB) Construction Apprenticeship Scheme in Wall and Floor Tiling.
- The Construction Industry Training Board (CITB) Construction Award in Wall and Floor Tiling allows those who have difficulties in gaining the work experience to train for an NVQ. You can apply straight to the CITB before or after finding employment or gaining a place on a training scheme.

CRCI:BB

CLCI:UF

Other related opportunities

- Building Technician p40
- Carpet Fitter p42
- Designer p136
- Floor Layer p54
- Labourer p60

Advantages/disadvantages

- You will be on your hands and knees, sometimes working in dusty, dirty or cramped conditions.
- The work is varied and you can achieve spectacular results using coloured and textured tiles to decorate walls and floors.

Earnings guide

- Salaries start between £12,000 and £17,000 per year while training.
- This can rise to £18,000–£24,000 for skilled tilers. With experience this rises to £25,000+.
- £40,000 is possible for the highest earners.
- Overtime is often available, and on some projects there are bonuses based on outputs, which can lead to higher earnings.

Further information

ConstructionSkills
Bircham Newton
King's Lynn
Norfolk
PE31 6RH
01485 577577
www.cskills.net
www.bconstructive.co.uk

The Tile Association
Forum Court
83 Copers Cope Road
Beckenham
Kent
BR3 1NR
020 8663 0946
www.tiles.org.uk

www.cityandguilds.com/myperfectjob

Water Distribution / Sewerage Operative

What the work involves

- Water distribution/sewerage operatives lay, maintain and repair the pipework that carries drinking water, waste water and sewage.
- Your tasks might include digging trenches in roads and relaying them afterwards, putting up barriers and warning signs, laying pipes, repairing leaks, clearing blockages and installing water meters.
- You will use a range of tools such as welding equipment to join pipes together.
- You will also use machinery such as mechanical diggers.

The type of person suited to this work

You must have good practical skills and be mechanically minded so that you can use tools, equipment and machinery effectively. Working on-site can be dangerous, so a responsible attitude is essential. You will have to follow plans and instructions accurately, so that systems are installed correctly and safely.

You need to be physically fit for bending, kneeling and carrying materials and equipment.

You must be able to deal directly with members of the public, who might be upset that their water services are disrupted. You must also be able to work in a team with other water distribution/sewerage operatives. A driving licence may be required.

Working conditions

You will work outdoors in all weather conditions. The work can be dusty, dirty and wet, as well as smelly.

You will need to follow strict health, safety and hygiene regulations, which may include wearing breathing apparatus, a safety helmet, boots and gloves.

You may work normal working hours or shifts, but the particular hours you work will vary according to the needs of the job and the hours of daylight available. You may also be called out at weekends and at all times of the day and night to do emergency repairs.

The future outlook

There is currently quite a lot of work available for water distribution/sewerage operatives because the privatised water companies, who manage water supply and sewerage disposal, are investing money in developing their systems.

Work is available across the UK with water companies and construction firms.

With experience, you may be promoted to a team leader or supervisor post.

Some operatives move into related areas such as water distribution inspection work.

entry level

1

To both enter and train while working in this career, you will need qualifications at Level 1. Please refer to explanation on page vii.

Qualifications and courses

- There are no formal entry requirements, but water companies may ask for 4 GCSEs/S grades (A–C/1–3) including maths, English, science or technology.
- Relevant experience, for example in site maintenance work, is useful. Registration in an appropriate safety passport scheme could be required by many employers to be able to work on-site.
- Entrants are trained on the job, and may work towards vocational qualifications. An NVQ/SVQ Level 2 is available in Water Distribution. CABWI offers a range of relevant NVQs, including Distribution Control Level 2, Operating Process Plant (Water) Level 2, Leakage Control Level 3 and Maintaining Water Supply Level 3.
- Apprenticeships/Skillseekers may be available for people aged 16–24. The scheme starts with basic preliminary training, with apprentices usually working towards NVQs/SVQs at Level 2 in subjects such as customer care, water distribution, construction and technical drawing.

CRCI:BB

CLCI:UN

Other related opportunities

- Construction Plant Operator p49
- Gas Distribution Worker p211
- Labourer p60
- Plumber p65
- Road Worker p66
- Technician (Construction) p72

Advantages/disadvantages

- The work can be physically demanding for some people, and it can get smelly if you are working on sewerage systems.
- It can be satisfying to know that you are helping to provide people with an essential service.

Earnings guide

- As a trainee you can earn around £11,000–£13,000 a year.
- This can rise to £14,000–£16,000+ for fully trained operatives with one year's experience.
- With additional experience earnings can increase further to £18,000 or more.
- Earnings vary depending on your employer and which part of the country you work in.

Further information

www.cityandguilds.com/myperfectjob

Energy & Utility Skills (Sector Skills Council for the electricity, gas, waste management and water industries)
Friars Gate Two
1011 Stratford Road
Solihull
B90 4BN
0845 077 9922
www.euskills.co.uk

CABWI Awarding Body
1 Queen Anne's Gate
London
SW1H 9BT
020 7957 4523
www.cabwi.co.uk

Water UK
1 Queen Anne's Gate
London
SW1H 9BT
020 7344 1844
www.water.org.uk

Window Fitter

What the work involves

- Apprenticeship/Skillseekers may be available for candidates aged 16–24.
- Once you have fixed a new window into the surrounding brickwork, you will need to give it a weatherproof seal.
- Many employers on construction-sites require workers to have a Construction Skills Certification Scheme (CSCS) card. This demonstrates that the holder has health and safety training, as well as aiming for or competence in a particular occupation (usually requiring an appropriate NVQ/SVQ or the equivalent).

entry level

To both enter and train while working in this career, you will need qualifications at Level 1–2. Please refer to explanation on page vii.

The type of person suited to this work

You will need good practical hand skills for using tools and as you will be lifting and carrying windows you will need to be physically fit. Also, as you will be using ladders, you will need to have a head for heights, and be aware of your own safety and that of those around you.

You must be able to measure accurately so that the window frames fit properly.

You may work on your own for some jobs, but you will often work with one other window fitter or in a small team, so you must be able to work with others. You should also be able to get on with customers, because you will spend a lot of time on their premises.

Working conditions

You will work indoors and outdoors in a variety of locations, and you will be working in most weather conditions. A driving licence may be useful or required.

You will need to pay attention to health and safety when working with glass and be happy clearing up after your work has finished.

You are likely to work normal working hours during the week, but overtime may be available at weekends.

The future outlook

Work is available with window and conservatory fitting companies of all sizes throughout the UK. Increasing awareness of energy issues, and the need for all houses to have an energy assessment before sale, has increased demand for more energy efficient replacement windows.

Conservatories are also growing in popularity in the UK.

After gaining sufficient experience, you may progress to team leader or supervisory positions. You could also run your own window-fitting business. There are also openings within the sales and marketing sides of the industry.

Qualifications and courses

- There are no formal entry requirements, but you may need some GCSEs/S grades, or equivalent vocational qualifications such as a Foundation GNVQ/GSVQ Level 1. Maths, English and design and technology subjects are useful.
- Apprenticeship/Skillseekers may be available for people aged 16–24. Applicants normally need GCSEs/S grades (A–E/1–5), or an equivalent qualification such as Intermediate GNVQ or First Diploma.
- Initial training is provided by employers and covers removing and fitting window frames, health and safety, customer relations and relevant paperwork. Entrants then work with experienced window installers before being allowed to work alone.
- You can gain vocational qualifications while you work. You will be taught practical skills and may spend time off-site at a college or training centre. You may work towards NVQs/SVQs in Fenestration Installation at Level 2, Fenestration Installation and Surveying at Level 3, and Glazing Installation and Maintenance at Levels 2–3.
- Details of centres offering assessment for glazing and installation NVQs/SVQs are available from Glass Training Limited and from the Glass Qualifications Authority.

CRCI:BB

CLCI:UF

Other related opportunities

- Carpenter / Joiner p41
- Carpet Fitter p42
- Ceiling Fixer p45
- Glazier p55

Advantages/disadvantages

- Lifting and carrying windows and working at heights may be difficult for some people.
- You will get to travel to many different locations in your job.
- It is satisfying to make customers happy by improving the appearance, value and function of their buildings by installing new windows.

Earnings guide

- Whilst training you will earn around £12,500 a year.
- Once trained, you can expect an average salary of around £14,500–£18,000.
- £22,000–£26,000 is likely to be earned by a competent fitter.
- Earnings will depend on where you work and the size of the organisation.

Further information

Proskills UK (Sector Skills Council for process and manufacturing industries)
Centurion Court
85b Milton Park
Abingdon
Oxfordshire
OX14 4RY
01235 833844
www.proskills.co.uk

Glass Qualifications Authority
Provincial House
Solly Street
Sheffield
S1 4BA
0114 272 0033
www.glassqualificationsauthority.com

Glass and Glazing Federation
44–48 Borough High Street
London
SE1 1XB
0870 042 4255
www.ggf.co.uk

www.cityandguilds.com/myperfectjob

Do you like meeting new people, enjoy preparing food and like keeping places clean and tidy? The catering and hospitality industry has lots of opportunities in these sorts of jobs:

- **Bar Person**
- **Chef**
- **Hotel Manager**
- **Kitchen Porter**
- **Receptionist**

But what's it like working in this area?

Here's Jonathan Cox's story

Bar Manager/Owner

Jonathan's love of food and the catering trade started at an early age as his mother owned a restaurant. He took a degree in Hotel Management and worked for several large catering firms before running his own restaurant/hotel in Wales. On returning to London he helped a friend with the opening of the Havelock Tavern in the late 1990s and this first-generation gastropub proved to be a great success. Jon then opened, and now manages, another establishment, The Earl Spencer, in South London, a gastropub aimed at the local community that won the prestigious 2004 London Evening Standard Pub of the Year award.

WHAT MAKES A GREAT MANAGER

'You have to be people-oriented; you have to enjoy being in a social environment where people are coming out to have a good time. You have to be prepared to work at unsocial times, which is crucial to anyone coming into this job because it plays havoc with your social life, and you have to be prepared for longish hours. You need to be aware and practical and be able to act on your own initiative because dealing with people is different all the time, and remember this is a service industry so you must believe in good service. You also need stamina and enthusiasm because there's that old cliché of you've got to love what you do. Having an interest in what I do is absolutely fundamental to me.'

Jon's duties include a lot of deskwork as he has five separate wine suppliers as well as other drink and food suppliers. He must coordinate his 20 members of staff including bar staff, waiters and waitresses and kitchen staff. Each day he must check the premises to make sure everything is in good order, then he orders in supplies, sorts out the money in the tills, opens the post, checks that day's menus with the chef and deals with any problems. He also spends a lot of time talking to his customers getting feedback on the bar and the food.

THE DRAWBACKS TO THE JOB

'To start off with, it is a lowly income for the hours you work; you are not going to generate the same level of income at the beginning as you would do in other jobs, and the hours you have to work if you want to succeed are very long.'

WHY ENTER THE INDUSTRY THEN?

'If you want to come into this industry then do think about it carefully. However, if you want to go into something where you can rise through the ranks pretty quickly, where there's a lot of opportunity to travel and where you can have an awful lot of fun and fulfilment then this is a good thing to do because you are not sitting at a computer thinking about things – this is really hands-on.'

In the future, Jon would like to build on the success he has already had at The Earl Spencer and to that end he is currently in the process of expanding by opening a second bar on the first floor of his premises.

Bar Manager / Licensee

What the work involves

- Your will manage a bar, pub or other establishment that is licensed to sell alcohol. Your duties will include the recruitment and training of staff, dealing with the accounts, ordering stock and maintaining links with suppliers.
- You will need to keep up to date with any changes to licensing laws and other legal requirements such as health and safety or fire safety regulations, and make sure your customers and staff keep to them.
- In addition, you will deal with customers and make sure they enjoy their visit.

The type of person suited to this work

You must enjoy meeting and speaking to people of all ages and have excellent communication skills. A practical and flexible approach is important, because you will undertake a variety of tasks. As you may have to deal with problems with customers or suppliers, you should have a confident, professional attitude.

You will be managing cash on a daily basis so you will need to have good numeracy skills. A well-organised approach is important as you must ensure that all pub activities are properly staffed.

Finally, you should keep up to date with legal requirements and enforce those that affect you. Being physically fit and able to stay on your feet all day is helpful.

Working conditions

Although pubs, clubs and bars can remain open for 24 hours a day, most have chosen to only extend their hours at weekends or for special events. You will work long hours, during which you will do lifting and carrying of heavy items.

You may have to deal with demanding or difficult customers.

The future outlook

This is a growing and changing industry. There are 60,000 pubs in the UK with lots of opportunties to enter and then progress within the industry.

A publican can own, lease or become a tenant of their premises. You can also be a manager on behalf of a brewery of different premises such as one of the high street pubs and bars, family establishments, café-type bars or themed pubs and restaurants across the country.

With experience, you could progress to a larger establishment or even consider managing a bar overseas.

CRCI:C

CLCI:IB

Qualifications and courses

- No formal entry qualifications are required for this work and there are various routes into the profession.
- You can start work as a bar person from the age of 18, and then work your way up to supervisory or management positions. NVQs/SVQs are available in Bar Service (Level 2), On-Licensed Premises Supervision (Level 3) and On-Licensed Premises Management (Level 4).
- You could study for an HNC/HND, Foundation degree or degree in a related subject such as hospitality management or licensed retail.
- Larger companies run management training programmes for people with a degree or HND. This need not be in a pub- or catering-related subject. Trainees start at assistant manager level, and training may include study as well as practical training.
- New entrants to the profession can take the Professional Barperson's Qualification of the British Institute of Innkeeping (BII). This is for bar staff working in on-licensed premises in England and Wales. The Award in Beer and Cellar Quality is also available. For people wishing to progress to management, the National Certificate in Licensed Retailing and the National Certificate for Personal Licence Holders are available. In Scotland, the BII offers the Scottish Licensee's Certificate for on-licensed and all other premises and the Scottish Licensee's Certificate (Off-Sale).
- Alcohol Focus Scotland offers various levels of the ServeWise course depending on staff requirements.

entry level

To both enter and train while working in this career, you will need qualifications at Level 1. Please refer to explanation on page vii.

Other related opportunities

- Bar Person p84
- Brewer p176
- Catering / Restaurant Manager p85
- Hotel Manager p95
- Nightclub Manager p371

Advantages/disadvantages

- This work combines meeting and working with people, with management skills.
- The hours will be long and might affect your personal life.
- You will have to deal with people who can be the worse for alcohol.
- You can own your pub.

Earnings guide

- Earnings vary according to the location, type and size of the premises you work in.
- The average starting salary for a trainee manager is £14,000–£15,000, but with experience this can increase to between £22,000 and £30,000.
- If you work within a very successful and large establishment, it is possible to earn up to £50,000.

Further information

British Institute of Innkeeping
Wessex House
80 Park House
Camberley
Surrey
GU15 3PT
01276 684449
www.bii.org

People 1st
2nd Floor
38 Market Square
Uxbridge
UB8 1LH
0870 060 2550
www.people1st.co.uk

Springboard UK
3 Denmark Street
London
WC2H 8LP
020 7497 8654
www.springboarduk.org.uk

Institute of Brewing and Distilling
33 Clarges Street
London
W1J 7EE
020 7499 8144
www.ibd.org.uk

British Beer and Pub Association
Market Towers
1 Nine Elms Lane
London
SW8 5NQ
020 7627 9191
www.beerandpub.com

Scottish Licensed Trade Association
10 Walker Street
Edinburgh
EH13 7LA
0131 225 5169
www.slta.co.uk

www.cityandguilds.com/myperfectjob

CRCI:C

CLCI:IB

Bar Person

What the work involves

- Your work will include taking orders and payments from customers, serving drinks and snacks, cleaning up and working as part of a team.
- If your bar provides meals you will also take and serve food orders and then clear tables.
- You will be expected to help keep the bar areas clean and tidy, and be aware of any arguments or situations arising amongst the customers.

The type of person suited to this work

This job involves providing a friendly, quick service to customers, so you will need to be friendly and efficient. You will need good customer care and communication skills as you will have to deal with difficult customers.

Working behind a bar is a very active job so a good level of physical fitness is helpful. Numeracy skills and being honest are very important as you will be handling cash and taking card payments.

You will work as part of a team so will do a range of cleaning tasks as needed.

Working conditions

You will be on your feet in a busy and noisy environment for long periods.

Some people can be rude and aggressive, you will have to maintain a friendly, professional and polite manner at all times.

Some premises have chosen to open 24 hours a day, whilst others have extended their opening hours. You will normally work a number of sessions starting in the mid-morning until late at night.

The future outlook

There are around 64,000 licensed premises across the UK including pubs, clubs, bars and cafés. This variety means that you have lots of choice when choosing where you would like to work when you start and progress your career.

Larger companies provide training schemes to help staff develop their careers. With experience, you could become a bar supervisor and then progress to management or choose to work overseas or on cruise ships.

entry level

To both enter and train while working in this career, you will need qualifications at Level 1. Please refer to explanation on page vii.

Qualifications and courses

- There are no minimum qualifications. A friendly manner, an interest in customer care and communication and numeracy skills are desirable. You can work as a bar person from the age of 18.
- Previous experience in catering or kitchen work can be useful. The basic food hygiene certificate can be helpful.
- Apprenticeships/Skillseekers are available in this area for candidates aged 16–24.
- Most employers provide basic in-house training for new staff. This would cover areas such as using cash tills, working with the bar equipment and health and safety.
- You may also be able to work towards NVQ/SVQ Levels 2 and 3 in Food and Drink Service and Level 2 in Bar Service.
- With experience and further training, you could work towards NVQ/SVQ Level 3 in On-Licensed Premises Supervision. On completion of this, you could work in a supervisory role or start a management training scheme, depending on your employer.
- The British Institute of Innkeeping (BII) offers a variety of awards for specific requirements.

CRCI:C

CLCI:IC

Other related opportunities

- Bar Manager / Licensee p82
- Cellar Technician p86
- Holiday Centre Work p364
- Waiting Staff p100

Advantages/disadvantages

- Bar work is great for meeting and working with lots of people.
- There are many opportunities to work on a flexible, part-time basis.
- The unsociable working hours can affect your personal life.

Earnings guide

- Earnings will vary according to the size, type and location of the premises.
- Wages for bar work are normally paid hourly, in line with minimum hourly wage.
- Instead of an hourly rate you may start on a salary of around £10,500 per year
- With experience you could progress to a supervisory role and oversee the work of bar staff and receive around £17,000.

Further information

www.cityandguilds.com/myperfectjob

British Institute of Innkeeping
Wessex House
80 Park House
Camberley
Surrey
GU15 3PT
01276 684449
www.bii.org

People 1st
2nd Floor
38 Market Square
Uxbridge
UB8 1LH
0870 060 2550
www.people1st.co.uk

Springboard UK
3 Denmark Street
London
WC2H 8LP
020 7497 8654
www.springboarduk.org.uk

British Beer and Pub Association
Market Towers
1 Nine Elms Lane
London
SW8 5NQ
020 7627 9191
www.beerandpub.com

Catering / Restaurant Manager

What the work involves

- You will manage and employ staff in a kitchen or restaurant.
- Your duties will include preparing meals, serving food and making sure everything is produced to a high standard.
- Part of your work will involve planning menus, checking stocks of food and drink and ordering fresh supplies when needed.
- Paperwork is a part of the job too, so you will manage budgets and organise staff rotas.
- You will be responsible for the health and safety of both your staff and customers.

The type of person suited to this work

You will be dealing with kitchen staff, suppliers and those from other areas of the business, so you should be confident and have excellent communication skills. You should be interested in providing good customer care.

As you will be involved with preparing food for the public you will need to follow and keep up to date with health and safety laws. You will also need a good knowledge of food, an understanding of the different roles of your staff, have management skills and be well organised.

You will also need good numeracy skills as you will be managing a budget and working out stock quantities.

Working conditions

Much of your time will be spent in your kitchen or restaurant, which can get very hot and busy. You might be using cutting tools and knives and be on your feet for long periods.

As you will be managing and preparing food for the public, you will always need to follow high standards of food safety and hygiene.

Finally, expect to wear a uniform or protective clothing and regularly work unsociable hours.

The future outlook

There are around 106,500 restaurants employing 500,000 people in the UK. The sector offers a wide range of career opportunities and is one where you can progress quickly. However, it will help your career if you work in increasingly bigger and well-known premises.

In some parts of the UK – the major cities and south-east of England – where there are lots of restaurants, employers are finding it difficult to get staff with good skills. This means that if you do well your future prospects are very positive.

entry level

3

To both enter and train while working in this career, you will need qualifications at Level 3. Please refer to explanation on page vii.

Qualifications and courses

- You can start in a job as a kitchen assistant, waiter/waitress, chef or cook and work your way up. People working in the industry can take NVQs/SVQs, for example Hospitality Supervision Level 3 or Hospitality Management Level 4.
- The Institute of Hospitality (formerly the Hotel and Catering International Management Association) offers a selection of courses for staff in specific roles.
- Communication and numeracy skills are useful. A second language may also be helpful.
- If aged 16–24, you could also undertake Apprenticeships/Skillseekers in Hospitality.
- Many hotels and hotel chains offer training schemes. It may be possible to join a scheme with A levels/H grades or equivalent, but the usual requirement is a degree or HND/C in a relevant subject (for example hospitality management, hospitality and catering, hotel management, international hospitality management). Minimum requirements for degree entry are usually 5 GCSEs/S grades (A–C/1–3) and 2 A levels or 3 H grades. Postgraduate courses are also available.

CRCI:C

CLCI:IB

Other related opportunities

- Air Cabin Crew p555
- Airline Customer Service Agent p557
- Chef p87
- Contract Catering / Functions Manager p88
- Cruise Ship Work p560
- Fast Food Service Manager p90

Advantages/disadvantages

- This can be a very busy job where you will be doing several tasks at the same time.
- Hours are long and will involve unsociable hours including weekend or evening work.
- The job can provide the chance to work creatively with food.
- You may live on-site.

Earnings guide

- Salary rates vary depending on the type and size of restaurant, location and level of responsibility.
- Trainee starting salaries are £16,000–£20,000. With experience, and in a large restaurant, this can rise to £30,000–£40,000.
- A senior manager in the most successful premises can earn up to £60,000+.

Further information

People 1st
2nd Floor
38 Market Square
Uxbridge
UB8 1LH
0870 060 2550
www.people1st.co.uk

Institute of Hospitality
Trinity Court
34 West Street
Sutton
Surrey
SM1 1SH
020 8661 4900
www.hcima.co.uk

Springboard UK
3 Denmark Street
London
WC2H 8LP
020 7497 8654
www.springboarduk.org.uk

www.cityandguilds.com/myperfectjob

Cellar Technician

What the work involves

- You will set up and maintain the systems that provide alcoholic and soft drinks in pubs, hotels and other sites.
- Visiting a range of locations, you will install equipment and deal with emergencies or problems.
- You will undertake regular maintenance checks to make sure that everything works properly and train the staff on how to operate it.
- You might work from home or be based within a brewery.

The type of person suited to this work

Because of the technical nature of the work, you will need good practical skills and the confidence to work and operate different systems quickly and efficiently. As you will be handling heavy equipment, a good level of physical fitness is helpful. The ability to speak to lots of different people is useful, as is a confidence in your ability to do the job well.

You will need to be sociable and friendly and be willing to do lots of driving from site to site. As you will be providing a service on behalf of your company for lots of different licensed premises you will need to have excellent customer care skills.

Working conditions

You will spend lots of time driving from site to site. Some of your work will be attending emergency call-outs which could include evenings and weekends that might affect your personal life. The extended pub opening hours might mean this includes 24-hour call-out duties.

You will work in dark, cramped conditions using specialist tools and equipment.

The future outlook

Because of the steady growth in hospitality venues and the need for branded drinks, the number of jobs is expected to grow steadily. Many applicants come from the licensed trade who have watched the job and become interested. It is therefore useful to have pub experience or relevant qualifications before applying.

With experience you can apply for senior/managerial posts or move into other areas of the licensed or food and drink sector.

entry level

To both enter and train while working in this career, you will need qualifications at Level 1. Please refer to explanation on page vii.

Qualifications and courses

- There are no minimum entry requirements for this job, though some employers prefer candidates with a good general education, particularly with GCSEs in maths, science or technology subjects.
- The following qualifications are also useful: NVQ/SVQ Levels 2 or 3, City & Guilds or BTEC First or National awards. Some employers in particular may prefer electrical or electronic engineering.
- Employers provide training that covers areas such as health and safety, customer care, refrigeration, checking systems and working with equipment.
- You could work towards the NVQ/SVQ Levels 2 and 3 Drinks Dispense Systems (Installation and Maintenance).
- The British Institute of Innkeeping (BII) offers a Level 2 award in Cellar Service Installation.

GRCI:C

CLCI:IC

Other related opportunities

Advantages/disadvantages

- This job combines meeting and training people and lots of practical work.
- You will have to travel from your base to customers over a geographical area.
- You may work in uncomfortable conditions, for example when fitting a new dispensing system in a cellar.

Earnings guide

- The starting salary is normally around £12,000 per year.
- With experience this can increase to £20,000+. When fully qualified you could get up to £25,000.
- You may also be paid overtime for emergency call-out duties or for working in the evenings or at weekends.

Further information

www.cityandguilds.com/myperfectjob

British Soft Drinks Association
20–22 Stukeley Street
London
WC2B 5LR
020 7430 0356
www.britishsoftdrinks.com

People 1st
2nd Floor
38 Market Square
Uxbridge
UB8 1LH
0870 060 2550
www.people1st.co.uk

Scottish Licensed Trade Association
10 Walker Street
Edinburgh
EH13 7LA
0131 225 5169
www.slta.co.uk

Chef

What the work involves

- You could work in restaurants, cafés, bars and cruise ships. Some chefs also work for specialist food companies, helping to create new products.
- Your role will be to coordinate kitchen activities and supervise the preparation of food by your team of kitchen staff.
- Planning new menus and dishes, checking stocks of food and drink and dealing with suppliers are also included.

entry level

To both enter and train while working in this career, you will need qualifications at Level 1. Please refer to explanation on page vii.

The type of person suited to this work

You will be working in a kitchen preparing food to order. You must be able to keep calm under pressure and do lots of tasks at once. As you are responsible for the health and safety of everyone in your kitchen, you must be able to stay alert at all times.

You will need excellent cooking skills, be very creative and have a love of food. It is also helpful if you want to try out new things and set trends.

Kitchens work best when everyone works together as a team, so team-working skills are useful, as are good communication skills.

Finally, measuring ingredients and managing a budget and stock levels are included, so good numeracy skills are helpful.

Working conditions

Most of your work will be within a kitchen, which will be hot, busy and noisy. Kitchens are also full of equipment and cutting tools that can be dangerous if not used correctly.

As you will be preparing food you will be expected to wear protective clothing and pay attention to health and hygiene.

You will work unsociable hours including evening and weekends, which might affect your personal life.

The future outlook

In many areas of the country there is a shortage of chefs. This is due to an increasing number of establishments opening and fewer chefs with the skills needed.

Starting as an assistant or commis chef you will help in different sections of the kitchen. With experience, you can progress to sous chef where you act as deputy to the chef and manage a section of your own.

Once you have gained significant experience you can apply to be a chef in locations at home and abroad.

Qualifications and courses

- It is possible to work your way up with enough kitchen experience. Some employers will allow you to be trained up by an experienced chef whilst you work in the kitchen. It can be helpful to gain a food hygiene certificate whilst working towards becoming a chef.
- Communication skills and a good standard of numeracy are useful.
- You can study for NVQs/SVQs (Levels 2–3) in Food Preparation and Cooking. You do not usually need academic qualifications.
- Apprenticeships/Skillseekers may be available for people aged 16–24.
- Further qualifications are also available, including Foundation HNCs in Professional Cookery or Professional Patisserie which require NVQ/SVQ Level 3 or a National Certificate in Catering, or HNDs in Culinary Art, Patisserie, Food Service or Kitchen and Larder Work. Scotland has a variety of qualifications available.
- Chefs may work their way up to become an executive head chef, which requires extensive training. Chefs generally begin as a commis chef (assistant), then progress to become a chef de partie (section leader), then as a sous chef (deputy chef), followed by a head chef and finally an executive head chef.

CRCI:C

CLCI:IC

Other related opportunities

- Catering / Restaurant Manager p85
- Contract Catering / Functions Manager p88
- Home Economist p93

Advantages/disadvantages

- This type of work means long hours including weekends and evenings.
- You will be working on your feet for much of the time in a hot and busy environment.
- Preparing high-quality food is very rewarding and will be a memorable event for your customers.

Earnings guide

- Salaries vary according to the type of employer and geographic area. Where there are chef shortages, salaries are higher.
- Salaries start at £12,000 per year for a junior commis chef, rising to £17,000 then to £25,000 as a second chef with experience.
- Head chefs can earn up to £30,000+.
- Famous and successful chefs can earn £40,000–£60,000+. However, your earnings will be based on your experience, reputation and size and type of premises.

Further information

People 1st
2nd Floor
38 Market Square
Uxbridge
UB8 1LH
0870 060 2550
www.people1st.co.uk

Institute of Hospitality
Trinity Court
34 West Street
Sutton
Surrey
SM1 1SH
020 8661 4900
www.hcima.co.uk

Springboard UK
3 Denmark Street
London
WC2H 8LP
020 7497 8654
www.springboarduk.org.uk

www.cityandguilds.com/myperfectjob

Contract Catering / Functions Manager

What the work involves

- The types of contract/functions that you will plan and deliver include business meetings, corporate events, weddings and other family occasions.
- Your role will be to check, plan and order the supplies of kitchen equipment, food and drinks for each event.
- You might also be involved with managing the waiting and kitchen staff, and budgets.
- The level to which you will get involved in these aspects will depend on whether you run your own company or work for a large organisation.

entry level

To both enter and train while working in this career, you will need qualifications at Level 1–3. Please refer to explanation on page vii.

The type of person suited to this work

Being able to communicate well with staff and with customers is important. Numeracy skills are also useful as you will be dealing with budgets and checking stocks of food, drink and equipment. A good knowledge of health and hygiene is vital as you will be preparing food for the public.

Due to the contact with people, such as serving or dealing with clients you must be presentable at all times. Because of the varied and often busy nature of this work, you will need to be flexible, confident and enjoy food! Finally, to help you oversee many activities at once you will need to be well organised and be able to plan lots of different aspects.

Working conditions

This is tiring work which can take days of preparation before the actual event when the guests arrive. It includes evening and weekend working.

There could be some travelling involved, perhaps away from home for overnight stays. You will be working at different locations including outdoors in marquees or indoors in kitchens, people's homes or other community settings.

You will be expected to wear protective clothing and be aware of health and hygiene regulations.

The future outlook

Function and event catering is a growing but competitive industry. There is increasing demand from businesses for good quality catering support. There are good opportunities for those with experience to work for well-known clients that might include celebrities. There is also a lot of demand for catering services at weddings and other private events.

If you are very successful you could progress to one of the larger national contract firms or start your own business.

Qualifications and courses

- It is possible to gain work in this area without qualifications, with experience and training gained whilst working.
- Communication and numeracy skills are important.
- Some catering companies offer formal training schemes. It may be possible to join a scheme with A levels/H grades or equivalent, but an HNC/HND, Foundation degree or degree in a relevant subject (for example hospitality management, hospitality and catering, hotel management, international hospitality management) is often preferred.
- You can also take NVQs/SVQs, for example Hospitality Supervision Level 3.
- The Institute of Hospitality (formerly the Hotel and Catering International Management Association) offers a selection of courses for staff in specific roles.
- You could also undertake an Apprenticeship/Skillseekers to enter this area.

CRCI:C | CLCI:IC

Other related opportunities

- Catering / Restaurant Manager p85
- Chef p87
- Hotel Manager p95

Advantages/disadvantages

- As you will be attending a range of events, the work provides the chance to meet different people.
- You will work in different types of locations and are likely to have a varied and long working day.
- You could provide the catering at a celebrity wedding!

Earnings guide

- Salaries differ depending on the employer and your location. Your earnings can also depend on the numbers you cater for.
- £15,000–£18,000 per year is a normal starting salary as an assistant.
- This rises to £19,000–£25,000 with experience.
- At senior management level expect £35,000–£50,000+.

Further information

www.cityandguilds.com/myperfectjob

People 1st
2nd Floor
38 Market Square
Uxbridge
UB8 1LH
0870 060 2550
www.people1st.co.uk

Springboard UK
3 Denmark Street
London
WC2H 8LP
020 7497 8654
www.springboarduk.org.uk

Institute of Hospitality
Trinity Court
34 West Street
Sutton
Surrey
SM1 1SH
020 8661 4900
www.hcima.co.uk

Fast Food Service Assistant

What the work involves

- You will take food orders from customers and serve food over the counter.
- Your duties will include taking food payments, providing the correct change and working with a cash till.
- Some of your work will be in the kitchen area preparing food.
- You will be expected to help clean the kitchen, customer and serving areas.
- The range of outlets which employ fast food assistants include take-aways, pizza and burger restaurants, fish and chip shops and cafés.

The type of person suited to this work

As you will be working directly with customers, you will need good people skills and a polite and positive attitude. Team-working skills are useful as you are likely to be part of a small team. You should be able to work quickly and accurately under pressure and have good practical, hands-on skills.

You will need to be confident handling cash and be honest. Finally, as you will be working closely with food for the public, you should have a high standard of personal hygiene and be aware of the health and safety of yourself and others.

Working conditions

As you will be serving food for people at all times of the day, you might have to work weekends and evenings on a regular basis. You are likely to work sessions or on a part-time basis.

You will probably wear a uniform or protective clothing. This is a busy and potentially dangerous environment.

Some members of the public are rude and aggressive, which can be difficult to deal with.

The future outlook

Fast food restaurants and cafés are found across the UK. There are therefore a variety of opportunities which makes this an easy area to enter whether you have experience or not.

Some of the larger chains offer excellent training which can help you progress into management positions or obtain work within other areas of the catering or service sectors.

This work can fit around family or educational commitments.

entry level

To both enter and train while working in this career, you will need qualifications at Level 1. Please refer to explanation on page vii.

Qualifications and courses

- There are no minimum qualifications, but previous experience in a catering environment, particularly in dealing with customers, can be helpful.
- A basic food hygiene certificate is useful.
- Apprenticeships/Skillseekers may be available for people aged 16–24.
- Employers may provide the opportunity to gain qualifications and hygiene certificates as part of your training. Others may offer the chance to gain catering and customer service qualifications as you progress in experience. Training in how to work with cash tills is usually provided by employers.
- You may also receive training which leads to qualifications such as NVQ/SVQ Level 1 in Food and Drink Service or Preparing and Serving Food, or Level 2 Hospitality Quick Service.
- With further training, you could work towards a BTEC National Diploma in Hospitality Supervision.
- You can take general catering courses which include NVQs/SVQs Levels 2 and 3 in Customer Service, Level 1 and 2 in Food and Drink Service, and Levels 1–3 in Food Preparation and Cooking.

CRCI:C

CLCI:IC

Other related opportunities

- Fast Food Service Manager p90
- Kitchen Assistant p98
- Waiting Staff p100

Advantages/disadvantages

- Because you are dealing with customers and working as part of a team, this can be a sociable job.
- You will probably be required to work some weekends and evenings.
- It is flexible work that can fit around other commitments.

Earnings guide

- Earnings can vary according to the type of fast food outlet and where you work.
- £10,000 per year is generally the starting salary. This increases £14,000–£16,000 with experience and training.
- In larger companies, it is possible to earn up to £16,000+

Further information

People 1st
2nd Floor
38 Market Square
Uxbridge
UB8 1LH
0870 060 2550
www.people1st.co.uk

Institute of Hospitality
Trinity Court
34 West Street
Sutton
Surrey
SM1 1SH
020 8661 4900
www.hcima.co.uk

Springboard UK
3 Denmark Street
London
WC2H 8LP
020 7497 8654
www.springboarduk.org.uk

www.cityandguilds.com/myperfectjob

Fast Food Service Manager

What the work involves

- Your job will be to manage the staff and profits of a fast food outlet. There are lots of different types including take-aways, pizza and burger restaurants, fish and chip shops and cafés.
- You will maintain stocks of food and drink, oversee budgets and talk to suppliers.
- Some of the work will include recruiting staff, organising rotas and dealing with the wages of your assistants.
- You will monitor the standard of health and safety across all areas of the premises.
- In busy periods, you might also take orders and serve food.

The type of person suited to this work

You will be working with customers so you will need good communication skills and a polite and positive manner. As people expect their food to be delivered quickly, being able to work under pressure is helpful. The ability to manage and motivate staff is very important.

Some outlets operate targets which means you will need business skills and business sense. As you will be responsible for managing budgets and increasing profits numeracy skills are also helpful.

You will be overseeing the production and serving of food, so you will need a good knowledge of health and hygiene regulations and to be able to operate to them.

Working conditions

As people want to buy food from fast food outlets at all times of the day, you will have to work weekends and evenings on a regular basis.

Serving and kitchen areas can be very busy and hot, so you will have to do a lot of activities at the same time.

When working in the kitchen you will need to work to a high standard of health and hygiene and wear protective clothing.

The future outlook

This is a fast growing area of the catering industry. Fast food restaurants and cafés can be found across the UK which means there are a variety of opportunities available. To enter this job you will normally have either management or previous food service experience.

The larger outlets provide training opportunities which could help you progress to regional level posts in training or sales, or you could look to use your skills in other catering companies.

entry level

To both enter and train while working in this career, you will need qualifications at Level 1–3. Please refer to explanation on page vii.

Qualifications and courses

- It is possible to work your way up to this job by gaining experience and training as a fast food service assistant. However, as well as experience, you will need to have gained your food hygiene certificate and customer service qualifications.
- The types of qualifications needed can vary between companies.
- Relevant degree courses including hospitality management, hotel and catering management and culinary arts management are available through many universities. Other qualifications available include a BTEC National Certificate or Diploma in Hospitality Supervision, NVQs Levels 2–4 in Customer Service, or a 1-year Hotel and Catering Management postgraduate conversion course.
- Relevant catering and fast food service Apprenticeships/Skillseekers can help you gain the experience to progress up to a management job.
- Larger companies offer management training programmes that you would complete whilst working closely with an experienced manager.
- Key Skills in communication and application of number are important.

CRCI:C

CLCI:IC

Other related opportunities

- Catering / Restaurant Manager p85
- Fast Food Service Assistant p89
- Kitchen Assistant p98
- Waiting Staff p100

Advantages/disadvantages

- Because you are dealing with customers and working as part of a team, this can be a sociable and active job.
- You will probably be required to work some weekends and evenings.
- This is a relatively easy area in which to gain a management-level post.

Earnings guide

- Earnings can vary according to the type of fast food outlet you work in and geographic location.
- As a trainee manager you could earn around £18,000 per year.
- This can rise to £25,000–£30,000 with experience.
- £35,000–£55,000 is possible for senior managers.

Further information

www.cityandguilds.com/myperfectjob

People 1st
2nd Floor
38 Market Square
Uxbridge
UB8 1LH
0870 060 2550
www.people1st.co.uk

Institute of Hospitality
Trinity Court
34 West Street
Sutton
Surrey
SM1 1SH
020 8661 4900
www.hcima.co.uk

Springboard UK
3 Denmark Street
London
WC2H 8LP
020 7497 8654
www.springboarduk.org.uk

Food Safety Officer

What the work involves

- You will advise those working in catering/food premises by providing information on healthy eating and the presentation, preparation and storage of food for public consumption.
- Your role will be to investigate outbreaks of food-related illnesses and implement hazard warnings.
- Some of your work will include liaising with colleagues across the country and specialists in disease control and microbiology.
- If you work for a food business you will provide training and advice to other employees.

The type of person suited to this work

You should have an interest in both food and science. This job involves helping people to put into place safe ways to prepare, produce, store and package food. To do this, you will need a high level of knowledge about environmental health.

You will also need a good understanding of law and be confident – especially if you have to shut down a business. You should enjoy doing lots of different jobs at once and be flexible and happy to travel.

Some of your work might involve giving presentations to audiences that range from school children to company managers, so you should be happy talking to people of differing ages and backgrounds.

Working conditions

Although you will have an office, most of your time will involve visiting people in their workplaces or homes following up complaints and giving advice.

This could involve seeing things which could be smelly and unpleasant. You will spend time driving and will wear protective clothing such as masks, hair protection and boots.

You might have to work evenings and weekends.

The future outlook

Due to the rise in mass manufacturing of food, take-aways and fast food outlets, the need for food safety officers has remained steady.

Outside of Scotland, most food safety officers begin as environmental health officers and specialise later. In Scotland, inspection and food hygiene is undertaken by registered food safety officers.

With experience you can progress to senior positions within food safety or return to other areas of environmental health or enter self-employment/consultancy.

CRCI:JD | CLCI:COP

Qualifications and courses

- To become a food safety officer outside Scotland, you will need to train as an environmental health officer.
- Candidates need a BSc or MSc in environmental science accredited by the Chartered Institute of Environmental Health (CIEH) or the Royal Environmental Health Institute of Scotland (REHIS). Entry to a first degree normally requires 2 A levels/3 H grades including a science subject, plus 5 GCSEs/S grades (A–C/1–3) including English, maths and science. Entry to the MSc requires a first degree in a relevant science or technology subject accredited by the CIEH or REHIS, or equivalent. Before qualifying as an environmental health officer, graduates must undertake a minimum of 48 weeks' practical training. Students complete a logbook accompanied by a portfolio of evidence, before taking a professional examination.
- In England and Wales, at least 50% of the training must be with a local authority. Training can be incorporated into a first degree through a sandwich year, and entrants are often part-sponsored by local authorities. Successful completion of all the training requirements leads to the Environmental Health Officers' Registration Board Certificate and graduate membership of the CIEH.
- In Scotland, there is a separate training route for food safety officers, although you can also train as an environmental health officer before specialising in food safety.
- Food safety officers working in Scotland must meet the requirements of the Scottish Food Safety Officers' Registration Board. Candidates for the Higher Certificates in Food Premises Inspection and Food Standards Inspection must have a minimum of an HND in food science or food technology.
- New entrants undertake a minimum of 6 months' practical training with a Scottish local authority. On successful completion of the practical training and professional examinations, trainees will be awarded the appropriate professional qualification.

entry level

To both enter and train while working in this career, you will need qualifications at Level 4–8. Please refer to explanation on page vii.

Other related opportunities

- Dietitian p277
- Environmental Health Practitioner / Officer p280
- Health and Safety Adviser p19
- Health Promotion / Education Specialist p281
- Home Economist p93
- Meat Inspector p445
- Pest Control Technician p427
- Trading Standards Officer p460

Advantages/disadvantages

- This job offers flexibility, variety, challenge and some travelling.
- You might be responsible for closing down businesses.
- You might see things which are unpleasant and smelly.
- You will be involved in protecting public health.

Earnings guide

- Future earnings depend on the size and type of organisation worked for, for some small companies its £20,000–£25,000 per year. Within local authorities range from £26,000–£31,000+ per year.
- Senior positions range from £35,000–£65,000 (for those with extensive experience and responsibility).
- If you are self-employed, daily rates range from £250 to £460 per day.

Further information

Chartered Institute of Environmental Health
Chadwick Court
15 Hatfields
London
SE1 8DJ
020 7928 6006
www.ehocareers.org

Royal Environmental Health Institute of Scotland
3 Manor Place
Edinburgh
EH3 7DH
0131 225 6999
www.rehis.org

CRCI:JD

CLCI:COP

Home Economist

What the work involves

- You will work in a wide range of areas, including laboratories, kitchens and supply companies, providing specialist information and advice on many aspects of food.
- Your duties will be to provide services, possibly on a self-employed basis, such as menu testing for a food company, doing food presentations at specialist exhibitions or assessing new cookery equipment.
- Home economists also work in education and other areas, informing others about nutrition and developing awareness of healthy eating and living.

entry level

To both enter and train while working in this career, you will need qualifications at Level 3. Please refer to explanation on page vii.

The type of person suited to this work

As you may be developing new food and food products, you will need a good scientific and technical awareness. To be able to provide complicated and specialist knowledge, you will need to enjoy communicating with others. Having confidence in handling and preparing food is very important. Some jobs such as styling and producing food for magazines require flair and creativity.

Because you will be supporting different clients, you will need to have a strong interest in people and their needs. Patience and attention to detail are also important.

You will need to be very self-motivated if you work as a consultant.

Working conditions

You will work for much of your time in kitchens which are hot and have lots of dangerous equipment and cutting tools. You will therefore need a high standard of health and safety awareness and the ability to make sure guidelines are followed by yourself and others.

This is physically demanding work that involves lifting, carrying and standing for long periods.

The future outlook

Home economics/consumer science is a wide area that provides opportunities in food development, appliance testing, education and other areas. The range of opportunities is currently growing due to the current drive encouraging healthy eating and reducing obesity.

With experience, many home economists go on to run their own businesses and provide freelance support to other organisations. There is also the option to work overseas in developing countries that need your specialist knowledge and skills.

Qualifications and courses

- Home economists/consumer scientists usually enter the profession with relevant educational qualifications and/or practical experience.
- Communication and numeracy skills are important.
- You can gain HNCs, HNDs and degrees in relevant subjects, such as consumer studies/science, food studies/science, food and nutrition, food and marketing, food technology, catering management. The usual entry requirements for an HNC/D are 4 GCSEs/S grades (A–C/1–3) and 1 A level/Advanced Higher or equivalent. For a degree, 5 GCSEs/S grades (A–C/1–3) and 2 A levels/Advanced Highers or equivalent are normally required.
- Relevant courses at further education level include NVQs/SVQs in Food Preparation or Food and Drink Manufacturing Operations.
- Employers may offer in-house training leading to NVQs/SVQs.

Other related opportunities

- Brewer p176
- Chef p87
- Contract Catering / Functions Manager p88
- Dietitian p277
- Food Safety Officer p91

Advantages/disadvantages

- This job is a combination of cooking skills, science, technical ability and developing new products.
- You can be a specialist in one area or a generalist across many.
- This role lets you work with food without always being in a kitchen all day.

Earnings guide

- Earnings vary between employers.
- You can expect to get £21,000–£23,000 per year as a starting salary.
- This can rise to £25,500–£35,000 after several years' experience. However, the most senior earn more than this.
- Some jobs also offer benefits such as a company car and/or pension.

Further information

People 1st
2nd Floor
38 Market Square
Uxbridge
UB8 1LH
0870 060 2550
www.people1st.co.uk

Hotel / Accommodation Room Attendant

What the work involves

- You will clean, tidy and prepare guest rooms to a high standard using cleaning materials and equipment. This could include cleaning bathroom and toilet areas and other parts of the hotel.
- Work involves stocking up levels of supplies as they are used and keeping records of any items of lost property left in rooms.
- Using a trolley or cart, you will move supplies of linen, towels and other items around the hotel.
- You will also check for maintenance problems or damage to hotel property.

The type of person suited to this work

Because much of the work involves cleaning areas of the site and moving supplies around, you will need a good level of physical fitness. You will also need to be well organised, enthusiastic and able to work quickly to get all your tasks completed on time. Although you will need good individual skills, team-working skills are also helpful.

You must have a polite and friendly manner, because you will meet hotel guests. In order to keep up standards of cleanliness for guests, you must have a good eye for detail. As you will be cleaning areas around guests' personal belongings, you should be very honest and trustworthy.

Working conditions

This is physical work so expect to be on your feet for much of the time, using cleaning equipment and pushing a cart with your equipment from room to room.

You will be working with cleaning fluids and other cleaning equipment on a daily basis, which could affect those with skin problems.

You will probably work shifts and it is sometimes possible to live in.

The future outlook

There are around 48,000 hotels in the UK employing 280,000 people. However, these figures do not include the other options in this area such as bed and breakfasts or leisure facilities. Larger employers provide staff with good training and development support. The number of top level hotels is increasing, and is expected to grow further as we get nearer to the London Olympics in 2012.

You could also work abroad, for an international hotel or in a resort. With experience, you could go on to work as an accommodation manager or housekeeper.

entry level

1

To both enter and train while working in this career, you will need qualifications at Level 1. Please refer to explanation on page vii.

Qualifications and courses

- There are no minimum entry requirements for this job. Some companies prefer to employ people aged over 18.
- Employers provide on-the-job training when you first start work, usually under the supervision of a more experienced member of staff. This could include aspects such as safe lifting methods and furniture and carpet cleaning.
- It may be useful to gain an NVQ/SVQ Level 2 in Housekeeping or Levels 1 and 2 in Cleaning Support Services.
- You could undertake Apprenticeships/ Skillseekers to enter this area of work.
- To progess into accommodation manager or staff supervisor work, you could gain an NVQ/SVQ Level 3 in Hospitality Supervision.

CRCI:C

CLCI:IC

Other related opportunities

- Cleaner p418
- Cruise Ship Work p560
- Hotel Manager p95
- Housekeeper p97

Advantages/disadvantages

- In some jobs, you can live on-site and have some meals provided.
- There are opportunities to gain seasonal and holiday work. This type of job is also available on a part-time basis.
- On the days when lots of guests are arriving and leaving this is very busy work.

Earnings guide

- Earnings vary according to employer and location and may be based on hourly rates from the minimum rate up to £7–£8 per hour, which might include your room and meals.
- This can rise to between £10,000 and £11,000 per year with experience and training.
- Guests often leave tips for room attendants, which you may share with other staff or be allowed to keep yourself.

Further information

www.cityandguilds.com/myperfectjob

Institute of Hospitality
Trinity Court
34 West Street
Sutton
Surrey
SM1 1SH
020 8661 4900
www.hcima.co.uk

Springboard UK
3 Denmark Street
London
WC2H 8LP
020 7497 8654
www.springboarduk.org.uk

Hotel Manager

What the work involves

- You will manage the services and staff of your hotel making sure that it is a successful business and gains new customers to make a profit.
- As the manager, you will be responsible for checking that the buildings and grounds of your hotel meet health and safety and other standards.
- Your work could also involve promoting and developing the hotel to increase numbers of customers.
- You could work in all types of hotel from a small private one up to large national or international chain.

entry level

To both enter and train while working in this career, you will need qualifications at Level 2–8. Please refer to explanation on page vii.

The type of person suited to this work

As you will manage budgets and cash flow, you will need a good level of numeracy and the confidence to handle large quantities of money. Communication skills are very important as you will be organising staff and dealing with guests. You will be working in a sociable, busy environment so you will need to enjoy meeting lots of different people.

You should be well organised and able to work to targets. Strong customer care and good business skills are essential and because the working hours can be long, you will need to be flexible.

A knowledge of tourism is useful, as is being able to speak another language.

Working conditions

This work involves working long hours that include evenings and weekends. You might spend some of your evenings living-in so you can be on-site in case of emergencies. You are also likely to work shifts.

Some members of the public can be rude and aggresive so you will need to maintain a calm professional manner at all times.

You will also need to have a smart appearance at all times and might have to wear a uniform.

The future outlook

Hospitality is a developing sector and there are about 48,000 hotels of all kinds throughout the UK employing over 280,000 people. After a difficult period the hotel sector is showing signs of growth which should continue up until 2012. There is currently a strong demand for hotel management staff.

With experience, you could work overseas or progress from hotel management into other areas of a company such as human resources, finance and IT.

Qualifications and courses

- There are a number of routes into this job.
- No specific academic qualifications are required, as it is possible to enter the industry at a lower level and work your way up. You can study part time towards NVQ/SVQ Level 1 and 2 in Catering and Hospitality and Level 3 Supervisory Management.
- Apprenticeships/Skillseekers may be available for candidates aged 16–24. Apprentices undertake on-the-job training and work towards NVQ/SVQ Level 1 and 2 in Catering and Hospitality and Level 3 Supervisory Management.
- It is possible to join with previous hotel experience and through attending fast-track training schemes. Knowledge of a second language can be useful.
- The Institute of Hospitality (formerly the Hotel and Catering International Management Association) offers a selection of courses for staff in specific roles.
- Many entrants to this profession have a degree, HNC/D or postgraduate qualification, and enter as management trainees. Relevant degree subjects include Hospitality Management and Hotel and Catering Management.

CRCI:C

CLCI:IB

Other related opportunities

- Bar Manager / Licensee p82
- Catering / Restaurant Manager p85
- Holiday Centre Work, p364
- Holiday Representative, p365
- Housekeeper p97

Advantages/disadvantages

- Because of the nature of the work, this is a very sociable job.
- Live-in accommodation within the hotel is offered with some jobs.
- There are opportunities to travel and work overseas.
- You can progress to be a manager of a large hotel relatively quickly.

Earnings guide

- Salaries will depend on the size, reputation and location of the hotel in which you work. London and the south-east of England pay the highest.
- As an assistant trainee manager you could get £15,000 per year.
- As trainee manager £16,000–£18,000 per year.
- £55,000–£100,000+ is possible for those in the largest London hotels.

Further information

People 1st
2nd Floor
38 Market Square
Uxbridge
UB8 1LH
0870 060 2550
www.people1st.co.uk

Institute of Hospitality
Trinity Court
34 West Street
Sutton
Surrey
SM1 1SH
020 8661 4900
www.hcima.co.uk

Springboard UK
3 Denmark Street
London
WC2H 8LP
020 7497 8654
www.springboarduk.org.uk

www.cityandguilds.com/myperfectjob

Hotel Porter

What the work involves

- As a porter, you will greet hotel guests, answer the phone, take reservations and deal with general enquiries.
- You will also be responsible for moving guests' luggage to and from rooms.
- You may transport large equipment and objects around the hotel site when required.
- If you work as a night porter, you will look after the security and safety of the hotel site.
- As a head porter in a large hotel, you will be responsible for a team of porters that will include night, conference and kitchen porters.

entry level

To both enter and train while working in this career, you will need qualifications at Level 1. Please refer to explanation on page vii.

The type of person suited to this work

As you will be working with hotel guests, you will need good customer-care skills and a smart appearance. Good communication skills and an ability to work as part of a busy team are also important.

Because you will be required to undertake duties as and when required, you will need a flexible and enthusiastic attitude. Being responsible for the security of the hotel site and guests' belongings means that you must be aware of security issues and be honest and reliable.

As the work regularly includes lifting and carrying, you will need a good level of physical fitness. The ability to drive is useful.

Working conditions

This work can be physically demanding as you will spend a lot of time on your feet.

Even though you will be doing a lot of physical work, you will need to keep up a smart appearance and may have to wear a uniform.

You could work shifts or standard hours. You may live in and possibly be on call. If you work as a night porter you will work throughout the evening which can affect your personal life.

The future outlook

There are many opportunities to work as a porter in hotels all over the country. You could also gain part-time or seasonal portering work to suit you. You could also work in portering roles abroad.

Smaller hotels tend to employ one porter so you would need to move to larger hotels if you want to progress, so being mobile can be helpful. In larger companies, you could work towards a job as a head porter or a reception-based role.

Qualifications and courses

- There are no minimum entry requirements for this job although some employers prefer individuals with a good general education.
- Communication skills and confidence with numbers are useful.
- A driving licence and experience of driving a car can be helpful. Some employers prefer individuals to be over 18 years of age as you may be required to serve alcohol.
- Many hotels will provide training to new staff, whether or not they have previous experience. This is usually gained over a few weeks or longer, under the supervision of a more experienced member of staff.
- It is possible to gain qualifications whilst working, including the NCFE Level 2 Certificate in Customer Service for Hospitality, NVQs Level 1 and 2 in Front Office, or SVQ Level 1 in Porter Service.
- You could undertake an Apprenticeship/ Skillseekers to enter this area of work.
- With experience, it is possible to progress to working as Head Porter.

CRCI:C | CLCI:IC

Other related opportunities

- Airport Baggage Handler p558
- Cleaner p418
- Hotel / Accommodation Room Attendant p94
- Receptionist p25

Advantages/disadvantages

- In some hotels, you would be able to live in on-site.
- This job can fit educational commitments by offering to seasonal opportunties.
- This is a job which provides the opportunity to meet many different people.
- Some hotels prefer to employ mature individuals.

Earnings guide

- Salary levels vary according to the type of hotel you work for and geographic location.
- When starting you can earn around £11,000 per year.
- This can rise to £12,000–£15,000 with experience. Head Porters in large hotels could earn up to £22,000.
- You can also earn more through tips from guests.

Further information

www.cityandguilds.com/myperfectjob

Institute of Hospitality
Trinity Court
34 West Street
Sutton
Surrey
SM1 1SH
020 8661 4900
www.hcima.co.uk

People 1st
2nd Floor
38 Market Square
Uxbridge
UB8 1LH
0870 060 2550
www.people1st.co.uk

Housekeeper

What the work involves

- Working in hotels, conference centres and other sites you will be responsible for a high standard of cleanliness and hygiene at all times in areas such as bedrooms and meeting rooms.
- You will manage a housekeeping budget and oversee staff salaries.
- You will also manage a team of room attendants and other housekeeping staff. This includes organising work rotas and allocating staff duties.
- You may carry out staff training in the safe use of equipment and company standards.

entry level

1–2

To both enter and train while working in this career, you will need qualifications at Level 1–2. Please refer to explanation on page vii.

Qualifications and courses

- It is possible to enter this career without academic qualifications. Many people work their way up from a job as a room attendant.
- Good communication and organisation skills are important for this type of work.
- Training usually takes place on the job. Candidates can work towards NVQs/SVQs or can study for qualifications through The Institute of Hospitality, including Leisure and Tourism (Level 3), the Diploma in Management for Hospitality, Leisure and Tourism (Level 4) or the Certificate in Management for Hospitality.
- Some people enter Housekeeping as trainees, otherwise A levels/H grades or HNCs/HNDs in Hospitality may be required.
- Apprenticeships/Skillseekers placements may be available for those aged 16–24.

The type of person suited to this work

As you will be managing a team of staff, you will need strong management skills. You will be responsible for making sure that housekeeping staff work to a high standard, so good verbal communication skills are also important.

You will need to be confident in things such as explaining working procedures or training new staff. Good business sense and an ability to manage budgets are useful.

So that you can undertake different administrative tasks, business and management skills are useful.

Your role will be focused upon providing good customer care, so enthusiasm and an interest in good service are also helpful.

Working conditions

You will be on your feet for much of the time as this job involves a wide range of tasks.

You will use a range of cleaning chemicals and equipment that could cause problems if you have skin problems.

Although you will have an office, during your work you will visit many parts of the hotel.

You might be expected to live in and work unsociable hours.

The future outlook

This is a key role within the hotel sector but is often overlooked. There is some scope for developing a career in management in this area but opportunities do not come up often and you will have to work your way from junior or deputy housekeeper to senior housekeeper. In larger hotels, you could go on to a role in head office, in areas such as human resources or training.

International companies could provide the opportunity to work overseas. With enough experience, you could go on to own and run a hotel.

CRCI:C

CLCI:IB

Other related opportunities

- Cruise Ship Work p560
- Hotel / Accommodation Room Attendant p94
- Hotel Manager p95
- School Matron p182

Advantages/disadvantages

- There is a lack of promotional opportunities as people stay in their jobs for many years.
- You will have to work some unsociable hours, which could affect your personal life.
- Some larger hotel and leisure companies provide leisure and restaurant discounts to staff.

Earnings guide

- A salary starting at £11,000 per year is usual for a junior housekeeper.
- This can rise to £14,500–£18,000 with experience.
- As housekeeper in a small hotel, you could get up to £28,000
- Salaries up to £35,000 are possible head housekeepers working in the largest London-based hotels.

Further information

People 1st
2nd Floor
38 Market Square
Uxbridge
UB8 1LH
0870 060 2550
www.people1st.co.uk

Institute of Hospitality
Trinity Court
34 West Street
Sutton
Surrey
SM1 1SH
020 8661 4900
www.hcima.co.uk

Springboard UK
3 Denmark Street
London
WC2H 8LP
020 7497 8654
www.springboarduk.org.uk

www.cityandguilds.com/myperfectjob

Kitchen Assistant

What the work involves

- Working in the kitchen, you will prepare food, clean, wash up equipment and undertake general kitchen duties for hotels, restaurants and other sites.
- You will prepare meals for customers quickly and to a high standard. You will also prepare the kitchen before cooking and clean it afterwards. This will include mopping floors and keeping facilities extremely clean.
- You might also assist the chef to plan menus and check that there are adequate supplies of food and drink.

entry level

To both enter and train while working in this career, you will need qualifications at Level 1. Please refer to explanation on page vii.

The type of person suited to this work

As you will be preparing food for customers, you will need good time-keeping skills and be able to cope with working under pressure. An enthusiastic and flexible approach is also helpful.

Because you will be working with other staff in a hot and crowded kitchen, you will need good team-working skills. You will also need verbal communication skills, and an awareness of food safety and health and hygiene are important for this work. As you will be preparing food for public consumption you will need to have an interest in providing good customer care.

A good standard of personal hygiene and a tidy appearance are also important.

Working conditions

You will undertake most or all of your work in kitchens, which can be noisy, hot and crowded.

You will spend a lot of time on your feet undertaking a range of tasks, sometimes using potentially dangerous kitchen equipment.

You will work to a high standard of hygiene, and will be required to wear protective clothing and, in some cases, a company uniform.

This job includes unsociable hours and weekend working.

The future outlook

Across the UK there are about 106,000 restaurants employing 500,000 staff, which means there is a high demand for kitchen assistants in a wide range of food preparation organisations and settings. If you work for a larger company it might be easier to progress or move around the company and work in different areas.

With experience, you could go on to work as an assistant chef and then, with further experience or qualifications, go on to be a head chef.

Qualifications and courses

- There is no minimum qualification for this type of work. The basic food hygiene certificate can be useful and some previous catering experience is helpful.
- The ability to work with your hands so that you can prepare food and work with equipment is very important.
- Communication and numeracy skills are useful.
- You will be trained whilst working, usually with the support of a more experienced member of staff. Training could include food hygiene, food preparation methods and working with kitchen equipment.
- Some employers will provide the chance for you to gain a basic food hygiene certificate.
- You could undertake Apprenticeships/ Skillseekers opportunities in this area of work.
- You may also receive on-the-job training, which can lead to qualifications such as NVQ/SVQ Level 1 in Hospitality or NVQ/ SVQ Level 2 in Food Processing.
- You can take general catering courses, which include NVQ/SVQ Levels 1 and 2 in Food Preparation and Cooking or Food and Drink Service. You can also take City & Guilds certificate in Food Preparation before you start work, or while in work. In Scotland the SQA National Qualification in Health and Food Technology is available.

CRCI:C

CLCI:IC

Other related opportunities

- Fast Food Service Assistant p89
- Kitchen Porter p99
- Meat Process Worker p215
- Waiting Staff p100

Advantages/disadvantages

- Some employers provide subsidised accommodation and free meals.
- You will be required to work long shifts at unsociable times, such as evenings and weekends.
- There are many options to gain this type of work on a part-time, flexible basis.

Earnings guide

- Many employers pay at an hourly rate that varies between the minimum hourly rate and £8 per hour.
- You could be required to work part time, from 10 hours up to 25 hours a week.
- Annual salaries for working a 35–40 hour week range between £9,500 and £16,000 per year.

Further information

www.cityandguilds.com/myperfectjob

People 1st
2nd Floor
38 Market Square
Uxbridge
UB8 1LH
0870 060 2550
www.people1st.co.uk

Institute of Hospitality
Trinity Court
34 West Street
Sutton
Surrey
SM1 1SH
020 8661 4900
www.hcima.co.uk

Springboard UK
3 Denmark Street
London
WC2H 8LP
020 7497 8654
www.springboarduk.org.uk

Kitchen Porter

What the work involves

- Kitchen porters work in hotels, restaurants, leisure centres and all other facilities providing meals and catering services.
- As a kitchen porter, you will move heavy equipment and furniture around the kitchen and other sites as required. This may include transporting equipment by car.
- You will help to prepare food, wash and chop vegetables, and undertake the washing-up of dishes and kitchen equipment.
- Your responsibilities will include cleaning and clearing the kitchen area and disposing of kitchen waste safely and hygienically.

The type of person suited to this work

This is physical work that involves being on your feet in a hot and busy kitchen environment. You will move equipment around and provide other support for your fellow kitchen staff. This means good team work and a flexible outlook is helpful.

You will need a good knowledge of health and hygiene, and a high standard of personal cleanliness, as you will be working with food and will have to keep the kitchen areas clean. You will also use equipment and tools that can be dangerous.

A hard-working approach and being able to work on your own are both important. You will also need attention to detail with the ability to work to high standards.

Working conditions

This job involves moving equipment, preparing food and being on your feet, so it can be very physically demanding. Some of the equipment you will use can be dangerous.

The types of kitchen you might work in could vary between spacious modern facilities and crowded sites in older buildings. All kitchens get noisy and busy.

Some of your work will involve unsociable hours and weekend working.

The future outlook

There are around 106,000 restaurants, 60,000 pubs and 20,000 other food outlets across the UK, most of which employ kitchen porters. You could progress to work as an assistant chef and then to a head chef or catering manager role. There is a strong demand in the industry for people with the right attitude and practical skills.

You may progress quicker in a large organisation than in a smaller company. You could gain work abroad in a holiday resort or hotel.

entry level

1

To both enter and train while working in this career, you will need qualifications at Level 1. Please refer to explanation on page vii.

Qualifications and courses

- There are no minimum qualifications. Previous catering or kitchen experience and the basic food hygiene certificate can be useful.
- A clean driving licence is helpful.
- Good practical skills and a good level of physical fitness are important.
- Employers usually provide training in basic cookery techniques, food hygiene and manual lifting and handling. This is usually with the support of a more experienced member of staff.
- You could undertake an Apprenticeship/Skillseekers if you are aged 16–24.
- You may also receive training, which leads to qualifications such as NVQ/SVQ Level 1 in Preparing and Serving Food.
- With further experience and training, you could take general catering courses, which include NVQ/SVQ Levels 1 and 2 in Food Preparation and Cooking and NVQ/SVQ Hospitality Levels 1–3.
- You can also take a City & Guilds certificate in Food Preparation before you start work, or while in work. In Scotland the SQA National Qualification in Health and Food Technology is available.

CRCI:C

CLCI:IC

Other related opportunities

- Fast Food Service Assistant p89
- Kitchen Assistant p98
- Meat Process Worker p215

Advantages/disadvantages

- There are many opportunities to gain seasonal work to suit you. There are also options to work part time.
- In some jobs such as within restaurants and hotels, long hours including evenings and weekends times are involved.
- This can be hard, physical work.

Earnings guide

- Earnings vary according to the size, reputation and location of your employer.
- Earnings start from £9,500 per year for those with little or no experience.
- With experience and some training, you could earn up to £16,000.

Further information

People 1st
2nd Floor
38 Market Square
Uxbridge
UB8 1LH
0870 060 2550
www.people1st.co.uk

Institute of Hospitality
Trinity Court
34 West Street
Sutton
Surrey
SM1 1SH
020 8661 4900
www.hcima.co.uk

Springboard UK
3 Denmark Street
London
WC2H 8LP
020 7497 8654
www.springboarduk.org.uk

Waiting Staff

What the work involves

Waiting and banqueting staff

- You will take food orders from customers and provide meals, through table or counter service.
- Working with kitchen staff you will ensure that customers receive the food that they ordered.
- You will provide accurate bills for meals and take payment from customers. Before and during your shift you will probably have to keep the eating area clean and prepare tables for customers.
- Waiting staff work in a wide range of locations, including cruise ships, pubs, hotels and holiday camps.

Butler

- You will work in a private household where you will be responsible for arranging travel and security, providing and serving food and welcoming visitors.
- It is likely that you will work within a wealthy household, including those of famous celebrities or even royalty.

The type of person suited to this work

Waiting and banqueting staff

As you will be providing a service to customers, you will need a polite attitude and good customer care skills. A neat appearance is also important.

You might have to explain parts of the menu to customers, so an interest in food and drink is useful.

Because you will be taking food orders from customers and passing them on to kitchen staff, you will need a good memory and communication skills. You should be happy to work as part of a team.

The ability to work with numbers and deal with cash is important. You must work to a high standard of health and hygiene at all times.

Butler

In addition to the above skills, you should be very well presented, honest and reliable. Your employers will expect you to be dedicated, loyal and 100% trustworthy as you will be responsible for the security of them and their home when the family is away.

Working conditions

Waiting and banqueting staff

You will be on your feet for most of the time, carrying heavy plates and dishes.

Most waiting staff work a number of tables at once and have to remember different customer requests. You will be expected to work to a high standard of cleanliness at all times.

Butler

You will probably work within luxurious surroundings in the UK or abroad. You will normally live in and have your own quarters. Although you may stay and care for the home whilst your employer is away, you might also escort them and travel extensively.

The future outlook

Waiting and banqueting staff

The food and catering industry is growing in the UK, with further expansion predicted. This means there is a strong demand for waiting staff with good customer-service skills and experience in the UK and overseas. With experience, you could become junior or head waiter.

Larger employers such as hotel chains increasingly provide formal training and support for staff. These types of employers may also allow staff to move to other facilities within the same company.

Butler

Opportuntiies to become a butler are increasing. You are more likely to get a job if you are willing to be flexible and take on other responsibilities, such as those of a personal assistant, or provide some childcare services. Many catering firms provide butler services and there is demand from contract caterers, hotels and financial institutions.

Many of the jobs are overseas and the most successful butlers will have to be willing to travel.

Other related opportunities

- Bar Person p84
- Cruise Ship Work p560
- Fast Food Service Assistant p89
- Holiday Centre Work p364
- Kitchen Assistant p98

Advantages/disadvantages

Waiting and banquetting staff

- Catering staff are often provided with free meals and uniforms whilst on duty.
- Large employers such as hotels sometimes provide the option to live in on-site.
- There may be the chance to earn extra income through customer tips.
- It is possible to gain part-time and seasonal waiting work.

Butler

- You could work for a famous celebrity or royalty.
- Your job could include lots of travelling and living in luxurious homes.
- This job can affect your personal life as it is difficult to be off duty.

Earnings guide

Waiting and banqueting staff

- Salaries will depend on the location, size and reputation of the organisation you work for. Starting out you can expect around £10,000 per year. With experience this rises to £14,000.
- If you become a section head, or specialist wine waiter/sommelier, this will increase to £19,000–£25,000+. In most jobs you would receive tips from customers in addition to your salary.

Butler

- Your salary will depend on your experience and your employer. Starting salaries are around £17,000–£20,000 per year. With experience this can increase to £26,000. The most successful can achieve £50,000. In addition, you will be provided with free accommodation and meals.

Qualifications and courses

entry level

To both enter and train while working in this career, you will need qualifications at Level 1. Please refer to explanation on page vii.

Waiting and banqueting staff

- There are no minimum qualifications. Key Skills in communication and application of number are important.
- Awareness of food hygiene and a basic food hygiene certificate can be useful.
- It is possible to gain NVQs/SVQs Levels 1 & 2 in Catering and Hospitality
- You could also work on a part-time basis towards NVQs/SVQs in Food and Drink Service Level 1 & 2. Further on, you could gain an NVQ/SVQ in Food Service Advanced Craft at Level 3.
- Higher profile employers may require staff with experience in specialist areas such as Fine Dining and Silver Service. Some employers would train you in these areas.
- Work-based learning providers and colleges may provide introductory silver service training courses. Formal qualifications are not usually required for these courses.

Further information

Institute of Hospitality
Trinity Court
34 West Street
Sutton
Surrey
SM1 1SH
020 8661 4900
www.hcima.co.uk

People 1st
2nd Floor
38 Market Square
Uxbridge
UB8 1LH
0870 060 2550
www.people1st.co.uk

Springboard UK
3 Denmark Street
London
WC2H 8LP
020 7497 8654
www.springboarduk.org.uk

www.cityandguilds.com/myperfectjob

Here's Colin Gray's story:

Party Organiser

Colin works for a company called By Word Of Mouth that does event design and catering for everything from private dinner parties for 12 to huge functions held in marquees or in such august locations as the V&A Museum or the Royal College of Art. Colin, aged 23, studied Event Management at university and worked for a year with another company before joining By Word Of Mouth.

WHAT HE DOES

'To start off with, I have to meet the clients to discuss the kind of event they want and where they want to hold it. We discuss the catering with them and talk them through what they would like, and if they don't have any ideas then I will come up with some for them. I show them photographs of other parties we have done and then we will plan a menu. After that, if the party is for quite a few people we get the clients in for a tasting and give them a couple of options to see what they would prefer.'

Colin is also responsible for the look of the party – everything from the lighting, the crockery and glassware, and how the food is presented, through to the colour scheme and design concept. His duties vary depending on the scale of the event. For instance, if he is catering and organising a party for 100 people he will need at least 12 staff. For dinner parties in people's own homes they often use the facilities already available, but for a marquee event they have to bring in everything from ovens (from 2 to 20), to hot cupboards and even freezers. It's hard work but Colin loves it.

'I don't like being in an office all day long, so I love the variety of what I do and I get to see so many beautiful locations; for example tomorrow night I am doing a big dinner at the London Aquarium. I also love working with a close team where there is so much enthusiasm and where everyone is working towards the same goal. I never sit back and think, "Oh, this job is boring!"'

THE DOWNSIDE

'During the summer the unsocial hours you work (evenings and weekends) can be a bore when you could be out enjoying the sun, and sometimes at 4am when you are still working you do kind of ask yourself the question, "Why am I doing this?". You do have to put in the extra hours and be prepared to work extremely long shifts.'

As far as Colin is concerned it is worthwhile however, and eventually he would like to run his own events company. This is his advice to anyone wanting to enter the industry:

'Be passionate about it. You've got to be willing to start at the bottom as a waiter or waitress and work your way up, and if you put the work in then it can become very rewarding both personally and financially.'

Are computers or ICT your thing? Some of the jobs in this cluster are so new they are still developing. Here are some ideas to start you thinking:

- **Computer Games Designer**
- **IT Operator**
- **Multimedia Designer**
- **Software Developer**
- **Website developer**

But what's it like working in this area?

Here's Tony Bickley's story

Computer Games Designer

Tony has always been interested in computers and computer games, so, having studied maths and four sciences at school, he was intrigued when he saw a job advert asking 'do you take computer games seriously?'. He answered the advert and got the job as an apprentice programmer and started to work his way up through the programming hierarchy all the way to being a computer game designer. He is now Head of Development for Konami, a company that specialises in all computer games including those for mobile phones and online. Brands include the football game Pro Evolution, Metalgearsolid and Yu Gi Oh.

HOW TONY GOT STARTED

'Someone once said to me that the power of computer games is, if you want gravity to go up instead of down, you can make it go up. As I have always been fairly imaginative I loved the idea of creating my own universes and living within them – and just think, in this business I get to play with toys!'

When he began as a game designer Tony would start from scratch, working from the design concept up. Having climbed the career ladder, he now spends 50 per cent of his time doing spreadsheets and admin such as working out licensing deals with companies, but he still pitches design ideas and works closely with the whole design team to work out new concepts. One of the games he is most proud of is based on the *Star Trek* TV and movie series. He spends a lot of his time travelling around Europe and America pitching new game ideas.

THE SKILLS YOU NEED TO SUCCEED

'You need to be imaginative and open-minded and also very creative. Designers should spend at least 30% of their time studying the marketplace finding out what are the best games in the world and then asking why they are the best. What have they got that I can put into my own games? If you have an art skill it can be useful, but creativity is more important. You need reasonable technical background skills and because there is some fantastic talent out there you need to be highly competitive.'

Tony loves what he does and is highly paid for it, but he is also aware that if you don't keep upgrading your skills and knowledge you can fall by the wayside in an industry that is constantly transforming itself.

WHAT TONY LOVES ABOUT HIS JOB

'What I do is fun, it's exciting, it's innovative. It gives you a warm, slushy feeling to think you have created something that a million people will enjoy playing. It's a good job, a job for life, but companies do go bankrupt so you may find yourself working for a lot of different companies during your career. You just can't afford to sit on your laurels.'

Computer Business Analyst

What the work involves

- You will meet with your clients to find out how their businesses work and what they want to achieve with ICT.
- Making suggestions about the types of technology that could be used to improve clients' profitability and efficiency will also be part of your job.
- It will be your responsibility to produce a brief for the project to assist colleagues, such as software developers, in designing the best systems solution.
- You will keep in touch with your client at all times during the project.
- You may also train staff to use the new system.

The type of person suited to this work

Your understanding of how businesses work is the key to being a successful business analyst – you will be aware of the need to balance costs with solutions.

You will also need to be a good negotiator, able to influence managers who may not understand how the new solutions or products you are suggesting can benefit their businesses.

Excellent communication skills are crucial because you will need to put across your ideas in meetings and in written reports.

You will also need a strong knowledge of what is available in the technology market and how it works in order to develop project briefs.

Working conditions

You will spend time at your office base, meeting and working with other members of the project team.

It is likely that your job will also involve travelling to meet clients at all stages of the project and you may be away from home for several days at a time.

Although your hours will be usually Monday to Friday, when projects are near to completion you will need to work some evenings and weekends.

The future outlook

Employers include specialist ICT consultants, software houses and computer companies.

There is a growing market for ICT analysts with the right combination of skills and talents. Analysts with e-commerce technology skills and experience are in particular demand, due to the continued growth of internet use in business.

Progression is possible into senior analyst jobs and on to project management or consultancy work.

entry level

4–8

To both enter and train while working in this career, you will need qualifications at Level 4–8. Please refer to explanation on page vii.

Qualifications and courses

- You may need a degree, Foundation degree or HNC/D in a relevant subject, for example e-business/commerce, accountancy, business or computer science to enter this job.
- A new sponsored degree from e-skills – information technology management for business – is available. This is focused on learning through project work in compact teams with external mentors from sponsoring organisations such as BT, CA, Ford, Fujitsu, Hewlett Packard, IBM, Lehman Brothers, Morgan Stanley and Norwich Union.
- The normal minimum entry requirements for degrees are 2 A levels/3 H grades and 5 GCSEs/S grades (A–C/1–3), and for Foundation degrees or HNC/Ds, 1 A level/2 H grades and 3 GCSEs/S grades (A–C/1–3). Maths may be a required subject.
- Another funded route that may be on offer in your area is the Higher Apprenticeship in IT. This leads to a full Honours degree in addition to vocational, technical and Key Skills qualifications and work experience.
- Training programmes on offer for graduate entrants include the Graduate Professional Development Award (GPDA). This offers training and accreditation to IT professionals working in the industry. It includes e-skills, internet services delivery and industrial management and practice.
- The new 14–19 Diploma in IT is available at Levels 1–3 and focuses on competencies relevant to IT professional work. Level 3 is equivalent to A levels.

CRCI:D

CLCI:CAV

Other related opportunities

- Engineer: Professional p205
- IT Marketing Manager p112
- Software Architect / Developer p119
- Systems Analyst p120
- Technical Sales Specialist p121

Advantages/disadvantages

- You can get a real sense of satisfaction from producing successful solutions that transform a business.
- There often has to be a trade-off between the solution you would like to recommend and the limitations put down by your client who has a tight budget.

Earnings guide

- £21,000–£25,000 per year is usual for starting salaries.
- This can rise to £25,000–£45,000 with experience.
- Senior business analysts can earn £60,000 or more.
- Additional benefits may include profit sharing, performance-related pay and a car.

Further information

British Computer Society
North Star House
North Star Avenue
Swindon
Wiltshire
SN2 1FA
01793 417424
www.bcs.org

Institute for the Management of Information Systems
5 Kingfisher House
New Mill Road
Orpington
Kent
BR5 3QG
0700 002 3456
www.imis.org.uk

e-skills UK (Sector Skills Council for information technology, telecommunications and contact centres)
1 Castle Lane
London
SW1E 6DR
020 7963 8920
www.e-skills.com

Institute of ICT Training
Westwood House
Westwood Business Park
Coventry
CV4 8HS
0845 006 8858
www.iitt.org.uk

Computer Engineer / Scientist

What the work involves

- Working as an expert, you will be developing the solutions and products for tomorrow's computer industry.
- You may work as a researcher in industry or in an academic institution.
- You may be working as a hardware research engineer or a programming specialist developing fifth-generation artificial intelligence languages.
- You will use facts, data measurements, tools and methodologies to research and build solutions in a logical manner.
- You may share your findings by writing research papers and giving lectures.

The type of person suited to this work

You will need technical, practical and creative ability. It will be useful if you write your own programs or have built your own computer system.

You should be an excellent problem-solver, able to use information to come up with solutions. You will need to be able to anticipate problems and work out ways to stop them happening.

You must have enough patience to be able to produce accurate work when your deadline is close and your tests are not going well.

Your teamwork and communication skills should also be strong as you will be working with a project team, and at higher levels you will be giving presentations or lectures.

Working conditions

You may be based in a laboratory, a research and development unit, or a workshop.

At project management level you may travel nationally and internationally to meetings and conferences.

You will work a 37- to 40-hour week but you will need to be flexible and put in extra hours at key times.

The future outlook

There is a strong demand for computer scientists in many sectors, including academia, government research, computer manufacturing, software development and electronics and telecommunications.

There is a particularly strong need for talented computer engineers or scientists who are both technical and creative.

You will start work as a junior member of a project team. With experience you could move into lecturing or project management.

entry level

3–8

To both enter and train while working in this career, you will need qualifications at Level 3–8. Please refer to explanation on page vii.

Qualifications and courses

- The usual entry qualification is a degree or a Master's degree in a relevant subject, for example computer science, artificial intelligence or electronic engineering. Some employers will expect a doctorate.
- The normal minimum entry requirements for degrees are 2 A levels/3 H grades and 5 GCSEs/S grades (A–C/1–3). Required subjects usually include maths and physics.
- Should you have no formal qualifications, there may be the opportunity of an Apprenticeship in IT within your area. Otherwise Access courses are generally available if you wish to progress to a degree.
- Training programmes are on offer for graduate entrants from any discipline. Engineers must ensure their technical knowledge is always up to date by completing the Continuing Professional Development course.
- Computer engineers can gain professional engineering qualifications. To become an incorporated engineer you will need an engineering degree (BEng) plus experience and a professional review. To become a chartered engineer you will need a Master's degree in engineering (MEng), plus experience and a professional review.
- The new 14–19 Diploma in IT is available at Levels 1–3 and focuses on competencies relevant to IT professional work. Level 3 is equivalent to 3.5 A levels.

CRCI:D | CLCI:CAV

Other related opportunities

- Computer Hardware Technician p107
- Engineer: Professional p205
- Multimedia Designer p115
- Physicist p485
- Software Architect / Developer p119

Advantages/disadvantages

- Your team's work could make the headlines. New products and cutting-edge research, such as the building of world-class supercomputers, are of international interest.
- Solutions to problems do not happen quickly. It can be really frustrating to retest hundreds of times and still not get the result you are looking for.

Earnings guide

- Starting salaries are usually from £18,000 to £25,000 per year.
- With experience you can expect to get between £29,000 and £35,000.
- At senior levels you can earn between £40,000 and £60,000+.

Further information

British Computer Society
North Star House
North Star Avenue
Swindon
Wiltshire
SN2 1FA
01793 417424
www.bcs.org

e-skills UK (Sector Skills Council for information technology, telecommunications and contact centres)
1 Castle Lane
London
SW1E 6DR
020 7963 8920
www.e-skills.com

Engineering Careers Information Service
SEMTA House
14 Upton Road
Watford
Hertfordshire
WD18 0JT
0800 282167
www.enginuity.org.uk

Computer Games Designer

What the work involves

- Using storyboards and flowcharts, you will present your ideas for a new computer game to a panel for acceptance or rejection.
- If it is accepted you will manage all aspects of the playing experience, from scripts to programming and from animation to sound effects and music.
- You will work with a team of specialists, such as programmers and graphic artists, to produce a prototype.
- Once a computer games play-tester has picked out any flaws and if the panel think it is a winner, it will go into full development by your team.

entry level

3–8

To both enter and train while working in this career, you will need qualifications at Level 3–8. Please refer to explanation on page vii.

Qualifications and courses

- The computer games industry generally requires relevant experience. Many employers will ask for a degree, Foundation degree or HND plus a portfolio of game projects or design.
- Useful degree subjects include computer games technology, computer arts, or computer animation. At least 2 A levels/3 H grades or equivalent may be required or preferred for entry to related degrees.
- A funded route that may be on offer in your area is the Higher Apprenticeship in IT. This leads to a full Honours degree in addition to vocational, technical and Key Skills qualifications and work experience.
- If you are aged 16–24 you could enter IT work directly through an Apprenticeship/ Skillseekers and work for the qualifications needed for higher-level IT work.
- Training programmes are on offer for graduate entrants from any discipline.
- The new 14–19 Diploma in IT is available at Levels 1–3 and focuses on competencies relevant to IT professional work. Level 3 is equivalent to 3.5 A levels.

The type of person suited to this work

To be a top-class computer games designer you will need creativity and an ability to see how ideas could work together. You will also have a passion for and knowledge of the computer games market.

Your ideas need to be technically viable and cost-effective, so you will need a broad understanding of computers and games consoles, multimedia and the internet.

You will need to be a team player to work with specialists such as graphic designers to make sure that their part of the project fits in with your vision of the final version of the game.

Working conditions

You will be mainly based in an office or studio working with other members of the games project team.

Although your hours will be usually Monday to Friday, when there is a deadline for your game you will need to work some evenings and weekends.

The future outlook

Employers are specialised companies producing games for PCs or games consoles such as the Xbox or PS2. This is a growth area as the computer games industry is a profitable global business.

It is a popular career choice so entry is competitive. You will need to be talented and may need to get experience in games programming or testing first.

There may be opportunities to work abroad. Progression is possible into management or consultancy work.

CRCI:D

CLCI:CAV

Other related opportunities

- Multimedia Designer p115
- Multimedia Programmer p116
- Software Architect / Developer p119
- Website Designer p122

Advantages/disadvantages

- Games designers say it is enjoyable creating entertainment for a living.
- It is a young business and the rewards can be high.
- It can be tough when a game does not sell or has poor reviews.
- It is stressful producing a game for a timed release such as the Christmas market.

Earnings guide

- £19,000–£22,000 per year is usual for starting/training salaries.
- This can rise to £25,000–£35,000 with experience.
- £35,000–£55,000 is possible for senior games designers.
- Additional benefits usually include profit sharing and performance-related pay or a bonus.

Further information

British Computer Society
North Star House
North Star Avenue
Swindon
Wiltshire
SN2 1FA
01793 417424
www.bcs.org

e-skills UK (Sector Skills Council for information technology, telecommunications and contact centres)
1 Castle Lane
London
SW1E 6DR
020 7963 8920
www.e-skills.com

Skillset (Sector Skills Council for the audiovisual industries)
Prospect House
80–110 New Oxford Street
London
WC1A 1HB
08080 300900
www.skillset.org

Institute of ICT Training
Westwood House
Westwood Business Park
Coventry
CV4 8HS
0845 006 8858
www.iitt.org.uk

Computer Hardware Technician

What the work involves

- You will be responsible for installing and repairing computer hardware – the computer itself rather than the applications or software.
- You may go out to repair on-site or in a workshop.
- To find out more about the fault you will use a set of diagnostic CDs.
- When repairing a fault or upgrading a machine you will open up the computer and use tools to install upgrades or replace faulty parts.
- You may specialise in installing new computer systems and training the people who use them.

The type of person suited to this work

You will need both technical and practical ability. Building your own computer system and repairing friends' machines is something you will probably already be doing in your spare time.

You should be a good problem-solver. You will need to be able to identify what is wrong and put it right quickly as your customer may be losing money while you do the repair.

Your verbal and listening skills should be strong because you will have to find out what is wrong and then explain what needs repairing to the computer user who may have no technical knowledge.

Often working on your own you will also need to be reliable and able to work unsupervised.

Working conditions

You may be based in a workshop, or be repairing hardware for one firm, but many technicians travel to customers' premises or homes.

You may need to drive a vehicle to each job and cover a large area of the UK.

You will work a 37- to 40-hour week, but as businesses need major work to be done on evenings and weekends you will have to work shifts or be on a call-out rota.

The future outlook

Computer hardware technicians are employed by computer manufacturers, computer service firms and by a range of large organisations such as banks, hospitals and universities.

This is a stable area of work because computers need regular repairs or upgrades to improve performance or capacity.

Promotion could be to team leader or supervisor and then on to senior engineer.

Self-employment as a freelance/consultant engineer is possible.

entry level

2–8

To both enter and train while working in this career, you will need qualifications at Level 2–8. Please refer to explanation on page vii.

Qualifications and courses

- A degree, Foundation degree or HND/C is sometimes required, but previous experience in other areas can be just as important. Useful degree subjects include computer systems engineering or electronic engineering.
- The normal minimum entry requirements for degrees are 2 A levels/3 H grades and 5 GCSEs/S grades (A–C/1–3). For technical degrees, maths, technology or a science subject may be required.
- If you are aged 16–24 you could enter computer engineering work directly through Apprenticeships/Skillseekers and work for the qualifications needed for higher-level work.
- You will need a driving licence to work for the majority of employers.
- Training programmes are on offer for graduate entrants from any discipline. Engineers must ensure their technical knowledge is always up to date by completing the Continuing Professional Development course.
- The new 14-19 Diploma in IT is available at Levels 1–3 and focuses on competencies relevant to IT professional work. Level 3 is equivalent to 3.5 A levels.

CRCI:GE

CLCI:RAK

Other related opportunities

- Computer Engineer / Scientist p105
- Computer Technical Support p109
- Engineer: Technician p208

Advantages/disadvantages

- There is lots of variety as few problems are the same.
- It is rewarding to get a computer up and running again.
- Your customer may have a service agreement requiring you to put the problem right in a fixed period of time, which can be stressful.

Earnings guide

- Starting/trainee salaries are usually from £13,500 to £17,000 per year.
- You could earn £19,000–£25,000 with experience.
- Earnings can rise to between £35,000 and £40,000 at supervisory level.
- Additional benefits may include a car.

Further information

British Computer Society
North Star House
North Star Avenue
Swindon
Wiltshire
SN2 1FA
01793 417424
www.bcs.org

e-skills UK (Sector Skills Council for information technology, telecommunications and contact centres)
1 Castle Lane
London
SW1E 6DR
020 7963 8920
www.e-skills.com

Engineering Careers Information Service
SEMTA House
14 Upton Road
Watford
Hertfordshire
WD18 0JT
0800 282167
www.enginuity.org.uk

Institute of ICT Training
Westwood House
Westwood Business Park
Coventry
CV4 8HS
0845 006 8858
www.iitt.org.uk

Computer Helpdesk Adviser

What the work involves

- You will answer telephone calls or emails from computer users who are having technical problems.
- Listening carefully to the person and asking them questions, you will try to work out what the problem is.
- You will then ask the customer to take certain actions to try to correct the fault.
- You will log the query and give the customer a job number.
- If the problem is too complex to sort out by phone or email you may arrange for a technician to repair faulty hardware or arrange delivery of a replacement software disk.

entry level

2–8

To both enter and train while working in this career, you will need qualifications at Level 2–8. Please refer to explanation on page vii.

The type of person suited to this work

You should have lots of tact and patience. When people are impatient or angry they will think they have checked the basics, for example the wiring, but the problem may be caused by user error.

Your verbal and listening skills need to be first class to be able to guide a customer to take the action they need to put a problem right.

You will need to enjoy a challenge as well as be able to think quickly and logically. To solve a problem you may have to move from idea to idea and approach it from different directions.

You will need to be keen to learn and keep up to date with your employer's new products.

Working conditions

You will be sitting in front of a screen wearing a headset to talk to customers. You may be based in a call centre with lots of activity and background noise.

Employers usually give frequent breaks from the screen for advisers to make the job less stressful.

You will work 37–40 hours a week usually in shifts often including weekend and evening work.

The future outlook

The main employers are computer hardware and software manufacturers and internet service providers who offer support to their customers.

Support work has grown rapidly in recent years, but helpdesks are sometimes sourced outside the UK by employers looking for lower costs.

This is a job with a high turnover as it is often used as a stepping stone to move into the competitive software industry.

Promotion to supervisory and management work is possible.

Qualifications and courses

- It may be possible to enter as a trainee or apprentice with GCSEs/S grades, including English, maths, science and IT. It is also possible to enter with an Applied A level or BTEC National qualification in IT or Computing.
- Many people enter this career with no formal qualifications but with relevant computer knowledge and good customer service experience. However, employers generally prefer you to have a qualification such as a degree, HNC/HND in computing, BTEC National Diploma or C&G in IT Practitioners. A degree would be an advantage in entering a training scheme as a specialist.
- A funded route that may be on offer in your area is the Higher Apprenticeship in IT. This leads to a full Honours degree in addition to vocational, technical and Key Skills qualifications and work experience.
- The Help Desk Institute offers recognised qualifications for people working in the sector. The Customer Support Specialist qualification is aimed at new entrants; the Help Desk Analyst qualification is for people with at least 9 months' experience; Service Desk Manager is available to people with 3–5 years' experience.
- The new 14–19 Diploma in IT is available at Levels 1–3 and focuses on competencies relevant to IT professional work. Level 3 is equivalent to 3.5 A levels.

CRCI:D

CLCI:CAV

Other related opportunities

- Computer Technical Support p109
- Customer Services p442
- Database Operator p110
- IT Operator p113
- IT Trainer p114
- Technical Sales Specialist p121

Advantages/disadvantages

- You will get useful training in computers and software.
- It is rewarding to resolve a problem.
- Your work will be very closely monitored by managers.
- The job can be stressful because customers can be angry and frustrated by the time they ring you.

Earnings guide

- £13,000–£16,000 per year is usual for starting/trainee salaries.
- This can rise to £18,000–£23,000 with experience.
- £28,000+ is possible at supervisory level.

Further information

British Computer Society
North Star House
North Star Avenue
Swindon
Wiltshire
SN2 1FA
01793 417424
www.bcs.org

e-skills UK (Sector Skills Council for information technology, telecommunications and contact centres)
1 Castle Lane
London
SW1E 6DR
020 7963 8920
www.e-skills.com

Institute of ICT Training
Westwood House
Westwood Business Park
Coventry
CV4 8HS
0845 006 8858
www.iitt.org.uk

information about ICT jobs and Training
Help Desk Institute
21 High Street
Orpington
BR6 6BG
01689 889100
www.hdi-europe.com

Computer Technical Support

What the work involves

- You will work for an organisation which has lots of ICT equipment, offering specialist technical support to its computer users.
- You may install new systems and upgrades and train staff in their use.
- You may be responsible for supporting staff with hardware or software problems.
- Initially, you may try to resolve the problem by telephone or email, only going out to the user's workstation if necessary.
- You will try to fix the problem but if the hardware is under guarantee you will call out the manufacturer's service engineer.

entry level

2–3

To both enter and train while working in this career, you will need qualifications at Level 2–3. Please refer to explanation on page vii.

The type of person suited to this work

You should be interested in knowing how technology works. You may have tried building or upgrading a PC. You will need to be both technical and practical to resolve hardware or software problems.

You will also need to be a good communicator – able to explain technical stuff to users who may not be clear about what it means.

You need to cope well with stress and deadlines. You will be under pressure to get the problem sorted in the shortest possible time so that staff can get back to work.

A keenness to keep learning and stay up to date is vital – you will be expected to be the expert.

Working conditions

You will probably be based in an office with a technical workshop attached.

Your employer may have several sites you need to travel between, sometimes in different parts of the UK.

You may have to work shifts to cover your employer's hours of operation, which may be 24/7, or to install or repair equipment outside office hours.

The future outlook

The main employers of computer support technicians are large organisations such as banks, retail chains, hospitals, airlines and universities, who are dependent on their large computer networks to be functional during working hours.

This is a growth area of work with increasing numbers of organisations becoming dependent on ICT to operate efficiently.

With experience, promotion could be to network manager/administrator or on to network development.

Qualifications and courses

- The majority of technical support staff are expected to have a degree with relevant work experience. Access courses are available for those with no qualifications or an alternative option is for those with little IT experience or more than 1 year's work experience to obtain qualifications from The Help Desk Institute (HDI).
- It is possible for school-leavers to enter this work as trainees or via an Apprenticeship/ Skillseekers.
- Acceptable entry qualifications include BTEC National Diploma in IT, SQA National Certificate in IT or BSC Information Technology Management for Business. Some candidates enter with a degree or HNC/D in computing, computer science or a related subject.
- Entrants are trained on the job, and may work towards further qualifications.
- Some IT companies offer certification courses in their own products. The CompTIA (Computing Technology Industry Association) A+ Certificate is recognised by the industry as an entry-level qualification.
- The new 14–19 Diploma in IT is available at Levels 1–3 and focuses on competencies relevant to IT professional work. Level 3 is equivalent to 3.5 A levels.

CRCI:D

CLCI:CAV

Other related opportunities

- Computer Hardware Technician p107
- Computer Helpdesk Adviser p108
- Network Designer p117
- Technical Sales Specialist p121

Advantages/disadvantages

- If you take advantage of the training on offer, this broad-based job can be a stepping stone to jobs at a higher level in the ICT industry.
- By the time you arrive at a colleague's workstation you will be under pressure to sort out their problem quickly.

Earnings guide

- £14,000–£17,000 per year is usual for starting/trainee salaries.
- This can rise to £18,000–£23,000 with experience.
- £30,000+ is possible at supervisory level.
- Additional benefits may include a car.

Further information

British Computer Society
North Star House
North Star Avenue
Swindon
Wiltshire
SN2 1FA
01793 417424
www.bcs.org

e-skills UK (Sector Skills Council for information technology, telecommunications and contact centres)
1 Castle Lane
London
SW1E 6DR
020 7963 8920
www.e-skills.com

Institute of ICT Training
Westwood House
Westwood Business Park
Coventry
CV4 8HS
0845 006 8858
www.iitt.org.uk

Database Operator

What the work involves

- If lots of information needs to be stored with the capacity to search and access specific parts of the data, a database will be used. For example, a hospital uses a database to manage information about its patients.
- You would be responsible for making sure that your databases are accurate, accessible and secure.
- To keep the data secure you will issue staff with passwords, train users and back up the contents regularly.
- You will need to identify and resolve problems.
- You may be responsible for setting up a new database.

The type of person suited to this work

Databases operate to give people the information they require to do their jobs, so you will need strong communication skills. You will be offering support to staff using the database and preparing reports and guidelines for managers and staff.

You should be a good negotiator. To train users to input or access a new or modified database you will need to be able to convince them the changes will benefit them.

To set up or develop a database you will need to be very technical with a high level of programming knowledge. You will also need to be a good listener, able to find out what the database users want the new design to achieve.

Working conditions

You will be based mainly in your own office although in some cases the work can be carried out away from the office base using laptops and broadband wireless technology.

Your employer may have several sites you need to travel between, sometimes in different parts of the UK.

You may have to be on-call to deal with problems outside your normal working hours.

The future outlook

The main employers of database managers are large organisations, such as banks and retailers. You could also work for a specialist ICT firm providing a complete database service to customers.

This is a growth area because increasing numbers of businesses are developing databases for their websites to allow customers to look at information about their goods online and then go on to buy them.

With experience, promotion could be to network development or into consultancy work.

entry level

3–8

To both enter and train while working in this career, you will need qualifications at Level 3–8. Please refer to explanation on page vii.

Qualifications and courses

- The usual entry qualification for this work is a degree, Foundation degree or HNC/D in a relevant subject, for example computer science, software development, operational research, e-commerce technology or maths. Other qualifications may be acceptable, such as BTEC National Diplomas and NVQs/SVQs.
- The normal minimum entry requirements for degrees are 2 A levels/3 H grades and 5 GCSEs/S grades (A–C/1–3), and for Foundation degrees or HNC/Ds, 1 A level/ 2 H grades and 3 GCSEs/S grades (A–C/1–3). For technical degrees, maths/science may be required.
- A funded route that may be on offer in your area is the Higher Apprenticeship in IT. This leads to a full Honours degree in addition to vocational, technical and Key Skills qualifications and work experience.
- Entry without a degree may be possible if you have got significant programming experience and knowledge.
- Training programmes are on offer for graduate entrants from any discipline including the Graduate Professional Development Award (GPDA).
- Database managers may also take manufacturers' courses in particular operating systems/packages.
- The new 14–19 Diploma in IT is available at Levels 1–3 and focuses on competencies relevant to IT professional work. Level 3 is equivalent to 3.5 A levels.

CRCI:D

CLCI:CAV

Other related opportunities

- IT Trainer p114
- Network Designer p117
- Network Manager p118
- Software Architect / Developer p119

Advantages/disadvantages

- If you are methodical and analytical, you will enjoy the complex job of writing a new database.
- It can be frustrating when database users cause problems by not keeping their information up to date or leaving vital parts out.

Earnings guide

- £16,500–£21,000 per year is usual for starting salaries.
- This can rise to £22,000–£35,000 with experience.
- £50,000+ is possible at supervisory level.

Further information

British Computer Society
North Star House
North Star Avenue
Swindon
Wiltshire
SN2 1FA
01793 417424
www.bcs.org

e-skills UK (Sector Skills Council for information technology, telecommunications and contact centres)
1 Castle Lane
London
SW1E 6DR
020 7963 8920
www.e-skills.com

Institute for the Management of Information Systems
5 Kingfisher House
New Mill Road
Orpington
Kent
BR5 3QG
0700 002 3456
www.imis.org.uk

Internet / Web Professional

What the work involves

- You will be responsible for managing and maintaining an internet site.
- You may supervise a team of staff who design and program the various pages that make it up.
- In a small company, you may be the programmer, designer and master/manager of the site.
- Maintaining the site may be complex, especially on a shopping site that handles sales queries, sales and payment, delivery and after-sales arrangements.
- You may write content or develop a content management program for authorised staff to contribute material.

The type of person suited to this work

You should be the kind of person who always carefully checks their work. You will need to set up secure data entry checking systems and regularly test them for faults. If your shopping site's database starts matching the wrong prices to the wrong goods, you will need to spot the problem and pull the plug fast!

You will probably have set up your own website or have helped maintain one for a group you belong to.

Your creative skills are important but you will have to make sure you do not make it difficult for visitors to your site to find the information they want.

Strong communication skills are vital – you will be required to lead a project team at senior level.

Working conditions

You will be mainly office-based, using a computer to manage the site.

You may have to move around your company's site to train, meet with managers and discuss site improvements.

You will work a 37- to 40-hour week, normally Monday to Friday, but if you are working to maintain and support a 24/7 shopping site you will work shifts as part of a team to cover all hours.

The future outlook

Websites are big business, with growing numbers of organisations using them to share information, market themselves, sell goods or services and advertise jobs.

Employers of web professionals include web-based retailers, travel companies, the multimedia industry, local and central government and financial companies.

Promotion could be to project management level.

A talented web professional could move into freelance or website development consultancy work.

Entry level

3–8

To both enter and train while working in this career, you will need qualifications at Level 3–8. Please refer to explanation on page vii.

Qualifications and courses

- The usual entry qualification for this work is a degree, Foundation degree or HNC/D in a relevant subject, such as e-business/commerce, e-systems design and technology, three-dimensional design, graphic design, computer science or other related areas.
- A new sponsored degree from e-skills, information technology management for business, is available. This is focused on learning through project work in compact teams with external mentors from sponsoring organisations.
- The normal minimum entry requirements for degrees are 2 A levels/3 H grades and 5 GCSEs/S grades (A–C/1–3), and for Foundation degrees or HNC/Ds 1 A level/2 H grades and 3 GCSEs/S grades (A–C/1–3).
- Another funded route that may be on offer in your area is the Higher Apprenticeship in IT. This leads to a full Honours degree in addition to vocational, technical and Key Skills qualifications and work experience.
- Training programmes are on offer for graduate entrants from any discipline, including the Graduate Professional Development Award (GPDA). This offers training and accreditation to IT professionals working in the industry. It includes e-skills, internet services delivery and industrial management and practice.
- The new 14–19 Diploma in IT is available at Levels 1–3 and focuses on competencies relevant to IT professional work. Level 3 is equivalent to 3.5 A levels.

Other related opportunities

- Database Operator p110
- Multimedia Designer p115
- Network Manager p118
- Software Architect / Developer p119
- Website Designer p122

Advantages/disadvantages

- If you have got the right skills, this is an expanding market with high rewards on offer.
- Being responsible for the world wide web window of your company can be stressful. Not only did a well-known e-retailer's site collapse when it advertised a hand-held computer at £7 instead of £300, but it faced huge legal bills to deal with the consumer backlash.

Earnings guide

- £18,000–£22,000 per year is usual for starting salaries.
- This can rise to around £32,000 with experience.
- £40,000+ is possible for senior web managers with additional responsibilities.
- £50,000+ is achievable for project managers.

CRCI:D

CLCI:CAV

Further information

British Computer Society
North Star House
North Star Avenue
Swindon
Wiltshire
SN2 1FA
01793 417424
www.bcs.org

e-skills UK (Sector Skills Council for information technology, telecommunications and contact centres)
1 Castle Lane
London
SW1E 6DR
020 7963 8920
www.e-skills.com

British Interactive Multimedia Association
Briarlea House
Southend Road
Billericay
CM11 2PR
020 7436 8250
www.bima.co.uk

IT Marketing Manager

What the work involves

- You will have responsibility for every aspect of a particular product or family of products (hardware, software or communications).
- Working with the developers in your company, you will make sure they have the right information about what the market needs to guarantee a profit.
- You will prepare detailed plans for packaging, pricing, selling, advertising and delivering the product.
- Forecasting demand for the product, liaising with the product team, suggesting any modifications needed and overseeing the sales drive will also be involved.

entry level

3–8

To both enter and train while working in this career, you will need qualifications at Level 3–8. Please refer to explanation on page vii.

The type of person suited to this work

This job requires marketing skills and good technical and business aptitude. You will have to promote, price and place the product but you will also have to understand the ICT market and keep up to date with technological advances.

You will also need to be a good negotiator, able to influence developers who may not be keen to take on board your suggestions for changes to the product.

Excellent communication and networking skills are crucial because you will be a key player in your company, working not only with all staff but also with external contacts such as packaging specialists, retailers and the media.

Working conditions

You will spend time at your office base, meeting and working with members of product project teams and sales staff.

You may have to travel a lot to market your products and may be away for several days at a time.

Although your hours will be usually Monday to Friday, when products are near to completion you will need to put in the overtime needed.

The future outlook

Employers include large ICT companies producing products such as mobile phones, hardware and software. Smaller companies may buy in an external consultant for this role.

This is rarely a first job. Entry is usually after gaining experience first as a marketing assistant or technical sales specialist.

Promotion prospects depend on how good you are at your job. You may be able to move into a higher level of management or set up as a consultant.

Qualifications and courses

- You may need a degree, Foundation degree or HNC/D in a relevant subject, for example marketing, accountancy, business and finance, e-business/commerce or computer science to enter this job. A new sponsored degree from e-skills – information technology management for business – is available.
- The normal minimum entry requirements for degrees are 2 A levels/3 H grades and 5 GCSEs/S grades (A–C/1–3), and for Foundation degrees or HNC/Ds, 1 A level/ 2 H grades and 3 GCSEs/S grades (A–C/1–3). Maths may be a required subject.
- A funded route that may be on offer in your area is the Higher Apprenticeship in IT. This leads to a full Honours degree in addition to vocational, technical and Key Skills qualifications and work experience.
- You will probably be required to drive for this job.
- Training programmes on offer for graduate entrants include the Graduate Professional Development Award (GPDA). This offers training and accreditation to IT professionals working in the industry.
- The Communication, Advertising and Marketing Education Foundation also offers a qualification, the Advanced Diploma in Marketing Communications.
- The new 14–19 Diploma in IT is available at Levels 1–3 and focuses on competencies relevant to IT professional work. Level 3 is equivalent to 3.5 A levels.

CRCI:O

CLCI:OB

Other related opportunities

- Computer Business Analyst p104
- Marketing p151
- Technical Sales Specialist p121

Advantages/disadvantages

- If the product you are working on achieves or improves on the profits you predicted, you will probably earn a bonus.
- It can be stressful having to push the team to get the right product out before your competitors beat you to the finish line!

Earnings guide

- £16,000–£25,000 per year is possible as a marketing assistant.
- This can rise to £30,000–£40,000 with experience.
- You could earn £60,000+ as a senior manager.
- Additional benefits may include profit sharing, performance-related pay and the use of a company car.

Further information

British Computer Society
North Star House
North Star Avenue
Swindon
Wiltshire
SN2 1FA
01793 417424
www.bcs.org

Chartered Institute of Marketing
Moor Hall
Cookham
Maidenhead
Berkshire
SL6 9QH
01628 427500
www.cim.co.uk

e-skills UK (Sector Skills Council for information technology, telecommunications and contact centres)
1 Castle Lane
London
SW1E 6DR
020 7963 8920
www.e-skills.com

Communication, Advertising and Marketing Education (CAM) Foundation
Moor Hall
Cookham
Maidenhead
Berkshire
SL6 9QH
01628 427180
www.camfoundation.com

IT Operator

What the work involves

- ICT or computer operators work for organisations that operate a multi-user computer system to store, manage and present their data.
- Your main responsibility will be starting up, running, backing up data, closing down and cleaning your employer's multi-user computer system.
- You will be updating and running database programmes and tasks prepared by programmers or database managers.
- Routine recording and reporting of any errors you spot to your manager or ICT specialist will also be your responsibility.

entry level

1–3

To both enter and train while working in this career, you will need qualifications at Level 1–3. Please refer to explanation on page vii.

The type of person suited to this work

Attention to detail and a responsible attitude are vital in this job. The data you enter needs to be accurate and if you do not spot errors they may lead to costly problems and delays.

Routine tasks such as backing up data, cleaning the equipment and putting the data in using a keyboard are central to this job, so you will need good keyboard skills and be practical and methodical.

You will also need to be good with figures as most databases have lots of data in number format.

The computer system you will be dealing with is complex and you will need to be keen to understand how both the hardware and software operate.

Qualifications and courses

- You do not need specific entry qualifications for this job, but GCSEs/S grades (A–C/1–3) in such subjects as maths, English and IT are an advantage. Employers may prefer Customer Service skills.
- Useful qualifications include BTEC National Awards in computer- and business-related subjects.
- The Help Desk Institute (HDI) offers recognised qualifications for people with or without experience working in the sector.
- If you are aged 16–24 you could enter IT work through an Apprenticeship/Skillseeker route. You would then work towards NVQs/SVQs Levels 2 or 3 in information technology.
- Trainee computer operators can start as an Apprentice and develop skills as they work. The British Computer Society (BCS) offer professional qualifications for those who wish to improve their existing skills.
- Training is usually provided by employers on the job.
- The new 14–19 Diploma in IT is available at Levels 1–3 and focuses on competencies relevant to IT professional work. Level 3 is equivalent to 3.5 A levels.

CRCI:D

CLCI:CAV

Working conditions

You will be working in an office, possibly in the same room as a noisy computer server. For long periods you will sit at your workstation. You will have to be aware of health concerns such as eye strain and your sitting position.

You will probably work office hours, Monday to Friday. You may have to work shifts.

The future outlook

IT operators work for large organisations using large multi-user databases. Examples include banks, retailers, universities, hospitals and government departments.

Job opportunities are decreasing. ICT systems are now usually networked and data put in by authorised computer users with support from a specialist database or network manager.

With experience and training, you may be able to gain promotion to technical support, database or network management.

Other related opportunities

- Clerk p12
- Database Operator p110
- Network Manager p118
- Secretary p28

Advantages/disadvantages

- With extra study you can train up to database or network management level.
- This job is starting to disappear as content management programs become more user-friendly and more employees at all levels input data as one of their work tasks.

Earnings guide

- Starting salaries are around £14,000–£18,000 per year.
- Once trained as an operator and with experience, you could earn around £25,000+.
- At managerial level an operator can earn between £30,000 and £50,000.

Further information

British Computer Society
North Star House
North Star Avenue
Swindon
Wiltshire
SN2 1FA
01793 417424
www.bcs.org

e-skills UK (Sector Skills Council for information technology, telecommunications and contact centres)
1 Castle Lane
London
SW1E 6DR
020 7963 8920
www.e-skills.com

www.cityandguilds.com/myperfectjob

IT Trainer

What the work involves

- IT trainers give people user skills, for example in applications such as Word, Excel or desktop-publishing packages.
- You may train in advanced computer skills such as programming languages.
- Planning courses, preparing learning materials and setting up the computers ready for a session will all be involved.
- You will do presentations and network some materials. You will walk around the room to support individuals in your group.
- Evaluating what has been learned and changing future learning materials as required will also be part of your job.

The type of person suited to this work

The constant release of new ICT products guarantees a future for trainers but only if you are keen to stay up to date. You will need lots of self-discipline to do research and prepare learning materials.

As e-learning and virtual classroom technology expands, more learners are being taught over the internet. Therefore, you will need to be up to date with e-learning tools, technologies and processes.

This job is about helping others to learn. Whether you train face to face or by virtual technology, you will need strong interpersonal and communication skills. All learners are sensitive to criticism and need to be motivated and encouraged.

Working conditions

You may be based in a modern office training room or you may travel to clients' premises to train their staff on-site.

Although your hours will be usually Monday to Friday, you will have to prepare learning materials and keep up to date by working some evenings and weekends.

The future outlook

Employers such as hardware and software manufacturers, ICT consultancies, training organisations and colleges employ ICT trainers. There is a strong demand for trainers and there are currently over 60,000 ICT trainers in the UK.

This job is rarely a first job. Most trainers have gained experience in other areas of computing first.

Experienced ICT trainers can move into self-employment as consultants. Promotion into supervisory or management roles may be possible.

entry level

3–8

To both enter and train while working in this career, you will need qualifications at Level 3–8. Please refer to explanation on page vii.

Qualifications and courses

- To work as an IT trainer you need to first gain the relevant skills and experience in IT yourself.
- Although no set qualifications are required, it may be an advantage to have a degree, Foundation degree or HNC/D in a relevant subject, for example computer science, e-business/commerce or software engineering.
- The normal minimum entry requirements for degrees are 2 A levels/3 H grades and 5 GCSEs/S grades (A–C/1–3), and for Foundation degrees or HNC/Ds, 1 A level/ 2 H grades and 3 GCSEs/S grades (A–C/1–3).
- You could enter this job without a degree if you have got significant experience and training in IT.
- The Institute of IT Training is the certification awarding body for a range of courses in e-learning training skills offered by the Training Foundation.
- You can qualify as an assessor by taking the Assessors Award. This would be needed to assess learners working towards NVQs/SVQs.
- The new 14–19 Diploma in IT is available at Levels 1–3 and focuses on competencies relevant to IT professional work. Level 3 is equivalent to 3.5 A levels.

CRCI:F

CLCI:FAP

Other related opportunities

- Computer Business Analyst p104
- Lecturer, p178
- Network Manager p118
- Teacher, p184
- Training Officer p33
- Work-based Training, p188

Advantages/disadvantages

- You can get a real feeling of achievement when your learners succeed in understanding a difficult subject.
- This job can be badly affected when the economy is depressed as training is often the first thing businesses cut back on in difficult times.

Earnings guide

- Starting salaries are usually £16,000–£19,000 per year.
- With experience, you could earn £20,000-£25,000+.
- At senior levels, with management responsibilities, it is possible to earn £35,000.
- Self-employed trainers work for set fees either per day or per training course and can earn over £30,000.

Further information

Institute of ICT Training
Westwood House
Westwood Business Park
Coventry
CV4 8HS
0845 006 8858
www.iitt.org.uk

British Computer Society
North Star House
North Star Avenue
Swindon
Wiltshire
SN2 1FA
01793 417424
www.bcs.org

e-skills UK (Sector Skills Council for information technology, telecommunications and contact centres)
1 Castle Lane
London
SW1E 6DR
020 7963 8920
www.e-skills.com

Training Foundation Ltd
Foundation House
University of Warwick Science Park
Coventry
CV4 7HS
024 7641 1288
www.trainingfoundation.com

Multimedia Designer

What the work involves

- You will help clients look at how they can use multimedia to improve their marketing, information or learning resources.
- You will work out the right medium to use, for example an interactive website or a virtual reality training program.
- Meeting to agree a solution, you will develop a brief and then create prototypes or simulations to show the customer your ideas.
- Your role will also involve planning, coordinating and overseeing the whole project.
- You will test, integrate and, if needed, install at the customer's site.

The type of person suited to this work

Your creative skills need to be outstanding if you are thinking about this job. Every project will be different and you will need the vision to be able to think about what a client wants to achieve with a multimedia project and then develop ideas to produce a solution.

You need to be good at working in a team and motivating others to achieve tight deadlines. This job is never done alone – you will be working with both artistic and technical colleagues, all trying to put your vision into practice.

You should have excellent presentation and communication skills, as you may need to bid against other designers to win contracts for new projects.

Working conditions

You will spend time working in an office at your workstation, but you will also be working with your project team and meeting customers.

You may have to travel regularly to clients, to meet and present your solutions to them.

Although your hours will be usually Monday to Friday, when you are preparing a bid or projects are near to completion you will need to put in extra hours.

The future outlook

Employers include specialist multimedia consultancies, internet service providers, e-learning specialists, software houses and hardware manufacturers.

Multimedia is a growth industry and designers who have an understanding of both the technical and creative sides of the industry are currently in demand.

Once experienced you could move into self-employment, or work on a contract or consultancy basis. You could also move into management or training.

entry level

3–8

To both enter and train while working in this career, you will need qualifications at Level 3–8. Please refer to explanation on page vii.

Qualifications and courses

- Entry is often by means of a degree, Foundation degree or HNC/D in a relevant subject, for example computing, software development, business information systems, multimedia design or graphic and media design.
- The normal minimum entry requirements for degrees are 2 A levels/3 H grades and 5 GCSEs/S grades (A–C/1–3), and for Foundation degrees or HNC/Ds, 1 A level/two H grades and three GCSEs/S grades (A–C/1–3). For technical degrees, mathematics/science may be required.
- A funded route, which may be on offer in your area, is the Higher Apprenticeship in IT. This leads to a full Honours degree in addition to vocational, technical and Key Skills qualifications and work experience.
- Entry without a degree, Foundation degree or HNC/D usually requires practical experience in the field and a portfolio of relevant samples.
- Training programmes are on offer for graduate entrants from any discipline including the Graduate Professional Development Award (GPDA). This offers training and accreditation to IT professionals working in the industry.
- The new 14–19 Diploma in IT is available at Levels 1–3 and focuses on competencies relevant to IT professional work. Level 3 is equivalent to 3.5 A levels.

CRCI:D

CLCI:CAV

Other related opportunities

- Computer Engineer / Scientist p105
- Film and TV Staff p143
- Internet / Web Professional p111
- Multimedia Programmer p116
- Software Architect / Developer p119

Advantages/disadvantages

- This job uses cutting-edge technology and is a young, vibrant industry to work in.
- The pace of development means you will never be able to stand still. You will have to keep up to date and keep learning to stay on top of the game.

Earnings guide

- £20,000–£25,000 per year is usual for starting salaries.
- The average salary for an experienced multimedia designer is £30,000+, more in London
- Highly experienced, you could earn £50,000+.
- The more skills and experience you have to offer, the more you can earn.

Further information

British Computer Society
North Star House
North Star Avenue
Swindon
Wiltshire
SN2 1FA
01793 417424
www.bcs.org

e-skills UK (Sector Skills Council for information technology, telecommunications and contact centres)
1 Castle Lane
London
SW1E 6DR
020 7963 8920
www.e-skills.com

British Interactive Multimedia Association
Briarlea House
Southend Road
Billericay
CM11 2PR
020 7436 8250
www.bima.co.uk

Multimedia Programmer

What the work involves

- Multimedia, in ICT, means a system that combines a number of different formats, such as text, data, graphics, sound, images and animation.
- You will be part of a team working together to build a multimedia project such as a website or interactive program.
- You will use specific languages such as HTML, Lingo and Java, and use tools for multimedia applications such as FrontPage, Visual Tools and Illustrator.
- You will test and sort out any technical bugs in your program.

The type of person suited to this work

Knowledge of specific multimedia programming languages is essential, as is a broad understanding of how multimedia works. If you are planning to go on a course to learn these skills, you will need to be a logical and analytical thinker.

Your communication and team-working skills will also need to be as good as your technical ability, because you will be working alongside other professionals, such as graphic designers, sound engineers and scriptwriters.

If you are creative – able to write scripts or to visualise how screens should look – as well as technical, you will be able to set your sights on project management.

Working conditions

You will be mainly working in a software development laboratory or office at your workstation, but you will also be working with your project team.

Although your hours will be usually Monday to Friday, when projects are near to completion you will need to work some evenings and weekends.

The future outlook

Employers include specialist multimedia product development consultancies, internet service providers, website development firms, software houses and e-learning specialist companies. Multimedia is one of the growth industries of the decade.

If you are creative as well as technical, you will be able to progress up to project management level. You could also move into self-employment, or work on a contract or consultancy basis.

entry level

To both enter and train while working in this career, you will need qualifications at Level 3–8. Please refer to explanation on page vii.

Qualifications and courses

- Entry is usually by means of a degree, Foundation degree or HNC/D in a relevant subject, for example multimedia technology, software engineering or computer science, or a degree with modules in computer graphics or Hypertext and Java programming.
- The normal minimum entry requirements for degrees are 2 A levels/3 H grades and 5 GCSEs/S grades (A–C/1–3), and for Foundation degrees or HNC/Ds, 1 A level/ 2 H grades and 3 GCSEs/S grades (A–C/1–3). For technical degrees, maths/science may be required.
- A funded route that may be on offer in your area is the Higher Apprenticeship in IT. This leads to a full Honours degree in addition to vocational, technical and Key Skills qualifications and work experience.
- Entry without a degree, Foundation degree or HNC/D is unusual unless you have substantial experience in programming work and experience of designing or programming websites using new media. A strong portfolio will be required.
- Training programmes are on offer for graduate entrants from any discipline, including the Graduate Professional Development Award (GPDA). This offers training and accreditation to IT professionals working in the industry.
- The new 14–19 Diploma in IT is available at Levels 1–3 and focuses on competencies relevant to IT professional work. Level 3 is equivalent to 3.5 A levels.

CRCI:D

CLCI:CAV

Other related opportunities

- Internet / Web Professional p111
- Multimedia Designer p115
- Software Architect / Developer p119
- Website Designer p122

Advantages/disadvantages

- You will get a buzz from using your skills to make a project come alive.
- This is a young industry, developing at a rapid pace, so you will need to keep up to date with technological change.
- If you are creative as well as technical, rewards are high.

Earnings guide

- £19,000–£25,000 per year is usual for starting salaries. Some companies may offer less.
- £28,000–£38,000 is possible with experience.
- Senior multimedia programmers can earn £45,000.
- Additional benefits may include profit sharing, performance-related pay and a car.

Further information

British Computer Society
North Star House
North Star Avenue
Swindon
Wiltshire
SN2 1FA
01793 417424
www.bcs.org

e-skills UK (Sector Skills Council for information technology, telecommunications and contact centres)
1 Castle Lane
London
SW1E 6DR
020 7963 8920
www.e-skills.com

British Interactive Multimedia Association
Briarlea House
Southend Road
Billericay
CM11 2PR
020 7436 8250
www.bima.co.uk

Network Designer

What the work involves

- IT networks allow people to work together, communicate and share information by linking their computers.
- You may be designing a local area network, linking computers in one building, or a wide area network, linking computers across a large geographical area.
- You will find out from your customer the size and likely demands on the network plus the area to be covered, in order to come up with the right network design.
- You will use the best solution and the right technology for the network you are designing.

The type of person suited to this work

You must have technical ability and a passion for computers. If you are able to invent, solve technical problems, think logically and pay attention to detail then you would enjoy this job.

Excellent communication skills and an understanding of how businesses work are also vital as you will be attending meetings, giving presentations and keeping in contact with customers and suppliers by email and telephone.

You will also need to be good at dealing with the information you find out, for example putting together comments made at a series of meetings with your network brief and technical specifications.

Working conditions

You will be mainly office-based, using a computer to produce, model and test design solutions.

You may have to travel, possibly internationally, to meet and present to customers.

Although your hours will be normally Monday to Friday, deadlines and keeping up to date with new networking technologies will mean working some evenings and weekends.

The future outlook

The network design industry is developing rapidly but is competitive with lots of specialist companies fighting for business. Despite this, there are opportunities for talented designers with strong communication skills and business acumen.

Network designers usually work for a specialist ICT networking firm or a large computer services company. You could move on from this work into technical consultancy, project management or general management.

entry level

4–8

To both enter and train while working in this career, you will need qualifications at Level 4–8. Please refer to explanation on page vii.

Qualifications and courses

- The usual entry qualification for this work is a degree, Foundation degree or HNC/D in a relevant subject, for example control and network computing, computer engineering, software engineering or computer science.
- The normal minimum entry requirements for degrees are 2 A levels/3 H grades and 5 GCSEs/S grades (A–C/1–3), and for Foundation degrees or HNC/Ds, 1 A level/ 2 H grades and 3 GCSEs/S grades (A–C/1–3). For technical degrees, maths/science may be required.
- A funded route that may be on offer in your area is the Higher Apprenticeship in IT. This leads to a full Honours degree in addition to vocational, technical and Key Skills qualifications and work experience.
- A strong portfolio in IT skills can compensate for a lack of qualifications.
- Training programmes are on offer for graduate entrants from any discipline including the Graduate Professional Development Award (GPDA). This offers training and accreditation to IT professionals working in the industry. It includes e-skills, internet services delivery and industrial management and practice.
- The new 14–19 Diploma in IT is available at Levels 1–3 and focuses on competencies relevant to IT professional work. Level 3 is equivalent to 3.5 A levels.

CRCI:D

CLCI:CAV

Other related opportunities

- Computer Business Analyst p104
- Multimedia Designer p115
- Network Manager p118
- Website Designer p122

Advantages/disadvantages

- This is a competitive business but rewards are high if you do succeed.
- The skills you will develop in this work will be transferable into any other sector of the ICT jobs market.
- You will get a buzz from using your own ideas to produce working solutions.

Earnings guide

- Starting salaries are usually from £19,000 to £25,000 per year.
- With experience you could earn from £28,000 to £50,000.
- Very successful network designers can earn £60,000+.
- Additional benefits may include profit sharing, performance-related pay and a car.

Further information

e-skills UK (Sector Skills Council for information technology, telecommunications and contact centres)
1 Castle Lane
London
SW1E 6DR
020 7963 8920
www.e-skills.com

British Computer Society
North Star House
North Star Avenue
Swindon
Wiltshire
SN2 1FA
01793 417424
www.bcs.org

Institute for the Management of Information Systems
5 Kingfisher House
New Mill Road
Orpington
Kent
BR5 3QG
0700 002 3456
www.imis.org.uk

Network Manager

What the work involves

- You will be responsible for a network of computers and any linked equipment such as printers. This could be a network in just one building or extending right across different sites.
- Managing access to and the security of your network, you will put in place and monitor firewalls, password systems and antivirus software.
- You will support any network users experiencing problems and track down and fix the problem.
- In large organisations you may be responsible for a team of computer technicians.

The type of person suited to this work

Your communication and interpersonal skills need to be top-notch for this job. You will be dealing with computer users with little technical knowledge and you will need to be able to clearly explain any actions they may need to take to get back onto the network.

You should have technical ability as well as determination. You may develop and write software programs for your network and need to be determined and logical to work out how to sort out any problems.

Network solutions are developing very quickly so you will need to be prepared to carry on learning to keep up your expert status.

Working conditions

You will be mainly office-based, using a computer to manage the system. You may need to work in the same room as a noisy mainframe server.

You may have to move around your company's site to attend meetings, train staff and resolve problems.

You will work a 37- to 40-hour week, normally Monday to Friday, but may need to work outside these hours to install systems or be on call.

The future outlook

Most organisations use networks to enable their staff to work together, communicate and share information and resources from their own workstations. Employers of network managers include industry, retailers, schools and universities, hospitals, local and central government and financial companies.

Promotion could be into the job of senior network manager. A talented network manager could also move into freelance or network design consultancy work.

entry level

To both enter and train while working in this career, you will need qualifications at Level 3–8. Please refer to explanation on page vii.

Qualifications and courses

- The usual entry qualification for this work is a degree, Foundation degree or HNC/D in a relevant subject, for example control and network computing, software engineering, artificial intelligence or computer science.
- The normal minimum entry requirements for degrees are 2 A levels/3 H grades and 5 GCSEs/S grades (A–C/1–3), and for Foundation degrees or HNC/Ds, 1 A level/ 2 H grades and 3 GCSEs/S grades (A–C/1–3). For technical degrees, maths/science may be required.
- A funded route that may be on offer in your area is the Higher Apprenticeship in IT. This leads to a full Honours degree in addition to vocational, technical and Key Skills qualifications and work experience.
- A strong portfolio in IT skills and relevant work experience is essential to most employers who often assist with continued training. Courses are available for those wishing to obtain professional qualifications.
- Training programmes are on offer for graduate entrants from any discipline including the Graduate Professional Development Award (GPDA). This offers training and accreditation to IT professionals working in the industry. It includes e-skills, internet services delivery and industrial management and practice.
- The new 14–19 Diploma in IT is available at Levels 1–3 and focuses on competencies relevant to IT professional work. Level 3 is equivalent to 3.5 A levels.

CRCI:D

CLCI:CAV

Other related opportunities

- Computer Hardware Technician p107
- Computer Helpdesk Adviser p108
- Computer Technical Support p109
- Database Operator p110
- Network Designer p117

Advantages/disadvantages

- You will feel valued – a key person in your company – because communication and the sharing of information are central to the effective running of any organisation.
- The network you are responsible for is so crucial that when it goes wrong users and managers will put you under lots of pressure to sort out the problem as soon as it happens.

Earnings guide

- Starting salaries are usually from about £23,500 to £30,000 per year.
- With experience you could earn from £33,000 to £45,000.
- Senior network managers can earn £55,000+.
- Additional benefits may include profit sharing or performance-related pay.

Further information

British Computer Society
North Star House
North Star Avenue
Swindon
Wiltshire
SN2 1FA
01793 417424
www.bcs.org

e-skills UK (Sector Skills Council for information technology, telecommunications and contact centres)
1 Castle Lane
London
SW1E 6DR
020 7963 8920
www.e-skills.com

Institute for the Management of Information Systems
5 Kingfisher House
New Mill Road
Orpington
Kent
BR5 3QG
0700 002 3456
www.imis.org.uk

Software Architect / Developer

What the work involves

- All ICT systems depend on software to operate, for example the software that runs an internet-based airline booking system.
- You will find out what the customer needs the software to do and then translate this into efficient, reliable code using programming languages such as C++, Java and Assembler.
- To check that it is the right solution, you will build a prototype for testing, and then modify, build, install and final-test the product.
- You will write instructions or a manual for users and may train staff.

3–8 **entry level**

To both enter and train while working in this career, you will need qualifications at Level 3–8. Please refer to explanation on page vii.

Qualifications and courses

- Entry is usually by means of a degree, foundation degree or HNC/D in a relevant subject, for example software development or engineering, computer science, electronics, maths or physics. A postgraduate IT conversion course can be useful if you have a qualification in a non-relevant subject.
- The normal minimum entry requirements for degrees are 2 A levels/3 H grades and 5 GCSEs/S grades (A–C/1–3), and for Foundation degrees or HNC/Ds, 1 A level/ 2 H grades and 3 GCSEs/S grades (A–C/1–3). For technical degrees, maths/science may be required.
- A funded route that may be on offer in your area is the Higher Apprenticeship in IT. This leads to a full Honours degree in addition to vocational, technical and Key Skills qualifications and work experience.
- Entry without a degree, Foundation degree or HNC/D is unusual unless you have substantial experience and proven ability in programming.
- Training programmes are on offer for graduate entrants from any discipline including the Graduate Professional Development Award (GPDA). This offers training and accreditation to IT professionals working in the industry. It includes e-skills, internet services delivery and industrial management and practice.
- The new 14–19 Diploma in IT is available at Levels 1–3 and focuses on competencies relevant to IT professional work. Level 3 is equivalent to 3.5 A levels.

The type of person suited to this work

Knowledge of computer programming languages is essential, as well as a good understanding of how computer hardware, software products and the internet operate.

Central to the writing of a good software solution for a customer is your understanding of their business and an ability to listen to what they want it to achieve.

Your communication and persuasive skills will also need to be strong to meet, give presentations to and train customers and their staff.

All products are developed in a team so you will need to be keen to work alongside other ICT specialists.

Working conditions

You will be mainly based in an office or laboratory, working with other members of the project team.

You may have to travel to clients to meet and present your solutions to them.

Although your hours will be usually Monday to Friday, when projects are near to completion you will need to work some evenings and weekends.

The future outlook

Employers include software and systems houses, ICT consultants and the aerospace, instrumentation and telecommunications industries. This is a growth area, especially for software developers offering technical and programming skills combined with strong interpersonal skills.

You may be able to progress into senior development or analyst jobs, into ICT training or on to project management.

CRCI:D

CLCI:CAV

Other related opportunities

- Computer Engineer / Scientist p105
- Internet / Web Professional p111
- Multimedia Programmer p116
- Systems Analyst p120
- Training Officer p33

Advantages/disadvantages

- No two projects are ever the same.
- Software developers say they enjoy developing a program that will be used in a very practical way.
- Programming is one of the best overall foundations for a career in ICT and will open up entry into any specialist ICT sector.

Earnings guide

- Starting salaries are usually from £20,000 to £25,000 per year.
- With 5–10 years experience you could earn £35,000–£50,000.
- Senior programmers can earn £60,000+.
- Additional benefits may include profit sharing, performance-related pay and a car.

Further information

British Computer Society
North Star House
North Star Avenue
Swindon
Wiltshire
SN2 1FA
01793 417424
www.bcs.org

Institute for the Management of Information Systems
5 Kingfisher House
New Mill Road
Orpington
Kent
BR5 3QG
0700 002 3456
www.imis.org.uk

e-skills UK (Sector Skills Council for information technology, telecommunications and contact centres)
1 Castle Lane
London
SW1E 6DR
020 7963 8920
www.e-skills.com

British Interactive Multimedia Association
Briarlea House
Southend Road
Billericay
CM11 2PR
020 7436 8250
www.bima.co.uk

Systems Analyst

What the work involves

- You may work with a business analyst to prepare a brief of what your client wants a computer system to do.
- You will be responsible for translating this brief into recommendations.
- To determine the system needed you will use performance monitoring or sizing tools. You will then design, cost and recommend suitable hardware/software solutions.
- If purpose-built software is needed, you may write it or brief a programmer on your team.
- You will then go on to install and test the configuration you have developed.

The type of person suited to this work

An excellent all-round knowledge of ICT, including hardware and software, is vital. You will also have to be keen on learning, as new ICT products continue to be developed and produced at a rapid pace and you will be expected to be the technical expert.

Your teamwork and communication skills will need to be good as you will be working with business clients and colleagues such as business analysts and programmers to produce the best value system as a team.

To make systems that work well and enhance profitability and efficiency for your customer, you will also need to be a problem-solver who understands how businesses work.

Working conditions

You will be mainly based in an office, working with other members of the project team.

You will have to travel to clients at all stages of the project and may be away for several days when installing and testing the new system.

Although your hours will be usually Monday to Friday, when projects are near to completion you will need to work some evenings and weekends.

The future outlook

Employers include software and systems houses, ICT consultants and large organisations. This is an expanding job area especially for systems analysts who have a business understanding as well as a broad technical knowledge.

You could move from this broad-based job to specialise either in offering ICT solutions for business, or a technical area such as software or website development.

Progression is possible into project management or consultancy work.

entry level

2–8

To both enter and train while working in this career, you will need qualifications at Level 2–8. Please refer to explanation on page vii.

Qualifications and courses

- A degree, Foundation degree or HND/C is usually required, but previous experience in other areas can be just as important. Useful degree subjects include computing or e-systems design and technology. A level/H grade maths may be required or preferred for these degrees.
- A new sponsored degree from e-skills, information technology management for business, is available. This is focused on learning through project work in compact teams with external mentors from sponsoring organisations.
- Another funded route that may be on offer in your area is the Higher Apprenticeship in IT. This leads to a full Honours degree in addition to vocational, technical and Key Skills qualifications and work experience.
- If you are aged 16–24 you could enter IT work directly through Apprenticeships/ Skillseekers and work for the qualifications needed for higher level IT work.
- Late entry is often possible for those who have developed computer skills working in other fields.
- Training programmes are on offer for graduate entrants from any discipline including the Graduate Professional Development Award (GPDA).
- A new 14–19 Diploma in IT is available at Levels 1–3, focusing on competencies relevant to IT professional work. Level 3 is equivalent to 3.5 A levels.

CRCI:D

CLCI:CAV

Other related opportunities

- Computer Business Analyst p104
- Database Operator p110
- Network Designer p117
- Software Architect / Developer p119

Advantages/disadvantages

- It is rewarding to put together hardware and software to create a unique solution designed for your customer.
- Clients tend to set very stressful, demanding briefs to deliver the right solution both at the lowest cost and in the shortest time possible.

Earnings guide

- Starting/training salaries are usually from £20,000 to £25,000 per year.
- With experience, you could earn from £26,000 to £45,000.
- Successful systems analysts can earn £50,000+.
- With management responsibilities £80,000 is possible in the south-east of England.
- Additional benefits may include profit sharing, performance-related pay and a car.

Further information

British Computer Society
North Star House
North Star Avenue
Swindon
Wiltshire
SN2 1FA
01793 417424
www.bcs.org

e-skills UK (Sector Skills Council for information technology, telecommunications and contact centres)
1 Castle Lane
London
SW1E 6DR
020 7963 8920
www.e-skills.com

Institute for the Management of Information Systems
5 Kingfisher House
New Mill Road
Orpington
Kent
BR5 3QG
0700 002 3456
www.imis.org.uk

Institute of ICT Training
Westwood House
Westwood Business Park
Coventry
CV4 8HS
0845 006 8858
www.iitt.org.uk

Technical Sales Specialist

What the work involves

- Anyone investing in an expensive ICT product usually wants to find out what it does and how it compares with other models before buying it.
- You will talk to customers interested in your product, finding out what they are looking for, explaining how it works, and hopefully selling it to them.
- Once you have clinched the deal you will take payment and arrange delivery dates.

The type of person suited to this work

You should be a people person who is mad about technology. You will also need good communication skills as you will be dealing with customers face to face and on the telephone.

You will have to be able to clearly explain technical jargon to customers who may have no technical knowledge. Equally, you will need to understand all the technical specifications of your products as some of your customers will be experts.

It is a competitive market so you will need to be good at selling, persuading and building customer loyalty. You will also need to be bang up to date with all the products out there so that you know what you are up against.

Working conditions

You may be based in an office, dealing with customers by phone or email, or in a retail outlet, selling direct.

If you specialise in selling to retail chains or organisations, you will spend lots of time driving and in meetings.

Your hours will depend on your customers. Your employer may operate a shift system to deal with queries and sales from early until late, seven days a week.

The future outlook

Employers include large ICT companies producing and retailing products such as mobile phones, computer hardware and software. Large specialist ICT retailers also employ technical sales staff.

The demand for new ICT products continues to grow but new competitors are always entering the market. Strong areas of demand include secure wireless broadband and mobile working.

You may be able to gain promotion to a supervisory or sales management role.

entry level

3–8

To both enter and train while working in this career, you will need qualifications at Level 3–8. Please refer to explanation on page vii.

Qualifications and courses

- You will usually need a degree, Foundation degree or HNC/D in a computer-related subject to enter this job.
- The normal minimum entry requirements for degrees are 2 A levels/3 H grades and 5 GCSEs/S grades (A–C/1–3), and for Foundation degrees or HNC/Ds, 1 A level/ 2 H grades and 3 GCSEs/S grades (A–C/1–3). Maths may be a required subject.
- A funded route that may be on offer in your area is the Higher Apprenticeship in IT. This leads to a full Honours degree in addition to vocational, technical and Key Skills qualifications and work experience.
- Some people move into sales from a technical job in design or production.
- A thorough understanding of the products to be sold is essential, and may be more important than formal qualifications.
- You will normally need to hold a driving licence for this job.
- Initial training is usually intense as you will need to gain a thorough technical knowledge of your employer's products and their preferred communication style.
- The new 14–19 Diploma in IT is available at Levels 1–3 and focuses on competencies relevant to IT professional work. Level 3 is equivalent to 3.5 A levels.

CRCI:D

CLCI:CAV

Other related opportunities

- Computer Business Analyst p104
- Computer Helpdesk Adviser p108
- IT Marketing Manager p112
- Marketing p151
- Specialist Shop Assistant p455

Advantages/disadvantages

- If you close a deal at a good price or sell extras such as a service contract, you may be paid a bonus.
- Selling can be very stressful, with high sales targets to achieve.
- It is frustrating if you have spent lots of time with a customer without it resulting in a purchase.

Earnings guide

- £20,000 per year is usual for starting salaries.
- This could rise to £25,000–£35,000 with experience.
- Sales managers can earn more than £50,000.
- Additional benefits may include profit sharing, performance-related pay and a car.

Further information

British Computer Society
North Star House
North Star Avenue
Swindon
Wiltshire
SN2 1FA
01793 417424
www.bcs.org

e-skills UK (Sector Skills Council for information technology, telecommunications and contact centres)
1 Castle Lane
London
SW1E 6DR
020 7963 8920
www.e-skills.com

Institute of Sales & Marketing Management
Harrier Court
Lower Woodside
Bedfordshire
LU1 4DQ
01582 840001
www.ismm.co.uk

Website Designer

What the work involves

- You may work for a specialist web-design company or on a self-employed basis.
- You will find out what a customer needs to achieve with a new or updated website and what the budget is.
- You may need to do a presentation in competition with other developers to win the contract.
- Creating a specification for how the site needs to look and work would be done by interviewing and meeting with your client's staff.
- You will have regular review meetings to try out web ideas and pages you have developed, and test for bugs.

The type of person suited to this work

Creativity is central to this job. You will need to listen to what the client wants to achieve and then turn your vision into a unique, working website.

As sites increasingly use a complex mixture of text, graphics, data, music and interactive functions, your technical skills are as important as your creativity.

Your communication and presentation skills need to be excellent to take your client with you from winning the contract to launching the site.

You will be working as part of a team, especially if developing a complex web project, so you will need to be a team player.

Working conditions

You will need to travel to meet clients on a regular basis. At certain key times in the project, such as building the specification and launch of the site, you may be away from home for long periods.

You will be working on a computer with internet access to develop your client's site. You will probably work remotely, at home or in an office base.

You will work a 37- to 40-hour week, normally Monday to Friday, but as deadlines loom you will have to put in extra hours.

The future outlook

Website development is expanding. There are growing numbers of even quite small businesses using the web to share information, market themselves, sell goods or services or advertise jobs.

Work is competitive for website consultants who often have to bid for projects against other website developers. You need to be talented to stay in the business.

Promotion could be to project management level. Website developers can specialise in the growing interactive or multimedia business.

entry level

3–8

To both enter and train while working in this career, you will need qualifications at Level 3–8. Please refer to explanation on page vii.

Qualifications and courses

- The usual entry qualification for this work is a degree, Foundation degree or HNC/D in a relevant subject, for example e-commerce technologies, e-systems design and technology, multimedia design or graphic design. A new sponsored degree from e-skills, information technology management for business, is available.
- Another funded route that may be on offer in your area is the Higher Apprenticeship in IT. This leads to a full Honours degree in addition to vocational, technical and Key Skills qualifications and work experience. You can also start an Apprenticeship at a lower level and build up the qualifications you need for higher-level work.
- If you have not got a degree but have lots of experience and training, for example in interactive programming languages, and a strong portfolio of web-design work, you should be able to enter this field.
- Training programmes are on offer for graduate entrants from any discipline including the Graduate Professional Development Award (GPDA). This offers training and accreditation to IT professionals working in the industry.
- The new 14–19 Diploma in IT is available at Levels 1–3 and focuses on competencies relevant to IT professional work. Level 3 is equivalent to 3.5 A levels.

CRCI:D

CLCI:CAV

Other related opportunities

- Computer Business Analyst p104
- Internet / Web Professional p111
- Multimedia Designer p115
- Multimedia Programmer p116

Advantages/disadvantages

- If you create a top-class site, not only will it generate more business for your client, it will also build your future success.
- It is stressful; you cannot ever do a poor job. Consultants say that 70% of new business comes from recommendations from existing clients.

Earnings guide

- £18,000–£25,000 per year is usual for starting salaries.
- With experience this can rise to £30,000 or more.
- Senior web developers with specialist skills can earn up to £45,000.
- £55,000+ is possible for successful consultants.

Further information

British Computer Society
North Star House
North Star Avenue
Swindon
Wiltshire
SN2 1FA
01793 417424
www.bcs.org

British Interactive Multimedia Association
Briarlea House
Southend Road
Billericay
CM11 2PR
020 7436 8250
www.bima.co.uk

e-skills UK (Sector Skills Council for information technology, telecommunications and contact centres)
1 Castle Lane
London
SW1E 6DR
020 7963 8920
www.e-skills.com

Do you care about design and colour, enjoy communicating with others – perhaps making things? This cluster of jobs all have a creative aspect, such as:

- **Artist**
- **Advertising Account Executive**
- **Marketing Manager**
- **Printer**
- **Designer**
- **Signwriter**

But what's it like working in this area?

Here's Tammi Walker's story

TV Researcher

A freelance TV and radio researcher, Tammi always knew she wanted to work in the media. Her careers adviser suggested journalism, but while studying two A levels in Communication and Film Studies, Tammi worked for a temp agency that sent her to the BBC. Realising that this was what she wanted to do, Tammi took a degree in Media Studies and English at De Montfort University in Leicester. During summer holidays she still temped at the BBC and a month before graduation they asked Tammi if she wanted a contract job. She took the role of Producer's Assistant and worked on Cold Lazarus*, a highly accredited TV drama. When the contract ended, Tammi worked for a while in development research before being appointed as Senior Researcher on the Trisha daytime talk show. Tammi is currently between jobs but will soon take up a research job on drama development for the BBC.*

WHAT DOES A RESEARCHER ACTUALLY DO?

'It depends on the company you are working for, but you will be asked to come up with ideas and develop a good story. You will have to find useful contributors and sometimes even interesting locations. However, the job is not only about people research, there is also subject research. Your company may be making a documentary on obsessions and you will have to find out as much about the subject as you can. In small companies, you can even be out shooting with a crew or finding archive clips to insert into a programme.'

WHAT SKILLS DOES A PERSON NEED TO BRING TO THE JOB?

'You need to be interested in TV and you need to be objective. People skills are key as you have to be very persuasive, extremely persistent and tenacious! A good researcher never takes no for an answer. Often, you will have to find people at very short notice.'

Tammi enjoys meeting new people and finding out about their lives. She also likes the fact most research jobs teach you new skills so you are constantly learning on the job. A downside is most researchers work on short contracts and so you never have real job security. Although there is no structured career progression through television, ultimately Tammi would like to learn enough to become a producer, but she could move sideways into more radio work.

TAMMI'S ADVICE TO THOSE WHO WOULD LIKE A CAREER IN TV

'Be passionate about TV and TV programmes, and come up with lots of ideas because they are your currency. Keep up with MediaGuardian – published on Mondays; perhaps subscribe to Broadcast or MediaNews magazines online. Do work experience or TV workshops if you can; and when you are actually in the industry, network like mad – if I had not kept in contact with people I met while temping at the BBC I would never have got my first job.'

Account Executive

What the work involves

- You will plan and develop strategies for campaigns to suit different clients' requirements, working for advertising, PR or media agencies.
- Project-managing several client briefs at the same time, you will be making sure that all the campaigns run smoothly, are within budget and run to schedule.
- Your work will involve liaising between clients and the agency staff, such as designers and budget planners.
- Identifying, approaching and engaging potential clients will also be important.

entry level

4–8

To both enter and train while working in this career, you will need qualifications at Level 4–8. Please refer to explanation on page vii.

The type of person suited to this work

Because much of your work involves discussions with clients and agency staff, you will need to be flexible, with good communication skills. Being good with record-keeping and having a well-organised approach are essential because you will be running a number of campaigns at the same time.

In order to help develop ideas for campaigns, you will need a strong creative flair and a resourceful attitude. A key ability will be to manage clients' campaigns within budget.

You will need to be confident and enjoy negotiating – sometimes with high-profile clients. Being a strong team player with a flexible and enthusiastic attitude is valuable.

Working conditions

You will work mostly in an office, spending a lot of time at your computer, when not attending campaign planning meetings and speaking on the phone. It is almost certain that at times you will have to work under pressure to complete projects within limited time-scales.

It will be possible to work normal office hours in the quieter periods, but during busy times you will have to work late if required. Also, you may travel on business.

The future outlook

Across the UK, including web-based companies, there are around 2040 advertising businesses mainly centred in London and major cities, so the industry is quite small, with around 21,000 people currently employed. Due to the popularity of this sector, competition for jobs is tough and there can be 15 graduate applicants – all with media-related qualifications – for every person employed in the industry. You will need to have particular skills or work experience that make you stand out.

Even with a job in the advertising industry it can be difficult to progress due to a lack of higher-level opportunities. Consult the IPA's online magazine *Campaign* for opportunities (see Further information). Only a few of the largest agencies employ more than 300 people – the majority have less than 100 employees.

However, if you are unable to find advertising work, the skills you will gain through your training will be relevant to the related industries of marketing, market research, business or retail and commerce.

Qualifications and courses

- There are no minimum educational requirements, but entry into advertising is very competitive and most entrants are graduates. A degree or Higher National Diploma (HND) is often required by large agencies, while smaller agencies also look for relevant work experience.
- A range of related courses are available at universities and colleges at HND, Foundation degree, Honours degree and postgraduate levels. Subjects include advertising, marketing, English, communications or advertising/marketing combined with another subject; a sandwich course can be particularly useful.
- Training tends to be done on the job. Staff may enrol on an Institute of Practitioners in Advertising (IPA) course if their employer is a member. Some staff may be required to study towards Communications Advertising and Marketing Education Foundation (CAM) qualifications.

CRCI:O

CLCI:OD

Other related opportunities

- Account Planner p125
- Advertising Media Executive p128
- Marketing p151
- Recruitment Agency Consultant p27
- Store Manager p459

Advantages/disadvantages

- The job is fast-paced, with hectic periods of work which you will need to log.
- There are opportunities to meet and work with a wide range of people.
- It is a very competitive career to enter, so you will have to be very determined.
- It can be rewarding when your clients' campaigns are successful.

Earnings guide

- Salaries vary according to employer and geographical location, although London agencies tend to pay the highest.
- Starting as a graduate you can expect to earn £18,000–£24,000 a year.
- £34,000–£45,000 can be expected at senior levels, with the most successful earning £60,000+.
- In some jobs you can earn commission in addition to your salary.

Further information

Advertising Association
7th Floor North
Artillery House
11–19 Artillery Row
London
SW1P 1RT
020 7340 1100
www.adassoc.org.uk

Communication, Advertising and Marketing Education (CAM) Foundation
Moor Hall
Cookham
Maidenhead
Berkshire
SL6 9QH
01628 427120
www.camfoundation.com

Institute of Practitioners in Advertising
44 Belgrave Square
London
SW1X 8QS
020 7235 7020
www.ipa.co.uk

Account Planner

What the work involves

- You will research public opinion and interest in a client's product or service to develop new advertising and media campaigns.
- Market research, positive and negative, will form a starting point from which you will plan and develop new advertising strategies for your clients.
- You will need to be very clear when interpretating your clients' intentions.
- The work will require close cooperation with your clients and your creative team in order to create strong and successful advertising.

entry level

To both enter and train while working in this career, you will need qualifications at Level 4–8. Please refer to explanation on page vii.

The type of person suited to this work

As you will be developing fresh advertising ideas, you will need to have creative ideas that meet the clients' requirements.

To understand and make use of a range of facts and figures in support of your work, you will need an ability to interpret and analyse trends in data.

As you will have to make presentations to your clients and colleagues at progress meetings, excellent verbal and written communication skills will be essential. Being self-motivated and confident is also important.

Good business skills are helpful and you will need to use clear verbal reasoning when stating your point of view: an air of self-possession – even assertiveness – can be an asset at times, tempered by a sense of humour and a flexible approach to working.

Working conditions

Most of your work will be undertaken in an office or at clients' premises. You will be expected to dress formally and be well presented at all times. Although you will work mainly in normal office hours, you can expect to work overtime and at weekends during busy periods.

You will have to travel to attend meetings on a regular basis, perhaps staying overnight.

The future outlook

The majority of job opportunities in advertising are based in London although the number of companies in other large cities is growing. Despite this, there are still only around 21,000 people working within the sector of advertising and media, making entry highly competitive. Realistically, account planning makes up only a very small part of the overall advertising/media sector.

If employed by one of the few larger companies – with over 300 employees – it is occasionally possible to work abroad in areas such as Europe. With experience, you could work on a freelance basis or move into market research, design or management.

Qualifications and courses

- Although there are no minimum educational requirements to becoming an account planner, competition is high and most entrants will have a degree. It is rare to get into the profession with less than an HND. Smaller agencies also tend to require relevant work experience, and a sandwich course can be a particular advantage.
- Useful Key Skills include application of number, communication and people skills.
- Training tends to be done on the job. New account planners may train with the Account Planning Group and Market Research Society, or work towards NVQ/SVQ Levels 3 or 4 in Advertising and Public Relations. You may enrol on a course run by the Institute of Practitioners in Advertising (IPA) if your employer is a member, or take qualifications with the Communications Advertising and Marketing Education Foundation (CAM).

CRCI:O

CLCI:OD

Other related opportunities

- Account Executive p124
- Advertising Media Executive p128
- Market Researcher p150
- Marketing p151

Advantages/disadvantages

- This type of work can provide the opportunity to work for high-profile companies with a Europe-wide or global reach.
- You will have to develop new ideas, often at relatively short notice.
- This is a very competitive career and only the most determined will succeed.
- Besides reflecting positive opinion you will sometimes have to pass negative information to clients about how their products are currently viewed.

Earnings guide

- Starting salaries range from £18,000 to £23,000 per year.
- Experienced account planners can earn between £30,000 and £45,000.
- At the most senior level £60,000+ is possible.
- Some employers provide bonuses if you develop successful campaigns or gain new business. The highest salaries are in London.

Further information

Advertising Association
7th Floor North
Artillery House
11–19 Artillery Row
London
SW1P 1RT
020 7340 1100
www.adassoc.org.uk

Communication, Advertising and Marketing Education (CAM) Foundation
Moor Hall
Cookham
Maidenhead
Berkshire
SL6 9QH
01628 427120
www.camfoundation.com

Account Planning Group
16 Creighton Avenue
London
N10 1NU
020 8444 3692
www.apg.org.uk

Institute of Practitioners in Advertising
44 Belgrave Square
London
SW1X 8QS
020 7235 7020
www.ipa.co.uk

Advertising Art Director

What the work involves

- You will design and create effective brand styles and images, with immediate impact, for advertising campaigns to suit clients' requirements.
- Working with specialist software, you will develop new designs, often at short notice, to convey the required mood or tone of a particular campaign.
- Working closely with colleagues, especially copywriters and reprographic specialists, you will make sure your ideas come together.
- You may also be involved in selecting photographers and other professionals to create additional visuals for use in a campaign.

The type of person suited to this work

You will need visual design skills and creative strengths, but also the know-how and skills to develop commercial ideas. The capacity to understand and adapt to a client's requirements is also important.

As you will be using software to create new designs, you will need to have up-to-date computer skills. However, the ability to get ideas across with pen and paper is also important.

Much of your time will be spent working as part of a team, so you will need excellent communication and people skills. You may have to deal with your ideas being rejected or changed so a flexible yet confident attitude is essential.

Finally, it is important to be able to work to exacting standards, paying close attention to detail.

Working conditions

Most of your tasks will be office-based, sometimes in a studio; you will be seated for long periods at a workstation using a number of computers, and may often be on the phone.

The majority of your work will be done in normal office hours. However, you will be under a lot of pressure to complete jobs in the lead-up to contract deadlines and at these times will be expected to work late. Your job will involve attending meetings and visiting your clients which could involve travel and overnight stays.

The future outlook

This is a highly competitive area of work to enter. There are currently around 1000 office-based advertising agencies across the UK, over half of which are in London. Although newer agencies exist in some of the larger cities (Manchester, Bristol and Newcastle), the numbers of creative art directors employed are still low.

With experience – and some successful campaigns in your portfolio – you could move up to work as a senior art director. Some established art directors go on to work on a freelance basis.

entry level

4–8

To both enter and train while working in this career, you will need qualifications at Level 4–8. Please refer to explanation on page vii.

Qualifications and courses

- While there are no specific entry requirements, most art directors are usually graphic designers trained to HND, degree or postgraduate level. Courses combining elements of graphic design and advertising are particularly useful.
- Students generally require at least 2 A levels/3 H grades and 5 GCSEs/S Grades (A–C/1–3) to get a place on a degree course. Foundation courses are also available
- Advertising or marketing and other relevant postgraduate degrees may improve chances of entry in a very competitive industry.
- Getting a job as an art director is dependent upon an impressive, well-presented portfolio of campaigns.
- D&AD runs workshops in which participants develop skills and build up a portfolio of work. See www.dandad.org for details.

CRCI:O

CLCI:OD

Other related opportunities

- Account Planner p125
- Advertising Copywriter p127
- Designer p136
- Marketing p151
- Publisher p162

Advantages/disadvantages

- This job is rewarding as it offers creative, design-conscious individuals the chance to influence the images of major companies and their brands.
- As there is a constant need to develop new ideas, the job can be high-pressured – even stressful at times
- It is a very competitive area to enter with more creative graduates wanting work than available vacancies. These tend to appear in *MediaGuardian* or *Campaign* – the IPA's online magazine (see Further information)

Earnings guide

- Salaries vary according to employer and geographical location. The highest earnings are normally with London-based agencies.
- Starting salaries at junior art director level are around £18,000–£25,000 per year.
- With experience and success this can rise to £35,000–£65,000.
- At senior and very senior levels you could earn £50,000–£150,000.
- A very few progress to Creative Arts Director and have salaries of around £300,000.

Further information

Communication, Advertising and Marketing Education (CAM) Foundation
Moor Hall
Cookham
Maidenhead
Berkshire
SL6 9QH
01628 427120
www.camfoundation.com

Design and Art Directors Association (D&AD)
9 Graphite Square
London
SE11 5EE
020 7840 1111
www.dandad.org

Institute of Practitioners in Advertising
44 Belgrave Square
London
SW1X 8QS
020 7235 7020
www.ipa.co.uk

Advertising Copywriter

What the work involves

- You will create ideas and write text (known as 'copy' in the industry) for use in adverts on TV, film, radio, posters and the internet or published in the press.
- You will make changes to your work in response to client feedback.
- Working closely with art directors, you will create a campaign tailored to promote a product or service.
- You will be working for a mix of clients, so you will write text and dialogue on a range of factual or emotive subjects and from different perspectives.

entry level

To both enter and train while working in this career, you will need qualifications at Level 4–8. Please refer to explanation on page vii.

The type of person suited to this work

As you will be developing the tone and style of the advertising, you will need very strong writing skills. For certain campaigns, an injection of humour can contribute a hook or slogan to engage viewers' or listeners' attention. The ability to describe a subject concisely can also be important. You will need to be creative and able to adapt to the demands of varied campaigns.

In discussing innovative ideas with your colleagues, you will make valuable use of your strengths in verbal and written communication skills.

You will have to stay flexible and ready to change what you think are good ideas to meet clients' requirements.

Working conditions

You will work a normal Monday to Friday week within an office or studio environment, where you will work at your computer and attend meetings. However, to meet contract deadlines you will often have to produce work to a deadline, so you will be expected to work late to get projects completed. Your firm might offer flexible working conditions, meaning you will be able to get some project work completed at home.

When visiting clients you might have to stay away overnight.

The future outlook

As with other areas of advertising, copywriting is a competitive area to enter with demand from graduates outstripping vacancies by fifteen to one. However, getting involved and producing strong work can lead to wider job opportunities and career progression. From a junior position you could go on to work as a creative director

With experience, some copywriters progress to be freelance. You could work in partnership with other 'creatives', setting up your own agency. Other copywriters go on to work in related areas such as public relations and publishing.

Qualifications and courses

- There are no formal entry requirements to be an advertising copywriter, but most entrants have a degree or HND. Relevant subjects include advertising or design, or disciplines such as English, journalism, communications or media. A postgraduate qualification in copywriting or creative advertising can be useful for graduates without a relevant background.
- Students generally require at least 2 A levels/3 H grades and 5 GCSEs/S Grades (A–C/1–3) to get a place on a degree course. Foundation courses are also available.
- The most common entry route involves producing a high-quality portfolio ('book') and showing this to agencies.
- You will probably need to complete several unpaid work experience placements as a copywriter before being taken on.
- Entry-level jobs are seldom advertised and there are currently no graduate training schemes into the creative side of advertising.
- D&AD runs workshops in which participants develop skills and build up a portfolio of work. See www.dandad.org for details.

Other related opportunities

- Advertising Art Director p126
- Commissioning Editor p134
- Copywriter p135
- Marketing p151

Advantages/disadvantages

- Your work can affect how a product or service is seen and thought about – with far-reaching effects if the campaign is for a government agency or charity.
- You will have to keep developing fresh ideas, which can be challenging.
- This is a very difficult and competitive industry to enter.
- You will be working alongside imaginative colleagues which can be stimulating.

Earnings guide

- Salaries vary according to employer and geographical region. Generally, London-based agencies pay higher salaries than elsewhere. Some employers also pay commission.
- As a starting salary outside London you can expect £10,000–£17,500 per year.
- With three to five years' experience this can rise to £25,000–£45,000.
- At senior levels you can expect to earn up to £150,000 depending on location.

Further information

Advertising Association
7th Floor North
Artillery House
11–19 Artillery Row
London
SW1P 1RT
020 7340 1100
www.adassoc.org.uk

Communication, Advertising and Marketing Education (CAM) Foundation
Moor Hall
Cookham
Maidenhead
Berkshire
SL6 9QH
01628 427120
www.camfoundation.com

Institute of Practitioners in Advertising
44 Belgrave Square
London
SW1X 8QS
020 7235 7020
www.ipa.co.uk

Design, Arts, Media, Marketing, Advertising and Printing

CRCI:O

CLCI:OD

Advertising Media Executive

What the work involves

- You will work with clients to select the most appropriate forms of media to advertise their products or services which might be the national/local press, TV, video or radio, poster campaigns, direct marketing and/or the internet.
- Your understanding of media and your knowledge of the public's media interests, will help clients make the best choices
- You will need to demonstrate a strong financial and business sense as you will handle clients' budgets: buying media space and liaising between media sources and your clients to agree terms.

entry level

4–8

To both enter and train while working in this career, you will need qualifications at Level 4–8. Please refer to explanation on page vii.

The type of person suited to this work

As you will be dealing with media providers and clients, you will need to be confident and assertive, with excellent written and verbal communication skills. The ability to work quickly – while handling pressure – is invaluable! You will need to have a real interest and knowledge concerning media interfaces, keeping up to date with new developments across the industry. An ability to understand and get under the skin of a particular advertising brief is helpful, while accuracy with figures is essential.

Finally, in order to juggle a number of projects, you will need to be well organised.

Working conditions

Most of your work will be undertaken during normal office hours within an office environment. However, at busy times you will be expected to work late. Some of your time will involve attending meetings and presentations with clients, which could involve overnight stays away from home.

Most of the day you will be seated at a computer console, speaking on the phone or attending meetings.

The future outlook

With new media developments, such as 'Web 2.0' and digital television, opportunities in web-based, digital advertising are increasing. However, this is still a very competitive area to enter with few opportunities for graduates. Unpaid work experience – often, simply shadowing an advertising media executive or director – is a highly recommended option for applicants keen to enter the industry.

Once in, and with experience, you could progress to a senior executive director role and then branch into other areas of advertising. Some media executives enter related jobs such as sales and marketing.

Qualifications and courses

- There are no formal entry requirements to be an advertising media executive; however, the majority of entrants are graduates. Subjects that can be particularly useful are communication and media studies, business/management, marketing, psychology and statistics.
- Experience gained pre-entry is desirable and any relevant work experience is considered favourably.
- There are very few vacancies for media executives advertised each year, so many candidates apply for other posts in the advertising sector as a way into the industry.

Other related opportunities

- Account Executive p124
- Account Planner p125
- Film and TV Staff p143
- Marketing p151

Advantages/disadvantages

- This job allows you to meet and work with a wide range of different people
- It is possible to earn commission – even bonuses – in addition to your salary.
- The work can be high-pressured due to limited time-scales.
- Seeing the final outcome of an advertising brief can be rewarding.

Earnings guide

- Salaries vary according to employer and geographical location. The highest are likely to be in London.
- £15,000–£24,000 per year is usual at entry level.
- With some experience salaries can rise to £25,000–£35,000. This increases with further experience.

Further information

Advertising Association
7th Floor North
Artillery House
11–19 Artillery Row
London
SW1P 1RT
020 7340 1100
www.adassoc.org.uk

Communication, Advertising and Marketing Education (CAM) Foundation
Moor Hall
Cookham
Maidenhead
Berkshire
SL6 9QH
01628 427120
www.camfoundation.com

Institute of Practitioners in Advertising
44 Belgrave Square
London
SW1X 8QS
020 7235 7020
www.ipa.co.uk

Animator

What the work involves

- You will create animations by developing cartoons, drawings, images on computer-assisted drawing (CAD) programmes or 3-D forms and figures into a continuous story using film or digital animation techniques
- You may also plan speech and music soundtracks for animated films.
- Working in fine detail, you will ensure that the animation works as smoothly and convincingly as possible.
- Animators produce creative and commercial work for use by TV companies, in computer games, advertising and films.

entry level

To both enter and train while working in this career, you will need qualifications at Level 4–8. Please refer to explanation on page vii.

The type of person suited to this work

You will need strong creative flair and imagination to develop new ideas for animated stories and characters.

You must have excellent computer skills: able to work with design packages. Although computerised animation is increasing in popularity, the ability to draw forms and figures and to model is still important.

Problem-solving skills are important in a job where you may need to adapt to technical challenges. An ability to work in a team with others, contributing equally while working patiently towards the finished product, are also an important attributes for an animator.

Working conditions

Your working environment will depend on the type of animation you do. In some jobs, you will work with tools to hand-create images or forms in different materials. You could be on your feet (using your hands) all day: bending, lifting and shaping models.

Many new animation jobs involve work with specialist CAD packages at a PC console – sometimes with colleagues. Most of your work will be done during normal office hours except when projects have tight deadlines!

The future outlook

This is a competitive area to enter. Although there are some opportunities for traditional drawing-based animators, the growth area is within computer-generated areas. WAP technology, the popularity of computer games and TV work have contributed more opportunities.

Once within the industry, contracts are usually short-term, but it is possible to move from working as a key animator, to an animation director role. At senior levels, you would have more creative input and be less directly involved with the technical side. With experience, you could set up as a freelance animator or start your own company.

Qualifications and courses

- Entry usually requires an HND, Foundation degree or degree in animation, art and design, or a related area; a relevant postgraduate qualification can be an asset. A portfolio of relevant work is also normally required.
- In England, Wales and Northern Ireland many students take a 1-year foundation course as preparation for entry to an art and design degree; 5 GCSEs (A–C) and a relevant A level are also usually required.
- In Scotland the first year of a degree course equates to the Foundation year.
- Entry to the profession without a degree/HND may be possible, in which case a good portfolio is essential.
- Gaining unpaid experience as a general or animation assistant for a company is a good way to build up relevant skills.
- With experience, you could work towards an NVQ/SVQ Level 3 in Animation Assistance; Skillset vocational courses for the industry are also available in Design for the Moving Image at Levels 2, 3 and 4.

Other related opportunities

- Cartoonist p133
- Designer p136
- Film and TV Staff p143
- Illustrator p147
- Sculptor p164

Advantages/disadvantages

- This type of work can be highly satisfying, providing opportunities to develop your own creative ideas and style.
- In more commercial jobs, you would need to produce work under pressure to meet a client's requirements.
- Animation is rising in popularity amongst the public. Many animated films are highly successful at the box office.

Earnings guide

- BECTU, the union for broadcasting, film, theatre, entertainment, leisure, interactive media and allied sectors, sets minimum wage guidelines for the industry, but animators negotiate their own rates and may receive more depending on the project.
- A new animator can expect to earn £70–£150 a day.
- An experienced animator could earn £556 a week.
- Senior animators can expect to earn £725+ a week.
- Contact BECTU for details of current freelance salaries.

Further information

Skillset (Sector Skills Council for the audiovisual industries)
Focus Point
21 Caledonian Road
London
N1 9GB
08080 300900
www.skillset.org/animation

Guild of British Animation
26 Noel Street
London
W1T 9PV
020 7434 2651
Provides job alerts

Broadcasting Entertainment Cinematograph and Theatre Union
373–377 Clapham Road
London
SW9 9BT
020 7346 0900
www.bectu.org.uk

Art Restorer

What the work involves

- You will protect and conserve the life of works of art by using your specialist skills to clean, restore or repair them.
- Applying knowledge of art history, you will assess the condition of pieces by visual observation or by using sophisticated digital imaging techniques.
- Art restorers/conservators oversee the upkeep of art in museums, stately homes and historic houses. Many work for themselves and provide specialist services to keepers of art collections.
- Besides historic art pieces, you can be asked for information and advice on how to preserve modern art installations composed of unusual materials (toast or elephant dung, as examples).

The type of person suited to this work

As you handle fragile objects, you will need a patient nature, plus conscientiousness and a sense of responsibility for the work's outcome. Paying attention to fine detail is essential. You will need good vision to check the condition of pieces at close range.

An art history background, and the ability to apply this knowledge to your work, is essential. You must be confident in working with your hands and using a range of tools and materials.

Being able to communicate clearly is helpful, as you may need to explain complex issues to clients or the public.

Working conditions

Your working environment will depend on the pieces you restore and the type of employer you work for. You could work in a museum, gallery, auction house or private house/estate. As with many conservators, you may work freelance from your own studio or home.

For different tasks, you will use specialist, volatile chemicals which can adversely affect people with skin conditions and respiratory problems.

Mainly, you will work normal office hours.

The future outlook

This is a highly skilled and competitive area of work. Gaining experience within a restorer's studio will help you acquire the essential technical and business skills. With time and increasing experience, you could then run your own business, offering services in painting or frame restoration. Freelance art restorers provide services for antique dealers, members of the public, art galleries and museums. Experienced British conservators can be contracted to work overseas on important collections or pieces.

A small number of restorers are permanently employed in UK museums, national galleries and stately homes. There is increasing, complex restoration work with modern artworks.

3–8

entry level

To both enter and train while working in this career, you will need qualifications at Level 3–8. Please refer to explanation on page vii.

Qualifications and courses

- Entry is normally through a professional apprenticeship or a specialist postgraduate qualification.
- You could take a City & Guilds Creative Skills Certificate in Picture Restoration, which provides a range of basic skills in this area. The course allows candidates to develop samples of work.
- You could then complete a City & Guilds Creative Studies Certificate in Picture/Frame Conservation/Restoration.
- Degree courses are available in conservation and restoration or restoration and decorative studies. Entry requirements are 2 A levels/3 H grades or the equivalent, and a GCSE/S grade or equivalent in a science is normally required. Degrees in other subjects such as fine art, ceramics and glass, textiles or science subjects are also helpful.
- Voluntary experience is useful, and can be gained through the National Association of Decorative and Fine Arts Societies (NADFAS) volunteer scheme.
- Following a qualification, it may take several years of experience before you are considered a fully competent restorer. Organisations such as the Guild of Master Craftsmen run seminars and courses, which can be a useful way of picking up skills.

CRCI:K

CLCI:FAE

Other related opportunities

- Antiques Dealer p434
- Art Exhibition Organiser p317
- Museum / Art Gallery p325
- Picture Framer p159
- Restorer / Conservation Officer p329

Advantages/disadvantages

- You will have the opportunity to work with valuable, beautiful and historic pieces of art.
- This is precise and detailed work and, because of the value of the pieces you could be restoring, there is no room for error.

Earnings guide

- Salaries vary according to employer and geographic location.
- You are more likely to earn a higher salary working on a self-employed basis than in museums or art galleries.
- Starting salaries are around £14,500–£18,000 per year.
- With experience you could earn £24,000.
- Senior restorers can earn £28,000–£35,000+.

Further information

Institute of Conservation (Icon)
3rd floor, Downstream Building
1 London Bridge
London
SE1 9BG
020 7785 3807
www.icon.org.uk

Fine Art Trade Guild
16–18 Empress Place
London
SW6 1TT
020 7381 6616
www.fineart.co.uk

National Association of Decorative and Fine Arts Societies
NADFAS House
8 Guilford Street
London
WC1N 1DA
020 7430 0730
www.nadfas.org.uk

Artist (Fine)

What the work involves

- You will create original works of art to sell to customers directly or through art galleries.
- Depending on your own interests, you will work with a range of media such as oil paints, charcoal or stone to create small or large pieces of work.
- Part of your time will be spent promoting your work to sponsors, galleries and other organisations, by networking or issuing publicity material.
- You may also organise solo or joint exhibitions in all sorts of venues to showcase your work.

The type of person suited to this work

As you will be creating original works of art, you will need strong artistic and technical skills, well-developed powers of observation and vivid imagination.

It takes perseverance and application to turn an original idea into a finished piece of artwork.

Many artists set up their own businesses, so having good business sense and the ability to organise your work is important.

Good communication skills will help you to convince galleries to show and sell your work. An ability to network and make contacts in the art world is also useful.

Working conditions

Most of your time will be spent within your studio working on pieces, or on location researching your work. You will spend much of your time alone which can be isolating for some people.

Many artistic materials are dusty, oily or staining and, even wearing overalls, you can expect to get dirty.

You may have to work with solvents and other chemicals, which can adversely affect those with sensitive skin, allergies or respiratory problems.

The future outlook

This job demands confidence and persistence and very few fine artists earn their full living from art alone. Many earn additional income by working in related areas where their skills are needed; these include arts education, community development and art galleries.

There is a range of networks supporting developing artists. It is possible to sell work through a number of galleries, shops, workshop cooperatives, studios and increasingly the internet. Larger cities or tourist hotspots with more of these venues do provide more opportunities to sell artwork. Some art institutions also provide self-employment support and information to students, both during and after courses.

entry level

3–8

To both enter and train while working in this career, you will need qualifications at Level 3–8. Please refer to explanation on page vii.

Qualifications and courses

- Most artists have formal qualifications such as a degree in fine art, or an HNC/HND or degree in art and design. Postgraduate qualifications in fine art are also available.
- It is possible to gain NVQ/SVQs in the following subjects: Arts Development and Teaching (Levels 3 and 4) and Visual and Applied Arts Practice Level 4.
- In England, Wales and Northern Ireland many students take a 1-year foundation course as preparation for entry to an Art and Design degree; 5 GCSEs (A–C) and a relevant A level are usually required.
- In Scotland, the first year of a degree course equates to the Foundation year.
- Entry requirements vary. Some institutions require A levels/H grades in relevant subjects, while others accept students on the strength of their portfolio.

CRCI:E

CLCI:ED

Other related opportunities

- Animator p129
- Cartoonist p133
- Designer p136
- Illustrator p147
- Sculptor p164

Advantages/disadvantages

- You will have the pleasure of seeing customers enjoy and appreciate your work.
- It can be an isolated way of life and may not always lead to recognition.
- There can be hard times as it can be difficult to earn a living as a fine artist.
- You will be doing personally fulfilling work.

Earnings guide

- It is possible to earn a regular income from your work but this is more likely with experience.
- Many artists have another job to provide a more stable source of income. Some teach part time, while others may work on a commission basis on community projects.
- A single work of art could sell for anything between £45 and £30,000 or more! However, the higher ranges are usually paid to well-known artists.
- Selling for a high price will depend on experience and the popularity of your work. Some trained fine artists work as book or medical illustrators to obtain an income.

Further information

Arts Council of England
2 Pear Tree Court
London
EC1R 0DS
0845 300 6200
www.artscouncil.org.uk

Scottish Arts Council
12 Manor Place
Edinburgh
EH3 7DD
0131 226 6051
www.scottisharts.org.uk

Department for Culture, Media and Sport
2–4 Cockspur Street
London
SW1Y 5DH
020 7211 6000
www.culture.gov.uk

Author

What the work involves

- You will write the text for books, magazines and ICT resources. This can involve developing initial ideas to create a complete piece or, simply rewriting sections.
- As part of the work, you will undertake research using resources such as the internet and libraries. Also, you may research publishers and send them samples of your work.
- Authors often specialise in a particular subject area such as technical writing, science, medicine, cookery, travel or education.
- A small number of authors write and publish creative works of fiction, poetry or drama.

entry level

To both enter and train while working in this career, you will need qualifications at Level 1. Please refer to explanation on page vii.

The type of person suited to this work

You will need to cope with working alone for much of the time. Having a good imagination and a creative approach is important.

The ability to write convincingly, with your reader or audience in mind, is very important! As you will be explaining project ideas to publishers, you will need strong communication skills.

Many authors work on a self-employed basis, so business awareness and numeracy are very helpful. To manage projects independently, you should be self-motivated and well organised. You will also need to be able to handle rejections from publishers.

Qualifications and courses

- Authors are not required to have any specific qualifications, although many are graduates.
- Communication and application of number are useful Key Skills. The ability to use a computer is also helpful.
- There are a variety of English and creative writing courses available. These range from degree and postgraduate courses to evening classes designed to improve a writer's technique.
- Arts Council grants may be available to new authors for work in literature and drama. It is necessary to request such a grant in the form of a written proposal.

Working conditions

Most of your work will be undertaken alone, which can be isolating.

Most authors work at a computer for long periods, researching and writing. Many work from home, but the work can be performed in any suitable setting.

Most authors are employed on a project-by-project basis, so the work provides very little job security.

The future outlook

There are opportunities to write and share your work with others, including writers' circles and amateur drama Making a living as a professional can be more challenging and it usually takes time to develop both your writing expertise and your specialist areas. It helps if you have established a network of useful contacts.

A variety of support groups, writers' groups and courses exist to help people develop their writing skills. Some writers' groups are using the internet to publish their works. At present, short dramas for radio broadcast are actively sought.

Other related opportunities

- Advertising Copywriter p127
- Commissioning Editor p134
- Copywriter p135
- Journalist p148

Advantages/disadvantages

- This type of work can provide the satisfaction of being creative and seeing your completed work in print.
- Not all authors succeed in publishing their work and you may need to take on other types of work to make a living.

Earnings guide

- Earnings vary widely depending on the nature of the writing project, your experience, and your popularity as a writer.
- Publishers may give a one-off payment for a piece of work or will pay you royalties (a percentage of the income from sales of the book). Royalties can be profitable if a book sells well.
- Salaries can be £15,000–£30,000 for authors employed in a commercial environment
- You may have a higher income if you are well known and your work is popular.

Further information

www.cityandguilds.com/myperfectjob

Arts Council of England
2 Pear Tree Court
London
EC1R 0DS
0845 300 6200
www.artscouncil.org.uk

Scottish Arts Council
12 Manor Place
Edinburgh
EH3 7DD
0131 226 6051
www.scottisharts.org.uk

Society of Authors
84 Drayton Gardens
London
SW10 9SB
020 7373 6642
www.societyofauthors.net

Cartoonist

What the work involves

- You will plan and draw original cartoons and captions. These can be single images, whole cartoon strips or entire books.
- You will promote and market your work, for example by sending out samples to newspapers and advertising through the internet.
- Cartoonists create images for greetings cards, adverts, book illustrations, magazines, newspapers and websites.
- A small number of cartoonists are employed to run regular cartoon features in newspapers or other media. but most maintain a 'web comic' of their work.

entry level

To both enter and train while working in this career, you will need qualifications at Level 4–8. Please refer to explanation on page vii.

The type of person suited to this work

You will need a streak of imaginative humour and strong creative flair to come up with new ideas – sometimes, on a day-by-day basis. Cartoon ideas often draw on situation humour or arise in quick response to headline news.

Even if you use a software art package, good drawing skills are very important. You may have to work to deadlines – creating cartoons for a variety of clients – so need to be well organised, with good business management skills. A good standard of numeracy is useful if you are self-employed.

You must also be able to adapt your drawing style to different projects. As you will be sending out examples of your work to potential employers, you will need to be able to deal with rejection.

Working conditions

Most professional cartoonists work on a freelance basis, either in a studio or from home. This can be isolating as many work alone. Much of your time will be spent at a drawing board or a PC console where you will either sit or stand using the materials required.

Sometimes you may need to attend meetings with clients or potential employers, which could involve travelling long distances.

The future outlook

Most cartoonists work on a freelance basis for a number of employers at the same time. Because it can be difficult to make a living initially, most cartoonists do related work such as design, art teaching and illustration. Some work as animators for companies that develop games and other ICT resources.

It has become usual to develop and promote your own work with the use of home computer design software and the internet. Many cartoonists maintain webcomics – strips and archives of their past work which are freely accessible. Very few webcomic artists receive financial reward. If numerous surfers access their webcomic pages, internet advertisers may pay cartoonists to promote their goods alongside.

Qualifications and courses

- A strong portfolio and relevant experience are usually more important than formal qualifications.
- Most entrants have an HNC/D or degree in an art and design subject.
- There are a small number of cartooning qualifications available through distance learning courses, including a Cartoon Diploma course. These can help you develop your cartooning skills and provide feedback on your work.
- In England, Wales and Northern Ireland, many students take a 1-year Foundation course as preparation for entry to an art and design degree course. 5 GCSEs (A–C) and a relevant A level are usually required.
- In Scotland the first year of an Art and Design degree course equates to the Foundation year.

Other related opportunities

- Animator p129
- Artist (Fine) p131
- Designer p136
- Illustrator p147

Advantages/disadvantages

- Because cartoonists are usually paid for individual pieces of work, they have little job security especially at the start of their careers.
- You would have the satisfaction of creating original work and seeing it in print.

Earnings guide

- Salaries vary widely. It is possible to earn higher levels of pay by doing commercial work for greetings cards and adverts.
- Cartoonists starting out in full-time employment can expect to earn around £15,000–£20,000 per year.
- If you become established, well known, and are in demand for your work, you could earn up to £50,000.
- Cartoonists are usually paid on a freelance, one-off basis. Cartoonists creating work to illustrate books can earn royalties from sales.

Further information

Arts Council of England
2 Pear Tree Court
London
EC1R 0DS
0845 300 6200
www.artscouncil.org.uk

Scottish Arts Council
12 Manor Place
Edinburgh
EH3 7DD
0131 226 6051
www.scottisharts.org.uk

ccskills – Creative & Cultural Skills
4th Floor
Lafone House
The Leathermarket
Weston St
London
SE1 3HN
020 7015 1800
www.ccskills.org.uk

Commissioning Editor

What the work involves

- You will develop the range of books and other publications produced by publishers. This could include researching the books people want to buy and identifying gaps in your company's list of books. Also, you will manage new editions of existing publications.
- Authors will send you publication ideas and manuscripts, and you will need to respond to their submissions.
- You will coordinate the development of individual publications from an original idea to completed book. This will involve meetings with authors and designers.

entry level

To both enter and train while working in this career, you will need qualifications at Level 4–8. Please refer to explanation on page vii.

The type of person suited to this work

It is essential that you enjoy working with people, as you will be meeting agents, authors and others on a regular basis.

The ability to encourage people to complete tasks to deadlines is very useful. Good verbal and written communication skills are important in a job where you will need to get across a clear message.

It is helpful if you have a creative flair when it comes to thinking up new ideas for books. However, you must also have a commercial approach to ensure that your publications will sell and projects keep to budget. As you will be planning new books while managing ongoing projects, you will need to be able to think ahead to prioritise and balance your workload.

Working conditions

Commissioning editors work as part of a team and are based in publishers' offices. They spend some of their time at meetings. This may include travel to other parts of the country or overseas.

In addition to normal office hours, you may have to work late when the job demands it, for example when a publication deadline is coming up.

This type of work can be stressful because of strict publication deadlines.

The future outlook

This is a competitive career area to enter, with most opportunities being located around London, Oxford or Edinburgh. If you enter the profession there are several progression routes to follow.

With experience you could move into a senior commissioning editor role, or take over management of the book list in a different part of your company. You could choose to take on a more general editorial role. A very small number of commissioning editors go on to manage their own publishing companies.

Qualifications and courses

- Commissioning editors are normally graduates with publishing experience gained over a number of years.
- A relevant postgraduate qualification is not essential for publishing but is certainly an advantage given the competition for places.
- As this is a senior role, it is unlikely that a new graduate would enter the publishing trade as a commissioning editor. Most start as an editorial assistant before seeking promotion to editor and then commissioning editor.
- Specialist training centres such as the Publishing Training Centre provide short courses on different areas of publishing and organisations such as Women in Publishing can provide advice and support to women entering the field.
- Entry into the industry is highly competitive and it is important to learn as much as possible about publishing from trade magazines or people in the industry before applying. Experience of writing or editing at a non-professional level can be useful.

CRCI:PD

CLCI:FAD

Other related opportunities

- Advertising Copywriter p127
- Copywriter p135
- Editor p141
- Literary Agent p149
- Publisher p162

Advantages/disadvantages

- You will have the satisfaction of seeing the results of your work in print as a book or publication.
- Developing new publications can take a long time so you will need to be patient.

Earnings guide

- Salaries vary according to employer and geographic location.
- As an Editorial Assistant salaries begin at around £15,000–£17,000 per year.
- As a Commissioning Editor earnings can increase to £27,000–£32,000.
- At senior levels, with several years of experience you could earn around £40,000 or more.

Further information

Publishers Association
29b Montague Street
London
WC1B 5BW
020 7691 9191
www.publishers.org.uk

Society of Young Publishers
Endeavour House
189 Shaftesbury Avenue
London
WC2H 3TJ
www.thesyp.org.uk

Publishing Training Centre at Book House
45 East Hill
Wandsworth
London
SW18 2QZ
020 8874 2718
www.train4publishing.co.uk

Women in Publishing
www.wipub.org.uk

Copywriter

What the work involves

- You will write informative, well-constructed text (or 'copy') on a wide range of subjects.
- You will create copy for websites, company magazines/publications, direct mail, brochures and product information guides.
- Design companies, sales promotion organisations and other companies employ copywriters to write text that promotes their services or products and helps to increase sales.

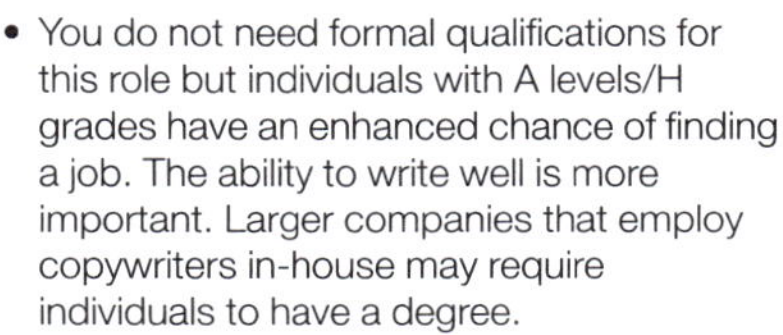

To both enter and train while working in this career, you will need qualifications at Level 4–8. Please refer to explanation on page vii.

Qualifications and courses

- You do not need formal qualifications for this role but individuals with A levels/H grades have an enhanced chance of finding a job. The ability to write well is more important. Larger companies that employ copywriters in-house may require individuals to have a degree.
- Qualifications in areas such as design, business and English can be useful. A qualification or background in journalism can also be helpful.
- Previous experience in an advertising copywriter role or communications role can be of benefit if setting up on your own.
- Distance learning courses are provided by the Institute of Copywriting and other organisations.

The type of person suited to this work

As you will be writing copy for a range of uses, you will need a strong creative flair and a good imagination.

Your copy may be used to promote companies or services, so you will need good business sense. You should be well organised with a flexible approach to your work.

The ability to see projects through from start to finish is important. Clear verbal communication skills are important as you will need to explain ideas, products and services to others.

You will have to accept alterations being made to your work!

Having a good level of numeracy is helpful if you work on a self-employed basis.

Working conditions

Many copywriters work on a freelance basis for a number of employers. Some work from home – others from offices. You will spend long periods of time sitting typing, which can be tiring.

Although you will spend a lot of time using a computer, you will also attend meetings with clients.

You may have to work long hours to complete projects, especially during busy periods.

The future outlook

There are some interesting opportunities available as many organisations need to promote their services and products.

Increased use of websites for promotional purposes means that the need for powerful, catchy text is growing.

However, there is a lot of competition. With good contacts, a strong writing style and a knowledge of your market it is possible to make a living in this area.

Other related opportunities

- Advertising Copywriter p127
- Author p132
- Journalist p148

Advantages/disadvantages

- This job provides the satisfaction of seeing your work in print.
- Copywriting can be stressful because of the need to produce new ideas to tight deadlines.
- There may be some job instability if working on a self-employed basis.

Earnings guide

- Earnings vary according to employer and project. Self-employed copywriters may charge hourly rates, by the day, or for individual projects.
- Starting salaries outside London are around £14,000 per year. London-based, you could start on £17,000.
- With 3–5 years' experience, and when employed by individual companies, you could earn between £32,000 and £40,000.
- Senior level salaries can range between £45,000 and £200,000+.

Further information

Institute of Copywriting
Overbrook Business Centre
Poolbridge Road
Blackford, Wedmore
Somerset
BS28 4PA
0800 781 1715
www.inst.org/copy

Society of Authors
84 Drayton Gardens
London
SW10 9SB
020 7373 6642
www.societyofauthors.net

Designer

What the work involves

- There are many different areas of design to specialise in, all of which require creativity. Here are the major areas for you to consider:

Ceramic designer

- You will design and create ceramic objects on a one-off basis for manufacture or sale in shops.
- Using your knowledge of a range of materials and technologies, you will produce practical and decorative items from clay.

Costume designer

- From original ideas and background research, you will design the clothes and accessories worn by the cast in films, plays and TV dramas. You will make decisions about which fabrics and materials to use
- You could also be involved with making or overseeing the production of costumes.

Exhibition designer

- You will plan and mount temporary exhibitions to display museum or gallery collections or to publicise organisations, their specialist products and services.
- You will promote and enhance the subject of the exhibition by displaying it in an innovative and attractive way.

Fashion/clothing designer

- Using your design sense and knowledge of textiles and other materials you will develop clothing and accessories. This could include articles such as footwear, babywear or sports clothes.
- As well as creating the initial drawings, you may also oversee the manufacture of these items.

Graphic designer

- This area includes producing original images and designs for use in published or other materials, such as leaflets, brochures, websites and stationery.
- You will create designs to meet clients' needs and develop ideas to suit the demands of specific projects.

Hat designer/milliner

- You will create original designs for hats, either on a one-off design basis or for sale in shops.
- The process includes drawing clear plans for construction of hats which you will then either create by hand or have made up in a factory. hand or send to be produced in a factory.

Industrial/product designer

- You will create new products or items as required by commercial, manufacturing and other organisations ranging from household items to specialist technical equipment.
- Using your knowledge of materials, you will devise and develop items to strict requirements.

Interior designer

- You will create a specific coordinated style or look for homes, commercial spaces and other areas.
- Your work will include assessing individual spaces, selecting upholstery, wallpaper, furniture and decorative objects to meet a client brief.

Jewellery designer

- You will create one-off pieces of jewellery such as earrings and necklaces using materials such as gold, silver and gemstones.
- You may design pieces for sale through shops or to meet clients' specific requirements.

Stage/set designer

- You will create original sets and scenery for theatrical productions, film and television.
- Working closely with the production team you will oversee the development and installation of the sets.

Textile designer

- You will create designs for items made out of printed, woven and knitted materials. You could plan and design the work by hand or use specialist equipment and ICT software.
- You may specialise in items such as knitwear, fashion or decorative objects.

Three-dimensional designer

- Three-dimensional designers tend to specialise in one particular area. They may work on the more commercial design side, for example in product or furniture design, or undertake more crafts-based work, for example designing and producing glassware.
- You may also oversee the production of your designs.

Wallpaper designer

- You will create original patterns and styles for wallpapers that are produced to be sold in shops or as one-off commissions. As well as creating the design, you may also have to select the most appropriate production process for creating the intended effect of the wallpaper.
- You may be required to produce a wallpaper design to suit the house style of the company for which you work or create your own designs.

Qualifications and courses

- Entry to this profession is rare without an HNC/HND or degree. A portfolio is also required.
- Mature entry is possible, and a good portfolio can sometimes substitute for qualifications.
- There are many specialist design areas. Some, such as graphic design, interior design or fashion and costume design, can require a degree in the specific subject. Courses with a strong technical element are usually needed to enter three-dimensional design, industrial, engineering or product design, or some of the craft-based fields, such as ceramics or jewellery design. Other available areas of work include costume design, exhibition design, millinery, stage set design, textiles and wallpaper design.
- In England, Wales and Northern Ireland many students take a 1-year Foundation course as preparation for entry to an Art and Design degree; 5 GCSEs (A–C) and a relevant A level are usually required.
- In Scotland, the first year of a degree course equates to the Foundation year.
- With some of the more craft-based design fields, entry may be possible via vocational qualifications including Apprenticeships/Skillseekers. Some of the more technical disciplines, such as product design, may require specialist postgraduate qualifications.

entry level

To both enter and train while working in this career, you will need qualifications at Level 4–8. Please refer to explanation on page vii.

The type of person suited to this work

Regardless of the type of design you specialise in, an ability to develop original designs, a strong creative flair and imagination are all essential skills. Although some of the technical skills needed to operate the different machines such as kilns, sewing machines or engraving tools can be taught, you will still need excellent manual and practical skills, and problem-solving abilities.

Having the skills to draw designs by hand and to use specialist ICT software when required are very important. You should also be able to create objects to scale, using exact measurements of a design, and be able to model or describe them, both from a visual and a practical viewpoint, to your clients.

Patience can be helpful when creating new designs or pieces of work! The ability to see a project through from start to finish is important. Good business sense and the ability to budget are helpful. You will also need to be able to promote your work by communicating with a wide range of people.

Finally, you should be the type of person who does not give up if, initially, people do not like your work!

Working conditions

The type of environment you will work in will be dependent on the area of design you specialise in. You could work in a studio, a workshop, a factory or from home. Many designers work on a self-employed basis and will work the hours needed to finish the job.

Ceramic designer

Most ceramic designers use a kiln to fire their pots, which can make the studio very hot. Clay is a dirty material to work with and some of the chemicals used within the firing process can be harmful. Working with clay is physically demanding work.

Costume designer/hat designer/milliner

After you have researched your ideas and designed them using drawings or computer software, you will either oversee their construction or do the work yourself. You will normally work within a studio with your drawing table, computer, cutting tables and sewing machines. This can be dusty work and the cutting required can be dangerous. As some of the work could involve intricate beading and embroidery, good eyesight and manual dexterity are required.

Exhibition designer

You are likely to work within a studio, designing the exhibition layout and stands, and then spend periods out of the studio overseeing the setting up and dismantling. With smaller exhibitions, you will use a range of cutting and power tools, and different materials, some of which could be dangerous if used incorrectly.

Fashion/clothing designer

This can be very stressful work, especially during the time leading up to the shows. Expect to work very long hours, changing ideas and meeting different people up until the last minute!

During your work you will work within a studio which will include large cutting tables and sewing machines. This can be dusty work and the cutting required can be dangerous. You will also spend some of your time visiting textile producers and clients at their premises.

Graphic designer

You will do most of your work within a studio where you will use the different techniques and materials needed to produce your work. You will combine your time at your computer and drawing board with visiting clients and undertaking research.

If you suffer from certain allergies, some of the materials you will use could affect you, due to their chemical nature and fumes.

Industrial/product designer

Some of your work will be undertaken in lab conditions where you will do experiments and test different materials and designs. You will combine your scientific and design interests to produce different products, ranging from boats to household equipment. Your work environment will be determined by the kind of products and their size.

Interior designer

Your work will be divided between meeting clients in their own homes or premises and working in your studio, or other work space. It could take several meetings before a design is finalised and agreed, and you could be working on a number of contracts at the same time which can be stressful.

Jewellery designer

Jewellery designers often work on very intricate pieces which incorporate precious and/or semi-precious gems. Although you will use magnifying equipment you should have excellent eyesight and keep your work area very clean and tidy.

You will use a range of different metals and shaping, cutting and heating tools.

Stage/set designer

Your work will be divided between being in a studio designing and building models of the sets, and then supervising or being involved in their creation. This part will normally happen behind the scenes in theatres, television studios or purpose-built warehouses. Many of the pieces you will work on will be very large, so you will use ladders and scaffolding.

When creating the original models you will use computer software and different materials to represent your ideas.

Textile/wallpaper designer

You will use computer software and your drawing skills to create textile or wallpaper designs. You will then oversee production of a sample either made to order, or as a design to sell to the different fabric or wallpaper producers. You could spend part of your time visiting or sending samples to different producers which could be frustrating if rejected.

Three-dimensional designer

Your workspace will depend on the materials you work with and the size of your designs. You could work in a small craft workshop or a large studio. It is likely that you will use a range of different cutting and construction tools, some of which could be dangerous to use and handle. Your finished products could be plastic, metal, wood or glass. These can also be dangerous if used incorrectly.

The future outlook

The contribution of art and design towards the national economy is very important. This is because if goods are not attractive, they will not sell, whether they do the job correctly or not. The manufacturing sector now recognises this fact and industrial and three-dimensional designers are very important to these types of businesses.

This importance can be measured by numbers of designers employed today. Around 2.4 million people work in the UK design and creative sector, which is continuing to grow by roughly 6% a year. This is an expanding area of the economy which had a turnover of nearly £70,000 million in 2007.

Around 5% of all UK exports are created and produced by the design and creative sector.

All of this means that design is growing at a steady rate, which is good news for new entrants and existing designers! Also, the UK industry has an excellent international reputation offering progression to work overseas if desired.

Since 2004, design has been the second highest area of employment growth across the whole creative sector, after software and interactive program design. This is the category incorporating all of the jobs listed within this entry.

Although many designers work for design companies, studios or other industrially-based organisations, many choose self-employment, either immediately after graduation or after gaining work experience.

Designers who specialise in crafts tend to set up their own company producing and marketing their own products. This could include running a small studio or shop, for example in jewellery design. A very small number of professionals in this area, such as clothing and fashion designers, gain a high profile through their work. Others work on a freelance basis for large design companies or manufacturing and retail businesses, providing support on a project-by-project basis.

Regardless of the area you specialise in, your long-term success will depend on your talent, drive and tenacity.

The most talented UK designers can choose to work abroad, while others decide to reduce their professional work and take on other related work such as teaching or consultancy.

Other related opportunities

- Animator p129
- Clothing and Fabric Production p198
- Display Designer / Window Dresser p139
- Gold / Silversmith p146
- Illustrator p147
- Model Maker p155
- Sculptor p164
- Teacher p184
- Toymaker / Designer p167

Advantages/disadvantages

- Whether you work in crafts, three-dimensional or product design, this job can provide the satisfaction of creating original work and seeing your ideas being used in a practical or decorative way.
- In many jobs, you will have to develop your own ideas around the requirements of your customer.
- It can be tough to succeed as a designer, particularly in areas such as textiles, jewellery and hat/millinery.
- Working as a freelance designer can mean a variable income, especially at the start.

Further information

Design Council
34 Bow Street
London
WC2E 7DL
020 7420 5200
www.designcouncil.org.uk

CERAMIC/JEWELLERY/TEXTILE

Crafts Council
44a Pentonville Road
Islington
London
N1 9BY
0207 806 2500
www.craftscouncil.org.uk

Department for Culture, Media and Sport
2–4 Cockspur Street
London
SW1Y 5DH
020 7211 6000
www.culture.gov.uk

COSTUME

Costume Society of Great Britain
28 Eburne Road
London
N7 6AU
www.costumesociety.org.uk

EXHIBITION

Association of Exhibition Organisers
119 High Street
Berkhamstead
Hertfordshire
HP4 2DJ
01442 285810
www.aeo.org.uk

TEXTILE/ CLOTHING/FASHION/HAT/ MILLINER

SkillFast-UK (Sector Skills Council for the apparel, footwear and textiles industries)
Richmond House
Lawnswood Business Park
Redvers Close
Leeds
LS16 6RD
0113 239 9600
www.skillfast-uk.org

GRAPHIC

Design and Art Direction
9 Graphite Square
Vauxhall Walk
London
SE11 5EE
020 7840 1111
www.dandad.org

JEWELLERY

Jewellery & Allied Industries Training Council
10 Vyse Street
Hockley
Birmingham
B18 6LT
www.jaitc.org.uk

STAGE/SET

Society of British Theatre Designers
4th Floor
55 Farringdon Road
London
EC1M 3JB
020 7242 9200
www.theatredesign.org.uk

GENERAL/INTERIOR/INDUSTRIAL/ PRODUCT/THREE DIMENSIONAL/ GRAPHIC

The Society for Professional Designers
5 Bermondsey Exchange
175–181 Bermondsey Street
London
SE1 3UW
020 7357 8088
www.csd.org.uk

INTERIOR/WALLPAPER/TEXTILE

British Interior Design Association
3–18 Chelsea Harbour Design Centre
Chelsea Harbour
London
SW10 0XE
020 7349 0800
www.bida.org

Earnings guide

- Earnings vary according to employer and design area. Salaries for designers employed by large companies tend to be higher.
- In addition, industrial/product and exhibition design can provide high-level salaries.
- In contrast, earnings for self-employed designers can be very low, particularly at the beginning.

Ceramic designer

- Like many crafts designers, most ceramics designers begin work part time whilst establishing themselves. Salary levels can be low at the beginning.
- Full-time starting salaries begin at around £12,000, rising to £17,000, but it is possible to earn £20,000+.

Costume designer/hat designer/milliner

- New entrants earn around £14,500–£18,000, rising to £20,000–£30,000 with experience. Working freelance you could get £800 per week.

Exhibition designer

- Starting salaries are around £18,500 rising to £27,000–£35,000 with 3 years' experience. £50,000–£60,000 is possible if you run your own successful business.

Fashion/clothing designer

- Your salary will be determined by your success and the most famous earn huge amounts. However, those starting out can expect around £15,000–£22,500, rising to an average of £30,000–£40,000 with five years' experience. At senior level you could earn up to £60,000.

Graphic designer

- Starting salaries range from £12,000–£16,000 per year. With experience earnings are between £19,000 and £26,000. Seniors can earn £50,000+.

Industrial/product/three-dimensional designer

- New entrants can earn around £15,000–£22,000, rising with experience to £35,000+. The most skilled and experienced can achieve £50,000+. However, most industrial/product designers will earn more than those within three-dimensional design.

Interior designer

- Many interior designers are freelance and earn from £30 to £60 per hour. New entrants can expect to earn from £16,000 to £23,000, rising with experience to salaries that exceed £30,000.

Jewellery designer

- Your salary will be determined by the size of the organisation you work for and your experience. Salaries are normally within the range of £18,000–£25,000. The most successful can earn much more.

Stage/set designer

- This area is very competitive and most stage/set designers are freelance or self-employed. Earnings will be dependent on individual ability and the size of different contracts. They can range from £14,000 to £18,000 when starting. With experience you can earn anything from £22,000 to £40,000.

Textile/wallpaper designer

- Salaries for new entrants start at around £17,500 rising to £30,000 with experience. £30,000–£40,000 is possible if you are a Design Director. If you work freelance, your salary will be based on individual success, reputation and the type of contracts you win.

Display Designer / Window Dresser

What the work involves

- You will plan and design eye-catching window or shop front displays for shops, businesses and other organisations.
- You will work closely with clients to make sure that your designs meet their requirements.
- First identifying materials and props for a window display, you will design an arrangement to create a striking theme or effect.
- You may also provide advice and information to other shop branches or organisations on successful display design.

entry level

2

To both enter and train while working in this career, you will need qualifications at Level 2. Please refer to explanation on page vii.

Qualifications and courses

- There are no minimum qualifications for this type of work. However, many entrants will have done an accredited course.
- Many different courses are available. Degree courses in Visual Merchandising usually require 2 A levels/H grades and 5 GCSEs/S grades (A–C/1–3). Foundation degrees typically require 1 A level/H grade and 5 GCSEs/S grades (A–C/1–3). Other courses include City & Guilds Level 2 award in Visual Merchandising, the Fashion Retail Academy Diploma in Fashion Retail at Levels 1 and 2 and various British Display Society certificates and diplomas.
- A portfolio of art and design work is usually required. Experience in display and the retail or exhibition sector can also be helpful.
- It is possible to gain NVQs/SVQs in Visual Merchandising Levels 2–4 and Design Level 3.
- You could also undertake Apprenticeships/ Skillseekers opportunities.

The type of person suited to this work

As the job involves a lot of hands-on design work, you will need strong creative flair. Your ideas will need to be balanced with those of your client. Planning displays that succeed in attracting customers and visitors requires a strong awareness of what interests people. As your work will often be used to promote services or products, you need to have an interest in business.

The ability to work with a wide range of people is also important. You may have to manage project budgets so you will need to be numerate. Physical stamina is helpful, as putting displays together can be tiring.

Some displays, such as fashion shop windows, require designers who are very aware of trends.

Working conditions

Normally, you will be working indoors with different hand tools, materials, fabrics and the products to be displayed in the window or display. The work can often be pressured due to strict deadlines.

The job can involve a great deal of physical activity and manual work. You will do lots of lifting and be on your feet for long periods, which can be very tiring.

You may have to work late especially in the build-up to holiday seasons such as Christmas.

The future outlook

This is an area of work which is looking for talented new entrants. There are a range of opportunities, for example working for specialist display consultancy firms, large retailers, museums, theme parks and other visitor attractions. You will probably start as a junior and progress to a more senior position. You could also go on to teach or lecture in design-related subjects.

With experience, some display designers set up their own businesses or provide consultancy support to other organisations.

Other related opportunities

- Designer p136
- Model Maker p155
- Store Demonstrator p458
- Store Manager p459

Advantages/disadvantages

- This type of work can be pressured due to tight deadlines.
- You will have the satisfaction of seeing very visible results from your work.
- Many people will enjoy your displays and give you positive feedback.
- You could get the chance to work with animatronics or other special effects.

Earnings guide

- Junior display staff entering the profession can earn around £15,000 per year.
- Earnings can rise to £20,000–£27,000 with experience.
- £45,000+ is possible for top designers at the most senior levels.

Further information

British Display Society
12 Cliff Avenue
Chalkwell
Leigh-on-Sea
Essex
SS9 1HF
020 8856 2030
www.britishdisplaysociety.co.uk

ccskills – Creative & Cultural Skills
4th Floor, Lafone House
The Leathermarket
Weston St
London
SE1 3HN
020 7015 1800
www.ccskills.org.uk

Design Council
34 Bow Street
London
WC2E 7DL
020 7420 5200
www.designcouncil.org.uk

Skillsmart Retail Ltd.
4th Floor 93 Newman Street
London
W1T 3EZ
020 7462 5060
www.skillsmartretail.com

DTP Operator

What the work involves

- You will work with desktop publishing (DTP) software, such as QuarkXPress and Adobe InDesign CS3 to develop publications such as newsletters and leaflets.
- Using software programs, you will lay out pages and organise images and text so that it is easy to read. Depending on where you work, you may help make design decisions and develop entire publications, or work to directions of designers.
- You may also be responsible for checking that the information is free from spelling mistakes and grammatical errors.

The type of person suited to this work

The ability to work with computer design packages is essential. You should also be able to cope with long periods of working at a computer.

An eye for design and the ability to lay out text and images attractively is important. As you are likely to work as part of a team in this role, you will need good people and communication skills.

You could be following instructions from your team or clients, so the ability to listen carefully is important. You will also need to be well organised with good time-management skills as you could be working on more than one project at a time. Paying attention to detail is important to ensure that your work is of a high standard.

Working conditions

You will work within an office environment at a workstation that has a computer. Many DTP operators work in specific design studios while others are employed within offices.

You will spend most of your time at your computer and you will be seated for long periods at a time.

You will usually work normal office hours but at busy times you may have to work late to complete projects.

The future outlook

Companies of many kinds are looking to create high quality publications – often by employing their own staff rather than paying design studios to do it for them. There is a strong demand for ICT-literate people with the right combination of skills and personality, particularly in larger cities. You could progress to managing a team of DTP operators or move into more creative DTP operating. Some DTP operators work on a freelance basis.

With experience, an excellent portfolio and a graphic design qualification, you could go on to work as a graphic designer. It is also possible to work within related areas such as marketing or sales promotions.

entry level

4–8

To both enter and train while working in this career, you will need qualifications at Level 4–8. Please refer to explanation on page vii.

Qualifications and courses

- Minimum entry requirements to become a DTP operator are usually GCSEs/S grades (A–C/1–3) in English, maths and ICT. However, many DTP operators have graphic design or computing qualifications at HNC/HND level or higher. Gaining experience of the software used is also helpful.
- DTP operators who start work straight from school or college usually begin as an administrator or studio junior and work their way up.
- You could take a course in DTP. Colleges and other training centres offer courses in different DTP packages. A Desktop Publishing Skills Certificate at Basic and Advanced levels is also available. Entry requirements vary but the ability to use a computer is usually required. These types of courses can also provide the opportunity to create a portfolio of work.

Other related opportunities

- Designer p136
- Display Designer / Window Dresser p139
- IT Operator p113
- Marketing p151

Advantages/disadvantages

- This type of work can provide the opportunity to develop your design skills and interests, and help you move into other design-related work.
- The work can be high pressured due to strict deadlines.

Earnings guide

- Salaries vary according to employer and location, with the highest being within London and the south-east of England.
- You can expect a starting salary of around £15,000 per year.
- With experience you could earn £25,000–£30,000.
- Freelance DTP operators charge by the hour, by the day, or for individual projects. This can vary from £40+ an hour, or £150+ per day.

Further information

Design Council
34 Bow Street
London
WC2E 7DL
020 7420 5200
www.designcouncil.org.uk

Publishers Association
29b Montague Street
London
WC1B 5BW
020 7691 9191
www.publishers.org.uk

ccskills – Creative & Cultural Skills
4th Floor, Lafone House
The Leathermarket
Weston St
London
SE1 3HN
020 7015 1800
www.ccskills.org.uk

Editor

What the work involves

- You will prepare manuscripts for publication by checking for grammatical errors, spelling mistakes and inconsistencies in style.
- You may also proofread texts before they go to the production team for publication.
- Along with meeting authors and your team, you will also manage your paperwork and budgets.
- Editors are employed by companies or are self-employed, working on texts in subject areas such as science, health, cookery, travel and business. Some editors work on academic texts, for example, medical topics, which can mean spotting factual errors.

The type of person suited to this work

As you will be responsible for preparing texts for publication, you will pay great attention to detail and have a pride in your work.

Patience and a methodical approach to your work are also helpful. Because of the nature of the work, an excellent knowledge of English language and strong writing skills are expected.

If you are working in-house for a publishing or other company, you will need good team-working skills. However, wherever you work you will need to be able to deal tactfully with people, for example when explaining changes to authors' manuscripts.

The ability to manage budgets is useful, as is the ability to work to tight deadlines and cope with pressure.

Working conditions

Most editors work within offices or are self-employed and work from home. Many publishing companies are based around London and Edinburgh, although some are sited in other major towns and cities. You will spend your time attending meetings with authors, designers, printers, illustrators and colleagues, which may involve some travelling and overnight stays.

At the busiest times you may have to work late to meet copy or production deadlines, but mostly you will work normal working hours.

The future outlook

This is a very competitive area and many editors start off in an administrative or related role and work their way up. There is a clear career route within the sector which starts with junior editor and progresses up to commissioning and senior editor levels. You could also move into other areas of publishing such as senior management.

Increasingly, editors work on a freelance basis for a number of employers.

entry level

To both enter and train while working in this career, you will need qualifications at Level 3–8. Please refer to explanation on page vii.

Qualifications and courses

- Candidates may be taken on as editorial assistants or trainees to gain experience. Building a portfolio of work and experience is important.
- Although there are no set formal entry qualifications for this career, most editors are graduates. Relevant degree subjects include English and humanities, and degrees in publishing are also available. To work in specialist areas of publishing, a degree in a relevant discipline is an advantage; for example a science degree may be preferred by scientific publishers. It is also possible to study for a postgraduate qualification in publishing (PgDip or MA).
- The Society for Editors and Proofreaders (SfEP) offers introductory and advanced training courses on topics such as copy editing and grammar skills. Publishing training organisations also offer a range of editing courses which may be helpful. For entry, you are required to have a reasonable standard of English.

Other related opportunities

- Account Planner p125
- Author p132
- Commissioning Editor p134
- Journalist p148
- Publisher p162

Advantages/disadvantages

- The work provides the satisfaction of shaping and improving the style and tone of manuscripts.
- As you will be making sure a publication goes into production on time, this can be a high-pressured job.
- You will meet and work with lots of different types of people during your work.

Earnings guide

- Earnings vary according to employer and geographic location.
- Starting salaries are between £15,000 and £22,000 per year.
- Salaries for experienced editors employed in-house vary between £23,000 and £30,000.
- The most senior can earn £33,000+.
- Freelance rates vary between £15 and £35 an hour, with higher rates paid for more complex project management editorial work. However, the amount of work you have will vary.

Further information

Publishers Association
29b Montague Street
London
WC1B 5BW
020 7691 9191
www.publishers.org.uk

Society for Editors and Proofreaders
Riverbank House
1 Putney Bridge Approach
London
SW6 3JD
020 7736 3278
www.sfep.org.uk

ccskills – Creative & Cultural Skills
4th Floor, Lafone House
The Leathermarket
Weston St
London
SE1 3HN
020 7015 1800
www.ccskills.org.uk

Engraver

What the work involves

- Working with specialist equipment you will create and then insert or engrave images, words or patterns onto stone, glass, metal or wood.
- You could develop your own designs, or be commissioned by individuals to do one-off pieces of work. Sometimes, associations or societies order a whole series of newly engraved commemorative pieces.
- If you work on a self-employed basis, you will need to manage the financial side of the business and promote your work.

entry level

1

To both enter and train while working in this career, you will need qualifications at Level 1. Please refer to explanation on page vii.

Qualifications and courses

- There are no formal educational requirements, but academic courses are available through some institutions. These cover a variety of subject areas.
- For those interested in the creative side of engraving, there are degree courses in metalwork, jewellery making and silversmithing. Entry requirements usually include a portfolio of work, an Art and Design Foundation course and/or a BTEC national diploma in a relevant subject.
- Training is usually done on the job, working with an experienced engraver.

The type of person suited to this work

This is very detailed work so you will need to be patient and conscientious. A good eye for design is also useful in creating your own pieces.

For more specialist engravers who create purely artistic works, an individual style is essential. You will need to have good practical skills and enjoy working with different equipment.

An awareness of health and safety is important as some equipment and materials can be potentially dangerous. If you work on a self-employed basis, you will need the confidence to promote your own work and skills to manage the business side.

Working conditions

Engravers work in studios or factories, which can be draughty and noisy. The environment and tools you will use could depend on the material you engrave. You are likely to wear overalls and use goggles to protect your eyes, gloves to safeguard your skin and ear protectors if using noisy tools.

If you work on stone, engraving headstones with machine tools for example, there can be some heavy lifting involved.

Engravers employed by companies or working in shops generally work between 35 and 40 hours a week during normal office hours. If you are self-employed your hours will depend on your workload.

The future outlook

This is a competitive area as there is a limited demand for glass and metal engraving. Increasingly, the more commercial work is done in shops using machinery, though there are opportunities in larger companies.

Stone engravers are sought by stone masonry firms which are doing less hand-carving than formerly.

It is possible to make a living as an engraver producing work for sale through galleries and craft shops. It usually takes time to become established. There may be some opportunities to work overseas.

CRCI:E

CLCI:EG

Other related opportunities

- Engineer: Craft p203
- Gold / Silversmith p146
- Picture Framer p159
- Sculptor p164
- Stonemason p69

Advantages/disadvantages

- This type of work can provide the satisfaction of producing something attractive and lasting.
- Working with materials such as glass and metal can be challenging and time-consuming.

Earnings guide

- Salaries vary according to your employer and the type of engraving you specialise in.
- You may earn more by working on a commission basis.
- Salaries are likely to be higher and more stable if you are working for commercial organisations.
- Starting salary can be £10,000–£14,000 per year as a new engraver.
- With experience this can rise to £16,000–£20,000. Top earners can expect up to £30,000.

Further information

Crafts Council
44a Pentonville Road
Islington
London
N1 9BY
0207 806 2500
www.craftscouncil.org.uk

Jewellery & Allied Industries Training Council
c/o British Jewellers' Association
10 Vyse Street
Birmingham
B18 6LT
www.jaitc.org.uk

ccskills – Creative & Cultural Skills
4th Floor, Lafone House
The Leathermarket
Weston St
London
SE1 3HN
020 7015 1800
www.ccskills.org.uk

Film and TV Staff

What the work involves

Producer

- Your role will be that of the lead person in film, TV, radio and video production. You will originate ideas, have creative input, get involved in casting decisions and script editing and will generally oversee the complete production.
- Many producers also play a financial role, approaching initial backers and managing the budget throughout production. All producers need a detailed knowledge of the industry and sound business skills.

Director

- Your job will be to manage the process of creating TV programmes and films. This involves overseeing the work and schedules of the team behind the production.
- You will define the presentation and style of films and productions by making decisions about camera work, editing and acting.
- By coordinating the production process you will ensure that the programme or film stays true to its original aim. You will also handle any problems with acting or production staff.

Programme/script editor

- You will define the presentation and style of TV programmes and films by developing content and ideas.
- You will also write and check scripts and programme plans. In the planning stages for a new series, you may also undertake background research.

Film/television editor

- You will create the flow and pace of a production by using ICT editing equipment to put shots together in a smooth sequence.
- You will ensure the continuity and order of TV programmes and films.

Floor manager

- You will be responsible for ensuring that the floor or set in film or television is fully prepared for filming. You will check that technical equipment is in place and that the correct scenery or props are set up for each scene.
- This includes coordinating presenters and actors to ensure that they enter the floor at the right times.
- You will also provide instructions and information to lighting, props and other staff before and after filming.

Production assistant

- You will provide support to the producer and director to help ensure that productions run smoothly and to schedule.
- You will manage a range of key administrative activities, such as organising scripts and filming updates, booking hotels and hiring equipment.
- You may also be responsible for managing budgets for productions.

Sound technician

- You will ensure that the sound quality of productions is of the highest possible standard by managing recording levels from the start to the end of filming.
- You will set up and organise equipment in preparation for filming in a variety of locations, even outside. You will also be responsible for maintaining and repairing sound equipment.

Video recording operator/cameraperson

- You will use camera equipment to accurately film and record a range of television programmes and films. You will work with other technical staff such as lighting and sound technicians to ensure that filming meets production aims.
- You will manage and monitor camera equipment in studios and on location during filming and move cameras around to follow scenes, as required.
- You will select the appropriate camera equipment for each project. Your work will include setting up equipment before each shoot, and dismantling it when a session is finished.

Art director

- You will ensure that TV productions such as films or dramas have the right feel and presentation by finding appropriate shoot locations and helping to create appropriate sets and scenery for films and TV programmes.
- You will support the production team by overseeing staff activities within the art department and manage a budget.
- Working with construction staff, you will plan and develop sets. You could create drawings and plans by hand or on a computer. You will also create new design ideas for productions, as required.

Runner

- Your job will be to provide a wide range of practical help and support to all members of the production team.
- As well as some administrative work, you will pass messages and carry equipment and scripts between offices and sets – often, with no prior notice.

Qualifications and courses

Producer

- Producers need extensive industry experience and most will have worked their way up the ladder. A degree is an almost essential starting point. Some producers may have a financial or legal background.

Director

- There are no specific entry requirements, but most entrants will have a degree or postgraduate qualification.
- Although a media-related degree is not essential, many directors take a postgraduate course in directing or gain valuable practical work experience. Relevant academic qualifications are available, but good experience is essential.

Programme/script editor

- There are no specific entry requirements; however, experience of writing and editing in related areas is important.

Film/television editor

- Candidates may be taken on as assistants or trainees to gain experience. A portfolio of work can be helpful.

Floor manager

- Applicants do not need formal educational qualifications, but GCSEs/S grades including English or equivalent are useful. NVQ/SVQ Levels 2, 3 and 4 in Broadcast, Film and Video Production are available.
- There are also industry-based training schemes.
- For television, experience as a theatre stage manager may be required. It may be possible to take a job as a trainee or floor assistant to gain more experience.
- Some floor managers move to their first jobs after working in another area of broadcasting. In film, many people start as runners, and experience can be very important.

Production assistant

- No formal qualifications are required but entry is highly competitive, and many entrants have qualifications ranging from A levels/H grades up to degrees. Specific vocational qualifications are also available. Good secretarial skills are often required. Understanding of the production process is very important and relevant previous experience is an advantage. Many production staff begin as runners and work their way up.

Sound technician

- No formal educational qualifications are specified, but GCSEs/S grades in maths, physics and English would be useful.
- Practical experience is very useful in wiring and soldering, as well as relevant work experience. It is good to build up a portfolio of work.
- NVQs/SVQs Levels 2, 3 and 4 and industry-based training schemes are available.

Video recording operator/cameraperson

- Any graduate can apply but degree courses in the following are useful: media studies, performing arts, photography and media production.
- Experience and knowledge of photography is important.
- Entry is possible without a degree/HND, and many start as trainees.

Art director

- There are no formal qualfications. However, most applicants will have relevant qualifications in areas such as media or design or the equivalent experience.

Runner

- There are no formal entry requirements for this role and it is often a key starting point into the TV and film industry. However, a good level of general education may be useful, as well as an understanding of the production process.

entry level

To both enter and train while working in this career, you will need qualifications at Level 4–8. Please refer to explanation on page vii.

The type of person suited to this work

Working in the world of film and TV can be very demanding and stressful. It is also very competitive so you will need to be very self-motivated, determined to succeed and able to cope under pressure. Depending on the area that you choose to enter, you will need excellent technical skills and an understanding of the different roles of your team

It will be important for you to be confident, have good verbal communication skills and be able to react quickly and calmly to any crises that may arise. Interpersonal skills and having a sense of humour can help. Team working is very important as on some jobs you could be away from home on location for weeks at a time.

An adaptable and flexible approach to your work is helpful. The ability to keep to budgets can be useful for some jobs. Some also require people who have strong design skills and a creative flair.

Everyone within this sector needs to have a good awareness of health and safety issues as you will be working with electrical equipment, heavy cameras and cables.

Working on set can involve very long days, so a good level of physical stamina and fitness will help you to cope.

Working conditions

You will work in a variety of locations and, if outdoors, you will have to cope with muddy, wet and cold conditions. You will also be expected to work at night, both during- and post-production, in some of the jobs.

You may have to spend long periods of time working on your feet. You could also have to carry, lift and erect equipment, which will be heavy and physically demanding. The hours can be very long in this industry and often include regular evening and weekend work.

This type of work can be pressured due to strict time and financial limits.

Technical and production roles in TV and film often demand high levels of concentration and patience.

You will work both on set and on location and would have to travel as required. This could affect your personal life.

The future outlook

Within the design and creative industries, work in the film and TV sector is growing at a rate of 5% a year. This means it is one of the top three growth areas across the whole sector (interactive games and software design being the other two). The UK film industry provides excellent technical, computerised and special effects to filmmakers across the world. Equally, the TV industry sells programmes to broadcasting companies around the world.

Despite this, entry to the industry is still very competitive and excellent technical skills are expected from all applicants. Perseverance and a determination to succeed will also help with the rejections! Once in the sector, many people successfully work their way through the levels of technical or production crew. Today, there is a strong demand for skilled technologists within the industry.

Many professionals work freelance on a project-by-project basis. Others gain longer-term work within television or film production companies.

You could gain your first vital experience of the industry by getting involved with projects on a voluntary basis or by creating your own films or productions. The sector skills council – Skillset – may provide information on project funding and sources of support (see Further information).

If you are considering entering this sector it is advisable to first consider the differences between the worlds of film and television.

Due to the increase and ongoing development in areas such as digital television, in the recent past TV has expanded more than film. There are around 110,000 people now working in TV and radio. Recent financial unrest and high on-costs for TV companies is leading to a slow-down in the industry with fewer new productions in the pipeline. The British film industry is coping well and still expected to grow, but obtaining finance backing to develop larger productions will get harder.

Other related opportunities

- Engineer: Technician p208
- Lighting Technician p398
- Photographer p157
- Producer (Theatre) p403
- Researcher (Media) p163
- Roadie p406
- Stagehand p408

Advantages/disadvantages

- This type of work provides the satisfaction of seeing the results of your work.
- This is a fast-moving and varied industry which can provide exciting opportunities.
- Increasingly, television and film staff are employed on a freelance or short-term contract basis which can lead to job instability.
- Although you will work with many celebrities, this is not glamorous work!

Earnings guide

- Earnings in this sector vary greatly according to employer and project.

Producer/director/programme/script editor/film television editor/art Editor/runner

- Many TV and film staff are employed on a freelance or contract basis. Rates vary between roles and media area but are usually paid on a daily basis.
- It is possible to gain short or longer-term contracts with television and production companies. Your individual reputation can affect your earning capacity.

Floor manager

- Your earnings could start at £16,000–£22,000 per year. With experience, £23,000–£36,000 is possible. Working freelance you could get £150 per day.

Production assistant

- Starting salaries range between £14,000 and £20,000 per year; with experience, £24,000–£30,000 is possible. Working freelance you could expect around £520 per week.

Sound technician

- Starting salaries are around £15,000 per year; with experience, £24,000–£30,000 is possible.

Video recording operator/cameraperson

- Starting salaries begin at around £15,000 per year; with experience £18,000+ is possible. Experienced seniors can earn up to £35,000.

Further information

Skillset (Sector Skills Council for the Audiovisual Industries)
Focus Point
21 Caledonian Road
London
N1 9GB
020 7713 9800
www.skillset.org

Broadcasting Entertainment Cinematograph and Theatre Union
373–377 Clapham Road
London
SW9 9BT
020 7346 0900
www.bectu.org.uk

TELEVISION WORK

BBC Recruitment
PO Box 48305
London
W12 6YE
www.bbc.co.uk/jobs

Department for Culture, Media and Sport
2–4 Cockspur Street
London
SW1Y 5DH
020 7211 6000
www.culture.gov.uk

FILM RELATED

Scottish Screen
249 West George Street
Glasgow
G2 4QE
0845 300 7300
www.scottishscreen.com

GENERAL FILM RELATED

UK Film Council
10 Little Portland Street
London
W1W 7JG
020 7861 7861
www.ukfilmcouncil.org.uk

Here's Elizabeth Todd's story:

Fashion Designer

Elizabeth was exceptionally good at art and needlework at school and knew she wanted a job that was artistic and so became a window-dresser. She continued to make her own clothes and 16 years ago opened her first womenswear shop, in Blackpool, selling evening wear made by other designers. However, it soon became apparent her clients wanted something unique and so she began to design her own evening dresses. Elizabeth had made her own wedding dress, and when she was asked to design a wedding gown for a customer's daughter she readily agreed. This is when her business really took off. She now has two Elizabeth Todd Bridal Wear shops, in Blackpool and London, specialising in wedding gowns that incorporate corsetry in their bodices, and Elizabeth still does the occasional evening gown to special order.

'At any one time we could have up to 15 clients on the go from first design to final fitting. My company now employs about six people and we also do bridesmaids' gowns, grooms' waistcoats and even some outfits for the mother of the bride. It is hard work but I always knew I could never work for someone else.'

WHAT DOES SHE FEEL MAKES HER JOB WORTHWHILE?

'I love the creation part of it. If it was possible, that is what I would do all of the time: just sitting designing different things. I get so proud of my dresses, I like my customers to get really close up to the shop window when they come for a fitting so passers-by can see them! It is so rewarding. The downside, however, is the stress of having to always watch the cash flow and doing the admin side of things because I'm useless at anything like that.'

Elizabeth is making a good living from her business but is very aware that competition in the fashion industry is becoming fiercer and more cut-throat by the day. She says anyone entering the business should be very aware of this.

'People go into fashion with all these romantic dreams but you really have to be gifted to start with, and these days if you want to go out on your own you absolutely have to have a backer. So many people go into fashion and then find they can't get a job at the end of it, so you have to be totally realistic about your chances. Be single-minded, be prepared to go for it and have the courage to design with your own individual voice because that is the only way you can make an impact on the market.'

Gold / Silversmith

What the work involves

- You will create large and small items in silver and gold. These could include boxes, figures, picture frames and clocks.
- Working with your hands you will use sheet silver and gold, and specialist equipment.
- You may create objects to a commission for jewellers or individual clients or develop your own craft pieces to sell through galleries and craft shops.

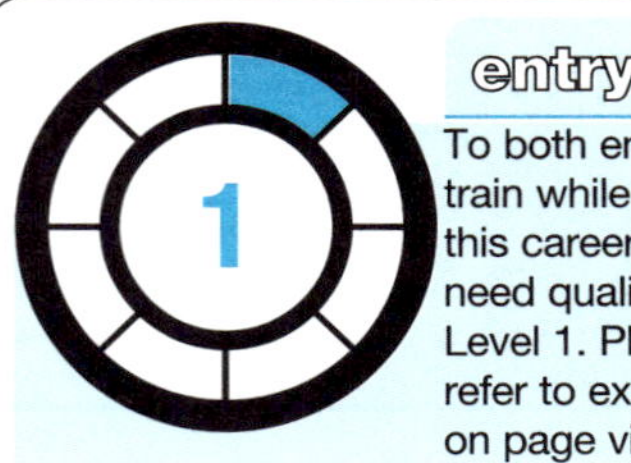

entry level

To both enter and train while working in this career, you will need qualifications at Level 1. Please refer to explanation on page vii.

Qualifications and courses

- No formal educational qualifications are required, but GCSE/S grades in art and design or design and technology are useful. A variety of formal qualifications are available, from City & Guilds certificates to postgraduate courses.
- Training is usually done on the job, working with an experienced goldsmith or silversmith.
- One possible entry point for those aged 16–24 is through an Apprenticeship/ Skillseekers.

The type of person suited to this work

This job demands tremendous dexterity and specialist equipment. A technical and creative approach is useful to help you to plan a piece and decide on the amount of material needed. You will also need to be confident in handling and working with precious metals.

An artistic flair is essential in this type of work, as is the ability to see a project through from start to finish. You will need considerable patience to undertake delicate and sometimes repetitive work.

If you run your own business you will need a confident and determined approach so that you can promote yourself and your products. Financial and business skills are also needed.

Working conditions

You will probably work in a workshop or studio – either with other craftspeople or on your own. You will use specialist tools for heating, cutting, bending and shaping the metals, which can be dangerous if used incorrectly. You will therefore need to wear eye, face and hand protection for some jobs.

Some gold/silversmiths work in jewellery shops and will have meetings with customers to discuss pieces of work.

The future outlook

Most goldsmiths and silversmiths are employed within London, Birmingham and Glasgow. This is a competitive area and the cost of silver and gold means that there is a relatively small market for this type of work. You could work for a specialist company or a jeweller's shop.

With experience and funding, you could set up your own studio/shop to sell individual pieces such as jewellery and ornaments. If you choose this route, your future success will be determined by your ability to produce products that sell and your personal reputation, as well as a strong business sense.

Other related opportunities

- Art Restorer p130
- Designer p136
- Engraver p142
- Sculptor p164
- Watch / Clock Repairer p226

Advantages/disadvantages

- This type of work provides the intense satisfaction of creating attractive and lasting objects.
- Because you will be working with expensive materials, there is very little room for mistakes.

Earnings guide

- Salaries vary widely.
- Payments for individual pieces of work or commissions vary.
- Many goldsmiths/silversmiths work on a part-time basis either for themselves or for jewellers.
- As a guide you could start out as a full-time employed designer earning £12,000+ per year, rising to £20,000–£25,000.

Further information

Crafts Council
44a Pentonville Road
Islington
London
N1 9BY
0207 806 2500
www.craftscouncil.org.uk

Institute of Professional Goldsmiths
PO Box 668
Rickmansworth
WD3 0EQ
www.ipgold.org.uk

British Jewellers' Association
Federation House
10 Vyse Street
Birmingham
B18 6LT
0121 237 1110
www.bja.org.uk

Jewellery & Allied Industries Training Council
c/o British Jewellers' Association
10 Vyse Street
Birmingham
B18 6LT
www.jaitc.org.uk

National Association of Goldsmiths
78a Luke Street
London
EC2A 4XG
020 7613 4445
www.jewellers-online.org

Illustrator

What the work involves

- You will create original illustrations for published material such as books, magazines and greetings cards. You may also create images for TV and the internet.
- You will work with design software, pen and ink and other media to develop strong designs.
- Your work will include attending meetings with clients, agreeing payments and contracts and working to fulfil specific clients' orders.
- Promoting your work to publishers and other potential clients through the internet and through speculative applications will also be necessary.

entry level

To both enter and train while working in this career, you will need qualifications at Level 4–8. Please refer to explanation on page vii.

Qualifications and courses

- Most professional illustrators have formal qualifications, usually an HNC/HND, Foundation degree or degree in art and design. A good portfolio is also required and an excellent portfolio can be a substitute for academic qualifications.
- In England, Wales and Northern Ireland, many students take a 1-year foundation course as preparation for entry to an art and design degree; 5 GCSEs (A–C) and a relevant A level are also usually required.
- In Scotland, the first year of a degree course equates to the Foundation year.
- Training is provided on the job, and can lead to specialisation in such areas as technical illustration or medical illustration.

The type of person suited to this work

You will need strong design skills, a creative flair and imagination for this type of work. The ability to work with computer design packages is increasingly useful but having strengths in traditional artistic skills, such as drawing from life, can be helpful. Sharing ideas and working around another person's vision or 'brief' demands good communication skills.

You will need to approach potential employers for work so a confident attitude is very important. In order to protect your copyright and licence rights to your work, you will need a good knowledge of legal issues. Working on a self-employed basis also demands strong business and financial sense.

Working conditions

You are likely to work in a studio either within a workspace or unit with other crafts people and designers or at your own premises. A few illustrators work in publishing or design houses, but this practice is reducing as more become freelance.

You will work at a drawing board or work station, possibly using a computer. Other materials and equipment you use will depend on the type and style of the work. You will probably use paints and adhesives which may cause respiratory problems or skin allergies for susceptible people.

The future outlook

The internet and email have made it easier for illustrators to promote themselves and find work. It is possible to gain work from clients based overseas. Some people choose to specialise in medical, botanical or technical illustration.

However, this is a very competitive area of work. To subsidise their income, some illustrators also teach, lecture or work in other related areas. A small number write and illustrate their own books. Others make an additional living by selling illustrations and paintings through galleries.

Other related opportunities

- Artist (Fine) p131
- Cartoonist p133
- Designer p136
- Medical Illustrator p153
- Technical Illustrator p166

Advantages/disadvantages

- This type of work provides the satisfaction of seeing your work in print.
- Working on a freelance job-by-job basis can be an insecure way to make a living. Generally, illustrators have a second job to support them during quiet periods.

Earnings guide

- Salaries vary according to employers and individual projects. Projects can range from one image to a series of illustrations. Illustrators may be paid per project, by the hour or by the day. Hourly pay is around £35.
- Income for employed new entrants is around £15,000–£18,000 per year.
- Experienced illustrators could earn £20,000–£32,000.
- The best known can earn in excess of £40,000 per year.

Further information

Design Council
34 Bow Street
London
WC2E 7DL
020 7420 5200
www.designcouncil.org.uk

Association of Illustrators
2nd Floor, Back Building
150 Curtain Road
London
EC2A 3AT
020 7613 4328
www.theaoi.com

ccskills – Creative & Cultural Skills
4th Floor, Lafone House
The Leathermarket
Weston St
London
SE1 3HN
020 7015 1800
www.ccskills.org.uk

Journalist

What the work involves

- Journalists research, write and digitally present stories on subjects such as current affairs, business, health and culture.
- These stories can immediately become live news articles or features for local and national newspapers, magazines, TV and radio.
- You will visit different locations and conduct interviews with a wide range of people as part of your research.
- You will be planning, writing and editing articles to a house style, usually to very short deadlines.

The type of person suited to this work

As you will be producing articles on a regular basis you will need to enjoy working under pressure for much of the time. Also, you should be highly self-motivated and enthusiastic. Strong written and verbal communication skills are essential for this job.

You could be working on a number of projects at the same time so you will need to be very well organised. Having an interest in people and what motivates them is often key to success in journalism. You should also have a good instinct for a potential story. Being able to undertake research through interviews and contacts is very important. You will use your ICT skills constantly.

You will be expected to research sad stories and meet people who are grieving or upset, who will not want to speak to you. This can be stressful so you need to be understanding but persuasive.

Working conditions

Your work will be dictated by the story you are following. You could visit a range of locations in the working day, often at short notice as news stories unfold.

Overnight travel is often part of this job when chasing a story or undertaking research. In addition, you will have to work long, sometimes irregular hours in order to meet publication deadlines. These elements combined could disrupt and affect your personal life.

Whilst you may be part of a wider team, you could work alone for much of the time, or in the company of a photographer.

The future outlook

This is a highly competitive area to enter and approximately a third of all journalists work freelance. Many full-time journalists started work as freelancers to establish their reputations. Most jobs are within London and the south-east of England, although opportunities do arise in regional or local newspapers and other local/national media (radio and television).

It is possible to cross over from newspaper/magazine journalism into broadcast journalism as a reporter or presenter. There may be opportunities to work abroad.

Entry level

4–8

To both enter and train while working in this career, you will need qualifications at Level 4–8. Please refer to explanation on page vii.

Qualifications and courses

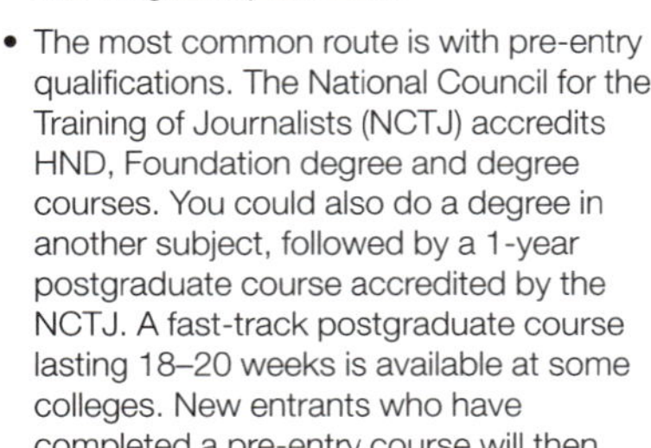

- There are two main routes into newspaper and magazine journalism.
- The most common route is with pre-entry qualifications. The National Council for the Training of Journalists (NCTJ) accredits HND, Foundation degree and degree courses. You could also do a degree in another subject, followed by a 1-year postgraduate course accredited by the NCTJ. A fast-track postgraduate course lasting 18–20 weeks is available at some colleges. New entrants who have completed a pre-entry course will then complete an 18-month training period with their employer.
- It may also be possible to gain direct entry into the profession from school or university, although this route is becoming increasingly rare. Direct entry candidates need a minimum of 5 GCSEs/S grades (A–C/1–3) including English. Candidates directly entering into journalism will often be required to study for professional qualifications. Newspapers often require trainees to study toward the National Certificate of the National Council for the Training of Journalists. Magazines tend to have their own training courses accredited by the Periodicals Training Council. NVQs/SVQs are also available.

Other related opportunities

- Author p132
- Copywriter p135
- Editor p141
- Film and TV Staff p143
- Researcher (Media) p163

Advantages/disadvantages

- You will be responsible for creating news and features that could be read, heard or seen by many thousands of people – often beyond the UK.
- Due to very short deadlines, you will have to produce work under pressure on a regular basis. This can be stressful and highly demanding.
- You might have to get information or photographs to support very sad and distressing stories, which could make you unpopular.

Earnings guide

- Salaries start at £10,000–£15,000 per year at trainee level on a local newspaper. Around £17,000 is usual if starting at a magazine.
- Experienced journalists can earn £22,000–£45,000.
- The most successful and well-known journalists can earn in excess of £100,000.

Further information

National Union of Journalists
308–312 Gray's Inn Road
London
WC1X 8DP
020 7278 7916
www.nuj.org.uk

National Council for the Training of Journalists
The New Granary
Station Road
Newport
Saffron Walden
Essex
CB11 3PL
01799 544014
www.nctj.com

BROADCAST JOURNALISM
Broadcast Journalism Training Council
18 Millers Close
Rippingale
Lincolnshire
PE10 0TH
01778 440025
www.bjtc.org.uk

National Union of Journalists Training
www.nujtraining.org.uk

Literary Agent

What the work involves

- You will respond to publication ideas and manuscripts from authors. Part of your job will be assessing the quality and commercial potential of book ideas.
- You will represent certain authors and will promote your authors' work to publishers and TV, radio and film producers. It will be your responsibility to develop publication and rights agreements on their behalf.
- You will also support and advise the authors you represent.
- Literary agents provide services to writers in a range of areas. These include sport, travel, film and drama, fiction and children's books.

The type of person suited to this work

As you will be acting as the link between authors and the publishing or production world, you will need excellent communication skills. The ability to develop good contacts and a name for reliability is essential.

An assertive approach will be helpful when it comes to agreeing contracts and rights on behalf of authors. You should have a good knowledge of the law and how it applies to publishing as your authors will rely on you for professional advice in this area.

You should also be able to develop good working relationships with authors. It is also imperative to have good business/financial skills and an enthusiasm for books and publishing.

Working conditions

Literary agents are office-based. Some work for themselves whilst others are employed in larger agencies. Although, theoretically, they could work anywhere, most literary agents are based near London or Edinburgh as the UK publishing industry is largely centred around these two capitals.

You should expect to work 30–40 hours a week, including evening and weekends, as some of your work will involve attending social events to network and raise the profile of your authors.

A fair proportion of your time will also be spent in meetings with publishers and authors agreeing terms and contracts.

The future outlook

This is a competitive area. However, publishers increasingly prefer to respond to new publication ideas through agents. After gaining experience in a literary agency you could work for yourself or in partnership in a specialist area such as children's books, science fiction or crime fiction.

Some literary agents move into a related area such as editorial work, rights or sales within publishing. Your success will be determined partly by the standard of the writers you represent but, also, by the quality of the advice you can provide to them.

entry level

4–8

To both enter and train while working in this career, you will need qualifications at Level 4–8. Please refer to explanation on page vii.

Qualifications and courses

- Entrants usually have a degree which can be in any subject.
- Most agents have substantial work experience and/or qualifications in publishing. This may be in an editorial or similar role.
- A degree or postgraduate qualification in publishing can be an advantage for initial entry into the profession of literary agent.

Other related opportunities

- Account Planner p125
- Commissioning Editor p134
- Editor p141
- Publisher p162

Advantages/disadvantages

- You will have the satisfaction of supporting new authors and helping them to succeed.
- As you will earn your income from commissions, you will be under pressure to identify and promote new authors to publishers.

Earnings guide

- Salaries vary widely according to the nature of the agent, the number of authors they work with and the success they have in selling their books.
- Literary agents are paid commission which is usually between 10% and 25% of authors' earnings.

Further information

Publishers Association
29b Montague Street
London
WC1B 5BW
020 7691 9191
www.publishers.org.uk

Association of Authors' Agents
AP Watt Ltd
20 John Street
London
WC1N 2DR
020 7405 6774
www.agentsassoc.co.uk

Market Researcher

What the work involves

- You will undertake research to obtain people's opinions on specific products, services or issues and then analyse the results.
- Developing surveys to analyse public opinion on a wide range of subjects or issues will be part of your job. You may also interview small groups of people, known as focus groups or panels, to assess in more detail their views on a specific topic.
- You will compile the results of your research in the form of detailed reports or summary analyses to be used by your clients, businesses and other organisations.

The type of person suited to this work

This job is all about people and their opinions, so verbal communication skills are essential. You will also need strong writing skills to create surveys, plan interviews and write reports.

You will need to understand exactly what your client wants to know and think up ways to get this information. A logical and deductive approach to your work is important.

Also, as you will be working with facts and figures and a lot of paperwork you will need to be well organised. Confidence in working with numbers will be useful in helping you to perform statistical analyses. Being aware of the marketplace and what sells is also important.

Working conditions

Market researchers work from offices and attend meetings, presentations and interviews. You could work in a specialist market research agency or department within a larger organisation. Some market researchers work freelance.

The job can involve frequent daily and overnight travel.

This can be a pressured role as you will be required to produce detailed information at short notice. It can be difficult working with the public if they do not want to help you.

The future outlook

The market research industry is worth over £1 billion a year. As well as businesses, many other organisations increasingly depend on market researchers to provide up-to-the-minute facts and figures concerning public opinion on everything from train services to trainers!

After gaining experience as a market research interviewer you can move up to research executive, and then progress to senior research executive. With sufficient experience you could enter a senior management role or set up your own agency.

entry level

To both enter and train while working in this career, you will need qualifications at Level 4–8. Please refer to explanation on page vii.

Qualifications and courses

- There are no set qualifications for this role. Employers tend to look for an outgoing personality and enthusiasm for the job, rather than academic qualifications. However, most new entrants are graduates.
- Training will usually be in-house. This generally comprises a 2- or 3-day intensive course, which may award a certificate.
- NVQs/SVQs are available in Customer Service at Levels 2 and 3 and Marketing Research (Interviewing) at Level 1. These may be useful and some companies may support further study.
- The Market Research Society (MRS) awards an Introductory Certificate in Market and Social Research. This can be upgraded to an Advanced Certificate. The MRS also offers a Market Research Society Diploma and, if this is successfully completed, the candidate will be eligible for full membership of the Market Research Society.
- MA courses are available in social and market research or in marketing management specialising in market research. Candidates would need to hold a first degree.

CRCI:O

CLCI:OB

Other related opportunities

- Marketing p151
- Researcher (Media) p163
- Statistician p489

Advantages/disadvantages

- You will work on a variety of projects and meet many different types of people, which can be very interesting.
- You will have to work antisocial hours (at weekends or evenings) on a regular basis.
- The public may not want to speak to you and getting the information needed may be difficult.

Earnings guide

- Starting salaries for interviewers range from £15,000 to £18,000 per year.
- With 3–5 years' experience this can rise to £26,000.
- Agencies pay £10–£13 per hour.
- A very experienced market researcher could earn between £35,000 and £45,000.

Further information

Market Research Society
15 Northburgh Street
London
EC1V 0JR
020 7490 4911
www.mrs.org.uk

Marketing

What the work involves

Marketing executive

- You will coordinate activities and events to promote or raise awareness of a particular product or service through poster and leaflet campaigns, website promotions, developing newsletters and setting up special events.
- Your work will involve a lot of communication with designers, media contacts and venue managers.
- You may also be responsible for planning events and overseeing budgets.

Marketing manager

- You will create marketing campaigns to promote and increase sales of specific products or services. You will also manage the image of particular products.
- A lot of your time will be spent seeking new opportunities to increase profits for companies and finding ways to put these into action. You will evaluate past marketing strategies and use this information to develop new campaigns.
- You will manage marketing executives and other members of staff.

The type of person suited to this work

As marketing is all about getting a message across to people, you will need strong written and verbal communication skills. You will also need to enjoy meeting and working with people. You should have a well-organised approach to your work.

High levels of ICT skills are invaluable for these roles, as you will be using specialist software which will need to interface with the programs used by designers and printers. Having a strong sense of what sells, and why, will help you be successful in this work. Financial know-how will also help you to manage sometimes sizeable budgets. You will need an assertive and confident approach to ensure that projects are completed to deadlines.

Marketing roles demand a well-presented and professional appearance so you will need to dress formally. You also must feel comfortable attending public meetings and different social events such as those of the Chamber of Commerce, to promote yourself and your clients.

Working conditions

Marketing executive

Most of your time will be spent in an office, working normal office hours. You may have to travel to meet clients and possibly have overnight stays. This could be difficult if you have family commitments.

Some executives undertake part or all of their work from home.

Marketing manager

As your work will involve overseeing marketing campaigns you will do a lot of travelling to meet clients and speaking to other professionals (designers, printers, the press, venue/conference managers).

The remainder of your time will be spent in the office. You will work at a computer and speak to clients on the telephone. This can be very stressful work, especially during the lead up to a new campaign launch. You will need to work extra hours, possibly even weekends and including some overnight stays. In some areas of marketing international travel may be required.

The future outlook

Marketing executive

Many organisations and companies who produce products or services that they want others to buy employ marketing executives to promote them. The success of the company can depend on the skills of the marketing staff, so this is an important role within the overall organisation.

Most graduates enter marketing as executives and then progress to either marketing management or into other related work offering more challenges, such as export marketing. This role offers international travel and wider career experience. Others opt for self-employment.

Marketing manager

As a marketing manager your main progression routes will be: to move to other organisations that will offer increased career challenges and higher-profile contracts; to become self-employed or to aim for promotion to a marketing director post.

It is possible to work for companies who are based overseas, or who have offices abroad, if you want international experience. If this is an attractive option to you, then export marketing could be an area to consider.

Qualifications and courses

Marketing executive

- Employers tend to look for candidates with HNDs and degrees, although it is possible to enter the profession through relevant work experience and on the strength of your personal qualities.
- A BTEC National Certificate/Diploma, in Business (Marketing) is available.
- HNDs and Foundation degrees are available in business and marketing. There are numerous degree courses in marketing, and in marketing combined with another subject such as economics, accounting or a foreign language. Other useful degree subjects include business, maths and computing.
- The Chartered Institute of Marketing (CIM) offers qualifications to enable school-leavers and graduates of different disciplines to enter the profession. There are no formal entry requirements for the Introductory Certificate; 2 A levels are required for the Professional Certificate; a degree or equivalent is required for the Professional Diploma.
- The Communication, Advertising and Marketing Foundation also offers a qualification, the Advanced Diploma in Communication Studies. It is aimed at candidates with a degree, but experience in the industry of more than 2 years is also considered.

Marketing manager

- Entry may be via a degree or work experience and professional qualifications. Graduates can go straight into marketing on a graduate trainee scheme. The Chartered Institute of Marketing offers qualifications at four levels.
- The Introductory Certificate in Marketing requires no previous experience. Applicants need to be over 17. The Professional Certificate in Marketing requires 2 A levels or equivalent and candidates must be over 18. Professional Diploma in Marketing requires a CIM Certificate, a degree or 3 years' work experience (one of which should be at managerial level).
- For the Postgraduate Diploma, the Advanced Certificate, a Marketing degree or 6 years' marketing management experience is required.
- Many employers prefer candidates to have a degree.
- Graduates can take a 1-year postgraduate course in marketing or management studies.
- The Communications, Advertising and Marketing Foundation (CAM) offers an Advanced Diploma in Communication Studies aimed at graduates.
- NVQs/SVQs in Marketing Communications at Level 2 and Marketing Products and Services at Levels 3 and 4 are available for people working in marketing.

entry level

To both enter and train while working in this career, you will need qualifications at Level 4–8. Please refer to explanation on page vii.

Other related opportunities

- Account Executive p124
- Copywriter p135
- Customer Services p442
- Importer / Exporter p567
- Public Relations Officer p161
- Purchasing Administrator p577
- Store Manager p459

Advantages/disadvantages

- If you are successful, you will have the satisfaction of increasing people's use of services and levels of product sales, and raising company profits.
- This type of work can be very fast-paced and stressful, particularly around the time of a new campaign launch.

Earnings guide

Marketing

- Salaries will depend on where you work, and the size and type of your organisation. It is possible to increase your earnings by commission or bonuses. Generally, salaries are higher in major cities, London and the south-east of England.

Marketing manager

- Starting salaries for new graduates as a marketing assistant/executive range from £16,000–£25,000 per year.
- This rises to £30,000–£40,000 with experience and additional responsibilities.

Marketing executive

- £35,000–£65,000+ is possible at executive/senior/director levels.

Further information

Chartered Institute of Marketing
Moor Hall
Cookham
Maidenhead
Berkshire
SL6 9QH
01628 427500
www.cim.co.uk

Communication, Advertising and Marketing Education (CAM) Foundation
Moor Hall
Cookham
Maidenhead
Berkshire
SL6 9QH
01628 427120
www.camfoundation.com

Medical Illustrator

What the work involves

- You will create annotated or labelled images to provide visual information to professionals and trainees working in medical care, research and education.
- Developing accurate graphics using media such as photography, video and computer design packages will be part of your job. You will also work as a medical photographer and video producer (digital technician) or, combine all these functions in one role.
- You will have to record images of patients and develop graphics for health/medical publications. You could work in wards, operating theatres, pathology labs, mortuaries and clinical exam centres.

The type of person suited to this work

Depending on your role, you may need excellent technical skills to be able to work with equipment such as videos and cameras. For other roles, you should be able to work creatively yet accurately with computer design packages. Good visual sense and attention to detail is very important.

As you will have to record images of patients, a sensitive and tactful approach is very important. Also required is the ability to communicate with all sorts of people, some of whom could be very ill. You must be able to cope with upsetting situations and sights, for example, if visiting someone who is very ill or if working in a mortuary or operating theatre. An ethical approach to your work is also essential.

Working conditions

You may be based within a group of hospitals and other centres and have to travel regularly between these. During the day you will visit theatres, wards, training centres and mortuaries – all of which could involve distressing sights and intense odours.

You will work within an office or studio to prepare and produce images and visual information. You will also use a computer and software design packages.

Depending on your role, you may need to be able to cope with photographing operations or recording the results of laboratory research.

The future outlook

Whilst this is a relatively small and quite competitive area of work, there is a steady need for accurate medical visual information. Gaining a range of technical skills and experience rather than specialising in one area could open more opportunities. After training, it is possible to progress within one organisation or, you could go on to provide freelance services for medical establishments or medical and scientific publications.

The profession operates a clear progression structure and it is possible to reach the post of Head of Department or Chief Medical Illustrator.

entry level

4–8

To both enter and train while working in this career, you will need qualifications at Level 4–8. Please refer to explanation on page vii.

Qualifications and courses

- Most professional illustrators have formal qualifications, usually an HNC/HND or degree in art and design. Recent government proposals mean that most medical illustrators will normally require a first degree.
- Specialist medical art courses include the MPhil in Medical Art at Manchester University and the MSc in Forensic and Medical Art at Dundee University. Entry requirements for both are an HND or degree in an art and design subject or a degree in a medical or life science along with a high level of artistic ability.
- Medical illustrators usually enter the profession as trainees and learn on the job while working towards a medical illustration qualification.

Other related opportunities

- Designer p136
- Illustrator p147
- Photographer p157
- Technical Illustrator p166

Advantages/disadvantages

- You will work with sick and sometimes distressed patients. You may also have to deal with upsetting sights.
- This job gives the satisfaction of providing valuable visual information to help medical professionals and their patients.

Earnings guide

- £16,500–£19,000 per year is usual for starting salaries.
- With experience, senior medical illustrators can earn around £30,000+.
- Up to £40,000 is possible for a Head of Department in a university teaching hospital.
- Medical illustrators in large universities could be employed on a number of pay scales covering technicians, medical laboratory officers, or sterile services technicians. Check with the universities for more details.

Further information

Institute of Medical Illustrators
29 Arboretum Street
Nottingham
NG1 4JA
01216 272336
www.imi.org.uk

Association of Illustrators
2nd Floor, Back Building
150 Curtain Road
London
EC2A 3AT
020 7613 4328
www.theaoi.com

Model

What the work involves

- Depending on the contracts agreed by your model agency, you could be involved in different types of modelling, such as fashion, photographic or demonstration work.
- You could work in a studio, on location outdoors, at fashion shows or at events such as car shows or conventions.
- Your job will be to show off new clothing or products to their best advantage in order to help potential customers visualise them being worn or in use.

The type of person suited to this work

This is a very competitive area to find consistent work, so you will have to be determined and prepared to deal with disappointment if contracts do not come your way. Above all, you will have to believe in your own uniqueness and take rejections.

Most fashion model agencies have set physical requirements that you will have to meet before you are accepted onto their books. Most models tend to be tall, slender, young and female – however, you can be of either sex and there are opportunities for people who do not meet the traditional size, height and age requirements. There is also scope for models with one particularly good feature, such as hands, feet, eyes or hair, to model specific items.

During your work you will meet a great mix of people from many different countries and cultural backgrounds, so you will have to be confident and have good communication skills.

In some contracts (such as those within glamour or lingerie modelling) you may be expected to reveal private parts of your body, so you should be happy to work with strangers and not be embarrassed easily.

Working conditions

The places you will work will depend on the type of modelling that you do and the nature of the contracts you are offered. You might work indoors within a studio, which can be hot and can involve many hours to get the correct shot, or you could be on location doing catalogue work. You might also work at large events demonstrating cars or safety equipment, or helping to launch a new product.

You will be on your feet for long periods at a time and will always have to look your best, even if you have been travelling from one country to another.

The future outlook

Only the most successful models are always in work. Most are self-employed and have to take up temporary or part-time work when necessary. Although most model agencies are based in or around London, there has been growth in other cities.

To build your reputation, you will have to create a portfolio of work using photos from previous contracts. As you win new and interesting assignments, the quality of your portfolio should improve and more agencies will take you on. This is an industry where fame equals success – both in the work offered and in the financial rewards.

Whilst top models are very famous and can be rich, there are hundreds more who struggle to find work and pay their bills. Most models have to finish their career in their early 30s.

entry level

To both enter and train while working in this career, you will need qualifications at Level 2. Please refer to explanation on page vii.

Qualifications and courses

- There are no formal entry qualifications, but an excellent appearance and personality are beneficial. Most employers also require entrants to have clear and healthy skin, and good teeth, hair and hands.
- A portfolio of photographs is normally required for modelling agencies.
- Female models should be at least five feet eight inches (1.72m) tall and around 34–24–34 inches (86–61–86cm). Male models should be at least six feet (1.83m) tall with at least a 38–40 inch (97–102cm) chest and a 30–32 inch (76–81cm) waist. However, some photographic models are required to be smaller or larger than the usual sizes, depending on employer requirements.
- There are modelling courses which focus on diet, health and figure correction, deportment, fashion coordination, grooming, catwalk turns and movements, photographic modelling techniques and how to work with agents. There are also fashion-related courses which include business aspects.
- Any young person under 16 years of age and carrying out modelling work is required to be licensed by the local Education and Welfare Authority.

CRCI:O

CLCI:O

Other related opportunities

- Beauty p412
- Designer p136
- Image Consultant p425
- Marketing p151
- Store Demonstrator p458
- Wardrobe Assistant p410

Advantages/disadvantages

- Only a few models get the top contracts.
- You could get to see other parts of the world.
- You will be standing for long periods while always having to look your best.
- Although the job has a glamorous side, it can be also boring and hard work.

Earnings guide

- You will probably be self-employed so your earnings will depend on your success in finding regular, well-paid work. Most agencies keep 20% of earnings as commission.
- You can expect to start on around £50–£70 per day, rising to £250–£500+ per day for the most successful.

Further information

Alba Model Information
PO Box 588
Southport
PR8 9BR
0871 717 7170
www.albamodel.info

Association of Model Agents (AMA)
122 Brompton Road
London
SW3 1JD
020 7584 6466

London College of Fashion
20 John Prince's Steet
London
W1G 0BJ
0207 514 7400
www.fashion.arts.ac.uk

Model Maker

What the work involves

- Working with materials such as fibreglass, resin, wood and rubber you will create three-dimensional images or models.
- You will construct detailed and accurate models of buildings and other architectural sites. Also, you might make figures for museums, TV or film companies.
- You will work with clients to develop their ideas into a convincing and practical model, deciding which materials to use.
- Finally, you will plan models using technical drawings or computer software

The type of person suited to this work

You will need a strong creative flair and imagination to visualise and develop models. Producing detailed models out of fragile materials demands tremendous patience You will also need good technical skills. In addition, you should have a logical approach, in order to plan and create accurate work

The tasks will demand great attention to detail. Good eyesight is important in this role. A feel for and interest in design will enable you to create well-planned models. create well-planned models.

You will also need a basic knowledge of maths and the ability to understand technical drawings. The capacity to work effectively with computer design packages is increasingly important in this area of work.

Working conditions

Your work will be carried out in a studio, where you will wear protective clothing to suit the materials and tools you are using. This could include eye, ear and skin protection. Sometimes you may be based in an office, planning models with specialist design software.

As this job involves a great deal of close eye-work, it may not be suitable for those with even slight visual impairment.

Model makers work with chemicals, which can affect people with skin or respiratory conditions.

The future outlook

Most model makers work within London and the south-east of England. Whilst this is quite a small area of work, there are a number of career routes and demand is stable.

You could focus on architectural model making and work for a large architectural practice. Other organisations requiring model makers include museums, creating historical models for display purposes. However, most model makers work on a freelance basis and are paid on a contract-by-contract basis.

Model makers also create the props and figures in all kinds of films including animations, adverts and TV programmes which offers other job opportunities.

entry level

2

To both enter and train while working in this career, you will need qualifications at Level 2. Please refer to explanation on page vii.

Qualifications and courses

- There are no formal entry requirements for this job. However, most entrants complete a model-making course and a portfolio of work is usually required.
- The ability to work with your hands, using specialist tools, is required.
- There are a wide variety of courses available, from a City & Guilds Level 2 Progression Award in Applying Engineering Principles to degrees in 3-dimensional design. Entry requirements vary, but entry is very competitive and most institutions will expect at least some GCSEs/S grades in subjects such as maths, design and technology, and physics.
- Entry via an Apprenticeship/Skillseekers programme may be possible.

Other related opportunities

- Designer p136
- Sculptor p164
- Toymaker / Designer p167

Advantages/disadvantages

- This job can provide the satisfaction of using your creativity and developing original work.
- You may need to create highly detailed work to fairly limited deadlines, which can be stressful.

Earnings guide

- Starting salaries begin at around £13,000–£17,000 per year.
- With experience this rises to around £23,000.
- At senior level with many years of experience you could earn up to £45,000.

Further information

Design Council
34 Bow Street
London
WC2E 7DL
020 7420 5200
www.designcouncil.org.uk

Crafts Council
44a Pentonville Road
Islington
London
N1 9BY
0207 806 2500
www.craftscouncil.org.uk

ccskills – Creative & Cultural Skill
4th Floor, Lafone House
The Leathermarket
Weston St
London
SE1 3HN
020 7015 1800
www.ccskills.org.uk

Musical Instrument Maker / Repairer

What the work involves

- You will repair and service musical instruments such as pianos, flutes and violins. This can involve replacing worn-down or broken parts or checking for the cause of specific faults.
- Most musical instrument makers and repairers specialise in a particular group of instruments – woodwind, percussion, strings, brass, piano, etc.
- Your work will include meeting customers and dealing with requests for repairs or commissions for new instruments. You will take responsibility for customers' instruments whilst they are in your care.

The type of person suited to this work

Musical instruments are complex objects so you will need a good eye for detail and a patient approach. Strong technical skills will enable you to design, create or repair instruments. You will need to be dextrous and confident in working with your hands and in using materials such as wood and glue. A practical understanding of how musical instruments function is essential.

As a maker, you will need good design skills. Your work will involve dealing with and meeting customers so the ability to work with people and good verbal communication skills are important.

Being able to provide information to customers about how to care for and maintain their instruments, along with an interest in music and a good ear for tone and pitch, are also helpful attributes.

Working conditions

You could work in the workshop of a specialist company or from home if self-employed. You will work with a range of specialised tools.

With larger instruments, such as pianos, organs or timpani, you will need to visit private homes and other locations (such as concert halls, theatres or music studios) to do repairs on-site. A driving licence and your own transport will be helpful.

The work requires strong manual handling skills. Some of the specialist materials used in the work could affect people with skin or respiratory conditions.

The future outlook

This is a specialised area of work, but the services of musical instrument repairers/makers are needed by educational music departments, major orchestras, opera houses and theatres, rehearsal studios, retailers, individual musicians and others.

Many repairers/makers work on a self-employed basis and specialise in a specific area such as early musical instruments or classical guitars. Some make more unusual instruments to customer requests. You could work for a specialist company or music shop, making or repairing instruments. Some music shops will publicise local repairers and instrument makers, rather than employing their own.

There will be opportunities to work abroad.

entry level

1–2

To both enter and train while working in this career, you will need qualifications at Level 1–2. Please refer to explanation on page vii.

Qualifications and courses

- Applicants should have GCSEs/S grades in relevant subjects, such as design and technology, plus a professional qualification. These range from City & Guilds certificates to degrees.
- It is useful to be able to play a musical instrument.
- Specific vocational qualifications are available in music technology, musical instrument making, and musical instrument technology and repair. Some courses allow specialisation in certain types of instruments such as strings or woodwind.

CRCI:NJ

CLCI:SAB

Other related opportunities

- Engineer: Craft p203
- Music p400
- Piano Tuner p158
- Teacher p184

Advantages/disadvantages

- This job provides the satisfaction of creating new instruments or restoring an instrument to its former condition.
- Many musical instrument repairers/makers work on a project-by-project basis, which can create some job insecurity.
- If you enjoy making or listening to music, this career has excellent fringe benefits as you could work for some of the best musical talents in the UK.

Earnings guide

- In some parts of the country there is not sufficient work for full-time employment. The following is a guide only, as earnings will depend on your location, the local music scene and your specialism.
- You could earn £16,000–£20,000 per year once trained and experienced.
- £33,000 is possible at senior levels and with lots of experience.
- With few on-the-job training opportunities, most people gain their own experience before setting up a business, or advertising their services.

Further information

Crafts Council
44a Pentonville Road
Islington
London
N1 9BY
0207 806 2500
www.craftscouncil.org.uk

National Association of Musical Instrument Repairers
48 Gallants Farm Road
East Barnet
Hertfordshire
EN4 8ES
01303 269062
www.namir.org.uk

Institute of Musical Instrument Technology
Northfield House
11 Kendal Avenue South
Croydon
CR2 0QR
www.imit.org.uk

Photographer

What the work involves

- You will create photographic images using technical lighting and equipment. By using your eye for design and knowledge of photographic techniques you will create images for a specific project or brief.
- Today, many photographers work with digital enhancing techniques to modify and improve, add interest or illusions to the images they produce.
- Photographers' services are used in commercial and other sectors. These include press reportage for newspapers, fashion/beauty for magazines, food photography for specialist publications, wedding and portrait photography, science and medical photography, and service photography attached to the Police or Armed Forces.

The type of person suited to this work

Whatever type of photography you do, you will need a strong visual sense and an eye for what makes a good picture. Attention to detail is also important. You will need the technical knowledge and skills to get the most from lighting, studio set-ups and, of course, camera equipment! To use the best editing software, computing skills are increasingly important.

Having strong communication skills and a flexible attitude come in useful when discussing projects or 'briefs' with clients or putting nervous subjects at ease. To work on a freelance basis, business skills and self-confidence are essential.

Working conditions

Your working environment will depend on the type of photographs you produce. You will generally either be studio- or location-based. In a studio you could work with still-life, portraiture or a combination. Lighting equipment can be heavy and the work can be physically tiring as you will be on your feet for long periods.

If you work outdoors you could record images for advertising, photo-journalism or more pictorial styles. This can require patience if the weather or light conditions are not correct for your shot.

Commercial photography is often completed to tight deadlines which can be stressful.

The future outlook

This is a very competitive profession. You could start, as many photographers did formerly, by gaining experience as a photographer's assistant. This could provide you with the essential skills and an understanding of commercial and other types of photography, but there are few openings as digital photography has reduced the work of professionals.

When you do gain experience in the profession, you could then progress into freelance work or specialise in a particular area such as press, medical, industrial or food photography. Some photographers work in related areas, such as graphic design or progress into teaching or lecturing.

If you choose press or fashion photography you will normally operate on a freelance basis. However, some newspapers do employ their own photographers. Your success will depend on your ability to take pictures that sell.

entry level

2

To both enter and train while working in this career, you will need qualifications at Level 2. Please refer to explanation on page vii.

Qualifications and courses

- There is no set route from training to employment in this sector. Applicants will need a portfolio of work.
- Candidates wishing to pursue careers as police, medical or press photographers will need 5 GCSEs/S grades (A–C/1–3) including English and maths. One A level/Advanced Higher and relevant work experience may be required.
- A variety of college courses are available. City & Guilds offer awards in Photography at Level 1 (6922), Level 2 (6923) and Level 3 (6924). They also offer Photo Imaging Level 4 (4448).
- NVQ/SVQ Photography is available at Levels 2–4 and Photo Imaging and Photo Processing at Levels 2–4.
- BTEC National Certificates and Diplomas are available in Art and Design (Photography). HNC/HND, Foundation degree and degree courses are available in photography.
- There are GCSE and AS/A2 qualifications in Art and Design (Photography).
- The British Institute of Photography's professional qualifying exam requires an HND or a degree.
- Apprenticeships/Skillseekers opportunities may be available for those aged 16–24.

Other related opportunities

- Artist (Fine) p131
- Designer p136
- Film and TV Staff p143
- Illustrator p147
- Medical illustrator p153

Advantages/disadvantages

- You will have the satisfaction of using your creativity and technical skills to create original images.
- It takes time in this competitive industry to develop contacts, so if you work on a freelance basis you may need a second job to support yourself.

Earnings guide

- As a trainee assistant photographer you can earn £9000–£12,000 per year.
- This rises to £16,000–£30,000 with experience.
- £50,000+ is possible at senior levels.
- Earnings will vary if you are self-employed or freelance.

Further information

Skillset (Sector Skills Council for the audiovisual industries)
Focus Point
21 Caledonian Road
London
N1 9GB
020 7713 9800
www.skillset.org

Association of Photographers
81 Leonard Street
London
EC2A 4QS
020 7739 6669
www.the-aop.org

British Institute of Professional Photographers
1 Prebendal Court
Oxford Road
Aylesbury
Buckinghamshire
HP19 8EY
01296 718530
www.bipp.com

www.cityandguilds.com/myperfectjob

Piano Tuner

What the work involves

- You will check the condition and tonic range of different types of pianos. You will do this by undertaking assessments using specialist equipment.
- You will be making minor or major technical adjustments to pianos depending on the nature of the task. This could range from fine tuning to obtain 'concert pitch' for an imminent performance to significant maintenance work.
- Smaller jobs are often undertaken in people's homes whilst larger tasks are completed at a concert venue or in workshops or studios.

entry level

To both enter and train while working in this career, you will need qualifications at Level 1. Please refer to explanation on page vii.

The type of person suited to this work

You will need a good ear for sound so you can accurately assess the state of different types of pianos. Although it is not essential, a number of piano tuners have 'perfect pitch'.

A practical understanding of how pianos function is also useful. You will use your technical abilities to bring pianos into tune. The ability to communicate is very important as you will visit and work in people's homes, theatres and other venues.

Having lots of patience is needed if you are to identify the cause of technical faults within instruments. Larger-scale repair work is usually carried out in a workshop. This also demands good manual skills and the ability to use a range of tools.

If self-employed you will need financial, marketing and business skills.

Working conditions

You will work between a range of different venues, including people's homes, schools and your workshop or studio. For minor repairs, tuning and maintenance checks you will make regular scheduled visits which will require access to transport for carrying your tools and equipment across a wide work area.

Your studio could be cold and noisy.

Working on a self-employed basis can create some job insecurity, particularly at the start.

The future outlook

There are a number of employment opportunities in this career area. Piano tuners or technicians work in instrument manufacturing companies, music or piano shops. You could work on a self-employed basis, providing repair and tuning services to a range of customers.

Some piano tuners specialise in travelling anywhere that their services are needed, including overseas. Others progress into piano sales and renovation to expand their business services and to supplement their income.

Qualifications and courses

- Piano-tuning courses are available. No formal qualifications are required. An interview and practical test needs to be passed.
- Key Skills in communication and application of number are useful.
- London Metropolitan University runs a Foundation degree and a degree in Musical Instruments which includes the option to specialise in piano tuning and repair. Entrance to the Foundation degree requires 1 A level/2 H grades, while 2 A levels/3 H grades are necessary for the degree. The University also runs a part-time evening course in piano tuning.
- The Royal National College for the Blind runs the VIEW National Diploma for Piano Tuners. Students learn about the tuning and repair of pianos as well as the practicalities of running a small business.

CRCI:E

CLCI:GAD/S

Other related opportunities

- Music p400
- Musical Instrument Maker / Repairer p156
- Specialist Shop Assistant p455
- Teacher p184

Advantages/disadvantages

- You will have the satisfaction of enhancing the condition and quality of pianos.
- Working on pianos in private homes can be challenging, as you will need to be able to make a quick decision about how much work needs doing.

Earnings guide

- Starting salaries are low, but with several years' experience you could earn up to £20,000.
- At senior levels you could earn up to £40,000.
- Piano tuners employed in specialist shops can earn £16,000–£23,000.

Further information

Pianoforte Tuners' Association
www.pianotuner.org.uk

Association of Blind Piano Tuners
31 Wyre Crescent
Lynwood
Darwen
Lancashire
BB3 0JG
www.abpt.org.uk

Picture Framer

What the work involves

- You will plan and create attractive and protective surrounds or frames for prints, paintings, photographs and three-dimensional objects.
- Working with specialist equipment and materials you will create strong, high-quality frames.
- Helping customers choose the most suitable style and size of frame will be part of your job, as will advising them on the most practical and appropriate method of framing and glazing the artwork.
- If you work on a self-employed basis you will need to promote your services to potential customers.

entry level

To both enter and train while working in this career, you will need qualifications at Level 1. Please refer to explanation on page vii.

Qualifications and courses

- There are no formal educational requirements. However, an interest and experience in woodwork or metalwork would be useful. Some GCSEs/S grades (A–E/1–5) can also be an advantage; relevant subjects include art and design and Craft, Design and Technology.
- Training is usually done on the job. Some specialist training courses are also available.
- Picture framers are able to work towards the Fine Art Trade Guild Commended Framer (GCF) qualification, which involves both practical and written assessments. In order to work with high-value items, framers need to be trained to conservation standards.

The type of person suited to this work

Framing services are used to protect valued or valuable works of art, so an interest in art is essential. You will also need good customer service skills. Technical skills and the ability to work safely with potentially dangerous equipment are highly important. You should be able to carry out a range of framing techniques.

Paying attention to detail and taking a pride in your work will ensure that you produce high-quality frames. You will need to be able to work under pressure as short deadlines can be a part of this job. You should also be commercially aware. If self-employed, you will require business, financial and marketing skills to be successful.

Working conditions

You could work in a shop or workshop. When working in the shop you will have to deal with customers who can sometimes be rude or confrontational, if dissatisfied. Workshops can be noisy and busy.

Picture framers generally work 37 hours a week, with overtime during busy periods. Some picture framers work on a part-time basis.

Picture framers work with potentially dangerous equipment such as specialist cutting machinery so you will need to be aware of health and safety requirements.

The future outlook

As there are less than 10,000 picture-framing businesses across all of the UK, opportunities for new entrants can be limited.

Many picture framers set up their own studios or shops and often sell works of art and artists' materials as well as providing framing services. Others work solely in framing and are employed in larger workshops – mass-producing framed prints and mirrors. With experience and additional training in conservation techniques and materials, some framers progress into art and furniture restoration work.

Other related opportunities

- Antiques Dealer p434
- Art Restorer p130
- Gold / Silversmith p146
- Model Maker p155
- Specialist Shop Assistant p455
- Store Manager p459

Advantages/disadvantages

- This job provides the satisfaction of creating enduring and high-quality items.
- This is precise, careful work that demands a lot of patience.
- You will sometimes have to take responsibility for highly valuable works of art whilst they are in your care.

Earnings guide

- Your salary will depend on where you work and your employment situation.
- As a trainee picture framer you could earn around £10,000 per year.
- This rises to £16,000 with experience.
- If working in a workshop or specialist shop in a management role you could earn £20,000–£26,000.
- Earnings for self-employed framers vary depending on location and expertise.

Further information

Fine Art Trade Guild
16–18 Empress Place
London
SW6 1TT
020 7381 6616
www.fineart.co.uk

Institute of Conservation (Icon)
3rd floor, Downstream Building
1 London Bridge
London
SE1 9BG
020 7785 3807
www.icon.org.uk

ccskills – Creative & Cultural Skills
4th Floor, Lafone House
The Leathermarket
Weston St
London
SE1 3HN
020 7015 1800
www.ccskills.org.uk

Printer

What the work involves

- There are different types of printer for each of the range of jobs which are involved in taking the initial text or designs all the way up to producing and folding the finished item.
- How many of those tasks you do and to what degree you will do each of them will depend on the size and type of print company that you work for.
- You could scan images into the text, set artwork using computers and desktop publishing software, proofread sample pages, make the plates for the printing press or maintain the press.

The type of person suited to this work

You will need to be able to work under pressure, have an eye for detail and be able to focus on the job at hand for long periods.

Printing requires people who can work in teams and communicate with each other. It is usual that your work will involve computers and other types of machinery and equipment so you will need good practical skills and understanding of ICT, as well as problem-solving abilities. Print runs do not always go smoothly!

Good colour vision is important and you will need to demonstrate art and design skills to convince customers that you can make finished products look good, whether it be a CD cover, page of pure text or a full-colour brochure.

Working conditions

You will normally work office hours but at busy periods you could do additional hours. Overtime and shift work are available. Your working environment will depend on your role and the firm's size. For example, if you work at the printing press it will be noisy and dirty. In the office/studio it is likely to be clean.

You will have to wear protective clothing when handling inks or maintaining the machinery. Some paper finishes contain hazardous chemicals, so you must observe health and safety regulations.

The future outlook

The printing, packaging and design industry is the UK's sixth largest manufacturing sector. 316,000 people are employed in over 15,000 companies mostly around London, south-east England, Bristol and Leeds.

Opportunities will depend on your skills and the size and type of your company. Although printers cover all the stages of production, the job of folding machine operator (at the finishing end of the process) is becoming a skills shortage area.

With experience and additional design skills, you could work for a specialist press production company, a design or reprographic house or general printers. To run a printing business takes high-level business skills, including accounting and sales.

entry level

1–2

To both enter and train while working in this career, you will need qualifications at Level 1–2. Please refer to explanation on page vii.

Qualifications and courses

- Although there are no set entry requirements for this career, GCSEs/S grades (A–C/1–3) in English, maths, science and computer studies are an advantage.
- You can study a relevant college course prior to entry. A BTEC First Diploma and National Award, Certificate and Diploma are available in Printing. GCSEs/S grades (A–C/1–3) are required for entry to these courses. Degrees, HNDs and Foundation degrees are available in subjects such as digital media for publishing and print, print management, print media and digital design, graphic communication. The normal minimum entry requirements are 1 A level/2 H grades or equivalent for an HND/Foundation degree, 2 A levels/3 H grades or equivalent for a degree course.
- Apprenticeships/Skillseekers may be available for candidates aged 16–24.
- New entrants receive on-the-job training and may also be able to study part time towards a qualification. City and Guilds offer an NVQ at Levels 2 and 3 in Printing, and a vocational certificate (C&G 5261) in Printing and Graphic Communication. NVQs/SVQs are available in Pre-Press and Machine.

CRCI:PD

CLCI:SAR

Other related opportunities

- CAD Draughtsman / Woman p197
- DTP Operator p140
- Publisher p162
- Signwriter / Signmaker p165

Advantages/disadvantages

- This job combines creative and artistic skills with technical and computer aided design.
- You might have to move to other parts of the country for promotion.
- Some printing jobs have become skills shortage areas.
- Many companies now produce high quality publications in-house, so printers need to work with large volumes or specialist niche markets to make a profit.

Earnings guide

- As a trainee you can expect to earn between £12,000 and £16,000 per year.
- With experience you could expect to earn £20,000–£27,500.

Further information

www.cityandguilds.com/myperfectjob

British Printing Industries Federation
Farrindon Point
29/35 Farringdon Road
London
EC1M 3JF
0870 240 4085
www.britishprint.com

Institute of Paper, Printing and Publishing
Runnymede Malthouse
off Hummer Road
Egham
Surrey
TW20 9BD
0870 330 8625
www.ip3.org.uk

Scottish Print Employers Federation
48 Palmerston Place
Edinburgh
Scotland
EH12 5DE
0131220 4353
www.spef.org.uk

Public Relations Officer

What the work involves

- You will manage the image and reputation of organisations by writing publicity materials, studying and advising clients and responding to enquiries or complaints.
- It will be important that you develop and maintain positive working relationships with the local, national and relevant trade press and TV news reporters.
- Your job may also involve giving presentations and organising events to increase public awareness of the company or organisation you work for.
- Public relations (PR) officers work in public relations or communications departments in large organisations and PR companies. Some work on a freelance basis.

The type of person suited to this work

PR is all about maintaining a positive image, so you will need a confident approach and a well-presented appearance. You will be a strong communicator and enjoy liaising with a wide range of people, although you may rely on a team to keep you up-to-date with activities and successes within your organisation. Written communication and research skills are essential, so good ICT skills are highly important.

You will need to be able to cope with pressure. You should also have a flexible approach in a job where you will manage several projects at once. Being well organised will help you keep on top of a variety of phone-calls, information enquiries and other tasks. Financial management skills are also useful.

Working conditions

Most of your work will be within an office where you will have a workstation with computer, access to office equipment and your phone. You will have meetings with clients, colleagues or other professionals.

Although you will work normal office hours, longer hours are common in this job, particularly in busy periods.

On a regular basis, you will need to travel to attend meetings, special events and presentations. These could be in the evenings or at weekends and might involve an overnight stay. Working for global companies or high-profile charities may mean some overseas travel.

The future outlook

With businesses, major corporations, the government and other organisations seeking to promote their services and products, PR is a growing industry. However, competition in this area is strong, with often hundreds of well-qualified applicants for one post. The normal progression route within PR is to work as a PR assistant and then as an account executive, followed by a move into a senior role.

It is possible to work abroad either within an existing organisation or by moving to one based overseas or with offices abroad. With experience, some PR professionals set up their own companies or work freelance for other organisations.

Other related opportunities

- Account Executive p124
- Account Planner p125
- Copywriter p135
- Journalist p148
- Marketing p151
- Road Safety Officer p583

Advantages/disadvantages

- There can be opportunities to take part in high-profile campaigns.
- This job can be pressured due to the speed of information releases and the range of activities you will have to juggle.
- If working for a high-profile organisation, you may have to be on call to respond to unexpected situations or emergencies.

entry level

To both enter and train while working in this career, you will need qualifications at Level 4–8. Please refer to explanation on page vii.

Qualifications and courses

- Most entrants to this profession are graduates.
- Degrees are available in relevant subjects, such as public relations and marketing. There is also a Foundation degree in business (public relations).
- Entry is highly competitive and a postgraduate qualification and previous work experience are an advantage. Work experience may be gained with a charity or voluntary organisation.
- Employers provide training, and some have graduate training schemes.
- The Chartered Institute of Public Relations (IPR) offers professional qualifications. Entry requirements for the CIPR Advanced Certificate are a first degree or 2 years' experience and 5 GCSEs/S grades (A–C/1–3), including English language.
- The Public Relations Consultants Association offers a Diploma in Public Relations Consultancy Management. A degree or 2 years' experience in a senior role is required.
- The Communication, Advertising and Marketing Foundation (CAM) offers qualifications. The Advanced Certificate requires a degree or relevant experience and 5 GCSEs/S grades (A–C/1–3), including English and maths or equivalent. For the Higher Diploma, experience and a good educational background are required.

Earnings guide

- Starting salaries are usually around £14,000–£24,000 per year.
- This rises to £26,000–£36,000 with experience.
- £40,000–£100,000 is possible as a senior manager/director in a large company.
- The type of organisation you work for will affect your earnings. The voluntary and charity sector tend to pay less than public or government organisations.

Further information

Chartered Institute of Public Relations
CIPR Public Relations Centre
32 St James's Square
London
SW1Y 4JR
020 7766 3333
www.ipr.org.uk

Communication, Advertising and Marketing Education (CAM) Foundation
Moor Hall
Cookham
Maidenhead
Berkshire
SL6 9QH
01628 427120
www.camfoundation.com

Publisher

What the work involves

- You will plan and manage ranges or lists of books, magazines or ICT resources produced by your department or company.
- You will develop ideas for new publications and respond to book proposals from authors. You will also oversee the entire process of developing new publications.
- Responsible for keeping individual projects to budget, you will ensure that items are produced on time.
- You may also be responsible for developing marketing strategies to increase publication sales from your catalogue.

entry level

To both enter and train while working in this career, you will need qualifications at Level 4–8. Please refer to explanation on page vii.

The type of person suited to this work

You will need a strong interest in producing books and publications that people and businesses will buy. As you will liaise closely with authors and colleagues, you should enjoy meeting and working with a variety of people. You will also need strong written and verbal communication skills.

An assertive and confident personality can be useful in making sure that projects are completed to schedule. A strong interest in publishing and a creative flair will help you to develop new publications to occupy small niches in the market. You must be well organised and able to plan ahead. Financial management skills will help you to ensure that publications are produced within budget.

Qualifications and courses

- The majority of entrants into publishing have gained a degree. Relevant experience can be very helpful, although some publishing companies do advertise for trainees with no experience necessary.
- Given the competition for places in the publishing industry, a relevant postgraduate qualification may be helpful.
- A growing number of NVQ/SVQ qualifications are becoming available in this area.
- Specialist training centres such as the Publishing Training Centre provide short courses on different areas of publishing, and organisations such as Women in Publishing can provide advice and support to women entering this field.

Working conditions

Most of your work will take place within an office of a company or organisation. You will attend meetings and work at a computer. Much of your work will involve talking to authors, colleagues, designers, ICT specialists and printers either face to face, by email or on the phone.

Although your working week will be normal office hours, you can expect to work late at times, occasionally attending evening events. Business trips, including overnight stays, are a possibility and you could travel abroad.

The future outlook

Publishers are employed by specialist business, professional and educational companies as well as publishing houses, to develop and sell publications. In all sectors, publishing can be a competitive area to get into.

Some people go into this area from a sales/marketing background. With experience, you can move from publishing into a number of related business, marketing or sales roles.

It is possible to set up your own publishing company, although the market is well covered and profit margins narrow. Currently, the area of greatest expansion is that offered by the internet and digital publishing.

CRCI:PD

CLCI:FAD

Other related opportunities

- Commissioning Editor p134
- Editor p141
- Film and TV Staff p143
- Literary Agent p149

Advantages/disadvantages

- This type of job provides the satisfaction of seeing the results of your work in print.
- Because of strict deadlines, this job can be demanding.
- In many positions, you will be responsible for coming up with strategies to increase your company's publications sales, which can be stressful.
- You will meet and work with an interesting cross-section of people.

Earnings guide

- Salaries can vary depending on the size and type of employer. Commission and productivity bonuses can be paid, so the more books that are sold, the higher potential earnings can be.
- Starting salaries in editorial roles can be around £16,000–£25,000 per year (depending on the role).
- With experience you could earn up to £35,000.
- Senior managers and directors of a large publishing company can earn between £48,000 and £80,000.

Further information

Publishers Association
29b Montague Street
London
WC1B 5BW
020 7691 9191
www.publishers.org.uk

Society of Young Publishers
Endeavour House
189 Shaftesbury Avenue
London
WC2H 3TJ
www.thesyp.org.uk

Publishing Training Centre at Book House
45 East Hill
Wandsworth
London
SW18 2QZ
020 8874 2718
www.train4publishing.co.uk

Women in Publishing
www.wipub.org.uk

Researcher (Media)

What the work involves

- Researchers develop TV and radio programmes and documentary films by gathering and checking information on specific subjects, people or places.
- You will use the internet and phone, conduct face-to-face interviews and visit different locations to do your research.
- It will be your job to research guests and programme contributors as well as to find relevant images, film clips and music. You could also write and edit programme scripts.
- You will brief the production team on the specific subjects covered by your research in preparation for filming.

The type of person suited to this work

The ability to find accurate, relevant information quickly is central to this role. To do this you will need a creative flair and the ability to think big to develop programme ideas. A flexible approach will help you balance varied tasks and unsociable hours.

Strength in written and verbal communication will enable you to work as part of a production team and to get the most from your research. Tight deadlines require the ability to work well under pressure. You will also need to be well organised to be able to manage your work. As you will be responsible for gaining permission to access and make use of information, you will need a clear understanding of the law.

Working conditions

Media researchers are based in offices or studios to undertake their desk research. They also spend time on research trips to locations in the UK or overseas.

The work usually needs to be completed to strict deadlines which can create a pressured, but fast-moving and interesting working environment.

It is likely that you would have to work at weekends and in the evenings on a regular basis.

The future outlook

Whilst this is a competitive area to get into, researchers are employed in many areas of the media including radio, production companies, television and film companies. Researchers normally provide the information for factual rather than drama-based productions; this can limit the volume of work available.

With experience, you could progress into a role as an assistant producer and then on to working as a producer/programme director.

Many researchers work freelance, getting paid on a contract-by-contract basis.

Others specialise in areas such as documentaries on wildlife, architecture, social history, travel, while others concentrate on picture research.

entry level

4–8

To both enter and train while working in this career, you will need qualifications at Level 4–8. Please refer to explanation on page vii.

Qualifications and courses

- Graduates are preferred, and subjects such as legal studies, history, journalism and media studies are useful. Relevant work experience and evidence of research skills can be accepted in some cases.
- Work experience is very important.
- IT skills and a driving licence are essential.
- Many researchers have experience in other areas of the industry or journalism. A good knowledge of current affairs and media practice can be an advantage.

Other related opportunities

- Film and TV Staff p143
- Historian p320
- Journalist p148
- Researcher p328

Advantages/disadvantages

- You will have to work long and often unsociable hours, which can affect family and personal life.
- This is a varied job in a fast-moving industry. You could get the opportunity to travel to a range of places.

Earnings guide

- Trainee starting salaries are around £14,000–£16,000 per year.
- £22,000–£26,000 is possible with experience. Specialists could earn up to £38,000.
- Freelance researchers can earn from £180 to £420 a day, depending on experience and employer.

Further information

Skillset (Sector Skills Council for the audiovisual industries)
Prospect House
80–110 New Oxford Street
London
WC1A 1HB
08080 300900
www.skillset.org

Research Centre for Television and Interactivity
227 West George Street
Glasgow
G2 2ND
0141 568 7113
www.researchcentre.co.uk

Sculptor

What the work involves

- You will plan, develop scale-models and create small or large three-dimensional works of art (or sculptures).
- You will use different artistic techniques, depending on your style, to develop sculptures.
- You will promote and sell your work through art galleries, studios and specialist shops. Recognised, acclaimed sculptors specialise in creating pieces to commissions, for public spaces or company buildings.
- Sculptors create work with a variety of materials to suit their style, such as wood, clay, stone, bronze, steel and marble.

entry level

To both enter and train while working in this career, you will need qualifications at Level 4–8. Please refer to explanation on page vii.

Qualifications and courses

- There is no set career path, but an HNC/HND or degree in art and design can be an advantage. Degrees in fine art, specialising in sculpture, are available.
- In England, Wales and Northern Ireland, many students take a 1-year Foundation course as preparation for entry to an art and design degree. Five GCSEs (A–C) and a relevant A level are usually required.
- In Scotland, the first year of a degree course equates to the Foundation year.
- Very few paid positions or commissions are available, and a strong portfolio is essential.

The type of person suited to this work

You will be creating original works of art, so will need a strong creative flair, imagination and your own style. It can take intense focus over long periods to develop a sculpture from an original idea to the completed work. Some technical processes and materials are challenging to work with, so patience is essential. You will also need good practical and design skills and an understanding of different materials.

As you are likely to be self-employed, you will need good financial and business skills. Confidence and a belief in yourself will be essential. The ability to communicate clearly with gallery owners and potential clients will be very useful.

Working conditions

You will spend most of your time working in your studio developing and creating your work. How clean that environment is will depend on your chosen materials. Many sculptors use plaster or clay to create their prototypes, which can be dusty.

As you will be using your hands, specialist tools and equipment, manual dexterity is essential. You may also use scaffolding, ladders and heavy lifting equipment so an awareness of health and safety will be essential.

You will need to work with some products that can affect those with skin and respiratory conditions.

The future outlook

It is often difficult to make a living from sculpting, especially at the beginning. You will need to make the most of arts support networks and agencies that exist to develop and promote your work. You could sell work through galleries, shows, shops and studios, or a dedicated website.

Some sculptors have second jobs teaching art or sculpture. Others work with community organisations, building up portfolios and contacts in specialist areas such as public art.

CRCI:E

CLCI:E

Other related opportunities

- Artist (Fine) p131
- Designer p136
- Model Maker p155

Advantages/disadvantages

- This type of work provides the satisfaction of creating unique and lasting objects.
- It can be tough starting a career in this area and you may need a second job to support yourself.

Earnings guide

- It is possible to earn a regular income from your work but this is more likely with experience. Most sculptors have another source of income.
- As a full-time trainee you can expect to earn around £14,000+ per year.
- Experienced masons could get up to £24,000, with senior stonemasons earning £27,000+.
- A sculpture can sell for anything between £50 and £30,000 or more. However, the higher ranges are usually paid to well-known sculptors.

Further information

Arts Council of England
2 Pear Tree Court
London
EC1R 0DS
0845 300 6200
www.artscouncil.org.uk

Scottish Arts Council
12 Manor Place
Edinburgh
EH3 7DD
0131 226 6051
www.scottisharts.org.uk

Royal British Society of Sculptors
108 Old Brompton Road
London
SW7 3RA
020 7373 5554
www.rbs.org.uk

Crafts Council
44a Pentonville Road
Islington
London
N1 9BY
0207 806 2500
www.craftscouncil.org.uk

Signwriter / Signmaker

What the work involves

- You will design, plan and produce signs with graphic images, lettering and logos to publicise companies, attract customers and draw attention to specific locations.
- You will work closely with customers to develop appropriate, attractive designs that match their requirements.
- Signwriters/signmakers work for a range of companies and organisations, producing signs for shop fronts, roadsides, hospitals, vehicles and even boats!

entry level

To both enter and train while working in this career, you will need qualifications at Level 1. Please refer to explanation on page vii.

The type of person suited to this work

As you will be creating signs to attract, interest or warn people, you will need strong graphic design skills. A creative flair and good drawing skills are also important. You will need a good understanding of the materials you work with and good practical and manual skills.

You will need to pay attention to detail and have a logical approach to ensure that your signs are well produced and precise. Technical skills will allow you to work with a range of equipment. ICT skills are increasingly important in this area. Good written and verbal communication skills will help you to meet clients' requirements accurately and avoid expensive errors.

Working conditions

You could work within a studio or manufacturing site, which can get messy and noisy. You may attend meetings with customers. Much of your time will be spent drafting signs at a computer using special software.

You may work with large or small-scale specialist equipment, with printing inks and chemical finishes, which can affect people with skin or respiratory conditions.

Sometimes, you will make site visits to ensure that your signs will be highly visible.

The future outlook

This is a fairly competitive area; however, the demand for high-quality signs from a range of organisations means that there are many opportunities. You could work in the more commercial side of signwriting, within a specialist company on the design or manufacturing side. Or you could work within the more creative, hand-crafted side of the industry.

Some signwriters go into set design for theatre. With experience, you could start your own business – perhaps specialising in pub or restaurant signs.

Qualifications and courses

- There are no formal educational requirements, but relevant vocational qualifications can be useful. NVQs/SVQs are available in Signmaking.
- Training is usually done on the job.
- Many employers offer Apprenticeships/ Skillseekers for people aged 16–24. Applicants normally require 4 GCSEs/S grades (A–D/1–4), including maths, English language, a science and an art and design subject, or other evidence of aptitude and achievement.
- It is also possible to take a full- or part-time course in signwriting and signmaking. Or you can specialise in this area after taking a general Art and Design course.

Other related opportunities

- Cartoonist p133
- Designer p136

Advantages/disadvantages

- This kind of work can provide some opportunities to work creatively and use your imagination to help customers, for example when designing a company logo.
- You may travel to visit a range of locations, to take measurements or photographs.
- You can work abroad as a signwriter.

Earnings guide

- Trainees are most likely to start on the national minimum wage.
- With experience, signwriters can earn £17,000–£24,000 per year.
- With management responsibilities you could earn up to £30,000.
- Self-employed signwriters will earn more.

Further information

British Sign and Graphics Association
5 Orton Enterprise Centre
Bakewell Road
Peterborough
Cambridgeshire
PE2 6XU
01733 230033
www.bsga.co.uk

ccskills – Creative & Cultural Skills
4th Floor
Lafone House
The Leathermarket
Weston St
London
SE1 3HN
020 7015 1800
www.ccskills.org.uk

Technical Illustrator

What the work involves

- You will design graphics or illustrations to accompany and clarify often complex technical information.
- Creating technically accurate images using specialist IT design software to suit clients' requirements will be part of your job.
- You will meet with clients to discuss individual projects and provide suggestions about the clearest ways to illustrate their information.
- Technical illustrators create key visual information for product and systems manuals, training information, presentations and technical websites.

The type of person suited to this work

You will need strong design and technical drawing skills to plan and create exact images. In order to create accurate, specific images it will be essential to pay close attention to detail. You should also be able to work well with computer design software. As you will create images of a variety of systems and products, you will need a strong interest in how and why things work. An ability to understand the aim of a particular project is very important.

As many technical illustrators work on a self-employed basis, you will need the confidence to promote your services as well as good business sense.

Working conditions

For most of your work you will be based in an office where you will do your 2-D designs and visual images and attend meetings with clients and colleagues. When doing your illustrating, it is likely that you will spend a lot of time working on a computer or possibly at a drawing board.

For some jobs you may make site visits to view the systems or equipment that you are illustrating.

The future outlook

This is a competitive area. You could work, as many technical illustrators do, on a self-employed basis. However, it can take time to build up contacts and regular work. Some technical illustrators work as team members within specialist publishing or graphics/illustrations companies.

There are a very limited number of opportunities working for scientific or technical publishers. Some technical illustrators go into teaching and lecturing, while others take further qualifications and become packaging and product designers.

entry level

To both enter and train while working in this career, you will need qualifications at Level 4–8. Please refer to explanation on page vii.

Qualifications and courses

- Most professional illustrators have formal qualifications, usually an HNC/HND or degree in Art and Design.
- In England, Wales and Northern Ireland, many students take a 1-year Foundation course as preparation for entry to an art and design degree; 5 GCSEs (A–C) and a relevant A level are also usually required.
- In Scotland, the first year of a degree course equates to the Foundation year.
- Training is provided on the job, and can lead to specialisation in such areas as technical illustration or medical illustration.
- There are two specialist 3-year degrees in Technical Illustration: Information Illustration, and Scientific and Natural History Illustration run by Blackpool and the Fylde College. 2 A levels/3 H grades may be required, but applicants without academic qualifications who can demonstrate sufficient aptitude are also considered.

CRCI:E

CLCI:ED

Other related opportunities

- Architect p36
- Architectural Technician / Technologist p38
- Designer p136
- Illustrator p147
- Medical Illustrator p153
- CAD Draughtsman/woman p197

Advantages/disadvantages

- Many technical illustrators work on a self-employed basis. It can be difficult to make a full-time living from this, especially at the beginning.
- You may have to work to short deadlines, which can be stressful.

Earnings guide

- Salaries vary according to employer.
- In a full-time job after training, you could be earning £15,500+ per year.
- With 5 to 10 years' experience this can rise to £45,000 depending on the work available.
- If working on a self-employed basis, you would be paid on an hourly or project-by-project basis to be agreed between yourself and the contractor. This is normally around £35 per hour.

Further information

Institute of Scientific and Technical Communicators (ISTC)
PO Box 522
Peterborough
PE2 5WX
01733 390141
www.istc.org.uk

Toymaker / Designer

What the work involves

- You will design, plan, test and create toys for babies, children and even adults! Your products could be eye-catching and ornamental, educational or just for fun.
- As a traditional toymaker, you could use early designs to make traditional toys by hand, such as doll's houses and rocking horses.
- You may plan and create modern toys that are sold in high-street shops for toy manufacturing companies.
- You will spend time promoting your work and design services to clients and customers. Your work could be sold in shops or at craft fairs and toy fairs.

The type of person suited to this work

As you will be developing original ideas, you will need a strong creative flair. Practical design skills and an active imagination will help you create long-lasting and functional toys from your designs. A genuine interest in how individuals respond to toys will help you design appealing items that sell well.

If creating objects by hand, as many toymakers do, you will need good manual handling skills and an understanding of the materials you work with. It is important to work to a high standard to ensure that your toys meet legal safety requirements. If self-employed, you will also need good business and financial skills and the confidence to promote your work.

Working conditions

Most toymakers/designers spend a lot of time in a workshop, planning and developing their products. Here you will use your tools, equipment and different materials. Some of them can be dangerous so you will need to be aware of health and safety regulations and of the need to wear protective clothing and masks.

If employed as a toy designer by a toy production company, you may work purely with computer design software and create, rather than construct, your designs.

The future outlook

Public interest in traditional toys and games is growing. You could work on a self-employed basis, making and designing toys. Some toymakers/designers own shops where they sell unusual and traditional toys as well as their own handmade toys. A growing number sell their products at craft fairs, on the internet or by mail order. With rising concerns for the environment, you may have to ensure your materials are from sustainable sources and eco-friendly.

A small number of toymakers also restore antique toys. There is steady demand for innovative toys in high street shops and you will always have an emerging potential market for new products!

entry level

4–8

To both enter and train while working in this career, you will need qualifications at Level 4–8. Please refer to explanation on page vii.

Qualifications and courses

- There are no formal entry requirements, but many entrants have a background in art and design, and HND or degree qualifications can be an advantage. Relevant subjects include art and design, graphic or three-dimensional design, creative arts and craft and model making.
- In England, Wales and Northern Ireland many students take a 1-year Foundation course as preparation for entry to an art and design degree; 5 GCSEs (A–C) and a relevant A level are also usually required.
- In Scotland the first year of a degree equates to the Foundation year.
- A good portfolio is an advantage, and can be a requirement for entry to certain courses.
- There are various courses available, such as Foundation degrees in 3-dimensional design and creative arts, and degrees in craft studies. Institutes sometimes have links with toy manufacturers, which can provide a useful first step into the industry. Degree entry requirements are usually 2 A levels/3 H grades or equivalent.

Other related opportunities

- Carpenter / Joiner p41
- Designer p136
- Model Maker p155
- Sculptor p164
- Technical Illustrator p166

Advantages/disadvantages

- This work provides the enjoyment of creating fun, attractive objects.
- It can take time to build up a business, if working on a self-employed basis.
- If self-employed you will need both creative and business skills to succeed.

Earnings guide

- Salaries vary according to the type of work you specialise in.
- Starting salaries for toy designers working for toy manufacturers range from £12,000–£16,000 per year.
- With experience and working in a large company this can increase to £23,000–£35,000. As a top designer you could get up to £45,000.
- Traditional toymakers are usually self-employed and salaries will depend on the success of the business.

Further information

British Toymakers Guild
124 Walcot Street
Bath
BA1 5BG
01225 442440
www.toymakersguild.co.uk

Design Council
34 Bow Street
London
WC2E 7DL
020 7420 5200
www.designcouncil.org.uk

Crafts Council
44a Pentonville Road
Islington
London
N1 9BY
0207 806 2500
www.craftscouncil.org.uk

ccskills – Creative & Cultural Skills
4th Floor
Lafone House
The Leathermarket
Weston St
London
SE1 3HN
020 7015 1800
www.ccskills.org.uk

Do you want to get involved within the world of teaching, learning or education? This section includes job ideas involving helping people of all ages.

- **Education and Childcare Inspector**
- **Nursery Nurse**
- **Playworker**
- **Teacher**
- **Training Manager**

But what's it like working in this area?

Here's Sue Modeva's story

Crèche Manager

When Sue, now aged 35, left school she went to Southport College to do her Nursery Nurse training via the National Nursery Examination Board (NNEB). However, she left after a year and did not take up childcare again until after her son was old enough to go to primary school. She then started to work in the nursery at his school and was later offered a position to assist with children with special needs. She was working part time and earning, but she also started to train on the job to become a Specialist Teacher's Assistant. A high percentage of the children she worked with not only had special needs but also had English as a second language. Her duties included building relationships with the children and implementing play strategies. Five years ago she became the crèche manager at a Cannons gym in London and she updated her qualifications by attending a part-time evening course for two years, giving her a CACHE Level 3 Certificate of Professional Development in Work with Children and Young People.

'Here I am still very hands-on with the children, but I now have to deal with legal requirements, monitoring my staff, recruiting, doing performance evaluations and liaising with outside agencies such as Child Protection. Five hundred children between the ages of 3 months and 5 years are registered here and we probably get between 44 and 50 children a day, as their mums come into the gym.'

For Sue, the interaction with the children is the highlight of the day and she says it keeps her young, although she emphasises the work can be extremely tiring both emotionally and physically, especially as having eye contact with the children requires a lot of bending down and a lot of picking up.

WHAT YOU NEED TO SUCCEED

'You really need to be patient to do this job, and have self-confidence and be committed and caring. Above all, you have to have the right attitude and be responsible and reliable. Liking babies is not enough because in this job you have to constantly develop and update your skills in line with new legislation.'

SUE'S ADVICE FOR PROSPECTIVE NURSERY NURSES

If you are interested in becoming a nursery nurse Sue suggests contacting your local Early Years Development Partnership (EYDP) who will have a list of nurseries who may be willing to give you work experience, or get involved with your local Brownies, Cubs or Rainbow group. She also suggests babysitting, or joining a drama group, as role play and reading stories are key areas in childcare. As far as progression through the industry is concerned you can always move up by becoming a manager, but also think about branching out into child psychology, or into education through drama. Ultimately, Sue would like to have her own small nursery.

Adult Education Organiser / Tutor

What the work involves

Organiser

- You will evaluate and organise adult education programmes by reviewing courses, numbers of students and checking their achievements.
- As your job will also involve creating courses that meet the needs of the community, you will talk to tutors, advisers, guidance workers, heads of departments, others working in further education and local employers.
- To make sure that courses can run, you will advertise for tutors who represent a range of interests – such as the arts and crafts field, things like canework and glass painting or more academic interests like local history, ancient walking routes, etc. You will also oversee the publishing of each new prospectus.

Tutor

- You will have to submit a proposal to teach your sessions. These can be half-/whole-day or weekend courses, that run from a few days up to a whole year. If enough adults choose your course, you will then agree a contract with the adult education organiser.
- Part of your job will involve preparing sessions by printing materials and ordering resources.
- So that your students can learn and work at their own pace, you will provide lots of feedback and support.
- Finally, so that they are rewarded for their achievements, you will enter your students and learners for their exams or assessment.

The type of person suited to this work

To teach adult education programmes, you must be friendly, interesting and be able to stimulate your students to want to learn. To do this, you willl need to be interested in and know your subject. It is vital that you have a combination of experience and passion for your subject.

As an organiser, previous experience of teaching or tutoring are useful along with the same requirements for the tutor. Experience of administering courses as a programme leader, key stage coordinator, or head of department will also be useful.

For both posts, communicating with students and colleagues, is essential – therefore, excellent verbal, written and organisational skills are required.

Working conditions

Depending on your subject, you could spend your time in- or outdoors. However, most tutors deliver classes indoors in a classroom. The style of the classroom can range from very formal such as a lecture theatre or to more relaxed positions, sitting at easels or craft tables, etc.

The majority of classes run as either twilight or evening sessions – when most adults have finished work. Twilight sessions can start at 4.30pm or 5.00pm, while evening sessions usually begin at 7.00pm and finish up to 10.00pm.

As an organiser, you will work within an office, although you will visit students and tutors in their learning centres.

The future outlook

It is very important that adults across the UK increase their level of Key Skills (communication, literacy, numeracy and ICT skills). Because of this, adult education is increasing in importance and there are new tutors of all types of subjects across the country.

As well as increasing academic qualifications and Key Skills, adult education also provides cultural awareness and vocational courses. There are lots of reasons for people to continue learning, for example changing career, returning to work or for leisure. Adult education helps all types of individual to reach their potential by offering local courses.

Because of the importance that the government is giving to all types of learning, the need for individuals to work within the adult education sector is expected to continue to rise. However, if you choose to become a tutor it is more likely that you will operate on a part-time sessional basis alongside your permanent work rather than it becoming your full-time job.

CRCI:F

CLCI:FAB

Qualifications and courses

- There are no set entry requirements for this work, and no upper age limit.
- Candidates normally have a qualification in teaching adults such as the City & Guilds Certificate in Further Education Teaching and/or experience of teaching adults. Many also have a degree.
- Although not essential, a Certificate in Education (CertEd) in Further Education or Post-Compulsory Education is offered by many colleges and universities and can be studied for part time whilst working as a tutor or organiser.
- Adult education practitioners who already hold a degree can study for a postgraduate qualification in subjects such as adult and continuing education and lifelong learning.
- People with experience as adult education tutors may transfer into organiser roles.

entry level

To both enter and train while working in this career, you will need qualifications at Level 4–8. Please refer to explanation on page vii.

- NVQs in Training and Development and SVQs in Learning and Development are available at Levels 3–5.

Other related opportunities

- Learning Mentor p177
- Lecturer p178
- Special Needs Learning Support Assistant p183
- Teacher p184
- Teaching / Classroom Assistant p187
- Work-based Training p188

Advantages/disadvantages

- You will meet interesting people with special talents and gifts.
- Tutoring offers you the opportunity to give something back to the community.
- You might have to work late hours and travel in bad weather during winter.
- Some of the locations that you will visit might be in isolated premises which could be dangerous if you travel alone.

Earnings guide

- Adult education organisers can earn at the same level as course coordinators and sometimes heads of department. Starting pay, if you have an adult education qualification, is around £20,000–£22,000 per year.
- This rises to £25,000–£30,000 with experience. More if you supervise staff.
- Most tutors receive an hourly rate and have part-time contracts. Rates vary between individual providers. You could be offered anything from £15 per hour up to £30 per hour with travel expenses. This depends on the level of the subject, numbers of students involved and if the subject is assessed for nationally recognised qualifications.

Further information

Training and Development Agency for Schools
Portland House
Stag Place
London
SW1E 5TT
020 7925 3700
www.tda.gov.uk

Information, Advice and Guidance for Adults
www.lifelonglearning.co.uk

City & Guilds
1 Giltspur Street
London
EC1A 9DD
020 7294 2800
www.city-and-guilds.co.uk
enquiry@city-and-guilds.co.uk

Institute for Learning
5th Floor
St Andrews House
18-20 St Andrew Street
London
EC4A 3AY
0870 757 7894
www.ifl.ac.uk

Training, Adult Literacy, ESOL and Numeracy Teachers
www.talent.ac.uk

CRCI:F
CLCI:FAB

Bursar / School Business Manager

What the work involves

- You will be responsible for the financial planning and accounts of a school or college. Although the term 'bursar' is common in independent schools, in the state sector you might also be called a school business manager or finance manager.
- Your role will include the staff pay, some recruitment and managing contracts such as cleaning and maintenance companies. You will also have to keep all the school premises insurance documents up to date.
- In independent schools, you will also set fees and distribute bursaries, scholarships and awards.

entry level

To both enter and train while working in this career, you will need qualifications at Level 4–8. Please refer to explanation on page vii.

The type of person suited to this work

Before becoming bursars, most people are financial managers in large commercial organisations. It will be helpful if you have worked with different people, as you will deal with the head teacher and senior staff, other professionals (auditors, company managers, etc), parents and, occasionally, students! You need a polite yet firm approach and excellent communication skills.

As bursar, you will need a head for figures and be happy using computers and financial software. There will always be lots of jobs needing your attention so you should be a good organiser and enjoy keeping busy.

Working conditions

Normally, you will work in an office sitting at a desk. Here, you will have access to a computer and spend lots of time talkng to people – both in or outside of your organisation.

You will attend lots of meetings with the headteacher and other professional staff – sometimes staying late to give reports to your school's governing body.

You may also need to work during the evenings and in school holidays.

The future outlook

Most bursars progress to the job after working in either a private financial organisation, after being an accountant or occasionally after working the way up from within a school/college.

With experience, bursars can move to larger organisations or return to the private sector. It is also possible to work in British schools overseas.

Posts are advertised in local and national level publications such as the *Times Educational Supplement*. Jobs are also posted on the National Bursars Association (NBA) website.

Qualifications and courses

- There are no fixed entry qualifications for this role.
- Most entrants have experience in related fields, and many hold a degree or professional qualification.
- Management experience in education, accountancy, business, commerce and industry, personnel or the armed forces is of value.
- Some people gain promotion from a school administration post. Qualifications such as NVQ Level 3 or 4 in Administration or Management, or SVQ Level 3 or 4 Business Administration or Management, may be an advantage
- For people already in posts, the National College for School Leadership offers a Bursar Development Scheme. The Certificate of School Business Management is aimed at newly-appointed bursars or those in school administration posts, and the Diploma of School Business Management is intended for experienced bursars/business managers. These qualifications are available to both state and independent school bursars.
- The Independent Schools' Bursars Association offers training for those working in independent schools.
- The National Bursars Association (NBA) Registration Scheme is also aimed at experienced bursars. The scheme can be completed in 1 year and leads to a postgraduate-level qualification.
- The NBA also offers the Institute of Administrative Management (IAM) Diploma by distance learning. Postgraduate courses in subjects such as education business management are available.

Other related opportunities

- Accountant p2
- Accounting Technician p4
- Administrator p6
- Financial Adviser p18

Advantages/disadvantages

- You will have lots of opportunity to use your own initiative.
- This is a job that offers the chance to work in a school without being in the classroom.
- You will meet people of all ages and from different backgrounds.

Earnings guide

- The salary range for bursars differs greatly depending on where you work and the size and type of institution you work in. The average starting salary in a state school or college is £25,000–£27,000 per year, rising to £40,000+ with experience.
- In the independent sector, salaries are higher and it is possible to earn between £60,000 and £90,000 at the top end of the scale.

Further information

National Bursars Association
Top Floor Offices
140 Wood Street
Rugby
Warwickshire
CV21 2SP
01788 573300
www.nba.org.uk

Independent Schools' Bursars Association
Units 11–12 Manor Farm
Cliddesden
Basingstoke
RG25 2BJ
01256 330369
www.isba.uk.com

Financial Services Skills Council
51 Gresham Street
London
EC2V 7HQ
020 7216 7366
www.fssc.org.uk

National College for School Leadership
Triumph Road
Nottingham
NG8 1DH
0878 001 1155
www.stage.ncsl.org.uk

Local Government Careers
www.lgcareers.com

Education and Childcare Inspector

What the work involves

- You will use your extensive experience gained from working in schools, colleges, nurseries or youth service settings (normally at management level), to undertake inspections.
- You might inspect early years learning, or focus on secondary education and preparation for work. Inspections cover special schools and out-of-school learning units.
- Although inspectors work within a team of 2–3, you will spend some of your time alone.
- During the visit, you will contribute to the inspection report, which is then made available for everyone to read on the internet.

The type of person suited to this work

Inspectors need to know about the types of organisation that they inspect very well, so they know what things to look out for. You should enjoy meeting people of all ages and backgrounds, and know how to put them at their ease. You will need to explain to very young children what you are doing in ways that are easy to understand.

Inspectors have to examine all levels of practice in educational establishments. You should be confident and happy to stand by your decisions, which can be difficult if the organisation you have inspected is not doing well.

Finally, you should be happy writing reports, using a laptop and speaking to large groups of people explaining what you have found out.

Working conditions

As you will be visiting organisations all over the country, you should be happy to spend periods away from home.

Most of the work takes place in classrooms or offices where you will speak to head teachers, pupils, parents, governors and the other professionals linked to the organisation.

This job involves lots of listening, watching, reading reports and studying the work of the students and tutors/teachers.

The future outlook

Recently, the way in which inspections are undertaken has changed, resulting in them now lasting a few days rather than the 2–3 weeks that they previously took. As a result, fewer inspectors are needed. If you are interested in this type of work, any future openings are likely to be on a part-time basis.

Inspectors are now recruited by private companies, so you should approach them for information on their recruitment schemes.

entry level

4–8

To both enter and train while working in this career, you will need qualifications at Level 4–8. Please refer to explanation on page vii.

Qualifications and courses

- Team and registered inspectors in England and Wales, and Inspectors in Scotland, must be qualified teachers.
- Qualified Teacher Status (QTS) is gained through Initial Teacher Training (ITT). The two main routes are a first degree followed by a Postgraduate Certificate in Education (PGCE) or a first degree (BEd/BA/BSc) leading to QTS.
- Registered inspectors in England and Wales must be experienced Team Inspectors. Inspectors in Scotland must have 5 years' teaching experience, including experience in a senior position.
- Registered inspectors need inspection experience and should have been the lead inspector for some subjects and aspects of teaching. Registered inspectors usually begin their training as team inspectors.
- Lay inspectors are members of the team who have not had paid teaching experience. Non-teaching experience in the education sector and/or management experience is useful. In Scotland, inspection teams also include practising teachers and lecturers.
- Training for inspectors is provided by the Office for Standards in Education (Ofsted) in England, Estyn in Wales, HM Inspectorate of Education in Scotland, and the Department of Education for Northern Ireland.

CRCI:F

CLCI:FAB

Other related opportunities

- Teacher p184
- Work-based Training p188

Advantages/disadvantages

- This job offers you the chance to use your experience to make sure that the correct quality is in place.
- It offers the opportunity to visit different organisations around the country.
- There is rarely any follow-up in the role of inspector as you are unlikely to repeat an inspection of the same institution or home.

Earnings guide

- Inspectors generally earn the same as advisers employed by local authorities. Pay varies, depending on the level of work.
- Childcare inspectors are usually employed by private organisations, salaries vary but as a guide starting salaries are around £25,000.
- HMI's can earn £48,000–£60,000 per year for full-time employment, with pro rata for part time.

Further information

Ofsted (Office for Standards in Education)
www.ofsted.gov.uk

Association of Professionals in Education and Children's Trusts (Aspect)
Woolley Hall
Woolley
Wakefield
West Yorkshire
WF4 2JR
01226 383420/8
www.aspect.org.uk

Department for Children, Schools and Families
www.standards.dfes.gov.uk

Local Government Careers
www.lgcareers.com

Department for Employment and Learning (Northern Ireland)
Adelaide House
39/49 Adelaide St
Belfast
BT2 8FD
www.delni.gov.uk

Estyn
Anchor Court
Keen Road
Cardiff
CF24 5JW
029 2044 6446
www.estyn.gov.uk

HM Inspectorate of Education in Scotland
01506 600 200
www.hmie.gov.uk

Education Officer

What the work involves

Education officer

- You will prepare interesting educational materials and resources for visits of school students to your museum, gallery or other organisation.
- It will be your responsibility to tell the public about new exhibitions and shows, with eye-catching publicity, newsletters and flyers.
- You might also update the educational sections of your website by producing lesson materials, careers information or the pages designed for young people.

Education administrator

- You have to interpret education policies, working with a team of educational advisers, helping divide up the education budget across a local authority.
- You are responsible for making sure that the local authority complies with all new government legislation.
- Troubleshooting is a regular task – you are the one who sorts out any problems for schools in your local authority.

The type of person suited to this work

As an education officer, you will need self-confidence and an ability to talk to young people in a way that will interest and excite them. You must be bright, interesting, humorous, have lots of patience and a willingness to listen.

You will always be busy, so you will need good organisational skills and written and verbal communication skills. An understanding of ICT and confidence in handling budgets will also be useful.

Your work will involve preparing lesson materials for use before, during and after visits, so you will need an understanding of the National Curriculum and teaching methods.

Working conditions

Your time will be spent in an office or lecture room, on the exhibition floor of a museum or gallery, or visiting local schools where you will represent your organisation. You might wear a uniform or protective clothing.

Depending on your organisation, you might spend some of your time outdoors in all weathers, for example at a zoo or community farm. You might do some evening work.

The future outlook

More people in Britain visit museums, galleries, exhibitions and other attractions every year than go to football matches. Both adults and young people want to gain more from their visits to national collections and interactive experiences are increasing in popularity. Alongside the traditional exhibition, demonstrations, videos, talks and other presentations are being introduced under the guidance of education officers.

This is an area of work that attracts many applications, so getting in can be competitive. However, there will be a steady increase in the number of educational jobs, many of which will be taken up by ex-teachers.

With experience you could diversify to produce curriculum materials, and help to create and produce websites or other learning resources.

CRCI:F

CLCI:FAB

Qualifications and courses

- To work as an education officer in a museum or gallery, a degree is required. Useful degree subjects include history, archaeology, anthropology, museum studies, cultural studies, history of art and education.
- Qualifications and/or experience in teaching or community education are useful, and may be required.
- Experience in a museum or gallery is essential.
- Postgraduate qualifications are available in relevant subjects such as museum studies and heritage management. Entry to these courses requires a degree in any subject, and, normally, some related work experience.

entry level

To both enter and train while working in this career, you will need qualifications at Level 3–8. Please refer to explanation on page vii.

Other related opportunities

- Administrator p6
- Adult Education Organiser / Tutor p170
- Learning Mentor p177
- Teacher p184

Advantages/disadvantages

- You will be juggling lots of different tasks at once.
- This offers an opportunity to be involved in teaching without being in the classroom.
- You will contribute to making a visit to your organisation a more memorable one for everyone.

Earnings guide

- Education officers working in large prestigious museums or educational adventure establishments in full-time positions can earn £19,000–£28,500 per year.
- Education assistants who work alongside education officers can earn £16,000–£21,000.

Further information

Cultural Heritage National Training Organisation
7 Burnett Street
Little Germany
Bradford
BD1 5BJ
01274 391087
www.chnto.org.uk

Department for Culture, Media and Sport
2–4 Cockspur Street
London
SW1Y 5DH
020 7211 6000
www.culture.gov.uk

Campaign for Learning through Museums and Galleries
Gooseham Mill House
Gooseham
Bude
Cornwall
EX23 9PQ
01288 331615
www.clmg.org.uk

GEM – Group for Education in Museums
Primrose House
193 Gillingham Road
Gillingham
Kent
ME7 4EP
01634 312409
www.gem.org.uk

www.cityandguilds.com/myperfectjob

CRCI:F

CLCI:FAB

Education Officer (LA)

What the work involves

- You will be responsible for making sure that your local authority (LA) provides a successful education service.
- Your role will be to develop and put into place education plans and monitor school services.
- As part of your role you might also manage budgets, write reports, manage staff and interpret data and changes to education legislation.
- You will meet and write reports for head teachers, governors and parents to explain the changes to the educational services in your authority.

The type of person suited to this work

You will need a thorough understanding of education, normally gained by being a teacher with senior management level experience. As you will be describing how to implement education plans in presentations and reports, you will need excellent communication skills and confidence in your knowledge and ability.

An interest in quality improvement, educational practices and legislation are vital. You should be able to make decisions and have business planning and data analysis skills.

Depending on your role you might also have to manage staff and a budget, so good team-working and negotiating skills are also helpful.

Working conditions

You will have an office base where you will spend some of your time. However, you will also attend meetings, visit schools and make presentations to members of the public and teachers.

Although you will normally attend during office hours, you might have to work occasional evenings.

It might be possible to operate on a job-share or flexible working basis.

The future outlook

There are approximately 175 local authorities across England and Wales, with a further 34 councils in Scotland. Across these, around 5000 education officers are employed.

This role requires extensive teaching/education experience, and is a post that many teachers who have worked at a senior level want to progress into. Depending on the location, there can be stiff competition for posts.

3–8

entry level

To both enter and train while working in this career, you will need qualifications at Level 3–8. Please refer to explanation on page vii.

Qualifications and courses

- A minimum of a degree is required for entry to this career. Other entry qualifications include a teaching qualification, a Master's qualification in education or educational management, or management experience in education.
- Some posts require a teaching qualification and experience. To qualify as a teacher, you can take a BEd, BA or BSc degree leading to Qualified Teacher Status (QTS), or a degree in another subject followed by a PGCE. Your degree should normally be in the subject you wish to teach, or a closely related subject. All candidates for teacher training must have GCSEs at grade C or above, or the equivalent, in English and maths. Candidates for primary or Key Stage 2/3 teaching born after 1 September 1979 also need GCSE science. There are also employment-based routes to QTS for people who wish to qualify while working in a school.
- For other posts, it is possible to enter with administrative experience in the education sector. Entrants to educational administrator posts will normally be graduates.

CRCI:F

CLCI:FAB

Other related opportunities

- Consultant p16
- Education and Childcare Inspector, p173
- Training Officer p33

Advantages/disadvantages

- This offers the opportunity to work in education without being in the classroom.
- You might have to make decisions that are unpopular.
- You will travel around your area meeting lots of different people.

Earnings guide

- Your salary will depend on the location of your job. However starting salaries are around £30,000 a year.
- With experience you could get up to £45,000. At the top end with a senior position you may get up to £50,000.

Further information

Local Government Careers
www.lgcareers.com

Convention of Scottish Local Authorities
Roseberry House
9 Haymarket Terrace
Edinburgh
EH12 5XZ
0131 474 9200
www.cosla.gov.uk

Learning Mentor

What the work involves

- You will support different people whilst they are learning.
- Working on a one-to-one basis, you will listen to their difficulties, offer solutions and suggest different ways to approach problems.
- You will help everybody you work with to succeed, enjoy their learning experience and want to keep trying.

entry level

To both enter and train while working in this career, you will need qualifications at Level 4–8. Please refer to explanation on page vii.

The type of person suited to this work

To be a good learning mentor, you will need to have experience of the subject you mentor, along with an understanding of different styles of studying. You should enjoy helping and listening to people and have good communication skills. You should be patient and willing to listen.

The best mentors are those who can be a critical friend and know the benefits of learning and can explain them to the people you will work with.

It will also help if you have had first-hand experience of the issues yourself, probably whilst you were learning as this will help you to appreciate the difficulties people face.

Working conditions

You can work on a part- or full-time basis with people at school, home or sometimes at a college, university or training centre. You might be employed on a term-time only basis or all year round. Some of your work might involve weekends and evenings – this will depend on the organisation you work for.

You will meet in a quiet confidential area where you will examine workbooks and essays, talk over any issues and give help.

The future outlook

Mentoring is one way to help students who might otherwise drop out or may not achieve their qualifications. At every level of learning, mentors have been proved to be key workers and operate alongside other teaching professionals.

The government initiative 'Excellence in Cities' requires every participating secondary school to employ at least one mentor. The role has been so successful that Ofsted reported that '95% of all surveyed schools' showed that mentoring had played a positive contribution to the school's development.

Qualifications and courses

- There are no formal entry requirements for this career. However, most entrants have a degree, HND or equivalent vocational qualification.
- Relevant degree subjects include social sciences, psychology and National Curriculum subjects, particularly English and maths.
- Experience of working with young people is required, and experience in a related area such as social work, counselling or teaching is useful.
- Experience on a voluntary mentoring scheme is also useful.
- Newly-appointed learning mentors take part in a 5-day national initial training programme provided by the DCSF. The Mentoring and Befriending Foundation also provides training opportunities.
- It may be possible to work towards a Foundation degree or NVQ/SVQ Level 3 or 4 in Learning, Development and Support Services. The Level 4 NVQ/SVQ is normally required to become a learning mentor coordinator.
- All candidates are required to undergo a Criminal Records Bureau check.

CRCI:F

CLCI:FAB

Other related opportunities

- Adult Education Organiser / Tutor p170
- Careers Adviser p526
- Personal Adviser – Connexions p539
- Special Needs Learning Support Assistant p183
- Teacher p184
- Teaching / Classroom Assistant p187
- Youth and Community Worker p551

Advantages/disadvantages

- This job involves lots of different roles – friend, confidence builder and motivator.
- Results have shown how important this job can be in helping learners to succeed.
- You will be working with students without being a teacher.

Earnings guide

- Within schools, salaries for newly appointed mentors range between £14,000 and £19,000 per year. With experience, you can expect this to increase to £23,000, and as a senior mentor up to £25,000.
- Other organisations may pay more. For example, mentoring a company's chief executive or operations manager, means your pay could reach £30 per hour.

Further information

Department for Children, Schools and Families
www.standards.dfes.gov.uk

Local Government Jobs
www.lgjobs.com

Mentoring and Befriending Foundation
1st floor, Charles House
Albert Street
Eccles
Manchester
M30 0PW
0161 787 8600
www.mandbf.org.uk

Learning Mentors
www.standards.dfes.gov.uk/learningmentors

Lecturer

What the work involves

Lecturer in further education (FE)

- You will teach students aged 16+, on vocational (work-based) or academic (general) courses at a further education college, the information and skills needed to achieve their qualifications.
- As well as teaching your main subject you will also be a pastoral tutor helping students with their personal development and career planning.
- You will also arrange work placements with local companies, visit students to monitor and assess their progress, act as a student mentor and meet your colleagues to develop courses.

Lecturer in higher education (HE)

- As a higher education lecturer you will teach undergraduate or postgraduate students at a university or franchised college.
- As well as delivering lectures you will take tutorials, act as a consultant for individual research projects and run seminars on topics related to the department's research interests.
- To maintain your professional knowledge you will also carry out research in your specialist area, submit papers for publication in academic journals and periodicals.

The type of person suited to this work

Lecturers need to be patient and interested in helping people of all ages to learn and increase their knowledge by developing their ability, skills and interests. It is also important to be comfortable talking to large groups of students.

If you choose to lecture in HE, you are likely to have already done research work and completed a thesis. You must be very interested in your subject and how facts support hypotheses and theories. To be able to help your students learn you will also need to enjoy debating and arguing different ideas and concepts.

FE lecturers often have extensive practical experience of their specialist area before entering the profession.

Working conditions

Most of your time will be teaching in either lecture theatres, classrooms, labs or workshops. For some practical subjects you might spend some of your time outdoors.

When not teaching you will be office-based, using a computer for research, writing papers, storing data, reports and analyses, and recording students' progress, etc.

Although you are likely to work mostly during the day you will also work at night and occasional weekends. Depending on your institution, you will mostly work term time although FE conditions are changing to all year round.

The future outlook

There are around 500 colleges and universities across the UK with over 4 million students aged 16+. Around 39% of jobs are held by women. In a bid to increase national competitiveness, the government is promoting lifelong learning as an important requirement for all individuals. Both universitiies and FE colleges are being expected to talk to employers to make sure their courses meet the needs of companies as well as individuals.

All of this means that lecturers are playing a vital role in helping to increase the skills levels of the country.

There are a number of progression routes open to both type of lecturer.

For FE lecturers there are opportunities to enter other areas of teaching including HE, financial work, quality improvement and human resources. In addition, you could also look to take more senior positions within your current or another college.

As an HE lecturer, some of your options will depend on the size and financial status of your institution. There is evidence to show that taking a career break can be a disadvantage as this can reduce your ability to do the research work which is so important if you are to build your reputation. Sabbaticals, however, are considered to be positive as they will enable you to spend time doing research. HE lecturers can apply for promotion within their own or other institutions, undertake consultancy, enter the media or do public speaking. You could also find part-time work providing advisory or training services or start your business.

CRCI:F

CLCI:FAB

Qualifications and courses

entry level

To both enter and train while working in this career, you will need qualifications at Level 4–8. Please refer to explanation on page vii.

Lecturer in further education

- All new lecturers in FE must have Qualified Teacher, Learning and Skills (QTLS) status.
- The minimum qualification you will need to work as a full lecturer is the Level 5 Diploma in Teaching in the Lifelong Learning Sector, which leads to QTL status. The Diploma is roughly equivalent to the PGCE/CertEd in Further or Post-Compulsory Education, and many institutions will continue to use the old qualification names, referenced against the new Diploma.
- You will generally need an NQF Level 4–6 qualification for entry to a Diploma or CertEd programme, and a degree for entry to a PGCE. You will normally also need at least a Level 3 qualification in the subject you wish to teach.
- In Scotland, further education lecturers can take a Further Education Teaching Qualification (TQFE) through an approved university. Entrants must be in employment for a minimum of 120 hours during the course and must hold an HNC, HND, relevant professional qualification, or a degree.
- In Scotland, further education lecturers can take a Further Education Teaching Qualification (TQFE) at certain universities, or a Professional Development Award in further education teaching. Both types of qualification are normally studied part time, while in the post.

Lecturer in higher education

- HE lecturers need a 1st or 2.1 Honours degree and a postgraduate qualification. A PhD is normally required, but a Master's may be acceptable, and candidates working towards a PhD may be considered.
- For posts in academic subjects, a record of research and publication is required. Teaching experience whilst working towards a PhD is also valuable. Lecturers in vocational subjects should have several years of relevant work experience.
- Opportunities to study for a postgraduate qualification followed by a fellowship or lecturing post can arise for research assistants.
- Lecturers normally receive further training from their employer institution. The Higher Education Academy accredits in-service programmes for lecturers.

Other related opportunities

- Consultant p16
- Education and Childcare Inspector p173
- Teacher p184
- Work-based Training p188

Advantages/disadvantages

- You will be working in an area that has great importance to the government.
- You are a professional teacher, but in a less-structured, formal environment than a school.
- In HE, it can be hard to follow up your own research interests when you have to set up and help run demonstrations or tutorials for undergraduates, while marking essays and assignments.
- In FE, you could teach students of all ages with many different reasons for studying.

Earnings guide

- Most full-time FE lecturers start their career within the range of £16,200–£22,000 per year. With several years experience or promotion to senior level this rises to £31,000+. Those employed on part-time or sessional basis earn £16–£25+ per hour.
- HE lecturers are paid more, with starting salaries after a PhD ranging between £25,826 and £42,000. At senior lecturer level, salaries can be between £38,000 and £48,000.
- Salaries for both jobs are dependent on the research of your department, links with local businesses and the size and status of your university/college.

Further information

Lifelong Learning UK
5th floor, St Andrew's House
18–20 St Andrew Street
London
EC4A 3AY
0870 757 7890
www.lifelonglearninguk.org

Association of University Teachers
Egmont House
25–31 Tavistock Place
London
WC1H 9UT
020 7670 9700
www.aut.org.uk

NATFHE (University and College Lecturers' Union)
27 Brittania Street
London
WC1X 9JP
020 7837 3636
www.natfhe.org.uk

Play Worker

What the work involves

- You will be responsible for making sure that children between the ages of 5 and 15 play in a safe environment.
- Your job will be to encourage children and young people to learn through play by giving them the freedom to explore and get to know themselves.
- Some of your time might include sourcing the materials for young people to use in their play and checking the level of use of the different types of equipment.

entry level

To both enter and train while working in this career, you will need qualifications at Level 1. Please refer to explanation on page vii.

The type of person suited to this work

To do this job well, you will need to be imaginative and creative. It is also essential that you like being with children of all ages, understand what they like to do and recognise how they change as they develop.

You will need to be positive and patient with lots of energy and stamina. As the safety of the children will be your responsibility, you will have to have high levels of concentration and stay alert at all times.

This work suits those who were themselves teenagers only recently, but it can also be a marvellous job for mature, even retired, workers who enjoy being around young people.

Working conditions

As many opportunities operate after school or during holidays you will normally work in the early evening, at weekends and in school holidays. Many jobs are seasonal and most are part time.

You might work indoors, in a hall, gym or community centre – although if you are involved in sports play, you can expect to spend some of your time outdoors.

Some play workers work with hospitalised children.

The future outlook

This area of work is rising in importance and is part of the National Childcare Strategy, which recognises the importance of giving young people opportunities to make the most of their lives through education, sport and leisure.

With the increased number of working parents, the need for out-of-school carers – such as play workers – has grown.

With experience as a play worker, you could consider further training to work as a creative or play therapist, youth worker, teacher or work in play development.

Qualifications and courses

- No formal qualifications are required, but all candidates are subject to a Criminal Records Bureau (CRB) police check.
- Voluntary or paid work experience with children in useful. Most play workers start with some relevant experience and achieve qualifications whilst working.
- Relevant courses include the CACHE Certificate in Playwork and NCFE Certificate in Playwork, both at Level 2, and the CACHE Certificate and Diploma in Child Care and Education.
- Many play workers have qualifications at a higher level. HNCs/Ds, Foundation degrees and degrees are available in subjects such as playwork or community, play and youth studies.
- NVQs/SVQs are available in Playwork at Levels 2 and 3 and Early Years Care and Education. Experienced play workers can also work towards the Level 3 Certificate in Work with Children offered by CACHE.
- Apprenticeships/Skillseekers opportunities may be available for those aged between 16 and 24.

CRCI:V

CLCI:KEB

Other related opportunities

- Childminder p528
- Outdoor Pursuits Instructor p372
- Therapist p309
- Youth and Community Worker p551

Advantages/disadvantages

- This work can be very tiring as many young people get bored quickly and need lots of variety.
- Many local authorities employ play workers on play buses or in adventure play areas.
- It will be up to you to stimulate and encourage children of all ages.

Earnings guide

- As most play workers are employed on a part-time or sessional basis, pay rates are lower than in some similar types of work. Starting salaries for newly recruited staff range between £11,500 and £15,000 per year.
- With experience or promotion, salaries can increase to £20,000+.
- As a senior manager, it is possible to achieve salaries up to £35,000.

Further information

www.cityandguilds.com/myperfectjob

Children's Play Information Service
National Children's Bureau
8 Wakley Street
London
EC1V 7QE
020 7843 6303

CACHE (Council for Awards in Children's Care and Education)
Beauort House
Grosvenor Road
St Albans
Hertfordshire
AL1 3AW
01727 818616
www.cache.org.uk

SkillsActive (Sector Skills Council for active leisure and learning)
Castlewood House
77–91 New Oxford Street
London
WC1A 1PX
08000 933300
www.skillsactive.com

School Lunchtime Supervisor

What the work involves

- You will supervise children and students at lunchtimes, making sure that their behaviour is good and that everyone eats their meals in an orderly and relaxed way.
- As some younger children have difficulty eating their meals, you might have to cut up their food or give other help.
- Once the children have eaten their food, you might also supervise outdoor areas making sure the play does not become too dangerous and that no child is being bullied or is lonely.

entry level

To both enter and train while working in this career, you will need qualifications at Level 1. Please refer to explanation on page vii.

The type of person suited to this work

This is a part-time job that will suit you if you like working and being with young people. It is an excellent option if you want to return to work or need a part-time job to fit around your family commitments and school holidays.

You will have to be confident and able to discipline young people but have a friendly, relaxed approach. During lunchtime, the safety of the pupils will be your responsibility so you will have to be aware and prevent any potential accidents.

Good communication skills are vital, along with a good sense of humour!

If you have a basic understanding of First Aid, this can be an advantage.

Qualifications and courses

- No set qualifications are needed for this role.
- Experience with children is an advantage, as are First Aid skills.
- Candidates must be over 18 and will undergo a police Criminal Records Bureau (CRB) check.
- Training generally takes place on the job, and there may be opportunities to study towards vocational qualifications such as NVQ/SVQ Level 2 Award in Support Work in Schools, CACHE Level 3 Award, Certificate or Diploma in Support Work in Schools, or City & Guilds Level 3 Award in Safeguarding Children and Young People.
- Some local authorities offer a Certificate in Midday Supervision.
- Some local authorities employ people to run play activities during breaktimes. To enter these posts, it can help to have experience or qualifications in playwork.

Working conditions

Your normal hours will be between 12.00pm and 3.00pm and will cover a combination of indoor work, whilst the students eat their meals, and outdoor, when they have finished and go out to play.

Some schools provide meals and uniforms for their lunchtime staff.

You will work during term time only, often on a renewable temporary contract.

The future outlook

With changes to the terms and conditions of teachers working in schools, fewer permanent staff members have supervisory roles during the lunch breaks. There are many more opportunities to perform this essential role in schools.

With training, this can be a step towards other jobs such as youth and community worker, play worker or childminder, or you can apply to be a manager of the team of supervisors within your own or a different school.

CRCI:F

CLCI:FAB

Other related opportunities

- Play Worker p180
- Road Crossing Assistant (Schools) p582
- Teaching / Classroom Assistant p187
- Youth and Community Worker p551

Advantages/disadvantages

- This job is great if you want to combine family responsibilities with work.
- The role is all about being a friend for the pupils.
- Young people can be noisy and exhausting!
- It is great work if you have a family and want to have school holidays with them.

Earnings guide

- Generally, you are paid just above the minimum wage for adults: rates range from £6.50 to £7.50 per hour.
- As supervisor, you have responsibility for organising a team of lunchtime assistants and your pay may be between £8.00 and £10.00 per hour.
- Sometimes free meals are provided.

Further information

CACHE (Council for Awards in Children's Care and Education)
Beauort House
Grosvenor Road
St Albans
Hertfordshire
AL1 3AW
01727 818616
www.cache.org.uk

www.cityandguilds.com/myperfectjob

School Matron

What the work involves

- You will normally work within boarding and special schools, residential care homes and sometimes universities, looking after the young people who stay there.
- Your work will involve making sure they stay healthy and happy. You will not provide healthcare (other than non-prescription medicines) unless you are a trained nurse.
- Much of the time will involve listening to problems, helping them to settle in or talking to them when they are lonely or worried.
- Other duties include keeping clothes clean and checking laundry.

The type of person suited to this work

You should be responsible, caring, friendly and hard-working with a real concern for the mental and physical well-being of the young people in your care. As they are living away from home, you will become a parental figure providing the care and affection that otherwise would be missing. You have to care for students when they are at their most vulnerable – ill, depressed or worried, and sometimes in pain, so you must be understanding, patient and have excellent communication skills.

You will need good organisational skills and have the ability to get on with young people and other professionals.

Working conditions

Your day will start very early and finish late. You will normally live and work on-site within your own accommodation. Depending on the type of organisation, you may work term time only but will have access to your accommodation all year round.

There are odd times during the day when you get some rest. This is a tiring, but rewarding job, as young people will rely on you.

The future outlook

A school matron is a vital link between home and school. Where boarders have family abroad and no near relative, the role is vital. The school – and, in particular, school matron – is in *loco parentis*, which means the school has the responsibilities of the absent parents.

This is a job which is not expected to see growth in the near future so current numbers will stay the same.

With experience you could apply for a more senior post, find a position abroad or transfer to another social care job.

entry level

3

To both enter and train while working in this career, you will need qualifications at Level 3. Please refer to explanation on page vii.

Qualifications and courses

- Although there are no formal requirements for this role, many schools will expect qualifications or experience in fields such as childcare or nursing.
- A recent First Aid certificate is an advantage, and may be required.
- Relevant childcare qualifications include the CACHE Diploma in Childcare and Education or the BTEC National Diploma in Care or Children's Care, Learning and Development. The entry requirements are 2 GCSEs/S grades (A–C/1–3) including English language for the CACHE Diploma and 4 GCSEs/S grades for the National Diploma.
- The main nursing qualifications are a diploma or degree in nursing. The usual entry requirements for a nursing diploma or 5 GCSEs/S grades (A–C/1–3) or an equivalent, such as NVQ/SVQ Level 3 or an Access course. Entry requirements for a nursing degree are usually 2 A levels/3 H grades or equivalent, plus GCSEs/S grades. See the 'Nurse (Registered)' entry for detailed information.

CRCI:F

CLCI:FAB

Other related opportunities

- Counselling Work p529
- Home Care Assistant p534
- Housekeeper p97
- Nurse (Registered) p289
- Warden (Accommodation) p549

Advantages/disadvantages

- You will have the freedom to run the job in a way that suits you and those in your care.
- You may deal with bullying, effects of separation, criminal acts or drug-taking, and sometimes the staff also need care and attention.
- There are long holidays when you can stay at the school or are free to travel.

Earnings guide

- Starting salaries will depend on the type of organisation you work for, but are normally around £15,000 per year.
- This rises with experience up to £22,500. In addition to your salary, it is normal to have your accommodation and some or all of your meals provided.

Further information

Boarding Schools' Association
Grosvenor Gardens House
35–37 Grosvenor Gardens
London
SW1W 0BS
020 7798 1580
www.boarding.org.uk

Scottish Council for Independent Schools
21 Melville Street
Edinburgh
EH3 7PE
0131 220 2106
www.scis.org.uk

Special Needs Learning Support Assistant

What the work involves

- You will help learners with learning difficulties or disabilities in support units, either in mainstream schools, special educational schools or in colleges.
- During your work you will offer lots of one-to-one support to your students by attending classes and practical sessions with them.
- You will help them by offering extra help such as explaining difficult ideas or reading things to them.
- Part of your work will be to follow the learning programmes designed to help them progress.

The type of person suited to this work

You will need to be a patient and caring person with an interest in young people who have special needs. You should be interested in school subjects and have a strong desire to help your students progress by achieving the most that they can.

You will need to be able to notice the different reactions of your students and be comfortable talking over the things which concern them.

Written and verbal communication skills are also important as you will spend some of your time writing reports and notes, giving feedback on progress and possibly attending case conferences with other professionals.

Working conditions

Many learning support assistants work in mainstream schools, but some are employed in independent schools, in residential institutions for students with special needs or specialist colleges working with several students at a time.

You will normally work between 8.30am and 4.30pm, although you might have to attend meetings after this and sometimes at weekends. If you work in a residential institution, your hours could be longer and involve shifts that include evenings and weekends.

The work is intensive and tiring, with only short rests and breaks in a busy day.

The future outlook

Due to the decision to support more young people with special needs in attending mainstream schools and colleges there has been an increase in the number and need for learning support assistants.

If you choose to work in this area, you could progress into a unit manager role or decide to train as a teacher. You could also decide to specialise with young people with a particular disability.

entry level

To both enter and train while working in this career, you will need qualifications at Level 2. Please refer to explanation on page vii.

Qualifications and courses

- There are no set qualifications for this role. Previous relevant experience, for example in nursery nursing, is an advantage. Candidates need to be at least 18.
- Pre-entry qualifications at Level 2 are available. Level 2 Certificates for teaching assistants are offered by CACHE, NCFE, Edexcel (BTEC) and ABC. These qualifications are also available to people already working in childcare. CACHE, NCFE and Edexcel (BTEC) also offer a Level 3 Certificate, aimed at experienced teaching assistants. GCSEs/S grades (A–C/1–3) including English and maths are normally required for entry to a Level 3 course.
- Learning support and teaching/classroom assistants are trained on the job. Local authorities in England and Wales may provide additional training.
- People already working in a learning support role can work towards NVQ Level 2 and 3 in Teaching Assistants or SVQ Level 2 and 3 in Classroom Assistants. A City & Guilds qualification in Learning Support (Level 2) is available. There are also NVQs/SVQs in Early Years Care and Education.
- A number of colleges and universities offer Foundation degrees for teaching assistants and learning support assistants. Typical entry requirements are GCSEs/S grades (A–C/1–3), relevant work experience, and a Level 3 qualification such as an A level/2 H grades.
- For those aged 16–24, Apprenticeships/Skillseekers may be available in this area.
- Anyone who will be working with children must undergo a CRB police check.

CRCI:F

CLCI:FAB

Other related opportunities

- Home Care Assistant p534
- Learning Mentor p177
- Teacher p184
- Teaching / Classroom Assistant p187

Advantages/disadvantages

- It is very satisfying helping young people who have learning or physical needs gain a wider understanding of the world and their place in it.
- You might help students take steps towards independent living.
- This is demanding work, requiring patient, calm support in all situations.

Earnings guide

- Pay starts around £12,400–£15,000 per year.
- With experience this rises to £16,000+.
- If you work with young people or learners who have the most severe difficulties, or you become a unit manager, you could earn between £18,000 and £21,000.

Further information

CACHE (Council for Awards in Children's Care and Education)
Beauort House
Grosvenor Road
St Albans
Hertfordshire
AL1 3AW
01727 818616
www.cache.org.uk

NCFE national awarding body
Citygate
St James' Boulevard
Newcastle upon Tyne
NE1 4JE
0191 239 8000
www.ncfe.org.uk

Lifelong Learning UK
5th floor, St Andrew's House
18–20 St Andrew Street
London
EC4A 3AY
0870 757 7890
www.lifelonglearninguk.org

www.cityandguilds.com/myperfectjob

Teacher

What the work involves

Teacher of English to speakers of other languages (TESOL)

- You will teach students of every age who want to learn to speak English, for educational, cultural or business reasons.
- Your students will often wish to learn English for reasons linked with their careers – possibly in finance, ICT, medicine or engineering.
- You might also help immigrants, refugees or international students to develop English language skills, sometimes on a one-to-one basis.

Teacher of music

- You will teach young musicians within large classes, in small groups, as individuals or in bands to develop vocal and instrumental skills and performance technique.
- This involves teaching an appreciation of musical theory and composition, musical development and different composers' works.
- As a music teacher, you will be helping others to appreciate musical compositions and developing their listening skills.

Teacher: primary school

- Your work will include preparing materials and resources for structured play and social development work within early years classes.
- Responding to the National Curriculum, you will teach young children reading, writing and number work, following frameworks for literacy and numeracy.
- You will work with children from age 4 until the time that they leave your school and transfer to the next level, which changes depending on where you work.

Teacher: secondary school

- At secondary level, you will teach pupils the requirements of Key Stages 3 and 4 of the National Curriculum, following the standards laid down by the Department for Children, Schools and Families.
- Some of your work will be acting as a form tutor, encouraging personal development, forward planning, good patterns of behaviour and social awareness amongst your students.
- You will stimulate and encourage high levels of performance from pupils of every ability, assessing their progress towards national awards.

Teacher: special educational needs

- Your work will involve helping children with disabilities and/or learning difficulties to achieve their maximum ability using special programmes, aids and resources to convey ideas and concepts.
- Working with educational psychologists, social workers, other teachers and learning support workers, you will assess their individual needs and draw up an Individual Education Plan.
- In each of these teaching jobs, you will accompany students on visits and trips, help them understand the world around them, and teach life skills to give them greater independence.

The type of person suited to this work

To teach, you need to have a number of well-developed skills – patience and a caring attitude towards others, excellent communication skills, firmness and commitment, fitness and stamina, imagination and creativity, and an interest in drawing out and developing individuals' potential in learning.

You have to be well organised, flexible and able to change plans and the sequence of lessons to accommodate unexpected events. You must be able to recognise and praise efforts and achievements, however small.

Finally, you should be comfortable in maintaining discipline and be confident when speaking to large groups of young people and other professionals.

Qualifications and courses

entry level

To both enter and train while working in this career, you will need qualifications at Level 4–8. Please refer to explanation on page vii.

Teacher of English to speakers of other languages (TESOL)

- There are no set entry requirements for this work, but some employers prefer a degree. Useful subjects are English, linguistics, modern foreign languages and education. It is normally necessary to undertake a training course. Courses include:
- CELTA (Cambridge Certificate in English Language Teaching to Adults) and CELTYL (Cambridge Certificate in English Language teaching to Young Learners). Two A levels/Advanced Highers or equivalent are required and candidates should be over 18. An Extension Certificate is available for holder of CELTA who wish to gain CELTYL.
- TESOL (Trinity College London Certificate in Teaching English to Speakers of Other Languages) has the same entry requirements as CELTA.
- Higher-level courses are also available for people with a Certificate qualification and TEFL/TESOL experience: DELTA (Cambridge Diploma in English Language Teaching to Adults) and the Trinity Licentiate Diploma. Experienced teachers with a degree and/or TESOL qualification can also study for a Master's in TESOL.
- If candidates wish to teach in a state school, a teaching qualification must be held (degree or PGCE).

Teacher of music

- Music teachers working in state schools must have Qualified Teacher Status (QTS).
- There are two main routes to QTS. A first degree, such as a music degree, followed by a Postgraduate Certificate in Education (PGCE) qualifies candidates to teach. A BEd degree such as Music with Primary Teacher Training combines a degree and QTS training.
- In addition, music teachers must be able to demonstrate a good standard of musicianship, usually grade 7/8 from an Associated Board on a first instrument and grade 6 on a second.
- Graduate diploma courses offered by conservatoires are equivalent to degrees but would need to be followed by a 1-year PGCE.
- If you are not teaching in state schools then entry routes can vary.

Teacher: primary/secondary school

- Teaching in primary and secondary schools is a graduate profession. There are two main routes into teaching:
- You can take a BEd, BA or BSc degree leading to QTS over 3 or 4 years of full-time study. QTS is awarded subject to passing skills tests in numeracy, literacy and information and communications technology. Shortened degrees are available at some institutions for candidates with previous study at higher education level (eg HND or DipHE) and for candidates who are qualified to teach overseas.
- There are also employment-based routes to QTS for people who wish to qualify while working in a school. The Graduate Teacher Programme, for people with a degree, takes between 3 months and 1 year. The Registered Teacher Programme, for people with an HND, Foundation degree or equivalent, normally takes 2 years. You can do a BA or BSc degree in another subject (preferably a National Curriculum subject) and then a PGCE at a university or college. Most PGCEs take 1 year of full-time study, but part-time and flexible routes are available. Some institutions offer a 2-year conversion route for candidates whose degree is in a different subject from the one they wish to teach. School-Centred Initial Teacher Training offers the option of PGCE study based in and run by schools. PGCE candidates must pass the skills tests to obtain Qualified Teacher Status.
- Newly qualified teachers must complete an induction period and register with the General Teaching Council.

Teacher: special educational needs

- Only those with QTS can move into this role.
- It is generally necessary to have 2 years' teaching experience in a mainstream school before training to become a teacher for pupils with special educational needs.
- You must have a relevant qualification within 3 years if you are teaching children with visual, hearing or multi-sensory impairments.
- Postgraduate qualifications are available in subjects such as special educational needs, specific learning difficulties (dyslexia), and visual impairment. Courses can usually be studied part time or by distance learning.
- Qualified teachers of hearing impaired pupils require CACDP Stage 1 in sign language, or equivalent. Qualified teachers of visually impaired pupils must be proficient in Braille.

CRCI:F

CLCI:FAB

Working conditions

Teachers work in all kinds of settings within public and private sector schools and learning centres, and in their own or pupils' homes as tutors or music teachers.

You must be prepared to travel, as there are school trips, visits to students on work placements, band tours, and overseas visits for modern foreign language and PE teachers.

If you teach ESOL, you may work in this country or abroad, teaching in community and learning centres, commercial and industrial settings.

There are opportunties for promotion within your own or another school, initally to department head, and later up to management level, although you may have to move schools to take up your next post.

The future outlook

There is always a need for teachers. At present, there are shortages of maths, physics and chemistry teachers. It is also hard to recruit modern foreign language and design technology teachers in some parts of the country.

Although budgets have meant that some schools have been forced to increase class sizes and have therefore recruited additional teaching assistants, there is now more money coming to schools and additional teachers are being recruited.

Music teaching has suffered, but more music teachers are predicted to be needed.

There are many ways to enter teaching today, encouraging late-starters – graduates and non-graduates – to take up a teaching career, sometimes, with a 'golden handshake'. There may be further salary increases for teachers who are effective in helping their students achieve good results, besides the Advanced Skills Teachers who advise on classroom practice.

If you join as a probationary teacher, there is a well-designed progression route that should enable all teachers, who want to, to move into more responsible positions such as head of a department, subject or year group. They can then move on to deputy headship or even become head teachers.

Some teachers decide to leave direct classroom work to enter support or advisory roles with local authorities, or become an inspector or trainer.

Other related opportunities

- Adult Education Organiser / Tutor p170
- Education and Childcare Inspector p173
- Lecturer p178
- Road Safety Officer p583
- Teaching / Classroom Assistant p187
- Work-based Training p188

Advantages/disadvantages

- Time is short – there is preparation, classes, marking and assessing, analysing coursework, communicating with examining bodies, meetings and ordering materials.
- Work starts the moment you enter the building and continues until you leave, but it does mean that you value your holidays.
- In teaching, there are rewards from unexpected quarters – a gleam of understanding from a child with severe disabilities, or a top GCSE result from an outsider are all moments to remember.

Further information

Cambridge ESOL
1 Hills Road
Cambridge
CB1 2EU
01223 553355
www.cambridgeesol.org
Former UCLES:
www.cambridgeassessment.org.uk

Training and Development Agency for Schools
Portland House
Stag Place
London
SW1E 5TT
020 7925 3700
www.tda.gov.uk

Can Teach
www.useyourheadteach.gov.uk

Eteach
www.eteach.com

MUSIC TEACHER

Associated Board of the Royal Schools of Music
24 Portland Place
London
W1B 1LU
020 7636 5400
www.abrsm.org.uk

Music Teachers
www.musicteachers.co.uk

Earnings guide

Teacher of English to speakers of other languages (TESOL)

- If you work within the UK you can earn approximately £13,000–£18,000 per year, but short-term contracts are usual and opportunities are often seasonal. Senior positions attract salaries of between £18,000 and £27,000. If you work outside the UK, your salary is likely to be much lower.

Teacher of music

- Generally, wages are between £20 and £30 per hour depending on reputation, experience and location.

Teacher: primary school

- There are strict guidelines governing teachers' pay. In England, Wales and Northern Ireland, primary level salaries begin at £20,627 per year and rise to £30,148 – more if working in London. In Scotland, they are £19,440–£31,008.
- With promotion, in all areas salaries can be in excess of £33,444. Advanced Skilled Teachers (ASTs) can earn £34,083–£51,819.

Teacher: secondary school

- Newly qualified teachers (NQTs) start at £20,627 in England and Wales, or £24,168+ if they work in inner London.
- With experience, skills and passing different thresholds, this can rise to £30,148–£35,121. More if working in London or the south-east of England.

Teacher: special educational needs

- This job also has fixed salary scales. Salaries start at £20,627 per year and rise to £30,148 with experience. With added responsibility and additional points, you can achieve up to £33,926.
- Special Educational Needs (SEN) teachers starting salaries depend on the employer, level of qualifications and responsibilities.

CRCI:F

CLCI:FAB

Teaching / Classroom Assistant

What the work involves

- You will help individual pupils to learn by supporting their teacher and sometimes by describing the work in a more visual way or reading questions aloud.
- Teaching assistants can plan and deliver parts of a lesson for the main teacher, working together to make the best use of time and resources.
- You have to check the progression of students, often in small groups. This can be important if it is a large class where there is little time for the teacher to give pupils' individual attention.

The type of person suited to this work

In this work, you need to like children and be able to work with them to help them make the most of their time in school. You should be interested in children and their social and educational development. You will need lots of patience and be able to stay calm, as all pupils have their off-days when they are noisy or upset.

Sometimes, you will work with the students who need extra help so you should be confident and be able to get young people motivated.

Working conditions

Nearly every school or college has a team of classroom or teaching assistants working in different departments, under a line manager.

If you are attached to a particular group of students, you may have to hurry about between their timetabled classes.

You will also do lots of different tasks such as photocopying, preparing materials for artwork, taking out and putting away equipment, listening to reading, checking sums, putting up wall displays and completing records.

The future outlook

Recent changes to the workload of teachers have involved freeing them from some administrative tasks so they have more classroom time. This has increased the need for teaching assistants working across the UK.

One response has been the introduction of the new post of higher level teaching assistant. In 2007, over 8000 people had achieved HLTA Status.

Often, teaching assistants train to become teachers themselves, and there are Initial Teacher Training courses specially for teaching assistants.

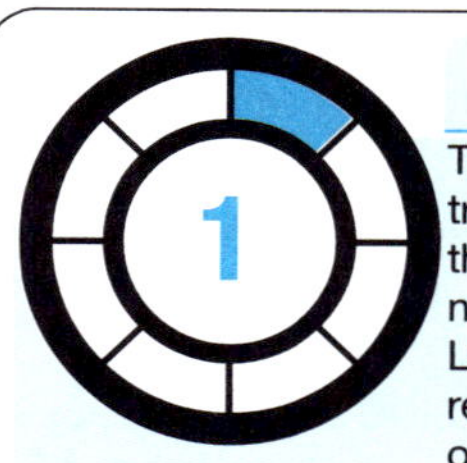

entry level

To both enter and train while working in this career, you will need qualifications at Level 1. Please refer to explanation on page vii.

Qualifications and courses

- There are no set qualifications for this role, but applicants are encouraged to have a good general education, including English and maths skills. Previous relevant experience, for example in nursery nursing, is an advantage. Candidates need to be at least 18.
- Pre-entry qualifications at Level 2 are available. Level 2 Certificates for teaching assistants are offered by CACHE, NCFE, Edexcel (BTEC) and ABC. These qualifications are also available to people already working in childcare.
- CACHE, NCFE and Edexcel (BTEC) also offer a Level 3 Certificate, aimed at experienced teaching assistants. GCSEs/S grades (A–C/1–3) including English and maths are normally required for entry to a Level 3 course.
- Teaching/classroom assistants are trained on the job. Local authorities in England and Wales may provide additional training.
- People already working as teaching or classroom assistants can work towards NVQ Level 2 and 3 in Teaching Assistants or SVQ Level 2 and 3 in Classroom Assistants. There are also NVQs/SVQs in Early Years Care and Education.
- Teaching assistants in England can work towards Higher Level Teaching Assistant (HLTA) status. Literacy and numeracy qualifications at Level 2 are required to begin training.
- A number of colleges and universities offer Foundation degrees for teaching assistants and learning support assistants. Typical entry requirements are GCSEs/S grades (A–C/1–3), relevant work experience, and a Level 3 qualification such as an A level/2 H grades.
- For those aged 16–24, Apprenticeships/ Skillseekers may be available in this area.
- Anyone who will be working with children must undergo a CRB police check.

CRCI:F | CLCI:FAB

Other related opportunities

- Nursery Nurse p538
- Play Worker p180
- Road Crossing Assistant (Schools) p582
- Special Needs Learning Support Assistant p183
- Teacher p184

Advantages/disadvantages

- Working with children and young people can be exhausting but fun!
- This can be a very rewarding job as you will see the pupils in your class develop and grow.
- You will be very busy, so you may have to snatch meetings with colleagues to share information.

Earnings guide

- Pay levels are set by local authorities or sometimes by school governors, so the rate can vary across regions.
- The starting salary is normally between £11,000 and £16,000 per year. With experience, this can rise to between £16,000 and £21,000.
- The rate for a HLTA is set by the local authority.

Further information

Training and Development Agency for Schools
Portland House
Stag Place
London
SW1E 5TT
020 7925 3700
www.tda.gov.uk

CACHE (Council for Awards in Children's Care and Education)
Beauort House
Grosvenor Road
St Albans
Hertfordshire
AL1 3AW
01727 818616
www.cache.org.uk

NCFE national awarding body
Citygate
St James' Boulevard
Newcastle upon Tyne
NE1 4JE
0191 239 8000
www.ncfe.org.uk

Lifelong Learning UK
5th floor, St Andrew's House
18–20 St Andrew Street
London
EC4A 3AY
0870 757 7890
www.lifelonglearninguk.org

www.cityandguilds.com/myperfectjob

Work-based Training

What the work involves

- Work-based training offers individuals the chance to gain a work skill whilst doing the job. Alongside learning about the job and getting practical experience, vocational (work-based) qualifications are taught, normally for one day a week or a block period, in a training centre or at a local college. The following illustrates the different jobs in work-based learning:

NVQ/SVQ Assessor

- Working alongside the trainees, you will offer feedback on their progress as they gain experience and take their NVQ/SVQ qualifications. Most of your work will involve watching individuals, asking them questions and then signing off modules as they progress towards achieving their NVQs/SVQs.
- You will observe how trainees do different tasks and measure their achievements against the standards for the qualification. You will also read through each trainee's portfolio of evidence, checking that tasks are undertaken.

Instructor

- As an instructor you will work alongside trainees teaching them how to gain their skills.
- You will visit trainees in their workplace or training centre, giving them support and training them to improve their skills.
- You might provide people with expert knowledge in a new skills area.

Manager

- Working for a training company, you will predict the present and future skills needs of your workforce and identify what is needed to improve them.
- You will develop your company's training policy, manage a budget, review staff levels and record your employees' or trainees' training progress.

The type of person suited to this work

For each of these jobs you will need a real interest in other people and a commitment to helping them to progress. This is not a fixed area of work – the need for new skills arises all the time, particularly in ICT. Therefore, you must be interested in new technology, efficiency and cost-effectiveness.

You will need excellent people skills as you will deal with all kinds and ages of individuals whom you will need to motivate and encourage – some of whom will not have enjoyed school and find training difficult.

You will need excellent communication skills for the large amount of speaking, questioning, listening and reporting that are involved. In addition you should be extremely organised and able to interpret the different standards in ways that are helpful to those who are learning.

Working conditions

You will have access to an office where you will update learner records, check learners' portfolios and work at your computer. However, you will also spend a lot of your time travelling to meet employers and learners at their places of work.

Depending on your specialist area you could have very early starts (for example assessing bakers at work) or late finishes (assessing people serving in a restaurant or car finishers working nights).

To help those that you work with, you will need to stay up to date with the changes and developments in your occupational area by attending national employers' meetings or researching on the internet.

The future outlook

The arrival of new technologies, new companies and different ways of working means that there is a continual need to help businesses and industry develop the right people to carry out new work tasks. All of these jobs are playing a vital role in achieving this.

All companies today are expected to develop their workforces and the government is determined to raise skills levels across Britain. Training is important and there will be increasing need for instructors, NVQ/SVQ assessors and training managers in the future. This may result in more firms and organisations having a team of specialists who train other employees in their particular area of expertise – health and safety, information and communications technology, marketing, management practices, etc.

More young people are being encouraged to consider Apprenticeships, National Traineeships or Skillseekers opportunities upon leaving school or college. These all require staff to support them through their programmes. As the government intends to further encourage learning through work-based qualifications the situation will continue to be positive for those looking to work in the field.

Qualifications and courses

- There are no set entry requirements to work as a training instructor. Candidates must have knowledge and experience in the subject or work area to be taught, and normally a relevant academic or vocational qualification.
- You can work towards relevant qualifications whilst in employment, including the Chartered Institute of Personnel and Development (CIPD) Certificate in Training Practice (CTP) and NVQs/SVQs in Learning and Development at Levels 3, 4 and 5. The CTP is equivalent to NVQ/SVQ Level 3, and has no formal entry requirements.
- The higher level NVQs/SVQs and the CIPD Professional Development Scheme are appropriate for people in training manager posts.
- Postgraduate qualifications are available in subjects such as education and training management, training and development, mentoring and coaching. These programmes can usually be studied part time or by distance learning, and entry requirements are a degree or equivalent professional qualification.
- Training practitioners can also work towards NVQ/SVQ assessor qualifications. Entry requirements are at least 2 years' occupational experience in the subject or work area to be assessed.
- Assessor qualifications are A1 (assess candidates using a range of methods) or A2 (assess candidates' performance through observation). To obtain the qualification, you need to build up a portfolio of evidence from your work with NVQ/SVQ candidates.
- Qualified assessors can do further training to work as NVQ/SVQ verifiers. Verifier qualifications are V1 (conduct internal quality assurance of assessment process) or V2 (conduct external quality assurance of assessment process).

entry level

To both enter and train while working in this career, you will need qualifications at Level 4–8. Please refer to explanation on page vii.

Other related opportunities

- Driving Examiner / Driving Instructor p565
- Human Resources / Personnel Officer p20
- Lecturer p178
- Teacher p184
- Training Officer p33

Advantages/disadvantages

- You will spend lots of your time meeting, speaking to and getting to know other people.
- This work involves being at the centre of improving the skills levels of the workforce.
- These jobs offer people with experience the opportunity to train and dvelop others.

Earnings guide

NVQ/SVQ Assessor

- Average starting salaries are between £16,000 and £20,000. More experienced assessors can expect to earn £17,000–£25,000 per year which can increase beyond £35,000 for the most senior. It is also possible to do this work on a freelance basis. Rates start at £225 or more per day.

Instructor

- Salaries for instructors are between £21,000 and £26,000.

Manager

- Many work-based learning organisations are a part of larger private training companies who are profit orientated. Many managers are paid on the success of the learners and course results and can get bonuses in addition to their basic salary. Others are paid a fixed amount.
- For those on fixed salaries, these start at around £27,000+. The most experienced can achieve up to £45,000.

Further information

City & Guilds
1 Giltspur Street
London
EC1A 9DD
020 7294 2800
www.city-and-guilds.co.uk
enquiry@city-and-guilds.co.uk

OCR
9 Hills Road
Cambridge
CB2 1PB
01223 553311
www.ocr.org.uk

Chartered Institute of Personnel and Development
CIPD House
151 The Broadway
London
SW19 1JQ
020 8971 9000
www.cipd.co.uk

Qualifications and Curriculum Authority
83 Piccadilly
London
W1J 8QA
020 7509 5555
www.qca.org.uk
info@qca.org.uk

NVQ/SVQ ASSESSOR

Institute of Assessors and Interval Verifiers (IAV)
PO Box 148
Wirral
CH62 7W
0151 334 8215
www.iavitd.co.uk

MANAGER

ENTO
4th floor
Kimberley House
47 Vaughan Way
Leicester
LE1 4SG
0116 251 7979
www.ento.co.uk

CRCI:F

CLCI:FAP

Here's Charlotte Adams's story:

Teaching Assistant

Charlotte, who is 29, always wanted to work with children but had never considered working with children with special needs. However, she got a job at the Greenmead School, Putney, for children with special needs, by doing work experience there when she left school. That was 14 years ago and Charlotte is still at Greenmead. She has done a childcare course that lasted 2 years on a youth training scheme, giving her NVQ Levels 1 and 2 qualifications. This enables her to feed children who have had gastrostomies, to replace gastro tubes, to administer Rectal Valium (an emergency drug for epilepsy) and to use suction machines for children with tracheotomies or who have poor swallowing control.

WHAT THE JOB ENTAILS

'I support the teacher in a classroom of six children and there are another three assistants working with me. The children are aged between 3 and 11 years old and all have severe disabilities. In a day we will work with computers, standing frames, physiotherapy groups and music groups. We have a sensory room and do a lot of sensory work, including swimming. I and the other assistants also provide bus escorts for the children.'

WHAT'S GOOD ABOUT THE JOB

Charlotte enjoys what she does so much she says she will never change her profession. She is always busy and says she learns something new every day. However, one of the occupational hazards of working with children with disabilities is all the lifting and hoisting that it entails, leading to back pain and muscular strain, and people need to be physically fit to do what Charlotte does. This has not put her off, though, and she would like to progress to taking further qualifications in childcare such as NVQ Levels 3 and 4 to achieve her ultimate ambition of managing a caring agency or a respite centre for people with special needs.

WHAT YOU NEED TO SUCCEED

'Being patient, understanding and willing to learn. You should be prepared to be pleasantly surprised because there is more to life than just a wheelchair. If you are seriously considering doing what I do, you should visit a school or set up a work placement so you can prepare yourself. It will help you to decide if you feel up to the task.'

Are you interested in how and why things work? Do you enjoy using your hands and working with different tools or machinery? Engineering, manufacturing and production is a huge and varied section. Here are some of the careers included:

- **Engineer – Craft**
- **Motor Vehicle Body Repairer**
- **Packer**
- **Production Worker**
- **Sheet Metal Worker**

But what's it like working in this area?

Here's Steven Sharpe's story

Gas Distribution Worker

In a way, gas distribution is in the blood for Steven – his father has always worked for TRANSCO, the safety arm of the gas trade that deals with emergency leaks. Steven studied Maths, English, Geography, Physics and Metalwork at GCSE before joining TRANSCO where you get training on the job. He is now a TRANSCO Senior Operative and is currently going through the Gas Network Operations (GNO) scheme to become a TRANSCO Craftsman.

WHAT THE JOBS ENTAILS

'I work as part of a two-man team repairing gas escapes and renewing the gas pipes in the London Network. For example, we were recently called in after the big fire in east London that destroyed the art warehouse storing works by the likes of Tracey Emin and Damien Hirst.'

WHAT'S HOT AND WHAT'S NOT ABOUT THE JOB

'The downside of working for TRANSCO is that it is a 24-hour emergency call-out service, so you can be out at all hours and in all weather conditions. Working through the night digging up roads in the middle of winter isn't much fun, but I do like the variety of the work, where you are always doing something different, and the people I work with are great.'

Although Steven says he has not thought about where he would eventually like to end up in his career, he is progressing via the training scheme he is now undertaking and there is the possibility of further progression by going into further education at some point.

WHAT YOU NEED TO SUCCEED

'You have to be genuine and hardworking to get on in this job. People don't necessarily realise just how hard it is and you need to be prepared for the physical aspect of it. You also need to be genuine and you must have respect for the people you work with.'

Assembler

What the work involves

- You will work on an assembly line within a large or small factory or workshop, or at a bench. You could work on products within sectors as diverse as: engineering, furniture production, soft-furnishings, domestic electrical equipment, vehicles, electrical circuit boards and more.

Assembly line

- You will help to produce products or components as they arrive at your work area. Sometimes they may not stop, but keep moving along a belt or route in the factory.
- You could either work as part of a team where everyone has a different part to play, or on your own being responsible for a range of tasks.
- As the line needs to keep going at a set speed, you will be required to work at the same pace as everyone else.

Bench

- Batches of items will be brought to you for assembly at your bench or workstation.
- Using handtools, and in some cases simple machinery, you will carry out specific assembly tasks or create a finished product.

The type of person suited to this work

You will need to have practical skills and enjoy making or repairing items.

Depending on the type of assembly work and the products created you will spend much of your time working as part of a team – although at a bench you could be on your own.

In order to construct your product or components you will have to follow diagrams and instructions and be able to work quickly and precisely. If you are slow, others further up the line will not be able to do their work.

You will need to be able to get on with people and be responsible and hard working.

As it can be repetitive work you must be able to do the same task many times a day.

Working conditions

Assembly line

You can expect to be in a large factory type of environment – in some sectors this could be noisy, dirty and busy and in others, such as the electronics industry, it would be clean and dust-free.

Some assembly lines require 24/7 production; if so, you willl normally work a shift pattern. You will need to be physically fit.

Bench

You will be sitting or standing using the tools and machinery positioned around you. This could be physically demanding work.

You will need to be fast and accurate to keep production operating.

If you need to use a soldering iron for assembly it can be hot work and may cause fumes.

Part-time work is possible.

The future outlook

Assemblers are required in all types of companies producing all sorts of products and components across the UK. The largest employers of assemblers are the electrical, electronic and information technology industries.

As machines are increasingly replacing some of the assembly work that used to be done by people, jobs are reducing and will continue to do so. However there is still demand for assemblers to work on assembling products that are too intricate to be done by machine, or for assembling very small batches of goods.

Your opportunities will be dependent on the make-up of your local employment market.You should find out more about local manufacturing companies and check for vacancies in local newspapers, Connexions centres, careers centres and Job Centre Plus offices.

With experience, you may be able to progress into other areas of manufacturing such as quality control, or go on to train as an engineering craft worker.

CRCI:NJ

CLCI:SAB

Qualifications and courses

- There are no formal entry requirements for this work.
- Key Skills, GCSEs/S grades in English, maths and practical subjects or vocational qualifications in engineering/manufacturing can be useful.
- Apprenticeships/Skillseekers may be available to enter this area of work.
- You will need to have excellent manual skills. A practical entry test may be required for some jobs.
- For industries where parts are colour coded, such as electronics assembly, you will need good eyesight and normal colour vision.

entry level

To both enter and train while working in this career, you will need qualifications at Level 1–2. Please refer to explanation on page vii.

Other related opportunities

- Clothing and Fabric Production p198
- Engineer: Craft p203
- Motor Vehicle Work p217
- Warehouse p586

Advantages/disadvantages

- You will need to concentrate and work quickly for long periods of the day whilst doing repetitive work.
- You could be working in a dirty and noisy environment.
- The number of vacancies will continue to drop as more machines replace people.
- This type of work is available on a part-time basis, which is attractive to people with families wanting to supplement their income.

Earnings guide

- This will depend on the product and type of company you work for. Starting salaries for assemblers are on average £10,000–£12,000 per year.
- For experienced assemblers salaries can range from £12,000 to £16,000.
- Very skilled and experienced assemblers in certain parts of the industry, such as automotive assembly, can earn £18,000+.
- Assemblers in some industries receive a basic salary based on minimum wage rates.
- Productivity bonuses are commonly used as an incentive and will increase salaries.

Further information

Engineering Council UK
10 Maltravers Street
London
WC2R 3ER
020 7240 7891
www.engc.org.uk

www.cityandguilds.com/myperfectjob

CRCI:NJ

CLCI:SAB

Blacksmith

What the work involves

- By using traditional and modern forging techniques to heat, and then shape and join a wide range of different metals, you will create or repair different products and objects.

Artist blacksmith

- You will produce architectural and decorative pieces such as gates, garden features and furniture.
- You may create specially commissioned pieces such as a large sculpture or a stairway for a building project.

Industrial blacksmith

- You will produce functional objects for use by companies such as fire escapes, security screens or specialist tools.
- You may specialise in an area such as agricultural engineering, security or the mining industries.

entry level

To both enter and train while working in this career, you will need qualifications at Level 2–3. Please refer to explanation on page vii.

The type of person suited to this work

You should enjoy using practical skills and not mind getting hot, dirty and physically tired. As you will mostly work alone, you should enjoy your own company and be able to use your initiative.

Much of your time will be spent on your feet using different hand tools, often near to the forge which will be very hot.

Although you will be wearing protective clothing you will need to be very responsible. The tools and materials that you will be working with can be very dangerous.

Having a creative and artistic flair will help you to use your materials imaginatively.

Working conditions

To be able to work with the different metals you will be using different hand and bench tools and a forge. This will result in conditions that can be noisy, dirty and sometimes cramped.

You will spend much of the time on your feet working with your tools. This is physically demanding work, so you will need to be fit.

You will wear protective clothing such as gloves, ear protectors and goggles.

You may need to travel to meet customers or to install pieces of work 'on-site'.

The future outlook

There are around 900 blacksmiths working in the UK, most of whom are sole traders working for themselves. Those who work within a company might progress to supervisory or managerial posts.

If you are self-employed, future success will rely on your ability to gain orders. You will need to build your reputation based on the quality and creativity of your work.

Recently, blacksmithing has become recognised by architects and the building industry as offering creative structural opportunities.

Artist blacksmith

The current interest in decorative metalwork and its use in building projects has led to a slight increase in work for artist blacksmiths.

Industrial blacksmith

Often employed by engineering companies and the mining industry, there is a decline in opportunities for industrial blacksmiths.

Qualifications and courses

- Training can be by an apprenticeship or college course. Some courses may require specific GCSEs/S grades and forgework experience. These are available throughout the country.
- HNDs and degrees in creative aspects of blacksmithing are available. Two A levels/3 H grades and 5 GCSEs/S grades(A–C/1–3) are required for degree entry. A previous qualification in a craft-related subject is required for entry to some courses.
- The Countryside Agency operates a National Crafts Training Programme, in partnership with Herefordshire College of Technology. This combines on-the-job training with periods of block-release study at the college, and lasts from 2 to 3 years. Students can gain a range of awards at different levels from the Worshipful Company of Blacksmiths. The Scheme is primarily designed for trainees aged between 16 and 25, employed in firms in rural areas of England. Other professional bodies also offer a range of short specialist courses in blacksmithing.
- Industrial blacksmiths can train through an Apprenticeship/Skillseekers in engineering, which combines NVQ/SVQs in fabrication and welding with on-the-job blacksmith training.

CRCI:SAW

CLCI:N

Other related opportunities

- Engineer: Craft p203
- Farrier p243

Advantages/disadvantages

- Much of the work is done alone in a forge or workshop. This can be isolating.
- The work is tiring, hot and dirty, but when you have created what a customer requires it can be satisfying too.
- if you are involved in a creative project such as a commissioned sculpture, it can be very rewarding.
- If self-employed your long-term future could be uncertain.

Earnings guide

- There are currently no agreed minimum rates for apprentice blacksmiths so salaries can vary widely. Most blacksmiths are self-employed.
- Starting salaries generally range from £10,000 to £16,000 a year.
- Once training has been completed you could earn £25,000+ a year depending on regional differences.

Further information

British Artist Blacksmiths Association
60 Buchanan Street
Balfron
Glasgow
G63 0TW
01360 440830
www.baba.org.uk

National Association of Farriers, Blacksmiths and Agricultural Engineers
The Forge, Avenue B
10th Street
Stoneleigh Park
Warwickshire
CV8 2LG
024 7669 6595
www.nafbae.org

Worshipful Company of Blacksmiths
48 Upwood Road
Lee
London
SE12 8AN
020 8318 9684
www.blacksmithscompany.org.uk

Crafts Council
44a Pentonville Road
Islington
London
N1 9BY
020 7278 7700
www.craftscouncil.org.uk

Brewer

What the work involves

Technical brewer

- Your job will be to manage the production of beers and lagers in a brewery. You will also manage the brewery workers.
- In a large brewery you may have responsibility for one part of the brewing process such as mixing the ingredients, fermentation or quality control. In a small brewery you may manage the whole process.
- You will be responsible for checking the consistency and quality of the beer or lager, keeping records, and the ordering of stock and raw materials. Some technical brewers also develop new beers.

Brewery worker

- As making beer is a practical job that has many stages, you could be involved in the whole process, or just one aspect.
- Depending on your role, you will operate computerised machinery and monitor the quality and temperature of the beer.
- You will sterilise your equipment, clean your work area and keep records.
- You might also work outside, loading the beer and unloading deliveries.

The type of person suited to this work

Technical brewer

You will need to be scientific, with an enquiring mind and a particular interest in biochemistry. In addition, the brewery process involves lots of different machinery, much of it computerised, so both a practical ability and an interest in engineering are useful. As you will be managing both the process of making the beer and the people working in the brewery, excellent management and communication skills are needed.

Brewery worker

You will need to be practical, physically fit and able to be on your feet for long periods at a time. Good communication and team-working skills are important as you will be working with all the staff involved in the production process. As you will use many types of machinery and carry out different tasks you will also need to be flexible, have normal colour vision and good manual skills.

Working conditions

The process of brewing involves working in a hot, steamy, noisy and often smelly envionment. The brewery will need to operate 24/7, so expect to work on average 39 hours a week on shifts, including evenings and weekends.

You will have to wear overalls, a mask, boots and ear protection.

Technical brewer

Some of your work may take place in an office or a laboratory.

Brewery worker

You will be operating machinery, so you will need health and safety awareness.

The future outlook

Twenty-eight million pints of beer are drunk in the UK each day and about 90% of this beer is produced in this country. There are in the region of 2000 different brands of beer, and every day 1.5 million pints are exported to over 120 countries. There are currently about 21,000 people employed in the brewing industry in the UK.

Sales and exports of beers and lagers remain good, but increasing automation of the production process, larger breweries and low turnover of staff has resulted in an industry with few vacancies. First jobs in brewing can be very difficult to secure.

Technical brewer

Most technical brewers are recruited through graduate training programmes and positions can be competitive. Most vacancies are advertised locally or on company websites, so you will have to be very proactive in searching the jobs out. With experience, you could progress to positions such as senior/head brewer, or enter self-employment running your own specialised microbrewery. You could also move into related areas such as production, health and safety or retail and distribution.

Brewery worker

Increased use of machines has also reduced the numbers of brewery workers now working in the industry. It is likely that you would need to live near a brewery to obtain work, as most jobs are advertised locally. If successful you could then progress into supervisory levels or transfer to other breweries for promotion. If you obtain degree-level qualifications you could apply for technical brewer positions.

Qualifications and courses

entry level

To both enter and train while working in this career, you will need qualifications at Level 2–8. Please refer to explanation on page vii.

Technical brewer

- Entrants to this career need a degree in brewing/distilling, a pure or applied science such as biological science, microbiology, chemistry, chemical/mechanical engineering or food science/technology.
- Specialist degrees in brewing are offered by Heriot-Watt University. The BSc in Brewing and Distilling requires 3 A levels/H grades, including at least one science subject. Heriot-Watt University also offers a postgraduate diploma and an MSc in Brewing and Distilling. A degree in a biological science, chemistry or chemical engineering is required for entry to the course.
- Trainee brewers must achieve the professional qualifications of the Institute of Brewing and Distilling. The Diploma in Brewing qualifies you to work as a technical brewer. Candidates who have studied brewing at Heriot-Watt are exempt from the examination. The Diploma Master Brewer is taken by brewers with at least 4 years' experience in the industry.

Brewery worker

- There are no specific entry qualifications for this career, but GCSEs/S grades in English and maths are helpful. Apprenticeships/ Skillseekers may be available for candidates aged 16–24.
- Brewery workers are trained on the job, and may work towards NVQs/SVQs in Food and Drink Manufacturing Operations at Levels 1 and 2.
- The Institute of Brewing and Distilling offers a General Certificate in Brewing and Packaging and a General Certificate in Distilling, both of which equate to NVQ/SVQ Level 2.

Other related opportunities

- Bar Manager / Licensee p82
- Biotechnologist p471
- Cellar Technician p86
- Engineer: Professional p205
- Home Economist p93
- Scientist p486

Advantages/disadvantages

- Due to automation and low staff turnover, competition for vacancies can be high.
- The work includes lots of different aspects that include science, production, engineering, retail and distribution.
- Working in a brewery can be smelly, hot and physically demanding.
- You can feel a strong sense of satisfaction in being involved in producing a high-quality product.

Earnings guide

Technical brewer

- As a new entrant you can expect to earn on average £20,000 per year, rising with experience to £28,000. Middle managers on average earn £30,000–£40,000. Head brewers and production directors of large breweries can earn from £45,000 to £60,000+.

Brewery worker

- Your starting salary would be around £18,000 rising to up to £21,000 with experience. With promotion and additional responsibility, £26,000–£35,000 is possible. You are likely to earn additional pay for working shifts.

Further information

Institute of Brewing and Distilling
33 Clarges Street
London
W1J 7EE
020 7499 8144
www.ibd.org.uk

British Beer and Pub Association
Market Towers
1 Nine Elms Lane
London
SW8 5NQ
020 7627 9191
www.beerandpub.com

Improve Ltd (Sector Skills Council for food and drink manufacturing and processing)
Ground floor, Providence House
2 Innovation Close
York
YO10 5ZF
0845 644 0448
www.improveltd.co.uk

CRCI:NJ CLCI:SAB

CAD Draughtsman / Woman

What the work involves

- You will produce the drawings and instructions that will enable others to create structures, equipment or components.
- Using a a CAD workstation or PC, in a design and drawing office, you will draw up technical drawings for components or sections of a structure or piece of equipment.
- You will work from instructions or specifications or sometimes from a computer model of the whole project.
- Depending on the specialism of the company you work for, you may design part of a structure as large as a factory or bridge, or a component as small as an electronic circuit.

entry level

2–3

To both enter and train while working in this career, you will need qualifications at Level 2–3. Please refer to explanation on page vii.

The type of person suited to this work

You will have to be patient and accurate, and have a good understanding of different engineering processes.

Much of your time you will be working at your computer but you will also have to visit and instruct other staff and talk to supervisors. This means you should be happy working with people of all levels, and be confident and articulate.

Although an art ability is not necessary, an interest in technical drawing, ICT, maths and science is.

You will be creating the drawings and instructions that will aid production so you will look for creative solutions to problems. You will design using manual or computerised equipment, so you should be happy using both styles.

Working conditions

Most of your work will be done sitting in front of your computer or drawing board in an office or design area.

You will work office hours but you may need to work overtime when deadlines are close.

Sometimes you will visit the shop floor or factory area where the product you are designing is being made – which could be noisy, hot and dirty.

The future outlook

A wide range of employers recruit CAD draughtsmen and women, including aeronautical, civil, electrical, mechanical and marine engineering companies, central and local government and the public utilites such as water and electricity supply.

Due to the recent advancements in CAD work, there is currently a shortage of draughtspeople across the country

You can progress on to senior, supervisory and team-leader work with experience and training.

There are opportunities to work abroad.

Qualifications and courses

- You can enter this job as a trainee technician with an employer, through an Apprenticeship/Skillseekers scheme. Most entrants are aged 16–19, but entry is possible up to the age of 24. Applicants require four 4 GCSEs/S grades (A–C/1–3) or equivalent including maths and science or technology.
- Alternatively, you can take relevant pre-entry qualifications such as a BTEC First Certificate in Engineering or First Diploma in Manufacturing Engineering, National Certificate/Diploma in Manufacturing Engineering, or a City & Guilds Level 2 award in CAD.
- Some gain entry at technician level, after attaining a BTEC National Certificate or Diploma in a subject like engineering or manufacturing.
- It is possible to work as an engineering operative, craftsperson or CAD operator whilst studying part-time.
- Apprenticeships/Skillseekers are available for candidates aged 16–24.
- Qualifications that can be obtained through on-the-job training include NVQs/SVQs at Level 3, BTEC National Certificates or Diplomas, an SQA National Certificate Group Award or a City & Guilds certificate.

CRCI:GH | CLCI:RAX

Other related opportunities

- Architectural Technician / Technologist p38
- Surveyor / Surveying Technician p70
- Town Planning Technician p76

Advantages/disadvantages

- As much of your work involves using your drawing board or computer, your eyes could get tired and strained.
- Currently there is a shortage of skilled CAD draughtsmen and women.
- If you want to progress you can move to supervisor level within your own company or elsewhere.
- With experience, it may be possible to do this work on a freelance basis, being contracted by smaller companies who do not employ their own draughtsperson.

Earnings guide

- Earnings will be affected by the type of industry you work in and your location.
- General starting salaries are around £15,000–£19,500 per year.
- With experience, and working in one of the higher paying industries, you can earn up to £26,000.
- At senior level you can earn more than £40,000.

Further information

Engineering Careers Information Service
SEMTA House
14 Upton Road
Watford
Hertfordshire
WD18 0JT
0800 282167
www.enginuity.org.uk

Scottish Engineering
105 West George Street
Glasgow
G2 1QL
0141 221 3181
www.scottishengineering.org.uk

Chartered Institute of Architectural Technologists
397 City Road
London
EC1V 1NH
020 7278 2206
www.ciat.org.uk

www.cityandguilds.com/myperfectjob

Clothing and Fabric Production

What the work involves

Clothing packer

- You will pack or re-pack various items of clothing for distribution.
- Manual packing will include folding, arranging and packaging individual items of clothing, or batches of clothes, so that they are displayed well and can be safely dispatched.
- Some mass-produced garments are packed by a machine that you would load with garments and packaging materials, and then unload the packaged items for dispatch.

Clothing pattern cutter/grader

- You may specialise in either pattern cutting or grading, or do both these jobs.
- If working as a pattern cutter, you will produce patterns from designers' drawings and concepts.
- If working as a pattern grader, you will use computer-aided design technology to adapt the pattern to fit different sizes.

Clothing presser

- You will use steam pressing machines to finish a garment.
- Different machines, usually computerised, will be operated depending on the type of fabric and the garment.
- If working in a small workshop, you may hand press garments using steam irons and vacuum presses.

Clothing sewing machinist

- You will make all or part of a garment or item by stitching together pre-cut fabric pieces.
- Some processes may be computerised so that you will just need to load part of a garment into a machine, which will then be programmed to stitch automatically.
- Your machine will need to be maintained by cleaning, oiling and changing needles and threads.

Footwear manufacturing operative

- You will make shoes and boots as part of a production process.
- You will probably work in one part of production: cutting out leather or fabric, stitching together the uppers, moulding the upper shoe, or completing the shoe with sprays, laces or dyes.
- You may work with your hands or use mechanical, computerised, or electronic equipment.

Knitting machinist

- You will operate machines that knit yarn into fabric or garments, and carry out basic maintenance, such as cleaning, on your equipment.
- You may need to supervise the smooth running of several machines and deal with minor problems.
- If you are employed by one of the smaller, specialist manufacturers you may produce individual items with some handcrafting.

Tailor/dressmaker

- You will produce made-to-measure clothes for individual customers.
- Meeting each customer you will discuss what they would like made, agree style, fabric and costings, measure them, and later do regular fittings.
- If working as a dressmaker, you will make a range of clothing, including dresses, skirts, trousers and blouses for children and adults. If working as a tailor, you will specialise in making suits and coats for men and women.

Textile operative

- Working in a textile factory, manufacturing products such as carpets, you may work preparing the yarns of fibres to be woven or knitted (this may involve carding and combing, or with synthetic fibres, chemical processing), or on a machine spinning the yarn onto cones or bobbins, or making the fabric on a loom.
- You will carry out basic maintenance on your machinery, make sure you have a supply of raw materials and keep your work area clean and tidy.
- You may work on finishing processes such as dyeing or waterproofing.

Textile technician

- You will be responsible for the maintenance of all machinery and equipment in the textile factory.
- Once a fault has been identified you will be responsible for the entire repair, working out what is wrong and getting the machinery back in service.
- You may specialise in repairing a specific type of machine, or have a more multi-skilled general maintenance role.

Qualifications and courses

Clothing packer

- Apprenticeships/Skillseekers are the normal route for career entry. The entry requirements for these are usually 4 GCSEs/S grades (A–C/1–3) including English and maths, whilst design and technology and/or art and design are also useful subjects. Computer literacy is becoming increasingly important in this industry.
- Training qualifications, gained on the job, are available as follows: NVQ/SVQ Level 2 in Manufacturing Sewn Products, ABC Levels 2 and 3 Certificates in Pattern Cutting, or NVQ/SVQ Level 2 in Manufacturing Sewn Products.

Clothing pattern cutter/grader

- A qualification in a clothing-related subject is required by many companies. Experience in fashion can be helpful.
- Apprenticeships/Skillseekers are the normal route for career entry. The entry requirements for these are usually 4 GCSEs/S grades (A–C/1–3) including English and maths, whilst design and technology and/or art and design are also useful subjects.
- Training qualifications, gained on the job, are available as follows: NVQ/SVQ Level 2 in Manufacturing Sewn Products, ABC Levels 2 and 3 Certificates in Pattern Cutting, or NVQ/SVQ Level 2 in Manufacturing Sewn Products.

Clothing presser

- There are no formal entry requirements for this job although you would need to be able to follow instructions carefully as most clothes pressing operations involve heavy machinery.
- Clothing pressers can work either within textile and clothing manufacturing companies or in dry-cleaning companies. You will be expected to be able to use a variety of different pressing machines.
- Training is usually on the job. NVQs/SVQs are available in Manufacturing: Sewn Products at Levels 1 and 2. Apprenticeships/Skillseekers are available for those aged 16–24.

Clothing sewing machinist

- Whilst there are no formal entry requirements, employers invariably seek sewing experience and there might well be an 'eye' test to undertake. Where Apprenticeships/Skillseekers are offered, then some GCSEs/S grades could be required.
- NVQ/SVQs at Levels 1 and 2 can be achieved. The qualification covers the main areas of cutting, sewing, sealing and pressing. NVQ Level 3 in Apparel Manufacturing Technology can then be taken. City & Guilds qualifications are available at Level 1, covering the basic skills for sewing and at Level 2 in clothing and knitting crafts.

Footwear manufacturing operative

- Entrants may be required to show potential practical skills and the ability to use machines and other computerised equipment. A manual dexterity test is sometimes needed.
- Apprenticeships/Skillseekers are available for candidates aged 16–24
- NVQs are also available: Levels 1 and 2 in Footwear Manufacture, and Level 3 in Footwear and Leather Products Manufacture.

Knitting machinist

- Whilst there are no formal entry requirements, most employers seek GCSEs/S grades, including English and maths.
- Most training is usually done on the job under the supervision of a trained knitter.
- Apprenticeships/Skillseekers are a typical route for those seeking to train as a Savile Row tailor, learning under the supervision of a master tailor.
- NVQs/SVQs at Levels 1 and 2 in Manufacturing Textiles are offered to applicants with some experience.

Tailor/dressmaker

- Whilst there are no formal entry requirements, most employers seek GCSEs/S grades, including English and maths.
- A relevant BTEC National qualification can be studied on a full-time or part-time basis, either before entry or while working.

entry level

To both enter and train while working in this career, you will need qualifications at Level 1–2. Please refer to explanation on page vii.

- Apprenticeships/Skillseekers are a typical route for those seeking to train as a Savile Row tailor, learning under the supervision of a master tailor.
- Learning is carried out on the job. NVQ/SVQs at Levels 1 and 2 in Manufacturing Sewn Products are available. These cover certain areas of cutting, sewing, sealing and pressing. NVQ Level 3 in Apparel Manufacturing Technology can then be achieved.
- Other relevant qualifications include ABC Level 3 awards in Pattern Cutting and Construction Techniques: Handcraft Tailored Trousers and Construction Techniques: Handcraft Tailored Jackets.
- Apprenticeships/Skillseekers are available for candidates aged 16–24.

Textile operative/Technician

- There are no formal entry qualifications, but some employers prefer GCSEs/S grades (A–C/1–3) in English and maths, or the equivalent.
- An eye test and colour vision test may be required.
- Apprenticeships/Skillseekers may be available for people aged 16–24. A technician apprenticeship is a common entry route for young people.
- Apprentices work towards NVQs/SVQs in Manufacturing Sewn Products at Levels 1–2 and Manufacturing Textiles at Levels 1–3.
- Some people enter at technician level with an HNC/D or Foundation degree in textiles.

The type of person suited to this work

You will need an interest in clothing and textiles and how they are made.

Working in places where dangerous tools and machines are used, you will also need to be practical, responsible, reliable, methodical, and health-and-safety conscious.

Working well within a team, you also need to be able to concentrate and work on your own to meet production deadlines.

You will need good manual dexterity as many jobs in this industry require good practical skills.

For many jobs it would be helpful to be physically fit, as you may be required to lift heavy materials, tools or finished products as part of your daily work.

Creativity, with a strong eye for colour and design, and sewing skills are essential if the job includes handcrafting skills, for example the job of tailor/dressmaker.

Working conditions

Many of these jobs are based in a clothing or textiles manufacturing factory, which can be quite noisy, busy and sometimes stuffy or dusty, although they are usually clean and well lit.

Working as a clothing presser you will need to be willing to stand for long periods of time and work in a hot and damp atmosphere.

Technological advances have reduced the noise levels of machinery in many clothing and textiles factories, but where noise is a problem you will be provided with ear protectors.

Workers in the industry generally work a 35–40 hour week, which may involve shift work and some overtime. Saturday and evening work is common for tailors/dressmakers.

The future outlook

Around 90,000 people are employed in the manufacture of clothing and other textile-related goods in the UK. Many employers are small companies but one in five people in this sector work for organisations with 200 or more employees.

The manufacture of clothes, shoes and textiles increasingly takes place overseas because of lower production costs, but the UK still has a significant clothing and textiles industry. The UK industry maintains its foothold in the market by producing good quality shoes, textiles and clothes to target the high end of the market.

Numbers of unskilled opportunities are decreasing. Firms use modern equipment and there is a demand for multi-skilled staff especially at technician level.

The clothing and textiles industry values staff who become highly-trained or multi-skilled, and there are good progression opportunities to supervisory, training, quality control and management roles.

Other related opportunities

- Assembler p192
- Designer p136
- Engineer: Craft p203
- Engineer: Technician p208
- Shoe Repairer p453

Advantages/disadvantages

- Operative level jobs in the industry can be very repetitive, especially if you are involved in only a small part of the process.
- Some jobs can be creative, for example tailors/dressmakers use their creativity to produce individual garments for customers.
- More jobs are becoming multi-skilled – this makes the job more interesting and there is a demand from employers for workers with a range of skills.
- It is a sizeable industry and you may be able to progress onto supervisory, training, or management work within a larger company.

Earnings guide

Clothing packer

- Starting salaries are around £10,000 a year and with experience you could earn from £12,000 to £18,000.

Clothing pattern cutter/grader

- Salaries start on around £12,000 and rise to £20,000 with experience. Supervisors in some large companies and fashion houses may earn more than £25,000.

Clothing presser

- Starting salaries are around £10,500 rising after training to around £11,000. Experienced clothing pressers earn around £12,500–£14,000.

Clothing sewing machinist

- Starting on average at £10,500 a year, with experience you can earn around £12,500–£15,000. Some employers pay piece rates. This means that the more items you make, the more you earn.

Footwear manufacturing operative

- New entrants earn around £10,000–£12,000 a year. Once trained and experienced, operatives can earn £12,500–£18,000 including overtime and shift payments.

Knitting machinist

- Starting salaries are around £10,000 a year rising with experience to £13,000–£20,000 a year.

Tailor/dressmaker

- Training salaries are around £10,500–£12,500 a year. An experienced tailor/dressmaker can earn £18,000–£25,000 a year. Some senior tailors/dressmakers may be able to earn up to £50,000+ a year.

Textile operative

- You could start on £10,000–£12,000 per year. An experienced worker can earn up to £20,000 a year.

Textile technician

- As a trainee you may get £7500–£9000. When trained and with experience salaries range from £16,000–£20,000. A technician with wide experience and responsibility for complex machinery can earn up to £25,000.

Further information

Carpet Foundation
MCF Complex
60 New Road
Kidderminster
Worcestershire
DY12 1AQ
01562 755568
www.comebacktocarpet.com

Confederation of British Wool Textiles
Merrydale House
Roysdale Way
Bradford
West Yorkshire
BD4 6SB
01274 652207
www.cbwt.co.uk

Textile Centre for Excellence
Textile House
Red Doles Lane
Huddersfield
West Yorkshire
HD2 1YF
01484 346500
www.textile-training.com

Textile Institute
1st floor, St James's Buildings
Oxford Street
Manchester
M1 6FQ
0161 237 1188
www.texi.org

Textile Services Association
7 Churchill Court
58 Station Road
North Harrow
Middlesex
HA2 7SA
020 8863 7755
www.tsa-uk.org

IoP: The Packaging Society c/o Institute of Materials, Minerals and Mining
Springfield House
Springfield Business Park
Grantham
Lincolnshire
NG31 7BG
01476514590
www.iop.co.uk

CRCI:SAS

CLCI:N

Electricity Generation Worker

What the work involves

- Staff working within power stations install, repair, operate and maintain the machinery and equipment involved in generating electricity.
- You will be using a range of practical enginering skills, diagnosing faults and working to correct them.
- Craft workers often work in a specialism such as mechanical, control and instrumental (C&I), or electrical. They can also be multi-skilled across a range of different engineering craft areas.

Mechanical

- You will specialise in the repair and upkeep of apparatus and equipment like boilers and turbines.

Electricity

- Within this area you will deal with electrical plant and equipment like transformers, generators and electrical switchgear.

Control and Instrumentation (C&I)

- Operating and maintaining all of the control equipment and instruments that monitor the plant within the power station will be your main responsibility.

The type of person suited to this work

If you want to work within an electricity generating station you should be very methodical in your approach to work and be able to read and understand technical drawings, instructions and diagrams. You will also need to be practical, as you will use a range of hand and power tools.

As you will normally be working as part of a team, it is important to have good communication skills.

This work can be dangerous, so you will also have to be both responsible and aware of health and safety regulations for yourself and your team.

If you are working with electrical plant and equipment you will need normal colour vision.

Working conditions

Your working hours will depend on the area that you specialise in. You could do a basic Monday to Friday working week but it is more common to work in shifts to include weekends. You may also be on-call for emergencies. You should expect to have to work overtime if necessary.

You will normally work within a power station. This means that the type of environment will depend on the individual power station. You could be working in a cramped space, dirty workshop or clean work area.

You will probably wear protective headgear and overalls.

The future outlook

A range of fuels are used in the electricity generation industry including, coal, oil, nuclear, gas, wind, marine and biomass (a mix of renewable woodbased materials). Power stations are often built in isolated parts of the UK because of the fuel sources. However there are a range of changes taking place exploring different types of plants and renewable fuels, such as the recent investment in a project to build a number of windfarms on large industrial sites. These windfarms would enable a power generating company to make and supply electricity directly to a few large industrial consumers.

There are around 40 companies operating as major electricity producers who provide the bulk of the oportunities, and you need to apply for vacancies directly from these companies. Entry into this work can be competitive and work experience is recommended.

With experience you could progress into technician, supervisory or managerial positions.

Qualifications and courses

- To enter this work you will normally have completed your training as an engineering craftsperson and have been trained to NVQ/SVQ Level 3.
- This is achieved by training on the job and through part-time study.
- There are a number of routes into craft engineering, and formal qualifications are not always necessary.
- It is possible to enter through the Apprenticeship/Skillseeker route. Some employers may require up to 5 GCSEs/S grades (A–E/1–5) and look for English, maths, science and technology, or equivalent Level 2 qualifications.
- During or after qualification as a craft engineer it is possible to take NVQ/SVQs at Level 2 and 3 in Maintaining Electricity Generating Systems and Operating Electricity Generation Systems.

entry level

To both enter and train while working in this career, you will need qualifications at Level 2–3. Please refer to explanation on page vii.

Other related opportunities

- Engineer: Craft p203
- Engineer: Technician p208
- Gas Distribution Worker p211
- Oil and Gas Drilling Industry p219

Advantages/disadvantages

- This can be dangerous work – care and attention to your personal and colleagues' safety is important at all times.
- Entry into the work is competitive.
- Some electricity generating power stations are in very isolated areas – this may mean a long commute to work.
- Training and progression routes are good in engineering – with further training and experience you will be able to aim at technician level.

Earnings guide

- Salaries will depend on your location and your experience.
- As a trainee staring out you can expect to get £10,000–£15,000 a year.
- With experience and supervisory responsibility this could increase to £17,000–£22,000.
- Senior technicians can earn £35,000–£40,000.
- Extra payments are made for overtime and emergency call-outs.

Further information

www.cityandguilds.com/myperfectjob

Engineering Careers Information Service
SEMTA House
14 Upton Road
Watford
Hertfordshire
WD18 0JT
0800 282167
www.enginuity.org.uk

Engineering Council UK
10 Maltravers Street
London
WC2R 3ER
020 7240 7891
www.engc.org.uk

Scottish Engineering
105 West George Street
Glasgow
G2 1QL
0141 221 3181
www.scottishengineering.org.uk

AFAQ-ETA
185 Park Street
Bankside
London
SE1 9DY
020 7922 1630
www.afaq-eta.com

Institution of Engineering and Technology
Michael Faraday House
Stevenage
Hertfordshire
SG1 2AY
01438765586
www.theiet.org

Institution of Mechanical Engineers
1 Birdcage Walk
Westminster
London
SW1H 9JJ
020 7222 7899
www.imeche.org.uk

CRCI:GE
CLCI:RAK

Engineer: Craft

What the work involves

- You will be producing, repairing or designing different types of product constructed from a range of materials such as metal, plastic or wood.
- You will need to be able to operate a number of hand and power tools and possibly specialise and gain knowledge in one type of product or engineering area.
- The following list includes the most common opportunities and covers the different engineering areas:

Aerospace

- You will be producing or repairing aircraft or aircraft engine parts. Due to the importance of air safety you will have to be highly skilled and be able to work to extremely fine tolerances, being very accurate at all stages of your work whether measuring or using tools and equipment.

Agricultural

- You will mainly repair and service agricultural or land-based machinery and equipment, such as grass-cutting equipment, tractors and rotavators.

Electrical (Operator)

- You may work in maintenance and repair. Some operators work in homes repairing domestic equipment such as washing machines, tumble dryers or freezers. Others are involved repairing office or ICT equipment like photocopiers, computers, scanners or fax machines.
- Power supply/electrical installation: you would either work outdoors, ensuring external supply lines and cabling from the power station to the customers' premises are safe and efficient, or indoors installing, testing or repairing electrical supplies and equipment.
- Production: normally employed within the manufacturing industry working on production lines, you would be assembling or checking different electrical equipment.

Domestic appliances – gas

- You would repair, service and maintain gas-powered domestic appliances such as central-heating systems, cookers and fires.

Mechanical – general

- To encourage flexibility in the workplace many mechanical craftspeople are becoming more multi-skilled than specialists. This means you would gain the necessary skills in fabrication, welding, machining and fitting skills suitable for your employer's business.
- However, the following specialist roles are also available:

Machinist (turner/miller/lathe operator)

- A skilled job involving operating the different types of engineering equipment or tools such as CNC, turning, lathes, milling, grinding and drilling machines, cutting equipment and presses.

Sheet metal worker

- By using advanced manual and hand-tool skills, sheet-metal workers bend, cut, fold and join different metals to create and assemble products or components that are then used in the aerospace, mechanical, heating or car industries.

Toolmaker

- A specialised role involving building, designing and creating the tools which are needed to help production processes mostly within the manufacturing field.

Welder

- There are two types of welder. The most common are able to do any of the following different types of welding: oxygen and acetylene, electric arc and inert gas. They can select the correct technique for the specific job.
- Less common are welders who become specialists in one of the above types and are working in specialist areas like shipbuilding.

Maintenance fitter

- Fitters work within the following engineering areas: electrical, mechanical, aerospace or computers. They maintain, repair and service industrial machinery and equipment within factories or production lines.

The type of person suited to this work

Whichever area of engineering you choose to work in, you will be using lots of different hand or machine tools, so you should enjoy practical tasks and have good hand-eye coordination. An interest in knowing how and why things work, and what to do if they don't, is also useful. You should also be able to work on your own or as part of a team.

Within many areas of engineering you will have to work to very precise measurements and use technical diagrams, so being able to work accurately and patiently are both very important skills. Interest in maths, science and technology is also helpful, as is an ability to do mental arithmetic and having good computer skills.

Qualifications and courses

- Engineering craftspeople are trained to NVQ/SVQ Level 3. Training is usually done on the job and through part-time study. There are a number of routes into this work, and formal qualifications are not always necessary.
- The typical entry route to a career in craft-level engineering is by completing an Advanced Apprenticeships/Skillseekers in engineering. Most apprentices enter between the ages of 16 and 18, with 4–5 GCSEs/S grades (A–C/1–3), particularly in English, maths, science and technology, the new GCSE in engineering, or equivalent.
- Apprentices work towards at least NVQ/SVQ Level 3 in Engineering Production, and may go on to study for a national or higher national certificate or diploma.
- Many people who wish to work in this area take a degree in an engineering subject such as materials or mechanical engineering. Three A level/4 H grades (A–C/1–3) usually including maths and/or a science subject will be required.

entry level

To both enter and train while working in this career, you will need qualifications at Level 1–2. Please refer to explanation on page vii.

Working conditions

The type of environment that you work within will be very dependent on your chosen area of engineering, the type of products being produced or repaired, and the tools required to do so.

In many areas of engineering you will be indoors in a hot, noisy and sometimes dirty work space. However, in areas such as computer engineering you will work in workshops that have to remain clean and temperature controlled.

You will need to be physically fit, to be able to stand and to use the machines and tools that your chosen engineering area requires.

You might also need to pass a colour blindness test.

The future outlook

In the UK there are approximately 1.8 million people working in engineering. There is a steady demand for engineers at all levels including craft – especially for those with good levels of skills with a keeness to gain engineering qualfiications and experience.

If the sector is to continue to be successful and competitive, the new people entering the industry need to have the right skills, experience and qualifications.

Due to the lack of available craft engineers in some areas of the country, and the fact that companies are increasingly competing for contracts at both national and international levels, employers need their staff to be multi-skilled, flexible and happy to undertake ongoing training.

With experience, you could look to progress to a team leader or supervisory role either within your existing company or elsewhere, move into more specialised functions such as design, start your own business or look at taking additional qualifications to work at technician level.

Other related opportunities

- Assembler p192
- Blacksmith p194
- Electricity Generation Worker p201
- Engineer: Technician p208
- Gas Distribution Worker p211
- Locksmith p212
- Marine Engineering / Marine Industry p213
- Motor Vehicle Work p217
- Oil and Gas Drilling Industry p219
- Quarry Worker p221
- Railway Fitter / Electrician p223
- Thermal Insulation Engineer p225
- Watch / Clock Repairer p226

Advantages/disadvantages

- Not all of the areas of engineering are available at the same level throughout the country, and much will depend on where you work or live as to the range of options available.
- Whilst there are many specialised job areas, many employers increasingly want staff to be multi-skilled. This means that you might learn a range of skills rather than becoming specialised in one role.
- Salaries in the engineering sector are traditionally high.
- It is possible to take additional qualfications and training and progress on to technician level.

Earnings guide

- The industry has introduced suggested minimum salaries that are increasingly being used across the country.
- There may also be regional variations especially within London and the Midlands area, so use the following as a guideline only.
- First-year craft apprentices start around £8,000–£10,000 per year.
- Newly qualified craft engineers earn on average £17,000.
- It is possible to earn £23,000–£30,000 with qualifications and experience in some geographical and engineering areas.

CRCI:G

CLCI:R

Further information

www.cityandguilds.com/myperfectjob

GENERAL/MECHANICAL
Engineering Council UK
10 Maltravers Street
London
WC2R 3ER
020 7240 7891
www.engc.org.uk

AEROSPACE
Royal Aeronautical Society
4 Hamilton Place
London
W1J 7BQ
020 7670 4326
www.aerosociety.com/careers

AGRICULTURAL
Institution of Agricultural Engineers
West End Road
Silsoe
Bedford
MK45 4DU
01525 861096
www.iagre.org.uk

Engineering Careers Information Service
SEMTA House
14 Upton Road
Watford
Hertfordshire
WD18 0JT
0800 282167
www.enginuity.org.uk

Engineer: Professional

What the work involves

- If you work in engineering at professional level your work will involve managing other staff, making project decisions and undertaking research and development of existing or new products or services.
- At professional level you are more likely to ask members of your team to undertake practical tasks than do them yourself.
- Here are the major areas available for you to consider:

Aerospace

- Also known as aeronautical, you will work on different types of fixed or rotary winged civilian or military aircraft. Aerospace engineering recruits people with different engineering specialisms – so you can join having acquired chemical, electrical and mechanical skills and use them to meet the specific requirements of developing, maintaining or designing aircraft.

Agricultural

- To ensure that the agricultural and horticultural industries continue to be both profitable and efficient, they are increasingly using and developing technological equipment. You would develop, design and maintain new equipment, machines and processes. Your projects could be varied and include working on areas like crop protection, irrigation, building construction or forestry machinery.

Biomedical/Clinical

- This specialist area concentrates on using your engineering skills and experience to treat or rehabilitate patients with serious diseases or disabilities. Working alongside medical staff you will design things such as replacement joints or surgical equipment.

Chemical

- Using significant engineering skills you would be involved in the production and control of the chemical plant and machinery used in the manufacture of chemicals, plastics, pharmaceuticals and petroleum products.

Communications/Telecommunications

- Having an understanding of electronics engineering, you will specialise in the different methods used within the telecommunications field, such as fibre optics, satellite, video and telephone systems. You could also be involved in developing and installing telecommunications equipment in businesses.
- As a telecoms engineer you would be involved in installing, repairing and maintaining equipment.

Electrical

- Working at the 'front-end' of the industry; you would be researching, designing and developing new electronic products or innovations to deliver power supplies to the consumer.
- As you will probably operate in a team supervising and advising colleagues, you would need a thorough understanding of all aspects of the work of your organisation and other fields of engineering and science.

Energy/Environmental

- You will help to lead developments into alternative power sources such as those using wind, sea, sun and tidal energies.
- Other interest areas would include energy conservation in buildings.

Manufacturing – production

- You will oversee the different types of manufacturing operations in the manufacturing sector. Your role could depend on the size of the company you work for, as generally the smaller the organisation the wider range of skills you will need. You would be involved in controlling production – making sure equipment operates, stock and supplies are available, as well as liaising with the workforce and problem solving.

Manufacturing – quality control

- This is an important function as you would be responsible for the safety and effectiveness of the materials or products produced by your organisation. Your testing of equipment will range from purely visual to using high-level technical equipment like X-ray or ultrasonics. When faults are found you would have the power to either refer back to the designers, refuse to pass the product or even stop future production.

Materials

- Normally working within the development and testing side of a variety of engineering fields (for example, aerospace, construction or telecommunication), you will design, develop and improve the metals, products and different materials which surround us at home, work and play. Recognising environmental issues would be important, as would an understanding of both your own specialist engineering area and others.

Mechanical

- One of the broadest engineering areas, your work would probably be focused on the progressive and management sides of the mechanical engineering industry such as research and development, design, installation, marketing, manufacture or a combination of these.
- You will help to solve complex issues, so you will gain a feel for this sector, knowing which processes, tools and materials to use for which job.

Mining

- You would normally work within a team of other professional engineers designing and managing new or improving existing systems to extract ore from quarries or mines.
- Some of your work would involve the equipment and plant, as well as exploring the environmental impact of each system.

Nuclear

- Working within the production and use of nuclear fuels to generate electric power, your job could include skills from many engineering fields, including mechanical, civil or electrical, each adapted to handle and control the extremely dangerous radioactive materials.

Oil/Gas

- Involved in the specialised field of mining engineering, you will be concerned with exploration of oil and gas reservoirs within the earth. Once a potential source of oil or gas has been identified you would work alongside other experts, including geologists to determine the appropriate drilling processes required to extract the fuel and gauge the potential size of each field. Some of your work would be laboratory based.

Qualifications and courses

- Professional engineering (Chartered or Incorporated engineer) is usually a graduate profession, although there are opportunities to progress from craft or technical level in some branches of engineering.
- The main route to becoming a professional engineer is a degree in the relevant branch of engineering, for example chemical engineering, civil engineering, electrical/electronic engineering, manufacturing, materials or mechanical engineering, marine engineering, or a closely related subject. The normal minimum entry requirements for an engineering degree are 3 A levels or 5 Scottish Highers including mathematics and a science, usually physics or chemistry. Some employers offer sponsorship to students on degree courses and professional institutions also run scholarship programmes for relevant degree programmes.
- Candidates who do not have the relevant A levels or equivalent may gain entry to an engineering degree by taking a 1-year Foundation course. Foundation courses are offered by universities, and are sometimes taught at local partner colleges.
- Professional engineers can be Chartered or Incorporated members of one of the engineering professional bodies, for example the Institution of Chemical Engineers, the Institution of Civil Engineers, the Institute of Marine Engineers, the Institution of Mechanical Engineers, or the Institution of Engineering and Technology. The professional bodies accredit BEng and MEng degrees. The usual requirement for chartered status is an accredited MEng degree, or equivalent. For incorporated status, a 3-year accredited BEng or BSc degree or an HND or equivalent plus an additional period of learning in the relevant area is required.
- It is possible to enter engineering after taking GCSEs and progress to technician or professional level by studying part time for an HNC/D or NVQ/SVQ Level 4 or 5.

entry level

To both enter and train while working in this career, you will need qualifications at Level 4–8. Please refer to explanation on page vii.

The type of person suited to this work

To be an engineer at this level, you will need to have an analytical mind and be excited by finding out how and why things work or react in the way they do. You will normally work in a team consisting of other engineers representing all levels. This means you will need good verbal and presentation skills and the ability to get on with lots of different people.

If you are interested in science, maths, computer science and technology, engineering at this level applies skills and knowledge from all these subject areas. It will be useful to have a genuine interest in the specific area you choose.

Professional engineers (Chartered and Incorporated) generally work at the forefront of future developments – in lots of different industries. You should be an adaptable person interested and excited by the challenge of taking existing projects further or starting new ones.

Working conditions

Your working conditions will depend on your specialism, as you could work in large or small factories, workshops, laboratories, mines, quarries, indoors or outdoors. However, at professional level, much of your work is likely to be office- or laboratory-based.

Some working areas will be dirty and cramped, while other places like laboratories have to be clean and often temperature controlled. Although you could be working a standard 37–40 hour Monday to Friday week, you may do shifts, or be on 24-hour call out.

Many areas of engineering can be dangerous, involving work with hazardous chemicals and equipment, at height, underground or using large machines.

You will be provided with protective clothing reflecting your individual risk. Many engineering sectors require full-colour vision, so check this carefully before choosing your area.

The future outlook

During the 20th century, engineering has moved from being a clearly defined discipline to something that impacts on many sectors. Some of this has been due to the impact of technology and has resulted in increasing numbers of experienced engineers being required. In the UK currently there are more than 1.8 million people working in engineering. A recent survey showed that half of the top 1500 companies depended extensively upon engineering for the creation, development, manufacture or distribution of their products, services or processes.

There are around 600,000 engineers qualified at Chartered or Incorporated level in the UK. In many areas of engineering there are severe shortages of people with the necessary skills to sustain competitiveness.

All of this is good news for those entering the engineering sector. Your skills will be in demand and the number of employers at home and abroad requiring them are on the increase.

There are excellent promotion prospects. Experienced engineers can progress into management positions either managing a specfic project or a whole department. Some engineers move into marketing and sales, research or teaching. It is also possible to move into self-employed consultancy work. There are opportunites to work overseas and a wide range of international engineering companies.

CRCI:G

CLCI:R

Other related opportunities

- Air Traffic Controller p556
- Brewer p176
- Civil / Construction Engineer p46
- Engineer: Technician p208
- Marine Engineering / Marine Industry p213
- Pilot p573
- Quarry Worker p221
- Scientist p486

Advantages/disadvantages

- The range of jobs included within engineering is enormous, offering you the opportunity to change direction throughout your career to either progress or acquire new skills.
- Salaries within engineering are high in comparison to similar occupational sectors.
- Although engineering is at the forefront of most technological, production, research and development, and is therefore a very creative sector, many people still consider engineering to be an old-fashioned, dirty industry concerned with different machines.
- If science, maths and problem solving are your things, engineering could be the career for you!
- There are opportunities to work abroad.

Earnings guide

- Salaries across the engineering sector have risen steadily, especially with the impact of recruitment problems. With experience you should see your earnings increasing very quickly. The following should be used as a guide only as there will be regional differences.

Aerospace

- After graduation, expect £21,000–£26,000 per year. With 3–5 years' experience, this will rise to £35,000–£45,000. For those highly qualified salaries range between £45,000 and £60,000.

Agricultural

- After graduation, expect £21,000–£25,000. With experience this will rise to £27,000–£36,000. If chartered you can earn up to £50,000.

Biomedical/Clinical

- The NHS average training grade should expect around £24,000. Once registered and with experience this can rise up to £28,000–£36,000. Chartered status can bring £50,000+. Senior grades can be consultant level grades – £75,000+ is possible.

Chemical

- After graduation expect about £24,000–£27,000. With experience, and chartered, this will rise to £35,000–£60,000. For those highly skilled, the salary can go up to £150,000.

Communications/telecommunications

- After graduation, expect £23,000–£26,000. With experience the average salary is about £35,000. The salary for those highly skilled is £37,000–£45,000.

Electrical

- After graduation, expect around £23,000. With experience, the average salary is £35,000. The salary for those highly skilled is around £45,000.

Energy/Environmental

- Starting out expect £21,000–£23,000. With experience, this will rise to £27,000–£35,000. Highly skilled and with chartered status the salary range is £40,000–£50,000.

Manufacturing – production

- After graduation, expect around £22,000–£25,000. With experience, this will rise to around £26,500–£36,000. The salary for those highly skilled is around £50,000.

Manufacturing – quality control

- After graduation, expect around £23,000–£25,000. With experience, this will rise to around £36,000. The salary for those highly skilled is £37,000–£45,000.

Materials

- After graduation, expect around £22,000–£25,000. With experience, this will rise to around £27,000–£38,000. The salary for those highly skilled is £40,000–£50,000.

Mechanical

- After graduation, expect around £23,000-£25,000. With experience, this will rise to around £26,000–£37,000. Highly skilled and with chartered status you can expect to get up to £45,000.

Mining

- After graduation, expect around £23,000–£30,000. With five or more years' experience, expect up to £60,000+. The salary for those highly skilled can be up to £100,000.

Nuclear

- After graduation expect around £23,000–£26,000. With experience, this will rise to around £35,000–£40,000. Highly skilled and with chartered status expect around £55,000+.

Oil/Gas

- After graduation, expect around £26,000–£30,000. With a PhD, expect a salary of £33,000+. With experience, the salary is around £30,000–£35,000. The salary for those highly skilled is £50,000–£70,000.

Further information

Institution of Engineering and Technology
Michael Faraday House
Stevenage
Hertfordshire
SG1 2AY
01438 765586
www.theiet.org

Scottish Engineering
105 West George Street
Glasgow
G2 1QL
0141 221 3181
www.scottishengineering.org.uk

Engineering Careers Information Service
SEMTA House
14 Upton Road
Watford
Hertfordshire WD18 0JT
0800 282167
www.enginuity.org.uk

AEROSPACE

Royal Aeronautical Society
4 Hamilton Place
London
WCJ 7BQ
020 7670 4326
www.aerosociety.com

AGRICULTURAL

Institution of Agricultural Engineers
West End Road
Silsoe
Bedford
MK45 4DU
01525 861096
www.iagre.org.uk

BIOMEDICAL

National Centre for Training and Education in Prosthetics and Orthotics
University of Strathclyde
Curran Building
131 St James Road
Glasgow
G4 0LS
0141 548 3298
www.strath.ac.uk/prosthetics

CHEMICAL

Institution of Chemical Engineers
Careers Liaison Department, Davis Building
165–189 Railway Terrace
Rugby
CV21 3HQ
01788 578214
Main website: www.icheme.org
Careers website: www.whynotchemeng.com

COMMUNICATIONS/ TELECOMMUNICATIONS

Communications Information Technology Association
Douglas House
32–34 Simpson Road
Fenny Stratford
Bletchley
Milton Keynes MK1 1BA
01908 645000
www.cita.org.uk

ENERGY

Energy Institute
61 New Cavendish Street
London
W1G 7AR
020 7467 7100
www.energyinst.org.uk

MANUFACTURING/ MECHANICAL

Institution of Mechanical Engineers
1 Birdcage Walk
Westminster
London
SW1H 9JJ
020 7222 7899
www.imeche.org.uk

MATERIALS/MINING/ PETROLEUM

Institute of Materials, Minerals and Mining (IOM^3)
1 Carlton House Terrace
London
SW1Y 5DB
020 7451 7300
Main website: www.iom3.org
Careers website: www.materials-careers.org.uk

NUCLEAR

Institution of Nuclear Engineers
Allan House
1 Penerley Road
London
SE6 2LQ
020 8698 1500
www.inuce.org.uk

Engineering Council UK
10 Maltravers Street
London
WC2R 3ER
020 7240 7891
www.engc.org.uk

CRCI:G
CLCI:R

Engineer: Technician

What the work involves

- Technicians work in all aspects of engineering. They normally work as part of a team alongside other engineers working at professional (those who are Chartered or Incorporated) and craft levels.
- Although your duties as an engineering technician will be dependent on the particular field of engineering that you enter, the work generally falls into the following categories: design, research and development, building and testing, or repair and maintenance.
- Here are the major available options:

Aerospace

- This involves the design, repair and manufacture of aircraft. You could work on civilian or military aircraft, as well as missiles, satellites and space vehicles.
- You will normally work in a specialised section concentrating on one aspect of production or repair, for example engines, fuel storage, hydraulics, avionics and airframes. However, in some smaller companies you might work on a range of aspects of production and specialisms.

Chemical

- This deals with extracting raw materials and chemicals from all kinds of products. You could work in a number of industries including food and drink, textiles, aerospace and mining.
- You will help to design new plant (machinery) and products in a laboratory before introducing them into the workplace.

Electrical

- You would make sure that electricity reaches homes and businesses from the originating power station. To do this you could work in one of the following types of area: installing and testing wiring systems, repairing equipment or producing electronic appliances.

Engineering maintenance

- You will be responsible for making sure that the machinery and equipment in your organisation works efficiently and continuously. You could work on a range of equipment depending on what your employer produces, including office and laboratory, aircraft, telecommunications, computer and others. Your work will involve identifying faults and drawing up procedures to prevent further faults occurring.

Materials

- Working in a team with other engineering staff and scientists, you will design new products or improve existing ones. You will test materials for strength, reliability, environmental impact and cost-effectiveness.
- To be a successful materials technician you will need to have a broad knowledge of lots of engineering fields.

Measurement and control

- This area of work involves overseeing the instruments that control production and make sure that it can continue. You could work in lots of different organisations from light engineering through to heavy machinery. The work involves carrying out necessary maintenance and repair and adjusting the equipment accordingly.

Mechanical

- You will design, construct and operate different machines in all aspects of engineering. For example, you could work within chemical, electronic or mechanical areas. You will work in a team with other engineers and need a broad understanding of different engineering areas.

Telecommunications

- You will install different telecommunications equipment in homes and businesses. As well as installing, you will repair, test and set up the equipment using cables, fibre optics, satellite or digital television systems and lots of other new technology.

The type of person suited to this work

To be an engineering technician you will need to have an analytical mind and want to know how and why things work. An interest in maths, science and technology as well as computer literacy is also important.

Lots of technicians work in a team. This means you will need good verbal and presentation skills and the ability to get on with different people.

In most areas you will be either managing craftspeople to do the work, or using the tools and equipment yourself to measure, cut, design and produce things. As you will also be using materials such as wood, metal and chemicals you should be able to recognise which tools will work best for which material. Practical hand skills would also be helpful.

You should be happy working on your initiative and be able to provide creative solutions to problems.

Qualifications and courses

entry level

To both enter and train while working in this career, you will need qualifications at Level 2–3. Please refer to explanation on page vii.

- Engineering technicians should hold at least a Level 3 qualification such as an NVQ/SVQ, BTEC National Certificate or Diploma, or equivalent City & Guilds Certificate. Full-time, part-time and work-based routes are available.
- You can gain the required qualifications through full-time study at college. For entry to a BTEC National Diploma or Certificate, four GCSEs/S grades (A–C/1–3) are usually required, including English, maths and science. Alternative entry qualifications include BTEC First Certificate/Diploma or SQA national certificate.
- If aged 16–24 you could undertake work-based training through an Advanced Apprenticeship/Skillseekers. You could then work towards an NVQ/SVQ Level 3, and can study part time at college for BTEC National and City & Guilds qualifications.
- Engineering technicians with a Level 3 or 4 qualification and 3 years' responsible work experience are eligible to become technician members of one of the engineering professional bodies. It is also possible to continue to HNC/D or degree-level study.
- Specific qualifications are also available in some branches:

Aerospace

- NVQ/SVQs are available in Aircraft Maintenance Engineering at Levels 2 and 3.

Electrical

- An electrical installation apprenticeship usually takes four years.
- During this you will normally work to achieve City & Guilds (2381) Electrical Installation and NVQ/SVQ Level 3 Electrotechnical Services.
- Other relevant qualfications include a BTEC National Certificate/Diploma in Electrical/Electronic Engineering, or NVQ/SVQ in Electrical and Electronic Servicing at Level 3.

Materials

- Materials technicians can take distance learning modules offered by the IOM Academy, which can lead to an IOM Academy Training Certificate.

Working conditions

Your working conditions will depend on the specific area you choose to work within, as you could work in large or small factories, workshops, laboratories, indoors or outdoors.

Some working areas will be dirty and cramped, while other places like laboratories have to be clean and sometimes temperature controlled.

Many areas of engineering can be dangerous and involve working with hazardous chemicals and equipment. You will be provided with protective clothing such as overalls, head and foot protection.

Although you could be working a standard 37–40 hour Monday to Friday week, you may do shifts, or 24-hour call-out rotas.

The future outlook

Aerospace

The UK aerospace industry employs around 275,000 people, making it the second largest in the world. Most of the work is in the civilian and military aircraft industries. Employers include aerospace manufacturers and airline operators as well as the armed forces. As air safety is so important, there are prospects in both civilian and military areas for the foreseeable future. With experience, opportunities for progression to senior or managerial positions will be available within the UK or abroad.

Chemical

The chemical industry employs 250,000 people in the UK and there is a steady demand for technicians in the industry. As chemical technicians work in so many industries, you will be able to progress in your own area or move into another. You could consider local government, the armed services, water, gas and electricity or jobs in customer support, marketing or sales.

Electrical

There has been an ongoing skills shortage within this branch for several years. Expansion in demand for technicians with electical expertise has been fuelled by the increasing use of computer technology by industry. Recent surveys have shown that 35% of employers are experiencing recruitment difficulties. This means that if you enter this area your future prospects are good. Opportunities are available throughout the country but especially in London, the south-east of England and Scotland.

Engineering maintenance

Demand in this area remains steady. To make the most of your skills, ongoing learning and up-skilling is recommended. This will help you adapt to the changes experienced by the sector and make you more employable. With experience you will be able to progress to managerial opportunities within the UK or abroad.

Materials

There is an ongoing demand for skilled staff in all the sectors requiring materials technicians. With experience you will be able to progress into different branches or move into specialist areas like sales, marketing or management. You could also find work within consultancy firms.

Measurement and control

There are opportunities to progress into the installation and maintenance of monitoring equipment, design and development of new control components, supervisory and managerial positions. You could also move into a different sector, as many use measurement and control technicians.

Mechanical

This is an area with long-standing skills shortages. With experience and qualifications you will be able to progress within your own sector or move easily into others requiring mechanical engineers. You could also look at opportunities within sales, marketing and customer support.

Telecommunications

Around 260,000 technicans work within the telecommunications industry – one of the fastest changing sectors in the UK. The full potential of this industry is unknown as it is still growing and developing. However, with experience and qualifications your opportunities for advancement should be good.

Generally there are good opportunites for promotion for technicians. If you are willing to train and qualify as an incorporated or chartered engineer you can move into management.

Other related opportunities

- Civil / Construction Engineer p46
- Electricity Generation Worker p201
- Engineer: Craft p203
- Engineer: Professional p205
- Marine Engineering / Marine Industry p213
- Motor Vehicle Work p217
- Quarry Worker p221
- Rail p578
- Railway Fitter / Electrician p223
- Thermal Insulation Engineer p225
- Watch / Clock Repairer p226

Advantages/disadvantages

- As engineering covers many diverse areas the biggest advantage is having a career that can be flexible, letting you move from industry to industry.
- Salaries are relatively high in comparison to other sectors.
- You could be working in dirty and cold work places.
- Although the engineering industry has tried hard to rid itself of its old-fashioned image, this still exists.
- Not every company has invested in new technology to the same extent – so look around at different employers before taking up your first job.
- With training and qualfiications you can progress to professional engineer level.

Earnings guide

- Salaries will vary depending on the particular sector and many are affected by regional differences.
- The following should be used as a guide only.

Aerospace

- Apprentices normally start at around £12,000–£14,000 per year, rising to £20,000–£25,000 with experience and qualifications. Senior technicians can earn £30,000+.

Chemical

- £15,000 is typical for new entrants, rising to £20,000 with qualifications and experience. Senior technicians can earn £30,000+.

Electrical

- Those starting out can expect £15,000–£18,000 which will rise with experience and qualifications to £24,000–£28,000. Senior technicians can earn £30,000+.

Engineering maintenance

- New entrants receive around £18,000. With experience this rises to £20,000–£24,000. Senior technicians have the potential to earn £30,000–£35,000.

Materials

- Apprentices normally start at around £14,000–£17,000, rising to £20,000–£25,000 with experience and qualifications. Senior technicians can earn £30,000+.

Measurement and control

- £13,000–£16,000 is usual for new entrants, rising to £20,000–£25,000 with qualifications and experience. Senior technicians can earn £35,000+.

Mechanical

- New entrants normally earn around £14,000–£16,500, rising to £19,000–£24,000 with qualifications and experience. Senior technicians can earn up to £30,000.

Telecommunications

- Starting salaries are around £12,000–£15,000. With qualifications and experience this rises to £25,000. At senior level you can get £35,000+.

Further information

www.cityandguilds.com/myperfectjob

Engineering Council UK
10 Maltravers Street
London
WC2R 3ER
020 7240 7891
www.engc.org.uk

Engineering Careers Information Service
SEMTA House
14 Upton Road
Watford
Hertfordshire
WD18 0JT
0800 282167
www.enginuity.org.uk

AERONAUTICAL

Royal Aeronautical Society
4 Hamilton Place
London
WCJ 7BQ
020 7670 4326
www.aerosociety.com

CHEMICAL

Institution of Chemical Engineers
Careers Liaison Department, Davis Building
165–189 Railway Terrace
Rugby
CV21 3HQ
01788 578214
Main website: www.icheme.org
Careers website: www.whynotchemeng.com

MATERIALS

Institute of Materials, Minerals and Mining (IOM^3)
1 Carlton House Terrace
London
SW1Y 5DB
020 7451 7300
Main website: www.iom3.org
Careers website: www.materials-careers.org.uk

MEASUREMENT AND CONTROL

Institute of Measurement and Control
87 Gower Street
London
WC1E 6AA
020 7387 4949
www.istmc.org.uk

MECHANICAL

Institution of Mechanical Engineers
1 Birdcage Walk
Westminster
London
SW1H 9JJ
020 7222 7899
www.imeche.org.uk

TELECOMMUNICATIONS

e-skills UK (Sector Skills Council for information technology, telecommunications and contact centres)
1 Castle Lane
London
SW1E 6DR
020 963 8920
www.e-skills.com

Communications Information Technology Association
Douglas House, 32–34 Simpson Road
Fenny Stratford
Bletchley
Milton Keynes
MK1 1BA
01908 645000
www.cita.org.uk

Institution of Engineering and Technology
Michael Faraday House
Stevenage
Hertfordshire
SG1 2AY
01438 765586
www.theiet.org

Scottish Engineering
105 West George Street
Glasgow
G2 1QL
0141 221 3181
www.scottishengineering.org.uk

ELECTRICAL

Institution of Engineering and Technology
Michael Faraday House
Stevenage
Hertfordshire
SG1 2AY
01438 765586
www.theiet.org

SEMTA (Science, Engineering, Manufacturing Technologies Alliance)
14 Upton Road
Watford
Hertfordshire
WD18 0JT
01923 238441
www.semta.org.uk

Gas Distribution Worker

What the work involves

- Gas is transported from its supply points (called beaches) to domestic and industrial customers by a network of pipes and meters that it will be your responsibility to maintain.
- To gain access to pipework you will probably need to dig a hole in a road, garden or pavement.
- You will also repair the damage after you have installed or replaced the pipework.
- You will be responsible for the safety of yourself and others when carrying out work. This will include putting up warning signs, barriers and traffic control if needed.
- You may have to deal with emergency gas leaks.

The type of person suited to this work

You will normally work in a small team, so you should enjoy working with and be able to get on with people. Before you start work you might have to knock on customers' doors informing them of who you are, so being polite and courteous are also important skills.

This can be a physically demanding job. You will be using digging and excavating tools and pipe-laying equipment. To make sure you do the job correctly you will have to understand and follow technical instructions and drawings.

When the job is complete, you will have to make sure the finished surface is safe and as good as it was when you started, so you should be tidy and efficient.

Working conditions

You will be working in a team outdoors in all weathers. You will normally work a 37–40 hour week, overtime and weekend work will be expected on a rota basis.

You will be using equipment which can be physically demanding and you will get dirty.

As this can be dangerous work you will wear protective clothing such as high-visibility and fireproof clothing, steel toe-capped boots and head gear.

The future outlook

The National Grid coordinates and monitors the gas distribution network in the UK. There are four gas distribution companies; National Grid Distribution, Wales and West Utilities, Northern Gas Networks and Scotia Gas Networks (operating in the south of England as Southern Gas and in Scotland as Scotland Gas Networks). There is currently a national shortage of gas distribution workers, particularly in cities and industrial areas.

With experience and training, you could progress to a technician, supervisory or management position where you would be responsible for a number of teams.

entry level

1–2

To both enter and train while working in this career, you will need qualifications at Level 1–2. Please refer to explanation on page vii.

Qualifications and courses

- You will normally start as a trainee or an apprentice.
- There are no formal qualifications required, however, employers look for good GCSEs/S grades in maths, science, English and a practical technical subject.
- It's also useful to have some experience in engineering or building work. A lot of adults are recruited through this route.
- You can also enter through an Advanced Apprenticeship with the National Grid. You will need 4 GCSEs/S grades (A–C/1–4) including maths and English.
- Once employed you can work towards NVQ Gas Appliances Installation and Maintenance at Level 2 and Gas Network Engineering at Level 3, or SVQ Domestic Natural Gas Installation and Maintenance at Levels 2 and 3. Once you have completed an NVQ/SVQ Level 3 it is possible to apply for HND/degree or higher level NVQ/SVQs.
- Having a clean driving licence is increasingly important.

Other related opportunities

- Construction Plant Operator p49
- Electrician (Installation) p51
- Electricity Generation Worker p201
- Engineer: Craft p203
- Oil and Gas Drilling Industry p219
- Plumber p65
- Thermal Insulation Engineer p225
- Water Distribution / Sewerage Operative p78

Advantages/disadvantages

- Being outside in all weathers can be a positive or negative depending on the time of year!
- You might get verbal abuse from angry customers complaining about holes in their road.
- It can be satisfying to know that you are helping members of the community receive power for their homes and businesses.

Earnings guide

- Whilst training, workers can earn from £11,000 to £15,000 per year.
- Upon qualification and with experience this rises to between £17,000 and £21,000.
- As a team leader or with more responsibility you can expect your salary to increase to £25,000–£27,000.

Further information

National Grid Plc
National Grid House, Warwick Technology Park
Gallows Hill
Warwick
CV34 6DA
01926 65 3000
www.nationalgrid.com/uk

Northern Gas Networks
1100 Century Way
Colton
Leeds
LS15 8TU
0113 397 5300
www.northerngasnetworks.co.uk

Scotland Gas Networks
Inchcolm House
11 West Shore Road
Edinburgh
Scotland EH5 1RH
0131 559 6000
www.scotiagasnetworks.co.uk

Southern Gas Networks
2 Leesons Hill
Orpington
Kent BR5 2TN
01689 881300
www.scotiagasnetworks.co.uk

Wales & West Utilities Limited
Lambourne House
Cardiff Business Park
Llanishen
Cardiff CF14 5GL
0845 605 6677
www.wwutilities.co.uk

www.cityandguilds.com/myperfectjob

Locksmith

What the work involves

- You will sell, install and maintain the locks of houses, cars and businesses for your customers.
- You will use specialist machinery to cut replacement keys for locks.
- Advising on, repairing and installing security and closed-circuit television systems may be part of your job.
- You may be a specialist offering just one of these services such as key cutting or security systems, or you may work for a company offering a range of services.
- You may also provide a 24-hour call-out service for those who have lost keys or locked themselves out of their home, car or business.

The type of person suited to this work

If you have ever been locked out of your home or a car you will know how distressing it can be. As a locksmith you will have to be calm and patient – reassuring your customers whilst providing a prompt and reliable service. Good communication skills are important in this job.

Your customers and employer will also expect you to be totally trustworthy and honest.

To do this job you will have to enjoy using your hands, different tools and equipment. You should enjoy practical tasks and be able to offer solutions to security problems. Carpentry or general engineering skills are also helpful.

A driving licence may be required.

Working conditions

If you work in a shop you will probably have a 37–40-hour Monday–Saturday week. Self-employment is possible.

If you, or your employer, offer a 24 hour call-out service, you could be working at all times of day or night. This can be difficult if you have family commitments.

Where you work will depend on your customers and could include working outdoors in all weathers.

You may work mainly from a van that holds your tools, and do lots of driving.

The future outlook

As worries about home and business security have increased, the demand for more secure locks and security systems to be fitted by qualifed locksmiths has grown too. Currently there are around 2000 qualified locksmiths in the UK.

Employers include independent small locksmiths, larger national companies offering a 24-hour call-out emergency service, specialist security companies, DIY hardware stores and shoe repairers which offer a key-cutting service.

Progression for locksmiths is mainly achieved by becoming self-employed and building up a profitable business. It is also possible to progress into more specialist areas of work such as safe engineering.

entry level

1

To both enter and train while working in this career, you will need qualifications at Level 1. Please refer to explanation on page vii.

Qualifications and courses

- There are no formal educational requirements, but most applicants will be required to hold GCSE/S grades in English, mathematics and preferably a practical subject like craft or technology.
- Some locksmiths offer apprenticeship opportunities – contact local locksmiths to see if they require new staff or trainees. You might be able to gain an Apprenticeship/ Skillseeker opportunity if you are aged 16–24.
- The Master Locksmiths Association (MLA) offers a General Locksmithing Course at their training centres. Contact the MLA for details.
- To apply you will have to be a member of the British Locksmithing Institute (BLI). Individuals can apply for student membership of the BLI without any prior experience, and then study for 3 years to be become an Advanced Student; further examinations are available after this.
- NVQs/SVQs are available in Providing Security or Emergency and Alarm Systems.

CRCI:G

CLCI:R

Other related opportunities

- Carpenter / Joiner p41
- Engineer: Craft p203
- Motor Vehicle Work p217
- Security p518
- Watch / Clock Repairer p226

Advantages/disadvantages

- This can be a varied job. You willl never know what your next job will be, or where you will have to go.
- Meeting the public can be interesting and knowing you've helped people can be rewarding.
- Working all hours of the day and night can be difficult and call-outs to replace locks after burglaries can be distressing.

Earnings guide

- As a trainee you can expect to earn around £13,500 per year.
- With experience this can increase to £20,000–£23,000.
- Many locksmiths choose to become self-employed. Earnings will then depend on individual charges and company success.
- Earnings will be affected by regional differences; more can be expected in the larger cities as 24-hour call-outs will be more common.

Further information

Master Locksmiths Association
5D Great Central Way
Woodford Halse
Daventry
Northamptonshire
NN11 3PZ
01327 262255
www.locksmiths.co.uk

Security Systems and Alarms Inspections Board
Suite 3
131 Bedford Street
North Shields
Tyne and Wear
NE29 6LA
0191 296 3242
www.ssaib.co.uk

British Security Industry Association
Security House
Barbourne Rd
Worcester
WR1 1RS
01905 21464
www.bsia.co.uk

Marine Engineering / Marine Industry

What the work involves

Marine engineer: craft/boat builder

- If you work in boat building you will be working with small commercial and pleasure craft. The majority of new small craft are built using glass fibre or new composite materials in a factory unit.
- If you work in shipbuilding you will be working with larger vessels such as warships, submarines or specialist vessels such as tankers. You will probably work in an assembly type of ship yard using metal based skills like welding, cutting, bending, and others used in engineering manufacture.
- In both boat building and shipbuilding you may work repairing or converting older vessels.
- As well as the external parts of the vessel you could also install and repair engines, the internal living quarters and sea-safety equipment.

Marine engineer: technician

- You will work with marine engineers building, servicing, operating and repairing the engineering equipment and machinery used in ships and offshore installations.
- You could work in shipbuilding and repair, as a seagoing technician for the Royal Navy or Merchant Navy, or for the oil and gas industry. If seagoing, you will work with the Engineering officer with responsibility for the operation and maintenance of all equipment and machinery when a vessel is at sea.

Marine engineer: professional

- There are a range of opportunities for professional marine engineers. You could work in shipbuilding and repair, as a marine enginering officer for the Royal Navy or merchant navy, or for the oil and gas industry.
- You will design, build, operate and maintain the engineering equipment and machinery used in ships and offshore installatiions.
- If working as an engineering officer for the Royal Navy or merchant navy you will be seagoing and responsible for all the equipment and machinery whilst the vessel is at sea.

Naval architect

- You will work as a specialist engineer responsible for designing, producing plans and constructing boats and ships.
- Sourcing and obtaining the right materials for constructing the vessel will also be part of your job.
- You will work closely with marine engineers who design the vessel's equipment and machinery.
- You may specialise in research and development, construction and repair, or act as a consultant advising on how best to repair or reconstruct boats and ships.

The type of person suited to this work

Your main interest should be in water transport from huge tankers to jetskis – their design, repair and construction. If you are involved in the practical work of building or repair you will need to use different hand and machine tools, sometimes using very traditional woodworking skills.

You should have a pride in your work and be willing to learn lots of different skills. For example, some craftspeople use a range of skills including carpentry, plumbing and even kitchen fitting! You could work with fibreglass or other materials so you will have to be happy working with lots of different products.

Whichever area you enter, people skills are really important – you willl have to be able to work with both colleagues and customers.

Other things that you will need are an interest in science, being able to look for creative solutions to problems and being physically fit.

Qualifications and courses

entry level

To both enter and train while working in this career, you will need qualifications at Level 1–8. Please refer to explanation on page vii.

- The qualifications and training will depend on the area that you want to enter:

Marine engineer: craft/boat builder

- Candidates are usually required to have 3–5 GCSEs/S grades (A–C/1–3) in English, maths and a science or technology subject.
- Most people take an apprenticeship, training on the job whilst attending college studying for NVQs/SVQs at Levels 1 and 2.
- If you are aged 16–24, Apprenticeships/ Skillseekers opportunities are available.
- Most companies require multi-skilled employees so your training will be varied, covering all aspects and skill requirements.

Marine engineer: technician

- The normal entry route is through an apprenticeship lasting three to four years. Some programmes lead to EngTech status registration with the Engineering Council UK (ECUK). Typical entry requirements are 4 GCSEs/S grades (A–C/1–3, including maths, science or technology.
- If you are aged 16–24, Apprenticeships/ Skillseekers may be available. Some programmes lead to EngTech status registration with the Engineering Council UK (ECUK). Typical entry requirements are 4 GCSEs/S grades (A–C/1–3, including maths, science or technology.

Marine engineer: professional

- Applicants will need a degree in a relevant area of engineering. To qualify as an incorporated marine engineer, you will need to have an accredited 3-year degree, complete a period of professional development, pass a review, and gain corporate membership of the Institution of Engineering and Technology. To qualify as a chartered marine engineer, you will need to have an MEng degree or equivalent, complete a period of professional development, pass a review and gain corporate membership of the Institute of Marine Engineering, Science and Technology.

Naval architect

- You will need a degree in a relevant subject accredited by the Royal Institution of Naval Architects (RINA). Universities prefer applicants with voluntary or work experience in any area of engineering or design work.
- Most training occurs on the job, under the mentorship of a senior engineer. Trainees might also participate in RINA and The Institute of Marine Engineering, Science and Technology (IMarEST) accredited training programmes.

Working conditions

You may be based in or around a shipyard, marina, on board a ship or submarine (if seagoing), or in a factory or workshop if building or repairing leisure craft.

If you are in a design office you will sit at your work station using drawing boards and ICT equipment. It may be necessary to meet and brief the staff who undertake the practical work in the yard or workshops.

Upon the ships or in the yard, you could work undercover or out in all weathers. Some of the work will take place in cramped conditions, requiring you to be physically fit. Some materials, like fibreglass will require you to wear protective clothing.

If you are involved in sea trials or work as seagoing technician or engineer you could work in dangerous conditions.

Most work normal office hours, except for seagoing technicians and officers. Longer hours may be needed to meet deadlines.

The future outlook

There has been a decline in the UK shipbuilding industry over the past 20 years but the surviving shipyards are doing well – building specialist ships mainly for the offshore industry and the Royal Navy. There are large commercial shipyards in the north-west and north-east of England, around Portsmouth and Southampton and on the Clyde in Scotland. Whilst the number of traditional boats that are being built from new is small, there are hundreds around the country requiring repair and maintenance. This part of the industry is thriving.

The leisure boating industry is very diverse, from large luxury powerboats through sailing boats and narrowboats to jet skis, and it is a growth industry. There are about 1600 boatbuilding companies in the UK mainly based on the south coast and in the south-west of England, East Anglia, Wales, West Scotland, the Midlands and the Thames Valley.

There is no set pattern to the industry. Many people specialise in particular areas and expand their experience as they progress. This might mean moving from company to company or developing in one firm. The boating industry requires people who have a wide range of skills, who work hard and use their initiative.

As the industry covers a diverse range of areas there are lots of opportunities available for the different skills needed. For example, marine engineers and naval architects with experience may move into marine surveying working for marine classification companies, or for the Maritime and Coastguard Agency, work as consultants, or gain employment overseas.

Other related opportunities

- Engineer: Craft p203
- Engineer: Professional p205
- Engineer: Technician p208
- Lock Keeper p570
- Merchant Navy p571
- Oil and Gas Drilling Industry p219
- Royal Navy p516

Advantages/disadvantages

- The marine industry values staff who are multi-skilled with good people and communication skills.
- Because of the range of skills needed across the marine industry, you will be able to progress within the marine sector or move outside where your skills will be equally valued. For example, you could be a kitchen fitter within a boat or in a house!
- You could be working on some boats that cost millions of pounds or a small weekend dinghy. Both require the same high standards of work to ensure safety at sea and comfort for the owner.

Earnings guide

- In some areas of the industry, nationally agreed salaries are being introduced, especially in the first few years of training.
- The following should be used as a guide only, as there will be regional differences.

Marine engineer: craft/boat builder

- Starting salaries for craft engineers/boat builders are around £12,000–£16,000 per year. With qualifications this rises to around £18,000–£22,000.
- With experience you could earn up to £30,000.

Marine engineer: technician

- Starting salaries for qualified technicians are £12,000–£16,000, rising to £17,000–£23,000 with experience. Highly qualified and experienced staff can earn £25,000–£35,000.

Marine engineer: professional

- Immediately after graduation, salaries are around £21,000 per year. With experience, this rises to £28,000–£37,000. A fully qualified and experienced marine engineer can earn £40,000+.

Naval architect

- New graduates can expect around £23,000–£26,000. With experience you can get £35,000–£60,000.
- You may be self-employed. This means earnings will be dependent on personal success.

Further information

British Marine Federation
Marine House
Thorpe Lea Road
Egham
Surrey TW20 8BF
01784 473377
www.britishmarine.co.uk

Institute of Marine Engineering, Science and Technology (IMarEST)
80 Coleman Street
London
EC2R 5BJ
020 7382 2600
www.imarest.org

Engineering Careers Information Service
SEMTA House
14 Upton Road
Watford
Hertfordshire
WD18 0JT
0800 282167
www.enginuity.org.uk

MARINE ENGINEER-PROFESSIONAL

Institution of Engineering and Technology
Michael Faraday House
Stevenage
Hertfordshire
SG1 2AY
01438 765586
www.theiet.org

NAVAL ARCHITECT

Royal Institution of Naval Architects
10 Upper Belgrave Street
London
SW1X 8BQ
020 7235 4622
www.rina.org.uk

Merchant Navy Training Board
Carthusian Court
12 Carthusian Street
London
EC1M 6EZ
020 7417 2800
www.mntb.org.uk

Armed Forces Careers Navy
22 Unthank Road
Norwich
NR2 1AH
01603 620033
www.royalnavy.mod.uk

Meat Process Worker

What the work involves

Abattoir operative

- You will be part of the process that slaughters animals for food.
- After the animals have been humanely killed, you will remove the skins, internal organs and inedible parts of the dead animal – separating the edible meat from the waste.
- You will cut up and bone carcasses ready for delivery to meat wholesalers and meat manufacturing companies.

Meat manufacturing operative

- You will work as part of the manufacturing process that produces meat products.
- Working on a production line you will be responsible for one of the processes that make products such as pies, sausages, burgers and bacon.
- You may weigh, wrap and label meat products.
- If working in a specialist chicken plant you may use machinery to kill and prepare poultry.
- You may need to cut and bone meat using saws, knives and machinery.

The type of person suited to this work

This can be distressing and smelly work, so you should be aware of what the job involves and be prepared to cope with blood and mess. You will be part of a team, so you should be happy to work with others. As you will have to do lots of lifting, carrying and operating machinery, you will need to be physically fit and able to be on your feet for long periods at a time.

It will be important that you pay attention to strict hygiene and health and safety laws. You should have a responsible attitude as you may use dangerous knives, cutting tools and machinery. You also need to be aware of your personal cleanliness as you are part of a food production process.

Working conditions

Refrigerated areas are cold and all areas need frequent cleaning and so may be wet. You will be expected to wear protective clothing, including footwear, hairnets and warm clothing if needed.

Automated areas can be very noisy but you will be provided with ear-protectors.

This can be physically demanding work and there may be unpleasant smells in some areas.

You will normally do a 40-hour week, although shift and part-time work are possible.

The future outlook

The meat industry is a significant employer with opportunities in abattoirs and in manufacturing and processing plants. About 97% of the UK population eats meat and consumption is about the same as 20 years ago.

Abattoir operative

Around 11,000 people work within abattoirs and 30,000 within poultry slaughterhouses. There are approximately 145 slaughterhouses/abattoirs across the UK. Many abattoirs specialise in one group of animals, such as cattle or sheep or pigs. Due to high staff turnover, there are currently lots of opportunities in the industry.

With experience you could apply for senior internal positions or look to move to related areas such as butchery, retail, food marketing or preparation. Quality control, health and safety consultancy or self-employment are also possible.

With training and registration with the Department for the Environment, Food and Rural Affairs (DEFRA) you could work as a slaughterman/woman.

Meat manufacturing operative

About 60,000 people work in the meat manufacturing, processing and bacon curing industries. There is a steady demand for operatives in the industry – with a high turnover of staff.

With experience you could apply for supervisory, quality control and management jobs or move into related areas of work such as butchery, food preparation or retail.

With the right experience, qualifications and training you may be able to progress into work on the meat inspection teams employed by the Meat Hygiene Service (MHS) – part of the Food Standards Agency.

Qualifications and courses

entry level

To both enter and train while working in this career, you will need qualifications at Level 1. Please refer to explanation on page vii.

- There are no formal entry qualifications for these jobs. However, GCSEs/S grades in English and maths are useful, particularly if you want to move up to supervisory, inspection or technical level.
- To work as a slaughterman/woman, you must be aged 18 or over, and be licensed with the Department for the Environment, Food and Rural Affairs (DEFRA).
- Abattoir workers and meat manufacturing operatives may be able to work towards NVQs/SVQs at Levels 1–3 in Meat and Poultry Processing or Meat and Poultry Plant Operations and then onto an NVQ/SVQ at Level 4 in Meat Processing Management. NVQs/SVQs are accredited by the Meat Training Council and include health, safety and hygiene training.
- The Meat Training Council offers other courses, including the Meat Safety Certificate, and Intermediate and Advanced Certificates in Meat and Poultry.

Other related opportunities

- Kitchen Assistant p98
- Kitchen Porter p99
- Meat Inspector p445
- Specialist Shop Assistant p455

Advantages/disadvantages

- This can be cold, smelly and dirty work.
- You will be part of a team and often there is a good working atmosphere within a production team.
- It is possible to do this job on a part-time basis and many returners to work find it an easy industry to enter.
- Many employers welcome mature entrants.
- The job can be repetitive and monotonous especially if you are based for long periods on one part of the production line or working on one process in the abattoir.

Earnings guide

Abattoir operative

- As shift-working can increase earnings, the following should be used as a guide.
- The minimum salary for trained adults is around £11,500 per year, rising to £17,000 with experience. Very experienced abattoir workers with supervisory duties may earn up to £25,000.

Meat manufacturing operative

- The starting salary is usually about £11,000 per year.
- Experienced meat manufacturing operatives earn up to £18,000 per year.

Further information

www.cityandguilds.com/myperfectjob

Meat Training Council
PO Box 141
Winterhill House
Snowdon Drive
Milton Keynes
MK6 1YY
01908 231062
www.meattraining.org.uk

Worshipful Company of Butchers Guild
Butchers' Hall
87 Bartholomew Close
London
EC1A 7EB
020 7600 4106
www.butchershall.com

Improve Ltd (Sector Skills Council for food and drink manufacturing and processing)
Ground floor
Providence House
2 Innovation Close
York
YO10 5ZF
0845 644 0448
www.improveltd.co.uk

Food Standards Agency
Aviation House
125 Kingsway
London
WC2B 6NH
020 7276 8000
www.food.gov.uk

Scottish Meat Training
8–10 Needless Road
Perth
PH2 0JW
01738 637785
www.foodtraining.net

CRCI:NC
CLCI:SAC

Motor Vehicle Work

What the work involves

Auto-electrician

- Using different tools and testing equipment you will install or repair faults in the electrical circuits and components inside different vehicles. You might also specialise in installing audio equipment such as CD players or alarms.
- There is a move towards auto-electricians being mechanics as well as electrical specialists, so general skills are important.

Body repairer/paint sprayer

- You will work assessing and then repairing the damage to any of the structural and cosmetic parts of a vehicle by using hand bending, shaping and forming techniques including welding. Once repaired you will prepare the surface and paint using a spray gun and finish off with a coat of lacquer.

Motor vehicle mechanic – light

- If you work at craft level you will repair, maintain and service cars, motorbikes and small vans.
- At technician level your work will be more based around diagnosis, road testing and fault finding. However, you will also be involved in many of the areas undertaken at craft level too. You will use a range of tools including computerised equipment and might undertake or prepare vehicles for MOTs.

Vehicle maintenance patroller

- Working for organisations like the AA or RAC you would attend breakdowns. You will diagnose and if possible repair at the roadside. If the car requires too much work to do the job quickly, you will transport your customers and their car home or to the nearest garage.

Motor vehicle mechanic – heavy

- This role is similar to that of the motor mechanic – light, except the vehicles will be larger and more diverse! You could work on tractors, building and construction equipment, trucks, lorries or buses.
- As well as repairing and maintaining, you will undertake day-to-day servicing to ensure everything remains mechanically sound and safe.

Tyre and exhaust fitter

- Using tools like hydraulic jacks and other hand tools you will remove worn or damaged tyres or exhausts from vehicles and replace with new ones.
- Sometimes you might also work on brakes and do oil changes.

Valet

- Working mainly in car showrooms or second-hand car sales, you will valet (clean and polish) the inside and outside of the vehicles for sale. You could also work in some garages who valet vehicles after a service or other work – as part of the service to customers.

Windscreen repairer/fitter

- Due to the damage that stones or other objects can cause to windscreens, you will repair or replace the damaged screen by using different tools and chemicals.

The type of person suited to this work

You should enjoy working on and being around different vehicles – repairing, maintaining and improving their performance and appearance. Being able to work in a team and talk to people from all backgrounds is important. You will need to have good listening and understanding skills, as translating your customers' descriptions of their cars' problems and faults isn't always easy.

If you choose to start your own business you will need to have good customer care and administrative skills.

You should also be good at problem solving and enjoy using hand, power and other tools.

You will be working with oil, grease and for some jobs chemicals or paint and this may not be suitable if you have allergies or skin conditions.

A driving licence is useful or required for many types of vehicle-related work.

Working conditions

You will often be working with dangerous chemicals, fuels or paints so the wearing of protective clothing is important. You might also have to use eye protection, a mask and gloves.

Many in this industry will work Monday to Saturday morning – with other weekend and evening work required, especially if your organisation provides 24-hour emergency cover for insurance companies, or services such as valeting or windscreen replacement.

You will normally work in or close-by to a garage or workshop. If mobile or self-employed, you could work at a customer's premises taking your tools with you in a van.

You could be working in a noisy, dirty and sometimes cold environment, often in cramped conditions. Being physically fit and having good colour vision are essential.

The future outlook

Across the vehicle industry there is a steady demand for new recruits and a strong demand for trained vehicle professionals to repair and maintain vehicles. However, there is often competition for the places in the more popular areas, like light vehicle, so considering all of the other opportunities available is recommended. Many of the skills are similar from one aspect to another, so it is possible to move across later.

Currently there are more than 30 million vehicles in the UK and jobs to support this industry are on offer at a range of places including car-servicing workshops and repair garages, specialist windscreen or tyre and exhaust companies, vehicle manufacturing companies, public transport operators and roadside rescue organisations.

Within all of the areas, with the possible exception of valeting, it is possible to progress on to management or supervisory posts. Some people also look at entering training posts to help develop new recruits.

Another growing area is self-employment, for example as a mobile mechanic or running a small business such as mobile valeting.

There is a push in the industry for people to become multi-skilled in lots of different areas. This means that you would be able to look for other opportunities later in your career.

Opportunities will be dependent on where you live and the nature of the local employment scene. In some parts of the country there are more openings than in others. Generally the bigger cities and towns will have more.

Qualifications and courses

entry level

To both enter and train while working in this career, you will need qualifications at Level 1–3. Please refer to explanation on page vii.

Auto-electrician

- Most employers will require applicants to pass an aptitude test and have 4 GCSEs/S grades in maths, English and a science, preferably physics. These qualifications will provide entry to a BTEC/SQA qualification.
- Apprenticeships/Skillseekers are available for people aged 16–24.

Body repairer/paint sprayer, tyre and exhaust fitter, windscreen repairer/fitter

- GCSEs/S grades in English, mathematics, and science or technology can be helpful. They are normally necessary for body repair workers and often higher passes are required (A–C/1–3).
- Entry is normally through an Apprenticeships/Skillseekers scheme, or a recognised full-time training course in a relevant area of vehicle repair and servicing. Courses can lead to NVQs in Vehicle Body and Paint Operations, Automotive Glazing or Vehicle Fitting Operations.

Motor vehicle mechanic – light, vehicle mechanic – heavy

- Entry is normally through an Apprenticeship/Skillseekers. An aptitude test may be required. Good literacy and numeracy skills are an advantage.
- You can enter at either Level 2 or Level 3.
- For Level 2 you will need GCSEs/S grades in English, maths and a science or a vocational equivalent such as a BTEC First or SQA National qualification at Intermediate II.
- For Level 3 you will need 4 GCSEs/S grades including English, maths and science or a vocational equivalent. You can then take a BTEC/SQA National qualification in Vehicle Repair and Technology, Motor Vehicle or similar.
- The Retail Motor Industry Federation runs REMIT – the training organisation for motor mechanics, who offer Apprenticeship/Skillseeker opportunities across the country.

Vehicle maintenance patroller

- You will need to be a qualified mechanic with several years' experience, normally be over 21 and hold a clean driving licence. Each organisation then has its own variety of selection and practical tests – normally including a driving test.

Valet

- You don't normally need formal qualifications to enter this area of work. However, employers will look for keenness and Key Skills in verbal communication and a good level of personal presentation.

Other related opportunities

- Assembler p192
- Car Salesperson p440
- Courier p559
- Driver p563
- Engineer: Craft p203
- Engineer: Technician p208
- Locksmith p212
- Vehicle Parts Operative p461

Advantages/disadvantages

- This is a competitive area to enter, both to initially find a job and then to remain employed. The vehicle industry has a large turnover of garages every year with closures due to local competition or high car prices.
- Once you have reached a high level of training and skill there is a strong demand in the motor vehicle industry for trained and experienced vehicle professionals.
- If you love vehicles you will enjoy working on them!
- Once qualified and with experience it is possible to set up your own business offering a mobile service or buying your own garage.

Earnings guide

Auto-electrician

- At entry as a trainee you will earn up to £11,000 per year. After training and with experience you can earn up to £17,000. With lots of experience you could get up to £25,000+.
- If you choose to become self-employed your earnings will depend on contracts, but £20,000+ is possible.

Motor vehicle mechanic

- As a trainee you can get between £7,000 and £11,000 per year. When qualified this rises to around £13,000. With experience £20,000–£26,000 is possible.

Body repairer/paint sprayer, motor vehicle mechanic – light and heavy

- Trainees earn between £7,000 and £13,000. When qualified you can get £14,000–£18,000.
- With additional skills, experience and supervisory skills earnings can be up to £26,000.

Vehicle maintenance patroller

- Pay is normally between £21,000 and £24,500 depending on where you work and live. With experience you can get up to £30,000. Overtime and bonuses are available.

Tyre and exhaust fitter, windscreen repairer/fitter

- Salaries start at about £11,000 for trainees. This rises to around £16,000 with qualifications and experience.
- Earnings of £20,000+ are possible for the most skilled.

Valet

- You can expect a starting salary of around £11,000.
- With experience you can earn more than £13,000. This can be boosted with overtime or shift payments.
- If you choose to run a self-employed car valeting business, earnings could increase.

Further information

City & Guilds

www.cityandguilds.com/myperfectjob

Retail Motor Industry Federation
201 Great Portland Street
London
W1W 5AB
020 7580 9122
www.rmif.co.uk

DTI Automotive Unit
151 Buckingham Palace Road
London
SW1W 9SS
020 7215 1066
www.autoindustry.co.uk
info@autoindustry.co.uk

Automotive Skills
93 Newman Street
London
W1T 3DT
020 7436 6373
www.automotiveskills.org.uk

Institute of the Motor Industry
Fanshaws
Brickendon
Hertford
SG13 8PQ
01992 511521
www.motor.org.uk

Automotive Academy
2410 Regents Court
The Crescent
Solihull Parkway
Birmingham Business Park
B37 7YE
0121 717 6655
www.automotiveacademy.co.uk

Oil and Gas Drilling Industry

What the work involves

Derrickman or woman

- A derrick is the tower structure that supports the oil or gas rig's drilling assembly on an oil or gas production platform.
- As a derrickman or woman, you will be looking after the pipe to which the drill is attached.
- Using hoisting equipment, you will handle and stack sections of the drill pipe, as well as controlling and supervising the condition of the mud pumps and the system that circulates the mud.

Driller

- You will supervise and control the drill operations team (the roustabouts, roughnecks and the derrickman/woman).
- Your main responsibilty will be operating and maintaining the machinery that you raise and lower, to ensure the tension and speed of the drill remains constant.
- You will also keep records of the drilling and its progress.

Rig superintendent

- Supervising the overall production and drilling process, you will also be responsible for the recruitment, retention and training of staff on the production platform.
- You will have to meet visitors, senior managers and representatives from the oil or gas production companies who visit your platform.
- Checking staff rotas and overseeing the upkeep and supply of equipment will be part of your responsibility.

Roughneck

- The drill is the most important part of any platform and your job will include adding additional lengths to the drill as it goes deeper into the rock.
- You will maintain, de-sand, de-silt and keep everything in order.

Roustabout

- Doing most of the labouring work, you could work in either the oil or gas drilling industries.
- You will be cleaning, painting, scraping and repairing the platform – and helping to offload supplies from delivery boats and then storing them away using specialist lifting equipment when needed.

Tool pusher

- You will be responsible for managing all drilling operations, checking the work in progress and dealing with any problems – such as when the drill hits harder rock.
- Responsiblity for safety standards in your team will be a vital part of your job.

The type of person suited to this work

Working in this industry will mean spending long periods of time away from your home and family, so being independent and happy to get along with lots of different people is important.

This can be physical, dangerous work so you must be fit and healthy. You will also need to be responsible and safety conscious as safety is the number one priority when you are working offshore.

To get to the rigs you will normally fly in by helicopiter. You cannot be afraid of flying, nor should you be late for your flight as missing it means you cannot undertake your duty and therefore reduces the available numbers in your team.

Working conditions

A typical large drilling platform complex houses a staff of around 100, but smaller floating production facilities can have a staff as small as 30. Facilities on platforms vary according to size but generally include cabins, canteens and recreational facilities such as gyms. Meals and accommodation are provided but for safety reasons you will not be allowed to drink alcohol on the platform.

Working offshore for two weeks at a time, in a 12-hour shift pattern, is followed by a two-week break on shore.

You will need to wear protective clothing such as thermal suits, ear protectors and helmets as you will be working in dirty, cold and often noisy conditions. You will also sometimes work from heights.

The future outlook

There are about 6000 companies involved in the oil and gas industry in the UK and around 200 offshore installations producing gas and oil. Companies include operating ones that explore and produce oil and gas, drilling ones contracted to do the drilling and contract service ones that supply all the services needed by the offshore platforms.

The overall employment picture is stable, with more looking to enter the sector than actual opportunities. There is however, a high turnover of roustabouts – so there may be opportunities in this area.

Work can be available off- and onshore or abroad.

Most of the opportunities in the UK are based in the North Sea – around north-east England and Scotland. There are also newer fields close to the Shetland Islands and in the Irish Sea.

Your future employment will depend on the demand for gas and oil and many contracts can be for only a few months at a time.

There are progression opportunities. It is possible with training and experience to move to more senior posts, for example from roustabout to roughneck and then on to derrickman/woman, assistant driller and driller. Progression from tool pusher is to rig manager. Rig managers can move on to manage larger platforms or into other management work onshore.

Qualifications and courses

- There are no formal educational entry requirements, as full training is given by the employer. However, you can enter through an Apprenticeship scheme. For this you will need 4 GCSEs/S grades (A–C/1–3) including maths and English.
- Entrants must be 18 years old and at least 163cm tall.
- Candidates generally enter as roustabouts and progress to become roughnecks.
- All offshore workers must complete an offshore safety, survival and firefighting course. NVQ/SVQ Levels 1, 2 and 3 in Offshore Drilling Operations are available.
- You will also have to pass a fitness examination, including sight and hearing tests.
- The position of toolpusher/rig superintendent is achieved by progressing through the ranks, starting as a roustabout. From this you will progress to roughneck and then driller. On average it takes around 5 years to progress from roughneck to toolpusher.

entry level

To both enter and train while working in this career, you will need qualifications at Level 1–2. Please refer to explanation on page vii.

Other related opportunities

- Electricity Generation Worker p201
- Engineer: Craft p203
- Marine Engineering / Marine Industry p213
- Quarry Worker p221

Advantages/disadvantages

- If you are only offered short-term contract work you may have periods of time when you are not earning and this can be difficult – especially if you have financial commitments.
- You may have to travel long distances from your home base and spend weeks away from your family.
- There are financial advantages to working offshore – your contract will probably include free food and board so you should have few costs when you are working. Also wages are higher in the industry to compensate for offshore work.

Earnings guide

Derrickman or woman
- Starting salary is normally in the range of £25,000–£31,000 a year.

Driller
- This is a key job on the platform and earnings of £30,000 up to £48,000 are possible.

Rig superintendent
- Salaries can be more than £55,000 a year depending on the size of the offshore installation you are managing.

Roughneck
- Starting salary is usually around £23,000 rising to £26,000 with experience.

Roustabout
- Starting salary is usually around £19,000 rising to £25,000 with experience.

Tool pusher
- Starting salaries are around £40,000 per year. With experience this can rise to £55,000+. £73,000–£77,000 is possible for the most experienced.
- Your earnings will depend on the organisation you work for. However, it is likely that in addition to your salary you will also receive free meals and board when offshore. If you work at an onshore site, expect your earnings to be reduced by 70–80%.

Further information

www.cityandguilds.com/myperfectjob

Cogent (Sector Skills Council for the chemical, nuclear, oil and gas, petroleum and polymer industries)
Unit 5, Mandarin Court
Centre Park
Warrington
Cheshire
WA1 1GG
01925 515200
www.cogent-ssc.com

Energy Institute
61 New Cavendish Street
London
W1G 7AR
020 7467 7100
www.energyinst.org.uk

Oilcareers
The Westhill Business Park
Westhill
Aberdeen
Aberdeenshire
AB32 6UF
0870 870 4564
www.oilcareers.com

UK Offshore Operators Association
3rd floor, The Exchange 2
62 Market Street
Aberdeen
Scotland
AB11 5PJ
01224 577250
www.oilandgas.org.uk

Quarry Worker

What the work involves

- Quarrying involves opencast mining to extract various minerals from the ground. In the UK the principal ones are coal, gypsum, crushed rock, clay and sand.
- Explosives and heavy machinery are used within most quarries during the process.

Quarry worker

- As a quarry worker you could work in a variety of roles including: operators of machines such as excavators or cranes; plant and process operators working on the crushers, grading and screening plant; maintenance workers – undertaking maintenance on the different machinery and plant, including electrical, mechanical and fitting work; drilling holes for exploration or explosives; shotfirers, working mostly with the explosives; drivers who operate tipping machines and move and collect the staff on buses; technicians working in the laboratories undertaking quality control and sampling excavated minerals.

Quarry engineer

- As a qualified engineer you will be responsible for the management, organisation and planning of all the work undertaken in your quarry.
- You will need an understanding of both the scientific aspects of the work and the business and management sides.

The type of person suited to this work

This can be dangerous work, so in all aspects you will have to be able to follow instructions and keep to health and safety guidelines.

Quarry worker

Much of your work will involve being physically active, so you should be very fit and healthy. You will have to respect the dangers that you will be working in – your own and your colleagues' safety will rely on this.

You will probably work in a team so getting along with others will be an important requirement. Being able to read written instructions and use measuring or other numerical skills will be essential.

Quarry engineer

Maths and physics are important aspects to this work, so an interest in both will be essential.

Although you will not use the machinery and equipment yourself, you should understand how each machine operates and what it can do. You will also need to understand technical drawings and plans.

You should be able to work in a team, with good communication skills.

Working conditions

The working conditions will be dusty, noisy and dangerous.

The sites are often in the country so travelling could be involved.

Your working hours may be worked in shifts and could include weekends and evenings.

Quarry worker

You will be working outside in all weathers sometimes climbing, carrying and bending. You will be expected to wear protective clothing such as hard hats, boots, gloves and ear protection. You might also have to wear goggles.

Quarry engineer

Recently the work has moved from being mostly on-site to a more office-based function with some on-site work.

The future outlook

There are over 2000 quarries across the UK operated by a range of companies – from small to very large international quarrying operations. The employment situation is good with opportunities for both quarry workers and quarry engineers.

Quarry worker

If you are working as an operative, driver, mechanic or fitter it is possible to train to be a driller or shotfirer by taking specialist training courses. With experience, supervisory posts may also become available or you can choose to work abroad.

You could also take additional qualifications and apply for technician level work.

Quarry engineer

Quarry engineers can look for promotional opportunities within their existing organisation, with a competitor or abroad. The industry has a strong professional development system in place which is supported by the Institute of Quarrying (IOQ). This ranges from student to fellowship levels. Ongoing study is recommended if you want to progress in the quarrying industry.

There are good opportunites to work abroad and many engineers have found undertaking a period abroad has added to their progression opportunities.

Qualifications and courses

entry level

To both enter and train while working in this career, you will need qualifications at Level 1–8. Please refer to explanation on page vii.

Quarry worker

- There are no formal educational requirements, but the majority of employers seek 5 GCSEs/S grades (A–C/1–3), and the ability to drive or willingness to attain LGV status would prove useful.
- If you have experience in other aspects of the construction, mining or mobile plant operations your skills would also be suitable for quarrying work.
- There are NVQ/SVQ Level 1–2 opportunities in drilling, mobile plant, process plant, road building, shot firing and laboratory operation.
- Courses are provided by EPIC (the training organisation and awarding body for the extractive and mineral processing industries).
- To be a shot firer you must complete a Shot Firing Certificate.
- It is possible to enter as an Apprentice/Skillseekers if aged 16–24.

Quarry engineer

- A degree, Foundation degree or HND in a relevant subject is required. Degree courses are available in subjects such as minerals and mining engineering, minerals surveying, and mining engineering. It is also possible to enter from another branch of engineering such as civil engineering. The Institute of Quarrying (IOQ) recognises qualifications in chemistry, earth sciences, construction, mechanical engineering, materials science and related fields, as well as specialist mining/minerals courses, for professional membership.
- Training is normally provided on the job, and graduate apprenticeships may be available for candidates with a first degree.
- Entrants will normally gain professional accreditation with a relevant body – either the IOQ or the Institute of Materials, Minerals and Mining.
- Some companies offer funding or sponsorship through your degree with financial support and/or work experience placements during your vacations. Contact the IOQ for details.

Other related opportunities

- Engineer: Craft p203
- Engineer: Professional p205
- Engineer: Technician p208
- Oil and Gas Drilling Industry p219

Advantages/disadvantages

- Many engineers have found their prospects improved by a period working abroad. As many companies have quarrying operations overseas, particularly in developing countries, it is realistic to aim for overseas experience.
- The industry has an excellent training and development structure in place for staff of all levels.
- There are good employment opportunites at all levels.
- If you have a good aptitude and undertake training you will be able to advance to supervisory or management work in the industry at a relatively young age.

Earnings guide

- All earnings will be dependent upon additional payments such as overtime, bonuses and shift pay.

Quarry worker

- Unskilled starting salaries are around £12,500 a year.
- At craft level and with experience this rises to £15,000–£20,000.

Quarry engineer

- Upon graduation salaries are around £19,500–£24,000.
- With experience you can earn £25,000–£35,000.
- The most senior can earn £35,000–£50,000.

Further information

www.cityandguilds.com/myperfectjob

Institute of Quarrying
7 Regent Street
Nottingham
NG1 5BS
0115 945 3880
www.quarrying.org

EPIC Training and Consulting Services Ltd
Alban Row
27–31 Verulam Road
St Albans
Hertfordshire
AL3 4DG
01727 869008
Main website: www.epicltd.com
Careers in quarrying website: www.careersinquarrying.com

CRCI:G

CLCI:R

Railway Fitter / Electrician

What the work involves

- Keeping the railway stock maintained and working efficiently involves a lot of people all doing different work with a range of skills.
- This entry focuses upon the following main engineering functions:

Railway mechanical fitter

- You will maintain and service the traction and rolling stock, plant, machinery and passenger coaches. You could also repair station equipment like customer lifts and hoisting equipment.
- Responding to the team supervisor you will diagnose and cure faults, undertake safety checks and sometimes work on new locomotives or tractions by using a range of skills such as those used in welding, mechanical and maintenance engineering.

Railway electrical fitter

- You will work alongside mechanical fitters and other craft and technician level engineers. You will specialise in the electrical side of the maintenance and servicing work. You will work on the traction and rolling stock, plant machinery and passenger coaches.
- When required, you will also repair the electrical aspects of station equipment like customer lifts and hoisting equipment as well as installing or repairing overhead power lines and supply cables.

Multi-skilled railway fitter

- You will have a combination of both of the sets of skills held by mechanical and electrical specialists – and you will be able to work in either aspect.

The type of person suited to this work

You should enjoy working with your hands, diagnosing faults and working out solutions. You will be comfortable using different hand tools and equipment and enjoy working in a team alongside other fitters.

Physically fitness is important as you will be on your feet, working at your bench or directly within the various railway stock.

You should be happy to follow verbal and written instructions, be able to read and understand technical drawings and diagrams and have a responsible attitude to health and safety.

An interest in maths, science and practical subjects will also be useful.

Working conditions

Much of your work will take place within heated workshops or depots. Depending on your work you might have to visit jobs which are outdoors, for example near to railway sidings or within a station. On these occasions it might be cold and dark.

As many of the work places are in remote or difficult areas to access, having your own transport is often essential.

You will have to wear protective clothing and be happy working in cramped places, using lots of bending and lifting.

Good colour vision will be essential too.

Yor normal working week will be 37 hours worked in shifts that cover early, late, evening and weekend working.

The future outlook

There are about 8000 railway fitters and electricians in the UK. Employers include train, light rail and metro operating companies and London Underground. In addition there are a number of specialist maintenance companies carrying out work for operating companies and engineering companies making new traction units and carriages.

Currently there is an expansion and modernisation programme of the railway industry and network underway, so opportunities in the railway industry are good. Railway fitters are sometimes recruited once they have qualified in other areas of the engineering industry.

Once within the industry, there are well-developed promotional and in-service training programmes which help fitters to progress to supervisor, technician, team leader and, finally, management level if they want to.

CRCI:GE

CLCI:RAB/RAK

Qualifications and courses

- It is sometimes possible to start as a trainee straight from school, but a better route of entry is through an Apprenticeship/Skillseekers scheme.
- Requirements for the Apprenticeships/ Skillseekers are usually 3–5 GCSEs/S grades (A–C/1–3) including English, maths, science and technology. An Intermediate GNVQ/GSVQ may also be accepted.
- The selection process will also depend on the satisfactory outcome of medical examinations, eye tests (normal colour vision is required), hearing tests and alcohol and drug screenings. An aptitude test may be set.
- Induction training for qualified recruits is followed by on-the-job training. Those qualified as fitters may receive electrical training and vice versa to make candidates more versatile.
- NVQs/SVQs in Rail Transport Engineering: Maintenance (Traction and Rolling Stock) or (Plant) at Levels 2 and 3 are available.
- An ability to drive, with access to personal transport, is often required.

entry level

To both enter and train while working in this career, you will need qualifications at Level 2–3. Please refer to explanation on page vii.

Other related opportunities

- Engineer: Craft p203
- Engineer: Technician p208
- Rail p578

Advantages/disadvantages

- The rail industry is beginning to expand – so there will be an increasing need for new recruits.
- The training and career routes are well developed.
- Due to the range of jobs within the railway industry it is possible to move sideways into other related job areas.

Earnings guide

- Each railway company sets its own rates of pay so you will always find slight differences across the country.
- During an Apprenticeship you will receive around £9,500–£13,000 per year. With experience and qualifications you can get £17,000–£22,000.
- Very skilled and experienced railway fitters can earn up to £30,000 per year.
- Overtime and free or reduced rail travel are also common.

Further information

www.cityandguilds.com/myperfectjob

Network Rail
40 Melton Street
London
NW1 2EE
020 7557 8000
www.networkrail.co.uk

Careers in Rail
www.careersinrail.org

GoSkills (Sector Skills Council for passenger transport)
Concorde House
Trinity Park
Solihull
B37 7UQ
0121 635 5520
www.goskills.org

CRCI:GE

CLCI:RAB/RAK

Thermal Insulation Engineer

What the work involves

- You will use various types of insulation to either prevent heat loss or keep heat out within different types of products and equipment, such as boilers, pipe-work, refrigeration or air conditioning.
- The types of insulation you will use will be dependent on the actual project but could involve silicate or foam.
- You will measure, cut and shape insulating materials to fit around pipes, boilers and duct work.
- Once the item is insulated, you will cover it using sheet metal or another cladding material.
- You could work on existing systems or help in the building of new structures and equipment.

The type of person suited to this work

Some of the materials you will be exposed to will have the potential to be dangerous, so you will have to be aware of your own safety and that of others.

Much of the work involves strenuous lifting, balancing and some climbing up scaffolding, so you will have to be physically fit.

The ability to work in a team and get on with other people will be important as you will often work alongside other professionals from the construction and engineering industries.

You should be able to understand instructions, have a practical approach to your work and enjoy using manual skills.

Working conditions

You could be working indoors or outside at heights, in places that are cramped or difficult to access.

You may be exposed to harmful substances and be working in dusty and dirty environments, so you will wear protective clothing, like goggles and sometimes a face mask.

You will normally work a standard 38-hour week, but overtime and evening or weekend working might be required.

You will probably need to travel around the country to different sites and projects.

The future outlook

The energy conservation industry is expanding and there is a growth in demand for qualified thermal insulation engineers to work on a wide range of engineering and construction projects.

With training and experience your main opportunities will be within building, building service engineering or specialised energy conservation companies.

Within the larger companies it might be possible to progress into supervisory posts and work abroad can be available.

entry level

2

To both enter and train while working in this career, you will need qualifications at Level 2. Please refer to explanation on page vii.

Qualifications and courses

- Although no formal qualifications are required, employers usually require GCSEs/S grades in English, maths, science and an engineering or construction subject.
- It is possible to enter this career from an Apprenticeship/Skillseekers opportunity if you are aged 16–24.
- You will have to pass an entry test after which you will undertake on-the-job and off-the-job training at college. Your employer could use a training programme provided by the Insulation and Environmental Training Agency (IETA).
- It is also helpful if you can evidence some practical work experience when applying.
- NVQs/SVQs in Thermal Insulation Engineering are available in relevant subjects at Levels 2–3.

Other related opportunities

- Engineer: Craft p203
- Engineer: Technician p208
- Gas Distribution Worker p211
- Heating and Ventilating Engineer p56
- Plumber p65

Advantages/disadvantages

- You will be working alongside people from different industries.
- The skills needed to be able to start and finish a job will be varied.
- You may need to stay away from home – this could be difficult if you have family commitments.
- Opportuniites are good and overseas work may be possible.

Earnings guide

- Whilst training, your earnings will range from £9,000–£16,000 a year.
- With qualifications this rises to between £17,000 and £21,000
- Senior thermal insulation engineers can earn up to £27,000.
- Expenses may be paid when you need to live away from your home base during a project.

Further information

Insulation and Environmental Training Agency
Tica House, Allington Way
Yarm Road Business Park
Darlington
Co Durham
DL1 4QB
01325 466704
www.tica-acad.co.uk

CITB–ConstructionSkills
Bircham Newton
King's Lynn
Norfolk
PE31 6RH
01485 577577
www.constructionskills.net
www.citb-constructionskills.co.uk

www.cityandguilds.com/myperfectjob

Watch / Clock Repairer

What the work involves

- You will be using very precise and accurate hand and machine tools to clean, service and repair watches and clocks.
- If you need to replace or repair damaged parts, you will also clean and oil the mechanisms, reassemble and then adjust and test the timepiece.
- You may replace watch batteries, straps or bracelets.
- If you work in a shop selling watches and clocks you may also sell jewellery.
- If you work in specialist antique clock restoration and repair you may have to design and make replacement parts.

The type of person suited to this work

As many repairers work alone from within a workshop or shop, you should be happy with your own company. You will need good eyesight, practical ability and excellent hand skills as the tools you will be working with can be small and delicate.

This can be slow and complex work, so as well as having lots of patience, you should also be able to keep your work area clean and tidy.

During your work you will be giving advice to customers and possibly serving in a shop, so being able to talk to people who will sometimes be difficult is important.

Working conditions

Your work environment will have to be clean and dust free. You will normally be based within a workshop which could adjoin either a jewellery or a craft shop.

You may also need to visit customers when giving estimates for the repair and or restoration of some pieces like larger clocks.

Depending on your work, you might need to work Saturdays with a day off in the week.

The future outlook

Horology (the art or science of measuring time, often used as the formal name for repairing watches and clocks) is a small profession but it has a long history.

Employers are usually small specialised repair or restoration firms or retail jewellers.

Self-employment is common.

There is a worldwide shortage of experienced and qualified watch and clock repairers.

Progression opportunities include retail management, training, teaching, specialisation in the restoration of antique timepieces or setting up your own business.

entry level

2

To both enter and train while working in this career, you will need qualifications at Level 2. Please refer to explanation on page vii.

Qualifications and courses

- There are no formal educational requirements, although some employers will require GCSEs/S grades (A–C/1–3) in maths, science and technology. An aptitude in craft and technology subjects is an advantage.
- Apprenticeships lasting three years are sometimes available, although opportunities are very limited. It is advisable to contact members of the British Horological Society (BHI) for local vacancies. Details are available on the BHI website.
- Courses accredited by the BHI are also available. Training opportunities are posted on the BHI website.
- Other relevant courses are available, including an HND in Horology, and the internationally recognised qualifications run by WOSTEP (the Watchmakers of Switzerland Training and Education Programme), specialising in the repair of mechanical and quartz watches. Entry requirements for such courses are typically 4–5 GCSEs/S grades (A–C/1–3) including English language.

CRCI:G

CLCI: R

Other related opportunities

- Engineer: Craft p203
- Engineer: Technician p208
- Gold / Silversmith p146
- Locksmith p212
- Shopkeeper p454

Advantages/disadvantages

- You will receive lots of satisfaction from knowing you've repaired and restored a valuable or precious family heirloom.
- Restoration or repair work can be complex, and care is needed as some of the pieces will be fragile but very valuable.
- Because of the worldwide shortage of good repairers it is possible to find work abroad.

Earnings guide

- Your earnings will depend on your type of employment and location.
- If working for a private company, you would earn around £14,000–£17,000 a year.
- Experienced watch and clock repairers can earn up to £29,000.
- If you are self-employed, your earnings will depend on your success in attracting customers – but earnings can be high for experienced repairers.

Further information

British Horological Institute
Upton Hall
Upton
Newark
Nottinghamshire
NG23 5TE
01636 813795
www.bhi.co.uk

Worshipful Company of Clockmakers
Salters' Hall
Fore Street
London
EC2Y 5DE
0207 638 5500
www.clockmakers.org

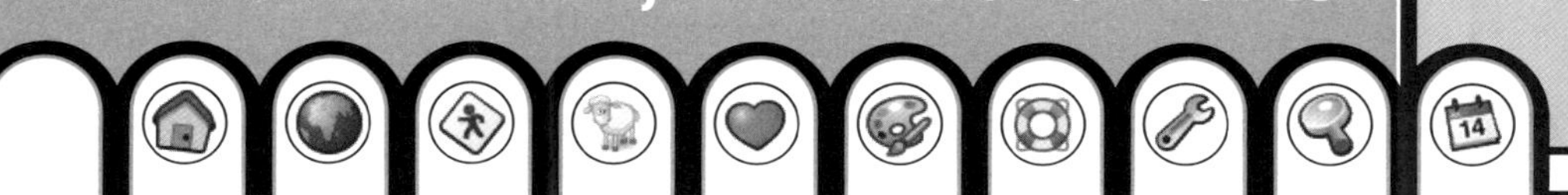

If you care about the environment or the welfare of animals, or enjoy helping things to grow, this could be the cluster for you. Try some of these ideas:

- **Animal Technician**
- **Farmer**
- **Forest Worker**
- **Gamekeeper**
- **Veterinary Surgeon**

But what's it like working in this area?
Here's Annabelle Bray's story:

Horticulturalist (Gardener)

Thirty-three-year-old Annabelle read maths at university before doing a variety of office jobs, including being a Technical Administrator at the Environment Agency. When she was 27, she applied for a Careership with the National Trust and was awarded a place on this 3-year course. She was based in the garden of Antony House, at Tor Point, Cornwall, and for 10 weeks each year she attended Bickton College in Devon. She gained NVQ Levels 2 and 3 in Amenity Horticulture and has a Royal Horticultural Society (RHS) General qualification as well as qualifications in the use of pesticides. Two weeks before her course finished Annabelle learned she had got a job at the Eden Project in Cornwall and has been there ever since.

WHAT THE JOBS ENTAILS

'I don't work in the Biodomes here, but in the outside area known as The Pit. I work with a team of 7 and we start at 7.30am when we meet to discuss what tasks we need to do that day. We have to get all our heavy machinery work done before 9.30am when the public arrives. We have a break at 10.15am and after that we do general maintenance such as weeding, planting, mulching and pruning, depending on the season. There's still a lot of development going on at the Eden Project so we could be working on new displays and because of the contours of the site I do a lot of my work on slopes. We also recording and label our plants as this is an educational site, and also liaising with the visitors and answering their questions.'

WHAT'S HOT AND WHAT'S NOT ABOUT THE JOB

'The nicest thing is working out in the open air and being part of nature. I also like working in a dynamic team, I find that very inspirational. However, sometimes in the winter the weather does get to you. We have something called Bulb Mania each year and have to plant many thousands of bulbs and it's not such fun when you are planting in the pouring rain.'

Annabelle says you need a sense of humour to do what she does and it is essential to have a love of plants. She also thinks enthusiasm and a keenness to learn are key. Because she is working in the public arena she says attention to detail is essential.

WHAT THE FUTURE HOLDS

'Because I love what I do I want to progress and the Eden Project is very supportive of its employees' personal development and gives us time out to get more qualifications. I'd like to specialise more in the scientific side of plant identification and would like to work on surveying the wild flowers of Cornwall.'

'At present there's a shortage of young, qualified gardeners so I would say to anyone wanting to do this get some work experience because then when you apply to do qualifications you can show how keen you are.'

Agricultural Scientist

What the work involves

- Agricultural scientists use biology, biochemistry and chemistry to research and develop more efficient ways to breed and manage livestock and/or increase plant or crop production. You could be employed by a range of employers including private chemical or agricultural companies and national or local government.
- Your work might include teaching and informing farmers or other growers about the results of your research on aspects like fertilisers, using chemicals, animal genetics or fungicides.

Agronomist

- Agronomists specialise in improving the quality of soil to raise the quality and productivity of crops.
- Your areas of expertise would include irrigation, drainage, plant breeding, soil classification, soil fertility and weed control.

The type of person suited to this work

You will need an interest in and in-depth knowledge of the environment and science, particularly biology and chemistry. More importantly however, will be how you use your science background in your work. You will spend a lot of time communicating and listening to growers' problems before researching solutions within the laboratory or in the field to meet their needs.

You should be able to handle lots of complex problems and be patient and organised in the way you approach them, as some of your work will take a long time to develop.

This job requires you to work both alone and as part of a team, so you should be happy to work with people from different backgrounds and have excellent communication skills.

Working conditions

Depending on the area of your research or work you could be indoors within a laboratory, outdoors on farms and nurseries or a combination of both. You are likely to work with hazardous equipment, so protective clothing will be provided.

If you suffer from allergies related to animals, pollen or dust this work could be difficult for you. Some jobs will also require good colour vision.

You might have to travel, so a driving licence could be useful.

The future outlook

General research opportunities are reducing but some areas like genetic engineering are increasing. Although small, the main openings for applicants continue to be as consultants within manufacturing companies which produce animal feed, chemicals, fertilisers and seeds, research organisations and national or local government offices. Recently there have been openings within international organisations such as the United Nations to help to develop Third World economies by improving their food production and farming ability.

With experience you could lecture or teach within universities, colleges or schools and there are opportunities to work abroad.

As a lot of this work involves selling and communicating to different people, sales-related work for the production companies is also possible.

entry level

4–8

To both enter and train while working in this career, you will need qualifications at Level 4–8. Please refer to explanation on page vii.

Qualifications and courses

- The normal entry is by a Foundation degree, HND or degree in a relevant discipline such as agriculture/agricultural science, biochemistry or a horticultural, biological or related subject. Some jobs will also require a higher degree or postgraduate qualification in a specialist area like seed production or agricultural development.
- To enter a degree you will need A levels/H grades including science subjects and GCSEs/S grades including English, maths and science subjects.
- Some farm or horticulture experience is preferred. For adults wishing to enter this field but lacking normal entry requirements, most colleges and universities are flexible and will consider relevant experience. Qualifications gained at work such as NVQs/SVQs may be acceptable, or an Access course could be taken in preparation for a degree course.

Agronomist

- Newcastle University offer a degree in Agronomy which requires 3 A levels grade BCC plus GCSE biology and chemistry, or equivalent.

Other related opportunities

- Biologist p468
- Chemist p472
- Earth Sciences p475
- Ecologist p478
- Farm Work p241
- Forestry p246

Advantages/disadvantages

- This job offers the opportunity to combine scientific research with practical work.
- Some jobs are in decline.
- It is a great career if you love plants, animals or the land.

Earnings guide

- Pay will depend on the location and type of employer. Some private companies and most public organisations have structured pay scales in place.
- Generally new graduates can expect between £22,000 and £25,000 per year.
- This can rise to around £33,000–£40,000 with experience.
- People in senior positions such as department heads, can earn £60,000+.

Further information

Lantra (Sector Skills Council for the environmental and land-based industries)
Lantra House
Stoneleigh Park
Kenilworth
Warwickshire
CV8 2LG
024 7669 6996
www.lantra.co.uk

Department for Environment, Food and Rural Affairs (DEFRA)
Nobel House
17 Smith Square
London
SW1P 3JR
020 7238 6000
www.defra.gov.uk

Institute of Biology
9 Red Lion Court
London
EC4A 3EF
020 7936 5900
www.iob.org

Animal Protection / Charity

What the work involves

- Organisations like the Royal Society for the Prevention of Cruelty to Animals (RSPCA) and Scottish Society for the Prevention of Cruelty to Animals (SSPCA) and Dogs Trust provide 24-hour protection for animals suffering cruelty. Alongside the work of veterinary surgeons, nurses and kennel assistants who are employed to provide aftercare and medical support, organisations require front-line staff to rescue the animals and bring them into local rescue centres. The following jobs focus on the removal and rescue of animals in danger or suffering abuse:

Animal inspector

- You will work for an animal protection organisation or local authority offering a 24/7 service for animals across the UK. Some of your work will involve undertaking rescue work, but you will also visit and advise pet and animal owners so they can improve their care.
- Other duties also include managing staff from the other public services at rescues, taking cases to court, checking conditions within animal establishments like auctions and kennels and administering First Aid.

Animal collector

- You will be on-call and have to be able to move quickly to rescue animals at risk, possibly from a dangerous location. This involves working alongside vets and other emergency services.
- You need to be confident handling all types of animals and know how to transport them safely.

The type of person suited to this work

You will have to be committed to the safety and protection of animals. This can be challenging work as many of the situations you will find yourself in could be potentially dangerous, so you will have to be aware of your own, the public's and the animals' health and safety. Some of your work will be distressing and may be sad, especially if you have to carry out euthanasia. Although you will often work on your own, you may well work within a team, especially in rescue situations. You will need excellent communication skills with the ability to remain calm in a crisis.

This is physical and active work. You will spend lots of your time meeting and talking to people from lots of different backgrounds, some of whom will be abusive.

Working conditions

Each day will be different as you will never know where you will be needed. You could be in a factory, private house, animal establishment or outdoors up to your waist in water.

You will spend a lot of your time travelling around your area driving a van. You will probably have to work shifts including evenings and weekends.

Animals can bite and kick, especially when they are frightened, so you will have to use your skills to make sure they remain safe and that you do not put yourself at risk. You will not be able to do this work if you suffer from animal or dust-based allergies.

The future outlook

This type of work is very competitive and applicants outnumber vacancies.

Animal inspector

Every year the RSPCA receives around 2000 applications for approximately 20 inspector places.To enter it is essential that you have practical experience of working with a range of animals. Applicants with security, armed services or animal health backgrounds are often at an advantage.

Animal collector

Animal collection officer vacancies are advertised locally as and when they arise. With experience you can apply for other related work or other opportunities such as an inspector's job. With experience, you can move into other related jobs such as local authority dog and animal warden, kennel, cattery and veterinary work or animal inspector.

CRCI:HC

CLCI:WAM

Other related opportunities

- Animal Work p231
- Dog Handler p500
- Dog Work p237
- Police p506
- Trading Standards Officer p460
- Veterinary Nurse p261

Advantages/disadvantages

- You will have the satisfaction of rescuing animals that are being abused and mistreated.
- Some people will be abusive and you may come across dangerous situations.
- It is rewarding to know you have made a difference to the quality of animals' lives and give them a chance to be rehomed.

Earnings guide

- Salaries will depend on the size of each charity/employer. The RSPCA/SSPCA rates are given as a guide:

Animal inspector

- Starting salaries as a trainee are around £15,750 per year.
- Fully-trained inspectors are paid from £23,360 to £26,121.
- The salaries of the SSPCA are slightly higher. A newly qualified inspector can earn up to £17,000 per year. A chief superintendent can earn £30,000+.

Qualifications and courses

entry level

To both enter and train while working in this career, you will need qualifications at Level 1–2. Please refer to explanation on page vii.

Animal inspector

- This job is not suitable for school leavers, as the minimum age for entry is 22. You will need a full driving licence, experience of working with animals and excellent communication skills.
- GCSEs/S grades including English and a science subject are required. However, physical fitness is as important as academic qualifications; you have to be able to swim 50 metres fully clothed.
- The RSPCA has its own 6-month training course including animal welfare legislation, basic veterinary training, rescue situation techniques, interview and communication techniques, animal handling and public speaking.
- Once qualified you can be posted anywhere in the UK.

Animal collector

- There are no formal qualifications required for this work, but GCSEs/S grades in English and science would be helpful. You also need to have held a driving licence for at least 3 years and have previous experience of working with animals.
- The RSPCA provides on-the-job training and certificates in animal rescue techniques and providing euthanasia.

Further information

www.cityandguilds.com/myperfectjob

Royal Society for the Prevention of Cruelty to Animals
Wilberforce Way
Southwater
Horsham
Sussex
RH13 9RS
0870 333 5999
www.rspca.org.uk

Scottish Society for the Prevention of Cruelty to Animals
Braehead Mains
603 Queensferry Road
Edinburgh
EH4 6AE
0131 339 0222
www.scottishspca.org

Dogs Trust
17 Wakely Street
London
EC1V 1NA
020 7837 0006
www.dogstrust.org.uk

Here's Valerie Selby's story:

Conservation Officer

Although she never had a specific job in mind, Valerie was always interested in plants and conservation work and had done a lot of voluntary conservation work from the age of 14. She took a degree in Amenity Horticulture and during her year out she got a work placement at the Sussex Wildlife Trust. After graduating she worked voluntarily with her local council conservation officer before getting a short-term contract to work on a nature reserve. She then worked for the London Wildlife Trust before getting her current job as the Principal Parks Officer (Biodiversity) for Wandsworth Borough Council.

CRCI:HC

CLCI:WAM

WHAT THE JOB ENTAILS

'I give advice on wildlife and habitat management. I comment on planning applications that may have an impact on wildlife or on specific habitats, giving advice to the developers on how to maintain features on-site that are of benefit to wildlife. I also advise on how to create new habitats as part of the development. Part of my brief is to write and implement the Biodiversity Action Plan for Wandsworth that involves working with local people on specific habitats and species of importance for Wandsworth.'

Valerie's job may sound ideal for someone who loves nature so much, but she says one of the biggest downsides is having to sit at a desk looking at a computer screen instead of being out on-site. She finds it frustrating that nature conservation is not a statutory provision for local councils such as Wandsworth and so often comes bottom of the council's list of priorities, after social services, education and housing. However, there are other things she loves about what she does.

WHAT'S HOT ABOUT CONSERVATION

'I love knowing I can influence how we manage land to encourage more and different species into the area. I can walk past marshland at the end of one of our lakes, for example, see water birds nesting and watch a dragonfly, and know that I helped create and manage that whole area and provided a home for those animals.'

WHAT YOU NEED TO SUCCEED

A love of the outdoors will obviously help you get on in this career, but Valerie says you must also be patient and have the ability to compromise on occasions and be realistic about the wider situation you are in – it is not about living in trees to protect them, but about working out the existing value of those trees compared to additional new habitats that may be gained from a new development. For anyone interested in a career in conservation, Valerie advises the best thing to do is to get some practical experience.

'When we employ people, we need to be confident they have done practical work such as coppicing or meadow mowing, so do some voluntary work with your local conservation group or Wildlife Trust as well as getting your qualifications.'

Animal Work

What the work involves

Animal behaviourist/psychologist

- Animal psychologists advise owners whose pets have developed inappropriate and dangerous behaviour. Although working with all domestic animals, you would probably focus on dogs, cats and horses. Typical problems include aggressive behaviour, soiling or destructiveness. You will combine your academic knowledge of the theory of behaviour by supporting the owners to help solve their pets' problems. You could be connected to a veterinary practice, work in kennels, catteries and welfare societies or be freelance.

Animal pathologist

- This highly specialised role provides an essential service to vets, the livestock industry and government agencies by reporting on causes of illness and death of commercial livestock, pets and domestic animals. Jobs are within pharmaceutical companies, research organisations and commercial veterinary pathology laboratories.

Animal physiotherapist

- Animals suffer from joint and muscular pain in the same way that humans do. As a result, animal physiotherapy has become a regular part of animal care. After gaining your qualifications and extensive practical experience as a human physiotherapist you would take additional qualifications to enable you to treat and work with animals. You would be used by many domestic pet owners but especially horse owners.

Animal technician

- Technicians are responsible for the welfare of the animals used in universities and research establishments for biomedical research. The majority of these animals are rats, mice and other rodents. However, work can include domestic, farm and other animals.

The type of person suited to this work

To do any of the jobs in this area you will need a strong interest in animals, their care and welfare. However, as some of these jobs also involve working with the owner, you will have to be able to communicate with people too!

Working with animals can be messy and smelly work, so you must be prepared to get dirty. You will also need to have lots of patience and remain calm. You should expect the work to be occasionally distressing, especially if the animal is injured or has died, so you will have to be able to avoid getting emotionally involved.

If you choose to work as a pathologist or technician, you will primarily be a scientist – so you will need to be methodical, able to use technical equipment and analyse results.

Working conditions

Depending on your specialism, you could be in a clinic, laboratory, animal centre or be out and about visiting customers. You could be indoors or outside in all weathers. A driving licence is essential for some posts and you will normally wear protective clothing.

Some jobs will involve evening and weekend working, especially if you visit your clients and animals in their own homes.

The work can be dusty, dirty and physically demanding, so you will need to be fit and active. This work can be difficult for those who suffer from allergies.

The future outlook

Many of these jobs are competitive to enter and employ very small numbers. It is strongly recommended to gain some voluntary or paid work experience before applying for employment, education or training.

Animal behaviourist/psychologist/ physiotherapist

There are very limited career opportunities for these jobs although demand across the canine and equine areas has increased due to television programmes and press coverage. Some of the larger animal welfare charities are starting to employ staff with these skills, however, most are self-employed running their own practices. To be successful you will need to build up a client list and have good business skills. There is not a structured career path in place.

Animal pathologist

There are fewer than 100 qualified animal pathologists employed within the UK, so this area is extremely competitive. Once qualified many graduates look to work within one of the seven universities offering veterinary science across the UK, but this can be difficult. Other openings can be in a commerical laboratory doing diagnostic work for the Veterinary Laboratories Agency (VLA). The VLA provide services to vets across the country.

Animal technician

Animal research is a controversial subject and the number of technicians has declined in recent years. Many of those working in the area choose to keep it secret to avoid any reprisals. There are now a few thousand employed across the UK working mostly within universities, teaching hospitals, pharmaceutical companies and research institutions. Most work is in London, the south-east of England, major cities and remote areas across the UK.

To progress people tend to move from one employer to another, into a different sector or up to senior technician level posts.

Qualifications and courses

Animal behaviourist/psychologist

- There is no fixed route into this career, but there are an increasing number of pet behaviour/counselling courses available including some on-line opportunities. A degree in behavioural science, veterinary medicine, psychology or biological sciences will all be useful. There are specific animal behaviour degrees.
- Depending on the degree subject and institution, entry requirements will require A levels/H grades in sciences and/or mathematics.
- When entering this area, a relevant qualification is desirable along with practical, on-the-job experience such as kennel or cattery work, stables work, veterinary practice, or work with one of the animal welfare societies.

Animal pathologist

- To become a member of the Royal College of Pathologists (RCP) you need to hold a recognised veterinary degree and take the RCP examinations in animal pathology.
- Before applying, contact each veterinary school or the RCP to ensure your chosen courses are recognised. You will need the highest level A levels/H grades including sciences and maths to enter veterinary school.

Animal physiotherapist

- To qualify as a chartered animal physiotherapist, you first need a degree in human physiotherapy. You will need the highest level A levels/H grades in maths and science for entry. This is a very competitive degree choice.
- Upon completion of the degree you then can choose to either spend a further minimum of 2 years gaining work experience with a practising chartered animal physiotherapist, or study part time for the PG Dip or MSc in veterinary physiotherapy with the Royal Veterinary College.

entry level

To both enter and train while working in this career, you will need qualifications at Level 2–8. Please refer to explanation on page vii.

Animal technician

- There are no required entry qualifications for this work; however, employers prefer those with 4–5 GCSEs/S grades at level A–C/1–3. Preference will be given to those with scientific, research, laboratory or animal welfare experience.
- The Institute of Animal Technology (IAT) offers several certificates and diplomas in animal technology work. NVQs/SVQs Levels 2 and 3 in the subject are also available. Technicians involved in laboratory testing may need an appropriate Home Office licence, usually gained after a minimum of 1 year's experience and after completion of a module course.

Other related opportunities

- Animal Protection / Charity p229
- Dog Work p237
- Equine / Horse Work p239
- Pathologist p297
- Physiotherapist p301
- Therapist p309
- Veterinary Nurse p261
- Veterinary Surgeon p262

Advantages/disadvantages

- You will be working with animals, perhaps helping them to have a better quality of life.
- Pet owners can be more difficult than their pets!
- Animal technicians may be harassed by animal rights activists.
- Many of these jobs offer opportunities for self-employment.
- It can be difficult to build up a client list as a behaviourist.

Earnings guide

Animal behaviourist/psychologist
- Many working in this area are self-employed, average fees are around £20–£50 for each consultation.

Animal pathologist
- Salaries are similar to those of a veterinary surgeon. Starting rates are between £15,000 and £27,000 per year. With experience this rises to £30,000–£40,000.

Animal physiotherapist
- Many working in this area are self-employed, average fees are around £45–£80 for each consultation.

Animal technician
- Typical trainee starting salaries range from £12,000 to £15,000 per year. With experience this rises to £23,000. Senior technicians with substantial experience can get £28,000+.

CRCI:HC | CLCI:WAM

Further information

www.cityandguilds.com/myperfectjob

ANIMAL BEHAVIOURIST
Association of Pet Behaviour Counsellors
PO Box 46
Worcester
WR8 9YS
www.apbc.org.uk
£3.50 for an information pack

ANIMAL PATHOLOGIST
Royal College of Pathologists
2 Carlton House Terrace
London
SW1Y 5AF
020 7451 6700
www.rcpath.org

ANIMAL PATHOLOGY/PHYSIOTHERAPY
Royal Veterinary College
Hawkshead Lane
North Mymms
Hatfield
Hertfordshire AL9 7TA
01707 666333
www.rvc.ac.uk

ANIMAL PHYSIOTHERAPIST
Association of Chartered Physiotherapists in Animal Therapy
Morland House
Salters Lane
Winchester
Hampshire SO22 5LP
01962 844390
www.acpat.org

Chartered Society of Physiotherapy
14 Bedford Row
London
WC1R 4ED
020 7306 6666
www.csp.org.uk

ANIMAL TECHNICIAN
Institute of Animal Technology
5 South Parade
Summertown
Oxford
OX2 7JL
www.iat.org.uk

ANIMAL TECHNICIAN/PATHOLOGIST
Department for Environment, Food and Rural Affairs (DEFRA)
Nobel House
17 Smith Square
London
SW1P 3JR
020 7238 6000
www.defra.gov.uk

Land-force.com
www.land-force.com

Arboricultural Worker / Manager

What the work involves

- Working in private estates, public parks, national forests or woodland areas, you will look after the spaces for current and future generations. You should have an interest in the environment, plants and wildlife.

Worker

- Under the direction of your manager you would use specialist cutting and lifting equipment, plant new trees, cut down old and diseased trees or thin down dense areas.

Manager

- Your job would be to manage and supervise your staff to care for the forest, trees or woodland areas in your care. As some of these areas are open to the public you will need to be aware of the health and safety of both your employees and visitors.
- You will also plan new or existing spaces, handle budgets and be responsible for your team of staff.

The type of person suited to this work

This work needs people who enjoy being outdoors and love the countryside.

Worker

You should be happy working in potentially dangerous situations using specialised lifting and cutting equipment. You will need to be aware of both your own health and safety and that of your team and members of the public. Good communication and teamworking skills are essential. As this can be physically demanding you should be fit and healthy.

Manager

You will need good communication, leadership and organisational skills. Some of the work will involve being responsible for heavy lifting and cutting equipment. This job combines practical outdoor work with management, planning and financial budgeting so you will need to be able to handle several projects at the same time, remain focused and enjoy hard physical work.

Working conditions

You will be outdoors in all weathers, which can be hot, cold and wet! You will also be using equipment and undertaking some heavy lifting so you will need to be fit and active. If you suffer from pollen or dust allergies this job could be difficult for you.

Manager

Some of your work will include working indoors at a computer where you will plan new projects or undertake administrative tasks.

The future outlook

Although there are jobs available with a range of employers and organisations, most are very competitive. To increase your employment opportunities, undertaking work experience is helpful.The total number employed in all aspects of forestry, arboriculture and wood processing is 45,000. Approximately 10,000 of these people work within forestry and wood processing.

Possible organisations/employers include the National Trust, public parks, private estates, local authority amenity departments, garden centres and commercial contractors. With experience it is also possible to work abroad, become a trainer or undertake freelance consultancy work.

entry level

To both enter and train while working in this career, you will need qualifications at Level 1–8. Please refer to explanation on page vii.

Qualifications and courses

Worker

- There are no set entry qualifications for this work. A driving licence is normally required, and candidates should be physically fit. Many courses require relevant work experience, and for some courses, entrants need to be at least 17.
- Some people enter with relevant qualifications studied full time at college, such as a BTEC National Diploma in Forestry and Arboriculture (Arboriculture) or Countryside Management (Woodland Management). The City & Guilds National Certificate in Horticulture has arboriculture options.
- It is also possible to enter without qualifications and train as you work. The essential skills are covered by National Proficiency Tests Council (NPTC) and Scottish Skills Testing Service (SSTS) certificates of competence and Lantra Awards. Apprenticeships/Skillseekers may be available for those aged 16–24.
- People working in the industry can work towards NVQs/SVQs at Level 2 in Arboriculture and Level 3 in Treework (Arboriculture) and the Royal Forestry Society's Certificate in Arboriculture.

Manager

- It is also possible to take relevant degrees or HNDs in subjects like horticulture, forestry or arboriculture. To enter you will need 2 A levels/H grades including science and maths with 5 GCSEs or 3–4 S grades at A–C/1–3.
- The Institute of Chartered Foresters also offers professional qualifications that can lead to Chartered Forester status.

CRCI:HB

CLCI:WAF

Other related opportunities

- Countryside Work p235
- Forestry p246
- Landscape p255

Advantages/disadvantages

- You will be outdoors in all weathers.
- If you suffer from allergies this work could be difficult.
- It is satisfying to know you have made a difference to the environment for current and future generations.

Earnings guide

- Due to the competitive nature of the work, salaries will vary across the country and depend on your employer.

Worker

- Starting salaries are between £15,000 and £17,000 per year. With experience this could increase to £25,000.

Manager

- New managers earn around £16,000–£18,000 per year.
- This rises to £30,000+ for someone with experience.

Further information

Lantra (Sector Skills Council for the environmental and land-based industries)
Lantra House
Stoneleigh Park
Kenilworth
Warwickshire CV8 2LG
024 7669 6996
www.lantra.co.uk

Arboricultural Association
Ampfield House
Ampfield
Romsey
Hampshire
SO51 9PA
01794 368717
www.trees.org.uk

Forestry Commission
Silvan House
231 Corstorphine Road
Edinburgh
EH12 7AT
0845 367 3787
www.forestry.gov.uk

Institute of Chartered Foresters
7a St Colme Street
Edinburgh
EH3 6AA
0131 225 2705
www.charteredforesters.org

www.cityandguilds.com/myperfectjob

Beekeeper

What the work involves

- Most professional beekeepers keep at least 100 beehives.
- During the spring and summer you will be working with the hives, checking the progress of each colony and making sure that they have enough space for honey collection.
- Several times a year you will take off the honey.
- In the autumn you will prepare the hives for winter and collect, extract and process the honey and fill and label jars.

entry level

To both enter and train while working in this career, you will need qualifications at Level 1. Please refer to explanation on page vii.

The type of person suited to this work

This is very practical work so you will need to be good with your hands and be fit and active. To avoid upsetting your bees you will need to be calm and methodical. You also need to be confident around potentially aggressive insects.

You should enjoy being outdoors, and due to the heavy lifting involved you will need to be strong in your back and arms.

If you want your honey to do well you will also require sales and marketing skills.

Working conditions

This job combines working outdoors in the spring and summer with being indoors preparing new hives and processing honey and wax in the winter. You might move hives to take advantage of nectar in orchards in spring and perhaps heather in the late summer so you could have to travel to different locations.

This work will not be suitable for those who suffer from certain allergies.

The future outlook

There are only a small number of full-time professional beekeepers in the UK. The main prospect is self-employment, probably after first gaining experience from keeping bees as a hobby.

To be successful you will have to be able to sell and market your honey, so being able to talk to customers and maintaining high standards of taste and quality are important. With the increasing popularity of farmers' and rural markets and the initerest in organic and natural products, opportunities for selling honey is increasing.

Qualifications and courses

- There are no set entry requirements for beekeeping; however, practical experience is vital and can be gained through joining a local beekeeping association. It may also be possible to train on the job with an experienced bee farmer, but opportunities are rare.
- Beekeeping courses are available through local associations, providing practical knowledge of the industry as well as increasing your existing knowledge. The British Beekeepers' Association (BBKA) runs examinations leading to Basic Assessment, General and Advanced Certificates in Beekeeping.
- Some agricultural colleges and institutions run a National Diploma in Beekeeping.
- A driving licence is essential to transport hives from site to site, and to make deliveries.
- The Scottish Beekeepers' Association runs courses that include the Scottish Basic Beemaster Certificate and Scottish Honey Judge Certificate.

CRCI:HA

CLCI:WAB

Other related opportunities

- Countryside Work p235
- Fish Farmer p244

Advantages/disadvantages

- You will be working on your own a lot.
- You can sometimes develop an allergy to bee stings, which could result in a change of career.
- You will probably get stung regularly.
- Working with bees is fascinating.
- This is a great job if you enjoy being outdoors.

Earnings guide

- Earnings vary depending on the spring and summer weather and your success as a beekeeper. Most beekeepers make a modest living but you are unlikely to become wealthy.
- As a guide only, a self-employed person could expect to earn around £8,000–£15,000 per year.

Further information

Lantra (Sector Skills Council for the environmental and land-based industries)
Lantra House
Stoneleigh Park
Kenilworth
Warwickshire
CV8 2LG
024 7669 6996
www.lantra.co.uk

British Beekeepers' Association
National Beekeeping Centre
Royal Agricultural Showground
Stoneleigh
Warwickshire
CV8 2LG
www.bbka.org.uk

Scottish Beekeepers' Association
www.scottishbeekeepers.org.uk

Countryside Work

What the work involves

Conservation officer

- You would be responsible for an area of the countryside, such as a nature reserve or country park. Your work would involve putting into action the plans of your employer who could be a land owner or organisation such as the National Trust.
- You will manage the work of a team of rangers, wardens and possibly volunteers. You could manage all of the public rights of access and perhaps give talks to visitors who might be adults or schoolchildren.
- The ecology and long-term survival of your area will be your responsibility, so you will use your specialist knowledge of animals and plants to secure their future.

Ranger/warden

- By patrolling the countryside throughout the year you will monitor the success and progress of the plants, animals, fencing and buildings in your care.
- You will be responsible for the safety and enjoyment of any visitors, answer their queries and help them get the most from their visit.
- If you have any rare plants or protected animals like nesting birds in your area you will be responsible for creating suitable protection.

The type of person suited to this work

To do these jobs you will need to enjoy being outdoors and have a strong interest in wildlife and the countryside. You will be working in all weathers and although you will wear protective clothing you may still get very cold and wet or hot and dusty!

To ensure the future of your area you will need to provide information to the public which could include talking to potential funding organisations or local politicians. You will therefore have to be confident talking in public and have excellent written and spoken communication skills.

You might have to write reports and sometimes undertake research.

To find work you may have to start with some voluntary or community-based work, so it's important that you are keen and willing.

Working conditions

Most of your work will be outdoors, driving or walking around your area. This is physically demanding work and is likely to involve walking over difficult terrain.

You are likely to work longer hours during the spring and summer, especially if there are animals or plants that require protection.

This work can be difficult if you suffer from pollen or dust allergies.

The future outlook

Most countryside/environment jobs are offered by government agencies such as English Nature or Scottish National Heritage, local government, charities or large organisations such as the National Trust. There are 5000 people currently employed within the local authority sector. Due to current interest in the countryside and conservation, and the increasing numbers of graduates completing related further and higher education courses, competition for all jobs is very high.

Once employed within the industry it is likely that you will need to move from employer to employer to gain career progression.

Due to the short-term funding situtation within this area of work, many jobs are offered on temporary contracts or on a seasonal basis. To help you to find your first job, voluntary or community-based projects are recommended.

After gaining significant experience, it is possible to enter lecturing, consultancy or research work.

Qualifications and courses

entry level

To both enter and train while working in this career, you will need qualifications at Level 2–8. Please refer to explanation on page vii.

Conservation officer

- The usual entry requirement for a conservation officer is a degree or HND in a relevant subject such as rural resource management, countryside management, environmental studies or conservation management. A relevant postgraduate qualification can be an advantage.
- It is possible to enter as a ranger or warden and progress to a conservation officer post through experience and professional training.

Ranger/warden

- There are no set entry qualifications to be a countryside ranger, but GCSEs/S grades or higher-level qualifications in science and geography may be required.
- Relevant courses include NVQs/SVQs at Levels 2 and 3 in Environmental Conservation and BTEC/SQA National Certificates or Diplomas in Countryside and Forestry, Conservation, Countryside Skills or Countryside Management.
- Some people become countryside rangers after doing a relevant degree or HND.
- Most training for conservation officers and rangers is done on the job.
- Courses for professional development are provided by Lantra National Training Organisation. NVQs/SVQs may be available for people working in the industry.

General

- A driving licence is essential. These jobs are not normally suitable for school leavers as employers prefer applicants aged 21 or over.
- The National Trust offers a salaried careership scheme for people aged 16–19 for countryside wardens or gardeners leading to NVQ at Level 3.

Other related opportunities

- Beekeeper p234
- Fish Farmer p244
- Forestry p246
- Gamekeeper p248

Advantages/disadvantages

- You will spend a lot of time in the open air combining your interest in the countryside with work!
- You could be working in remote areas.
- This job also includes administration and office work.
- It is a very competitive area to enter so unpaid experience can be vital.

Earnings guide

Conservation officer

- Starting with a government agency, you would probably earn around £17,500–£19,000 per year. This rises to around £26,000 with experience. Senior posts attract £30,000–£35,000.
- Local authorities offer salaries between £17,200 and £21,500.

Ranger/warden

- Initial salaries are between £16,000 and £19,000 per year. With experience this rises to around £22,000. The most senior can earn £25,000+.

Further information

www.cityandguilds.com/myperfectjob

Lantra (Sector Skills Council for the environmental and land-based industries)
Lantra House
Stoneleigh Park
Kenilworth
Warwickshire
CV8 2LG
024 7669 6996
www.lantra.co.uk

English Nature
Northminster House
Peterborough
PE1 1UA
01733 455000
www.english-nature.org.uk

Wildlife Trusts
The Kiln, Waterside
Mather Road
Newark
Nottinghamshire
NG24 1WT
0870 036 7711
www.wildlifetrusts.org

National Trust
PO Box 39
Warrington
Cheshire
WA5 7WD
0870 458 4000
www.nationaltrust.org.uk

Countryside Agency
John Dower House
Crescent Place
Cheltenham
Gloucestershire
GL50 3RA
01242 521381
www.countryside.gov.uk

Land-force.com
www.land-force.com

CRCI:HC

CLCI:WAR

Dog Work

What the work involves

Dog groomer

- Working from home, in a grooming salon, pet shop or veterinary practice you will bath, groom, trim, clip nails and clean the teeth of your clients' dogs.
- You will work with the owners of all sorts of dogs from family pets to top pedigree show animals so, in addition to good dog grooming skills you will need communication skills too.

Kennel worker

- There are lots of types of kennels including: boarding, pet sanctuary, breeding and quarantine kennels for dogs brought from overseas.
- As well as cleaning the kennels, you will feed, exercise and keep a check on the dogs' health.

Trainer

- As a trainer of dogs, dog handlers or dog owners you could support security staff, the police force or animal charities like the Guide Dogs for the Blind. Your work will be divided between training the dogs and their human carers.

Warden

- Wardens normally work for local government authorities collecting stray or abandoned dogs and controlling dog fouling in parks and public areas.

The type of person suited to this work

To work in this area you will have to love dogs and want to work with them for hours at a time. However, many of these jobs also include working with people, so you will need excellent communication skills and be very enthusiastic.

Working with animals requires great patience and understanding. You will need to wait for results and be happy repeating tasks many times until the dog and owner/handler understands what is expected.

As you could be on your feet for a lot of the day you will have to be physically fit. If you suffer from allergies this work could be difficult for you.

Working conditions

Depending on the job you choose you could work indoors or outside, or a combination of the two. Animals don't have days off, so expect to work evenings, weekends and public holidays. All dogs have the potential to bite so you will have to be aware of the safety of all involved.

Dog groomer

You will be on your feet in hot and humid conditions. As you willl be using shampoo and other treatments, those with skin conditions will need to wear protection.

Kennel worker

This is physically demanding work involving walking dogs and cleaning the kennels using equipment and chemicals. You may work shifts.

Trainer

If you work for a large organisation you are likely to receive excellent terms and conditions, including hours of work and pension rights.

If you choose to work with domestic owners you will probably be self-employed and work from a community setting like a village hall or playing field during evenings or weekends.

Warden

You will travel around in a van collecting the stray or unwanted dogs in your patch. A driving licence is essential and you will have to work evenings and weekends.

Many dogs will be frightened and confused so they could be aggressive, so you will have to be aware of your own and others' safety.

The future outlook

Dog groomer

Demand for dog grooming has increased recently. There are now around 3000 grooming centres across the UK. However, there may not be sufficient work yet for full-time employment for all. This work can be seasonal as during the winter months many owners choose to keep their dogs' coats longer than in the summer.

Kennel worker

There are approximately 3500 kennels, but with recent changes in quarantine laws numbers employed within this job have reduced. However, you could work for national charitable organisations like the RSPCA, Guide Dogs for the Blind Association or a private dog breeder. The Army and Police recruit both service and civilian kennel staff.

Trainer

Most people working in this role have progressed from working in other dog-related work as a dog handler or pet behaviourist to specialise as a trainer. Before you can undertake this job you will need to have substantial experience of working with both dogs and people to do well.

Organisations such as the Guide Dogs for the Blind Association train their own trainers. There is normally a long waiting list to enter, with numbers working in the area still small. For example Guide Dogs for the Blind employs 500 trainers, but the Hearing Dogs for the Deaf employs 50.

Warden

Wardens are employed by most local government authorities to reduce the number of abandoned and stray dogs within their areas. Competition for this work can be high and mature applicants are welcomed. Previous experience of working with animals is recommended.

Qualifications and courses

entry level

To both enter and train while working in this career, you will need qualifications at Level 1–2. Please refer to explanation on page vii.

Dog groomer/kennel worker

- There are no formal educational requirements. NVQ/SVQ Levels 1–3 or BTEC National Qualifications in Animal Care may be useful. Many grooming parlours prefer to employ those with the City & Guilds Dog Grooming certificate. It is also possible to attend a fee-paying course at a private dog-grooming training centre.
- Applicants must be aged over 16. The Guide Dogs for the Blind Association accept work experience and volunteering requests at their local offices, for applicants aged over 18. They also require a full UK driving licence for all Puppy Walkers. Hearing Dogs for the Deaf also recruit volunteer puppy socialisers from people who have experience of looking after young dogs and have an approved home.
- Apprenticeship/Skillseekers available for those aged 16–24.
- Training covers health and safety, handling dogs, dog breeds, coat condition and care, canine diseases, First Aid and setting up and managing a salon. Experience with dogs is usually required.

Trainer

- For most jobs you will have to first join the organisation of your choice, and undertake general training before applying to specialise with dogs. After working as a handler you will then be able to apply for this senior post. Some organisations require 3 GCSEs/S grades (A–C/1–3) or equivalent, including English language. A full driving licence is often required. A training course usually needs to be passed.
- If you work as a domestic dog trainer you will need experience gained through working with dogs or specific canine or animal behaviourist qualifications.

Warden

- Applicants do not always require formal qualifications, although GCSE/S grades including English and maths are useful. Age, maturity and experience of working with dogs and people can be more important.
- Training courses are run by Lantra (the Sector Skills Council for the environment and land-based sector). They also have developed several Apprenticeship/Skillseekers schemes for those aged 16–24.

Other related opportunities

- Animal Protection / Charity p229
- Animal Work p231
- Dog Handler p500
- Veterinary Nurse p261
- Zookeeper p263

Advantages/disadvantages

- If you really are a dog enthusiast, this might be your idea of heaven.
- Your employer might be in a remote location so personal transport could be essential.
- Dog owners can be as difficult as their dogs.
- Some jobs can be part time or seasonal.

Earnings guide

Dog groomer

- Rates can vary from £2,000–£5,000 per year if part time, to up to £11,000–£14,000 if full time. With experience or if working on an employed basis within an organisation, £15,000–£25,000 is possible. Self-employed groomers earn around £20–£50 per hour.

Kennel worker

- Pay will depend on the nature of your employer however, most start at levels around the minimum wage. If you are working for a private kennels £12,000–£15,000 is likely. For animal charities and larger organisations you may get more.

Trainer

- Pay will depend on the nature and type of your employer. As an example the Guide Dogs for the Blind offers a starting salary of £14,123 rising to £15,500 after 6 months. With experience rates rise from £17,628 to £18,549. If you are self-employed your earnings will depend on your success.

Warden

- Salaries vary across the country but range between £16,000 and £21,000 per year. A vehicle is often provided.

CRCI:HC

CLCI:WAM

Further information

www.cityandguilds.com/myperfectjob

British Dog Groomers' Association/Pet Care Trust
Bedford Business Centre
170 Mile Road
Bedford
MK42 9TW
08700 624400
www.petcare.org.uk

British Institute of Professional Dog Trainers
The General Secretary
Bowstone Gate
Disley
Cheshire
SK12 2AW
www.bipdt.com

Guide Dogs for the Blind Association
Burghfield Common
Reading
Berkshire
RG7 3YG
0118 983 5555
www.guidedogs.org.uk

Police recruitment information
0845 608 3000
www.policecouldyou.co.uk

Equine / Horse Work

What the work involves

Groom/stablehand

- You would be responsible for the health and welfare of the horses in your care. You would groom, feed, muck out and tack up.
- You could be based within a riding school, competition or livery yard, racing stable, veterinary hospital or breeding stud. You may be able to ride and even compete, but this depends on the type of yard and your experience.

Jockey

- Starting as an apprentice groom and helping to groom, care for and exercise the horses, your main aim would be to become a jockey and race-ride.
- You will need to meet the weight restrictions as jockeys are small and light. You would then have to build up your number of winners so you can keep racing.

Racehorse trainer

- Trainers usually own or lease their stables and train horses for owners as well as owning horses themselves. Most trainers start as jockeys or assistant trainers and progress to running their own yard.
- Not only will you have to train the horses but you will have to manage a business, and attract and retain owners. To be successful you will work closely with all of those in your team including other professionals like vets and farriers.

Stud hand

- This is a specialised area of work and although the tasks are similar to those of a groom/stablehand you will be working with stallions, brood mares and young stock.
- You will use your understanding and knowledge of breeding lines to help owners breed a foal that meets their requirements.

The type of person suited to this work

If you choose to work with horses you will have to love being around and caring for them. As well as having lots of patience and the right temperament to be with the horses, you will need communication and team-working skills to work with your colleagues, owners and stable visitors.

Most of your work will be outdoors undertaking hard physical, dirty work. You will have to be happy to get your hands dirty by mucking out, grooming and cleaning tack.

The hours are long and the pay can be low!

As a trainer or yard manager, you will need to manage staff, maintain budgets, market your services and have business skills.

Working conditions

You will spend most of your work outdoors lifting heavy bags of feed, hay and bedding. Some of your work will include carrying tack, cleaning up the yard or riding. In the summer the work can be hot, dusty and smelly. In the winter it is cold, wet and muddy. You will need to wear protective clothing and, as this work can be dangerous, be aware of your own and others' safety.

Horses can kick and bite, and you can fall off! You can expect to work 24/7 especially if you live-in. You will probably be required to work shifts covering weekends and public holidays.

The future outlook

Riding and taking care of horses is a very popular activity with different types of stables across the country. There are an estimated 250,000 people working in all the related areas such as saddlery and farrier work. Regarding horse-care work there are approximately 6000 businesses employing over 54,000 people, 75% of whom are female. This totals 5.7% of all animal-based work in the UK.

Groom/stablehand

All stables need the help of grooms and although they have traditionally been at the bottom of the career ladder, there is now a growing awareness amongst owners and yard managers of the vital role they play.

With experience it is possible to specialise in one of the different equestrian activities. Competition grooms (show-jumping, dressage and eventing) are especially in demand. Gaining your HGV driving licence can open up increased opportunities. Most grooms progress to more successful yards that compete internationally or keep more expensive and quality horses.

Jockey

Horseracing is the second largest spectator sport in the UK and employs over 100,000 people – very few of whom actually become jockeys. If you are good enough to be offered an apprenticeship and become first an amateur and then a professional jockey, you are likely to retire by the age of 45. Competition for rides is fierce and the lifestyle demanding. You will have to stay fit and injury free.

Racehorse trainer

There are around 500 licensed trainers in the UK. Before you are granted a licence the Jockey Club expects several years' experience as an assistant trainer. Your success will then depend on attracting and retaining the owners of good quality horses, and lots of luck!

Stud hand

Currently, interest in breeding quality British horses and ponies has increased due to European competition. Stud work is therefore rising in importance and those with the best skills are in demand.

Qualifications and courses

- As well as the qualifications detailed below some people choose to enter as a working pupil; this option is especially popular within competition yards. Vacancies for working pupils are advertised within the national horse press.

Groom/stablehand

- Applicants must be 16 years old. Some employers ask for GCSE/S grades, especially in maths and English. Some employers may include weight restrictions.
- Full-time courses include BTEC National Diploma in Horse Care or Equine Studies and NVQ in Equine Studies.
- Nationally recognised qualifications may be required, such as NVQ/SVQ Levels 1–3 in Horse Care and Horse Care Management, the British Horse Society (BHS) stage 1–4 exams or the Association of British Riding Schools (ABRS) certificates and diplomas.
- Apprenticeships/Skillseekers may be available for those aged 16–24. Apprentice grooms can gain NVQ/SVQ Level 2 Horse Care, apprentice riding instructors can aim for NVQ/SVQ Level 3 Horse Care and Management.
- A driving licence is useful.

Jockey

- No formal qualifications are required. Applicants should be about 51kg (8st) for flat racing and 60kg (9st 7lbs) for jump racing, and under 25 years old. You will also need to be small and extremely fit.
- The British Racing School offers a free 9-week Foundation Apprenticeship which includes food and accommodation in Newmarket; students then move to a training yard and are assessed periodically for the remaining 25% of their course. The Apprenticeship takes around 1 year to complete.
- Candidates must pass a medical examination.

Racehorse trainer

- Racehorse trainers need to be licensed with the Jockey Club. There are three types of licence: a Combined Jump and Flat Licence, a Jump Only Licence and a Flat Only Licence.
- All candidates for a trainer's licence must attend three 1 week modules held at the British Racing School: Racehorse Management (achievement of NVQ Level 3 in Racehorse Care and Management prior to attendance on this module is compulsory); Business Skills for Racehorse Trainers; and Staff Management. In exceptional circumstances, the Jockey Club Licensing Committee may award exemptions from modules 2 and/or 3 to those who can prove substantial experience and/or qualifications in those areas.

entry level

To both enter and train while working in this career, you will need qualifications at Level 1–2. Please refer to explanation on page vii.

- Trainers must have spent at least 2 years in an assistant trainer position.
- To start as an assistant trainer, previous experience in a racing yard or as a jockey is desirable. Assistant trainers should also work towards NVQ Level 3 Racehorse Care and Management.

Stud hand

- There are no formal entry requirements for this job. Some knowledge of stable work and horse care is expected.
- Candidates under the age of 19 may enter as a trainee stud hand and work towards an NVQ Level 2. Training is free and starts with a residential course at a Centre, then continues in the workplace (either a racing yard or stud).

Other related opportunities

- Animal Work p231
- Dog Work p237
- Farrier p243
- Horse Riding p366

Advantages/disadvantages

- You really need to be a horse lover. If you are you will put up with the disadvantages!
- Pay can be low and stables can be in remote locations.
- Injury risks are high in all horse activities. This could affect your long-term career security.
- Looking after horses is not a 9 to 5 job.

Earnings guide

Groom/stablehand/stud hand

- The horse industry has a reputation for low salaries and long hours. As a starting salary you can expect to be on the minimum wage up to around £10,500 per year.
- This can rise to £15,000–£16,000 for the most experienced. As head groom you can expect £20,000+. If you live-in, free or supplemented board and lodging is common.

Jockey

- A trainee jockey starts at around £10,500 per year. With experience this can rise to £20,000+. The most successful earn £50,000–£60,000.

Racehorse trainer

- As you are likely to be self-employed your earnings will depend on the size and success of your yard.
- As a guide, a trainer can earn anything from £15,000 per year to £50,000 if very experienced and with a good record of winning.

Further information

Association of British Riding Schools
Queen's Chambers
38–40 Queen Street
Penzance
Cornwall
TR18 4BH
01736 369440
www.abrs-info.org

British Horse Society
Stoneleigh Deer Park
Kenilworth
Warwickshire
CV8 2XZ
08701 202244
www.bhs.org.uk

British Racing School
Snailwell Road
Newmarket
Suffolk
CB8 7NU
01638 665103
www.brs.org.uk

Farm Work

What the work involves

Farm manager

- As a manager you will be responsible for the overall running of a farm. This includes making the decisions about which crops to grow or livestock to raise.
- You will supervise the work of your staff, keep up to date with farming developments and oversee the economic side of the business.
- You will have to communicate with goverment officials, farming suppliers and feed merchants and your customers who could be major supermarkets or small local shops.

Farmhand

- You will undertake the practical duties on a farm.
- This will include the feeding and care of livestock, driving and maintaining machinery, planting crops, fencing and operating tools and equipment.

Shepherd/shepherdess

- Working mainly in remote locations across the UK, you will care for a flock of sheep.
- You will be responsible for the health and safety of the animals, feed them, administer injections, clean their fleeces and make sure they remain disease free.

Stockman/stockwoman

- This work involves caring for dairy herds, beef cattle, pigs and/or poultry.
- You will be responsible for the feeding and healthcare of your animals to make sure they remain fit and healthy.
- Your duties will depend on the animals in your care but could include milking dairy herds, preparation for slaughter and general maintenance.

The type of person suited to this work

You must enjoy being outdoors in the countryside, working in all weathers. As you will be caring for animals or getting things to grow you should have an interest in the environment. If you are allergic to pollen or animals this work will be very difficult for you.

You will have to be fit and active, able to be on your feet all day and prepared to work very long hours, especially during the summer months. If your animals become ill, you will have to be prepared to be with them and administer drugs when needed.

As a manager you will have to be able to recruit, develop and retain your staff, as well as run the business of the farm.

Working conditions

All these jobs involve a lot of time outdoors, so you will be out in the wind and the rain, summer and winter. Farming is not a 9–5 job and is very physical work. It can also be dangerous, as a lot of the equipment is hazardous.

Managers will spend a lot of their time doing accounts and making sure the farm is operating profitably, but will need to muck in with general farm work during busy periods, like harvest.

The future outlook

The overall number of people employed across UK farms has dropped during the last decade to just under 300,000. This fall is due to international competition and falling prices. There are more staff employed within livestock agricultural than crop agriculture. Across the UK the types of farming changes due to differences in the environment so your opportunities would depend on your location.

Farm manager

Competition for jobs is intense and career progression is likely to involve moving from one part of the country to another. With substantial experience and qualifications it is possible to progress into other related areas of agriculture such as plant breeding, crop protection, plant trials or genetics. These opportunities are available within private companies or academic/research organisations. Training or research opportunities are also possible.

Farmhand/stockman/stockwoman

The kinds of farming opportunities available will vary depending on the part of the country where you live. The eastern side of the UK has mainly arable farming, whilst the west concentrates on livestock. Experienced workers with training can become managers without having to buy their own farms but opportunities are scarce and promotion unlikely unless you work on a very large farm.

Shepherd/shepherdess

Fewer shepherds are now being employed and those who do find employment can expect to do general farm work duties as well. Pure shepherding jobs are generally within the most remote areas of the country and on the larger estates.

Qualifications and courses

Farm manager

- There are no formal entry requirements but most who enter this area do so with an HND, degree or other higher level qualification. Courses are available in agriculture, agricultural science, land and property management, and agricultural engineering. A levels/H grades or their equivalent, often including a science subject will be required. Postgraduate courses are also available.
- It is possible to enter with an NVQ/SVQ in Agriculture Crop Production or Livestock Production Level 3, Agriculture (Livestock Management) Level 4 or Agricultural and Commercial Horticulture (Crop Management) Level 4. Candidates should also have previous experience of farm work, and most degree-level courses include sandwich placements for this purpose.
- In order to maintain skills and knowledge, ongoing study is expected. Courses are provided within the land-based colleges of further education or by Lantra across the UK.
- A driving licence is essential.
- Apprenticeships/Skillseekers may be available for those aged 16–24.

Farmhand/stockman/stockwoman

- Formal qualifications are not normally needed but relevant work experience is useful. BTEC and City & Guilds National Qualifications are available in Agriculture, Mixed Farming and Crop Production.
- You would normally train on the job. NVQ/SVQ Levels 1–4 in Agriculture, Agriculture Crop Production, Mixed Farming and Livestock Production are available.
- A driving licence is normally required. CITB or NPTC accredited tractor driving, chainsaw use and pesticide use courses are also recommended.
- Apprenticeships/Skillseekers may be available for those aged 16–24.

Shepherd/shepherdess

- Formal qualifications are not normally needed, but an interest or work experience in animal-based work is useful.
- There are short courses available covering specialist areas like shearing and lambing at land-based colleges and further education centres across the UK.

entry level

To both enter and train while working in this career, you will need qualifications at Level 1–8. Please refer to explanation on page vii.

Other related opportunities

- Animal Work p231
- Countryside Work p235
- Fish Farmer p244
- Forestry p246
- Horticultural / Garden Centre p253
- Poultry Worker p258

Advantages/disadvantages

- You will spend a lot of time in the open air caring for living and growing things.
- At some times of the year your social life may be restricted.
- You could be alone for long periods of the day.
- Your future can depend on things outside of your control such as bird flu or foot and mouth disease.
- You might have to stay up through the night to care for animals that are ill or giving birth.

Earnings guide

- All earnings will depend on the size and success of the farm and its location.

Farm manager

- Average salaries are around £20,800. The most successful can be between £25,000 and £40,000.

Farmhand/stockman/shepherd

- Many starting salaries are at the minimum wage levels. With experience this can increase from £11,000 to £14,000. The most experienced staff achieve £20,000.
- Some jobs include accommodation with subsidised rent. At busy times you may get overtime payments which can make a significant addition to pay.

Further information

www.cityandguilds.com/myperfectjob

Lantra (Sector Skills Council for the environmental and land-based industries)
Lantra House
Stoneleigh Park
Kenilworth
Warwickshire
CV8 2LG
024 7669 6996
www.lantra.co.uk

Farming and Countryside Education
The National Agricultural Centre
Stoneleigh Park
Warwickshire
CV8 2LZ
024 7685 8261
www.face-online.org.uk

Department for Environment, Food and Rural Affairs (DEFRA)
Nobel House
17 Smith Square
London
SW1P 3JR
020 7238 6000
www.defra.gov.uk

Land-force.com
www.land-force.com

Farrier

What the work involves

- Farriers shoe, trim and care for the feet of horses.
- You could work from a blacksmith's forge or a mobile workshop and go to the horses in a converted vehicle.
- As well as the skills of removing and fitting new shoes, you will have to keep up to date with new practices and know about horse anatomy, illnesses and how the two are linked.
- You would often work in partnership with vets to treat leg and joint problems.

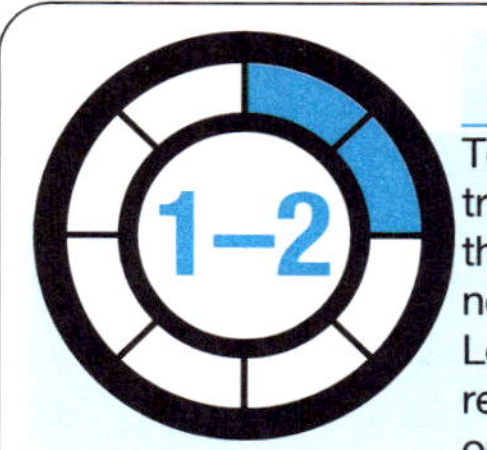

entry level

To both enter and train while working in this career, you will need qualifications at Level 1–2. Please refer to explanation on page vii.

Qualifications and courses

- Younger trainee farriers are required to take a 4-year Advanced Apprenticeship with an FRC Approved Training Farrier (ATF). They must be at least 16 years old, have 4 GCSEs/S grades (A–C/1–3), including English language, and hold a Forging Certificate. Candidates should contact the Farrier Training Agency (FTA) for information regarding the FRC Approved Training Farrier list and colleges running approved block-release courses.
- Applicants will need 4 GCSEs/S grades (A–C/1–3) or equivalent including English language, NVQ Level 2, Key Skills Level 2 in communication and application of number, or to pass an entrance exam.
- They will then complete an apprenticeship while working for the approved training farrier; this takes 4 years and 2 months. An NVQ/SVQ is available at Level 3 and the course combines on-the-job training with periods at a college.
- By law farriers must be registered with the Farriers' Registration Council and have passed the diploma of the Worshipful Company of Farriers (DipWCF) in order to practise.
- A driving licence is required.

The type of person suited to this work

You should enjoy being around horses and have the right temperament to handle them. As you are providing a service you will need to get on with your customers and deliver high-quality care to them and their horses.

You will have to enjoy being outdoors working in all weathers, often in a muddy environment. This work is both practical and physical, so you will need to be strong and able to do manual work using lots of hand tools.

Working conditions

Your days will involve driving to each customer, working with the horses and returning to your forge to prepare shoes and collect materials. In the summer months your hours will be long, especially when more people are riding their horses. This can be hot, tiring work, especially if fitting shoes to a difficult horse.

The future outlook

Riding is a very popular activity and there are stables all round the country. There are about 2900 farriers who are mostly self-employed. There are always more young people interested in entering the profession than vacancies, resulting in high competition for each apprenticeship. On average 80–100 apprentices are recruited annually.

Some farriers supplement their earnings by undertaking blacksmithing whilst they build up their farriery client list.

Other related opportunities

- Blacksmith p194
- Engineer: Craft p203
- Equine / Horse Work p239
- Horse Riding p366

Advantages/disadvantages

- You should enjoy being around horses.
- It's a satisfying skill to have; using your hands.
- The work is physically demanding and can result in back injuries.
- This is a great job if you want to work with horses without riding.

Earnings guide

- The Farriers Registration Council sets minimum wages. When starting you can expect a salary of around £8,500 per year.
- Once qualified, earnings range from £10,000 to £20,000, depending on success and the number of customers.
- Some experienced and popular farriers can earn over £40,000.

Further information

Farriery Training Agency
Sefton House
Adam Court
Newark Road
Peterborough
PE1 5PP
01733 319911
www.farrier-reg.gov.uk

National Association of Farriers, Blacksmiths and Agricultural Engineers
The Forge, Avenue B
10th Street
Stoneleigh Park
Warwickshire
CV8 2LG
024 7669 6595
www.nafbae.org

Worshipful Company of Farriers
19 Queen Street
Chipperfield
Kings Langley
Hertfordshire
WD4 9BT
01923 260747
www.wcf.org.uk

Fish Farmer

What the work involves

- As a fish farmer you will raise fish from small (juvenile) fry until they reach saleable size. The most common fish to raise are salmon and trout.
- You will feed, check for disease and protect them from predators. You will finally net the catch and pack them for market.
- Some farms specialise in producing the breeding stock: the fingerlings (the tiny fish that other farmers bring to saleable size).
- Some shellfish farms in coastal locations also produce oysters, scallops and mussels.

entry level

To both enter and train while working in this career, you will need qualifications at Level 1–8. Please refer to explanation on page vii.

Qualifications and courses

- Applicants do not necessarily require formal educational qualifications, but fish-related qualifications and previous related work experience are useful.
- A BTEC First Diploma in Fish Husbandry is available to those with 4 GCSE/S grades (A–C/1–3); students can then progress to the National Diploma in Fish Management or the Scottish group Award in Fishery Studies.
- BTEC and SQA Higher National qualifications can be taken in Fish Farm Management, Aquaculture or Fishery Studies.
- Training can be done on the job with attendance at short courses. Entrants may work towards NVQs/SVQs at Levels 2 and 3 in Fish Husbandry, or may study by distance learning for the Institute of Fisheries Management Diploma.
- Degrees in aquaculture/fisheries studies, biology, marine and freshwater biology are available.
- In Scotland, entry is available through Skillseekers.

The type of person suited to this work

You will need to be a practical type with the ability to learn a lot about fish and be happy to get wet and dirty. Much of this work is scientific in approach, so you should have good observational skills, to be able to identify anything that might affect the quality and success of the fish in your care.

You will need to be patient, hard working and persevere if things are tough. This work is difficult and long-term security is not guaranteed.

If you become a manager, in addition to your practical ability, you will also have to have good business and administrative skills.

Working conditions

Working with fish is the same as any animal-based work, which means they need care and attention 24/7. You are likely to work on a rota basis with 2 days off every week and work very long hours including early mornings, late evenings and weekends.

You will be outdoors in damp, cold conditions having to cope with all types of weather. Some of the work will be unpleasant and will involve the sight of blood.

The future outlook

With the problems related with sea fish stocks, fish farming is becoming quite important as a source of fish. There are plans to farm other kinds of fish such as turbot and cod.

Like other farming enterprises, fish farms are vulnerable to price fluctuations, so predicting the future is risky. Around 7500 people are employed in the industry, most of whom are based in Scotland. Of these, half are managers mainly with a scientific background.

There are 300 trout farms located in Scotland, southern and central England and north Yorkshire.

Other related opportunities

- Beekeeper p234
- Biologist p468
- Countryside Work p235
- Farm Work p241
- Fisherman / Woman p245
- Gamekeeper p248

Advantages/disadvantages

- You will spend a lot of time in the open air.
- You may spend a lot of time working on your own.
- There are only limited areas where the work is available.
- This work can affect your social life.
- Fish farming is a risky business as fish can be very affected by disease.

Earnings guide

Fish farm worker

- Starting out you can expect to earn around £9,500 per year. Average earnings for those with experience are between £12,000 and £17,000.

Manager

- Experienced managers can expect up to £30,000.

Further information

Institute of Fisheries Management
22 Rushworth Avenue
West Bridgford
Nottingham
NG2 7LF
0115 982 2317
www.ifm.org.uk

Sparsholt College Hampshire
Sparsholt
Winchester
Hampshire
SO21 2NF
01962 776441
www.sparsholt.ac.uk

British Trout Association
The Rural Centre
West Mains
Ingliston
EH28 8NZ
0131 472 4080
www.britishtrout.co.uk

Fisherman / Woman

What the work involves

- You will spend anything from a few days to several weeks at sea.
- During your work you will drop the nets, wind them in, sort the catch and then box it up.
- If your vessel has the facility you might help to process fish on board by gutting and filleting.
- You might keep watch, steer the ship and use winching gear.

entry level

To both enter and train while working in this career, you will need qualifications at Level 1. Please refer to explanation on page vii.

The type of person suited to this work

This work is very practical, physically demanding and can involve being away from home for periods of time. You will have to be hardworking, able to use your initiative and enjoy working within a very close team of people.

As you will be at sea in dangerous and treacherous conditions, experiencing all types of weather, you should be able to cope with whatever you come up against but remain positive and focused.

You will need a good sense of humour and excellent team working skills. You should be willing to muck in and help your colleagues as you will spend a lot of time in their company.

Working conditions

This is a very tough outdoor job. You will be out in the wind and the rain, summer and winter getting wet and cold. Fishing is the most dangerous industry in the UK, with of big machinery and rough seas producing a combination of risks which must be treated with great caution. You will have to work long hours at sea, often for substantial periods away from home.

The future outlook

With all the problems with fish stocks, the UK fishing industry is in decline. Boats are being taken out of service and fish quotas for many species are being cut. However, there are still around 20,000 part- and full-time employees working on approximately 7000 vessels. Most managers are self-employed.

Jobs are located around the coasts of Scotland, the south-west and eastern England. Many are part of family-owned businesses which have been in existence for generations, making it difficult to find work. Some are seasonal meaning long-term security can be difficult.

Qualifications and courses

- New entrants must take the Marine Coastguard Agency approved basic Safety Training course. They must have good eyesight and be physically fit. New entrants usually start as deckhands.
- Most people enter through one of 18 Catching Sector Group Training Associations (GTAs) in the UK. These run free or EU-funded short practical courses. The Seafish Industry Training Division also provides new entrant training programmes.
- Apprenticeships/Skillseekers opportunities might be available for those aged 16–24.
- Skippers have to take the Marine Coastguard Agency certificates which cover different levels of competence, before they can take charge of a fishing vessel.
- With experience it is possible to progress to NVQ/SVQ Level 4 in Marine Engineering Operations or Marine Vessel Operations.
- Open Learning Modules are available allowing fishermen, from deckhands to skippers, to develop their skills and knowledge on board rather than in the classroom.

CRCI:HA

CLCI:WAF

Other related opportunities

- Fish Farmer p244
- Merchant Navy p571
- Oil and Gas Drilling Industry p219
- Royal Navy p516

Advantages/disadvantages

- You will spend a lot of time onboard your boat at sea working as part of small team.
- Due to periods at sea, your social and family life may be difficult.
- Jobs are limited to certain locations in the UK.
- Pay can be variable.

Earnings guide

- Earnings from fishing can be very variable, as pay often includes a share of the profit. Good weather and good catches mean good money. Winter storms spent sheltering in harbour results in no income. The following should be used as a guide:
- New entrants can expect to receive £11,000 per year as a starting salary.
- With experience this rises to around £30,000.
- Skippers are generally self-employed so their earnings will depend on the success of their team and good weather. Some very experienced skippers earn as much as £65,000.

Further information

Sea Fish Industry Authority
Training department
St Andrew's Dock
Hull
HU3 4QE
01482 327837
www.seafish.org

Scottish Fishermen's Federation
24 Rubislaw Terrace
Aberdeen
AB10 1XE
01224 646944
www.sff.co.uk

Forestry

What the work involves

Forestry officer/manager

- Forestry officers or managers care for forests across the UK that are used for timber production and increasingly, recreational activities.
- You would plan and manage the annual programme of your forest. This would include organising the clearing of areas, planting and felling trees, and overseeing the general maintenance.

Forestry worker

- You would do all of the practical jobs in your forests, woodland and amenity areas. This would include planting trees, felling trees, managing weeds and undergrowth, maintaining fencing and carrying out tree surgery.
- In addition, you would use hand and power tools, drive vehicles and repair any broken fences or pathways.

The type of person suited to this work

Forestry officer

You will have to be an excellent organiser and administrator as you will be planning jobs months in advance. You will need both technical skills and theoretical knowledge of forests and wildlife. You will require management, communication and teamworking skills so that the business is successful.

Forestry worker

This can be dangerous work as you will be using heavy machinery and hand tools. It is important that you can follow instructions, enjoy being outdoors and want to work with nature. Trees take a long time to grow, so you will need to combine lots of patience with your physical, practical skills.

Working conditions

You will probably work a standard Monday–Friday week with overtime and weekend work during the busier summer months. You will have to be aware of health and safety legislation as this can be dangerous work, using potentially hazardous tools. Although you are likely to be working in cold, damp conditions, protective clothing will be provided.

Forestry officer

Much of your time will be spent outdoors but you will also work indoors planning and creating jobs for your staff to follow. You are likely to do a lot of travelling, whilst you check the different areas under your responsibility.

The future outlook

This is a competitive area of work and voluntary or relevant work experience will be useful before attending a course or applying for employment. Forestry is one of the smallest areas of environmental work, employing only around 3000 people across the UK.

The range of employers open to you includes the Forestry Commission, private landowners and estates, local authorities and large companies. Career progression is likely to involve moving, as promotion is rare within all but the largest employers.

There tend to be more applicants than vacancies, although this trend is beginning to show slight improvement due to the growing awareness of the importance of leisure time and being out in the country. Many contracts are short term so you need to have a flexible approach to employment opportunities.

With significant experience, self-employment as a consultant or trainer is possible.

CRCI:HB

CLCI:WAF

Qualifications and courses

entry level

To both enter and train while working in this career, you will need qualifications at Level 1–8. Please refer to explanation on page vii.

Forestry worker

- There are no formal entry requirements but at least 2 GCSE/S grades (A–C/1–3) or a forestry qualification would be an advantage. Experience is often more important, and organisations such as the Woodland Trust, The National Trust, and the British Trust for Conservation Volunteers (BTCV) all accept volunteer applications.
- NVQs/SVQs are available in Forestry (Establishment and Harvesting) Level 2 and Treework (Forestry Establishment or Forestry Harvesting) Level 3. The National Proficiency Tests Council offer the Chainsaw Competency Certificate and Large Tree Felling Certificate.
- BTEC/SQA offer a National Diploma in Forestry and Arboriculture and Countryside Management (Woodland Management). BTEC First Certificates are available in Countryside and Environment, Introduction to Woodlands and Forestry, Countryside and Forestry, and Forestry Mechanisation.
- Once in employment, forest workers will gain skills to use forest tools and machinery safely. The National Proficiency Tests Council (NPTC), the Scottish Skills Testing Service (SSTS) and Lantra award competence certificates in skills such as operating chainsaws and carrying out chemical spraying.
- Apprenticeships/Skillseekers opportunities may be available to those aged 16–24.
- The Forestry Commission offers 2-year apprenticeships that include NVQ Level 3 Trees and Timber. Applicants require at least 2 GCSE's (A–C, 1–3 passes) including maths and English and have a good working knowledge of computers. A proven interest in a forestry career is also required.

Forestry officer

- Entry is with a Foundation degree, HND, degree or postgraduate qualification in forestry. For entry to a degree, 2 A levels/3 H grades, normally including maths or a science, and 3 GCSEs/S grades (A–C/1–3) are required. At least 1 A level/H grade or equivalent is required for entry to an HND or Foundation degree. Relevant work experience is essential. This can be achieved through voluntary work with the National Trust or Forestry Commission.
- The Institute of Chartered Foresters has several levels of membership for those who are studying, working in or supportive of the industry. Each individual application must be supported and endorsed by two Chartered Foresters who are personally acquainted with the applicant and their work. Students will be full time at college or university and undertaking courses approved by the Institute, in a relevant subject.

Other related opportunities

- Arboricultural Worker / Manager p233
- Countryside Work p235
- Gamekeeper p248
- Gardener / Garden Designer p249
- Tree Surgeon p260

Advantages/disadvantages

- If you want to make a difference in the countryside this could be the job for you.
- As in all jobs with plants, you are often at the mercy of the weather.
- Some jobs are in remote areas.
- It can take a long time to see the results of your work.

Earnings guide

Forestry officer

- Forestry Commission salaries for officers start at £19,800 per year, with experience it can rise to £30,000.

Forestry worker

- You are likely to earn around £12,200 per year when starting out.
- This rises to around £17,000 with experience. Some employers also provide subsidised accommodation.

Further information

Forestry Commission
Silvan House
231 Corstorphine Road
Edinburgh
EH12 7AT
0845 367 3787
www.forestry.gov.uk

Royal Forestry Society
102 High Street
Tring
Hertfordshire
HP23 4AF
01442 822028
www.rfs.org.uk

Institute of Chartered Foresters
7a St Colme Street
Edinburgh
EH3 6AA
0131 225 2705
www.charteredforesters.org

Land-force.com
www.land-force.com

www.cityandguilds.com/myperfectjob

CRCI:HB

Gamekeeper

What the work involves

- As a gamekeeper you would work on a large country estate, where shooting for sport is part of the estate business.
- You will be responsible for providing birds and other animals such as deer or hares for the clients to shoot, or possibly fish to catch.
- This is usually achieved by raising pheasants and other game birds and releasing them into the wild once they are mature enough.
- You will control predators by shooting and trapping (rats, foxes and crows are some of the birds' principal enemies).
- You will be responsible for booking additional help such as beaters.

The type of person suited to this work

You must have an unsentimental approach to wildlife as this job involves the killing of animals for sport. To enable the clients to get the most from their day of sport you will have to be a good communicator and able to offer advice about using their guns and how to be successful.

You will have to be physically fit with lots of stamina and happy to work on your own for long periods of time. You should enjoy being outdoors but as some of your work will also involve preparing the guns, you will spend some time indoors too. This is a varied job with lots of responsibility – your success will be measured by the enjoyment of the clients.

Working conditions

You will be outdoors in all weathers all through the year. Your hours will be flexible and will involve weekend working and late/early starts. You will spend long periods of time on your own, doing lots of walking checking the estate and the progress of the game.

As you will be handling and using guns, traps and poisons, you will have to be confident using them and very aware of your own safety and that of others.

This work will be difficult for those who suffer from allergies to animals, pollen or dust.

The future outlook

Most of this work is within remote parts of the country or on large country estates. This work is in decline as trends have changed resulting in many gamekeepers being expected to combine this work with other estate jobs, such as maintenance and general forestry/conservation duties.

If you are able to find work there is a formal promotion path in place which most have followed, from trainee gamekeeper to underkeeper, up to beatkeeper and then finally head keeper.

entry level

To both enter and train while working in this career, you will need qualifications at Level 1–2. Please refer to explanation on page vii.

Qualifications and courses

- No formal qualifications are needed for this role. However, 2/3 GCSEs/S grades (A–E/1–5) may be an advantage. Voluntary or relevant work experience is very useful.
- Training is generally on the job, but there are some courses available to applicants who wish to progress.
- City & Guilds offer the National and Advanced National Certificate in Environmental Conservation (Countryside Management); National Certificate in Gamekeeping Level 2 and the Certificate in Land-based Studies Level 1.
- NVQs/SVQs are available in Gamekeeping and Wildlife Management at Levels 2 and 3.
- A BTEC National Award is available in Gamekeeping.
- An HNC is available in Gamekeeping and Wildlife Management. Candidates would need practical experience and/or the National Award in Gamekeeping.
- Foundation degrees are available in Countryside and Environment (Gamekeeping) at several colleges. These generally require a National Diploma or 2 or more A levels for entry.
- Apprenticeships/Skillseekers may be available for those aged 16–24.

CRCI:HC | CLCI:WAM

Other related opportunities

- Countryside Work p235
- Farrier p243
- Forestry p246

Advantages/disadvantages

- This job combines outdoor physical work with lots of practical skills.
- You will be on your own a lot.
- You might be provided with a house.
- The industry is in decline and jobs are difficult to find.

Earnings guide

- Starting salaries for new entrants are around £10,000 per year.
- Single-hand gamekeepers earn between £13,000 and £18,500.
- Head gamekeepers can expect up to £21,500.

Further information

British Association for Shooting & Conservation
Marford Mill
Rossett
Wrexham
Clwyd
LL12 0HL
01244 573 000
www.basc.org.uk

Lantra (Sector Skills Council for the environmental and land-based industries)
Lantra House
Stoneleigh Park
Kenilworth
Warwickshire
CV8 2LG
024 7669 6996
www.lantra.co.uk

Game Conservancy Trust
Fordingbridge
Hampshire
SP6 1EF
01425 652381
www.gct.org.uk

National Gamekeepers Trust
PO Box 3360
Stourbridge
DY7 5YG
www.gamekeeperstrust.org.uk

Gardener / Garden Designer

What the work involves

Gardener

- Gardeners work in a wide range of settings from large gardens such as those in stately homes and National Trust properties to small urban parks and private gardens.
- As a skilled gardener you will be able to tell a cultivated plant from a weed, and will know how to grow it, how to prune it and when it flowers.
- At first you would do the routine jobs before moving on to the more skilled jobs such as propagating plants and running a greenhouse.

Garden designer/landscaper

- You would advise clients on how to improve the look and planting of their garden, such as paths, flower beds, water features, etc and the planting scheme – the best plants to grow and where to put them.
- You would present your ideas as a series of plans and drawings and you would probably supervise a landscape contractor to turn your design into reality.

The type of person suited to this work

You will need to be physically fit and confident in using hand tools. Depending on your employer, you will probably spend periods driving to different locations, so a driving licence would be useful.

Gardener
You will need to have practical skills with an interest in plants and different landscaping materials. You will need to have a lot of patience when talking to your customers and while you wait for your gardens to look their best. You will have to love being outdoors and working with plants, with a strong eye for colour.

Garden designer
You will need to be a creative person who can picture how a piece of bare or neglected ground can be transformed into something beautiful. Drawing and ICT skills will be useful as is extensive knowledge of plants and the environments they need to grow well.

Working conditions

Gardener

Gardeners will mostly be working outdoors but if you are lucky there will be a greenhouse to retreat into in the worst of the winter. There will be quite a lot of physical work lifting large pots and bags of peat and digging and clearing beds. You will often have to get out in the wind and the rain, particularly in the winter, when much of the preparation for the main gardening season is done.

Garden designer/landscaper

You will spend as much time in your studio designing and researching your design as you spend working outdoors overseeing the practical tasks.

The future outlook

Gardener

Due to the current boom in people wanting to improve their homes and gardens there are plenty of opportunities available at the moment. There are around 90,000 gardeners working in all types of gardens. Many are self-employeed offering services to both the public and private sectors. With experience, you could move on to supervisor or manager jobs, especially if you get some further qualifications.

Garden designer/landscaper

Half of all designers work in private practice, which can be small businesses providing services to the public and private sectors. Some specialise in certain types of design such as planting, landscaping, etc. Some designers choose to be self-employed offering services to private home owners who may contract in other professionals as needed. Success for both types will be based on reputation and the types of contracts won.

Qualifications and courses

entry level

To both enter and train while working in this career, you will need qualifications at Level 1–8. Please refer to explanation on page vii.

Gardener

- There are no set requirements for entry to this career. GCSEs/S grades (A–C/1–3) would be useful. Courses are available to those who wish to progress.
- A BTEC First Certificate, National Certificate, National Diploma and Higher National Certificate and Diploma are all available in Horticulture.
- Apprenticeships may be available to those aged between 16 and 24.
- NVQs/SVQs are available in Horticulture Level 1, Commercial and Amenity Horticulture Levels 1–4 and Agriculture and Commercial Horticulture Level 4.
- City & Guilds offer the Certificate/Practical Certificate in Gardening Levels 1 and 2, Horticulture Skills Test, National and Advanced National Certificate in Horticulture Levels 2 and 3 and the Certificate in Land-based Studies Level 1.
- The Royal Horticultural Society (RHS) have a general examination, which allows entry onto the Advanced National Certificate in Horticulture.
- Self-employed gardeners usually require a driving licence.

Garden designer

- Although there are no formal requirements for this job, a design-orientated qualification is an advantage. Professional qualifications are often obtained.
- Many garden design courses are offered via distance learning from colleges such as the Regent Academy and the KLC School of Design, but lots of other land-based and some art colleges offer options too.
- City & Guilds offer the Certificate/Practical Certificate in Gardening at Levels 1 and 2, which encompasses modules in garden design.
- It is possible to study for NVQs/SVQs at Levels 2–3 in Constructing and Restoring Landscapes, Level 3 in Designing and Specifying Land Designs, and Level 4 in Designing Landscapes and Planning their Management.
- Degrees in garden design and related subjects are available at some universities and colleges. The Society of Garden Designers offers registered membership to those who can demonstrate knowledge in relevant areas and with two years' practical experience.
- A driving licence is usually required.

Other related opportunities

- Arboricultural Worker / Manager p233
- Biologist p468
- Designer p136
- Groundsperson / Greenkeeper p251
- Horticultural / Garden Centre p253
- Parks Officer p257

Advantages/disadvantages

- Designers can mix creative, practical and outdoor work.
- Your work will depend on the weather.
- You may work in beautiful places (or create them if you are a designer).
- If you like plants and people this could be the job for you.
- Some contracts can be seasonal.

Earnings guide

Gardener

- Gardeners start at around £10,000–£12,000 per year.
- With experience this can rise to £18,500+. A growing number of gardeners are choosing to become self-employed. Earnings will depend on their success.

Garden designer/landscaper

- Your salary would depend on the type and size of the business you work for. As a guide, trainee rates start at between £10,000 and £20,000 per year.
- Designers' pay will depend entirely on how well they can market themselves and generate work; many are self-employed and charge around £30–£60 per hour.

Further information

www.cityandguilds.com/myperfectjob

Institute of Horticulture
14–15 Belgrave Square
London
SW1X 8PS
020 7245 6943
www.horticulture.org.uk

Lantra (Sector Skills Council for the environmental and land-based industries)
Lantra House
Stoneleigh Park
Kenilworth
Warwickshire
CV8 2LG
024 7669 6996
www.lantra.co.uk

Royal Horticultural Society – Education Department
Wisley
Woking
Surrey
GU23 6QB
www.rhs.org.uk

Groundsperson / Greenkeeper

What the work involves

Groundsperson

- Your main role will be to prepare and maintain the grounds used for different sports. Although you might work on synthetic surfaces for games like tennis and hockey, most of the time you will be working with grass.
- You will cut, treat, weed and prepare the surface before each game, match or event.
- During your work you will use a range of equipment including sit-on mowers and machines for marking out pitches.
- You might work for a professional golf, football, cricket or rugby club, or you could work for the amenities department of a local authority.

Greenkeeper

- In this role you will focus on the condition of the grass surfaces that the sports people will use. You will ensure the surface is flat and extremely well prepared before each game or event.
- By using your horticultural skills you will improve the quality of each playing surface.

The type of person suited to this work

Both of these jobs require people who can combine specialist horticultural knowledge with an understanding of the different sports and what the competitors of each sport require. You might also be expected to care for the flower beds, walls and paths close to the ground, so you should have a pride in your work and an appreciation of how plants and materials can improve the environment.

You will probably work in a team so you should enjoy being with others. As well as the horticultural side, you will also have to be prepared to do a range of other jobs from putting up nets, to preparing seating and applying fertilisers. You will need lots of stamina and be willing to work unsocial hours.

Working conditions

You will have to work flexible hours including evenings and weekends. You will need to be fit, strong and active with a strong eye for detail. If you suffer from an allergy to pollen this work might be difficult for you.

You will spend a lot of your time outdoors working in all weathers, although when repairing and maintaining the equipment you will probably be in a workshop. You will need to wear protective clothing.

The future outlook

The range of potential places for you to work is increasing and demand for staff is growing. You could work in a professional sports club, local authority education or sports and leisure department, hotel, university or college.

With additional qualifications and experience you could apply for promotion to head ground staff positions or become an area manager looking after a large number of sites.

Some of this work may be seasonal and part time, so you may need additional work to supplement your earnings.

CRCI:HB

CLCI:WAD

Qualifications and courses

Groundsperson

- There are no set qualifications required for this role. Training generally takes place on the job, but it is possible to study relevant courses on a day-release basis to gain qualifications. Some of these could be NVQ Level 1 in Horticulture, NVQ Levels 2, 3 and 4 in Amenity Horticulture (Sports Turf Management), BTEC and NPTC qualifications in Horticulture.
- Apprenticeships/Skillseekers opportunities may be available for those aged between 16 and 24.
- The Institute of Groundsmanship (IOG) offers three levels of courses covering practical greenkeeping, scientific principles of groundsmanship, and grounds management. For 14 to 16 year olds in Nottingham, the IOG run a Pathfinder course which is curriculum-based. For IOG members who have a minimum of 5 years' practical management experience, there are City & Guilds Level 4 (Licentiateship) and 5 (Graduate) awards available.
- A BTEC National Certificate/Diploma in Horticulture or Amenity Horticulture and a City & Guilds qualification in Horticulture at Levels 2 and 3 are available. Higher level courses are available including Foundation degrees in sports turf and golf course management. There are also degrees in sports turf science and management. Entry requirements are 2 A levels/3 H grades and 5 GCSEs/S grades (A–C/1–3).

Greenkeeper

- No formal requirements are needed for this role. However 2/3 GCSEs/S grades at A–C/1–3 or equivalent would be an advantage.
- NVQs/SVQs are available in Greenkeeping and Sports Turf Management at Levels 2 and 3 and Horticulture and Greenkeeping at Levels 1 and 2.
- An HNC is available in Sports Turf and Greenkeeping. There are also HNDs and Foundation Degrees available and a top-up degree is offered at Guildford College of Further and Higher Education in Horticulture (Sports Turf) Management.
- Most greenkeepers join the British and International Golf Greenkeepers Association (BIGGA) which offers various certificates, diplomas, subsidised training courses, scholarship opportunities and Continuing Professional Development (CPD). It also operates a Master Greenkeeper Certificate Scheme which recognises qualifications, skills and experience in golf course management.

entry level

To both enter and train while working in this career, you will need qualifications at Level 1–2. Please refer to explanation on page vii.

Other related opportunities

Advantages/disadvantages

- This job offers the opportunity for your work to be seen by thousands of people!
- It offers non-sportspeople a chance to get involved with sport.
- At lower levels of sport you might get the opportunity to play your favourite sport having prepared the ground first!

Earnings guide

- Institute of Groundsmanship recommends the following rates.
- A trainee groundsperson will start at around £10,500.
- Unskilled staff can expect £14,190-£17,340.
- Skilled staff can expect £17,715–£21,640. A head groundsperson earns £21,640–£28,400. Staff who are responsible for the major sporting venues can receive higher salaries.

Further information

Lantra (Sector Skills Council for the environmental and land-based industries)
Lantra House
Stoneleigh Park
Kenilworth
Warwickshire
CV8 2LG
024 7669 6996
www.lantra.co.uk

Institute of Groundsmanship
28 Stratford Office Village
Walker Avenue
Wolverton Mill East
Milton Keynes
MK12 5TW
01908 312511
www.iog.org

British International Golf Greenkeepers Association
BIGGA House
Alne
York
YO61 1UF
01347 833800
www.bigga.org.uk

CRCI:HB

CLCI:WAD

Horticultural / Garden Centre

What the work involves

Horticultural manager

- You will work for either a specialist or a general grower of different plants, shrubs and trees. As manager you will supervise, train and recruit staff as well as looking after the day-to-day running of the organisation.
- You will look after the stock, making sure it is in good condition and that you have the right plants available.
- In addition, controlling pests and diseases, and making decisions about which plants to grow will be your responsibility.
- For the business to be succesful, you will also manage the budgets and administration, speak to customers and make sure deliveries are despatched on time.

Horticultural worker

- You will look after the plants, check for disease, feed, water, prune and spray them.
- To produce new stock, you will plant out cuttings and seedlings. You will also pot-up and pack plants ready for despatch.

Garden centre worker/manager

- Working in a garden centre or nursery involves stocking shelves, maintaining outdoor display areas and giving advice to customers.
- You will look after the stock, water and feed the plants, make sure the public spaces are safe, unload deliveries and spend time on the tills.

The type of person suited to this work

These jobs, need people who love plants and are interested in science and the environment. Much of your day will involve lifting, carrying and working with the plants, so you will need lots of stamina and have to be physically fit. You will also do lots of bending.

You will need patience, as you will get asked the same questions by different customers and you will have to remain polite and help them. Some of your time will be spent indoors. However, you will be outdoors for much of the time working in all weathers, doing dirty and dusty work. These jobs could be difficult if you suffer from allergies to pollen or dust.

Working conditions

You will spend time indoors and outdoors sometimes in wet and windy conditions as much of the preparation for the main gardening season is done during the winter. Some garden centres have jobs where you are indoors in the sales area for some of the time, and if you are a manager you will have an office. You could spend some of your time in greenhouses, these can be cold and/or humid.

Horticultural manager/worker
You will generally do a 40-hour Monday to Friday week, with additional hours at busy times. You will be doing lots of carrying, lifting and bending over.

Garden centre worker/manager
You will do shift work which will include working at weekends and occasional late evenings. Part-time work is possible.

The future outlook

The horticultural and nursery sector is the largest industry in the UK. There are 13,000 businesses employing 70,000 workers many of whom are employed on a casual seasonal basis. The total market for gardening products is now worth over £3.5 billion every year and is expected to continue to rise. Horticulture is a growth area and it is expected to grow further.

Horticultural jobs are available within major plant producers, national parks, public gardens and local and national garden shops/nurseries. As competition for manager jobs is strong, you might have to move to gain promotion, but as the sector is improving so quickly this might change.

CRCI:HB | CLCI:WAD

Qualifications and courses

entry level

To both enter and train while working in this career, you will need qualifications at Level 1–3. Please refer to explanation on page vii.

Horticultural manager

- NVQs/SVQs in Management or Supervisory Management and qualifications such as HND/BSc in Horticulture with Business Management are available. Once you are in employment, you may be able to work towards NVQ Level 3 or 4 in Amenity Horticulture, or NVQ Level 3 in Production Horticulture.
- The Royal Horticulture Society (RHS) offers the General Examination in Horticulture, the RHS Advanced Certificate and RHS Diploma.
- The Royal Botanical Gardens at Kew offer International Diploma courses in Botanic Garden Management; Herbarium Techniques; Plant Conservation Strategies; Botanic Garden Education; plus a 3-year full-time Kew Diploma in Horticulture.

Horticultural worker

- There are no formal entry requirements for horticultural work, but GCSEs/S grades (A–C/1–3) in science subjects or a BTEC First Diploma in Land-based Industries are useful.
- Apprenticeships may be available to those aged between 16 and 24. NVQ/SVQs in Commercial and Amenity Horticulture Levels 1–4 and Agriculture and Commercial Horticulture at Level 4 are available. NVQs/SVQs are also available in Horticulture at Level 1.
- City & Guilds offer the Horticultural Skills test and the National /Advanced National Certificate in Horticulture Levels 2 and 3. For unemployed women in the Crystal Palace area of London, Capal Manor College offers the City & Guilds certificate in Horticultural Skills.
- BTEC National Qualifications are available in Horticulture. There are also Foundation Degrees and Degrees covering Horticulture, Retail Horticulture and Amenity Horticulture.

Garden centre worker/manager

- To work within a garden centre, qualifications in both horticulture and customer service are an advantage.
- If working in a garden centre, NVQs/SVQs in Customer Service Levels 1 to 3 may be taken.

Other related opportunities

- Arboricultural Worker / Manager p233
- Gardener / Garden Designer p249
- Groundsperson / Greenkeeper p251
- Landscape p255
- Parks Officer p257
- Tree Surgeon p260

Advantages/disadvantages

- There is a good mix of practical and managerial work, so if you like working with plants and people this could be for you.
- Watching plants grow can take time and you will need lots of patience.
- These jobs combine lots of skills and can be very rewarding.
- This is an expanding market with lots of opportunities.

Earnings guide

Horticultural worker/garden centre worker/garden centre manager

- Pay varies depending on the area and type of employer.
- Starting salaries for trainee workers is around £12,000 per year.
- With experience this rises to around £20,000. Overtime pay might be available.

Horticultural manager

- Starting salaries are around £16,000 per year rising to £21,000 for graduates.
- Qualified and experienced managers can earn between £25,000 and £40,000.

Further information

www.cityandguilds.com/myperfectjob

Institute of Horticulture
14–15 Belgrave Square
London
SW1X 8PS
020 7245 6943
www.horticulture.org.uk

Growing Careers Partnership
Writtle College
Chelmsford
Essex
CM1 3RR
01245 424200
www.growing-careers.com

Lantra (Sector Skills Council for the environmental and land-based industries)
Lantra House
Stoneleigh Park
Kenilworth
Warwickshire
CV8 2LG
024 7669 6996
www.lantra.co.uk

Royal Horticultural Society – Education Department
Wisley
Woking
Surrey
GU23 6QB
www.rhs.org.uk

Land-force.com
www.land-force.com

Landscape

What the work involves

- Landscape architects, landscapers and managers create and maintain gardens, parks, public spaces and commercial developments. These areas could be in the country or in towns.

Landscape architect

- You will design or develop a new or existing outside space. You will then make a plan and drawings and calculate the cost.
- Your plan would show the layout of the site and say what plantings should be included. You would then see the project through to completion by supervising the work on-site.
- Although you will understand garden design you will also have an understanding of civil engineering, horticulture and planning law.

Landscaper/manager

- As a landscaper you will do the practical work of turning a landscape architect's plan into the finished thing.
- You will operate machinery, carry out planting schemes, put up fences, create ponds, lay paths, build walls, construct decking and make terraces.

The type of person suited to this work

You will have to enjoy being outdoors and want to make a difference to the environment. You will be interested in making, building and constructing hard landscaping but will appreciate and understand the impact that different plants can have. You will need to be physically strong and able to use machinery and hand tools. You will need to be happy in the open in both the summer and the winter and be prepared to spend time away from home on some jobs.

Working conditions

Landscape architect

Architects spend a lot of time in the design studio sitting at a computer and drawing board or attending meetings on-site at clients' premises. You could spend about a quarter of your time at the project site, supervising operations. Some of your time will also be spent on the phone dealing with contractors and suppliers.

Landscaper/manager

You will be outdoors creating the design and working on landscape maintenance. Managers will work in an office for a lot of their time, but also go out for meetings to check and supervise work on-site.

The future outlook

Due to the impact of home improvement programmes, designing and developing gardens is now a popular and growing business. However, it can be a competitive area to find employment in, so many choose self-employment.

The types of organisations who recruit landscape staff are local authorities, botanical gardens, large private estates, the National Trust, English Heritage, building contractors and landscape design houses.

If you choose to become self-employed your success will depend upon finding customers, the quality of your work and how quickly you can build your reputation.

Qualifications and courses

Landscape architect

- You will need a degree in landscape architecture or a degree in any subject with a relevant postgraduate qualification. Useful subjects at A level/H grade include art, biology, botany, graphic design, environmental studies and geography.
- Entrants who have completed a course accredited by the Landscape Institute (LI) can work towards chartered membership of the LI through the Professional Practice Examination.
- Mature entry may be possible with sufficient relevant work experience.
- Courses are also available at land-based colleges of further education, who offer a range of HND/HNC/BTEC National qualifications in relevant subjects.

Landscaper/manager

- There are no required qualifications but relevant GCSEs/S grades, National Proficiency Tests Council (NPTC) certificates, BTEC and RHS certificates/diplomas are useful. A driving licence is often required.
- NVQ/SVQs are available in Amenity Horticulture with options for landscaping at Levels 3–4. Managers often enter with a Level 4 qualification in horticulture, civil engineering, or landscape engineering.

entry level

To both enter and train while working in this career, you will need qualifications at Level 1–8. Please refer to explanation on page vii.

- Useful subjects at A level/H grade include maths, sciences, art, biology, botany, graphic design, environmental studies and geography.
- Apprenticeships/Skillseekers may be available for those aged 16–24.

Other related opportunities

- Arboricultural Worker / Manager p233
- Architect p36
- Dry Stone Waller p50
- Ecologist p478
- Fence Erector p53
- Gardener / Garden Designer p249
- Horticultural / Garden Centre p253

Advantages/disadvantages

- There is a good mix of practical hands-on work with planning, design and meeting people.
- You will get satisfaction from knowing your work will have an impact on future generations.
- You could get wet, cold, hot and dusty.
- You will not be able to do this work if you suffer from pollen or dust allergies.

Earnings guide

Landscape architect

- Starting salaries are around £20,000 per year.
- Salaries then range from between £25,000 and £40,000.

Landscaper/manager

- Starting rates are generally £12,000–£16,000 per year and range from £19,000 to £25,000 for those with experience.
- Senior managers with additional responsibilities, can get up to £40,000.
- Rates for those who are self-employed will depend on their personal success. Work may be seasonal.

Further information

www.cityandguilds.com/myperfectjob

Lantra (Sector Skills Council for the environmental and land-based industries)
Lantra House
Stoneleigh Park
Kenilworth
Warwickshire
CV8 2LG
024 7669 6996
www.lantra.co.uk

British Association of Landscape Industries
Landscape House
Stoneleigh Park
Warwickshire
CV8 2LG
02476 690333
www.bali.co.uk

Landscape Institute
33 Great Portland Street
London
W1W 8QG
020 7299 4500
www.landscapeinstitute.org

Institute of Horticulture
14–15 Belgrave Square
London
SW1X 8PS
020 7245 6943
www.horticulture.org.uk

Royal Horticultural Society – Education Department
Wisley
Woking
Surrey
GU23 6QB
www.rhs.org.uk

CRCI:HB | CLCI:UL

Parks Officer

What the work involves

- You will supervise the gardeners and horticulturists who maintain and look after local parks, sports and recreation centres, gardens and public places.
- As well as planning new planting schemes you will organise staffing rotas and plan annual work programmes.
- You will be responsible for the recruitment and monitoring of your team, and budget control.
- You will have to liaise with your employer, which is normally local government, and other department colleagues.

The type of person suited to this work

To do this work you will have to be very organised, be able to plan ahead and manage people. You will need to use your technical and practical horticultural skills, have an understanding of budgets and an ability to meet and negotiate with those who work in different departments.

You will also combine outdoor practical work with indoor planning and administration. You should have a good understanding of plants and how to present outside spaces so they look good all year round.

To do this job you will need to be physically fit. If you suffer from asthma, pollen-based allergies or some skin conditions this work might be difficult for you.

Working conditions

You will normally work for a local authority who often adopt a flexible Monday–Friday system of attendance. At busier times, particularly in the spring and summer you may do extra hours.

You will be provided with protective clothing and will have to ensure health and safety rules are followed by your teams.

Some of your work will be indoors at a computer in an office where you will spend time ordering plants and materials.

The future outlook

Most parks officers are employed by a local or county council. A small number are employed by companies who win park management contracts.

It is likely that you will start your career as a gardener or horticulturist and then progress to parks officer once you have gained sufficient experience. Additional management training may be required.

You might have to move for career progression. Some move into department or divisional management within local/county authorities.

entry level

1–2

To both enter and train while working in this career, you will need qualifications at Level 1–2. Please refer to explanation on page vii.

Qualifications and courses

- No formal qualifications are required for this work although GCSEs/S grades at A–E/1–5 are helpful. Employers also look for practical skills.
- Many parks officers begin as gardeners/horticulturists. NVQs/SVQs in Amenity Horticulture at Level 1–2 are available and are useful qualifications to take at the early stages of your career.
- Land-based colleges offer a range of horticulture qualifications which will be useful, including the Royal Horticultural Society (RHS) General Examination, City & Guilds Advanced National Certificate in Horticulture (ANCH), BTEC and SQA National qualifications.
- Once you are employed as a parks officer, NVQs/SVQs in Amenity Horticulture and training skills are available at Levels 3–4.
- A driving licence may be required.
- Apprenticeships/Skillseekers opportunities may be available for those aged 16–24.

CRCI:HB | CLCI:WAD

Other related opportunities

- Countryside Work p235
- Gardener / Garden Designer p249
- Groundsperson / Greenkeeper p251
- Horticultural / Garden Centre p253
- Landscape p255
- Tree Surgeon p260

Advantages/disadvantages

- This is a mixture of indoor and outdoor work, using lots of different skills.
- You will use your experience and knowledge to make a difference in your community.
- You might have to wait for opportunities to become available or be willing to move.

Earnings guide

- As a parks officer your earnings will depend on the size of your employing authority and the number of sites you are responsible for. If you work for a local authority you will normally receive around £17,000–£18,000 per year.

Further information

Local Government Careers
www.lgcareers.com

Institute of Leisure and Amenity Management
ILAM House
Lower Basildon
Reading
Berkshire
RG8 9NE
01491 874800
www.ilam.co.uk

Convention of Scottish Local Authorities
Roseberry House
9 Haymarket Terrace
Edinburgh
EH12 5XZ
0131 474 9200
www.cosla.gov.uk

www.cityandguilds.com/myperfectjob

Poultry Worker

What the work involves

- Poultry workers are involved in producing of chickens, ducks, turkeys and geese for human consumption or breeding.
- Your job will be to keep the animals healthy and productive. This means feeding, watering and providing basic healthcare.
- In mechanised operations, you will keep a check on the machinery controlling their water, feed and environment.
- You will have to keep the houses and cages clean using high-pressure cleaning equipment.

The type of person suited to this work

Much of this work is repetitive, so it will suit you if you like doing the same things every day. You will be around birds, looking after their welfare and making sure they grow well. Because of worries about diseases such as avian flu you will also have to keep a check for signs of illness by being alert and observant.

You will have to be happy handling and checking the birds, which can be dirty and smelly work. Some birds may bite so you must be confident and aware of your own safety.

You will also need to be free of asthma and other allergies.

Working conditions

Most poultry operations are based in large purpose-designed buildings where the temperature and humidity are closely controlled. Expect there to be a lot of dust and unpleasant smells as many poultry are kept in confined areas. You will wear protective clothing and footwear and the work includes lots of bending over. You might have to do shift work.

If you work for a meat producer you will not be able to be squeamish.

The future outlook

There is a steady source of employment in the poultry industry, although most jobs are located in the rural parts of the country, particularly in the east of England. With experience you could become a unit manager.

Although the high-density factory farm still exists, there are more free-range and small-scale operations than there used to be, but these tend to be smaller concerns so career progression will be more limited. Some producers breed more exotic birds such as quail and guinea fowl. However, there are still a lot of large poultry operations in the UK where birds are raised on a factory scale.

Some firms will specialise in hatching chicks, or growing birds for meat or laying.

entry level

1

To both enter and train while working in this career, you will need qualifications at Level 1. Please refer to explanation on page vii.

Qualifications and courses

- There are no minimum entry requirements for this job although experience of agriculture would be helpful.
- Some GCSEs/S grades can be an advantage for career progression.
- The Scottish Agricultural College (SAC) runs a specialist HNC in Poultry Production and there is a BTEC National Award in Agricultural Production (Poultry).
- Apprenticeships/Skillseekers opportunities might be available if you are aged 16–24.
- It is possible to take full- and part-time poultry husbandry courses at local land-based colleges, although applicants are usually required to be in relevant employment. There are also independent training providers such as Progressive Poultry Training, who offer short courses to those employed in the industry.

Other related opportunities

- Beekeeper p234
- Farm Work p241
- Fish Farmer p244
- Gamekeeper p248

Advantages/disadvantages

- You may spend a lot of time working on your own.
- This can be noisy, dusty and smelly work.
- You will be responsible for the health and welfare of the birds in your care.
- Recent avian flu scares have affected the need for additional levels of hygiene and cleanliness.

Earnings guide

- Poultry workers receive about £12,000–£14,000 per year once they reach craftworker level.
- This rises to around £16,000–£18,000 with experience.
- Overtime payments may be available.

Further information

www.cityandguilds.com/myperfectjob

Lantra (Sector Skills Council for the environmental and land-based industries)
Lantra House
Stoneleigh Park
Kenilworth
Warwickshire CV8 2LG
024 7669 6996
www.lantra.co.uk

CRCI:HC
CLCI:WAM

Taxidermist

What the work involves

- As a taxidermist you would make lifelike representations of animals, birds and fishes using the skin of a dead creature. You could spend time observing the animal in its natural environment taking photographs or drawing them.
- You would skin and cure the skin to preserve it, while keeping as much of the original colour and texture as possible.
- The body of the animal is then modelled by using a range of rather sculptural techniques, sewing and glueing pieces into place and then stretching the finished skin over the model.

entry level

To both enter and train while working in this career, you will need qualifications at Level 2. Please refer to explanation on page vii.

Qualifications and courses

- There are no set qualifications for this work, but at least 3 GCSEs/S grades including English, maths, art, biology and/or a technical subject or equivalent are normally needed for entry to a junior museum post in taxidermy.
- Lengthy on-the-job training, by watching an experienced taxidermist, is required. Some commercial taxidermy firms may offer apprenticeships which are generally over 3–5 years.
- Courses in subjects such as animal anatomy, biology, natural sciences or specimen conservation would prove useful for this work, as would good knowledge of wildlife.
- If you want to be a professional taxidermist you need to register with the Department for the Environment, Food and Rural Affairs (DEFRA) and follow their strict guidelines for the collection of specimens.
- The Guild of Taxidermists runs seminars and demonstrations suitable for those with some taxidermy experience. Independent taxidermists also occasionally offer short and residential courses for varying fees.
- There is a 2-year Master's course in conservation offered by the Royal College of Art/Victoria and Albert Museum which specialises in natural history. Essential entry requirements are a good knowledge of natural history along with a degree in a relevant subject, such as conservation or natural sciences.

The type of person suited to this work

This is very time-consuming work, which requires an understanding and appreciation of wildlife. You will have to be good with your hands, be patient and have an eye for colour and detail.

You will have good observation skills, but you will not be able to be squeamish as it can involve working on animals who have been in accidents. This can be lonely work, so you will need to like your own company.

Working conditions

You could work in your own home, within the conservation department of a museum or at a workshop. If you are working from home you will be able to do flexible hours to suit; however, if you choose to work for an employer you will probably do 37 hours, Monday–Friday.

You will use different hand tools and materials from real animal products like teeth and claws, to man-made products.

The future outlook

This is a very small profession and there are only a handful of professional taxidermists. Many people do this as a hobby rather than for employment.

You could work for a national or local museum or a national taxidermy company. If you work within a museum you might also do other conservation work with biological specimens. It is likely that you would have to move into managerial jobs to get promotion.

In recent years there has been a slight growth as opportunities abroad – particularly in the US and Africa – have become available.

CRCI:HC | CLCI:FAE

Other related opportunities

- Biologist p468
- Designer p136
- Embalmer p422
- Museum / Art Gallery p325
- Pathologist p297
- Restorer / Conservation Officer p329
- Sculptor p164

Advantages/disadvantages

- This combines using your artistic and practical ability with your understanding of animal anatomy.
- The general public can learn a lot about species by looking at your work.

Earnings guide

- Those who are self-employed can expect a low income that may need to be supplemented with additional part-time work.
- As a trainee you could expect to get around £12,000 per year.
- If you are employed by a museum, earnings are generally between £15,000 and £21,000.
- Higher salaries around £40,000 are available for senior managers.

Further information

Guild of Taxidermists
c/o Glasgow Museums Resource Centre
200 Woodhead Road
South Nitshill
Glasgow
G53 7NN
0141 267 9445
www.taxidermy.org.uk

Department for Environment, Food and Rural Affairs (DEFRA)
Nobel House
17 Smith Square
London
SW1P 3JR
020 7238 6000
www.defra.gov.uk

Museums Association
24 Calvin Street
London
E1 6NW
020 7426 6910
www.museumsassociation.org

Tree Surgeon

What the work involves

- You will carry out all kinds of work on the trees in private and public gardens, parks, roadsides and on paths.
- During your work you will trim and prune healthy trees, treat diseased trees, remove dead branches or cut down the tree completely.
- Using chainsaws, hand tools, ropes, ladders and other specialised climbing equipment, you will use your practical skills and knowledge of trees to make them safe, help them grow or increase the light available for other species.

entry level

To both enter and train while working in this career, you will need qualifications at Level 1–2. Please refer to explanation on page vii.

The type of person suited to this work

You will need to have practical skills and be happy using potentially dangerous machinery and tools. You will also have to be interested in trees and want to learn about them and the problems that can occur with them.

This job involves lots of physically demanding work, including lifting, bending, cutting and climbing so you will need to be strong and agile. You would need to understand and observe health and safety rules and be happy working in a team or on your own. As you will be dealing with customers and explaining what work needs to be done, you will need excellent communication skills.

Working conditions

This is a real outdoor job, summer and winter. You will be out in all weathers, hanging from ropes and using dangerous tools like a chainsaw.

If you suffer from an allergy to pollen and dust, or vertigo, this work would be difficult for you. You will have to wear protective clothing and be very safety conscious.

In the summer your working hours might be long, and they would be shorter in the winter.

The future outlook

As with other areas of garden design and improvement, there are reasonable opportunities in town and country. Around 2000 people are employed within local authorities and 10,000 work for the private employers whose focus is on tree care.

If you choose to take further qualifications you could enter senior or managerial positions, but this might involve moving to larger organisations.

There are opportunities to work abroad.

Qualifications and courses

- Entry into this profession is through a combination of on-the-job work experience and qualifications. Some employers require a degree for which specific A levels/H grades may be needed. There are NVQs/SVQs available in Forestry and Arboriculture at Levels 1 and 2, which include workplace assessment.
- The National Trust can help in organising work experience placements. The Woodland Trust and the British Trust for Conservation Volunteers (BTCV) provide opportunities for volunteer experience.
- Degrees are available in arboriculture but a degree in a related horticultural subject may be accepted.
- There are short part-time and full-time courses available at land-based colleges of further education in chainsaw use, maintenance of equipment, health and safety and climbing techniques. Tree surgeons must obtain a Competency Certificate from the National Proficiency Training Council or Scottish Skills Testing Service before working on their own or with machinery.
- The Royal Horticultural Society (RHS) also offers short courses leading to Arboricultural Association certificates.
- Candidates must be physically fit and a driving licence is normally needed.
- Lantra-accredited apprenticeships are also available

Other related opportunities

- Arboricultural Worker / Manager p233
- Countryside Work p235
- Forestry p246
- Horticultural / Garden Centre p253
- Landscape p255

Advantages/disadvantages

- The work can be hazardous so you have to obey safety regulations.
- You will be outside working in all weathers.
- You could do very long hours in the summer and shorter hours in the winter, which may affect your earnings.
- You will be making a difference to the environment which will affect future generations.

Earnings guide

- Salaries will depend on whether you are working for a contractor or are self-employed. You will probably earn more in the south-east of England.
- Starting salaries are around £12,000–£16,000 per year.
- This rises to around £18,000 with experience.
- The most experienced can earn between £20,000 and £29,000.

Further information

www.cityandguilds.com/myperfectjob

Arboricultural Association
Ampfield House
Ampfield
Romsey
Hampshire
SO51 9PA
01794 368717
www.trees.org.uk

Lantra (Sector Skills Council for the environmental and land-based industries)
Lantra House
Stoneleigh Park
Kenilworth
Warwickshire
CV8 2LG
024 7669 6996
www.lantra.co.uk

Royal Horticultural Society – Education Department
Wisley
Woking
Surrey
GU23 6QB
www.rhs.org.uk

Land-force.com
www.land-force.com

Veterinary Nurse

What the work involves

- Veterinary nurses assist vets in their work by helping to treat animals suffering from disease and injury.
- As well as carrying out simple treatments such as dressings and nail trimming, you will give injections, prepare and help in the theatre and sterilise the instruments after use.
- You might also work in reception giving an initial assessment of animals, order drugs and arrange future appointments.
- Most nurses also undertake the day-to-day care of animals recovering from treatment within veterinary hospitals.

entry level

3–8

To both enter and train while working in this career, you will need qualifications at Level 3–8. Please refer to explanation on page vii.

The type of person suited to this work

You will have to be passionate about animals and want to help them. To do this, you will need to learn about different diseases and treatment. Although lots of animals get better, some of this work will be sad and distressing. This means you will have to work in a practical and unsentimental way.

As much of your work will also involve working with the animals' owners, you will need to be sympathetic and have excellent communication skills to explain what is happening in the treatment.

If you do not like the sight of blood, or suffer from an animal-based allergy, this job will be difficult for you.

Working conditions

Although there are still lots of general practices that deal with small animals (dogs, cats, rabbits, etc), many more are becoming specialist centres as animal hospitals or large animal practices (cows, horses, sheep), and some are working with just horses or zoo animals. Your working conditions will depend on the type of practice you work in.

You are likely to have to do emergency out-of-hours cover during evenings and weekends.

The future outlook

Due to the rise in the number of specialist practices and more organisations like the Blue Cross and RSPCA employing veterinary nurses, job opportunities are improving. If you are really keen and jobs are difficult where you live, you could try starting as a veterinary receptionist and wait for a vacancy to come up in your practice or you could gain experience with a local animal charity. 75% of all staff are female.

With experience you could progress to be a practice manager or head nurse, or move into related areas like research or work for a drugs firm.

Qualifications and courses

- You can follow a Veterinary Nursing training scheme recognised by the Royal College of Veterinary Surgeons (RCVS). This is available as an Apprenticeship/Skillseekers if you are aged 17–24. In Scotland, Lantra-accredited apprenticeships are available.
- The scheme lasts 2 years, and consists of practical training and attendance at college. It leads to NVQs/SVQs at Levels 2 and 3 and, following 2 years' approved employment, the RCVS Certificate of Veterinary Nursing.
- Entry requirements are 5 GCSEs/S grades (A–C/1–3) including English language and 2 science or maths subjects. Trainees must be at least 17. For those without these qualifications, an alternative route may be through a National Qualification in Animal Nursing Assistant, Animal Management, or the NPTC Veterinary Care Assistant National Certificate.
- Candidates without the minimum qualifications can take a pre-veterinary nursing course before proceeding to the Veterinary Nursing scheme.
- You can do a 3- or 4-year degree course in Veterinary Nursing, which includes the full RCVS training. A level/H grade biology is normally required. Equivalent qualifications such as National Diploma in science may also be accepted.

CRCI:HC | CLCI:WAM

Other related opportunities

- Animal Protection / Charity p229
- Animal Work p231
- Dog Handler p500
- Dog Work p237
- Equine / Horse Work p239
- Horse Riding p366
- Veterinary Surgeon p262

Advantages/disadvantages

- You will get to help sick animals which will rely on you for their care.
- It is an interesting job with lots of variety.
- It can be stressful and distressing.
- You may have to work irregular hours which will affect your social life.

Earnings guide

- New entrants can expect to earn about £10,500–£12,000 per year.
- With experience this rises to around £17,000.
- Head nurses generally earn £19,000–£24,000, depending on the size and type of their practice.

Further information

British Veterinary Nursing Association
Suite 11, Shenval House
South Road
Harlow
Essex
CM20 2BD
01279 408644
www.bvna.org.uk

Royal College of Veterinary Surgeons
Belgravia House
62–64 Horseferry Road
London
SW1P 2AF
020 7222 2001
www.rcvs.org.uk
Send an A5 SAE for details.

British Equine Veterinary Association (BEVA)
Mulberry House
31 Market Street
Ely
Cambridgeshire
CB7 5LQ
01638 723555
www.beva.org.uk

www.cityandguilds.com/myperfectjob

Veterinary Surgeon

What the work involves

- A vet treats animals that are suffering because of disease or injury.
- You might carry out surgical operations and be involved in the inspection of livestock and meat.
- Some vets work like human GPs in local practices and others become specialists carrying out complex surgery on a certain part of the anatomy or become an expert for a particular animal.
- You might specialise in small-animal treatment, zoo animals, farm livestock or horses.

The type of person suited to this work

To work as a vet you will need to be able to learn large amounts of complex scientific information about animal diseases and treatment. You will use this knowledge to treat and care for the sick or injured animals in your practice, hospital or animal centre.

Some of your work will be sad or distressing so you will have to work in a practical and unsentimental way. Vets have to agree to put animals first, which includes putting them down when they are too sick or old to treat. You must have good communication skills to talk to the owners.

Working with large animals is physically demanding work, so you will need to be fit and active. If you dislike the sight of blood or suffer from animal allergies this job will not suit you.

Working conditions

Your working conditions will depend on the type of practice that employs you. In small-animal practice you will spend a lot of time in the surgery. Working with farm livestock and horses, you will be out on the road visiting your patients. Some of this work will be unpleasant or smelly and involve travelling long distances to get to the animals.

You will work long hours and be on call to cover emergencies.

The future outlook

There are around 9000 registered vets in the UK. About half are employed in a practice, training university or other animal centre with the other half being self-employed and having a share in a practice. Getting started as a vet involves a very competitive entry process, with far more people applying to courses than there are places, so high A level grades are essential.

Once you are qualified, finding a first job is not too difficult. You will normally join an established practice and would hope eventually to become a partner (effectively part-owner) of a practice. This would probably involve buying your way in.

Some vets work for the government or for firms researching and producing animal pharmaceuticals.

entry level

4–8

To both enter and train while working in this career, you will need qualifications at Level 4–8. Please refer to explanation on page vii.

Qualifications and courses

- Competition for entry is very stiff. All universities recommend that potential applicants gain practical work experience before applying for a degree in veterinary science/veterinary medicine approved by the Royal College of Veterinary Surgeons (RCVS).
- Entry requirements depend on the university, but the normal minimum requirement is 3 A levels at grades AAB including chemistry and 1 or 2 from biology, physics and maths, or 5 H grades at AAABB including chemistry and 2 from biology, physics or maths. A good range of GCSE/S grades (A*–A/1) are also required.
- Courses may include an optional additional year in which students gain an Honours degree in a related science subject. All courses include the 38 weeks of practical experience required by RCVS.
- Degree courses last 5 years. The Degree at Cambridge University lasts 6 years and is a combination of two degrees, which on completion allows membership of the Royal College of Veterinary Surgeons (MRCVS).
- Before being able to work as a veterinary surgeon, it is essential to be registered with the Royal College of Veterinary Surgeons (RCVS), the UK regulatory body. To qualify for registration, you must have a veterinary degree from a UK university approved by the RCVS or an equivalent overseas qualification recognised by the RCVS.

Other related opportunities

- Animal Protection / Charity p229
- Animal Work p231
- Biologist p468
- Doctor p278
- Dog Work p237
- Equine / Horse Work p239
- Veterinary Nurse p261

Advantages/disadvantages

- The training is long and very competitive to enter.
- It can be a very stressful but rewarding job, with lots of responsibility.
- In this career you will never stop learning – more experience will make you a better vet.
- Animal producers and farmers will rely on your expertise.

Earnings guide

- Newly qualified vets earn around £30,500–£39,000 per year, depending on the location and type of practice. This might also include a car and free accommodation.
- With 4–5 years' experience, this rises to £48,000+.
- A senior partner can expect £53,000+.

Further information

Royal College of Veterinary Surgeons
Belgravia House
62–64 Horseferry Road
London
SW1P 2AF
020 7222 2001
www.rcvs.org.uk

British Equine Veterinary Association (BEVA)
Mulberry House
31 Market Street
Ely
Cambridgeshire
CB7 5LQ
01638 723555
www.beva.org.uk
Send an A5 SAE for details.

Zookeeper

What the work involves

- You could work in a safari, wildlife or birdlife park where you would care for and treat the animals.
- You will feed the animals, look for signs of disease or injury and clean out the cages of the animals in your care.
- As zoos have changed, now placing more importance on conservation and education, some of your work could involve talking to visitors.
- You will keep records of feeding, health and behaviour and check the safety of the animals and visitors.

entry level

To both enter and train while working in this career, you will need qualifications at Level 1–3. Please refer to explanation on page vii.

The type of person suited to this work

As with every job working with animals, you will have to be patient and like handling and being around them. Some of this work is physically demanding so you will have to be fit and active.

Some animals you will work with could be dangerous, so you will have to respect them and be aware of your own and others' safety.

With the importance placed upon promoting conservation and education within modern zoos, you might have to speak and give presentations to visitors. This means verbal communication skills are also very important.

Working conditions

Your working conditions will depend on the type of animal park and the animals in your care. However, as animals require 24/7 care, you will work 5–6 days a week, normally on a shift system including early mornings, late evenings, weekends and bank holidays, especially during the busiest periods.

You will be doing physically demanding and dirty work so you will be provided with protective clothing. If you suffer from allergies this work will be difficult for you.

Some centres close for parts of the year which means your work could be seasonal.

The future outlook

There are 350 zoos and animal parks throughout the UK employing around 3000 people. Expect to move for work or promotion. Jobs can be very competitive meaning work experience is highly recommended. Many zoos offer a volunteer work experience scheme: contact your local park for details.

The work might be part time or seasonal so you may need to have additional work to supplement your earnings.

With experience you can progress to head keeper or related work with organisations like the RSCPA/SSPCA, kennels or animal inspection.

Qualifications and courses

- No specific qualifications are required although an interest in biology or natural sciences is useful. GCSEs/S grades (A–C/1–3), especially in English and science subjects, will be useful.
- Previous experience of zoo work is useful, through a volunteer programme or holiday job.
- General animal care and management courses available include City & Guilds Advanced Certificate in Animal Care, NVQs/SVQs in Animal Care Level 2, BTEC First Diploma and National Diploma in Animal Care, Foundation degree or BSc Honours degree in animal management.
- The National Extension College runs an Animal Management course in conjunction with recognised zoological bodies including the Association of British Wild Animal Keepers (ABWAK).
- Sparsholt College in Hampshire offers a Foundation degree in Zoo Resource Management for people in relevant employment.
- Apprenticeships/Skillseekers opportunities may be available if you are aged 16–24.
- Practical on-the-job training is provided by experienced keepers for new staff.

CRCI:HC

CLCI:WAM

Other related opportunities

- Animal Protection / Charity p229
- Animal Work p231
- Dog Work p237
- Farm Work p241
- Horse Riding p366
- Veterinary Nurse p261

Advantages/disadvantages

- This can be difficult work to enter and progress in.
- The rewards can be small.
- You will be working with the most unusual or exotic animals.
- The role of zoos as centres of breeding and supporting conversation has increased recently, so you could underatke important work.

Earnings guide

- Pay will depend on the location and type of animal park. Many jobs include free or subsidised accommodation.
- As a guide salaries are likely to be £12,000 a year at trainee level.
- With experience, this can rise to £15,000–£16,000.
- Senior keepers can earn up to £24,000.

Further information

Association of British Wild Animal Keepers
Chessington Zoo
Leatherhead Road
Surrey
KT9 2NE
01372 731555
www.abwak.co.uk

Federation of Zoological Gardens of Great Britain & Ireland
Zoological Gardens
Regents Park
London
NW1 4RY
020 7586 0230
www.zoofederation.org.uk
Write for details with an A5 SAE.

British and Irish Association of Zoos and Aquariums (BIAZA)
Regents Park
London
NW1 4RY
020 7449 6351
www.biaza.org.uk

Do you want to help people to recover from illness by treating and caring for them? The healthcare cluster includes jobs you may not be aware of, so research your ideas carefully:

- **Acupuncturist**
- **Dietitian**
- **Health Promotions Specialist**
- **Nurse**
- **Reflexologist**

But what's it like working in this area?

Here's Janet Ginnings's story:

Aromatherapist

Janet originally trained as a hairdresser and now has her own hair and beauty salon in Curzon Street in London's Mayfair. Twelve years ago she decided to train to be an aromatherapist and she took an ITEC (International Therapy Examination Council) course in aromatherapy. ITEC is the major awarding body in the field of beauty and complementary therapies in this country. She now splits her time between looking after her hair customers and seeing six aromatherapy clients a week. Janet comes from India and it was here that her interest in fragrant oils began.

'I remember my mother always wore jasmine flowers in her hair and I just loved the smell of them; also the whole family had recipes that were handed down for making beauty products like body scrubs which included sandalwood oil, so for me learning to be an aromatherapist was just taking it one step further.'

QUALIFICATIONS YOU WILL NEED

In order to train to be an aromatherapist you must first take courses in anatomy and physiology, and holistic massage. Once you have completed these you must then complete another year-long course in the use of the aromatherapy oils, their properties and their side effects.

'There are so many oils you really have to have knowledge of each one. Some of them are very powerful, so you cannot use them if your client is pregnant or has high blood pressure. Learning them all takes a long time and you never stop learning. I have a reference book with all the oils in it and I am always looking up new things and trying different oils out on myself.'

Janet believes that in order to be a good aromatherapist you must get the best training possible and also become a member of a professional body such as HABIA (Hair and Beauty Industry Authority – its Level 3 NVQ/SVQ in Beauty Therapy includes aromatherapy massage). She also believes that training to do other therapies or hairdressing gives the best therapists an added string to their bow, as clients are increasingly turning to natural therapies. It also ensures they can make a decent wage.

'It is hard to make a living just doing aromatherapy, but, remember, you are a trained masseuse anyway, so you could do Swedish massage or other holistic massages in order to make ends meet. Other good therapies to learn are reflexology, Indian head massage and reiki. There are always new therapies to learn about and new courses to take and the more things you can do the better your chances of making good money.'

WHAT JANET LOVES ABOUT HER JOB

'I love doing this – it is so rewarding. I find it very interesting treating people, and also very gratifying. It is nice to see your clients relax. When I massage I have very calming music playing and I close my eyes and it relaxes me too, it helps me to get in tune with my clients' bodies and minds. Some of them even say I have got magic in my hands!'

Ambulance

What the work involves

Paramedic

- Paramedics attend medical emergencies and accidents as quickly and as safely as possible.
- Using your knowledge and skills, you will then assess the patient's condition, give them immediate treatment and care for them until they reach hospital.
- You will use medical equipment and supplies such as oxygen and drugs.
- The job involves keeping accurate records and maintaining the ambulance and equipment.

Ambulance technician

- Ambulance technicians assist paramedics in attending medical emergencies.
- Your work will include driving to and from the scene, giving drugs and using medical equipment.
- You will also transport patients from one hospital to another when necessary.

Ambulance care assistant

- Ambulance technicians assist paramedics in attending medical emergencies.
- As an ambulance care assistant, you will drive frail or elderly people to and from hospitals, clinics and day-care centres.
- Your job will involve helping patients into and out of the ambulance, looking after them on the journey and driving the ambulance.

The type of person suited to this work

All ambulance staff must have a responsible and mature attitude. You must also be caring and patient when dealing with people who may be upset or distressed. You will need to be able to work well in a team, follow instructions and have excellent communication skills for reassuring and talking to patients. Common sense and an ability to keep calm in an emergency are also necessary.

You must be physically fit to move and lift patients and will need to be able to learn how to use medical equipment and other supplies carefully and accurately in high pressure situations.

Ambulance technicians and paramedics need to be able to deal with serious injuries and very distressing situations. Paramedics also have to think quickly, be decisive and take control of events.

Working conditions

You will spend a lot of time in your ambulance, be outdoors in all weathers, be lifting patients and will wear a uniform. These jobs involve working with all kinds of people who may be stressed, frightened or in pain. The work can be emotionally and physically demanding.

Ambulance technician/paramedic

You will use specialist equipment and drugs to care for patients whilst they are travelling in your ambulance.

Ambulance technicians and paramedics work shifts, including nights, weekends and bank holidays. You will probably be expected to drive the ambulance safely at speed.

Ambulance care assistant

You will spend most of your time taking people to and from hospital, but may also care for people in their homes or whilst they are in hospital.

The future outlook

Most jobs are with the NHS throughout the UK. Each ambulance service does its own recruitment and competition is high. There are also some opportunities to work for private hospitals and the armed forces.

Recent changes in the ambulance service mean more highly trained staff are able to offer an increasingly effective level of care.

Paramedic

As well as opportunities within the control room, training and recruitment, there is a growth in clinical roles for paramedics to work within doctors' surgeries and as emergency care practitioners.

Ambulance technician

It is common for ambulance technicians with experience to train as paramedics. Others choose to work in the control room, or in related areas such as training and health and safety.

Ambulance care assistant

Ambulance care assistants may progress to advanced levels, transporting patients with special clinical needs. Working as an ambulance care assistant is also a recognised route to a career as an ambulance technician and from there to paramedic.

It is also possible to move into other roles within the ambulance service such as emergency call handling, training and human resources. With experience, you can also gain promotion to senior management positions.

CRCI:JI

CLCI:JOC

Qualifications and courses

- The usual entry is through becoming an ambulance care assistant. Candidates must be at least 18 years old (21 in some services) and have held a clean driving licence (including C1 and D1 categories) for at least a year. Candidates are required to pass entrance exams, including a medical examination. At least 4 GCSEs/S grades (A–C/1–3), including English and maths, may also be required. You will also need a clear police check.
- Direct entry as an ambulance technician is possible with some services. Trainee technicians spend up to 12 weeks undertaking intensive training in pre-hospital emergency care, physiology and anatomy, and emergency driving.

Paramedic

- To become a paramedic, you normally need at least 1 year's experience as an ambulance technician and to be registered with the Health Professions Council.
- It is possible to study for a degree in paramedic science. Graduates of these courses may gain direct entry to some ambulance services. For entry to a degree course, at least 2 A levels/3 H grades or equivalent are required, including biological subjects/chemistry.

entry level

To both enter and train while working in this career, you will need qualifications at Level 2–8. Please refer to explanation on page vii.

Other related opportunities

- Coastguard p495
- Firefighter / Officer p502
- Healthcare Assistant p284
- Nurse (Registered) p289
- Police p506
- Social Worker p545

Advantages/disadvantages

- The demands of dealing with serious injuries and with people in distress as well as the need to work quickly but accurately can make this a stressful role.
- It is rewarding to be able to help people, ranging from reassuring a patient who is worried about a hospital appointment to saving someone's life.
- The NHS offers training opportunities and a variety of career options.
- The nature of the job means that no two working days will ever be the same.

Earnings guide

- Pay levels vary between geographical areas, but are usually within the NHS pay rates.
- Allowances are available for staff working overtime or on standby duty, and for staff working in London and parts of the south-east of England.

Paramedic

- Paramedics earn between £19,683 and £25,424 per year in NHS band 5.
- Emergency Care Practitioners are on NHS band 6: £23,458– £31,779.

Ambulance technician

- Ambulance technicians on band 4 earn between £16,853 and £20,261.

Ambulance care assistant

- Fully qualified NHS ambulance care assistants earn between £12,177 and £16,405 per year.

Further information

Skills for Health
2nd floor
Goldsmiths House
Broad Plain
Bristol
BS2 0JP
0117 922 1155
www.skillsforhealth.org.uk
office@skillsforhealth.org.uk

NHS Careers
0845 606 0655
www.nhscareers.nhs.uk

Ambulance Service Association
London
SE1 8RT
020 7928 9620
www.asa.uk.net
reception@asa.uk.net

British Paramedic Association
28 Wilfred Street
Derby
DE23 8GF
01332 746356
www.britishparamedic.org

City & Guilds

www.cityandguilds.com/myperfectjob

CRCI:JI

CLCI:JOC

Anaesthetist

What the work involves

- Anaesthetists are doctors who have undergone further training in anaesthesia.
- You will prepare and administer drugs to make patients unconscious and pain free during surgery, you will monitor them during the procedure and bring them back to consciousness afterwards. You will also give local anaesthesia to specific areas of the body.
- You will also give pain relief after surgery, to seriously ill patients or during procedures such as childbirth.
- Anaesthetists also work in intensive care, resuscitation and pain management.

entry level

To both enter and train while working in this career, you will need qualifications at Level 4–8. Please refer to explanation on page vii.

The type of person suited to this work

Anaesthetists need excellent communication skills to care for patients, listening to them and reassuring them about the procedures they are having. You should also be able to work well in a team with other medical staff and be able to both give and follow instructions.

You should be able to stay calm in an emergency and make decisions under pressure. You will need to be able to use complicated equipment and administer powerful drugs safely and accurately.

Finally, you must be prepared to undergo a long programme of education and training in order to gain the in-depth knowledge and skills necessary to become an anaesthetist.

Qualifications and courses

- The initial training is the same as that required to become a hospital doctor (see p 278); candidates must complete a medical degree recognised by the General Medical Council (GMC). This requires very high A level/H grade results, including chemistry and other science subjects. Competition for a medical school place is very high.
- After completing a medical degree, candidates must undergo specialist postgraduate training for around 7 years in anaesthesia, intensive care medicine and pain management while working under supervision. After completing the training programme, trainees receive a Certificate of Completion of Training (CCT) and become eligible to have their names added to the General Medical Council's register.

Working conditions

Anaesthetists work in operating theatres, wards, clinics and accident and emergency departments within hospitals.

You will work directly with patients and as part of a medical team and will handle potentially dangerous drugs and equipment.

You will work shifts and be on an on-call rota, which includes working at nights, at weekends and on bank holidays.

The future outlook

There are opportunities throughout the UK, mainly within the NHS but also in private hospitals and clinics. Promotion to consultant posts is very competitive. Anaesthetists may work in sub-specialities such as paediatrics, obstetrics, cardiac surgery, resuscitation or intensive care.

Once fully qualified, you will probably be expected to teach and examine students and trainees and to carry out research. With experience you could move into teaching and research within medical schools.

CRCI:JH

CLCI:JAB

Other related opportunities

- Doctor p278
- Nurse (Registered) p289
- Pathologist p297
- Psychiatrist p304
- Radiologist p306
- Surgeon p260

Advantages/disadvantages

- Being responsible for the safety of patients in your care and dealing with emergency situations means that this is a very demanding job.
- It is rewarding to be able to help patients through surgery and other medical procedures by giving them pain relief.

Earnings guide

- Salary levels in the NHS may vary in different locations, the figures below are a guide.
- Junior hospital doctors usually earn a supplement on top of their basic salary. Most earn £32,087 in their first year of training and £39,798 in their second year. A doctor training as a specialist could earn between £43,000 and £67,000.
- Consultants can earn from £71,000 upwards.
- Some senior consultants can earn up to £161,000.
- Earnings are often more through private practice work.

Further information

Skills for Health
2nd floor
Goldsmiths House
Broad Plain
Bristol
BS2 0JP
0117 922 1155
www.skillsforhealth.org.uk
office@skillsforhealth.org.uk

NHS Careers
0845 60 60 655
www.nhscareers.nhs.uk

British Medical Association
BMA House
Tavistock Square
London
WC1H 9JP
020 7387 4499
www.bma.org.uk

Association of Anaesthetists of Great Britain and Ireland
21 Portland Place
London
W1B 1PY
020 7631 1650
www.aagbi.org
info@aagbi.org

The Royal College of Anaesthetists
Churchill House
35 Red Lion Square
London
WC1R 4SG
020 7092 1500
info@rcoa.ac.uk

Audiologist

What the work involves

- Audiologists examine patients to identify and assess hearing and balance disorders.
- As an audiologist, you will use specialist equipment to test patients and assess their problems and needs.
- You will also fit hearing aids and give treatment and advice to patients on how to improve and manage their conditions.
- Audiologists usually work in one of four main areas: paediatrics, adult assessment and rehabilitation, special needs groups, and research and development.

entry level

To both enter and train while working in this career, you will need qualifications at Level 4–8. Please refer to explanation on page vii.

Qualifications and courses

- The professional qualification for audiologists is a 4-year BSc degree in audiology. The entry requirements for an audiology degree are 3 A levels/5 H grades or equivalent including at least 1 science subject, maths or psychology.
- You will spend the first 2 years of the course at university. During year 3, you will work in a placement in an audiology setting. The final year will be spent back at university learning about more advanced aspects of audiology.
- It is also possible to enter this profession with a degree in another appropriate subject and a Master's in audiology. Relevant degree subject areas include medical sciences, life sciences, physical sciences, or mathematical/applied sciences. The best entry route into the MSc is as an NHS regionally funded trainee.

The type of person suited to this work

As an audiologist you will need to speak clearly and be easily understood by people who are lip reading. You will need to be a caring person with excellent communication skills to deal sensitively with patients of all ages and backgrounds, listening to them and explaining the tests and procedures you are doing. You should also be flexible and able to work as part of a team.

You will need to be practical to operate specialist equipment and take a logical, scientific approach to your work and be able to assess patients' needs and conditions correctly, keep accurate records and provide solutions and practical help.

Working conditions

Most audiologists work as part of hospital team but you could also be based in a clinic or visit patients in their homes or in care homes or schools. You could also be involved in teaching and research work in a university.

You will probably work Monday to Friday but could have to be on call and cover shifts including nights, weekends and bank holiday.

The future outlook

Audiology is a rapidly developing area of healthcare, there is a shortage of qualified staff so job prospects are good

There are opportunities within the NHS throughout the UK. There are also jobs available in research and in private hospitals.

You could specialise in one area such as paediatrics or adult rehabilitation.

Within the NHS you could progress to higher grades, where you will have more responsibility including managing and training others.

CRCI:JF

CLCI:JOB

Other related opportunities

- Occupational Therapist p292
- Physiotherapist p309
- Speech and Language Therapist p309

Advantages/disadvantages

- Working face to face with patients can be challenging.
- It is satisfying to use your knowledge and skills to improve people's hearing and balance conditions. A National Study of Hearing showed that about 16% of the population have a significant hearing loss, so work in this field is important.

Earnings guide

- The NHS sets rates for audiologists. There are extra payments available, for example if you work in London.
- Trainees start on NHS band 6: £23,458–£31,779 per year. Once qualified this rises to band 7: £28,313–£37,326.
- Senior posts have a salary range at bands 8–9 of £36,112–£90,607.

Further information

Skills for Health
2nd floor
Goldsmiths House
Broad Plain
Bristol
BS2 0JP
0117 922 1155
www.skillsforhealth.org.uk
office@skillsforhealth.org.uk

NHS Careers
0845 60 60 655
www.nhscareers.nhs.uk

British Academy of Audiology
PO Box 346
Resources for Associations
Association House
South Park Road
Macclesfield
Cheshire
SK11 6SH
01625 504066
www.baaudiology.org
admin@baaudiology.org

British Society of Audiology
80 Brighton Road
Reading
Berks
RG6 1PS
01189 660622
www.thebsa.org.uk
bsa@thebsa.org.uk

Chiropodist / Podiatrist

What the work involves

- Chiropodists (also known as podiatrists) deal with problems of the feet and lower limbs.
- The work involves diagnosing and treating problems that can occur in the foot and leg. Common problems include in-growing toenails, verrucas, foot ulcers, overuse or sports injuries.
- Tasks include using specialist equipment, carrying out surgery, managing wounds, removing corns and analysing the way people walk in order to find out what is causing their problems.
- You will treat people with disabilities and long-term illnesses.

The type of person suited to this work

Chiropodists need to be caring and understanding. You will be talking and listening to patients of all ages and with a wide range of problems, and who could be distressed or in pain. You should be able to reassure them and explain their treatment clearly and simply. You will also need good communication skills to be an effective part of a healthcare team. You should be able to apply your skills and knowledge to diagnose and solve problems.

You should be good with your hands as you will be using equipment and performing surgery, dealing with wounds or foot ulcers or removing corns with a scalpel.

Working conditions

You may work in a range of locations such as hospitals, clinics, nursing homes, schools, chemists and gyms or may visit people in their own homes.

You will work within a team and will probably do normal hours from Monday to Friday.

If you are self-employed you may need to work in the evenings or at weekends to treat people at times to suit them.

The future outlook

Most opportunities are within the NHS but you could also work in private clinics, high street chemists and sports and leisure centres.

Job prospects are good. Around 85% of students are employed within 4 months of finishing their degree and 100% within 8–9 months.

If you want to set up a chiropody practice, you should make sure that there will be enough work available for you and any other chiropodists already working in your area.

After you have qualified as a chiropodist within the NHS, you could be applying for a more senior post within a couple of years.

You may choose to specialise in one area of chiropody such as diabetes, biomechanics (musculo-skeletal disorders), forensic podiatry, working with children or surgery. You could also go on to teach and do research in a university or move into management.

entry level

4–8

To both enter and train while working in this career, you will need qualifications at Level 4–8. Please refer to explanation on page vii.

Qualifications and courses

- To work as a chiropodist/podiatrist in the NHS, you need to have passed a BSc degree in podiatry approved by the Health Professions Council (HPC). You must be registered with the HPC in order to practise.
- For entry to a podiatry degree, 5 GCSEs/S grades (A–C/1–3), including English language and science(s), and 2 A levels/3 H grades or equivalent, including a science subject, are usually required. Chemistry or biology may be preferred. Only a small number of institutions offer podiatry courses, so places are extremely limited.
- Mature entry to a podiatry degree is via a science-based Access course or A levels or equivalent.
- Entrants must pass a police background check, and are medically screened.
- Employment can also be found as a podiatry assistant, where training is offered by the employer.

CRCI:JG

CLCI:JAT

Other related opportunities

- Complementary Health Practitioner p271
- Physiotherapist p301
- Prosthetist / Orthotist p303

Advantages/disadvantages

- The idea of working with other people's feet may not appeal instantly, but chiropodists generally get great satisfaction from their work.
- You will have to deal with people who may be badly injured or very ill and who are distressed and in pain.

Earnings guide

- Salary levels in the NHS may be subject to change. Additional allowances are available for those living in or near London.
- Starting salaries for NHS chiropodists range from £19,683 to £25,424 per year. With experience this can rise to £31,799.
- Specialists can earn up to £37,326. Consultants can earn up to £73,000.
- There are also higher grades for chiropody teachers and chief members of staff, as well as extra payments available, for example if you work in London.
- Earnings as a self-employed chiropodist in private practice vary widely, depending on how much you charge and how many clients you see, but could be £50,000+.

Chiropody assistant

- Starting salaries in the NHS are £14,437–£17,257 per year. With a relevant NVQ and some experience this rises to £20,261.

Further information

Skills for Health
2nd floor
Goldsmiths House
Broad Plain
Bristol
BS2 0JP
0117 922 1155
www.skillsforhealth.org.uk
office@skillsforhealth.org.uk

NHS Careers
0845 60 60 655
www.nhscareers.nhs.uk

Society of Chiropodists and Podiatrists
1 Fellmonger's Path
Tower Bridge Road
London
SE1 3LY
020 7234 8620
www.feetforlife.org

Complementary Health Practitioner

What the work involves

- Complementary health practitioners treat the patient holistically, which means treating them as a whole person rather than treating specific symptoms. A wide range of techniques are used in complementary health.

Acupuncturist

- Acupuncturists insert fine needles into the client's body at particular points to stimulate the natural energy that circulates within the body. Acupuncture is used for pain relief and to treat a wide range of conditions.

Alexander technique practitioner

- Alexander technique practitioners take clients through movements that improve posture, increase mobility and reduce tension in the body. The Alexander technique helps a range of conditions including joint and muscle problems, breathing disorders, coordination problems and stress-related conditions.

Aromatherapist

- Aromatherapists use essential oils taken from aromatic plants to treat a variety of conditions such as skin problems, anxiety, aches and pains and digestive problems. As an aromatherapist, you will choose and blend oils to suit the client and their condition. You will often massage the oils into the client's body and may also give the client the oils to use at home.

Chiropractor

- Chiropractors use their hands to make adjustments to the joints of the spine and other parts of the body. As a chiropractor, you will diagnose and treat patients with problems such as back pain, poor mobility, headaches and digestive problems.

Crystal therapist

- Crystal therapists place crystals on the body to heal a vast range of conditions. Crystals contain energies and you will choose the best type to suit your client and their condition.

Healer

- Healers channel energy to help to heal any condition caused by stress, illness or injury. The energy balances the body and helps to trigger the client's own healing process. As a healer you will channel the energy by placing your hands lightly on or around different areas of the client's body.

Herbalist

- Herbalists use herbal remedies to treat medical conditions and to rebalance the body. As a herbalist, you will decide which plants and plant extracts to use for each client and their condition. You may provide the remedies in many forms, such as tablets, liquids or ointments.

Homeopath

- Homeopaths treat the causes of illnesses by using remedies that stimulate the body's own healing process. Homeopathy is based on the idea that 'like cures like', so you will give your client tiny doses of natural substances that if given in larger doses to a healthy person, would produce similar symptoms to those that the client is experiencing.

Masseur/masseuse

- Masseurs/masseuses use their hands to knead, stroke and pummel different areas of the body including skin, muscles and joints. Massage stimulates circulation, relaxes muscles, relieves pain and promotes a feeling of well-being in your client.

Naturopath

- Naturopaths use a variety of natural methods to help the body to heal itself. For example, as a naturopath you may give advice on nutrition, exercise or relaxation techniques. You may also provide or suggest a range of treatments such as massage, homeopathy or counselling. The advice and treatments you give will vary to suit each client.

Osteopath

- Osteopaths deal with the muscular-skeletal system of the body. They mainly treat problems such as back pain, headaches and injuries, but they may also treat other conditions such as digestive problems. As an osteopath, your work will include using your hands to massage muscles and manipulate joints.

Reflexologist

- Reflexologists deal with a wide range of health conditions by putting pressure on certain parts of their clients' feet to stimulate healing. The different parts of the foot link to various parts of the body. As a reflexologist, you will press the relevant reflex points on the foot to heal the particular area of the body.

Reiki therapist

- Reiki therapists transfer healing energy to their clients. As a Reiki therapist, you will use a sequence of hand positions over the whole body to encourage the energy flows to the areas that need it. The energy restores balance, reduces pain and supports the body's natural ability to heal itself. It can help the client physically, emotionally and spiritually.

CRCI:JA/JB | CLCI:JOD

Qualifications and courses

entry level

To both enter and train while working in this career, you will need qualifications at Level 1–8. Please refer to explanation on page vii.

- Acupuncturist, chiropractor, osteopath, herbalist, homeopath, naturopath: entry requirements for relevant courses usually include 2–3 A levels/4 H grades, including a science, and 5 GCSEs/S grades (A–C/1–3) including English and maths. Alexander technique, aromatherapist, crystal therapist, healer, masseur/masseuse, reflexologist, reiki therapist: there are now National Occupational Standards for most of these careers, either already in existence or in development. There are no set entry requirements for courses, but it is useful to have some GCSEs/S grades or equivalent.

Acupuncturist

- The British Acupuncture Accreditation Board accredits courses. College courses lead to a professional qualification in acupuncture, and some also award a degree. The universities of Salford and Westminster run degrees in traditional Chinese medicine (acupuncture). Entrants who have completed one of the above courses are eligible for full membership of the British Acupuncture Council or, in the case of traditional Chinese medicine, with the British Register of Complementary Practitioners.

Chiropractor

- Practising chiropractors must be registered with the General Chiropractic Council (GCC). To register, a chiropractor must have completed a recognised degree course. For entry to a degree in chiropractic, A levels/H grades or equivalent including a science are required. Preliminary chiropractic courses are available for applicants without the usual entry requirements. After qualifying, chiropractors need to do a 1-year period of provisional registration undertaking supervised clinical work, prior to final registration with the GCC.

Herbalist

- The National Institute of Medical Herbalists (NIMH) accredits BSc (Hons) courses in the UK. Entry requirements vary, but generally 3 A levels/4 H grades including biology are required.

Homeopath

- There is no set path to becoming a homeopath, but a wide range of training courses, from vocational to degree level, are available. Entry requirements vary significantly.

Naturopath

- To become a registered naturopath with the General Council and Register of Naturopaths, an accredited degree or diploma is required. A diploma is offered by the British College of Osteopathic Medicine. Entry to the diploma requires 3 A levels/4 H grades, usually including biology and chemistry, and 5 GCSEs/S grades (A–C/1–3), including English.

Osteopath

- Practising osteopaths must be registered with the General Osteopathic Council. Candidates must complete an accredited degree course in osteopathy/osteopathic medicine. Degree entry requirements are 2 A levels/3 H grades in science subjects, including chemistry and biology, and at least 5 GCSEs/S grades (A–C/1–3), or equivalent.

The type of person suited to this work

Complementary health practitioners must be sensitive and caring with strong communication skills to gain the trust of their clients and put them at ease. You should have a strong belief in your therapy and be able to explain your treatments clearly.

Most practitioners undertake detailed consultations with clients so you should be able to listen carefully and assess conditions before deciding on a course of treatment and may need to refer people to conventional medicine. You must be responsible and practical and comfortable with giving hands on treatment.

Good business sense is important if you are self-employed.

Working conditions

You could work in a range of locations, such as complementary therapy centres, clinics, hospitals, your own or other people's homes, health farms and fitness centres. A driving licence is useful.

You will work with different kinds of equipment, remedies or substances, depending on your therapy. Some therapies can be physically demanding and most involve standing. You may see some people only once or twice and others over long periods. Working closely with clients can be emotionally intense and working as a self employed therapist you can feel isolated.

You will probably have to work in the evenings or at weekends to treat people at times that suit them.

The future outlook

Complementary health is a growing area. Demand rises for therapies as they become better known and people are increasingly looking for new ways to deal with their physical and emotional problems.

Most practitioners are self-employed and work in private practice and you will need to spend time advertising and promoting your services. Some areas will have more potential clients than others, and if you want to set up a practice it is important to make sure that there will be enough work available for you and any other practitioners already working in the area. It takes time to develop a private complementary health practice and you are unlikely to earn much at first. It is important to get a recognised qualification and register with the relevant professional body.

Interest in certain types of complementary therapies is increasing within mainstream health care so opportunities are likely to increase within the NHS. Currently a limited number of practitioners of therapies such as homeopathy and acupuncture already work in NHS hospitals and healthcare centres. There can also be jobs available in leisure centres.

With experience, you could choose to move into teaching or research.

Other related opportunities

- Art Therapist p284
- Dietitian p277
- Doctor p278
- Nurse (Registered) p289
- Physiotherapist p301
- Therapist p309

Advantages/disadvantages

- You will need to be able to cope with the fact that it is not always possible to completely cure people of their conditions.
- However, you will often be able to improve people's health or cure conditions, which can be very satisfying.
- You can work flexibly and fit your work round other commitments.
- The job can offer a lot of variety because of the range of clients you will see and the different places where you may work.
- Working closely with people can be both demanding and rewarding.

Earnings guide

- Most complementary health practitioners are self-employed and charge clients for each session. So earnings vary widely, depending on how much you charge and how many clients you see. As it usually takes time to develop a client base, your earnings may be very low to start with.
- Fees for individual sessions can range widely, from £25 to £100 and in some cases even more. Practitioners who can offer their clients a great deal of experience and knowledge in their field usually charge higher fees.
- Some practitioners supplement their income by selling products relating to their field to individual clients to complement their treatments.
- Earnings for new practitioners may start at anything between £10,000 and £25,000 per year, depending on the number of clients they have, and the location in which they work.
- Experienced practitioners may earn £30,000+.

Further information

Skills for Health
2nd floor
Goldsmiths House
Broad Plain
Bristol
BS2 0JP
0117 922 1155
www.skillsforhealth.org.uk
office@skillsforhealth.org.uk

Institute for Complementary Medicine
Unit 25
Tavern Quay Business Centre
Sweden Gate
London
SE16 7TX
020 7231 5855
www.i-c-m.org.uk
info@i-c-m.org.uk

City& Guilds

www.cityandguilds.com/myperfectjob

Critical Care Technologist

What the work involves

- Critical care technologists support other medical staff caring for critically ill patients by maintaining and operating life-support equipment in intensive care units.
- As a critical care technologist, your work will include setting up equipment, taking readings and checking the equipment is working correctly.
- You will work closely with patients and their relatives.

entry level

To both enter and train while working in this career, you will need qualifications at Level 1–8. Please refer to explanation on page vii.

The type of person suited to this work

You will need maturity and excellent communication skills to work with patients and their relatives at a time of intense stress, and be able to explain things simply and clearly. You will need to be practical with good technical skills to operate complex equipment and will need to be able to concentrate and pay attention to details for long periods of time as patients' lives will depend on your skills. You will need to be able to work as part of a team, follow instructions accurately, take responsibility and be able to remain calm and work quickly under pressure.

Working conditions

Critical care technologists mainly work as part of a team in the intensive care unit of a hospital using specialist equipment and machinery.

You will need to work to strict health and safety regulations ensuring that infections and diseases are safely contained.

You will need to work shifts on a rota basis, which includes nights, weekends and bank holidays.

The future outlook

This is a small but growing profession with opportunities within the NHS throughout the country. Job prospects are good as there is a shortage of applicants for job vacancies.

You may progress your career by applying for higher grades. The higher grade posts involve more responsibility for managing and training others.

Many critical care technologists are involved in research and teaching, as well as in practice.

Qualifications and courses

- There are no formal entry requirements, but most hospitals expect a good general education and may prefer 4 GCSEs/S grades (A–C/1–3). Critical care technology is moving towards becoming a degree-entry career.
- Many candidates enter with higher qualifications, for example A levels, Advanced Highers or a BTEC National qualification in science subjects or electronics.
- Degrees in life sciences, science, maths or electronics are a good grounding for this type of work. A degree in physiological measurement is available.
- Trainee technicians follow a 2-year training programme based in a hospital with day-release to a local college. Qualifications include a BTEC National Certificate in Science: Medical Physics and Physiological Measurement or NVQ/SVQ Level 3 in Medical Physics and Physiological Measurement.
- Apprenticeships/Skillseekers may be available to those between the ages of 16 and 24.

CRCI:JF

CLCI:JOB

Other related opportunities

- Audiologist p269
- Healthcare Assistant p284
- Operating Department Practitioner p294
- Radiographer p305

Advantages/disadvantages

- Working under pressure in emergency situations is emotionally and physically demanding.
- It is extremely rewarding to help patients recover.
- You will have a varied working day, be using your technical skills and have contact with patients.

Earnings guide

- The NHS sets pay rates for critical care technologists (on the sterile services technician pay scale).
- Critical care technologist trainees earn up to £17,257 per year. Once qualified and with experience this rises to £25,424.
- Specialists can earn up to £31,779.
- As a team manger you could get £36,112.
- There are extra payments available, for example if you work in London.

Further information

www.cityandguilds.com/myperfectjob

Skills for Health
2nd floor
Goldsmiths House
Broad Plain
Bristol
BS2 0JP
0117 922 1155
www.skillsforhealth.org.uk
office@skillsforhealth.org.uk

NHS Careers
0845 60 60 655
www.nhscareers.nhs.uk

Society of Critical Care Technologists
6 South Bar
Banbury
Oxfordshire
OX16 9AA
023 8079 6123
www.criticalcaretech.org.uk

Dental

What the work involves

Dental hygienist

- Dental hygienists aim to improve the oral health of their patients. As a hygienist, your duties will include scaling and polishing patients' teeth, and advising them about how to look after their teeth and gums.

Dental nurse

- Dental nurses help dentists in their work. You will carry out a range of tasks such as taking notes for patient records, preparing mixtures for fillings, processing X-rays and passing instruments to the dentist during treatments.

Dental technician

- Dental technicians make crowns, bridges, dentures and braces for dental patients. You will use impressions of a patient's teeth and gums to make each fitting. You will work with a range of materials such as gold, porcelain and plastic.

Dental therapist

- Dental therapists carry out many of the same duties as hygienists, but they are also qualified to do straightforward dental treatments such as simple fillings and the removal of decayed baby teeth. Most of your work is likely to be with children, older people and people with special needs.

Dentist

- Dentists examine patients' teeth and gums to find out if there are any problems. They will decide what needs to be done and then carry out the treatment. The work includes drilling teeth, filling cavities, removing decayed teeth and fitting dentures.

Orthodontist

- Orthodontists are dentists with specialist training who can treat complex cases such as crooked or missing teeth or problems with the jaw. Much of their work involves improving the appearance of teeth and includes fitting and adjusting braces.

The type of person suited to this work

All dental professionals must have excellent manual skills and good eyesight to use instruments carefully and accurately in patients' mouths. You should also be caring and patient and able to reassure people who are often anxious about treatment.

Dental nurse
Dental nurses need to be able to follow instructions and have a sympathetic manner for dealing with patients who might be nervous or in pain.

Dental technician
Dental technicians use laboratory equipment in their work and finish each fitting by hand, so you will need excellent manual skills and good eyesight. You must also pay attention to detail, because each fitting must be made perfectly to suit each patient.

Working conditions

Dental practitioners work in local dental surgeries, clinics and hospitals. You may also visit schools and people's homes. Many dentists are self-employed.

You may work a normal working week, but you may also need to work evenings or weekends and to be on call to carry out emergency work.

Most roles involve working closely with patients, advising them and working on their teeth. You will spend much of the time on your feet and should be able to concentrate for long periods.

You will use specialist equipment to undertake patient treatment and will need excellent manual skills.

The future outlook

The number of dentists has increased in recent years so it is becoming more competitive but there are still shortages of NHS dentists and job prospects are good. Many dentists are self-employed.

Dental hygienist

This is a growing career with a shortage of qualified staff so prospects are good. You could become a practice manager or go on to train others.

Dental nurse

There is a lack of dental nurses across the UK, so prospects are good. You could go on to specialise in an area such as orthodontic nursing. You could also go into a management role or take further qualifications to become a dental hygienist or dental therapist.

Dental technician

There is competition for jobs but a shortage of qualified staff in some areas. Dental technicians normally specialise in creating one kind of fitting, such as braces. You may progress to senior technician grades.

Dental therapist

This is a growth area with competition for training places but a shortage of trained staff. You could specialise or go into training or research.

Dentist

Most dentists work in local surgeries and do a mixture of NHS and private work. With experience, dentists often go on to become a partner in a practice or buy their own practice.

Hospital dentists usually specialise in an area of dentistry such as surgery or children's dentistry and, with postgraduate qualifications, can become consultants.

You could go into research or teaching in a university and there are also opportunities to work within the armed forces or in industry.

Orthodontist

You could work in a dental practice or set up your own business. There are also opportunities for orthodontists in hospitals and community clinics. With a good level of experience, you could go on to train others in orthodontics.

CRCI:JC | CLCI:JAF

Qualifications and courses

entry level

To both enter and train while working in this career, you will need qualifications at Level 1–8. Please refer to explanation on page vii.

Dental hygienist

- To qualify, dental hygienists must obtain a Diploma in Dental Hygiene or Combined Diploma in Dental Hygiene and Dental Therapy. Applicants must be at least 18 to start training. After qualifying, they must enrol with the General Dental Council.
- Entry requirements for a Diploma are typically 5 GCSEs/S grades (A–C/1–3), including English language and a science, and either a recognised dental nurse qualification or 2 A levels/three H grades.

Dental nurse

- There are no formal academic entry requirements to start work in a dental practice or clinic, but a good general education is normally required. GCSEs/S grades or equivalent in English and biology are an advantage.
- In order to practise, dental nurses must be registered with the General Dental Council (GDC). Registration requires the National Certificate of the National Examining Board for Dental Nurses, NVQ/SVQ Level 3 in Oral Healthcare, or a Certificate of Proficiency in Dental Nursing awarded by a recognised dental hospital.

Dental technician

- Dental technicians must be registered with the General Dental Council. To qualify for registration, one of the following qualifications is required: BTEC National Diploma in Dental Technology, Foundation degree or degree in dental technology, or SQA HNC in Dental Technology. Entry to a National Diploma, HNC or foundation degree requires 4 GCSEs/S grades (A–C/1–3), including English, maths and science, or equivalent.
- Entry to a dental technology degree requires 2 A levels/4 H grades or equivalent; appropriate prior learning and experience may also be acceptable.

Dental therapist

- Dental therapists must be registered with the General Dental Council in order to practise. To qualify for registration, a Diploma in Dental Therapy or Combined Diploma in Dental Hygiene and Dental Therapy is required.
- Candidates for the Diploma require 5 GCSEs/S Grades (A–C/1–3) including English, maths and a science, and either 2 A levels/4 H grades or equivalent, or a nationally recognised dental nurse qualification.

Dentist

- A degree from a dental school is needed to qualify as a dentist in the UK. Entry requirements for the degree are high, typically 3 science A levels (AAA–ABB) or 5 H grades (AAAAB), including chemistry, or equivalent. Candidates also normally require GCSE/S grade (A–C/1–3) English, and many dental schools ask for physics, maths and biology at this level. A standard dental degree takes 5 years full time.
- A degree incorporating a 1-year pre-dental course may be available for applicants without the required science qualifications.

Orthodontist

- All orthodontists are qualified dentists. After qualifying as a dentist, you will need to study for the Diploma of Member of the Faculty of Dental Surgery (MFDS); this takes at least 2 years.
- After achieving the MFDS, you will need a place on an orthodontic training scheme, which lasts 3 years, and combines academic study with clinical training in a hospital. You will then take the Membership in Orthodontics (MOrth) exam to qualify as an orthodontist. Orthodontists wishing to enter hospital consultancy work need to train for 2 further years towards the Fellowship of Dental Surgery in Orthodontics (FDS Orth).

Other related opportunities

- Doctor p278
- Healthcare Assistant p284
- Nurse p289

Advantages/disadvantages

- Dentistry is not for you if you think you would be uncomfortable working with unhealthy teeth and gums.
- It is satisfying to be able to play a part in improving patients' oral health and to free them from any pain.
- If based in a dental practice, you will have patients who you will see regularly.
- Dental practitioners can work nearly anywhere in the country, often at hours to suit them.
- This career area provides opportunities to work overseas or be self employed.

Earnings guide

- Salary levels in the NHS may be subject to change due to the Agenda for Change programme.

Dental hygienist

- Dental hygienists earn around £18,600–£25,000 per year in the NHS. This can rise to £30,000–£35,000 with experience. Earnings can be much higher in private practice.

Dental nurse

- Training rates vary but are around £9,000–£14,500 per year. Dental nurses in the NHS get around £14,033–£16,799 per year when first trained. With experience, this rises to around £19,730. Top earners with staff responsibilities get up to £30,000. Wages in private practice vary widely depending on the employer.

Dental technician

- Dental technicians can earn up to around £24,000 a year once qualified. With experience and further qualifications or as a specialist you can earn over £35,000.

Dental therapist

- NHS dental therapists earn from £16,500 per year when starting to over £30,000 with experience. They can earn more in private practice.

Dentist

- Dentists working in NHS dental surgeries start on around £28,000 per year when qualified. At senior levels salaries can be over £80,000.
- Hospital dentists start on £25,800+ per year as a house officer. This can rise to £96,000+ for consultants.

Orthodontist

- Orthodontists working within the NHS can earn £35,000+ per year. Salary levels are usually higher in private practice.

Further information

City & Guilds

www.cityandguilds.com/myperfectjob

Skills for Health
2nd floor
Goldsmiths House
Broad Plain
Bristol
BS2 0JP
0117 922 1155
www.skillsforhealth.org.uk
office@skillsforhealth.org.uk

General Dental Council
37 Wimpole Street
London
W1G 8DQ
0845 222 4141
www.gdc-uk.org
ces@gdc-uk.org

NHS Careers
0845 60 60 655
www.nhscareers.nhs.uk

DENTAL HYGIENIST
British Society of Dental Hygiene and Therapy
3 Kestrel Court
Waterwells Business Park
Waterwells Drive
Gloucester
GL2 2AT
01452 886365
www.bsdht.org.uk

DENTAL TECHNICIAN
Dental Technologists Association
Waterwells Business Park
Waterwells Drive
Gloucester
GL2 2AT
0870 243 0753
www.dta-uk.org
sueadams@ta-uk.org

DENTAL NURSE
British Association of Dental Nurses
PO Box 4
Room 200
Hillhouse International Business Centre
Thornton-Cleveleys
FY5 4QD
0870 211 0113
www.badn.org.uk
admin@badn.org.uk

DENTAL THERAPIST
British Association of Dental Therapists
www.badt.org.uk

DENTIST
British Dental Association
64 Wimpole Street
London
W1G 8YS
020 7935 0875
www.bda.org
enquiries@bda.org

ORTHODONTIST
12 Bridewell Place
London
EC4V 6AP
020 7353 8680
www.bos.org.uk

Dietitian

What the work involves

- Dietitians use their scientific knowledge of food to provide information and advice about diet and nutrition.
- As a dietitian, you will give advice to a broad range of people, such as hospital patients, caterers, sports professionals and the general public.
- You will help people improve their health and prevent disease by making changes in their diet.
- Dietitians prevent and treat food-related disorders, illnesses and diseases. Some work in industry developing food products and others in the media.

The type of person suited to this work

Dietitians need to be able to develop expert knowledge of the science of nutrition and how the body works. They must also have excellent communication skills to be able to give practical information and advice to a range of people from school children to food manufacturers.

If you are working with patients, you will need to be caring, supportive and non-judgemental, and able to understand the needs and issues of individual patients. You should also be able to motivate people so that they can follow your advice and make the changes that you recommend.

Working conditions

You may work in a range of locations such as hospitals, laboratories, offices and sports centres.

You are likely to work a normal working week from Monday to Friday, although in hospitals you may be called in to work at weekends and on bank holidays.

In most jobs you will be working directly with patients who can be ill, distressed or reluctant to take your advice.

The future outlook

The British Dietetic Association (BDA) has over 5000 members, and the profession is growing. There are opportunities across the UK and abroad but jobs can be competitive.

A lot of dietitians work in the NHS, but there are also many opportunities in areas like sports nutrition, the food and pharmaceutical industries, scientific research, education and journalism. You could become self-employed working as a consultant or seeing private clients.

In the NHS, you could go on to specialise in areas such as cancer care, or with particular groups such as children or the elderly. You could also move into management.

entry level

4–8

To both enter and train while working in this career, you will need qualifications at Level 4–8. Please refer to explanation on page vii.

Qualifications and courses

- To become a dietitian, an approved degree or postgraduate qualification (PgDip/MSc) in dietetics or human nutrition and dietetics is required. You must then register with the Health Professionals Council in order to practise in the NHS. You will need 2–3 A levels/3 H grades including chemistry and another science and 3 GCSEs/S grades (A–C/1–3) including English and maths, or equivalent, for entry to a degree in dietetics.
- Entry requirements for a postgraduate diploma are typically an Honours degree in a science subject with an acceptable level of biochemistry and human physiology, along with a good command of spoken and written English.
- Mature applicants can complete an Access course in science to be accepted into a degree programme.
- Some institutions expect applicants to have visited a dietetic department before applying for a place.

CRCI:JG

CLCI:JAV

Other related opportunities

- Complementary Health Practitioner p271
- Health Promotion / Education Specialist p281
- Scientist p486

Advantages/disadvantages

- People may be unable or unwilling to take on your advice, which can frustrating.
- It is rewarding to see improvements in people when they put into practice the information and advice you have given them.

Earnings guide

- Starting salary for an NHS dietitian is around £19,683, rising to £25,424 per year.
- Salaries for senior grade dietitians can be £28,313–£37,326.
- A district chief dietitian can earn up to £43,335 and a consultant £50,000+.
- There are higher grades for chief members of staff, or for work outside the NHS. There are also additional payments available, for example if you work in London.

Further information

Skills for Health
2nd floor
Goldsmiths House
Broad Plain
Bristol
BS2 0JP
0117 922 1155
www.skillsforhealth.org.uk
office@skillsforhealth.org.uk

NHS Careers
0845 60 60 655
www.nhscareers.nhs.uk

British Dietetic Association
5th Floor Charles House
148–9 Great Charles Street
Queensway
Birmingham
B3 3HT
0121 200 8080
www.bda.uk.com
info@bda.uk.com

Doctor

What the work involves

General practitioner (GP)

- General practitioners (GPs) diagnose people's health problems in local communities. A GP's job involves talking to and examining patients to find out what is wrong with them and then deciding on the best course of treatment. This might include giving advice, prescribing medicine or referring patients to a specialist hospital doctor for further tests.

Hospital doctor

- Hospital doctors diagnose patients' health problems by talking to them and carrying out tests. Once you have diagnosed a patient's problem, you will then recommend or provide treatment. As a hospital doctor, you will specialise in one of around 60 possible areas such as accident and emergency medicine, psychiatry or paediatrics.

Surgeon

- Surgeons operate on patients in hospital operating theatres. Your work will also include diagnosing problems, talking to and advising patients and checking them after surgery. As a surgeon, you will specialise in operating on specific conditions or diseases, or particular parts of the body, such as the heart.

The type of person suited to this work

As a doctor you must be interested in science and able to absorb a lot of information and use your knowledge and skills to diagnose and solve problems. You should be caring, with excellent communication skills to work as part of a team and listen carefully to patients and explain their conditions and treatments simply and clearly. You will have to take responsibility, work accurately under pressure and be able to cope with work that is physically and emotionally demanding. You will be dealing with drugs and technical equipment so should be able to concentrate and pay attention to detail. You will also need to be good with your hands for carrying out treatments, particularly if you want to become a surgeon.

Working conditions

General practitioner (GP)

GPs are based within general practices in towns and rural areas. They see patients from all backgrounds with a huge range of problems. The work can be stressful and demanding.

GPs usually work Monday to Friday, covering Saturday surgeries on a rota. They may be on an on-call rota, visiting people at home at nights, weekends and bank holidays.

Hospital doctor

You will work with a team of healthcare professionals based in a hospital department such as, accident and emergency, neurology or cardiology.

Hours can be long, you will work shifts and be on an on-call rota. Again, the work can be stressful and physically and emotionally demanding.

Surgeon

You will work in a hospital department for your specialist field. You will deal with patients on the wards as well as in the operating theatre.

Surgeons usually work on a shift basis and also on an on-call rota.

The future outlook

Throughout the UK most opportunities are with the NHS. You can also work in private hospitals, the pharmaceutical industry or in teaching and research. There is a shortage of doctors so prospects are good. There is usually a lot of competition for consultant posts but recent changes to training should make progression easier.

Once qualified, you can specialise further in particular areas of work. It is also possible to work abroad, perhaps using your skills to help people in developing countries.

General practitioner (GP)

Changes in the way the healthcare system works means that it is likely that GPs will have more involvement with how health is promoted in their local communities in the future.

Qualifications and courses

- After the Foundation programme, GPs train for a further 3 years. They will then be awarded the Certificate of Completion of Training and entered on the GP register by the General Medical Council.
- A 4-year graduate entry degree is available for candidates with a first or good second-class degree in a relevant subject.
- Graduation is followed by the new 2-year Foundation Programme (combining the 1-year pre-registration house officer training with the first year of senior house officer training under the old system). Successful completion of the first year leads to full membership of the GMC. At the end of the second year, doctors decide which speciality to follow.

General practitioner (GP)

- To become a GP, doctors follow a 3-year Vocational Training Scheme (VTS). The training includes 1 to 2 years as a GP registrar and time with other specialisms. After this, a doctor is required to apply for the Joint Committee on Postgraduate Training for General Practice certificate to work as a GP.

Hospital doctor

- After the Foundation programme, hospital doctors train for up to 8 years depending on their chosen area of specialisation.
- Training leads to the Certificate of Completion of Training (CCT) and eligibility for entry on the GMC's Specialist Register. It then becomes possible to apply for work as a consultant.

Surgeon

- Initial training as a surgeon is gained as a senior house officer. This is followed by a further 5 to 7 years' training to become a specialist registrar, including higher surgical training in one of the nine surgical specialities. This leads to the Certificate of Completion of Training (CCT), and eligibility for entry on the GMC's Specialist Register. It then becomes possible to apply for work as a consultant.
- After 4 years' training, doctors can take the Intercollegiate Speciality exam leading to the Fellow of the Royal College of Surgeons Diploma. The Member of the Royal College of Surgeons (MRCS) Diploma is awarded on the completion of all levels of training.
- Surgeons can do research projects during training and obtain a higher degree (MD or ChM).

entry level

To both enter and train while working in this career, you will need qualifications at Level 4–8. Please refer to explanation on page vii.

Other related opportunities

- Anaesthetist p268
- Dental p275
- Nurse (Registered) p289
- Pathologist p297
- Psychiatrist p304
- Radiologist p306

Advantages/disadvantages

- The work can be very physically and emotionally demanding, especially during emergency situations or complex operations.
- It is fulfilling to be able to help patients and make a difference to people's lives.
- This career offers a lot of variety and the option of working in one of many specialist areas.
- You will have to undergo a long programme of education and training in order to gain the in-depth knowledge and skills required to be a doctor.
- The training is long and demanding and you will have to continue to learn and develop your skills and knowledge throughout your career.

Earnings guide

- Salary levels in the NHS have a national rate, but this can also vary in some areas.
- Most junior doctors and senior house officers earn around £32,000 in their first year of training, rising to £39,798 in the second. Doctors on specialist training can earn up to £67,000.
- Specialists with experience can earn up to £78,000.
- Consultants earn from £71,000 and with additional payments and merits it is possible for consultants to earn anything up to £161,000.

General practitioner (GP)

- Most GPs' salaries are around £80,000 to £120,000.
- Extra earnings may be available through private practice work. Working in the private sector you could earn higher salaries.

Further information

Skills for Health
2nd floor
Goldsmiths House
Broad Plain
Bristol
BS2 0JP
0117 922 1155
www.skillsforhealth.org.uk
office@skillsforhealth.org.uk

NHS Careers
0845 60 60 655
www.nhscareers.nhs.uk

British Medical Association
BMA House
Tavistock Square
London
WC1H 9JP
020 7387 4499
www.bma.org.uk

Royal College of General Practitioners
14 Princes Gate
Hyde Park
London
SW7 1PU
0845 456 4041
www.rcgp.org.uk
info@rcgp.org.uk

Environmental Health Practitioner / Officer

What the work involves

- Environmental health practitioners work to improve public health. Some are responsible for all aspects of environmental health in their local areas, while others specialise in either food safety, housing conditions, workplace health and safety, or environmental conditions (for example pollution).
- As an environmental health practitioner, your tasks might include developing public health policies, carrying out inspections in premises such as restaurants, houses and workplaces to identify any hazards and ensure that relevant laws are being followed, and educating and advising the public and businesses.

The type of person suited to this work

You must be interested in finding ways of improving public health, and will need a scientific and logical approach to work to collect and assess evidence and use it to identify and solve problems. Excellent written and verbal communication skills are vital for explaining regulations clearly and simply to a wide range of people from directors of large companies to members of the public.

You have to be able to handle challenging situations and deal with difficult people, for example when confronting noisy neighbours or investigating unsafe food. And you must be able to enforce the law when necessary.

You need to be comfortable working both alone and as part of a team.

Working conditions

You will be office-based, but spend a lot of time visiting homes and businesses such as restaurants and factories in your local area.

Some of the places you visit will be smelly, dirty or potentially dangerous and you will sometimes have to wear protective clothing.

You will probably work a normal working week from Monday to Friday, but you will occasionally need to work evenings and at weekends.

The future outlook

Job opportunities are good as there is a shortage of environmental health practitioners.

Most jobs are with local authorities, but you could also work for central government agencies such as the Food Standards Agency or Environment Agency, or for environmental protection consultancies, the NHS, holiday companies or the food industry.

With experience, you could progress to higher levels such as senior, principal or chief environmental officer. Self-employment and working abroad are also options.

4–8

entry level

To both enter and train while working in this career, you will need qualifications at Level 4–8. Please refer to explanation on page vii.

Qualifications and courses

- To become an environmental health officer, you will need a BSc or MSc in environmental science accredited by the Chartered Institute of Environmental Health (CIEH) or the Royal Environmental Health Institute of Scotland (REHIS). Entry to a first degree normally requires 2 A levels/3 H grades including a science subject, plus 5 GCSEs/S grades (A–C/1–3) including English, maths and science, or equivalent. Entry to the MSc requires a first degree in a relevant science or technology subject accredited by the CIEH or REHIS, or equivalent.
- In Scotland, candidates take the BSc Honours degree in Environmental Health at the University of Strathclyde. Entry requirements for this are 4 H grades/3 A levels including chemistry, maths and preferably physics and/or biology.
- Before qualifying as an environmental health officer, graduates must undertake a minimum of 48 weeks' practical training. Students complete a logbook of practical training accompanied by a portfolio of evidence, before taking a professional examination.
- In England and Wales, at least 50% of the training must be with a local authority. Training can be incorporated into a first degree through a sandwich year, and entrants are often part-sponsored by local authorities. Successful completion of all the training requirements leads to the Environmental Health Officers' Registration Board Certificate and graduate membership of the CIEH.
- In Scotland, the whole of the training period must be with a local authority, supervised by REHIS. Training may be undertaken during university holidays or after graduation. Successful completion of all the training requirements leads to the REHIS Diploma in Environmental Health.

Other related opportunities

- Health and Safety Adviser p19
- Health Promotion / Education Specialist p281
- Meat Inspector p445
- Road Safety Officer p583
- Trading Standards Officer p460

Advantages/disadvantages

- It can be challenging dealing with people who are angry, for example when enforcing regulations.
- You will have the satisfaction of protecting the health and safety of people and improving their quality of life.
- You may have to face some distressing sights.

Earnings guide

- Starting salaries are around £25,000+ per year for local authority environmental health officers. This can increase to around £30,000 with experience.
- Senior staff can earn over £60,000 a year.
- Salaries in the private sector vary. Environmental health officers working for private companies may earn more than those in local authorities, but this is not always the case.

Further information

Chartered Institute of Environmental Health
Chadwick Court
15 Hatfields
London
SE1 8DJ
020 7928 6006
www.cieh.org

Royal Environmental Health Institute of Scotland
3 Manor Place
Edinburgh
EH3 7DH
0131 225 6999
www.rehis.org
contact@rehis.com

Environment Agency
National Customer Contact Centre
PO Box 544
Rotherham
S60 1BY
08708 506 506
www.environment-agency.gov.uk
enquiries@environment-agency.gov.uk

CRCI:JD

CLCI:COP

Health Promotion / Education Specialist

What the work involves

- Health promotion/education specialists aim to promote public health. You could work with organisations such as schools or directly with individuals, groups or communities or could be developing community policies.
- Your work might include advising individuals on how to make lifestyle changes such as taking more exercise or giving up smoking, encouraging organisations like workplaces, schools and hospitals to improve diets and promote health, and developing partnerships with communities to improve public health.

The type of person suited to this work

As a health promotion/education specialist you will need to be able to encourage and motivate individuals and communities. Good communication and negotiation skills are important for working with people from school children to community members and policy makers.

You should be able to research information, write clear reports and think of imaginative ways to encourage people and organisations to make changes. You will need to be understanding, supportive and non-judgemental and able to relate to the needs and problems of a wide range of people, communities and cultures. You will also have to have good organisational skills to run and manage projects.

Working conditions

You may work in a range of locations such as health centres, local authority buildings, hospitals, workplaces and fitness centres.

You are likely to have a normal working week from Monday to Friday. Some employers offer flexible working schemes.

The job often involves travel to and attendance at meetings, for example at local schools or community groups.

The future outlook

There are around 2000 health promotion specialists in the UK and public health is a priority for the government. Jobs can be very competitive though and you will probably need to do work experience.

Most health promotion/education specialists work for the NHS, health promotion agencies, local authorities, or in social and community settings. You can progress to management roles or go into research and lecturing in health promotion.

entry level

4–8

To both enter and train while working in this career, you will need qualifications at Level 4–8. Please refer to explanation on page vii.

Qualifications and courses

- Entrants to this field need a degree. This can be in any discipline, but courses in health promotion, health studies, public health, social science, environmental health or related subjects provide an advantage. Entry requirements for degrees are usually a minimum of 2 A levels/3 H grades. More senior posts generally require a postgraduate diploma or MSc in Health Promotion.
- It may be possible to train on the job for recognised qualifications. The Open University offers certificates in Health Promotion and Promoting Public Health: Skills, Perspectives and Practice. Some colleges run a Health Studies Access Course, which gives candidates the entry requirements needed to study in higher education.
- It is possible to enter the profession through related fields. It is advisable to undertake relevant voluntary work in order to gain experience.
- The Society of Health Education and Health Promotion Specialists (SHEPS) maintains a voluntary register for specialists in this field, and recommends degree and postgraduate courses to its members.

CRCI:J

CLCI:JOZ

Other related opportunities

- Dietitian p277
- Environmental Health Practitioner / Officer p280
- Health and Safety Adviser p19
- Nurse (Registered) p289

Advantages/disadvantages

- Changing people's habits can be difficult and take a long time.
- Seeing improvements in public health when people put into practice the information and advice you have provided is very rewarding.
- This job can provide the chance to work with many different people.

Earnings guide

- Pay varies among employers.
- In the NHS starting salaries when qualified are £19,683–£25,424 per year.
- More experienced and senior staff can earn up to £36,000 and managers £60,000+.
- With some employers, there may be extra payments available, for example if you work in London.

Further information

Skills for Health
2nd floor
Goldsmiths House
Broad Plain
Bristol
BS2 0JP
0117 922 1155
www.skillsforhealth.org.uk
office@skillsforhealth.org.uk

Faculty of Public Health
4 St Andrews Place
London
NW1 4LB
020 7935 0243
www.fphm.org.uk
enquiries@fph.org.uk

NHS Careers
0845 60 60 655
www.nhscareers.nhs.uk

Society of Health Education and Health Promotion Specialists
School of Health and Policy Studies
UCE
Birmingham
B42 2SU
0121 331 5511
www.hj-web.co.uk/sheps

Health Records Clerk

What the work involves

- Health records clerks prepare and maintain records of patients and information about their care.
- They also file the records and retrieve them when other members of hospital staff need them.
- As a health records clerk, you will organise and maintain paper and electronic records.
- You might also have other tasks such as making appointments and working at a reception desk to direct patients to different parts of the hospital.

The type of person suited to this work

Health records clerks need to be efficient, well organised and able to pay attention to detail, so that records are kept and filed correctly. You must also be discreet and responsible as you will be dealing with confidential information.

Good communication skills are important so that you can deal with patients, answer phone queries and work well as part of a team with other hospital or surgery staff.

You should be able to stay calm in busy situations as this job can get very pressured. ICT skills are essential. You will also need to be motivated and able to concentrate on work which can be repetitive.

Working conditions

You will probably work in a hospital or surgery, and may be based in an office, record storage area or ward. You may work alone or be part of a team.

You are likely to work a normal working week from Monday to Friday, but you may need to work shifts including nights, weekends and bank holidays.

The job involves working with detailed information and organising and maintaining computer and paper-based records.

The future outlook

There are plenty of opportunities for health records clerks across the UK and the number of members of the Institute of Health Record and Information Management (IHRIM) is increasing. However, you should check with hospitals in your area, as job prospects vary in different parts of the UK.

Most health records clerks work for the NHS or private hospitals.

Health records clerks may progress to junior, then senior management roles. It may also be possible to move into careers with patient contact. Alternatively, you may choose to use your administrative/information management skills in similar areas of work outside of healthcare.

entry level

1–2

To both enter and train while working in this career, you will need qualifications at Level 1–2. Please refer to explanation on page vii.

Qualifications and courses

- There are no set entry qualifications to become a health records clerk. However, employers usually ask for 5 GCSEs/S grades (A–C/1–3) including English and maths, or equivalent qualifications such as NVQ/SVQ Levels 1–2 in Administration.
- Administrative experience and keyboard skills are useful.
- Training is usually on the job, with supervision by experienced staff. You will learn about the operation of hospital administrative systems and how to maintain records.
- Apprenticeships/Skillseekers may be available for candidates aged 16–24.
- Whilst in the post you may work towards qualifications awarded by the Institute of Health Record and Information Management (IHRIM). The Institute offers Certificates of Technical Competence at basic and supervisory level, and a professional Certificate and Diploma. Health records clerks can also take the National Clinical Coding Qualification (UK).

CRCI:JE

CLCI:CAL

Other related opportunities

- Clerk p12
- Court Administrative Officer p335
- Receptionist p25
- Secretary p28

Advantages/disadvantages

- The work can be repetitive and demanding at busy times.
- This job is an important part of providing patients with a good level of care.
- There are opportunities for progression and jobs available in most areas.

Earnings guide

- Health records clerks starting in the NHS can expect £12,182–£13,253 per year. With experience this can rise to £15,107.
- Admissions clerks start at £12,577 and this rises with experience.
- Clinicical coding clerks can start at £14,437 rising to £17,257.
- Supervisors may earn up to £25,000.
- There are also higher grades if you move into management. Extra payments are available, for example if you work in London.

Further information

www.cityandguilds.com/myperfectjob

Skills for Health
2nd floor
Goldsmiths House
Broad Plain
Bristol
BS2 0JP
0117 922 1155
www.skillsforhealth.org.uk
office@skillsforhealth.org.uk

NHS Careers
0845 60 60 655
www.nhscareers.nhs.uk

Institute of Health Record and Information Management
141 Leander Drive
Castleton
Rochdale
OL11 2XE
01706 868481
www.ihrim.co.uk
ihrim@zen.co.uk

Health Service Manager

What the work involves

- Health service managers are responsible for the delivery of healthcare services. For example, you may run a hospital or be responsible for managing a section of the hospital, such as surgery or medicine.
- You could work in a specialist role such as human resources or financial management, or you might oversee the delivery of services in a whole regional health authority.
- As a health service manager, your tasks might include managing staff, organising day-to-day work, setting budgets and allocating resources.

The type of person suited to this work

Health service managers need to have a range of management skills. You will need to be able to plan delivery of services, organise work, solve problems as they arise, analyse financial information and plan projects.

Good verbal and written communication skills are important for working with colleagues at all levels and for report writing. If you specialise in a particular area, such as information technology or purchasing, you will also need skills specific to that role.

You should be committed to delivering a high level of healthcare to patients and able to take responsibility and make difficult decisions.

Working conditions

You are likely to be based in an office, but you may need to travel to meetings, so a driving licence is useful.

You will work normal working hours from Monday to Friday, but will probably have to work longer hours and may have to be on call in the evenings and at weekends on a rota basis.

This role often involves managing people, which can be very demanding.

The future outlook

There are opportunities for health service managers all over the UK, mainly within the NHS. The NHS Graduate Scheme recruits graduates to intensive training schemes in General Management, Human Resources and Finance. Competition for entry to these schemes is fierce.

There are also jobs available in private hospitals and with the Armed Forces.

With experience, you can progress to more senior posts. You will usually need higher management or specialist qualifications to gain promotion and will probably have to move area.

Experienced health service managers can go on to become consultants or use their skills to enter other management careers outside of healthcare.

entry level

4–8

To both enter and train while working in this career, you will need qualifications at Level 4–8. Please refer to explanation on page vii.

Qualifications and courses

- It is possible to join the NHS at an administrative level and progress into management. Entry at this level is usually with at least 4 or 5 GCSEs/S grades (A–C/1–3) or equivalent. Many health service managers enter the profession from other roles in the NHS having gained sufficient experience and qualifications. Others gain managerial experience elsewhere before progressing into the NHS.
- You can apply for a place on one of the NHS graduate management training schemes. Entry to the schemes requires a 2.2 degree in any discipline or a postgraduate qualification. Some equivalent qualifications are acceptable.
- The General Management Training Scheme in England and the NHS Scotland Management Training Scheme last for 2 years and include two placements and a project, leading to a Master's in Healthcare Leadership and Management.
- The Financial Management Training Scheme lasts up to 40 months. It includes a number of work assignments and leads to a professional accountancy qualification with the Chartered Institute of Management Accountants (CIMA) or the Chartered Institute of Public Finance and Accountancy (CIPFA).
- The Human Resources Management Training Scheme lasts 2 year. It includes three placements and an elective assignment, and leads to a postgraduate diploma in Human Resources and graduate membership of the Chartered Institute of Personnel and Development (CIPD).

CRCI:JE

CLCI:CAL

Other related opportunities

- Human Resources/Personnel Officer p20
- Practice Manager (GP) p302

Advantages/disadvantages

- You will have to deal with a variety of tasks at once, so the work can be pressured and demanding.
- It is rewarding to know that you are playing an important role in delivering a high level of care to patients.
- You will gain valuable skills and the NHS offers a range of career options.

Earnings guide

- The starting salary for a health service manager is around £20,000 per year.
- Salaries for experienced managers vary according the type of job and level of responsibility. They can range from around £35,000–£60,000+.
- Chief executives can earn £100,000+.
- There are extra payments available, for example if you work in London.

Further information

Skills for Health
2nd floor
Goldsmiths House
Broad Plain
Bristol
BS2 0JP
0117 922 1155
www.skillsforhealth.org.uk
office@skillsforhealth.org.uk

NHS Careers
0845 60 60 655
www.nhscareers.nhs.uk

Institute of Healthcare Management
18–21 Morley Street
London
SE1 7QZ
020 7620 1030
www.ihm.org.uk
enquiries@ihm.org.uk

NHS Graduate Management Training Scheme
www.futureleaders.nhs.uk

Healthcare Assistant

What the work involves

- Healthcare assistants help to look after patients under the guidance of a nurse or other health professional.
- The job is very varied and your exact role will depend on where you work.
- You might be on a hospital ward making beds, taking temperatures and helping patients eat, wash and use the toilet.
- You could be in a particular department, such as chiropody, where you might cut toenails or apply simple dressings.
- Some healthcare assistants look after people in their own homes.

The type of person suited to this work

You will be providing hands on care so will need to be friendly, caring, sympathetic and sensitive. Listening and talking to patients is important, so you will need good communication skills and to be able to relate to people from all backgrounds who may be distressed, in pain or unable to communicate clearly. You should be able to work with confidential information and enjoy being part of a team.

You should be practical and good with your hands and must be physically fit to move and support patients. You should be observant and able to stay calm under pressure.

Working conditions

You will be based in hospitals or nursing homes or within the community visiting patients at home, when a driving licence may be required.

You will usually work shifts, including nights, weekends and bank holidays.

You will be working closely with patients which can be very rewarding but can also be tiring and emotionally and physically demanding.

You will have to wear a uniform.

The future outlook

Job prospects are good as this is a growing area of work and healthcare assistants are increasingly encouraged to gain qualifications and take on more responsibility.

Most employment is available with NHS hospitals throughout the UK. There are also opportunities with other employers such as private hospitals and nursing homes.

As you gain experience and qualifications you can progress on to nurse training, or to training in other professional health careers, such as occupational therapy. Your employer may pay your salary while you are training.

entry level

1

To both enter and train while working in this career, you will need qualifications at Level 1. Please refer to explanation on page vii.

Qualifications and courses

- There are no minimum entry qualifications for this work, but good literacy and numeracy are required.
- Some employers ask for exam passes or NVQs/SVQs in Care.
- Healthcare assistants are trained on the job, and may attend in-house training courses or short college courses. It is possible to work towards NVQ/SVQ Levels 2–4 in Care whilst working.
- Apprenticeships/Skillseekers may be available for candidates aged 16–24.

CRCI:JI

CLCI:JAD

Other related opportunities

- Ambulance p266
- Care Assistant p525
- Home Care Assistant p534
- Nurse (Registered) p289
- Occupational Therapy Support p293

Advantages/disadvantages

- You will be dealing with the intimate care of patients and the work can be distressing.
- It is rewarding to look after patients and make them feel comfortable.
- This job can offer a lot of variety and be the first step to a range of health careers.

Earnings guide

- The starting salary for an NHS healthcare assistant is about £12,500 per year.
- This rises to around £14,000 for a healthcare assistant with qualifications and experience.
- Salaries progress up to around £17,000 with an NVQ Level 3. Additional payments may be available if you work unsocial hours.
- Extra earnings are available, for example if you work in London.

Further information

Skills for Health
2nd floor
Goldsmiths House
Broad Plain
Bristol
BS2 0JP
0117 922 1155
www.skillsforhealth.org.uk
office@skillsforhealth.org.uk

NHS Careers
0845 60 60 655
www.nhscareers.nhs.uk

Hospital Play Specialist

What the work involves

- Hospital play specialists use play to entertain children and teenagers and help them to deal with their experiences in hospital.
- The work includes organising and leading play activities in a playroom or at patients' bedsides, using play to prepare children for treatments, diverting children's attention from unpleasant procedures, encouraging friendships and observing children's play to assess development.
- You may also work with severely disabled children.

entry level

3

To both enter and train while working in this career, you will need qualifications at Level 3. Please refer to explanation on page vii.

The type of person suited to this work

As a hospital play specialist, you should get on well with children and teenagers, and be caring and patient with them. You need to be sympathetic to the needs and issues of each child, have some understanding of medical conditions, and must be able to cope with distressing situations.

Enthusiasm and creativity are important for preparing and leading play activities and you will need to assess how children are developing.

You will need to be able to communicate well with a range of people, including children and parents, and be able to work well with other healthcare staff such as doctors, nurses, physiotherapists and occupational therapists.

Working conditions

Play specialists work in children's hospitals, children's wards and outpatients' clinics. You may take children on trips or may visit children in their homes, so you may need a driving licence.

You will probably work as part of a team with other play or medical staff.

You will need to be fit and active and may have to work weekends and bank holidays.

The future outlook

Most employment is available with NHS hospitals throughout the UK and there is currently an increase in the number of posts available nationally. There are also opportunities with other employers such as hospices and community paediatric teams.

Employment opportunities vary locally. For example, there are more vacancies in areas that have large children's hospitals.

You may progress to senior positions such as senior hospital play specialist or play coordinator.

Qualifications and courses

- The minimum age for entry is 20, and maturity is seen as an advantage.
- To become a qualified hospital play specialist, you will need the Edexcel BTEC Professional Development Diploma in Specialised Play for Sick Children and Young People, approved by the Hospital Play Staff Education Trust (HPSET). This is offered at selected colleges. Applicants must have an appropriate qualification in a subject such as childcare, nursery nursing, drama or music therapy, occupational therapy, teaching or social work, and at least 3 years' recent experience of working with children in a group setting.
- For those students not working in a hospital setting, a 200-hour practical experience placement will be undertaken as part of the programme.
- To achieve registration as a hospital play specialist, all HPSET requirements must be met.
- It is possible that qualified hospital play specialists may be able to access Foundation degree courses following this programme of study.

CRCI:J

CLCI:J

Other related opportunities

- Childminder p528
- Nurse (Registered) p289
- Nursery Nurse p538
- Play Worker p180
- Therapist p309

Advantages/disadvantages

- The work can be physically and emotionally demanding.
- It can be very rewarding to help sick children to enjoy themselves and cope with being ill or in hospital.

Earnings guide

- The National Association of Hospital Play Staff (NAHPS) sets recommended salary rates, but employers are able to set their own.
- Hospital play specialists earn around £16,835–£20,261 per year.
- At team leader level you could expect to earn £19,683–£25,424 and as a team manager you can get £23,458–£31,779.
- At team leader level you could expect to earn £19,683–£25,424 and as a team manager you can get £22,458–£31,779.
- Extra earnings may be available, for example if you work in London.

Further information

Skills for Health
2nd floor
Goldsmiths House
Broad Plain
Bristol
BS2 0JP
0117 922 1155
www.skillsforhealth.org.uk
office@skillsforhealth.org.uk

NHS Careers
0845 60 60 655
www.nhscareers.nhs.uk

National Association of Hospital Play Staff
www.nahps.org.uk

Hospital Play Staff Education Trust
PO Box 1153
Postwick
Norwich
NR13 5WQ
01603 700353
www.hpset.org.uk

Hospital Porter

What the work involves

- Hospital porters transport patients, equipment and other items to where they need to go within the hospital.
- One of your main tasks would be to move frail and ill patients between departments and wards, while keeping them safe and comfortable. You will transport patients using wheelchairs and trolleys.
- You may also have a variety of other tasks such as delivering mail and moving medical equipment and supplies.

entry level

To both enter and train while working in this career, you will need qualifications at Level 1. Please refer to explanation on page vii.

The type of person suited to this work

Hospital porters need to be responsible and reliable with a positive attitude to make sure that people and equipment are transported to the correct part of the hospital on time. You will need to learn special techniques for lifting and handling patients and equipment, and should be able to follow instructions and work well as part of a team.

Patients may be distressed or in pain so you must be caring and sympathetic and be able to reassure them and keep them comfortable.

Physical fitness is important, because you will walk long distances during your shift and you will have to lift and move patients and equipment.

Working conditions

You will work with patients and other staff, mainly indoors, although you may need to travel to other hospital sites to make deliveries.

You will need to pay attention to health and safety when lifting and handling people and equipment.

Porters usually wear a uniform and often need to work shifts, which includes working nights, weekends and bank holidays.

The future outlook

Most jobs are within NHS hospitals, although there are also posts within private hospitals. There are opportunities throughout the country but they can be competitive in some areas.

With experience you could become a supervisor and then take management qualifications for promotion to head porter or porter manager. You could also do further training to move into related careers, such as healthcare assistant or ambulance work.

Qualifications and courses

- There are no formal entry requirements for this job, but applicants must be literate and have good all-round communication skills.
- There is no set minimum age, but most applicants are at least 18 years old, and there are good opportunities for mature entrants.
- Candidates usually have to pass a medical examination, and may be required to take a physical fitness test.
- Experience of volunteer hospital portering work, or of paid or voluntary work in another area of healthcare or another job that involves contact with the public, can be useful.
- A driving licence may be required.

CRCI:J

CLCI:JOZ

Other related opportunities

- Ambulance p266
- Healthcare Assistant p284
- Hotel Porter p96
- Kitchen Porter p99

Advantages/disadvantages

- The work can be physically demanding and stressful at times.
- You will meet people and the job is active and busy.
- It is satisfying to play a vital role within a hospital; without porters a hospital would not be able to function.

Earnings guide

- The NHS sets national pay rates for hospital porters.
- Earnings start at around £12,182–£13,253 per year.
- With experience this can rise to around £15,523. Team leaders can get up to £17,257.
- Extra payments are available, for example for working extra hours.

Further information

www.cityandguilds.com/myperfectjob

Skills for Health
2nd floor
Goldsmiths House
Broad Plain
Bristol
BS2 0JP
0117 922 1155
www.skillsforhealth.org.uk
office@skillsforhealth.org.uk

NHS Careers
0845 60 60 655
www.nhscareers.nhs.uk

Medical Laboratory Assistant

What the work involves

- Medical laboratory assistants support the work of biomedical scientists who analyse patients' medical samples to diagnose illnesses.
- As a medical laboratory assistant, you will carry out a variety of tasks, which might include sorting and labelling tissue samples, sterilising and disinfecting equipment, making up chemical solutions, separating blood serum and plasma from samples, maintaining laboratory stocks, recording laboratory information and using computers to analyse information.

entry level

To both enter and train while working in this career, you will need qualifications at Level 1–2. Please refer to explanation on page vii.

Qualifications and courses

- There are no formal entry requirements for this job, but 4 or more GCSEs/S grades (A–C/1–3) in English, maths and a science,or an equivalent qualification such as a BTEC First Diploma in Applied Science may be an advantage.
- Most training is done on the job under the supervision of experienced senior colleagues. Laboratory assistants can work towards qualifications such as NVQs/SVQs in Clinical Laboratory Support, or Laboratory and Associated Technical Activities.

The type of person suited to this work

Medical laboratory assistants need a careful, methodical approach to their work. You should be able to concentrate and pay attention to detail as mistakes can be critical.

You will also have to follow instructions and set procedures and work accurately under pressure to meet deadlines.

You should be good at practical, scientific tasks such as preparing chemical solutions, sorting and analysing samples and keeping detailed records. You will work in a team with other laboratory assistants and biomedical scientists so will need good communications skills.

Working conditions

Most medical laboratory technicians work in pathology laboratories within hospitals, but some work directly with patients.

You will need to work safely in the laboratory and wear protective clothing, such as a lab coat and gloves.

You are likely to work a normal working week from Monday to Friday, but could have to work outside of normal hours.

The future outlook

The demand for medical laboratory assistants varies. Most employment is available in NHS hospitals. There is similar work available with private hospitals, research and university laboratories and government research departments.

You may specialise in one area of the work such as haematology (study of blood), or move to a related career such as pharmacy technician. To train as a clinical or biomedical scientist you will need to study for a relevant degree.

CRCI:JF

CLCI:JAX

Other related opportunities

- Laboratory Technician p481
- Pharmacy Technician p298
- Phlebotomist p300

Advantages/disadvantages

- The work can be repetitive and you will probably need more qualifications to progress.
- You will be performing an important part of a hospital's medical work, because you will be helping to diagnose patients' illnesses.

Earnings guide

- As a trainee you would start at around £12,577–£15,523 per year.
- With experience this rises to £16,853–£20,261.
- With experience, and in management, you can expect to get around £30,000+.

Further information

Skills for Health
2nd floor
Goldsmiths House
Broad Plain
Bristol
BS2 0JP
0117 922 1155
www.skillsforhealth.org.uk
office@skillsforhealth.org.uk

NHS Careers
0845 60 60 655
www.nhscareers.nhs.uk

Institute of Biomedical Science
12 Coldbath Square
London
EC1R 5HL
020 7713 0214
www.ibms.org
mail@ibms.org

www.cityandguilds.com/myperfectjob

Medical Physicist

What the work involves

- Medical physicists have expert knowledge of the techniques and equipment used to diagnose and treat disease. For example, you would deal with X-ray diagnosis, radiography, ultrasound, infrared and radio-frequency radiation, and measurements of pressure and temperature in the body.
- This is a very varied career. You might design, develop and maintain equipment, and advise medical staff on its use.
- Your role may also involve patient contact, explaining procedures or supervising the doses of radiation for treatment.

entry level

To both enter and train while working in this career, you will need qualifications at Level 4–8. Please refer to explanation on page vii.

The type of person suited to this work

Medical physicists need to have a strong interest in science and want to use their skills and knowledge to solve problems and improve the diagnosis and treatment of disease.

You should have research skills, be able to work accurately and take responsibility for decisions which will have a direct effect on patients. You will need good communication skills to explain complex procedures clearly and simply to patients, and to work as part of a team.

You must also be prepared to keep up with the latest developments and continue to learn new skills.

Working conditions

Most medical physicists work in hospitals and laboratories and some have contact with patients on wards or in clinics.

You will need to work safely with the equipment and chemicals in the laboratory, some of which can be hazardous.

You are likely to work a normal working week from Monday to Friday, but may have to work outside normal hours and may have to travel to conferences.

The future outlook

The number of medical physicists is increasing although trainee posts are competitive and you may have to relocate for some specialist roles.

Most jobs are in the larger NHS hospitals throughout the UK. There are also some opportunities in the medical equipment industry, private hospitals and medical research institutes.

Within the NHS there is a recognised career path and you could even reach consultant level. Employment in the private sector is less structured.

Qualifications and courses

- Candidates will need a 1st or 2.1 degree in a physical science or engineering subject, such as physics, medical physics, electrical engineering, medical engineering, or computer engineering. Entry to a relevant degree course requires at least 2 A levels/ 3 H grades, plus 5 GCSEs/S grades (A–C/1–3), including English and maths, or equivalent qualifications. In practice, 3 A levels/4 H grades may be required. It is almost essential for medical physicists to have physics and maths at A level/H grade, or equivalent qualifications.
- An MSc, PhD or industrial experience may also be useful.
- Candidates go into the profession as Grade A trainees. The training programme lasts 2 years, and includes study for an MSc in medical physics. Successful completion of Grade A training also leads to the Diploma of the Institute of Physics and Engineering in Medicine (IPEM). Candidates may then apply for a Grade B post.
- Grade B medical physicists undertake 2 years of training in a specialist field. On completion, they are eligible for registration with the Health Professional Council to work in the NHS. Grade B also leads to Corporate Membership of the IPEM.

CRCI:JF

CLCI:JOB

Other related opportunities

- Engineer: Professional p205
- Radiographer p305
- Scientist p486

Advantages/disadvantages

- Some parts of the work may be routine at times.
- You will be playing an important role in the overall healthcare of the patients, because you will be contributing to the diagnosis and treatment of their diseases.

Earnings guide

- As a trainee you could expect a salary between £19,683 and £25,424 per year.
- With several years' experience and with training, you could earn around £35,000 per year.
- Senior posts can have a salary of around £50,000–£60,000+.
- Rates in the private sector are similar.

Further information

Skills for Health
2nd floor
Goldsmiths House
Broad Plain
Bristol
BS2 0JP
0117 922 1155
www.skillsforhealth.org.uk
office@skillsforhealth.org.uk

NHS Careers
0845 60 60 655
www.nhscareers.nhs.uk

Institute of Physics and Engineering in Medicine
Fairmount House
230 Tadcaster Road
York
YO24 1ES
01904 610821
www.ipem.ac.uk
office@ipem.ac.uk

Nurse (Registered)

What the work involves

Adult nurse

- As an adult nurse you would care for adult patients with a variety of illnesses and injuries. Your duties would include assessing need and planning care, giving medicines and injections, changing dressings and monitoring patients' conditions (for example checking blood pressure).

Children's nurse

- Children's nurses care for babies and children aged up to18. Although the duties you will carry out are similar to those for adult nurses, the patients you work with are very different. The bodies and minds of babies and children work in different ways to those of adults. Your job will involve an understanding of their particular needs, and you will also work closely with the children's families.

District nurse

- District nurses care for patients in the community. They usually work in people's own homes or in other locations such as nursing homes and health centres. Your tasks will be similar to those of a nurse in a hospital, but you may also have more of a role in teaching patients and their families how to administer healthcare themselves.

Health visitor

- Health visitors work in the community, seeing patients in their own homes and in health centres. You will promote healthcare by educating, advising and counselling people. For example, you may be advising new mothers on how to look after themselves and their babies, or supporting someone who wants to give up smoking.

Learning disability nurse

- Learning disability nurses work with people with learning disabilities to teach and support them to live as independently as possible. You will work with people in a range of locations such as people's own homes, residential care homes and schools. Your job will include helping people with everyday tasks such as dressing, making tea, going shopping, budgeting or bringing up a family.

Mental health nurse

- Mental health nurses care for people with mental health problems in hospitals and in the community. You will help patients to overcome or cope with their illness, so they can lead as normal a life as possible. Your role will include listening to patients, helping them to find ways of coping with their problems, and involving friends, family and other professionals in patients' care.

Midwife

- Midwives work in hospitals, clinics and people's homes. As a midwife, your role will include helping a pregnant woman and her partner prepare for the birth of their baby, monitoring the pregnancy, delivering the baby and offering support and advice to the parents after the birth.

Occupational health nurse

- Occupational health nurses look after the health of people at work. Your job might include giving advice on healthy working conditions and using equipment safely, training people in First Aid, carrying out health assessments and helping people who are returning to work after illness or injury.

School nurse

- School nurses look after the health of children in schools. This involves carrying out health checks on pupils, delivering health education, supporting parents and helping pupils to cope with their health problems. You may be based in one school or make visits to a number of schools.

Qualifications and courses

entry level

To both enter and train while working in this career, you will need qualifications at Level 2–8. Please refer to explanation on page vii.

Adult nurse/children's nurse/ learning disability nurse/mental health nurse

- All nurses must be registered with the Nursing and Midwifery Council. There are two main routes to professional registration: the diploma or the degree.
- Nursing diplomas are usually studied full time over 3 years. Candidates must normally have 5 GCSEs/S grades (A–C/1–3), preferably including English and a science subject or equivalent. Minimum age of entry is 17 years and 6 months in England (17 in Scotland, 18 in Northern Ireland and Wales) upon commencement of the course.
- Nursing degrees (BN/BNurs/BA/BSc) usually take 3 or 4 years of full-time study. Typical entry requirements are 2–3 A levels/H grades, possibly including a biological science, and 5 GCSEs/S grades (A–C/1–3) including English, or equivalent. Shortened degrees are available for graduates in health-related or biological science subjects. It is sometimes possible for diploma students to top up their qualifications to degrees by undertaking further study after registration.
- Some institutions offer a route to nurse registration for graduates in health-related or biological science subjects. The postgraduate diploma in nursing is studied over 2 years full time.
- Candidates with few or no formal qualifications may be able to enrol on a Nurse Cadet scheme, a 2-year training programme leading to a pre-registration nursing programme.
- You will choose which of the four branches of nursing you want to specialise in during your nursing course.

Midwife

- All midwives must be registered with the Nursing and Midwifery Council. There are three main routes to professional registration: the diploma, the degree, or a shortened course for qualified nurses.
- Midwifery diplomas are usually studied full-time over 3 years. Candidates must normally have 5 GCSEs/S grades (A–C/1–3), preferably including English, maths and a science subject. Minimum age of entry is 17 years and 6 months in England (17 in Scotland, 18 in Northern Ireland and Wales) upon commencement of the course.
- Midwifery degrees (BMid/BMidwif/BA/BSc) usually take 3 or 4 years of full-time study. Typical entry requirements are 2–3 A levels/H grades, preferably including a science subject, and 5 GCSEs/S grades (A–C/1–3) including English, maths and science or equivalent. It is sometimes possible for diploma students to top up their qualifications to degrees by undertaking further study after registration.
- Shortened midwifery diplomas and degrees are available for registered nurses. These courses are studied full time for 18 months.

District nurse/health visitor/ occupational health nurse/school nurse

- Entrants to these nursing specialisms must already hold a nursing qualification (DipHE or degree) and be registered with the Nursing and Midwifery Council (NMC).
- To qualify as a district nurse, health visitor, occupational health nurse or school nurse, you need to study part time towards a relevant diploma or degree. In addition to being a registered nurse, you will usually need at least 2 years' post-registration experience, and may require 120 academic credits at Level 1 for a diploma and 120 at Level 2 for a degree.

The type of person suited to this work

You will spend most of your time with patients from all backgrounds and with a wide range of problems, disabilities and illnesses. They could be very distressed so you will need to be non-judgemental, caring and sympathetic, with excellent communication skills, able to follow instructions and work in a team. You should be observant and will need to listen to your patients, assess their needs and monitor their progress. You will need to be practical and sensitive as you will be giving injections, using equipment and helping patients with things like washing and toileting.

You must be able to take responsibility and remain calm in an emergency.

Working conditions

You could be based in a hospital, clinic or in the community and may need a driving licence for some jobs.

Working hours are usually 37.5 hours a week. Most nurses work shifts, which includes working at nights, at weekends and on bank holidays.

This can be physically and emotionally demanding work. You could be lifting or leaning over patients and be on your feet for much of the day.

Some of your work will be unpleasant and distressing and involve preparing patients for surgery or providing post-operative or general care, for example changing dressings, cleaning up and making beds.

The future outlook

You will need relevant work experience and entry to training for children's nurse and midwifery is particularly competitive.

Most employment is available with NHS and private hospitals throughout the UK. There are also opportunities with other employers such as private nursing homes, businesses, schools and the armed forces. Nursing agencies also provide short-term and longer-term work opportunities.

With experience, you may move up the grades to more senior positions, leading teams of nurses and other staff. Some nurses move into high-level management positions. Alternatively, you could eventually become a nurse consultant, with expertise in a clinical area. There are also opportunities to carry out research or move into training nurses.

Other related opportunities

- Ambulance p266
- Counselling Work p529
- Doctor p278
- Health Promotion / Education Specialist p281
- Healthcare Assistant p284
- Hospital Play Specialist p285
- Therapist p309

Advantages/disadvantages

- Nursing can be stressful and emotionally and physically demanding.
- However, you will get great satisfaction from reducing suffering and improving the health of patients in your care. Working as part of a team of healthcare professionals can also be very rewarding.
- In general, patients and communities value the work of nurses.
- When people are unwell they can become rude, aggressive, frightened and difficult. You will have to learn to deal with all types of behaviour.

Earnings guide

- The starting salary for a newly qualified nurse in the NHS is £19,683–£25,424 per year.
- With experience or as a specialist you could earn around £23,458–£37,326 per year.
- As a modern matron you could get up to £43,335 per year.
- Nurse consultants may earn up to £62,402 per year.
- Extra earnings are available, for example if you work at nights or weekends, or if you work in London. Many nurses supplement their pay by undertaking agency work covering shifts in areas where there is staff shortage due to holidays or sickness.

Further information

Skills for Health
2nd floor
Goldsmiths House
Broad Plain
Bristol
BS2 0JP
0117 922 1155
www.skillsforhealth.org.uk
office@skillsforhealth.org.uk

NHS Careers
0845 60 60 655
www.nhscareers.nhs.uk

Royal College of Nursing
20 Cavendish Square
London
W1G 0RN
020 7409 3333
www.rcn.org.uk

Nursing & Midwifery Council
23 Portland Place
London
W1B 1PZ
020 7637 7181
www.nmc-uk.org

Here's Maxine Holder-Critchlow's story:

CRCI:JI

CLCI:JAD

Nursing Assistant

Maxine started her career as a qualified Nursery Nurse and went on to work for a series of nurseries while being employed by an agency. The agency asked Maxine to go and help out the nurses at the famous children's hospital Great Ormond Street (GOS) who had a very heavy workload. Initially, she was responsible for entertaining the children, taking them down to the X-ray department or to have scans, and bottle- or tube-feeding the babies. Her manager decided it would be better if she worked with the long-term patients, and she became an Associate Carer or Nursing Assistant learning to care for patients with tracheotomies and even accompanying them on visits home. The longer she stayed the more experienced she became, and when she reached the point where she was on the highest level of pay for an Associate Carer she decided to train to be a nurse. She has just started her training at South Bank University in London, and in 3 years she will qualify as a Registered Children's Nurse (RCN).

WHAT MAXINE LOVES ABOUT NURSING

'The best part is if you have been nursing a child who has been really poorly and they come back to the ward and ask to see you, and you realise the difference in them, just how well they have become – that's what makes the job worthwhile. I'm getting to do the thing I love the most and that is working with children.'

Although she is enjoying her training, Maxine says she does miss being at the hospital and is really looking forward to her upcoming 6-week block release placement at GOS.

'It's really interesting because before I only had the practical experience; now with what I am learning it is all making sense to me – now I know why I do what I do.'

WHAT YOU NEED TO MAKE A SUCCESS OF NURSING

'First and foremost you have to want to do it; your heart must be in it because the biggest downside of this business is if one of your patients doesn't make it – that is the hardest, hardest thing and some people can't take that. You need to be very kind, very patient with people, and you have to be very understanding and have good listening skills. Nursing is hard work and you are on your feet a lot but you get so focused on what you are doing you look at the clock and think "where has the time gone?".'

In 5 years' time Maxine would like to be an S Grade nurse, which is a Senior Staff Nurse, because then she would have the opportunity to actually take charge of a ward, and she wants to further her career by doing more training in order to keep up with new procedures.

'Being black myself, I want to be a role model to other black nurses to show them that they can attain the top positions in nursing.'

Occupational Therapist

What the work involves

- Occupational therapists help people overcome physical, psychological or social problems arising from illness or disability. They focus on what patients can achieve, rather than on their disabilities helping them with everyday tasks like washing or cooking so that their lives are as full and independent as possible.
- Your job will include writing treatment plans, giving advice on practical issues such as disability equipment, teaching coping strategies and using activities to stimulate clients.

entry level

To both enter and train while working in this career, you will need qualifications at Level 4–8. Please refer to explanation on page vii.

The type of person suited to this work

You must enjoy working with people as your clients will have a range of problems and could be difficult, anxious or unpredictable. You will need to be practical, creative and good at solving problems. You also have to be patient, caring, and sensitive to your clients' needs, concerns and expectations.

You will need good communication skills for listening and talking to clients and their families and to work effectively in a team. You have to be able to encourage and motivate your clients, and be observant so that you can assess them and monitor their progress.

Working conditions

You may work in a variety of locations, such as hospitals, people's own homes, residential homes and workplaces. A driving licence may be useful.

Most occupational therapists work a normal working week from Monday to Friday, although you may have to work evenings and weekends.

Working with clients can be emotionally demanding and physically tiring.

The future outlook

This is a growing profession but competition for jobs can be high and you will need relevant work experience for entry to degrees.

Employers include NHS and private hospitals, local authorities, charities and voluntary agencies and equipment companies. You may also work in private practice. UK-qualified occupational therapists may also work overseas.

With experience, you could gain promotion to more senior positions or move into teaching or research.

Qualifications and courses

- To become an occupational therapist, you need a degree or postgraduate diploma in occupational therapy approved by the College of Occupational Therapists. You must also be registered with the Health Professional Council in order to practise in the NHS. For entry to a degree course, you will normally need 2 A levels/3 H grades including a science, preferably biology, human biology or psychology and 5 GCSEs/S grades (A–C/1–3), or equivalent.
- A degree in occupational therapy normally takes 3 years. An accelerated 2-year diploma programme is available for graduates in other subjects who have experience in health or social care.
- In-service courses are available for those employed as occupational therapy support workers or technical instructors. Courses are studied part time on a day-release basis and lead to professional qualification as an occupational therapist.

Other related opportunities

- Art Therapist p309
- Counselling Work p529
- Health Promotion / Education Specialist p281
- Nurse (Registered) p289
- Occupational Therapy Support p293
- Physiotherapist p301
- Therapist p309

Advantages/disadvantages

- The work can be emotionally and mentally demanding.
- It is very rewarding to be able to help people to overcome difficulties and achieve their goals.
- You could specialise in a variety of areas such as rehabilitation, learning disability or paediatrics.

Earnings guide

- After qualifying you can earn between £19,683 and £25,424 per year.
- With experience this can rise to around £31,779.
- Senior grade occupational therapists earn up to £37,326, with consultants earning more.

Further information

Skills for Health
2nd floor
Goldsmiths House
Broad Plain
Bristol
BS2 0JP
0117 922 1155
www.skillsforhealth.org.uk
office@skillsforhealth.org.uk

NHS Careers
0845 60 60 655
www.nhscareers.nhs.uk

British Association/College of Occupational Therapists
106–114 Borough High Street
London
SE1 1LB
020 7357 6480
www.cot.org.uk

Occupational Therapy Support

What the work involves

- Occupational therapy support workers assist occupational therapists and work directly with clients helping them to overcome physical, psychological or social problems that arise from illness or disability.
- You might help clients find new ways of dealing with everyday tasks such as washing, dressing and cooking after an accident or illness. You will also monitor clients' progress, write reports and help the occupational therapist to plan treatment.

entry level

To both enter and train while working in this career, you will need qualifications at Level 1–2. Please refer to explanation on page vii.

The type of person suited to this work

You must enjoy working closely with a wide range of people with a variety of problems. You have to be patient and caring, and be able to see things from your clients' points of view. You will need good communication skills for listening and talking to clients and you have to be encouraging and motivating to help them reach their potential.

Practical skills are important for carrying out activities such as cookery. You will also need good observational skills to be able to record your clients' progress.

You should enjoy working in a team with other healthcare staff, including occupational therapists.

Qualifications and courses

- There are no set entry requirements for this role, but a good standard of education is required. Experience of working with people may also be an advantage.
- Four GCSEs/S grades (A–C/1–3), including maths, English and a science subject, or equivalent qualifications, may be required for more advanced work.
- Qualifications and experience in anatomy, physiology and body massage, or an NVQ/SVQ Level 2 in Care or Health and Social Care, (formerly known as NVQ/SVQ in Care) may be useful.
- Training will generally be done on the job by senior staff.
- NVQ Level 3 in Health: Allied Health Profession Support or SVQ Level 3 in Health and Social Care are available for people working in this area.

Working conditions

You may work in a wide variety of locations, such as hospitals, people's homes and residential homes and will work closely with an occupational therapist. A driving licence may be useful.

Most occupational therapy support staff work a normal working week from Monday to Friday, and can often work part time.

This is a practical job which can be physically and emotionally demanding.

The future outlook

The demand for occupational therapy support workers varies locally, so contact employers for information.

The demand for occupational therapy support workers varies locally, so contact employers for information.

You could go on to train as an occupational therapist by taking a degree in occupational therapy either full time or whilst you are employed as a support worker.

CRCI:JG | CLCI:JAR

Other related opportunities

- Healthcare Assistant p284
- Hospital Play Specialist p285
- Nurse (Registered) p289
- Occupational Therapist p292

Advantages/disadvantages

- The work can be emotionally demanding at times because you need to deal with clients' frustrations.
- It is very satisfying to help your clients achieve their goals and improve their lives.

Earnings guide

- The starting salary for an occupational support worker is around £12,577–£15,523 per year.
- With experience and NVQ qualifications you can get around £17,257.

Further information

www.cityandguilds.com/myperfectjob

Skills for Health
2nd floor
Goldsmiths House
Broad Plain
Bristol
BS2 0JP
0117 922 1155
www.skillsforhealth.org.uk

NHS Careers
0845 60 60 655
www.nhscareers.nhs.uk

British Association/College of Occupational Therapists
106–114 Borough High Street
London
SE1 1LB
020 7357 6480
www.cot.org.uk

Operating Department Practitioner

What the work involves

- Operating department practitioners work alongside surgeons, anaesthetists and other staff before, during and after operations.
- As well as playing a vital role in the preparation of the operating theatre, you will be involved with assessing and monitoring the well-being of patients before, during and after surgery.
- Your role will include preparing equipment and drugs, transferring patients to operating theatres and passing instruments and dressings to surgeons during operations.

entry level

3

To both enter and train while working in this career, you will need qualifications at Level 3. Please refer to explanation on page vii.

Qualifications and courses

- Entry into this work requires a Diploma of Higher Education (DipHE) in Operating Department Practice approved by the Health Professions Council (HPC). Courses are available throughout the UK and generally last 2 years. The normal minimum entry requirements are 5 GCSEs/S grades (A–C/1–3) preferably in English, maths and/or a science based subject or equivalent, but some institutions may require AS levels or A levels/H grades.
- The minimum age for entry is 18, and adult entry is common. Access courses may be taken prior to diploma programmes.
- Entrants often have experience of other types of hospital work, for example as a healthcare assistant, and apply to become operating department practitioners later.

The type of person suited to this work

Operating department practitioners need the scientific knowledge and practical skills to prepare specialist equipment and drugs. You will be helping with operations so cannot be squeamish.

It is important to pay close attention when monitoring patients because their lives depend on it. You must be able to react quickly and accurately if the patient experiences any complications.

You will talk and listen to patients before and after operations, so must be caring and sensitive. You will also need good communication skills to follow instructions and work well as part of a team with other medical staff.

Working conditions

You will mainly work in operating theatres, anaesthetic areas and recovery rooms in hospitals.

You will need to follow hygiene procedures closely and wear a sterile gown and gloves during operations and be able to stand for long periods.

You will usually work shifts which may include working at nights, at weekends and on bank holidays. You may also have stand-by or on-call duties.

The future outlook

There is a growing area of work and there is a shortage of trained operating department practitioners, so job prospects are excellent. Most employment is available with the NHS throughout the UK and there are also opportunities in private hospitals.

You could progress into higher grade posts which involve more responsibility for managing and training others. There are also opportunities to enter research or teaching.

CRCI:J

CLCI:JOZ

Other related opportunities

- Ambulance p266
- Critical Care Technologist p274
- Healthcare Assistant p284
- Sterile Services Technician p308

Advantages/disadvantages

- The work can be stressful at times and it's important not to be squeamish as you will see some unpleasant things.
- It is rewarding to be part of a team improving people's health and saving lives.
- You could work in a range of areas, such as resuscitation, intensive care or day surgery.

Earnings guide

- Starting salaries for qualified staff with the NHS are around £16,853–£20,261 per year.
- With experience you can earn up to £31,779 per year.

Further information

Skills for Health
2nd floor
Goldsmiths House
Broad Plain
Bristol
BS2 0JP
0117 922 1155
www.skillsforhealth.org.uk
office@skillsforhealth.org.uk

NHS Careers
0845 60 60 655
www.nhscareers.nhs.uk

College of Operating Department Practitioners
197–199 City Road
London
EC1V 1JN
0870 746 0984
www.aodp.org
office@codp.org.uk

Optician

What the work involves

- Dispensing opticians use prescriptions from optometrists to supply and fit glasses. The work includes measuring the patient's face to ensure the glasses will fit and advising on lenses and frame styles to suit them and their prescription.
- The optician checks the finished glasses meet the original specifications and supplies them to the patient and will also do repairs.
- Some dispensing opticians take further training to supply and fit contact lenses.

The type of person suited to this work

You will need to be able to develop the scientific knowledge needed to interpret prescriptions.

You will need good communication skills to listen and talk to patients of all ages and backgrounds when advising them, and to work well in a team with other staff such as optometrists.

Manual skills are important for taking measurements and for adjusting and repairing glasses.

If you run your own opticians business, you will also need sales and business skills.

Working conditions

Most dispensing opticians work in high-street opticians. Some run their own practices so have to deal with the financial and management challenges of being self-employed.

You may work 35–40 hours a week from Monday to Friday, but will probably have to work on Saturdays as well (with some time off during the week instead).

The future outlook

This is a growing field with most dispensing opticians working for high-street companies. There is also some work available in hospitals.

With experience, you may specialise, for example in supplying and fitting contact lenses or low vision aids.

You may also be promoted into a management position within a high-street optical chain. With experience, some opticians choose to run their own practices. Success in this depends on a good choice of location and strong business skills.

entry level

To both enter and train while working in this career, you will need qualifications at Level 2–8. Please refer to explanation on page vii.

Qualifications and courses

- The only route into this role is through professional qualifications.
- In order to practise as a dispensing optician, you must be registered with the General Optical Council (GOC). To qualify for full registration, you must complete an appropriate training course, pass the Professional Qualifying Examinations of the Association of British Dispensing Opticians (ABDO), and undergo a pre-registration year working under the supervision of a qualified optician.
- There are a number of training routes available. It is possible to study full time before starting work. You could take a 3-year degree course in optical management, ophthalmic dispensing, or a related area. Alternatively, 2-year diploma courses or Foundation degrees in ophthalmic dispensing are available. Typical entry requirements for a degree or Foundation degree are 2 A levels/3 H grades, normally including relevant science subjects, and 5 GCSEs/S grades (A–C/1–3) including English, or equivalent. For a diploma, you will normally need at least 5 GCSEs/S grades (A–C/1–3) including English, maths and a science, or equivalent.
- It is also possible to start work as a trainee with a qualified optometrist and work towards part-time qualifications. ABDO offers a 3-year distance learning course and certain colleges offer a 3-year day-release programme for those in suitable employment. Typical entry requirements are 5 GCSEs/S grades (A–C/1–3) including English, maths and a science, or equivalent. ABDO runs a series of Access courses for those lacking these qualifications.
- ABDO also offers a Continuing Education and Training (CET) scheme for qualified opticians.

Other related opportunities

- Dental p275
- Optometrist p296
- Pharmacy p298

Advantages/disadvantages

- It can be stressful having to meet sales targets in some opticians.
- If you enjoy combining scientific knowledge with working with the public, this job could be good for you.

Earnings guide

- Salary levels vary enormously and are usually higher for opticians with management responsibility for an outlet within an optical chain.
- Starting salaries are around £14,000 per year which can rise to around £30,000 per year.
- Some dispensing opticians can earn up to £80,000.

Further information

Skills for Health
2nd floor
Goldsmiths House
Broad Plain
Bristol
BS2 0JP
0117 922 1155
www.skillsforhealth.org.uk
office@skillsforhealth.org.uk

NHS Careers
0845 60 60 655
www.nhscareers.nhs.uk

Association of British Dispensing Opticians
199 Gloucester Terrace
London
W2 6LD
0207 298 5100
www.abdo.org.uk
general@abdo.org.uk

General Optical Council
41 Harley Street
London
W1G 8DJ
020 7580 3898
www.optical.org
goc@optical.org

Optometrist

What the work involves

- Optometrists examine patients' eyes for disease or abnormalities, and carry out sight tests.
- Your work will include using instruments to look into the eye, using various tests to check how well a patient can see, asking the patient questions about any problems, and placing lenses in front of the eye to work out a patient's prescription. You may also supply and fit glasses or contact lenses.
- Optometrists working in hospitals often deal with the more complex eye conditions.

entry level

To both enter and train while working in this career, you will need qualifications at Level 4–8. Please refer to explanation on page vii.

The type of person suited to this work

You will need to be able to pay close attention to detail and apply your scientific knowledge and skills in order to examine eyes accurately and diagnose problems correctly.

Manual skills are important for using instruments, handling lenses and fitting contact lenses.

You must also be able to listen and talk to patients of all ages when examining them and explaining procedures. You will need good communication skills to work as part of a team with other staff, such as dispensing opticians.

Working conditions

Optometrists work in high-street opticians and hospitals, in examination rooms which usually have no natural light and often have to be quite dark.

You will probably have a normal working week from Monday to Friday, but may need to work on Saturdays as well.

The future outlook

Job prospects are good but vary throughout the UK. You may work for a chain of opticians, an independent practice, or a hospital. You could also do related work with lens manufacturers.

With experience, you may specialise, for example in children's vision, low vision or contact lenses. You may choose to run your own practice. There are opportunities to move into research and university teaching.

Qualifications and courses

- The only route into optometry is through professional qualifications.
- The Professional Qualification Examination of the General Optical Council (GOC) is in two parts.
- Part 1 of the Professional Qualifying Examination involves gaining a degree.
- Accredited degrees are offered at several universities. Entry requirements may vary according to the institution. Candidates are normally expected to have 5 GCSEs/S grades (A–C/1–3), including English language, maths and physics or double award science, and 3 A levels/5 H grades including at least 2 from biology, maths, physics and chemistry, or equivalent.
- After graduation, new entrants must follow a pre-registration year of supervised clinical experience. Part 2 of the Professional Qualifying Examination is taken during the training year. After qualification, trainees are eligible to register with the GOC and as Members of the College of Optometrists.
- There are many advanced courses that allow qualified optometrists to specialise in other areas. Courses can include paediatric vision, vision therapy and sports vision.

CRCI:JJ

CLCI:JAL

Other related opportunities

- Dental p275
- Doctor p278
- Optician p295
- Physiotherapist p301

Advantages/disadvantages

- The work can be routine and repetitive at times.
- If you enjoy combining scientific knowledge with working with the public, this job could be good for you.
- Working closely with patients can be demanding.

Earnings guide

- Optometrists in private practice start on around £16,500 per year and can earn up to around £36,000 with experience, but salaries can be a lot higher.
- Qualified and experienced optometrists can earn up to £37,000 in NHS hospitals.
- Consultants can earn up to £75,000 in NHS hospitals and more in the private sector.

Further information

Skills for Health
2nd floor
Goldsmiths House
Broad Plain
Bristol
BS2 0JP
0117 922 1155
www.skillsforhealth.org.uk
office@skillsforhealth.org.uk

NHS Careers
0845 60 60 655
www.nhscareers.nhs.uk

General Optical Council
41 Harley Street
London
W1G 8DJ
020 7580 3898
www.optical.org
goc@optical.org

College of Optometrists
41–42 Craven Street
London
WC2N 5NG
020 7839 6000
www.college-optometrists.org
optometry@college-optometrists.org

Pathologist

What the work involves

- Pathologists are doctors who have undergone further training to specialise in pathology.
- As a pathologists you will detect and diagnose diseases and help to identify sources of disease and reduce the risk of it spreading further.
- You could work in one of many branches including haematology (studying diseases of the blood), histopathology (studying tissue samples removed for diagnosis, and determining cause of death by performing post mortems) and immunology (studying diseases and conditions of the immune system).
- You will spend a lot of time in a laboratory, but will also work directly with patients.

The type of person suited to this work

To be a pathologist you should be able to use your medical knowledge and training to diagnose patients' conditions accurately. You must have problem-solving skills and pay close attention to detail when carrying out laboratory assessments.

You need to be caring and interested in patients, with excellent communication skills to be able to listen to them carefully and explain their conditions and treatments in a clear, simple way. You should be able to make decisions and work well as part of a team with other medical staff such as doctors and biomedical scientists.

Becoming a pathologist involves a long programme of education and training in order to gain the in-depth knowledge and skills necessary.

Working conditions

You will normally work within a hospital as part of a medical team working both in a laboratory and with patients. You will need to work safely in the laboratory and wear protective clothing such as a lab coat and gloves.

Hours can be long and you will probably work shifts and be on an on-call rota, which includes working at nights, at weekends and on bank holidays.

The future outlook

Most pathologists work within the NHS throughout the UK. There are also opportunities in industry, working for private companies.

You may decide to specialise further in particular areas of the work such as forensic pathology or transfusion medicine. You may also move into academic work, carrying out research or teaching students.

There are also similar careers in pathology for clinical and biomedical scientists, but they do not treat patients.

entry level

4–8

To both enter and train while working in this career, you will need qualifications at Level 4–8. Please refer to explanation on page vii.

Qualifications and courses

- As for hospital doctors (see p 278), candidates complete a medical degree recognised by the General Medical Council (GMC).
- Following a medical degree and the 2-year Foundation programme, pathologists begin specialist training, which can last from 5–8 years.
- On completion of the training, pathologists are awarded the Certificate of Completion of Specialist Training (CCST), which enables them to work as consultants.

Other related opportunities

- Anaesthetist p268
- Doctor p278
- Nurse (Registered) p289
- Psychiatrist p304
- Radiologist p306
- Scientist p486

Advantages/disadvantages

- The work can be emotionally demanding because it includes dealing with patients who have life-threatening conditions.
- Your work can be vital in finding an accurate and early diagnosis for patients, which can help to save lives.

Earnings guide

- Salary levels in the NHS have a national rate, but this can also vary in some areas.
- Most junior doctors and senior house officers earn around £32,000 in their first year of training, rising to £39,798 in the second. Doctors on specialist training can earn up to £76,000.
- Specialists with experience can earn up to £78,000.
- Consultants earn from £71,000 and with additional payments and merits it is possible for consultants to earn anything up to £161,000.

Further information

Skills for Health
2nd floor
Goldsmiths House
Broad Plain
Bristol
BS2 0JP
0117 922 1155
www.skillsforhealth.org.uk
office@skillsforhealth.org.uk

NHS Careers
0845 60 60 655
www.nhscareers.nhs.uk

British Medical Association
BMA House
Tavistock Square
London
WC1H 9JP
020 7387 4499
www.bma.org.uk

Royal College of Pathologists
2 Carlton House Terrace
London
SW1Y 5AF
020 7451 6700
www.rcpath.org
info@rcpath.org

Pharmacy

What the work involves

Pharmacy technician

- Pharmacy technicians prepare, supply and dispense medicines and give advice on how to take them. They work under the supervision of a qualified pharmacist.
- Pharmacy technicians also monitor stocks of medicines, check expiry dates and reorder stock when necessary.

Pharmacist

- Pharmacists work in one of three areas: hospital, community or industry.
- Hospital pharmacists are responsible for buying, manufacturing, dispensing and supplying medicines for in-patients and out-patients. They work closely with other healthcare staff to make sure that patients receive the most appropriate treatment and the right dosage, and they provide advice to patients about their medicines.
- Community pharmacists work in high-street, local and rural pharmacies. They supply medicines either over the counter or following doctors' prescriptions and give advice on how to take them and any side effects they may have. They also give advice on general health issues such as giving up smoking.
- Industrial pharmacists work in the pharmaceutical industry, discovering, developing, manufacturing, testing and marketing new drugs.

Pharmacologist

- Pharmacologists study the effects of drugs on the body. As a pharmacologist, your work might include discovering, researching, developing and testing new drugs and medicines. You will study the actions of drugs in computer simulations, in cells and tissues, in animals and in human volunteers. You will measure the effectiveness, safety and duration of the effect of drugs on people.

The type of person suited to this work

If you work with patients or members of the public, you must be able to explain things simply and accurately. You must also be able to work in a team with other pharmacy staff.

You will need to use technical equipment and computers and pay close attention to detail. You will need to be able to work in a team and write accurate records and reports.

Pharmacist
Pharmacists need to use their scientific knowledge and problem-solving skills when preparing medicines for patients. Accuracy and attention to detail are essential for pharmacists and pharmacy technicians when selecting, preparing, measuring and labelling medicines.

Pharmacologist
Pharmacologists need to be able to analyse the effects of drugs accurately, so you must be able to carry out experiments carefully and methodically, and have good problem-solving skills. You need to be prepared to carry out some of the tests on animals and people.

Working conditions

You may work in locations such as pharmacy departments in hospitals, high-street pharmacies and pharmaceutical laboratories. You will need to wear protective clothing such as a lab coat and gloves.

Industrial pharmacists and pharmacologists normally have a typical working week from Monday to Friday. Pharmacists and pharmacy technicians in hospitals and community pharmacies often work some evenings and weekends on a rota.

The future outlook

There is good demand for pharmacists, pharmacy technicians and pharmacologists and shortages in some areas. Employers include NHS and private hospitals, community pharmacies, pharmaceutical companies and government departments.

Pharmacy technician

Pharmacy technicians can become specialists or move into management positions.

Pharmacist

With experience, hospital pharmacists may choose to specialise in areas such as production pharmacy (preparing medicines) or preparing radioactive medicines (which diagnose and treat disease). You may also choose to move into a teaching or management role.

Community pharmacists may become self-employed, owning and running their own pharmacies.

Industrial pharmacists may specialise in areas such as animal medicine or clinical trials.

There are increasing opportunities for pharmacists in Primary Care Trusts, the organisations that manage healthcare services and resources within each specific geographical area. This could involve helping develop services or working with individual general practices.

A small number of pharmacists go into education, teaching healthcare professionals.

Pharmacologist

Pharmacologists may specialise in a particular area of their work or move into a research or teaching role. Some are involved in the legal aspects of developing drugs or you could become a scientific journalist or train as a doctor.

CRCI:JK/TD | CLCI:JAG/QOB

Qualifications and courses

To both enter and train while working in this career, you will need qualifications at Level 1–8. Please refer to explanation on page vii.

Pharmacy technician

- There are no set entry qualifications for training as a pharmacy technician. In practice, though, employers often ask for at least 4 GCSEs/S grades (A–C/1–3), including English, maths and at least 1 science subject, or equivalent. Applicants need to be over 16 and have normal colour vision.
- Those already working in a pharmacy can follow a distance learning course offered by the National Pharmaceutical Association leading to NVQ Level 3 in Pharmacy Services, or work towards a part-time college course such as NVQ/SVQ Level 3 in Pharmacy Services, or BTEC/SQA National Certificate in Pharmacy Services. In Scotland, an HNC in Pharmaceutical Sciences is available for qualified pharmacy technicians with 2 years' experience. There is also an SQA National Certificate in Pharmaceutical Sciences which can be studied full time prior to entry.
- Apprenticeships/Skillseekers may be available to those aged 16–24.

Pharmacist

- The only route into pharmacy is through professional qualifications. It is necessary to gain a degree accredited by The Royal Pharmaceutical Society of Great Britain (RPSGB), leading to the Master of Pharmacy (MPharm) degree. Entry requirements are 5 GCSEs/S grades (A–C/1–3) or equivalent, including English and maths, and 3 A levels/4 H grades including chemistry and at least 1 other science (preferably biology). Equivalent qualifications such as National Diplomas and science-based Access courses may also be accepted, provided there is sufficient chemistry content, or a chemistry A level is offered alongside the qualification.
- Graduates must complete a pre-registration year of practical training in a community or hospital pharmacy and pass the RPSGB's registration examination. At least 6 months of this time must be spent in the community or hospital sector.
- Opportunities are available to study for postgraduate courses and further study is seen as an essential part of a pharmacist's career development.

Pharmacologist

- A degree is essential for entry to this profession. Many universities offer degrees in pharmacology, or pharmacology combined with another biological subject. Entry is also possible with a degree in a related subject such as biology, biochemistry or pharmacy.

The normal entry requirements for a pharmacology degree are 3 A-levels/3 or 4 H grades, normally including chemistry and at least 1 other science, together with 5 GCSEs/S grades (A–C, 1–3), including English and maths. Many people enter the profession with a postgraduate qualification, e.g. MSc in a related subject.

- Training is generally on the job and update courses are available through employers.
- It is possible to work as a technician in pharmacology, and there may be opportunities to study for a relevant science-based qualification such as a BTEC National Award in Science. NVQs/SVQs for technicians are available in Clinical Laboratory Support and Laboratory and Associated Technical Activities at Levels 2 and 3. Technicians may be able to gain enough qualifications to undertake a degree.

Other related opportunities

- Biochemist p467
- Biotechnologist p471
- Chemist p472
- Doctor p278
- Scientist p486

Advantages/disadvantages

- Some of the work may involve standing for long periods.
- Your work will help people in many ways, for example to prevent and treat diseases and illnesses, and to give relief from pain.

Pharmacy technician/pharmacist

- Working in the community can be demanding because it involves dealing with the public and working to time limits.

Pharmacologist

- Pharmacologists may be harassed by animal rights activists.

Earnings guide

- Salary levels in the NHS are set annually; those below are a guide only.

Pharmacy technician

- Pharmacy technicians in the NHS start at £14,037 per year. This increases to £16,405–£19,730 when qualified. Team leaders can earn up to £36,416. There are also extra payments available if you work in London.
- Earnings for pharmacy technicians outside the NHS may vary depending on the employer. They generally start on around £13,000 per year.

Pharmacist

- Hospital pharmacists in the NHS earn £19,166 in their pre-registration year. Qualified pharmacists earn £22,886–£31,004. Consultants can earn £73,000+.
- Earnings for community pharmacists start at around £25,000 a year. A pharmacist in a senior, managerial position may earn over £55,000.

Pharmacologist

- Earnings for pharmacologists start at around £23,500 per year. With experience you could earn around £28,000 and up to £70,000 if you are a manager. You will probably earn less if you work for a university. You can receive 25% extra in senior positions if you have a PhD.
- There are extra payments available, for example if you work in London.

Further information

Skills for Health
2nd floor
Goldsmiths House
Broad Plain
Bristol
BS2 0JP
0117 922 1155
www.skillsforhealth.org.uk
office@skillsforhealth.org.uk

NHS Careers
0845 60 60 655
www.nhscareers.nhs.uk

Royal Pharmaceutical Society of Great Britain
1 Lambeth High Street
London
SE1 7JN
020 7735 9141
www.rpsgb.org.uk
enquiries@rpsgb.org

National Pharmacy Association
Mallinson House
38–42 St Peter's Street
St Albans
Hertfordshire
AL1 3NP
01727 832161
www.npa.co.uk
npa@npa.co.uk

PHARMACOLOGIST

British Pharmacological Society
16 Angel Gate
City Road
London
EC1V 2PT
020 7417 0110
www.bps.ac.uk

PHARMACY TECHNICIAN

Association of Pharmacy Technicians UK
4th Floor
1 Mabledon Place
London
WC1H 9AJ
020 7551 1551
www.aptuk.org

CRCI:JK/TD CLCI:JAG/QOB

Phlebotomist

What the work involves

- Phlebotomists are specialist medical laboratory assistants who collect blood samples for analysis to help diagnose diseases. They take blood samples from patients as painlessly as possible, label them and make sure they are taken promptly and safely to a laboratory for examination.
- Some phlebotomists combine this work with the various other duties of a medical laboratory assistant within laboratories, such as sterilising equipment and maintaining laboratory stocks.

The type of person suited to this work

Phlebotomists need to be practical and good with their hands to take blood without harming the patient or disturbing nursing care. You will also have to work accurately and pay attention to detail to ensure that samples are taken and labelled correctly and not contaminated during collection, as this could affect results.

It is important that you are able to communicate well with a range of people from children to the elderly. Some people are scared of having their blood taken, so you need to be able to reassure them.

You will also need good communication skills to work well in a team with colleagues, such as other medical laboratory assistants and biomedical scientists (who analyse the blood samples that you collect).

Working conditions

You will carry out your work in hospital wards, out-patient departments and in the community. You will also spend time working in laboratories.

You will need to pay close attention to health and safety to prevent infection, and will wear a uniform and protective clothing such as gloves.

You are likely to work a normal working day during the week, but you may also need to work at weekends.

The future outlook

Most employment is available in NHS hospitals throughout the UK. There is also similar work available in the blood transfusion services, government research departments and university laboratories.

The demand for phlebotomists varies locally, so contact your local hospital for more information.

Although there is no route for phlebotomists to progress to a career as a biomedical scientist, you may be encouraged to gain the qualifications that you need to train as a biomedical scientist. You may also train to enter other areas of healthcare, such as nursing.

entry level

1–2

To both enter and train while working in this career, you will need qualifications at Level 1–2. Please refer to explanation on page vii.

Qualifications and courses

- There are no formal entry requirements for this job, but 4 or more GCSEs/S grades (A–C/1–3), English, maths and science, or equivalent, may be an advantage, and are essential for more advanced work.
- Training is usually done entirely on the job. After training, you may be awarded a Certificate of Competence, which will allow you to work without close supervision throughout the hospital. You will be trained to National Occupational Standards.
- Phlebotomists may be able to work towards related qualifications, such as NVQ/SVQ Medical Assistance Level 2 or City & Guilds Level 2 in Medical Assistance. The National Association of Phlebotomists offers short training courses and workshops.

CRCI:JF

CLCI:JAX

Other related opportunities

- Healthcare Assistant p284
- Medical Laboratory Assistant p287
- Nurse (Registered) p289
- Scientist p486

Advantages/disadvantages

- Some of your patients will be scared of blood and needles which can be stressful.
- It can be rewarding to work with patients and pay a vital role in helping to diagnose illnesses.

Earnings guide

- The NHS sets national pay rates for phlebotomists each year; those listed below are a guide only.
- Salaries start at £12,577 per year and generally go up to £15,523.
- Seniors can earn £16,853–£20,261. Managers can get up to £31,779.
- There are also extra payments available if you work in London.

Further information

Skills for Health
2nd floor
Goldsmiths House
Broad Plain
Bristol
BS2 0JP
0117 922 1155
www.skillsforhealth.org.uk
office@skillsforhealth.org.uk

NHS Careers
0845 60 60 655
www.nhscareers.nhs.uk

National Association of Phlebotomists
12 Coldbath Square
London
EC1R 5HL
020 7833 8784
www.phlebotomy.org
phlebotomy@btinternet.com

Physiotherapist

What the work involves

- Physiotherapists treat patients with problems affecting their muscles, bones, heart, circulation and lungs caused by accidents, illness and ageing.
- Your work will include assessing the patient and then planning and giving treatment. This might include exercise, movement, hydrotherapy, massage and manipulation. You will also educate people to prevent health problems.
- Physiotherapists focus on improving people's health and quality of life and work in many different areas, such as mental health, occupational health and intensive care.

The type of person suited to this work

You will be giving hands on treatment to a range of patients from premature babies to people in intensive care and the elderly so must be caring and sympathetic.

You must be able to communicate well with patients so that you can understand their needs, explain treatments, teach them exercises and encourage them to help themselves. You will also need good communication skills to work well in a team with other healthcare staff such as doctors and nurses.

Manual skills and physical fitness are important for carrying out treatments. An ability to assess and treat patients' conditions is necessary, so you have to be able to think logically and be able to apply your scientific knowledge and skills in a clinical setting.

Working conditions

You may work in a range of locations, such as hospitals, health centres, doctors' surgeries and people's homes.

You are likely to work a normal week from Monday to Friday, but, if you work in a private practice, you may need to work in the evenings or occasionally at weekends to treat people at times that are suitable for them. You may also need to be on an on-call rota for some jobs.

This job can be physically and emotionally demanding.

The future outlook

Physiotherapy is developing a wider role in public and community health. There is strong competition for places on degree courses and for junior positions. Once you are experienced though, employment prospects are very good, with a range of possible career areas. There are opportunities in NHS hospitals and GP surgeries, and in private hospitals, clinics and nursing homes.

Promotion prospects for qualified physiotherapists within the NHS are good and you could be applying for a more senior post within a couple of years.

With experience, you may specialise, for example in respiratory physiotherapy or care of the elderly, or you could move into a management position.

You may also decide to own and run your own clinic. If you want to set up a clinic in a particular area, you should make sure that there will be enough work available for you and any other physiotherapists already working there.

There are also opportunities to move into research and teaching in universities.

entry level

4–8

To both enter and train while working in this career, you will need qualifications at Level 4–8. Please refer to explanation on page vii.

Qualifications and courses

- To be state registered, physiotherapists must have a degree approved by the Health Professions Council. Those with an approved degree are eligible for membership of the Chartered Society of Physiotherapy. Full- and part-time courses are available. Candidates who wish to practise will have to undergo a police check.
- Minimum entry requirements for a degree are 5 GCSEs/S Grades (A–C/1–3), including maths, English and a science, plus 3 A levels/5 H grades, including a biological science. In practice, competition is high, so higher grades are often needed and relevant experience can prove advantageous.
- Equivalent qualifications accepted include BTEC HND in Health Studies (Science), Applied A level/Scottish Group Award in Health and Social Care/Science, NVQ Level 3, Access courses and the Open University Foundation course in science.
- Graduates with a good Honours degree in a related subject, for example biological science, psychology or sport science, can study on an accelerated Master's degree programme, such as the MSc in physiotherapy, which can enhance career prospects.
- Adults can complete Access courses in health science to be considered for degree-level study.

Other related opportunities

- Complementary Health Practitioner p271
- Occupational Therapist p292
- Sports Physiotherapist p307
- Therapist p309

Advantages/disadvantages

- All patients and their conditions are different so the job is varied and interesting.
- The work can be physically and emotionally demanding.
- It's very rewarding to be able to use your knowledge and practical skills to improve people's quality of life.

Earnings guide

- Salary levels in the NHS are set on a yearly basis; those listed below are a guide only.
- Starting salary for a newly qualified physiotherapist with a 4-year degree is £19,683–£25,424 per year.
- Senior grade and team leader physiotherapists earn from £27,622–£34,416.
- Senior managers and consultants earn between £35,232 and £50,733.
- There are also higher grades for physiotherapy teachers and chief members of staff. There are extra payments available, for example if you work in London. Earnings as a self-employed physiotherapist in private practice vary.

Further information

Skills for Health
2nd floor
Goldsmiths House
Broad Plain
Bristol
BS2 0JP
0117 922 1155
www.skillsforhealth.org.uk
office@skillsforhealth.org.uk

NHS Careers
0845 60 60 655
www.nhscareers.nhs.uk

Chartered Society of Physiotherapy
14 Bedford Row
London
WC1R 4ED
020 7306 6666
www.csp.org.uk
enquiries@csp.org.uk

Practice Manager (GP)

What the work involves

- Practice managers run local doctors' surgeries and health centres.
- As a practice manager, you will be responsible for managing finances, resources and staff.
- Your work may include duties such as managing reception and clerical staff, organising patients' records, controlling the stock of equipment and supplies, monitoring budgets, planning new services and arranging work rotas for staff.
- You may have responsibility for more than one practice.

The type of person suited to this work

Practice managers have a range of management skills. You will need to be able to lead and motivate staff, supervise and organise their work, solve problems as they arise, make decisions and manage financial information and budgets. ICT skills are also useful.

You must also have a responsible attitude, because you will be dealing with confidential patient information. Good communication skills are important for working with doctors, nurses, other staff and patients.

Good business sense and a commitment to delivering a high level of healthcare to patients in the local community are also essential, as well as decision-making and planning skills.

Working conditions

You are likely to be based in an office within a surgery or health centre, but you may work in more than one practice, so a driving licence is useful.

You will work normal working hours from Monday to Friday, though you may need to work longer hours if you are busy.

General practices and clinics can be very busy working environments with many different activities demanding your attention.

The future outlook

There are employment opportunities for practice managers in NHS surgeries and health centres throughout the UK.

With experience you may progress to more senior posts, for example running a larger practice. It may also be possible to move into other areas of health service management, such as in hospitals or health authority offices.

Alternatively, you could use your skills to progress into management careers outside of healthcare.

entry level

3–8

To both enter and train while working in this career, you will need qualifications at Level 3–8. Please refer to explanation on page vii.

Qualifications and courses

- There are no formal requirements for entry to this career, but experience as an administrator or manager in a health or social care setting is essential, which means that most new entrants are in their mid-to-late twenties or older. Qualifications in management or a related area can also be an advantage.
- People in posts as practice managers or assistant practice managers can work towards the main professional qualification in this field, the Association of Medical Secretaries, Practice Managers, Administrators and Receptionists (AMSPAR) Diploma in Primary Care Management.
- Candidates for the Diploma must be educated to Level 3 (A level/H grade, National Certificate/Diploma or equivalent). Candidates should normally have 2 years' relevant experience.

CRCI:JE

CLCI:CAL

Other related opportunities

- Accountant p2
- Administrator p6
- Health Service Manager p283

Advantages/disadvantages

- This is a high level, responsible job so can be stressful and demanding.
- It is satisfying to be able to run a practice effectively and efficiently, to provide a good working environment for staff, and to give good service to patients in the local community.

Earnings guide

- Salary levels in the NHS are set each year; those below are a guide only.
- The starting salary for managers of a small practice is around £19,686–£25,424 per year.
- Managers in a group practice can earn up to £31,779 and senior practice managers can earn £70,000 depending on size and location of the practice.
- There are extra payments available, for example if you work in London.

Further information

Skills for Health
2nd floor
Goldsmiths House
Broad Plain
Bristol
BS2 0JP
0117 922 1155
www.skillsforhealth.org.uk
office@skillsforhealth.org.uk

NHS Careers
0845 60 60 655
www.nhscareers.nhs.uk

Association of Medical Secretaries, Practice Managers, Administrators and Receptionists
Tavistock House North
Tavistock Square
London
WC1H 9LN
020 7387 6005
www.amspar.co.uk

Institute of Healthcare Management
18–21 Morley Street
London
SE1 7QZ
020 7620 1030
www.ihm.org.uk
enquiries@ihm.org.uk

Prosthetist / Orthotist

What the work involves

Prosthetist

- Prosthetists design and fit artificial limbs (prostheses) for patients who have lost a limb, have a deformity or who were born without a limb.
- Your work will include taking a plaster cast of the area where the artificial replacement limb will fit and modelling it so that it will be safe and comfortable for the patient. You will also fit and adjust the replacement limb and teach the patient how to use it so that they are as mobile and independent as possible.

Orthotist

- Orthotists provide surgical appliances (orthoses) such as braces, collars, splints and special footwear for patients. For example, a patient might need special shoes because of arthritis or someone with back problems might need a brace.
- Your work will include assessing the patient's problem, designing, fitting and adjusting the orthosis, and helping the patient to use it.

The type of person suited to this work

Prosthetists and orthotists need a high level of technical knowledge and aptitude in areas such as biomechanics and movement.

You must be good with your hands to take measurements, design devices and do fittings and make adjustments. You must be good at using technical skills to solve problems and be able to work accurately because each device must be made perfectly to fit each individual patient.

You also need excellent communication skills for working with patients. You have to be caring, patient, tactful and able to reassure and encourage patients and explain procedures to them. You need to be able to work well as part of a team that includes doctors, nurses, physiotherapists and occupational therapists.

Working conditions

Prosthetists and orthotists work in locations such as hospitals, clinics and centres for people with disabilities. You will also spend some time in workshops where the prostheses and orthoses are made.

You will generally work normal hours from Monday to Friday, although you may have to work late at busy times. A driving licence is useful if you are working in a number of different locations.

The future outlook

With a shortage of prosthetists and orthotists, job prospects are generally excellent in most areas of the UK. Most prosthetists and orthotists work within the NHS but there are also opportunities in private practice and with commercial companies that make devices for NHS hospitals.

With experience, you may specialise in a particular area of the work such as upper or lower limb prosthetics or spinal orthotics; you could also move into management or carry out research and teaching.

There are also many opportunities to work all over the world. Prosthetic and orthotic work is especially important in parts of the world where development programmes are working with communities affected by war.

entry level

To both enter and train while working in this career, you will need qualifications at Level 4–8. Please refer to explanation on page vii.

Qualifications and courses

- Training to become a prosthetist and orthotist takes 4 years, leading to a BSc (Honours) degree. The degree qualifies the student to practise in both prosthetics and orthotics. Graduates can either specialise in one area or practise both specialities.
- The BSc (Hons) in Prosthetics and Orthotics is only available at the University of Salford and the University of Strathclyde. The entry requirements for Salford are 240 UCAS points, including A levels in biology and, preferably, maths or physics, plus 5 GCSEs/S Grades (A–C/1–3) including English and maths. For entry to the Strathclyde degree, 3 H Grades at B or above in maths and either physics or technological studies, and grade C or above in either biology or chemistry are required. Equivalent qualifications may be acceptable.
- The University of Strathclyde also offers an MSc in rehabilitation studies with specific modules for professional prosthetists and orthotists. The normal entry requirement is a relevant Honours degree.
- Graduates must register with the Health Professions Council before being allowed to practice.

CRCI:JF

CLCI:JOL

Other related opportunities

- Chiropodist/podiatrist p270
- Engineer: Professional p205
- Occupational Therapist p292
- Physiotherapist p301

Advantages/disadvantages

- Working with ill and injured patients who are upset and in pain can be emotionally demanding.
- It is satisfying to be able to see the positive effects that the artificial limbs and surgical appliances have on people's lives. For example, you can help people to move around more easily or relieve them from discomfort.

Earnings guide

- There is no set salary scale for NHS prosthetists and orthotists, but salaries tend to be similar to those in commercial companies.
- The starting salary for prosthetists and orthotists is around £19,000 per year.
- Experienced prosthetists and orthotists can earn up to £36,000.
- Consultants can earn up to £45,000. Some seniors in the NHS can get up to £50,000.
- Earnings are generally higher in London. There may also be higher earnings for those with management responsibilities.

Further information

Skills for Health
2nd floor
Goldsmiths House
Broad Plain
Bristol BS2 0JP
0117 922 1155
www.skillsforhealth.org.uk
office@skillsforhealth.org.uk

NHS Careers
0845 60 60 655
www.nhscareers.nhs.uk

British Association of Prosthetists and Orthotists
Sir James Clark Building
Abbey Mill Business Centre
Paisley PA1 1TJ
0845 166 8490
www.bapo.com

Psychiatrist

What the work involves

- Psychiatrists are doctors who have undergone further training in psychiatry.
- As a psychiatrist, you will diagnose mental health problems by talking to patients and carrying out tests. You will then decide on a course of treatment which could include prescribing drugs and talking to patients to help them deal with their problems.
- You will treat people with a range of mental health problems. These include depression, schizophrenia, eating disorders, anxieties, phobias, drug and alcohol abuse, and post-traumatic stress disorder.
- You will probably specialise in one area such as child and adolescent psychiatry, forensic psychiatry or learning disabilities.

The type of person suited to this work

As a psychiatrist you need to be patient and caring. You will need excellent communication skills to listen carefully to people who might be confused or withdrawn. You will help them talk through and come to terms with their problems or illness and should be able to explain their conditions and treatment in a clear, simple way. You will work with relatives and carers, and as part of a team with other medical staff such as psychiatric nurses and occupational therapists.

You will need to be prepared to undergo a long programme of education and training in order to gain the in-depth knowledge and skills necessary to become a psychiatrist.

Working conditions

You could work in a range of locations, including hospitals, people's own homes, schools, residential homes and prisons.

You are likely to work shifts and be on an on-call rota, which includes working at nights, at weekends and on bank holidays.

Working closely with patients can be emotionally demanding.

You will work as part of a team of healthcare professionals.

The future outlook

Most psychiatrists work within the NHS throughout the UK. There is also a small amount of work available in private hospitals, care homes and rehabilitation centres. The armed forces also employ psychiatrists.

There are six specialist areas of psychiatry that you may work in: adult psychiatry; child and adolescent psychiatry; forensic psychiatry; psychiatry of learning disability; old age psychiatry; and psychotherapy.

Entry to psychotherapy is competitive, but there is currently a shortage of psychiatrists in other specialities.

You could move into academic work, either carrying out research or teaching medical students.

entry level

4–8

To both enter and train while working in this career, you will need qualifications at Level 4–8. Please refer to explanation on page vii.

Qualifications and courses

- To become a psychiatrist you need to qualify as a doctor first. You will therefore need to complete a medical degree recognised by the General Medical Council (GMC).
- After graduating, candidates undertake a 2-year foundation programme before applying for specialist training in psychiatry.
- Training as a specialist registrar takes up to a further 6 years, spent training in general adult and old age psychiatry and gaining experience of other specialisms. This leads to the Certificate of Completion of Specialist Training (CCST), and eligibility for entry on the GMC's Specialist Register. It then becomes possible to apply for work as a consultant.

CRCI:JH

CLCI:JAB

Other related opportunities

- Doctor p278
- Nurse (Registered) p289
- Psychologist p541
- Therapist p309

Advantages/disadvantages

- Your patients could be confused or aggressive with a range of difficult problems so the work can be demanding.
- It is rewarding to be able to make a difference to people's lives by helping them to regain their self-respect and happiness.

Earnings guide

- Salary levels in the NHS have a national rate, but this can also vary in some areas.
- Most junior doctors and senior house officers earn around £32,000 in their first year of training, rising to £39,798 in the second. Doctors on specialist training can earn up to £67,000.
- Specialists with experience can earn up to £78,000.
- Consultants earn from £71,000 and with additional payments and merits it is possible for consultants to earn anything up to £161,000.
- Extra earnings may be available through private practice work.

Further information

Skills for Health
2nd floor
Goldsmiths House
Broad Plain
Bristol
BS2 0JP
0117 922 1155
www.skillsforhealth.org.uk
office@ skillsforhealth.org.uk

NHS Careers
0845 60 60 655
www.nhscareers.nhs.uk

British Medical Association
BMA House
Tavistock Square
London
WC1H 9JP
020 7387 4499
www.bma.org.uk

Royal College of Psychiatrists
17 Belgrave Square
London
SW1X 8PG
020 7235 2351
www.rcpsych.ac.uk
rcpsych@rcpsych.ac.uk

Radiographer

What the work involves

- There are two types of radiographer: diagnostic and therapeutic.
- Diagnostic radiographers produce and interpret images of organs, limbs and other parts of the body that are used to diagnose injury and disease. As a diagnostic radiographer, you may use a variety of methods such as X-ray, computed tomography (CT) scanning and ultrasound.
- Therapeutic radiographers treat patients, mostly those who have cancer, by delivering controlled doses of radiation. As a therapeutic radiographer, you will usually be involved in every aspect of the treatment, including pre-treatment preparation, planning, the delivery of the radiation and follow-up care of patients.

entry level

To both enter and train while working in this career, you will need qualifications at Level 4–8. Please refer to explanation on page vii.

The type of person suited to this work

As a radiographer, you will work with a range of patients from children to the elderly. You need to be caring and able to focus on each patient's needs. You must be able to listen and talk to patients and reassure them when carrying out diagnostic tests or treatments. Therapeutic radiographers, in particular, get to know patients because they see them regularly through the course of their treatment.

An ability to assess and treat patients' conditions accurately is vital, so you have to be able to concentrate and pay attention to detail. You should also be interested in science and technology and be confident when operating sophisticated computerised equipment.

You will also need good communication skills to work well in a team with other medical staff such as doctors.

Working conditions

You will work mainly in hospitals, in departments such as radiography, accident and emergency, or oncology (study of tumours).

Working with radiation is potentially dangerous, but you will be trained in how to work safely.

You may have a normal working week from Monday to Friday, but might have to work shifts on a rota basis, particularly if you are a diagnostic radiographer. This may include working at nights, at weekends and on bank holidays.

The future outlook

Although this is a growing area, there is a shortage of radiographers, so employment prospects are excellent. Most employment is available with the NHS throughout the UK. There is also work available in private hospitals and clinics and in industry. When you first qualify as a diagnostic radiographer, you will probably spend a lot of your time working in the accident and emergency department.

Promotion prospects in radiography are excellent. Diagnostic radiographers can move into specialist areas such as MRI, ultrasound or nuclear medicine. Therapeutic radiographers may specialise in areas such as treatment planning or treatment review.

Radiographers could move into management, teaching or research. There are also good opportunities to work abroad.

Qualifications and courses

- Radiographers must be registered with the Health Professions Council to be able to work in the NHS. Candidates who complete a degree approved by the Health Professions Council or Society of Radiographers are eligible for registration.
- Degree courses are available in diagnostic and therapeutic radiography. Typical minimum entry requirements are 2 A levels/3–4 H grades including at least 1 science subject plus 5 GCSEs/S grades (A–C/1–3) including maths, English and science subjects.
- Most degree courses accept mature candidates and encourage qualifications other than A levels, including science-based Access courses.
- Healthcare professionals or others with a relevant first degree may qualify as a therapeutic radiographer by studying for a postgraduate pre-registration qualification.
- Specialist postgraduate courses allow graduates to specialise in subjects such as ultrasound, computed tomography (CT) scanning, magnetic resonance imaging (MRI) or research.

CRCI:JF/JG | CLCI:JAP

Other related opportunities

- Medical Physicist p288
- Nurse p289
- Radiologist p306

Advantages/disadvantages

- The work can be challenging when working with patients who are frightened or distressed, particularly in therapeutic radiography.
- It is extremely fulfilling to be able to use your knowledge and skills to diagnose or treat patients' conditions.

Earnings guide

- £19,683–£25,424 per year is the starting salary for NHS radiographers.
- Senior grade and supervisory radiographers earn from £23,458–£37,326.
- Consultants can earn £52,000+.
- There are also higher grades for radiography teachers and chief members of staff. And there are extra payments available, for example if you work in London. Earnings for radiographers working outside the NHS are similar.

Further information

Skills for Health
2nd floor
Goldsmiths House
Broad Plain
Bristol
BS2 0JP
0117 922 1155
www.skillsforhealth.org.uk
office@skillsforhealth.org.uk

NHS Careers
0845 60 60 655
www.nhscareers.nhs.uk

Society of Radiographers
207 Providence Square
Mill Street
London
SE1 2EW
020 7740 7200
www.sor.org
ifno@sor.org

Radiography Careers
www.radiographycareers.co.uk

Radiologist

What the work involves

- Radiologists are doctors who have undergone further training in radiology.
- As a radiologist, you will diagnose patients' diseases by using information gained from images such as X-rays, and computed tomography (CT) or magnetic resonance imaging (MRI) scans.
- Radiologists increasingly perform interventional procedures such as biopsies, using image guidance.
- You will also play an important role in identifying sources of disease and reducing the possible risks of it spreading further.

entry level

To both enter and train while working in this career, you will need qualifications at Level 4–8. Please refer to explanation on page vii.

The type of person suited to this work

As a radiologist, you need to care about patients, and you must be able to explain things to them simply and clearly so that they understand their health conditions and any treatments they may need. You will also need good communication skills to work well as part of a team with other medical staff.

Scientific and technical knowledge and an ability to diagnose patients' conditions accurately are also necessary. You will need good eyesight and excellent attention to detail for interpreting images and practical skills for caring for patients and operating equipment.

Radiologists undergo a long programme of education and training in order to gain the in-depth knowledge and skills necessary.

Working conditions

You will work within a hospital, mainly in the radiology department.

Scientific and technical knowledge and an ability to diagnose patients' conditions accurately are also necessary. You will need good eyesight and excellent attention to detail for interpreting images and practical skills for caring for patients and operating equipment.

Radiologists undergo a long programme of education and training in order to gain the in-depth knowledge and skills necessary.

The future outlook

Career prospects are excellent due to an international shortage of radiologists. Most radiologists work within the NHS throughout the UK. There is also some work available in private hospitals.

You may decide to specialise further in particular areas of the work, or you could move into management. You may also move into academic work, either carrying out research or teaching medical students.

Qualifications and courses

- Entry to radiology is initially the same as for hospital doctors (see p 278). To enter, candidates complete a medical degree recognised by the General Medical Council (GMC).
- Candidates require at least 2 years' post-qualifying experience to enter training as a radiologist, but in practice, competition for training positions is very intense, and many new entrants have more than 3 years' clinical experience and a postgraduate qualification. New entrants must enrol as Members of the Royal College of Radiologists.
- Specialist training as a radiologist takes at least 5 years, and leads to the Certificate of Completion of Specialist Training (CCST). At least 4 years of the training are spent in clinical posts, and 6 months' research in any aspect of diagnostic imaging is also included. Trainees must pass all 3 parts of the Fellowship of the Royal College of Radiologists (FRCR) examination.
- The Royal College of Radiologists operates a Continuing Professional Development scheme for qualified radiologists to update their knowledge and skills.

CRCI:JH

CLCI:JAB

Other related opportunities

- Anaesthetist p268
- Doctor p278
- Nurse (Registered) p289
- Pathologist p297
- Psychiatrist p304
- Radiographer p305

Advantages/disadvantages

- The work can be emotionally demanding because you will be dealing with patients who may have life-threatening conditions.
- Your work can be vital in finding an accurate and early diagnosis for patients, which can help to save lives.

Earnings guide

- The salary for senior house officers with 5 years' experience could earn up to £67,000 per year.
- Specialists and consultants can earn from £71,000 to £120,000+.
- Salary levels in the NHS have a national rate, but this can vary in some areas. Extra earnings may be available through private practice work.

Further information

Skills for Health
2nd floor
Goldsmiths House
Broad Plain
Bristol
BS2 0JP
0117 922 1155
www.skillsforhealth.org.uk

NHS Careers
0845 60 60 655
www.nhscareers.nhs.uk

British Medical Association
BMA House
Tavistock Square
London
WC1H 9JP
020 7387 4499
www.bma.org.uk

Royal College of Radiologists
38 Portland Place
London
W1B 1JQ
020 7636 4432
www.rcr.ac.uk
enquiries@rcr.ac.uk

Sports Physiotherapist

What the work involves

- Sports physiotherapists specialise in helping sportspeople, and people who play sport as a hobby, to recover from sports injuries and return to full fitness.
- Your work will include assessing the patient, and deciding on and giving treatment, which might include exercise, movement, hydrotherapy, massage and manipulation.
- You will also give advice on how to prevent injuries and maintain health.
- You might specialise in a particular sport such as football, or work with sportspeople from a range of areas.

entry level

To both enter and train while working in this career, you will need qualifications at Level 4–8. Please refer to explanation on page vii.

The type of person suited to this work

You should be interested in sport and in helping people to recover from injuries and maintain their fitness. You need to be tactful and sympathetic and be able to explain treatments to clients, teach them exercises, give advice and motivate and encourage them to help themselves to recover from their injuries.

Manual skills and physical fitness are important for carrying out treatments. An ability to assess and treat patients' conditions is necessary, so you must be able to think logically and be able to apply your scientific knowledge and skills to solve problems.

You also need to be able to act quickly if you are working at a sports ground while sport is being played.

Working conditions

You will work in locations such as sports clinics, sports and fitness centres and sports clubs. You will usually work indoors, but some sports physiotherapists work outdoors at sports grounds too.

You will probably need to work at evenings and weekends.

This is a hands-on job and it can be very physically demanding. It can be stressful working with people who are in pain and frustrated by their injuries.

The future outlook

Competition for places on physiotherapy courses is fierce and you will need relevant experience and proof of your commitment. Once you are qualified you will need to get experience in general physiotherapy, and moving from there into sports physiotherapy is also very competitive.

There is no set career route for sports physiotherapist but with experience you could move from working with a reserve team to the first team or to a bigger club.

You may also decide to open your own sports clinic. If you want to set up a clinic in a particular area, you should make sure that there will be enough work available for you and any other sports physiotherapists already working there.

Qualifications and courses

- Sports physiotherapists are registered physiotherapists who have chosen to specialise in sport. To be state registered, physiotherapists must have a degree accredited by the Health Professions Council. Those with an approved degree are eligible for membership of the Chartered Society of Physiotherapy. Candidates who wish to practise will have to undergo a police check.
- The normal entry requirements for a physiotherapy degree are 5 GCSEs/S grades (A–C/1–3), including maths, English and science subjects, 3 A levels at grade C, including a biological science, or 5 H grades (AABBB), including at least 2 science subjects.
- Equivalent qualifications include BTEC National Certificate/Diploma in Health Studies, Applied A level in Health and Social care, Scottish Group Award in Science, NVQ Level 3, or a science-based Access or Open University Foundation course.
- Graduates with a good Honours degree in a related subject, for example biological science, psychology or sport science, can study on an accelerated Master's degree programme, such as the MSc in sport or rehabilitation science.
- A valid First Aid certificate must be held.

CRCI:JG

CLCI:JAN

Other related opportunities

- Complementary Health Practitioner p271
- Occupational Therapist p292
- Physiotherapist p301
- Sports p374
- Therapist p309

Advantages/disadvantages

- It can be challenging to develop a career in this area, because it is very competitive and does not offer clearly defined career routes.
- This job could be good for you if you want to use your skills in a sports environment. It's very rewarding to be able to help bring sportspeople back from injury so that they can play at full fitness again.

Earnings guide

- Salary levels in the NHS are set on a yearly basis; those listed below are a guide only. During training, sports physiotherapists are often on NHS pay and carry out their extra work in sports physiotherapy for no pay or just expenses.
- Newly qualified physiotherapists in the NHS earn £19,683–£25,424 per year.
- Senior physiotherapists can earn £27,622–£34,416.
- Consultant physiotherapists can get up to £50,733.
- Earnings as a qualified sports physiotherapist vary widely, depending on your employer or, if self-employed, how much you charge and how many clients you see. Earnings start from about £25,000 and may be much higher for sports physiotherapists working with top sports teams or individuals.

Further information

Skills for Health
2nd floor
Goldsmiths House
Broad Plain
Bristol
BS2 0JP
0117 922 1155
www.skillsforhealth.org.uk
office@skillsforhealth.org.uk

NHS Careers
0845 60 60 655
www.nhscareers.nhs.uk

Chartered Society of Physiotherapy
14 Bedford Row
London
WC1R 4ED
020 7306 6666
www.csp.org.uk
enquiries@csp.org.uk

Sterile Services Technician

What the work involves

- Sterile Services Technicians work as part of a team responsible for helping to prevent infections spreading by making sure that hospital equipment is sterile.
- Your work will involve collecting and cleaning a range of instruments from things like syringes to larger pieces of equipment. Some things will have to be dismantled and examined through a microscope before being sterilised and then reassembled and tested afterwards.
- You will work to national standards, operating highly technical machines, and must keep accurate records of your work.

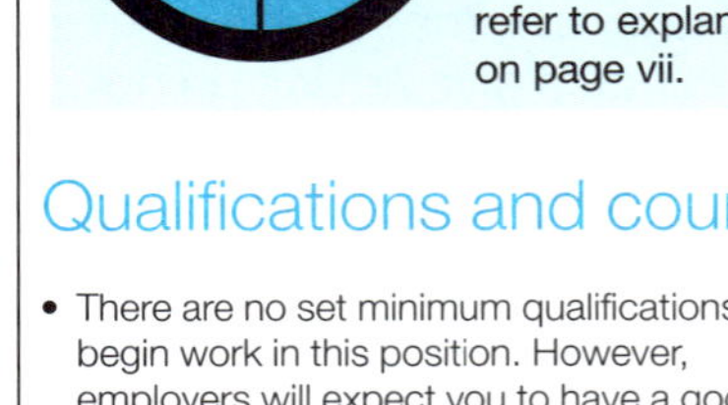

entry level

To both enter and train while working in this career, you will need qualifications at Level 4–8. Please refer to explanation on page vii.

The type of person suited to this work

You will need to be good with your hands to operate complex equipment and must be able to work accurately, pay attention to detail and follow instructions and set procedures carefully.

Sterile Services Technicians should be very careful about hygiene and interested in keeping hospitals and equipment clean and safe for patients and staff. You will work in a team so will need good communication skills. You should also be well organised and able to keep clear, detailed records.

You will be collecting and dismantling machinery so will need to be fit.

Qualifications and courses

- There are no set minimum qualifications to begin work in this position. However, employers will expect you to have a good general standard of education, to have strong reading skills and neat handwriting (for labelling materials and equipment clearly and correctly).
- Some employers may prefer you to have 5 GCSEs (A–C). Qualifications such as a BTEC National Certificate or Diploma in Applied Science could also be an advantage.
- Whilst on the job, you may be encouraged to train for an ASET Level 2 Certificate in Control of Infection and Contamination, or an NCFE Level 2 Certificate in Infection Control.

Working conditions

You will work in a hospital as part of team and will also have contact with doctors, nurses and other staff. Based in the sterile services department, you will collect equipment from all parts of the hospital and this will involve lifting and pushing trolleys.

You will have to wear protective clothing and may have to work shifts.

The future outlook

Most jobs are in NHS hospitals throughout the UK, but you could also work in a private hospital. Opportunities are good, as there is a shortage of applicants for vacancies.

With experience, you could get promotion to senior technician or supervisor. You could then take professional qualifications and become a Sterile Services Manager. As a manager you could move in to management in other areas of the NHS.

Other related opportunities

- Hospital Porter p286
- Medical Laboratory Assistant p287
- Nurse p289

Advantages/disadvantages

- The work can be routine and physically demanding.
- You will be making a vital contribution to controlling the spread of potentially deadly infections.

Earnings guide

- Starting salaries are from £12,577–£15,523 per year.
- As an assistant manager you can expect to earn £19,683–£25,424.

Further information

Skills for Health
2nd floor
Goldsmiths House
Broad Plain
Bristol
BS2 0JP
0117 922 1155
www.skillsforhealth.org.uk
office@skillsforhealth.org.uk

NHS Careers
0845 60 60 655
www.nhscareers.nhs.uk

Institute of Decontamination Sciences
Chesterfield Royal Hospital NHS Foundation Trust
Calow
Chesterfield
Derbyshire
S44 5BL
01246 513069
www.idsc-uk.co.uk
idsc.admin@googlemail.com

CRCI:JG
CLCI:JAN

Therapist

What the work involves

Art therapist

- Art therapists use art to enable their clients to communicate, express their feelings and explore their lives and problems. They use a range of techniques in their work, such as painting, working with clay or producing collages. The process can bring feelings to the surface, which can then be worked with. Art therapists work with a range of patients, including children, the elderly and people with learning disabilities, either in groups or on a one-to-one basis.

Drama therapist

- As a drama therapist you would use drama to help people to deal with a range of problems. You would provide a safe, non-judgemental environment in which people can examine their beliefs, attitudes, feelings and experiences, and try out new ways of living their lives. You will use techniques such as role-play, storytelling and movement. You could work with a variety of patients, either in groups or individually.

Music therapist

- Music therapists encourage clients to use a range of instruments, including their own voices, to explore the world of sound and music. This can have a number of benefits, such as improving communication, increasing self-awareness and confidence, and promoting well-being. You will work with patients with a variety of needs or problems, either one to one or in groups.

Nutritional therapist

- You would take your scientific knowledge of nutrition and apply it to the care of patients to promote or improve health and to prevent disease. As a nutritional therapist, your work will include assessing the patient by asking them questions and carrying out tests such as food allergy tests. You will then recommend treatment, which may include eliminating certain foods from the diet, adding other foods, or using supplements.

Play therapist

- Play therapists use play to help children to explore, understand and communicate their feelings about past and present experiences that are affecting their lives. You could work with children with a variety of problems. For example, they may have been abused, experienced loss or witnessed violence, or they may be ill or disabled.

Speech and language therapist

- Speech and language therapists work with patients who have problems with speaking, chewing or swallowing. As a speech and language therapist, your work will include assessing each patient and planning a course of individual treatment. You will work with a range of patients including children who need help to develop their speech, people with a speech defect such as a stammer, and those who have trouble eating because of an accident or illness.

The type of person suited to this work

As well as having in-depth knowledge and skill in your particular area of therapy, you must be interested in helping people with their problems. You will be working with people of all ages and backgrounds and with a wide range of issues, so need a practical, creative approach to problem solving.

You also have to be patient and caring, and sensitive to your clients' needs and issues.

You should be able to communicate well with clients and their families and be able to understand their problems and situation and encourage and motivate them to make positive changes. You should enjoy working with other staff and have initiative and business skills if you run your own practice.

Working conditions

You may work in a wide range of locations, such as hospitals, day centres, schools, people's own homes, hospices and prisons. A driving licence may be useful.

Some people are self-employed or combine part-time paid work with running their own business. If you are self-employed, you may work from home or from a clinic.

You may work a normal working week from Monday to Friday, although many therapists work at evenings and weekends at times to suit their clients.

You might work on your own or as part of a team, so the ability to communicate with others will be important.

Working closely with people with mental health issues can be stressful and emotionally demanding.

The future outlook

Employers of therapists include NHS and private hospitals, local authority social services departments, prisons and voluntary agencies. You may also work in private practice. With experience, you may progress to more senior positions. You may also choose to specialise in one area of your work or move into a training, supervisory or management role.

Art therapist
Art therapy is a growing area but there is competition for posts.

Drama therapist
The number of drama therapists is rising so employment opportunities are reasonable but can be competitive.

Music therapist
Music therapy is a relatively small but growing career area and prospects in the NHS are quite good.

Nutritional therapist
Most nutritional therapists are self-employed, so your success will depend on developing your business and gaining a good number of clients.

Play therapist
The number of play therapists is increasing but opportunities vary regionally. With experience you could move into teaching play therapy.

Speech and language therapist
There is a shortage of speech and language therapists in the UK. With experience you could specialise, perhaps with children or move into teaching or research.

Qualifications and courses

entry level

To both enter and train while working in this career, you will need qualifications at Level 4–8. Please refer to explanation on page vii.

Art therapist

- To work as an art therapist you need a postgraduate diploma in Art Therapy. Art therapists must be registered with the Health Professions Council and have undertaken training accredited by the British Association of Art Therapists (BAAT).
- For entry to a postgraduate therapy course, you normally need to have a degree in an art and design subject plus at least 1 year's work experience in a relevant area of health, education or social care. A degree in another subject, such as teaching, psychology or social work, may also be accepted.

Drama therapist

- To become a drama therapist, you need to have a degree in a related subject such as drama or psychology, plus experience of working with people with problems, as well as practical drama experience. You can then apply for a place on a course approved by the British Association of Dramatherapists and then register with the Health Professions Council.
- Approved courses can take 1 year of full-time study or 2–3 years' part-time study, and may lead to a Postgraduate Diploma in Dramatherapy or Drama and Movement Therapy, or a Master's degree in Dramatherapy.

Music therapist

- Music therapists must complete a postgraduate course accredited by the Association of Professional Music Therapists (APMT) and recognised by the Health Professions Council in order to gain state registration. Minimum entry requirements are usually 3 years of musical training with a diploma or graduateship from a college of music or a degree from a university.
- Occasionally, students with a degree in a subject such as education or psychology, who have also reached a high standard of musical competence, are accepted on postgraduate courses.

Nutritional therapist

- To be registered with the British Association for Nutritional Therapy (BANT), it is necessary to do either a degree or a diploma in nutritional therapy. The diploma can take up to 3 years of part-time intensive study. Entry to a degree courses usually requires 2 A levels/3 H grades preferably including biology, human biology, physics or chemistry, and 5 GCSEs/S grades (A–C/1–3). Entry to a diploma will normally require GCSEs/S grades or equivalent, including relevant subjects.
- Training courses in nutritional therapy can vary in length, cost and content. Courses accredited by BANT must include 50 hours of supervised clinical practice as well as academic study.

Play therapist

- Play therapists need to hold a postgraduate qualification recognised by the British Association of Play Therapists (BAPT).
- The usual requirements for entry to a BAPT-accredited course are a degree or equivalent in social work, teaching, psychology, occupational therapy or another relevant area and 2 years' experience of working with children.
- Entrants must be at least 25 and must undergo personal therapy to ensure they are emotionally stable.

Speech and language therapist

- Speech and language therapists qualify by taking an approved 3- or 4-year full-time degree course in speech and language therapy, or a degree in another subject followed by a 2-year postgraduate course. They are then eligible for state registration with the Health Professions Council.
- Successful completion of the first degree or postgraduate course plus 1 year's supervised practise permits graduates to obtain registration with the Royal College of Speech and Language Therapists (RCSLT), which is essential for employment in the National Health Service.

Other related opportunities

- Actor / Actress p390
- Artist (Fine) p131
- Audiologist p269
- Counselling Work p529
- Dietitian p277
- Hospital Play Specialist p285
- Music p400
- Nurse (Registered) p289
- Occupational Therapist p292
- Psychologist p541
- Social Worker p545

Advantages/disadvantages

- The work can be emotionally and mentally demanding at times because you will be dealing with patients' problems, and sometimes powerful emotions.
- If you are self-employed it can take time to build up a client group and earn a reasonable wage.
- Many people find this an excellent way to combine their interests and specialist knowledge to help people feel better, recover from illness or improve their lives.
- Working on a self-employed basis can provide a flexible way of working for people with other commitments.

Earnings guide

- Earnings for therapists working in private practice may be similar to those in the NHS, but will vary depending on the employer.
- Earnings for self-employed therapists depend on how much they charge and how many clients they can see.

Art/drama/music therapists

- £22,886 per year is the starting salary for NHS art, drama and music therapists. As a senior grade therapist you could earn £36,000+.

Speech and language therapists

- £19,683 is the starting salary for NHS speech and language therapists. Experienced speech and language therapists can earn up to £37,326. Heads of departments or consultants can earn £70,000+.

Play therapists

- Newly qualified play therapists usually earn around £22,143. With experience you could earn £30,000+. In private practice, play therapists can earn from £30 to £80 a session.

Nutritional therapist

- Nutritional therapists are mainly self-employed and charge between £50 and £100 for sessions.

Further information

Skills for Health
2nd floor
Goldsmiths House
Broad Plain
Bristol BS2 0JP
0117 922 1155
www.skillsforhealth.org.uk
office@skillsforhealth.org.uk

NHS Careers
0845 60 60 655
www.nhscareers.nhs.uk

ART THERAPIST
British Association of Art Therapists
24-27 White Lion Street
London
N1 9PD
020 7686 4216
www.baat.org
info@baat.org

DRAMA THERAPIST
British Association of Dramatherapists
Waverley
Battledown Approach
Cheltenham
Gloucestershire
GL52 6RE
01242 235 515
www.badth.org.uk
enquiries@badth.org.uk

MUSIC THERAPIST
Association of Professional Music Therapists
61 Church Hill Road
East Barnet
Hertfordshire EN4 8SY
020 8440 4153
www.apmt.org
APMToffice@aol.com

NUTRITIONAL THERAPIST
British Association for Applied Nutrition & Nutritional Therapy
27 Old Gloucester Street
London
WC1N 3XX
0870 606 1284
www.bant.org.uk
theadministrator@bant.org.uk

PLAY THERAPIST
British Association of Play Therapists
1 Beacon Mews
South Road
Weybridge
Surrey
KT13 9DZ
01932 828638
www.bapt.uk.com
www.bapt.uk.com

SPEECH AND LANGUAGE THERAPIST
Royal College of Speech and Language Therapists
2 White Hart Yard
London
SE1 1NX
020 7378 1200
www.rcslt.org
info@rcslt.org

Trichologist

What the work involves

- Trichologists diagnose and treat diseases and disorders of the scalp and hair such as hair loss, hair breakage and dandruff.
- As a trichologist, your role will include talking to the patient about their medical history, health and diet and closely examining the patient's hair and scalp.
- You will give advice and recommend any necessary treatment, such as creams or shampoos. You may also refer patients on to other healthcare professionals if appropriate.

entry level

To both enter and train while working in this career, you will need qualifications at Level 4–8. Please refer to explanation on page vii.

The type of person suited to this work

Trichologists need good communication skills to talk to patients about their concerns and explain their condition and any treatments they may need. You should be sympathetic and tactful and able to reassure patients, put them at their ease and listen carefully to their concerns.

You will need to apply your scientific knowledge and experience to your work, have a methodical approach and pay attention to detail so that you can assess patients' conditions accurately and plan appropriate treatment.

Working conditions

Most trichologists work in clinics, but those who are involved in research and teaching work in universities and colleges, or in pharmaceutical and cosmetics companies.

You may have normal working hours from Monday to Friday, but if you work in private practice you will probably need to work in the evenings, or occasionally at weekends, to treat people at times that suit them.

The work involves close contact and hands-on treatment of patients.

The future outlook

Most trichologists are self-employed and run their own clinics, usually working on their own. Dermatologists are doctors who have trained in trichology and are usually employed in hospitals.

Trichologists may also go on to work as lecturers in colleges or universities, often in hair and beauty departments.

There are also a small number of opportunities to work in research in pharmaceutical and cosmetics companies.

Qualifications and courses

- The main route into trichology and entry to the register of qualified members of The Institute of Trichologists is by successful completion of the Institute's 2-year training course in trichology (there are limited exceptions to this, for example for doctors (dermatologists) and graduates of HND trichology courses at selected colleges).
- Entrants are often mature, though there is no set minimum age. There are no set minimum entry requirements, but the course is academic and scientific in nature and the progress of students is closely monitored.
- Successful completion of the Institute's course makes you eligible for admission as an Associate Member of the Institute (AIT). Progression to full membership (MIT) is available upon further study and a minimum of 2 years' professional practise as a trichologist.
- To become a doctor (dermatologist), candidates complete a medical degree recognised by the General Medical Council (GMC) as outlined in the doctor entry (see p278).

Other related opportunities

- Doctor p278
- Hairdresser / Barber p424

Advantages/disadvantages

- Working with patients can be challenging and stressful.
- It is rewarding to be able to use your knowledge to treat patients successfully.

Earnings guide

- Most trichologists are self-employed and charge clients by the session. Earnings vary widely, depending on how much you charge and how many clients you see. How much you earn can depend on which area of the country you are working in
- Earnings for newly self-employed practitioners may start from about £12,000–£13,000 a year. Experienced practitioners may earn up to £30,000.
- For NHS (doctor) dermatologists,you must complete a medical degree, and the salary for these posts is outlined in the medical doctor information page.
- Extra earnings may be available through private practice work.

Further information

Skills for Health
2nd floor
Goldsmiths House
Broad Plain
Bristol
BS2 0JP
0117 922 1155
www.skillsforhealth.org.uk
office@skillsforhealth.org.uk

NHS Careers
0845 60 60 655
www.nhscareers.nhs.uk

Institute of Trichologists
24 Langroyd Road
London
SW17 7PL
0870 607 0602
www.trichologists.org.uk
admin@trichologists.org.uk

CRCI:RC

CLCI:IL

Do you enjoy history, researching information or want a job that involves using another language? The information and culture section is not very big, but includes some unusual job ideas, for example:

- **Anthropologist**
- **Arts Administrator**
- **Historian**
- **Museum Attendant**
- **Translator**

But what's it like working in this area?
Here's Pavel Pietrzak's story:

Interpreter

A native of Poland, Pavel studied English at school before going on to do a degree in English Philology at university. This was basically a course looking at both English literature and linguistics. Pavel came to England 18 years ago at the age of 23 and became an interpreter/translator. While here he has taken an Open University degree in Computer Studies and Database Design. Because of his degree and experience he was accepted by both the Institute of Linguistics (IOL) and the Institute of Interpreters (ITI), the two governing bodies for the profession. He now runs his own company, Polished Words Ltd, which specialises in translating English into Polish and he owns a 50% share in Opius Ltd, a company dealing with multilingual translation and interpretation.

WHAT THE JOB ENTAILS

'I take enquiries from potential clients (mostly private companies and businesses) and look at the job to see whether it is something either I or one of my associates can deal with. I then go back to the client with a quote and ask about deadlines. Most clients set tight deadlines and this can be stressful. You have to be accessible, otherwise clients will go elsewhere, and it takes a while to build up a good reputation and a client base. You also need to keep up with your own language and your second language because although you can interpret and translate word for word, the best interpreters rise above that and convey the more general meaning of the words, so you need to be able to switch your linguistic thinking into another language effortlessly.'

THE GOOD AND BAD SIDES TO WHAT HE DOES

'I like the language aspect of it the most. I find it quite challenging to get it right. I also like being my own boss and having a degree of flexibility because I work from home. However, that can be a mixed blessing because you can feel cut off from people and the short deadlines can be really stressful.'

In order to progress in his career, Pavel is now about to sit for his Public Service Interpreters (PSI) exam. If you want to work for the police, courts, hospitals or any other public body in Britain, you have to pass your PSI exam and get on its register. You may then find you are offered large amounts of work.

Ultimately, Pavel would like to expand his business so he oversees other people's work.

WHAT YOU NEED TO SUCCEED

'The bottom line is you have to know the language, but you also need patience, analytical thinking and attention to detail. How you talk to your clients is also important: Are you courteous? Are you prepared to sort out problems? Keep up with your own language and your second language by reading newspapers, talking to native speakers and by visiting the country. Finally, I think computer skills are very important and above all, do get recognised by one of the governing bodies such as the ITI or the IOL because you can never have too many qualifications and they will help give you access to many more clients.'

Anthropologist

What the work involves

- You will study and research the behaviour and beliefs of people and social groups.
- You will investigate specific issues and areas that make up part of everyday culture in the UK and other parts of the world.
- You will apply specialist knowledge and research skills to find out about differences between human cultures and societies.
- Anthropologists undertake their research around a wide range of areas such as archaeology, the arts, the environment, biology and religion.

The type of person suited to this work

Whatever job you do as an anthropologist, you will need a strong interest in people and a respectful, flexible attitude to other people's beliefs and customs. You should also enjoy meeting new people and going into different social situations. You will need to be able to deal with travelling, living and working away from home for periods at a time for some jobs.

Good communication skills are also very important. Strong research skills and an organised approach are useful. ICT skills and a good level of numeracy are also helpful. You will need an observant approach with an interest in a wide range of subjects.

Working conditions

For research-based work, you may need to visit and stay in different areas. Spending time in other places means that anthropology is not generally a 9–5 office-based job.

The work can involve travel in the UK and overseas.

Some physical or biological anthropologists work in laboratories analysing and researching samples.

The future outlook

You could gain employment as a researcher on specific projects. Many anthropologists progress within academia by undertaking research and teaching around their specialist interests. You could also work for government bodies and charities. There are some opportunities to work overseas.

Anthropologists also apply their research skills and training to their work in other areas such as social care, teaching and the health service.

4–8

entry level

To both enter and train while working in this career, you will need qualifications at Level 4–8. Please refer to explanation on page vii.

Qualifications and courses

- Entry to this area is usually gained with degree-level or postgraduate training or qualifications. Voluntary or paid work experience can be useful.
- There are limited opportunities to gain qualifications in this area before degree level. Sociology A levels and GCSEs cover some aspects of anthropology. For biological anthropology, an A level in biology may be useful.
- Access and degree courses in this area cover subjects such as social anthropology and physical/biological anthropology. Anthropology can also be studied as part of a combined Honours degree with subjects such as social anthropology or psychology.
- It is also possible to study for a Master's or other postgraduate degree in anthropology following a first degree in any subject.
- The Association of Social Anthropologists runs seminars and conferences, and information on bursaries and awards for anthropology students. Some universities such as Wolverhampton and Brighton have Centres for Learning and Teaching which run courses on sociology, anthropology and politics, although these are aimed at applicants with some knowledge of the subject.
- Professionals using their anthropology training in another area are likely to have gained a qualification or degree in another subject.
- Researchers in this area are often required to have a relevant postgraduate qualification or the equivalent practical experience.

CRCI:K

CLCI:FAH

Other related opportunities

- Archaeologist p315
- Historian p320
- Researcher p328

Advantages/disadvantages

- This job can provide opportunities to develop and research theories about people and cultures.
- Anthropology can also provide the chance to meet a variety of people and visit different places.
- Field research can be physically demanding and spending time away can be difficult if you have family commitments.

Earnings guide

- Anthropologists work in a wide range of sectors, so salaries vary widely.
- Starting salaries for graduates are around £21,000+ per year, rising to £26,000 for research assistants/researchers, depending on experience.
- £24,000–£28,000 per year is usual for lecturers.
- £28,000–£40,000 is the range for senior lecturers.

Further information

Royal Anthropological Institute of Great Britain and Ireland (RAI)
50 Fitzroy Street
London
W1T 5BT
020 7387 0455
www.therai.org.uk

Higher Education Academy Subject Network for Sociology, Anthropology and Politics (C-SAP)
The University of Birmingham
Edgbaston
Birmingham
B15 2TT
0121 414 7919
www.c-sap.bham.ac.uk

Association of Social Anthropologists of the Commonwealth
50 Fitzroy St
London
W1T 5BT
www.theasa.org

Archaeologist

What the work involves

- Using your specialist knowledge and skills you will investigate and record physical evidence of the past and develop public understanding of history.
- You will provide practical support on archaeological excavations or 'digs', which may include undertaking basic digging work, project-managing an excavation or researching evidence found on-sites.
- You could manage and oversee historic buildings and monuments.
- You may provide information and advice on how to protect and maintain historical sites.

The type of person suited to this work

You will need a strong interest in history and how people lived in the past. For practical work you will need a patient and careful approach. You should also be observant with an eye for detail. A good level of physical fitness and manual dexterity will be needed when working on digs and handling objects.

The ability to work as part of a team is useful. In more senior jobs, you will need to explain your work to others so communication skills are important. Writing skills will help you to be able to write up reports and keep detailed records. ICT skills are also useful.

Working conditions

Archaeologists often work on-sites or digs that are outdoors. Varying weather conditions and the nature of the work make this job physically demanding.

You will need good manual handling skills and a conscientious approach when working with historical artefacts.

Some archaeologists are based in offices within government bodies, heritage organisations and museums.

The future outlook

Whatever route you follow, this is a very competitive area in which to develop a career. You will need to gain practical experience on a voluntary or paid basis. With further experience you could project-manage site excavations or work as a researcher analysing excavation findings.

Some archaeologists work for heritage organisations to help preserve the historic monuments and buildings. Others go into teaching or follow an academic career.

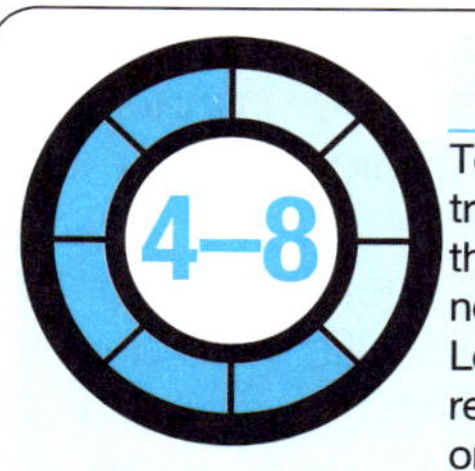

entry level

To both enter and train while working in this career, you will need qualifications at Level 4–8. Please refer to explanation on page vii.

Qualifications and courses

- Most professional archaeologists have a degree or postgraduate qualification.
- Degree entry usually requires 5 GCSEs/S grades (A–C/1–3) or equivalent, with a good mix of arts and sciences. High grades in 3 A levels/4 H grades are often needed. There are no specific subject requirements at A level/H grade. NVQs Level 3 and 4 are available in archaeological practice.
- Archaeology can be studied as a single Honours degree or in combination with another degree subject. A small number of HNCs, HNDs, Foundation degrees and DipHEs are available in archaeology.
- Entry to postgraduate courses requires a good first degree.
- Voluntary experience on digs is very useful. The key professional bodies can provide details of holiday work experience opportunities. The Archaeology Training Forum (ATF; a consortium of professional bodies involved in archaeology) develop and offer short courses in Continuing Professional Development, including the programme at Oxford University Department of Continuing Education, and others at the Institute of Archaeology and Antiquity at Birmingham University, the Ironbridge Institute and the School of Archaeology and Ancient History at Leicester University.

CRCI:K

CLCI:FAH

Other related opportunities

- Anthropologist p314
- Archivist p316
- Historian p320
- Restorer / Conservation Officer p329

Advantages/disadvantages

- It is likely that you will need to move around different geographical areas to gain practical experience.
- There are opportunities to work overseas.
- Archaeologists with a good level of experience in a specialist area can go on to work as consultants.

Earnings guide

- £14,300–£15,500 per year is usual for starting salaries.
- With experience and some supervisory responsibilities this can rise to around £18,000.
- Project managers can expect a salary of around £28,000.

Further information

Creative and Cultural Skills
4th Floor
Lafone House
London
SE1 3HN
020 7015 1847
www.ccskills.org.uk

Institute of Field Archaeologists
PO Box 227
University of Reading
Reading
RG6 6AB
0118 378 6446
www.archaeologists.net

Council for British Archaeology
St Mary's House
66 Bootham
York
YO30 7BZ
01904 671417
www.britarch.ac.uk

Archivist

What the work involves

- You will manage and organise stored sets of historical information, or archives. This could include records such as documents, maps, films and other items.
- Many archivists deal with information enquiries and advise on the availability of specific records.
- You will ensure that archives are maintained and managed in the most appropriate way. You may also conserve documents and prepare them for storage.
- Your work could involve setting up new archives and assessing, recording and cataloguing information.

entry level

To both enter and train while working in this career, you will need qualifications at Level 4–8. Please refer to explanation on page vii.

The type of person suited to this work

As an archivist, you will manage a range of information so a well-organised approach is essential. An interest in preserving historical records is also important. Working within specialist information systems requires a methodical attitude.

You may provide information and advice to members of the public so strong communication skills are useful. You will also need good customer-care skills and enjoy helping people with their enquiries. As you will need to locate information quickly, research skills are very important. Attention to detail is also helpful. You should be able to work as part of a team.

Working conditions

Working environments vary. Record/archive centres can be modern and spacious, but if based in older buildings space may be limited.

Accessing records from cramped storage rooms or high shelves can be physically demanding.

This job may not suit people with dust allergies.

In roles dealing with enquiries from visitors, the working environment can be very busy.

The future outlook

Public records offices, private companies and other organisations need skilled information professionals. With experience, you could progress from an assistant archivist role into senior management. You could work on a consultancy basis, managing specific projects.

You may also work with historical material to undertake promotional or educational activities. You could specialise in conservation and move into museums and heritage work.

Qualifications and courses

- Entrants to this profession need a 2.1 Honours degree followed by a postgraduate qualification in archives and records management or archival studies. A first degree in history, languages, classics or information studies/science may be useful, but degrees in any discipline are accepted.
- The Society of Archivists recognises postgraduate courses in archives and records management/archival studies at certain UK universities. The Society's website provides a list of accredited courses.
- Relevant work experience is an advantage in gaining a place on a postgraduate course, and the Society of Archivists provides information about work experience placements.
- Once qualified, records managers can join the Society of Archivists' Registration Scheme.

CRCI:F

CLCI:F

Other related opportunities

- Archaeologist p315
- Public Records Officer p327

Advantages/disadvantages

- This job allows you to preserve and protect historical documents.
- Employers often offer short-term contracts which can create job instability.
- For people with experience, there are opportunities to undertake this role on a consultancy basis.

Earnings guide

- £17,000–£24,000 per year is typical for starting salaries (before gaining a professional qualification).
- The Society of Archivists recommends £20,295 as a minimum salary for starting.
- When qualified and with some experience and a specialism you could earn up to £28,000.
- As a manager it is possible to earn £40,000.

Further information

Society of Archivists
Prioryfield House
20 Canon Street
Taunton
Somerset
TA1 1SW
01823 327030
www.archives.org.uk

Creative and Cultural Skills
4th Floor
Lafone House
London
SE1 3HN
020 7015 1847
www.ccskills.org.uk

National Archives
Kew
Richmond
Surrey
TW9 4DU
020 8876 3444
www.nationalarchives.gov.uk

Art Exhibition Organiser

What the work involves

- You will plan, organise and produce art exhibitions in galleries, museums and other locations.
- You will organise exhibition spaces before and after shows. This could involve overseeing technical and other staff during the installation and dismantling of exhibitions.
- Your work may also involve managing budgets as well as writing text to accompany and publicise exhibitions.
- Art exhibition professionals tend to specialise in a particular area such as textiles, contemporary art and historical art.

entry level

3

To both enter and train while working in this career, you will need qualifications at Level 3. Please refer to explanation on page vii.

Qualifications and courses

- There are no set entry requirements to become an art exhibition organiser. Many entrants to this profession are graduates, although relevant experience and an interest in the arts are often seen as equally important to qualifications.
- A degree in an art or design subject can be useful. Postgraduate qualifications, degrees, Foundation degrees and HNDs are available in subjects such as museum and exhibition design, exhibition and retail design and events management.
- NVQs/SVQs Levels 4 and 5 in Cultural Heritage Management are available.

The type of person suited to this work

You will need a good knowledge of the area of art in which you specialise. You should also have a creative approach and an eye for design to create informative exhibitions. ICT design skills are useful. You will ensure that exhibitions are designed to be accessible to all visitors. You will also enjoy meeting and working with a range of people.

Your flexible attitude will allow you to deal with planning and practical problems! Attention to detail is also helpful. The ability to manage people will be useful for overseeing the work of technical and other staff. You will need numeracy skills to manage exhibition budgets.

Working conditions

If you work in providing consultancy as an art exhibition organiser, you will normally work from home or from the contractors' own offices.

You will spend some of your time at the site of the exhibition.

Working hours can be long, especially just before and after an exhibition opens.

You may need to help with setting up exhibitions, which can be physically demanding.

The future outlook

Art exhibition work often forms part of other roles in a museum, art gallery or community organisation. Freelance work is usually only available to those with a good level of arts management or administrative experience.

There are a small number of opportunities in larger galleries to work as an exhibitions assistant. With experience, you could progress to a role as a senior exhibition organiser or head of department.

Other related opportunities

- Arts Administrator p318
- Museum / Art Gallery p325

Advantages/disadvantages

- Due to the nature of the work and the need to meet deadlines, this can sometimes be a very pressured job.
- This job provides the opportunity to produce exhibitions on subjects that interest you.
- Opportunities to do this on a full-time basis are fairly limited.

Earnings guide

- Art exhibition organisers can work as consultants, for which they earn a project-based salary or daily fee.
- The work can form part of a role such as arts officer/administrator.
- As a starting salary assistant exhibitions officers in museums or galleries earn £13,000–£15,000 per year.
- Once experienced, exhibition officers can earn up to £30,000.
- Senior managers could earn as much as £50,000.
- Many of the highly paid jobs are in London and the south-east of England and in the largest cities.

Further information

EQ
Suite E229
Dean Clough
Halifax
West Yorkshire
HX3 5AX
01422 381618
www.thinkeq.org.uk

Arts Council of England
2 Pear Tree Court
London
EC1R 0DS
0845 300 6200
www.artscouncil.org.uk

Scottish Arts Council
12 Manor Place
Edinburgh
EH3 7DD
0845 603 6000
www.scottisharts.org.uk

Arts Administrator

What the work involves

- You will support the development and operation of activities and events in areas such as visual arts, drama and music.
- You will undertake a range of administrative tasks including coordinating facilities and office management. You may be responsible for managing funding applications and budgets.
- Your job could also involve arts marketing activities such as writing press releases.
- Arts administrators are employed within galleries, arts centres, community arts groups and one-off arts projects.

entry level

To both enter and train while working in this career, you will need qualifications at Level 4–8. Please refer to explanation on page vii.

The type of person suited to this work

Enthusiasm for the arts is essential for this role. You will need a committed approach and to be able to take the initiative. A good range of administrative, office and ICT skills are also essential. You will be able to communicate well in person and in writing. Because it is likely that you will have to manage project budgets, numeracy skills are also useful.

As you will coordinate a number of activities at once, you will need a well-organised approach. You should enjoy working with a range of people including artists and members of the public. You should be able to work independently and as part of a team. A flexible outlook is useful.

Working conditions

Working hours can vary but it is likely that you will need to work some evenings and weekends to attend events.

Working environments vary according to employer. You may be based in a spacious office or have to work in more cramped conditions.

Within roles that have an arts development aspect, you will be required to travel between locations to attend meetings and make contacts.

The future outlook

As with many aspects of arts management, this is a competitive area to get into. Developing expertise in a specific area such as community arts or theatre can be helpful. With experience, you could progress from an assistant administrator role into a more senior job.

With higher levels of experience, you could provide freelance support to arts groups and projects. You could specialise in a particular area such as arts marketing and management.

Qualifications and courses

- There are no specific entry requirements, but most arts administrators have a degree in an arts subject or business studies.
- At degree level, arts management can be studied on its own, or in combination with related subject such as events management and heritage management. There are no particular subject requirements for entry to these degrees.
- Postgraduate courses in arts administration/arts management are available. A degree and/or relevant work experience is required for entry to these programmes.
- NVQs are available in Cultural Venue Operations and Support at Level 2 and Cultural Venue Administration or Cultural Heritage Operations at Level 3, Cultural Heritage at Level 4 and Cultural Heritage Management at Level 5.
- Some entrants to this profession take the Institute of Chartered Secretaries and Administrators (ICSA) professional examinations. Candidates without formal qualifications can take the Certificate in Business Practice and then progress to the Diploma and Professional Programme. Degrees, professional and vocational qualifications give exemption from some parts of the qualifying programme.
- Experience in the arts, in administration or business, and ICT skills can be an advantage.

GRCI:E

CLCI:E

Other related opportunities

- Art Exhibition Organiser p317
- Museum / Art Gallery p325

Advantages/disadvantages

- This job provides the satisfaction of working in the arts.
- Many roles are available on a part-time or project basis which can create job insecurity.
- You may have to move geographic areas to gain work.

Earnings guide

- Salary levels vary according to the type of organisation you work for.
- £13,000 per year is a normal starting salary for an assistant or trainee.
- When qualified this rises to £15,500.
- This can rise to £20,000+ with experience.
- Senior managers may earn between £25,000 and £60,000.
- Salaries are higher in London and in other large cities.

Further information

EQ
Suite E229
Dean Clough
Halifax
West Yorkshire
HX3 5AX
01422 381618
www.thinkeq.org.uk

Arts Council of England
2 Pear Tree Court
London
EC1R 0DS
0845 300 6200
www.artscouncil.org.uk

Scottish Arts Council
12 Manor Place
Edinburgh
EH3 7DD
0845 603 6000
www.scottisharts.org.uk

Arts Marketing Association
7a Clifton Court
Clifton Road
Cambridge
CB1 7BN
01223 578078
www.a-m-a.co.uk

Genealogist

What the work involves

- You will organise and plan research into the history or ancestry of individual families (genealogy) and write reports from your findings.
- You will work with a range of historical information such as newspapers and directories to trace specific facts about family histories.
- Your work could also involve liaising with or supervising the work of researchers.
- Meeting with clients and keeping them updated with your research would also be part of your job.

entry level

To both enter and train while working in this career, you will need qualifications at Level 2. Please refer to explanation on page vii.

Qualifications and courses

- There are no formal qualifications needed to be a professional genealogist. However, a good basic education along with a sound knowledge of social and local history sources are necessary. Knowledge of palaeography (the study of ancient writing and scripts) and Latin are also essential.
- Direct entry to this profession is not usual. Entrants normally have qualifications and experience in a related field such as archive administration, librarianship or historical research.
- A degree in history provides a useful first step, while University Campus Suffolk has a degree in Family and Community History. Blackpool and the Fylde College runs a Foundation degree in History and Heritage Management Studies, which covers genealogy.
- The Society of Genealogists provides short courses in genealogy and palaeography both for beginners and for those already working in the field. The Institute of Heraldic and Genealogical Studies provides qualifications for genealogists, including a certificate, higher certificate and diploma in genealogy. People who complete these qualifications may be able to progress to Licenciateship of the Institute.

The type of person suited to this work

As you will be investigating family history, a strong enthusiasm for historical research is essential. You will also need excellent research skills and the ability to understand detailed information. ICT skills will help you work with specialist research and information management software. You will also need writing skills to produce reports.

You should enjoy meeting a range of people. You will also need a good knowledge of historical resources and subject areas. An organised, thorough approach to your work is important. Working with unique historical documents demands good manual handling skills.

Working conditions

Most genealogists are self-employed and work from home or from offices. However, they spend a lot of their time in public records offices or in other sites, undertaking research.

The job can involve some travel, for example to public records offices or archive collections.

You will spend a lot of time reading and assessing detailed information.

The future outlook

Genealogy is usually followed as an interest rather than as a profession. The number of opportunities for work in this area is very small so there is a lot of competition.

Most genealogists work on a self-employed basis whilst a small number work for specialist research companies. They develop specialist knowledge on a specific subject or geographical area. Genealogists often undertake additional work such as teaching genealogy.

CRCI:K

CLCI:FAF

Other related opportunities

- Archivist p316
- Historian p320
- Public Records Officer p327
- Researcher p328

Advantages/disadvantages

- There are very few job opportunities. Most genealogists have additional employment.
- The work is often project-based, which creates some job insecurity.
- This work gives the satisfaction of providing people with information about their family history.

Earnings guide

- Freelance genealogists are usually paid at an hourly rate which can range from £16 to £35.
- For more complex projects, genealogists may charge a total fee. This can range from £35 to £100 depending on the amount of work involved.
- Genealogists with a postgraduate qualification can expect to earn £26,500–£33,000 per year.
- Very experienced/senior genealogists can earn £50,000+.

Further information

Creative and Cultural Skills
4th Floor
Lafone House
London
SE1 3HN
020 7015 1847
www.ccskills.org.uk

Society of Genealogists
14 Charterhouse Buildings
Goswell Road
London
EC1M 7BA
020 7251 8799
www.sog.org.uk

Institute of Heraldic and Genealogical Studies
79–82 Northgate
Canterbury
Kent
CT1 1BA
01227 768664
www.ihgs.ac.uk

Historian

What the work involves

- You will undertake historical research using ICT and paper-based information and other resources to broaden public and academic understanding of the past.
- You may teach and lecture on specific historical subjects. You could also write articles for professional journals and other publications.
- Heritage organisations sometimes employ historians.
- Professional historians usually specialise in a specific area of history such as women's history, the history of science or industrial history.

entry level

To both enter and train while working in this career, you will need qualifications at Level 4–8. Please refer to explanation on page vii.

The type of person suited to this work

For any job in this area, you will need a strong enthusiasm for history. You should also have a good knowledge of your specialist subjects. The ability to work with ICT and paper-based resources is also important. Good attention to detail will ensure that you undertake accurate research.

As you may need to explain complex issues to others, good verbal communication skills are important. Writing skills will help you write up research and articles. Historians need to consider a wide range of theories, so an open-minded approach is important. You should also be well organised to manage and plan your research.

Qualifications and courses

- An MA in history or historical archaeology is usually required for work as an archival or historical researcher.
- Entry requirements for postgraduate degrees are a first degree in history. Entry requirements for first degrees are generally 3 A levels/5 H Grades including history (A–C).
- For a position in a university faculty, a PhD is usually required.
- Training courses in historical research are available through the Institute of Historical Research, the Society of Genealogists and the Institute of Heraldic and Genealogical Studies.

Working conditions

You will undertake some of your work in libraries and archive centres. This will involve reading and assessing information. Some historical researchers are based in public records offices.

Historians in an academic role spend time lecturing and teaching students.

Undertaking historical research on a self-employed basis can create some job insecurity.

The future outlook

As a professional historian you could go into historical research or follow an academic career path. Many historians combine both roles and write, teach and research on their specialist area of interest. Others combine historical research with other related areas such as genealogy.

A small number of historians are employed by heritage organisations to provide expert advice and support.

CRCI:K

CLCI:FAG

Other related opportunities

- Archaeologist p315
- Archivist p316
- Genealogist p319
- Museum / Art Gallery p325
- Researcher p328

Advantages/disadvantages

- This type of work provides the satisfaction of undertaking original research and finding out about the past.
- It takes time to get established as a specialist on a specific historical period or subject either in research, writing or academic work.

Earnings guide

- Earnings vary according to your job.
- Historical researchers usually charge by the hour; rates vary from £16 to £35.
- Starting salaries for academic posts range from £21,000 to £27,000 per year.
- With experience this rises to around £33,000.
- At senior academic levels, this could increase to £35,000–£50,000.

Further information

Institute of Historical Research
University of London
Senate House
Malet Street
London
WC1E 7HU
020 7862 8740
www.history.ac.uk

Royal Historical Society
University College London
Gower Street
London
WC1E 6BT
020 7387 7532
www.rhs.ac.uk

Creative and Cultural Skills
4th Floor
Lafone House
London
SE1 3HN
020 7015 1847
www.ccskills.org.uk

Information Scientist

What the work involves

- You will develop, manage and coordinate information systems in a range of organisations and companies.
- You will utilise information systems and resources to locate and provide information in response to enquiries. You may work with ICT or paper-based information.
- You could work in a range of sectors, including law, education and business.
- Information scientists are employed in a variety of job roles and work as information analysts, information officers, information managers and librarians.

entry level

To both enter and train while working in this career, you will need qualifications at Level 4–8. Please refer to explanation on page vii.

The type of person suited to this work

Managing and working with information requires a range of skills. You should be able to work with different forms of information such as databases, the internet and paper resources. You may provide information for members of the public or staff within an organisation so strong communication skills are important. An interest in customer care is useful.

You will need writing skills for some roles and ICT skills are increasingly important. Managing information demands an organised, methodical approach. A good level of numeracy can be useful. You will need a resourceful approach when undertaking detailed research.

Working conditions

Information scientists work in offices, resource centres, libraries and other sites.

You may be based in a public centre and work face to face with members of the public or staff within your organisation. You may also deal with information enquiries over the phone and through email.

You will need to attend meetings with colleagues and managers.

The future outlook

Information science is a very broad area. You could begin in an assistant or junior information job. With experience, you could progress to working in an information management role.

Some information scientists with experience in a specialist area work on a consultancy basis. Some specialise in undertaking research whilst others organise new information systems. There are also opportunities to work abroad on a short-term or longer-term basis.

Qualifications and courses

- Most professional information scientists are graduates.
- The fastest route to professional qualification is via a first degree in subjects such as information management, information studies and information and library studies, which are accredited by the Chartered Institute of Library and Information Professionals (CILIP).
- An alternative route to professional qualification is via a degree in any subject, followed by a CILIP-approved postgraduate qualification. Experience of information-related work is advantageous, and may be a requirement for some postgraduate courses. Graduate training opportunities are available for people who wish to pursue a career in this area, and need to gain relevant experience before studying for a postgraduate qualification. Details are available through CILIP.
- It is also possible to become a qualified information scientist from a library/information assistant post. CILIP offers a Certification scheme for people with 5 years' experience of information work, or 2 years' experience plus relevant work-based training.
- Entrants through both the educational and certification routes may have the opportunity to work towards Chartered membership of CILIP. Candidates for Chartership must have completed an approved period of professional experience.

CRCI:K

CLCI:FAF

Other related opportunities

- Archivist p316
- Librarian p323
- Public Records Officer p327
- Researcher p328

Advantages/disadvantages

- Depending on the sector you work in, this job can be very fast paced.
- Information science skills are transferable to a wide range of job areas, allowing you to develop a career in areas that interest you such as the public sector or business.

Earnings guide

- £17,000–£20,000 per year is usual for starting salaries.
- When qualified you can get up to £26,000.
- With experience this rises to £35,000.
- £60,000 is possible at senior levels in large commercial organisations.
- Information consultants can earn around £400–£500 a day.

Further information

Chartered Institute of Library and Information Professionals
7 Ridgemount Street
London
WC1E 7AE
020 7255 0500
www.cilip.org.uk

Aslib, The Association for Information Management
Holywell Centre
1 Phipp Street
London
EC2A 4PS
020 7613 3031
www.aslib.com

Interpreter

What the work involves

- Interpreters convert words spoken in one language into conversation or speech in another language.
- Using your knowledge of foreign languages, you will enable speakers of different languages to communicate with each other.
- You may interpret while a person speaks or make notes and then interpret their statements.
- Interpreters provide services for international political conferences, court hearings, business meetings and public services.

entry level

To both enter and train while working in this career, you will need qualifications at Level 4–8. Please refer to explanation on page vii.

Qualifications and courses

- Most interpreters have a degree in languages or in translation and interpreting, or a combined degree in languages with a subject such as business, law or engineering. For modern language degrees, a modern language A level/H grade is normally required.
- Fluency in two languages including English is usually required to work as an interpreter.
- The Chartered Institute of Linguists (IoL) offers vocational qualifications in a wide range of languages, including the Certificate in Bilingual Skills (equivalent to A Level/H grade), the Diploma in Public Service Interpreting at NQF Level 6, and the Diploma in Translation at Level 7. Examinations are open entry, but candidates are expected to have achieved the required level of competence before sitting an exam.
- CILT, the National Centre for Languages, has developed National Occupational Standards for professional linguists. The Standards form the basis of NVQ/SVQ units, which may be awarded individually or may lead to NVQ/SVQ Level 4 or 5 in Public Service Interpreting.
- Qualified interpreters can work towards membership of the IoL or Institute of Translation and Interpreting. These professional bodies provide further training and development opportunities.

The type of person suited to this work

As an interpreter you will need a strong grasp of at least one and preferably two foreign languages. An understanding of the culture of the languages you are working in is important. You will also need to be able to listen well and speak clearly.

A confident approach is useful when interpreting in conferences and courts. You will interpret on areas such as business and law, so you will need a good knowledge of a range of subjects and of current affairs. You may have to interpret confidential information so a discreet approach is important. A good memory is useful. This type of work requires a good standard of health.

Working conditions

Intepreters have to concentrate continuously for long periods, which can be physically demanding.

The nature of the job demands the ability to travel to different geographic locations at fairly short notice, either abroad or within the UK.

Interpreters work in a range of environments, including high-profile conferences and formal meetings.

The future outlook

This area of work is very competitive with a limited number of full-time opportunities. A small number of interpreters work for international or European agencies. Others are employed by local governments and interpret in courts, hospitals and police stations.

You may choose to work within community organisations, helping people gain access to public services. Many interpreters work on a freelance basis for organisations or individuals.

CRCI:K

CLCI:FAL

Other related opportunities

- Importer / Exporter p567
- Secretary p28
- Teacher p184
- Translator p330

Advantages/disadvantages

- This type of work provides the opportunity to travel and live abroad.
- Due to tight schedules and high levels of travel, this can be a pressured job.
- Freelance interpreters often need to take on additional work to support themselves.

Earnings guide

- Newly qualified interpreters can expect a salary of around £20,000 per year.
- This can rise to £30,000 with experience and £60,000 at senior levels.
- Working freelance, you could charge between £275 and £400 per day.

Further information

CILT – The National Centre for Languages
20 Bedfordbury
London
WC2N 4LB
020 7379 5101
www.cilt.org.uk

Chartered Institute of Linguists
Saxon House
48 Southwark Street
London
SE1 1UN
020 7940 3100
www.iol.org.uk

Institute of Translation and Interpreting
Fortuna House
South Fifth Street
Milton Keynes
MK9 2EU
01908 325250
www.iti.org.uk

Librarian

What the work involves

- You will manage collections of books, newspapers and documents and ICT resources in libraries and information services to make them available to visitors.
- You may also choose new resources to suit the library or information service you work in.
- Your work will also involve helping visitors look for information and use ICT and other resources.
- Librarians are employed in libraries and in information and resources centres in schools, colleges, public libraries, private companies and government bodies.

entry level

To both enter and train while working in this career, you will need qualifications at Level 3–8. Please refer to explanation on page vii.

The type of person suited to this work

All library services exist to provide information and resources to visitors, so you should enjoy helping people with enquiries. Customer care skills are essential. You will also need good research skills and the ability to use resources to locate information. You should be able to communicate with a range of people.

The ability to work with ICT software, the internet and databases as well as explaining these to others is increasingly important. Management skills are useful, as is the ability to work as part of a team. Financial skills will help you manage budgets. You will need an organised approach to your work.

Working conditions

In many roles, you will work face to face with members of the public or staff within an organisation. Working on a counter, dealing with information enquiries, and lifting and carrying books can all be physically demanding.

Library work can be pressured, as you will need to locate and provide information to meet specific requests.

Regular weekend or evening work may be part of your job. It is also possible to do this job on a part-time basis.

The future outlook

Librarians play an important role in helping people access information. Your career path would depend on the area you choose to work in. After gaining experience you could progress into a senior role, taking responsibility for a specific subject or part of the library service.

At a senior level, you could manage a branch library or department. Some librarians move into information management roles within public services or private companies.

Qualifications and courses

- The fastest route to becoming a qualified librarian is via a degree accredited by the Chartered Institute of Library and Information Professionals (CILIP). The usual entry requirements are 2 A levels/3 H grades (any subjects), but people with experience as library assistants are often admitted to the degree courses with vocational qualifications.
- An alternative route is via a degree in another subject followed by a CILIP-accredited postgraduate qualification. Such courses usually last 1 year full time or 2–3 years part time. Prior experience of library or information work is advantageous, and is a requirement for some postgraduate courses. Graduate training opportunities are available for people who wish to pursue a career in this area and, and need to gain relevant experience before studying for a postgraduate qualification. The majority of trainee posts are in academic libraries, but there are also opportunities with legal and professional organisations. Details are available through CILIP.
- It is also possible for people working as library assistants to qualify as a librarian. CILIP offers a Certification scheme for people with 5 years' experience of library and information work, or 2 years' experience plus relevant work-based training.
- Entrants through both the educational and certification routes may have the opportunity to work towards Chartered membership of CILIP. Candidates for Chartership must have completed an approved period of professional experience.

CRCI:K

CLCI:FAF

Other related opportunities

- Archivist p316
- Information Scientist p321
- Library Assistant p324
- Public Records Officer p327

Advantages/disadvantages

- The job can be physically demanding.
- You may need to move geographic locations to develop your career.
- This type of work provides the satisfaction of helping people access information and other services.

Earnings guide

- Salaries vary according to the sector (public or private) in which you are employed, but CILIP recommends the following minimum salaries.
- Starting salaries for librarians range from £18,500 to £22,500 per year.
- At chartered librarian level, it is possible to earn up to £28,000.
- A senior academic librarian can earn up to £40,000, and a head of service £61,000.

Further information

Chartered Institute of Library and Information Professionals
7 Ridgemount Street
London
WC1E 7AE
020 7255 0500
www.cilip.org.uk

Aslib, The Association for Information Management
Holywell Centre
1 Phipp Street
London
EC2A 4PS
020 7613 3031
www.aslib.com

Library Assistant

What the work involves

- You will organise and reshelve books and other resources. You may also work on the library counter to help visitors with enquiries and check books in and out of the library.
- Administrative activities, such as dealing with petty cash, cataloguing new library resources and maintaining databases may also be part of your work.
- Library assistants work in libraries and in information and resources centres in schools, colleges, public libraries, private companies and government bodies.

entry level

To both enter and train while working in this career, you will need qualifications at Level 2. Please refer to explanation on page vii.

The type of person suited to this work

All library services exist to provide information and resources to visitors, so you should enjoy helping people with their enquiries. Customer care skills are useful. You should also be able to communicate well with a range of people. You should enjoy working as part of a team and providing support to librarians.

The ability to work with ICT software, the internet and databases can be helpful. Administrative and office skills are also useful. A flexible attitude will help you to manage a variety of tasks. You should also have an organised approach to your work.

Working conditions

You may work face to face with members of the public or staff within an organisation.

Library work can be pressured and physically demanding as you will be on your feet, lifting, carrying and re-shelving books.

Depending on your job, you may have to work some regular weekends or evenings. Some people in this job are also employed on a part-time basis.

The future outlook

Library assistants are employed in library and information services in businesses, community library services and government. Larger organisations provide opportunities to progress into senior library assistant roles and take on additional responsibilities.

At this stage, you could choose to work at the senior level of library assistant work. Some library assistants gain a library qualification in order to move on to working as librarians.

Qualifications and courses

- Library assistants are often expected by employers to have at least 5 GCSEs/S grades (A–C/1–3) or the equivalent, usually including English. Some assistant posts, for example in commercial libraries or information centres, may require A levels/H grades.
- Training usually takes place in the workplace under the supervision of experienced staff. Assistants may be encouraged to study towards a City & Guilds qualification or NVQs/SVQs in Information and Library Services at Levels 2 and 3.
- In Scotland, it is possible to work towards the 2-year SQA National Certificate in Library and Information Science.
- Apprenticeships/Skillseekers in Information and Library Services may be available for candidates aged 16–24.
- Senior library assistants can study for a librarianship qualification (degree or postgraduate qualification) accredited by the Chartered Institute of Library and Information Professionals (CILIP).
- The Chartered Institute of Library and Information Professionals (CILIP) provides a wide range of courses for those already working in library services.

CRCI:K | CLCI:FAF

Other related opportunities

- Archivist p316
- Information Scientist p321
- Librarian p323

Advantages/disadvantages

- The job often involves working on your feet and dealing with people, which can be physically demanding.
- Library/information work provides the satisfaction of supporting services which provide information and other important facilities to people.

Earnings guide

- Salaries vary according to employer and geographic location.
- Librarians start at around £13,000 per year.
- You can get £17,000–£15,000 with experience.
- Senior assistants can earn up to about £20,000.

Further information

www.cityandguilds.com/myperfectjob

Chartered Institute of Library and Information Professionals
7 Ridgemount Street
London
WC1E 7AE
020 7255 0500
www.cilip.org.uk

Aslib, The Association for Information Management
Holywell Centre
1 Phipp Street
London
EC2A 4PS
020 7613 3031
www.aslib.com

Museum / Art Gallery

What the work involves

Assistant/attendant

- You will work face to face with visitors to galleries and museums, deal with enquiries and provide information.
- Your role will also involve attending and watching over the security of exhibitions and displays.
- You will help set up and dismantle exhibitions. You may also be responsible for museum/gallery security and fire safety.

Curator

- You will manage and maintain collections of artworks, historical objects or documents. Curators usually have specialist knowledge of a specific historical or cultural field such as women's history, textiles or archaeology.
- You will write and research on the collections in your care.
- You may also give talks to members of the public at special events.
- You will work with other museum/gallery staff to plan exhibitions using items and information from your collection.

Technician

- You will help prepare gallery and museum spaces for temporary exhibitions and collection displays.
- Your work will involve installing audio-visual equipment, such as lighting to suit specific exhibitions. You will also transport objects and artworks to and from exhibition spaces.
- You will provide general technical support to the museums/gallery team as required.

The type of person suited to this work

Assistant/attendant

You should enjoy meeting and helping people, because you will deal with members of the public on a regular basis. You will need a patient and friendly approach when responding to enquiries and protecting fragile exhibition pieces from over-enthusiastic visitors! You will need a good understanding of fire and security issues. Manual handling skills are useful for setting up and taking down exhibitions. As you may deal with money in a museum or gallery shop, cash-handling skills are useful. You should also be able to work well as part of a team.

Curator

As you will be responsible for managing and caring for collections of historical objects, you will need a good knowledge of history and of your specialist area. You will also need to be able to communicate this information to other staff and to members of the public. You may speak at educational events, so enthusiasm for your subject is essential. You will also need good written communication skills for writing reports. ICT skills are increasingly important in this area, for example when managing collection information through specialist databases. Manual handling skills will help you to handle objects carefully when assessing them.

Technician

You will need a good range of technical skills to meet the varied practical demands of a museum/gallery environment. As well as providing support for setting up new exhibitions, you will have to deal with practical problems as they arise. The ability to handle fragile or valuable objects and artworks is also useful. You will also need a good knowledge of building security and maintenance. You may also be responsible for the fire safety of the gallery/museum. You will be a good team player and have a strong interest in helping people get the most out of their visits to galleries and museums.

Working conditions

You may have to be on call to respond to emergencies at the gallery/museum.

Many jobs in the museum/galleries sector involve weekend or evening work. You may have to work long hours to set up and install new exhibitions.

Assistant/attendant

You will have to spend a lot of your time on your feet when undertaking security at exhibitions, which can be physically demanding.

The future outlook

Whilst museum/gallery work is a competitive area in which to develop a career, it offers a variety of interesting roles. You could work your way up in some larger organisations, but often you will need to move employers in order to move up the career ladder.

Whatever job role interests you, gaining relevant work experience is very important. It is also helpful to focus on the subjects that interest you, such as modern art, natural history or archaeology.

Assistant/attendant

With experience, you could go on to work as a senior attendant/assistant, managing a team of attendants/assistants.

Curator

From working as an assistant curator, you could progress into a curator's role. From here you could move on to work as a senior curator or go into managing museums/galleries or historic buildings.

Technician

It is possible to progress to working as a senior or head technician. In larger organisations, you could manage a team of technicians.

Qualifications and courses

Assistant/attendant

- Experience of working with the public and an interest in museums are more important than formal qualifications for these roles. A good general education is usually required and some museums/galleries require 5 GCSEs/S grades (A–C/1–3).
- You may be able to gain NVQs/SVQs in Heritage Care and Visitor Services at Level 2 and Cultural Heritage Operations at Level 3 whilst working.

Curator

- Entrants should normally have a relevant degree and/or a postgraduate qualification in museum, gallery or heritage studies. Voluntary experience in a museum, gallery or other heritage site is also important.
- A wide range of degree subjects are relevant to museum work, including history, fine art, history of art, biology, botany, chemistry, anthropology and textiles. Some degrees include modules/placements specifically relevant to museum studies. Some specialised degrees such as museum and gallery studies, art gallery and heritage management are available
- NVQs/SVQs offer an alternative route for people with relevant work experience. NVQs/SVQs are available at Levels 3, 4 and 5 in Cultural Heritage Operations, Cultural Heritage and Cultural Heritage Management.
- People working in museums can also work towards Associateship of the Museums Association. This qualification is available to people in all areas of museum work, and takes 2 years to achieve.

entry level

To both enter and train while working in this career, you will need qualifications at Level 2–8. Please refer to explanation on page vii.

Technician

- Technical knowledge and experience of working with the public is usually required.
- Specific craft skills such as carpentry can be useful.
- For some roles, people with a knowledge of art and artistic techniques may be preferred.

Other related opportunities

- Archaeologist p315
- Art Exhibition Organiser p317
- Arts Administrator p318
- Restorer / Conservation Officer p329

Advantages/disadvantages

- These jobs provide the satisfaction of working closely with works of art and historical objects, some of which can be very valuable.
- Because of the public nature of attendant/assistant roles, this can be a sociable job.
- This is a competitive area of work, so you may have to change jobs to receive promotion.

Earnings guide

Assistant/attendant

- £11,000–£13,000 per year is usual for starting salaries.
- With experience or progression to a senior assistant/attendant role you could earn £15,000–£16,000.

Curator

- £16,000–£17,000 is usual for a starting salary.
- This can rise to £21,000–£26,000 with experience.
- £27,000–£36,000 is possible at senior levels.

Technician

- £15,000–£17,000 is the usual rate for those with experience.
- £20,000+ is possible at senior levels.

Further information

Creative and Cultural Skills
4th Floor
Lafone House
London
SE1 3HN
020 7015 1847
www.ccskills.org.uk

Museums Association
24 Calvin Street
London
E1 6NW
020 7426 6910
www.museumsassociation.org

National Association of Decorative and Fine Arts Societies
NADFAS House
8 Guilford Street
London
WC1N 1DA
020 7430 0730
www.nadfas.org.uk

CRCI:K

CLCI:FAE

Public Records Officer

What the work involves

- You will work on reception and respond to information requests from members of the public. You may also work in reading rooms helping people use resources.
- You will help manage collections of records and prepare, catalogue and archive new records.
- National and local public records offices collect and preserve historical and modern documents. These include central government records, court records and documents about a specific geographical area and its activities, such as maps, account books and photographs.

entry level

To both enter and train while working in this career, you will need qualifications at Level 4–8. Please refer to explanation on page vii.

Qualifications and courses

- Public records officers need to be trained as archivists.
- A good Honours degree and a postgraduate qualification in archive studies/records management are required. Your first degree should usually be in a history, language or information science-related subject, but most courses are acceptable provided you can show a keen interest in history.
- Relevant experience is an advantage for gaining a place on a postgraduate course.
- The National Archives provides short training courses in Records and Information Management which are specific to public records.

The type of person suited to this work

As you will work directly with visitors, you will need good customer service skills and an interest in helping people with their research. Strong communication skills are important at all levels of public records office work.

The ability to write will help you to accurately record documents and keep track of enquiries. You will use your ICT skills on a regular basis. You should be able to work within professional classification systems. Cash-handling skills are useful when working on reception. Financial skills will help you manage budgets in more senior jobs. A well-organised approach is important.

Working conditions

At junior levels particularly, you will have to work some evening and weekend shifts.

Depending on your role, you will be based on reception dealing with enquiries from members of the public. You may also work in centre reading rooms, helping people use resources.

At more senior levels you would spend time in meetings, planning and overseeing public records services.

The future outlook

Opportunities exist within local records centres and the National Archive (Public Records Office). You could start in a general support role and then progress with experience and further qualifications, into a records management/archive position. You may choose to move into related areas, such as libraries/archives management or work in a records or information role for a private company.

CRCI:AC | CLCI:CAG

Other related opportunities

- Archivist p316
- Information Scientist p321
- Librarian p323
- Researcher p328

Advantages/disadvantages

- This job can be pressured as it combines working with the public with providing information on request.
- You will work with documents of historical and cultural interest.
- Many public records offices offer flexible working schemes.

Earnings guide

- Starting salaries for staff providing reception and reading room support range from £15,000 to £20,000 per year.
- This can rise to £22,000 with experience.
- £27,000–£40,000 is possible at senior levels.

Further information

Creative and Cultural Skills
4th Floor
Lafone House
London
SE1 3HN
020 7015 1847
www.ccskills.org.uk

Society of Archivists
Prioryfield House
20 Canon Street
Taunton
Somerset
TA1 1SW
01823 327030
www.archives.org.uk

National Archives
Kew
Richmond
Surrey
TW9 4DU
020 8876 3444
www.nationalarchives.gov.uk

Records Management Society
Woodside
Coleheath Bottom, Speen
Princes Risborough
Buckinghamshire
HP27 0SZ
01494 488566
www.rms-gb.org.uk

Researcher

What the work involves

- You will undertake research on specific areas, such as family history and the history of specific geographic locations on behalf of members of the public.
- You may undertake large research projects or smaller projects to locate specific pieces of information.
- Researchers work with records and documents in public records offices, archives and libraries. They also research family or personal documents.
- Some researchers write special-interest books and give public talks.

The type of person suited to this work

Researching detailed historical information requires a conscientious and well-organised approach. You will also need the skills to research and assess a range of records and documents. As many records and historical documents are stored electronically, ICT skills are essential.

It is important that you can communicate well with clients to assess exactly the kind of information that they require. Written communication skills will help you to create accurate and informative research reports for your clients. You will need good business sense and the confidence to promote your service, to work on a self-employed basis.

Working conditions

Most researchers work on a self-employed basis from home. However, they spend a lot of their working day based in public records offices, archive centres and local studies libraries.

This work involves a lot of close reading of detailed information on paper and computer.

You will work alone most of the time, which may not suit some people.

The future outlook

In order to develop a career, you will need to decide which areas to focus on. Most researchers have knowledge of a specific geographical location and of the record centres that hold relevant information. Some work as record agents, undertaking research in specific records centres on behalf of clients.

Whatever area you decide to work in, you will need to undertake a range of projects to make a living in this competitive area.

entry level

3

To both enter and train while working in this career, you will need qualifications at Level 3. Please refer to explanation on page vii.

Qualifications and courses

- There are no formal qualifications for gaining work as a freelance researcher or record agent, but a good level of experience and general education is very helpful.
- For genealogy research, a thorough knowledge of social and local history sources and knowledge of palaeography and some Latin is essential.
- An MA in history or historical archaeology is usually needed for work as an archival or historical researcher.
- Training courses in historical research are available through the Institute of Historical Research, the Society of Genealogists and the Institute of Heraldic and Genealogical Studies.

CRCI:K

CLCI:F

Other related opportunities

- Archivist p316
- Genealogist p319
- Historian p320

Advantages/disadvantages

- Working on a self-employed basis can lead to job insecurity. You may need to take on other work to make a living.
- This job enables you to undertake original research, which can be a challenging, but interesting process.

Earnings guide

- Researchers usually work on a freelance basis and charge by the hour. Hourly rates vary from £18 to £40.
- For larger projects, they may charge a total fee that can vary from £35 to £100, depending on the amount of work involved.

Further information

Creative and Cultural Skills
4th Floor
Lafone House
London
SE1 3HN
020 7015 1847
www.ccskills.org.uk

Institute of Historical Research
University of London
Senate House
Malet Street
London
WC1E 7HU
020 7862 8740
www.history.ac.uk

Institute of Heraldic and Genealogical Studies
79–82 Northgate
Canterbury
Kent
CT1 1BA
01227 768664
www.ihgs.ac.uk

Restorer / Conservation Officer

What the work involves

- You will manage the preservation of historical objects and artworks, applying your specialist knowledge of subjects such as textiles and furniture.
- You may undertake conservation work, treating objects to protect them against wear and tear, or restore objects to as close to their original state as possible. Your job may involve managing freelance restorers/conservators.
- As well as objects in museums and galleries, restoration/conservation officers manage the care of historic houses and stately homes.

entry level

To both enter and train while working in this career, you will need qualifications at Level 3. Please refer to explanation on page vii.

Qualifications and courses

- Entry is usually by degree or postgraduate qualification, though candidates with relevant craft qualifications and experience may be eligible.
- Degrees and Foundation degrees are available in various restoration and conservation areas such as furniture and buildings. For Foundation degrees, work experience or a range of GCSEs are usually required. For degree entry, a Foundation degree or HND or 2 A levels/3 H grades (including chemistry) are normally required.
- For postgraduate courses a relevant degree, such as science, fine art or art history, is usually required.
- Voluntary experience is useful, and can be gained through the National Association of Decorative and Fine Arts Societies (NADFAS) volunteer scheme.
- Restorers/Conservation Officers can work towards NVQs/SVQs in Cultural Heritage Operations (Level 3), Cultural Heritage (Level 4) and Cultural Heritage Management (Level 5).

The type of person suited to this work

The role of preserving and protecting valuable collections or buildings requires a good knowledge of conservation and restoration issues. In some jobs, you will undertake conservation/restoration work yourself so you will need excellent practical skills and good attention to detail.

In other jobs you will manage other professionals to do the work, so communication skills are essential. These skills will also be useful when advising colleagues and providing information at public events. Writing skills are also helpful and ICT skills are increasingly important. The ability to work as part of a team is essential.

Working conditions

Your work is likely to involve handling and treating fragile objects, so good practical skills are important.

You may have to work with specialist materials and equipment, which can affect people with skin conditions.

In most jobs, you will spend much of your time assessing and researching collections. You will also attend meetings with colleagues.

The future outlook

Restoration/conservation officers work in museums, galleries and historic houses, often with alternative job titles such as Collections Manager or Curator. Many will have worked as craft conservators/restorers or have gained extensive experience in caring for collections.

Having geographic mobility will help you to gain work. With experience, you could progress into managing a historic house or into a senior management role in a museum or gallery.

Other related opportunities

- Archaeologist p315
- Art Restorer p130
- Museum / Art Gallery p325

Advantages/disadvantages

- This type of work offers the chance to protect and care for valuable historical collections.
- Most galleries/museums employ only one person in this type of role, so you may have to move around to develop your career in this area.

Earnings guide

- Salaries vary according to your employer.
- New entrants may start at £16,000–£18,000 per year.
- This can rise to £20,000–£30,000 with experience.
- £35,000+ is possible at senior levels.
- Your salary will depend on the high quality of your work and it may be easier to get work in London and the larger cities.

Further information

Creative and Cultural Skills
4th Floor
Lafone House
London
SE1 3HN
020 7015 1847
www.ccskills.org.uk

National Association of Decorative and Fine Arts Societies
NADFAS House
8 Guilford Street
London
WC1N 1DA
020 7430 0730
www.nadfas.org.uk

Institute of Conservation (Icon)
3rd floor, Downstream Building
1 London Bridge
London
SE1 9BG
020 7785 3807
www.icon.org.uk

Translator

What the work involves

- You will convert written text from one language to another. You will ensure that your translation matches the tone and style of the original text and has a high standard of grammar.
- You will translate documents such as letters, reports, leaflets and brochures.
- Your work will also involve meetings with employers to agree projects.
- Translators provide services to specialist translation agencies, private companies, local government bodies and international organisations.

The type of person suited to this work

Translators must work to a high standard of accuracy, so attention to detail is important. The ability to write in your chosen languages in a range of styles is essential. You should also be able to understand and translate complex documents. ICT skills are very useful. Your verbal communication skills will help you to discuss and agree projects with employers.

Discretion is important as you may translate confidential information. Being well organised will help you to meet project deadlines. You will need a confident approach to work on a freelance basis and promote your services. Numeracy skills are also useful.

Working conditions

Translators are usually based in offices at home, if self-employed, or in companies.

You may attend meetings with employers and colleagues.

This type of work involves close working at a computer and the use of resources such as dictionaries and technical reference books.

The future outlook

As a translator you could work for a variety of employers, translating medical, technical, legal and other documents. This is a competitive area, but the increase in internet-based business and the communication needs of organisations offers some interesting opportunities. Many translators work on a freelance basis.

There are opportunities to work for private companies and international organisations on a permanent basis, in the UK or abroad.

entry level

To both enter and train while working in this career, you will need qualifications at Level 4–8. Please refer to explanation on page vii.

Qualifications and courses

- Most translators have a relevant degree. These include degrees in one or more foreign languages (preferably applied), a foreign language combined with a specialist subject such as business, law, engineering, computer studies, Asian or European studies, or translation or interpreting.
- For modern language degrees, a modern language A level/H grade is normally required.
- Postgraduate courses in translation are available, and usually require a degree in a modern language. The Chartered Institute of Linguists (IoL) offers vocational qualifications in a wide range of languages, including the Certificate in Bilingual Skills (equivalent to A Level/H grade) the Diploma in Public Service Interpreting at NQF Level 6, and the Diploma in Translation at Level 7. Examinations are open entry, but candidates are expected to have achieved the required level of competence before sitting an exam.
- Fluency in two or more languages is required to work as a translator.
- Qualified translators can work towards membership of the IoL or Institute of Translation and Interpreting. These professional bodies provide further training and development opportunities.

CRCI:K | CLCI:FAL

Other related opportunities

- Interpreter p322
- Secretary p28

Advantages/disadvantages

- This area of work can provide opportunities to travel and work abroad.
- Working on a self-employed project-by-project basis can create some job instability.
- Translation can be very demanding due to short deadlines and the constant demand for accuracy.

Earnings guide

- Translators may be paid between £75 and £180 per 1000 words, depending on the language they are translating.
- Translators employed by business, for example in technical translation, can earn £18,000 per year as a starting salary.
- This can increase to £25,000–£50,000 with experience.
- Translators employed by business, for example in technical translation, can earn £18,000 per year as a starting salary.

Further information

CILT – The National Centre for Languages
20 Bedfordbury
London
WC2N 4LB
020 7379 5101
www.cilt.org.uk

Chartered Institute of Linguists
Saxon House
48 Southwark Street
London
SE1 1UN
020 7940 3100
www.iol.org.uk

Institute of Translation and Interpreting
Fortuna House
South Fifth Street
Milton Keynes
MK9 2EU
01908 325250
www.iti.org.uk

Are you interested in fairness and justice? Law and politics includes jobs that make sure everyone is given an equal voice. This cluster includes:

- **Barrister**
- **Crown Prosecutor**
- **Legal Executive**
- **Member of Parliament**
- **Patent Attorney**

But what's it like working in this area?

Here's Leanne Nuttall's story:

Legal Executive

Having failed to get the A level grades she needed to study Law at university, and also disheartened by how much such a degree would cost, Leanne, 24, decided to become a Legal Executive instead (a position with duties very similar to those of a solicitor). Leanne went the vocational route by working with the law firm Clyde & Co. in the City by day and studying at college one night a week. Her course, with the Institute of Legal Executives (ILEX), lasted four years and she is now a Member of ILEX. However she cannot call herself a Legal Executive until she has become a Fellow of ILEX, which she will achieve by working for her law firm full time for a further two years. In the meantime her title is Legal Assistant.

WHAT LEANNE ACTUALLY DOES

'I started out as Clyde & Co.'s Outdoor Clerk, going to the court every day and taking all the papers that needed to go down, but now I am office-based and have my own cases I deal with under supervision from my department. In the beginning you are given all the jobs no one else wants to do, like the filing and photocopying, getting bundles together, sending the bills out to clients and chasing clients for payment. But if you stick with it, it soon becomes interesting. Every day can be different as you will be working on a case and a fax comes in and you will think "I must go and sort this out". Because we all work on different cases, everyone is really interested in what everyone else is doing. There are always emails flying about saying "does anyone know about this?".'

WHAT SHE LOVES ABOUT HER JOB

'I've wanted to go into law since I was about five. I love talking to clients, debating with the other side and trying to agree and get the best settlement for my client. When you work on a case for two years and you finally win at the end of it, that's a great feeling.'

One of the downsides of being a Legal Executive rather than having a law degree and being a solicitor is that you don't earn the same money or respect, and you also cannot become a Partner in your firm. However, you can continue studying with ILEX and qualify as a solicitor by doing two courses (the CTE and the LPC) that take a further two to five years. This may seem a long time, but Leanne says there are advantages to doing it this way round.

'You do need determination and persistence because you won't get the money or the perks straight away being a Legal Executive. But if you don't want to go to university and get a law degree you can join a firm and earn as you learn. Just think, I'm not £15,000 in debt like many law students and I already have four years' experience of working in the industry. It may take me two years longer to qualify, but I want to stay with Clyde & Co. as long as I can, because I like the City life and ultimately I want to become a Partner.'

Bailiff / Enforcement Agent

What the work involves

- Court bailiffs deliver legal documents such as court summonses to people who owe money and might also take steps to get the money paid.
- Certificated/private bailiffs visit people in debt to recover the money they owe, arranging for removal of their property where necessary.
- In Scotland, officers of court deliver legal documents to people who owe money and take all the legal steps required to get the money paid.
- You might also give advice on how to pay debts.

entry level

To both enter and train while working in this career, you will need qualifications at Level 1–2. Please refer to explanation on page vii.

The type of person suited to this work

As there are strict legal procedures connected with recovering debt, you will need to enjoy dealing with information to make sure you are completely up to date and need to be thorough in your work so that you do everything correctly and legally. Good communication skills are needed to make sure people understand what they have to do.

The work will bring you into contact with many different types of people, so it's important that you are able to deal with all sorts of people. You may need to be assertive to deal with people's resistance and be persistent to get the job done. Being tactful and able to cope with people under stress are also important.

Qualifications and courses

- In England, employers tend to look for 4 GCSEs/S grades (A–C/1–3), including English and maths. Applicants must be aged between 21 and 62 but mature candidates, without a criminal record or debt, are often preferred because their life experience may help them deal with difficult situations.
- To become a certificated bailiff, candidates need to obtain a Bailiff's General Certificate. This is issued by a circuit judge who will ask candidates questions on bailiff law and procedures. The necessary legal knowledge can be gained by taking the examinations of the Certificated Bailiffs' Association.
- In Scotland, at least 5 GCSEs/S grades, including English and maths, are required. Applicants should be under 70.
- To be commissioned as a sheriff officer, candidates need to pass the examinations of the Society of Messengers-at-Arms and Sheriff Officers. The minimum age to be commissioned is 20 but training, which normally takes 3 years, can begin earlier.
- In England and Wales, bailiffs work in both the public and private sector (high court and civil service bailiffs, as well as private/ certified bailiffs). Training is comprised of a mixture of on the job and short courses.
- A clean current driving licence is useful. Maturity and experience are an advantage.
- A bond up to the value of £10,000, plus two references will be required for insurance purposes.

Working conditions

You will spend a lot of time travelling and so will need a clean driving licence. Although you will be based in an office, you might have to visit people's homes in the evenings and early mornings to make sure that someone is there.

If you have to remove furniture in payment of debt, you could have to do a lot of heavy lifting, so you will need to be physically fit.

The future outlook

In England and Wales, court bailiffs generally work for the county courts and private bailiffs with magistrates' court orders.

In Scotland, officers of court are called sheriff officers in the sheriff court and messengers-at-arms in the Court of Session.

There are few openings for this kind of work and you are unlikely to start straight from school. You could become self-employed or work part time. Promotion prospects are also limited. You could progress into other types of work, for example security.

CRCI:L

CLCI:LAG

Other related opportunities

- Administrator p6
- Court Administrative Officer p335
- Court Usher / Officer / Macer p338
- Debt Counsellor / Money Adviser p531
- Security p518
- Welfare Rights Officer / Worker p550

Advantages/disadvantages

- The work is varied and no two days will be the same.
- You will not spend all your time in one place.
- You will meet many different people, some of whom may be difficult to deal with and threatening.
- The hours can be long and unsocial.

Earnings guide

- Starting salaries are around £14,000–£16,000 per year.
- This rises to £20,000–£25,000 with experience.
- Around £30,,000 is possible for the very experienced.
- Private firms may pay you a basic salary plus some form of commission or commission only.
- In Scotland you could start at around £17,000; with experience you could get £26,000–£28,000.

Further information

www.cityandguilds.com/myperfectjob

Enforcement Services Association
Park House
10 Park Street
Bristol
BS1 5HX
0117 907 4771
www.ensas.org.uk

Society of Messengers-at-Arms and Sheriff Officers
11 Alva Street
Edinburgh
EH2 4PH
0131 225 9110
www.smaso.org

Barrister's / Advocate's Clerk

What the work involves

- The job involves managing the day-to-day work for a group of barristers (England and Wales) or advocates (Scotland).
- An important task will be liaising with solicitors to encourage them to give work to your business.
- You will estimate how much work is involved in a case to see how much time it will take, allocate cases to barristers/advocates and negotiate fees.
- When you first enter this career, you will prepare accounts, do filing and photocopying, and answer the phone.

The type of person suited to this work

As your work will involve meeting people and talking to them, you will need excellent speaking skills. Good writing skills are useful for writing letters and preparing notes and reports. Being good with figures is essential when negotiating fees and preparing accounts.

You will need to be businesslike and have good negotiating skills to bring in work, and confidence to deal with solicitors, court officials and clients.

Your work will involve handling confidential information, which means discretion and tact are necessary. It is also important to be a good team worker and flexible in your approach to work.

Working conditions

You will work mainly indoors in an office, probably using computers and spending a lot of time on the telephone. However, you may travel in connection with your work so a driving licence is useful.

As you will also be meeting other professionals, you will have to be smartly dressed at all times.

Most of your work will be Monday to Friday during standard office hours with evenings and weekends during busy periods.

The future outlook

There are very few vacancies for this job. Barristers are based in offices known as 'chambers' with one clerk serving more than one barrister. Advocates work in groups known as 'stables' in the Advocates' Library in Edinburgh. You would start as a junior clerk (England and Wales) or deputy (Scotland) and progress to clerk with experience. Training will be ongoing throughout your career. With experience you could train for another legal profession or move into general administrative work.

You normally start work as a deputy in Scotland and either apply elsewhere or gain internal promotion from deputy to advocates' clerk.

entry level

3–8

To both enter and train while working in this career, you will need qualifications at Level 3–8. Please refer to explanation on page vii.

Qualifications and courses

- In England and Wales, barristers' clerks usually require a minimum of 4 GCSEs/S grades (A–C/1–3), including maths and English. A levels are an advantage. In Scotland (for the Advocate's clerk post) applicants will be at a distinct advantage if they offer H grades.
- Candidates may join the Institute of Barristers' Clerks (IBC). After completing an appropriate BTEC course and 5 years' service in Chambers, a student can apply for qualified membership of the IBC.
- IBC provide training courses, such as the BTEC Advanced Award in Chambers Administration, Level 3 for junior clerks with approximately 3 years of experience.
- In Scotland, advocates' clerks are usually employed from age 17–18 or after several years' legal experience and require a minimum of an H grade in English, and evidence of computer literacy and numeracy.
- Most training is on the job but candidates are encouraged to take courses organised by Faculty Services Ltd.

Other related opportunities

- Barrister / Advocate p334
- Court Administrative Officer p335
- Court Legal Advisor / Court Clerk / Sheriff's Clerk p336
- Legal Executive p342
- Secretary p28
- Solicitor / Notary Public p349

Advantages/disadvantages

- Your work will be interesting and varied.
- You will have a lot of responsibility.
- You will meet many different people.
- You might have to work long hours and stay late in the evenings to meet deadlines.
- With extra training you can progress into other legal careers.

Earnings guide

- Salaries start at around £12,000–£16,000 per year.
- With experience clerks can earn between £30,000 and £50,000.
- Senior clerks sometimes can earn up to £100,000.
- With further experience, self-employment might be an option for you. Once self-employed you could earn around £24,000 to £30,000.
- In Scotland you can earn between £24,000 and £28,000. As a senior you can earn up to £45,000.

Further information

Institute of Barristers' Clerks
289-293 High Holborn
London
WC1 7HZ
020 7831 7144
www.ibc.org.uk

Faculty Services Ltd
Advocates' Library
Parliament House
Edinburgh
EH1 1RF
0131 260 5636
www.advocates.org.uk

Barrister / Advocate

What the work involves

- Barristers (in England and Wales) and advocates (in Scotland) give legal advice to solicitors and other professionals either in writing or face to face, and act for clients in certain cases in the high courts.
- You will research information and past cases before giving advice to solicitors and also advise them on whether a case should come to court.
- In court, you will examine witnesses and present the case for the prosecution or the defence.
- You will also act for clients at tribunals or enquiries if asked to act by a solicitor.

The type of person suited to this work

As you will need to research large amounts of information, including past cases, before giving legal advice, an interest in research and the ability to handle information are essential. You will need to be able to think logically to work out what's important in the case and apply the law to it.

You will need to be confident to speak in court and convince a jury with your arguments, and be able to think quickly when questioning witnesses or defendants. Good writing and speaking skills are needed to deal with people and prepare your case.

Keeping an open mind is important and you must be able to gain people's confidence.

Working conditions

Barristers usually work in offices called 'chambers', and advocates in groups known as 'stables' in the Advocates' Library in Edinburgh.

If you specialise in criminal law, you will spend more time in court than civil law specialists would. As you will travel widely, a driving licence is useful.

You will use computers for research and reports, and wear robes in court.

The future outlook

Most barristers/advocates are self-employed and it can take around 5 years to establish a practice and become known. After 10–15 years' experience you can apply to 'take silk' to become a Queen's Counsel. This is essential if you want to become a judge in the higher courts. Some people work in central or local government where there is a clear promotion structure. Undertaking continuous professional development is important.

entry level

To both enter and train while working in this career, you will need qualifications at Level 4–8. Please refer to explanation on page vii.

Qualifications and courses

England and Wales

- For the academic stage, you will need either an approved law degree (minimum 2.2) or another degree (minimum 2.2) followed by a postgraduate law conversion course, known as the Common Professional Examination (CPE), or a Postgraduate Diploma in Law.
- For the vocational stage, you must become a student member of one of the 4 Inns of Court and undertake the Bar Vocational Course (1 year full-time, 2 years part-time). You must also complete two 6-month pupillages working in Chambers.
- Training for the 'bar' continues for 3 years, working in one of the Inns of Court.

Scotland

- For the academic stage, you will need either an Honours degree in Scottish Law from a Scottish University (minimum 2.2); an Ordinary degree in Scottish Law from a Scottish University with an Honours degree from a UK university (minimum 2.2); or a Scottish Ordinary degree with distinction. You must also undertake a 1-year full-time postgraduate Diploma in Legal Practice at a Scottish university.
- For the vocational stage, you will need to work for 12–21 months in a solicitor's office and 'devilling' to a member of the bar for 9 and a half months, before taking the entry examinations of the Faculty of Advocates.
- Advocates will normally practice as a solicitor for 10 years, prior to acting as an advocate.

Other related opportunities

- Barrister / Advocate's Clerk p333
- Court Legal Advisor / Court Clerk / Sheriff's Clerk p336
- Crown Prosecutor / Coroner / Procurator Fiscal p339
- Judge / Sheriff p341
- Legal Executive p342
- Solicitor / Notary Public p349

Advantages/disadvantages

- The work is varied and you will get satisfaction when you win a case.
- You will work with a wide range of people.
- Some cases may put you under pressure, particularly if they attract media attention.
- You will sometimes work long hours to meet deadlines.

Earnings guide

- During pupillage £11,000–£20,000 per year is the average salary.
- Earnings between £25,000 and £56,000 are normal in the Crown Prosecution Service in England and Wales.
- As an Advocate in Scotland you may start at around £11,000; moving up to £24,000–£56,000 in the Procurator Fiscal Service.
- Top barristers earn up to £250,000, sometimes more.
- The majority of practising barristers in both England and Scotland are self-employed. Earnings can be anything between £25,000 and £1,000,000 depending on experience, location and reputation.

Further information

General Council of the Bar of England and Wales
289-293 High Holborn
London
WC1V 7HZ
020 7242 0082
www.barcouncil.org.uk

Faculty of Advocates
The Clerk of Faculty
Advocates' Library, Parliament House
Edinburgh
EH1 1RF
0131 226 5071
www.advocates.org.uk

Court Administrative Officer

What the work involves

- You will organise all the papers and information for a court hearing so that everything is ready for the judge or magistrate when the hearing starts.
- Booking dates, times and courtrooms for court hearings will be part of your job and you will prepare the timetable for each day.
- You will make sure everyone arriving at court knows where to go.
- After the hearings, you will carry out court orders, for example endorsing driving licences, writing adoption orders or collecting fines.

entry level

To both enter and train while working in this career, you will need qualifications at Level 2–3. Please refer to explanation on page vii.

Qualifications and courses

- Qualification requirements vary within different regions, but a good general education is required, with 2–5 GCSEs/S grades, including maths and English, depending on the type of court and location. Some areas require administrative, typing, office or computing experience with others also requiring a minimum of 1 year of relevant office-based experience. Contact your local courts to research their requirements. Applicants without formal qualifications may be able to sit an aptitude test. New recruits tend to hold A levels/H grades and will usually need 5 GCSEs/S grades (A–C/1–3) or equivalent qualifications.
- On-the-job qualifications are offered through locally based short courses. NVQ/SVQ Level 2 Administration may be available. Many officers start as Administrative Assistants.
- Many people who work as court administrative officers are already completing articles or undertaking other legal training.

The type of person suited to this work

As you will be responsible for making sure that court hearings run smoothly and everything is ready on time, it's important to be methodical and thorough in your work and pay attention to detail.

As many different people come to court, you need to be polite, friendly and helpful so that you can put them at ease and explain things clearly. Some people may be nervous or aggressive.

If you are working in a finance section, you need to be able to work with figures to deal with fines and costs.

Working conditions

Most of your time will be spent indoors in courtrooms and offices in the court.

You will be sitting down for most of the day.

You may have to travel to different courts, so a driving licence is useful.

The future outlook

Court administrative officers in England and Wales are employed by the Magistrates' Courts and move through promotion grades. In Scotland they are often known as court officers and are employed by the Scottish Court Service. Most training is on the job. You may have to move courts to widen your experience. You could move into similar work in the legal field or into general administrative work.

CRCI:L

CLCI:LAG/CAT

Other related opportunities

- Administrator p6
- Barrister / Advocate's Clerk p333
- Clerk p12
- Court Legal Advisor / Court Clerk / Sheriff's Clerk p336
- Court Usher / Officer / Macer p338
- Receptionist p25

Advantages/disadvantages

- The work is varied and no two days will be the same.
- You will meet and work with many different people.
- Some people could be aggressive and threatening.
- You may have to start early or work late at busy times.

Earnings guide

- Salaries for administrative assistant/court officers start at around £12,000.
- With experience you could earn around £14,000 –£17,000.
- Senior clerks or team leaders could earn £20,000+.

Further information

Law Society of England and Wales
The Law Society's Hall
Chancery Lane
London
WC2A 1PL
0870 606 2555
www.lawsociety.org.uk

Department for Constitutional Affairs
Selborne House
54 Victoria Street
London
SW1E 6QW
020 7210 8614
www.dca.gov.uk

Scottish Court Service
Hayweight House
23 Lauriston Street
Edinburgh
EH3 9DQ
0131 229 9200
www.scotcourts.gov.uk

www.cityandguilds.com/myperfectjob

Court Legal Adviser / Court Clerk / Sheriff's Clerk

What the work involves

Court clerk (England and Wales)

- Court clerks are qualified solicitors or barristers with responsibility for advising magistrates in magistrates' courts.
- You will use your specialist legal knowledge to advise magistrates (who aren't legally qualified) on points of law, procedures, penalties and other issues including licensing law.
- You will deal with paperwork such as warrants and licences, legal aid and adoption procedures.
- Other duties could include attending meetings, liaising with police and social workers, keeping statistics and organising staff training.

Sheriff's clerk (Scotland)

- Sheriff's clerks carry out a wide range of duties which will vary according to the size of court and their experience.
- You may advise on points of law and procedures in any court (civil or criminal), or you may have a more general administrative role.

The type of person suited to this work

As you will be expected to advise on a wide range of issues, it is important to have a keen interest in law and enjoy dealing with large amounts of information. You will need to be thorough and pay attention to detail to be sure you give accurate information.

You will deal with many different people so it's important to be tolerant and remain detached from emotionally demanding cases. You will also need to be discreet to deal with confidential information and remain impartial.

Court clerks must be organised to deal with a number of tasks whilst being able to think logically and communicating well with others.

Working conditions

You will normally have an office in one court building.

You may travel around different courts and might spend some time travelling in rural areas, so a driving licence is useful.

You may use computers in your work.

Court buildings vary from very old to very new.

The future outlook

There are about 400 magistrates' courts in England and Wales, employing around 1,000 court clerks. There's a career structure in the HM Court Service and you could become a justices' clerk responsible for running a number of courts in an area or a justices' chief executive. In England and Wales, court clerks are increasingly known as judicial advisers.

In Scotland, sheriff's clerks are employed by the Scottish Court Service. Small rural courts may have only one clerk, while a court in a big city such as Edinburgh or Glasgow will have several. There is a clear promotion structure within the Scottish Court Service.

entry level

3–8

To both enter and train while working in this career, you will need qualifications at Level 3–8. Please refer to explanation on page vii.

Qualifications and courses

Court clerk (England and Wales)

- Candidates must be either barristers or solicitors, or have successfully completed the examinations for one of these professions.
- Barristers need an approved law degree or a non-law degree followed by the Common Professional Examination (CPE), Postgraduate Diploma (PgDL) in Law. They then complete a Bar Vocational Course followed by two 6-month 'pupillages' with an experienced barrister. In Scotland, advocates need a law degree followed by the Diploma in Legal Practice and 21 months' experience with a solicitor and 9 months' 'devilling' experience.
- In England and Wales, solicitors need an approved law degree or a non-law degree followed by the CPE PgDL. They can also qualify through ILEX. They must then take a Legal Practice Course followed by 2 years' training with a solicitor. In Scotland, the normal route is a law degree followed by the Diploma in Legal Practice and 2 years' training with a solicitor.
- Clerks then follow training programmes organised by their courts. They might begin by 'clerking' one area before covering the full range of work.
- Clerks usually start their careers as Administrative Assistants or Officers.

Sheriff's clerk (Scotland)

- There are no minimum entry requirements but a good standard of education is expected.
- Fast-track entry is sometimes available to those with a degree.

Earnings guide

- You can expect around £19,000–£24,000 per year on entry as a court legal adviser
- With experience you can earn £30,000+.
- Justices clerks earn around £43,000–£65,000+.
- Sheriffs' clerks can expect to earn £24,000 on entry, rising to £28,000–£35,000 with experience and seniority.

Other related opportunities

- Barrister / Advocate p334
- Barrister / Advocate's Clerk p333
- Crown Prosecutor / Coroner / Procurator Fiscal p339
- Judge / Sheriff p341
- Legal Executive p342
- Solicitor / Notary Public p349

Advantages/disadvantages

- The work is varied and no two days will be the same.
- You will work with a wide range of people.
- You might have to work unsocial hours at times.
- You might find it hard not to be the decision-maker.

Further information

Her Majesty's Courts Service
5th Floor
Clive House
Petty France
London
SW1H 9HD
020 7189 2000
www.hmcourts-service.gov.uk

Scottish Court Service
Hayweight House
23 Lauriston Street
Edinburgh
EH3 9DQ
0131 229 9200
www.scotcourts.gov.uk

CRCI:L

CLCI:LAG

Court Reporter / Verbatim Reporter

What the work involves

- As a court reporter, also known as a verbatim reporter, your job could involve attending court hearings, listening and reporting what is said.
- Using a stenotype machine, or sometimes other recording equipment, you will write down everything a witness says, but you may edit other speakers to correct the grammar.
- Mostly you will work on your own, but in complex cases where lawyers may want a daily transcript of proceedings, you will work in a team of three on a rota basis.
- You may also record proceedings within other legal meetings such as industrial tribunals.

The type of person suited to this work

As the main part of your job is listening, you need to be able to concentrate for a long time and listen carefully to what is said. It's essential to pay attention to detail to make sure your record is accurate.

You will need fast typing skills, good grammar and punctuation and to be able to speak clearly so you can read back what you have written.

If you do not catch what is said or get behind, it's important to have the confidence to stop proceedings or ask for something to be repeated.

You need to be able to work on your own and in a team, depending on whether you are taking the complete record or working a rota.

Working conditions

Your work would be indoors, mainly in a courtroom.

You will operate a steno machine, a machine with a keyboard layout which enables whole words and phrases to be typed at one stroke. You may also use other equipment.

You will be sitting down for most of the time.

You may have to travel to different courts, so a driving licence is useful.

The future outlook

In England and Wales, verbatim reporters attend some criminal cases in the crown courts. In Scotland they work at civil cases in the Sheriff Court and in the High Courts. They are also present at other events, including industrial tribunals, public enquiries and in Parliament to record proceedings for Hansard. Some reporters also provide the media industry with captions and subtitles. Most court reporters are self-employed and there is no defined promotion ladder.

Many work for companies contracted to service courts. This is a small but growing profession with a shortage of trained staff.

Other public sector organisations, such as the police force, are also beginning to use reporters to record interviews.

entry level

To both enter and train while working in this career, you will need qualifications at Level 3–8. Please refer to explanation on page vii.

Qualifications and courses

- Candidates are usually required to have 3–5 GCSEs/S grades (A–C/1–3), including English. Thorough knowledge of English language, grammar and punctuation is required.
- Maturity and work experience is an advantage.
- Applicants need to have qualifications in using shorthand machines, and may need to be accredited as having a shorthand speed of 160 words per minute by the British Institute of Verbatim Reporters (BIVR). For real-time court reporting you will be expected to have shorthand at 200 words per minute.
- Courses are available through the BIVR on both a full-time and a distance-learning basis. Courses are not available in Scotland as all training is done on the job with a mentor.
- It is possible after training and 3 years' experience to become a member of the BIVR by taking an examination. Qualified members of the BIVR with Deaf Awareness training can become accredited Speech to Text (STT) Reporters. In Scotland, court Reporters are usually trained on the job.
- Training for real-time reporting takes approximately 2 years.

CRCI:L

CLCI:LAG

Other related opportunities

- Administrator p6
- Clerk p12
- Court Administrative Officer p335
- Personal Assistant p24
- Secretary p28
- Translator p330

Advantages/disadvantages

- The work is varied and interesting.
- You will have contact with a wide range of people.
- You will have to concentrate for long periods so the work is demanding.
- You might have to work in the evenings at very short notice to complete reports for the next day.

Earnings guide

- Starting salaries are around £12,000–£15,000 per year.
- You could earn £20,000+ as an experienced real-time reporter, i.e. working in a team of three. In Scotland you could earn up to £18,000.
- You can expect a daily rate of around £165–£185 if you work freelance.
- Real-time reporters working freelance can earn £300+ a day.

Further information

British Institute of Verbatim Reporters
73 Alicia Gardens
Kenton
Harrow,
Middx HA3 8JD
020 8907 8249
www.bivr.org.uk

Court Usher / Officer / Macer

What the work involves

- You will make sure that everything in the courtroom is ready for court proceedings to begin, for example that all papers are ready, glasses and water are on tables and fire exits are clear.
- When people arrive at court, you will meet them and direct them to the right courtroom.
- In court, you will tell people to stand when the judge comes in, call witnesses and administer the right oath to witnesses.
- In Scotland, you will be known as a court officer in the sheriff court and a macer in the supreme courts.

entry level

2

To both enter and train while working in this career, you will need qualifications at Level 2. Please refer to explanation on page vii.

Qualifications and courses

- Whilst no formal qualifications are required, a minimum of at least 4 GCSEs/S grades (A–C/1–3), or the equivalent, including English, is strongly recommended. Training is conducted on the job, as well as through short courses.
- The stated minimum age is 21 (16 in Scotland), but most courts prefer to recruit mature people under the age of 63 (60 in Scotland).
- A background in the police or armed forces can be an advantage. A driving licence may be required.

The type of person suited to this work

As courtrooms must be properly prepared with everything ready at the beginning of the day, court ushers need to be thorough in their work and pay attention to detail. They need to be organised and methodical to have everything in the right place at the right time.

All kinds of people come to court, some of whom may be nervous, and it is important to have good speaking skills to explain what is happening and put people at ease. You will also need to be confident to call witnesses and sound in control in court.

It is important to stay calm at all times and be impartial to deal with people from both sides of a case.

Working conditions

Most of your work will be in a courtroom but you might also have an office in the courthouse. In certain jury cases, you may have to stay away from home overnight and you will have to be smartly dressed at all times.

You might have to travel between courts, so a driving licence is useful.

The future outlook

There are not many jobs for court ushers and getting in can be competitive in some areas of the UK. Most people have experience of other work first, for example within the police or armed services.

You can be promoted to senior and supervisory grades. You could also progress into other administrative jobs within the legal profession or outside.

Overall, promotion prospects can be difficult due to the competitive nature of the career.

Other related opportunities

- Administrator p6
- Clerk p12
- Court Administrative Officer p335
- Receptionist p25

Advantages/disadvantages

- The job will be varied and no two days will be the same.
- You might have to stay late or start early if proceedings overrun.
- You will meet many different people.
- Some people may be difficult to deal with.

Earnings guide

- As a starting salay in England and Wales you can expect to earn between £12,099 and £14,300 per year.
- This rises to around £16,000 with experience.
- Around £12,000–£13,500 is usual as a macer in Scotland.
- Overtime payments for late nights or early starts are often paid.

Further information

www.cityandguilds.com/myperfectjob

Her Majesty's Courts Service Headquarters
5th Floor
Clive House
Petty France
London
SW1H 9HD
020 7210 8500
www.hmcourts-service.gov.uk

Scottish Court Service
Hayweight House
23 Lauriston Street
Edinburgh
EH3 9DQ
0131 229 9200
www.scotcourts.gov.uk

Crown Prosecutor / Coroner / Procurator Fiscal

What the work involves

Crown prosecutor

- You will look at reports from the police and other agencies and decide whether or not crimes in England and Wales should be prosecuted.
- Using evidence including what witnesses have said, you will prepare the prosecution's case for court and make sure everything is ready on time.
- You will take statements from witnesses before a trial and examine witnesses in court, asking questions to guide them through their evidence and listening carefully to what they say.
- When all the evidence has been heard, you will sum up the case for the prosecution.

Coroner

- You will investigate sudden and suspicious deaths in England and Wales, and decide whether or not an inquest is required.
- Coroners preside at inquests and make decisions on whether or not further action such as prosecution is required.

Procurator fiscal

- Your work will involve preparing the case for the prosecution of criminal cases in Scotland.
- You will carry out similar duties to crown prosecutors in England and Wales, based on the Scottish legal system.
- In Scotland, sudden and suspicious deaths are investigated by the Procurator Fiscal Service, which has responsibility for fatal accident enquiries.

The type of person suited to this work

Preparing cases involves looking at statements and reports so you need to be able to read and analyse a lot of information. In some cases, you will need to check points of law and ask for more information, so you must be able to spot gaps and pay attention to detail.

As much of your work will be talking to people, listening to what they say and writing reports, you need to have very good speaking, listening and writing skills. Being confident to speak in court and argue logically are also important.

As cases must come to court in time, you must be organised, able to meet deadlines and work under pressure.

Working conditions

You will be based in an office but will spend time in court.

Although most of your work will be indoors, you will spend time outdoors at scenes of crime and accidents, depending on your job.

Smart dress is essential at all times and you will wear a gown in court.

You may have to travel to different courts, so a driving licence is useful.

The future outlook

Crown prosecutor

Crown prosecutors are employed by the Crown Prosecution Service, the government department responsible for prosecuting crime in England and Wales. They are responsible for prosecution of the majority of cases tried in the Magistrates' Courts and Crown Court. There is a clear promotion structure within the service but very few top senior posts. Competition for jobs in the CPS is very keen.

Coroner

Coroners are appointed and paid for by local councils but hold office under the crown. Many appointments are part time and are combined with other legal or medical work.

Procurator fiscal

Procurators fiscal in Scotland are employed by the Crown Office and Procurator Fiscal Service. They work in one of 49 districts and are civil servants working under the direction of the Lord Advocate. They work in District and Sheriff Courts but not the High Court of Justiciary. There are around 335 deputies and procurators fiscal but jobs are very competitive. There are very few top senior posts.

Crown prosecutors and procurators fiscal can transfer into other areas of law such as private practice. You will have opportunities for further training.

Qualifications and courses

Crown prosecutor

- To be a candidate, you must be either a solicitor admitted in England and Wales with a full current practising certificate, or a barrister called to the English Bar who has completed pupillage.
- The Crown Prosecution Service offers a limited number of 2-year training contracts to solicitors who have completed their Legal Practice course, and 1-year pupillages to barristers who have completed their BVC.
- Administrative Officers or caseworkers with at least 12 months' qualifying service with the CPS can apply for the internal Law Scholarship Scheme and Legal Trainee Scheme. This is the only scheme that the CPS will fund LPC and BVC qualifications.

Coroner

- Candidates usually start as deputy or assistant deputy coroners and must be qualified lawyers or legally qualified medical practitioners with at least 5 years' experience.
- Aldermen and councillors of local authorities are not eligible for appointment as coroners in their counties or districts until 6 months after the end of their service.
- Useful Key Skills include communication, decision making, problem solving and working with others.

Procurator fiscal

- All procurators fiscal are qualified solicitors in the Scottish legal system. An LLB degree in Scottish law (or 3 years of pre-diploma training and a pass in the Law Society of Scotland's exams) is required, followed by a Diploma in Legal Practice and 2 years working as a trainee solicitor.

entry level

To both enter and train while working in this career, you will need qualifications at Level 4–8. Please refer to explanation on page vii.

- Once qualified, candidates apply to join the Procurator Fiscal Service through the Crown Office. Applicants start as deputes, working under guidance of senior colleagues and gradually taking more responsibility. Once several years' experience has been accrued, they can apply to become procurator fiscals but promotion is not automatic.
- The Procurator Fiscal Service offers a limited number of places for the 2-year traineeship, the final stage in qualifying as a solicitor.

Other related opportunities

- Barrister / Advocate p334
- Judge / Sheriff p341
- Solicitor / Notary Public p349

Advantages/disadvantages

- The work is varied, carries responsibility and can be satisfying.
- You will have contact with many different types of people, some of whom may be difficult to deal with.
- There will be a lot of administration and paperwork.
- You will be on an on-call rota for evenings, weekends and bank holidays.
- You will have good career prospects.

Earnings guide

Crown prosecutor

- Crown prosecutors start at £28,662 per year.
- As a Senior Crown Prosecutor you could earn around £35,568.

Coroner

- Coroners receive an agreed fee, and as a guide, if you work full time as a deputy coroner, you can earn around £25,000 per year. As a coroner you can expect between £55,000–£72,000.

Procurator fiscal

- As a procurator fiscal you can earn around £28,000 a year after 2 years as a trainee.
- You could expect to earn around £40,000–£47,000 with more experience, rising to around £58,000 at the top level.

Further information

Crown Prosecution Service
50 Ludgate Hill
London
EC4M 7EX
020 7796 8000
www.cps.gov.uk

The Coroners' Society of England and Wales
HM Coroner's Court
The Cotton Exchange
Old Hall Street
London
L3 9UF
0151 233 4708
www.coronersociety.org.uk

Law Society of Scotland
26 Drumsheugh Gardens
Edinburgh
EH3 7YR
0131 226 7411
www.lawscot.org.uk

Crown Office Scotland
25 Chambers Street
Edinburgh
EH1 1LA
0131 226 2626
www.crownoffice.gov.uk

CRCI:I

CLCI:LAZ

Judge / Sheriff

What the work involves

- Judges (sheriffs in Scotland) preside over courts and make judgements on what should happen based on the evidence from both sides.
- You will listen to all the evidence and decide on procedures, including whether a piece of evidence can be used, and keep order in court.
- In jury cases, you will instruct and advise the jury on the strength of the evidence before the jury leaves court to consider the verdict.
- You will decide on penalties in criminal courts and on settlements in civil cases.

The type of person suited to this work

As judges make the final decisions in any court case, it is important to be able to grasp facts quickly and analyse the evidence to help make your decision. Judges must think logically and not become emotionally involved.

You will need to have good speaking skills to explain things to the jury and to consult with other legal professionals, and good listening skills to pay careful attention to the evidence. You will also need to have confidence to speak in public.

It is important to have the confidence to make difficult decisions and stick by them. Discretion is needed to deal with confidential information.

Working conditions

You will spend much of your time in court but will also have an office with support staff to help you. You will travel between courts and may have to spend time away from home.

You will dress smartly at all times and wear robes in court. Courts are also very formal and have traditions which you must observe.

The future outlook

There are very few openings for judges and sheriffs, which means entry is competitive, and they have normally followed a long career in law as a barrister/advocate.

Most judges work in one type of court, such as a Crown Court or Court of Appeal. Senior positions, such as Lord Chief Justice and Master of the Rolls, are made on the recommendation of the Prime Minister.

In Scotland, most sheriffs work in sheriff courts. A few with experience become supreme court judges in the High Court of Justiciary or the Court of Session.

entry level

To both enter and train while working in this career, you will need qualifications at Level 4–8. Please refer to explanation on page vii.

Qualifications and courses

- Candidates are almost always qualified barristers or advocates who have 5–7 years' experience and have progressed to working as a deputy district judge or a recorder. District or circuit judges are usually appointed after 10–15 years' court experience. Judges are appointed by The Lord Chancellor.
- After 10–15 years' experience, barristers may apply to become a Queen's Counsel and may eventually become a High Court judge or a Court of Session judge in Scotland.
- Judicial office holders must retire on their 70th birthday.
- Sheriffs are required to be qualified advocates (members of the Scottish Bar) of 10 years' experience.

CRCI:L | CLCI:LAF

Other related opportunities

- Barrister / Advocate p334
- Crown Prosecutor / Coroner / Procurator Fiscal p339
- Legal Executive p342
- Solicitor / Notary Public p349

Advantages/disadvantages

- The work is varied and no two days will be the same.
- It's a very responsible job.
- You will meet many different people and hear some cases which will have a high media interest or involve upsetting or distressing evidence.
- Some courts work into the evenings.

Earnings guide

- Salaries can vary according to region, but start at around £96,500–£113,170 per year as a senior district judge.
- You could earn £123,300+ as a circuit judge.
- Sherrifs earn around £117,000 per year.
- Around £162,000 + is possible as a High Court judge.
- Around £230,400 a year is the salary as Lord Chief Justice, the highest legal position in the land.

Further information

Judicial Communications Office
Office of the Lord Chief Justice
11.07 Thomas More Building
Royal Courts of Justice
Strand
London
WC2A 2LL
www.judiciary.gov.uk

Judicial Appointments Commission
11 Tothill Street
London
SW1H 9LJ
020 7210 1453
www.judicialappointments.gov.uk

Legal Executive

What the work involves

- Your job will be to work with solicitors, preparing complex cases for them and dealing with straightforward cases yourself.
- You will interview clients, asking questions to help you give them legal advice and explain legal points to them clearly.
- You will write letters on their behalf, checking points of law and paying close attention to detail.
- In certain cases, you may represent clients in court or at tribunals.

The type of person suited to this work

As much of the work involves talking and listening to all sorts of people, it is important to have very good speaking and listening skills. Excellent writing skills are also important for producing letters and taking statements.

Clients will give you confidential information and tell you very personal things so it is important to be discreet and tactful. You will also need patience as legal points can be difficult to grasp.

When preparing cases, you will be handling large amounts of information, which means it is useful to enjoy research and be a thorough worker. You will need to be well organised.

Working conditions

You will be based in an office but you may attend court. You will be sitting down for most of the time but will stand when speaking in court. You will be expected to dress smartly at all times.

You may have to travel to visit clients or legal libraries, so a driving licence is useful.

Excellent communication skills will be important because you will need to get along with your clients, colleagues and other professionals.

The future outlook

There are around 23,000 Institute of Legal Executives (ILEX) members in the UK. Most people work for solicitors in private practice but there are jobs in local and central government and industry. Legal executives usually specialise in one area, for example property or business law.

You can train to qualify as a legal executive advocate, which allows you to follow a case right through to court. There will be ongoing training opportunities to keep you up to date with changes in the law.

This is a very competitive career. Due to the number of degree courses now offering professional qualifications, it is becoming even more difficult to enter for those with Level 3 qualifications.

entry level

3–8

To both enter and train while working in this career, you will need qualifications at Level 3–8. Please refer to explanation on page vii.

Qualifications and courses

- The normal minimum requirements are 4 GCSEs/S grades (A–C/1–3) in academic subjects, including English. City & Guilds/ILEX Paralegal Programmes Level 2 Certificate in Vocational Paralegal Studies is a suitable alternative to GCSEs for older candidates.
- Students may begin their training with the Institute of Legal Executives' certificate in Law and Practice Level 3, which requires 4 GCSEs/S grades (A–C /1–3) including English language or literature, or equivalent (including the C&G/ILEX Level 2 Vocational Paralegal Studies Certificate). Trainees then take the Level 3 Professional Diploma in Law and Practice (which replaces the Level 3 Professional Diploma in Law). An extended diploma is also available.
- Trainees then progress to the Higher Diploma in Law. Full training at Levels 3 and 4 takes 3–4 years (while working full time) and leads to ILEX Membership. ILEX qualifications can also be taken as part of a Modern legal Apprenticeship scheme.
- Some qualifications, for example A levels and/or degrees (especially in law), may provide exemption from some academic parts of the ILEX qualifications. People with relevant experience can also apply to have their experience approved by ILEX.
- ILEX Fellows, working as legal executives, can take the Legal Practice Course (LPC) and become a qualified solicitors.
- In Scotland, staff are known as paralegals or solicitors' assistants. Generally 4 GCSEs/S grades (A–C/1–3) including English and maths, followed by office experience, are required. There is no equivalent to ILEX in Scotland.

CRCI:L

CLCI:LAD

Other related opportunities

- Administrator p6
- Barrister / Advocate's Clerk p333
- Court Legal Advisor / Court Clerk / Sheriff's Clerk p336
- Solicitor / Notary Public p349

Advantages/disadvantages

- This is a very competitive area to enter.
- You will have the chance to work in a legal environment while studying part time and earn a good salary
- You may have to work under pressure to meet deadlines and possibly work evenings and weekends.

Earnings guide

- Starting salaries once you have passed ILEX exams and are a fully qualified legal executive are around £20,000–£25,000, depending on where you work.
- Legal executives with a bit more experience can earn around £30,000.
- Senior ILEX Fellows can earn over £45,000, depending on location and experience.

Further information

Institute of Legal Executives
Kempston Manor
Kempston
Bedford
MK42 7AB
01234 841000
www.ilex.org.uk

Law Society of Northern Ireland
40 Linenhall Street
Belfast
BT2 8BA
028 90 231614
www.lawsoc-ni.org

Law Society of England and Wales
The Law Society's Hall
Chancery Lane
London
WC2A 1PL
0870 606 2555
www.lawsociety.org.uk

Licensed Conveyancer

What the work involves

- Licensed conveyancers deal with the legal side of buying and selling houses, flats, business premises and other property.
- You will draw up the legal documents, known as contracts, that buyers and sellers exchange to make a sale legal.
- You will deal with enquiries from clients by phone and in person, explaining legal phrases in contracts in simple language.
- Other work will include liaising with lawyers and estate agents involved in the sale and researching details in the contract.

entry level

To both enter and train while working in this career, you will need qualifications at Level 3–8. Please refer to explanation on page vii.

The type of person suited to this work

Dealing with people is a big part of the job, requiring good communication skills and the ability to put legal language into everyday words. Being a good team worker is useful to liaise with others involved in a contract.

As legal contracts must be completely accurate, you will need to be very thorough in your work and pay close attention to detail. It is important to be able to handle large amounts of information when drawing up contracts.

You will be dealing with several properties at the same time, which will need good organisation and being able to do several jobs at once. You will need to be able to meet deadlines.

Working conditions

Most of your work will be office-based. You will normally work Monday to Friday office hours, but may be required to work some late evenings or Saturday mornings to meet your clients. Your job may be salaried or commission only.

The future outlook

Conveyancing is a very small profession with under 1000 licensed conveyancers in England and Wales, and very few qualified conveyancers in Scotland. Job opportunities are mainly with legal practices. You could become self-employed and run your own business.

Training is ongoing to ensure you keep up to date with developments in property law. You could progress into other legal professions or the property world.

Qualifications and courses

England and Wales

- Candidates must pass the Council for Licensed Conveyancers (CLC) training and exams. To begin the training they must be 21 years old and have 4 GCSEs including English. An A level in law is useful. Many applicants will hold a law degree or might have undertaken the Institute of Legal Executives (ILEX) course.
- They must have at least 2 years' practical training with a 'qualified employer' and pass the Council of Licensed Conveyancers (CLC) examination, which is taken by over half of all students as a correspondence course, and is also offered at some colleges on a part-time basis.
- After passing the course, candidates apply for a limited licence. After a further 3 consecutive years you can apply for a full licence.

Scotland

- Qualified conveyancers generally require a degree in law from a Scottish university or a Diploma/Certificate in legal studies which lasts at least 2 years.
- They then undertake a training contract of at least 1 year with an independent qualified conveyancer. After 6 months of training, trainees are required to attend a Professional Competence Course, which comprises 36 hours of core requirements and 18 hours of electives. Attendance at the course is an integral part of the traineeship.
- Candidates for law degrees usually need 5 GCSEs/S grades (A–C/1–3) and 3 A levels/H grades. Alternatively, some universities require applicants to take the National Admissions Test for Law (LNAT).

CRCI:L | CLCI:LAZ

Other related opportunities

- Barrister / Advocate p334
- Estate Agent p52
- Legal Executive p342
- Solicitor / Notary Public p349
- Surveyor / Surveying Technician p70

Advantages/disadvantages

- The work is varied and you will meet different people.
- You will get satisfaction when clients get their dream home.
- There may be stress when you are trying to meet deadlines or clients feel things are moving too slowly.
- Some people may be difficult.

Earnings guide

- Salaries for qualified conveyancers start at around £18,000–£22,000.
- This rises to £25,000–£35,000 after gaining further experience.
- With 5 years' experience this rises to £68,000–£95,000+.

Further information

Council for Licensed Conveyancers
16 Glebe Road
Chelmsford
Essex
CM1 1QG
01245 349599
www.conveyancer.org.uk

Law Society of Scotland
26 Drumsheugh Gardens
Edinburgh
EH3 7YR
0131 226 7411
www.lawscot.org.uk

Patent Agent / Examiner

What the work involves

Patent agent/attorney

- You will advise clients with an invention they want patented on the law of intellectual property, and others with questions about this branch of law.
- The work involves checking that an invention is a new one and not one which already exists.
- After checking, you will prepare specifications for the Patent Office, carrying out any negotiations required and representing the client before the patent examiner.
- As there are many different types of invention, you will probably specialise in trademarks, designs or electronics.
- Patent attorney is another name for patent agent and you will carry out the same type of work.
- You can take an additional European Qualifying Examination to become a European Patent Attorney.

Patent examiner

- You will examine patent applications submitted by patent agents for new inventions, trademarks or a design.
- The work involves carrying out a search to check that each application is a new invention.
- You will carry out a detailed examination of the application to ensure it is clear and meets legal requirements.
- Finally, you will grant or refuse the patent.

The type of person suited to this work

As the work involves applying the law of intellectual property to inventions, you will need a thorough knowledge of this area of law and the ability to apply it to the invention you are dealing with. You will need to enjoy and be good at researching and handling information to check all work thoroughly.

You will come into contact with many people, which will mean you need good speaking and listening skills. You will be required to explain legal points to people in simple language. Good writing skills are also needed.

Good organisation is important to deal with several jobs at once and you will need to be able to make decisions.

Working conditions

Most of your work would be based in an office although patent agents do some travelling in the UK, for which a driving licence is useful, and may travel abroad.

A lot of the work involves using computers to research and write reports. You are also likely to do a lot of work by phone, email and the internet. Most of your work will be during office hours, Monday to Friday.

The future outlook

It takes a long time to qualify for patent work and it is a very small profession. There are around 1750 registered agents in the UK. Around 80% of these work in private practices, mostly in the larger towns and cities. Around 20% work with industrial companies or local government agencies.

Patent examiners are civil servants, mostly based in the Patent Office in Newport with a few working in London. The civil service has a formal promotion structure leading to senior patent examiner.

There may be opportunities to work for the European Patent Office.

CRCI:L

CLCI:LAK

Qualifications and courses

entry level

To both enter and train while working in this career, you will need qualifications at Level 4–8. Please refer to explanation on page vii.

Patent agent/attorney

- All patent agents need a scientific or technical background, usually a degree in a science or engineering subject. Students usually need 5 GCSEs/S grades (A–C/1–3) including English and maths, and at least 2 A levels/H grades.
- Patent agents receive specialist training in intellectual property law. Qualified solicitors with experience of working in an intellectual property department or those training to become patent agents and similar professions may apply to join the Chartered Institute of Patent Agents (CIPA).
- A high level of skill in the English language is required, and a knowledge of other languages, particularly French and/or German, is an advantage.
- Admission to the Register of Patent Agents and the Register of Trade Mark Agents requires a training period and the passing of examinations. It usually takes 4–5 years to qualify.
- Postgraduate qualifications in intellectual property law are available at a few universities. The Certificate in IP Law, offered by several universities as a short course (typically 1–3 months) gives exemption from all the Foundation Papers of the CIPA examinations.

Patent examiner

- Candidates normally require a good Honours degree in science, maths, engineering or technology and a knowledge of French and/or German.
- An equivalent professional qualification or corporate membership of a relevant major professional institution may be accepted as an alternative.
- Candidates must also meet the civil service's nationality and residency requirements.
- Key Skills are communication, decision making, information handling, organising, problem solving and working with others.

Other related opportunities

- Information Scientist p321
- Researcher p328
- Solicitor / Notary Public p349
- Translator p330

Advantages/disadvantages

- The work is varied, responsible and intellectually demanding.
- You will get satisfaction from helping new inventions become recognised and being involved at an early stage of the job.
- You will work with many different people.
- The work can be stressful and you could feel under pressure.

Earnings guide

- As a trainee you could earn around £23,000 to £28,000 per year.
- Technical assistants nearing qualification can expect £28,000–£47,000.
- Once qualified you could get £52,000–£72,000.
- With 5 years' experience this rises to £68,000–£95,000+.

Further information

Chartered Institute of Patent Agents
95 Chancery Lane
London
WC2A 1DT
020 7405 9450
www.cipa.org.uk

Patent Office
Concept House
Cardiff Road
Newport
NP10 8QQ
0845 950 0505
www.patent.gov.uk

Political Work

What the work involves

UK

- MPs represent the people in their local constituencies in Parliament, usually as a member of a political party.
- You will hold 'surgeries' in your local constituency and deal with issues raised by local people at local and national level.
- In Parliament, you will join committees, attend meetings and take part in debates.
- You may specialise in a particular area, for example health or education, and may hold office in the government or for the Opposition.

Scotland

- MSPs represent the views of their local constituents in the Scottish Parliament.
- You will be involved in policies for Scotland in certain areas of government, including health and education.

Wales

- AMs represent the views of local people on Welsh affairs in the National Assembly for Wales.
- You will help to formulate policies on Welsh affairs on matters devolved from the UK Parliament.

Europe

- MEPs' work includes scrutinising proposals for new EU laws.
- Other work includes monitoring spending and approving international agreements.

Constituency agent

- Your job will be to organise the running of the constituency for your political party including election campaigns.
- As secretary to the local office, your duties will include managing local membership, fundraising and organising volunteer helpers.
- You will arrange meetings and appointments, coordinate PR and marketing, and deal with enquiries from constituents.

The type of person suited to this work

As the work will bring you into contact with many different people, it's essential to have good speaking and listening skills. A pleasant manner and the ability to gain people's confidence are important, as is being persuasive to bring people round to your viewpoint.

You will be expected to keep up to date with party policies and legislation, which requires being able to deal with large amounts of information quickly and thoroughly. An interest in research is helpful to deal with enquiries and gather information for committees.

You must be able to think quickly, argue logically and be confident to speak in public.

Working conditions

Your time will be split between your local constituency and Parliament/Scottish Parliament/Welsh Assembly. MEPs spend most of their time in Strasbourg.

You will work late at night in the House of Commons, and long hours in any MP role.

Parliaments have traditions and procedures that you will be expected to observe.

You will spend a lot of time travelling.

Constituency agent

Most of your work will be based in the party office which will be open to the public. However, you will be expected to do lots of travelling both locally and nationally, so a driving licence and car will be useful.

You could work evenings, weekends or during the day. Hours could increase during national or local events like elections.

The future outlook

You will need work and life experience before you can become an MP. Your job in any parliament will depend on being re-elected, which means it is important to have another career option to fall back on.

There are about 646 MPs in the UK Parliament, 129 MSPs in the Scottish Parliament, 60 Welsh Assembly members and around 87 UK members in the European Parliament.

Although most MPs represent the local people in their constituencies, they are also very much involved in the government of their country. You could be offered a post in a ministry, which may lead to appointment as a minister in a particular area. In exceptional circumstances, you could become the leader of your party and the Prime Minister or First Minister.

Constituency agent

Competition for this kind of job is keen and it is important to have relevant work or voluntary experience in areas like administration, organising, marketing and dealing with people. Local voluntary campaign experience is extremely useful.

There are many political parties in the UK, varying in size and strength. Your prospects could depend on the size of the party you support. Later, you could become a local councillor or Member of Parliament.

Qualifications and courses

Member of Parliament

- Any British citizen, citizen of a British overseas territory or member of a Commonwealth country or the Republic of Ireland may stand for election as long as they are over 21 years old.
- Those disqualified from election are undischarged bankrupts, prisoners of more than 1 year, members of the House of Lords and people holding offices listed in the House of Commons Disqualification Act 1975. The Representation of the People Act 1983 disqualifies those found guilty of various election-related offences for a period of 10 years. Members are not permitted to resign their seats; they must request appointment to one of two ceremonial offices which exist solely to enable 'resignations' by MPs.
- In Scotland and Wales there are regional members as well as constituency members.
- There are no formal minimum educational requirements but many MPs are graduates or hold other professional qualifications.
- Qualifications in business, law or economics are particularly useful.
- It is essential to be actively involved in a political party and experience in areas such as trade union work is helpful.
- There is a series of selection interviews before candidates can be 'adopted' by their party and their local constituency to stand for election. Candidates must then carry out a successful electoral campaign and be elected by the votes of the local people.
- Key Skills are communication, decision making, information handling, organising, supervisory and management skills, and working with others.

Constituency agent

- There are no set entry requirements for this work, although many entrants have a degree in politics, industrial relations, social policy, economics, marketing, public relations or journalism.
- Training varies depending on the party you work for, and may include on-the-job training and distance learning.
- Experience of working for the party on a voluntary basis is useful. Most agents are members of the party they work for with significant voluntary experience.
- Experience in other areas is also useful, for example involvement with a trade union or employer's organisation, holding office in a students' union or parent teacher association, or campaign work for a charity or pressure group.
- In general, candidates must be at least 20 years of age.
- Key Skills are communication, information handling, IT, organising, managing money, management and supervisory skills, numerical skills, problem solving and working with others.

entry level

To both enter and train while working in this career, you will need qualifications at Level 2–8. Please refer to explanation on page vii.

Other related opportunities

- Marketing p151
- Public Relations Officer p161
- Trade Union Official p547
- Welfare Rights Officer / Worker p550

Advantages/disadvantages

- The work is varied and challenging, and no two days will be the same.
- You will get satisfaction, particularly if your party is in power, but also frustration when votes do not go your way.
- You will be constantly in the public eye.
- You will meet lots of different people.
- You will need plenty of stamina to handle the long hours and the job can be very pressurised.

Earnings guide

- Basic salary for an MP in the in the House of Commons is £61,820. Additional allowances are also available for things like travel and communications.
- Salaries depend on the types of responsibilities. You could earn £138,724 as a cabinet minister.
- You could earn around £189,994 a year as Prime Minister.
- MEPs are paid the same salaries as national MPs in their own countries. Parliamentary under secretaries in the commons can earn £92,100.

Constituency agent

- You could expect to earn around £16,000 per year as a starting salary.
- This can rise to £28,000–£35,000, depending on experience and level of responsibility. You may be provided with a car.

Further information

House of Commons Information Office
House of Commons
Westminster
London
SW1A 0AA
020 7219 4272
www.parliament.uk

Scottish Parliament
Edinburgh
EH99 1SP
0131 348 5000
www.scottish.parliament.uk

National Assembly for Wales
Cardiff Bay
Cardiff
CF99 1NA
029 2082 5111
www.wales.gov.uk

European Parliament
2 Queen Anne's Gate
London
SW1H 9AA
020 7227 4300
www.europarl.org.uk

www.cityandguilds.com/myperfectjob

Registrar of Births, Deaths, Marriages and Civil Partnerships

What the work involves

- Registrars record all births, stillbirths, marriages, civil partnerships and deaths in an area, making sure all details are accurate.
- After a birth, you will interview parents, record the baby's name and date of birth and issue a birth certificate.
- After a death, you will interview relatives before issuing a death certificate and inform the coroner or procurator fiscal if anything seems suspicious.
- You will interview people planning to marry or enter a civil partnership to check they can legally do so, and conduct civil ceremonies.
- Some registrars also conduct baby-naming ceremonies and reaffirmation of vows.

The type of person suited to this work

As most of the work involves talking and listening to people, you will need good speaking and listening skills. It is also important to judge how people are feeling and be sympathetic if need be, without becoming emotionally involved.

Handling information and attention to detail are vital to be sure that all legal requirements are carried out. You may need patience to explain procedures to people who are unclear about them.

Confidence is important when conducting marriage and civil partnership ceremonies, and good judgement to decide if people are telling the truth. It's important to be flexible to deal with different situations.

Working conditions

You will be based in the registrar's office for your district.

You may travel to some religious marriages to complete the legalities connected with them so a driving licence is useful. You might attend ceremonies within a hotel or other public places.

Computers are becoming increasingly important but good handwriting is often a requirement.

You will be sitting down for most of the time.

The future outlook

There are about 1750 registrars in England and Wales and about 500 in Scotland. There are very few vacancies for this kind of work. Part-time work may be possible.

You would usually start as an assistant and be promoted to registrar, but promotion opportunities are limited. You will have opportunities for in-house training and could move into other administration-based careers.

entry level

2

To both enter and train while working in this career, you will need qualifications at Level 2. Please refer to explanation on page vii.

Qualifications and courses

- In England and Wales, there are no set entry requirements for this career. A good general standard of education is expected, including English and maths. GCSEs are increasingly preferred and if working in Wales, candidates require GCSE Welsh.
- Applicants from certain professions are prohibited from becoming registrars, including doctors, midwives, ministers of religion, funeral directors and anyone working in the life assurance industry.
- Register office staff take the Registrar General's Certificate of Competence in Registration Law and Practice.
- In Scotland, candidates need 3 GCSEs/S grades (A–C/1–3), including English. Assistant registrars must be 18 and registrars must be 21.
- Candidates take the examination of the Association of Registrars in Scotland and obtain a Certificate of Proficiency in the Law and Practice of Registration. At least 2 years' experience is required before the certificate can be awarded.
- Key Skills are communication, information handling, ICT and working with others. Experience of public speaking and a driving licence may also be useful.

CRCI:L

CLCI:LAZ

Other related opportunities

- Administrator p6
- Clerk p12
- Court Administrative Officer p335
- Court Legal Adviser / Court Clerk / Sheriff's Clerk p336
- Court Usher / Officer / Macer p338
- Legal Executive p342

Advantages/disadvantages

- The work is varied and no two days are the same.
- You will meet many different people at their happiest or saddest moments.
- You will work some weekends and bank holidays and may be on call at other times.
- This is seen as an important community position to hold.

Earnings guide

- You would earn around £16,000–£18,000 per year when starting.
- £20,000–£30,000 is usual as an experienced superintendent.
- Up to £45,000 is possible at the most senior levels.

Further information

www.cityandguilds.com/myperfectjob

Association of Registrars of Scotland
Secretary, Registration Area Office
Municipal Buildings, College Street
Dumbarton
G82 1NR
01389 738350

Local Government Careers
www.lgcareers.com

Solicitor / Notary Public

What the work involves

Solicitor

- A major part of your job will be giving clients advice on legal matters, for example buying and selling a house, making a will or setting up a business.
- You will carry out legal work on their behalf, including writing letters and checking carefully to see that all the requirements are in place.
- In certain circumstances, you may represent clients in court.
- You may have to instruct a barrister or advocate to act for your client.

Notary public

- Your main job will be to certify deeds and other documents so that they will be accepted by judicial and public authorities anywhere in the world as authentic and legally binding.
- Notaries public are generally solicitors who combine this function with other legal work.

The type of person suited to this work

As legal work involves looking at vast amounts of information and legal documents, it is important that you are good at reading and analysing information. A keen interest in law (which can often be very dry) is essential. You will need to be thorough in your work and pay attention to detail.

Solicitors work with all sorts of people which means you must be able to explain legal points to them clearly. Good writing skills are also needed to write letters and reports. You may have to speak in public.

When dealing with clients, you will need to be discreet to deal with confidential information. It is important to remain impartial.

Working conditions

Most of your work is indoors in an office.

You might spend time in court.

You might have to visit clients at home or other places, for example a police station or prison.

You may have to travel around, so a driving licence is useful.

The future outlook

There is keen competition for every traineeship vacancy, but there are good prospects for qualified solicitors in private practice, local and central government and industry. You will usually specialise in one area of law, for example property or company law.

Solicitors are encouraged to keep up to date with training and professional development. There's a promotion structure in central and local government. Solicitors in private practice often become partners.

entry level

4–8

To both enter and train while working in this career, you will need qualifications at Level 4–8. Please refer to explanation on page vii.

Qualifications and courses

England and Wales

- Candidates with either an approved law degree, or a non-law degree followed by the Common Professional Examination (CPE), the Postgraduate Diploma in Law (PgDL) or the Senior Status Law degree. Some universities require entrants to take the National Admissions Test for Law (LNAT).
- Candidates without a degree can take examinations to become Members or Fellows of the Institute of Legal Executives (ILEX).
- A Legal Practice Course (LPC) must be completed followed by 2 years of training with a solicitor.

Scotland

- Candidates need either and approved Scottish Law degree, or a good non-law degree followed by a 2-year graduate law degree. Entry is usually with 5 H grades (A–B) including English.
- Candidates can take 3 years' pre-diploma training and pass the Law Society of Scotland exams.
- Entrants must complete a 26-week Diploma in Legal Practice followed by a 2-year training contract with a practising solicitor in Scotland.

Northern Ireland

- Solicitors must complete an apprenticeship programme of 2–4 years, depending on the academic route taken.

Notary public

- In England and Wales qualified and experienced solicitors can take a Postgraduate Diploma in Notarial Practice and be approved by the Master of the Faculties to act within a specific area. A notary public in the City of London takes the professional qualification of the Worshipful Company of Scriveners.
- In Scotland solicitors can apply to be enrolled as notaries on qualifying as solicitors.

CRCI:L

CLCI:LAC

Other related opportunities

- Barrister / Advocate p334
- Crown Prosecutor / Coroner / Procurator Fiscal p339
- Judge / Sheriff p341
- Legal Executive p342

Advantages/disadvantages

- The work is varied and no two days will be the same.
- You will meet many different people.
- You might have to work long hours, including evenings, weekends and even bank holidays.
- Some people may be difficult and unpleasant.

Earnings guide

- As a trainee you can expect to earn a minimum of £15,820 per year in England; in Scotland you start at £15,000 for the first year rising to £18,000 in the second.
- This rises to £30,000–£55,000 once you are qualified and have experience.
- Up to £100,000+ is possible as a partner/senior with lots of experience and depending on the size and location of the practice.
- Notaries public are paid a fee for their work.

Further information

Law Society of Northern Ireland
Law Society House
98 Victoria Street
Belfast
BT1 3JZ
028 9023 1614
www.lawsoc-ni.org

Law Society of Scotland
26 Drumsheugh Gardens
Edinburgh
EH3 7YR
0131 226 7411
www.lawscot.org.uk

Law Society of England and Wales
The Law Society's Hall
Chancery Lane
London
WC2A 1PL
0870 606 2555
www.lawsociety.org.uk

The Administration Department
The Notaries Society
PO Box 226
Melton
Woodbridge
IP12 1WX
www.thenotariessociety.org.uk

Worshipful Company of Scriveners
HQS Wellington
Temple Stairs
Victoria Embankment
London
WC2R 2PN
020 7240 0529
www.scriveners.org.uk

Here's Sarah Teather's story:

Member of Parliament

At 32, Liberal Democrat Sarah is one of Britain's youngest MP. It wasn't until she was studying Natural Sciences at Cambridge University that she actually joined the Lib Dem Party. On graduation, she gained work drafting advice to government on scientific issues, and her experience of working in policy fed her ambition to become a politician because she realised the only way you can really get things done is by changing the system. She then worked as a policy analyst at a cancer care charity and had to take unpaid leave from her job in order to campaign for the Brent East by-election. She became MP for Brent East on 19 September 2003.

For Sarah the most rewarding thing about her job is being able to make a difference. She says it is a great feeling being able to get something done for someone either by writing a letter or by standing up for something in Parliament. She also loves the variety of what she does.

WHAT THE JOB ENTAILS

'Some days there will be lots of media (TV, radio, newspapers) to do, then the next day I will be visiting a local temple or community group. Other days I'll be out campaigning with local Lib Dems or there might be a really exciting debate or close vote in the House of Commons. The downside of all this is a complete lack of personal time in which to see friends and family – it really is a 24/7 job.'

Sarah has already progressed rapidly in her career; in 2003–4 she was the party's Spokesperson on Health, in 2004–5 she was Spokesperson for London, in 2005–6, Shadow Secretary for Community & Local Government, and now she is the Shadow Education Secretary. Brent East is one of the most ethnically diverse constituencies in the country and so to communicate better with her constituents Sarah is taking Gujarati and Urdu lessons.

HOW YOU BECOME AN MP

'Get involved and stay involved. It takes a long time and an awful lot of hard work. You have to be approved by your own party, then you have to enter a contest to be your party's candidate. If you are successful you get to fight that seat. It can take years. Often when you are young there is a temptation for local parties to use you as leaflet fodder, delivering the party's message around the constituency. However, don't be down-hearted by this as it is the key to success – telling people about the Lib Dems and what they believe in. I hate to think how many leaflets I have delivered over the years, and I am still delivering them now!'

Are you sporty or interested in aspects of the leisure and tourism industry? The types of jobs included here are:

- **Aerobics Teacher**
- **Entertainment Manager**
- **Leisure Centre Assistant**
- **Professional Sportsperson**
- **Tourist Guide**

But what's it like working in this area?
Here's Lorraine Dean-Grundy's story:

Fitness Instructor

Lorraine has always been sporty, attending aerobic classes at her local leisure centre and representing both her school and then Richmond-upon-Thames College in South London at netball and hockey. She initially trained to be a film editor but in 1994, after the birth of her first child, she re-trained as a fitness instructor passing the Royal Society of Arts 'Exercise To Music' intensive course. Since then she has undertaken further training to teach different forms of exercise including aqua, spin and bodypump. 41-year-old Lorraine now works as a freelance fitness instructor for various gyms and sports clubs such as Cannons, Esporta, The Harbour Club and Virgin Active in and around South London.

WHAT SHE FEELS IS IMPORTANT ABOUT THE JOB

'Basically, I try to move people forward to attain the results they desire. I like to think I offer the motivation to others to enjoy exercise whatever their size, shape or even age. Everyone exercises for different reasons but ultimately the motivation (the reason for coming back week after week) rests with the instructor's ability to relate to the class. I want to help inspire others to reach their goals, whether those are physical or mental. If someone feels they are achieving their aerobic potential and are feeling good about themselves, then I feel I am doing my job well.'

WHAT'S HOT AND WHAT'S NOT ABOUT THE JOB

'I love the interaction I have with my classes. The banter and fun work hand-in-hand with the way I teach – and you really do have to have fun. You have to be willing to make a fool of yourself and to entertain your class; you really can't take yourself too seriously. One of the downsides to the job is feeling tired because often you don't have enough recovery time between classes and you really can't allow yourself to have an "off" day.'

Lorraine sees herself continuing to grow as an instructor and constantly strives to gain greater knowledge of different forms of exercise and teaching methods. She is especially interested in all aspects of good nutrition and she wants to extend the range of classes she teaches to include Pilates and yoga so she can continue as an instructor even as her body changes due to ageing.

WHAT YOU NEED TO SUCCEED

'You have to be confident and you cannot be judgemental in any way because you must build a relationship with your class. I feel total loyalty to my classes (you have to show the class the loyalty they show you) and hope I imbue a sense of belonging in my regulars. Ultimately you must be willing to listen, learn, educate and entertain. But the most important thing of all is you have got to have fun and enjoy what you do.'

Aerobics Teacher

What the work involves

- Planning exercise routines that stimulate and stretch experienced class members, while not overtaxing newcomers.
- Picking a range of dance music to motivate aerobics students during warm up, exercise and warm down.
- Taking an active role in leading and instructing the class – demonstrating and explaining particular exercise sequences.
- Maintaining continual vigilance during the class, assessing each individual's performance and watching out for signs of tiredness or strain.
- Developing and practising new aerobic exercises that aim to flex and extend different muscle groups.

The type of person suited to this work

Aerobics instructors can take eight or nine classes each week, so you have to be extremely fit and well-organised. Learners watch you closely, so you need to be practised and professional with oodles of confidence and enthusiasm! Most instructors are cheerful extroverts who inspire people to perform at their best.

Instructions have to be given in clear, positive tones that carry over music. Some individuals take time to learn the routines, so you need to be patient, offering friendly encouragement.

Aerobics instructors are interested in body tone and know how to exercise different muscle groups safely. Being alert to the latest techniques also means using new equipment correctly!

Working conditions

Aerobics instructors take classes in all sorts of locations and may travel considerable distances each week.

Usually, you are in a fitness studio, gym or sports hall – possibly outdoors in good weather.

Leading aerobics classes on a regular basis is highly demanding, but you are relaxed and stress-free after sessions!

Dress is comfortable sportswear; often, you can use other facilities in the fitness centre.

The future outlook

Interest in sport and fitness has never been higher, and many people choose to exercise indoors all year round.

This is an expanding area of work. Many fitness centres employ an aerobics trainer to take two or more weekly sessions.

Besides local authority and privately-run health and fitness centres, adult and community education programmes offer aerobics classes.

You can progress to taking several aerobics sessions in the area – even to training new aerobics teachers.

Training as a fitness instructor in additional exercise regimes could expand your career options.

entry level

To both enter and train while working in this career, you will need qualifications at Level 1. Please refer to explanation on page vii.

Qualifications and courses

- No formal educational qualifications are necessary for teaching aerobics, but you must be 18 and hold an exercise teaching qualification at Level 2, such as the YMCA Qualifications (CYQ) Certificate in Fitness Instructing or OCR's Certificate in Teaching Exercise and Fitness. There is also an NCFE Level 2 Certificate in Fitness Industry Studies. Nationally recognised certificates lead to entry in the Register of Exercise Professionals; this is essential to obtain public liability insurance.
- The CYQ and OCR qualifications are available in a range of exercise specialisms including exercise to music, Pilates, aqua, gym and more.
- Workplace qualifications include NVQ/SVQ Level 2 in Instructing Exercise and Fitness. You can also gain Level 3 Advanced Instructor qualifications, for example, NVQ/SVQ in Instructing Physical Activity and Exercise, or, Coaching, Teaching and Instructing for exercise and fitness. NCFE offers a Level 3 Certificate in Fitness instructing, CYQ, in Advanced Fitness Instructing.
- Employers usually require a first-aid qualification covering cardiopulmonary resuscitation (CPR) techniques, such as the CYQ First Aid at Work.
- Working as an aerobics teacher, you need to keep ahead with new exercise regimes through SkillsActive-approved short courses. These are offered by YMCA centres and Further Education colleges.

Other related opportunities

- Health and Fitness Instructor p362
- Leisure Centre p368

Advantages/disadvantages

- Your busiest work times are when others are relaxing. Classes may be at lunchtime or in the evening and are often at weekends. This flexible work pattern could suit if you have another job or caring responsibilities.
- As a freelancer, you can build up a programme of classes at different centres to suit yourself, but may need to hire a suitably large heated exercise room.
- This job involves travel – moving between classes held at different venues. Weigh up the time and costs involved before committing yourself.

Earnings guide

- In local authority fitness centres, earnings start at around £12,500 per year for full-time work.
- With experience, pay can rise to £16,000.
- You could work freelance, charging around £25 per hour.
- Rates of pay are higher in private health clubs where it is possible to earn up to £30 + per hour.

CRCI:MB | CLCI:GAG

Further information

www.cityandguilds.com/myperfectjob

YMCA Fitness Industry Training
111 Great Russell Street
London
WC1B 3NP
020 7343 1850
www.ymcafit.org.uk

KeepFitAssociation
Astra House
Suite 1.05
Arklow Road
London
SE14 6EB
020 8692 9566
www.keepfit.org.uk

Register of Exercise Professionals
8–10 Crown Hill
Croydon
Surrey
CR0 1RZ
020 8686 6464
www.exerciseregister.org

SkillsActive (Sector Skills Council for active leisure and learning)
Castlewood House
77–91 New Oxford Street
London
WC1A 1PX
08000 933300
www.skillsactive.com

Betting Shop Cashier

What the work involves

- Being a counter cashier in a betting shop, handling bets made by individuals on the outcome of sporting fixtures and other events.
- Recording bets, calculating and taking the correct money.
- Working out any winnings and counting out cash.
- Talking to customers about sporting fixtures, negotiating calmly with winners and losers.
- Taking bets made over the phone, or by email, in between dealing with clients at the counter.

The type of person suited to this work

Only people aged 18 and over can work in betting shops. As you will handle large sums of cash, you have to be absolutely reliable and honest. Some larger betting organisations take younger entrants as support staff.

It is vital to do rapid mental sums to cross-check the electronic calculators – usually doing rough percentages and fractions. Consider whether you can work calmly under pressure, because betting shops are very busy and noisy at times. Experience of shop work or counter service is valued by betting firms.

Staff in the gaming industry usually know a great deal about sporting events. It creates a good atmosphere if you and the customers share an interest in some of the fixtures.

Working conditions

Inside a betting shop, there can be considerable noise and a real press of people placing bets when major sporting events are on.

Betting shop cashiers stand or sit behind a counter. The work is all indoors, and it can be difficult to leave the counter once the betting heats up.

When business is slack, you may do tasks such as cleaning counters, data entry or revising the fixtures listings and displays.

The future outlook

With more gambling and financial transactions taking place via the internet, the total number of betting shops across the UK has decreased – but, there is still at least one medium-sized outlet in every large town.

The work does not attract everyone, so those that choose to enter the gaming industry are usually successful.

Increasingly, ICT skills will be needed for this work.

Counter service may become a less significant part of the work, but it is still essential to have good interpersonal skills and phone manner.

A few fully trained cashiers become self-employed and run their own, independent bookmaking business.

entry level

To both enter and train while working in this career, you will need qualifications at Level 1. Please refer to explanation on page vii.

Qualifications and courses

- No formal qualifications are needed to start this work, although some employers look for a GCSE/S grade (A–C/1–3) in maths.
- Key Skills in ICT, numeracy and communication are valued, but larger employers set their own entry tests in number work.
- Cashiers can be trained on the job. Training covers areas such as counter operations, cash handling, customer service and how to calculate winnings. You may have the opportunity to work towards NVQs/SVQs Levels 2–3 in Customer Service.
- Larger firms have graduate training programmes for staff.
- After further weeks of in-house training in health and safety, security, company policy, merchandising and promotion and the processing of betting transactions, you can become a betting shop manager. With time, you can raise your level of NVQ/SVQ qualifications in Customer Service.
- Promotion can be rapid for keen entrants. Able cashiers can be appointed shop manager, but not before the age of 20.
- You will have a head start as a trainee manager in larger betting firms entering with a BTEC Higher National Diploma, NVQ/SVQ Level 4, or a degree in Business Management.

Other related opportunities

- Bingo Caller p354
- Bookmaker p355
- Croupier p359
- Entertainments Manager p361

Advantages/disadvantages

- In the peak sporting season – between April and August – there are late finishes and early starts. You might have to work split shifts, taking a day off midweek.
- Betting shops are open 7 days a week, so you will be working at weekends and on bank holidays when others are relaxing.
- You are well placed to learn everything about sporting fixtures.
- Your job may bring you into contact with a narrow sector of the public. This can be a limitation of the work.

Earnings guide

- This work is not highly paid.
- Starting out and working full time, you could earn up to £12,500 per year.
- With experience you can expect up to £15,500.
- If you become a betting shop manager, pay can rise to £22,000.
- Higher salaries are paid in the London area.

Further information

Gambling Commission
Victoria Square House
Victoria Square
Birmingham
B2 4BP
0121 230 6666
www.gamblingcommission.gov.uk

National Association of Bookmakers
PO Box 2442
East Molesey
Surrey
KT8 2WE
01884 841859

Association of British Bookmakers Ltd
Regency House
1–4 Warrwick Street
London
W1B 5LT
020 7434 2111
www.abb.uk.com

www.cityandguilds.com/myperfectjob

Bingo Caller

What the work involves

- Being in charge of running bingo games in social clubs, holiday centres and bingo halls.
- Using a computer to select random numbers for the game of bingo and announcing them in a clear, confident and friendly manner.
- Keeping up a flow of cheerful banter to amuse the players.
- Checking completed bingo cards against the computer and presenting prizes to the winners.
- Organising linked-up local and regional bingo contests.

The type of person suited to this work

You cannot be someone who shuns the limelight! A bingo caller is the absolute focus of attention for players, so you need to be well groomed and smartly dressed.

You need good eyesight and normal colour vision, excellent hearing and a clear speaking voice to chat with people of all ages and backgrounds. It is important to think on your feet, maintaining a stream of patter and changing tactics as the game progresses.

A flair for numbers and skill with computers are both vital assets, as you have to respond to ushers moving amongst the players signalling the winning cards which you check against the computer.

Dealing with bingo players takes tact and diplomacy. You have to be fair, consistent and honest. At times, you will make unpopular decisions when it is necessary to be assertive.

Working conditions

Bingo halls are dimly lit places and they can get hot and stuffy when full.

Games are played during the afternoon and evening – in some places, seven days a week.

You could be working a roster of split shifts during most afternoons and nights of the week, as well as at weekends, only occasionally getting a full day off.

The future outlook

Although bingo has lost some of its popularity, there were still 639 licensed bingo clubs across the UK in 2006, with plenty of openings to start work as a bingo caller. The smoking ban in public places and the rise of online bingo has resulted in some large chains selling off vulnerable premises.

Many people gain bingo-calling skills through volunteering work in care homes or community centres. This is a good way to find out if you have a flair for bingo calling and enjoy the work.

There are bingo halls and social clubs in every major town, where opportunities arise to progress to hall or club manager, gaining the essential skills and qualifications in the workplace.

Experienced bingo callers are often in demand to work on cruise liners and in holiday camps and parks.

With ability in numeracy, you could make a sideways career move to train as a croupier in one of Britain's growing number of casinos.

entry level

1

To both enter and train while working in this career, you will need qualifications at Level 1. Please refer to explanation on page vii.

Qualifications and courses

- There are no formal entry qualifications to work as a bingo caller. It is usual for bingo callers to be at least 18 years of age, in compliance with the gambling and licensing laws. However, bingo game assistants – or ushers – can be aged 16.
- Employers prefer some GCSEs/S grades, mainly in English, maths and ICT.
- Training can be carried out on the job by learning from in-house skilled bingo callers and floor managers, or there may be an opportunity for trainees to attend a calling school.
- You have to learn the gaming regulations set out in the Gambling Act, and keep up to date with any changes to the rules controlling bingo.
- The only specific professional qualification available within the Bingo business is the SVQ Level 2 in Bingo Operations. This covers topics including customer service, bingo calling, and bingo games support.

Other related opportunities

- Betting Shop Cashier p353
- Bookmaker p355
- Croupier p359
- Entertainments Manager p361
- Holiday Centre Work p364
- Holiday Representative p365

Advantages/disadvantages

- In this type of work, you have to mix a great deal with older, retired people. Going to a bingo hall is the weekly social highlight for some players, so you need to be upbeat, enthusiastic and humorous, whatever your mood.
- Being at work while others are relaxing and socialising may be difficult to juggle with your own home and social life.

Earnings guide

- Trainee bingo callers earn a low salary, but you will be paid more as you gain experience and become better known.
- There are variations in earnings, depending on the region and the playing capacity of the bingo centre where you work.
- Pay starts at around £10,000 per year, but you can earn up to £20,500+ if you become a popular regional or national bingo caller.
- In the more sophisticated gaming halls and on cruise liners, earnings are in the range of £24,000–£28,000. Also, callers working on liners have no living expenses while aboard ship.

Further information

www.cityandguilds.com/myperfectjob

Gambling Commission
Victoria Square House
Victoria Square
Birmingham
B2 4BP
0121 230 6666
www.gamblingcommission.gov.uk

Bingo Association of Great Britain
Lexham House
75 High Street North
Dunstable
Bedfordshire
LU6 1JF
01582 860921
www.bingo-association.co.uk

People 1st (Sector Skills Council for hospitality, leisure, travel and tourism)
2nd floor, Armstrong House
38 Market Square
Uxbridge
Middlesex
UB8 1LH
0870 060 2550
www.people1st.co.uk

CRCI:MA | CLCI:GAK

Bookmaker

What the work involves

- Taking bets from punters (clients) on the outcomes of sporting events and contests in the world of entertainment, and issuing betting cards.
- As a licensed bookmaker: running a betting shop, or your own or employer's 'bookie's pitch' at different racing events all over the country.
- Working out the betting odds for every race entrant and communicating with other bookies via the internet or by 'tic-tac' semaphore at racing events.
- Writing up and adjusting the changing odds for each track event on a display board.

The type of person suited to this work

Successful bookmakers have a flexible mix of skills and aptitudes.

You need to be alert – listening, reading and observing – gathering vital information about race entrants' recent performance ratings and handicaps. Also, you consider factors such as the stable (or kennel) and trainer, the jockey and the track conditions, to calculate betting odds for all race entrants. This will be the amount you pay out if they win, or are placed second or third.

The odds you offer will be influenced by those of competing bookmakers, and you need to make rapid adjustments as the odds shorten just before 'off'.

Confidence and good verbal and negotiating skills are vital for contact with punters and others in the racing world – track officials, race administrators and government officials making sure the 2007 Gaming Act regulations are being observed.

Successful bookmakers usually have excellent recall of relevant details.

Working conditions

As a bookie setting up pitch on racecourses, you cover large distances to attend all major sporting events.

Much of your work is outdoors – perhaps standing on a stepladder for visibility. You are exposed to the elements!

Bookmakers who work only in betting shops may find the environment restricting, especially at times when punters become agitated and excited. You may have to handle difficult, even menacing, punters who have lost their stake.

The future outlook

People enjoy placing bets and gambling on all manner of outcomes. This line of work will not disappear, as long as businesses comply with the Gaming Act revisions. You can make a good living as a bookmaker.

Some bookies only do a short stint on a mobile pitch before moving into a more settled job, such as, working for the national Tote (Horserace Totaliser Board), as a betting shop manager, or as a games host in a social club or holiday camp.

Successful bookmakers often prefer to move into self-employment and many experienced bookies work well beyond normal retirement age.

Other related opportunities

- Accounting Technician p4
- Betting Shop Cashier p353
- Bingo Caller p354
- Croupier p359
- Entertainments Manager p361

Advantages/disadvantages

- Bookmakers are involved with betting and gambling – with people taking risks. You have to be calm and collected, keeping your head when others lose theirs.
- The lifestyle is not an easy one, especially if you have to follow all the racing action to make a living.
- Some people find the long hours (past 6.30pm in winter and up to 9.30pm in summer) – with or without travelling to race meetings – do not fit easily with a normal family life.

entry level

To both enter and train while working in this career, you will need qualifications at Level 1. Please refer to explanation on page vii.

Qualifications and courses

- There are no formal entry requirements for bookmakers, although the large betting shop chains may ask for 3 GCSEs/S grades (A–C/1–3), including English, ICT and maths. Other employers will probably not ask for particular entry qualifications, but GCSE/S grade maths is useful. You may have to take a basic maths test at interview, focusing on the calculation of percentages, odds and payments.
- Some entrants – particularly to trainee management positions – have a degree, HND or Foundation degree. Business or mathematical subjects can be useful.
- A high level of numeracy, good customer service including being able to handle troublesome customers, excellent knowledge of betting opportunities and basic computer skills are all essential for this work.
- Experience of customer service and reliability with handling money is an advantage. Betting shop employees may have opportunities to work towards NVQs/SVQs at Levels 2 and 3 in Customer Service or in Licensed Bookmaking.
- Training is provided on the job, and covers areas such as calculating betting odds and payouts, administration, customer service, business skills, managing staff, betting laws and company policies. Large companies may provide training in their own training centres.
- By law, you have to be 18 to work in a betting office and you have to be at least 20 to start as a manager.

Earnings guide

- Starting as a trainee you could earn £13,300–£16,000 per year.
- Bookmakers managing betting shops can earn up to £25,000+ in their own shop or in an outlet of a major employer.
- Earnings of bookies on race courses fluctuate with racing conditions, the number of entrants and punters, and the number of events in the calendar.

CRCI:MA | CLCI:GAK

Further information

Gambling Commission
Victoria Square House
Victoria Square
Birmingham
B2 4BP
0121 230 6666
www.gamblingcommission.gov.uk

Association of British Bookmakers Ltd
Regency House
1–4 Warwick Street
London
W1B 5LT
020 7434 2111
www.abb.uk.com

National Association of Bookmakers
PO Box 2442
East Molesey
Surrey
KT8 2WE
01884 841859

People 1st (Sector Skills Council for hospitality, leisure, travel and tourism)
2nd floor
Armstrong Housee
38 Market Square
Uxbridge
Middlesex
UB8 1LH
0870 060 2550
www.people1st.co.uk

www.cityandguilds.com/myperfectjob

Cinema

What the work involves

Projectionist

- Showing films in cinemas, multiplexes, IMAX movie theatres and entertainment halls during afternoons and evenings until late – in some venues, very late.
- Operating and maintaining the equipment to show long-playing DVDs and sometimes, older reel films. Dispatching and receiving film orders and returning films, to deadlines.
- Managing the running of films and features to the advertised programme times, and adjusting focus, sound quality and volume – always observing local licensing agreements for showing films.
- Taking charge of all technical operations in the cinema – the lighting, heating and ventilation, fire alarms and utility services – being aware of health and safety regulations.

Cinema/theatre attendant

- Stocking the kiosk, cafe/bar, shop and trays with sweets, drinks and ices for sale to cinema-goers. Selling programmes, magazines, food and drink to the audience.
- Checking tickets and showing or helping people to their seats.
- Handling problems and complaints during the performance as a customer service assistant; sometimes working as front-of-house usher before and after shows.

The type of person suited to this work

Projectionist
As you work alone much of the time, you need to enjoy working independently and on your own initiative. Although you may have seen the film several times, you have to be alert and vigilant to trouble-shoot.

A good eye for detail, and excellent hand-eye coordination are usual. As programmes must run to time, you have to be reliable and methodical in managing the work.

You should be interested in film formats and sound, as well as in how things work. When technical hitches arise in the cinema, you have to take immediate action to solve and fix the problem – whether it is splicing an older reel film or fixing the boiler.

Cinema/theatre attendant
If you are working front of house, you need a friendly and helpful disposition towards people. You may have to solve difficulties and handle the situation if people become unruly or unwell in the cinema – usually by getting the manager. You have to be good at mental arithmetic when selling items and giving change.

Film classification laws mean that you may not be accepted for work in the cinema if you are under 18 years old.

Working conditions

Projectionist

Projectionists work in small, windowless rooms which are sometimes air-conditioned.
The job is not a sociable one and you might only converse with the manager, the caretaker and the cleaner.

Periodically, you may have to change xenon projection bulbs and must observe safety procedures, using the correct mask, gloves and leather coat, in case the bulb explodes.

Cinema/theatre attendant

It is always dim in cinemas but, as an attendant, you have to stay in touch with problems and the needs of the audience.

At times, you may sell programmes or work at a kiosk in the main foyer where there may be more contact with other cinema workers.

The future outlook

The entertainment industry is buoyant at the moment, with a steady resurgence in cinema-going and lively interest in the medium. The British film industry is benefiting from an increased flow of revenue, making more films in the UK today than at any time since the 1960s.

Large leisure companies own and run most of the biggest cinemas in Britain. Many of these are modern multiplexes showing a range of films of varying styles targeted at different age groups. There are more shows per evening than in single-screen cinemas, so there continues to be increasing work for projectionists and cinema attendants. Newer multiplexes have larger projection rooms where projectionists may work as a team.

Projectionists need more training in digital technology for showing DVDs in the latest IMAX cinemas where – with enhanced 3D effects and Dolby surround-sound – the audience feel a part of the action. As yet, these facilities are too costly to introduce very widely.

New opportunities are arising for projectionists and attendants with the trend for large-screen showings of films and live events on satellite TV in attractive outdoor settings – courtyards of stately homes, National Trust gardens and so on.

Qualifications and courses

entry level

To both enter and train while working in this career, you will need qualifications at Level 1. Please refer to explanation on page vii.

Projectionist

- There are no minimum requirements for entry to this work, but technical skills and qualifications which show aptitude are an advantage. Projectionists must be 18 years or over if showing an 18-rated film.
- Relevant qualifications include a City & Guilds award in Electrical and Electronic Servicing, or any further education course in the field of electronics. Projectionists must be ICT-literate to work with DVD technology.
- Training is provided on the job and through in-house training courses. BKSTS (The Moving Image Society) provides projectionist training seminars covering topics such as projector maintenance, image quality, sound quality and emerging techniques. Occasionally, relevant short courses are offered by the National Film and Television School.
- Projectionists can work towards the Projectionist Certificate currently run by BKSTS, or attend a training programme run by The British Film Institute (BFI).
- Apprenticeships/Skillseekers may be available in this area for people aged 16–24.

Cinema/theatre attendant

- Attendants need no qualifications to start, but experience as a barperson, counter service assistant in retail or catering, or retail assistant is useful. You may progress to work in the box office, gaining NVQs at Levels 1–3 in Customer Service.

Other related opportunities

- Film and TV Staff p143

Advantages/disadvantages

- You will have unsocial working hours but may get an evening off mid-week.
- There is considerable job independence as a projectionist and you may not start work until the afternoon.
- You get first view of all the latest films, becoming very knowledgeable about films and film-making.
- It is exciting to screen a new release. You are the last technical contact with a film's production – showing the completed result in the best possible conditions. It can be interesting to observe the audiences' reactions.

Earnings guide

Projectionist

- Trainee projectionists earn up to £12,000 per year.
- With experience you could earn up to £16,000.
- If you are managing projection equipment and different films in a multiplex, you can be paid up to £20,000.

Cinema/theatre attendant

- Pay is low in this work.
- Most attendants and front of house assistants work part time and do shift work. As a guide, you could expect to get £10,000–£12,000 per annum.

Further information

Skillset (Sector Skills Council for the audiovisual industries)
Prospect House
80–110 New Oxford Street
London
WC1A 1HB
08080 300900
www.skillset.org

BKSTS – The Moving Image Society
Pinewood Studios
Iver Heath
Buckinghamshire
SL0 0NH
01753 656656
www.bksts.com

City Screen – The Picturehouse Cinema
Recruitment Division
Hardy House
16–18 Beak Street
London
W1F 9RD
www.picturehouses.co.uk

BFI – British Film Institute
21 Stephen Street
London
W1T 1LN
020 7255 1444
www.bfi.org.uk

National Film and Television School
Beaconsfield Studios
Station Road
Beaconsfield
Bucks
HP9 1LG
01494 671234
www.nftsfilm-tv.ac.uk

www.cityandguilds.com/myperfectjob

CRCI:MA

CLCI:GAN

Coach Tour Manager

What the work involves

- Researching coach tours and new itineraries – liaising with travel companies, hoteliers, restaurants, European-wide venues and theatre box offices.
- Travelling on tour with holidaymakers to destinations in the UK and abroad.
- Welcoming travellers, checking paperwork and noting special requirements. Accompanying the party and informing them about places of interest en route.
- Ensuring that the tour covers the publicised route, communicating ahead to check that facilities and services are ready.

The type of person suited to this work

A friendly, outgoing personality is a must. Well-organised, methodical people who inspire confidence make good tour managers.

You need stamina to keep on the go, logging reports and making onward contact when your party is resting. Long hours on coaches are tiring and you may have to help some passengers with their luggage. You are on call 24 hours a day, but have to stay calm, clear-headed and friendly when under pressure.

There are always adjustments to the schedule – route alterations, parking difficulties, double bookings, illness or even death of a tourist – so you have to be cool in a crisis and highly flexible.

If you are excited at visiting new places, your enthusiasm will infect the party! This job suits someone who loves to learn and recount intriguing facts and stories.

Working conditions

You must enjoy being on the go: it might be the Eden Project on Sunday, collecting and returning home an out-of-town party attending a London show on Tuesday and Wembley on Wednesday. Then, there might be a trip to Norway's fjords starting early on Friday.

Travelling abroad a great deal means you are constantly adjusting to different climates. You may also have to live out of a suitcase for much of the time.

There is almost no 'off duty' time when on a tour, as you are responsible for every individual in the party and for a successful outcome.

The future outlook

The coach tour is a highly popular, traditional holiday with people who are retired, who enjoy being in others' company or who share an interest.

This is a relatively cheap means of travel, so coach tours are a top holiday choice for many British travellers. Not everyone wishes to fly and with increasing numbers of short leisure breaks and long weekends, it is probable that coach trips will retain their popularity. Future work for a coach tour manager will be to design novel, ecotourist trips that excite the interest of younger holidaymakers.

entry level

To both enter and train while working in this career, you will need qualifications at Level 1. Please refer to explanation on page vii.

Qualifications and courses

- People who become coach tour managers start from quite different educational backgrounds, as there are no formal entry requirements.
- It is a help if you had a good general education, but GCSEs/S grades (A–C/1–3) in English, maths, ICT, geography and a modern foreign language would provide firm proof.
- The majority of entrants start as travel consultants or in similar roles, to gain knowledge and experience with structured on-the-job training.
- There are usually some Apprenticeship/Skillseekers opportunities available.
- Some employers prefer applicants with a degree or a good qualification. Applicants with little or no relevant qualifications may wish to study a full-time GCSE/S grade, an A level/H grade, or BTEC National/SQA qualification in Travel and Tourism Management or International Tour Management.
- ABTA – Association of British Travel Agents – offers a professional Certificate in Travel (Tour Operations) at Levels 2 and 3, recognised by the industry sector. A new Level 3 Certificate in Tour Management is offered by NCFE.
- Weekly trade magazines carry frequent advertisements for coach tour managers; search online or ask in a local travel firm.

CRCI:MC

CLCI:GAX

Other related opportunities

- Entertainments Manager p361
- Holiday Centre Work p364
- Tour Guide p379
- Tour Manager p381
- Transfer Representative p384

Advantages/disadvantages

- Coach tour managers find out a great deal about different countries – their landscapes, towns, people and cultures.
- You cannot 'leave the party'. Once embarked, barring major incidents, you are there as the manager for the tour's duration.
- Much of your time is spent in the company of the travellers or holidaymakers, so it is essential to get on with all kinds of people.
- As the constant travelling is unsettling, this is a job that best suits people between careers or with no family obligations. Mature, fit, tour managers are welcomed.

Earnings guide

- Starting pay is around £13,000–£14,000 per year.
- This can rise to £20,000 with experience, and there are benefits, such as free accommodation and meals when travelling.
- You may boost your earnings with tips.
- As tour manager, you can earn £23,000+, but the rate depends on individual tour operators.

Further information

www.cityandguilds.com/myperfectjob

People 1st (Sector Skills Council for hospitality, leisure, travel and tourism)
2nd floor, Armstrong House
38 Market Square
Uxbridge
Middlesex
UB8 1LH
0870 060 2550
www.people1st.co.uk

IATM – International Association of Tour Managers Ltd (British Region)
397 Walworth Road
London
SE17 2AW
020 7703 9154
www.iatm.co.uk

ABTA – Association of British Travel Agents Ltd
68–71 Newman Street
London
W1T 3AH
020 7637 2444
www.abta.com
Jobs for tour managers

Croupier

What the work involves

- Setting up gaming tables, preparing packs of cards and selling gaming tokens to casino-goers.
- Greeting customers, inviting them to join games of roulette, black jack or baccarat and explaining the rules if necessary.
- Spinning the roulette or money wheel, shuffling and dealing cards, shaking mini dice cages and encouraging players to place their bets.
- Announcing and paying out wins and collecting in lost bets.

The type of person suited to this work

People who become successful croupiers have engaging personalities. A considerable part of the work is making customers feel happy and relaxed, so a croupier who is amiable and fun will be a success. If you are good with people and able to talk to all types of people into the small hours, you will be a positive asset to a casino.

Good appearance is highly important in casino work. You have to take great care to be smartly dressed in evening clothes, clean and manicured, with immaculately groomed hair.

You have to enjoy games and be happy watching others win. You are at work!

There may be difficult moments, when people are emotional, distressed, even angered by losing, so you must be confident, firm and assertive if necessary.

Although you must be aged 18 to enter the gaming industry, most casino-operating companies encourage early entry.

For greeting visitors to the UK and for croupier work in metropolitan centres and across the EU, language skills are a great asset.

Working conditions

Casinos open 7 days a week and on all the usual holidays from 2pm to 6am, so staff work shifts, from 2pm–10pm and from 10pm–6am.

On cruise liners, croupiers spend up to 12 months on board, with about 6 weeks' vacation. Casinos close when in port, so you do get some time ashore in exotic locations!

Casinos are well-appointed venues, and you mix mainly with a smartly dressed clientele.

The future outlook

Gambling has become better regulated in recent years, and you will find that employers do value their staff. With a growing number of casinos in Britain in 2007 – 140 at present – experienced croupiers no longer need to move abroad for work. There are fewer than 400 main casinos across Europe.

Significant numbers of croupiers are needed to fill jobs on cruise liners, and this can be a favourite choice for experienced croupiers seeking management-level experience.

Many certificated gaming staff from Britain now work abroad, particularly in the USA.

CRCI:MA | CLCI:GAK

Qualifications and courses

- All casino staff – from trainee croupier or dealer up to management level – must be vetted for a clean criminal record by the Gambling Commission which sets strict gaming rules and controls practices across the gaming industry. Unless you hold their Red Licence, you will be barred from the work.
- You have to be 18 to start, but there are no specific entry requirements. Good GCSEs/S grades are useful, but not essential. You must be very quick at mental arithmetic, with good manual dexterity for work at the gaming tables. Prospective employers may set you tests at interview.
- Most major casino operators run a training scheme for entrants both in-house and externally. To gain a BTEC Advanced Diploma in Casino Operations, entrants may attend a 12-week course available at Blackpool and the Fylde College.
- As a croupier of 2-years' experience, with additional training you can progress to supervise a number of gaming tables. Floor managers have additional security responsibilities in counting, checking and locking away all the money taken by close of business.

entry level

To both enter and train while working in this career, you will need qualifications at Level 1. Please refer to explanation on page vii.

- You can progress to become an inspector and, finally, manager of a casino.
- Croupiers who have 2 years' or more experience or who enter the work with a BSc (Hons) in Business Economics and Gambling Studies may fast-track to management responsibilities.

Other related opportunities

- Bingo Caller p354
- Entertainments Manager p361

Advantages/disadvantages

- Croupiers work while others play! This job suits people without family commitments, as the hours are unsocial.
- Croupiers stand for several hours, concentrating on running the games without error, while talking to customers. This can be tiring.
- The atmosphere can be quite stuffy and rooms dimly lit.
- Casino-goers drink alcohol, so feelings and emotions can be heightened during gaming. Arguments sometimes break out and accusations are made, so you must observe all the rules and regulations governing gaming.
- If you are quick and ambitious, you can make rapid progress from croupier to casino manager.

Earnings guide

- Starting salaries are £12,000 per year for trainee croupiers.
- After two years, experienced croupiers can earn £20,000–£27,000, but salaries are higher abroad.
- Casino inspectors earn between £24,000 and £29,000, casino managers – slightly more.
- Pay scales for casino staff on cruise liners are similar, but accommodation is free and salaries are often boosted by tips.
- Salaries in London are higher.

Further information

www.cityandguilds.com/myperfectjob

Gambling Commission
Victoria Square House
Victoria Square
Birmingham
B2 4BP
0121 230 6666
www.gamblingcommission.gov.uk

British Casino Association
38 Grosvenor Gardens
London
SW1W 0EB
020 7730 1055
www.britishcasinoassociation.org.uk/careers

Casino Operators' Association of the UK
PO Box 55
Thorncombe
Chard
TA20 4YT
01297 678312
www.casinooperatorsassociation.org.uk

CRCI:MA | CLCI:GAK

Entertainments Manager

What the work involves

- Having responsibility within an organisation or venue for the schedule of visiting entertainers, achieving a balance of activities that engage the age and gender balance and reflect the cultural interests of the audience.
- Planning, organising, advertising and overseeing a full calendar of social events to amuse and entertain groups of people; acting as a Master of Ceremonies (MC), social secretary, events rep or entertainments manager.
- Contacting acts and agents to make bookings by phone, fax and email.
- Costing out the entertainment plan to see if the social budget will cover the proposals.
- Agreeing the best possible terms with agents, and when the events listing is finalised, publishing and promoting the programme on a weekly and daily basis.

entry level

To both enter and train while working in this career, you will need qualifications at Level 1. Please refer to explanation on page vii.

The type of person suited to this work

You have to be the type that doesn't get fazed.

Entertainments managers are full of good cheer; they are people who enjoy life, can think on their feet and can make audiences cry with laughter, if need be. They are skilled communicators, who also make good use of ICT.

This job requires high-level skills in problem solving. It is no easy task to put together a programme of entertainment to suit all tastes. Your organisation depends on you to find reliable acts – often, to a new formula. You have to make quick appraisals to drive home a deal. You need persuasive powers, imagination and considerable personal initiative.

Qualifications and courses

- There are no formal entry requirements for this career, and relevant experience can be more important than qualifications.
- Useful courses at further and higher education level include hospitality management, leisure management, events management, management and travel and tourism.
- You could enter with a degree, HND or Foundation degree in a subject such as hospitality, leisure management, business studies, marketing or events management. The minimum entry requirements for a degree are 2 A levels/3 H grades and 5 GCSEs/S grades (A–C/1–3) or equivalent, and for an HND or Foundation degree, 1 A level/2 H grades and 4 GCSEs/S grades (A–C/1–3).
- People working in the industry can work towards NVQs/SVQs in Cultural Venue Operations at Level 2, Cultural Venue Administration at Level 3 or Arts Development and Teaching at Level 3.
- NCFE offers Certificates at Level 2 in Event Planning and in Event Management at Level 3.

CRCI:Q

CLCI:GAB

Working conditions

Your job might be a permanent post in a grand hotel based in a popular resort, on a cruise liner, or with a large company that frequently entertains important clients.

Entertainments managers work invisibly in an office during daylight hours, emerging only after 6pm to manage the flow of evening entertainment, introducing the artists and ad-libbing between acts.

There is seasonal work for entertainments managers in all the major holiday centres.

The future outlook

Corporate hospitality is used to create a good relationship between client and service provider. As entertainments manager, you have a job with considerable responsibility.

As the travel and tourism industry is still growing at a fast rate, there will be increasing need for entertainment to fill evenings for holidaymakers. Memorable evenings – being entertained by stand-up comics or flamenco dancers – encourage them to rebook with the same cruise line, hotel or tour company.

Other related opportunities

- Bingo Caller p354
- Croupier p359
- Holiday Representative p365
- Theme Park Assistant / Manager p377

Advantages/disadvantages

- There is a great deal of camaraderie in the entertainments industry, and you will meet and mix with some interesting and entertaining artists.
- Almost every evening you have to work hard and stay focused while others are enjoying themselves and relaxing – including the weekends and public holidays.
- Pressure can build if an act does not show up, so you might need to do the occasional special turn to fill a gap and prevent the audience from getting irritable.

Earnings guide

- Generally, travel and recreation work is not well paid.
- Entertainment managers can expect to earn between £16,000 and £21,000 per year, depending on experience.
- If you hold this post with a large international company, pay and prospects could be much higher, so your earnings might be nearer to £25,000–£35,000.

Further information

People 1st (Sector Skills Council for hospitality, leisure, travel and tourism)
2nd floor, Armstrong House
38 Market Square
Uxbridge
Middlesex
UB8 1LH
0870 060 2550
www.people1st.co.uk

Creative & Cultural Skills (Sector Skills Council for advertising, crafts, cultural heritage, the arts and music)
11 Southwark Street
London
SE1 1RQ
020 7089 5866
www.ccskills.org.uk

NCFE national awarding body
Citygate
St James' Boulevard
Newcastle upon Tyne
NE1 4JE
0191 239 8000
www.ncfe.org.uk

www.cityandguilds.com/myperfectjob

Health and Fitness Instructor

What the work involves

- Giving clients fitness assessments and working out individualised exercise programmes to fulfil their goals.
- Training and supervising clients in the safe use of exercise equipment.
- Leading class exercises in keep fit, holistic body conditioning, circuits, cardio kick, aqua, step, Pilates, advanced gym, yoga, weights, etc.
- Setting up, putting away and maintaining all exercise equipment.
- Offering verbal support and encouragement to keep clients 'on task'.

The type of person suited to this work

An enthusiastic and energetic instructor can breed confidence in their clients. You need a strong personal interest in keeping fit and healthy which you are able to convey to others.

People with good communication skills can motivate and enthuse individuals from a range of different backgrounds and experiences. Some clients will be at a low level of physical and mental well-being; it will be your task to help them improve their overall health and fitness.

As an instructor, if you are well informed about nutrition and healthy diets, you will be able to offer guidance to others.

To be a successful instructor, your own fitness and stamina has to be maintained at a very high level through regular stretching and exercise. Taking an active part as instructor in regular classes will keep your personal level of fitness at a peak. Sometimes, committed instructors train together.

Working conditions

Health and fitness classes are run by local authorities in their leisure and sports centres; this often means travelling between locations.

Facilities and additional services are usually excellent. Exercising suites of a similar or higher standard are usual in private health and fitness clubs.

Fitness exercising is nearly always performed indoors, although some of the routines can be practised outdoors in fair weather, where this is feasible.

The future outlook

Keeping fit and healthy is a growth industry in the UK. There are several thousand privately run companies, besides local authority leisure and sports development centres, all offering fitness courses with opportunities for individual workouts.

This area of non-competitive personal exercising has gained in popularity – faster than team sports participation.

Health and fitness instructors will continue to be in demand, particularly if they regularly update their skills through professional development. This enables instructors to offer training in the very latest techniques for body-conditioning.

A growing number of health and fitness instructors prefer to be their own boss, acting as mobile personal trainers for a broad client group who they may visit in their own homes or at work.

CRCI:MB

CLCI:GAG

Qualifications and courses

- You have to be 18 to work as an instructor, and are expected to work towards NVQs/SVQs at Level 2 or above in Sport and Recreation or in Coaching, Teaching and Instructing (available in various exercise areas). To be employed as a health and fitness instructor, you need qualifications recognised by SkillsActive – the Sector Skills Council – and an entry in the Register of Exercise Professionals to obtain public liability insurance.
- Relevant vocational qualifications are offered by OCR and Central YMCA Qualifications (CYQ). Courses are available at Levels 1–3, and cover subjects such as exercise and fitness knowledge, fitness instructing, circuits, step, group indoor cycling, sports conditioning, improving personal exercise and nutrition, nutrition and weight management. A Level 2 qualification is required to work as an instructor, while Level 3 qualifications lead to advanced instructor status.
- You may choose to focus on teaching adults, working with people recovering from injuries, ante- or post-natal women or people with limited mobility, including older people. To specialise, you work towards an NVQ/SVQ Level 3 in Coaching, Teaching and Instructing Adults.
- There is a Level 2 Certificate in Fitness Industry Studies and new qualifications in Fitness Instructing offered by NCFE at Levels 2 and 3.
- You need a current First Aid certificate which incorporates the essential cardiopulmonary resuscitation (CPR) certificate.

entry level

To both enter and train while working in this career, you will need qualifications at Level 1. Please refer to explanation on page vii.

Other related opportunities

- Aerobics Teacher p352
- Leisure Centre p368
- Outdoor Pursuits Instructor p372

Advantages/disadvantages

- There is a relaxed atmosphere at leisure and fitness centres. People come to unwind and to give themselves a boost by working out.
- Regular classes are demanding and you must avoid pressure to take on more groups than is sensible.
- As a self-employed instructor, you can set your own hourly rates to cover the cost of hiring or providing suitable premises and all the recommended equipment for different exercise schemes.
- There is no upper age limit to working as a health and fitness instructor while you remain flexible and fit!

Earnings guide

- Part-time hourly rates are quite low. Rates start at £9–£11 per hour, rising to about £25 per hour for private fitness training.
- If you work for a local authority leisure centre, the full-time equivalent salary is £14,000 per year when starting out.
- With experience and additional responsibilities this can increase to £21,000+.
- You can work part time for a local authority and supplement your earnings with private sessions as a personal trainer.
- Health and fitness trainers employed by top sports clubs earn higher rates.

Further information

Register of Exercise Professionals
8–10 Crown Hill
Croydon
Surrey
CR0 1RZ
020 8686 6464
www.exerciseregister.org

YMCA Fitness Industry Training
111 Great Russell Street
London
WC1B 3NP
020 7343 1850
www.ymcafit.org.uk

Keep Fit Association
Astra House, Suite 1.05
Arklow Road
London
SE14 6EB
020 8692 9566
www.keepfit.org.uk

NCFE national awarding body
Citygate
St James' Boulevard
Newcastle upon Tyne
NE1 4JE
0191 239 8000
www.ncfe.org.uk

SkillsActive (Sector Skills Council for active leisure and learning)
Castlewood House
77–91 New Oxford Street
London
WC1A 1PX
08000 933300
www.skillsactive.com

CRCI:MB

CLCI:GAG

www.cityandguilds.com/myperfectjob

Holiday Centre Work

What the work involves

- Trying hard to make sure that every visitor to your holiday centre has the best holiday of their life.
- Doing a range of different tasks, from performing in cabaret and running entertainment shows for children, to cleaning out the chalets and changing the linen and towels.
- Looking after groups of youngsters in play areas, aqua-sports zones and gyms. Operating equipment, such as fun fairs, glide rides and sound systems.
- With experience you might perform other duties, from running shops or fast food outlets, to helping manage the site and recruiting and training staff, to managing the catering, cleaning, maintenance and on-site entertainment.

The type of person suited to this work

Holiday centre workers need stamina and a strongly developed sense of humour. The work suits people who are natural survivors and who enjoy mixing. Patience and humour are key qualities for holiday centre work, as you may be working with very young children, people with disabilities and the over-65s.

If you are naturally happy and optimistic, you will enjoy your work. Although tasks can be repetitive, the customers are constantly changing. If you are a cheerful and reliable member of a work team, this can help everyone maintain their energy levels.

A strong physique and good health are vital attributes for holiday centre workers. The hours can be long and you may have very early starts with late finishes.

Working conditions

Holiday centre workers usually live on-site during the holiday season, because of the pattern of early and late shift work. There are slack times during the day when you are free, but it might be impossible to travel far from the centre.

Work tends to stretch into 7 days, although larger centres do insist that their workers have one clear day off each week.

You will probably wear a highly visible uniform, so visitors can spot you easily.

Often, you are responsible for groups of children or adults doing an activity, so you have to be highly safety conscious, ready to use first-aid knowledge and problem-solving skills at all times.

The future outlook

The holiday centre will always be a great place to strike out from if you want to be an entertainer. Audiences can be relied on to give straightforward, honest criticism, so this will always be a good environment in which to test out new acts before transferring to city stages, clubs or cruise liners.

Changing leisure patterns have meant that more people take short and weekend breaks as well as annual leave, so the 'holiday season' extends through much of the year. Holiday centres do their best to attract 'out-of-season' trade by offering weekends with snooker champions, well-known comedians and performers.

There is a constant turnover of part-time casual workers in this field; therefore there are always opportunities advertised at nearby jobcentres and in local newspapers during the season. Holiday centres have become popular once more.

entry level

To both enter and train while working in this career, you will need qualifications at Level 1. Please refer to explanation on page vii.

Qualifications and courses

- There are no formal entry requirements for this work.
- Relevant qualifications will be required to work in specific areas, for example, in fitness instructing or child care. GCSEs/S grades are useful, especially maths and English, and are normal requirements for administrative posts.
- Other useful qualifications, depending on the particular job, include First Aid certificates and health and safety qualifications. A Criminal Records Bureau check is essential for jobs where you work with children.
- Relevant experience in areas such as customer service, catering or child care/youth work is an advantage. Knowledge of a foreign language is useful, and may be required for work on-sites in Europe.
- Training is provided on the job and through in-house courses.
- Holiday centre workers may be able to gain NVQs/SVQs in Customer Service at Levels 2–3, Catering and Hospitality at Levels 1–3, Food Preparation and Cooking at Levels 2–3, or in other relevant areas.
- CITO (Caravan Industry Training) provides qualifications for caravan park workers and managers. These include NVQ Level 2 in Operational Services (Caravan Parks) and NVQ Level 3 in Operations and Development. They also offer a Park Management Certificate by distance learning.

CRCI:MC

CLCI:GAX

Other related opportunities

- Entertainments Manager p361
- Holiday Representative p365
- Theme Park Assistant / Manager p377
- Tour Guide p379

Advantages/disadvantages

- Many workers are happy to live in some discomfort during the holiday season, when there may be little privacy, as you might have to share accommodation with other workers.
- Holidaymakers can be fun to work for, but there are always some complaints and problems to solve.
- It can be a strain keeping up a cheerful outlook and happy public face.

Earnings guide

- The casual nature of many of the jobs attracts shift-workers and students needing to earn money to fund their learning.
- When starting out, you may get around £10,000 per year, rising to £11,500–£12,500 between 18 and 21.
- With experience this can rise to £16,000–;£19,000.
- Administrative and catering jobs receive rather better pay, as do the croupier, entertainments manager and site manager – the last earning up to £22,000.

Further information

www.cityandguilds.com/myperfectjob

Institute of Hospitality
Trinity Court
34 West Street
Sutton
Surrey
SM1 1SH
020 8661 4900
www.hcima.co.uk

SkillsActive (Sector Skills Council for active leisure and learning)
Castlewood House
77–91 New Oxford Street
London
WC1A 1PX
08000 933300
www.skillsactive.com

CITO (Caravan Industry Training Ltd)
74–76 Victoria Road
Aldershot
Hants
GU11 1SS
01252 796085
www.cito.org.uk

Holiday Representative

What the work involves

- Meeting holidaymakers at airports, helping them to locate their luggage and board onward transport to their accommodation.
- Being at a holiday resort abroad, speaking the native language fluently, representing a travel company and looking after their holidaying customers.
- Informing customers about their accommodation and its immediate locality, giving out information about local bus routes and times, hire cars, local restaurants, sites of interest, etc. Selling tickets for excursions and helping with paperwork, lost items or people needing emergency medical care.
- Accompanying tourists on expeditions and sometimes entertaining the party with group ice-breakers and other activities.

entry level

To both enter and train while working in this career, you will need qualifications at Level 1. Please refer to explanation on page vii.

The type of person suited to this work

As a rep you will be well groomed and of smart appearance. Most are under 30, doing a holiday full-in job while on a break from studies, gaining fluency in the country's language. Reps may also take on this work between jobs, or when preparing for a career move in leisure and tourism.

It is important for the tour operator that all their holiday customers' needs are met and that the holidaymakers enjoy themselves. The holiday rep is there to make that happen. You will need to be a chatty and approachable person who enjoys meeting and helping different kinds of people at all times of the day and night.

Working conditions

Often, you are the first point of contact for your company abroad, and so you must always be ready to put work first.

Holiday reps work in every kind of climate, from extremely cold, snowy conditions to hot and dry environments. They work both outdoors and indoors, usually in small teams.

There are resorts where the holiday reps spend all their time with holidaying groups from arrival to departure. This can mean late finishes and early starts.

The future outlook

With travel abroad still increasing annually, there is an expanding need for people with these skills to work as resort or holiday reps.

For some holidaymakers, holiday reps play a vital role in introducing them to their accommodation and the local environment. Many people do not have foreign language skills, nor research the area they are visiting. Quite a number of visitors rely entirely on company reps to do interpretive tasks to ensure that they enjoy a trouble-free holiday experience.

Qualifications and courses

- Some companies like their recruits to have GCSEs/S grades in maths and English, humanities or geography, plus at least one modern foreign language.
- No formal educational qualifications are required by tour operators, but previous experience in customer service is often required.
- NVQs/SVQs at Levels 1 and 2 are available in Travel and Tourism, and Level 2 Certificates for Resort Representatives are offered by BTEC and NCFE.
- Travel reps have to be constantly updating their knowledge of the holiday destination area and country.
- It is recommended that you are conversationally fluent in the language of the country you wish to work in, but this is not always essential.
- Training is offered by most of the larger tour operators through an induction programme lasting 2–4 weeks.
- Some reps go on to take 2-year full-time courses – such as A levels or a National Diploma/SQA award in Travel and Tourism – while some start via this route, moving on to take a foundation or a BA Hons degree in Travel and Tourism at university.

CRCI:MC

CLCI:GAX

Other related opportunities

- Air Cabin Crew p555
- Airline Customer Service Agent p557
- Entertainments Manager p361
- Tour Guide p379
- Tour Manager p381
- Transfer Representative p384
- Travel Agency Sales Consultant p385

Advantages/disadvantages

- This is responsible work, where you will have to deal with serious problems, so you need to be prepared to face every possibility.
- There is time to learn about the people and culture of the country.
- Some reps work with specialist, independent companies and may find themselves more isolated when abroad.

Earnings guide

- Holiday reps earn between £9,500 and £10,500 per year when starting out.
- Reps have the advantage of free travel, accommodation and board so much of their pay can be saved.
- With experience, reps can earn up to £16,000.
- Some reps, if very experienced and working in a niche tourist destination, can get £18,000.

Further information

People 1st (Sector Skills Council for hospitality, leisure, travel and tourism)
2nd floor, Armstrong House
38 Market Square
Uxbridge
Middlesex
UB8 1LH
0870 060 2550
www.people1st.co.uk

NCFE national awarding body
Citygate
St James' Boulevard
Newcastle upon Tyne
NE1 4JE
0191 239 8000
www.ncfe.org.uk

TTC Training
The Quayside
4 Furnival Road
Sheffield
S4 7YA
0800 915 9348
www.ttctraining.co.uk

www.cityandguilds.com/myperfectjob

Horse Riding

What the work involves

Centre manager/leader

- You will have the day-to-day responsibility for running a riding centre where the focus is on training both horses and riders, as well as developing riding instructors. You will also monitor the condition and care of all the horses stabled at the centre.
- Dealing with all business and house-keeping matters – handling finance and accounts, insurance policies, dealing with suppliers, consulting with the vet, booking in riding pupils and entering riders for events and competitions.
- Keeping up with training initiatives, courses and qualifications and regularly updating the riding centre staff.

Riding instructor

- Leading out horses to grass, before mucking out and supplying stables with clean bedding, food and water; bringing in the next pupils' mounts.
- Consulting lists for the day, gathering together the necessary tack and hard hats, greeting riders, teaching them to tack up their mounts while developing consideration towards the horses.
- From a central point in a riding school, instructing pupils in a clear, positive voice on mounting, correct posture and actions for handling their horses at different paces, focusing on each individual's progress.
- During schooling, managing any alarms or accidents involving mounts or riders.

The type of person suited to this work

Centre manager/leader

Managers of horse-riding centres and their instructors are strong-willed, energetic people, not afraid of hard work. You have to be tough, enterprising and calculating to carry responsibility for the yard's success. You also have to love horses!

There are always practical problems to solve. This work takes someone of drive, ambition and focus, with good organisational skills, who is calm, clear headed and a good communicator, capable of directing the activities of others.

Riding instructor

Instructors have to work conscientiously, on their own initiative. As an instructor, you are always monitoring the condition and behaviour of riders and their mounts, with a steady focus on health and safety.

You need to sustain an adequate level of fitness to meet the physical demands of the job.

Working conditions

You will have to make early starts, as there is a great deal to do before the day's business starts. Work can go on until midnight!

You work in an enjoyable and healthy environment which can help to counter any stresses of the job. However, it can get hot and dusty in the summer and cold in the winter.

There's a great deal of physical, hard work each day which helps you to keep fit and active. You hardly ever sit down – except, perhaps, in a saddle.

Riding instructors may find that part-time work is available.

The future outlook

Numbers of riding establishments – schools for training pupils and horses and centres for trekking on horseback – are increasing as farmers develop new lines of business. There are now well over 3000 riding centres across Britain.

All these enterprises need experienced equestrian managers with a business background, so there are ample opportunities to find work, once trained. There is also increasing demand for instructors at every kind of riding centre.

Horse and Hound magazine carries job vacancies.

It is worth taking your training as far as you can as there are excellent opportunities in the horse-riding industry. An increasing number of people are choosing to spend periods abroad, especially in France and Germany. If you want to do the same, learning the appropriate language will be helpful.

When fully qualified as an instructor, you could be in demand to train individual riders for show-jumping, dressage and other competitive events.

CRCI:HC

CLCI:WAM

Qualifications and courses

Centre manager/leader

- To lead the activities of a riding school or centre, a manager must have substantial experience in equestrian work and may hold a BHS Principal's Diploma.
- Starting out, you can take NVQs/SVQs at Levels 1 and 2 in Horse Care, and at Level 3 in Horse Care and Management.
- There are full-time courses at specialist colleges which offer training leading to BTEC National Diploma in Horse Management, or the BHS (British Horse Society) or SQA National Certificate in Horse Management. The BHS and Association of British Riding Schools (ABRS) offer a range of useful qualifications for intending managers.
- A qualification in Riding Holiday Centre Management is offered by British Equestrian Tourism and is available for the more experienced, potential manager.
- Candidates training towards the Equestrian Tourism (ET) Riding Holiday Centre Manager qualification must be at least 22 years old, hold a certificate in First Aid, an ET Ride Leader Certificate, and have passed the BHS Riding and Road Safety Test.

Riding instructor

- To become a qualified horse-riding instructor, you have to work through graded qualifications of either the BHS or the ABRS.
- Most people qualify by training at a riding school and taking the progressively more demanding tests to gain accreditation. The lowest level for starters is BHS's Preliminary Teacher's Test that you can take aged 17 and a half.
- You have to log up many hours of teaching practice, while learning theory about horses, road safety, etc and gaining Health & Safety and First Aid at Work Certificates.
- You can also become an assistant riding instructor through a full-time course at a Further Education college, and then add on your BHS or ABRS credits with further experience in a job.
- Assistant/Ride Leader qualifications in hacking or trekking are available through the British Horse Society.

entry level

To both enter and train while working in this career, you will need qualifications at Level 1–3. Please refer to explanation on page vii.

Other related opportunities

- Equine / Horse Work p239
- Sports p374

Advantages/disadvantages

- There is no time off for managers as you live and breathe the life of the riding school or centre. Instructors, with early morning tasks and teaching duties until late, also spend a great deal of time at the stables.
- There is considerable responsibility for managers and instructors; riding schools are high-cost operations with heavy bills and insurance premiums to meet, so there is pressure on everyone to make a success of the enterprise.
- If you love horses and riding, these jobs can be very rewarding, whatever level of hardship is endured.

Earnings guide

Managers

- Pay for managers depends on factors such as size and location of the stables, and on turnover of business based on the school's reputation and number of riders.
- You may start at around £20,000, progressing to £28,000 or so with experience and further qualifications. Prestigious stables will pay considerably more for the services of a proven, top-class manager to run their business.

Instructors

- Instructors' starting pay is around £13,000 per year. With experience this rises to £20,000.
- Some senior instructors can earn up to £24,000.

Further information

Association of British Riding Schools
Queen's Chambers
38–40 Queen Street
Penzance
Cornwall
TR18 4BH
01736 369440
www.abrs-info.org

Riding for the Disabled Association
Lavinia Norfolk House
Avenue R
Stoneleigh Park
Warwickshire
CV8 2LY
0845 658 1082
www.riding-for-disabled.org.uk

Trekking and Riding Society for Scotland
Bruaich-Na-H'Abhainne
Maragowan
Killin
Perthshire
FK21 8TN
01567 820909
www.ridinginscotland.com

British Horse Society
Stoneleigh Deer Park
Kenilworth
Warwickshire
CV8 2XZ
08701 202244
www.bhs.org.uk

Lantra (Sector Skills Council for the environmental and land-based industries)
Lantra House
Stoneleigh Park
Kenilworth
Warwickshire
CV8 2LG
024 7669 6996
www.lantra.co.uk

Horse and Hound magazine
www.horseandhound.co.uk

Leisure Centre

What the work involves

Assistant

- Helping to run sports and exercise sessions in the leisure centre, often joining in activities with different age groups.
- Setting out any equipment, such as mats and benches, volleyball or badminton nets, and clearing everything away after sessions finish. Demonstrating the safe use of equipment and assisting learners to practise different techniques.
- Working on the reception desk issuing tickets and tokens, taking bookings, answering enquiries and doing other tasks specified by your line manager.

Manager

- Overseeing and managing the day-to-day work of all the staff running the leisure centre. Keeping in touch with all users of the centre, and responding to requests, complaints and concerns.
- Recruiting and arranging induction training and development for incoming leisure centre staff. Ensuring all staff have regular reviews and personal development training.
- Meeting with the company or council reps responsible for the leisure centre to discuss budgets, sources of funding and marketing issues, and for planning new activities and developments.

The type of person suited to this work

People working in leisure centres always have an active interest in sport and fitness. You have to convince recruiters that you are committed to keeping up a high level of personal fitness, and keen to work towards qualifications as an exercise instructor, coach or manager.

Employers look for people with obvious enthusiasm, but also with common sense and a responsible attitude towards others. If you are keen to progress to managerial level, you will need some examples of situations where you have taken a lead role.

Leisure centre staff should have excellent interpersonal skills, being friendly and helpful to all centre users. Often, they have to follow instructions to the letter. It is important to show that you can communicate clearly and are adaptable, and able to mix well with different kinds of people.

Working conditions

All your work time will be spent indoors – at the poolside, in a sports hall, in the weights room, at reception or in the office – unless you are training as an instructor of hockey, netball or tennis.

All leisure centre work involves some unsocial hours – early starts or late finishes – because the premises are open to suit the community at large. Because of the long hours of opening, managers and their assistants work shifts.

There will be a dress code, which might be sweatshirts and tracksuit bottoms, polos and shorts, or even suits for managers, all in bright corporate colours that are highly visible.

In leisure centres, often it is assistants who have to hose down pool sides, showers and changing rooms and do other cleaning tasks on a rota basis.

The future outlook

Currently, interest in sport and leisure centres is booming and this trend looks set to continue. People are becoming more aware of their personal levels of fitness.

New government legislation may try to counter the growing problem of obesity across Britain, and leisure centres will be working more intensely with school-age children, possibly planning and overseeing exercise programmes to promote individuals' health and fitness.

Leisure centre managers will give time to developing and offering new-interest sports and training routines, ahead of public demand.

CRCI:MA

CLCI:GAJ

Qualifications and courses

entry level

To both enter and train while working in this career, you will need qualifications at Level 1–3. Please refer to explanation on page vii.

Assistant

- Although there are no formal entry requirements, many leisure development organisations look for a good standard of education from potential assistants and managers. They may ask for GCSE/S grades in maths, English and a science as a minimum.
- Training is often given on the job, although a number of courses are offered through the Institute of Leisure and Amenity management (ILAM) and the Institute of Sport and Recreation Management (ISRM). Normally, assistants try for an instructor or coach award in their preferred sport or activity and are expected to gain a Lifeguard's Certificate and take on pool duties. The more technically minded can study towards NVQs/SVQs in operating Equipment and Facilities.
- With commitment and effort, you can progress from being a leisure centre assistant to supervisor, and then assistant manager, before becoming a leisure centre manager.

Manager

- Some young people work part time in leisure centres while taking full-time courses such as a GCSE/S grade, an A level in leisure and recreation, or a BTEC National or SQA National in Sports Studies. This is useful work experience if, later, they decide to train as centre managers.
- Trainee managers are expected to have relevant work experience and be working towards Level 3 and 4 qualifications (NVQ/SVQ, HND or degree) in Sports and Leisure Studies, or Sport and Recreation.
- ISPAL offers professional qualifications for managers in Leisure Management. The ISRM (Institute of Sport and Recreational Management) offers a continuous assessment route to a Management Certificate or a Diploma.

Other related opportunities

- Health and Fitness Instructor p362
- Holiday Centre Work p364
- Lifeguard p370
- Outdoor Pursuits Instructor p372
- Sports p374
- Watersport Instructor p386

Advantages/disadvantages

- You work while others play, but you have all the amenities to enjoy out of hours!
- Earnings can be low, unless you start on the trainee management route.
- The work is highly responsible.
- Most leisure centre staff are very relaxed, making pleasant colleagues and, normally, there is a good working atmosphere. The work style is busy but not hectic or pressurised.

Earnings guide

- For trainee leisure centre assistants, pay starts at around £11,000 per year rising to £15,000 with qualifications and experience.
- A trainee manager will start at around £17,000.
- When qualified, salaries rise to £22,000–;£25,000.
- £35,000+ is possible at the top end of the scale. Pay is dependent on the size of centre, number of customers and staffing levels.

Further information

ISPAL – Institute of Sport, Parks and Leisure
The Grotto House
Lower Basildon
Reading
Berkshire
RG8 9NE
0845 603 8734
www.ispal.org.uk

Sport England
3rd Floor
Victoria House
Bloomsbury Square
London
WC1B 4SE
0845 850 8508
www.sportengland.org

ISRM – Institute of Sport and Recreation Management
Sir John Beckwith Centre for Sport
Loughborough University
Loughborough
Leicestershire
LE11 3TU
01509 226474
www.isrm.co.uk

SkillsActive (Sector Skills Council for active leisure and learning)
Castlewood House
77–91 New Oxford Street
London
WC1A 1PX
08000 933300
www.skillsactive.com

www.cityandguilds.com/myperfectjob

CRCI:MA

CLCI:GAJ

Lifeguard

What the work involves

- Overseeing, patrolling and monitoring the water and weather conditions where people are swimming, surfing or boating, displaying warning flags if necessary.
- Keeping watch on stretches of shoreline, observing all activities to reduce the risk of tragic accidents occurring; taking rapid action to alert the public to danger.
- Monitoring the safety of swimmers doing training, diving or splashing about in public swimming pools.
- Rescuing people at risk from drowning, towing them to safety, assisting them ashore, carrying out mouth-to-mouth – sometimes CPR (cardiopulmonary resuscitation) – to revive victims of drowning.

The type of person suited to this work

Lifeguards are very fit, active people who have a deep interest in watersports – canoeing, sailing, swimming, surfing or fishing. They understand the level of unexpected danger in all watersport activities, and the need for swift action in an emergency.

Lifeguards have to be completely confident in the water and be fast, strong swimmers, able to cover 400 metres of a pool in less than 8 minutes. If you have been involved in rescue work, you will know how important good teamwork is in resolving potentially tragic situations.

It's a responsible job. You must have the capacity to give loud verbal directives, to become highly assertive, taking command and managing a dangerous incident in the pool, sea or surf, or on the beach.

You need to maintain a high performance level in swimming and in sprinting, for beach lifeguards.

Working conditions

Almost all work time is spent beside water, indoors or on a beach. If you work as an ocean/beach lifeguard, normally you wear a wetsuit in windy or cold conditions. Poolside lifeguards wear tracksuits or polo and shorts.

You have to like the ambience of a swimming pool or beach, and get satisfaction from watching others enjoy watersports, while keeping an alert and vigilant watch. You have got to be ready to act in seconds – not minutes.

It is important to get on with the other lifeguards in your team, and work well under instruction from the team's supervisor, for whom you log reports.

The future outlook

Interest in watersports has grown dramatically; they are popular as a leisure pursuit with the young and the not-so-young. More and more people own windsurfing boards or visit the popular surfing beaches, go kayaking or sailing. All trainers of these sports need to hold a lifeguard's certificate.

Swimming pools are always busy with club trainees, learners and keep-fit enthusiasts. Attendants working at a poolside must have a lifeguard certificate and over 32,000 are issued by the national governing body for lifeguarding (the RLSS) each year. There is increasing work for qualified lifeguards at all water sport facilities.

entry level

1

To both enter and train while working in this career, you will need qualifications at Level 1. Please refer to explanation on page vii.

Qualifications and courses

- If you work as a Leisure Centre Assistant, you will need to gain a lifeguard qualification as quickly as possible, in order to take on poolside duties.
- Lifeguard training, for the National Pool Lifeguard Qualification of the Royal Life Saving Society, is for those over 16. It is mandatory to take the 7th edition 1st revision NPLQ. Training is over 6 days and covers 2 assessed units: The Principles of Lifesaving and Swimming Pool Supervision, and The Application of Supervision and Rescue in a Swimming Pool.
- NPLQ training can only take place in a centre approved by the Institute of Qualified Lifeguards (over 1900 pools in Britain now have IQL). Entrants can receive a copy of IQL's training handbook, The Lifeguard, directly from Lifesavers.
- All lifeguards need to hold a valid First Aid Worker Certificate.
- Lifeguard qualifications must be renewed every 2 years.
- Ocean/beach lifeguards can take additional, intensive courses covering practical ocean rescue skills involving the use of boards and tubes. You must be 18 years or over to train as a Beach/Ocean lifeguard. The NaRS Beach Lifeguard award covers sea-rescue, professional management skills, practical lifeguarding and managing beaches.

Other related opportunities

- Leisure Centre p368
- Outdoor Pursuits Instructor p372
- Sports p374
- Watersport Instructor p386

Advantages/disadvantages

- You have to work without distraction, surrounded by people enjoying leisure time.
- There can be periods of boredom that you have to work through, maintaining vigilance. Accidents can happen at any time.
- Although you can gain a glowing tan while keeping watch, there are dangers of overexposure to sunlight.

Earnings guide

- Pay levels vary, depending on employer and patrol times involved.
- Many qualified ocean/beach lifeguards work as voluntary Beach Rescue Lifeguards for the RNLI (Royal National Lifeboat Institute) which can help arrange training.
- Starting salaries are around £11,500–£15,000 per year. With experience this can rise to £16,000+.
- Some lifeguards work for local authorities on a part-time basis when hourly rates of pay vary.

Further information

ISRM – Institute of Sport and Recreation Management
Sir John Beckwith Centre for Sport
Loughborough University
Loughborough
Leicestershire
LE11 3TU
01509 226474
www.isrm.co.uk

Royal Life Saving Society UK
River House
Broom
Warwickshire
B50 4HN
01789 773994
www.lifesavers.org.uk

Swimming Teachers' Associaton
Anchor House
Birch Street
Walsall
WS2 8HZ
01922 645097
www.sta.co.uk

SkillsActive (Sector Skills Council for active leisure and learning)
Castlewood House
77–91 New Oxford Street
London
WC1A 1PX
08000 933300
www.skillsactive.com

Saltwater Training
23 Grenville Road
Padstow
Cornwall
PL28 8EX
01841 533076
www.saltwatertraining.com

Nightclub Manager

What the work involves

- Having responsibility for the smooth running of a late evening entertainment venue which offers music and is licensed to sell alcohol and food.
- Helping to hire and train staff to operate the club's techno-equipment – sound system, DVD and lighting – to run the bar and wait at tables, to look after the premises and trouble-shoot within the club and on the door.
- Drawing up future nightly listings, booking and paying artists and DJs to perform in the nightclub.
- Overseeing the club, ensuring it runs as a profitable concern, each night until late, including every weekend.

The type of person suited to this work

You have to be a night owl to work as a nightclub manager, and, this is not a job for the shy, retiring or unconfident.

You must appear open and attentive, with an alert but calm appearance, demonstrating that you are watchful and aware. You have to be high profile throughout the opening hours and be available to defuse issues before they start. You also have to get on well with accountants, licensing authorities, environmental health inspectors and fire officers, suppliers and performers.

You need to be able to maintain a nightclub with a fun and stimulating atmosphere, where people have no concerns about coming in for a good time.

Working conditions

You will be the lead person and direct the activities of a support team of nightclub workers. This means putting in longer hours than most. You may be on-site from early afternoon until after 2.30am – even 4.00am or later at weekends.

The dim lighting, high-volume sounds and stuffy atmosphere, together with the late nights, can harm your health over time.

It is essential to be of good appearance, dressed extremely smartly. Never appear without looking sharp because it is you that sets the style code for the club.

There will be plenty of occasions when you have to talk down high-spirited nightclub goers – sometimes, insisting on guests leaving.

The future outlook

There are various styles of nightclub meeting the needs of quite different club-goers – especially in large cities.

Outside big cities, there is more emphasis on dance clubs which appeal mainly to a younger clientele, but there are usually one or two late-night venues where someone older can spend a good evening.

There is a constant turnover of nightclub staff, including managers, so there will be plenty of job opportunities in different kinds of nightclubs for the foreseeable future.

Some managers move to work abroad in resorts, or on cruise liners, and there is similar work in holiday centres across Britain.

entry level

1

To both enter and train while working in this career, you will need qualifications at Level 1. Please refer to explanation on page vii.

Qualifications and courses

- There are no formal educational qualifications which are essential to starting work as a nightclub manager, but employers do look for a number of qualities and skills.
- Problem solving is an important skill in nightclub work – thinking on your feet, to come up with instant, practical solutions.
- You should be able to demonstrate high levels of the other Key Skills, for example an ability with numbers is useful for budget management. Good verbal and written communication skills are also helpful, as is being confident, a good organiser, and having a knowledge of health and safety.
- Being a manager means leading the team of nightclub workers, so any qualifications you can gain in human resource management are useful.
- Accountancy or amenity management qualifications are useful: Edexcel offers NVQs/SVQs for Accounting Technicians at Levels 2 and 3, and NCFE offers a Certificate at Level 2 in Event Planning and 3 in Events Management.

CRCI:MA

CLCI:GAN

Other related opportunities

- Entertainments Manager p361
- Theme Park Assistant / Manager p377
- Tour Manager p381

Advantages/disadvantages

- Being in a nightclub, evening after evening until the early hours, has an appeal for some people. However, the majority who leave manager positions say the work pattern was their main reason for going.
- You rub shoulders with many interesting and well-known people; this is certainly not a dull job if you enjoy socialising.
- There can be a good ambience in the club, between customers and staff, but creating that magic atmosphere is largely down to you.

Earnings guide

- Nightclub managers may start at around £20,000+ per year.
- With experience this can rise to £25,000. You may receive bonuses from the owning leisure organisation if your club does well.
- In London and other cities, pay may be higher, possibly rising to £32,000 for those with the qualities and skills sought by owners of more exclusive nightclubs.

Further information

Edexcel
Customer Service
One90, High Holborn
London
WC1V 7BH
0870 240 9800
www.edexcel.org.uk

NCFE national awarding body
Citygate
St James' Boulevard
Newcastle upon Tyne
NE1 4JE
0191 239 8000
www.ncfe.org.uk

EQ
Suite E229
Dean Clough
Halifax
West Yorkshire
HX3 5AX
01422 381618
www.thinkeq.org.uk

www.cityandguilds.com/myperfectjob

Outdoor Pursuits Instructor

What the work involves

- Living and or working in an outdoor education or outward bound centre, you will instruct and train children and adults to learn new skills and overcome challenges – while enjoying themselves!
- You can be involved with a wide range of outdoor activities from canoeing, fell walking and orienteering, rock climbing, caving and abseiling to snowboarding and skiing.
- Joining with other instructors, you will take parties out to learn downhill skiing, mountaineering or one of a range of watersports.
- There will be evening work, instructing and training visitors in the theory side of each pursuit – also covering care of the environment, reading the weather and orienteering – while reinforcing safety and emergency procedures.
- You may plan and timetable a range of activities to meet the needs of different visiting parties.

The type of person suited to this work

All outdoor pursuits enthusiasts are independent, capable people who enjoy testing themselves against the elements. They like encouraging others to share their feelings of challenge and achievement. Of course, there are essential qualities you must have, besides a high level of fitness and stamina.

You have to be completely reliable and conscientious as you will have responsibility for the safety and welfare of others – assessing risks and individuals' capabilities. Besides personal competence in various activities, you need to be able to work as part of a team, taking the lead where necessary.

Your instructions have to be understood by everyone in the group, and you will need to be able to motivate and encourage individuals who find the going tough.

Working conditions

One day, you might be on a mountainside or working up a rock chimney; the next, you could be in a flat meadow with targets and a group of archers.

You will work mainly during spring to autumn, but some centres offer a limited range of outdoor pursuits through the winter, such as kayaking and rock wall climbing.

There are long hours in this work – it is not 9 to 5. If there is a hike, you may have to be up and away by 5.30am and might not be back until 9pm. And then, there is always paperwork.

You may not be a great mixer, but you have to be able to communicate easily and pleasantly with all kinds of people on a daily basis; most will be staying in the shared accommodation for up to a week. Humour always helps!

The future outlook

There is a continued and growing interest in adventure sports, where people tackle challenges that are outside their normal experience, and there will be increasing job opportunities in the future. 75,000 people work in this area of sport in Britain today, across 2500 outlets for outdoor pursuits!

To be a successful instructor, you have to want to teach young people. There are growing numbers of disabled youngsters and adults being introduced to outdoor pursuits as a new challenge.

Instructors with considerable experience are needed to train newly recruited instructors – some even start their own centre.

You will get opportunities to work abroad – so polishing up a foreign language could give you an advantage!

CRCI:MB

CLCI:GAG

Qualifications and courses

- There are no set qualifications for entry to this career, but entrants must normally be at least 18 holding proficiency or coaching awards in relevant outdoor sports. Each sport's National Governing Body offers these awards which you can train for in a Further Education college or through a youth club.
- A First Aid certificate is also essential, and a life-saving qualification is required for some posts. It is also an advantage if you drive and can gain a DVLA minibus driving licence.
- Some people start as volunteers, working towards NVQs/SVQs at Level 2 in Outdoor Activity Leadership, while other relevant qualifications include: the British Sports Trust (Sports Leaders UK) Sports Leadership and Basic Expedition Leadership awards.

You can take an A level in Sport and Physical Education; a BTEC National Certificate or Diploma in Sport (Outdoor Education); or the SQA National qualification in Leading Sports Activities or Sports Coaching Studies.

- A Sports Leaders UK Level 2 award in Basic Expedition Leading is required by most local authorities to lead Duke of Edinburgh Award groups.
- There are relevant higher education degree, HND and Foundation degree courses available in adventure education, outdoor activities management, outdoor education or outdoor leadership.

entry level

To both enter and train while working in this career, you will need qualifications at Level 1–3. Please refer to explanation on page vii.

- Some people become outdoor pursuits instructors following experience as a teacher, youth worker or sports coach.
- Further training is done on the job, and instructors work towards NVQ/SVQ Level 3 in Outdoor Education and Development Training or Outdoor Recreation. Experienced instructors can gain professional accreditation from the Institute for Outdoor Learning (IOL).
- Apprenticeships/Skillseekers may be available for people aged 16–24.

Other related opportunities

- Health and Fitness Instructor p362
- Leisure Centre p368
- Teacher p184
- Watersport Instructor p386

Advantages/disadvantages

- Many instructors work on short-term contracts covering the season.
- There are opportunities to work with university sports clubs and youth clubs, and some leisure and fitness centres employ part-time outdoor pursuits instructors, so you may be able to build up to working throughout the full year.
- This can be a highly responsible job, where many other people are trusting you to make the right decision for all the party.

Earnings guide

- Earnings are certainly not high in this line of work, but free accommodation and food in the centre are benefits.
- Starting salaries are around £10,000 per year.
- With experience, this rises to £12,000–;£18,000.
- Some senior instructors can earn up to £25,000.

Further information

Institute for Outdoor Learning
Plumpton Old Hall
Plumpton
Penrith
Cumbria
CA11 9NP
01768 885800
www.outdoor-learning.org

Mountain Leader Training England
Siabod Cottage
Capel Curig
Conwy
Gwynedd
LL24 0ES
01690 720314
www.mltb.org

SkillsActive (Sector Skills Council for active leisure and learning)
Castlewood House
77–91 New Oxford Street
London
WC1A 1PX
08000 933300
www.skillsactive.com

Sports Leaders UK
23–25 Linford Forum
Rockingham Drive
Milton Keynes
MK14 6LY
01908 689180
www.bst.org.uk
(part of British Sports Trust)

www.cityandguilds.com/myperfectjob

CRCI:MB

CLCI:GAG

Sports

What the work involves

Exercise scientist

- Using scientific knowledge to assess the relative benefits of different exercise regimes aimed at providing high-level performance training for sports professionals and assisting recovery from serious injuries, promoting personal fitness – particularly in older people – and improving general health and movement.

Coach

- Working with people of all ages and at every level of expertise to develop their skill in a particular field of sport.
- Devising and continually refining personal training programmes for top sports professionals, working through the programme with them and monitoring changes in their level of performance.

Development officer

- Helping to popularise particular sports, such as rugby or tennis, and encouraging people to actively take up the particular sport, or sport in general.
- Through publicity drives – using every media format – working to increase the uptake of programmes offered by local leisure and sports development centres; one immediate aim being to develop skills of more young British athletes by the London Olympics in 2012.

Sports psychologist

- Working to boost the self-image, self-esteem and confidence of professional sportspeople.
- Assisting top-class team players to understand how to play an improved tactical game through being more alert to conscious and unconscious signals from other players.
- Helping team players and single professionals learn mental defences that keep up morale and boost their confidence to win, as well as tactics to undermine and destabilise the confidence of their opponents.

Professional sportsperson

- Exercising and training to maintain high levels of personal fitness and stamina, besides polishing individual specialist skills. Travelling to events and taking part in competitions, which may be held anywhere in the world.

Cricketer

- Playing as a professional during the cricket season in Britain, but returning to other employment out of season. Alternatively, as a top team player selected from a county team, touring and playing at professional level all year round, in this country and abroad.

Footballer/rugby player

- Playing as a paid professional in one of the top division teams in Britain, but not always amongst the team players selected to compete in matches. Boosting earnings with sponsorship money, if sufficiently well known.

Professional horse rider

- Taking part in equestrian sports, showing and competing for horse trainers, breeders and owners. Training with individual horses, developing an excellent working partnership.

Golfer

- Competing as a professional golfer in tournaments held in this country, Europe and wider.

CRCI:MB

CLCI:GAG

The type of person suited to this work

Professional players have reached the top of their sport only through a single-minded effort to 'be the best'. Without exception, they have all spent long hours exercising and training in their preferred sport, and have devoted time to competitions, tournaments and galas, while schoolmates may be still in bed, playing computer games or out socialising. Sportspeople have 'stickability', willpower and dedication.

People try to reach the peak in their chosen sport for many different reasons, but those who do succeed feel that all the sacrifices and effort have been worth it. Success can be measured in events won, income and sponsorship offers.

Not everyone becomes famous or fabulously wealthy. There are vast numbers of professional players who only gain a sense of personal achievement and, perhaps, self-fulfillment. This is clearly the case for some of the magnificent disabled champions.

Qualifications and courses

Exercise scientist

- Entrants are usually graduates with sports science degrees. Related degrees, such as physical education, sport fitness, sport physiotherapy or sport medicine, may be acceptable.

Coach

- Sports coaches should have a recognised qualification in coaching, which can be gained through a relevant course or through the relevant national governing body for the sport concerned. Experience in the work is also vital.
- Candidates may need to be over 18 and hold a First Aid certificate.

Development officer

- Entrants usually have a degree in sports development, sports education, sport studies, sports science, physical education or recreation and/or leisure management.

Sports psychologist

- A degree or postgraduate course in sport psychology is required.

Professional sportsperson

- No formal educational qualifications are required, except for golfers.

Golfer

- The Professional Golfers' Association requires players to have 4 GCSEs/S grades (A–C/1–3) or equivalent qualifications.
- The PGA also runs a 3 year course called the Trainee Diploma Programme.
- The Sports Academy runs a 2-year full-time course in Golf Development and the PGA runs a 3-year Foundation degree programme.

entry level

To both enter and train while working in this career, you will need qualifications at Level 1–8. Please refer to explanation on page vii.

Working conditions

In most sporting activities, competing, events and training take place outdoors and have to go ahead, regardless of conditions.

Most professionals spend long hours exercising and preparing to train through warm-up sessions and body-conditioning routines, often with a personal or team trainer and sports coach. Once finished, there is also a lengthy warm down period.

Part of the training programme will include receiving physiotherapy treatments, massage or sessions with the sports psychologist or team's dietitian in the professional association's club.

The future outlook

Sports and sporting fixtures are big business for the competing clubs, professional associations, the media, the government and, of course, the professionals themselves. There is a huge industry devoted to supporting sports at their top level because, in all countries of the world, they hold fascination and interest for so many. Governments foster this interest, recognising that sports do unite people and can also contribute to the wealth of a nation. Countries worldwide compete quite desperately to host prestigious competitive events, such as the Olympic Games.

The entire leisure and sports industry has a turnover of several billion pounds in the UK alone – boosted over the next few years in preparing for the London Olympics in 2012.

For sporting professionals, although feted and admired for a short time, their careers usually have an early peak, and the majority turn to training or coaching other rising stars in their field. Some sportspeople make good sports commentators, reporters and media personalities, while others work on the edges of the sporting world in other capacities.

After their playing career is finished, some famous sports professionals set up their own training academies to encourage and train young sports enthusiasts.

Other related opportunities

- Equine / Horse Work p239
- Health and Fitness Instructor p362
- Horse Riding p366
- Leisure Centre p368
- Outdoor Pursuits Instructor p372
- Watersport Instructor p386

Advantages/disadvantages

- To be a top sportsperson brings considerable rewards in terms of fame and, possibly, fortune.
- Famous players are dogged by the media as all the world is interested in their day-to-day lives, as well as their sporting performance.
- Keeping on top as a sports professional takes work, work and work, with little time away from the sport for other things in life.
- Your routine is carefully scheduled, particularly in the run-up to important events or fixtures; you may have to include regular dope tests in your diary.
- Hard training programmes, long-distance travel and the stress of top-level competition lowers immunity and professional players readily become prone to passing infections.

Earnings guide

- Professional sportspeople usually earn appearance fees, and they can win prize money which may be modest, or run to six figures, depending on the sport and the particular event.
- Most sportspeople supplement their earnings with a second job which they continue after their career as a professional fades, and many get money from advertising products.
- Only a few tennis players, golfers and boxers – plus a relatively small number of footballers and rugby players – earn vast sums from winnings. Most professional players have a short-term seasonal contract to support them through competitions.

Coach

- A coach employed full time may earn between £15,000–£25,000 per year depending on experience.
- Hourly rates can be £14–£25 per hour.

Development officer

- Full-time salaries range between £18,500 and £26,000+ depending on experience.

Further information

Sport England
3rd floor
Victoria House
Bloomsbury Square
London WC1B 4SE
0845 850 8508
www.sportengland.org

Sports Coach UK
114 Cardigan Road
Headingley
Leeds
LS6 3BJ
0113 274 4802
www.sportscoachuk.org

Sport Scotland
Caledonia House
South Gyle
Edinburgh
EH12 9DQ
0131 317 7200
www.sportscotland.org.uk

SkillsActive (Sector Skills Council for active leisure and learning)
Castlewood House
77–91 New Oxford Street
London
WC1A 1PX
08000 933300
www.skillsactive.com

Sports Council for Northern Ireland
House of Sport
Upper Malone Road
Belfast
BT9 5LA
028 9038 1222
www.sportni.net

Sports Council for Wales
Sophia Gardens
Cardiff
CF11 9SW
0845 045 0904
www.sports-council-wales.co.uk

UK Sport
40 Bernard Street
London
WC1N 1ST
020 7211 5100
www.uksport.gov.uk

SPECIFIC SPORTS

England and Wales Cricket Board
Lord's Cricket Ground
London
NW8 8QZ
020 7432 1200
www.ecb.co.uk

Football Association
25 Soho Square
London
W1D 4FA
020 7745 4545
www.thefa.com

British Horseracing Education and Standards Trust
Suite 16, Unit 8, Kings Court
Willie Snaith Road
Newmarket
Suffolk CB8 7SG
01638 560743
www.bhtb.co.uk

Royal Yachting Association
RYA House
Ensign Way, Hamble
Southampton
Hampshire SO31 4YA
0845 345 0400
www.rya.org.uk

Professional Golfers' Association
Centenary House
The De Vere Belfry
Sutton Coldfield
West Midlands B76 9BT
01675 470333
www.pga.info

Rugby Football League
Red Hall
Red Hall Lane
Leeds
LS17 8NB
0844 477 7113
www.therfl.co.uk

Lawn Tennis Association
The National Tennis Centre
100 Priory Lane
Roehampton
London SW15 5JQ
020 8487 7000
www.lta.org.uk

Rugby Football Union
Rugby House
Rugby Road
Twickenham
Middlesex TW1 1DS
0870 405 2000
www.rfu.com

Theme Park Assistant / Manager

What the work involves

Assistant

- Greeting customers at the rides, checking ticket holders' ages and heights. Sometimes, you will need to issue ride mats, ensuring only safe numbers enter the rides.
- As part of a team, operating and supervising big rides in a theme park, such as Alton Towers, Thorpe Park, Legoland or Chessington World of Adventure.
- Closing safety barriers and running the rides at varying speeds – always observing the safety rules and watching the progress of the riders.
- Keeping a close eye on the environment surrounding rides you work at, ensuring there are no hazards.

Manager

- As manager, you will need to oversee all the different operations within a theme park, ensure the smooth running of all the attractions and amusements, the catering operations, the maintenance and surveillance of the park, etc.
- A large part of your job will be recruiting and training staff for special areas of operation, and being responsible for the health and safety of visitors and staff. You will also have to manage customer services.
- You will be held responsible for any failures or problems that might arise, so this job does require a high level of vigilance. Out of season, there will be repairs and upgrading to organise, plus the planning and introduction of new rides.
- In smaller concerns, much of your time will be spent overseeing the finances of the operation and in planning marketing strategies to attract customers. In larger theme parks, a specialist business manager will carry out this function.

The type of person suited to this work

Those involved in running an entertainment attraction that draws people in large numbers have to enjoy working in the public eye. Theme park workers should be happy relating to the public, wanting them to have an exciting and memorable experience, but also being aware of and concerned for their safety.

Except for the managers and a few experienced assistants, this is seasonal work, carried out by people who move around the country between casual work opportunities. Because of the potential hazards for the public at theme parks, workers must be trustworthy and dependable, with good practical and mechanical skills, able to follow instructions carefully and safely.

Working conditions

Theme park assistants often do their own repairs and maintenance during the mornings, working in supervised teams when the rides are shut down.

This is an outdoor job and, although some areas are under cover, you will be exposed to the elements much of the time.

Theme parks are open 7 days a week, and on bank holidays, so you work shifts and get a full day off each week.

The manager must inspect the whole site before opening time, taking responsibility for seeing all the necessary safety checks have been done, and that the rides and other facilities are fully staffed.

The future outlook

People with fairground jobs, or with travelling circuses, may be happy to join a fixed-site attraction and put down roots. There is always a high turnover of staff, but a core of workers stay on, benefiting from training and increased responsibility. People do move between big parks, but now have certificates as evidence of their transferable skills.

Theme parks have been going for over 30 years and their development has peaked.

Although they are fun venues for family outings, few groups make return trips to theme parks, so it is unlikely that many more proposed developments will get planning permission.

There is more work in Europe for trained, experienced theme park workers. You should contact individual attractions directly, to ask about job opportunities. It helps if you speak their language.

Qualifications and courses

Assistant

- You have to be 18 to start work in a theme park. No formal qualifications are needed, but if your aim is to become a supervisor or manager then it is best to have some GCSEs/S grades in maths, English, ICT and, possibly, DT and sports education.
- There are work-based qualifications available: there are NVQs/SVQs in Mechanical Ride Operations at Level 2, and you receive health and safety training from day one – formally as part of induction, and informally from the staff you work with, who can pass on useful information. NVQs/SVQs in customer care, catering and sales could also be relevant.

Manager

- With experience and qualifications, you can progress to team leader and then gain promotion to managerial jobs, taking the ISPAL (Institue of Sport, Parks and Leisure) Certificates and Diploma.
- Large parks, such as Alton Towers, need several specialist managers to plan and oversee all the catering, site cleaning and waste management, the ride operations, financial arrangements and marketing. Once aboard the team, there are plenty of opportunities for developing leadership skills.

entry level

To both enter and train while working in this career, you will need qualifications at Level 1–3. Please refer to explanation on page vii.

Other related opportunities

- Entertainments Manager p361
- Holiday Centre Work p364
- Leisure Centre p368

Advantages/disadvantages

- This is a specialised line of entertainment and leisure work and might not prove to be a stepping stone to other areas in the industry.
- Managers, with qualifications and experience in the leisure and entertainment industry, can move between employment areas more easily. You can transfer to running leisure or sports centres, amusement complexes or holiday parks.
- It is great to work in an area where everyone is having as much fun as they possibly can.

Earnings guide

Assistant

- Unqualified casual workers can be paid the national minimum wage and work quite unsocial hours, but this pay rate can rise with experience in the job.
- There might be a few benefits for employees, such as paid overtime, free health insurance and a cash bonus at the season's close.
- You might expect to get around £9,000 per year when starting out. With experience, this could rise to £15,000.

Manager

- Managers can earn £20,500–£23,500 per year.

Further information

www.cityandguilds.com/myperfectjob

ISPAL – Institute of Sport, Parks and Leisure
The Grotto House
Lower Basildon
Reading
Berkshire
RG8 9NE
0845 603 8734
www.ispal.org.uk

EQ
Suite E229
Dean Clough
Halifax
West Yorkshire
HX3 5AX
01422 381618
www.thinkeq.org.uk

SkillsActive (Sector Skills Council for active leisure and learning)
Castlewood House
77–91 New Oxford Street
London
WC1A 1PX
08000 933300
www.skillsactive.com

People 1st
2nd Floor
38 Market Square
Uxbridge
UB8 1LH
0870 060 2550
www.people1st.co.uk

CRCI:MB

CLCI:GAG

Tour Guide

What the work involves

- You will meet and greet parties of people taking a holiday journey, trip, visit or tour together – involving planes, rail or coach, or other mode of transport.
- Checking ahead with the tour manager – by yourself, if necessary – to make sure that all arrangements for the particular tour are in place.
- Accompanying the sightseers or tourists on their journey, keeping up a lively flow of informative chat about the area, the wildlife or the town – its history and architecture.
- Acting as assistant and helper to anyone experiencing difficulties in keeping up – climbing stairs, getting through doorways or in and out of transport with bags.

The type of person suited to this work

To be an interesting tour guide, you should have excellent communication skills and be happy and confident addressing parties of different people. You will need lots of stamina and energy, not just to physically withstand a long tour extending over days (or, perhaps, several tours in one day) but also, repeating the same narrative over and over again.

Popular guides are colourful, lively and slightly eccentric people, with good communication skills, who can hold the attention of a large group of strangers of different ages and educational backgrounds. Mature, retired people sometimes choose to become guides in gardens, museums, art galleries and historic buildings, to keep their interests and intellect alive, and to meet people. As a guide, you need to have an excellent memory for facts, as you can expect to be asked all manner of questions by visitors and tourists.

Enterprising undergraduates on arts and humanities higher education courses can develop tour guide skills to boost their vacation earnings.

Working conditions

Conditions do vary. You may work with a microphone on an open-topped bus travelling around an historic city, or you might be on the deck of a boat speaking through the PA system.

Many tour guides work indoors, guiding groups round historic houses, castles, churches, abbeys and cathedrals, but not necessarily in warm conditions.

It can be quite tedious being a guide who is fixed in one room or a suite of a large historic building, answering questions from individual visitors filing past.

Guides with a specialism such as ornithology, flora or music, can travel long distances by plane and coach accompanying themed tours, spending several days away from home. This might be difficult for those with family commitments.

The future outlook

With increasing leisure, more and more people are taking short breaks and long weekends away.

Often visitors have the option of a tour or trip, and so tour guides are in great demand in Britain's historic centres such as Bath, Stratford-upon-Avon and London. With nearly six million visitors coming to Britain each year, together with home tourists, there is a lot of scope for employment in the tourism industry.

The tourist boards across the UK all employ tour guides at heritage sites and this pattern of recruitment seems set to grow as the tourism season now extends to nearly the full year.

Themed walking holidays or tours of distant places for special groups are becoming increasingly popular and many travel companies employ guides throughout the year.

Qualifications and courses

- Most tour guides are aged over 18, and although you need no formal qualifications, some GCSEs/S grades (A–C/1–3) would be useful. You will need to know a great deal about the places where you are working. Tour guides can work towards NVQs/SVQs at Level 2 and 3 in Travel and Tourism.
- If you work in one particular locality, you can become the local expert on, for instance, a certain period of history, the ancestry of a well-known family, the architecture, furniture and artworks in a historic building, the background and lifestyle of famous people, species of plants in a tropical glasshouse, etc.
- You may have to do your own research, or you can accompany a more experienced and knowledgeable guide, until you have absorbed the information yourself. To both broaden your own knowledge base and add to your fund of interesting stories you could attend local historical society lectures. A background in history and local studies can be very useful.
- Fluency in a modern foreign language is an asset when speaking to groups of foreign visitors. Speaking and listening skills in German, French and Spanish are all useful to a tour guide.
- The Institute of Tourist Guiding accredits training courses at three levels: Level 2 covers fixed route commentary, interpretation and presentation; the Level 3 'Green Badge' covers flexible route commentary, heritage interpretation and presentation; the Level 4 'Blue Badge' in Tourist Guiding is the highest level of qualification and is required to work at certain tourist sites.

entry level

To both enter and train while working in this career, you will need qualifications at Level 1–2. Please refer to explanation on page vii.

Other related opportunities

- Air Cabin Crew p555
- Airline Customer Service Agent p557
- Coach Tour Manager p358
- Holiday Representative p365
- Tour Manager p381
- Tourist Information Centre Assistant p383
- Transfer Representative p384

Advantages/disadvantages

- Repetition of facts can make this a difficult job to stick at, long term. It is hard to repeat the same joke, or to be enthusiastic about a ghost or bloodstain after many tours.
- The workload is variable and tour guides are usually employed on a casual, seasonal basis.
- Some party members like to contradict, cross-question and argue a point.
- There may well be days when the weather is poor, which might dampen your enthusiasm.
- You can find yourself working in interesting historical settings or spectacular scenery.

Earnings guide

- Tour guides are paid by the hour to attend a group of tourists or sightseers. Many guides work part time in casual positions, often for The National Trust or similar organisations in Scotland, Ireland and Wales.
- Earnings vary as some guides are volunteers, but you can earn up to £15 per hour for a few hours each day. You might also receive tips from your audiences.
- In full-time employment your salary might be around £10,000–£12,500 per year.
- Working for a package tour company, your salary would be rather higher and your accommodation, travel and meals free.

Further information

www.cityandguilds.com/myperfectjob

Institute of Travel and Tourism
PO Box 217
Ware
Hertfordshire
SG12 8WY
0870 770 7960
www.itt.co.uk

Guild of British Coach Operators
PO Box 5657
Southend-on-Sea
Essex
SS1 3WT
www.coach-tours.co.uk

IATM – International Association of Tour Managers Ltd (British Region)
397 Walworth Road
London
SE17 2AW
020 7703 9154
www.iatm.co.uk

Institute of Tour Guiding
Lloyd's Court
1 Goodman's Yard
London
E1 8AT
020 7953 1257
www.itg.org.uk

TTC Training
The Quayside
4 Furnival Road
Sheffield
S4 7YA
0800 915 9348
www.ttctraining.co.uk

CRCI:MC
CLCI:GAX

Tour Manager

What the work involves

- Putting together proposals for complete tour packages, ranging from exciting day trips to stimulating or relaxing holidays. Often, tour managers dream up new ideas sparked by the media.
- Visiting destinations to research the airlines, coach operators, accommodation and pools, to investigate the restaurants, availability of car hire etc, before revising the proposed costs.
- Passing on details of all new excursions and holiday packages to the marketing team who prepare schedules and fresh brochures.
- Accompanying occasional tours to ensure that customers are satisfied with all the services and are enjoying the holiday package. In smaller companies, the tour manager always travels with the holidaymakers.

The type of person suited to this work

Tour managers tend to be very methodical people, passionate about detail.

Never leaving anything to chance, and keeping one step ahead means that they are always calm in a crisis.

If there are lessons to be learnt from a real-life situation, people who make good tour managers will always be the first to note down any changes that need to be made.

Most tour managers are concerned to offer their customers best value for money, and make strenuous efforts to have satisfied, happy customers who will rebook with their holiday company year on year.

Working conditions

You will be working for a large national or international company, or even for a small specialist tour operator, always following company policy and promoting the company's interests.

You will wear company livery (a uniform) that could be a fairly loud suit, shirt and tie, so that you stand out from the crowd in an airport concourse or big meeting room.

When travelling with a tour, you will be on call 24 hours a day to attend to customers' needs, complaints and worries.

The future outlook

There is great competition for managerial positions within travel and tourism companies. However, if you build a broad base of knowledge and experience over some years, and have well-developed people skills, your prospects of work in the future will be greater than those of a new entrant from a degree course who may not have done as much travelling.

The travel and tourism industry is huge and growing, both within the UK and abroad. To do well, travel companies will have to work hard at building reputations of offering good value for money, plus excellent care services for their customers. Today, many travellers are concerned to know if carbon emissions from their journeys can be offset through sustainable developments at home and in countries they visit.

As more British tourists experience travel abroad, their expectations of travel and holiday accommodation, entertainment and and customer service across the UK rise accordingly.

CRCI:MC

CLCI:GAX

Qualifications and courses

- There are no formal educational requirements to start work in this area, but many have a number of relevant qualifications.
- GCSEs/S grades (A–C/1–3) in English, maths and geography are very useful; as are A levels, a BTEC National Diploma or SQA National qualifications in Travel and Tourism Services.
- If aged 16–24, you might be able to enter with an Apprenticeship/Skillseekers. You will be able to study and gain qualifications in the workplace, such as NVQs/SVQs in Travel Services (Tour Operations) at Levels 1–3.
- There are full-time HND and degree courses offered at many universities in Travel and Tourism Management. Some are sandwich courses, where you spend a year working in the industry. You can also opt for international tourism management, adventure, sport and tourism or hospitality, and leisure and tourism as degree choices.
- NCFE offers a Level 3 Certificate for On-Tour Managers, a Level 3 in Travel and Tourism Management and Level 2 and 3 Certificates in Sustainable Tourism. For would-be managers, City and Guilds offer an HLQ at Level 4 in Travel and Tourism. These qualifications can be gained part time through study at a further education college.
- Tour managers who are active members of the International Association of Tour Managers (IATM) may obtain a free Certificate of Tour Management Accreditation.

entry level

To both enter and train while working in this career, you will need qualifications at Level 1–3. Please refer to explanation on page vii.

Other related opportunities

- Air Cabin Crew p555
- Airline Customer Service Agent p557
- Coach Tour Manager p358
- Holiday Centre Work p364
- Tour Guide p379
- Transfer Representative p384

Advantages/disadvantages

- This is a job where you can follow the project all the way from a highly original idea, to developing a new package deal, to gathering customers' views about their experiences.
- The constant travelling can disrupt home and family life.

Earnings guide

- As a tour manager, you start at around £14,000 per year.
- With experience this can rise to £25,000.
- Top flight travel companies, operating worldwide, pay better rates to managers with excellent, proven skills in the business.

Further information

www.cityandguilds.com/myperfectjob

People 1st (Sector Skills Council for hospitality, leisure, travel and tourism)
2nd floor, Armstrong House
38 Market Square
Uxbridge
Middlesex
UB8 1LH
0870 060 2550
www.people1st.co.uk

IATM – International Association of Tour Managers Ltd (British Region)
397 Walworth Road
London
SE17 2AW
020 7703 9154
www.iatm.co.uk

Tourism Management Institute
41 Chalton Street
London
NW1 1JD
01926 641506
www.tmi.org.uk

TTC Training
The Quayside
4 Furnival Road
Sheffield
S4 7YA
0800 915 9348
www.ttctraining.co.uk

NCFE national awarding body
Citygate
St James' Boulevard
Newcastle upon Tyne
NE1 4JE
0191 239 8000
www.ncfe.org.uk

CRCI:MC

CLCI:GAX

Tourist Information Centre Assistant

What the work involves

- You will be answering questions face to face, over the phone or via the internet, from adults, tourists from Britain and overseas, business people, local young people and researchers.
- Working in a team in a centre, you will provide information, make bookings and reservations, locate places and businesses, and inform people about forthcoming shows and events in the local area.
- From a counter in the centre, you will issue leaflets and sell maps, postcards and items of interest from the local area and region.

entry level

To both enter and train while working in this career, you will need qualifications at Level 1. Please refer to explanation on page vii.

The type of person suited to this work

To find the work enjoyable, you need to have a genuine interest in local matters and in promoting your local area. It helps if you have up-to-date knowledge about places that might interest different ages and groups of people.

A methodical approach to researching difficult questions to dig out answers is an asset in this work, where you will rarely use the words: 'I don't know.'

Other useful attributes are having customer-service experience, the ability to research information using the internet, and verbal communication skills.

Most TIC assistants jobshare and enjoy teamworking, when they can back each other up by answering the phone or fetching leaflets if another assistant is busy at the counter.

Working conditions

Usually, tourist information centres are modern, bright spaces that make pleasant work surroundings.

There is quite a lot of standing at the counter and moving to and from storage areas with piles of information leaflets and stock items.

You may spend some hours sitting at a computer, researching routes, or B&B facilities in distant locations. Although local TICs hold local and some regional information, you often have to find out facts about distant areas for travellers or people relocating.

The future outlook

It is quite difficult to move from being a casual part-time worker into a permanent full-time job in a Tourist Information Centre, unless someone either moves away or retires. There is a very slow turnover of jobs, although there are over 600 centres in England, 30 in Northern Ireland, 150 in Scotland and 80 in Wales. Every centre has to have an experienced permanent manager, but there is variation in hours – even days – of opening between the centres, depending on their size, location and frequency of use. Smaller centres may only have two paid employees. Large centres, in big cities, can have the equivalent of seven or eight full-time employees, some working a jobshare on a part-time basis.

The National Tourist Board supports and helps to sustain the presence of the Tourist Information Centres, so it is probable that in slowly restoring numbers of overseas visitors coming to Britain (which dropped after an outbreak of foot-and-mouth disease in 2001) these centres will be maintained for the foreseeable future.

Qualifications and courses

- No formal educational qualifications are required to work as a TIC assistant. In this type of work, it is personal qualities that are usually more important.
- Listening acutely and speaking clearly are essential skills, and it is very helpful if assistants can use ICT to research information and respond to enquirers via the internet.
- Applicants who have got GCSEs/S grades (A–C/1–3) may be at an advantage. A number of TICs are close to international airports or in popular destinations for overseas visitors. In these centres it is valuable if one or more TIC assistants have modern language skills to help newly-arrived tourists, business travellers and foreign visitors. British Sign Language will also be an advantage.
- Working as an assistant, you can be assessed for NVQs/SVQs in Tourist Information in the workplace, and many employees within TICs work towards these awards.
- There are also the part-time HLQ Level 4 or BTEC or SQA HNC qualifications in Leisure and Tourism which might be useful for career progression to become a TIC manager. However, it is possible to move into supervisory and managerial positions simply with experience in the work.

CRCI:MC

CLCI:GAX

Other related opportunities

- Holiday Centre Work p364
- Holiday Representative p365
- Tour Guide p379
- Tour Manager p381

Advantages/disadvantages

- There are busy and slack times at the counter in TICs.
- Much of the work may be done over the phone and not face to face.
- Today, TICs may be contacted via the internet from anywhere in the world.
- You will play an important role in promoting both the local region and its economy.

Earnings guide

- TIC staff mainly work part time, but for full-time equivalent staff, starting salaries are around £10,000 per year.
- With experience this can rise to £18,000.
- You can earn up to £22,000 as a full-time centre manager.

Further information

VisitBritain
Thames Tower
Black's Road
London
W6 9EL
020 8846 9000
www.tourismtrade.org.uk

VisitScotland
Fairways Business Park
Deer Park Avenue
Livingston
EH5 48AF
0131 624 9840
www.visitscotland.com

Travel Trade Wales
Brunel House
2 Fitzalen Road
Cardiff
CF24 0UY
0870 300306
www.traveltradewales.com

www.cityandguilds.com/myperfectjob

Transfer Representative

What the work involves

- As a travel firm's transfer rep you will be informally meeting and greeting the company's holidaymakers on their arrival at terminals close to holiday destinations.
- Solving any problems that have arisen for passengers, such as loss of passport, visa, wallet or baggage, or dealing with emergencies, such as severe illness in flight.
- Helping new arrivals to find their transfer coach – getting the visitors and their baggage safely aboard. Smoothing out problems with seating and answering coach drivers' queries about route changes, exact setting-down points, late baggage and so on.
- Checking all the details of transport and accommodation for the arriving parties, to make sure that everything is in place for their stay.

The type of person suited to this work

You will need a competent, calm and friendly manner to help tired and worried travellers. Travellers will be glad to find you, especially after a long – possibly, delayed – flight. Often, holidaymakers want to chat and find their bearings in the foreign airport and country. You must be helpful and supportive – happy to listen whatever the hour of day or night and despite having to respond to complaints and grumbles.

To meet each party and to assist with departures, you will have to stay well informed about incoming and departing flights and train schedules. You may need to liaise with the airport, the station and the coach operator(s) in order to make swift adjustments to collection times and hotel drops.

Finally, you will have to be forward-looking, efficient and capable, and be able to inspire confidence in a crisis.

Working conditions

You could be outdoors in all weathers and temperatures ranging from very hot to extremely cold, in coach parks, railway terminals or airport concourses from early to late.

You will also spend some time indoors speaking on the phone and working at a computer researching information.

There will be company 'livery' to wear – an eye-catching suit, shirt, tie, even hat – in the tour operator's colours which can be a source of discomfort in very warm conditions.

The future outlook

With cheap travel, more and more families, singles and groups, opt to take package holidays. Many retired people are willing to book longer, more explorative or more exotic trips and there's really no off-season in this work. Numbers of travellers have not been reduced by terrorist threats and continuing warfare in many areas of the world.

Transfer reps play a highly important public relations role for the companies they represent and, as the level of tourist traffic increases, problems with charter flights, package holiday deals and busy schedules will result in more rather than fewer reps being recruited.

entry level

1

To both enter and train while working in this career, you will need qualifications at Level 1. Please refer to explanation on page vii.

Qualifications and courses

- No formal educational qualifications are needed, but most tour operators employ young adults in this role who have at least a number of GCSEs/S grades (A–C/1–3) and who are already training to work in the travel and tourism industry. Generally, this job can provide an excellent vacation opportunity where you learn as you earn, exploring popular holiday destinations.
- Transfer reps should be fluent in the language of the country being visited.
- Although it is unusual for travel reps to undertake any formal training on the job, besides a short period of induction with a more senior rep, there are NVQs/SVQs available in Travel Services – Customer Services, which can be studied for independently.
- Transfer reps might work towards the NCFE Level 1 Certificate in Travel, followed by Level 2 Certificates for Airport Passenger Services Agents or Resort Representatives.

CRCI:MC

CLCI:GAX

Other related opportunities

- Air Cabin Crew p555
- Airline Customer Service Agent p557
- Coach Tour Manager p358
- Entertainments Manager p361
- Holiday Representative p365
- Tour Guide p379
- Tour Manager p381
- Travel Agency Sales Consultant p385

Advantages/disadvantages

- You get opportunities to practise your modern foreign languages.
- It can be a good way of taking a holiday – while staying in pocket!
- As a travel rep, you gain an intimate view of the people and culture of the country you are based in and may make useful contacts for later work.

Earnings guide

- As travel reps' accommodation, board and travel are paid for by their employer, the actual earnings are minimal, normally around £650–£750+ each month.

Further information

www.cityandguilds.com/myperfectjob

Institute of Travel and Tourism
PO Box 217
Ware
Hertfordshire
SG12 8WY
0870 770 7960
www.itt.co.uk

Institute of Tour Guiding
Lloyd's Court
1 Goodman's Yard
London
E1 8AT
020 7953 1257
www.itg.org.uk

TTC Training
The Quayside
4 Furnival Road
Sheffield
S4 7YA
0800 915 9348
www.ttctraining.co.uk

Travel Agency Sales Consultant

What the work involves

- Selling holiday packages to the public and trying to meet your company's sales targets.
- Putting together individual holidays for an independent customer or for an organisation that seeks travel, accommodation and entertainment arrangements that are distinct from the travel company's normal holiday packages.
- Contacting airline, ferry and rail sales operatives to arrange transport, and then making reservations for accommodation, meals, hire cars and entertainment with hotels, restaurants, car rental companies and box offices, whether in this country or abroad.

entry level

To both enter and train while working in this career, you will need qualifications at Level 1. Please refer to explanation on page vii.

The type of person suited to this work

Having agreed an outline plan together with your customer, you need to have excellent adminstrative and research skills to quickly track down, assemble and book all the component parts needed for their ideal journey or holiday.

A natural and friendly interest in other people is a plus in this work. Finding the right holiday package for each customer is an art, so you will need excellent listening and questioning skills to make considered decisions on what the person in front of you – or on the phone – may find entertaining, stimulating or relaxing.

If you are friendly, communicative and methodical, with excellent ICT skills, you will suit both your customers' and your employers' needs. It helps if you have a real interest in exploring new places yourself.

Working conditions

You work indoors, in a modern retail outlet, mainly at a desk or behind a counter.

There are numerous details to check over the phone and tickets, booking confirmations and insurance notes to post out to customers. Almost all the work is done at a computer screen, except for scanning through brochures for holiday deals and consulting transport timetables.

The agency can be very busy at lunchtimes, near to closing time and on Saturdays, before holiday periods. Many sales consultants work part time and there may be only two or three workers in the agency.

The future outlook

With growing interest in travel and holidays abroad – a fascination fed by the media – worldwide, the travel business has grown into a top-flight industry, with the highest turnover and numbers of employees of all major industrial sectors.

Despite the involvement of many overseas countries with war and terrorism campaigns, people want to experience distant places for themselves.

There are over 7000 travel agencies in Britain, each employing ten staff or fewer. There are plenty of opportunities to advance to a managerial position – even to start your own independent holiday company offering special-interest holidays.

You can move sideways into another area of tourism work, as a holiday rep, tour guide or tour manager for example, seeing more of the world than the local high street. This is useful background experience for running a tour operator business of your own!

Qualifications and courses

- Although no formal educational qualifications are needed, it's helpful to have a good standard of education with GCSEs/S grades (A–C/1–3) in English and maths as a minimum. Skills in geography and ICT are also sought.
- Young people aged 16–24 can train in travel agency work through an Apprenticeship/ Skillseekers training. You can start with very few GCSEs/S grades, taking work-based NVQs/SVQs Levels 2 and 3 in Travel Services. Some of the study is part time at a Further Education college.
- Full-time A level and National Diploma/SQA courses in Travel and Tourism also make an excellent starting point for this work.
- There are some full-time management courses offered by TTC Training for those who want to progress to travel agency manager.
- The travel industry offers its own examinations – the ABTA Travel Agents Certificate. ABTA Primary and Advanced Examinations take place in March, June and December.

CRCI:MC

CLCI:GAX

Other related opportunities

- Air Cabin Crew p555
- Airline Customer Service Agent p557
- Coach Tour Manager p358
- Holiday Representative p365
- Tour Guide p379
- Tour Manager p381
- Transfer Representative p384

Advantages/disadvantages

- There can be long periods sitting at the computer, answering emails and checking flight and booking details. You will spend a considerable amount of time 'on hold' at the end of a phoneline, confirming bookings. Sometimes you have to do this work under pressure, with a string of customers waiting their turn.
- Some consultants find the pace too slow in a travel agency and either move into other areas of work or set up a travel agency at home. There's information on how to go about it on Travel Hub's website.
- A real perk in this work is that you do get some free or discounted holidays.

Earnings guide

- Starting pay for a sales consultant is around £11,000 per year. Apprentices will get less.
- With experience and some NVQs/SVQs you can earn up to £14,000.
- Senior consultants can earn up to £19,000.

Further information

TTC Training
The Quayside
4 Furnival Road
Sheffield
S4 7YA
0800 915 9348
www.ttctraining.co.uk

City & Guilds

www.cityandguilds.com/myperfectjob

Watersport Instructor

What the work involves

- Introducing young and older people to the excitement and fun of watersports.
- Instructing starters and experienced watersport people in safe techniques of surfing, wave skiing, windsurfing, sailing, canoeing and kayaking.
- Driving watersport parties between their accommodation and the waterfront.
- Teaching trainees the essentials of personal health and safety on and in the water and how to ensure the safety of others, by avoiding collisions with other users of the water.

The type of person suited to this work

You should be fit and healthy, and be very enthusiastic about watersports!

Instructions must be delivered loudly and clearly, and often repeated, with additional signals, such as flags, bells, flashing lights, whistles or start guns. To teach people from very different backgrounds, you will need a flexible, friendly but firm approach. Also, you have to get on with other instructors, often working as a team.

Watersports are risky, so you have to be level-headed, constantly re-assessing factors such as the imminent weather forecast, the water or sea state and the times and heights of tidal change, because these will dictate the success of your watersports.

Working conditions

Watersport centres are in magnificent places, such as the Cornish coast or Lake District, where you could live for many weeks.

Being outdoors, all day long, is some people's ideal. But, remember, windsurfers and kayakers can be caught in snowstorms in May.

Hours are long, as there is theory to tackle during the evenings.

Some sailing instruction involves night passages and sea-crossings where conditions can be changeable.

The future outlook

For young people with leisure time and money to spend, watersports have become a firm favourite. Novices need instruction, and improving learners enjoy attending week-long or weekend courses to upgrade their skills.

There is increasing demand for watersport instructors.

Many jobs are part time, but there are full-time positions at sea-training centres around the British coast and at inland watersport centres. Local authority-run centres offer some full-time, permanent positions.

Out of season, many qualified watersport instructors teach part-time RYA theory courses at Further Education colleges, whilst some train other instructors. A number of inshore and offshore RYA practical courses continue all year – weather permitting.

CRCI:MB

CLCI:GAG

Qualifications and courses

- No formal educational qualifications are needed for this work, but to be an instructor, you need a professional instructor qualification in each of your chosen watersports.
- The Royal Yachting Association (RYA) offers Dinghy Instructor courses at basic, senior and advanced levels.
- The RYA also runs instructors' courses in Power Boating, Yachting and Windsurfing – Levels 1 and 2 Coach Awards.
- The British Canoe Union (BCU) runs Certificates in Coaching Paddlesports at Levels 1 and 2.
- You may need a full, clean driving licence to gain the DVLA licence to drive minibuses, as well as a current First Aid certificate.

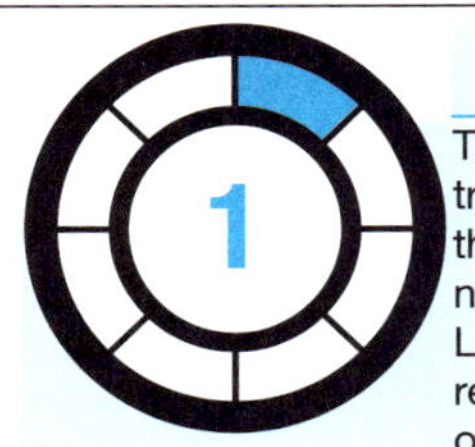

entry level

To both enter and train while working in this career, you will need qualifications at Level 1. Please refer to explanation on page vii.

Other related opportunities

- Aerobics Teacher p352
- Health and Fitness Instructor p362
- Horse Riding p366
- Lifeguard p370
- Outdoor Pursuits Instructor p372

Advantages/disadvantages

- You are responsible for the health and safety of all watersport trainees and may have to react rapidly in an emergency.
- The day's work can be strenuous and you may feel exhausted at the end.
- Living conditions are fairly basic at an outdoor centre or on board a yacht.
- It is great to spend all day doing the thing you love best – sailing, body boarding or kayaking, and getting paid for doing it!

Earnings guide

- £12,000–£15,000 per year is the average rate for instructors teaching watersports to juniors.
- This rises to £16,000+ if you have experience of teaching.
- Up to £25,000 is possible for experienced instructors, teaching novice instructors.
- Freelance instructorsearn around £60–£90 per day.

Further information

British Canoe Union
John Dudderidge House
Adbolton Lane
West Bridgford
Nottinghamshire
NG2 5AS
0115 982 1100
www.bcu.org.uk

Sports Coach UK
114 Cardigan Road
Headingley
Leeds
LS6 3BJ
0113 274 4802
www.sportscoachuk.org

Royal Yachting Association
RYA House
Ensign Way, Hamble
Southampton
Hampshire
SO31 4YA
0845 345 0400
www.rya.org.uk

Institute for Outdoor Learning
Plumpton Old Hall
Plumpton
Penrith
Cumbria
CA11 9NP
01768 885800
www.outdoor-learning.org

SkillsActive (Sector Skills Council for active leisure and learning)
Castlewood House
77–91 New Oxford Street
London
WC1A 1PX
08000 933300
www.skillsactive.com

City& Guilds

www.cityandguilds.com/myperfectjob

Do you want to appear on stage, singing, dancing or acting? Would you like to work behind the scenes supporting a production? This cluster includes:

- **Choreographer**
- **Dancer**
- **Make-up Artist**
- **Musician**
- **Stunt Performer**

But what's it like working in this area?
Here's Celia Grannum's story:

Dancer

Born in Barbados, 27-year-old Celia had spent her young girlhood doing the Royal Academy of Dancing syllabuses. She at one time thought of becoming an architect, but when she realised dancing was her life, she travelled to New York where she trained at the prestigious Tisch School of the Arts (part of New York University). After completing her dance studies in New York she worked freelance in the city before travelling to London where she is now involved with both The Jazz Exchange Music and Dance Company, and Ballet Black. She also works as both a dance teacher and a Pilates teacher.

HER PRESENT CIRCUMSTANCES

'In the past few years I have really got my feet (so to speak!) into the dance scene in London and I have met a lot of people, which really helps. I am really enjoying it at present because I have a lot of projects lined up for the future. However, I am really glad I still do teaching and the Pilates because they are my bread and butter when the dance jobs dry up. I have always had multiple interests and when you are freelancing you really need them. One of my friends is an usher when he's not working; another has done some very lucrative work with a major pop star (Kylie) and in that situation you have to be smart about it and bank the money and save it for the lean times.'

FUTURE PROSPECTS

'I love choreographing and so I want to do more of that. Maybe some opportunities will come up through the people I have met here.'

WHAT'S NOT SO HOT

Although she adores what she does, Celia is well aware of the dangers – both physical and mental – that are out there for anyone entering this most competitive of fields.

'Injury is a serious consideration for anyone who is working with their body. At Ballet Black we get free physical therapy, but freelance dancers normally have to pay for that themselves and it can get very expensive. The other thing that is dangerous about dancing is mental injury. This is because you are always aiming for a physical ideal and you can get to a place (in your head) where you believe you are never good enough. If you tell yourself that every day, it destroys your self-confidence.'

However, dancing is something Celia would never give up. For her it really is a vocation.

'This really is a spiritual experience. When I'm dancing it is almost as if I am not there, I go somewhere else. It's the physicality of it, moving and feeling free in your body. It's a joy and an exhilaration. It's also to do with communicating with the audience.'

So what advice would Celia give to anyone thinking about becoming a dancer?

'Follow your heart and don't be swayed. There are a lot of negatives attached to dancing, but give it a shot and if it isn't for you then you still have time to train to do something else. If you are 15 or 16 and have that burning desire to do it then you have to try it now because it is better to discover it is not working out while you are young rather than to be married with three kids and realise you can no longer give it a try because it's physically just too late.'

Actor / Actress

What the work involves

- Actors/actresses perform in front of audiences and this can sometimes include dancing and singing as part of the role.
- There are opportunities for acting parts in dramatic plays, comedies or musicals on stage or on TV.
- Actors/actresses need to have lots of stamina, as rehearsals can be long and hard in order to get things right before the show opens.
- Work is rarely permanent or regular and a lot of time may be spent looking for jobs and attending auditions.

entry level

To both enter and train while working in this career, you will need qualifications at Level 2–3. Please refer to explanation on page vii.

Qualifications and courses

- Although there are no specific requirements to enter this profession, it is very competitive and almost all actors have formal training.
- You can take an acting course (usually a Diploma/Professional Diploma) at a drama school. Courses last between 1 and 3 years. Entry is by audition and interview, and A levels/H grades or the equivalent are often required.
- The National Council for Drama Training (NCDT) accredits full-time vocational drama school courses and degrees. Graduates of NCDT-accredited courses who are legally entitled to work in the UK are eligible for Equity membership. Part-time courses and more academic degrees in, for example, drama or theatre studies, are not accredited.
- You can do a degree in acting (or a related subject like drama or performing arts). Acting degrees are offered by drama schools and by universities. Entry requirements vary, but always include an audition and interview, as well as A levels/H grades or the equivalent.
- Some courses may specify 5 GCSEs/S grades (A–C/1–3) and some may require 2 A levels/3 H grades or a BTEC Diploma in Performing Arts.

The type of person suited to this work

If you are thinking about acting, you must first be dedicated to this as a career as it is a very competitive area and only around 25% of actors are constantly in work. You will need lots of stamina and a good level of fitness, and it will help if you have self-confidence and a cheerful personality.

There will be many times when you will be rejected at auditions mainly because you are just not the right face for the part, and so you will need to be able to cope with this and keep trying.

It is a tough, demanding career to enter and to stay in, but once you get regular work it can be very satisfying.

Working conditions

You will work mainly indoors, in theatres, halls and sometimes studios. Each venue will vary in size, facilities available and levels of comfort.

Sometimes summer productions are performed in open-air theatres, arenas or stately homes and castles.

You could have to travel to different venues for your performances where you might spend time waiting for your part in the performance.

The future outlook

Prospects for success as an actor depend on talent, hard work and a bit of luck. Although age is not an issue, some leave the profession in their 50s and 60s, while others continue to get work well beyond that age.

Some actors go on to work as writers or directors, while others train to teach drama in schools and colleges.

CRCI:Q

CLCI:G

Other related opportunities

- Dancer p393
- Director (Theatre) p395
- Producer (Theatre) p403
- Stage Manager p407

Advantages/disadvantages

- The long travelling hours to get to performance venues and then waiting to perform could be boring.
- This area of work is very competitive.
- It is not all glamour and money, but can be great fun.

Earnings guide

- Basic rates of pay depend on experience; outside London you could earn up to £12,000 per year with regular employment, rising to around £13,300 for a few fortunates.
- An actor working in a London West End theatre could expect around £14,800 per year for a once-per-night performance, and £17,500 for twice-nightly performances.
- According to Equity, nearly 50% of actors earn less than £7,000 per year from their profession, and only about 6% can earn more than £30,000.
- As you build up your experience and reputation your income could be much more than this, but it may take many years.
- It is a good idea to join Equity, the union for the world of entertainment – this can help you to negotiate fair rates of pay and terms and conditions.

Further information

National Council for Drama Training
1–7 Woburn Walk
London
WC1H 0JJ
020 7387 3650
www.ncdt.co.uk

Creative & Cultural Skills (Sector Skills Council for advertising, crafts, cultural heritage, the arts and music)
11 Southwark Street
London
SE1 1RQ
020 7089 5866
www.ccskills.org.uk

Equity
Guild House
Upper St Martin's Lane
London
WC2H 9EG
020 7379 6000
www.equity.org.uk

National Arts Youth Theatres
Darlington Arts Centre
Vane Terrace
Darlington
DL3 7AX
01325 363330
www.nayt.org.uk

Choreographer

What the work involves

- As a choreographer, you will create, design and develop new dance movements for productions such as ballets, opera and musicals.
- Creating a dance means planning the way dancers move around the set to create beautiful and exciting routines which interpret the music.
- You will be on your feet a lot of the day and have to deal with many performers with different levels of expertise.
- Choreographers work closely with performance artists, musical directors, ballet dance teachers and trainers.

entry level

To both enter and train while working in this career, you will need qualifications at Level 2–3. Please refer to explanation on page vii.

Qualifications and courses

- There are no formal entry qualifications for this career. GCSEs/S grades and AS/A levels/H grades are available in dance, and some institutions offer a BTEC National Diploma in Performing Arts.
- Most choreographers have experience as dance performers prior to becoming choreographers.
- Choreography can be studied as an option on some full-time vocational dance courses accredited by the Council for Dance Education and Training, as part of a degree course in dance or as a postgraduate course.
- Work experience alongside an experienced practitioner offers a good introduction to choreography and will certainly be taken into account if applying for a dance or choreography-related course.

The type of person suited to this work

You will need to have a keen, lively interest in music and movement, and a very well-developed sense of rhythm and timing.

To develop new ballets, dances and shorter dance routines requires an excellent knowledge of past and present pieces, complete understanding of how the body works and of possible movements within dance and the creative imagination to interpret the significance of events and mood changes through physical expression.

Choreographers have responsibility for developing and teaching complicated movements and routines. You will need a good memory, clear communication skills, patience and an ability to get on well with others.

Working conditions

Your work will be mainly indoors in dance studios, theatres, TV or film studios.

Your initial contacts are likely to be producers, directors and musical conductors. Some choreographers work directly with modern composers, interpreting their music.

As production plans progress, you will start working directly with the performers and a repetiteur who plays rehearsal music.

The future outlook

Jobs and opportunities can be limited as this is a highly competitive area of work, where experience counts.

It is possible to find opportunities outside the mainstream ballet areas, for example in modern dance companies and developing international venues.

Opera and musicals are becoming reinvigorated through audience demand and both performance areas require choreographers to interpret dance music and contextual pieces as dance routines.

Other related opportunities

- Arts Administrator p318
- Dancer p393
- Producer (Theatre) p403
- Teacher p184

Advantages/disadvantages

- Many hours are spent traveling to different venues – even overseas.
- Seeing your finished routine beautifully performed will boost your morale.
- Enthusiastic reviews will help your career progression.
- It will be hard going, and you will need patience and enthusiasm to get the best from dancers.

Earnings guide

- Equity recommends a minimum daily sum of up to £100.
- You could earn round £12,500 per year if you have just finished at a dance college, or completed a degree or other college courses.
- Your salary will reach £20,000 if you have moved into choreography as an experienced dancer.
- Experienced, well-known choreographers can earn £50,000, but good salaries will depend on your skills and experience.

Further information

Council for Dance Education and Training
Toynbee Hall
28 Commercial Street
London
E1 6LS
020 7247 4030
www.cdet.org.uk

Dance UK (includes British Association of Choreographers)
Battersea Arts Centre
Lavender Hill
London
SW11 5TF
020 7228 4990
www.danceuk.org

Creative & Cultural Skills (Sector Skills Council for advertising, crafts, cultural heritage, the arts and music)
11 Southwark Street
London
SE1 1RQ
020 7089 5866
www.ccskills.org.uk

Circus Performer

What the work involves

- You will be performing on stage, in a theatre, at a festival site or in the big top of a traditional travelling circus.
- You will need to ensure your techniques are perfect before a performance and this will take many hours of repetitive training.
- Your performances need to appeal to a wide age range of people, so costumes and props must be humorous or dazzling to an audience.
- Good fitness and stamina levels are essential if you are to perform well.

entry level

2

To both enter and train while working in this career, you will need qualifications at Level 2. Please refer to explanation on page vii.

Qualifications and courses

- There is no defined entry route into this profession. Circus performers may belong to traditional family-run circuses and train on-site.
- There are various institutions offering courses in this profession. Circus Space offers a 2-year Foundation degree in Circus Arts (successful students may, on audition, progress to a BA (Hons) degree, taking a further year); Circomedia in Bristol offers a 1-year professional training programme and a 2-year BTEC National Diploma in Performance; Circus Maniacs offers 6-months to 3-years full-time professional circus training; Greentop Community Circus offers a 12-week, full-time Circus in Performance Foundation Course (accredited through the Open College Network to Levels 2 and 3); NoFit State Circus and Zippo's Academy offer on-the-job training programmes to students.
- Some performing arts and theatre degrees include strands in mime, acrobatics, physical theatre, etc.
- Skylight Circus Arts offers a range of opportunities to work with young people with physical and learning disabilities.
- Qualified, experienced circus performers (also students) can apply for Equity membership.

The type of person suited to this work

Circus performing is not just a job – it is a way of life. Those working in a travelling circus need to be committed to a nomadic lifestyle. You will be continually moving between performance sites and carrying out different tasks – besides perfecting your performing skills.

From the clown to the trapeze artist, performers work together to put on the best show possible, and everyone needs to be fit and train hard each day to keep up their skills-level and perform well.

All performers need to be confident about their abilities, with positive, cheerful personalities, considerable energy and enthusiasm.

Working conditions

You could be working in television/video studios, theatres, in arts centres, at promotional events or as part of a travelling circus, when you will live in mobile accommodation. This sounds exciting, but can also be difficult.

You may be on the roads all night, spending mornings catching up on sleep.

You will perform in the evenings and at weekends, practising during the day.

The future outlook

Good circus performers will always be in demand and not only in the traditional circus. More opportunities are emerging in contemporary circus fields, including circus skills work for videos and advertising.

Increasingly, Arts Councils are supporting development of circus skills, but the industry is tight – many European performers come to the UK – so work and income can be unpredictable. However, it seems 60% of recent circus school graduates were fully employed in circus performance.

CRCI:Q

CLCI:G

Other related opportunities

- Entertainer p397
- Lighting Technician p398
- Music p400
- Stunt Performer p409

Advantages/disadvantages

- This type of work can lead to injury if you are careless.
- You will have to travel for long periods as part of a circus troupe or as an independent performer.
- Giving highly skilled performances which are greatly appreciated can give you a terrific buzz.

Earnings guide

- Wages and employment opportunities fluctuate in circus work, but the better your performances and skills, the more you can earn.
- Most performers are self-employed and charge by performance. However there are some full-time employed performers and salaries can start at around £10,000 per year, rising to £16,000 with experience and up to £25,000 for the very experienced.
- Charging by performance, new performers can expect £150–£160 for a performance.
- Aerialists are paid £300+ for a single performance act. Equity recommends up to £350 per week for performers.
- Experienced, skilled performers can get £600–£900 per performance.

Further information

Circomedia – Centre for Contemporary Circus and Physical Performance
Britannia Road
Kingswood
Bristol
BS15 8DB
0117 947 7288
www.circomedia.com

The Circus Space
Cornet Street
London
N1 6HD
020 7613 4141
www.thecircusspace.co.uk

Skylight Circus Arts
Broadwater Centre
Smith Street
Rochdale
OL16 1HE
01706 650676
www.skylight-circus-arts.org.uk

Equity
Guild House
Upper St Martin's Lane
London
WC2H 9EG
020 7379 6000
www.equity.org.uk

Circus Arts
020 7401 8866
www.circusarts.org.uk

Dancer

What the work involves

- Dancing is an exhilarating but physically demanding career – you will need to be very fit!
- You need a keen interest in dance and may have attended lessons from an early age.
- Dancers at every level of the profession spend long hours in classes – exercising, practising routines, working with choreographers and other dancers. Some dancers now do fitness training alongside dance, to reduce the risk of injury.
- You will find work in theatres, cabaret clubs, cruise ships or video/TV studios, in performances as diverse as ballet, stage musicals, jazz and contemporary dance.

The type of person suited to this work

Anyone entering this area of work must love dancing and be very talented to succeed.

Dancers must be dedicated to improving technique through daily practice – sometimes, for as long as 10 hours each day.

To be a successful dancer, you need musicality – a good sense of rhythm and timing. Being creative and imaginative with routines and choreography is, of course, an additional boost.

Dancers spend far more time practising than performing. Often, dancers have spells without work, so it is important that you can cope with setbacks and remain positive and focused.

Working conditions

Most of your rehearsals and performances will take place indoors in studios, schools, theatres or other performance venues.

While training, most dancers work closely with others in small or larger groups for long hours each day, so it is important that you get on well with all kinds of people. Also, you need patience to handle the strains of working within the same competitive group for a long time.

The future outlook

Your future prospects as a dancer will largely depend on talent, hard work and luck, because competition is always strong. Only a very few individuals become top performance artists in solo roles.

Dancers with dance companies can progress from chorus to solo parts, but this is dependent on the individual dancer – their dedication, skills and training, and to some extent age and general suitability for the role. Although dancing is a career for younger people, dance teachers can continue long after they are no longer professional performers, and many leave dancing to set up private dance schools.

Qualifications and courses

- Training in dance usually begins in childhood and graded exams are offered by the Royal Academy of Dance and the Imperial Society of Teachers of Dancing.
- Classical ballet dancers must start training by age 12 for girls and 14 for boys.
- You can do a vocational dance performance course at a specialist school such as the Royal Academy of Dance. These courses (Diploma, National Diploma or degree) are usually 3 years in duration. There are general dance courses and more specialised courses in ballet, contemporary dance or musical theatre. Entry is by audition, interview and a medical, and the educational standard equivalent of 5 GCSEs/S grades (A–C/1–3) are normally required. For ballet, there are also physical requirements which include height restrictions, having a strong back and legs and good body proportions. The Council for Dance Education and Training accredits full-time courses at vocational dance schools.
- You can do a degree in dance at a university or college of higher education. A levels/H grades or the equivalent are usually required, and candidates attend an audition. Some courses are performance-oriented, while others are more theoretical.
- Students normally enter vocational dance schools at age 16–18. However, some dance schools take pupils from 10 onwards and offer National Curriculum study alongside dance training.

entry level

To both enter and train while working in this career, you will need qualifications at Level 2–3. Please refer to explanation on page vii.

- Some courses offer a teacher-training element. The Royal Academy of Dance and Imperial Society of Teachers of Dancing offer specialist teacher training programmes.
- The British Ballet Organisation and the British Theatre Dance Association also offer dance and teacher training qualifications.

Other related opportunities

- Choreographer p391
- Director (Theatre) p395
- Producer (Theatre) p403
- Teacher p184

Advantages/disadvantages

- Getting paid work can sometimes be difficult.
- You will need to stay fit and healthy: injuries can necessitate a complete career change.
- Dance shoes and practice clothing are a big expense.
- Dance can be a fantastically rewarding career.
- Your career as a top soloist can be finished by the age of 30.

Earnings guide

- Salaries for dancers depend on length, type and location of the job. Most dancers are members of the British Actors Equity Association – a body which negotiates for minimum salaries. Some dancers are self-employed and set their own rates per contract. Equity sets a minimum rate per week of around £305.
- Starting out in full-time employment you may get around £19,000 per year. As a soloist this can rise to £23,000–£25,000.
- Top performers can earn £30,000+. Dancers in the Royal Ballet corps earn £14,000–£17,500+.
- Dance teachers are mainly self-employed and receive salaries dependent on the type and size of dance school they work in.

CRCI:Q
CLCI:G

Further information

Council for Dance Education and Training
Toynbee Hall
28 Commercial Street
London
E1 6LS
020 7247 4030
www.cdet.org.uk

Royal Academy of Dance
36 Battersea Square
London
SW11 3RA
020 7223 0091
www.rad.org.uk

Royal Ballet School
White Lodge
Richmond Park
London
TW10 5HR
020 8876 5547
www.royal-ballet-school.org.uk

Director (Theatre)

What the work involves

- As director of a drama season or single play, you will have control over artistic interpretation.
- You will coordinate all creative elements of a production – design, stylistic presentation and interpretative work of artists – overseeing any musical/choreographic inputs.
- There will be daily conferences with the producer, the musical director, technical teams, theatre managers, financial backers and, of course, rehearsing artists.
- Your enthusiasm and creative vision must transfer to everyone involved in the production.

The type of person suited to this work

To work as a director requires a strong, creative individual with good interpretative skills, energy and drive. Persuading financiers to back your innovative ideas for a particular season or single production takes excellent communication skills. Directors are problem solvers who can critically analyse technical or artistic issues and come up with novel solutions.

Building your career on short, fixed-term contracts, where you will work very long hours on particular jobs, you will need to be dedicated to your profession and a risk-taker! Be prepared to put in hours of unpaid work early in your career while you are building your reputation.

Working conditions

Theatre directors work indoors, often in cramped conditions in theatres. The atmosphere can be dusty and gloomy during daytime hours. Venues vary in terms of size, age of the facilities and quality of accommodation.

Occasionally, you will be directing summer productions performed in outdoor venues or on tour abroad.

Your job may last for several weeks or for a period of 2 or 3 years.

The future outlook

Prospects as a director depend on future funding of the arts (i.e. the level of support from government and financial backing) as well as successful theatre management and individual artistic talent, hard work and enthusiasm. Age is not an issue in this profession – successful directors are headhunted for contracts well beyond normal retirement age.

Once their name is known, successful directors often move into work in film and TV, where the pay is considerably better.

entry level

To both enter and train while working in this career, you will need qualifications at Level 3–8. Please refer to explanation on page vii.

Qualifications and courses

- There are no specific qualifications required to become a theatre director but an appropriate degree may help with work opportunities. Relevant subjects could include English, drama/theatre studies, music, creative/performing arts, languages or humanities-based subjects such as philosophy, history or psychology. HNDs or Foundation degrees in creative/performing arts, drama/theatre studies, music and arts in the community may also be useful. Entry without any of these is also possible for those who have built a reputation and can demonstrate experience as an actor, writer, assistant director or stage manager.
- For entry to a degree course, you need 5 GCSE/S grades at (A–C/1–3) and a minimum of 2 A levels/H grades or the equivalent. Skills in foreign languages can be an asset to a theatre director.
- A 2-year full-time Master of Fine Arts in Theatre Directing is offered by the NCDT.
- Practical experience of acting, stage management or directing is usually more valuable than attendance on a postgraduate course, so build your portfolio in school/college drama clubs, local dramatic societies and fringe theatre.
- Each year, three students with theatre experience, aged 20+, are offered a 1-year placement on Channel 4's Theatre Director Scheme.

Other related opportunities

- Actor / Actress p390
- Producer (Theatre) p403
- Stage Manager p407

Advantages/disadvantages

- Interpreting great or new works of drama requires emotional and creative intelligence.
- The work can be highly satisfying and exhilarating, if your creative vision translates into a successful production on stage.
- At times, you will have no work, so try not to be reliant on earnings as a theatre director when you start out.

Earnings guide

- Your level of pay will depend on the contract being offered – this will vary between direction of one play to a full season's work.
- Networking and negotiation will form part of your working life; this will also apply to your own earnings. It is sensible to join Equity.
- As you build experience and reputation, your income should increase in step, but this can take years.
- As a general guide you could earn £17,000+ per year starting out, and with ten years or more experience you could earn up to £40,000.

Further information

Arts Council of England
2 Pear Tree Court
London
EC1R 0DS
0845 300 6200
www.artscouncil.org.uk

Arts Council Wales
9 Museum Place
Cardiff
CF10 3NX
029 2037 6500
www.artswales.org.uk

Arts Council Northern Ireland
77 Malone Road
Belfast
BT9 6AQ
028 9038 5200
www.artscouncil-ni.org.uk

Broadcasting Entertainment Cinematograph and Theatre Union
373–377 Clapham Road
London
SW9 9BT
020 7346 0900
www.bectu.org.uk

National Council of Drama Training
1–7 Woburn Walk
London
WC1H OJJ
020 7387 3650
www.ncdt.org.uk

Equity
Guild House
Upper St Martin's Lane
London
WC2H 9EG
020 7379 6000
www.equity.org.uk

Channel 4 Theatre Director Scheme
www.c4tds.co.uk

Disc Jockey

What the work involves

- Working as a club DJ, you use a wide variety of equipment including multimedia and specialist lighting.
- You may entertain live audiences at events and parties and may act as the master of ceremonies.
- As a radio DJ, you work in a studio playing records and chatting to listeners – with some stations, this could include a phone-in option.
- VJing is a new way forward using a good PC and software to mix/inter-splice sounds with images from video clips and loops, in real time.

entry level

To both enter and train while working in this career, you will need qualifications at Level 2–3. Please refer to explanation on page vii.

The type of person suited to this work

To succeed, you must have a passion for music and skills in music technology. The work requires excellent coordination, good communication and listening skills, and a lively outgoing personality.

DJs use the latest in turntables, amplifiers and multimedia – and practice techniques such as mixing, scratching, beat mixing and cross fading to make their live performance interesting.

Sheer hard work and persistence are keys to success. As most DJs are self-employed, basic business skills are an advantage. Initially, time will be spent promoting your skills in a search for work; well-known DJs are invited to perform!

Working conditions

As a DJ, you may work in clubs, on radio, in hotels, in holiday camps or at festivals and gigs – even on boats.

You will work unsocial hours in a noisy atmosphere, travelling long distances to events.

Keeping up with the latest technology and music genres is time-consuming.

High noise levels are an occupational hazard for DJs; you need to take steps to protect your hearing.

The future outlook

Some DJs stay in the job only a short time before moving on. Many work part time alongside a daytime job.

You have to be a self-starter, looking for opportunities, as jobs are rarely advertised. Experienced DJs can get seasonal work in holiday camps. Some move into careers in music production or retail.

Increasingly, DJs are finding opportunities working with VJs who create pop videos, while some experienced DJs find work abroad.

Qualifications and courses

- There is no specific entry route to this job, and no formal qualifications are required, but a love of music is vital.
- An Edexcel/BTEC National award in DJ Technology is offered at some colleges of further education, often combined with music technology. The normal entry requirements are 4 GCSEs/S grades (A–C/1–3). There are also BTEC qualifications in Popular Music, Music Technology and Performing Arts that can be useful.
- NCFE and City & Guilds also award qualifications in DJ skills/DJ Technique/DJ – Mix, offered as short, full-time courses by a few colleges and specialist training centres.
- There are many degrees, HNC/Ds and Foundation degrees available in related areas, e.g. creative music technology, music production, as well as NVQ Level 3 in Radio Production.
- Training in radio skills is offered by CSV Media which runs Media Clubhouses around the UK.
- Work experience is highly advisable. A technical career in radio is a good start to becoming a radio DJ and there are many college and hospital radio networks where you can practise.
- Some top DJs offer masterclasses; some club DJs allow work-shadowing to gain technical skills.

CRCI:Q

CLCI:G

Other related opportunities

- Lighting Technician p398
- Music p400
- Nightclub Manager p371

Advantages/disadvantages

- You will be working late nights and at weekends, and over public holidays.
- There can be heavy equipment to move around, often in the early hours.
- You may travel considerable distances between venues.
- Set-up equipment costs from £300 to well over £1000.

Earnings guide

- Income varies with the event; your reputation will determine your fee.
- Your charges/pay should reflect local DJ rates; initially, expect a little less!
- DJs can charge between £50 and £300+ per session, with experience this can rise to £1000+.
- There are a few top DJs in Europe earning around £100,000 per year.
- Many DJs do other work to boost their income.

Further information

SAE Institute
United House
North Road
Islington
London
N7 9DP
020 7609 2653
www.sae.edu

School of Sound Recording
10 Tariff Street
Manchester
M1 2FF
0161 228 3072
www.s-s-r.com

Access to Music
Lionel House
35 Millstone Lane
Leicester
LE1 5JN
0800 281 842
www.accesstomusic.co.uk

Arts and Entertainment Technical Training Initiative
Lower Ground
14 Blenheim Terrace
London
NW8 0EB
020 732 86174
www.touchlondon.co.uk

Entertainer

What the work involves

- Entertainers perform in front of audiences, and include comedians, circus performers, street artists, nightclub cabaret comics and singers, dancers, musicians, magicians and lots more.
- You could be entertaining on your own or with a troupe.
- Most of your performances will take place in the evenings and at weekends, unless you become a street artist, but you will have to spend many hours during the day practising your skills, developing your fitness and maintaining equipment.

entry level

To both enter and train while working in this career, you will need qualifications at Level 2–3. Please refer to explanation on page vii.

The type of person suited to this work

Entertainers are paid for being skilled in their chosen performance areas, and you will need to be very experienced in your specialist field. Not only will you need innovative, high-level skills in performance, self-confidence and an outgoing, lively personality but you will also create ideas that make you unique within your area of work.

You will need to be hard-working, with the ability to take criticism if the audience is less than enthusiastic about your act.

In performance work, you have to be self-motivated and dedicated to achieving your own success.

Working conditions

You will mainly perform indoors – quite often in noisy atmospheres. Working venues may be pubs, clubs, cruise ships, holiday camps, festivals and shows.

Most performances are in the evening, leaving daytimes for travelling, rehearsing or creating new material.

You may have to spend time away from home. Entertainers are usually self-employed: you will need to be able to keep accounts.

The future outlook

The entertainment industry is very competitive and many entertainers work part time or just at weekends, alongside their day job.

As technology takes a bigger hold on public entertainment, there are more opportunities for entertainers to make videos, CDs, contribute to animation films and be part of promotional events.

In the future, your knowledge of the industry could prove useful in a role as entertainments manager or events organiser.

Qualifications and courses

- There are no formal entry requirements for entertaining; some people enter a career following an early interest in magic, clowning, etc.
- If you intend to specialise in a specific entertainment area, you can access formal training courses at school/college or through private training providers. You should check out local courses and higher education options at an early stage if you are interested, because these courses tend to fill up early.
- There are many appropriate courses available in performing arts, performance studies, music, dance and so on. Entry usually includes an audition and interview with a minimum of 2 A levels/H grades and 5 GCSEs/S grades (A–C/1–3), or the equivalent.
- Courses in dance require high grades in music or dance at entry.
- CCSkills (Creative and Cultural Skills) are developing nationwide Creative Apprenticeships, which cover a variety of creative fields.

CRCI:Q

CLCI:G

Other related opportunities

- Actor / Actress p390
- Choreographer p391
- Circus Performer p392
- Dancer p393
- Disc Jockey p396
- Nightclub Manager p371

Advantages/disadvantages

- You will be working unsocial hours which can affect your private life.
- There is lots of travelling between venues.
- Occasionally, you could be in noisy environments.
- Positive feedback from audiences can be a good confidence booster.

Earnings guide

- Earnings in the entertainment industry mainly depend on skills, experience and reputation.
- As a part-time entertainer you could earn £50–£250 for each performance.
- Working full time, you could earn up to £16,000 per year.
- Successful, full-time entertainers can earn £30,000–£60,000.

Further information

Arts Council of England
2 Pear Tree Court
London
EC1R 0DS
0845 300 6200
www.artscouncil.org.uk

The Circus Space
Cornet Street
London
N1 6HD
020 7613 4141
www.thecircusspace.co.uk

The Magic Circle
12 Stephenson Way
Euston
London
NW1 2HD
020 7387 2222
www.themagiccircle.co.uk

EQ
Suite E229
Dean Clough
Halifax
West Yorkshire
HX3 5AX
01422 381618
www.thinkeq.org.uk

Register of Stage Schools
www.stageregister.co.uk

Lighting Technician

What the work involves

- You will be responsible for creating stage lighting effects, working closely with the set designer and producer.
- You will do lighting for advertising sets, in video production, animation and broadcasting work.
- During performances, you will be in charge of the correct working of the lights and doing any essential maintenance of equipment.
- Making sure the power system is suitable for amplifiers and sound equipment will be a part of your job.
- It is important to visit venues before productions start, watching rehearsals to get the lighting effects right for live performances.

The type of person suited to this work

Anyone entering this career must have an interest in electrical work and electronics, have a strong interest in theatre and performance, or live concerts. You will also need to be physically fit and work well in a team.

Lighting technicians need to have a creative flair as the main aim of this job is to create the atmosphere required by the producer.

In some situations, for example changing or operating spotlights, the tasks could involve working at heights, and would not suit a person who suffers from vertigo.

Many lighting technicians have to travel long distances to do their work.

Working conditions

Most of your work will be indoors, usually working afternoons, evenings and weekends. You will work with lots of heavy equipment and you may sometimes need to wear protective steel toe-capped boots.

You may have to work in cramped spaces with computerised control systems.

You will often be away from home for weeks and months if you are travelling with a roadshow.

The future outlook

Theatre lighting is being covered by specialist companies who employ technicians on a short-term contract basis. However, once you are experienced and known in the trade, your opportunity to join the backstage crew of a particular theatre group is increased.

Progression as a lighting technician relies on skills and dedication. When in demand, you can become a senior or chief lighting technician and, in some cases, technical manager.

entry level

To both enter and train while working in this career, you will need qualifications at Level 2–3. Please refer to explanation on page vii.

Qualifications and courses

- A lighting technician may start work as an assistant electrician and gain skills on the job.
- All lighting technicians must be fully qualified electricians. Relevant qualifications include the City & Guilds Certificate in Electrotechnical Technology (2330), or SVQs Levels 2 and 3 in Lighting (Live Performance). Full-time or part-time college courses are available or you may find a traineeship with a specialist lighting company.
- Colleges and universities offer courses in subjects such as technical theatre, theatre design and theatre production, which include the study of lighting. Relevant courses include BTEC National Certificate/ Diploma in Production Arts, BTEC HNC/ HND in Performing Arts (Production), accredited drama school diplomas in technical theatre, degrees in lighting design, lighting technology or technical theatre.
- Specialist degrees in lighting design are offered by Rose Bruford College and Central School of Speech and Drama. Drama schools offer degrees and vocational training courses in technical theatre or stage management which include lighting. Many of these are accredited by the National Council for Drama Training.
- The BBC offers a central work experience scheme, but places are limited.
- The Association of British Theatre Technicians and Skillset offer professional qualifications in Lighting and Lighting Direction.
- Apprenticeships/Skillseekers may be available to those aged 16–24.

CRCI:Q

CLCI:G

Other related opportunities

- Cinema p356
- Disc Jockey p396
- Roadie p406
- Stage Manager p407
- Stagehand p408

Advantages/disadvantages

- You will have irregular working hours, including evening and weekend work – usually, away from home.
- Salaries for this work are not high.
- Seeing your skills and experience light up a set or production will be a great confidence booster.

Earnings guide

- Trainee technicians start at around £10,000 per year.
- With experience, this rises to £13,000–£20,000.
- A qualified electrician working in television could earn up to £25,000.

Further information

Association of British Theatre Technicians
47 Bermondsey Street
London
SE1 3XT
020 7403 3778
www.abtt.org.uk

National Electrotechnical Training
34 Palace Court
London
W2 4HY
020 7313 4846
www.net-works.org.uk

National Electrotechnical Training – Scotland
Bush House
Bush Estate
Penicuik
Midlothian
EH26 0SB
0131 445 9225
www.net-works.org.uk

Make-up Artist

What the work involves

- Your work will involve applying make-up and arranging hair for male and female artists and performers in films, TV and stage productions.
- You will need to listen to the director in order to create the desired finished look for the individual characters or troupe.
- Most of your work will be done off stage in a make-up or dressing room.
- You could be employed in TV, by a video production company or by a theatre or film company, or be self-employed, perhaps as part of a backstage team.

The type of person suited to this work

Anyone who considers doing make-up work needs to be creative, with the imagination to visualise the finished effect. You will have to pay great attention to detail. The job requires excellent communication and listening skills, as advising colleagues or clients on their image will need a sense of tact and clarity.

At times, there will be many people all of whom need to be made up for a particular scene, and you could be working flat out, under intense pressure. Self-confidence, an outgoing personality and the ability to stay calm in a crisis are all positive factors in building relationships and succeeding at work.

Working conditions

Most of your work will be indoors in theatres, in studios and, at first, possibly in retail outlets. Try to get work experience as a make-up artist with local amateur dramatic or operatic groups.

Doing make-up involves many busy hours spent standing and bending over customers and you will need to be physically fit.

If you are self-employed, you will probably need to provide your own cosmetics.

The future outlook

Although this is not a huge area for employment there will always be a demand for make-up artists. The larger towns and cities present the best opportunities. Although limited, some work could be available in the larger hotels or on cruise ships.

Securing full-time work in TV or video, on a cruise ship, in a hotel, a retail store or with a theatre company are all possible, once you have gained experience.

It will be possible to set up your own beauty salon.

entry level

2–3

To both enter and train while working in this career, you will need qualifications at Level 2–3. Please refer to explanation on page vii.

Qualifications and courses

- Make-up artists in theatre/TV/film are usually trained in beauty therapy, and may have an NVQ/SVQ or a Diploma of the Vocational Training Charitable Trust (VTCT) or equivalent qualification.
- There are a range of specialist further education courses in theatrical and/or media make-up. VTCT offers a Diploma course, and BTEC National awards and Certificates and SQA modules are also available. These courses can be studied at college on a full- or part-time basis.
- Greasepaint offers short courses in make-up for TV, film, fashion and theatre.
- A number of universities and colleges run HND courses in theatrical and/or media make-up or make-up artistry. A degree course in costume, technical effects and make-up for performing arts is offered at London College of Fashion, and allows students to specialise in make-up. The usual entry requirements for HND and degree courses are 2 A levels or equivalent (for example an Edexcel National Diploma). Their 2-year full-time Foundation degree course in specialist make-up design has lower entry requirements.
- Apprenticeships/Skillseekers may be available to those aged 16–24.

Other related opportunities

- Beauty p412
- Body Artist / Tattooist p414
- Hairdresser / Barber p424
- Image Consultant p425

Advantages/disadvantages

- Handling some cosmetics could cause skin irritations.
- Working hours may be irregular and unsociable, especially if you do make-up both before and during performances.
- Make-up is a highly satisfying job when you see your work on stage or set.

Earnings guide

- Self-employed make-up artists can earn around £15,000 per year. With experience this can rise to £25,000. The highest paid earn up to £45,000.
- Employed by a company, you can start on £14,000–£16,000 earning more with specialist skills.
- Artists employed on a full-time basis by broadcasting or film companies to do make-up, hair and wigs for actors/actresses can earn over £25,000.

Further information

British Association of Beauty Therapy and Cosmetology Ltd
Ambrose House
Meteor Court
Barnett Way
GL4 3GG
0845 065 9000
www.babtac.com

Make Up Artist magazine
www.makeupmag.com

The Stage
Stage House
47 Bermondsey Street
London
SE1 3XT
020 7403 1818
www.thestage.co.uk

Greasepaint
Greasepaint Studio
143 Northfield Avenue
Ealing
W13 9QT
www.greasepaint.co.uk

www.cityandguilds.com/myperfectjob

Music

What the work involves

- To be successful as a musician, you will need lots of talent, a love and understanding of music and mental stamina.
- You will need to work hard – perhaps focusing on the theories behind evolving musical tradition or instrumental and notational developments and differing styles.
- In all fields, being a musician means practising for long hours – alone, with teachers and in groups – learning techniques to give polished performances in front of audiences.
- All career musicians have a good sense of pitch, rhythm, timing and musicality, to be able to understand and then interpret the sense or theme explored by individual musical compositions.

Composer

- You will be producing original music, such as popular songs, television, video and radio themes or advertising pieces, film music, works with a religious theme, operas or symphonies.
- You will need to be creative, and to have a good ear for melody and an excellent knowledge of musical notation and instrumentation.
- You could be using manuscript paper and pencil, electronic keyboard linked with computer software programs, or video to record your pieces.
- Unless you perform solo or in a band, it may take a little time to start having your own compositions performed and recorded.

Conductor

- Conducting a small ensemble or an orchestra is a big challenge, and it is a huge responsibility to present the work of great composers.
- You will perform on stage or in an orchestra pit, conducting the musicians – sometimes with singers, a choir or chorus – ensuring that everyone plays or sings their piece perfectly during a performance.
- You will need to be dedicated to music, with great knowledge and understanding of many pieces and different musical genres.
- You may need to examine and mark scores or rehearse different classical works and newly composed pieces for many hours every day.

Musician – classical

- You will play an instrument in an orchestra, as a member of an ensemble group, or as a solo performer – often, across the UK and on tours abroad.
- You might also teach music to boost your income.
- Classical musicians would normally start at an early age and continue to take graded exams in playing their instruments, or in performing to audiences.
- Sessional musicians need to be excellent sight readers as they may not have played or heard a particular piece before rehearsal.

Musician – popular

- You will probably work in a small band or with one other person – sometimes, on your own.
- As a popular musician you might play more than one instrument, dance and/or sing during a performance.
- It is likely that you will be travelling and performing one-night gigs throughout the year, or playing for a whole season in one venue.
- You could specialise in rock, jazz, the blues, pop, country, folk, indie, rap or a combination of any of these.

Singer

- You will be performing in clubs, at gigs, on television or radio, in a recording studio, in an opera house, as a solo artist on stage, as part of a small group or in a choir or chorus.
- You will need to understand every word of the pieces you sing – sometimes in translation – in order to get the meaning across.
- You will spend many hours practising – also, developing and strengthening your breathing and vocal movements, your diction and pronunciation of foreign languages.
- Good presentation and well-developed acting skills will always help your stage performance.

CRCI:Q | CLCI:G

Qualifications and courses

- There are a variety of routes into careers in music.
- People interested in music usually take lessons from childhood. Graded examinations in the different musical instruments and in singing are offered by the Associated Board of Royal Schools of Music (ABRSM), the Guildhall Examinations Service, Trinity College London, and London College of Music Examinations. These form part of the entry requirements for most music courses.
- The ABRSM offers a Certificate of Teaching for people who have completed the graded examinations and wish to become music teachers. To enable private teachers to keep updated with current syllabuses, the Incorporated Society of Musicians (ISM) offers part-time professional development courses including the Music Teaching in Professional Practice.
- Popular musicians do not necessarily need any formal training. BTEC National qualifications and HND/Cs in popular music/modern musicianship are available at colleges. These courses cover composition as well as ensemble playing and stage performance.
- Several further education colleges offer full-time BTEC National courses in music technology and there are other certificates available, for example in audio technology and the music industry.
- Classical musicians are formally trained, and usually have a degree (BMus) from a conservatoire.
- Universities and colleges of higher education also offer degrees in music. These may be more theoretical and less performance-oriented than courses offered by conservatoires.
- Undergraduate music courses often include elements of composition and/or conducting. More specialised postgraduate courses are available in these areas.
- Military band courses, offered by the Army, Royal Air Force and Royal Marines, provide an alternative career route. Applicants should have Grade 8 standard on a wind, percussion or stringed instrument, and are selected by audition. The course combines musical training with a basic military training.
- A Postgraduate Certificate in Education (PGCE) in Music is available for those who want to teach – see Teacher: Teacher of Music.
- Adults without formal entry requirements who wish to study modern music can take a 1-year full-time Access to Music course at certain further education colleges. This course can be a preparatory step for progression to a degree course.

entry level

To both enter and train while working in this career, you will need qualifications at Level 2–3. Please refer to explanation on page vii.

The type of person suited to this work

As getting paid work will depend on experience, popularity and individual contracts, anyone aiming to succeed in the music field will need to be dedicated. Musicians do have to practise to maintain their skills level, as well as rehearsing performance works and polishing their presentation.

Many musicians are self-employed and so will benefit from developing their marketing and business skills. Sometimes musicians work on their own and at other times as part of large or small groups, so they need to be flexible and self-motivated, and work well as part of teams.

Musicians need to be comfortable meeting lots of new people, working unsociable hours and travelling to and from rehearsals and performances. They should see music as a way of life and not just a career. The music business can be tough in many ways and most people who go into it tend to regard their work as a vocation rather than just a salaried job.

Working conditions

The type of environment you work in will vary greatly with the different areas of music and the expected audience. Most musicians travel away from home a great deal – sometimes, for long periods.

Composer

Composers normally work on their own, either from home, in a college setting or private music studio.

Conductor

Conductors mainly work in large theatres, concert halls or auditoriums.

Musician – classical

Classical musicians and singers are likely to perform in a theatre and these will vary in size from small scale to the Albert Hall. The better-known classical orchestras and symphonias spend part of each year touring.

Musician – popular

As part of a band you will work in clubs, theatres, halls, arenas and stadiums or in recording studios. Your lifestyle will be unsettled as most bands travel widely.

Singer

As a singer you could find yourself performing in a variety of venues such as recording studios, places of worship, nightclubs, opera houses, in TV or radio studios and in theatres and concert halls.

The future outlook

Working in the music industry is very competitive and many people now make a successful living through combining short-term contracts with other areas of work such as sessional recording, or by teaching their particular skills to young and older people. More and more people have an interest in relaxing through joining musical societies or learning to play instruments.

As a composer, there has been a recent surge of interest in modern composition and new works are allotted far more air time than previously. Digital broadcasting and the increase in channels and stations has assisted focus on new and different genres.

Many classical players and performers are trying to make names for themselves with small group/ensemble work, as several of the larger employing orchestras in the UK are finding it harder to fund their usual programmes due to a lack of incremental rises in the level of Arts Council funding.

Popular music players, singers and composers have new media to raise company and public awareness of their talents. Many bands are able to self-promote using their own websites, with video and soundbites. The industry is transferring to web-based platforms which enables the sale of MP3s through online music stores.

Popular singers who compose their own material and work with a cross-cultural range of instruments or musicians are increasingly given airtime.

Classical singers continue to find paid work as there has been a cross-fertilisation of musical knowledge and interest between popular open-air events and classical concerts and festivals.

The music industry is vast, with unknown numbers of people working in some small way within this sector. As it develops, through television coverage, video and electronic sound, this industry is attracting more young people than ever before.

Other related opportunities

- Actor / Actress p390
- Disc Jockey p396
- Musical Instrument Maker / Repairer p156
- Piano Tuner p158
- Roadie p406
- Teacher p184

Advantages/disadvantages

- Pay can be low when you start.
- Not all areas of music have unions to back them up with minimum pay rates.
- Venues vary from nightclubs to prestigious opera houses, although players' conditions may not reflect the glitz of front of house.
- Musicians in every field work long hours away from home.
- It is very competitive, and contracts may be difficult to get and to hold.
- You will have to spend long hours practising your skills, journeying to venues and working weekends.
- It can be a rewarding career, if you love music.
- Most musicians experience feelings of real exhilaration from performing to appreciative audiences.

Earnings guide

- Musicians' incomes vary greatly according to experience, talent and type of work, and earnings can be low when you first start your career.
- The Incorporated Society of Musicians (ISM) works with musicians unions to agree basic rates for professional musicians. Details can be found on the ISM website.

Composer

- There are no set rates of pay for composers. Much depends on the popularity of your work, the publisher and the number of users.

Musician – classical

- Musicians in orchestras normally get around £75–£90+ per concert.
- Experienced musicians earn more, but only around 2000 classical musicians work full time in the UK in established orchestras, receiving a salary. Contracted players start at around £23,000–£26,000 but can earn £27,000–£35,000 as a section leader.
- Soloists and orchestra leaders can earn around £180+ for a concert and rehearsal time.
- Freelancers can expect to earn about £35,000+ per year and rather more in London. Many classical musicians work freelance and have incomes from a variety of jobs in the industry.
- Musicians in the Royal Air Force earn from £16,900, going up to £35,000 for leading bandmasters.
- Royal Marines musicians, starting training at 16, earn from £11,432–£13,461, rising to £24,312 after training.
- Army musicians starting at 17 will earn from £11,200, rising after basic training to £13,350 and going up to £36,500 as a leading bandmaster.

Musician – popular

- Pay rates for musicians vary widely. Earnings depend on the number of hours and weeks worked, a performer's reputation, the setting and the contract.
- In television entertainment, the income for a performance is around £150–£300.
- Musicians in a successful rock band may get a very high income from live performances and royalties from recordings and merchandising.
- Some successful musicians earn performance or recording fees that far exceed the average, but this is only after you have become recognised as a top performer.

Singer

- There are no set rates for this work, and income can depend on your experience, popularity, venue and contract. But if you are in full-time employment you could start on £11,500 rising to £25,000 with experience, and up to £100,000 for those in great demand.
- Experienced singers backing a professional album or track can earn £350+ for 3 hours' work.
- Working in a range of venues such as clubs, at weddings or celebrations, or with a band, a soloist could expect to get anything between £75 and £175 (plus expenses) per performance of around 2 and a half hours – often including an afternoon rehearsal.
- A professional singer performing in the background for a television programme can earn between £95 and £145 per performance. In addition they may be paid rehearsal fees of around £50+ per 3 hours.

Further information

Incorporated Society of Musicians
10 Stratford Place
London
WC1 1AA
020 7629 4413
www.ism.org

British Phonographic Industry
25 Savile Row
London
W1S 2ES
020 7534 5300
www.bpi.co.uk

Musicians' Union
60–62 Clapham Road
London
SW9 0JJ
020 7840 5534
www.musiciansunion.org.uk

Access to Music
Lionel House
35 Millstone Lane
Leicester
LE1 5JN
0800 281 842
www.accesstomusic.co.uk

Directorate Corps of Army Music
Kneller Hall
Twickenham
Middlesex TW2 7DU
020 8744 8638

EQ
Suite E229
Dean Clough
Halifax
West Yorkshire HX3 5AX
01422 381618
www.thinkeq.org.uk

Association of British Orchestras
20 Rupert Street
London
W1D 6DF
020 7287 0333
www.abo.org.uk

Producer (Theatre)

What the work involves

Producer

- Your role will be that of a lead person in the production of plays, radio drama broadcasts – and sometimes films.
- You will be responsible for raising interest in future programmes to get financial backing to cover production costs.
- Producers select the key performers, choose a suitable director, adapt scripts, coordinate and supervise the work of different departments as well as the artists; you will have to make policy decisions.
- Usually, you will have a production assistant who will work closely to your instructions.

Production assistant

- Assisting the producer, you will have a coordinating role on the production.
- You will be involved in distributing scripts, keeping the production team informed about relevant issues and arranging rehearsing schedules.
- You will need to be very well organised with good administrative skills.
- You could be dealing with records of expenses and working on other detailed figures needed by the producer or production team.

The type of person suited to this work

Producer

You will need to be highly organised, creative and a good communicator. You will take a flexible approach and will have fully developed management skills. As part of the role is securing funds for the production, a background in finance or business could be helpful.

Production assistant

Production assistants must be efficient, pay attention to detail and able to work under pressure.

You will need to be good at problem-solving and have excellent communication skills, be methodical and have the ability to prioritise your work.

The job will involve long hours, and often evening and weekend work, and this requires a high level of stamina.

CRCI:Q

CLCI:G

Working conditions

Producer

The stress of overseeing a production, while continually exploring future work, can play a big part in a producer's life. In addition, the organising of rehearsals and constant round of meetings with writers, designers, financial backers and production technicians can add stress to the job. The irregular and long hours with spells away can put a strain on family life.

Production assistant

You will work long irregular hours – possibly, away from home on location for days or weeks at a time.

The future outlook

Producer

Employment for producers is expected to remain stable, although there are fewer opportunities than there are job-seekers. As most producers are self-employed and work on a contract basis, they will need to keep up to date with developing areas of work such as cable and satellite television, increasing production of independent films, and the growth and development of interactive media such as web films and video. Increasingly, there are jobs to be found in theme parks and other leisure venues. This is a very competitive area of work and many producers leave the field after a number of years in the production industry.

Production assistant

This is a popular and competitive area of work and there are few vacancies compared with numbers of those seeking employment.

Production assistants can find work in areas such as television, independent production companies, films, theatre and radio. With experience, there may be opportunities for promotion to a senior production assistant and, with skills in management and budgets, you could progress to become a producer.

Qualifications and courses

Producer

- Producers usually have extensive experience in the industry – often, in commercial theatre. They may have progressed from roles such as production assistant, or even runner. A number will have obtained degrees or HNDs.

Production assistant

- There are no specific entry requirements for this job. However, it is highly competitive and most entrants have relevant academic qualifications and/or experience.
- Administrative skills – including keyboard skills, high levels of computer literacy, even shorthand – are required. Production assistants may be promoted from secretarial or administrative roles.
- A range of related courses can be studied full time at college or university. A levels and BTEC National qualifications are available in media production. There are HNDs and degrees in relevant areas, for example broadcasting or media production.
- It is useful to gain relevant experience, for example in student or hospital radio, or working from early on within amateur theatre and operatic production.
- Film and Television Freelance Training (FT2) offers training for technical and production careers. Applicants for production training should have secretarial skills, including the ability to touch-type at 40 words per minute. The training is apprenticeship-based, and includes attachments with different production crews. Trainees also undertake short courses and work towards Skillset NVQs.
- People already employed within the industry can work towards the Skillset qualifications at Levels 2, 3 and 4. Most training is done on the job.
- Apprenticeships/Skillseekers may be available to those aged 16–24.

entry level

To both enter and train while working in this career, you will need qualifications at Level 3–8. Please refer to explanation on page vii.

Other related opportunities

- Administrator p6
- Director (Theatre) p395
- Entertainments Manager p361
- Stage Manager p407

Advantages/disadvantages

Producer

- Producers work under constant pressure. Many face stress from a continual need to find their next jobs.
- To succeed, they need patience and commitment to their area of expertise.
- Hours are long and there is evening and weekend work.
- This job requires negotiating and communication skills – you will be a link between the company's management structure, their backers, the artists and technical staff.

Production assistant

- As an assistant you will work long hours.
- You need to be patient and calm to work with team members who may be under pressure.

Earnings guide

Producer

- Established producers can earn good salaries of £40,000, but earnings will depend on experience, talent, regular work and the type of production they are working on.

Production assistant

- £18,000–£20,000 per year is a typical salary as a trainee production assistant, but can be lower for radio.
- You could earn up to £26,000 with some experience.
- £27,000–£40,000 and over is possible at senior levels with lots of experience.

Further information

Skillset (Sector Skills Council for the audiovisual industries)
Prospect House
80–110 New Oxford Street
London
WC1A 1HB
08080 300900
www.skillset.org

Film and Television Freelance Training (FT2)
4th Floor, Warwick House
9 Warwick Street
London
W1B 5LY
020 7734 5141
www.ft2.org.uk

BBC Recruitment Services
PO Box 7000
London
W12 8JG
0870 333 1330
www.bbc.co.uk/jobs

Moving Image Society
www.bksts.com
Information on a range of jobs in the film industry

Props Maker

What the work involves

- You will be responsible for designing, producing and finishing the props used in stage, theatre, circus, video, film or television work.
- You could be involved in making changes to existing props.
- You will link with outreach workers – artists, multimedia workers and designers – who may construct props for you.
- The work needs a wide range of practical and design skills in carpentry, model-making, sewing and computer-aided design.

The type of person suited to this work

This job is suited to a creative, practical person with technical and craft skills such as model-making, electronics, lighting, computer-aided design and carpentry. As well as an understanding of materials and their uses, an interest in historical and different cultural backgrounds is extremely helpful.

Jobs may have to be completed at the last minute before a performance, so you will need patience and determination. Many props makers have been carpenters or joiners, metalworkers, interior decorators, etc.

As the job involves linking with many external agencies and tradespeople, excellent verbal communication skills will be essential.

Working conditions

Most of your work will be carried out in studios, backstage or in specially designed workshops.

Some projects will require you to go out to suppliers and negotiate prices for suitable resources.

Working conditions vary and you could be working weekends and evenings.

The future outlook

There is not a huge demand for props makers in the UK. Employment has remained the same for a number of years with no expected change to opportunities available.

It is rare for a props maker to be on a permanent employment contract; most are self-employed working on short-term contracts.

You should keep a portfolio of past work to show potential employers. Props makers develop experience as volunteers in local repertory/amateur dramatic companies or fringe theatre.

entry level

To both enter and train while working in this career, you will need qualifications at Level 2–3. Please refer to explanation on page vii.

Qualifications and courses

- There are no formal entry requirements, but many people start by studying courses in stage management or design.
- Some higher education courses include modules on props-making; however, you will need to research carefully before applying. Getting a work experience placement with a theatre company or in amateur dramatic clubs will give you valuable experience before and during training.
- You could start training on a relevant course, such as performing arts, art, design, theatre technician or model making. Qualifications include BTEC National Diploma in Production Arts, BTEC HNC/HND in Performing Arts (Production), a degree or Foundation degree in an appropriate subject, or a drama school Diploma in stage design or technical theatre.
- A number of universities and colleges of higher education offer HNDs in model-making, stage design and prop-making. The usual entry requirements for HND and degree courses are 2 A levels/Highers or equivalent (for example National Diploma or NVQ/SVQ at Level 3).
- Skillset, the training organisation for the film, television and broadcasting industries, offers courses and NVQ/SVQ Levels 2–4.

Other related opportunities

- Carpenter / Joiner p41
- Model Maker p155

Advantages/disadvantages

- Backstage conditions could be dirty, cramped and smelling of paints and adhesives.
- Work hours are long, especially towards the opening night of a production.
- Seeing props you have created having a key role in a production can be very rewarding.

Earnings guide

- There are no set rates of pay for props makers and income can be quite low. BECTU recommends rates around £195–£375 per day, but as a rule most prop makers set their own fees.
- Income depends on experience, quality of previous jobs and your ability to get work.
- With a relevant qualification, and some experience, you can expect to earn £18,000 per year.
- Contracts for larger projects could be £20,000–£35,000.

Further information

Association of British Theatre Technicians
47 Bermondsey Street
London
SE1 3XT
020 7403 3778
www.abtt.org.uk

Skillset (Sector Skills Council for the audiovisual industries)
Prospect House
80–110 New Oxford Street
London
WC1A 1HB
08080 300900
www.skillset.org

Society of British Theatre Designers
4th Floor
55 Farringdon Road
London
EC1M 3JB
020 7242 9200
www.theatredesign.org.uk

www.cityandguilds.com/myperfectjob

Roadie

What the work involves

- You will have to lift, move and set up heavy equipment, load and unload vans and trailers and do lots of driving around.
- You will be responsible for setting up a range of equipment including amplifications systems, electric cabling, stage and special effects lighting, videos and other media.
- You will need to maintain and fine-tune your equipment on a regular basis.
- Your work could include handling pyrotechnics, laser displays, computers – as well as videos.

entry level

To both enter and train while working in this career, you will need qualifications at Level 1–2. Please refer to explanation on page vii.

The type of person suited to this work

You will need to have a strong interest in music, technology and electrics. It is essential for anyone working in this career to have good communication skills and an interest in people, and to be creative and practical.

Physical fitness and stamina will be essential, and a sense of humour is a bonus in this work. You should be able to work whilst under pressure. Because many roadies are self-employed, a well-organised person with some business skills will do well with maintaining their accounts, keeping records and dates of bookings.

Working conditions

You will have exceptionally long working hours, mainly evenings, nights and weekends, and if you are on a tour, you might be working 7 days a week.

You will be working in clubs and other venues which can be noisy and hot.

The work is very physical and there is lots of heavy lifting involved, and sometimes you could be working at heights on electrical cabling.

The future outlook

There are more roadies looking for work than there are jobs. The work is unpredictable and you may need another job to boost your income. Work can be seasonal, with more roadies needed for summer festivals and gigs.

Marketing your services will be essential for getting gigs; many roadies now use websites to advertise.

Expanding your areas of expertise to include technical skills such as sound or lighting will certainly improve your chances of employment.

Qualifications and courses

- There are no formal entry qualifications for becoming a roadie. Most people enter this career through experience of working with a friend or other contacts. If you are under 18 you may not be able to work in some licensed premises.
- If you are planning to do the more technical work you may need qualifications. Suitable courses would be in lighting, pyrotechnics, video work and sound production. Details of suitable courses are available from the Production Services Association and British Phonographic Industry and many of these do not require formal entry qualifications.
- The majority of roadies will learn the trade from working with other more experienced people. Although the job has no specific training route, courses such as electrics and video, and music technician courses, would be a useful addition to help expand job prospects.
- Useful skills and qualifications include a health and safety certificate, a First Aid certificate, a Light Goods Vehicle or Passenger Service Vehicle driving licence and the ability to speak one or more foreign languages.

CRCI:G

CLCI:Q

Other related opportunities

- Disc Jockey p396
- Lighting Technician p398
- Music p400
- Removals Operative p581
- Stagehand p408

Advantages/disadvantages

- Roadies work long unsociable hours and there is lots of travelling.
- You will have to do heavy lifting, sometimes working in dusty, cramped conditions.
- You will stay throughout the concert or gig, as equipment may need moving onto/off stage.
- Very loud sounds will damage your hearing if your ears are unprotected.

Earnings guide

- There is no set earning scale and pay will depend on the gig, your experience and general availability of roadies.
- As a starter, you could earn around £12,000–£13,000 per year.
- A roadie with electrical, audio or video skills can earn £20,000+. With technical skills this can rise to £30,000–£32,000.
- With a big touring band, you could earn £35,000+, depending on contract.

Further information

www.cityandguilds.com/myperfectjob

Production Services Association
Centre Court
1301 Stratford Road, Hall Green
Birmingham
B28 9HH
0121 639 7127
www.psa.org.uk

British Phonographic Industry
25 Savile Row
London
W1S 2ES
020 7534 5300
www.bpi.co.uk

Stage Manager

What the work involves

- Working with designers, directors and producers, you will discuss what props, lighting and other stage support are needed for the production.
- You will be in charge of everything that happens on stage during a production including calling actors, giving technical cues and moving scenery.
- If you are working on a large production, you may have an assistant.

entry level

To both enter and train while working in this career, you will need qualifications at Level 3. Please refer to explanation on page vii.

The type of person suited to this work

You will need to have artistic flair, be practical, communicate instructions clearly and manage others confidently, working as part of a team with artists, directors, the production team and technical and backstage staff. Good time management skills are crucial.

The work is demanding and stressful as the successful running of the backstage support for the performance rests with you. A cool head and a sense of humour – while still being assertive – will make the work easier for you. An excellent stage manager can help create a good team atmosphere backstage between artists, props manager and stagehands.

Working conditions

You will spend long hours in theatres and studios, sometimes working into the night to meet deadlines. In addition, you will have to travel to different venues.

The atmosphere backstage during rehearsals and performances can be very enclosed, hot and dusty.

Finding work is not easy and can take up a huge amount of your time, so be prepared for rejection and periods without work.

The future outlook

The employment demand for stage managers has remained stable for some years. This is a competitive area of work and the opportunities for employment are not extensive. Opportunities exist in theatre companies, opera, theatre in education and touring companies.

Experience in amateur theatre – with student productions and drama clubs – shows commitment and gives you valuable experience.

Most stage managers work to specific contracts and are normally interviewed and employed by the producer or director.

Qualifications and courses

- Usually, entrants to this job have undertaken professional training. Also, it may be possible to enter with relevant practical experience.
- Stage managers have usually taken a stage management course at drama school. The National Council for Drama Training accredits some vocational stage management courses. Diplomas and degrees are studied over 2 or 3 years full time, and entry is by interview and portfolio of practical work.
- Some universities offer degrees and HNDs in technical theatre or theatre production which include study of stage management. Candidates should also aim to gain practical experience in student productions or fringe theatre as a degree is not recognised as vocational training.
- You could be employed as a stagehand and work your way up.
- The Stage Management Association runs a variety of short courses for people already working as stage managers or assistant stage managers.
- NVQs/SVQs are available in Stage Management, and there are BTEC/SQA qualifications in relevant subjects. Some drama schools offer short, part-time courses in stage management.

Other related opportunities

- Entertainments Manager p361
- Props Maker p405
- Stagehand p408

Advantages/disadvantages

- You will work long, unpredictable hours to meet production deadlines.
- Permanent contracts are difficult to find.
- The work is both creative and practical.
- There is a great sense of achievement at the end of a successful run when everything has operated smoothly.

Earnings guide

- Starting out as a trainee manager you will earn about £14,000–£16,000+ per year. With experience, your annual salary can rise to £20,000+.
- With a lot of experience, you can expect to be earning £26,000–£40,000.

Further information

EQ
Suite E229
Dean Clough
Halifax
West Yorkshire
HX3 5AX
01422 381618
www.thinkeq.org.uk

Arts and Entertainment Technical Training Initiative
Lower Ground
14 Blenheim Terrace
London
NW8 0EB
020 732 86174
www.touchlondon.co.uk

Stage Management Association
47 Bermondsey Street
London
SE1 3XT
020 7403 6655
www.stagemanagementassociation.co.uk

Broadcasting Entertainment Cinematograph and Theatre Union
373–377 Clapham Road
London
SW9 9BT
020 7346 0900
www.bectu.org.uk

Stagehand

What the work involves

- Working backstage with others in a team, you will be supporting the stage manager in the run-up to a production.
- You will have to be alert to take cues from the stage manager, as each performance may be slightly different.
- You will help to move scenery and equipment on and off stage during rehearsals and productions, and may operate the stage curtain.
- You will be expected to act as a runner – picking up props from designers/makers and transferring them to the theatre.

entry level

1–2

To both enter and train while working in this career, you will need qualifications at Level 1–2. Please refer to explanation on page vii.

The type of person suited to this work

If you decide to work as a stagehand, you will need to have a real interest in theatre work, including front of house, acting and behind scenes. The work can be very physically demanding, so physical fitness, stamina and an understanding of health and safety will all be necessary for the work.

Long hours will be spent waiting around, listening to the rehearsals and the productions many times over, and this could become boring, so patience and control, plus an ability to remain interested will be essential.

Qualifications and courses

- There are no formal entry requirements for this job.
- Practical skills, such as carpentry, and experience of using tools and machinery are useful.
- Candidates would usually have experience of working in theatre, for example on amateur productions.
- Casual employment on a theatre production may lead to full-time employment.
- Stagehands are trained on the job, but may also undertake part-time study in subjects related to theatre work. The Association of British Theatre Technicians (ABTT) runs relevant short courses for stagehands and backstage technicians. There are BTEC Certificates and Diplomas, or HNCs and HNDs in appropriate subjects such as Performing or Production Arts, Technical Theatre and Stage Management.

Working conditions

Working as a stagehand within theatre involves lifting and carrying heavy equipment. Theatres can be dusty and you may work in cramped, dark conditions.

As theatres open in the evening, expect late nights, weekend working and lots of time away from home.

You will have to be aware of your own and colleagues' health and safety as theatres can be dangerous places.

The future outlook

There are limited opportunities in theatres, touring companies, and theatre in education. Experience with student productions or local amateur groups shows commitment and gives valuable experience.

Many starting out as stagehands and finding it difficult to progress to stage manager can move into other areas of backstage work, perhaps becoming props makers, lighting technicians and sometimes set designers.

Lots of stagehands work freelance for individual productions.

CRCI:Q

CLCI:G

Other related opportunities

- Carpenter / Joiner p41
- Entertainments Manager p361
- Lighting Technician p398
- Props Maker p405
- Stage Manager p407

Advantages/disadvantages

- You will spend time waiting around backstage during rehearsals and productions.
- Low pay is usual when starting out.
- You need to be able to handle possible rejection and some time out of work.
- It is rewarding that your skills play a role in a production's success.

Earnings guide

- Starting out as a stagehand you will earn about £12,000–£15,000 per year in large theatres. With experience your annual salary can rise to £18,000. If you are freelance you could earn anything between £15,000 and £25,000.
- With technical skills you could get £20,000–£30,000.
- Working freelance you could earn anything between £18,000 and £25,000.
- Pay is pro rata for casual employment and you could get overtime for working longer hours.
- See Stage Manager on the previous page for information about potential salaries if you progress from stagehand work.

Further information

www.cityandguilds.com/myperfectjob

EQ
Suite E229
Dean Clough
Halifax
West Yorkshire
HX3 5AX
01422 381618
www.thinkeq.org.uk

Arts and Entertainment Technical Training Initiative
Lower Ground
14 Blenheim Terrace
London
NW8 0EB
020 732 86174
www.touchlondon.co.uk

Stage Management Association
47 Bermondsey Street
London
SE1 3XT
020 7403 6655
www.stagemanagementassociation.co.uk

Broadcasting Entertainment Cinematograph and Theatre Union
373–377 Clapham Road
London
SW9 9BT
020 7346 0900
www.bectu.org.uk

Stunt Performer

What the work involves

- You will plan, design, practise and perform stunts in areas such as motorbike riding, car driving, diving, flying, paragliding, bungee jumping, skiing and horse riding.
- Standing in for actors in TV, film or video productions, you will enter flaming buildings, crash vehicles, drive at speed or do dangerous stunts at sea.
- Sometimes, performances are in front of live audiences.
- You may advise other performers on health and safety issues.

entry level

To both enter and train while working in this career, you will need qualifications at Level 1–2. Please refer to explanation on page vii.

The type of person suited to this work

Being skilled in a range of sports, including gymnastics, trampolining, parachuting, wrestling, fencing and some of the well-known martial arts, is often useful.

This is dangerous work – so you will need to be a risk-taker.

Stunt performers are dedicated to their art, and committed to ensuring that their skills are highly developed.

You will be happy to practise every aspect of your stunts over and again until they are reproducible in all details, so, you must be a perfectionist. You must always be aware of the dangers you face, practising long hours to make the performance appear easy!

Working conditions

Part of your working day could be spent within a studio, on location or on a film set.

You could be working indoors or out, in cramped spaces, at heights, or sometimes in bad weather conditions.

The hours could be very long, often up to 16 hours per day depending on the production, with weekend work and travelling to distant places being the norm.

The future outlook

Opportunities for live stunt work are decreasing, as digital graphics and new media can simulate stunts. There are 300–400 UK stunt performers, but only 30% are in full-time employment, so competition for work is fierce. Jobs with stunt firms are advertised in Contacts, the online version of *The Stage* magazine.

Stunt artists work anywhere in the world, with main employers being film, TV and video production companies. You will need a high level of stamina and fitness; this is a young person's career.

Some stunt performers progress into advisory work, helping film directors or advising and training other stunt artists.

Qualifications and courses

- There are no academic entry requirements for this work. Stunt performers may have trained as actors.
- Stunt performers should have skills in areas such as martial arts, fencing, horse riding, boxing, diving and climbing. Qualifications should not be more than 5 years old.
- Stage combat is taught on professional acting courses at drama schools.
- Organisations such as the British Academy of Dramatic Combat, the British Academy of Stage and Screen Combat, and YoungBlood Ltd run year-long courses, workshops and classes in stage combat for practising actors.
- Most stunt performers are self-employed and look for contract work with film or TV companies, but to work as a stunt artist in the UK, you need to be accepted on the Joint Industry Stunt Committee (JISC) register, and should be aged 18 or over. To register, you must present your skills qualifications to the JISC, together with evidence that you have spent a minimum of 60 days in front of a camera. Equity recommends that film and TV producers only draw up contracts with stunt performers who are on the JISC register.

Other related opportunities

- Actor / Actress p390

Advantages/disadvantages

- You will be doing difficult and dangerous work, involving many risks.
- You will be out in all weathers, working in blazing buildings, enclosed spaces or at great heights.
- Long hours will be spent practising or away on location.
- This is a very competitive area of work with poor prospects.

Earnings guide

- There is no formal pay scale for stunt performers, and income varies greatly. Equity sets fees for stunt work with television companies and independent producers.
- Recommended daily rates are £250–£368 for TV work, and £420+ a day for film work.
- Although not the usual route, you could start in full-time employment at around £11,000 per year.
- A very experienced performer may earn £25,000+ per year.

Further information

EQ
Suite E229
Dean Clough
Halifax
West Yorkshire HX3 5AX
01422 381618
www.thinkeq.org.uk

Skillset (Sector Skills Council for the audiovisual industries)
Prospect House
80–110 New Oxford Street
London
WC1A 1HB
08080 300900
www.skillset.org

British Academy of Dramatic Combat
www.badc.co.uk

YoungBlood Ltd
16 Gunnersbury Close
Chiswick High Road
London
W4 4AH
0845 644 9418
www.youngblood.co.uk

British Academy of Stage and Screen Combat
Suite 280
14 Tottenham Court Road
London
W1T 1JY
020 8352 0605
www.bassc.org

Joint Industry Stunt Committee
c/o Equity
Guild House
Upper St Martin's Lane
London WC2H 9EG
Full details on application to join the JISC register are contained in a document called 'Rules of the stunt register', which is available by writing to Equity at the address above.

Wardrobe Assistant

What the work involves

- Working within the production team, you will make sure actors/actresses are dressed authentically for the performance.
- You may have to help artists dress for performances, making sure they are wearing their costumes and props correctly.
- In charge of the dress of several performers, you will have to clean, iron and repair costumes, look after accessories and keep the stockroom clean and tidy between performances.
- You have to keep records and catalogue all the items in stock.

The type of person suited to this work

Wardrobe assistants should have a strong interest in the theatre. You will need to be creative, with an eye for detail and have strong practical skills, including sewing. Much of the work will involve dressing and communicating with artists who may be under stress just before, or during, a performance when quick costume changes are demanded.

It will be important to have good communication skills, know how to be tactful and diplomatic, and have the ability to stay calm in a crisis.

Working conditions

You will spend most of your time backstage, often in dusty conditions. You will be using sewing or cleaning equipment to clean, iron or repair costumes. Costumes need to be taken to artists for quick changes mid-performance. You may help artists dress/undress.

Your working hours will be daytime for rehearsals and evening for performances – working public holidays and weekends. Some wardrobe assistants are attached to touring companies and work away for several weeks a year.

The future outlook

This area of employment remains as it has been for the past few years, with just a few opportunities in theatre, film or in TV. However, a young person starting out can get experience of costume work in local amateur operatic, drama or opera groups, or with a school/college productions.

With good training and experience in dressmaking and theatrical work, you may become wardrobe assistant with a company, or work in a costume museum or National Trust venues.

entry level

1–2

To both enter and train while working in this career, you will need qualifications at Level 1–2. Please refer to explanation on page vii.

Qualifications and courses

- There are no formal entry qualifications for this work. Wardrobe assistants should have skills/experience or a qualification in areas such as dressmaking, hand- and machine-sewing and pattern cutting.
- Many colleges offer part-time courses such as City & Guilds Certificates in fashion, pattern cutting, theatre costume, dressmaking, etc.
- It could be an advantage to have an HND, degree or postgraduate qualification in a relevant subject. Wardrobe skills are taught on most drama school technical theatre courses. The National Council for Drama Training accredits full-time vocational training courses.
- Universities, colleges and art schools offer HNDs and degrees in theatre costume and related areas. You would need 5 GCSEs/S grades (A–C/1–3) for entry.
- Other qualifications available include: City & Guilds Certificates/Diplomas in Design and Craft, BTEC National Certificates/Diplomas in Production Arts, BTEC Certificates/Diplomas in Fashion and Clothing (Levels 1–2), and the BTEC Level 5 Professional Diploma in Costume Management.

Other related opportunities

- Display Designer / Window Dresser p139
- Museum / Art Gallery p325

Advantages/disadvantages

- You will receive low pay for skilled work that has big responsibilities associated with the work.
- Evening work is a regular part of this job.
- Working with a touring company, you will live in rented accommodation for many weeks.
- You will work in an exciting environment – perhaps, with famous dancers, singers and actors.

Earnings guide

- Salaries are initially low; a wardrobe assistant with good sewing skills could expect a starting salary of around £11,000–£14,500 in the theatre, more in film and TV.
- An experienced wardrobe assistant could earn up to £18,000–£21,000.

CRCI:Q

CLCI:G

Further information

www.cityandguilds.com/myperfectjob

CAPITB Trust
80 Richardshaw Lane
Pudsey
Leeds
LS28 6BN
0113 227 3345
www.careers-in-clothing.co.uk

Film and Television Freelance Training (FT2)
4th Floor, Warwick House
9 Warwick Street
London
W1B 5LY
020 7734 5141
www.ft2.org.uk

Museum of Costume
Bath
www.museumofcostume.co.uk

EQ
Suite E229
Dean Clough
Halifax
West Yorkshire
HX3 5AX
01422 381618
www.thinkeq.org.uk

FT2 (Film and Television Freelance Training)
18-20 Southwark Street
London
SE1 1TJ
020 7520 5757
www.ft2.org.uk

Do you want to work with people but not sure how? This broad cluster includes jobs that provide both personal services like hair or beauty and cleaning and cleaning services. It includes jobs such as:

- **Beauty Consultant**
- **Chimney Sweep**
- **Dry Cleaning Assistant**
- **Nail Technician**
- **Wigmaker**

But what's it like working in this area?
Here's Vicky Robinson's story:

Nail Technician

Vicky started out in ladies' fashion but had always been fascinated by having her nails done and so, when she wanted to change careers, she trained to be a Mobile Nail Technician (one who visits clients in their own homes rather than treating them at a salon). She trained with a variety of different companies in and around Liverpool, all using different techniques, and when she heard about the gel technique practised by Alessandro International (recommended by the Federation of Holistic Therapists) she went to them for further training. She found she quickly progressed through the company and, having started as a Trainee Mobile Nail Technician just eight years ago, she is now Alessandro's Chief of Operations and has an NVQ Assessors Award and an NVQ Teaching Award. In the process, the company as a whole has become a recognised NVQ Centre.

THE DOWNSIDE TO THE MOBILE LIFE

'When I was a mobile technician the thing I found the hardest was being able to fit enough appointments into the day. You can start at 8am and not finish until 11pm and find you have spent most of the time on the road.'

WHY NAILS ARE NICE

Vicky loved the fact that so many clients became her friends through their regular appointments. She says seeing them in their own homes made for a much less formal, friendlier atmosphere than seeing them in a salon. For those who are considering a career in this fast-growing industry, Vicky says the future looks bright.

'I think the phenomenal growth we have seen in the industry in the last ten years may slow down but the bubble isn't about to burst yet. The beauty industry as a whole is thriving because people have got more money to spend on leisure. This is still a young industry where you can move up the career ladder very quickly, so now is the right time to join it.'

Vicky's advice to would-be nail technicians is to get as much and as varied experience and training as possible.

'You absolutely have to get professional training because there are things like contra-indications, health and hygiene, and you will need to get insurance and only professional courses are recognised by insurance companies. Ask around, read professional magazines such as Hair and Beauty***, talk to a good nail technician and learn about all the different systems such as acrylic, fibreglass and gel because you need to base yourself in a number of systems. If you want to travel you will need training with acrylic because it is still the most popular system in America while Europe is increasingly turning to gel systems. The more systems you know the more money you can make, and you really can make good money – you just have to invest in the training to get maximum profits.'***

Beauty

What the work involves

Consultant

- You will work in department stores and other public locations promoting and selling beauty products such as make-up and facial and body lotions on behalf of cosmetics companies.
- You will provide product demonstrations to individual customers or groups, including facials, make-up applications and manicures. You will give advice and information on cosmetic products to customers.
- Your work may also involve selling items and taking cash or card payments, managing stock levels and keeping the demonstration area attractive and presentable.

Therapist

- You will provide a range of face and body treatments, depending on your specific skills and training. This could include facials, massages, electrolysis and waxing treatments.
- Your work will involve cleaning and tidying the treatment room before and after each client.
- Beauty therapists provide services in beauty salons, health clubs and hotels. They also work on a self-employed basis in rented treatment rooms or from treatment rooms in their homes.

The type of person suited to this work

Consultant

A sociable and professional approach is important because you will meet and greet many customers. Working on a store counter can be fast-paced so you should be able to stay calm in busy situations. You will use your communication skills to encourage customers to find out more about your products. You should also have a strong interest in helping people make the best of themselves. For applying make-up and other products you will need an eye for design and good practical skills. Numeracy skills will help you manage stock and take payments. You should enjoy the challenge of working towards sales targets.

Therapist

People often choose to have a beauty therapy treatment to help them relax, so you will need a calm, confident approach. An interest in helping people with a range of therapies is essential. You will need good communication skills when advising clients about the treatments they can have. You should be comfortable with having regular hands-on contact with people. A well-presented appearance and a good level of physical fitness is also important. You will work to a high standard of health and hygiene. If you work for yourself, you will need good business skills as this area of work can be competitive. You will also be well organised when booking appointments and keeping records.

Working conditions

Consultant

You could work between 37 and 40 hours a week, with some weekend hours.

Shop environments can get busy and you will spend a lot of time on your feet. Depending on where you work, you may wear a uniform.

Therapist

Beauty therapists work in salons or health clubs. Freelance beauty therapists work from adapted areas of their own homes or hire out treatment rooms. You could also visit clients in their homes.

Beauty therapists usually wear a uniform.

The future outlook

Consultant

Beauty consultancy offers a flexible career to people who want to combine their interest in beauty with working in sales. As well as employment within department stores, there are opportunities to work in airports and hotels. You may choose to promote and sell products from your own home. With experience, you could progress to working as a team manager and then move on to an area management role.

Therapist

With the increase in public awareness of the benefits of holistic therapies, people are increasingly seeking beauty treatments. You could be based in a beauty salon or hotel, working as part of a team. With experience you could progress into a management role. You may choose to set up your own beauty therapy business or, with further experience, move into training and lecturing in beauty therapy. There are opportunities to work on cruise ships and in resorts overseas.

CRCI:RC

CLCI:IK/OFM

Qualifications and courses

- Most beauty therapists enter with relevant qualifications. Courses include NVQ/SVQs, Vocational Training Charitable Trust (VTCT) awards, BTEC Certificate/Diploma in Retail Beauty Consultancy, International Therapy Examination Council (ITEC) awards, and C&G qualifications in a range of therapies and salon management. Universities and higher education colleges offer HNCs/Ds, Foundation degrees and degrees in beauty therapy, cosmetic science and beauty combined with hospitality or travel and tourism.

Consultant

- Beauty consultants may have previous experience in retail or sales.
- The VTCT offers Level 2 Certificates in Cosmetic Make-up and Beauty Consultancy, and NVQ/SVQs are available in Retail Operations, Customer Services, and Beauty Therapy (Make-Up). These qualifications may be taken prior to employment as a beauty consultant or whilst working.
- The Hairdressing and Beauty Industry Authority (HABIA) validate various beauty, hairdressing and barbering courses.

Therapist

- Trainee beauty therapists work towards NVQs/SVQs at Levels 2 and 3. Candidates are usually required to have some GCSEs/S grades (A–C/1–3). Level 3 is the usual qualification for a professional beauty therapist.

entry level

To both enter and train while working in this career, you will need qualifications at Level 1–3. Please refer to explanation on page vii.

- Apprenticeships/Skillseekers are available for candidates aged 16–24.
- Beauty therapists often extend their knowledge into holistic or alternative treatments such as massage and aromatherapy. The International Federation of Professional Aromatherapists (IFPA) accredit courses at private schools and colleges in the UK.

Other related opportunities

- Hairdresser / Barber p424
- Make-up Artist p399
- Nail Technician p426

Advantages/disadvantages

Consultant

- This type of work is often available on a part-time or flexible basis which may suit people with other commitments.

Therapist

- Therapists working in health and beauty companies or clubs may be provided with free club membership and reduced cost treatments. If based in a hotel, you could get free accommodation (but with a reduction in pay) as well as meals on and off duty.

Earnings guide

Consultant

- Starting salaries range from £11,000 to £13,000.
- With experience you could earn £19,000.
- At senior/management levels you could earn £20,000–£30,000.
- There are usually opportunities to earn extra income through sales of beauty products.

Therapist

- Once qualified as a beauty therapist you could earn around £10,000 per year.
- With experience you could earn up to £15,000.
- At senior/management levels you could earn £25,000+.

Further information

Hairdressing And Beauty Industry Authority
Oxford House
Sixth Avenue, Sky Business Park
Robin Hood Airport
Doncaster
DN9 3GG
08452 306080
www.habia.org.uk

Guild of Professional Beauty Therapists
Guild House
320 Burton Road
Derby
DE23 6AF
0870 000 4242
www.beautyguild.com

Vocational Training Charitable Trust
Third Floor
Eastleigh House
Upper Market Street
Eastleigh
SO50 9FD
02380 684 500
www.vtct.org.uk

British Association of Beauty Therapy and Cosmetology Ltd
Ambrose House
Meteor Court
Barnett Way
GL4 3GG
0845 065 9000
www.babtac.com

www.cityandguilds.com/myperfectjob

Body Artist / Tattooist

What the work involves

- You will produce tattoos and other forms of body art for customers using specialist equipment. You may offer specific tattoo styles or create new designs for customers.
- You will draw the design onto the skin and use specialist equipment to tattoo the design on with inks.
- You must prepare and maintain your equipment to a high standard of hygiene and safety and you will also clean and tidy the treatment area between customers.
- You may offer additional body modification services such as piercing.

entry level

To both enter and train while working in this career, you will need qualifications at Level 1. Please refer to explanation on page vii.

The type of person suited to this work

As a professional body artist/tattooist you must work to a high standard of health and safety at all times. You will need excellent manual handling skills when undertaking body art. Creating tattoos and preparing your equipment can be a slow process so you will need to be patient. A confident but careful attitude is essential.

You will have a strong creative flair with knowledge of a wide range of tattoo designs. Drawing skills are useful when putting together new tattoo designs for customers. You will use your communication skills to meet customers and discuss the type of tattoo or body art they want.

Working conditions

Tattooists usually work in studios or shops with a waiting area and treatment room.

This type of work demands a high level of concentration and good visual and manual skills. You may be on your feet for long periods which can be physically demanding.

Whilst undertaking body art work you will wear latex gloves and other protective clothing.

The future outlook

Tattooing/body art has grown in popularity both as a form of accessory and as a means of self-expression. With tattooists based throughout the country, this is a very competitive area.

With experience you could set up your own studio, providing tattoo services and selling body art products. Body artists with a lot of experience also work as guest artists in body art studios. There are opportunities to work abroad.

Qualifications and courses

- There are no formal entry requirements for this job. Entrants should be 18 or over, and qualifications in art or related areas may be useful.
- Training is usually done through an apprenticeship with a registered tattooist. It can be difficult to find apprenticeships. A good portfolio of artwork will help demonstrate your commitment to working in this area. The apprenticeship lasts 2 to 3 years.
- In order to work legally as a tattooist, you need to be registered with the Environmental Health Department.
- The Vocational Training Charitable Trust (VTCT) Certificate and Diploma in Body Piercing and Body Art are offered by some private colleges and training centres. Trainees can obtain these qualifications through part-time study and workplace assessment.
- VTCT also offers a Level 2 Certificate in Ear Piercing, if you wish to specialise in this area.

CRCI:R

CLCI:IZ

Other related opportunities

- Designer p136

Advantages/disadvantages

- This type of work can provide the chance to work creatively by designing unique body art.
- Because of the nature of the work, there is no room for error!
- Due to the limited number of vacancies, you may have to move locations to gain experience.

Earnings guide

- Starting salaries for trainees are around £11,000 per year.
- With experience you could earn up to £15,000.
- At senior levels you could earn £20,000–£32,000.
- It can be difficult to find a training place and some people pay to learn through an experienced tattooist.

Further information

www.cityandguilds.com/myperfectjob

Tattoo Club of Great Britain (incorporating the British Tattoo History Museum)
389 Cowley Road
Oxford
OX4 2BS
01865 716877
www.tattoo.co.uk

Car Valet

What the work involves

- You will clean and finish car exteriors and interiors using specialist equipment.
- You may clean every part of a vehicle or the exterior only. You may also clean the engine and help prepare cars for bodywork repairs.
- You will clear the interior of rubbish and polish the surfaces and windows. You will also clean the seats. For exteriors you will clean the bodywork and wheels.
- Car valets work for vehicle service centres, new and used car centres, crash repair centres and valeting companies.

entry level

To both enter and train while working in this career, you will need qualifications at Level 1. Please refer to explanation on page vii.

The type of person suited to this work

Car valets must be physically fit with good manual skills. Stamina is also helpful for a role in which individual valeting jobs can take from 1 to 4 hours. You should be able to use different types of cleaning equipment and apply your knowledge of health and safety to your work.

As you will be providing a service to customers, you should be able to work to a consistently high standard. You will be reliable and a good team player. You will also need to be a quick but thorough worker with an eye for detail. As with all cleaning and maintenance jobs, you should be able to cope with messy or dirty working conditions.

Working conditions

The work is very hands on and can be tiring because it involves reaching into and across vehicles. Car valets also spend a lot of time on their feet.

You may be based outside, cleaning cars on a forecourt, sometimes in poor weather conditions.

This job requires regular contact with cleaning chemicals, so it may not suit people with allergies or skin conditions.

The future outlook

Car valeting is a key part of the sales and services end of the motor vehicle industry. You could work for a large vehicle repair company or service centre as part of a valeting team.

You may choose to set up your own valeting company. Some professional car valets offer a mobile service, going out to visit customers at their premises. With experience and further training, you could progress into a technical or sales role.

Qualifications and courses

- No formal qualifications are required for entry to this job. Qualifications in practical or technical subjects, or previous experience in the motor trade or in cleaning work, can be an advantage.
- Entrants are usually aged 17, as a full driving licence is almost always required.
- Training is done on the job. In addition to practical training, car valets may be sent on short courses run by the manufacturers of cleaning products. The British Institute of Cleaning Science offers a Car Valeting Certificate.
- NVQs/SVQs Level 1 in Vehicle Maintenance and related areas include modules on valeting.

Other related opportunities

- Cleaner p418

Advantages/disadvantages

- Car valeting jobs may include some regular travel, either when providing services to customers on their premises, or when returning vehicles to customers.
- This type of job offers the chance to work in close contact with a range of cars and other vehicles.

Earnings guide

- Starting salaries begin at £10,000 per year.
- With experience you could earn £13,000+.
- Working overtime could possibly increase your salary to around £17,000.

Further information

British Institute of Cleaning Science
9 Premier Court
Boarden Close
Northampton
NN3 6LF
01604 678710
www.bics.org.uk

Automotive Skills
93 Newman Street
London
W1T 3DT
020 7436 6373
www.automotiveskills.org.uk

www.cityandguilds.com/myperfectjob

Caretaker

What the work involves

- Caretakers manage the security, cleaning and general maintenance of sites such as schools, colleges and office blocks.
- In some jobs, you would combine caretaking with other roles such as cleaner, gardener, porter or security attendant.
- You will be responsible for opening and locking the premises and checking building security. You will repair broken equipment and reorder supplies.
- Your work may also involve some gardening. You may also clean parts of the site or manage the work of the site cleaners.

entry level

To both enter and train while working in this career, you will need qualifications at Level 1. Please refer to explanation on page vii.

The type of person suited to this work

Caretakers need good communication skills, because they have a lot of contact with the people based on their premises. You may be responsible for the security of an entire site and all its contents, so it's important to have a mature, honest attitude. The ability to work independently is essential, for example when repairing broken equipment or dealing with emergencies. You should also be able to work as part of a team.

Physical fitness is essential for lifting and moving equipment, gardening work and other activities. You will work to a high standard of health and safety at all times.

Working conditions

Whilst some caretakers work full time, many work on a split-shift basis with some evening and weekend work.

Caretaking work is physically demanding. Some of your work will be based outside using ladders and other tools.

Caretakers work with cleaning chemicals and wear protective clothing such as gloves and overalls. The job may not suit people with allergies or skin conditions.

The future outlook

Caretaking is an essential part of premises management. Being the only person on a whole site early in the morning with responsibility for security can be challenging.

Many locations, such as schools, only employ one caretaker, so you may need to change employers and locations to progress. Larger employers may employ a small team of caretakers. With experience you could work up to senior caretaker level.

Qualifications and courses

- No formal qualifications are required for entry to this job. Some GCSEs/S grades (A–E/1–5), particularly English, maths and practical subjects, may be an advantage. However, hands-on skills and experience in basic DIY, carpentry, painting and decorating or glazing are more important.
- Experience in maintenance or security work is useful, as is a driving licence. Within some areas, for example schools and colleges, you will need to pass a police check.
- Maturity is an advantage and employers often prefer older applicants with relevant experience.
- Caretakers are trained on the job. It may be possible for entrants to work towards an NVQ/SVQ Level 3 in Property and Caretaking Supervision. Caretakers can also work towards the Chartered Institute of Housing's Level 3 Certificate in Housing, specialist pathway in Caretaking and Concierge Services. This can be achieved in 1 year through part-time study, distance learning, or in-house training with an employer.

CRCI:RB

CLCI:IJ

Other related opportunities

- Cleaner p418
- Hotel Porter p96
- Labourer p60
- Security p518

Advantages/disadvantages

- As the premises keyholder, you may be on call for emergencies.
- This job can be sociable and caretakers often build up a good working relationship with the people based on their premises.
- It is possible to do this kind of work on a part-time basis.

Earnings guide

- Starting salaries range from £11,000 to £12,000 per year.
- With experience it is possible to earn £22,000+.
- You could earn a higher salary as a senior or mobile caretaker.
- In some work, for example education, caretakers are offered on-site subsidised housing as part of their contract.

Further information

www.cityandguilds.com/myperfectjob

Chartered Institute of Housing
Octavia House
Westwood Way
Coventry
CV4 8JP
024 7685 1700
www.cih.org

Chartered Institute of Housing – Scotland
6 Palmerston Place
Edinburgh
EH12 5AA
0131 225 4544
www.cih.org/home_scotland

The Caretakers' website
www.thecaretakers.net

Chimney Sweep

What the work involves

- You will help prevent chimney fires and dangerous fuel emissions by inspecting and cleaning chimney and flue systems, heating appliances and vents.
- Your work will involve using brush and vacuum equipment to clear chimneys and vents of blockages.
- You will provide information and advice to customers on the repair and maintenance of their chimneys.
- Chimney sweeps visit customers in their homes and undertake inspections and cleaning on-site.

The type of person suited to this work

Chimney sweeps combine their professional knowledge with practical skills to protect public safety. You will need a good knowledge of different types of chimney and flue systems. Operating brush and vacuum chimney cleaning equipment requires good manual skills.

You will visit customers in their homes, so you should have a friendly, professional attitude. Your communication skills will help you to provide advice on correctly maintaining chimney systems. In a job that involves travelling and working alone, a good level of physical fitness is essential.

Working conditions

When clearing chimneys, you will wear protective clothing, such as overalls, gloves, helmet, eye guard and respiratory protection.

Travel to different locations is a regular part of the work, so holding a driving licence is essential.

You may work unsocial hours, at weekends or evenings, to suit customers.

This job can involve working in dusty environments and may not suit people with allergies or skin conditions.

The future outlook

Chimney sweeping is a specialist but essential service. After gaining the relevant experience and professional qualifications, you could set up your own business, providing services within your local area. Most chimney sweeps build up a network of loyal and regular customers. You could also offer additional roofing or ventilation services. There may be opportunities to work with another professional or to join a small specialist company.

entry level

To both enter and train while working in this career, you will need qualifications at Level 1. Please refer to explanation on page vii.

Qualifications and courses

- There are no formal entry requirements, but basic qualifications in English and maths are useful. Previous experience of practical/manual work is an advantage. You would normally be trained on the job by an experienced chimney sweep.
- Trainee chimney sweeps can work towards membership of the National Association of Chimney Sweeps (NACS). NACS provides an induction course accredited by CITB and City & Guilds, covering basic chimney sweeping techniques and health and safety. On completion of the training, sweeps become probationary members of NACS until they have gained sufficient experience and on-site training to work as professional sweeps.
- NACS also provides an NVQ Level 2 in Chimney Engineering based on assessments in the workplace and at the NACS centre.
- The other professional body for chimney sweeps is the Guild of Master Sweeps. To become a member, you must hold a City & Guilds 7641 qualification in Chimney Cleaning and successfully complete the Guild entrance exam.
- NACS also provides short courses in particular areas of the work. To be qualified to carry out inspections and work on gas appliances you need to gain a certificate of competence through the Accredited Certification Scheme (ACS), leading to registration with CORGI (Council of Registered Gas Engineers).
- A driving licence is required for driving and transporting equipment to customers' homes.

Other related opportunities

- Heating and Ventilating Engineer p56
- Roofer p67

Advantages/disadvantages

- Whilst the job involves meeting different people, the actual work is usually undertaken alone.
- Most chimney sweeps work on a self-employed basis, which can lead to some job insecurity, particularly at the start of their careers.

Earnings guide

- Most chimney sweeps are self-employed and are paid on a job-by-job basis.
- If working full time you could expect to earn between £15,000 and £24,000 per year.

Further information

Asset Skills (Sector Skills Council in property services, housing, cleaning services and facilities management)
2 The Courtyard
48 New North Road
Exeter
Devon
EX4 4EP
01392 423399
www.assetskills.org

National Association of Chimney Sweeps
Unit 15, Emerald Way
Stone Business Park
Stone
Staffordshire
ST15 0SR
01785 811732
www.chimneyworks.co.uk

Guild of Master Sweeps
www.guild-of-master-sweeps.co.uk

www.cityandguilds.com/myperfectjob

Cleaner

What the work involves

Carpet/upholstery

- You will use specialist equipment to clean carpets, curtains and furniture in private homes, offices and other locations.
- You may specialise in cleaning specific types of carpets or offer additional carpet and upholstery repair services.

Domestic

- You will clean, dust and tidy the floors and surfaces of private homes.
- To undertake your job you will work with a vacuum cleaner, mop and other equipment.

Industrial

- You will use specialist equipment to clean and clear the surfaces and interiors of industrial systems in factories and other sites.
- Industrial cleaners usually work in a team for cleaning companies that provide services for businesses such as chemical manufacturers and engineering companies.

Street

- Working as part of a team you will maintain the clean appearance of streets, car parks and other large areas. This will involve sweeping away rubbish and emptying council bins.
- Street cleaners work as part of street-cleansing teams employed by local councils or for the companies that provide these services to councils.

Window

- You will clean the exterior windows of private homes, offices, shops and other buildings.
- You will use a ladder and other equipment to reach and clean windows.

Hospital

- Your job will be to make sure all areas of the hospital are kept clean, free of germs and safe for patients, staff and visitors.
- You will use special cleaning equipment and chemicals and you may work in theatres and wards.

The type of person suited to this work

Cleaners provide an important public service, so you should enjoy working to a high standard. You will also need a down-to-earth, practical attitude to your work. You should be able to cope with dirty or messy conditions. Practical skills are very important when using your hands to clean or to operate cleaning equipment. A good knowledge of health and safety is essential. If you are self-employed, you will need good financial management skills.

You should enjoy meeting a wide range of people and providing a public service. You will also be a good team player. A well-motivated, reliable and highly trustworthy approach is essential.

Working conditions

Cleaning is physically demanding work which involves carrying equipment and working on your feet.

Because the job often involves the use of specialist cleaning chemicals it may not suit people with skin conditions or allergies.

You will have to deal with messy or dirty conditions on a regular basis.

Window
As a window cleaner, you will need a head for heights.

Hospital
You might have to clean theatres and wards. Some of this can be distressing. Your work will fit around the needs of the nurses and doctors, and could include speaking to patients and their families.

The future outlook

Cleaning is a growing industry and there is currently a shortage of skilled cleaners in a range of areas. There are opportunities to work on a temporary basis, to suit other commitments. Increasingly, there are routes to develop a career as a professional cleaner on a permanent basis. You could work for a large cleaning company as an industrial cleaner, carpet cleaner or domestic cleaner. Or you could choose to set up your own domestic or window-cleaning business.

There has been interest in keeping hospitals clean due to the recent problems with MRSA. The role that cleaners and all hospital staff play in reducing this are now recognised and additional training is being offered to hospital cleaners.

Qualifications and courses

- No formal qualifications are required for these jobs although basic numeracy is useful for measuring cleaning fluids.
- Certain types of cleaning may have specific practical requirements, for example the ability to work at heights, physical fitness and (usually) a driving licence for window cleaners.
- Cleaners are trained on the job, and usually receive training from their employer in areas such as health and safety and use of equipment.
- Cleaners can work towards NVQ/SVQ Levels 1 and 2 in Cleaning and Support Services. Specialist options are available at Level 2 in Cleaning Building Interiors, Cleaning Carpets and Soft Furnishings, Cleaning Food Premises and Cleaning Windows, Glass and Facade Surfaces. City & Guilds offer Level 2 and 3 awards in Cleaning Science and Supervision. Cleaners can also work towards the British Institute of Cleaning Science (BICS) Cleaning Operators Proficiency Certificate and other specialist certified courses.

entry level

To both enter and train while working in this career, you will need qualifications at Level 1. Please refer to explanation on page vii.

- Apprenticeships/Skillseekers may be available for people aged 16–24.

Other related opportunities

- Caretaker p416
- Home Care Assistant p534
- Pest Control Technician p427
- Recycling Operative p428

Advantages/disadvantages

- This type of work is often available on a shift basis, which may suit people with other commitments.
- The work can be physically tiring, with the risk of injury from the equipment or environment you are in contact with. However, most employers provide health and safety training.
- You may have to work in poor weather conditions, if based outdoors, for example as a window or street cleaner.

Earnings guide

- Salaries vary according to the type of work you do.

Carpet/upholstery
- With experience and if employed by a large company, you could earn £16,000–£20,000 per year.

Domestic
- Domestic cleaners are often employed on an hourly basis, and may work for a number of employers. Working full time you could get £11,000–£12,500.

Industrial
- Salaries vary starting at £11,000. With experience and supervisory responsibilities, you could earn up to £16,000.

Street
- Salaries vary from £11,000 to £12,500. With experience, this can increase to £16,000.

Window
- Self-employed window cleaners can earn £11,000–£16,000.

Hospital
- Average salaries for hospital cleaners are between £11,000 and £14,000+.

Further information

Asset Skills (Sector Skills Council in property services, housing, cleaning services and facilities management)
2 The Courtyard
48 New North Road
Exeter
Devon
EX4 4EP
01392 423399
www.assetskills.org

British Institute of Cleaning Science
9 Premier Court
Boarden Close
Northampton
NN3 6LF
01604 678710
www.bics.org.uk

British Cleaning Council
PO Box 1328
Kidderminster
DY11 5ZJ
01562 851129
www.britishcleaningcouncil.org

CARPET/UPHOLSTERY

National Carpet Cleaners Association
62c London Road
Oadby
Leicester
LE2 5DH
0116 271 9550
www.ncca.co.uk

WINDOW

Federation for Window Cleaners
Summerfield House
Harrogate Road
Stockport
Cheshire
SK5 6HQ
0161 432 8754
www.nfmwgc.com

www.cityandguilds.com/myperfectjob

Crematorium Technician

What the work involves

- You will assist with the running of the crematorium and cemetery premises.
- Your work will involve operating cremation equipment to a high standard of health and safety. You will ensure that the cremated remains are stored and disposed of correctly.
- You will help manage the chapel and cemetery and attend cremation ceremonies.
- Crematorium technicians often combine their work with assisting with cemetery duties, such as excavating graves and grounds maintenance. However, grave digging work is mostly undertaken by contractors working for local authorities.

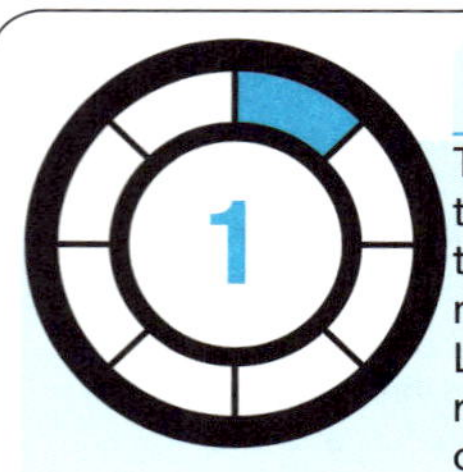

entry level

To both enter and train while working in this career, you will need qualifications at Level 1. Please refer to explanation on page vii.

The type of person suited to this work

Meeting and working with bereaved people requires a mature, sympathetic attitude. You will use your communication skills to liaise with people in the process of cremation ceremonies. A good level of physical fitness is helpful in a role that covers a wide range of activities. You should also have good manual handling skills to operate cremation equipment.

It's important that cremations are undertaken to a high standard of health and safety, so you should be able to follow strict working guidelines. Office and ICT skills can be helpful in this job. The ability to work as part of a team is also useful.

Working conditions

This can be a tiring job due to the range of activities involved and the physical requirements of operating cremation machinery.

Crematorium technicians need good practical handling skills to operate cremation equipment correctly.

You will normally work 37–40 hours a week, with some overtime.

The future outlook

Due to changing public attitudes, the number of cremations is increasing, as is the demand for skilled professionals.

Crematorium technicians are usually employed by local councils. Most are trained by more experienced colleagues whilst working. With experience, you could progress to working as a senior crematorium technician and manage a team of technicians.

Qualifications and courses

- There are no formal entry requirements for this type of work, and training is done on the job.
- Trainees follow the Crematorium Technicians' Training Scheme (CTTS) provided by the Institute of Cemetery and Crematorium Management (ICCM). The scheme consists of a BTEC Intermediate Certificate and a BTEC Advanced Certificate. Employees may also work towards NVQ/SVQ Level 2 in Amenity Horticulture (Cemeteries and Graveyards).
- Another work-based training route is provided by the Federation of British Cremation Authority's (FBCA) TEST scheme.
- Experienced crematorium technicians can progress to management roles. The ICCM Diploma in Cemetery and Crematorium Management can be studied by correspondence. The ICCM also operates a Continuing Professional Development scheme for crematorium staff at all levels.
- A driving licence is useful.

CRCI:RA | CLCI:IP

Other related opportunities

- Embalmer p422
- Funeral Work p423

Advantages/disadvantages

- This role provides the opportunity to provide support to people at an important and challenging time.
- The nature of the job means this work will be distressing at times.

Earnings guide

- Starting salaries are around £12,000 per year.
- With experience you could earn £16,500.
- At senior/management level you could earn £18,000+.

Further information

www.cityandguilds.com/myperfectjob

British Institute of Embalmers
21c Station Road
Knowle
Solihull
B93 0HL
01564 778991
www.bioe.co.uk

Institute of Cemetery & Crematorium Management
City of London Cemetery
Aldersbrook Road
London
E12 5DQ
020 8989 4661
www.iccm-uk.com

Dry Cleaning / Laundry

What the work involves

Assistant

- You will greet and serve customers. You will also take and return customers' dry cleaning and laundry orders, taking cash and keeping records.
- You will help to keep the shop premises clean and tidy.
- Your work will involve operating machinery, putting clothes through laundry and dry-cleaning processes, and folding and preparing the clothes and other items for collection.

Manager

- You will take customer orders and deal with queries. You will manage budgets, staff rotas and stock levels for your shop or premises.
- Your work could involve promoting your shop or business to potential customers.
- You will also be involved in maintaining the security and health and safety of the premises and buildings. You will manage the dry cleaning and laundry machinery.

The type of person suited to this work

Whether you will be working with customers face to face or taking care of their laundry behind the scenes, customer care and communication skills are essential. You will need a good knowledge of how to clean and process different types of materials as well as a good level of physical fitness.

To help you operate domestic and industrial cleaning machinery you will require manual handling skills and a thorough knowledge of health and safety.

You will be handling cash and managing budgets so you will need good money management skills and a well-organised approach to your work. You should also be reliable and self-motivated.

Working conditions

You may have to wear a uniform whilst working.

It is likely that you will have to work some weekend or evening hours.

This type of work can be physically demanding. In some jobs you will have close contact with potentially hazardous chemicals and cleaning processes, which may be unsuitable for people with allergies or skin conditions.

The future outlook

There is a growing demand for efficient, reliable laundry and dry-cleaning services. As an assistant, you could move into supervisory or management roles by gaining further experience and qualifications. You could also progress to running your own laundry or dry-cleaning business.

By choosing to be trained in, and then offering, other services such as repairs, alterations and ironing you would increase your career potential.

As a manager in a larger company, you could move into area management.

entry level

1

To both enter and train while working in this career, you will need qualifications at Level 1. Please refer to explanation on page vii.

Qualifications and courses

Assistant

- There are no formal minimum qualifications for this type of work. Communication and numeracy skills are useful. Training normally takes place on the job.
- You could gain Practical Laundry Certificates through the Guild of Cleaners and Launderers. You could also work towards examinations through the Guild's Qualification Star Scheme. This covers areas such as retail sales, stain removal and dry cleaning practice. It is also possible to work towards NVQs/SVQs in Laundry (Finishing) Level 1, Laundry (Washing) Level 1, Dry Cleaning Levels 1 and 2 and Laundry and Textile Cleaning Levels 1 and 2.
- If aged 16–24, you could undertake an Apprenticeship/Skillseekers opportunity.

Manager

- A good level of general education is usually required. With experience, laundry assistants can become supervisors and managers.
- It can be helpful to have gained Practical Laundry Certificates through the Guild of Cleaners and Launderers. NVQ/SVQ Level 2 in Team Leading and Level 3 and 4 in Management may be useful.
- You could go on to achieve a supervisory certificate and intermediate qualifications through the Guild of Cleaners and Launderers.
- Additional training courses are available through organisations such as the SATRA Technology Centre and the Textile Services Association.

Other related opportunities

- Cleaner p418

Advantages/disadvantages

- This type of work is often available part time which may suit people with other commitments.
- Some employers pay overtime for bank holiday and holiday period working.
- For staff based in high-street outlets or community laundrettes this can be a sociable role.

Earnings guide

- Earnings vary widely throughout the industry and will depend on the location and size of your employer.

Assistant

- As a dry cleaning assistant you could expect a salary of around £11,000 per year.

Manager

- Salaries range between £15,500 and £17,000.
- Senior managers in larger companies can receive £25,000+.

Further information

Textile Services Association
7 Churchill Court
58 Station Road
North Harrow
Middlesex
HA2 7SA
020 8863 7755
www.tsa-uk.org

Guild of Cleaners and Launderers
1 Wellfield Road
Offerton
Stockport
Cheshire
SK2 6AS
0845 600 1838
www.gcl.org.uk

SATRA Technology Centre
SATRA House
Rockingham Road
Kettering
Northamptonshire
NN16 9JH
01536 410000
www.satra.co.uk

www.cityandguilds.com/myperfectjob

Embalmer

What the work involves

- You will prepare the bodies of deceased people for funerals and for viewing by their relatives. Embalming also helps to reduce the spread of infection.
- You will use specialist equipment to remove all blood and gases from the deceased person's body and replace these with disinfecting fluid.
- Your work will involve preparing and cleaning the embalming equipment and treatment area.
- Embalmers work in operating rooms within funeral parlours.

entry level

To both enter and train while working in this career, you will need qualifications at Level 1. Please refer to explanation on page vii.

The type of person suited to this work

Because of the nature of this job, you must be able to cope with working with the bodies of deceased people. A respectful approach to your work is essential. You may have to deal with distressing sights so a mature, detached and down-to-earth attitude is very important.

You should be able to work to a high standard of health and hygiene. You will need good manual handling skills for undertaking embalming work because you will be using a range of equipment.

Embalming work involves presenting a deceased person in the most positive way for grieving relatives. A creative flair and attention to detail will help you to achieve this.

Working conditions

Embalmers work in operating rooms within funeral parlours. These are maintained to a very high standard of hygiene and kept at a low temperature.

Whilst embalming you will wear protective clothing such as latex gloves. The regular contact with chemicals means that this job may not suit people with skin conditions or allergies.

Embalming is physically demanding work and you should expect to work irregular hours and be on call.

The future outlook

Whilst embalming may be requested by relatives, it is often an integral part of the funeral care process. Funeral directors may also undertake embalming as part of their work. You could gain employment with a funeral care company or you may choose to work on a self-employed basis, providing services for a number of funeral companies.

There are opportunities to work abroad. With extensive experience, you could go into teaching or training.

There are around 1300 qualified embalmers in the UK, but the industry has a slow turnover of staff and getting in may be difficult.

Qualifications and courses

- There are no formal entry requirements for working as an embalmer, but GCSEs/S grades including English, maths, chemistry, biology and religious studies may be useful.
- Training is mainly on the job, with part-time tuition from a registered tutor at weekends or evenings, or through distance learning. Most embalmers work for qualifications awarded by the International Examinations Board of Embalmers (IEBE).
- The BIE training is modular, and trainees must pass the foundation module and test before proceeding with the rest of the training. Once you have passed the foundation module, you can register with the BIE as a student member.
- The main BIE training involves modules in anatomy, physiology, bacteriology and practical embalming, including examinations and practical work. Once you have passed these you can apply for full membership of the BIE.
- Some embalmers train to work in specialist areas, such as with disaster teams, embalming the bodies of victims.

CRCI:RA | CLCI:IP

Other related opportunities

- Crematorium Technician p420
- Funeral Work p423

Advantages/disadvantages

- There are opportunities for self-employment, working for a number of employers at the same time.
- There are also opportunities to work overseas.
- This can be distressing work, so you will need to be able to stay detached and professional.

Earnings guide

- Starting salaries begin at around £10,500 per year.
- With experience you could earn £15,000.
- At senior levels it is possible to earn £20,000+.

Further information

www.cityandguilds.com/myperfectjob

British Institute of Embalmers
21c Station Road
Knowle
Solihull
B93 0HL
01564 778991
www.bioe.co.uk

Funeral Work

What the work involves

- You will coordinate funeral and cremation arrangements. Much of your work will be focused on providing practical support to friends and relatives of the deceased person.
- By providing practical arrangements for the funeral you will assist in matters such as organising the funeral location. You will also attend at the funeral.
- Some funeral directors assist with preparing the deceased person's body for viewing by relatives or for the funeral itself. You might also undertake embalming work.

entry level

To both enter and train while working in this career, you will need qualifications at Level 1. Please refer to explanation on page vii.

The type of person suited to this work

Funeral directors need a flexible approach because of the varied activities that the job involves. A sensitive and mature attitude is essential.

You will need excellent communication skills for providing advice and support to bereaved relatives. Your management skills will help you to manage the work of funeral staff. You will need to be able to work to a high standard of health and safety at all times.

For liaising with local authorities and completing paperwork you will need a good knowledge of the relevant legal issues, and to be able to manage a business you will need good office and budgetary skills. A good knowledge of different cultures and religions is helpful.

Working conditions

Funeral directors work in funeral homes or centres based within high-street outlets or other areas.

As this job involves a wide range of activities it can be physically demanding.

You may work on call at weekends and in the evenings. You may also be required to work extra hours during busy times.

Funeral directors must dress smartly and usually wear suits.

The future outlook

Most people start a career in this area by gaining experience as a funeral operative or assistant. They learn the varied aspects of the job from more experienced colleagues and work towards professional qualifications.

You could work for one of the large funeral services companies or for a smaller company. With experience, you could work as a funeral director in the UK or abroad. With additional experience, you could set up your own funeral services company.

Qualifications and courses

- There are no minimum academic qualifications to work as a funeral director. You will normally start as funeral operative or assistant and learn whilst working. Your choice of qualifications and training will usually depend on the company you work for. For funeral operatives/assistants with driving duties, a driving licence is essential.
- BTEC and SQA offer vocational qualifications for people working as funeral operatives/assistants and directors. The Certificate in Funeral Services is for operatives/assistants, and the Advanced Diploma in Funeral Directing is for funeral directors.
- NVQs/SVQs are available in Funeral Services at Levels 2 and 3, and there is a Level 4 qualification in Funeral Services Management.
- Another route is to gain the National Association of Funeral Directors' (NAFD) Foundation Certificate in Funeral Directing. This is an introductory course which candidates must have completed before they can start the NAFD Diploma in Funeral Directing (DipFD). In order to work towards this professional qualification you must have a minimum of 2 years' employment in funeral services. This includes experience of personally arranging at least 25 funerals.
- Once working in funeral services you could choose to go on to gain the NAFD and Institute of Leadership and Management's Diploma in Funeral Service Management, or the Higher Certificate in Funeral Service Management of the British Institute of Funeral Directors (BIFD). To be eligible to do these you must have the NAFD Diploma in Funeral Directing or be a full member of the BIFD.

CRCI:RA | CLCI:IP

Other related opportunities

- Crematorium Technician p420
- Embalmer p422

Advantages/disadvantages

- Depending on the size of funeral company you work for, you may be on call on a regular basis, which can affect your personal life.
- Providing a professional sympathetic service to people experiencing a very difficult time can be rewarding.

Earnings guide

- Starting salaries are around £12,000 per year.
- With experience you could earn £15,000–£23,000.
- At senior/management level you could earn £32,000+.
- Additional benefits may include a car.

Further information

National Association of Funeral Directors
618 Warwick Road
Solihull
B91 1AA
0845 230 1343
www.nafd.org.uk

British Institute of Funeral Directors
41 Bridge Street
Tranent
East Lothian
EH33 1AH
0800 032 2733
www.bifd.org.uk

www.cityandguilds.com/myperfectjob

Hairdresser / Barber

What the work involves

- You will shampoo, cut and style clients' hair to a range of modern or classic looks. You may also provide dry or wet shaves and haircuts to male clients.
- You will discuss hair treatments with clients and may carry out colouring, tinting, perming and fixing hair extensions. You will also give advice on general haircare and hair products.
- At senior levels, you may provide training to junior hairdressers.
- Most hairdressers/barbers are based in salons in high streets and other areas. Some work as mobile hairdressers, providing services to clients in their own homes.

entry level

To both enter and train while working in this career, you will need qualifications at Level 1. Please refer to explanation on page vii.

The type of person suited to this work

Cutting and styling hair involves close personal contact with clients so hairdressers need to be able to make people feel relaxed. Good communication skills and a friendly manner are essential. You should also have an interest in fashion, a creative flair and an eye for detail. You will need manual dexterity when using specialist chemicals and equipment required to style, perm and colour customers' hair.

In smaller salons you may work on the reception desk booking appointments and taking cash, so you will have to be efficient, confident and numerate.

Some salons require staff to be able to offer a wider choice of services, such as nail and beauty treatments.

Working conditions

Most of your work will be indoors in salons or clients' homes.

If you work within a large, modern salon in a large town or city, the environment may be excellent. In a smaller salon, facilities and equipment may not be so up to date.

Hairdressing involves standing and bending over customers for long periods of the day, so you will need to be physically fit.

The future outlook

The demand for high quality hairdressing/barbering services is growing, with most areas likely to have a salon. You could work in a salon or set up your own business. If working as a mobile hairdresser, you could provide services to people in hospitals, care homes or prisons as well as private clients.

There are opportunities to work on cruise ships. With further beauty therapy training you could work in film, television or the theatre.

Qualifications and courses

- There are no minimum entry requirements for this job. Some people start as unqualified assistants/trainees and progress with experience.
- Hairdressing can be studied full time at college by taking an NVQ/SVQ (Levels 1–3 in hairdressing, Levels 2 and 3 in barbering). Some NVQs combine hairdressing with beauty therapy, and it is possible to specialise in ladies' or gentlemen's hairdressing.
- The Freelance Hair and Beauty Federation (FHBF) runs courses for hairdressers on planning, setting up and managing their business, and ongoing continuing personal development courses.
- NVQ/SVQs validated by the Hairdressing and Beauty Industry Authority (HABIA) can be taken part time whilst working in a hairdressing salon or barber's, or you can undertake an Apprenticeship/Skillseekers if aged 16–24.
- Qualified hairdressers can take more specialised courses through part-time study, for example City & Guilds certificates, NVQ units, VTCT/ITEC beauty therapy qualifications. It is possible to take an NVQ/SVQ Level 4 or HNC in Salon Management.
- A few Foundation degrees in Hairdressing and Salon Management are also available.

CRCI:RC

CLCI:IL

Other related opportunities

- Beauty p412
- Image Consultant p425
- Make-up Artist p399
- Nail Technician p426
- Wigmaker p431

Advantages/disadvantages

- Hairdressers/barbers have regular contact with beauty products and chemicals, which means that this type of work may not suit people with skin conditions or allergies.
- The demand for qualified and experienced hairdressers is increasing.

Earnings guide

- As a trainee at entry level you could earn the national minimum wage about £8,000–£9,000 per year at the age of 18.
- With experience and full training you could earn £12,000–£16,000.
- Top national hairdressers earn £20,000–£30,000+.
- Tips from customers will increase salaries at all levels.

Further information

www.cityandguilds.com/myperfectjob

Hairdressing And Beauty Industry Authority
Oxford House
Sixth Avenue, Sky Business Park
Robin Hood Airport
Doncaster DN9 3GG
08452 306080
www.habia.org.uk

Image Consultant

What the work involves

- You will advise people on how to make the most of their appearance using clothes, accessories and make-up. You will help them improve their confidence, body language and communication skills.
- You will undertake detailed consultations with clients to help them choose clothes and accessories that match their lifestyle and desired image.
- You may accompany clients on shopping trips or shop for them.
- Some image consultants are employed by businesses to advise on corporate image and staff presentation.

entry level

To both enter and train while working in this career, you will need qualifications at Level 3. Please refer to explanation on page vii.

Qualifications and courses

- There are no set entry requirements for this career, but experience in a related field is usual. Entrants come from backgrounds including beauty therapy, hairdressing, marketing, public relations or fashion retailing.
- Entrants may hold a degree or HND in a related area, such as beauty therapy, marketing or media. Candidates need at least 4 GCSEs/S grades (A–C/1–3) for HNC/D courses; for degrees, 2 A levels/H grades and 5 GCSEs/S grades (A–C/1–3) are required.
- Candidates coming from a background in hairdressing have usually attained NVQ Level 4.
- The professional qualification for image consultants is The Federation of Image Consultants (TFIC)/City & Guilds joint award in Image Consultancy. It is available at private training colleges. TFIC also offers seminars and workshops for the professional development of its members.

The type of person suited to this work

Image is as much about confidence as it is about looks, so a strong interest in helping people make the best of themselves is essential. Excellent communication skills are required for working in consultation with individual clients or large groups. As you will be working around clients' ideas and interests, you should be flexible.

You will have an eye for design, a good sense of colour coordination and a strong interest in clothes. A well-presented appearance is essential! For working on a freelance basis you will need financial management and business skills. A good level of physical fitness is useful.

Working conditions

Freelance image consultants usually have some flexibility in their working hours, but some evening or weekend work is likely.

Travelling to different locations is often a part of this job.

Image consultants work from home or from studios. Some meet and work with clients in their homes or workplaces. You may also visit shopping centres when on shopping trips with clients.

The future outlook

People are increasingly aware of the value of making the most of their image in their professional and personal lives. With experience, you could develop your own image consultancy or work for a specialist company or salon. Many freelance image consultants offer classes to companies as well as working with individual clients.

High-profile image consultants provide advice and support to celebrities, company managers and even politicians.

Other related opportunities

- Beauty p412
- Make-up Artist p399

Advantages/disadvantages

- This type of work provides the satisfaction of helping to build people's confidence and communication skills in the workplace and in their personal lives.
- Working closely with clients can be physically demanding.

Earnings guide

- Image consultants usually charge for individual sessions. This can vary from £35 to £80+ per session.
- Charges vary according to a consultant's experience and expertise.
- Very experienced image consultants can earn up to £30,000–£40,000 depending on location.

Further information

Hairdressing And Beauty Industry Authority
Oxford House
Sixth Avenue, Sky Business Park
Robin Hood Airport
Doncaster
DN9 3GG
08452 306080
www.habia.org.uk

Federation of Image Consultants
The Gables
Lammas
Norwich
NR10 5AF
07010 701018
www.tfic.org.uk

Nail Technician

What the work involves

- You will provide a range of nail treatments to clients, including manicures, nail extensions, nail art and nail jewellery.
- You will prepare clients' hands and nails for treatments. You may also provide advice on nail care and maintenance.
- Depending on the treatment you are providing, you will work with a range of beauty products and equipment such as brushes, stencils and airbrushes.
- You will clean and tidy the treatment area before and after each client.

The type of person suited to this work

Nail technicians work with many people so you should have good communication skills and a friendly manner. A professional appearance is also important. You will need excellent manual handling skills to undertake nail design work. In addition, a good knowledge of nail and beauty products is important. An eye for design and an interest in fashion are essential.

It will also be important that you are able to maintain a high standard of health and hygiene at all times.

If you work as a freelance technician you will need good financial management and business skills. You should also be able to cope with travelling to different work locations.

Working conditions

Nail technicians work in nail or beauty salons and other locations. Mobile nail technicians provide treatments to clients in their own homes.

Salon-based technicians usually work between 30 and 40 hours a week with some evening/weekend work.

Nail technicians come into regular contact with chemicals, so the job might not suit people with skin conditions or allergies. You may wear a uniform and face mask whilst working.

The future outlook

With nail salons opening in high streets throughout the country, nail technology is a popular area of beauty therapy. Beauty and hairdressing salons are increasingly offering nail treatments as a service.

You could work as a freelance nail technician, providing services to care homes and hotels as well as private clients. If you gain additional professional qualifications you could offer other therapies.

There are opportunities to work abroad or on cruise ships.

entry level

1

To both enter and train while working in this career, you will need qualifications at Level 1. Please refer to explanation on page vii.

Qualifications and courses

- There are no formal entry requirements for this career. However, in many areas nail technicians must be licensed by their local environmental health department. A nationally recognised qualification is required to become licensed, and some local authorities insist on an NVQ/SVQ.
- Relevant courses include the Vocational Training Charitable Trust (VTCT) Certificate in Nail Treatments with the option to specialise in Nail Technology or Nail Art and NVQ/SVQ in Nail Services at Levels 2 and 3. A nail services unit is included in NVQ/SVQ Beauty Therapy at Levels 2 and 3. The BTEC National Award, Certificate or Diploma in Beauty Therapy Sciences includes a specialist unit in nail technology.
- The qualification recommended by the Association of Nail Technicians (ANT) is the nail unit of NVQ/SVQ Level 3 in Beauty Therapy.
- Apprenticeships/Skillseekers are available to those aged 16–24.

CRCI:RC

CLCI:IK

Other related opportunities

- Beauty p412
- Hairdresser / Barber p424
- Make-up Artist p399

Advantages/disadvantages

- Working on a freelance basis can allow you to work flexible hours but unsocial hours are likely.
- Some salons provide bonus schemes and commission payments for product sales. Additional perks include free or reduced cost beauty treatments.

Earnings guide

- Freelance nail technicians usually charge per job. This varies according to the nature of the treatment, from £12 to £50+.
- Starting salaries are around £10,000 per year.
- With experience you could earn £15,000–£20,000.
- At senior/management level you could earn £25,000+.

Further information

www.cityandguilds.com/myperfectjob

Association of Nail Technicians
c/o Professional Beauty
3rd floor, Broadway House
2–6 Fulham Broadway
London
SW6 1AA
01322 555 724
www.professionalbeauty.co.uk/pm/346

Hairdressing And Beauty Industry Authority
Oxford House
Sixth Avenue, Sky Business Park
Robin Hood Airport
Doncaster
DN9 3GG
08452 306080
www.habia.org.uk

Pest Control Technician

What the work involves

- You will protect public health by treating and eradicating infestations of insects and vermin such as cockroaches and rats.
- Pest control technicians work in private homes, offices, shops and other sites.
- Your job may involve investigating or monitoring a site to check for pests.
- You will use a range of specialist chemicals and equipment. Your work may involve fitting traps or spraying areas with chemicals.
- In some situations you will provide advice to customers on the prevention of pest problems.

The type of person suited to this work

This job is all about protecting public health so you should be able to work to a high standard of health and safety. Working with chemical treatments and specialist equipment demands a professional approach. You will need to be calm when dealing with large numbers of insects, rodents and other pests. A strong stomach will also help you cope with working in unpleasant conditions.

Physical fitness and good manual handling skills are essential. You will need to be able to communicate and have a tactful approach when providing advice to customers. You will use your writing skills to keep records and write reports.

Working conditions

Whilst not all pest control work is unpleasant, dealing with dirty or unhygienic situations is a likely part of the job.

You will travel to different locations on a regular basis.

Pest control technicians must wear protective clothing, such as overalls and eye goggles. They work with a range of chemicals, so the job may not suit people with skin conditions or allergies.

The future outlook

Pest control technicians provide an important service to domestic homes, factories, offices and other locations in cities and rural areas. Many pest control technicians run their own businesses. Others gain work with local councils or with specialist companies.

With experience you could progress to supervising teams of staff, managing a large pest control company or working in a management role for local councils.

entry level

2

To both enter and train while working in this career, you will need qualifications at Level 2. Please refer to explanation on page vii.

Qualifications and courses

- A good standard of education is required, with GCSEs/S grades (A–E/1–5) in English, maths and science being useful. Because the job involves using specialist equipment and dangerous substances, some employers prefer candidates to be over 18.
- A driving licence is usually required.
- Training is undertaken on the job, supervised by an experienced technician. There may also be opportunities to attend training courses.
- The entry-level qualification for the industry is the British Pest Control Association/Royal Society for the Promotion of Health Certificate in Pest Control, which equates to NVQ Level 2.
- NVQs/SVQs are available in Pest Control Supervision at Level 3. The British Pest Control Association also offers a Pest Control Diploma and specialist short courses in fumigation, rodents, insects, bird management and field biology, and a Technical Inspector Certificate.
- The British Wood Preserving and Damp-Proofing Association offer short courses covering insect infestation. The National Proficiency Training Council (NPTC) offers Certificates in Competence in the use of pesticides in rural areas.

Other related opportunities

- Environmental Health Practitioer / Officer p280

Advantages/disadvantages

- Some employers provide extra pay for overtime.
- This type of work is sometimes available on a flexible basis.

Earnings guide

- As a trainee you could start at around £12,000 per year.
- With experience and qualifications this rises to £15,000–£22,000.
- At senior levels you could earn £30,000+.

Further information

British Pest Control Association
Ground Floor
Gleneagles House
Vernongate
Derby
DE1 1UP
0870 6092687
www.bpca.org.uk

National Pest Technicians Association
NPTA House
Hall Lane
Kinoulton
Nottinghamshire
NG12 3EF
01949 81133
www.npta.org.uk

Asset Skills (Sector Skills Council in property services, housing, cleaning services and facilities management)
2 The Courtyard
48 New North Road
Exeter
Devon
EX4 4EP
01392 423399
www.assetskills.org

Asset Skills Scotland (Sector Skills Council in property services, housing, cleaning services and facilities management)
Bank House
Bank Street
Aberfeldy
Perthshire
PH15 2BB
01887 829171
www.assetskills.org

Recycling Operative

What the work involves

- You will collect recyclable materials, such as paper, cans, cardboard, glass and organic waste, from homes and recycling banks and take them to recycling depots.
- Working as part of a team, you will travel round your area and empty recycling bins or collect recycling boxes.
- You may drive the collection vehicle or help the driver to move the vehicle around safely.
- Recycling technicians also work in recycling facilities, sorting through recycled materials in preparation for re-use.

The type of person suited to this work

A good level of physical fitness is essential for this type of work. You will also need manual handling skills to lift and move recycling collections. A knowledge of health and safety is very important. You should enjoy working well as part of a busy team. You may have to work to strict targets, so you will need a reliable and well-organised approach.

Working hands-on with rubbish will mean that you will have to be able to deal with unpleasant smells and sights. For work in a sorting facility, you will need good eyesight and attention to detail. A self-motivated attitude is useful.

Working conditions

Recycling operatives usually work around 40 hours a week with an early start and an early finish.

A good level of physical fitness is helpful.

You will wear protective clothing, such as gloves and overalls, and you will come into contact with dirt and rubbish on a regular basis.

This type of work may not suit people with skin conditions or allergies.

The future outlook

Protecting the environment and natural resources through recycling is increasingly important. It is likely that there will be a growth in the number of recycling jobs in local councils, contracting companies providing services to councils and recycling companies.

With experience in a recycling collection or sorting role, you could progress to a supervisory or management position.

entry level

To both enter and train while working in this career, you will need qualifications at Level 1. Please refer to explanation on page vii.

Qualifications and courses

- No formal qualifications are required for entry. The minimum age for entrants is 18.
- New entrants are trained in health and safety and the basic skills of the job. Further training is gained on the job. An LGV licence is needed for those who want to become drivers.
- Recycling operatives can work towards NVQs/SVQs in Recycling Operations at Levels 1 and 2 and NVQs/SVQs in Waste Management Operations at Levels 1 and 2, with specialist options in waste collection or recycling. An NVQ/SVQ in Community Recycling is also available.
- People working in supervisory roles can gain an NVQ/SVQ Level 3 in Management of Recycling Operations or an NVQ/SVQ Level 3 in Waste Management Supervision. It is also possible to work towards Level 3 and 4 qualifications in Environmental Conservation and Conservation Control.
- The University of Northampton offers Wastes Management as a combined degree subject. Entry is normally with 2–3 A levels/H grades. A few Foundation degrees in this subject are also available.

CRCI:RB

CLCI:IJ

Other related opportunities

- Refuse Collection Operative p429

Advantages/disadvantages

- Most recycling jobs start early in the morning but finish early in the afternoon.
- There are also opportunities to do this type of work on a part-time or flexible working basis, which may suit people with other commitments.

Earnings guide

- Starting salaries begin at around £11,500 per year.
- With experience and progress to a supervisory or management role, you could earn £15,000–£20,000.
- Seniors can earn up to £25,000.

Further information

www.cityandguilds.com/myperfectjob

Waste Management Industry Training and Advisory Board (WAMITAB)
Peterbridge House
3 The Lakes
Northampton
NN4 7HE
01604 231950
www.wamitab.org.uk

Asset Skills (Sector Skills Council in property services, housing, cleaning services and facilities management)
2 The Courtyard
48 New North Road
Exeter
Devon
EX4 4EP
01392 423399
www.assetskills.org

Energy & Utility Skills (Sector Skills Council for the electricity, gas, waste management and water industries)
Friars Gate Two
1011 Stratford Road
Solihull
B90 4BN
0845 077 9922
www.euskills.co.uk

Refuse Collection Operative

What the work involves

- You will collect rubbish and unwanted items and take them to an official rubbish tip or recycling depot.
- Working as part of a team you will travel round your area, emptying bins, removing plastic sacks of waste or picking up recyclable waste.
- You will throw sacks into the lorry or empty bins using an automatic lift. You will also help the driver to manoeuvre the vehicle safely.
- Recycling operatives may have additional duties, such as sorting rubbish or collecting hazardous waste.

entry level

To both enter and train while working in this career, you will need qualifications at Level 1. Please refer to explanation on page vii.

The type of person suited to this work

Walking nine miles and emptying 2000 bins a shift requires a good level of physical fitness. Although automated wheelie-bin loaders have been introduced in many areas, you will still need strength to lift bulky household waste. A strong stomach and a poor sense of smell are useful when dealing with rubbish. You should also be able to cope with getting your hands dirty.

Team-working skills are essential in this job. Most companies are required to complete their rounds to strict deadlines, so you should be able to work under pressure.

Working conditions

Most of your work will be undertaken outside in all types of weather conditions.

Protective overalls, footwear and gloves are provided.

The hours are 6am to 3pm, except for busy holiday periods when the amount of rubbish increases.

The future outlook

Britain produces 435 million tonnes of rubbish a year. Loaders will always be in demand as even recyclable rubbish has to be collected. However, there is keen competition for this job.

You could work for a contracting company providing services for a local authority. There are some jobs with specialist companies who collect paper or food waste. With experience, you could progress to supervisory or management work.

Qualifications and courses

- There are no specific educational qualifications required. You will need to be in good health and physically fit.
- You should be at least 18 and drivers must be over 21 to take an LGV licence.
- Apprenticeships/Skillseekers may be available for people aged 16–24.
- Key Skills in communication and working with others are useful.
- Many employers require a driving licence. Some will also expect you to have knowledge of your local area.
- On starting, you will have to take a short course on health and safety and then be trained on the job by an experienced colleague.
- Refuse operatives can work towards NVQs/SVQs at Levels 1 and 2 in Waste Management Operations and Level 3 in Waste Management Supervision. Refuse collection operatives can become drivers by gaining a LGV Large Goods Vehicle licence.

CRCI:WE | CLCI:YAD

Other related opportunities

- Recycling Operative p428

Advantages/disadvantages

- For most jobs, you will have to start very early in the morning. However, this means that you will be able to finish your working day quite early.
- The work is physically demanding and potentially unsafe. However, you will have protective clothing including gloves.

Earnings guide

- Salaries start at about £11,000 per year.
- With experience you could earn £17,000–£20,000.
- At senior levels it is possible to earn £18,000–£25,000.
- Drivers can earn between £17,000 and £20,000.
- There are usually opportunities to earn extra by working overtime or in holiday periods.

Further information

Waste Management Industry Training and Advisory Board (WAMITAB)
Peterbridge House
3 The Lakes
Northampton
NN4 7HE
01604 231950
www.wamitab.org.uk

Wedding Consultant

What the work involves

- You will organise wedding ceremonies, parties and other events to suit your clients' plans and budgets.
- Working closely with clients, you will help them decide on the type of wedding they want.
- Your work will also involve liaising with catering professionals, venue managers and suppliers.
- Depending on individual projects, you may be responsible for creating a whole look or style for a wedding. You could be responsible for all the practical arrangements such as catering, flowers, booking venues and guest transport.

entry level

To both enter and train while working in this career, you will need qualifications at Level 1. Please refer to explanation on page vii.

Qualifications and courses

- There are no set entry requirements for this career.
- Wedding consultants/planners/organisers may have a background in hospitality, design or business. The skills you bring to work are more important than the qualifications you might hold.
- Larger employers may require people with events planning experience.
- Degrees, Foundation degrees and HNDs are available in events management.
- Those with proof of more than 3 years' business trading, three client references and a satisfactory quality inspection can become members of the National Association of Professional Wedding Services. The Association can also provide details about the Advanced Certification in Wedding Design and Management, which is an intensive, in-depth course covering all aspects of wedding organisation.

The type of person suited to this work

Helping to create and plan the big day for clients requires excellent communication skills. A strong interest in helping people organise the wedding they want is important. To do this, you will need a combination of creative and practical skills to develop ideas and make them a reality.

You will have to have strong attention to detail and be a perfectionist to ensure that the weddings you plan run smoothly.

You should be able to negotiate agreements with suppliers on behalf of your clients, keep calm under pressure and be reliable with an outgoing, confident personality. Financial skills are useful.

Working conditions

Working hours can be long, especially in the period leading up to a wedding. You may also have to attend meetings with clients at evenings and weekends.

This type of work can be very highly pressured due to limited deadlines and the level of responsibility.

You will attend meetings at a variety of locations and your working day is likely to include some travel.

The future outlook

Professional wedding planning is a growing area. You could work on a freelance basis, offering planning services through your own company, or could work for a larger wedding planning company.

There are also opportunities to work within large hotels combining wedding consultancy and planning with other events-related work.

CRCI:R

CLCI:IZ

Other related opportunities

- Administrator p6
- Entertainments Manager p361
- Tour Manager p381

Advantages/disadvantages

- This is a sociable job which provides the opportunity to help clients have the kind of wedding they want.
- Having responsibility for ensuring that wedding days run smoothly means that there is little room for mistakes.
- When everything turns out well, it can be very rewarding!

Earnings guide

- You could earn £15,000+ working for a specialist wedding and events planning company.
- With a good level of experience, you could earn £25,000+.
- Freelance planners usually charge a percentage of the total cost of the wedding.

Further information

www.cityandguilds.com/myperfectjob

People 1st
2nd Floor
38 Market Square
Uxbridge
UB8 1LH
0870 060 2550
www.people1st.co.uk

National Association of Professional Wedding Services
Shelley Way
Wimbledon
London
SW19 1TH
020 8090 1921
www.theweddingassociation.co.uk

Wigmaker

What the work involves

- You will design and create a range of wigs and hairpieces using human hair or synthetic fibres.
- You may create or design wigs to suit individual customers.
- Your work could involve meeting with customers and helping them decide on the styles of wig to suit them. You may also provide advice to customers on caring for and maintaining their wigs.
- Wigmakers provide services for the entertainment industry, hospitals, wig supply companies, theatrical costume companies and private customers.

The type of person suited to this work

Wigmaking requires a combination of creative flair, practicality and people skills. You may work closely with customers requiring wigs due to illness or medical treatment, so a tactful approach is essential. You should also be able to understand the type of look an individual client wants. Your eye for design will help you create a variety of styles of wigs.

Wigmaking is a slow, detailed process so you will need excellent practical skills, attention to detail and a lot of patience! You must work to a very high standard at all times. As wigs are often made to order, you should be able to work to deadlines.

Working conditions

You may be based in a studio or workshop. Your work may also involve visiting private homes and hospital departments for customer fittings and consultations.

You will work with a range of equipment and chemicals and you will need manual handling skills and good eyesight.

This type of work may be unsuitable for people with skin conditions and allergies.

The future outlook

There are very limited employment opportunities in this area.

Wigmakers in entertainment and media usually provide additional make-up and hair services. They may run their own companies working for television, media and theatre companies or be employed in-house. Wigmakers also provide specialist care and services for clients experiencing hair loss due to a medical condition.

With experience, you could set up your own business or work for a wig supplier.

entry level

1

To both enter and train while working in this career, you will need qualifications at Level 1. Please refer to explanation on page vii.

Qualifications and courses

- There are no set entry requirements for this work.
- It is possible to study wigmaking part time at college. A City & Guilds Certificate (3013) is available in Wigmaking. The VTCT Diploma in Theatrical and Media Make-up includes study of wigmaking. NVQs/SVQs in Hairdressing may include units in wigmaking.
- Wigmaking can also be studied at higher education level, as part of an HND in media make-up or theatrical and media make-up.

Other related opportunities

- Hairdresser / Barber p424
- Make-up Artist p399

Advantages/disadvantages

- By creating and fitting attractive wigs for customers, you can help build their confidence.
- The level of contact you have with customers depends on your employer. In some jobs you may have minimum contact with clients and work solely in a studio.

Earnings guide

- Salaries vary according to sector and employer, you could start on £12,000 per year and rise to £20,000 with lots of experience
- Wigmakers working in theatre or the media will usually earn more than those working for companies supplying hospitals.
- Most wigmakers set a rate per job depending on the requirements of the client.

Further information

Skillset (Sector Skills Council for the audiovisual industries)
Prospect House
80–110 New Oxford Street
London
WC1A 1HB
08080 300900
www.skillset.org

Wigmakers' Association c/o The Hairdressing & Beauty Suppliers Association
Greenleaf House
128 Darkes Lane
Potters Bar
Herfordshire
EN6 1AE
01707 649499
www.hbsa.uk.com

www.cityandguilds.com/myperfectjob

Here's Deborah Gill's story:

Recycling Operative

Deborah has always been interested in environmental issues and after studying Geography, Chemistry and Biology at A level she went on to Southampton University to do an Honours degree in Environmental Science. She then started working for a London borough council on a temporary basis and then applied for and got the job as the borough's Waste Projects Officer.

WHAT THE JOB ENTAILS

'I look at how the recycling services in the borough are running and I work on projects to increase the amount recycled in the borough through the introduction of new collection schemes, publicity campaigns, and working with schools and residents associations. I also look at ways to encourage more people to reduce the amount of rubbish they throw away. In the last couple of months I have worked on a project to expand the number of recycling banks at blocks of flats and have been running a trial scheme in a small area to test the use of different containers for recycling.'

Deborah, 25, enjoys the fact she is not sat at a desk nine to five but is out and about meeting people and learning from other recycling officers what projects are going on around London. She also likes the fact that what she does benefits the environment directly: as collections increase, she can see just how much waste is saved from landfill sites. One of the downsides is that there is quite a lot of deskwork involved; what she does is not glamorous, and she often has to work early mornings.

WHAT YOU NEED TO SUCCEED

'I think there is a wide range of qualities that are useful for the job that could outweigh having a degree or other qualification. A good grasp of databases and spreadsheets would be an advantage, but much of the job is how you work with other people, so being able to communicate with the general public, contractors, councillors and other members of staff at all levels is a must. I also think a creative spark for publicity material helps. You really need to be enthusiastic and interested in environmental issues and have good customer service skills. At the end of the day you are trying to sell people the idea of recycling, so interest and enthusiasm go a long way.'

Deborah would now like to study for a specific waste management qualification and would like to broaden her experience by working in the private or charity sector.

THE LAST WORD

'Working with "rubbish" is much more interesting than it sounds, and enables you to get involved with much more than you would think!'

Do you enjoy meeting new people, helping them get what they need? The retail world includes lots of opportunities in areas such as:

- **Antique Dealer**
- **Customer Services Adviser**
- **Shelf Filler**
- **Specialist Shop Assistant**
- **Trading Standards Officer**

But what's it like working in this area?

Here's Jamie Farquhar's story:

Store Manager

Jamie has been a qualified tennis coach since the age of 17 and his ultimate aim is to become the manager of a tennis club. He studied Leisure Management and Sports Studies (BA Hons) at university and decided to go into retail on graduation to get as much experience as possible. His first job was as a receptionist at the famous Harbour Club in Chelsea, home to the biggest indoor tennis club in London. He left after a year to become a Sales Assistant at the Pro Shop within the Harbour Club, selling sportswear, training shoes and tennis rackets and balls, and after seven months was made Store Manager. Jamie is 23 years old.

THE PROS AND CONS OF BEING THE BOSS

'Sometimes we get freebies from the product reps who come into the shop which is nice, and I love the fact we are so busy all the time, although that can get quite tiring. But time goes so quickly I find I never worry about stupid things – the only thing you can think of is the job and that's brilliant because I really feel involved in it all. I love making the shop look nice and I love helping the customers. I take pride in making sure people are getting the right product for them. The downside with being the manager is the buck stops with me. If anything goes wrong it is down to me. I also have to ensure my staff are motivated and busy, and above all, happy. It does get stressful – there is a lot to do.'

Jamie's duties include sorting out stock discrepancies, emailing the buyers every day, keeping the stockroom in order, sending back faulty items, scanning deliveries, sorting out wages for the other three members of staff, doing staff reviews and delivering the monthly sales figures.

JAMIE'S ADVICE FOR THOSE WHO WANT TO MAKE ICT IN RETAIL

'It's mainly about hard work and discipline. You can move up the ladder very quickly as long as you are willing to learn, so get as much experience as you can. Get a Saturday job as a sales assistant while you are still at school or college. Get involved, get stuck in and learn everything you possibly can from the person on the next rung of the ladder up from you.'

There are 25 Pro Shops around the country, with Jamie's shop having a turnover of almost half a million pounds per annum. His next move could be to one of the bigger stores in the group, but he is keeping his options open.

'I am so happy at the moment working where I do that I don't really want to move! Hopefully, I will get a pay rise in the next few months but I believe I am getting so much experience here I will soon be equipped to achieve my dream of managing a tennis club because if I can do the management job I'm doing here I can definitely manage a club.'

Antiques Dealer

What the work involves

- You will be buying and selling things such as furniture, clocks, jewellery and pictures, which are either old (officially antiques must be at least 100 years old) or which people collect, for example a particular make of china.
- You will go to auctions and fairs to buy things to sell in shops, markets or antique salerooms.
- You will need to develop specialist knowledge so that you can assess an object's age and value and whether it will sell at a profit.
- You will advise customers on the value of their antiques.

The type of person suited to this work

You should be fascinated by antiques and working out where they come from and what they are worth.

You will need to be interested in history and dedicated enough to travel and visit fairs and auctions all over the country and possibly abroad, searching out bargains and objects to sell on. To do this you will need to develop good specialist knowledge to spot a bargain, know what is likely to be popular and then sell quickly at a profit.

Antiques and collectors' items do not have fixed prices so you will need to be able to make quick decisions, be good at negotiating over prices and cope with the stress of buying things at auction. You will need to have good all round business skills.

Working conditions

You will work in a shop, in an antiques saleroom or on a market stall. You could be outside in all weathers and will probably have to travel to different markets.

You will probably travel a lot to fairs and auctions and could be dealing with heavy objects like furniture or dusty and dirty things such as clothes and books.

Your working hours will vary a lot. Shops and stalls will be open at fixed times and on public holidays, and you could be visiting auctions or customers at any time.

The future outlook

Most antique dealers are self-employed or work in a family business, but you could start in an auction house or as a sales assistant in a larger shop.

Once you have developed contacts and a knowledge of antiques and their value, you could work for yourself, perhaps starting with a market stall and expanding your business from there, but you will need money to buy your first lot of stock.

Most dealers specialise in a particular period of history or type of antique.

entry level

2–8

To both enter and train while working in this career, you will need qualifications at Level 2–8. Please refer to explanation on page vii.

Qualifications and courses

- There are no formal qualifications needed for this work, but enthusiasm and sales skills are useful. GCSEs/S grades (A–C/1–3) in art, design and history are an advantage.
- Apprenticeship/Skillseekers may be available for those aged 16–24.
- Entry is normally through work experience or as a trainee. Many auction houses will employ people as general workers or assistants. An NVQ/SVQ in Retail Operations can be an advantage.
- The University of Central Lancashire offers a 3-year degree in Antiques and Design Studies and a Master's by distance learning in Antiques. There are also some relevant privately-run courses at institutions such as the Courtauld Institute of Art, Sotheby's, Christie's and West Dean College. Information about careers in antiques dealing and current vacancies with dealers may be available from the British Antique Dealers Association (BADA) or the Association of Art and Antique Dealers (LAPADA).
- There are some relevant privately run courses. The British Antique Dealers Association (BADA) will be able to offer advice about these, as well as information about current vacancies with dealers. The British Antique Dealers Association (BADA) may offer advice on these, as well as information about current vacancies with dealers. The Association of Art and Antique Dealers (LAPADA) also offers basic guidance on careers in antique dealing.

CRCI:SB

CLCI:OFM

Other related opportunities

- Archivist p316
- Market Trader p444
- Museum / Art Gallery p325
- Sales Assistant p450

Advantages/disadvantages

- You will be working with things that you love and have the thrill of finding bargains or rare items.
- It can be a very uncertain business and prices will rise and fall as things go in and out of fashion. You can make a lot of money but you can also lose a lot.

Earnings guide

- Earnings vary a lot depending on your success, contacts and luck.
- You can expect around £12,000 per year as an assistant.
- £20,000–£30,000 is usual for a dealer with experience.
- £50,000+ is possible for successful dealers or people with a high level of specialist knowledge.

Further information

British Antique Dealers Association
20 Rutland Gate
London
SW7 1BD
020 7589 4128
www.bada.org

Association of Art & Antiques Dealers (LAPADA)
535 King's Road
Chelsea
London
SW10 0SZ
020 7823 3511
www.lapada.org

Sotheby's
34–35 New Bond Street
London
W1S 2RT
020 7293 5000
www.sothebys.com

Christie's
8 King Street
St James's
London
SW1Y 6QT
020 7839 9060
www.christies.com

Bookseller

What the work involves

- You will be serving customers, taking money and answering queries, giving advice and ordering books.
- You will keep the shelves tidy and in order, putting new books out and arranging displays. You will be keeping records of books and sometimes adding a classification system.
- You will be ordering books from publishers and wholesalers and keeping stock information up to date.
- You might be working with local colleges or universities to make sure you have got the books needed for their courses.

entry level

2–8

To both enter and train while working in this career, you will need qualifications at Level 2–8. Please refer to explanation on page vii.

The type of person suited to this work

You will need to be genuinely interested in books and in keeping up to date with new publications so that you can help and advise customers.

You will need good communication skills for dealing with customers and sales reps and will work as part of a team, but should also be able to use your own initiative. You should be polite and helpful and able to stay calm when you are busy.

You will need to keep up to date with what books are selling well and when new books by popular authors are due out, and be able to research information for customers.

You will be taking cash and using tills and computers to check and order stock.

Working conditions

You will be working in a shop and most jobs are likely to be in large book chain stores. You will be dealing with customers, working in a team and you will have responsibility for a particular section.

You will be on your feet all day and could be carrying heavy books.

You will work 39–40 hours a week, and will probably have to work weekends on a rota basis and also do late and early shifts as large stores can be open long hours.

The future outlook

A lot of smaller book shops have closed due to competition from larger stores and the internet, so most opportunities are with the big chains.

You can get responsibility quite quickly as a supervisor or the person in charge of a section. You can go on to management level or to work for head office.

There is not much chance of promotion in smaller shops but you could use your knowledge and experience to open your own store, possibly specialising in antique or second-hand books.

Qualifications and courses

- There are no formal qualifications to enter this work, but most employers look for GCSEs/S grades (A–3/1–C) in English and maths. You can enter and train for this career with qualifications at Levels 2–3 or go in with higher qualifications at Level 3 and above.
- A degree in English or a degree/ HND/Foundation degree in retail, business management or retail marketing can be an advantage.
- Relevant courses at FE level include the Retail and Distributive Services, NVQs/SVQs in Retail Operations at Levels 2 and 3, Distributive Operations at Level 1, Customer Service at Levels 2, 3 and 4, Visual Merchandising at Level 2 and BTEC First and National qualifications in Retail/SQA National qualifications in Retail and Distribution.
- Apprenticeships/Skillseekers may be available to those aged 16–24.
- Membership of the Booksellers Association of the United Kingdom and Ireland may be useful.

Other related opportunities

- Librarian p323
- Publisher p162
- Sales Assistant p450

Advantages/disadvantages

- You could be using your knowledge and love of books to help other people and keep up to date with new publications.
- You could develop specialist knowledge, for example in children's books.
- You will be dealing with the public, which can be rewarding but also stressful!

Earnings guide

- Salaries vary a lot depending on the size of the shop. With some of the large chains you may get bonuses for good sales or meeting targets.
- You can expect £10,000–£12,000 per year when you start.
- With experience this can rise to £14,000.
- £30,000+ a year is possible as a manager of a large store.

Further information

Booksellers Association
Minster House
272–274 Vauxhall Bridge Road
London
SW1V 1BA
020 7802 0802
www.booksellers.org.uk

British Shops and Stores Association Limited
Middleton House
2 Main Road
Middleton Cheney, Banbury
Oxfordshire
OX17 2TN
01295 712277
www.british-shops.co.uk

www.cityandguilds.com/myperfectjob

Builders' Merchant

What the work involves

- You will be dealing with building materials such as wood, cement, tools and bathroom fittings.
- You will supply goods to building firms and individual builders – plumbers, electricians, plasterers – and members of the public, and taking payments and using tills.
- You will keep track of stock using computer or paper systems, order new stock, make special orders and take deliveries.
- You will work with customers and suppliers face to face and on the phone and offer specialist knowledge and advice.

entry level

To both enter and train while working in this career, you will need qualifications at Level 1–2. Please refer to explanation on page vii.

The type of person suited to this work

You will need to be interested in all aspects of the building industry but could develop specialist knowledge in one area as well. You should be able to learn about the things you sell and be able to give advice on how to use them.

You will need to be good at dealing with customers and suppliers. You will need to be well organised for ordering and sorting stock, able to use computer systems and deal with cash and other payments and be able to deal with paperwork.

You should be fit and active for carrying heavy things. Allergies to dust and chemicals can be a problem. You will need good numeracy skills to calculate amounts needed for different projects.

Qualifications and courses

- There are no formal entry qualifications for this work, You can enter and train in this career with qualifications at Levels 1 or 2. Most employers prefer applicants to have English and maths GCSEs/S grades (A–C/ 1–3).
- A qualification in retail or construction may also be useful. Relevant courses include BTEC Introductory Diploma in Construction, Retail and Administration, BTEC First Certificate/Diploma in Retail, and Vocational GCSE in Construction and Built Environment.
- Mature candidates may enter this career with experience in the retail or construction industries.
- Apprenticeships/Skillseekers may be available for those aged 16–24. The Builders' Merchants Federation (BMF) offers an Apprenticeship scheme leading to NVQs/SVQs at Levels 2 and 3.
- Builders' merchants can work towards NVQs/SVQs in relevant subjects such as Distribution and Warehousing, Customer Service and Retail Operations.
- Most training is on the job, learning from experienced staff.

Working conditions

You will work about 40 hours a week, usually on Saturdays and sometimes Sundays. You may start at about 7.30am so that builders can buy their materials on the way to their work.

You will be on your feet a lot and lifting heavy objects. You will be wearing overalls and protective boots or shoes.

Conditions can be cold and you could be working outside in all weathers.

The future outlook

There are job opportunities in all areas of the country, but these can vary depending on the strength of the building trade, and at present there are good opportunities.

The number of builders' merchants has increased with a lot of stores on out-of-town retail sites.

Some stores specialise, for example in plumbing supplies or wood and timber.

You can often work part time and if you work for large merchants, or a chain, you could become a supervisor or manager. You could also work for a supplier or as a sales representative.

CRCI:SD

CLCI:OK

Other related opportunities

- Builders' Yard Assistant p437
- Checkout Operator p441
- Sales Assistant p450
- Warehouse p586

Advantages/disadvantages

- The work can be a great way of using your interest in building and knowledge of materials, tools and equipment.
- There is quite a lot of paperwork involved in keeping track of the stock.
- You could be starting early in the morning and working outside in cold, wet weather.

Earnings guide

- You can expect £8,500–£9,500 per year as a trainee.
- This may rise to £11,000 when you have got some experience.
- Yard staff can earn £12,500 with experience, having perhaps taken some qualifications and gained more responsibility.
- Delivery van drivers can earn around £16,500.
- You could earn more as the manager of a department or store.

Further information

www.cityandguilds.com/myperfectjob

Builders' Merchants Federation
15 Soho Square
London
W1D 3HL
0870 901 3380
www.bmf.org.uk

British Shops and Stores Association Limited
Middleton House
2 Main Road
Middleton Cheney, Banbury
Oxfordshire
OX17 2TN
01295 712277
www.british-shops.co.uk

Builders' Yard Assistant

What the work involves

- You will work in a builders' merchants looking after the stock.
- You will handle a huge range of building materials like bricks, cement, wood, paint and bathroom fittings.
- You will take deliveries, checking the right things have arrived and store them properly so they do not get damp or damaged.
- You may be driving forklift trucks and moving stock using trolleys and ladders.
- You will keep the yard clean and tidy and help customers by answering questions, packing and loading their goods and possibly taking payments.

entry level

To both enter and train while working in this career, you will need qualifications at Level 1–2. Please refer to explanation on page vii.

Qualifications and courses

- You can enter and train in this career with qualifications at Levels 1 or 2.
- Mature candidates may enter with experience in the retail or construction industries.
- Apprenticeships/Skillseekers may be available for those aged 16–24. The Builders' Merchants Federation (BMF) offers an Apprenticeship scheme leading to NVQs/SVQs at Levels 2 and 3.
- Employees can work towards NVQs/SVQs in relevant subjects such as Distribution and Warehousing, Customer Service and Retail Operations.
- Most training is on the job, learning from experienced staff, but the Builders' Merchants Federation (BMF) offers an open learning programme leading to City & Guilds 6117 in Construction Materials Distribution. Candidates must complete five modules, from a list including subjects such as health and safety, customer care and specialist product knowledge.

The type of person suited to this work

You should be fit and healthy as you will be very active, lifting heavy things and working outside in all weathers.

Because you will be dealing with chemicals and dusty things such as wood and cement, asthma and allergies can be a problem.

You should be prepared to get dirty and will probably wear overalls and protective shoes or boots.

You will follow instructions from your supervisor and will need to use your initiative, making sure that you work in a safe and responsible way with heavy and possibly dangerous stock and equipment.

You should be able to check invoices and deal with customers and may have to handle payments.

Working conditions

You will be outside in all weathers and could be in stores which are dirty, cold and cramped. You will be lifting heavy objects and could be using a forklift truck and climbing ladders.

You will work around 40 hours a week and could start early, at around 7.30am. You may work Saturdays and possibly Sundays.

You will be working with the public, in a team, and taking instructions from your supervisor.

The future outlook

There are job opportunities in all areas of the country, but these can vary depending on the strength of the building trade.

The number of builders' merchants has increased with a lot of stores on out-of-town retail sites. You could work in a DIY store or become a supervisor or move on to delivery work.

Other related opportunities

- Builders' Merchant p436
- Sales Assistant p450
- Shelf Filler p452
- Warehouse p586

Advantages/disadvantages

- It is an active, physical, outdoor job and you could train to drive forklift trucks.
- The work can be repetitive, doing the same tasks each day.
- The work can be cold and dirty.

Earnings guide

- You can expect about £9,000 per year when you start.
- This could rise to £14,000 when you have gained more experience.
- As a manager you could earn £35,000+.

Further information

Builders Merchants Federation
15 Soho Square
London
W1D 3HL
0870 901 3380
www.bmf.org.uk

British Shops and Stores Association Limited
Middleton House
2 Main Road
Middleton Cheney, Banbury
Oxfordshire
OX17 2TN
01295 712277
www.british-shops.co.uk

www.cityandguilds.com/myperfectjob

Buyer

What the work involves

- Buyers work in all sorts of industries and organisations, but in retail you would probably work in the merchandising and marketing team.
- You will probably work for a large retail company and be looking for products which fit the company image and will appeal to their customers.
- You will visit manufacturers and suppliers to negotiate prices and decide on quantities and colours. You will also check on the quality of the products.
- You will help to predict and set trends, using computers to analyse sales figures and keep track of stock levels.

The type of person suited to this work

You will need to be confident and decisive because you will be dealing with large budgets.

You will also need to be assertive with good communication skills to negotiate prices and make presentations to managers and staff.

You will need to be able to analyse figures and use them to set prices and targets and check stock levels.

You should be creative, well organised and good at planning ahead, and have an eye for detail.

You will need to be able to work under pressure to meet deadlines.

You may need to work to set targets within a team of a large company.

Working conditions

You will be office-based but spend a lot of time visiting suppliers and manufacturers in this country and abroad, so will probably have to spend time away from home.

You will work office hours but probably need to work longer at busy times and to meet deadlines.

The future outlook

There are job opportunities all over the country but most will be in larger towns and cities, particularly London.

In a small company there may not be much chance of promotion, but in a larger company prospects are good. With additional experience, you can gain extra responsibility.

You could move into other areas of retail such as marketing or merchandising, or use your skills to work as a buyer in other areas, including manufacturing, the civil service and local government.

entry level

To both enter and train while working in this career, you will need qualifications at Level 4–8. Please refer to explanation on page vii.

Qualifications and courses

- There are no set qualifications for entry to a buyer job. However, entry is usually by degree, though an HND or equivalent can also be acceptable. Useful subjects include business, management, purchasing, logistics and marketing. Some specialist degrees are available in fashion buying. The minimum entry requirements for a degree course are normally 2 A levels/3 H grades or equivalent.
- Buyers are often required to study for the professional qualifications of the Chartered Institute of Purchasing and Supply (CIPS). CIPS offers a Certificate and Advanced Certificate for people employed in purchasing at a clerical level.
- Entrants with an HND or degree study towards the CIPS Graduate Diploma. CIPS-accredited degrees in purchasing or business are available at some institutions, and give exemption from part or all of the Graduate Diploma.
- People employed in buying can work towards NVQs/SVQs at Levels 2–4 in Procurement. The British Shops and Stores Association offers a Buying and Merchandising Foundation Course by distance learning, aimed at trainee or assistant buyers.
- Some companies offer their own training schemes, but only take on a few candidates each year.
- Employers often like you to be a member of the Chartered Institute of Purchasing and Supply (CIPS). CIPS runs qualifications from Level 2 (Introductory Certificate) to Level 7 (Executive Diploma).

CRCI:SB | CLCI:OP

Other related opportunities

- Marketing p151
- Merchandiser p446
- Purchasing Administrator p577
- Store Manager p459

Advantages/disadvantages

- This can be an exciting, challenging job and the decisions you make will directly affect what the public can buy and the image of the stores.
- You will have a lot of responsibility and will be making decisions and predictions involving large amounts of money which can be exciting, but also very stressful.

Earnings guide

- You can expect anything from £12,500 to £18,000 per year when you start as a trainee buyer. This variation is wide because it depends on the company you work for and the location.
- You can earn £20,000–£35,000 with experience.
- £50,000+ is possible as a successful, senior buyer for a large company.
- You could also earn large bonuses if you do well.

Further information

British Shops and Stores Association Limited
Middleton House
2 Main Road
Middleton Cheney, Banbury
Oxfordshire
OX17 2TN
01295 712277
www.british-shops.co.uk

Chartered Institute of Marketing
Moor Hall
Cookham
Maidenhead
Berkshire
SL6 9QH
01628 427500
www.cim.co.uk

Chartered Institute of Purchasing & Supply
Easton House
Easton on the Hill
Stamford
Lincolnshire
PE9 3NZ
01780 756777
www.cips.org

Call Centre Operative

What the work involves

- You may also be known as a contact centre operator and will be dealing with customers over the phone and using a computer to log details or find information.
- You may do telesales or telemarketing, selling, mail ordering, banking, or promoting goods and services, which could involve 'cold calling'.
- You could be doing market research, asking about people's buying habits or what services they would like from a company.
- You may be providing a service – receiving calls from customers who could be ordering goods, complaining about a service, or accessing their bank accounts.

The type of person suited to this work

You should have good spoken English, with a clear voice and good hearing. You will need excellent customer-service skills and must be able to be polite and calm when dealing with angry or impatient callers.

For telesales or telemarketing, you will need to be motivated and persistent as well as persuasive, but polite.

Good ICT skills are important so that you can input information quickly but accurately, whilst talking to the customer.

You will probably work to targets and could be very busy so should be able to stay calm under pressure and work on your own initiative, but also as part of a team.

Working conditions

You will be office-based, usually working 38–40 hours a week. You may work shifts which could include nights, weekends and evenings.

Call centre staff have their own workstations with a headset and computer and work as part of a team.

The work is usually based on targets and can be busy and stressful; calls are often monitored by supervisors and staff turnover can be fairly high.

The future outlook

There has been a huge growth in call centres recently as more services are available over the phone – such as mail order, banking and insurance – and more companies are using telesales and marketing to sell their goods and services.

Despite a number of companies taking the work out of the country, the UK still has the most call centres in Europe so there are lots of opportunities.

You could become a team leader or supervisor, training staff to improve their skills and checking their work and targets.

entry level

1–2

To both enter and train while working in this career, you will need qualifications at Level 1–2. Please refer to explanation on page vii.

Qualifications and courses

- Thre are no formal entry qualifications for this work, but some employers prefer English and maths GCSEs (A-C)/S grades You can enter and train in this career with qualifications at Levels 1 or 2.
- Call centre staff can work towards NVQ/SVQ Levels 2 and 3 in Telesales, NVQ/SVQ Levels 2 and 3 in Customer Service, NVQs Levels 2 & 3 in Call Handling Operations, Level 3 in Supervising Call Handling and Level 4 in Managing Call Handling, or SVQ Level 2 in Contact Centre Operations and Levels 3 and 4 in Contact Centre Professionals.
- BTEC offers a course in Contact Centre Skills and City & Guilds offers a certificate course in Contact Centre Techniques. Some colleges offer introductory courses in Contact Centre Skills. Call centre training and qualifications are also offered by e-skills UK.
- The Call Centre Association offers a Professional Certificate, achieved through completion of a call centre induction programme, and a Professional Diploma, which requires further CPD activities. A Higher Diploma, university Diploma and postgraduate qualification are available for team leaders and managers. The Chartered Institute of Marketing offers courses on telephone selling techniques.

CRCI:SA

CLCI:OM

Other related opportunities

- Customer Services p442
- Marketing p151
- Sales Assistant p450

Advantages/disadvantages

- Job opportunities are increasing and you can work flexible or part-time hours.
- You could use the customer-service and sales skills you will develop to move into other jobs.
- The work can be repetitive, busy and stressful; you will probably work to targets and be under pressure to make sales.

Earnings guide

- You can expect £11,000–£13,000 per year when you start.
- This can rise to £14,000–£17,000 when you have experience and depending on where you work. Financial services call centres tend to pay best and you will earn more in London.
- As a supervisor you could get £18,000–£22,000.
- You may get commission on sales or bonuses if you meet targets.

Further information

Marketing & Sales Standards Setting Body
Moor Hall
Cookham
Berkshire
SL6 9QH
01628 427106
www.msssb.org

Institute of Direct Marketing
1 Park Road
Teddington
Middlesex
TW11 0AR
020 8614 0277
www.theidm.com

Institute of Customer Service
2 Castle Court
St Peter's Street
Colchester
Essex
CO1 1EW
01206 571716
www.instituteofcustomerservice.com

City & Guilds

www.cityandguilds.com/myperfectjob

Car Salesperson

What the work involves

- You will be selling new or used cars, motorbikes or vans; greeting customers, finding out what they're looking for, advising them and explaining different models, features and prices, and demonstrating cars by going out on test drives.
- Your job will include arranging finance for customers and doing paperwork for the sale and the finance.
- Garages promote their cars through advertising, special events and direct contact with customers, which may also be part of your work.
- Sales staff help keep the forecourt, salesroom and cars clean and tidy.

The type of person suited to this work

You will need to be smart, confident and outgoing with a polite, friendly manner and an ability to deal with all types of people and be persuasive without being pushy. You will need good negotiation and numeracy skills.

You should be interested in cars, know a lot about the ones you are selling and be able to explain technical features clearly and simply.

Your wages will depend on how much you sell so you will need to be motivated and determined and able to deal with stress and pressure.

Your job will also involve working out prices and deals and completing forms and paperwork accurately.

You will need to be able to work without supervision.

Working conditions

You could be working in a small, local garage selling used cars or for a large main dealership. You will be based in a showroom but will also be outside on the forecourt and going on test drives.

You will spend most of your time dealing with customers but will also do paperwork.

Working on commission can be stressful and you will probably do quite long hours including evenings and weekends.

The future outlook

There are currently good opportunities in all parts of the country but it is a popular industry, so jobs can be competitive, especially with the large main dealers.

Prospects are good and you can earn a lot if you do well.

In larger dealerships you can progress to senior salesperson, sales manager or dealer principal.

At management level you will probably earn bonuses linked to the sales of the whole team.

You could go on and open your own showroom but will need a lot of money to get started.

entry level

1–2

To both enter and train while working in this career, you will need qualifications at Level 1–2. Please refer to explanation on page vii.

Qualifications and courses

- You do not need formal qualifications to enter and train in this career, but employers will expect GCSEs (A-C)/S in maths and English.
- Some employers look for previous sales or customer service experience. Some of the larger car manufacturers offer graduate traineeships, but these are usually limited to just a few places each year.
- A full, clean driving licence is usually required.
- Much of the training is done on the job, and trainees may be expected to attend short courses and training about the cars they are selling.
- Apprenticeships/Skillseekers may be available to those aged 16–24.
- Achieving a qualification is now very important in this area of work as applying for jobs is competitive.
- Car salespeople receive on-the-job training, and may also work towards NVQs/SVQs at Levels 2 and 3 in Vehicle Sales, or the Institute of the Motor Industry (IMI) Certificate and Diploma in Vehicle sales. The Level 2 Certificate leads to Licentiate Membership of the IMI and the Level 3 Diploma provides Associate Membership.
- Other suitable courses include the ISMM Level 2 course in Sales and Marketing and Level 3 course in Advanced Sales Skills.
- Sales people may also attend short courses run by vehicle manufacturers.

CRCI:SB

CLCI:OE

Other related opportunities

- Customer Services p442
- Motor Vehicle Work p217
- Sales Assistant p450
- Store Manager p459

Advantages/disadvantages

- You will be using your knowledge of cars to interest customers and persuade them to buy.
- You can do very well and earn a high salary.
- It can be very stressful working on commission and having to meet targets and you will probably work long hours.

Earnings guide

- Wages vary a lot. You may be on a fairly small basic salary plus commission and bonuses related to your sales.
- As a starting salary you could expect £9,500–£13,000 per year.
- With experience this can rise to £14,000–£17,000, up to £25,000 with bonuses.
- Top sales people can earn £30,000–£35,000.

Further information

Retail Motor Industry Federation
201 Great Portland Street
London
W1W 5AB
020 7580 9122
www.rmif.co.uk

Automotive Skills
93 Newman Street
London
W1T 3DT
020 7436 6373
www.automotiveskills.org.uk

Institute of the Motor Industry
Fanshaws
Brickendon
Hertford
SG13 8PQ
01992 511521
www.motor.org.uk

Scottish Motor Trade Association
Palmerston House
10 The Loan
South Queensferry
EH30 9NS
0131 331 5510
www.smta.co.uk

www.cityandguilds.com/myperfectjob

Checkout Operator

What the work involves

- You will work on a till, probably in a supermarket or large store receiving payments for goods being bought.
- You will pass goods over a scanner or enter the price onto the till using a keypad. You might weigh and price items such as fruit and vegetables.
- Working on a till involves taking payments using cash, cheques and credit/debit cards, and often giving cashback to customers.
- As part of serving the customers, you may help them pack their purchases into bags, and you will have to keep your area clean and tidy.

The type of person suited to this work

You will need to enjoy meeting people and working with the public to provide a good service, being polite, efficient and helpful.

You will need to have good listening and speaking skills.

You should be able to work accurately and quickly and handle cash and other payments, making sure you give the right change or checking details such as signatures or expiry dates on credit cards.

Checkout operators have to sit for quite long periods and do fairly routine, repetitive work. They also work under pressure and must stay calm when the queues get long and the customers impatient.

You should be well presented and be happy to wear an overall or uniform.

Working conditions

Shops are usually light, airy and warm but can be crowded and stressful.

Checkout operators usually work around 39–40 hours a week, often doing shifts.

You will be working on your own at a till with help from a supervisor who will sort out problems, empty the till and provide change.

A lot of the opportunities are part time. You will probably get staff discount and have a uniform provided.

The future outlook

Retail is a big industry employing around 3 million people in the UK and large stores are opening in out-of-town developments all over the country. There are opportunities in all areas but many of these are for part-time workers.

Most checkout operators work for large companies which usually offer good prospects for promotion and staff training.

You could go on to become a supervisor with responsibility for a particular section, for example the bakery, and even become a trainee manager.

entry level

To both enter and train while working in this career, you will need qualifications at Level 1–2. Please refer to explanation on page vii.

Qualifications and courses

- There are no formal qualification needed to enter and train in this career, although many employers are increasingly asking for good GCSEs/S grades in English and maths.
- You may need to pass a maths test at interview.
- Most training is done on the job working with experienced staff.
- A number of relevant qualifications are available in Retail and Distributive Services including NVQs/SVQs in Retail Operations at Levels 2 and 3, Distributive Operations at Level 1, Retail Sales Delivery at Level 2, Sales at Level 2 and Customer Service at Levels 2 and 3, or BTEC First and National qualifications in Retail/SQA National qualifications in Retail and Distribution.
- Apprenticeships are available for those under 24 years of age.

Other related opportunities

- Call Centre Operative p439
- Customer Services p442
- Petrol Service Sales Assistant p449
- Sales Assistant p450
- Shelf Filler p452

Advantages/disadvantages

- There are lots of job opportunities and you can work flexible and part-time hours and go on to work in other types of shops.
- You do not need qualifications and you could go on to become a supervisor and even move into management.
- The work can be routine and repetitive.

Earnings guide

- You can expect around £10,000–£11.500 per year when you first start work.
- This can rise to £13,000 when you have been working a while and have got some experience.
- £16,000–£19,000 is possible if you are working as a supervisor.

Further information

British Shops and Stores Association Limited
Middleton House
2 Main Road
Middleton Cheney, Banbury
Oxfordshire
OX17 2TN
01295 712277
www.british-shops.co.uk

Wholesale and Retail Training Council (WRTC)
10 Hydepark Road
Mallusk
Newtonabbey
Northern Ireland
BT36 4PY
www.wrtc.co.uk

www.cityandguilds.com/myperfectjob

Customer Services

What the work involves

- Many different types of companies employ customer service staff to provide a direct service to their customers and the public, to help promote their business and company image.

Customer services assistant

- You could be selling products or services or providing a service or information about the company.
- You will work with people face to face or over the telephone and will need a good knowledge of the company and its products.
- You might be displaying products, handling money and payments and dealing with complaints and you will probably work to targets.

Customer services manager

- As a manager you will be responsible for a team of customer service assistants, motivating them to meet their targets and making sure that they are working to company standards.
- Managers recruit and train staff, set and monitor targets, help staff to develop their skills and keep them informed about the company's products and services.
- Managers are expected to deal with more complicated queries or complaints and to make sure that the team is working well.

The type of person suited to this work

You should be friendly, helpful and polite, and enjoy meeting people. You will need to have a genuine interest in helping people. You could be dealing with difficult or angry customers, so will need to be patient and able to stay calm under pressure and when you are busy. You will need to have a lively quick-thinking mind to respond to a wide variety of queries.

Customer service staff must be flexible and able to work quickly and accurately, probably working to targets. They also use computers and may handle cash.

You will need to be able to work as part of a team, and somtimes on your own initiative.

You will need to learn about your company's products and be able to explain them clearly and simply to customers.

Manager

As a manager, you will also need to be able to take responsibility, motivate people and have good organisational and planning skills.

You will need to be good at interview skills, good with figures and computers, and be decisive and quick thinking.

Working conditions

You could be based in an office, mainly on the telephone, using a headset and computer.

You might be in a public office, perhaps behind a counter and a screen.

You will probably be sitting or standing in one place a lot.

The work can be busy and pressured. You will probably be working to targets and may get bonuses.

You could work normal office hours but may do shifts, including evenings, weekends and even nights.

The future outlook

There are a many opportunities in all types of organisations throughout the country, but especially in towns and cities. You might work for shops, banks, call centres, airports or tourist information centres.

Customer services assistant

You could go on to become a supervisor and then a manager.

Many companies, especially the larger ones, have good in-house training covering subjects such as product knowledge, customer service and sales skills.

You will develop skills which could be useful in other jobs or in other departments in the company. In smaller companies, you may be able to take on responsibility more quickly, but have less opportunity for promotion.

Customer services manager

Most opportunities for customer service managers are in larger companies, for example banks and chains of shops. You might be able to move into high-level jobs in the company's head office, perhaps as a customer service specialist, or use your skills and knowledge of the company to move into other management jobs.

In smaller companies you will probably take on a wider role if you get promotion.

CRCI:SA | CLCI:OFZ

Qualifications and courses

entry level

To both enter and train while working in this career, you will need qualifications at Level 1–2. Please refer to explanation on page vii.

Customer services assistant

- You can enter and train in this career with qualifications at Level 2, possibly Level 1. You will usually need 3–4 GCSEs/S grades (A–C/1–3), including maths and English. Some organisations may require higher qualifications such as NVQs/SVQs at Levels 3 and 4, HNCs/HNDs, A levels/other level qualifications or degrees.
- NVQ/SVQ Levels 2 or 3 in Customer Service would be an advantage. Training is often done on the job.

Customer services manager

- You can enter and train in this career with qualifications at Levels 2 or 3 but will need relevant experience. You will usually need 3–4 GCSEs/3–5 S grades (A–C/1–3), including maths and English. NVQ/SVQ Levels 2 or 3 in Customer Service or Management would be an advantage.
- Some employers ask for qualifications at a higher level, such as A levels/H grades or other Level 3 courses.
- Large organisations may have management training schemes, including fast-track schemes for graduates.
- Some entrants start work as customer service assistants or administrators and gain promotion.
- Experienced customer service managers can work towards NVQ/SVQ Level 4 in Customer Services, the Warwick Business School's (University of Warwick) Diploma in Service Leadership, or the University of Leicester's 2-year Diploma in Customer Service management.

Other related opportunities

- Bank / Building Society p9
- Insurance p21
- Sales Assistant p450
- Store Demonstrator p458
- Store Manager p459

Advantages/disadvantages

- You will be meeting people and providing a service, which can be interesting and rewarding.
- The work can be repetitive and dealing with difficult people or problems may be stressful.
- You can earn a good salary if you continually provide an excellent service.

Earnings guide

Customer services assistant

- You could earn £11,000–£12,000 a year when you start work.
- This may rise to £13,000–£18,000 when you have got some experience.
- £21,000+ is possible with experience and working in a large organisation.

Customer services manager

- You could earn £16,000–£20,000 as a trainee manager.
- £20,000–£27,000 is possible with experience and working in a large organisation.
- Experienced managers can earn £30,000+.
- Senior managers in large organisations could earn in excess of £40,000–£55,000.

Further information

Institute of Customer Service
2 Castle Court
St Peter's Street
Colchester
Essex
CO1 1EW
01206 571716
www.instituteofcustomerservice.com

British Shops and Stores Association Limited
Middleton House
2 Main Road
Middleton Cheney, Banbury
Oxfordshire
OX17 2TN
01295 712277
www.british-shops.co.uk

Institute of Leadership and Management (ILM)
1 Giltspur Street
London
EC1A 9DD
www.i-l-m.com

City & Guilds

www.cityandguilds.com/myperfectjob

Market Trader

What the work involves

- Market traders buy goods from a wholesaler or manufacturer, and then sell them from a market stall which they rent in an open-air or covered market.
- You might sell things you have made yourself, such as jewellery, pottery or clothes, at specialist craft markets.
- You will be dealing with customers, encouraging them to buy items on your stall, weighing and wrapping goods, and taking money and possibly cheques, credit and debit cards.
- As well as setting up the stall in the morning, arranging your things and keeping the stall clean and tidy, you will also pack up and clear away in the evenings.

The type of person suited to this work

You will need to be friendly and outgoing and enjoy working with the public in an informal way, persuading them to buy your goods. A good sense of humour is a big bonus when trying to get people to buy from your stall.

Market traders have to be fit and active to transport their goods, set up the stall, be on their feet all day and then pack up when the market closes. You should be prepared to work outside in all weathers, and even covered markets can be cold.

When you are buying goods you will have to know what will sell and negotiate a good price. You will deal with money and will have to do your own accounts, if you are self-employed.

You should be self-motivated and hard-working and, if you are selling your own things, be producing attractive, desirable products, and should be able to create an interesting display on your stall.

Working conditions

You will probably have a very early start and work from about 5am–6.00pm. You will probably have to work Saturdays and often Sundays.

Working on a market means being on your feet all day and outside in all weathers. You may have to travel to buy the goods you sell.

You could be working on your own or with one or two other people. You may work at the same market every day or move round to several different markets during the week.

The future outlook

It can be hard to do well with a market stall: there is a lot of competition and you will need good products.

On craft markets, it can be difficult to sell things at a competitive price.

For a while when you start, you may need to arrive very early in the morning to get a spare pitch, before an opportunity comes up to get your own, permanent stall.

Most market traders are self-employed and you could expand by taking on staff to run extra stalls or you could open a shop.

Local authorities often run weekly markets in town squares and on high streets.

entry level

1–2

To both enter and train while working in this career, you will need qualifications at Level 1–2. Please refer to explanation on page vii.

Qualifications and courses

- There are no formal entry requirements but you will need to have basic maths and English skills.
- You have to be over 18 to rent a market stall but can work as an assistant at 16.
- Most of the training is done on the job, learning from the person you work for or from other traders.
- There are some short courses you can take, usually run by the local authority, and the National Market Traders Federation (NMTF) can give advice.
- You could also do short courses on running your own business, provided by small business advice services.
- If you are selling things you have made, you will probably need to do a specialist course, for example jewellery making or a fashion course at university.
- A driving licence is usually essential.
- Many markets insist that traders have insurance for public liability. The National Market Traders' Federation can provide this.

CRCI:SB | CLCI:OM

Other related opportunities

Advantages/disadvantages

- You will be your own boss, working outside in an active, practical job with lots of contact with the public.
- Markets are often very lively, friendly places.
- The hours can be long and you will be out in all weathers.

Earnings guide

- Wages vary a lot depending on what you are selling and how busy the market is.
- You may earn around £7,000 per year if you have got a stall for 1 or 2 days a week.
- You could earn around £15,000–£22,000 a year if you are working 5+ days a week. If you are selling specialist goods you may earn more.
- A few market traders who are selling specialist goods can earn around £30,000–£40,000 a year.

Further information

www.cityandguilds.com/myperfectjob

National Market Traders' Federation
Hampton House
Hawshaw Lane, Hoyland
Barnsley
S74 0HA
01226 749021
www.nmtf.co.uk

British Shops and Stores Association Limited
Middleton House
2 Main Road
Middleton Cheney, Banbury
Oxfordshire
OX17 2TN
01295 712277
www.british-shops.co.uk

Meat Inspector

What the work involves

- Meat inspectors, sometimes also known as hygiene inspectors, visit slaughterhouses and meat stores to check that meat is being processed and produced safely and hygienically by following relevant laws and regulations.
- You will work with live animals and poultry to check that they are healthy and disease free, and also do post mortems.
- You will check that animals are cared for and transported properly and that meat plants and deliveries are run safely and hygienically, and that unwanted meat or carcases are destroyed properly.
- You will write detailed reports and make sure that any action you have recommended is taken quickly and to the right standards.

The type of person suited to this work

Meat inspectors have to have a good knowledge of the meat-processing industry and usually have worked somewhere like an abattoir or meat-processing plant first to get experience.

You will need to have a good deal of knowledge about the meat industry and the laws surrounding it. You will be dealing with people in lots of different organisations and at all levels, so will need to be able to establish good working relationships and deal calmly with problems.

You will need to have good written and communication skills in order to write clear, accurate, factual reports, understand and apply laws and regulations, know what you are looking for and have a good eye for detail.

It is a fairly active job so you will need to be fit and healthy, practical and good with your hands and able to work to strict safety guidelines.

Working conditions

You will spend most of your time travelling to farms and processing plants. You will be active and on your feet, wearing protective clothing, using tools and equipment and handling heavy meat carcasses.

Slaughterhouses can be cold and noisy and smell strongly, and on farms you will be working outdoors in all weathers.

Meat inspectors usually do normal office hours but may need to work evenings and weekends to work at short notice if there is a hygiene emergency.

The future outlook

Most meat inspectors work for the Meat Hygiene Service which is part of the government's Food Standards Agency. Others work for companies producing or selling food and meat products.

There are jobs in all parts of the UK but opportunities are limited with only around 2800 meat inspectors in the country.

You will need experience in the industry before you can become an inspector. You can then progress to be a supervisor or manager for the Meat Hygiene Service or go into management in a large food company.

entry level

2–3

To both enter and train while working in this career, you will need qualifications at Level 2–3. Please refer to explanation on page vii.

Qualifications and courses

- You can enter and train in this career with qualifications at Levels 2 or 3.
- You will need to get experience in the meat trade before you can become an inspector.
- All meat inspectors must hold the Royal Society for the Promotion of Health's Certificate in Meat Inspection or Poultry Meat Inspection.
- To get onto the course you will need to have at least 5 GCSEs/S grades (A–C/1–3), including English and maths or a science, or Associate membership of the Meat Training Council.
- NVQs/SVQs are available in Meat and Poultry Plant Operations at Level 2 and Meat and Poultry Processing and Meat Processing at Level 2. RSPH offers a Level 2 Certificate in Wild Game Meat Hygiene to meet the food hygiene laws. RSPH also offer Level 3 and Level 4 Awards in Food Safety Supervision for Manufacturing.
- Apprenticeships/Skillseekers may be available for people aged 16–24.

Other related opportunities

- Health and Safety Adviser p19
- Meat Process Worker p215
- Trading Standards Officer p460
- Veterinary Surgeon p262

Advantages/disadvantages

- You will need experience in the industry before you can become an inspector. You can then go on to be a supervisor or manager for the Meat Hygiene Service or go into management in a large food company.
- You need to be flexible with your working hours as you may be asked to respond to an emergency at anytime.

Earnings guide

- You can expect to earn £15,800–£16,500 per year as a trainee inspector.
- Up to £21,000 is the usual salary when you have got some experience.
- You could earn £23,000–£30,000 as a Senior Meat Inspector.

Further information

Meat Hygiene Service
Kings Pool
Peasholme Green
York
YO1 7PR
01904 455501
www.foodstandards.gov.uk

Meat Training Council
PO Box 141
Winterhill House
Snowdon Drive
Milton Keynes
MK6 1YY
01908 231062
www.meattraining.org.uk

Royal Society for the Promotion of Health
38a St George's Drive
London
SW1V 4BH
020 7630 0121
www.rsph.org

Food and Drink Qualifications
PO Box 141
Winterhill House
Snowdon Drive
MK6 1YY
01908 231062
www.meattraining.org.uk

FDQ
Food and Drink Qualifications
PO Box 141
Winterhill House
Snowdon Drive
MK6 1YY
01908 231062
www.meattraining.org.uk

Merchandiser

What the work involves

- You will probably work for a large chain of shops as part of their buying and marketing team, helping to create and maintain the brand image of the company, and to monitor how well their goods might sell.
- You will be involved in deciding what goods the stores will sell to get the best profits, and make sure they are displayed and presented in an attractive way that is consistent throughout the company.
- You may be responsible for a particular area of sales such as women's shoes or bathroom accessories.
- You will work closely with buyers, and help predict fashions and trends. You may also visit suppliers and manufacturers to find products which will appeal to your customers.
- You could work for a wide range of companies including fashion retailers, supermarkets or a chain of stores.

The type of person suited to this work

You will need to be interested in your product and in working out and predicting what will sell and how best to display it. You will need to understand what the customers want.

Merchandisers must be creative and self-motivated with initiative and confidence, because they make decisions involving large amounts of money and have to present their ideas to managers and staff.

You should be able to work well in a team and deal with people at all levels, including negotiating prices and arranging deliveries.

The job involves analysing statistics and sales figures and working under pressure to meet targets and deadlines. You will need excellent communication and negotiation skills.

Working conditions

You will mainly be based in an office in a large store, or in a head office and will probably visit other stores in your region.

You will also be visiting suppliers and manufacturers, so you may have to be away from home regularly.

As a senior merchandiser or with more experience, this will probably include going abroad.

You will probably work normal office hours, but might have to work much longer at busy times.

The future outlook

The retail industry employs a lot of people and is expanding and changing at quite a fast rate and so it is an exciting and challenging area.

Merchandising can be quite competitive – you will need creative, interesting ideas and probably experience in retail.

Most opportunities will be in large towns and cities, many in London.

In a large company, you could get promotion by specialising in a particular product or being responsible for all the stores in an area. Or you could move into related areas such as buying and marketing.

With experience, it is possible to travel and even work abroad.

entry level

To both enter and train while working in this career, you will need qualifications at Level 3–8. Please refer to explanation on page vii.

Qualifications and courses

- Most entrants to this career have a degree, or a Higher National Diploma (HND) but you may be able to start with qualifications at Level 3, and receive further training from your employer.
- Larger companies will accept degrees in any subjects, although retailing, marketing or business studies, economics or maths would be useful.
- You may be able to get a trainee post with Level 3 qualifications but these would be very competitive and you would probably have to have retail experience as well.
- You may be able to do an Apprenticeship/ Skillseekers if you are aged 16–24. NVQs/SVQs are available in Supply Chain Management at Levels 2–5, Retail Operations at Levels 2 and 3, Sales at Levels 2 and 3 or Sales Management at Level 4/5.
- You would probably start by working in all areas of the company as part of your training before specialising in merchandising.
- You could move into merchandising from a buying or marketing job.
- Merchandisers are trained on the job, and may also work towards the professional qualifications of the Chartered Institute of Purchasing and Supply or the Chartered Institute of Marketing. The British Shops and Stores Association offers a Buying and Merchandising Foundation Course by distance learning, aimed at trainee or assistant merchandisers and buyers.
- Some colleges and universities offer HNDs and Foundation degrees in relevant subjects.

Other related opportunities

- Buyer p438
- Marketing p151
- Purchasing Administrator p577
- Store Manager p459

Advantages/disadvantages

- You will be making decisions which will directly affect the image of your company and what the public can buy.
- You will have a lot of responsibility, making decisions involving large sums of money which can be stressful.
- Keeping your finger on the pulse of fashion, future trends and next year's 'must haves' can be exciting.

Earnings guide

- Your wages will vary according to the company you work for.
- As a starter you can expect £15,000–£18,000 per year.
- This could rise to £22,000–£40,000 for an experienced merchandiser.
- Senior merchandisers in large companies can earn up to £50,000.

Further information

British Shops and Stores Association Limited
Middleton House
2 Main Road
Middleton Cheney, Banbury
Oxfordshire
OX17 2TN
01295 712277
www.british-shops.co.uk

Chartered Institute of Marketing
Moor Hall
Cookham
Maidenhead
Berkshire
SL6 9QH
01628 427500
www.cim.co.uk

Chartered Institute of Purchasing & Supply
Easton House
Easton on the Hill
Stamford
Lincolnshire
PE9 3NZ
01780 756777
www.cips.org

Meter Reader

What the work involves

- You will be reading electric, gas or water meters at private homes or commercial buildings. You will be putting the information in to a portable computer or on to a form, to work out what the customer owes.
- You will visit houses and companies reading meters which are inside the building or outside in a box for which you will have a key.
- If the customer is out, you may need to estimate the reading or leave a card to say when you will be back.
- You will probably cover a particular area in a van, car or on foot, and have to work to targets, meet customers and answer questions about the service and the meters.

The type of person suited to this work

You will work mainly on your own and so will need to be able to use your initiative and be motivated and self-disciplined in order to meet your targets and get the work done.

Meter readers must work accurately with numbers and use computers and be happy to deal with the public.

You should be able to organise your own work and plan your routes to make sure you cover your whole area.

As you are out and about in all weathers and will do a lot of walking, you will need to be fit and healthy. You should also be polite, honest and trustworthy because you may be going into people's homes.

Working conditions

You will work alone and will spend most of your day driving or walking. You may need to crawl into small, dark places to find the meter.

The job involves meeting a lot of people and going into all sorts of homes and businesses.

Meter readers usually wear a uniform, always carry ID and may need safety clothing.

A normal week will be around 37–40 hours and you may be able to do overtime. You could have to work at evenings and weekends when people are at home to let you in.

The future outlook

There are job opportunities with companies which supply water, gas and electricity in all parts of the country.

The companies vary in size and some will pay bonuses if you meet or go over your targets.

You could get promotion and lead a team covering a particular area, become a supervisor or manager or become involved in training new staff.

entry level

To both enter and train while working in this career, you will need qualifications at Level 1–2. Please refer to explanation on page vii.

Qualifications and courses

- You can enter and train for this career with qualifications at Levels 1 or 2.
- There are no minimum entry requirements but you will need a good general education and may need GCSEs/S grades (A–C/1–3), usually including English and maths.
- You will probably need to be over 18 and have a clean driving licence, particularly in rural areas.
- Your employer will train you on the job. You will probably spend time learning about the services the company offers and health and safety issues. You will learn about the different meters and how to read them and how to enter the readings accurately on a handheld computer terminal.
- You will then spend time working with an experienced meter reader to learn how to do the job before you go out on your own.
- It is possible to get a relevant NVQ such as Level 2 Utilities Metering Operations or NVQ Level 3 in Revenue Protection.

CRCI:SA

CLCI:RAK

Other related opportunities

- Customer Services p442
- Milk Delivery Person p448
- Postal Delivery Person p576
- Sales Assistant p450

Advantages/disadvantages

- You will be out and about, doing active, practical work and meeting lots of different people.
- You will be working alone and will need to be motivated and self-disciplined to do the work and meet your targets.

Earnings guide

- You can expect around £12,000 per year when you start work.
- £14,000–£16,000 is usual when you have got some experience, and you could earn up to £20,000 with a few years' experience and some additional responsibilities.
- You may get bonuses for meeting targets.
- You would earn more as a supervisor or manager.

Further information

Office of Gas and Electricity Markets (Ofgem)
9 Millbank
London
SW1P 3GE
020 7901 7000
www.ofgem.gov.uk

Office of Water Services (Ofwat)
Centre City Tower
7 Hill Street
Birmingham
B5 4UA
0121 625 1300
www.ofwat.gov.uk

British Plumbing Employers Council Ltd
2 Walker Street
Edinburgh
EH3 7LB
0845 644 6558
www.bpec.org.uk

Milk Delivery Person

What the work involves

- You will drive a milk float to deliver milk, eggs, cream, yoghurt and other food, usually including potatoes, bread and fruit juice, to houses and businesses.
- Before you start you will need to collect the milk and other foods from a depot, you will then go on your round, delivering the things the customers have ordered and collecting empty milk bottles.
- When you have finished, you will go back to the depot to drop off leftover goods and the empty bottles.
- It is important to keep accurate records of what you have sold and how much customers owe so that you can collect the right payments from them. You will also have to keep your float clean and tidy.
- You may return to customers for payments later in the week.

The type of person suited to this work

You will be loading your float, carrying bottles and crates and working outside in all weathers so you will need to be fit and healthy.

You should enjoy meeting people but also be happy to work on your own.

To do a milk round you should be a safe driver and be able to get up very early in the mornings, even when it's cold and dark.

You have to be organised to work out what products you will need for the day based on customer orders, and to keep track of what you have sold, work out bills accurately and collect payments. You will also need to be able to keep records and accounts.

Working conditions

You will get up very early and probably finish your rounds by lunchtime. Expect to work Monday to Saturday delivering, probably visiting homes again on Saturday morning or a weekday evening to collect payments.

Doing a milk round means working outside in all weathers and probably on your own, meeting the public and keeping an eye on ill or elderly people on your round.

Most people are either self-employed or working for a franchise, where they pay a company to be able to sell their products.

The future outlook

Many people now buy most of their food, including milk, in supermarkets, so opportunities for milk rounds are reducing, especially in towns and cities. There are opportunities all over the country though, especially in rural areas.

You could work for a small, local dairy or for a large chain. Most people are self-employed, usually running a franchise.

To run a franchise you will probably need to invest money in a float or van, and learn about the company's products which you will then sell, paying them part of what you earn.

entry level

1–2

To both enter and train while working in this career, you will need qualifications at Level 1–2. Please refer to explanation on page vii.

Qualifications and courses

- You can enter and train for this career with qualifications at Levels 1 and 2.
- There are no formal entry qualifications, but GCSEs/S grades (A–C/1–3) in maths and English may be useful.
- You will usually need to be at least 18 years of age with a full clean driving licence.
- Large companies may offer short in-house induction courses or on-the-job training where you work in a depot and learn about the job and the products and then help out on a round before you work on your own round.
- You may be able to do NVQs/SVQs at Levels 2 and 3, including Customer Service and Sales, or NVQ Level 2 Carry and Deliver Goods.
- If you are working for a franchise, the company may give training on new products and business skills.
- Local colleges and small business advice services run courses on business skills for self-employed people, including book-keeping and selling.

CRCI:SB

CLCI:OM

Other related opportunities

- Driver p563
- Meter Reader p447
- Postal Delivery Person p576

Advantages/disadvantages

- It is a flexible job where you could work for yourself, be out and about meeting people and do active, practical work.
- You will be out in all weathers and will have to start very early in the mornings.

Earnings guide

- Earnings can vary but you could earn around £12,500–£13,500 a year when you start.
- Your wages could go up to around £17,000 when you have some experience.
- You could earn up to about £22,500 if you have additional responsibilities.

Further information

British Franchise Association
Thames View
Newtown Road
Henley-on-Thames
Oxfordshire
RG9 1HG
01491 578050
www.british-franchise.org.uk

Milk Development Council
Stroud Road
Cirencester
Gloucestershire
GL7 6JN
01285 646500
www.mdc.org.uk

Petrol Service Sales Assistant

What the work involves

- You will work at a till and use a console which activates the petrol pumps and displays the amount the customers have taken.
- You will be taking customers payments using cash, cheques, credit or debit cards. Many garages also sell groceries and a range of other products.
- Your job will involve keeping the shop clean and tidy, the shelves stocked up and the forecourt clean and tidy.
- In some petrol stations, you might be actually filling cars and vans with petrol or diesel for customers.
- It is important to follow health and safety guidelines and when you finish work, you will cash up your till and keep a log of how much petrol has been sold.

The type of person suited to this work

You should be someone who enjoys meeting people and working with the public, but who is also happy to work alone, without supervision or perhaps with one or two other people. You will need to be reliable and trustworthy and not be allergic to petrol or other fuels.

As well as serving customers, you will probably be asked for directions and will need to be responsible and reliable and able to use your initiative.

You will need to follow safety regulations and will have to take details of anyone who drives off without paying, and may have to speak to customers on the forecourt using a tannoy.

You should be able to handle money and payments, stay calm when you are busy and keep logs of how much petrol has been sold.

Working conditions

You will spend most of your time sitting at a till and serving customers, working on your own or with one or two others. You may be in quite a small kiosk, and at night, you will probably serve through a hatch.

If you are actually serving petrol you will be outside in all weathers.

You will work around 39–40 hours a week, usually doing shifts to cover evenings, weekends and sometimes nights.

You may be taking deliveries and garages can smell strongly of fuel.

The future outlook

There are petrol stations everywhere, especially in towns and cities, and job opportunities are good for part-time or full-time work, particularly in large garages and supermarkets.

You could use your sales and customer service experience to move into other shop work and from there progress to a supervisor's job and on to trainee management posts.

You could go on to work for the oil company which supplies the garage or supervise or manage several petrol stations in an area.

Other related opportunities

- Checkout Operator p441
- Customer Services p442
- Sales Assistant p450
- Store Manager p459

Advantages/disadvantages

- You will be meeting people and working with the public.
- You can work flexible hours and some people enjoy working shifts. Part-time work is common.
- The job is repetitive and you will probably spend most of your time sitting at a till.
- Most of the jobs are part time.

entry level

1–2

To both enter and train while working in this career, you will need qualifications at Level 1–2. Please refer to explanation on page vii.

Qualifications and courses

- You can enter and train for this career with qualifications at Levels 1 or 2.
- There are no formal entry requirements but you will need reasonable maths and English and may have to sit a test. Some employers may prefer a minimum of 4 GCSEs/S grades (A–C/1–3).
- You usually need to be at least 18 to sell petrol.
- Training is mainly on the job, working with experienced staff. You will probably start by doing an induction course to learn about the company and health and safety regulations. You can go on and do in-house courses on subjects such as security, customer care and dealing with fires.
- NVQs/SVQs are available in Forecourt Operations at Level 2, Customer Care at Level 2, Retail Operations at Level 2, and Customer Service at Levels 2, 3 and 4. There are also BTEC First and National qualifications in Retail and SQA National qualifications in Retail and Distribution, and various retail certificates offered by companies or local colleges.
- Some professional bodies offer courses. The Petrol Retailers Association offer a Certificate in Petrol Forecourt Safety at Level 2 and the Safe Unloading of Petrol from Road Tankers qualification.
- Apprenticeships/Skillseekers may be available to those aged 16–24.

Earnings guide

- You will probably earn £10,000–£13,000 per year when starting. You will get paid more for working shifts and doing overtime.
- Salaries could rise to £15,000–£17,000 as a forecourt supervisor or working nights.

Further information

Cogent (Sector Skills Council for the chemical, nuclear, oil and gas, petroleum and polymer industries)
Unit 5, Mandarin Court
Centre Park
Warrington
Cheshire
WA1 1GG
01925 515200
www.cogent-ssc.com

Retail Motor Industry Federation
201 Great Portland Street
London
W1W 5AB
020 7580 9122
www.rmif.co.uk

Scottish Motor Trade Association
Palmerston House
10 The Loan
South Queensferry
EH30 9NS
0131 331 5510
www.smta.co.uk

www.cityandguilds.com/myperfectjob

Sales Assistant

What the work involves

- You will deal with customers, offering them a polite and helpful and speedy service to sell a range of goods.
- You will help keep the shop tidy and well stocked, answer questions, deal with complaints and give suggestions and advice.
- Shops range from small specialist outlets to huge department stores, so your duties will vary. In small clothes shops, for example, you may help and advise people to find an outfit which suits them.
- You could be weighing food or advising on technical equipment such as TVs or computers. If your shop operates internet shopping, you might make up the orders that have been placed on-line.
- When you are working on the till, you will take payments, give change, deal with refunds, wrap goods and arrange orders and deliveries.

The type of person suited to this work

You will need to be well presented, outgoing, friendly and polite, enjoy meeting people and be able to deal with awkward customers and stay calm when you are busy.

Sales assistants have to learn about the things they are selling, which could involve in-house training, and they must be able to help and advise customers to find what they want.

You could be working to targets and earning bonuses according to how much you sell, so will need to be persuasive but not pushy.

You should be responsible and trustworthy, and fit and active to cope with being on your feet all day.

You should be able to work within a team and on your own when required.

Working conditions

Shops vary enormously. In small shops you could spend most of the time at the till/checkout. In large stores you could be working on the shop floor, helping and advising customers and fetching goods from stockrooms.

You may have to carry quite heavy things and will be on your feet all day.

You will keep the shop clean and tidy and may wear a uniform.

You could work early or late shifts and at weekends and evenings.

At peak times you will be very busy and at other times you may have very few customers.

The future outlook

There are shops in all areas of the country and opportunities are increasing as the retail industry is expanding. Large retail parks and shopping centres have meant that some smaller shops in town centres have closed.

Working in a small shop you may get to know your regulars well and be given responsibility quite quickly, but promotion prospects can be limited.

In large stores and chains you will probably get training and can quickly become a supervisor and then move into management jobs. Depending on your employer, you might have to move around from shop to shop gaining experience within different-sized shops and departments.

1–2 **entry level**

To both enter and train while working in this career, you will need qualifications at Level 1–2. Please refer to explanation on page vii.

Qualifications and courses

- You can enter and train for this career with qualifications at Levels 1 or 2.
- If you have a relevant qualification at Level 3 or above, you may be able to go straight into trainee management jobs. There are specific retail management degree and HND courses available.
- There are no minimum entry requirements for this work. However, larger companies may ask for 2–4 GCSEs/S grades (A–C/1–3).
- You may have to pass tests in basic maths and English.
- Most training is done on the job, learning from experienced staff.
- You could do an Apprenticeship/ Skillseekers if aged 16–24. You would get NVQs/SVQs at Levels 2 and 3, probably in Customer Service.
- Sales assistants can also work towards NVQs/SVQs in Retail Operations at Levels 2 and 3, or Distributive Operations at Levels 2 and 3, an OCR Certificate in Retail, or a C&G Certificate in Retailing.

CRCI:SB | CLCI:OE

Other related opportunities

- Beauty p412
- Checkout Operator p441
- Customer Services p442
- Receptionist p25
- Specialist Shop Assistant p455
- Store Demonstrator p458

Advantages/disadvantages

- There are lots of opportunities and you will be meeting new people.
- You will be on your feet all day and the hours can be long.
- You will have very busy times and very quiet times.

Earnings guide

- Wages vary a lot depending on the type and size of the shop.
- When you first start work you can expect a salary of around £11,500–£13,500 per year.
- With experience this rises to £18,000+ as a supervisor.
- You will get discounts and may get bonuses and commission on what you sell, and may get more money for working shifts.

Further information

www.cityandguilds.com/myperfectjob

British Shops and Stores Association Limited
Middleton House
2 Main Road
Middleton Cheney, Banbury
Oxfordshire OX17 2TN
01295 712277
www.british-shops.co.uk

Scrap Dealer

What the work involves

- Using equipment such as metal cutters and burners, you will collect and take apart metal machinery and vehicles – cars, vans and lorries.
- You will then sort the metal, taking out anything dangerous or unsuitable, grade it, clean it and bundle it together.
- The bundled metal is then fed into a crushing machine which forms it into bales.
- You will probably drive forklift trucks or cranes to move the metal and bales about the site and load it onto delivery lorries.
- You might drive the lorries as well, delivering the metal to steel works and foundries.

The type of person suited to this work

You will need to be fit, active and healthy, able to operate machinery and lift weights.

You should be prepared to work outside in all weathers and not mind getting dirty.

Scrapyards can be dangerous, so you will wear protective clothing and will need to work safely and responsibly.

You should be happy to work as part of a team, or on your own.

Working conditions

It is an active, physical job: you will be lifting heavy weights and operating machinery, hand-held cutters and other equipment.

You could be driving forklift trucks or lorries. You will work as part of a team and wear protective clothing, including boots and helmets.

You will probably work Monday–Saturday and may do overtime.

The future outlook

People are increasingly interested in recycling and local authorities have to meet government targets for recycling, so the demand for scrap metal is likely to rise.

You could be working for a small, local firm or a large company. Most scrap-metal dealers are near towns and cities.

Much of the work is now done using machinery and new techniques and methods are being developed all the time.

Once you have got some experience you could become a supervisor and even become self-employed and set up your own scrap dealer company.

entry level

1–2

To both enter and train while working in this career, you will need qualifications at Level 1–2. Please refer to explanation on page vii.

Qualifications and courses

- There are no minimum entry requirements for this job but you will need basic maths skills.
- You will be trained on the job, working with experienced staff.
- You will need to be very aware of health and safety issues and regulations which apply to scrapyards. The British Metals Recycling Association (BMRA) runs training courses specifically for the metal recycling industry, including health and safety, plant operator training, and preparation for the Environment Agency's technical competence tests.
- You must be 18 years old or over to drive a fork-lift truck without being supervised, and you need to be fully trained to drive a fork-lift truck by doing a course approved by the Health and Safety Commission. Several organisations run these, including the Association of Industrial Truck Trainers (AITT).
- You need to be fully trained to drive a forklift truck by doing a course approved by the Health and Safety Commission; several organisations run these, including the Association of Industrial Truck Trainers (AITT).

CRCI:SD | CLCI:OK

Other related opportunities

- Driver p563
- Lift Truck Operator p568
- Recycling Operative p428
- Refuse Collection Operative p429
- Warehouse p586

Advantages/disadvantages

- You do not need qualifications and it is an active, practical, outdoor job.
- The work can be dirty and dangerous, and you will be working outside in all weathers.

Earnings guide

- Wages will vary but you would probably start on around £11,500–£13,500 per year.
- An experienced forklift truck driver would earn around £19,500–£22,000.

Further information

British Metals Recycling Association
16 High Street
Brampton
Huntingdon
Cambridgeshire
PE28 4TU
01480 455249
www.recyclemetals.org

Fork Lift Truck Association
Manor Farm Buildings,
Lasham,
Alton,
Hampshire
GU34 5SL
01256 381441
www.fork-truck.org.uk

Association of Industrial Truck Trainers
The Spring Board Centre
Mantle Lane
Coalville
Leicestershire
LE67 3DW
01530 277857
www.aitt.co.uk

www.cityandguilds.com/myperfectjob

Shelf Filler

What the work involves

- Most shelf fillers work in supermarkets or large stores, loading trolleys in a stockroom or warehouse, before wheeling them in to the shop and arranging items on to the shelves. You may also be pricing goods using a price gun, and you might have to work on the till at the busiest times.
- You will check the shop to see where there are gaps or which things are running out, then collect the items from the stockroom and fill the shelves up from behind, bringing the older stock to the front to make sure things don't go past their sell-by dates.
- You will also help keep the store clean and tidy and will answer queries from customers, checking if the goods they want are in the stockroom or taking them to a different part of the shop to find what they are looking for.

entry level

To both enter and train while working in this career, you will need qualifications at Level 1–2. Please refer to explanation on page vii.

The type of person suited to this work

You will be loading and unloading trolleys and lifting fairly heavy weights, bending down to low shelves and may be using stepladders to reach higher shelves, so you will need to be fit and active.

You will need to have a neat appearance as you will be working in a public area.

You should enjoy meeting people as you will have a lot of contact with customers and will probably work on the tills as well, which means being polite and helpful.

Your job will include keeping stock records, on paper and computer, and repeating the same tasks all day. You will also be expected to make the sales items look good on the shelves, so a good eye for design will be useful.

Shelf fillers must be honest and reliable, able to concentrate and work as part of a team and be happy to wear a uniform or overall.

Qualifications and courses

- You can enter and train in this career with qualifications at Levels 1 or 2.
- There are no formal entry qualifications but you will probably need basic maths and English skills.
- Most of your training will be on the job, working with experienced staff.
- You might train to use the tills on the job, and could go on to take NVQs/SVQs in Retail at Levels 1, 2 and 3 or Retail Skills Level 2 or Customer Service Levels 1–4.
- With further training and qualifications, you could progress to a supervisor role, and may go on to become a trainee manager.
- If you work for a large company, you will probably start by doing an induction course for a few days before starting to work in the shop. This will cover things like health and safety and information about the company and its products.
- If aged 16–24 you may be able to do an Apprenticeship/Skillseekers where you would get NVQs/SVQs at Levels 2 and 3.

Working conditions

Shops are usually light, airy and warm but can be crowded and stressful.

Shelves are filled up all day but most of the work is done early or late and sometimes overnight, so you will probably work shifts, including weekends, doing around 39–40 hours a week.

A lot of the opportunities are part time. You will probably get a staff discount and have a uniform provided.

The future outlook

There are supermarkets and large stores in all areas of the country and job opportunities in shops are increasing. There is a trend towards out-of-town shopping areas where shops are often huge and so need many shelf fillers.

Large chain stores often have very good staff-training schemes and there are opportunities to get promotion to supervisor and then management level.

If you are working for a small store or company, you may need to move jobs to get promotion.

CRCI:SB

CLCI:OFM

Other related opportunities

- Checkout Operator p441
- Customer Services p442
- Petrol Service Sales Assistant p449
- Store Manager p459
- Warehouse p586

Advantages/disadvantages

- You may get staff discounts.
- You can work flexible hours, including evenings and weekends.
- You do not need qualifications to start, and could move up to become a supervisor and then into management jobs.
- The work can be repetitive and you may work unsocial hours.
- There are opportunities all over the country.

Earnings guide

- Wages vary a lot depending on the size and type of shop you work in.
- You will probably earn £11,000–£12,500 per year when you start.
- Your wages will go up when you have got experience or when you take on more responsibility, such as working on the tills or in a specialist department within the store.

Further information

www.cityandguilds.com/myperfectjob

British Shops and Stores Association Limited
Middleton House
2 Main Road
Middleton Cheney, Banbury
Oxfordshire
OX17 2TN
01295 712277
www.british-shops.co.uk

British Retail Consortium
2nd Floor
21 Dartmouth Street
London
SW1H 9BP
020 7854 8900
www.brc.org.uk

Shoe Repairer

What the work involves

- Shoe repairers mend and repair shoes boots and other footwear. They can also repair belts, bags and briefcases, using specialist tools and materials including nail and staple guns and stitching machines.
- You will replace soles and heels by stitching or gluing on new ones and finishing them off neatly.
- A lot of shoe repairers also use specialist machinery to cut keys and do metal engraving.
- You will be serving customers, labelling the shoes they leave, issuing customers with tickets, taking payments, using a till and probably selling things like shoe dyes and polishes, belts and handbags.

entry level

To both enter and train while working in this career, you will need qualifications at Level 1–2. Please refer to explanation on page vii.

The type of person suited to this work

It is important to be practical, good at working with your hands and able to do quite small, detailed work quickly and neatly. As the machinery and tools can be dangerous, you will need to be responsible and work safely, be happy wearing overalls and getting your hands dirty.

You might be dyeing shoes, so good colour vision as well as good eyesight for doing small repairs is essential. You will need to enjoy meeting people and be able to cope with being busy and working quickly whilst customers wait for their repairs. You should be happy to work on your own or in a small team, and be able to work out costs and deal with money and payments.

You will need to be able to work accurately and quickly, have good listening skills, and have business skills if you are self-employed.

Qualifications and courses

- You can enter and train in this career with qualifications at Levels 1 or 2.
- There are no formal entry requirements although customer service experience would be useful.
- NVQs/SVQs are available in Retail Operations at Levels 2 and 3, and a City & Guilds certificate in Retail Principles. City & Guilds also offer a Higher Professional Diploma in Retail Management.
- Training is done on the job, working alongside an experienced shoe repairer. It is possible to work towards an NVQ/SVQ Footwear Repair at Levels 2 and 3. Or a Vocationally Related Qualification (VRQ) in Footwear and Leather production.
- Apprenticeship/Skillseekers may be available to those aged 16–24.

Working conditions

You will be on your feet a lot, using a range of tools and equipment. You will be using dyes and glues and it can be noisy and dirty with strong smells, so you will wear an overall. Allergies can be a problem.

Shoe repairers usually work around 40 hours a week, including Saturdays.

You may work on your own or with one or two others and will be dealing with the public.

Some shoe repairers work in factories repairing goods which customers have returned.

The future outlook

There are around 8000 shoe repairers in all areas of the country but job opportunities can be limited as most are small shops only employing a few people.

Shoe repairers also work in small outlets in supermarkets or department stores.

You will learn a skill, probably including engraving, and could open your own business. You would need some money to start up, and business skills to plan your work and keep accounts.

In a large chain you could go on to management jobs.

CRCI:SB | CLCI:OFZ

Other related opportunities

- Clothing and Fabric Production p198
- Customer Services p442
- Sales Assistant p450
- Watch / Clock Repairer p226

Advantages/disadvantages

- You do not need qualifications and will be doing a practical, hands-on job and meeting lots of people.
- You could work for yourself, running your own shoe repair outlet.
- The work can be repetitive and fiddly.

Earnings guide

- Wages can vary a lot. Many shoe repairers are self-employed and so wages depend on how big the shop is, where it is and how well it is doing.
- Working for someone else, you will probably earn £10,500–£12,000 per year when you start.
- This could rise to £17,000 with experience and perhaps extra responsibility. Shop managers could get £21,000+.
- You might get paid bonuses and will probably get discounts.

Further information

SkillFast-UK (Sector Skills Council for the apparel, footwear and textiles industries)
Richmond House
Lawnswood Business Park
Redvers Close
Leeds
LS16 6RD
0113 239 9600
www.skillfast-uk.org

MultiService Association (Shoe Repairs, Watch Repairs, Engraving and Key Cutting)
St Crispin's House
Station Road
Desborough
Northamptonshire
NN14 2SA
01536 760374
http://somsr.msauk.biz/

British Shops and Stores Association Limited
Middleton House
2 Main Road
Middleton Cheney, Banbury
Oxfordshire
OX17 2TN
01295 712277
www.british-shops.co.uk

www.cityandguilds.com/myperfectjob

Shopkeeper

What the work involves

- A shopkeeper is normally self-employed running one or more specialist shops, selling anything from hardware to designer fashion.
- You will be finding manufacturers and suppliers, which can mean travelling in this country and abroad, for example to India to buy jewellery, or in your area to find craftspeople making pottery or specialist food such as homemade cheese or breads.
- In the shop, you will be serving customers, offering advice, helping them choose or order what they want and then wrapping the goods and taking payments.
- As well as keeping the shop tidy and well stocked, you will pay staff wages and keep books and accounts.
- You could be running a franchise store on behalf of a large retail chain.

entry level

To both enter and train while working in this career, you will need qualifications at Level 1–3. Please refer to explanation on page vii.

Qualifications and courses

- You can enter this career with qualifications at any level.
- There are no formal entry requirements although customer service experience would be useful.
- NVQs/SVQs are available in Retail Operations at Levels 2 and 3, and a City & Guilds certificate in Retail Principles. City & Guilds also offer a Higher Professional Diploma in Retail Management.
- Other qualifications available include the University Certificate in SME Retail Management which is offered by Manchester Metropolitan University. And some local colleges may offer evening courses in Marketing and Sales skills.

The type of person suited to this work

Anyone who is self-employed needs to be determined and motivated with a real interest in what they are doing; you should also be prepared to work long hours and to travel in order to find stock and suppliers.

You will need to be able to sell and market your goods and will need to be confident about finding products which people want to buy.

Excellent communication skills are essential for working with suppliers, building up good relationships with your customers and finding and supervising staff.

Also important is a good business sense and being able to plan your finances, keeping accounts and coping with the stress and uncertainty, as well as the rewards, of being your own boss.

You should be well organised, have some marketing, business and sales skills to succeed in this area of work.

Working conditions

Your hours and conditions will depend on what you are selling and how well you do.

Shops usually open at weekends and often in the evenings, with newsagents and convenience stores opening early and late.

You will be responsible for everything, so will work long hours. Being your own boss can be stressful and uncertain but also extremely satisfying and rewarding.

The future outlook

You could run any type of shop depending on what you are interested in.

One option is to operate a franchise, for example a local convenience store, paying a larger company to use their name and sell their products.

If you are successful, you could expand by opening more or larger stores.

The trend towards large shops, often in out-of-town developments, has meant that lots of smaller shops have closed. It's a very competitive business so you will need to find the right product, perhaps something unusual or very high quality.

Earnings guide

- Earnings can vary enormously and will depend on how successful you are, the size of the business, where it is and what you are selling.
- On average, shopkeepers earn £15,000–£30,000 a year but if you do well you could earn a lot more.

Other related opportunities

- Buyer p438
- Market Trader p444
- Merchandiser p446
- Sales Assistant p450
- Watch / Clock Repairer p226

Advantages/disadvantages

- There is a lot of freedom in being your own boss: you do not have to answer to anyone else and can make all your own choices and decisions.
- You will work long hours and have to take responsibility for everything, which can be very stressful.
- You will need to develop good business skills as success will depend on your abilities alone.

Further information

www.cityandguilds.com/myperfectjob

British Franchise Association
Thames View
Newtown Road
Henley-on-Thames
Oxfordshire
RG9 1HG
01491 578050
www.british-franchise.org.uk

Scottish Enterprise
5 Atlantic Quay
150 Broomielaw
Glasgow
G2 8LU
0141 248 2700
www.scottish-enterprise.com

Business Link
www.businesslink.gov.uk

CRCI:SB | CLCI:OE

Specialist Shop Assistant

What the work involves

- You will be dealing with customers, advising them, wrapping and serving goods and taking payments. You will need a knowledge of what you are selling and will keep the shop tidy, presenting the goods attractively.
- There is a huge range of different shops you could work in. Here are some of them:

Butcher

- Butchers prepare, store and sell meat and meat products such as pies and sausages, advising customers on different meats and how to cook them.
- They also bone and joint meat using knives and electrical equipment like mincing machines.
- It is important to store meat correctly and butchers work to strict hygiene regulations.

Computer sales assistant

- You will sell computers and software, for example word-processing packages and games, and related equipment such as printers, ink and paper.
- By talking to customers and finding out what they need, you can then advise them on the best products. To do this requires a lot of technical knowledge and the ability to demonstrate and possibly install equipment.

Florist

- Florists buy, display and sell flowers and plants, and often pots, containers and dried flowers.
- You will prepare flowers for special occasions – parties, weddings and funerals – making up table decorations, buttonholes, bouquets and wreaths.
- As well as arranging bouquets to sell, you will also make them up to customers' requests and will probably make deliveries, and could go to customers' houses or businesses to set up arrangements.

Fishmonger

- Fishmongers prepare and sell fish and seafood, advising customers about which fish are available and how to cook and serve them.
- You will use knives to skin, bone and gut fish and must work within strict hygiene guidelines.

Greengrocer

- Greengrocers buy and sell fresh fruit and vegetables and related things, including fresh herbs and flowers.
- Serving customers in a greengrocers includes weighing and packing goods and possibly advising on what's in season, where it was grown and how to prepare it.

Jeweller

- As well as jewellery, you will sell a range of other items, including ornaments, glassware, christening gifts and tankards.
- Jewellers serve and advise customers who may be spending large amounts of money on special items such as engagement and wedding rings.

Newsagent

- Newsagents sell newspapers and magazines and a range of other things which could include sweets, chocolate, books, stationery, cigarettes and basic food like bread and milk.
- You have to start very early in the morning in order to sort newspapers and arrange for them to be delivered to customers.

Pet shop

- Working in a pet shop includes looking after the animals, making sure they're clean and fed and sometimes breeding them for sale.
- As well as serving customers, you will also advise them on caring for and feeding the animals they buy.

Post office

- In a post office, you will sit at a counter, behind a screen, dealing with a range of products and services including parcels, stamps, car tax and passport applications.
- You will handle a lot of cash, paying out benefits such as pensions, dealing with gas and electricity bills, and servicing customers' personal Post Office accounts.
- A lot of time will be spent advising customers, helping them fill in forms, and completing a range of forms and paperwork yourself, some of which can be quite complicated.

Personal shopper

- You will help customers by collecting their purchases or helping them to choose which items to buy.
- Although you will probably work within a clothing or food outlet, you could work in all types of shop.
- You might also provide services to elderly and disabled shoppers who come to your store.

Qualifications and courses

- You can enter a career with qualifications at Levels 1 or 2, but you may have to pass tests in basic maths and English and larger companies may ask for some GCSEs/S grades (A–C/1–3). A Saturday or part-time job in a shop whilst you are still at school would be useful.
- With qualifications at Level 3 or above you may go straight into trainee management jobs.
- You might be able to enter via an Apprenticeship/Skillseekers if you are aged 16–24. You can work towards NVQs/SVQs at Levels 2 and 3, probably in Retail Operations and/or Customer Service.

Butcher

- You can take NVQs/SVQs at Levels 2–3 in relevant areas such as Meat and Poultry Butchering Operations, Meat Processing, Meat and Poultry Processing, Meat and Meat-based Products Sales and Distribution and a Foundation Certificate in Meat Safety and an Intermediate Certificate in Meat and Poultry.
- You can take management level qualifications and join the Worshipful Company of Butchers as an affiliate, associate or graduate member, depending on your qualifications and experience.

Computer sales assistant

- A qualification in ICT would be useful.
- You will do in-house courses to learn about the company you work for and about the products you are selling, including courses run by the manufacturers.

Florist

- You can do full-time courses in floristry before starting work. BTEC/SQA National qualifications are available in floristry, as are HNDs and Foundation degrees.
- You can take NVQs/SVQs in Floristry at Levels 2 and 3. A City & Guilds National Certificate in Floristry is also available.
- With experience you can take qualifications from the Society of Floristry – the Intermediate Certificate (ICSF) and the National Diploma (NDSF), which is the highest floristry qualification in this country and is recognised abroad.

Fishmonger

- You will be trained on the job in the correct way of cutting, preparing and storing fish and will take food hygiene and health and safety qualifications.

Greengrocer

- Training will be on the job and you will learn about how to store, prepare and advise customers on the fruit and vegetables you are selling.

Jeweller

- Training will be on the job. You will learn about the company you are working for and about the products you sell and may attend training and presentations from the companies which supply the products.
- The National Association of Goldsmiths offers the Professional Jewellers Diploma.

Newsagent

- You will be trained whilst you work, learning about the products you stock and how to handle orders and deliveries.
- You could take an NVQ in Business Start-up at Level 3 and Owner Management at Level 4.

Pet Shop

- You will be trained on the job in caring for the animals, feeding and cleaning them and advising customers on their needs.
- You could do a full-time course in animal care before you get a job or take NVQs/SVQs in animal care whilst you are working.
- Relevant pre-entry qualifications include a BTEC First Diploma in Animal Care, a National qualification in Animal Care (Pet Store Management), Animal Management (Care) or Fish Management (Ornamental). City & Guilds also offer a National Certificate in Aquatics and Ornamental Fish Management.

Post Office

- No formal qualifications are required but good numeracy, literacy and communication skills are essential. Previous experience within a retail position would be an advantage.
- You will initially work a 1-year probationary period during which you will either have training on the job or be required to attend a 4-week training programme. Staff may work towards an NVQ/SVQ Levels 2 and 3 in Customer Service.

Personal shopper

- There are no formal entry requirements for this job.
- You will normally have some experience in retail or fashion.

entry level

To both enter and train while working in this career, you will need qualifications at Level 1–8. Please refer to explanation on page vii.

The type of person suited to this work

You will need to be presentable, outgoing, friendly and polite, enjoy meeting people and be able to deal with awkward customers and stay calm when you are busy.

You could be working to targets and earning bonuses according to how much you sell, so will need to be persuasive but not pushy.

You should be responsible and trustworthy, and fit and active to cope with being on your feet all day.

Butcher/fishmonger

In a butchers or fishmongers, you will need to be able to work quickly and accurately with knives and other equipment.

Florist

Florists need to be artistic and good with their hands.

Pet shop

Pet shop assistants must enjoy working with animals.

Post office

In a post office, you will need to be good with numbers.

Personal shopper

As you will represent your store, you should be well presented and have good communication skills. You will need a good knowledge of the products within your shop and have a good idea of colour, fashion, style and trends.

Working conditions

Shops vary enormously. You will probably be on your feet all day and may have to carry quite heavy things.

Butchers, fishmongers, florists and greengrocers can be cold and messy and you will wear overalls and protective clothing, possibly including a hat.

In a jewellers, you will be expected to be smart and well presented.

In a post office, you will be sitting behind a counter for most of the day.

In a pet shop, you will be working with the animals including feeding and cleaning them out.

In a newsagents, you will probably have to start extremely early to deal with newspaper deliveries.

Whatever your work, you will keep the shop clean and tidy and may wear a uniform.

You could work early or late shifts and at weekends and evenings.

Personal shoppers often have access to special, more private customer facilities that may include fitting rooms or packaging services. You will spend a lot of your time on your feet escorting customers and fetching and carrying of products.

The future outlook

There are shops in all areas of the country and opportunities are increasing as the retail industry is expanding, but large retail parks and shopping centres have meant that some smaller, specialist shops in town centres have closed.

Large chain stores offer opportunities for some specialist retailers including butchers, fishmongers and florists, and training and prospects are good. You can get responsibility quite quickly and progress into management jobs.

Other specialist shops can either be individually owned, local shops or large chains. Again, the chains offer good prospects and training.

Working in a small shop you may get to know your regulars well and be given responsibility quite quickly, but promotion prospects can be limited.

You could use your specialist skills and experience to open your own shop but will need money to start you off.

With the Post Office, you could work in a large post office or run your own sub-post office, probably as part of another shop.

Other related opportunities

- Bookseller p435
- Checkout Operator p441
- Customer Services p442
- Meat Process Worker p215
- Receptionist p25
- Sales Assistant p450
- Store Manager p459

Advantages/disadvantages

- You do not need entry qualifications and there are good prospects for progressing into management level jobs.
- Pet shops can be a great way of working with animals. If you are artistic and interested in flowers and plants, floristry can be a rewarding career.
- If you are interested in food, you might enjoy working in specialist food shops advising customers.
- There are lots of opportunities and you will meet new people, and in small shops you will probably get to know your regulars well.
- You will be on your feet all day and the hours can be long.

Earnings guide

- Wages vary a lot depending on the type and size of the shop.
- Check the websites given below for more details.
- You could earn around £11,000 per year when you first start work.
- This could rise to £13,000–£15,000 when you have got some experience.
- You might earn £18,000+ as a supervisor.
- You will get discounts and may get bonuses and commission on what you sell. You may also get more money for working shifts.

Further information

British Shops and Stores Association Limited
Middleton House
2 Main Road
Middleton Cheney
Banbury
Oxfordshire OX17 2TN
01295 712277
www.british-shops.co.uk

BUTCHER
Meat Training Council
PO Box 141
Winterhill House
Snowdon Drive
Milton Keynes
MK6 1YY
01908 231062
www.meattraining.org.uk

Scottish Meat Training
8–10 Needless Road
Perth
PH2 0JW
01738 637785
www.foodtraining.net

FLORIST
Society of Floristry
0870 241 0432
www.societyoffloristry.org

FISHMONGER
Billingsgate Seafood Training School
Office 30
Billingsgate Market
Trafalgar Way
London
E14 5ST
020 7517 3548
www.seafoodtraining.org

JEWELLER
British Jewellers' Association
Federation House
10 Vyse Street
Birmingham
B18 6LT
0121 237 1110
www.bja.org.uk

NEWSAGENT
National Federation of Retail Newsagents
Yeoman House
Sekforde Street
London
EC1R 0HF
0207 253 4225
www.nfrn.org.uk

POST OFFICE
Post Office
80 Old Street
London
EC1V 9NN
0845 722 3344
www.postoffice.co.uk

JEWELLER
National Association of Goldsmiths
78a Luke Street
London
EC2A 4XG
020 7613 4445
www.jewellers-online.org

www.cityandguilds.com/myperfectjob

Store Demonstrator

What the work involves

- You could be in a supermarket, department store, shopping centre or exhibition hall, demonstrating or promoting a product or new line.
- You will set the products out attractively, for example cutting up food or pouring drinks, and clear up at the end of the session.
- Demonstrators give out leaflets, samples and vouchers for special offers, and encourage customers to try samples.
- You will also tell customers about the products, perhaps demonstrating how they work and what they can be used for, and encouraging them to buy.

entry level

To both enter and train while working in this career, you will need qualifications at Level 1–2. Please refer to explanation on page vii.

Qualifications and courses

- You can enter and train for this career with qualifications at Levels 1 or 2.
- There are no minimum requirements and you will need a good basic education and will need to be smart and have a good clear speaking voice. Some employers look for GCSE maths and English at grades A-C.
- You might need specialist knowledge, for example cooking and food hygiene qualifications to demonstrate food products, or beauty qualifications to work with cosmetics.
- There are no formal training courses: you will be trained on the job. An NVQ/SVQ related to the specialist area of your work such as Beauty Therapy can be useful. You might also find a Basic Certificate in Food Hygiene useful if you are demonstrating anything related to food.
- You will have training on the products you are working with from the company selling them. This could be leaflets and information or a demonstration of the products, including role-play and tips on selling and demonstration.
- If you work for just one company, they will probably have an in-house training programme.

The type of person suited to this work

You will need to enjoy meeting people, and be confident, friendly and outgoing, well presented and polite. You will need to be self-motivated and happy to approach people and encourage them to try new things.

You will need to have good communication and negotiation skills and be able to market the product, and explain why this product is better than others.

You should be able to learn about a product and be able to explain and demonstrate it clearly. You will need to be enthusiastic and persuasive, but not pushy. As a demonstrator you will be on your feet a lot and will need to stay positive and cheerful whatever response you get.

Working conditions

You might work full time for a company but most demonstrators are freelance, working through agencies and taking bookings, which can vary from half a day to a few weeks.

You could work in a supermarket, shopping centre or hotel or go to exhibitions such as motor shows. You might be outside in any weather, and stores and exhibitions can be crowded and noisy. Some demonstrators run evening parties within private homes, selling everything from chocolate to plastic goods.

You will be on your feet a lot and may have to wear a uniform. Your hours will vary a lot and many jobs will be at weekends.

The future outlook

There are 3000+ store demonstrators working in the UK at present. It's difficult to find full-time jobs, so you will probably be freelance, which is an uncertain and competitive way of working.

Prospects for promotion are limited but you could go on to work for an agency or to train other demonstrators.

You could use your skills to go into other areas of sales and marketing, for example as a beauty consultant.

Other related opportunities

- Beauty p412
- Call Centre Operative p439
- Customer Services p442
- Market Researcher p150
- Receptionist p25
- Sales Assistant p450

Advantages/disadvantages

- You will have variety and freedom and be meeting people. You will gain useful skills which you can use to go into other things.
- There are very few full-time jobs and there is lots of competition for those jobs. You will need to build up experience and be prepared to travel.

Earnings guide

- Wages vary a lot and it's unusual to find full-time work.
- You will probably be paid by the session and get, on average, around £40–£60 a day.
- In a few large stores you could get £100+ per day.
- A full-time demonstrator earns around £10,500–£18,000 per year.
- You may get commission and bonuses if you meet or go over your targets.

CRCI:SB

CLCI:OE

Further information

www.cityandguilds.com/myperfectjob

Institute of Sales Promotion
Arena House
66–68 Pentonville Road
Islington
London
N1 9HS
020 7837 5340
www.isp.org.uk

British Shops and Stores Association Limited
Middleton House
2 Main Road
Middleton Cheney, Banbury
Oxfordshire
OX17 2TN
01295 712277
www.british-shops.co.uk

Chartered Institute of Marketing
Moor Hall
Cookham
Maidenhead
Berkshire
SL6 9QH
01628 427500
www.cim.co.uk

Store Manager

What the work involves

- You will be running a shop, maybe a small store that is part of a chain or a large department store, overseeing a team of staff.
- Managers recruit, train and supervise staff, encouraging them to develop their skills and meet targets.
- You will monitor sales and look at ways of improving them through promotions, offers and displays, and oversee supplies by checking stock, placing orders and making sure you do not run out or over-order.
- The store manager has overall responsibility for everything that happens in the shop and must deal with any problems or complaints.

The type of person suited to this work

As you could be dealing with customers and complaints you will need excellent communication and negotiation skills. You will also need to manage, motivate, train, and sometimes discipline staff. You should be energetic and flexible, able to take responsibility and make quick decisions.

You will need an understanding of business, marketing and of relevant laws. You should be able to analyse sales figures and have creative ideas for selling and promoting goods to improve profits. As a store manager you will have to be organised and efficient and able to deal with paperwork whilst working to targets and deadlines.

You will need to have an interest in the retail and marketing industry.

Working conditions

Many stores are open long hours, at weekends and even overnight, so you will probably have to work shifts, usually over 5 days.

You will be on your feet a lot dealing with your staff and customers as well as doing administration and paperwork.

You may be based in one store, or be visiting several that you have responsibility for.

The future outlook

Retail is a big employer with over 158,000 store managers in the UK. There are lots of opportunities in all areas but trainee posts with large chains can be very competitive.

With a large retail chain your prospects can be good as they are likely to offer training and good progression and you can quickly take on more responsibilities.

You could move into other areas of the company, for example marketing or buying, and may be able to work abroad.

In smaller stores, you may have responsibility but limited chances for promotion.

You could work for yourself but will need money to start up your own store.

Other related opportunities

- Buyer p438
- Distribution Manager p562
- Marketing p151
- Merchandiser p446
- Shopkeeper p454

Advantages/disadvantages

- Retail is an expanding, developing business and so can offer you an exciting, challenging career with good promotion prospects.
- You will be under a lot of pressure to meet targets and will have a lot of responsibility quite early in your career.
- Working with the public can be demanding and stressful.

entry level

To both enter and train while working in this career, you will need qualifications at Level 2–8. Please refer to explanation on page vii.

Qualifications and courses

- You can enter and train in this career with qualifications at Levels 2, 3 or 4 and will probably need relevant experience as well. Some of the larger stores may require 5 GCSEs/S grades (A-C) including maths and English.
- NVQs/SVQs are available in Retail Operations at Levels 2 and 3. Other qualifications include BTEC Retail qualifications at Levels 2 and 3 and the City & Guilds Higher Professional Diploma in Retail Management at Level 4. Some professional courses are offered by the British Retail Consortium.
- You could join a management development scheme after gaining experience in the store. You could also consider a Diploma or Certificate Level 3 course in First Line Management offered by the Institute of Leadership and Management (ILM)
- With A levels/H grades or equivalent you could go directly onto a management training scheme. These are available with most of the major retail companies and are usually available on an annual recruitment basis. You should contact each organisation for their specific information.
- Fast-track training is usually available to graduates with a degree in any subject.
- Management degrees are offered by universities across the country. Other courses include a Graduate Apprenticeship Scheme offered by the University of Surrey which leads to a degree in professional development in retail management.

CRCI:SB

CLCI:OE

Earnings guide

- Wages vary with the company and the size of the store.
- You could earn £14,000–£20,000 per year when you start as a non-graduate trainee with a large chain.
- £11,000–£12,500 is more likely as a trainee with a smaller company.
- With experience this could rise to £21,000–£25,000.
- £45,000+ is possible if you are working for a large company with a lot of responsibility. This could be £60,000 if you are a manager in a large superstore.
- You will probably also get discounts, commission and bonuses related to sales.

Further information

British Shops and Stores Association Limited
Middleton House
2 Main Road
Middleton Cheney, Banbury
Oxfordshire
OX17 2TN
01295 712277
www.british-shops.co.uk

Chartered Institute of Purchasing & Supply
Easton House
Easton on the Hill
Stamford
Lincolnshire
PE9 3NZ
01780 756777
www.cips.org

Institute of Leadership & Management
www.i-l-m.com

www.cityandguilds.com/myperfectjob

Trading Standards Officer

What the work involves

- Trading Standards Officers (TSOs) work on behalf of local government to protect consumers. You will be checking that any individual or company selling products or services is keeping to the law and providing a fair and legal service.
- You will be working with a wide range of people and organisations, for example market traders, shops and factories. Your aim is to make sure customers get a fair deal.
- You will check that labels and adverts are accurate, for example checking that food products do contain what the label says, or that a company delivers the service they have promised.
- You will be enforcing the law, taking cases to court but also giving help and advice to companies and to consumers.
- You will travel to check pemises, or to follow up on a complaint from the public.

The type of person suited to this work

You will be enforcing a lot of different laws and regulations relating to a wide range of different industries, so will need to be able to take in and apply a lot of complex information.

You must have a good eye for detail and make sure the reports and records you write are accurate because they could be used in court.

Excellent communication and interpersonal skills are vital because you will be dealing with lots of different people, advising and helping them but also enforcing the law. You will need to be forceful but not aggressive.

You will need to be persistent, observant, trustworthy and able to stand up to people.

You will need to be able to remember lots of information, be efficient at using computers and spreadsheets, and be good at maths as you will be dealing with lots of statistics.

Working conditions

You would probably work for local government but could work for private industry advising on relevant legislation.

You will be office-based and part of a team but will spend a lot of time on your own, visiting places such as shops and factories, which could be dirty or cold.

TSOs work normal office hours and possibly evenings and weekends when shops and factories are open.

The future outlook

There are about 1500 qualified TSOs in the UK. There are jobs all over the country and the work varies: in rural areas you would spend a lot of time working with farm animals. If you work near a port or airport you could be checking imported goods.

There is a shortage of qualified staff but trainee jobs are competitive.

You can get promotion to the head of a section or division and could become the chief trading standards officer. As relevant laws and regulations are increasing, opportunities in private industry are also growing.

entry level

To both enter and train while working in this career, you will need qualifications at Level 3–8. Please refer to explanation on page vii.

Qualifications and courses

- This career has two main entry paths: you can enter as a graduate, or enter with qualifications at a lower level and follow a work-based route to qualification.
- To become a qualified trading standards officer, you need a Diploma in Consumer Affairs and Trading Standards (DCATS) awarded by the Trading Standards Institute, and you must be working for a local authority to achieve this. All applicants need to have 5 GCSEs/S grades (A–C) including English language, maths and a science, and 2 A levels or another Level 3 course.
- Non graduates can join a Trading Standards authority as an enforcement officer or consumer adviser and follow the Accreditation of Prior Experience Learning route (APEL) to the DCATS. The Trading Standards Institute also offers a Diploma in Consumer Affairs for people employed in these positions.
- Alternatively, you can follow a relevant degree course, such as a consumer protection degree. The normal entry requirements for a degree in trading standards or consumer protection are 2 A levels/3 H grades or equivalent. The degree provides exemption from certain parts of the DCATS.
- Some local councils run graduate training programmes. The Training Standards Institute (TSI) has introduced a new series of qualifications, for details visit their website.
- Apprenticeships/Skillseekers may be available in this area for people aged 16–24.

Other related opportunities

- Civil Service Scientific Officer p474
- Environmental Health Practitioner / Officer p280
- Health and Safety Adviser p19
- Police p506

Advantages/disadvantages

- This can be a varied and interesting job where you are helping the public to get a fair deal.
- It can be very satisfying when you have helped someone get compensation for poor goods or services.
- You could be dealing with difficult or aggressive people.

Earnings guide

- Salaries vary from one local authority to another and are different in private organisations. As a new enforcement officer or a trainee, you could expect £16,000–£20,000 per year.
- You would start on £25,000–£32,000 per year when newly qualified/graduated.
- You could earn £35,000–£50,000 as a senior trading standards officer.
- £70,000+ is possible for the head of a service, depending on the size of the local authority.

Further information

The Trading Standards Institute
1 Sylvan Court
Sylvan Way
Southfields Business Park
Basildon
SS15 6TH
0870 8729000
www.tscareers.org.uk

Local Government Careers
www.lgcareers.com

CRCI:SC
CLCI:COP

Vehicle Parts Operative

What the work involves

- This job involves ordering and looking after vehicle parts and accessories and selling them to the public, garages and mechanics.
- Vehicle parts operatives develop specialist knowledge of stock, and when ordering or supplying parts have to know the exact make, model and year of the car or van.
- You will do stock control to make sure you've got supplies of the most popular things, using computerised systems or possibly keeping paper records, and reordering from warehouses or manufacturers when stocks are low. You will be checking off parts that arrive against delivery notes before placing them in a stock room.
- As well as taking deliveries and taking orders over the phone and in person, you will use tills, take payments and sometimes invoice customers.

The type of person suited to this work

You should be interested in cars and be keen to learn about a wide range of parts and accessories and which makes of vehicles they are for. You will be dealing with stock from a number of different suppliers, so will need to be well organised and able to research where to find more unusual parts.

Vehicle parts operatives have to use computerised stock systems and deal with a lot of forms and paperwork; they also deal with mechanics and the public over the phone and in person and have to explain technical information clearly and simply.

You will need to have good communication skills, be good in a team situation or able to work on your own.

The job involves being on your feet a lot and you may be lifting and moving heavy things, so you will need to be fit and active.

Working conditions

You could be working in a large shop open to the public or a warehouse used by the motor trade. You could be in a fairly small, local garage or work for a large dealership.

You may have to lift weights, move trolleys and climb ladders to reach high shelves. You will work with the public and staff from the motor trade and probably as part of a team.

Normal hours are Monday to Friday from 8.30am–5.00pm, and you may work evenings and weekends.

The future outlook

There will probably be a shortage of skilled staff in the future so job opportunities are good and there are jobs available in all parts of the country.

If you work for a smaller company your promotion prospects might be limited but in larger companies you could get additional responsibility more quickly.

In a large organisation you could become a supervisor and then progress to management jobs.

You could become a trainee manager in other areas of the retail trade or move into car sales.

entry level

1–2

To both enter and train while working in this career, you will need qualifications at Level 1–2. Please refer to explanation on page vii.

Qualifications and courses

- You can enter and train in this career with qualifications at Levels 1 or 2. There is no upper age limit for entering this work.
- There are no formal entry requirements for this work, but GCSEs/S grades (A–C/1–3) in English, maths and ICT and science are useful.
- Training is mostly done on the job. You could do an Apprenticeship/ Skillseekers if you are aged 16–24. You would then take NVQs/SVQs at Levels 2 and 3.
- Trainee parts operatives can study for the Institute of the Motor Industry's Certificate (Level 2) and Diploma (Level 3) in Vehicle Parts Operations, or a City & Guilds award in Tyre Fitting. NVQs/SVQs at Levels 1–3 in Vehicle Parts Operations, Levels 1 and 2 in Vehicle Fitting, and Levels 2 and 3 in Vehicle Parts Distribution and Supply can be achieved in the workplace.
- You might want to study for a Certificate in Customer Service for the Motor Industry at Levels 2 or 3 available from The Institute of Motor Industry (IMI).

CRCI:SB

CLCI:OFM

Other related opportunities

- Car Salesperson p440
- Motor Vehicle Work p217
- Sales Assistant p450
- Stores Assistant p584
- Warehouse p586

Advantages/disadvantages

- It is a skilled job with training and you will be using your knowledge of, and interest in, cars and the motor trade.
- There is a lot of information to remember and the work can be repetitive.
- This is a good job for those wanting to work with vehicles who do not want to be mechanics.

Earnings guide

- You can expect £9,200–£11,000 per year when you start as a trainee.
- You might earn up to £18,000 when you have got some experience.
- £25,000+ is possible as a senior vehicle parts operative.
- Some employers offer performance related bonuses.

Further information

Automotive Skills
93 Newman Street
London
W1T 3DT
020 7436 6373
www.automotiveskills.org.uk

Retail Motor Industry Federation
201 Great Portland Street
London
W1W 5AB
020 7580 9122
www.rmif.co.uk

Institute of the Motor Industry
Fanshaws
Brickendon
Hertford
SG13 8PQ
01992 511521
www.motor.org.uk

www.cityandguilds.com/myperfectjob

Wine Merchant

What the work involves

- You will use your interest and knowledge of wine to buy from vineyards and suppliers and sell to the public or to shops, pubs and restaurants.
- As a buyer for a large merchant, you probably spend a lot of time abroad finding and tasting new wines, agreeing prices and checking quality. Other jobs include marketing, distribution or managing a shop.
- In a small, independent merchant, you will probably buy wine from companies who ship it in to the country, going to wine tastings to make selections, but probably not going abroad.
- You could work in a shop, ordering stock, managing staff and serving customers, or you might sell wine over the internet or by mail order and could be doing your own deliveries.
- You could be involved in producing marketing and sales materials to promote your wines.

The type of person suited to this work

Wine merchants are extremely interested in wine and keen to develop their knowledge and expertise, finding new wines and growers and keeping up to date with new developments and tastes.

You will need a good sense of taste and smell to be able to judge the quality of a wine. You will know about the different types and be able to advise people what goes well with what food.

The job involves dealing with the public and negotiating prices with growers and suppliers, and so requires excellent communication skills, and good customer service skills.

You should be good with numbers and have business skills if you are self-employed. A foreign language can be useful, and you will need to have an understanding of health and safety and the laws around buying and selling alcohol.

Working conditions

Conditions vary according to what you do. Working for yourself you will have freedom and flexibility, but will probably work long hours.

Wine shops are often open all day until 10pm so you might work shifts including weekends. You will be on your feet a lot and could be lifting heavy boxes and crates.

As a buyer you will travel a lot or you might be based in a head office.

You could be working with the public and will deal with people at all levels, sometimes even travelling to people's homes to sell wine.

The future outlook

The wine trade has grown a lot recently but it is a very competitive market with a lot of people buying wine from supermarkets, making it difficult for small shops to do well.

There are opportunities in off-licences and small wine merchants all over the country. There are good prospects for promotion to store manager and above if you work for a chain.

You could work in the head office of a large merchants, but there are very few jobs for specialist buyers.

To start your own business you will need experience, a good knowledge of wine, and money to buy stock and premises.

CRCI:SD

CLCI:OFM

Qualifications and courses

entry level

To both enter and train while working in this career, you will need qualifications at Level 1–3. Please refer to explanation on page vii.

- There are no formal entry requirements for this career but many new entrants have a degree or vocational qualification. Some employers prefer entrants to have 5 GCSEs/S grades (A–C/1–3) and experience in the retail industry.
- An interest in and knowledge of wine is essential and knowledge of one or more European languages can also be an advantage.
- Entry is usually at assistant or trainee manager level and candidates must be at least 18 years old. Some large companies recruit graduate management trainees.
- Higher education courses in wine studies are available. Trainee wine merchants can study for the Wine and Spirit Education Trust (WSET) Exams which range from a Foundation Certificate in Wines at Level 1to the Level 4 Diploma in Wines and Spirits. Once the Diploma has been completed, it is possible to progress to the Master of Wine qualification.
- Other relevant qualifications include BTEC Higher National Diploma (HND) in Hospitality Management (Licensed Retail), Advanced Certificate in Wines and Spirits qualifications offerd by WSET, or a Foundation degree in Wine Business.
- If you want to become an independent wine merchant, previous business experience and a wide knowledge of the industry and the product is essential. You will also need a premises licence and a personal licence to sell alcohol, which can only be obtained with an accredited qualification. This is the Level 2 National Certificate for Personal Licence Holders (provided by the professional bodies, the BIIAB, GOAL and GQAL), which is offered at various centres around the UK as a 1-day course or by self-study.

Other related opportunities

- Bar Manager / Licensee p82
- Buyer p438
- Store Manager p459

Advantages/disadvantages

- You will be using your knowledge and love of wine in your job and could get to travel and work abroad a lot.
- The wine trade is a very competitive business and jobs as a buyer, travelling abroad to find new wines, are scarce.

Earnings guide

- You could expect £12,000 per year starting out. Rising to £16,000 with some experience.
- You might earn £18,000–£25,000 as an experienced merchant or manager.
- £35,000 is possible if you are very successful, usually running your own business, or in a top job with one of the big wine merchants.

Further information

Wine & Spirit Education Trust
International Wine & Spirit Centre
39–45 Bermondsey Street
London
SE1 3XF
020 7089 3800
www.wset.co.uk

British Institute of Innkeeping
Wessex House
80 Park House
Camberley
Surrey
GU15 3PT
01276 684449
www.bii.org

City & Guilds

www.cityandguilds.com/myperfectjob

If you enjoy using numbers or science to solve problems, the range of opportunities available to you includes all levels and will require careful research, for example:

- **Astronomer**
- **Chemist**
- **Ecologist**
- **Food Scientist**
- **Laboratory Assistant**

But what's it like working in this area?

Here's Stephanie Sterling's story:

Laboratory Technician

Having always liked hospital environments and enjoyed human biology as well, Stephanie decided to combine both interests by studying for a degree in Biomedical Science at Wolverhampton University. As part of her degree she took a year out doing voluntary work in a hospital laboratory, but when she graduated she found it difficult to get a trainee position. Instead, she took a job as a phlebotomist at Birmingham Children's Hospital taking blood samples and working in the chemistry laboratory until a trainee position appeared. She went on to become a state registered Level 1 Biomedical Scientist (formerly known as a Medical Laboratory Scientific Officer) and now works at Great Ormond Street Hospital in London in the Haematology Laboratory.

WHAT THE JOB ENTAILS

'In this laboratory we analyse blood samples. We book the samples into the computer and then go on to analyse the sample depending on what the blood has been taken for. These days most analysis is done by machine, so there is not much hands-on work. We take routine tests for blood counts, to monitor leukaemias and to diagnose any abnormal blood. In coagulation tests we diagnose why the blood is not clotting or is clotting too much and we also deal with cross-matching blood for blood transfusions. Here at Great Ormond Street we also have a bone marrow laboratory where we do the diagnostics for bone marrow transplants.'

WHAT'S HOT AND WHAT'S NOT SO HOT ABOUT THE JOB

'I get a lot of satisfaction from working towards the healing process for somebody, and working with a team towards getting a patient well is really rewarding. However, it is not well paid considering we are all graduates, and as the nature of the job is a 24-hour service you will be working on call and at weekends and bank holidays. Also, because so much of the work in the lab is invisible, we don't get the recognition for what we do that nurses and doctors get.'

However, this situation may well change in the future because there is an acute shortage of biomedical scientists in this country. Those who are qualified are currently in great demand, so you may not get well paid but you will never be short of work.

WHAT YOU NEED TO SUCCEED

'You really need to be multi-faceted. You need to be patient, be able to think on your feet and when on call you need to be able to multi-task because you could well be the only person in the lab. You also need to be articulate as you will be talking to patients as well as the doctors and nurses, and you have to be a team player and be able to get on with your workmates.'

Stephanie could now go on to take her Master's degree on a day-release basis and would ultimately like to become a Biomedical Senior or even a Chief, bringing her up to Level 2 and 3. This can be gained with a Master's or by having the necessary experience.

Astronomer

What the work involves

- Astronomers investigate and study the universe. Astronomy covers a wide range of areas and astronomers usually focus on a specific subject, such as planets or stars.
- You will plan and coordinate projects using specialist equipment, such as telescope systems to observe the skies and collect information.
- You will analyse a wide range of information to identify specific characteristics of the natural world.
- You may work on mathematical and physics problems using specialist computer software.

entry level

To both enter and train while working in this career, you will need qualifications at Level 4–8. Please refer to explanation on page vii.

The type of person suited to this work

As a professional astronomer you should have a keen interest in the natural world. You will also need a good understanding of the sciences. Whether you are observing the skies or analysing detailed information, you should be able to take in a range of facts and figures. You will use your decision-making skills to make informed conclusions from the information you work with.

A patient and organised approach is essential. You should be confident in working with computers to complete a range of tasks. You will also need strong communication skills and enjoy working with numbers.

Working conditions

Late or antisocial working hours can often be a feature of this type of work, whether you are based in a university, observatory or research centre.

The job may involve spending time away from home as many of the major telescopes are in remote locations.

Close observation is often part of this job, so it may be unsuitable for people with visual impairments.

The future outlook

Employment as a professional astronomer is very competitive and demands a great deal of academic study.

Opportunities are starting to increase, particularly in industrial research and development.

If you followed the academic route you could undertake original research combined with a PhD-level degree and then progress to lecturing.

You may choose to work as part of a technical team providing support for astronomy research projects.

Qualifications and courses

- A degree in physics, maths, astrophysics, geophysics or a related science is required.
- Specialist degrees are available in astronomy, astrophysics and space science, and in astronomy combined with maths, physics or another science.
- Entry requirements for a relevant first degree are usually 3 A levels/4 H grades, including physics and mathematics, as well as 5 GCSEs/S grades (A–C/1–3), including English and possibly chemistry.
- Some degrees courses include fieldwork in the UK or overseas in countries such as Italy and Germany.
- Many institutions offer 1-year Foundation courses for candidates without the necessary scientific background. Foundation courses may be taught at the university or at a local partner college.
- Taught postgraduate courses in astronomy are available at some universities for people who have a degree in physics, maths or a related area.
- To work as a research astronomer, candidates should have a 1st or 2.1 MSci or MPhys degree, followed by further study for a PhD.
- University physics departments may include astronomical research groups, and some universities offer MPhil/PhD programmes specifically in astronomy. Specialist research areas vary between institutions.

CRCI:TD

CLCI:QOF

Other related opportunities

- Earth Sciences p475
- Geographer p480
- Mathematician p482
- Physicist p485

Advantages/disadvantages

- This job provides the opportunity to increase public understanding of the natural world.
- You may have to spend a lot of time undertaking observations, which requires patience and commitment.
- Undertaking research on-site can be physically tiring.

Earnings guide

- Starting salaries for academic research posts begin at approximately £22,000–£30,000 per year.
- With experience you could earn £30,000–£42,000.
- At senior levels you could earn £40,000–£60,000.

Further information

Royal Astronomical Society
Burlington House
Piccadilly
London
W1J 0BQ
020 7734 4582
www.ras.org.uk

British Astronomical Association
Burlington House
Piccadilly
London
W1J 0DU
020 7734 4145
www.britastro.org

Biochemist

What the work involves

- You will undertake scientific research into a range of living organisms and processes, using specialist equipment.
- Your work may involve collating detailed information and producing reports.
- Biochemists investigate the chemistry of a wide variety of living organisms. They use their investigations to plan experiments and undertake techniques to solve problems.
- Biochemists apply their knowledge and skills in many areas, including food and nutrition, agriculture, medicine, plant research and brewing.

entry level

To both enter and train while working in this career, you will need qualifications at Level 4–8. Please refer to explanation on page vii.

The type of person suited to this work

You will need to be curious about biological organisms and interested in improving systems and products. You will constantly use your problem-solving skills in this job. Your excellent observational skills will also come in very useful. You should enjoy working as part of a team.

You will be confident in using a range of scientific equipment to gain information. You will need a patient and methodical approach for sometimes repetitive but important activities. Your strong communication skills will help you explain and record your work. Confidence in working with numbers and detailed information is also essential.

Working conditions

You would normally work in a laboratory as part of a team. You may also do some of your work in an office environment.

In some sectors, biochemists work on a shift system.

The job involves the regular use of specialist equipment which requires good manual handling skills.

As you become more senior, it is likely you will be involved with managing staff or projects.

The future outlook

Many of the products you use on a daily basis have been developed by biochemists. Biochemists have an important role in organisations ranging from research institutes to multinational companies.

If you go into research and development, you would start by working as part of a team. With experience, you would progress to planning and managing experimental work. You may choose to undertake academic research and go into lecturing or teaching.

Qualifications and courses

- A degree in biochemistry or a related subject is required for entry to this profession. Many posts also require a postgraduate qualification. A levels/H grades including chemistry and/or biology are required for entry to a biochemistry degree. Some universities offer Foundation or bridging years as pre-degree courses for applicants who do not have the required qualifications.
- Biochemists with a degree and relevant work experience are eligible to join a professional body, the Biochemical Society or the Institute of Biology.
- Biochemists continue their training in service. Those with a first degree are often encouraged to study part time for an MSc or PhD.
- It is possible to enter as a technician with a minimum of 4 GCSEs/S grades (A–C/1–3), including English, maths and sciences.
- NVQs/SVQs are available in Laboratory and Associated Technical Activities at Levels 2, 3 and 4. A levels/H grades, or a National Certificate/Diploma or HNC/D in a science subject may be required.

Other related opportunities

- Biotechnologist p471
- Civil Service Scientific Officer p474

Advantages/disadvantages

- You may have to work very long hours in this job.
- This type of work is often project-based which provides job variety.
- Biochemistry offers a wide range of areas in which to specialise.

Earnings guide

- Starting salaries for trainees start at around £20,000 per year.
- Post registration and with experience, you could earn £27,500.
- At senior/management/consultancy level it is possible to earn £75,000–£100,000.
- Salary levels tend to be higher in industry compared with the NHS and universities, especially at junior levels.

Further information

Biochemical Society Membership Office
Portland Customer Services
Commerce Way
Whitehall Industrial Estate
Colchester
Essex
CO2 8HP
01206 796351
www.biochemistry.org

Association of Clinical Biochemists
130–132 Tooley Street
London
SE1 2TU
020 7403 8001
www.acb.org.uk

Institute of Biology
9 Red Lion Court
London
EC4A 3EF
020 7936 5900
www.iob.org

Biologist

What the work involves

- Biologists study, observe and investigate all kinds of life forms, from trees to bacteria.
- Whatever field of biology you work in, you will be involved with increasing public or academic knowledge of living organisms and how they interact with each other. As well as undertaking research and development, biologists are involved with helping develop products and managing natural resources.

Bacteriologist

- Bacteriologists study and analyse microscopic organisms, particularly ones that cause disease.
- Their research provides important information on protecting against illnesses and caring for people with specific kinds of diseases. Bacteriologists work in the National Health Service, research institutes and pharmaceutical companies.

Botanist

- Botanists study all kinds of plant life and plant biology, from trees to algae. You could use your specialist knowledge in a range of areas. Botanists are increasingly employed within industry and research in areas such as plant-cell technology and genetic engineering.
- Your work could involve managing rare plant collections, environmental conservation, horticulture, agriculture and other areas.

Entomologist

- Entomology is the study of insects of all shapes and sizes, including how they live and how they interact with their environment. Entomologists also observe the behaviour of insects to gain valuable information on the state of specific natural areas.
- As an entomologist, you could analyse and assess the effects of insect life on agriculture. Entomologists are also employed to undertake research in medicine or to support ecological and environmental conservation work.

Geneticist

- As a geneticist you will analyse and modify human, animal or plant DNA. If working as a human geneticist, you could be involved with medical genetics or human genetic research, researching and analysing the causes of specific conditions.
- You could undertake genetic engineering in agricultural research, for example developing plants that are drought-resistant. With growing recognition of the many potential uses of genetics, this is a fast-developing but sometimes controversial area.

Microbiologist

- Microbiologists study microorganisms such as bacteria and viruses. They research and analyse different types of microscopic organisms to support work in medicine, agriculture, food and milk production and pollution control.
- Your specialist skills and knowledge could be used in government defence departments, environmental conservation and medicine.

Marine biologist

- Marine biologists undertake practical research and analysis into animal and plant life in the world's seas and oceans. As well as academic research, you could apply your skills in fisheries, research or fish-farming development.
- For many roles, you will undertake practical research trips above or below the sea's surface and keep detailed research records.

Zoologist

- Zoologists are involved with classifying, studying and researching all kinds of animal life, from elephants to bacteria. You could be involved with protecting endangered species through practical work and raising public awareness.
- Some zoologists work in industry developing pharmaceuticals or enhancing agricultural products. Others are involved with research in their specific area of interest in academic or research institutions.

The type of person suited to this work

As a biologist you should have a real interest in science and a strong curiosity about living things. Jobs in this area often involve detailed analysis so you will need strong observational skills. You must also have a methodical approach to your work activities.

Many biologists work in a laboratory setting so you should be comfortable working with a range of scientific equipment. But you will also need to be happy undertaking practical research work, sometimes in unpleasant weather conditions. This could be in the countryside, in agricultural areas or by the sea. If you work in industry, you will need to understand the commercial applications of your work.

Zoologist

You will need to feel comfortable dissecting dead animals as part of your work for some roles in this area. Zoology degree courses may also include this kind of activity.

Qualifications and courses

entry level

To both enter and train while working in this career, you will need qualifications at Level 4–8. Please refer to explanation on page vii.

- Most entrants to these professions are graduates. A degree and often a postgraduate qualification in a biological science subject is required.
- The entry requirements for degrees usually include A level/H grade or BTEC National qualifications in the relevant science(s).
- Many institutions offer 1-year Foundation courses for candidates without the necessary scientific background. Foundation courses may be taught at the university or at a local partner college.
- After entry, biologists may study towards postgraduate qualifications or the examinations of professional bodies, for example the Institute of Biology.

Bacteriologist

- To work as a clinical bacteriologist, a 1st or 2.1 degree in a relevant subject is required and an MSc or PhD is an advantage.
- Clinical scientists start as Grade A trainees. The training lasts 2–3 years, and involves placements and formal study, often towards an MSc. On completion of the training, candidates are eligible for state registration, and can apply for Grade B posts. In-service training continues, and many clinical scientists work towards membership qualifications of professional bodies or a PhD.
- For entry to an academic research post, a postgraduate qualification is required. Applicants without a PhD may start as a research assistant and work towards a PhD.

Botanist

- Botanists may enter this career as laboratory technicians or technical assistants. The minimum requirement for these posts is a degree in a relevant subject, for example botany, plant biology, plant science, environmental science or ecology. A levels/H grades in biology and another science, often chemistry, are required for entry to botany degrees.
- To work as a researcher, a postgraduate qualification is required. Candidates may enter with a PhD, or enter as a trainee researcher in a university department and work towards a PhD.

Entomologist

- An Honours degree in biology or a related field is required. A level/H grade biology is usually required for entry to relevant degree courses. Candidates usually need at least 2 A levels/3 H grades including biology and 5 GCSEs/S grades (A-C/1–3) for entry to relevant degree courses.
- Entry at technician level requires GCSEs/S grades and A levels/H grades.

Geneticist

- An Honours degree in genetics, biomedical or biological sciences is required.
- Two science A levels/H grades are normally required for entry to relevant degree courses. Chemistry and/or biology may be specified.
- A postgraduate qualification is desirable.
- Training is undertaken in an accredited genetics laboratory, and follows the clinical scientist training programme lasting 2–3 years.

Microbiologist

- Most entrants to this profession have a degree, and sometimes also a postgraduate qualification, in microbiology or a related science subject.
- Relevant work experience is an advantage and may be required by employers.
- A levels/H grades in biology and 1 other science, usually chemistry, are required for entry to microbiology degrees.
- Many institutions offer 1-year Foundation courses for candidates without the necessary scientific background. Foundation courses may be taught at the university or at a local partner college.
- Microbiologists receive training on the job, and may study towards postgraduate qualifications or the examinations of relevant professional bodies.
- It is possible to work as a technician or medical laboratory technician. You will need 4 GCSEs/S grades (A–C/1–3) including 2 sciences, maths and English. NVQs/SVQs are available in Laboratory and Associated Technical Activities at Levels 2, 3 and 4.

Marine biologist

- Candidates can either take an Honours degree in marine, biology, marine science, or oceanography, or a degree in chemistry or physics followed by a postgraduate qualification. A levels/H grades in relevant science subjects are required for entry to degree courses. For degrees in marine biology, A level/H grade biology is normally required.
- A postgraduate qualification is an advantage.

Zoologist

- A degree and, often, an MSc or PhD is required for entry to this profession. Your degree can be in zoology or a related subject, such as wildlife biology, marine biology, parasitology, animal behaviour or ecology. An A level/H grade in biology is required for entry to these degree courses. Some courses ask for a second science, usually chemistry.
- The usual entry route is a post as a trainee researcher in a university research department. Trainees work towards a PhD.
- It is also possible to enter the profession at technician or trainee level with GCSEs/S grades, A levels/H grades, or equivalent qualifications including biology, maths, science and English.

Working conditions

As a biologist you could combine research and experimental work in an outside setting with laboratory and research centre-based projects.

If you work in industry, you could be based in a laboratory in a manufacturing plant. Your job may involve handling potentially dangerous chemicals and materials. You will be required to wear protective clothing and maintain a good standard of health and safety at all times.

Many biologists in research and academic roles are employed on a short-term project-by-project basis. This can create job instability.

In some sectors you may have to work on a shift basis.

Your job could involve fieldwork either in the UK or abroad for weeks or months at a time. This can affect your personal life and be physically demanding.

Research activities are increasingly undertaken with the use of computers and specialist software.

Senior roles in industry, research and academia usually involve management duties as well as liaising with colleagues and staff from other organisations.

The future outlook

Biology offers a wide range of interesting careers. Some are more financially rewarding than others, but all offer the chance to develop your personal interests into a profession, whether they involve animals, plants or bacteria!

You could choose to follow an academic or research-based career. You may need to gain a postgraduate qualification as part of the work and to further your career. There is usually a lot of competition for permanent university and research centre posts.

Opportunities for life science professionals are expanding within the agricultural and food industries, pharmaceuticals sector and biotechnology.

Bacteriologist

Bacteriology is a specialism that most people go into after gaining experience and professional skills in related areas such as microbiology. There are a small number of opportunities within the NHS, research institutes and industry.

Botanist

Growing recognition of the need to protect and care for the environment has also led to a development in career options for professionals such as botanists.

Entomologist

Entomologists work in a wide range of areas, including agricultural research and development, ecological protection and conservation, forensics and pest control. Others go on to develop their research interests as academic professionals after gaining postgraduate qualifications.

Geneticist

Genetics is a fast-developing area of science that offers the chance to work directly with patients as a medical geneticist within the NHS or directly within research in research centres and universities. You could also go on to work in research and development in industry.

Microbiologist

Microbiologists work in a range of fields. There are opportunities within the NHS and government laboratories and research centres.
Microbiologists also work for private companies developing food, drink, pharmaceuticals and other products. A smaller number undertake teaching and research in universities.

Marine biologist

Due to high levels of interest, there can be a lot of competition for jobs. Gaining a good level of practical experience in addition to the relevant training shows commitment and provides useful skills.

Zoologist

Whilst this is a specialist area, zoologists work for a variety of organisations such as environmental consultancies, conservation bodies, animal charities and local authorities. Others go into research and development in industry.

Other related opportunities

- Agricultural Scientist p228
- Biotechnologist p471
- Civil Service Scientific Officer p474
- Ecologist p478
- Scientist p486

Advantages/disadvantages

- There are opportunities to visit different types of outside locations on research trips. This can include short-term projects abroad.
- You will use your skills and knowledge to increase public understanding of many aspects of the natural environment.
- Research jobs are often offered on a short-term basis, which can create job insecurity.
- Employers such as the National Health Service can offer the chance to gain experience in different departments and provide well-structured career paths.

Earnings guide

- Starting salaries for graduates with a PhD begin at around £20,000–£27,000 per year. Starting salaries tend to be at the higher end of the scale for people with a higher or postgraduate degree.
- With experience, salaries can increase to £31,000.
- At senior university lecturer level, you could earn £31,000–£42,000. A professor can earn up to £60,000.
- Salary levels vary between areas of biology. They also differ from sector to sector, with jobs in industry sometimes paying more than those in public research and academic institutions.

Further information

Institute of Biology
9 Red Lion Court
London
EC4A 3EF
020 7936 5900
www.iob.org

BOTANIST

Botanical Society of the British Isles
www.bsbi.org.uk

ENTOMOLOGIST

Natural History Museum Department of Entomology
www.nhm.ac.uk/entomology

Royal Entomological Society
The Mansion House
Chiswell Green Lane
St Albans
AL2 3NS
01727 899387
www.royensoc.co.uk

GENETICIST

Genetics Society
Roslin BioCentre
Wallace Building
Roslin
Midlothian
EH25 9PS
0131 200 6392
www.genetics.org.uk

British Society of Human Genetics
Clinical Genetics Unit
Birmingham Women's Hospital
Birmingham
B15 2TG
0121 627 2634
www.bshg.org.uk

MICROBIOLOGIST

Society for General Microbiology
Marlborough House, Basingstoke Road,
Spencers Wood
Reading
RG7 1AG
0118 988 1800
Main website:
www.socgenmicrobiol.org.uk
Careers website: www.biocareers.org.uk

MARINE BIOLOGIST

Marine Biological Association
The Laboratory
Citadel Hill
Plymouth
PL1 2PB
01752 633207
www.mba.ac.uk

National Oceanography Centre
www.noc.soton.ac.uk

ZOOLOGIST

Institute of Zoology
ZSL, Regent's Park
London
NW1 4RY
020 7449 6601
www.zsl.org

Biotechnologist

What the work involves

- You will utilise biological organisms and processes to develop and adapt products. Biotechnologists work in a range of areas, many of which are very new, such as genetic engineering.
- You could work in research and development or in aspects of production such as quality control.
- Your work may involve enhancing existing products or developing new types of organisms.
- Biotechnology provides the scientific basis for agriculture, pharmaceuticals, waste management, food and medical care.

The type of person suited to this work

You will need a keen interest in science for working in any area of biotechnology. Strong observational skills and an organised approach are also essential. You will also be confident working with scientific equipment. You should be able to use computers to manage information and undertake research.

Most biotechnologists are employed as part of a group so the ability to work as part of a team is helpful. If you work as a technician, you should be able to cope with undertaking routine but required testing activities. Biochemists in industry also need to understand the commercial applications of their work.

Working conditions

Biotechnologists usually work in a laboratory or research centre in sterile conditions to undertake experimental and testing work.

Some jobs involve spending time in a noisy factory or manufacturing plant.

Your work is likely to involve using microscopes and electronic testing equipment, and spending time on a computer doing analysis work.

The future outlook

In this developing area of science, biotechnologists enable organisations to create and modify organisms for medical, environmental and commercial use.

They work within government research institutions whilst others play a central role in developing and enhancing products in commercial biotechnology companies.

There is also the option to develop an academic career – this may provide additional opportunities to undertake commercial research.

entry level

To both enter and train while working in this career, you will need qualifications at Level 4–8. Please refer to explanation on page vii.

Qualifications and courses

- A degree in biotechnology, bioscience or a related subject, such as microbiology, biochemistry or chemical engineering, is required for entry to this profession.
- A levels/H grades in chemistry and/or biology are required for entry to these degree courses.
- A postgraduate qualification is often required. For research posts, a PhD may be a requirement.
- School-leavers may start work as trainee technicians. The usual minimum entry requirements are 4 GCSEs/S grades (A–C/1–3), including a science and maths.
- Some posts require A levels/H grades, BTEC/SQA National qualifications, or an HNC/D.
- Technicians are mainly trained on the job. It is possible to work towards further qualifications, such as a degree or HND, through part-time study or day- or block-release.
- Graduates are also employed as technicians. In all cases, qualifications in science subjects are required.
- NVQs/SVQs are available at Levels 2–4 in Laboratory and Associated Technical Activities.

CRCI:TD | CLCI:QOD

Other related opportunities

- Biochemist p467
- Biologist p468
- Brewer p176
- Civil Service Scientific Officer p474

Advantages/disadvantages

- Laboratory work, particularly at technician level, can be time-consuming and requires a lot of patience.
- Biochemistry is a varied area of science which offers a variety of areas in which to work.
- This role requires a good level of manual dexterity.

Earnings guide

- As a graduate working in a university you could start on a salary of £20,000–£24,000 per year.
- Established senior lecturers can earn £31,000–£50,000.
- Professors with a great deal of experience can expect to earn up to £60,000.

Further information

BioIndustry Association
14–15 Belgrave Square
London
SWIX 8PS
020 7565 7190
www.bioindustry.org

Institute of Biology
9 Red Lion Court
London
EC4A 3EF
020 7936 5900
www.iob.org

Biotechnology and Biological Sciences Research Council
Polaris House
North Star Avenue
Swindon
SN2 1UH
01793 413200
www.bbsrc.ac.uk

Chemist

What the work involves

- Chemists work in many different sectors, undertaking the analysis and use of complex scientific processes and substances on a detailed molecular level.
- You will use scientific equipment to undertake research and analysis.
- As well as research and development, chemists also check that products are developed to a safe standard.
- Professional chemists are employed in a wide range of sectors, including the oil industry, pharmaceuticals, medical research and academia.

The type of person suited to this work

Whatever sector they work in, chemists need strong observational skills. They must also be able to think around complex scientific problems. You will have good manual handling abilities for undertaking research with a range of scientific equipment.

You should be well-organised with the patience to explain and record your work accurately. You will also be comfortable working with a lot of information and completing complex calculations. The ability to cope with undertaking sometimes repetitive activities in the laboratory is useful. You should also enjoy working as part of a team.

Working conditions

Your job could involve working in a laboratory as part of a research centre, but you may also undertake research outdoors on-site.

Because the job can involve working with potentially dangerous chemicals you may have to wear protective clothing.

If you are employed by a private company you maybe required to work on a shift system.

At senior levels, you may be involved with business development and managerial activities.

The future outlook

Professional chemists play an important role in developing and updating products and systems. Public research institutes, academic institutions and private companies employ chemists.

There are also opportunities in government research, health and education. Some chemists move into other areas, such as law, IT, science journalism and marketing. There are also opportunities to teach in schools and universities.

CRCI:TD

CLCI:QOF

Qualifications and courses

Graduate entry

- Most entrants to this career are graduates. For entry to a chemistry degree, A level/H grade in chemistry and at least one other science or maths is required. Degree courses are available in chemistry, biological chemistry, environmental chemistry, medical chemistry, and in chemistry combined with other subjects.
- Many institutions offer 1-year Foundation courses for candidates without the necessary scientific background. Foundation courses may be taught at the university or at a local partner college.
- Many chemists also have a postgraduate qualification in chemistry or in a specialist area such as materials chemistry, medicinal chemistry or pharmaceutical chemistry.
- Training is done on the job. Chemists often study for postgraduate qualifications (if not already held) or work towards professional membership of the Royal Society of Chemistry.

Technician

- It is possible to enter as a technician in a chemistry laboratory with a minimum of 4 GCSEs/S grades (A–C/1–3), including English, maths and sciences. A levels/H grades, a National Certificate/Diploma or HNC/D in a science subject may be required.
- Some posts require A levels/H grades, BTEC/SQA National qualifications, or an HNC/D. Graduates are also employed as technicians. In all cases, qualifications in science subjects are required.

entry level

To both enter and train while working in this career, you will need qualifications at Level 4–8. Please refer to explanation on page vii.

- NVQs/SVQs are available at Levels 2–4 in Laboratory and Associated Technical Activities and in Analytical Chemistry at Level 5.
- Technicians are mainly trained on the job. It is possible to work towards further qualifications, such as a degree or HND, through part-time study or day- or block-release.

Other related opportunities

- Biochemist p467
- Biotechnologist p471
- Civil Service Scientific Officer p474
- Scientist p486

Advantages/disadvantages

- Low numbers of entrants taking chemistry degrees means that there are many opportunities.
- Laboratory tasks can sometimes be repetitive and time-consuming.
- Many large companies employ chemists so promotion can be possible without moving employers.

Earnings guide

- Salary levels tend to increase with the level of academic qualification. At graduate entry you can earn £18,500–£30,000 per year.
- With experience, and when established, you can expect £30,000–£35,000.
- Salaries for chemists with a Master's degree/PhD can be up to £50,000.

Further information

Royal Society of Chemistry
Burlington House
Piccadilly
London
W1J 0BA
020 7437 8656
Main website: www.rsc.org
Careers and jobs website: www.chemsoc.org

Association for Clinical Biochemistry
130–132 Tooley Street
London
SE1 2TU
020 7403 8001
www.acb.org.uk

Science Council
32–36 Loman Street
London
SE1 0EH
020 7922 7888
www.sciencecouncil.org

Association of the British Pharmaceutical Industry
12 Whitehall
London
SW1A 2DY
0870 890 4333
Main website: www.abpi.org.uk
Careers website: www.abpi-careers.org.uk

Civil Service Scientific Officer

What the work involves

- You will manage and support scientific work to help the government make informed decisions about key issues such as transport, agriculture and health.
- Your work may involve planning and undertaking scientific research.
- You could be responsible for collecting and analysing different types of information.
- Scientific officers work in many government agencies, including the Ministry of Defence, the Department for Environment, Food and Rural Affairs and the Department of Trade and Industry.

The type of person suited to this work

Scientific officers need to combine a logical approach with a creative outlook to resolve complex scientific problems. You should also be able to use information to develop fresh answers to specific questions. You will use your scientific skills to undertake analysis and support government work.

As a scientific officer, you will also need to be a strong communicator with people and on paper. But you will be able to keep research work confidential at all times. You will apply your good observational and manual handling skills on a regular basis. Your well organised approach will help you manage and record your work.

Working conditions

Scientific officers undertake research activities in many different settings, including laboratories, hospitals and research centres.

In some roles you would work in direct contact with dangerous substances, such as radioactive materials, so you would need to wear protective clothing.

The nature of the job requires the ability to work well under pressure.

The future outlook

Professional scientists help shape strategy in many aspects of government work, including food production, environmental protection and defence. The Civil Service provides a clear career path, with opportunities to move into diverse areas.

You could start as an assistant scientific officer and, with experience, progress to working as a scientific officer, moving later on into a management job. This may involve working in a more strategic role, helping to define government policy.

entry level

To both enter and train while working in this career, you will need qualifications at Level 4–8. Please refer to explanation on page vii.

Qualifications and courses

- Specialist posts in the Civil Service usually require a degree in a relevant subject, relevant experience, or both. Candidates must pass selection tests.
- Scientific officers should have a minimum of a 2.1 degree in science, engineering, maths or another numerate discipline. Other relevant degree subjects include: chemistry, biochemistry, biological sciences and pharmacology. These will vary according to the agency that you want to work in.
- The Civil Service Fast Stream programme provides structured training for graduate entrants. This leads to a post as a Higher Scientific Officer and then to a Senior Scientific Officer role.
- The training programme may include a placement in Europe. There are also longer term employment opportunities within research centres in Europe.
- Government agencies such as the Ministry of Defence offer Graduate Development Programmes for which a minimum of a 2nd class degree in a relevant subject is required.
- It is possible to enter the scientific civil service as a Higher Scientific Officer with a relevant degree and 2 years' relevant postgraduate experience. This may vary between posts.

CRCI:TD | CLCI:Q

Other related opportunities

- Biochemist p467
- Chemist p472
- Physicist p485
- Scientist p486

Advantages/disadvantages

- The Civil Service offers job security and a well-structured career path.
- Because of the sensitive nature of the work, you will be required to maintain a high standard of confidentiality.
- With experience, you could move into other departments.

Earnings guide

- Salary ranges vary from department to department, but each department offers a clearly graded pay structure.
- Generally, starting salaries for graduates are £16,000–£24,000 per year. Individuals with relevant postgraduate qualifications may earn more.
- Once qualified you could earn £27,000–£45,000.
- At senior/management level, it is possible to earn up to £65,000.

Further information

MoD or BERR/DIUS
Civil Service Fast Stream
Pilgrims Well
427 London Road
Camberley
Surrey
GU15 3HZ
01276 400333
www.faststream.gov.uk

Civil Service Careers
www.careers.civil-service.gov.uk

Earth Sciences

What the work involves

- Earth scientists are involved with observing, analysing and understanding the many aspects that make up the natural world, including how we use and manage natural resources such as water, oil and gas. You could apply your specialist skills and knowledge in industry, education, management and development.

Climatologist

- Climatologists investigate and analyse long-term weather patterns in order to understand the causes of climate change.
- You will apply your knowledge of the climate and its conditions to help develop solutions to specific problems for environmental agencies, government bodies and research institutions. As well as applied climatology, your work may involve teaching others about the relationship between the climate and the environment.

Geologist

- Geologists analyse and study the planet earth, including its materials, structure and history.
- Your work may involve organising practical field and laboratory research to gain specific information. You may use your skills to support development work, for example in mineral mining and the oil industry.

Geological technician

- You will work closely with geologists, undertaking practical research work in the field and laboratory. You will collect and examine samples and produce test results.
- You will work with other sources, for example surveys and visual resources, to provide detailed information on specific geological features and aspects.

Geophysicist

- As a geophysicist or geoscientist, you will apply physics-based investigation techniques to explore and analyse the nature of the rocks, structures and minerals below the earth's surface. You would spend a lot of time undertaking practical work and writing up your results.
- Most geophysicists are involved with helping companies explore for oil and gas. You would help plan and organise exploration work and interpret detailed geological information.
- Geophysicists work in research in universities and research institutes and for companies involved in oil and mineral exploration.

Hydrologist

- As an invaluable natural resource, water needs to be monitored and managed by hydrologists. You will help ensure that water is available when and where it is needed and that it is safe to use and to drink.
- Your work could involve measuring river flows, rainfall, evaporation and ground water. You may assess water use in agriculture and forestry, or be involved with dealing with water-management emergencies, for example in droughts.

Meteorologist

- Information gained from observing the sky, the atmosphere and natural phenomena gives a picture of everyday weather conditions.
- As well as providing weather forecast information that is used throughout the media and to inform industries such as fishing, meteorologists undertake research into the earth's atmosphere. You could be employed by the Royal Navy, the RAF, the Meteorological Office and other employers.

Oceanographer

- Oceanographers study and analyse the many aspects of the world's oceans. They investigate how ocean organisms and structures work together. You could specialise in biological, chemical or geological oceanography.
- Your work could involve undertaking fieldwork above and below the sea's surface. You may also interpret the information you find and write research reports.

Vulcanologist

- Vulcanologists study the geology, chemistry and physics of volcanoes in order to increase the understanding of how they behave. As a vulcanologist you would undertake your research mainly within academic or research institutes.
- You may visit areas of volcanic activity to take samples and measurements. Away from the research site, you would interpret different types of information, create computer models and advise on the environmental effects of volcanoes.

Qualifications and courses

entry level

To both enter and train while working in this career, you will need qualifications at Level 4–8. Please refer to explanation on page vii.

- The normal entry route to these professions is a degree in a geoscience subject, such as geology, earth science, oceanography, meteorology, geophysics, geochemistry or engineering geology. A levels/H grades in science subjects and/or maths are usually required for entry to a degree.
- Taught postgraduate courses (MSc) are available, and may provide specialist academic and vocational training in areas such as environmental geology, petroleum geology and hydrology. Some employers prefer a postgraduate qualification. Research degrees (MPhil/PhD) are available, and may lead to a research appointment.
- School-leavers may start work as junior technicians. The usual minimum entry requirements are 4 GCSEs/S grades (A–C/1–3), including science and maths.
- Some posts require A levels/H grades, BTEC/SQA National qualifications or an HNC/D. Graduates are also employed as technicians. In all cases, qualifications in science subjects are required. Technicians are mainly trained on the job. It is possible to work towards further qualifications, such as a degree or HND, through part-time study, day- or block-release.
- NVQs/SVQs are available at Levels 2–4 in Laboratory and Associated Technical Activities.

Climatologist
- An Honours degree or above in physics, maths or am environmental science is usually required. In addition, a postgraduate qualification is increasingly demanded by employers.

Geologist
- The normal entry route to this profession is a degree in a geoscience subject, for example geology, earth science, geophysics, geochemistry or engineering geology. A levels/H grades in science subjects and/or maths are usually required.
- Taught postgraduate courses (MSc) are available and may provide specialist vocational training in areas such as environmental geology, petroleum geology or engineering geology. Some employers prefer a postgraduate qualification. Research degrees (MPhil/PhD) are available, and may lead to a research appointment.
- The British Geological Survey recruits assistant scientific officers with A levels/H grades and scientific officers with a relevant degree. There are also opportunities for voluntary work experience, and summer fieldwork placements for students on geology or earth science courses.
- It is possible to become a Chartered Geologist with the Geological Society, for which a minimum of 5 years' experience is required. Some degrees are also accredited by the society.

Geological technician
- There are varying entry levels to this work.
- School-leavers may start work as junior technicians. The usual minimum entry requirements are 4 GCSEs/S grades (A–C/1–3), including a science and maths. Technicians are mainly trained on the job. It is possible to work towards further qualifications, such as a degree or HND, through part-time study, day- or block-release.
- Some posts require A levels/H grades, AVCEs/GSVQ Level 3 or an HNC/D. Graduates are also employed as technicians. In all cases, qualifications in science subjects are required.
- NVQs/SVQs are available at Levels 2–4 in Laboratory and Associated Technical Activities.

Geophysicist
- An Honours degree in geoscience, geology, geotechnology or a related field is required. A levels/H grades in science subjects are normally required for entry.
- A postgraduate qualification is usually also required. Pre-entry experience is desirable.
- For entry at technician level, A level/H grade in physics is normally required. It may be possible to enter with an Intermediate GNVQ, SQA National at Intermediate 2, or BTEC First Certificate/Diploma in Science, or to undertake an Apprenticeship/Skillseekers.

Hydrologist
- The minimum requirement for entry to the profession is usually an Honours degree in geography, environmental science, civil engineering or mathematics. For entry to a degree, students usually require a minimum of 2 A levels/3 H grades or equivalent.
- A postgraduate qualification is usually also required. Pre-entry work experience is recommended.
- The Chartered Institution of Water and Environmental Management (CIWEM) accredits a number of undergraduate and postgraduate courses in the field.

Meteorologist
- Entrants to this profession need a degree. Degrees in meteorology are available, but other suitable subjects are physics, maths, computer science, oceanography and environmental science. Employers may also require A levels/H grades in maths and physics – these usually form part of the entry requirements for meteorology degrees.
- Relevant taught postgraduate courses are available. Subject areas include meteorology, climatology and atmospheric science. There are also opportunities to do a research PhD at some institutions.
- The main employer of meteorologists is the Met Office. The Met Office provides initial training for new entrants without a postgraduate qualification. The training consists of an 18-week Initial Forecasting Course, followed by 8 months' practical training at a weather station, and a 3-week Forecasting Consolidation Course.
- NVQs/SVQs in Meteorological Observation at Level 3 and Weather Forecasting at Level 4 are available for people working in meteorology.

Oceanographer
- Entrants to this profession need a degree. Degrees are available in oceanography and related areas, such as marine biology. Other relevant degree subjects include biology, chemistry, physics, mathematics and geology. A levels/H grades in sciences and maths are required.
- Most employers expect candidates to hold A level/H grade in maths. It is possible to join the Merchant or Royal Navy without a degree and take additional training to become an oceanographer.
- A postgraduate qualification is an advantage. Taught courses are available in oceanography and related/specialist areas. It is also possible to do research for an MPhil or PhD.

Vulcanologist
- For this highly specialised area of earth science, an Honours degree in geology or a related earth science is required. A relevant postgraduate qualification is usually also required.
- Although there are currently no specific vulcanology degrees in the UK, Lancaster University offers a degree in Earth and Environmental Science that allows for specialisation in vulcanology after the first year.

The type of person suited to this work

Whatever area they work in, earth scientists must combine their practical skills with scientific knowledge. The job calls for the ability to problem-solve and think creatively to resolve specific issues. With many roles in this area involving practical investigations, you should enjoy hands-on work in sometimes poor outside conditions, whether you're on on land or at sea! You'll also need to be confident in using technical equipment to get results.

The job demands excellent observational skills and attention to detail. For many roles in earth science you will need strong numeracy skills and the ability to work with detailed factual information. You should be comfortable in communicating your work to colleagues, managers and to people without a scientific background. Your team-working skills will be essential as many jobs in this area involve liaising, for example with other science, engineering and technical professionals.

Working conditions

Earth scientists employed in the oil and minerals industries may have to cope with uncomfortable working environments, for example on oil rigs at sea, on drill rigs and in remote mining areas.

Academic earth scientists may undertake more work in laboratories with some field trips to gather information.

The job often involves research activities which makes physical fitness and the ability to travel in the UK and abroad very important.

The working hours can be quite long, for example when involved with a research project on location.

For some jobs you will be based in an office environment, using a computer to analyse information, attending meetings and helping to manage staff and resources.

The future outlook

Earth scientists have an important role in helping to ensure the appropriate use, exploration and management of the natural environment and its resources. With growing public concern about the environment and new laws, many employers require the skills and knowledge of earth scientists.

Opportunities are increasing in organisations involved with managing natural resources and protecting the environment.

Construction, fuel and mineral exploration and development organisations within the public and private sectors need the skills of geoscience professionals. Developing a career in industry may mean having to move around to gain the relevant professional experience. For some jobs, this may involve spending time working overseas.

In some areas of earth science, you may need to work in a number of fairly low-paid or voluntary jobs before moving into a better paid role.

You may choose to develop an academic or research-based career. It can be fairly competitive to get into academic posts in universities and government research centres. A postgraduate qualification is usually required for these types of jobs.

Other related opportunities

- Agricultural Scientist p228
- Astronomer p466
- Engineer: Professional p205
- Geographer p480
- Physicist p485
- Scientist p486

Advantages/disadvantages

- In some areas of earth science you can live and work abroad while you undertake research work.
- The work can be physically demanding and may involve visiting potentially hazardous sites.
- You may have the opportunity to study and observe the natural world in a variety of locations.
- Some employment in this area is offered on a short-term contract basis only, which can lead to job insecurity.
- Employers increasingly require applicants to have a postgraduate qualification in a relevant subject.

Earnings guide

- Salary levels vary widely according to sector.

Climatologist

- Starting salaries begin at around £18,000 per year.
- With experience, you could earn £24,000-£37,000. This can increase to £50,000+ at senior levels.

Geologist

- Starting out as a graduate you can expect to get £20,000 per year.
- At senior levels this can increase to £35,000–£50,000, depending on your employer.

Geological technician

- Starting salaries begin at around £14,000 per year. With BTEC HND this is £16,000.
- With experience you can expect £23,000. At senior level expect £29,000+.

Geophysicist

- Starting salaries are around £22,000 per year. With a few years of experience expect £25,000–£45,000.
- At senior levels you could earn up to £50,000+.

Hydrologist

- Starting salaries range from £18,000 to £25,000 per year. With 5 years' experience this can be £25,000–£30,000.
- At senior levels you could earn up to £45,000+.

Meteorologist

- Starting salaries begin at around £18,000–£21,000 per year. With experience this rises to £30,000–£35,000.
- At senior levels you could earn up to £50,000.

Oceanographer

- Starting salaries begin at around £17,000–£21,000 per year; with a PhD you could start on £20,000–£22,000. A lecturer may get up to £37,000; an experienced oceanographer could get £56,000.
- At senior/management levels you could earn up to £55,000.

Vulcanologist

- Starting salaries begin at £19,000–£22,000 per year. With experience and qualifications you could earn £33,000–£38,000.
- At senior levels it is possible to earn up to £50,000.

Further information

CLIMATOLOGIST
Association of British Climatologists
www.royal-met-soc.org.uk/abcgroup.html

GEOLOGIST
British Geological Survey
Kingsley Dunham Centre
Keyworth
Nottingham
NG12 5GG
0115 936 3100
www.bgs.ac.uk

Geological Society
Burlington House
Piccadilly
London
W1J 0BG
020 7434 9944
www.geolsoc.org.uk

GEOPHYSICIST
British Geophysical Association
www.ras.org.uk

HYDROLOGIST
British Hydrological Society
c/o Institution of Civil Engineers
1–7 Great George Street
London
SW1P 3AA
020 222 7722
www.hydrology.org.uk

METEOROLOGIST
Royal Meteorological Society
104 Oxford Road
Reading
Berkshire RG1 7LL
0118 956 8500
www.royalmetsoc.org

Met Office
Fitzroy Road
Exeter
Devon EX1 3PB
0870 900 0100
www.metoffice.gov.uk

OCEANOGRAPHER
Institute of Marine Engineering, Science and Technology (IMarEST)
80 Coleman Street
London
EC2R 5BJ
020 7382 2600
www.imarest.org

National Oceanography Centre
www.noc.soton.ac.uk

VULCANOLOGIST
International Association of Volcanology and Chemistry of the Earth's Interior
www.iavcei.org

Ecologist

What the work involves

- Ecologists help to protect the natural world by investigating the relationship between living organisms and their environment.
- You will undertake ecological surveys of animals and plants and monitor the state of urban and rural environments.
- You may also write reports and analyse statistical information.
- Ecologists are employed by conservation charities, government departments, public bodies and environmental consultancies. A small number work in industry.

The type of person suited to this work

A keen interest in the natural world is essential for ecologists. You will collect detailed factual information about many aspects of the environment. Your observational skills and scientific knowledge will be an essential part of this. Your organised approach and ability to work to a high standard of accuracy will help you when collating statistics. You will use your manual handling skills to use scientific equipment.

You will need to be comfortable working outdoors in sometimes poor weather conditions. Your practical and hands-on approach will help you when undertaking this type of work. You will use your communication skills and your ability to complete complex calculations on a regular basis.

Working conditions

Ecologists work in laboratories or research centres when undertaking analysis activities.

You would work outside in all kinds of weather conditions when undertaking fieldwork such as surveys of plants or animals. For fieldwork you would need a good level of physical fitness and good observational skills. This may make the job unsuitable for people with visual impairments.

In the process of your job you may meet and work with other professionals, for example landscape designers, engineers and estate managers.

The future outlook

Ecology offers a wide range of opportunities and you could shape your career according to your interests . But there is a lot of competition for jobs. Some jobs are available only on a contract basis and it can take time to find a permanent role in this area.

Many types of organisations employ ecologists. You could go into scientific research, environmental management, teaching or conservation for organisations such as environmental consultancies, research bodies and private companies.

entry level

4–8

To both enter and train while working in this career, you will need qualifications at Level 4–8. Please refer to explanation on page vii.

Qualifications and courses

- Entrants require an Honours degree or above in the field of biological and earth sciences. Relevant subjects include ecology, environmental biology/ management; conservation or marine biology. Additionally, many employers seek experience (as a research assistant or a conservation project volunteer), and postgraduate qualifications are increasingly an advantage.
- A levels/H grades in sciences are required for entry to degrees in ecology or biological sciences. Biology A level or equivalent is a required or preferred subject for some degrees.
- NVQs/SVQs are available in Environmental Conservation at Levels 2 and 3 and Environmental Management at Level 4.
- A driving licence is useful.
- Ecologists with relevant qualifications and experience can become members of the Institute of Ecology and Environmental Management (IEEM). Different levels of membership are available depending on qualifications and experience. The IEEM also provides short professional development courses for its members.

Other related opportunities

- Countryside Work p235
- Forestry p246
- Geographer p480

Advantages/disadvantages

- This job provides the satisfaction of having a positive impact on the natural environment.
- It is likely that you will need to move around to develop your professional experience.
- Opportunities in areas such as environmental consultancy and management are increasing.

Earnings guide

- Salaries vary according to the type of organisation for which you work, but can be fairly low. Salaries can be higher in industry.
- Starting salaries range from £18,000 to £24,000 per year.
- With experience you could earn £25,000–£40,000.
- Senior/management roles in larger organisations can pay £45,000+.

Further information

British Ecological Society
26 Blades Court
Putney
London
SW15 2NU
020 8871 9797
www.britishecologicalsociety.org

Institution of Environmental Sciences
Suite 1
38 Ebury Street
London
SW1 0LU
020 7730 5516
www.ies-uk.org.uk

Council for Environmental Education
94 London Street
Reading
RG1 4SJ
0118 950 2550
www.cee.org.uk

Environment Council
212 High Holborn
London
WC1V 7BF
020 7836 2626
www.the-environment-council.org.uk

Institute of Ecology and Environmental Management (IEEM)
43 Southgate Street
Winchester
Hants
SO23 9EH
01962 868626
www.ieem.net

Education Technician

What the work involves

- Education technicians work in schools, colleges and universities helping teachers and lecturers give interesting and effective lessons and practical sessions.
- You will check and set up the equipment and materials needed for the teaching session. Afterwards, you will clean, organise and store them safely and securely.
- Your work may involve supporting and advising students with their experiments.
- You would be responsible for managing stock levels and ordering new supplies when required.

The type of person suited to this work

As a big part of your job will be managing the use and storage of scientific equipment, you must be well organised. Your eye for detail will help you make sure that the equipment is safe to use. You will need a good knowledge of science to set up a range of scientific experiments and exercises. You should be comfortable with undertaking a certain amount of routine and repetitive work.

Your communication skills will help you interact well with students, teachers and lecturers and support many different classroom activities. You will need to work to a high standard of health and safety at all times.

Working conditions

You will work in schools or colleges in laboratories, classrooms and equipment stores.

Depending on your employer, you may only have to work during term time.

You will have to wear protective clothing when handling and storing potentially dangerous chemicals and equipment.

A good level of physical fitness is useful because of the practical nature of the work.

The future outlook

There are job opportunities in schools and colleges throughout the country. In order to gain promotion, you would need to gain further qualifications.

With more experience and training, you could progress to working as a senior education technician, helping with planning lessons and providing information to groups of students.

As a senior technician in a large institution, your work could involve managing the work of junior technicians.

entry level

2–3

To both enter and train while working in this career, you will need qualifications at Level 2–3. Please refer to explanation on page vii.

Qualifications and courses

- There are no set entry requirements for this work, but GCSEs/S grades (A–C/1–3) in English, maths and science, BTEC or City & Guilds qualifications may be required. Nearly half of education lab technicians have an HNC/HND or a degree in a science or technology subject
- BTEC offer First Diplomas in science and applied science subjects. City & Guilds offer the Science Laboratory Assistants course.
- Technicians receive on-the-job training and may work towards NVQ/SVQ Levels 2 and 3 in Laboratory Technician Working in Education. Qualifications offered by The Institute of Science Technology (IST) are currently being changed to Certificates in Laboratory Technical Skills, available at Levels 1–3.
- Apprenticeships/Skillseekers may be available to those aged between 16 and 24.

Other related opportunities

- Laboratory Technician p481
- Lecturer p178
- Scientist p486
- Teacher p184
- Teaching / Classroom Assistant p187

Advantages/disadvantages

- You will spend most of your time based in a laboratory or classroom.
- The job is often only available on a part-time basis. This may suit people with other commitments.
- This role provides the job satisfaction of contributing to people's education.

Earnings guide

- Earnings vary according to employer, and some positions may offer a low salary.
- On average starting out in this work you could get around £12,000–£14,000 per year.
- With experience, you could earn up to £18,000.
- At senior level and with further qualifications you could earn up to £25,000.

Further information

Association for Science Education
College Lane
Hatfield
Hertfordshire
AL10 9AA
01707 283000
www.ase.org.uk

www.schoolscience.co.uk
Science Council
210 Euston Road
London
NW1 2BE
020 7611 8754
www.sciencecouncil.org

www.cityandguilds.com/myperfectjob

Geographer

What the work involves

- Geography combines the study of people and places, covering physical, environmental, human and economic issues.
- You will apply your specialist skills and knowledge in one or more of a variety of job areas, such as environmental management, planning, surveying, oceanography and travel and tourism.
- You could also teach and lecture on geography-related subjects.
- Your job could involve undertaking fieldwork and other types of research to increase public understanding of natural and human environments.

entry level

To both enter and train while working in this career, you will need qualifications at Level 4–8. Please refer to explanation on page vii.

Qualifications and courses

- An Honours degree or above in geography or a related field is required. Geography degrees cover varied aspects of human, economic and physical geography, but it is also possible to gain a first degree in one particular aspect, such as human or physical geography.
- Entry requirements for geography degrees vary, but often include an A level/H grade in geography. For science-based geography courses (BSc), science A levels/H grades may be required.
- Geography degrees usually include fieldwork at varied kinds of sites whilst some courses offer the chance to study abroad.
- For roles in environmental or conservation work, relevant voluntary experience can be useful. A driving licence can also be helpful.
- The Royal Geographical Society offers a Chartership scheme to members at fellowship level with a first degree in geography or equivalent and the required level of experience. The status of Chartered Geographer (CGeog) may benefit job applications and further career development.
- More specialised jobs may require a postgraduate degree in areas such as environmental management and applied geographic information systems.

The type of person suited to this work

As a geographer you need to be curious about the world around you, whatever area you work in. You also need the skills and knowledge to support your research. It's essential to have a practical and logical approach to your work.

You will be able to apply your problem-solving skills to analyse the information that you collect.

It is essential that you are comfortable undertaking fieldwork outside in sometimes poor conditions.

You will need good written communication skills for producing detailed reports and other forms of information. Your ICT skills will help you organise and manage this information. The nature of the job makes team-working skills essential for geographers.

Working conditions

The nature of jobs vary widely so working conditions could range from an office, to a research centre, to a college.

For jobs involving a high level of research, you may spend periods of time outside, sometimes in poor weather conditions. For research activities, a good level of physical fitness is helpful.

Fieldwork may involve spending periods of time away from home and working unsocial hours.

The future outlook

With a geography-based qualification, you could move into a wide range of areas. Because opportunities in geographical research are quite limited you may need a good level of voluntary experience before being taken on as a professional researcher.

Managing natural resources, protecting the environment or promoting places – these are some of the key areas you could choose to work in. You could also move into educating others about the varied aspects of geography.

CRCI:TD

CLCI:QOF

Other related opportunities

- Cartographer p43
- Countryside Work p235
- Earth Sciences p475
- Lecturer p178
- Surveyor / Surveying Technician p70
- Teacher p184
- Town Planner p75

Advantages/disadvantages

- There are opportunities to work overseas whilst undertaking geographical research.
- You may need to move around to gain professional experience in research.
- Geography is a good basis for careers in a range of areas.

Earnings guide

- Salaries vary according to the type of job you do.
- Environmental management professionals can earn from £24,000 to £35,000 per year.
- An academic research assistant could earn £15,000–£23,500.
- Salaries for geography teachers start at around £23,700 and go up to £35,000.

Further information

Geographical Association
160 Solly Street
Sheffield
S1 4BF
0114 296 0088
www.geography.org.uk

Royal Geographical Society (with the Institute of British Geographers)
1 Kensington Gore
London
SW7 2AR
020 7591 3000
www.rgs.org

Royal Scottish Geographical Society
Graham Hills Building
University of Strathclyde
Glasgow
G1 1QE
0141 552 3330
www.geo.ed.ac.uk/rsgs/

Laboratory Technician

What the work involves

- You will analyse samples of different types of substances and materials using specialist equipment.
- You could specialise in a particular area, such as microbiology or clinical chemistry.
- Your work may involve recording detailed information and developing and maintaining microbiological or other cultures.
- Laboratory technicians apply their scientific analysis and measurement skills in organisations such as the military services, the National Health Service, industry and scientific research institutions.

The type of person suited to this work

As you will provide important factual information through your work, you must complete all your activities to a high standard of accuracy. It is also essential that you pay attention to detail and take a methodical approach to your work at all times. Your patient attitude will help you undertake sometimes repetitive but important laboratory activities.

The job involves organising and setting up laboratory equipment so you will need good manual handling skills. As well as practical skills, you will also need to be confident in communicating with others. Your ICT skills will help you record and analyse a range of information. Because your work may involve handling potentially dangerous materials you must work to a good standard of health and safety at all times. You should also be able to work to deadlines.

Working conditions

You will spend most of your working day in a laboratory which has to be kept clean and sterile at all times.

You may work with specialist computer software in an office to complete some of your research and recording activities.

You will need to wear protective clothing when you are working in close contact with potentially harmful substances in the laboratory.

The future outlook

Scientific laboratory technicians play an important role in protecting public health. Their work also helps to make safe, high-quality products that many of us use every day.

Scientific laboratory technicians are employed within industry, health service organisations, public research and other areas.

With further experience, you could progress to supervising a team of technicians or managing a laboratory.

entry level

To both enter and train while working in this career, you will need qualifications at Level 2–3. Please refer to explanation on page vii.

Qualifications and courses

- At least 4 GCSEs/S grades (A–C/1–3), including English, mathematics and a science, are required for entry into this career. Equivalent qualifications such as an Intermediate GNVQ/SQA National at Intermediate 2, BTEC First Certificate or Diploma in science may be accepted.
- Qualifications at a higher level may be required. Entrants may have A levels/H grades, a BTEC/SQA National qualification, an HNC/D or a degree in science subjects.
- Work experience in a laboratory can be helpful to applications.
- Laboratory technicians are trained on the job, and may be able to study towards NVQs/SVQs at Levels 2–4 in Laboratory and Associated Technical Activities or Levels 2–3 in Laboratory Technician: Working in Education, or an HNC/D or degree in a science subject.
- Apprenticeships/Skillseekers may be available to those aged 16–24.

CRCI:TD

CLCI:QOB

Other related opportunities

- Biochemist p467
- Civil Service Scientific Officer p474
- Education Technician p479
- Medical Laboratory Assistant p287

Advantages/disadvantages

- Laboratory tasks can be repetitive and time-consuming and require patience.
- Because of the transferable nature of lab skills, you could move from one organisation to another quite easily.
- In some organisations you would work on a shift basis.

Earnings guide

- Salary levels vary between sectors. Organisations requiring more specialist skills may pay more.
- Starting salaries begin at around £11,000–£13,000 per year.
- With experience and qualifications, you could earn up to £25,000.
- At senior levels, in a team leader or laboratory manager role, it is possible to earn £32,000–£40,000.

Further information

Biochemical Society Membership Office
Portland Customer Services
Commerce Way
Whitehall Industrial Estate
Colchester
Essex
CO2 8HP
01206 796351
www.biochemistry.org

Science Council
210 Euston Road
London
NW1 2BE
020 7611 8754
www.sciencecouncil.org

www.cityandguilds.com/myperfectjob

Mathematician

What the work involves

- Mathematics is the study of measurements and quantities using numbers and symbols.
- Your work may involve undertaking research and analysis, planning and setting up research programmes and assessing research findings.
- You could work in job roles requiring mathematical skills and knowledge, for example actuary, operational researcher or statistician.
- As a mathematician you could work at all levels of industry, research and education and help to inform the work of different organisations.

entry level

To both enter and train while working in this career, you will need qualifications at Level 4–8. Please refer to explanation on page vii.

The type of person suited to this work

As a mathematician it is essential that you have a strong interest in working with numerical information to solve complex problems. You will also need to have a logical and methodical approach to your work. But your flexible and innovative approach will help you analyse a range of problems.

Your work may help shape the activities of your company so you must have good attention to detail. You should also be able to record your work accurately. Strong communication skills will help you explain mathematical ideas to people without a background in maths. As maths-related research can take time to plan and set up, a patient attitude can be helpful.

Working conditions

For many maths-related roles, you would work in an office and use computers to manage and analyse information.

If you work in education, you will spend time teaching in classrooms and in lecture rooms. You may also spend time undertaking research.

Mathematicians who work in business, such as accountants and finance consultants, will spend time in meetings with their clients.

The future outlook

Right now there is a lot of demand for professional mathematicians in many areas. From academic research, to teaching to a statistical research role as an operational researcher or statistician, there are a range of available careers

Other opportunities include working in business, finance or industry. There is a demand for professional mathematicians in companies that develop new products such as new computer software and pharmaceuticals.

Qualifications and courses

- A degree in maths is normally required to work as a professional mathematician in industry, business/finance, education or research. Degrees are available in general maths or in specific areas, for example, financial maths or business maths.
- Entry onto maths degree courses usually requires at least 2 A levels/3H grades (A–C/1–3), including maths, and 5GCSEs/S grades (A–C/1–3), including English and maths. Science and or computing-related subjects are also viewed favourably.
- Maths graduates are recruited directly by some companies and public sector organisations. Most mathematicians also have postgraduate qualifications, which require a first degree in mathematics, physics or another subject with a high mathematical content.
- To teach maths in primary and secondary schools, maths graduates need to study for a PGCE.
- It is possible to become a Chartered Mathematician with the Institute of Mathematics and its Applications. The requirements for chartered status are an Honours degree in maths or with more than two-thirds maths content, and 3 years in employment.

CRCI:TC

CLCI:QOJ

Other related opportunities

- Accountant p2
- Actuary p5
- Bank / Building Society p9
- Lecturer p178
- Software Architect / Developer p119
- Stockbroker p31
- Systems Analyst p120
- Teacher p184

Advantages/disadvantages

- Mathematical skills apply to many different sectors, so you could move across a range of areas.
- You may need to take a second degree to follow your chosen career.
- A shortage of qualified mathematicians means that there are a variety of opportunities.

Earnings guide

- Salary levels vary widely according to employer and sector, but maths graduates are known to earn the highest salaries of all graduates.
- Starting salaries for graduates range from £18,000–£25,000 per year.
- With several years' experience you could earn £30,000–£40,000.
- At senior levels it is possible to earn £55,000+.

Further information

Institute of Mathematics and its Applications
Catherine Richards House
16 Nelson Street
Southend-on-Sea
Essex
SS1 1EF
01702 354020
www.ima.org.uk

Mathematical Association
259 London Road
Leicester
LE2 3BE
0116 221 0013
www.m-a.org.uk

Maths Careers
www.mathscareers.org.uk
Council of Mathematical Sciences
Careers website

Metallurgist

What the work involves

- Metallurgists apply their materials science and engineering knowledge to support product and process development in areas such as aerospace, rail, construction and oil and gas.
- You may be involved with the metal extraction process, managing projects or researching metals and materials.
- You may help develop practical solutions for production problems.
- Whatever job you do, it is likely that your role will involve aspects of quality control, project management and process/product development.

The type of person suited to this work

Metallurgists need an excellent knowledge of metals and related materials, whatever area they work in. They must also be able to understand the uses for different materials. You will need to have good communication and team-working skills. But you will also have to be confident in making decisions that could affect major industrial processes and understand the commercial impact of your work.

Your flexible approach and attention to detail will help you adapt to the changing demands of different projects. Your ICT and numeracy skills will also be important. Because you may work with potentially dangerous materials you must have a good knowledge of health and safety.

Working conditions

You may have to work in a noisy location if you are employed by a large manufacturing company. In other roles you could be based in a laboratory-style setting.

Hours vary from employer to employer, but they can be long, for example if you are working to complete a specific project to a set deadline.

In many roles, you will be part of a team and may also meet with clients on a regular basis.

In some roles you may be required to write detailed reports.

The future outlook

Many industries are quite literally built on metals and related materials! With a strong demand for high quality materials in a wide range of industries, there are all kinds of opportunities.

You could undertake project management for individual companies. You may choose to work for companies that develop materials for industries such as automotive and aerospace engineering. Or you could directly manage the process of mining and extracting materials.

entry level

4–8

To both enter and train while working in this career, you will need qualifications at Level 4–8. Please refer to explanation on page vii.

Qualifications and courses

- The usual entry qualification for a professional materials scientist or metallurgist is a degree. Degrees are available in metallurgy and in materials science, materials technology and materials engineering. It is also possible to enter with a degree in a general science subject, such as physics or chemistry.
- Entry to a relevant degree course (such as physics, chemical engineering, metallurgy or materials science) usually requires a minmum of 2 A levels/3H grades and 5 GCSEs/S grades (A–C/1–3). BTEC/SQA National qualifications may be offered as alternatives. For those seeking entry to the profession with HNC/HNDs or Foundation degrees (in a subject such as metallurgy and materials, metals technology, manufacturing engineering or applied science) then at least 1 science A level/H grade will be required.
- The role can provide the satisfaction of developing new products and materials.
- There are opportunities to work and live abroad.

CRCI:TD

CLCI:QOS

Other related opportunities

- Engineer: Craft p203
- Engineer: Professional p205
- Engineer: Technician p208
- Quarry Worker p221
- Scientist p486

Advantages/disadvantages

- The role can provide the satisfaction of developing new products and materials.
- There are opportunities to work and live abroad.

Earnings guide

- Starting salaries range from around £20,000 to £25,000 per year.
- With experience and at a senior level it is possible to earn £30,000–£37,000.
- With chartered engineer status, and as a senior manager you could earn between £37,500 and £50,000.

Further information

Institute of Materials, Minerals and Mining (IOM[3])
1 Carlton House Terrace
London
SW1Y 5DB
020 7451 7300
Main website: www.iom3.org
Careers website: www.materials-careers.org.uk

Engineering Council UK
246 High Holborn
London
WC1V 7EX
020 7206 0500
www.engc.org.uk

Institute of Cast Metals Engineers
National Metalforming Centre
47 Birmingham Road
West Bromwich
West Midlands
B70 6PY
0121 601 6979
www.icme.org.uk

Operational Researcher

What the work involves

- Operational researchers use mathematical, scientific and other analytical methods to help improve the performance of organisations in business, industry and government.
- You will work closely with managers and other staff to develop practical solutions to very varied kinds of management and organisational issues.
- You will develop analytical models or strategies to improve a specific area or aspect of an organisation.
- You may also be involved with putting your ideas into practice within companies.

The type of person suited to this work

Operational research (which is also known as operations research or management science) is all about getting practical results from in-depth analysis. So you should enjoy solving problems and applying your analytical and mathematical abilities to develop practical solutions.

You will have a strong interest in helping organisations develop – and put your understanding of each company to practical use. You will need excellent communication skills for working closely with managers and other staff. Your flexible approach will help you cope with the varied demands of each project. Whilst you will need strong ICT skills, a creative flair can also benefit you in this job.

Working conditions

You will undertake most of your work in an office setting with meetings with managers, technical specialists and staff likely to be a regular part of your job.

In the course of your work you may undertake visits to different sites in an organisation to undertake research into specific problems.

Your job will involve collating, managing and analysing detailed information.

The future outlook

Operational researchers help many different organisations to develop successfully. There are increasing opportunities in manufacturing, finance and other sectors and you can build a varied career. You could move into managing an OR team or work in areas such as marketing. With more experience, you could develop a career as an OR consultant.

The Civil Service offers a well-structured career path and a range of opportunities in operational research.

entry level

To both enter and train while working in this career, you will need qualifications at Level 4–8. Please refer to explanation on page vii.

Qualifications and courses

- The normal entry requirement for this profession is an Honours degree in a mathematical subject, for example maths, physics, chemistry, engineering, computer science, statistics or economics. Specialist degrees in operational research are available at some institutions, and operational research is also offered in combination with certain other degree subjects, such as maths or statistics.
- For entry to a relevant degree course, applicants should expect to offer a minimum of 2 A levels/4 H grades, including mathematics. Applicants will need to check with individual institutions regarding additional foundation years, where the usual minimum entry requirements are not met
- It may be possible to become an operational researcher with a degree in a non-mathematical subject if you have a good A level/H grade in maths.
- Postgraduate courses are available in operational research.
- The Fast Stream Development Programme offers opportunities for graduates in the Civil Service. The government's Operational Research Service scheme is open to graduates with a degree or MSc in a numerate discipline.
- The Operational Research Society organises open days for undergraduates who may be interested in a career in this area. The society also offers a wide range of training courses and in-house training.

CRCI:TC

CLCI:COF

Other related opportunities

- Mathematician p482
- Statistician p489

Advantages/disadvantages

- Strong demand in many sectors means you can develop your career in varied types of companies.
- Operations research work is fast-moving and varied.
- Resolving production, resource or staffing problems for a company can be confrontational and stressful.

Earnings guide

- Salary levels vary between management consultancies, the Government Operational Research Service and other employers.
- Generally, starting salaries range from £20,000 to £28,000 per year.
- With experience, and some management responsibilities you could earn £32,000–£50,000.
- At operational research consultant level you could earn £50,000–£80,000+.

Further information

Operational Research Society
Seymour House
12 Edward Street
Birmingham
BH1 2RX
0121 233 9300
www.theorsociety.org.uk

Government Operational Research Service
www.operational-research.gov.uk

Physicist

What the work involves

- Physicists apply their understanding of matter and energy and how they work together, in industry, government research, academia and medicine.
- You could apply your specialist skills and knowledge to investigate diverse subjects, including space, nuclear, thermal, atomic and materials physics.
- You may be involved with research and development work or with designing projects.
- Your role could involve developing products and systems in areas such as computing, aeronautics, electronics and medicine.

The type of person suited to this work

Physicists must combine their scientific knowledge with strong problem-solving skills to develop knowledge of a range of issues. For this job you will need the confidence to work with complex numerical information. You should also have excellent attention to detail for undertaking research.

As your job may involve planning and setting up investigations with specialist equipment, you will need a well-organised and logical approach to your work. ICT skills are also important. You should have good written and verbal communication skills to explain your work. A patient approach for completing detailed projects can be useful.

Working conditions

You would be based in a laboratory, using specialist equipment when undertaking research. This work can involve handling potentially dangerous chemicals and wearing protective clothing.

Your work may also involve spending periods looking at and assessing information on a computer.

For some jobs you will have to do a certain amount of late or weekend working. Jobs in industry may involve working shifts.

The future outlook

Physicists work at the cutting edge of science and industry. They apply their skills in areas as varied as electronics, power, communications and defence. They are employed by research institutions, government bodies and private companies to improve and develop products and systems.

You could choose to go into research and development, based on your particular area of interest. You could choose to teach physics at school or university level.

entry level

To both enter and train while working in this career, you will need qualifications at Level 4–8. Please refer to explanation on page vii.

Qualifications and courses

- A relevant degree and a postgraduate qualification are required to work as a research physicist.
- Relevant work experience is an advantage, and may be required by employers.
- Entry to a degree course usually requires a minimum of at least 2 A levels/3–4 H grades, including physics and maths or equivalent, together with 5 GCSEs/S grades (A–C/1–3) including English, maths and science.
- Many institutions offer 1-year Foundation courses for candidates without the necessary scientific background. Foundation courses may be taught at the university or at a local partner college.
- Physicists are trained on the job, and often study towards postgraduate qualifications, a PhD or the membership examinations of relevant professional bodies. For example, medical physicists must work towards the Clinical Science Diploma of the Institute of Physics and Engineering in Medicine (IPEM).
- For entry at technician level, an A level/H grade in physics or an equivalent qualification such as a BTEC/SQA National in science is required. Some technicians may hold a science-based degree. Technicians can work towards NVQs/SVQs in Laboratory and Associated Technical Activities at Levels 2–4.

Other related opportunities

- Astronomer p466
- Civil Service Scientific Officer p474
- Engineer: Professional p205
- Medical Physicist p288

Advantages/disadvantages

- Physics offers the chance to develop public understanding of important scientific questions.
- The job can involve working with detailed information for long periods which can be very tiring.
- There is a strong demand for qualified physicists.

Earnings guide

- Salary levels vary according to employer and sector. You are likely to earn more with a relevant postgraduate degree.
- Starting salaries for graduates begin at £19,000–£25,000 per year.
- With further training and qualifications salaries increase to to £24,000–£35,000.
- At senior/management levels you could earn £40,000–£60,000.

Further information

Institute of Physics
76 Portland Place
London
W1B 1NT
020 7470 4800
Main website: www.iop.org
Careers website: www.careers.iop.org

Physics World
www.physicsworld.com

Physics news, jobs and resources
Institute of Physics and Engineering in Medicine
Fairmount House
230 Tadcaster Road
York
YO24 1ES
01904 610821
www.ipem.ac.uk

Scientist

What the work involves

- Scientists use specialist techniques and knowledge to increase our understanding of the world around us. Working in great detail or on a large scale, scientists observe, develop theories, plan experiments and bring together important information.
- Working in a huge variety of areas, scientists provide knowledge about the way we live. Many aspects of industry, medicine, education and other areas are influenced by the work of scientists.

Biomedical scientist

- Biomedical scientists (known as medical laboratory scientific officers in the National Health Service) undertake laboratory tests to help medical staff diagnose and treat disease.
- Your work may involve taking samples from patients or developing pharmaceutical products as part of a research team. You could be employed in the National Health Service, hospitals, the Health Protection Agency, the pharmaceutical industry or other government agencies.

Clinical scientist

- Clinical scientists work mainly for the NHS but are also employed in the Health Protection Agency, research centres and industry. They work in a range of scientific specialities.
- Your work may involve supporting doctors and other medical staff, suggesting suitable tests for diagnosing patients, reporting on results and recommending treatments. You may also research and test new methods of treatment and make recommendations on the best equipment or test materials.

Consumer scientist

- Consumer scientists or home economists provide support, information and specialist services related to healthy living and eating.
- Your work could involve developing new food products, educating people about healthy eating or assessing new cookery equipment.

Cosmetic scientist

- The cosmetics industry requires scientists to help develop, test and produce new and existing cosmetics and beauty products, such as make-up, perfumes and haircare products.
- You will apply your scientific skills and knowledge to ensure that cosmetic products used by many people are effective and safe.

Environmental scientist

- Environmental scientists apply scientific techniques to study and protect the natural environment.
- You could work in pollution monitoring, conservation, environmental consultancy and research and other areas.

Food scientist

- Food scientists undertake research, production and quality assurance work in all areas of the food industry.
- You could apply your knowledge of food chemistry, biology and nutrition and other areas to analyse food products, set up manufacturing processes and develop food labelling.

Forensic scientist

- You will use your skills to provide important scientific information and help resolve legal and criminal cases.
- By analysing samples and assessing accident and crime scenes, you will support the work of police and lawyers.

Materials scientist

- Materials scientists measure, define and process different kinds of materials. They help decide the types of materials to use in engineering, construction and product processing work.
- You will use your knowledge of the properties of metals and alloys, glass, ceramics and other materials in many areas of industrial research, development and production.

CRCI:T | CLCI:Q

The type of person suited to this work

Whatever their work involves, every scientist needs excellent observational skills. Your technical skills and ability to use scientific equipment to get results will be essential. A good level of numeracy is also important.

You will need an organised approach for undertaking practical work. A flexible attitude is also useful. You will be able to communicate well in writing and verbally to share your research with clients, colleagues and managers. You should also be able to interact well as part of a team. Scientists in every sector need to be able to work to set deadlines. They must also be able to work calmly under pressure. As a scientist you will get results by combining a logical approach with a creative flair.

If you are a scientist working in industry you will need an interest in the commercial use applications of your work.

Qualifications and courses

- Most entrants to this profession are graduates. A degree and often a postgraduate qualification in an appropriate science subject are required.
- The entry requirements for science-based degrees normally include A levels/H grades in sciences and or maths, or an equivalent such as BTEC/SQA National qualifications in the relevant science(s).
- Many institutions offer 1-year Foundation courses for candidates without the necessary scientific background.
- After entry, scientists may study towards postgraduate qualifications or the examinations of the relevant professional body.

Biomedical scientist

- The normal route into the profession requires a degree, accredited by The Institute of Biomedical Science (IBMS). It is possible to take other subjects, aside from biomedical science, such as chemistry or microbiology, and progress to a postgraduate qualification in biomedical science.
- A minimum of 2 A levels/3 H grades, including chemistry and biology, and 5 GCSEs/S grades (A–C/1–3) including English, science and maths are usually required for entry to a biomedical science degree. Those without formal entry requirements could present a range of alternatives or attend an Access course.
- To work in the NHS, it is necessary to be state registered. The requirements for registration are a degree approved by the Health Professionals Council and a year's in-service training.
- Following state registration, many biomedical scientists study part time for an MSc. This leads to Fellowship of the Institute of Biomedical Sciences.
- There may be some opportunities to start as a trainee biomedical scientist with A levels or the equivalent in life sciences. Trainees would then study for a biomedical science degree on a part-time basis.

Clinical scientist

- Entrants to this profession require a 1st or 2.1 class degree in a relevant subject, such as biochemistry, biology, chemistry, engineering, genetics, microbiology, physics or physiology. Enty to a degree typically requires a minimum of 2 A levels/3 H grades, including appropriate science subjects.
- An MSc or PhD in your specialist area is an advantage.
- Clinical scientists start as Grade A trainees. The training lasts 2–3 years, and involves placements and formal study, often towards and MSc. On completion of the training, candidates are eligible for state registration, and can apply for Grade B posts. In-service training continues, and many clinical scientists work towards membership qualifications of professional bodies or a PhD. After a minimum of 4 years in a training post scientists can register with the Health Professional Council allowing them to use their correct title of Clinical Scientist and work unsupervised.

Consumer scientist

- Entrants to this profession usually have relevant educational qualifications and/or industrial experience. HNDs and degrees are available in a variety of relevant subjects, for example consumer studies/science, food studies/science, food and nutrition, food and marketing, food technology. Degrees are also available in specialist areas of consumer science, such as consumer protection or consumer psychology.
- Relevant courses at further education level include NVQs/SVQs in Food Preparation or Food and Drink Manufacturing Operations and BTEC/SQA National qualifications in Hospitality. Employers may offer in-house training leading to NVQs/SVQs.
- Candidates with a relevant degree or HNC/D and 2 years' relevant work experience are eligible for corporate membership of the Institute of Consumer Sciences. People with experience and a position of responsibility in the industry are also eligible for membership.

Cosmetic scientist

- Career entry can be achieved at more than one level, including a relevant degree (cosmetic science, chemistry, chemical engineering, biology, microbiology, physics, medicine and pharmacy), Foundation degree or HNC/D. For degree entry, many colleges include a 1-year introductory course for students who have not studied the requisite science subjects at A level/H grade.
- The Diploma in Cosmetic Science can be attained by distance learning, after approximately 300 hours of study. A shorter course, particularly suited to those who have been working in the industry for some time, is the Principles and Practice of Cosmetic Science course, which is of use to those looking to move into supervisory or managerial roles and/or who are taking on a new field of expertise.

Environmental scientist

- A relevant environmental science degree is usually required. It is possible to gain work with a relevant HNC/D. Once qualified, you can apply for registration with the Council for the Registration of Forensic Practitioners.

Food scientist

- Entrants to this profession usually have a degree, HNC/D or Foundation degree. Relevant subjects include food science, food studies and food technology, as well as general science degrees. For entry to these courses, A levels/H grades in chemistry and/or biology may be required. Some people study for a postgraduate qualification in food science before entering work.
- You can enter with lower qualifications as a laboratory or quality control technician. Typical entry requirements include 4 GCSEs/S grades (A–C/1–3), including English, mathematics, chemistry and biology, or an Applied A level in science, or a BTEC National qualification in food science and manufacturing technology. Technicians can work towards NVQs/SVQs at Levels 1–4 in Food and Drink Manufacturing Operations, and at Levels 2–4 in Laboratory and Associated Technical Activities. They can also study part time for an HNC to gain promotion to food scientist. Once qualified, you can apply for registration with the Institute of Food Science and Technology (IFST), who run a Continuing Professional Development scheme.

entry level

To both enter and train while working in this career, you will need qualifications at Level 4–8. Please refer to explanation on page vii.

Forensic scientist

- To enter the profession as a forensic scientist, a good Honours degree (1st or upper 2 : 1) in biology, chemistry, forensic science or a related subject is usually required. Some employers may accept an equivalent professional qualification.
- An MSc in forensic science or a related subject is an advantage, as is laboratory experience.
- To enter as an assistant or technician forensic scientist in England and Wales 4 GCSEs (A–C), including a science or maths and at least one science A level or equivalent are required. In Scotland, a Higher National qualification in chemistry, biology or a related subject is normally required for technician/assistant entry.
- Forensic scientists are mainly trained on the job and through in-house courses. Once qualified, you can apply for registration with the Council for the Registration of Forensic Practitioners.

Materials scientist

- The usual entry qualification for a professional materials scientist or metallurgist is a degree. Degrees are available in metallurgy and in materials science, materials technology and materials engineering. It is also possible to enter with a degree in a general science subject, for example physics or chemistry. For entry to a relevant degree course, A level/H grade maths and a science are required. A Foundation year is available at some institutions for candidates without the required scientific background.
- To become a chartered materials engineer, you need to have studied a 4-year MEng degree or a 3-year BEng or BSc followed by a period of professional development.
- Postgraduate courses are available, and may be studied prior to entry, or through company training schemes.

Working conditions

Many scientists work in a laboratory or research centre. Your job may involve handling potentially dangerous materials, so you would need to wear protective clothing.

Some jobs in this area involve working outside in sometimes poor weather conditions to undertake fieldwork.

Some scientific jobs involve travelling to meetings, conferences and other events in the UK and abroad.

In addition to hands-on experimental work, your work may involve using computers.

Some jobs involve repetitive analysis work in the laboratory, which can be physically demanding.

Scientists working in industry at management level are increasingly involved in working directly with clients to agree and develop projects.

In industry, you might be employed on a shift basis.

Forensic scientist

As a forensic scientist working on a crime scene, you might have to deal with unpleasant or upsetting sights.

The future outlook

There is a growing demand for scientists in most sectors, with the need for professionals to undertake research, development and analysis work.

Scientists are needed to help ensure that the products we use and consume are safe. A career working in industry, for example as a cosmetic or materials scientist, can provide many opportunities.

Public research institutions also require support with research and development work. With experience, you could initiate and lead projects that could have a real impact on public quality of life.

You may choose to follow an academic career in your particular branch of science. This would involve teaching and working with students as well as undertaking your own research. Increasingly, scientists in universities are working closely with colleagues in industry and public research, which can lead to a career in other areas.

You may choose to apply your scientific knowledge in a related area, for example applying your environmental science skills to managing environmental or conservation projects.

With experience, you could progress to managing a team of scientists and developing and designing clinical trials and scientific research. At this level, your role would involve more management and development activities, with less time spent in the laboratory or research centre.

Further on in their careers, many scientists move into marketing, management and sales roles in their particular fields. Others work as consultants, providing specialist support to a range of companies.

Other related opportunities

- Biochemist p467
- Biologist p468
- Biotechnologist p471
- Brewer p176
- Chemist p472
- Civil Service Scientific Officer p474
- Earth Sciences p475
- Engineer: Professional p205
- Lecturer p178
- Metallurgist p483
- Physicist p485
- Teacher p184

Advantages/disadvantages

- Scientific careers provide the opportunity to apply your skills and knowledge to develop new products and provide important new scientific information.
- In some areas, a higher salary is gained by achieving a further postgraduate qualification.
- Scientists are constantly in demand in most areas of industry and medicine.
- At junior levels, some roles involve routine and repetitive laboratory-based work.
- As many roles in science are project based, it can offer varied and fast-moving careers.

Earnings guide

- Salary levels vary according to employer and sector.
- Salaries for scientists working in the National Health Service and other government health bodies are set annually.

Biomedical scientist

- Starting salaries vary from £19,000 to £25,000 per year. With experience this rises to £27,000–£35,000.
- At senior levels you could earn up to £60,000.

Clinical scientist

- Starting salaries vary from £19,000 to £25,000 per year. With experience this rises to £27,000–£35,000.
- At senior/consultant level this can increase to £55,000–£70,000.

Consumer scientist

- Starting salaries range from £17,500 to £22,000 per year. With experience, you could earn up to £30,000. At senior level you could get up to £50,000.
- Consumer scientists working on a consultancy basis can earn £150–£500 a day.

Cosmetic scientist

- Starting salaries are about £18,000–£23,000 per year. With experience, you could earn between £25,000 and £45,000.
- At senior levels it is possible to earn up to £50,000.

Environmental scientist

- Starting salaries range from £18,000 to £25,000 per year. With experience, you could earn up to £35,000.
- At senior levels it is possible to earn up to £55,000.

Food scientist

- Starting salaries range from £18,000 to £25,000 per year. This increases to £30,000–£40,000 with experience.
- At senior/management levels this can increase to £50,000+.

Forensic scientist

- Starting salaries are around £20,000 per year. This increases with experience to £30,000.
- At senior level you could earn up to £50,000.

Materials scientist

- Starting salaries range from around £18,000 per year. With experience, it is possible to earn £35,000–£45,000.
- At senior/management level you could earn £50,000+.

Further information

Science Council
32–36 Loman Street
London
SE1 0EH
020 7922 7888
www.sciencecouncil.org

BIOMEDICAL SCIENTIST

Institute of Biomedical Science
12 Coldbath Square
London
EC1R 5HL
020 7713 0214
www.ibms.org

CLINICAL SCIENTIST

Federation of Clinical Scientists
c/o Association for Clinical Biochemistry
130–132 Tooley Street
London
SE1 2TU
020 7403 8001
www.acb.org.uk/federation/

CONSUMER SCIENTIST

International Federation for Home Economics
www.ifhe.org

COSMETIC SCIENTIST

Society of Cosmetic Scientists
G.T. House
24–26 Rothesay Road
Luton
LU1 1QX
01582 726661
www.scs.org.uk

ENVIRONMENTAL SCIENTIST

Institution of Environmental Sciences
Suite 1
38 Ebury Street
London
SW1 0LU
020 7730 5516
www.ies-uk.org.uk

FOOD SCIENTIST

Institute of Food Science & Technology
5 Cambridge Court
210 Shepherd's Bush Road
London
W6 7NJ
020 7603 6316
www.ifst.org

FORENSIC SCIENTIST

Forensic Science Society
18a Mount Parade
Harrogate
North Yorkshire
HG1 1BX
01423 506 068
www.forensic-science-society.org.uk

MATERIALS SCIENTIST

Institute of Materials, Minerals and Mining (IOM^3)
1 Carlton House Terrace
London
SW1Y 5DB
020 7451 7300
Main website: www.iom3.org
Careers website: www.materials-careers org.uk

UK Centre for Materials Education
Materials Science and Engineering
University of Liverpool
Liverpool
L69 3GH
0151 794 5364
www.materials.ac.uk

CRCI:T

CLCI:Q

Statistician

What the work involves

- Statistics involves the use of mathematical techniques to collect, analyse and present large quantities of factual information.
- You will plan and undertake surveys using a range of mathematical research methods.
- You could apply your skills to investigate a range of subjects such as population levels, patterns of illness or national shopping habits.
- Statistical research plays a vital role in informing the activities of many areas such as government, advertising, medicine and scientific research.

The type of person suited to this work

Strong mathematical skills are essential for producing and analysing a range of statistical information. But you will also need excellent problem-solving abilities to create practical solutions and collect information on specific issues. Your organised approach will be essential in helping you to plan research and analyse the information it provides.

You will need to have excellent ICT skills as it is likely you will use specialist computer software. Your work could help to shape the work of different organisations, so you must work to a high standard of accuracy and attention to detail at all times. The ability to communicate with managers, staff and clients is essential.

Working conditions

You will be based in an office environment and spend a lot of time using computers. For some jobs you may work in a laboratory or research centre.

Statistical work demands a high level of concentration and the ability to take in a great deal of information.

The job involves working closely with other people on a consultancy basis or as part of a team.

The future outlook

With a strong demand for statisticians right now, there is a wide range of opportunities. Statisticians investigate and research issues within the environment, medicine, business, social science and many other areas.

You may choose to develop a career in the Government Statistical Service. There are many opportunities in scientific and medical research and pharmaceutical development. Or you could choose to research and lecture on statistics in academia.

entry level

To both enter and train while working in this career, you will need qualifications at Level 4–8. Please refer to explanation on page vii.

Qualifications and courses

- The usual entry qualification for this profession is a degree in statistics, or a combined degree in statistics and another subject such as maths, economics or computer science. It is possible to enter with degrees in other subjects, providing the degree has substantial statistics content. A level/H grade maths is required for entry to a statistics degree.
- Those with degrees in other mathematical subjects might enter after gaining a postgraduate qualification in statistics.
- The professional examinations of the Royal Statistical Society provide an alternative entry route for people already in relevant employment and for mature entrants.
- The Royal Statistical Society offers courses at three levels. The Ordinary Certificate requires a GCSE/S grade in maths or the equivalent and relevant work experience. The Higher Certificate is modular and follows on from the Ordinary Certificate. The Graduate Diploma is equivalent to an Honours degree. The courses can be studied by day-release, at evening classes or by distance learning.
- The Government Statistical Service has a fast-stream programme for assistant statistician recruitment. Candidates must have a 1st or 2nd class degree in a numerate subject.
- Statistical officer posts are also available to people with a 1st or 2nd class degree or 2 years' relevant work experience.
- The Government Statistical Service offers work experience placements for students.
- After 4 or 5 years' professional experience, statisticians with an approved degree or Graduate Diploma can qualify for Chartered Statistician status.

CRCI:TC | CLCI:QOJ

Other related opportunities

- Lecturer p178
- Mathematician p482
- Operational Researcher p484

Advantages/disadvantages

- Working to a high level of accuracy at all times can be very demanding.
- Roles in areas such as environmental or forensic statistics are more likely with a postgraduate qualification.
- As the job is often project-based, it offers a lot of variety.

Earnings guide

- Salary levels vary according to employer/sector.
- Starting salaries for graduates begin around £21,000 per year.
- With experience, you can earn £40,000, increasing to £50,000+ at senior levels.
- Government Statistical Service (GSS) starting salaries are around £18,500–£23,000.
- Senior level GSS salaries are £40,000–£53,000.

Further information

Royal Statistical Society
12 Errol Street
London
EC1Y 8LX
020 7638 8998
www.rss.org.uk/careers

Statisticians in Central government
www.statistics.gov.uk/recruitment/GSS

Office for National Statistics
Customer Contact Centre
Cardiff Road
Newport
NP10 8XG
0845 601 3034
www.statistics.gov.uk

Do you want a job involving security, helping or protecting people? This cluster includes many jobs that involve wearing a uniform, such as:

- **Army Officer**
- **Firefighter**
- **Police Officer**
- **Store Detective**
- **Traffic Warden**

But what's it like working in this area?

Here's Helen Peirce's story

Prison Officer

At the start of her working life 29-year-old Helen was toying with the idea of joining the police force. However, after careful consideration she decided joining the prison service would prove a far more interesting career. After gaining a higher diploma (HND) in Business, Administration, Finance and Secretarial Skills, she joined the prison service and now works at HM Prison Wandsworth, in South London. She is a Temporary Senior Officer (TSO) and currently works in the central resource unit of the establishment, managing the staff resources for the whole prison including sorting out any personal problems the staff may have.

WHAT YOU NEED TO SUCCEED IN THE PRISON SERVICE

'You need to have good life skills, for example being able to deal with crisis situations. You also need to have good communication and listening skills. Above all you need to be patient and have empathy. You need to be able to act as a role model. In my particular position you need to be able to assist both prison personnel and inmates with problem solving. One of the most important abilities you need is being able to "open" questions (explaining what the question actually means) in order for the prisoner to identify their own problem-solving skills.'

Dealing with so many different individuals on a daily basis is the thing Helen most likes about her job. She would definitely like to go on to gain more qualifications because these would help her with future chances of promotion within the service. Ultimately she aspires to being in charge of her own prison one day, effectively becoming 'The Governor'.

'The best thing I could say to people wishing to join the prison service is if you are looking for a long-lasting, interesting career where you are dealing with people on a daily basis then you will not find a better job, because that in essence is what we do.'

Army

What the work involves

- The Army plays an important role in Nato and UN operations and has three main branches: the combat arms (front-line troops), the combat support arms (who provide artillery, field engineering, signals and intelligence support) and the services (who provide all the supplies and services needed including administration, catering and medical care).

Officer

- You will lead, command and train a team of soldiers on day-to-day activities either on training exercises or on a range of combat, peacekeeping or disaster-relief missions.
- Your platoon's training, welfare and discipline will be your responsibility.
- You will also work in a specific professional or skill area, such as medicine, dentistry, engineering or intelligence.

Soldier

- To be ready for combat at any time, you will be involved in regular exercises or active duty, while maintaining a high level of fitness and military skills.
- You will also train and work in one of more than 130 different trade or skill areas, such as catering, transport and logistics, engineering or infantry.

The type of person suited to this work

You need to be self-disciplined, confident, with a talent for getting on with other people. Each army platoon is a team of 30, including soldiers, non-commissioned officers and a junior officer, all working, training and living together. Army life comes with high expectations of good conduct, behaviour and team work.

Initial training, with its physical and mental challenges, is often a shock, especially to young recruits who have not been away from home much before. You will need to have determination, courage and resilience as well as a good level of physical fitness.

Officers also need a flair for leadership and motivation along with an ability to inspire confidence in others.

Working conditions

Your main role will be military so you will be expected to go into dangerous war zones anywhere in the world.

You will be expected to wear a uniform and protective clothing when required. You will need to have criminal and identity checks, and be physically fit.

In barracks, hours are usually regular and worked in 8-hour duty shifts but on operational tours or exercises hours can be long and irregular.

The future outlook

The Army is the largest UK force and to retain its current strength of 111,000 personnel, it needs to recruit about 15,000 new entrants each year.

Officer

About 700+ new officers are recruited each year. Entry is competitive and 80% of current entrants are graduates. All non-graduate officers start as second lieutenants while graduates start as lieutenants. If you do well and pass promotion exams there is a clear promotion route from second lieutenant to lieutenant, captain, major, lieutenant colonel, colonel.

Soldier

The majority of new entrants join at this level. If you complete your training and do well there is a clear promotion route from private to lance corporal to sergeant and up to warrant officer. It is possible to be commissioned from the ranks provided that you pass the selection board.

Qualifications and courses

entry level

To both enter and train while working in this career, you will need qualifications at Level 1–8. Please refer to explanation on page vii.

- The minimum age is normally 17 years and 9 months, but apprentices and Army Foundation College students can join at 16. To qualify for a full 22-year career an applicant must be between 16 and 30 years old on the day of enlistment. Women can join all areas except the Household Cavalry, the Royal Armoured Corps and the Infantry. The upper age limit for enlisting is 33.

Officer

- The minimum entry requirements to join the Army as an officer are 7 GCSEs/S grades (A–C/1–3) and 2 A levels/3 Advanced Highers. Equivalent qualifications are accepted. English language and maths at GCSE/S grade are compulsory; science subjects and foreign languages are useful.
- 80% of successful entrants to officer level are graduates. Any UCAS-recognised degree is accepted but some specialist and technical corps may require specific degrees or professional qualifications.
- You will need to pass selection tests at the Regular Commissions Board, pass a medical test and meet the Army's nationality and residence requirements. Many training courses are offered and will help with preparation for promotion.
- As a general rule, all civilian candidates for Officer training should be over 17 years and 9 months and under 29 on application, although some specialisms have a higher upper age limit.

Soldier

- You may also join the Army as a non-commissioned officer/soldier. You will have to pass the Army Entrance Test, a physical assessment, a medical test and two interviews with the Army personnel selection officer, and meet the requirements of army nationality. Basic physical training normally lasts for 12 weeks.
- No particular qualifications are needed unless applying for a technical trade where GCSEs/S grades (A–C/1–3) in maths and English are needed. Otherwise, successful completion of a BARB test will be acceptable.

Other related opportunities

- Police p506
- Royal Air Force (RAF) p512
- Royal Marines p514
- Royal Navy p516
- Security p518

Advantages/disadvantages

- Initial training is tough; some soldiers regard it as one of the toughest times of their career. However, it is regarded as a real milestone and achievement to pass.
- If you are keen on keeping fit the Army offers lots of opportunities, including trying new sports and taking part in adventurous training exercises often in extreme terrain or weather conditions.
- You will live in a tightly knit community. Officers and soldiers say that they really enjoy and value the team spirit and the time spent with like-minded people.

Earnings guide

Officer

- On entry, second lieutenants earn £22,679 per year. Lieutenants earn from £27,980–£30,131. Captains earn from £37,768–£41,544. Colonels can earn up to £75,283.
- Brigadiers can earn up to £87,613.

Soldier

- Starting salaries are £12,571 per year. A private can earn from £15,677 rising to £18,963 as Lance corporal. Non-commissioned promotion grades range from £18,963 to £43,076 at warrant officer class 1 rank.

Further information

Armed Forces Careers Army
2 Magdalen St
Norwich
NR3 1HX
01603 624616
www.army.mod.uk

BRITISH ARMY
British Army
08457 300111
www.army.mod.uk

www.cityandguilds.com/myperfectjob

Bodyguard

What the work involves

- You will be guarding your client or group, keeping them safe from harm or unwanted attention. You may also be known as a Personal Protection Officer or a Close Protection Officer.
- Protecting an executive on a business trip to a dangerous region of the world, an overseas royal visiting the UK, or a celebrity during an autograph-signing session could all be part of your work.
- You will be planning how your client can go about their business without being at risk. For example, you will think about the best way to move them from a building into a car, or protecting from terrorist organisations or stalkers.
- It is possible to be a specialist in areas such as close protection, surveillance or defensive driving.

The type of person suited to this work

This is not a first job – most have related experience and the ones who win the most lucrative contracts have backgrounds in the Special Forces or specialist close-protection police units. Also, most of the work is on a self-employed basis, so you need to have a flair for business because you will need to sell your services, network and keep your accounts.

You will have to have exceptional planning skills because looking ahead and making sure that your client is free from harm or unwanted attention is crucial in this job.

You will also need to be confident, physically fit to cope with the demands of the work, and have good eyesight and hearing.

Your appearance, diplomacy and communication skills also need to be top level, because you will be with your client and need to blend into the background to observe at high profile events.

Working conditions

Your work will be wherever your client goes and so this could mean lots of travelling.

You may be at risk as you would protect your client if necessary with your own body – but this is more an issue when working in dangerous areas of the world.

You may work long and irregular hours during a contract as some clients may need 24 hour protection.

The future outlook

A lot of UK protection work is done by ex-armed military or police personnel. Most commercial officers work protecting high-profile business executives either in the UK or on projects overseas (especially in dangerous areas like parts of the former Soviet Union). Others work protecting celebrities and pop stars, usually from the constant media and public attention.

Very few officers are in long-term employment. The vast majority are self-employed. There is an increasing demand for good female officers.

Some progress into more mainstream security work, for example security guard or security manager.There may be opportunities to specialise in areas such as driving, and residential security.

entry level

1

To both enter and train while working in this career, you will need qualifications at Level 1. Please refer to explanation on page vii.

Qualifications and courses

- There are no formal entry requirements, but since 2006 there is a legal requirement for all Close Protection Officers (CPOs) to hold a Security Industry Authority Licence (SIA) which lasts for 3 years and covers some other security sectors which also require licences. The majority of successful CPOs have worked before either in the armed forces or as police officers. Knowledge of foreign languages is useful, and applicants should be physically fit.
- Training is through courses. There are a number of close protection agencies in the UK who offer courses. Many expect you to be over 21. This course covers terrorist methods of operation, trauma management and vehicle anti-ambush drills as well as elements such as driving skills and conflict resolution. It leads to a BTEC Level 4 Diploma in close protection.
- Buckingham Chilterns University College offers a Foundation degree in Protective Security Operations. Applicants need at least 2 A levels/H grades. Edexcel and City & Guilds also offer Level 3 certificates in Close Protection Operations and Close Protection.
- There is a shortage of female bodyguards.

Other related opportunities

- Army p492
- Police p506
- Royal Air Force (RAF) p512
- Royal Marines p514
- Security p518

Advantages/disadvantages

- This job is often done on a self-employed basis so your earnings may be high but could have to cover periods of unemployment.
- Training courses are residential and expensive. However, you could use your training to move into related security work.

Earnings guide

- New entrants can earn about £18,000 per year rising to £25,000-£30,000 with experience. With experience and working in high risk areas, you could earn up to £100,000.
- Many close protection officers earn daily or hourly rates for specific contracts. These could be from about £150 to £200 a day plus expenses for routine work, up to £500 a day in a very hostile environment.

Further information

Security Industry Authority
PO Box 9
Newcastle upon Tyne
NE82 6YX
0870 243 0100
www.the-sia.org.uk

Skills for Security
Security House
Barbourne Road
Worcester
WR1 1RS
08450 750111
www.skillsforsecurity.org.uk

Professional Bodyguard Association
72 New Bond Street
Mayfair
London
W1S 1RR
0800 585505
www.bodyguards-pba.com

Coastguard

What the work involves

- You will work as part of a team responding to vessels and people in distress. You will be policing over 10,500 miles of coastline and 1,000,000 square miles of sea and ocean.
- You will be dealing with 999 coastguard calls and radio distress calls, and may also be using the services of the Royal National Lifeboat Institution (RNLI).
- Using monitoring and communications equipment, you will make sure the right help is sent to the right location.
- You will keep records of all activity and weather conditions, giving information to vessels and reporting anything unusual.

Watch Officers

- Watch officers are involved in all areas of the work and may lead coastal, sea or cliff searches and rescues.

Watch Assistants

- Watch assistants work as administration support – keeping details of calls and rescues, and providing information to the general public.

The type of person suited to this work

You will need to enjoy working with computers, be able to concentrate for long periods and have a clear voice to make sure that you send the right rescuers to the right place. Eighty per cent of calls are from people taking part in leisure activities so your calm approach, local knowledge and clear instructions to the caller will make fatalities less likely.

If you are involved in active search and rescue work you will need a high level of physical fitness, because your work may include carrying heavy equipment, climbing and possibly working out at sea. Watch officers also lead and train groups of auxiliary coastguards, so will need good management and teaching skills.

You will need to have an interest in the sea, and the coastline.

Working conditions

Most of your work will be in an operations centre, using a computer and talking to others using hands-free communications equipment.

If actively involved in search and rescue work, you will be working outside in dangerous conditions.

Coastguards operate 24/7 – you will be working 12-hour shifts and a 42-hour week.

Uniforms and protective clothing are provided.

The future outlook

HM Coastguard is part of the Maritime and Coastguard Agency (MCA) and its employees are civil servants. There are about 1000 coastguards employed at centres around the UK coastline and a further 3000 auxiliary coastguards working as paid volunteers. This is a competitive job to enter.

It is possible to work up to officer or sector management level. However, there are a limited number of senior jobs in this fairly small service. It is also expected that numbers will continue to drop in some areas of the service in the next few years.

entry level

To both enter and train while working in this career, you will need qualifications at Level 1–2. Please refer to explanation on page vii.

Qualifications and courses

- Most people join HM Coastguard as a coastguard watch assistant (CWA). You will need a good standard of literacy and numeracy, hearing and eyesight, and interest in maritime affairs and the potential to use computer and communications equipment. There are no minimum entry qualifications, but maths and English to GCSE/S grade and Key Skills in communication and numeracy are useful. Most CWAs start as volunteers and you will need to be aged over 16 to apply.
- A few join at coastguard watch officer level (CWO). You will need a good standard of hearing and eyesight and a high level of fitness. Significant sea-going experience, preferably in a search and rescue capacity, and a driving licence are required.
- You would initially train for 7 weeks at the Coastguard Training Centre in Dorset. Training is then on the job with a further short course after 9 months. You have to pass a series of exams to be retained.
- Alternatively, you could become a CWA or CRO, which is a voluntary post. You will need to be over 16 and most volunteers work in a different career as well. You would be paid for the hours you work. The MCA welcomes mature entrants.

Other related opportunities

- Air Traffic Controller p556
- Merchant Navy p571
- Police p506
- Royal Navy p516

Advantages/disadvantages

- Satellite technology means that you will be able to organise the successful rescue of someone in distress even if they are hundreds of miles away from your control centre.
- However, the sea is more dangerous than the average leisure-user understands and you may arrive too late, which is an upsetting event for the whole team.

Earnings guide

- When starting out you could earn around £15,000 per year as a Coastguard Watch Assistant.
- Coastguard Watch Officers can earn up to £23,000.
- Shift allowances and overtime pay can increase earnings. Additional allowances are paid to those working in the Scottish Islands.

Further information

Maritime & Coastguard Agency- Human resources team
Bay 3/19 Spring Place
105 Commercial Road
Southampton
SO15 1EG
023 8032 9308
www.mcga.gov.uk

Port Skills and Safety Ltd
Room 220
Africa House
64–78 Kingsway
London
WC2B 6AH
020 2423538
www.portskillsandsafety.co.uk

Crime Scene Examiner

What the work involves

- You may also be known as a crime scene officer. You will be collecting, storing and recording evidence such as fibres, hair and blood to help investigate crimes like burglary or offences against the person, accidents and suspicious deaths.
- You will use equipment and materials to lift, package and preserve evidence, such as biological samples, paint, tyre marks and fingerprints.
- Your job will involve taking photographic and video evidence of both crime scenes and victims of crime.
- You will also need to keep thorough records and attend court when required to give evidence.

The type of person suited to this work

Sifting through evidence in minute detail is the main aspect of this job so you will need to be the type of person who has good attention to detail. You will need to be methodical and patient while sifting through evidence. Many samples are microscopic so you will also need to have good observation skills.

This job can be very distressing. You will need to be able to distance yourself emotionally from the crime, not be squeamish and be able to record the scene and collect evidence in an analytical, scientific way. Good team working is essential as you may be working on a project with many others.

An interest in science and technology is essential. You will need to keep up to date with developments in forensic science and technology as they will affect how you do your job.

Working conditions

You will work both outside and inside at crime scenes and inside back at base.

You will do a 37-hour working week, including shifts, but hours may be longer at times. You may also be on a 24-hour call out.

Conditions at crime scenes can be very difficult and unpleasant but you will be provided with protective clothing.You will usually need a driving licence.

The future outlook

Crime scene examiners are recruited by all regional police forces. Some forces only recruit civilians to do this work but a few also recruit specialist police officers. There are currently about 1800 crime scene examiners in the UK. Competition for vacancies is great.

It is possible to move into more specialised areas of work, such as the investigation of suspicious fires, or scenes where firearms have been used. There may be opportunities for promotion to senior examiner with management responsibilities.

entry level

To both enter and train while working in this career, you will need qualifications at Level 2–8. Please refer to explanation on page vii.

Qualifications and courses

- There are no minimum entry requirements but some forces require 3–5 GCSEs/S grades (A–C/1–3), including maths, English and science. Some forces may require A levels/H grades or equivalent. Others may specify that you need a GSCE, A level or HNC/HND in photography.
- You will need to be at least 18 with normal colour vision and no allergies to skin irritants. You will also have to pass a medical test and a background check. The majority of examiners start this job in their 20s and often have degrees or HNDs.
- Work experience is usually required, ideally in a related area such as photography or scientific work. Previous work dealing with the public would also be an advantage.
- Once in the job you would have a 1-month induction with your force, followed by a residential course at the National Training Centre (CENTREX NTC) in Durham. This course covers to photography, forensics and combined trace evidence, theory and practice. Specialist and refresher courses are also on offer. CENTREX organisation is now part of the National Policing Improvement Agency.
- Refresher courses must be taken every 5 years.

CRCI:UG

CLCI:MAB

Other related opportunities

- Environmental Health Practitioner / Officer p280
- Police p506
- Scientist p486

Advantages/disadvantages

- This is a job with an exciting image but it can be frequently repetitive, unpleasant and dirty.
- You will have the satisfaction of working with a team of investigating officers, forensic scientists and colleagues to find the evidence needed to trace, arrest and convict offenders.

Earnings guide

- £16,000–£17,000 per year is usual for starting salaries.
- This rises to £25,000 for experienced officers.
- £26,000–£32,000 is possible for senior officers.
- If you work in London you may get additional allowances.

Further information

National Training Centre for Scientific Support to Crime Investigation
Harperley Hall
Fir Tree
Crook
Co Durham
DL15 8DS
01388 762191
www.forensic-training.police.uk

Part of Centrex NTC; see www.centrex.police.uk
Police recruitment information
0845 608 3000
www.policecouldyou.co.uk

Scottish Police College
Tulliallan Castle
Kincardine
Fife
FK10 4BE
01259 732000
www.tulliallan.police.uk

Customs and Excise Officer

What the work involves

- You will be working as a civil servant for the Home Office. In 2005, Customs and Excise and the Inland Revenue Departments merged in some areas to provide a single tax collection agency.
- You will be enforcing tax regulations on all goods entering and leaving the country and all goods bought and sold in the UK.
- You may specialise in customs: searching baggage, people, freight and vehicles to check for anyone either not paying tax or smuggling in illegal items or substances.
- You may specialise in excise work: visiting traders, manufacturers and importers to check licences and accounts to make sure that the right duties are being paid on goods like petrol, alcohol and tobacco.
- You may specialise in VAT: visiting businesses to check their accounts and that the right amount of VAT is being collected.

The type of person suited to this work

If you are involved in front-line detection work, trying to detect illegal goods or entry into the UK, you will be involved in observing, questioning and challenging people, many of whom may not speak English. You will need top-notch communication skills plus a flair for observation, intuition and persistence. Knowledge of or a willingness to learn a foreign or minority language is useful.

If you work in VAT or excise, an aptitude for numbers and computers is a must, because you will be checking business accounts and watching out for sometimes quite sophisticated cover-ups. You will also need to be methodical, organised and logical.

Working conditions

Customs and immigration officers mainly work in airports, seaports and freight terminals but also may need to do some surveillance work outside. You will wear a uniform if working in front-line detection work.

Excise and VAT officers are based in offices but also travel around their local areas carrying out checks and interviews.

Customs and immigration officers work shifts and are expected to cover holidays and weekends on rota.

Excise and VAT officers generally work office hours, Monday to Friday.

The future outlook

There are about 23,000 staff based all over the country. Customs specialist staff are mainly located at air- and seaports and the Channel Tunnel.

It is possible to move on to senior or management posts. There are also specialist areas within customs, for example the job of detection officer or work with the operations and intelligence unit or the dog unit.

entry level

To both enter and train while working in this career, you will need qualifications at Level 2–8. Please refer to explanation on page vii.

Qualifications and courses

- Applicants can enter the job at several entry bands. For an Officer grade you will need 5 GCSEs/S grades (A–C/1–3) including English and maths, and 2 A levels/H grades. Many entrants at this level have a degree. You could join at a lower level into an administration job with a minimum of 2 GCSEs/S grades (A–C/1–3). If you do not have the minimum grades you could still enter if you sit and pass a selection test.
- For those with Honours degrees at 2.2 or above, fast-stream entry is possible. This is for entry into all Civil Service departments and although a preference can be expressed, entry into Customs and Excise is not guaranteed.
- Your training would last up to 9 months and may include some residential training courses. You would also learn on the job from more experienced officers.
- All fast-stream candidates must meet the requirements of Civil Service nationality. For all other entrants, you must be a British national, EU national or Commonwealth citizen.
- Once employed as a customs and excise officer, progression can be to dog handler.

CRCI:UE | CLCI:CAB

Other related opportunities

- Administrator p6
- Dog Handler p500
- Police p506
- Prison p509
- Private Investigator p511
- Security p518

Advantages/disadvantages

- When dealing with front-line detection work you may have to question or detain angry or abusive people, but you will have thorough training to help you deal with all eventualities.
- It can be a high-pressure job as large volumes of people arrive or depart at peak times.
- No two days are ever the same, especially in detection work, so expect the unexpected.
- It can be very rewarding to know that you have prevented dangerous items such as drugs and firearms getting into the country.

Earnings guide

- All staff working shifts or unsocial hours are paid additional allowances.
- Those working in and around London receive an additional allowance.
- Salaries for administration posts start at £12,734.
- A Customs and Excise Officer can earn £19,500–£25,200.
- Senior grades can earn up to £38,000.

Further information

Civil Service Careers
Unit 2–4 Lescren Way
Avonmouth
Bristol
BS11 8DG
0117 982 1171
www.civil-service.gov.uk/jobs

General Fast Stream Programme
Application Helpdesk:
Civil Service Fast Stream
Pilgrims Well
427 London Road
Camberley, Surrey
GU15 3HZ
01276 400333
www.faststream.gov.uk

HM Customs and Excise
www.hmce.gov.uk

Diver

What the work involves

- As a diver you will work underwater in a variety of places where work needs doing. You may do repair work on an oil rig, mend an underwater survey or recover a body.
- You may be an engineer or construction worker using tools to repair structures underwater, for example oil rigs, harbour walls or bridge supports.
- You could be a professional camera operator or photographer recording underwater structures or marine life.
- You may search rivers, canals and lakes for weapons, stolen property or missing people.

The type of person suited to this work

If your experiences of diving so far have been for pleasure, you may have the wrong idea of what is involved in commercial diving. The work is often done in difficult conditions and can be hazardous and exhausting. You will need to have lots of stamina and a responsible attitude.

You need to be an excellent swimmer and a good team player, but also be happy with your own company. When deep-water diving, you will need to spend days and sometimes weeks in a decompression chamber waiting for your body to readjust.

This work is so physically demanding that you will need very high levels of fitness and must accept that diving is a short career. You will need to be able to follow safety procedures carefully.

Working conditions

Most of your work will be in cold, wet, dark and possibly cramped conditions. You will wear protective clothing and breathing apparatus.

You could be based on a ship or an oil rig and may need to spend nights away from home. You may need to travel overseas for work.

This job is risky; decompression can be hazardous and there is also a risk of accidents when underwater.

The future outlook

Employers include construction or civil engineering companies, the police and the Navy. Most offshore work in the UK is in the North Sea fuel industries. Careers are short in diving. Some qualify as diving instructors, teaching other people to dive for work or leisure.

There is lots of competition and remotely operated technology is replacing some of the tasks that divers have done in the past, so there may well be even fewer opportunities in the future.

CRCI:U

CLCI:YAZ

Qualifications and courses

entry level

To both enter and train while working in this career, you will need qualifications at Level 1. Please refer to explanation on page vii.

- There are no minimum requirements for diver training but you will need to pass a medical test. A qualification in recreational diving would be an advantage. Candidates need to be strong swimmers and physically fit. Basic Maths and English skills can be a help.
- The Royal Navy train its divers at the Defence Diving School at Portsmouth on a 20-week course. Applicants are preferred to have previous diving experience. The Army also train divers at the Defence Diving School, although their course is in two parts: 6 weeks initial training and then a further 8 weeks advanced diving. Army divers are drawn from those serving in the Royal Engineers.
- Many divers gain academic and/or technical qualifications before they train to dive. Depending on the area in which the candidate wishes to work, training and requirements vary.
- Offshore industries often require divers. For this role, a science or engineering degree would be needed.
- A construction diver would need a qualification like an NVQ/SVQ Level 3 in Welding and Fabrication.
- Cranfield University offers Diving and Underwater Technology as an option on its Offshore and Ocean Technology MSc. Entry requirements are a good Honours degree in a relevant subject. Plymouth University offers diving as part of its Civil and Coastal Engineering degree and postgraduate courses.
- A relevant qualification approved by the Health and Safety Executive (HSE) must be held by anyone who dives professionally. A medical examination will have to be passed at regular intervals.
- Police officers must have been with the force for at least 2 years before applying to become a police diver. They must pass fitness and medical tests, as well as swimming skills tests. Police diver training lasts for 8 weeks.

Other related opportunities

- Civil / Construction Engineer p46
- Marine Engineering / Marine Industry p213
- Police p506
- Royal Navy p516

Advantages/disadvantages

- Skilled, experienced, fit divers are currently in demand, but it is often short-term contract work and diving careers are limited by your health.
- You may need to pay for your own training and equipment to become a commercial diver. These courses are expensive.

Earnings guide

- Pay varies according to employer. Most divers are paid by the day or by the job. Civil engineering divers an earn £65–£150 per day. Very experienced divers working in the oil industry could earn up to £270 per day, while those diving with a diving bell, could get around £1,000 per day.
- Inland divers can earn around £15,000 per year.
- Divers in the UK offshore industry earn about £30,000. Experienced divers can earn £46,000+.

Further information

Health and Safety Executive – Diving Operations
South Wing, Rose Court
2 Southwark Bridge
London
SE1 9HS
0845 345 0055
www.hse.gov.uk

Underwater Centre
An Aird
Fort William
Inverness-shire
PH33 6AN
01397 703786
www.theunderwatercentre.co.uk

Association of Diving Contractors
83 Boundary Lane
St Leonards
Ringwood
Hampshire
BH24 2SF
01202 855648
www.adc-uk.info

International Marine Contractors Association
5 Lower Belgrave Street
London
SW1W 0NR
020 7824 5520
www.imca-int.com/careers

Dog Handler

What the work involves

- Dog handlers work in a variety of security jobs including the police, the armed forces, customs and excise and private security firms.
- You will live and work with specially trained dogs and may be involved with training your own dog.
- Working as a team, you will search buildings, vehicles and open spaces for such things as people, illegal drugs, firearms or evidence.
- You may attend large-scale disturbances to control crowds or search for casualties at disaster scenes.
- You may search aeroplanes, ferries or people for explosives, drugs or goods brought into the country, and protect property including private property or military establishments.

entry level

To both enter and train while working in this career, you will need qualifications at Level 1–2. Please refer to explanation on page vii.

The type of person suited to this work

Many employers expect you to house and care for your dog from puppyhood right to the time it retires 7–10 years later. So not only will you need a passion for dogs, but you will also need a stable home life to get into this competitive job.

Dogs and their handlers are called in to specific situations. For example, 80% of all police dog work involves attending incidents, so you will need to be able to stay cool and calm in an emergency. You will need to be patient and self-confident, be alert and observant.

Dog-handling training courses are very stretching for both dog and handler. You will cover subjects such as canine psychology and veterinary practice, but also do lots of physical preparation work with your dog. So you will need to be fit and keen to learn.

Working conditions

Your working conditions will vary depending on your employer and the current job. For example, it may be inside a hot stuffy aeroplane hold, or out in severe weather on a mountainside.

Dogs are used in dangerous situations so you will be at risk of injury.

Working hours can be long and variable but usually include shift work and you may be on call for emergencies.

The future outlook

The main employers are the police, armed forces and customs and excise. Some other organisations employ a few dog handlers, for example the fire service, security companies and search and rescue services. The police force is one of the largest employers with an average of 20–30 dogs in smaller forces and more in larger ones.

This job is fiercely competitive as many handlers stay in the job for life, often training another dog when the first one retires.

Qualifications and courses

- Dog handling is almost always a second career, and you will probably need to be working within the organisation already. Employers such as HM Customs and Excise, the RAF, the police, the army and the fire service expect you to start your career in mainstream work first, for example as a police officer or immigration officer, before applying for dog handling work.
- You will need to meet the minimum requirements for the organisation you plan to join. The RAF, the army, the fire service and the police all have their own selection processes. For HM Customs and Excise you will need at least 2 GCSEs/S grades (A–C/1–3), including English language.
- Those in the police force will need police training before they can move into dog handling.
- You will also need to have good vision, be physically fit and have a love and affinity with dogs of all breeds. Any previous relevant work experience is an advantage.
- There is an ASET Level 2 National Award in Security Dog Handling and an NVQ/SVQ Level 1–3 in Animal Care.
- There is now a legal requirement for security guards, including dog handlers, to have a Security Industry Authority (SIA) licence and to get this you must attend an approved course, have recognised qualifications, and have had a criminal record check.

CRCI:U

CLCI:MAB

Other related opportunities

- Army p492
- Customs and Excise Officer p497
- Dog Work p237
- Police p506
- Royal Navy p516
- Security p518

Advantages/disadvantages

- You will form a really strong bond with your dog, working and living with it every day.
- All dog handlers fear that their dogs may be injured at any time.
- It is really rewarding when the dog you have trained catches a criminal, or finds dangerous drugs or explosives.

Earnings guide

- Starting salaries may be about £15,500 per year.
- Experienced dog handlers could expect to earn about £25,000+
- A few specialist dog handlers in very dangerous roles, such as searching for explosives, earn up to £30,000.
- Extra allowances are paid when the dog is expected to live with and be cared for by you.

Further information

Police recruitment information
0845 608 3000
www.policecouldyou.co.uk

Scottish Police College
Tulliallan Castle
Kincardine
Fife FK10 4BE
01259 732000
www.tulliallan.police.uk

Armed Forces Careers RAF
22 Unthank Road
Norwich
NR2 1AH
01603 614616
www.rafcareers.com

Armed Forces Careers Army
2 Magdalen St
Norwich
NR3 1HX
01603 624616
www.army.mod.uk

Armed Forces Careers Navy
22 Unthank Road
Norwich
NR2 1AH
01603 620033
www.royalnavy.mod.uk

HM Customs and Excise
www.hmce.gov.uk

Security Industry Authority
PO Box 9
Newcastle upon Tyne
NE82 6YX
0870 243 0100
www.the-sia.org.uk

Door Supervisor / Bouncer

What the work involves

- You will be standing at the entrance to a building, for example a nightclub, and will help to control people entering and leaving. You will be judging whether a person should be allowed into the premises.
- You may search customers' bags and clothing.
- You will refuse entry to anyone not meeting standards or conditions set by the management, such as a dress code.
- If trouble breaks out inside or outside the building, you will call the police if needed for assistance.
- You may collect tickets or entrance fees.
- When any incidents happen near to your club you will write short reports. You may need to use these in court if charges are made.

The type of person suited to this work

This is a high-profile job where you will be dealing with customers. You will need a smart appearance and excellent interpersonal skills as you will have to be firm enough to keep trouble-makers away from the venue but welcoming to most customers.

You will also need to have a calm, steady personality, not easily provoked in conflict situations which can be frequent when customers have been drinking and become argumentative.

You may be dealing with money or confiscating illegal items so you will need to be law abiding and trustworthy. With the introduction of licensing and training you will also need to be keen to learn about the industry.

You will need to be physically fit, be able to make quick decisions, know the law and health and safety regulations.

Working conditions

Most door supervisors work under cover outside the entrance but may be exposed to all weather conditions. You may need to wear a uniform or smart clothes.

Evening and night work is common in this job with shifts from early evening right into the early hours of the following day.

You may be at risk from aggressive customers.

The future outlook

There are opportunities throughout the UK but the majority are in large cities with thriving night-time economies. There are currently about 95,000 door supervisors employed in pubs, bars and clubs. This is a growth industry as the leisure industry continues to improve security.

Door supervisors can progress into related security work. Training and experience could be used to move into related areas such as security guard and security management.

entry level

1

To both enter and train while working in this career, you will need qualifications at Level 1. Please refer to explanation on page vii.

Qualifications and courses

- No academic qualifications are needed for this role. However, you will need to be over 18, be physically fit and have good knowledge of the licensing laws and customer service skills. You will also undergo a police check.
- The Security Industry Authority (SIA) exists to manage the licensing of the private security industry. The SIA endorses training providers through whom you can gain a Door Supervision Licence. To receive a licence you must have a Level 2 National Certificate in Door Supervision. BTEC Award in Level 2 Door Supervision or NOCN Level 2 Award in Door Supervision. As part of the Door Supervision licence scheme, you will have to undergo a criminal record check.
- The British Institute of Innkeeping, SITO and NCFE also run door supervision courses that may count towards qualifying for the SIA licence.
- Some employers will take you on as a trainee and support you through the training and licensing processes.

CRCI:UK

CLCI:MAG

Other related opportunities

- Bar Manager / Licensee p82
- Bodyguard p494
- Security p518

Advantages/disadvantages

- The introduction of licensing and qualifications is expected to improve the image of this job, so you will find it easier to progress into other areas of security management.
- You will be mainly working when other people are out having fun so your social life could be affected.

Earnings guide

- Wages are generally about £12,500 per year when starting out.
- Earnings for experienced, trained and licensed supervisors can be up to £30,000.
- Some door supervisors are paid an hourly rate between £9 and £15, sometimes more depending on the organisation you work for.

Further information

Security Industry Authority
PO Box 9
Newcastle upon Tyne
NE82 6YX
0870 243 0100
www.the-sia.org.uk

Skills for Security
Security House
Barbourne Road
Worcester
WR1 1RS
08450 750111
www.skillsforsecurity.org.uk

Door Superviser Training Organisation (DSTO)
Maurice House
2 Iddesleigh Road
Bournemouth
Dorset
BH3 7JR
01202 299969
www.dsto.co.uk

www.cityandguilds.com/myperfectjob

Firefighter / Officer

What the work involves

- You will be dealing with a range of emergencies, not only fires but also helping at incidents such as when people are trapped in lifts, handling chemical spillages and assisting at road, rail or air crash scenes.
- You will help to remove people from danger, such as burning buildings, accident sites, bomb alerts, and bring the situation under control.
- If your team arrives on the scene before the paramedics you will have to give First Aid.
- You may give advice to organisations on fire safety and check that buildings or public events meet fire regulations.

The type of person suited to this work

You will need to stay calm in dangerous situations. People in danger tend to react in extreme ways and you will need to be good at talking to them, giving instructions, reassuring them and leading them to safety.

You need to be an excellent team worker. You will be assigned to a 'watch' (a team) and need to work together to keep yourself and others safe.

You will need to have stamina and be very fit to deal with the demands of this work.

You will often need to work at heights, and in dark spaces, and you may need to rescue people from very confined spaces.

You may be the first to arrive at a nasty crash and have to administer First Aid. You will need to be able to deal with very stressful and disturbing situations.

Working conditions

You will be based at a fire station but go out to attend incidents. Fire stations have good facilities for eating and resting.

Working conditions can often be unpleasant and dangerous. You will wear a uniform and, when needed, protective clothing and equipment.

You will work 2 day shifts then 2 night shifts followed by 4 days off and work a total of 42 hours per week.

The future outlook

The main employers are regional fire services who employ about 41,000 firefighters. Airports, the Ministry of Defence, the RAF and the Royal Navy also recruit firefighters. Some firefighters start their career as retained firefighters to gain experience. Entry is competitive.

You could move into driving by taking an LGV licence. Promotion to supervisory and management roles is by clear grades and given on ability, but exams must also be passed.

entry level

1–2

To both enter and train while working in this career, you will need qualifications at Level 1–2. Please refer to explanation on page vii.

Qualifications and courses

- Each fire service can set its own entry requirements and the recruitment process may change between services. To be considered for selection as a firefighter you must be at least 18 years old, have good eyesight; with normal colour vision. Glasses or contact lenses occasionally may be permitted, and pass practical and written tests.
- A full UK driving licence is preferred.
- You will be required to pass certain rigorous physical and job-related tests (such as working within confined spaces and at heights).
- You will also be required to undergo stringent medical examinations to make sure you are fit enough to undertake arduous firefighting duties.
- You must have good colour vision (as tested by Ishihara plates). Your eyesight will also be tested. At present, laser treatment is unacceptable to some forces and entry is barred.
- Firefighters need a good general education. Some brigades may ask for specific GCSEs/S grades and some entrants have A levels/H grades or a degree.
- Firefighters need a good general education although no set qualifications are necessary. A numerical and written entrance test is required to ensure there is an understanding of problem solving and situation awareness. Apprenticeships/ Skillseekers may be available.

Other related opportunities

- Ambulance p266
- Police p506
- Royal Air Force (RAF) p512
- Royal Navy p516

Advantages/disadvantages

- This job can be very stressful and you cannot just leave an emergency situation if your shift has ended.
- You will get to know your watch really well and firefighters say they really enjoy the team spirit at work.
- There is demanding training but it will help to keep you safe.

Earnings guide

- As a trainee you will earn around £20,300 per year.
- With experience you can earn £21,245–£27,200.
- A leading firefighter can earn £29,600.
- A station officer can earn up to £31,000 and a senior divisional officer up to £45,000.
- Retained firefighters earn a retainer fee of around £2,500 per year. They also receive additional payments for attending fires.

Further information

Fire Service recruitment information
www.fireservice.co.uk

Details of all local fire services
Fire Brigade Union
www.fbu.org.uk

Information about pay rates
MOD Fire Services
Room 225, St Giles Court
1–13 St Giles High Street
London
WC2H 8LD

Armed Forces Careers Navy
22 Unthank Road
Norwich
NR2 1AH
01603 620033
www.royalnavy.mod.uk

Immigration Officer

What the work involves

- You will be working as a civil servant for the Home Office.
- Your job will be to control the entry of people into the UK by checking the passports and visas of passengers arriving at ports, airports or via the Channel Tunnel.
- You may ask questions to find out more about them and if suspicious, conduct a more detailed interview.
- As an assistant officer you would refer to a more senior officer if they are concerned about documentation or answers to questions.
- You may work in an office processing immigration applications and dealing with appeals.

The type of person suited to this work

You will need to be confident, assertive and have the ability to work under pressure and to deadlines. You will need to be well organised, reliable and have good report-writing skills. You will need a responsible attitude with excellent communication skills and an ability to get on with people from across the world.

This job is currently in the public eye, so you will have to be sure about your decisions and stick to them. You should enjoy investigating and collecting information very quickly with the ability to write up and pass on your concerns to others in your team or colleagues from other professions.

Working conditions

You could work in a range of places such as ports and airports where you will have access to a desk, PC, phone and interviewing area.

Some security officers have to undertake surveillance duties and work with other intelligence officers, but normally you will check documents and interview individuals within your office or interviewing booth.

You will work shifts that will include out of office hours and weekends.

The future outlook

The immigration service has expanded greatly in recent years. Half of all immigration staff are employed in the south-east of England at Heathrow, Gatwick and the Channel ports, because that is where the majority of people arrive. The numbers of people entering the UK and asking for asylum has increased over recent years. This has impacted on the service, which has grown in numbers from 1800 to more than 2500 employees. Entry is competitive at officer level and the majority of entrants are graduates.

It is possible to enter at assistant grade and work up to officer grade. Placements are also possible, for example, to Immigration Visa sections at the British Deputy High Commissions overseas or to police forces around the UK.

Assistant immigration officers work in over 50 airports and seaports around the UK and the Channel Tunnel.

entry level

2–8

To both enter and train while working in this career, you will need qualifications at Level 2–8. Please refer to explanation on page vii.

Qualifications and courses

- Applicants enter as either Assistant Immigration Officers or Immigration Officers.
- Assistant Immigration Officers have to sit a literacy and numeracy test and must attend interview.
- Immigration Officers need no formal qualifications although most employers expect a minimum of an A level/H grade or equivalent. Assistant Immigration Officers can apply for promotion to this level.
- Applicants with a minimum of a 2.2 Honours degree can apply for fast-stream entry. This is for entry into all Civil Service departments and although a preference can be expressed, entry into Immigration is not guaranteed.
- All fast-stream candidates must be UK nationals. For all other entrants, you must be a European Economic Area national, EU national or Commonwealth citizen. Swiss nationals, although Switzerland is not an EEA country, are also eligible to apply for non-reserved posts.
- After a period of 10 weeks initial training, entrants are placed with more experienced officers, usually at Dover, Heathrow or Gatwick. Financial support may be available for officers wishing to learn a foreign language.

CRCI:UC

CLCI:MAF

Other related opportunities

- Administrator p6
- Coastguard p495
- Equal Opportunities / Equalities Officer p17
- Police p506
- Welfare Rights Officer / Worker p550

Advantages/disadvantages

- You will play an important role in helping protect national security.
- This job is part of the civil service, so entry can be competitive.
- The civil service offers excellent conditions of service and training.

Earnings guide

- All staff working shifts or unsocial hours are paid additional allowances.
- Those working in and around London receive an additional allowance.
- When starting out as an assistant officer you could earn around £15,000 per year. With experience you can earn £17,200.
- Immigration officers start at around £20,000 and can rise with experience to £31,000+.

Further information

Civil Service Careers
Unit 2–4 Lescren Way
Avonmouth
Bristol
BS11 8DG
0117 982 1171
www.civil-service.gov.uk/jobs

General Fast Stream Programme
Application Helpdesk: Civil Service Fast Stream
Pilgrims Well
427 London Road
Camberley, Surrey
GU15 3HZ
01276 400333
www.faststream.gov.uk

Immigration and Nationality Directorate
www.ind.homeoffice.gov.uk

Home Office
Direct Communications Unit
2 Marsham Street
London
SW1P 4DF
020 7035 4848
www.homeoffice.gov.uk

Parking Attendant / Traffic Warden

What the work involves

Parking attendant

- You will be enforcing parking regulations for a local authority: patrolling and checking for illegal parking and non-payment of parking fees.
- Using a hand-held computer you will regularly check details of vehicles parked in limited-stay parking areas and issue fixed penalty tickets. You may take pictures of any illegally parked vehicles.
- You may need to arrange for vehicles to be clamped or sent to the pound. You will attend court to give evidence if any prosecution results from your work. You will have to report any suspected abandoned vehicles to the police.
- You will deal with queries from people asking for advice or information. In some areas parking attendants have now taken over the work of traffic wardens.

Traffic warden

- You will do the same tasks as a parking attendant but you will be working for the police.
- In addition, you may direct traffic at school crossings, temporary obstructions or major events, and if traffic lights fail, as well as assisting the police by watching out for stolen cars.

The type of person suited to this work

All employers look for a polite but firm manner as well as good customer handling and communication skills. You will need to be very good at dealing with people, many of whom may be feeling irate about the ticket you have just given them.

You need to be a good observer and able to follow rules and instructions. You will have to watch out at all times for illegal parking and enforce the rules even when you may feel sympathetic with the person you are issuing a ticket to.

You will meet a lot of people on your beat but you will also be working unsupervised and independently so you need to be confident, self-disciplined and reliable.

Working conditions

Most of your work will be out on the streets in all weathers. You will need to wear a uniform and carry a hand-held computer.

You will work shifts to a total of 36 hours over a 5-day week. Shifts cover early morning until late evening Monday to Sunday.

There is a risk of assault from aggressive members of the public.

The future outlook

Parking attendants now do most of the work that traffic wardens used to do, as most parking offences are no longer classified as criminal and so do not need to be enforced by traffic wardens who work for the police. There are government proposals to extend powers by decriminalising some public highway offences such as stopping in a yellow box junction. Although many of these offences will be monitored by cameras they will lead to an expansion of work for parking contractors. More than 100 local authorities now work in partnership with parking contractors to enforce parking legislation. Jobs are on offer with many of the main contractors.

Parking attendants and traffic wardens can be promoted into supervisory or training roles initially and then on into management if suitable. There are NVQ/SVQs in parking supervision and administration. However, prospects may be more limited in more rural areas.

CRCI:UG

CLCI:MAB

Qualifications and courses

entry level

To both enter and train while working in this career, you will need qualifications at Level 1. Please refer to explanation on page vii.

Parking attendant

- You do not need any particular qualifications to enter this work. However, English and maths GCSE/S grade or equivalent would be useful.
- Mature applicants are welcomed, as experience dealing with the general public is an advantage.
- Some employers prefer you to have had experience of working with the public. You can work towards City & Guilds Level 2 Certificate for Parking Attendants or an NVQ Level 2 in Controlling Parking Areas. On completion you could work towards a Level 3 course in Parking Management/Supervision or an NVQ Level 3 in Parking Clerical work.
- Training is always given on entry about parking legislation, to help you do your job well. You will then shadow a more experienced member of staff. Training covers on-street enforcement activity, car park patrolling and enforcement, clamping and towaway and CCTV operation.

Traffic warden

- There are no formal educational requirements in most areas, although GCSEs/S grades (A–C/1–3) are preferred by some employers. You will need to pass a written English, and in some areas a maths test. A medical exam is often required.
- There are different requirements for different areas throughout the country.
- Training is done on the job. In major cities, traffic wardens attend a training course at their police training centre. This may include First Aid.

Other related opportunities

- Police p506
- Road Crossing Assistant (Schools) p582
- Security p518
- Store Detective p521

Advantages/disadvantages

- You will keep fit, walking an average of 10 miles a day, 5 days a week carrying a 5kg pack (including your computer, printer and radio).
- There is no doubt that parking attendants and traffic wardens are not always popular and there has been a rise in the number of attacks on them.
- Illegal parking can cause real problems for most law-abiding motorists and many attendants feel a sense of satisfaction from keeping the roads clear.

Earnings guide

Parking attendant

- Starting pay is about £12,500 per year.
- Supervisors earn about £16,500. Top salaries are around £19,500.

Traffic warden

- Earnings can be in the range of £14,000–£20,000. Traffic wardens in London can earn between £17,000 and £22,000.
- There may be additional payment for shift work.

Further information

British Parking Association
Stuart House
41–43 Perrymount Road
Haywards Heath
West Sussex
RH16 3BN
01444 447300
www.britishparking.co.uk

Security Industry Authority
PO Box 9
Newcastle upon Tyne
NE82 6YX
0870 243 0100
www.the-sia.org.uk

Skills for Security
Security House
Barbourne Road
Worcester
WR1 1RS
08450 750111
www.skillsforsecurity.org.uk

Police recruitment information
0845 608 3000
www.policecouldyou.co.uk

www.cityandguilds.com/myperfectjob

Police

What the work involves

Police officer

- Patrolling your beat, usually on foot, you will be talking to members of the public, who may ask for help or tell you about suspicious behaviour or activity.
- You will need to respond to any situation that happens while you are out on the streets. You may be the first on the scene at a road traffic accident, a suicide attempt, an assault or a burglary.
- You will be keeping records, taking statements, writing reports and filling out forms. You may need to go to court to give evidence. You could be invited to give talks to students in schools.
- The police force has many specialised areas of work if you are fully trained and have experience including, CID, Mounted Police, Special Branch, Child Protection, Drugs Squad, Traffic Police and River Police.

Police family liaison officer

- You will be the main link between a family and investigating officers when someone has been murdered or has died in suspicious circumstances.
- Contact with the family will be more intense at certain times such as in the early days of bereavement, or when the case goes to court, but you will also keep in regular contact.
- You will coordinate any help needed by the family to recover, for example by arranging counselling. You will also help to protect the family from unwanted callers such as the media.

The type of person suited to this work

This is a people-centred job, so you will be keen to work with people from all backgrounds, have excellent communication skills and an ability to understand situations from different points of view. You will need to be honest, confident and have a mature attitude to help you weigh up situations. You will need courage, initiative and common sense.

Resilience is also vital as you will need to be able to remain calm and confident even in emergencies. Your problem-solving skills will also be good as you will need to gather information to help you understand situations, identify risks and make decisions about the right way to act.

Even if you are out there on your own you will need to talk to the control room, to seek advice and back-up, so you also need to be a team player.

Working conditions

Your working day as a police officer will be spent mainly outdoors in all weathers, with some desk work. Family liaison officers spend some time at the station and other times out visiting families.

You will wear a uniform and, when needed, protective clothing.

You may be at risk of assault.

Police constables usually work a 40-hour week on an 8-hour shift basis.

The future outlook

There is no national police force in the UK so you will need to apply to one of the 52 regional forces. Some forces have more vacancies than others, especially the ones policing large regional urban areas and in the south-east of England. All forces recruit every year and there is a government commitment to increase the number of police officers so prospects are good. However, entry is competitive.

After a 2-year probationary period the majority of officers carry on as beat officers but you can apply to specialise in areas such as traffic, CID, dog handling, firearms, river police, mounted police or crime prevention work. Specialisms are popular and some have extra entry or experience requirements. You may need to move to another force for some specialisms: for example, only a few forces now have mounted police units.

You could take your sergeant exams for promotion and then it is possible after you have gained more experience to move on in stages through the selection process of different grades right up to the highest levels.

A High Potential Development Scheme (HPD) exists that enables talented members of the force to enter a fast-track promotion opportunity. This programme is now open to new recruits as well as serving officers.

Qualifications and courses

- You will need to be at least 18 and be a British citizen, citizen of the EU or EEA, a Commonwealth citizen or a foreign national with indefinite leave to stay in the UK. Some colleges offer the BTEC National Diploma in Public Services which provides a good grounding for those who are not yet 18.
- There are no minimum qualifications required but you will have to pass literacy and numeracy tests and take a psychometric test as part of the selection process. There is no official upper age limit for joining for constables and sergeants but some forces in the UK set their own limits.
- The police probationer training scheme is known as Initial Police Learning and Development Programme (IPLDP). During the probationary period you will work towards NVQ Level 3 in Policing. Following this you will need to achieve NVQ Level 4 in Policing. Some degree courses in Policing are also being developed.
- All applicants are interviewed at a National Assessment Centre, and have to pass a medical examination and fitness test. Good eyesight is required. A police check is also carried out.
- Graduate applicants are selected on individual skills and abilities, not on their academic qualifications. However, high-calibre graduates are often placed on the HPD scheme.
- All officers serve a probation period of 2 years. After this period you can sit qualifying exams for promotion to the rank of sergeant. Or you can move into a specialist role such as family liaison officer.

entry level

To both enter and train while working in this career, you will need qualifications at Level 1–8. Please refer to explanation on page vii.

Other related opportunities

Advantages/disadvantages

- Officers say that they enjoy the variety and challenge in their work; that every minute of the day is different and that there is a feeling of personal satisfaction when they succeed in bringing a criminal to justice.
- This is a job where you can start as a constable and with training, the right qualities and experience, you can go right to the top.
- You do have to deal with distressing situations, but have support and training to help you cope.

Earnings guide

- Starting salaries are £ 20,000–£22,000 per year. With several years' experience, this can go up to £31,000.
- Sergeants earn up to £36,000. Inspectors earn £44,500.
- Allowances are paid for certain forces, for example in London.

Further information

Police recruitment information
0845 608 3000
www.policecouldyou.co.uk

Central Scotland Police
Randolphfield
Stirling
Scotland
FK8 2HD
01786 456000
www.centralscotland.police.uk

Police Service Portal
www.police.uk

www.cityandguilds.com/myperfectjob

Police: Community Support Officer

What the work involves

- You will support the work of the police and increase public safety by patrolling your local area.
- Your job will be to improve local communities by dealing with truancy, graffiti and abandoned vehicles, supporting the victims of crime and patrolling the streets.
- It will be your job to be a visible presence on the streets and reassure the general public that they are safe.
- Depending on your role you might also be given additional powers to detain someone, direct traffic, remove abandoned cars and issue fixed penalty notices.

entry level

To both enter and train while working in this career, you will need qualifications at Level 1. Please refer to explanation on page vii.

The type of person suited to this work

You will need to have excellent verbal communication and listening skills, and have the ability to remain focused and calm under pressure at all times. Members of the public can be rude and aggressive so you should be able to cope with all types of behaviour.

You will need to keep notes of everything suspicious and be able to describe to police constables the facts, especially if the situation is dangerous. You will need to have good team working skills, and be sympathetic and tolerant at all times.

You will also need to be able to make difficult decisions quickly and remain flexible as you will never know what your day will bring!

Qualifications and courses

- There are no formal entry qualifications, but a good standard of English literacy is required. Candidates take written and numeracy tests as part of the selection process, and local police forces may set their own entry requirements.
- The minimum age for entry to the police force is 18. Candidates must be British, EU or Commonwealth citizens with no residency restrictions. You will be selected for this job based on your application and interview.
- New entrants receive an intensive 3-week induction course. This is followed by on-the-job training.
- Community service experience is preferred. A BTEC First Diploma/National Diploma, a Foundation degree, or an NVQ Level 2 within the public services sector would be an advantage.

Working conditions

Much of your work will be walking the streets of the community where you are based. You will be outdoors in all weathers and may be involved in potentially dangerous situations. You will work shifts, including evenings, weekends and bank holidays. Part-time and jobshare working is available.

As well as wearing a uniform, you will be equipped with a radio for communication.

The future outlook

There are already around 14,000 community support officers in place, with plans to increase numbers to 25,000. Many community support officers use this job as a stepping stone to becoming a police officer. However, you will still need to achieve the necessary entry requirements to be a police officer, although the experience you will have gained should help your application.

Other related opportunities

- Firefighter / Officer p502
- Parking Attendant / Traffic Warden p504
- Police p506
- Road Safety Officer p583
- Security p518
- Store Detective p521

Advantages/disadvantages

- This can be a stepping stone to becoming a police officer.
- It will be satisfying to know that you will be helping to improve your community.
- Some police officers disapprove of the work undertaken by community support officers.

Earnings guide

- Individual forces can set their own rates of pay, so this is a guide only.
- Starting salaries begin at £16,000 per year. With experience, this rises to £19,000. In some areas this can be up to £25,000.
- Shift allowances and different levels of responsibility can affect earnings.

Further information

www.cityandguilds.com/myperfectjob

Police recruitment information
0845 608 3000
www.policecouldyou.co.uk

Police community support officers
www.national-pcsos.co.uk

Prison Work

What the work involves

- You will be working in a prison, remand centre or young offender institution looking after and rehabilitating those who have been put into custody by the courts.

Prison officer

- You will be supervising inmates by patrolling all areas of the prison and checking security systems.
- Prisoners taking part in education, work, training, visits or leisure activities will be supervised by you at all times. You may need to administer authorised physical control and restraint procedures.
- You will listen to prisoners' concerns, offering advice and guidance, and also keep records and report any problems or observations.

Prison governor (operational manager)

- You will be responsible for the overall running and security of your establishment. You will be supervising security, making inspections and carrying out disciplinary procedures.
- At times, you will walk through the prison to observe, listen and advise staff and inmates.
- You will deal with prisoner casework and administration, for example parole applications or complaints, and liaise with other professionals.

Prison instructor

- You may be a specialist prison officer qualified to train inmates or a civilian employed to train inmates and run work programmes.
- You will train prisoners in a vocational skill, for example hairdressing, ICT, building, horticulture or catering. You may teach basic or Key Skills.

The type of person suited to this work

You need to be able to work with a wide variety of people, helping them to improve their behaviour and skills to prevent them from reoffending. You will need excellent communication skills combined with the ability to maintain a relationship with them, but still keep order. You will need to be confident as you will be seen as a figure of authority.

You will need an encouraging attitude as well as an impartial and fair outlook. In addition, even senior operational managers operate within teams, so team-working skills are vital.

In prisons, situations can happen where you will need to be able to make quick but sound decisions, remaining calm and using your training to cope.

Working conditions

Prison officer

You will usually work in a prison and conditions vary according to level of security. You will always wear a uniform.

You will work an average of 39 hours a week in shifts, including nights and weekends.

Prison operational manager (governor)

You will have your own office but will also spend time in various parts of the prison.

Hours of work are variable and often long at senior levels. You will probably work some weekends and evenings and be on call.

Prison instructor

You will work in the best environment for you to train, for example an office, a workshop, a classroom – or outside if your subject is farming or horticulture.

You will work 37 hours in a 5-day week.

The future outlook

The Prison Service now has a staff of 47,080. Prison populations are expected to rise from the 89,285 in 2007. A new private women's prison opened in 2004 at Ashford (near Heathrow) and in 2005 a second prison opened at Peterborough, holding male and female inmates.

A National Offender Management Service (NOMS) has been set up to create a single system of management of offenders rather than the current dual prison and probation system. It is difficult to know how this is impacting fully at this point in time, but NOMS was set up to mean shorter prison stays for minor offenders (with community plus and minus programmes where offenders spend part of their week in detention and the remainder in community punishment). More intensive rehabilitation, treatment and education is in place for longer-stay prisoners.

Prison officer

You can progress to more senior grades after 4 years by taking an exam and going through a promotion board, and then possibly moving into operational management.

Prison operational manager (governor)

You can work through different grades and into managing more complex or larger establishments. You could also be promoted to area manager and operational director posts.

Prison instructor

There are currently about 1000 civilian instructional officers and this will probably increase with the even greater stress on the rehabilitation of offenders and the improvement of their basic skills. In Scotland most instructors are specialist prison officers.

Qualifications and courses

- You will need to be at least 18½ in England and Wales, and at least 20 in Scotland, and meet specific requirements concerning health, eyesight, physical fitness, nationality and criminal records for all posts.

Prison officer

- In England and Wales, applicants will need to pass an entry test regardless of their academic qualifications. In Scotland, unless you have 5 GCSEs/S grades (A–C/1–3) including English and maths, you will need at least 3 years' experience of managing people and then pass verbal reasoning and arithmetic assessments, and an interview. Undischarged bankrupts are not permitted to work within the Prison Service.
- New officers undergo a week's pretraining course at a prison before a 9-week residential training course. NVQ/SVQ in Custodial Care at Level 2 is available.

Prison governor (operations manager)

- Entry is usually through the Intensive Development Scheme for graduates or those with managerial experience outside the prison service, or staff within the prison service with supervisory experience. Entrants train for 12–18 months with periods away from home. Competition is fierce for the 20 places available annually.
- Prison officers can gain promotion to operational manager.

Prison instructor

- All instructors need to meet the same entry requirements as prison officers. For an instructional officer you will need relevant experience in the trade or subject you plan to teach. In addition you will have completed an apprenticeship or vocational qualifications such as a City & Guilds Advanced Certificate, BTEC, GNVQ, NVQ or SVQ, plus a health and safety qualification.

entry level

To both enter and train while working in this career, you will need qualifications at Level 2–8. Please refer to explanation on page vii.

- You will also need supervisory or teaching experience. Some posts require other qualifications and experience, for example further education teaching, literacy/numeracy teaching and NVQ/SVQ assessing qualifications.
- Training includes a 1-week induction course at the prison of employment, plus a further 4-week course held by a qualified training instructor.

Other related opportunities

- Adult Education Organiser / Tutor p170
- Customs and Excise Officer p497
- Probation Officer p540
- Security p518
- Work-based Training p188

Advantages/disadvantages

- This can be a challenging but very rewarding job. To know that you have worked towards helping a person to move back into the community, and be less likely to reoffend, can bring personal satisfaction.
- Prisons can be quite volatile places with challenging incidents and more rarely major disturbances. But you will be trained to deal with these incidents, and management can draft in outside help if needed in extreme situations.

Earnings guide

Prison officer

- Starting salaries are around £17,744 per year. After some years' experience this can rise to £27,530.
- Principal officers earn £30,926–£31,913.
- Extra allowances are paid for some establishments as well as for shift work.

Prison governor (operations manager)

- Governors pay at junior level starts at £29,371. This can rise to between £40,000 and £75,000 for a few senior managers running the largest and most complex prisons.

Prison instructor

- Prison officers (instructors) start around £17,744. With experience this can rise to £28,654.
- Rates of pay will depend on the size and type of prison and any extra responsibilities you have.

Further information

HM Prison Service
Room 329, Cleland House
Page Street
London
SW1P 4LN
020 7217 6437
www.hmprisonservice.gov.uk

Scottish Prison Service
Calton House
5 Redheughs Rigg
Edinburgh
EH12 9HW
0131 244 8745
www.sps.gov.uk

Skills for Justice (Sector Skills Council for custodial care, community justice, court and prosecution services, policing and law enforcement)
9–11 Riverside Court
Don Road
Sheffield
S9 2TJ
0114 261 1499
www.skillsforjustice.com

Home Office
Direct Communications Unit
2 Marsham Street
London
SW1P 4DF
020 7035 4848
www.homeoffice.gov.uk

Criminal Justice System virtual prison
www.cjsonline.gov.uk/offender/walkthrough

Northern Ireland Prison Service
www.niprosonservice.gov.uk

Private Investigator

What the work involves

- You will be collecting information for a private client or a solicitor by asking questions, researching, obtaining evidence and making sense of what you find out.
- Private investigators (PIs) do a variety of different jobs such as surveillance, tracing people, serving legal documents or investigating road accidents, suspected fraud and employee backgrounds. Some PIs specialise in a particular area, for example, insurance or domestic investigations.
- You could be recording your findings using a computer, and you may be asked to present your findings in court or to a large company. You will probably take witness statements, attend court hearings and give evidence.

The type of person suited to this work

Much of the day-to-day work of this exciting-sounding job is actually routine, so you will need to be patient and persistent and be happy with your own company. You may spend hours, sometimes days, watching and waiting for something to happen.

You need to be interested in learning about the law. The evidence you collect needs to be admissible in a court of law so you will need to know your stuff.

You will need to have excellent communications skills, both spoken and written in order to write reports and take witness statements. You may need to calm down anxious or aggressive people when you serve legal papers or repossess their car to pay a debt.

You will need to be able to work on your own, and be able to organise your time and evidence.

Working conditions

Most of your working hours will be spent driving or walking around. You may be in your vehicle for hours or out in all weathers.

Hours are irregular and in some cases they could be long and include evening and weekend work.

You may be at risk of assault from aggressive individuals who you are serving with legal papers.

The future outlook

Opportunites for this type of work have increased.

The majority of the 10,000 UK private investigators are self-employed or work for agencies. There is work but also competition and many PIs do not stay in the business for long. With the introduction of licensing there may be more opportunities for those with licences. A lot of the work is for legal, insurance or financial companies.

Some PIs go on to specialise in areas such as commercial piracy or insurance fraud. A few set up their own agencies and others move into supervisory or security management work.

entry level

1–2

To both enter and train while working in this career, you will need qualifications at Level 1–2. Please refer to explanation on page vii.

Qualifications and courses

- There are no formal entry qualifications for this work. However, many entrants have degrees or advanced level qualifications. Some employers like you to have some experience of work in the police or other security firms.
- You will need a driving licence and most successful PIs work in a related job such as the police, law, customs and excise or security work first.
- Applicants new to the role would benefit from having a relevant qualification, which may include an NVQ Level 3 in Intelligence Analysis, C&G in Security (Investigation) or a degree in an appropriate subject.
- Your training should be accepted by the Security Industry Authority (SIA), and include the topics of the law, investigative methods, equipment and legislation. Training can take place on the job, although this is rare and often proves difficult.
- A scheme is being introduced where a government licence issued by the SIA will be required to practise. Check with the SIA for the latest developments.
- Courses are available from a number of private companies and listed by the Association of British Investigators (ABI). Topics such as theft, court work, investigation and surveillance are offered. A City & Guilds Certificate in conflict management and communication skills is also available, offered through the National Investigations Group.

CRCI:UK | CLCI:MAG

Other related opportunities

- Bailiff / Enforcement Agent p332
- Customs and Excise Officer p497
- Police p506
- Store Detective p521

Advantages/disadvantages

- Private investigators are usually self-employed and so need to buy their own equipment such as a computer, car, and camcorder. Licences and training will also add to the expense.
- A lot of the work is routine, but PIs say that there is a lot of satisfaction when after months of patient work you manage to find the evidence your client needs.

Earnings guide

- Many PIs are self-employed and pay rates vary depending on the job and the area you are working in. Rates are higher in the south-east of England.
- Starting salaries are around £10,000–£12,000 per year. Experienced investigators could earn £14,000–£20,000. Well-qualified specialists can get £60,000+.
- If self-employed, you could expect to get £20,000–£25,000.
- Top salaries for a corporate investigator can be £55,000–£100,000.

Further information

Skills for Security
Security House
Barbourne Road
Worcester
WR1 1RS
08450 750111
www.skillsforsecurity.org.uk

Security Industry Authority
PO Box 9
Newcastle upon Tyne
NE82 6YX
0870 243 0100
www.the-sia.org.uk

Association of British Investigators
27 Old Gloucester Street
London
WC1N 3XX
0871 474 0006
www.theabi.org.uk

Institute of Professional Investigators
83 Guildford Street
Chertsey
Surrey
KT16 9JL
0870 330 8622
www.ipi.org.uk

Royal Air Force (RAF)

What the work involves

- The RAF is organised into three groups of personnel.

Airman/Airwoman

- You will train and work in one of more than 40 trades, for example catering, office work, medical support, fire-fighter or security.
- You will also carry out military duties, such as taking part in military exercises in the UK and overseas, or guarding RAF bases.

Non-commissioned aircrew

- You will work as a weapons system operator, specialising as an air loadmaster, an electronic warfare/acoustics technician or a linguist.
- Air loadmasters deliver troops and supplies around the world or work in search and rescue. Linguists use their language skills along with operational flying tasks.
- Electronic warfare/acoustics technicians use radar and sonar technology to search above and below the waves to identify targets.

Officer

- You will manage tasks and staff but also work as a specialist or professional. You will need to be able to inspire others, be confident and take responsibility for the decisions you make.
- You may work as a professional, for example as a pilot flying a Tornado in air-to-air combat or ground attack, or as a dental officer practising dentistry at an RAF base in the UK or overseas.
- You may also work as a specialist manager, for example as a supply officer managing the movement of the supplies needed, such as personnel, aircraft or explosives.

The type of person suited to this work

Your team-working skills need to be exceptional, as at all levels you will be operating as part of a team. This job is also a way of life for which you will need self-discipline, good fitness and interpersonal skills, and to be prepared to work where you are sent (including war zones). You will need to stay calm under pressure and be prepared to follow orders some of the time and use your initiative at other times.

Officers also need top-level communication and leadership skills along with good judgement and an ability to discipline and motivate.

You will have to join up for a minimum length of service. (For entrants under 17½ there is a short period after the first month when you can leave.) The average service length is 9 years, so you need to be sure it is for you.

Working conditions

Your work will be at an RAF base, on exercises or on a detachment, possibly overseas. You may have to go to dangerous war zones.

Your trade, profession or specialism will affect your usual day-to-day working conditions.

Hours of work can be irregular and include shifts and working at weekends and holidays.

You will need to wear uniform and protective clothing.

The future outlook

There are currently 54,000 personnel in full-time service with the RAF. The RAF regularly recruits for all levels and trades but some specialisms, for example pilots, are more competitive than others. For details of jobs available and training options visit the RAF website.

Promotion is possible if you perform well. For airmen and women, promotion is possible to corporal and sergeant. Warrant officer is the highest rank a non-commissioned officer can achieve. You can progress to become a commissioned officer. Commissioned officers can also be promoted, for example from flying officer, to flight lieutenant, squadron leader and beyond.

Qualifications and courses

- All candidates must pass the medical examination plus the pre-joining fitness test, and the RAF's aptitude tests, which cover verbal, numerical and special reasoning, electrical and mechanical reasoning, memory and work rate. There is also a basic interview, plus a specialism interview which may take two or more days to complete.

Airman/Airwoman

- You will need to be 16 years old and a British or Commonwealth citizen. There is a 9-week training course based at RAF Halton.
- Some trades require specific qualifications. For example, RAF weapons systems operators must be aged 17½ to 32 and have 5 GCSEs/S grades (A–C/1–3) including English language, maths and a physics-based science.

Non-commissioned aircrew

- Candidates initially enlist for 12 years and will need to be 17½ to 25 years old and a British or Commonwealth citizen with 5 GCSEs/S grades (A–C/1–3) including English language and maths. Linguistics specialists need language skills.
- Candidates must pass the aptitude and fitness tests conducted over 4 days at the Officers and Aircrew Selection Centre (OASC) at RAF Cranwell in Lincolnshire. Successful candidates then have a selection interview of around 45 minutes, and finally a set of four leadership tasks to perform with five or six other applicants working as a team. New recruits undergo 9 weeks basic training at RAF Halton plus 10 weeks Officer training at RAF Cranwell. A further period of specialist training must be completed before recruits are considered to be operational.

Officer

- You will need to be at least 17½ years old and a British or Commonwealth citizen. Entry requirements range from at least 5 GCSEs/S grades (A–C/1–3) to professional qualifications. Many officers are graduates.

entry level

To both enter and train while working in this career, you will need qualifications at Level 1–8. Please refer to explanation on page vii.

- Candidates must pass the aptitude and fitness tests conducted over 4 days at the Officers and Aircrew Selection Centre (OASC) at RAF Cranwell in Lincolnshire. Successful candidates then have a selection interview of around 45 minutes, and finally a set of four leadership tasks to perform with five or six other applicants working as a team. Entrants complete the 30-week Initial Officer Training course at the RAF College, Cranwell, in Lincolnshire. Professionally qualified Officers, such as Medical or Legal Officers, train at RAF Cranwell for 2 months.

Other related opportunities

- Air Traffic Controller p556
- Army p492
- Distribution Manager p562
- Pilot p573
- Royal Marines p514
- Royal Navy p516

Advantages/disadvantages

- The training on offer will be excellent. Many RAF staff retire at a relatively early age with vocational qualifications that enable them to move on into civilian jobs at a similar level.
- If you train to be a pilot with the RAF you will be paid to learn to fly – increasingly rare in commercial flying training. However, pilot officer vacancies are few in number and only one of 20 different officer careers so be prepared for competition; you will need to stand out from the crowd.

Earnings guide

- A charge for rent and food, if provided, will be deducted from your wages.

Airman/woman

- Training starting pay is about £12,575 per year, and £15,675 when qualified.
- Senior airmen/airwomen earn up to £26,650. With experience and promotion, you can earn up to £43,000.

Non-commissioned aircrew

- Entry-level pay on initial training is £12,575 during the first 6 months rising to £25,400 for the remainder of training.
- Sergeants earn up to £34,000, and flight sergeants up to £39,850.
- With experience and promotion, earnings can increase to £43,000.

Officer

- Entry-level pay for officer cadets is £21,881.
- Flight lieutenants can earn up to £40,190. Highest ranks can earn £80,000+.
- Flying officers earn from £27,250 to £32,700.
- With experience and promotion, earnings can rise to £86,000.
- Flight lieutenants can earn up to £40,190. Highest ranks can earn £80,000+.

Further information

Armed Forces Careers RAF
22 Unthank Road
Norwich
NR2 1AH
01603 614616
www.rafcareers.com

RAF4U
www.raf4u.com

Royal Marines

What the work involves

- Royal Marines are the Royal Navy's amphibious infantry and the UK's rapid response force. They operate in the air, on land and at sea. When in action or on exercises you will operate mainly in extreme conditions, such as in arctic, jungle, mountain or amphibious warfare.

Commando

- First and foremost you will be a commando and rifleman – ready to take immediate action in any emergency or threat to national security. You will need to work to a very high standard in front-line combat on land or at sea.
- Once you have passed your 30-week training course you can specialise either in general duties or in one of 26 trades, including assault engineer, mountain leader or swimmer canoeist.

Officer

- You will lead and manage a team of commandos, often in difficult situations, such as war zones, peace-keeping tasks or disaster areas.
- Once you have passed your training you can specialise in one of 10 areas including landing craft, signals, special boat service, mountain leader, weapons training, physical training or pilot.
- You will have responsibility for the training, welfare and discipline of your team.

The type of person suited to this work

This job and the training for it has no easy options or short cuts. You will need to be super-fit, committed, disciplined, resilient, brave and self-confident. Initial training is a tough 30-week course that will test you both mentally and physically. For example, a 30-mile march across Dartmoor with 14 kg of kit on your back, that has to be finished in 7 hours by officers and in 8 hours by commandos, needs real stamina and endurance.

Officers train even harder and five phases of training are essential. You will have an extra 14 months of training that can include exercises in mountain and arctic operations in Northern Europe and jungle warfare training in the Far East, or you may be sent to Northern Ireland. You will need to be prepared to take on lots of responsibility at an early stage and in extreme conditions.

Working conditions

A significant amount of your work will take place in potentially dangerous places and situations.

You will work irregular hours – especially when on active duty – but usually in shifts of about 8 hours each. You will also be on call at all times.

You will need to wear uniform and protective clothing.

You can be posted at short notice to serve wherever you are needed in the world.

The future outlook

Commando

Entry to commando work is very competitive. The majority of commandos specialise in general duties but it is possible to learn a trade.
Do note that vacancies vary and it is worth checking out with a local Forces Careers Office for vacancies and recruitment options.
Commandos can earn promotion up the ranks to warrant officer and apply for a commission to become an officer.

Officer

There are only about 700+ Royal Marine officers; entry is selective at both levels but this is the toughest.

Progression is excellent for the best – it is possible to become a major by the age of 30 and a lieutenant-colonel by your late 30s.

CRCI:UA

CLCI:BAB

Qualifications and courses

- For all entrants, minimum height is 151.5cm and weight should be in comparison to height.

Commando

- There are no minimum academic requirements, but the Royal Navy selection test, including reasoning, English language, numeracy and mechanical comprehension must be passed. To progress to Warrant Officer First Class level you will need to enter with GCSEs/S grades (A–C/1–3) in English and maths.
- You will need to pass an interview and medical check, be aged 16–33, and successfully complete both the three-day Potential Royal Marine Course (PRMC) and the 32-week Royal Marines Commando Recruits Course. You will need to be male (currently under review), with the exception of band service (which accepts females).
- The PRMC includes a written test, physical exercises including swimming and a personal interview. Band Service applicants must pass an audition.

Commando Officer

- You will need 5 GCSEs/S grades (A–C/1–3) including English language and maths and 2 A levels/H grades or equivalent (at least 180 UCAS points) and to be male, between 17 and 26 years old and a British citizen with at least 5 years' residency immediately prior to application. Candidates should be a minimum of 151.5cm tall and weight should be in proportion to height.
- Direct Entry Graduate candidates must be British citizens and have a minimum of 5 GCSEs/S grades (A–C/1–3) including English and maths. There are height and weight restrictions and currently only men may become commando officers. Good eyesight with colour vision is essential, and candidates must be aged under 26 on 1st September of year of entry.
- Candidates are required to attend a 3-day course in Devon followed by a 2-day interview in Hampshire if successful.

entry level

To both enter and train while working in this career, you will need qualifications at Level 1–8. Please refer to explanation on page vii.

Other related opportunities

- Army p492
- Bodyguard p494
- Police p506
- Royal Air Force (RAF) p512
- Royal Navy p516
- Security p518

Advantages/disadvantages

- All commandos and officers find the 30-week initial training course challenging – it is mentally and physically exhausting. But the feeling of achievement when you have coped with the challenges and achieved your Commando Green Beret is regarded as a once-in-a-lifetime experience.
- It is often a short career, because of the continued high fitness requirements and demands placed on this elite force, but your training will be well regarded when you leave the Marines.

Earnings guide

- Money is deducted for accommodation and food, if provided.
- When training your wages will be £12,575 per year, and as a marine you will get £15,677–£26,664.
- Corporals can earn £24,328–£30,357. Sergeants can earn £27,653–£34,025.
- Colour sergeants can earn up to £38,551 and warrant officers can earn up to £41,672.
- Officers at Level 2 earn £30,611–£39,851, and at Level 1 earn £35,565–£43,077.
- Majors can earn between £42,570 and £52,000.
- Lieutenant-colonels can earn up to £66,046 and colonels can earn up to £76,471.

Further information

Royal Marines
Careers information 0845 607 5555
www.royalmarines.mod.uk

Royal Navy

What the work involves

Rating

- You will work on board a ship or submarine, or in a Royal Navy (RN) establishment ashore in one of six main branches: warfare, engineering, supply, medical, Fleet Air Arm or submarine.
- Using your trade you will make sure that personnel, ships, aircraft, submarines and equipment are kept ready for action.
- You will take part in naval exercises both in UK and overseas waters.

Officer

- You will command and train ratings, looking after their welfare, development and discipline.
- Your day-to-day work will involve you in managing operations in one of four areas of duty: as a warfare officer, engineer officer, supply officer or specialist officer (for example chaplain, doctor or dentist).
- Your ship may be sent into a war zone, on peacekeeping duties, or be tasked to do a specific job such as policing the North Sea fishing grounds or helping out in a disaster situation.

The type of person suited to this work

Rating

You will need to be able to work as part of a team, have self-discipline and the ability to accept responsibility for your actions.

You should be physically fit, be able to take orders and have some practical and technical skills.

You should be keen on science and technology. Modern ships and weapon systems use highly sophisticated technology.

You will often be working in very dangerous conditions, so you need to be the calm and unflappable type.

Officer

Officers especially need top-level leadership and communication skills as well as good judgement. You will be required to inspire ratings, be resourceful and have excellent communication skills. You should have good levels of physical fitness and stamina. You may need to work in combat zones.

Working conditions

Most of your work will be on board a ship or submarine, or at land-based establishments in Britain or overseas. At sea, conditions can be cold, cramped and damp.

You will need to wear a uniform, and protective clothing when necessary.

Hours vary but you will usually work 8-hour turns of duty on a shift rota including weekends and holidays.

The future outlook

Rating

There are about 40,000+ ratings in the Royal Navy. The number recruited varies but there are annual vacancies or around 4500 per year. Once trained you can be promoted from junior rating to ordinary rating and then if you have got the right qualities you can progress through the ranks of able rating, leading rating, petty officer, chief petty officer and warrant officer. Ratings can apply for commissions (about 25% of officers start as ratings).

Officer

There are about 7500+ officers in the Royal Navy. There are annual vacancies but some specialisms are more competitive than others. A naval college entrant usually starts out as midshipman rising to sub-lieutenant after 2 years. A graduate starts as sub-lieutenant rising to lieutenant commander by their early 30s. If you have got the right qualities you can progress on to the ranks of commander, captain and, for a few, admiral.

CRCI:UA

CLCI:BAB

Qualifications and courses

entry level

To both enter and train while working in this career, you will need qualifications at Level 1–8. Please refer to explanation on page vii.

- You will need to be at least 151.5cm tall and be of proportionate weight. A medical, with strict eyesight standards, must be passed, and you must meet the Royal Navy nationality and residence requirements. Women can still not enter the submarine or mine clearance diving branches of the Royal Navy.

Rating

- You will be between 16 and 37 years old in most cases and must pass the Royal Navy selection test, an interview and a questionnaire. Formal qualifications may not be required but some trades require minimum qualifications and specific aptitude tests.
- Initial training lasts for 9 weeks at *HMS Raleigh* in Cornwall. Training includes practical exercises, a personal weapons test, a swimming test and general naval training. Specialist training for your chosen trade follows.

Officer

- There are several entry points for Officers: Non-Graduate Entry for those aged 17–26 who have at least 5 GCSEs/S grades and 2 A levels/H grades or 140 tariff points including English language and maths; Scholarship for those with 5 GCSEs/S grades and no break before continuing further education; Defence Technical Undergraduate Scheme (DTUS) for those under 23 with 5 GCSEs/S grades including English language and maths and 240 tariff points including grade C in maths and physics; Graduate entry for those with a UK degree. All candidates undergo a selection interview and medical examination before the Admiralty Interview Board AIB. Training takes place at Britania Royal Naval College, Dartmouth, Devon, and lasts for up to one year, including periods of sea training.

Other related opportunities

- Army p492
- Diver p498
- Marine Engineering / Marine Industry p213
- Merchant Navy p571
- Royal Air Force (RAF) p512
- Royal Marines p514

Advantages/disadvantages

- Few people stay in the navy until retirement age but you will be trained to a high level and will be offered a resettlement package to help you find work in civilian life.
- You will probably travel and sometimes may even make it ashore.
- You will be living in very cramped conditions with lots of other people. However, most naval ratings and officers say that they really enjoy the feeling of camaraderie on board and often make life-long friendships.

Earnings guide

- A bonus is paid for service at sea over 18 months. Where food and accommodation are provided, deductions are made from pay.

Rating

- New entrants earn £12,572 per year. Able ratings earn £15,677–£26,665.
- Warrant officers earn up to £43,077.

Officer

- Petty officers earn £27,653–£34,025. Chief Petty officers earn £30,611–£39,851, Warrant officers earn £35,565–£43,077.
- Lieutenant commanders earn up to £52,702 and captains earn up to £79,049.

Further information

Armed Forces Careers Navy
22 Unthank Road
Norwich
NR2 1AH
01603 620033
www.royalnavy.mod.uk

Royal Navy
Careers information 08456 075555
www.royal-navy.mod.uk

CRCI:UA | CLCI:BAB

Security

What the work involves

- Security work is about protecting organisations, people, places, valuable goods or money. The work can be at a place such as an airport, hospital or government building. You could also be protecting people or valuable items on the move, for example in security vans or on planes.

Manager

- You will be managing a team of security guards, and be responsible for their work, training and supervision.
- You will do security surveys, give advice on improvements and liaise with other organisations such as the local emergency services.
- You may have a specific task in a large organisation, for example managing internal investigations or surveillance work.

Officer

- If you are working at a base you may have specific tasks. You may work at reception monitoring visitors and deliveries. Or you may patrol a building or site, possibly with a dog, checking for intruders or fire risks.
- You may travel to lots of sites checking on security or you may collect money or items of value and move them in a secure vehicle.

The type of person suited to this work

This job can include tasks such as chasing intruders for which you will need a high level of fitness. However, a lot of the work can be routine; just by being there you will discourage law-breaking.

You should be keen on technology and be willing to do qualifications and training. As security systems become more complex and government regulations come into force, you will need to take part in learning and keep up to date. You will also have to keep records of all incidents, so you will also need to be happy to do paperwork.

To become a manager you will need lots of experience in security work as well as a talent for motivating a team of staff. You will need to be a mature, responsible and honest person. You will need to be good with written reports and confident with computers.

Working conditions

You will be working long hours, and you may be at risk of injury.

You may be based at one place which could be inside, or outside in all weathers.

Many security jobs involve driving and you will spend a lot of time in a security van.

You may need to wear a uniform or, if needed, protective clothing.

You will probably be working shifts of up to 12 hours covering days, nights and weekends. Some guards work permanent nights. Many security guards work a 48-hour week.

The future outlook

There are currently about 450,000 people employed in the wider security industry and a doubling in size is expected within the next 5 years. Jobs are on offer throughout the UK and you could be employed by any type of organisation. This area is one of massive growth with rising levels of fraud, theft and security breaches in organisations as well as increasing terrorist threats. It is also important to remember that the industry is currently being regulated and in the future many security guards and managers will need licences.

This work will increasingly use sophisticated technology with the growing use of computer security systems and also biometrics (fingerprint recognition systems) to control access to buildings and other secure areas. Security staff with training and technical ability are likely to be in demand in this growing industry.

Manager

Managers can progress with the right training and experience to overseeing security for a larger organisation, maybe covering an area or region, the whole of the UK or even a global management job.

Officer

Guards can move on to become a senior or chief security guard and then a supervisor. Previous training and experience is a requirement for management posts so there are good opportunities for progression.

CRCI:UK | CLCI:MAG

Qualifications and courses

- You will need to be numerate, literate, and aged over 18 (occasionally over 21) and may need a driving licence. You will also undergo a medical exam and police criminal check as part of the new licensing requirements plus possibly an employment history and credit check.

Manager

- You will need previous security work experience and training as a guard or actual work experience with the military or police. Specialist managers may need specific training and experience, for example in security systems, legislation and anti-terrorist or close protection work.
- Your employer may offer training. The International Institute of Security offers courses (some available by distance learning) and certificates in security management.

Officer

- All security guards require by law an industry licence, approved by the Security Industry Authority (SIA) which you must pay for. The licence is awarded to candidates who pass the two-part assessment process, usually delivered over 4 days.
- Employers may offer additional training such as NVQ/SVQ Level 2 Providing Security Services. Other qualifications available include a degree in Security and Risk Management or a Postgraduate Certificate in Maritime and Supply Chain Security.
- Apprenticeships/Skillseekers may be available for candidates aged 16–24.

entry level

To both enter and train while working in this career, you will need qualifications at Level 1–2. Please refer to explanation on page vii.

Other related opportunities

- Army p492
- Bodyguard p494
- Customs and Excise Officer p497
- Door Supervisor / Bouncer p501
- Locksmith p212
- Police p506
- Store Detective p521

Advantages/disadvantages

- As training becomes essential, and with the introduction of security licences, if you are willing to get qualified, your progression and earnings prospects are excellent.
- This work can put you in danger, but training is on offer to help you cope, and high-risk jobs often have higher salary and benefits packages.
- At high levels in large international organisations you may have the opportunity to travel or be based overseas.

Earnings guide

Manager

- On entry, managers earn £25,000–£28,000 per year, rising to £35,000+ with experience. Area managers can earn £40,000+ and international security managers can earn up to £66,000

Officer

- As a starting salary, guards can earn about £12,000–£15,000 per year. With experience this can rise to £20,800–£25,000.

Further information

Security Industry Authority
PO Box 9
Newcastle upon Tyne
NE82 6YX
0870 243 0100
www.the-sia.org.uk

Skills for Security
Security House
Barbourne Road
Worcester
WR1 1RS
08450 750111
www.skillsforsecurity.org.uk

International Institute of Security
Suite 8
The Business Centre
57 Torquay Road
Paignton
Devon
TQ3 3DT
01803 663275
www.iisec.co.uk

International Professional Security Association
Northumberland House Business
11 The Pavement
Popes Lane
Ealing
London
W5 4NG
020 8832 7417
www.ipsa.org.uk

www.cityandguilds.com/myperfectjob

Security Service Officer

What the work involves

- You will be a member of the Security Service, employed to protect the country from attack, terrorism and other forms of crime.
- Working alongside other security forces such as the police and other international law enforcement agencies, you will help to protect UK citizens and businesses across the world.
- You could be employed to undertake a number of roles depending on need and your skills. These include vetting investigation officers, suveillance officers, linguists and ICT specialists.
- In addition, the service also employs administrative and support staff.

entry level

To both enter and train while working in this career, you will need qualifications at Level 4–8. Please refer to explanation on page vii.

The type of person suited to this work

You will need an excellent range of skills across a range of areas. This job requires you to think on your feet and be aware of the full picture. You should be confident making decisions, be flexible and adaptable.

You will need good verbal and written communication skills with the ability to recall events accurately. You will also need commitment to your job and the ability to see everything through until it is finished. Some of your work will include informing and working alongside professionals from other national and international security services.

The skills you need will depend on your specialism, such as language or ICT ability.

Working conditions

Some of the posts operate shifts, which might include weekends. You could also be required to travel both nationally and internationally. It might be possible to work from home for some posts.

If you provide support services you will normally work in London and operate office hours.

This job can become more of a way of life than a career so you should be completely dedicated and be able to keep information totally confidential.

The future outlook

There are around 3,000 people working for the Service, many of whom are based in London. Although there are specialist jobs, 67% work within generalist roles. To increase the number employed up to 3,200 by 2008, there is currently a national recruitment scheme. Applicants should refer to the Security Service website for details on current vacancies, which change regularly.

The Service has a promotion programme that is based on performance and potential.

Qualifications and courses

- Applicants for any post within MI5 or the Secret Intelligence Service (SIS) must be British citizens and one or both of your parents must also be British or have substantial ties to the UK. You normally have to have been resident in the UK for 10 years prior to your application.
- MI5 applicants must be aged 18 or over. SIS applicants must be aged 21 or over and A-levels/H grades or degrees may be required by some organisations.
- Graduates from a wide range of disciplines are considered. Specialist areas may require more precise subject choices, for example linguistics or computer software development. Mature applicants and those with experience are also considered.
- Each applicant is considered individually during the rigorous vetting procedure, known as Developed Vetting (DV) clearance. Some candidates who already have clearance from previous employment may be exempt from some sections of the vetting process. Some applicants may require additional vetting, for example medical assessments.
- Specialist fields within MI5 include English Language Monitor, Intelligence Officer, Security Guard and Mobile Surveillance Officer.

CRCI:UK

CLCI:MAG

Other related opportunities

- Army p492
- Customs and Excise Officer p497
- Immigration Officer p503
- Police p506
- Security p518

Advantages/disadvantages

- You will be helping to protect national security.
- Some jobs involve lots of travelling for long periods at a time.
- This is not a normal 9–5 job!
- The current recruitment drive aims to attract people of all backgrounds.

Earnings guide

- Salaries are based on your role and the information below should be used as a guide only.
- Administrative assistants earn an average of £16,750 per year. Generalists, surveillance and linguist officers start at £24,200. Development vetting officers start at £33,500.
- In addition to pay there are excellent benefits including leisure and fitness facilities, childcare vouchers and travel assistance.

Further information

MI5
www.mi5.gov.uk

MI5 Careers
www.mi5careers.co.uk

Secret Intelligence Service
www.sis.gov.uk

Store Detective

What the work involves

- You will be preventing and detecting theft or fraud in a retail outlet.
- Working undercover, you will merge with shoppers, looking out for suspicious behaviour or theft. You will also have to assist other staff in the case of credit card fraud.
- Using a radio you will call for assistance and listen for alerts from other staff about known offenders entering the store.
- You may need to chase the suspected offender before you make a citizen's arrest.
- You will make notes of any incidents and may need to use these if a decision is made to prosecute.

entry level

To both enter and train while working in this career, you will need qualifications at Level 1. Please refer to explanation on page vii.

The type of person suited to this work

Your communication skills need to be excellent for this job. You will have to talk down customers who have become anxious or aggressive when challenged. Your written reports will be used in court if you prosecute and you will need to be fluent and precise to get a conviction.

Observation is also crucial: you need to be able to spot suspicious behaviour and also remember the faces of known shoplifters. You will need to be good at planning and thinking ahead so that when a situation happens you can act quickly.

You should be keen on technology as you will probably be using different types of surveillance equipment, for example closed-circuit TV and loop alarms.

You will also need to have a good level of physical fitness and stamina.

You will need to be mature, responsible and be able to handle difficult situations sensitively.

Qualifications and courses

- There are no formal entry requirements, but you will need to be able to write clearly and accurately. A GCSE/S grade in English or a Key Skill in communication would be useful.
- You will have to undergo a police check. Some employers may also do an employment history and credit check.
- Previous relevant work experience is preferred, especially within the police, prison or security industry.
- Training is through courses or on the job. Most companies run an induction course for new employees covering topics such as relevant criminal law and principles of investigation.
- The International Institute of Security and the International Professional Security Association both offer courses by distance learning.
- The Security Industry Authority (SIA) now has a requirement for you to be licenced to operate as a security guard.

Working conditions

Most of your work will be inside the store in pleasant, warm conditions.

A 40-hour week is common and you may work shifts to cover long opening hours and weekends. You will be on your feet most of your shift.

You may wear a uniform but the majority wear their own clothes to blend in.

The future outlook

Shoplifters cost stores more than £2 billion a year so most large stores in the UK employ store detectives to minimise their losses. Some retail chains employ their own detectives, while others use agencies on a contract basis.

You may be able to progress into supervisory work or move into more general security management.

CRCI:UK

CLCI:MAG

Other related opportunities

- Door Supervisor / Bouncer p501
- Police p506
- Private Investigator p511
- Security p518

Advantages/disadvantages

- Store detectives say they feel a sense of achievement when they manage to successfully prosecute an offender.
- This job can be a good stepping stone into jobs such as security management.

Earnings guide

- Starting wages are usually around £13,000 per year.
- Experienced store detectives can earn up to £22,500.
- £25,000+ is possible for top earners.

Further information

Security Industry Authority
PO Box 9
Newcastle upon Tyne
NE82 6YX
0870 243 0100
www.the-sia.org.uk

Skills for Security
Security House
Barbourne Road
Worcester
WR1 1RS
08450 750111
www.skillsforsecurity.org.uk

www.cityandguilds.com/myperfectjob

Here's Dean Butt's story:

Customs and Excise Officer

Dean, aged 25, was initially interested in joining the police force, but after serving four and a half years as a Special Constable he decided against it. While at college studying for a GNVQ in Business and Finance, and a BTEC National Diploma in Public Services and Society, he did some part-time work with someone who had a relation in Customs and Excise, who had told him how much he enjoyed his job and explained what type of work he actually did. After a chat with the Customs and Excise officer, Dean was really interested, so he wrote off to his local HMC&E (Her Majesty's Customs and Excise) to ask about jobs. They sent back an application form and he subsequently went for interview and was accepted. He is now an anti-smuggling officer at Nottingham East Midlands Airport.

WHAT THE JOB ENTAILS

'I am part of a team that detects prohibited, restricted and revenue goods including controlled Class A drugs such as cocaine and heroin. We also detect illegal firearms and explosives as well as other offensive weapons, and indecent and obscene material. In the course of our duties, we have to question people, search for drugs, take cases to court and as often as possible secure prosecutions.'

To be good at his job Dean says you must be a team player, be motivated and be passionate about what you do. He has just been promoted to band 5, and the next step up for him will be to senior officer within a passenger team or to move to a post in the Serious and Organised Crime Agency.

DEAN'S ADVICE FOR PROSPECTIVE CUSTOMS AND EXCISE OFFICERS

'You need to work within the law and follow the guidelines, make sure you work well within your team and concentrate on your yearly performance agreements with your line manager. You need to gain the right competencies throughout the year for the job you wish to pursue and try and get a secondment to the area you really want to specialise in.'

Interested in helping people by talking, caring and improving their quality of life? Advice, psychology and counselling services are part of many jobs in social care, for example:

- **Advice Centre**
- **Childminder**
- **Educational Welfare**
- **Money Adviser**
- **Youth and Community Worker**

But what's it like working in this area?
Here's Jo Amand's story:

Youth Worker

Jo, who is 25, had no initial interest in working in this profession, but she did the Duke of Edinburgh's Award scheme and part of that entailed community service and she started working with people with special needs. From there Jo branched out into working with youth clubs, play schemes and after-school clubs and after doing her A levels she left school to work part time at the London Borough of Harrow and did its in-house Youth Work qualification accredited through the Open College. When she was 22 she did a mature student course at Brunel University. This postgraduate national qualification in Youth Work was on a day-release basis. In September 2000 Jo started to work for Wandsworth Borough Council and she is now its Senior Youth Worker.

Jo's duties include supporting the tutoring staff and the careers advisors, doing a lot of work face to face with young people, and also having to cope with a lot of administration such as publicising the opportunities for young people in the borough.

'I started out coordinating the Duke of Edinburgh's Award scheme in the borough and my duties have progressed from there. Now I don't work so much with youth clubs but with special projects such as dance and drama courses and web design courses for young people aged 10 to 19. I also train teachers and other youth workers to get the qualification that will enable them to run outdoor trips, and one job I'm doing at the moment is organising a scheme over the summer months to supervise Year 11 pupils who are at risk of falling through the education net.'

WHAT'S HOT AND WHAT'S NOT ABOUT THE JOB

The diversity and challenging nature of the job are what Jo enjoys about it the most, along with actually being able to see young people progress because of the advice and support she gives them. But one of the downsides is she sometimes wants to help young people who don't want to accept her help. There are also a lot of guidelines and legal requirements she has to adhere to for her own safety and the safety of the people she works with, and this can be frustrating.

Ultimately Jo would like to progress into project development because she likes starting new things and watching them grow, and for this she will need to build up her levels of experience.

WHAT YOU NEED TO SUCCEED

'You need to have a very open mind to do what I do. You really have to have a good understanding of where other people are coming from. You definitely need patience and to be able to use your intuition and I would say it is very important to be consistent and deal with people in a consistent manner.'

Advice Centre / Benefits Adviser

What the work involves

- In this job you will help people cope with problems by listening, asking questions and giving impartial and confidential advice.
- You will explain people's rights on matters such as tenancy, employment, conflicts with neighbours, consumer law and finance, sometimes referring clients to other professionals.
- Helping people fill in forms to claim benefits and making phone calls on their behalf will be part of the job.
- Benefit advisers may represent their clients at tribunals, or act as advocates in a court of law.

The type of person suited to this work

As the work is mainly about dealing with people, it is essential to get on with all types of people and to remain impartial and non-judgemental. In order to explain issues very clearly to your clients, and help them to complete forms and documents, you will need excellent verbal and written communication skills.

You will be handling large amounts of information, often to find answers to queries, which means you must enjoy research and be able to grasp facts and analyse data quickly.

Clients may be upset and under stress. It is important to be sympathetic, tactful and discreet when handling these situations.

Working conditions

Benefit advisers are based in an open-access centre within a local community, town or city.

You will see clients on a one-to-one basis by appointment, but also liaise with colleagues and other professionals, such as social workers and solicitors.

You will do research using ICT to consult client records, access email and the internet. You might do shift work, including Saturdays and some evenings.

The future outlook

Advice centre work is not open to school-leavers; it suits mature people, experienced in other fields. Entry is competitive; you could gain experience in helping people through volunteering work.

Most jobs are with local authorities or charities. There are a few paid jobs with the Citizens Advice Bureau, but many posts are voluntary. Training will be given in counselling skills or benefits, for example.

Promotion prospects are limited, although every advice centre has a manager.

entry level

2–8

To both enter and train while working in this career, you will need qualifications at Level 2–8. Please refer to explanation on page vii.

Qualifications and courses

- There are no set minimum entry requirements for this job, but a good standard of education is desirable.
- Although a degree is not specified, many applicants have degrees in a range of subjects and/or professional qualifications.
- Life experience is essential, with applicants generally having a background of working with people.
- It will help if you have experience in advising/counselling work, communication, information handling, ICT, money management, problem-solving or working with others.
- Once in post, you will attend in-house training and updating courses.

CRCI:V

CLCI:KEB

Other related opportunities

- Counselling Work p529
- Debt Counsellor / Money Adviser p531
- Education Welfare Officer p532
- Equal Opportunities / Equalities Officer p17
- Social Worker p545
- Solicitor / Notary Public p349
- Welfare Rights Officer / Worker p550

Advantages/disadvantages

- You will work with many different people.
- Depending on your advisory area, you may work certain evenings and occasional weekends.
- Some clients may be angry and difficult to deal with; a few will have mental health problems.
- It is satisfying to help people sort out their difficulties and concerns.

Earnings guide

- Pay varies, depending on where you work and who you work for.
- Earnings are around £16,000–£18,500 per year on entry.
- Pay can rise to £22,000–£28,000+ with experience.
- Salaries can exceed £33,000 for those with a lot of experience. London rates are higher.

Further information

www.cityandguilds.com/myperfectjob

Citizens Advice Bureau
Myddelton House
115–123 Pentonville Road
London
N1 9LZ
020 7833 2181
www.citizensadvice.org.uk

Citizens Advice Scotland
2 Powderhall Road
Edinburgh
EH7 4GB
0131 550 1000
www.cas.org.uk

Advice UK
12th Floor, 2 London Bridge House
25 London Bridge Street
London
SE1 9ST
020 7407 4070
www.adviceuk.org.uk

Care Assistant

What the work involves

- Your clients could be children, elderly people or people with disabilities living in residential care or in their own homes.
- Care assistants help people who find it difficult to look after themselves with everyday tasks.
- You will help individuals to bathe, perhaps changing dressings, and to use the toilet or commode, and help with eating, washing, ironing, cleaning and shopping.
- Part of your time will be spent talking to clients, helping them to write letters, budget their money or pay bills.

The type of person suited to this work

As the job involves working with people who need individual support, you will have to work out what help they need and provide it in a sympathetic and tactful way. Care assistants need to be cheerful, outgoing and friendly, as their clients may be lonely or depressed.

The job usually involves domestic work so you need to be happy and skilled at doing housework and laundry.

Helping with handling money, and writing and reading personal and business letters, is work that must remain confidential, so care assistants need to be very trustworthy and discreet, able to keep clients' personal information private.

Working conditions

Most of your work is indoors but you may go out with people, for example to hospital appointments or on outings. You may have to live in for some jobs.

You need to be physically fit to help people who are unable to move around for themselves, and there could be heavy lifting.

You will be expected to be very careful about health and safety issues, such as fire and hot water.

The future outlook

There are over a million care assistants in the UK and demand is increasing. Many care assistants work in residential homes and day-care centres, but more people are being cared for in their own homes. The main employers are health authorities, social services, private homes and voluntary agencies.

Promotion depends on qualifications and experience. With experience in care work, you could train for related jobs such as social work or nursing.

entry level

To both enter and train while working in this career, you will need qualifications at Level 1–3. Please refer to explanation on page vii.

Qualifications and courses

- There are no fixed entry qualifications for this job.
- Previous experience, for example in voluntary work and/or an NVQ/SVQ in Care at Level 2 is useful, and may be required by some employers.
- You can study a range of relevant courses full-time at school or college, prior to entry. The First Diploma in Caring and Intermediate GNVQ in Health and Social Care are 1-year courses that do not require particular qualifications, although institutions may ask for some GCSEs/S grades. The National Diploma in Care and A level in Health and Social Care are 2-year courses, and usually require 4 GCSEs/S grades (A–C/1–3) or a BTEC First Diploma.
- Most training is work-based, and care assistants can work towards NVQs/SVQs in Care at Levels 1–3.
- Care Assistants must have good interpersonal skills and enjoy practical, physical and domestic abilities.
- Care assistants are required to be at least 18 years old.

CRCI:V

CLCI:KEB

Other related opportunities

- Childminder p528
- Cleaner p418
- Home Care Assistant p534
- Nurse (Registered) p289
- Nursery Nurse p538
- Social Worker p545

Advantages/disadvantages

- The work can be very satisfying but, occasionally, you may find that people are very demanding and not always pleasant.
- You may have to work shifts, evenings, weekends and public holidays, including Christmas Day.
- Some jobs can be messy and unpleasant.

Earnings guide

- Salaries are around £11,000–£14,000 per year at entry. With experience and qualifications you could get up to £17,000.
- You can earn £16,500+ in a residential post.
- Salaries can rise to £21,000 in a senior post.
- Managers can get up to £30,000 in some areas.
- You will be paid more for shift work and unsocial hours, i.e. for working late hours or providing overnight care.

Further information

General Social Care Council
Goldings House
2 Hays Lane
London
SE1 2HB
020 7397 5100
www.gscc.org.uk

Northern Ireland Social Care Council
7th Floor, Millennium House
19–25 Great Victoria Street
Belfast
BT2 7AQ
028 9041 7600
www.niscc.info

Scottish Social Services Council
Compass House
11 Riverside Drive
Dundee
DD1 4NY
01382 207101
www.sssc.uk.com

www.cityandguilds.com/myperfectjob

Careers Adviser

What the work involves

- You will help people make realistic choices about education, training and work by listening to their ideas, discussing their interests and skills, and providing information on different jobs.
- Researching information about job opportunities in different sectors from newspapers, the internet or through visits to employers is all part of the role.
- Advisory work is one to one, but you may work with large groups.
- Careers advisers work with young people in schools/colleges, but also with higher education students or adults.

The type of person suited to this work

Since much of the work involves talking and listening to people, careers advisers need to have excellent speaking and listening skills. They also need to be impartial, allowing people to come to their own decisions rather than making up their minds for them.

Careers information and guidance is largely ICT-based, so computer skills are essential, along with the ability to write reports and perform administrative tasks.

You will need to enjoy research, to keep up to date with changes in skills and opportunities across industrial sectors, with new qualifications and training routes.

Working conditions

Most of your work is office-based, either in a careers centre open to the public or an educational establishment.

You will travel between different educational establishments and visit employers and training organisations, which means that a driving licence is almost essential.

Some time will be spent in a careers centre or library, keeping up to date with job information. You might go on short training courses.

The future outlook

Careers advisers will continue to work in schools, colleges, universities and adult guidance services – some, will be based in one institution, others will work for several organisations. In England, Connexions provides a support service which includes careers advice and guidance for those aged 13–19. In Scotland, Wales and Northern Ireland, all-age guidance services are available.

In a careers service, you could move into managerial-level posts; you could become self-employed as a consultant or researcher. Ongoing professional development is essential.

entry level

4–8

To both enter and train while working in this career, you will need qualifications at Level 4–8. Please refer to explanation on page vii.

Qualifications and courses

- There are two main routes into this profession: the Qualification in Careers Guidance (QCG) or the work-based route leading to NVQ/SVQ Level 4 in Advice and Guidance, Guidance and Advocacy. Most candidates are graduates and are aged 21 or over. The new Foundation degree in Working with Young People and Young People's Services provides useful background.
- The QCG is a 1-year full-time or 2 years part-time course at university. Candidates must then achieve the NVQ/SVQ Level 4 in Advice, Guidance and Advocacy to become a qualified careers adviser.
- People already working in a careers guidance organisation can follow a work-based route to the NVQ/SVQ Level 4. The qualification is a combination of practical experience and taught sessions at college.
- You do not need a professional careers qualification to work as a careers adviser in higher education, although many candidates have qualified prior to working in HE. A specialist qualification for HE careers advisers, the Certificate/Diploma in Careers Education, Information and Guidance in Higher Education, is available.
- Qualified careers advisers who join the Connexions service must complete further in-service training.

CRCI:V

CLCI:KED

Other related opportunities

- Advice Centre / Benefits Adviser p524
- Counselling Work p529
- Employment Agency Consultant / Interviewer p533
- Human Resources / Personnel Officer p20
- Personal Adviser – Connexions p539
- Probation Officer p540
- Teacher p184
- Youth and Community Worker p551

Advantages/disadvantages

- The work is varied and can be highly satisfying.
- You will meet a wide range of people, always learning something new.
- You will work some evenings or weekends to attend school/college parents' evenings and for careers conventions.
- The job also includes a great deal of administrative work.

Earnings guide

- Pay is around £18,500–£20,500 per year when starting.
- Salaries rise to £24,500–£27,000 per year when fully qualified and with some experience.
- Salaries for middle management are around £35,000, and as a senior manager you can get £55,000+.

Further information

Institute of Careers Guidance
27a Lower High Street
Stourbridge
DY8 1TA
01384 376464
www.icg-uk.org

Connexions Service National Unit
Department for Children, Schools and Families
Moorfoot
Sheffield
S1 4PP
0114 259 1283
www.connexions.gov.uk

Careers Scotland
Scottish Enterprise
Atlantic Quay
Glasgow
G2 8LU
0141 228 2264
www.careers-scotland.org.uk

Careers Wales Associates Ltd
Suite 6, Block D, Van Court
Caerphilly Business Park
Caerphilly
CV83 3ED
029 2085 4880
www.careerswales.com

Careers Service Northern Ireland
Department for Employment and Learning
Adelaide House
39–49 Adelaide Street
Belfast
BT2 8FD
028 9025 7777
www.delni.gov.uk

Charity Fundraiser

What the work involves

- Your job will be to initiate and organise fundraising activities for your charity – from publicly-sponsored events to membership schemes with various benefits, besides corporate sponsorship.
- You will represent your charity at public events, such as dinners, giving talks to possible sponsors.
- There is administration and report writing – possibly, managing other staff and volunteers.
- You will prepare publicity material and liaise with broadcasters, the press and other media, keeping your charity in the public eye.

entry level

To both enter and train while working in this career, you will need qualifications at Level 3–8. Please refer to explanation on page vii.

The type of person suited to this work

As you will deal with people in every strata of society, it's important to get on with all types. Good spoken communication is essential to persuade people to support your charity; also, you will need confidence to speak engagingly in public.

People need to be persuaded to support your charity and it will require good negotiating skills and excellent writing skills to produce persuasive publicity material. You will have to be imaginative and creative to come up with novel fundraising ideas.

You will need to be able to organise your time and workload so you can keep running costs down to a minimum and save money for your charity.

Working conditions

You will normally be based in an office working on a computer, but you can be home-based, particularly if you work for a very small charity.

There may be pressure to hit deadlines for organising events and/or fundraising targets to meet.

You will travel fairly widely so a driving licence is useful.

You may spend time outdoors at fundraising activities.

The future outlook

It is not usual to become a charity fundraiser straight from school – most entrants have experience in sales or marketing and voluntary fundraising. Most jobs are with charities, pressure groups and non-profit-making organisations, including hospitals.

It may be necessary to move around – possibly to larger organisations – to progress your career. With experience you could move into management, become self-employed or offer consultancy advice.

Qualifications and courses

- There are no specific entry requirements for this work although you will need a good all-round background education and an interest in politics and social affairs. Many entrants are graduates and/or people with experience in marketing, sales or in working for other charities. Voluntary fundraising experience is useful.
- Large charities, such as Cancer Research UK, offer training schemes for entrants, while others, including Oxfam, run unpaid internships. Competition for places is fierce.
- The Institute of Fundraising runs an introductory course for charity fundraisers and a Certificate in Fundraising Management, equivalent to NVQ/SVQ Level 4, for experienced fundraisers. Short courses for people working as fundraisers/fundraising managers are also available.
- Skills in communication, information handling and ICT, money management and general numeracy, organising and supervision or leadership, plus an ability to work with others, are also required.

Other related opportunities

- Account Executive p124
- Account Planner p125
- Advertising Media Executive p128
- Marketing p151

Advantages/disadvantages

- There is office work plus talking to individuals and groups – sometimes, answering tough questions.
- You will get satisfaction from seeing your charity flourish, delivering positive outcomes.
- People who do not support your charity can be unpleasant.
- You will work evenings and weekends.

Earnings guide

- Your starting salary will be around £18,000–£21,000 per year depending on the charity.
- With experience and managerial responsibilities, you could be earning £25,000–£30,000.
- Senior managers in large charities can earn between £35,000 and £60,000.

Further information

Institute of Fundraising
Market Towers
1 Nine Elms Lane
London
SW8 9NQ
020 7627 3436
www.institute-of-fundraising.org.uk

Association of Chief Executives of Voluntary Organisations
83 Victoria Street
London
SW1H 0HW
0845 345 8481
www.acevo.org.uk

Directory of Social Change
24 Stephenson Way
London
NW1 2DP
020 7391 4800
www.dsc.org.uk

Childminder

What the work involves

- As a childminder, you will care for children in your own home, ensuring they are comfortable and happy while with you.
- You will plan the children's day – defined by play time, meals and rests – so your charges know what to expect.
- You may accompany children to and from playgroup, nursery or school.
- You will need to keep parents informed about their children, for example if a child has been unwell or if you have noticed anything important.

entry level

To both enter and train while working in this career, you will need qualifications at Level 1. Please refer to explanation on page vii.

The type of person suited to this work

Childminders must be good with young children, being patient, caring and able to communicate with them. You will need imagination to plan varied activities for children of different ages.

Childminders must share information with parents which means that good observation and communication skills are important. They must be prepared to make quick decisions if necessary.

Since childminders are self-employed, they need to be organised, with good administrative and numeracy skills to work out tax and invoices. ICT skills are useful for maintaining a database of relevant information about each child.

Working conditions

You will work in your own home which may have to be altered to meet childminding standards by fitting equipment such as gates on stairs and checking the security of garden fences and gates.

You may travel locally to take children to playgroup, so a driving licence is useful.

You will do a lot of bending, lifting and clearing up and will be on the go from very early morning into the evening.

The future outlook

Although the minimum age for entry is 18, most childminders are older, with experience of care work. The demand for childminders can vary regionally and at different times of the year. Your registration certificate will tell you how many children you can look after.

Childminders can move into jobs such as care assistant or home care assistant, or can go on to train for similar work as a nursery nurse or registered nurse.

Qualifications and courses

- There are no academic entry qualifications for this work but qualifications in childcare are useful. Candidates must be 18 or over. They, and everyone in their households over 16, must be police-checked.
- All childminders must hold a registered childminders' certificate. Registration and inspection of childminders is administered by Ofsted in England and the Care Commission in Scotland.
- There are various childminding courses which can be studied part-time or by distance learning. The Council for Awards in Children's Care and Education (CACHE) awards the Certificate in Childminding Level 3. It is also possible to work towards the NVQ/SVQ Level 3 in Children's Care, Learning and Development. The National Childminding Association of England and Wales (NCMA), the Scottish Childminding Association (SCMA) and the Northern Ireland Childminding Association (NICMA) all provide advice on training and qualifications.
- Short courses for childminders may be provided locally by the NCMA/SCMA or local authorities.

CRCI:V | CLCI:KEB

Other related opportunities

- Care Assistant p525
- Home Care Assistant p534
- Nurse (Registered) p289
- Nursery Nurse p538
- Play Worker p180
- Road Crossing Assistant (Schools) p582
- Special Needs Learning Support Assistant p183
- Teacher p184
- Teaching / Classroom Assistant p187

Advantages/disadvantages

- The work will be varied, fun and likely to be full of surprises.
- Working from home often suits people who have young children themselves.
- Some jobs can be messy and unpleasant.
- The hours can be very long and it can sometimes be hard work for low pay.

Earnings guide

- Your earnings will depend on the number of children you look after, how many hours you work and where you live.
- Most childminders charge an hourly rate of between £4.77 and £6.20 an hour plus expenses. Your income can vary at different times of the year: for example, your hours might go up or down during school holidays.
- If you are in full-time employment you can expect around £9,500 per year when starting and a rise to £13,000–£17,000 when experienced. Top rates in London can be £25,000+ for experienced childminders.

Further information

www.cityandguilds.com/myperfectjob

National Childminding Association
8 Masons Hill
Bromley
Kent
BR2 9EY
020 8464 6164
www.ncma.org.uk

Scottish Childminding Association
Suite 3
7 Melville Terrace
Stirling
FK8 2ND
01786 445377
www.childminding.org

Northern Ireland Childminding Association
16–18 Mill Street
Newtownards
Co Down
BT23 4LU
028 9181 1015
www.nicma.org

Counselling Work

What the work involves

Counselling worker

- By helping people explore and talk about their problems, you will listen to what they say and ask questions to help them think carefully about what is troubling them.
- You will help them to see things more clearly, perhaps from a different point of view.
- You will not tell people what to do but will help them work out their next steps themselves.
- You might work with people with a range of problems or specialise in a particular area, such as bereavement, gambling, relationship difficulties or eating disorders.

Psychotherapist

- You will help people to reduce stress levels and overcome emotional problems through talking and doing things together.
- You may specialise in work with children or adults; you can help individuals, groups, families or couples.

Psychoanalyst

- You will work on a one-to-one basis with people who experience problems such as depression, anxieties, phobias or obsessive problems.
- You will listen to patients describing incidents and episodes from their life, trying to uncover any emotional problems and traumas which may underlie their manifest behaviour, which can be neurotic or psychotic.

The type of person suited to this work

As most of the work involves talking and listening to people, excellent communication skills are essential. It is also important to be able to put people at their ease and help them to feel comfortable when talking about feelings which they may find difficult and upsetting. You need to be interested in how the mind works, and in people's welfare.

As clients come from a variety of backgrounds and have a wide range of problems, you must be able to work with people from different cultures and ethnic groups.

Counselling workers may not always agree with the views held by their clients which means they have to be patient, open-minded, tolerant and non-judgemental. You must also be a highly discreet individual, as you will be given a lot of confidential information.

Working in the area of 'talking therapies', you will spend time analysing the outcomes of sessions, reflecting and researching similar cases, and forming new action plans for individual clients attempting to take next steps to recovery.

Working conditions

You will work indoors, usually sitting in a quiet comfortable room in places such as advice centres, schools, colleges, outpatient clinics and health centres.

If you are self-employed, you might work from home, visit your clients at home, or both.

You will work mainly with people on a one-to-one basis but also, on occasions, with couples, families or groups.

Most therapy or counseling sessions last no longer than 1 hour. Psychoanalysis sessions and, occasionally, psychotherapy appointments can run on for longer than 1 hour.

Some counselling work is done exclusively over the phone.

The future outlook

Counselling worker
Most people gain voluntary experience before moving into part-time paid work. They usually have experience in a career such as social work, nursing or teaching. While the demand is increasing, there is keen competition for full-time posts. You could work in education or health, or with a specialist agency. People often combine counselling work with another role. Experienced counselling workers can become self-employed or train for a specialist area.

Psychotherapist
Most psychotherapists work within the NHS, in either child or adult areas. There is a dearth of fully trained psychotherapists in work at present and, although NHS jobs have been cut back, the 'talking therapies' offer a cost-effective way to treat large numbers of emotionally disturbed people, so more posts will become available in the longer term.

Psychoanalyst
There are only 450 fully trained psychoanalysts working in England, Wales and Northern Ireland, and the majority work in private practice. The training is long, costly and demanding, and the treatment is really only suitable for those who have suffered emotional trauma in childhood or early adulthood and who have not responded to alternative forms of counselling help.

Qualifications and courses

Counselling worker

- There are no formal entry requirements for this career. Most counselling workers gain accredited membership of a relevant professional body, for example, the British Association for Counselling and Psychotherapy (BACP), COSCA (which accredits in Scotland) or the British Psychological Society (BPS).
- Counselling is often a second career, and maturity and experience are beneficial. Entrants may have worked as teachers/ lecturers, personal tutors, careers advisers, social workers or nurses, or in other fields.
- Many private, voluntary and charitable counselling organisations have their own training programmes which focus on a particular client group.
- Certificate courses in counselling skills and theory take 1 year part time. A Diploma/ Advanced Diploma course lasts 2–3 years, studying part time.
- To obtain BACP accreditation, candidates need to have studied a course lasting 1 year full time or 2–3 years part time, and must have a certain number of hours in practice.
- Degrees, HNDs and Foundation degrees in counselling are offered at a number of universities and colleges.

Psychotherapist

- People who work as psychotherapists may have originally trained as a mental health professional or taken a degree in psychology and then undertaken further specialised training. A number of psychotherapists have no background training in mental health work, but have simply taken a specialist course to gain accreditation to practice.

entry level

To both enter and train while working in this career, you will need qualifications at Level 3–8. Please refer to explanation on page vii.

Psychoanalyst

- The majority of applicants for psychoanalysis training have a degree in medicine or clinical psychology. It is then necessary to complete a training course approved by the International Psychoanalytical Association (IPA), during which trainees must undergo psychoanalysis themselves to ensure they are fit to practice.

Other related opportunities

- Advice Centre / Benefits Adviser p524
- Careers Adviser p526
- Debt Counsellor / Money Adviser p531
- Doctor p278
- Nurse (Registered) p289
- Therapist p309
- Youth and Community Worker p551

Advantages/disadvantages

- The work can be very rewarding but also highly stressful.
- Starting salaries can be low, until you are fully trained and have gained some experience.
- You must be able to take constructive criticism from an experienced counselling worker, therapist or psychoanalyst – both during and after completing training.
- Some clients may become dependent on therapy or analysis sessions and will have to be carefully assisted to refocus.

Earnings guide

- Expect £19,000–£25,000 per year when newly qualified.
- Qualified and experienced counselling workers earn £35,000.
- Earnings can reach £40,000–£50,000 with management responsibilities.
- Counselling workers are paid £35–£50 an hour when consulted within a private practice.
- Trainee psychotherapists earn £19,600–£25,000 per year. Once trained and with experience you can earn up to £42,500. Senior psychotherapists in the NHS are paid around £60,000+.
- Psychoanalysts set their own fees of £30–50+ per session. When qualified, you can earn up to £25,000 per year. With experience this rises to around £30,000+. Very experienced psychoanalysts earn £46,000–£50,000.

Further information

British Association for Counselling and Psychotherapy
BACP House
35–37 Albert Street
Rugby
CV21 2SG
0870 443 5252
www.bacp.co.uk

COSCA
18 Viewfield Street
Stirling
FK8 1UA
01786 475140
www.cosca.org.uk

British Psychological Society
St Andrews House
48 Princess Road East
Leicester
LE1 7DR
0116 254 9568
www.bps.org.uk

UK Council for Psychotherapy
2nd Floor Edward House
2 Wakley Street
London
EC1V 7LT
020 7014 9955
www.psychotherapy.org.uk

British Psychoanalytic Council
West Hill House
6 Swains Lane
London
N6 6QS
020 7267 3626
www.bcp.org.uk

British Psychoanalytical Society
112a Shirland Road
Maida Vale
London
W9 2EQ
020 7563 5000
www.psychoanalysis.org.uk

Relate
www.relate.org.uk

Debt Counsellor / Money Adviser

What the work involves

- You will help people in serious debt by giving them free, impartial and confidential advice.
- If your clients are being taken to court, you can guide them through the legal procedures and may represent them in court.
- To make sure clients are claiming available tax allowances and benefits, you will list clients' income and expenditure, then try to help them plan their spending by devising a budget.
- By liaising with creditors, you will try to arrange realistic repayments over a reasonable timescale.

The type of person suited to this work

People experience money problems for reasons such as unemployment, redundancy and bad money management; you will need to work with very different people and be non-judgemental about their circumstances. You will need good writing and speaking skills and a confident manner so that people trust you.

Much of the work involves figures, so you do need high-level numeracy skills. It is important to be a quick-thinking negotiator to get the best deal for your clients.

Good time management and work planning are essential, as are excellent ICT skills. This job suits people who have worked in financial services.

Working conditions

You will work with a computer in an office, usually in an advice centre, but may also spend time in court, at meetings or visiting clients in their own homes.

You could travel around locally, so a driving licence is useful. You will have to work some evenings, to visit your clients at home, perhaps doing shift work.

Other agencies may contact you for advice on money matters.

The future outlook

You are unlikely to become a money adviser straight from school. Some entrants have degrees; others gain experience through paid or voluntary work. Although money advisers are in demand, there are more applicants than jobs. Most openings are town- or city-based, in advice centres, money advice units or with local authorities.

Prospects are very limited. You could move into other social care jobs or change to work in the financial sector.

entry level

To both enter and train while working in this career, you will need qualifications at Level 2–8. Please refer to explanation on page vii.

Qualifications and courses

- There are no fixed minimum entry requirements for this kind of work but it is preferable to have a good standard of general education, including a minimum of 3 GCSEs /S grades (A–C/1–3).
- Many applicants have training and/or experience in finance or accounting, consumer advice or volunteer work in an advice centre.
- Many candidates apply for paid posts after voluntary work giving general advice, during which they undertake short training courses.
- Money advisers need a clear understanding of the problems faced by people with low income and debt and also detailed knowledge of the relevant laws. Short courses in specialist areas such as court procedures, housing law or bankruptcy are available.
- NVQs/SVQs Levels 2–4 in Advice and Guidance are available. The Money Advice Trust and the Citizens Advice Bureau also provide training courses for debt counsellors.
- Additional skills such as advising/ counselling, communication, information handling, ICT, managing money and general numeracy skills, problem solving and working with others are also highly valued.

CRCI:V

CLCI:KEZ

Other related opportunities

- Accountant p2
- Accounting Technician p4
- Counselling Work p529
- Housing Manager p535
- Volunteer Organiser p548
- Welfare Rights Officer / Worker p550

Advantages/disadvantages

- Debt counsellors meet a tremendous range of people with varied financial difficulties to untangle.
- You will get satisfaction by helping people balance their affairs – some may be very distressed and frightened.
- You may work some evenings and weekends.
- Some people can be unpleasant, rude and difficult.

Earnings guide

- On entry, debt counsellors can expect to earn around £16,000–£18,000 per year.
- Earnings can rise to £25,000 with experience.
- £28,000 is an average salary for senior posts. Some self-employed debt counsellors with lots of experience can earn up to £30,000.

Further information

Citizens Advice Bureau
Myddelton House
115–123 Pentonville Road
London
N1 9LZ
020 7833 2181
www.citizensadvice.org.uk

Advice UK
12th Floor
2 London Bridge House
25 London Bridge Street
London
SE1 9ST
020 7407 4070
www.adviceuk.org.uk

Money Advice Scotland
Suite 306
Pentagon Centre
36 Washington Street
Glasgow
G3 8AZ
0141 572 0237
www.moneyadvicescotland.org.uk

www.cityandguilds.com/myperfectjob

Education Welfare Officer

What the work involves

- You will work with young people who are not attending school, and their families, to support them back into education.
- Often, you will help explore alternatives to school. If things do not work out, you may have to prosecute parents of children who are not attending school.
- You will help families get all the benefits they are entitled to, such as free school meals, clothing or transport.
- As a link between families and schools, you will try to improve existing relationships – writing reports, attending meetings and case conferences.

The type of person suited to this work

As there can be many reasons for poor attendance at school, such as fear of bullying, caring responsibilities at home or difficulty in coping with school work, it is important to be open-minded and to listen impartially to school staff and parents. You will also need to be strong enough to prosecute a family if it becomes necessary.

You must enjoy working with young people and see the value in education, because you may have to convince parents who do not share your views of its importance.

You will also have to keep up to date with relevant legislation and you must be able to work on your own and as part of a team.

Working conditions

You will have an office base, but most of your time will be spent visiting young people and their families at home or looking for young people in the local area, so a driving licence is useful.

You may go to other agencies' offices to attend meetings and case conferences.

Families may view your interventions as interfering rather than assisting; you must always consider your personal safety.

The future outlook

There are about 4000 education welfare officers in England, Wales and Northern Ireland. In Scotland, they are called attendance officers. Education welfare officers tend to be people with a considerable amount of life and work experience.

There is a promotion structure within local authorities and you can become a specialist, for example dealing only with primary school pupils. With further training, you can do similar work in care and social services.

entry level

To both enter and train while working in this career, you will need qualifications at Level 3–8. Please refer to explanation on page vii.

Qualifications and courses

- There are a number of routes into this profession. Candidates generally have relevant work experience, for example in special education, counselling or youth work.
- Some entrants are already qualified with degree-level qualifications in areas such as social work or teaching. Degree courses usually require a minimum of 2 A levels/3 H grades and 5 GCSEs/S grades (A–C/1–3), including English and maths. In Northern Ireland, 3 A levels/5 H grades are required for social work degrees.
- Entry requirements are flexible but a good standard of general education to A level/H grade is preferred. It is also possible to get a job and study for qualifications through in-service training.
- A number of additional skills and aptitudes are valuable for entry to this work, for example skills in advising/counselling work or caring for people, high-level skills in communication, decision-making, ICT and information handling, as well as working with others.

CRCI:V

CLCI:KEB

Other related opportunities

- Careers Adviser p526
- Counselling Work p529
- Personal Adviser – Connexions p539
- Probation Officer p540
- Psychologist p541
- Social Worker p545
- Teacher p184
- Youth and Community Worker p551

Advantages/disadvantages

- The job suits independent individuals who can self-organise and manage their own workload.
- You will have the satisfaction of helping people – sometimes quite profoundly.
- You may have to work in the evenings to find parents at home.
- Some people may be abusive and you may find yourself in stressful situations.

Earnings guide

- You will earn around £20,000 per year on entry.
- With experience you could earn £24,000–£28,000.
- For a head of service salaries are up to £50,000+.

Further information

General Social Care Council
Goldings House
2 Hays Lane
London
SE1 2HB
020 7397 5100
www.gscc.org.uk

Northern Ireland Social Care Council
7th Floor, Millennium House
19–25 Great Victoria Street
Belfast
BT2 7AQ
028 9041 7600
www.niscc.info

Scottish Social Services Council
Compass House
11 Riverside Drive
Dundee
DD1 4NY
01382 207101
www.sssc.uk.com

Employment Agency Consultant / Interviewer

What the work involves

- You will interview people looking for jobs to investigate their skills and interests, matching individuals with suitable vacancies.
- Part of the work could be giving aptitude tests to clients to explore their skills needs and to suggest suitable training.
- Working with employers, you will make contact to ask about their organisations' skills needs, encouraging them to use the agency's services.
- You will help employers draw up job descriptions and may also draft adverts for your agency.

The type of person suited to this work

To discuss individuals' job requirements and potential, you will need good speaking and listening skills. Also, you will have to gain people's confidence and put them at ease. There is administrative work and record-keeping, so good writing and ICT skills are useful.

It is essential that employers continue to use your agency, so you will need persuasive skills to convince them your agency is the best for them. You may need to be persistent if they do not respond after a first approach.

Some job vacancies placed with your agency may need to be filled quickly, so you will need to be flexible, adaptable and able to cope under pressure.

Working conditions

You will be based in an employment agency, usually in a town centre. You will work normal office hours, but expect to work evenings and weekends if there is an unusually large contract. Most agencies have 'shop front' premises open to job-seekers.

You may travel to visit employers, so a driving licence is useful.

You will need to be smartly dressed and well groomed at all times.

The future outlook

There are over 16,000 employment agencies in the UK, mainly in towns and cities. Many are around London. Most entrants have experience in areas such as retail and sales, personnel or administrative work. More agencies are specialising in particular sectors of employment.

You would normally start as a trainee consultant and progress with your existing employer. Larger agencies have more clearly defined promotion structures. Some people become self-employed or move into other areas such as personnel and sales.

entry level

3–8

To both enter and train while working in this career, you will need qualifications at Level 3–8. Please refer to explanation on page vii.

Qualifications and courses

- There are no specific entry qualifications for this work, and entrants come from a variety of backgrounds.
- Often, entrants to this job have previous experience in personnel, sales or administration.
- Employers may recruit graduates to trainee recruitment consultant positions. No specific degree subject is required.
- Trainee consultants receive training on the job, with larger agencies running their own internal training. The Recruitment and Employment Confederation (REC) offer courses which cover topics such as essential legislation, candidate management and recruitment processes. It may also be possible to study for an NVQ/SVQ at Level 3 in Recruitment.

Other related opportunities

- Careers Adviser p526
- Human Resources / Personnel Officer p20
- Personal Adviser – Connexions p539

Advantages/disadvantages

- The work brings you into contact with a range of employers and jobseekers, which can be interesting.
- You will get satisfaction from helping job-seekers and employers.
- You could work awkward hours in an agency specialising in jobs such as transport and distribution or nursing.
- Some people can be difficult to deal with.

Earnings guide

- Expect around £14,000+ a year upon entry.
- Pay rises to between £17,000 and £22,000 with 2–3 years' experience.
- It is possible to reach £40,000 in very large agencies.
- Many agencies will pay commission, based on how many jobs you succeed in filling and how many jobs/contracts you bring to the agency.

Further information

Recruitment & Employment Confederation
36–38 Mortimer Street
London
W1W 7RG
020 7462 3260
www.rec.uk.com

Chartered Institute of Personnel and Development
CIPD House
151 The Broadway
London
SW19 1JQ
020 8971 9000
www.cipd.co.uk

ENTO
4th Floor
Kimberley House
47 Vaughan Way
Leicester
LE1 4SG
0116 251 7979
www.ento.co.uk

Home Care Assistant

What the work involves

- Home carers help look after people who find it difficult to care for themselves in their own homes.
- You will do housework including cleaning, washing and ironing, but you could also be involved in personal care including bathing and dressing.
- Talking and listening to your clients is part of the job and you will also help with shopping, changing their library books, etc.
- Most work is with the elderly but you may be helping people of all ages who have disabilities or who have been in hospital.

entry level

To both enter and train while working in this career, you will need qualifications at Level 1–2. Please refer to explanation on page vii.

The type of person suited to this work

As keeping someone's home clean and tidy is important, you will need to be good at and enjoy housework and laundry. You will be handling someone else's money when you go shopping which means you must be honest and reliable.

Your clients will want to talk to you and may tell you very personal things, so it is important to be a good listener and to be very discreet. You will also need to be able to get on well with all kinds of people.

As your clients will be having difficulty looking after themselves, it is important that you can see jobs that need to be done and do them without making your client feel you are taking over.

Working conditions

Most of your work will be in other people's homes.

You may travel quite a distance in your local area, so a driving licence is useful.

The work can be quite hard physically, so it is important to be fit.

You might work with only one client or visit a number of different people depending on your job. You could work from very early in the morning until late at night.

The future outlook

Home care assistants are in great demand with more people being cared for in their own homes. Many jobs are with local authorities but you could also work in the private sector or for an agency. Training for this work is mainly given on the job with an experienced home care assistant.

You could move into residential care work or train for other caring professions, such as nursing or social work.

Qualifications and courses

- There are no fixed entry qualifications for this job.
- Previous experience, for example through voluntary work, may be required.
- You can study a range of relevant courses full time at college prior to entry. The First Diploma in Caring is a 1-year course and does not require particular qualifications, although institutions may ask for some GCSEs/S grades. The National Diploma in Care and A level in Health and Social Care are 2-year courses which usually require 4 GCSEs/S grades (A–C/1–3) or an Intermediate GNVQ/First Diploma. In Scotland, you can take an HNC/D in Care which normally requires H grades for entry.
- Most training is work-based, and home care assistants can work towards an NVQ/SVQ in Health and Social Care.
- Other requirements include a caring disposition, good communication skills, practical and physical capabilities and the ability to work well with others.

CRCI:V

CLCI:KEB

Other related opportunities

- Care Assistant p525
- Childminder p528
- Cleaner p418
- Nurse (Registered) p289
- Nursery Nurse p538
- Social Worker p545

Advantages/disadvantages

- The workload and clients are extremely variable, and you will get satisfaction from helping people.
- It is interesting to meet different people with different life experiences.
- Some jobs may be unpleasant.
- You may work unsocial hours, including weekends and public holidays; also, many jobs are part time.

Earnings guide

- You will start at £11,000–£12,300 per year if working for a local authority. With experience and holding a senior position you can get around £21,000.
- Expect to start on around £11,100 working in the private sector.
- You can earn up to £18,000 per year if you provide healthcare for people at home who have just been discharged from hospital (this role is called rehabilitation assistant).

Further information

www.cityandguilds.com/myperfectjob

General Social Care Council
Goldings House
2 Hays Lane
London
SE1 2HB
020 7397 5100
www.gscc.org.uk

Northern Ireland Social Care Council
7th Floor, Millennium House
19–25 Great Victoria Street
Belfast
BT2 7AQ
028 9041 7600
www.niscc.info

Scottish Social Services Council
Compass House
11 Riverside Drive
Dundee
DD1 4NY
01382 207101
www.sssc.uk.com

Housing Manager

What the work involves

- As a housing manager, you will deal with the day-to-day running of rented properties.
- Jobs include interviewing people to assess their housing needs and allocating vacant properties to tenants.
- You will advise tenants on issues about the property and on any benefits they may be entitled to, and take action if rents are not paid.
- Other duties include making sure housing estates are kept in good order, keeping records up to date and liaising with other agencies, including social work services.

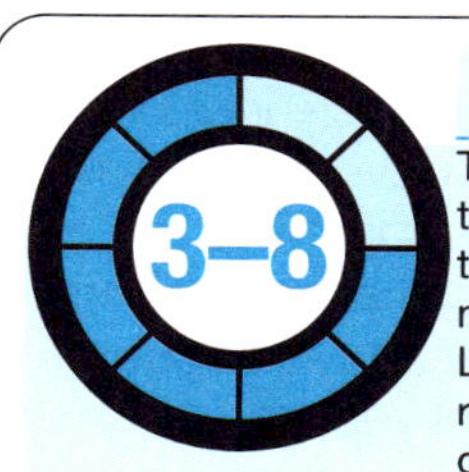

entry level

To both enter and train while working in this career, you will need qualifications at Level 3–8. Please refer to explanation on page vii.

The type of person suited to this work

As the job concerns people's homes, it is important to have a genuine interest in housing families and individuals. You need to be well organised, making sure that properties do not lie empty. You will need to get along with all sorts of people – tenants come from quite different backgrounds.

A good knowledge of housing (and other) benefits is important, including being thorough to check that your information is accurate.

You will need to be flexible to meet everyone's needs, for example allowing guide dogs in property where dogs are normally not allowed. The work will also involve a lot of administration; you will need good ICT skills.

Working conditions

You will be based in an office, but go out to visit tenants and properties, so a driving licence is useful. Work will follow the normal Monday to Friday working week, but you can be asked to provide emergency shift cover.

Mostly, your tasks will be indoors, but you may spend time outdoors looking at exterior repairs and general maintenance. You will need to use computer programs on the job, but training is usually given.

The future outlook

Most jobs are with local authorities but there are also opportunities with the large number of housing associations, housing trusts and private letting agencies. There is a clear promotion structure in local authorities but this can vary within other organisations. You may need to move around to widen your experience. There are opportunities for further training to keep up with developments in housing, in government policies, etc.

Qualifications and courses

- There is no standard entry route into housing. Many people gain qualifications from within the profession.
- The Chartered Institute of Housing (CIH) is the professional body with responsibility for housing.
- Entrants to the profession will be encouraged to study for qualifications recognised by the CIH. To become a corporate member of the CIH, candidates must gain the CIH Professional Qualification and pass the Test of Professional Practice.
- The CIH validates a range of Certificates in Housing at Levels 2–4. Students are usually part time and sponsored by their employer.
- There are also degree courses in social policy, housing and town planning, which normally require 2 A levels/3 H grades (A–C). Entry requirements are flexible for mature candidates. Postgraduate programmes at certificate and diploma level are available at a number of universities and colleges. NVQs/SVQs at Levels 2–4, taken on the job, are an alternative route to gaining qualifications in housing.
- In addition, skills in advising/counselling, communication, information handling, organising, money management, supervision/management and working with others are all valuable.

CRCI:V

CLCI:UH

Other related opportunities

- Social Worker p545
- Warden (Accommodation) p549
- Welfare Rights Officer / Worker p550

Advantages/disadvantages

- Housing managers are busy people who handle numerous different tasks each day.
- You will get great satisfaction from helping people find homes.
- Some tenants may be difficult and aggressive.
- Certain tasks as a housing manager could be unpleasant, for example dealing with rent arrears.

Earnings guide

- Expect around £17,900 per year on entry.
- £20,000–£27,000 is paid to those with experience.
- £60,000 is possible, but only at senior management/director level.

Further information

Chartered Institute of Housing
Octavia House
Westwood Way
Coventry
CV4 8JP
024 7685 1700
www.cih.org

Chartered Institute of Housing in Northern Ireland
Carmoney House
Edgewater Office Park
Belfast
BT3 9JQ
028 9077 8222
www.cih.org

Chartered Institute of Housing in Scotland
6 Palmerston Place
Edinburgh
EH12 5AA
0131 225 4544
www.cihscotland.org

Life Coach

What the work involves

- You will help people – independent clients or employees – to recognise and develop their special attributes and skills.
- You will coach individuals to become more successful in career matters, financial affairs or personal relationships.
- Using empathy and exceptional listening skills, you will establish a warm, personal yet professional relationship with clients.
- In one-to-ones – sometimes over the phone – you will help clients draw up realistic short- and long-term goals.
- With your client, you will enter cycles of agreement and commitment; later you will review and revise the action plans you have created.

entry level

To both enter and train while working in this career, you will need qualifications at Level 3. Please refer to explanation on page vii.

The type of person suited to this work

Once a bond of trust is established – that you are non-judgemental and hold personal information in strictest confidence – individuals will reveal their present feelings and frustrations, their future ambitions and their perceived restrictions to progress.

Besides integrity and discretion, life coaches need excellent interpersonal skills, patience and perseverance to allow clients the time to set themselves goals for change.

You will get satisfaction from seeing people fulfil their potential. Life coaching takes clarity of thought and firmness of purpose. You may need to overcome an inherent inertia (lack of drive to change) in your clients to get them to make progress!

Working conditions

You will agree timetables with clients for coaching sessions and hold one-to-ones at their work-base or in a neutral location. Later sessions are often by phone or email. Many life coaches work with busy, highly successful chief executives, usually outside normal business hours.

Coaching sessions can be weekly, fortnightly or monthly; the frequency may change.

You will review notes and recordings made during coaching to reflect on clients' progress.

The future outlook

Life coaching is a relatively new field, but interest has increased as more attention is paid to developing the whole person – both within and outside the workplace. A life coach can help to refocus individuals' goals and aspirations, improving work–life balance and job satisfaction, boosting productivity and creating good teamwork. All these factors can help companies with staff retention.

Life coaches work as independent consultants or for business consultancy agencies.

Qualifications and courses

- Although there are no specific requirements to enter this area of work, you need to have gained a great deal of life experience and to have tasted many different approaches to conducting business and managing an organisation's workforce performance and delivery.
- A degree in human resources work, organisations and structures, sociology or psychology would be helpful startpoints. For entry to a degree course, you need a minimum of 5 GCSEs/S grades at A–C/1–3, plus 2 or 3 A levels/H grades with an emphasis on the humanities.
- There are a number of private agencies and academies offering training in life coaching, for example the Coaching Academy, where you can take a 2-day fast-track course by distance learning to focus on corporate or individual (personal performance) life coaching.
- It is possible to take a longer diploma course in life coaching.
- Most life coaches plan and build unique, personalised coaching programmes which work best for the particular individual.

CRCI:Q

CLCI:G

Other related opportunities

- Careers Adviser p526
- Counselling Work p529
- Employment Agency Consultant / Interviewer p533
- Personal Adviser – Connexions p539
- Probation Officer p540
- Social Worker p545
- Teacher p184

Advantages/disadvantages

- There is great satisfaction in observing changes in your clients.
- If clients fail to implement action plans, it can be dispiriting and frustrating.
- You may have long-term coaching relationships with clients – who want to work on different aspects of their lives.

Earnings guide

- Pay is usually at sessional rates.
- Working for an agency, you can earn around £30 per session plus expenses. Hourly rates for private clients could be £40–£100+ for a coaching session lasting an hour.
- Life coaches who become well-known and sought out can charge higher fees for periods of life coaching lasting 6 months or longer.

Further information

Coaching Academy
0800 783 4823
www.the-coaching-academy.com

New Insights
Brightwire House
114a Church Road
Hove
East Sussex
BN3 2EB
0845 094 0212
www.life-coach-training-uk.com

Achievement Specialists Ltd
Achievement House
Southwick Road
Bournemouth
Dorset
BH6 5PU
01264 326229
www.achievementspecialists.co.uk

Mobility Officer – Visually Impaired

What the work involves

- You will visit blind and partially sighted people to explore the help they need to keep their independence, and then organise that support.
- A major part of your job will be showing your clients how to perform day-to-day tasks, such as cooking, as well as help with paperwork, sorting out benefits and finance.
- In addition, you will provide training in mobility – walking with a white cane and making journeys by public transport.
- Your role will be to provide ongoing support, to involve them in social activities.

The type of person suited to this work

As the work often involves dealing with people coming to terms with sight loss, you will need to be sympathetic, patient and understanding. Also, you will need to be a good listener because people may unburden themselves on you. Tact is essential when dealing with carers and families who may be over-protective.

You will be in contact with many different people and agencies, so you will need to get on with all sorts of people. There is a lot of report writing which needs good writing and ICT skills.

Clear decision making is needed to determine the best way to help, plus good organisational skills to manage your time and workload.

Working conditions

You will be based in an office but will spend most of your time visiting clients in their own homes.

You may have to travel widely in your area, so a driving licence is useful.

Some time will be spent out of doors doing mobility training, and some indoors, helping people learn ways to use their kitchens without sight.

You may accompany clients on outings and to appointments.

The future outlook

Most jobs are with local authority social work departments, statutory and voluntary agencies and schools and colleges providing specialist services for people with visual impairment.

There are few jobs and you may have to move to work, and to broaden your experience later in your career.

Prospects for promotion are limited. It is possible to retrain for jobs such as careers adviser, personal adviser (Connexions) or social work.

Other related opportunities

- Careers Adviser p526
- Counselling Work p529
- Personal Adviser - Connexions p539
- Social Worker p545
- Teacher p184

Advantages/disadvantages

- The work is challenging and each case requires individual consideration.
- It is very satisfying seeing people keep their independence and adjust to sight loss.
- The job may be emotionally demanding and you will need to remain impartial.
- Some clients may be reluctant to accept help.

Further information

Royal National Institute of the Blind
105 Judd Street
London
WC1H 9NE
0845 702 3153
www.rnib.org.uk

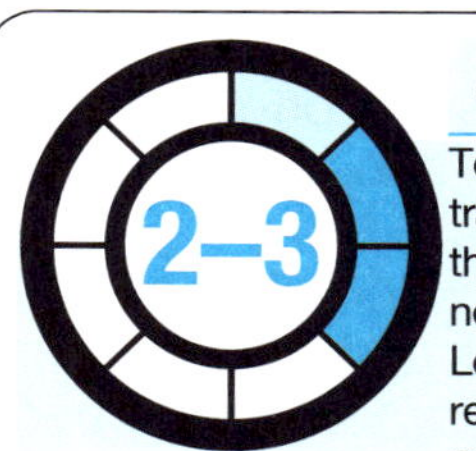

entry level

To both enter and train while working in this career, you will need qualifications at Level 2–3. Please refer to explanation on page vii.

Qualifications and courses

- To work as a mobility/rehabilitation officer for the visually impaired within social services, you will need the Diploma of Higher Education (DipHE) in Rehabilitation (Visual Impairment). The course is a 2-year distance-learning programme via UCE Birmingham and comprises specialist modules at certificate, diploma and degree level.
- You will be required to undertake an 80-day placement with a statutory or voluntary agency in the second year of the course.
- Candidates must be at least 18, preferably with some experience of care work. Entry requirements usually include GCSEs/S grades in English and maths (A–C/1–3) and A levels/H grades or BTEC National Diplomas. Entry for mature candidates is flexible but they must be able to demonstrate that they can already study at A level/H grade.
- In addition, employers will look for skills in counselling, caring for people, communication, organisation and working with others.

Earnings guide

- Salaries are around £18,600–£24,200 per year on entry.
- This can rise to £27,000 with experience.
- You can expect to earn up to £30,000 a year with promotion to a team leader post, but these opportunities are limited.

Nursery Nurse

What the work involves

- Within a nursery or private home, you will look after young children, from newborn babies to aged eight, ensuring they are safe and comfortable.
- Much of your work will involve feeding, changing, dressing and bathing babies and helping older children to develop in areas such as language, art, practical skills and music.
- You will plan the day to include play, exercise, meals and rest, to keep children healthy and mentally stimulated.
- You may work closely with hospitals, schools and other agencies, keeping them in touch with children's progress.

The type of person suited to this work

As nursery nurses spend most of their time with children, they need to enjoy caring for them, being outgoing, with a friendly manner towards children and adults. They also need to be patient and tolerant to deal with different types of behaviour.

You will need to be able to talk to children at their level and listen to what they say. Planning activities needs imagination and creativity, and it is helpful to be good at art, practical tasks and singing.

This job can be quite variable, so you will need to be flexible, enjoy team working and be comfortable working with many different types of people from all cultures and backgrounds.

Working conditions

Most of your work will be indoors in a nursery, school, hospital or private home. You may live in if you are a nanny in a private home. You might wear a uniform and protective clothing for some tasks.

If you have to travel locally with children in your care, a driving licence is useful.

The work involves bending, lifting and playing with children so you need to be physically fit.

The future outlook

Nursery nurses work in nurseries, schools and hospitals, and as nannies in private homes. With the large rise in working mothers, there is high demand for qualified childcare staff throughout the UK. Sometimes, there are opportunities to travel, particularly in private work.

You can start to train straight from school or after gaining experience in other types of work. Promotion prospects are limited. You could take further training to enter paediatric nursing or primary school teaching.

entry level

To both enter and train while working in this career, you will need qualifications at Level 2–3. Please refer to explanation on page vii.

Qualifications and courses

- Academic qualifications are not necessary to work as a nursery nurse, although a good general standard of education is an advantage.
- There is a framework of nationally-accredited nursery nurse qualifications in England and Wales. Typical qualifications include CACHE Level 3 Diploma in Child Care and Education; BTEC National Diploma in Children's Care, Learning and Development and NVQ/SVQ Level 3 in Children's Care, Learning and Development.
- In Scotland, registration of nursery workers has been introduced. From March 2007, early years practitioners with qualifications such as SVQ Level 3 or an HNC can register with the Scottish Social Services Council (SSSC). Support workers, qualified to SVQ Level 2 or equivalent, can register from October 2008.
- Supervised practical training forms an important part of all courses.
- If you are aged 16–24, it might be possible to train on the job with part-time attendance on a training course through an Apprenticeship/Skillseekers.
- Other useful skills and aptitudes for nursery nursing include caring for people, good communication and organisational skills, plus the ability to work with others.
- All applicants must pass a Criminal Records Bureau check before working with young people.

CRCI:V

CLCI:KEB

Other related opportunities

- Care Assistant p525
- Childminder p528
- Home Care Assistant p534
- Nurse (Registered) p289
- Special Needs Learning Support Assistant p183
- Teacher p184
- Teaching / Classroom Assistant p187

Advantages/disadvantages

- The work is varied and rewarding.
- As well as children, you will work with a wide range of adults.
- The hours can be long, particularly in nanny work, and you may have to work shifts and weekends.
- The pay is fairly low.

Earnings guide

- Expect to start on around £9,000–£11,500 per year.
- You can earn £14,000–£17,000 with experience.
- Salaries can rise to rise to £30,000+ for a senior post.
- £23,000+ a year, with accommodation and food, is possible for a nanny working in a private home.

Further information

www.cityandguilds.com/myperfectjob

National Training Organisation for Early Years
Pilgrims Lodge
Holywell Hill
St Albans
Hertfordshire
AL1 1ER
01727 738300
www.early-years-nto.org.uk

CACHE (Council for Awards in Children's Care and Education)
Beauort House
Grosvenor Road
St Albans
Hertfordshire
AL1 3AW
01727 818616
www.cache.org.uk

Care Commission
Compass House
11 Riverside Drive
Dundee
DD1 4DY
0845 6030890
www.carecommission.com

Personal Adviser – Connexions

What the work involves

- You will provide information, advice and guidance to young people in England aged 13–19 on their options in learning, personal development and future careers.
- You will work with young people whose circumstances prevent them making the best of their opportunities.
- With schools/colleges, training providers and employers, you will help design programmes to meet individuals' learning needs.
- Being a personal adviser also involves interaction with parents/carers and a range of other support agency professionals.

The type of person suited to this work

It is important to be able to gain young people's trust and confidence. Excellent communication skills are needed to talk with them, listening carefully to what they say.

You need to have a flexible approach and an ability to adapt quickly to unexpected situations. The job involves dealing with many different types of people. Patience and tolerance are vital since people develop in different ways. You must be non-judgemental, as you may not always agree with your clients, yet need to forge close links of trust.

The work involves administration and negotiation with other agencies, so report writing, ICT and communication skills are required.

Working conditions

You could be based in a school, college, Connexions centre or Connexions information resource area. You may meet clients in their home or a neutral setting such as a café.

You will travel locally to visit employers, young people you work with and representatives from other agencies working with young people. A driving licence and car are useful.

Work could include some evenings and occasional weekends.

The future outlook

Most entrants are at least 21 and have previous experience working with young people, through either voluntary or paid work. The Connexions service only operates in England.

Some personal advisers specialise in supporting a small number of young people with severe problems over a long period of time, while others work with a larger group over shorter periods. There is a promotion structure within Connexions, based on qualifications and experience.

entry level

To both enter and train while working in this career, you will need qualifications at Level 4–8. Please refer to explanation on page vii.

Qualifications and courses

- Many entrants to this work already hold the NVQ/SVQ Level 4 in Advice and Guidance, the professional qualification for careers advisers. To qualify as a personal adviser, they must then complete the Diploma for Connexions Personal Advisers or the Understanding Connexions Training Programme. Usually, the training programmes can be attended by day release, followed up with recording information, research and data analysis, and short theses based on your job.
- It is also possible to enter without the NVQ/SVQ Level 4 and work as a probationary personal adviser. You can become fully qualified by working towards the Diploma for Connexions Personal Advisers and the NVQ/SVQ.
- Both the Diploma and the Understanding Connexions Training Programme are accredited by universities.
- You need to be endorsed by a Connexions Partnership and vetted to work with young people.
- Other Key Skills are advising and counselling, communication, information handling and working with others.

Other related opportunities

- Advice Centre / Benefits Adviser p524
- Counselling Work p529
- Employment Agency Consultant / Interviewer p533
- Human Resources / Personnel Officer p20
- Probation Officer p540
- Teacher p184
- Youth and Community Worker p551

Advantages/disadvantages

- The work will be interesting and varied and bring you into contact with many different people.
- You will find it satisfying to see young people moving on.
- Some people may be unpleasant and difficult.
- You might have to work some evenings.

Earnings guide

- Expect to earn around £18,500–£22,000 per year while training.
- When qualified you can get £22,000–£27,000.
- Earnings can rise to £29,000–£35,000 with 5–10 years' experience and perhaps a specialism.
- You may receive an additional cost of living allowance if you work in and around London.

Further information

Connexions Service National Unit
Department for Children, Schools and Families
Moorfoot
Sheffield
S1 4PP
0114 259 1283
www.connexions.gov.uk

Probation Officer

What the work involves

- You will spend time interviewing offenders to provide courts with pre-sentence reports offering guidance on the kind of sentence the court should consider.
- Working on a regular basis with offenders, you will ensure court orders are carried out and try to help your clients not to re-offend.
- You will work closely with other agencies to solve practical problems that offenders have in obtaining work, benefits, housing, etc.
- You may also work with victims of crime, helping them recover from the experience.

entry level

To both enter and train while working in this career, you will need qualifications at Level 4–8. Please refer to explanation on page vii.

The type of person suited to this work

As you may work with particular offenders over a period of time, it is important to gain their trust and confidence so that you can help them. You will need to be able to cope under pressure when dealing with offenders who are non-compliant, aggressive or not coping well.

You will work with people of all ages and backgrounds, from colleagues to clients; this means you will need good speaking, listening and negotiating skills. It is important to be able to get on with all types of people.

A good knowledge of the criminal justice system is essential, as is the ability to research information and write clear, concise reports.

Working conditions

You will be based in an office but will move around to interview clients in prison or in their homes.

Much of your time will be spent in court, presenting pre-sentence reports and dealing with offenders once they are sentenced. Also, you will prepare reports and contribute to risk assessments for scrutiny by the Parole Board.

You may travel quite a bit locally, so a driving licence is useful.

The future outlook

In England and Wales, probation officers work for the National Probation Service. Crown Courts and some larger Magistrates' Courts have a probation team attached to them. There is a great need for new probation officers across England and Wales. In Scotland, the work is carried out by the Criminal Justice Team in local authority social work services. Court Teams are attached to the Sheriff and High Courts.

Promotion to senior grades is possible but management posts mean less contact with clients.

Qualifications and courses

- To qualify as a probation officer in England and Wales you will need a Diploma in Probation Studies (DipPS). Trainees are employed by individual probation services and follow a 2-year integrated course combining an NVQ Level 4 in Community Justice with a degree in Community Justice (Probation Studies). The minimum age to start the DipPS is 22.
- As a general guideline, the following qualifications are needed: candidates under 21 – 2 A levels and 3 GCSEs (A–C) or 3 A levels and 1 GCSE (A–C); candidates aged 21–25 – 5 GCSEs (A–C); candidates over 25 – formal qualifications may not be required but the recruitment and selection process includes written exercises designed to test the applicant's ability to study at a higher education level.
- Some experience of dealing with people in difficulties is essential. Voluntary work in a local youth club, young offenders' institution or with Millennium Volunteers could all count.
- In Scotland, trainees are required to be at least 22 and to hold a degree in social work.
- Other useful attributes include skills in advising or counselling work, communication, ICT and information handling, supervision and management, plus experience in working with others.

CRCI:V

CLCI:KEB

Other related opportunities

- Careers Adviser p526
- Counselling Work p529
- Education Welfare Officer p532
- Personal Adviser – Connexions p539
- Social Worker p545
- Solicitor / Notary Public p349

Advantages/disadvantages

- The work is varied, challenging and never dull.
- You will get satisfaction from helping people stay out of trouble.
- A considerable amount of time is spent preparing court reports.
- You may find it hard to remain impartial.
- You will be on call at weekends – on a rota basis.

Earnings guide

- Expect around £17,000–£18,400 per year while training.
- Your salary will rise to £22,299–£34,000 when qualified and experienced.
- Earnings can go up to around £38,000 as a chief probation officer.
- In Scotland, criminal justice social workers earn around £21,500–£26,000.

Further information

National Probation Directorate
Home Office, Horseferry House
Dean Ryle Street
London
SW1 2AW
020 7217 0659
www.homeoffice.gsi.gov.uk

National Association of Probation Officers
4 Chivalry Road
London
SW11 1HT
020 7223 4887
www.napo.org.uk

Scottish Social Services Council
Compass House
11 Riverside Drive
Dundee
DD1 4NY
01382 207101
www.sssc.uk.com

Psychologist

What the work involves

- Psychologists work scientifically, gathering information to establish how people act and to deduce why they act as they do.
- You will be talking to people about their behaviour and difficulties, using different interview techniques and psychometric tests depending on the client.
- You will work with a wide range of people, listening carefully to what they say, gathering accurate information to then analyse.
- Generally, you will specialise in a particular branch of psychology.

Clinical psychologist

- You will work with people whose health problems affect their behaviour, to learn what they do and why they do it.
- You will assess clients to identify problems and design a treatment programme or therapy, for example relaxation training to control their anxieties.

Counselling psychologist

- You will help individuals and groups deal with stressful times in their lives.
- You will help people make decisions for themselves, using psychological theories and techniques to help them deal with the difficulties in their lives.

Educational psychologist

- You will work with children with social, behavioural or learning difficulties to assess their progress and their academic and emotional needs.
- You will give them help and guidance, and design activities which will help them to learn.

Forensic psychologist

- You will apply psychology to the criminal and civil justice systems.
- Your job will involve direct contact with offenders to carry out assessments and you may design programmes to help in their rehabilitation.

Health psychologist

- This is a new and rapidly growing field of applied psychology which promotes changes in people's attitudes, behaviour and thinking about health.
- You will encourage people to adopt a healthier lifestyle, for example by taking more exercise, or help patients and their families to cope with illness.

Occupational psychologist

- Here, as a psychologist, you will explore how organisations function and how people behave at work to improve an organisation's efficiency and employees' job satisfaction.
- You will help managers plan how they recruit and train staff, and advise on matters concerning communication between individuals in the workplace, the most effective working environment and coping with change.

The type of person suited to this work

As the work is mostly about people and their behaviour, an interest in people, their personalities, abilities and interests is essential. The work involves contact with many different types of people which means you must be good at relating to others and have excellent communication skills.

As psychology involves using scientifically gathered information to analyse behaviour, an interest in science and problem-solving is fundamental.

Psychologists must think logically, analyse data and statistics, and work in an organised and methodical way. They need administrative and ICT skills for writing reports and analyses, and presenting information at case conferences or company meetings.

Qualifications and courses

- Entrants must be graduates with Graduate Basis for Registration (GBR) with the British Psychological Society (BPS).
- GBR can be obtained by taking a BPS-accredited degree in psychology or a non-accredited degree plus a conversion course.
- Additional postgraduate training is usually required to qualify in a specialist area.
- For entry to a degree course, you will need 2 A levels/3 H grades (A–C) including mathematics.

Clinical psychologist
- To specialise, you need to follow a BPS-accredited 3-year postgraduate training course, which is mostly hospital-based.

Counselling psychologist
- The BPS Diploma in Counselling Psychology (3 years full time or part-time equivalent), or a 3-year full-time BPS-accredited postgraduate training course in counselling psychology is necessary to achieve qualified status.

Educational psychologist
- Candidates must hold a BPS-accredited Honours degree in psychology and have had work experience with children and young people. This need not necessarily be in teaching; experience as a learning support assistant, educational social worker, learning mentor or care worker may also be acceptable.
- Candidates in England, Wales and Northern Ireland must also complete a 3-year, full-time BPS-accredited doctorate in educational psychology. In Scotland, candidates complete a 2-year Master's degree, followed by a year of supervised practice.

Forensic psychologist
- A BPS-accredited MSc or diploma in Forensic Psychology, followed by at least 2 years' supervised practice, are prerequisites for qualified status.

Health psychologist
- A BPS-accredited MSc and 2 years of appropriate supervised experience are essential for professional recognition.

Occupational psychologist
- Psychology graduates need to gain an accredited MSc followed by 2 years of supervised practice, or 3 years' supervised practice and the BPS Postgraduate Certificate in Occupational Psychology to become fully qualified.

entry level

To both enter and train while working in this career, you will need qualifications at Level 4–8. Please refer to explanation on page vii.

Working conditions

Your work will be mainly indoors in a school, college, hospital or business – depending on your job; however, you may be outdoors in some types of work.

You will probably have to travel between different locations, so a driving licence is useful.

You will be working with people on a one-to-one or group basis.

Some research work in laboratories will involve using specialist equipment.

The future outlook

Entry to psychology degrees is competitive and it takes a long time to become a chartered psychologist. Not everyone who leaves with a degree in psychology will find work within the area because there are more graduates than vacancies. The jobs available tend to be within government services, education and health, in the public and private sectors. Some people use a psychology degree as a way into other types of work, including careers guidance, human resources work and teaching. Ongoing professional development will be important throughout your career.

Clinical psychologist
Clinical psychologists, the biggest specialist area, work mainly in the Health Service but there are also opportunities in the Civil Service and private practice.

Counselling psychologist
Counselling psychologists are found mainly in health and social services but may also be found in private practice.

Educational psychologist
Most educational psychologists work for local authorities but there an increasing number are self-employed as independent consultants.

Forensic psychologist
Forensic psychologists work mainly in the legal system, for example within prisons or youth custody centres.

Health psychologist
Health psychology is a rapidly growing field with opportunities in many health-related areas.

Occupational psychologist
Occupational psychologists work in large companies in the public and private sectors. They can work with government and public services as private consultants. Some specialise in a certain area, for example ergonomics (the interaction of people with where they work), or health and safety – studying the causes of accidents and how to prevent them.

Other related opportunities

- Careers Adviser p526
- Counselling Work p529
- Health and Safety Adviser p19
- Human Resources / Personnel Officer p20
- Personal Adviser – Connexions p539
- Social Worker p545

Advantages/disadvantages

- The work is varied, interesting and challenging.
- You will meet many different types of people.
- Some people may be aggressive or even violent and you may sometimes have difficulty remaining impartial.
- You will have a lot of recording and administrative follow-up work to do.

Earnings guide

- As a graduate trainee in the NHS expect around £22,500 per year depending on the kind of work you do.
- This rises with experience to £27,500–£37,500.
- Up to £43,000 is possible in a senior post. Senior posts in the private sector can offer up to £80,000.
- You will be paid an additional allowance if you work in or around London and salaries throughout the country will vary, depending on your specialism.

Further information

British Psychological Society
St Andrews House
48 Princess Road East
Leicester
LE1 7DR
0116 254 9568
www.bps.org.uk

Religious Work

What the work involves

- While the work performed may change across different faiths, certain tasks are shared by most religions. The most common include:
  - Conducting meetings/services and prayers, reading from texts and taking the lead in set procedures and traditional forms.
  - Leading important ceremonies such as weddings, funerals and baptisms/naming ceremonies.
  - Listening to people's problems and giving support, advice and guidance.
  - Playing a key part in the local community, attending local events, focusing on the spiritual welfare of children, their parents/carers, the sick, the bereaved, etc, often paying home visits. A Jewish rabbi, Anglican vicar, Muslim imam or Roman Catholic priest can all be consulted on points of faith or law.
- Religious individuals can make a devotional career choice, dedicating their life to prayer, meditation or contemplation, while working to support the order of nuns, monks, Hari Krishna devotees, etc, within a local community. Some people of strong belief express their reverence and faith by doing voluntary work to sustain their local church, temple, mosque or synagogue.

The type of person suited to this work

You will need to have dedication and strong belief, as well as a thorough understanding of your religion's values and traditions. If you are the leader for your faith in the community, you will be expected to discuss and defend your faith.

You will meet and deal with many different kinds of people and will need excellent speaking and listening skills. It is important to be friendly, sympathetic and discreet when dealing with personal confidences and sensitive issues.

You will also spend time researching information and preparing talks, and you may have to learn long passages by heart which requires a good memory.

For most religious workers, the job is a vocation or calling.

Working conditions

Some of your work will be office-based, in your home or at your place of worship, but you may be expected to deliver or attend morning and evening worship.

You will travel locally a lot, so a driving licence may be useful.

You may spend time visiting people at home, in hospitals and in care homes, attending local meetings and events such as festivals and religious 'life cycle' events.

Many religions require particular forms of dress.

The future outlook

There are around 18 recognised religions in the UK. Each religion has a different structure and there is no set way of being promoted.

Most people become religious leaders after gaining substantial life experience, so you are unlikely to enter this career straight from school or university. Young people of religious faith frequently do volunteering work, in this country or abroad, helping disadvantaged young and older people improve their lives through education, their own efforts and moral purpose.

You may travel to holy places or do missionary work. Some religions move their leaders to other areas after a spell in one place.

Many religious leaders work at an international level to erase points of difference, reduce ignorance and intolerance, and find ways of living together to eradicate religious hatred.

Qualifications and courses

- There is no set route or standard entry requirements to become a religious worker, although a good general education is useful. The most important entry requirements are a strong belief in your faith and an active interest in its rules and traditions.
- In a number of religions, there are restrictions on who can become a religious leader, particularly in terms of gender, although some barriers have come down.
- Age is not a restriction to becoming a religious leader, and life experience, communicative ability and maturity can be the three most essential skills needed.
- It is possible to study religion, divinity or theology at universities or colleges. Degree and diploma courses are available across the UK, but it is important to check carefully that the course is acceptable to your religion.

entry level

To both enter and train while working in this career, you will need qualifications at Level 4–8. Please refer to explanation on page vii.

- Each religion has a different way of training its religious leaders, and this will often involve attending a specialist school or college for several years.

Other related opportunities

- Counselling Work p529
- Education Welfare Officer p532
- Funeral Work p423
- Lecturer p178
- Social Worker p545
- Teacher p184

Advantages/disadvantages

- This work provides variety and challenge.
- You will meet many different types of people.
- You will be on call 24 hours a day, seven days a week.
- You may have to make lifestyle changes, for example not getting married or eating only certain foods.

Earnings guide

- Religious leaders often work on a voluntary basis with expenses to cover costs.
- Some faiths provide accommodation.
- Stipends for those who are salaried may start low on around £8,000–£9,500 per year. When experienced you may get £23,000+.
- Some people also have other paid employment.

Further information

INFORM (Information Network Focus on Religious Movements)
Houghton Street
London
WC2A 2AE
020 7955 7654
www.inform.ac

Inter Faith Network
8A Lower Grosvenor Place
London
SW1W 0EN
020 7931 7726
www.interfaith.org.uk

Social Worker

What the work involves

Field social worker

- To help and support people at difficult times in their lives, you will assess people's needs, then plan and deliver a range of services to help them solve their problems.
- You will spend time listening to what they say, and may visit your clients at home to get a complete picture of their lives.
- Your work will be with health professionals, schools, the police, benefits agencies and the courts, depending on your clients, who could be of any stage of their lives and from any background.
- You will also attend meetings, conferences and perhaps court hearings, and prepare and write reports.

Residential social worker

- You will help people in residential care to be as independent as possible by caring for their physical needs and providing counselling, teaching and appropriate therapy.
- You will help clients to budget their money, you will probably have to sort out their benefits. This is all part of developing their personal and social skills.
- Your residents could be people of any age, many of whom may have physical disabilities, learning difficulties, or mental health or emotional problems.
- You will attend meetings and conferences, deal with administration and write reports.

The type of person suited to this work

Dealing with people and their problems requires being able to get on with a wide range of people and understand different attitudes and lifestyles. You need to have excellent communication skills to talk to people, listen to them and write reports.

You will have to have lots of patience as clients will not always be ready to accept your advice and support. You will need to be able to keep a clear head in very stressful situations.

Because social workers are bound by the law, you will have to be very thorough when checking and recording information to make sure you are completely up to date. This job requires people who are good time managers, to fit in all the administration work required by the courts, hospitals, etc.

Working conditions

Field social worker

Field social workers are office-based, but may move around between clients' homes, day centres, hospitals, health centres and the courts.

You could travel quite a lot, so a driving licence is useful.

Residential social worker

Residential social workers are based in residential establishments for children, the elderly or people with disabilities, but they do go out with their clients for outings and appointments, for example to a hospital.

The work can be physically tiring. Expect to work a basic 37-hour week, including weekend and evening shifts.

The future outlook

Field social worker

There are about 26,000 qualified field social workers in the UK and the demand is increasing. Main employers are local authority social services and the health service. Because social care covers so many areas, social workers are tending to specialise, for example in work with children, people with mental health problems or in criminal justice.

Residential social worker

Although recent trends are towards caring for people in their own homes, there is still a high demand for residential social workers. Main employers are local authorities, private nursing and residential homes, voluntary agencies and specialist employment agencies.

Social workers are generally at least in their twenties with social work qualifications and/or experience of care work. Social work offers many opportunities for training to achieve advanced qualifications. It is also possible to move into a range of caring careers with appropriate training, for example teaching, nursing or careers guidance. There is a clearly defined promotion path in the public sector and you will be able to widen your experience by transferring into different areas of work.

Qualifications and courses

Field social worker

- The 3-year social work Honours degree course has replaced the Diploma in Social Work (DipSW), and is required in order to become a social worker. For entry to a degree course you will need 2 A levels/4 H grades plus 5 GCSE/S grades (A–C/1–3) including English and maths. Other Level 3 qualifications may also be accepted.
- There are also postgraduate programmes. For further information, graduates should contact one of the following: the General Social Care Council (GSCC), the Scottish Social Services Council (SSSC), the Northern Ireland Social Care Council (NISCC) or the Care Council for Wales (CCW).
- There is no upper age limit for entry onto degree courses. Maturity and life and work experience are seen as an asset. Some universities are now offering a graduate-entry degree course that leads to a Master's qualification. Applications for these courses must be made through UCAS.
- An employment-based route is also available. Here, the candidate works full time as an unqualified social worker for a social services organisation which funds their training. To become qualified, you attend short training courses and follow a distance learning programme.
- Social workers are subject to a criminal record check and certain criminal convictions may prevent entry to this field.

Residential social worker

- Many residential social workers, also known as care officers, gain experience through voluntary work in a caring role.
- Residential social workers may be encouraged to undertake relevant NVQs/SVQs, which are available at Levels 2–4, in subjects such as Care, Caring for Children and Young People, and Promoting Independence.
- For career progression, it may be necessary to become a qualified social worker (see above).

entry level

To both enter and train while working in this career, you will need qualifications at Level 4–8. Please refer to explanation on page vii.

Other related opportunities

Advantages/disadvantages

- The job is varied, interesting and challenging.
- You will work with a wide range of people, one-to-one and in teams, and may work with a particular group of people over quite a long time.
- You may be torn between what you would like to do to help and what you are allowed to do.
- The job will often be very stressful and some people may be angry, difficult or even violent.
- You may work evenings, weekends and public holidays.
- Occasionally, as a field social worker, you have to be on call-out duty overnight.

Earnings guide

Field social worker

- Pay can be £19,800–£27,807 per year as a newly qualified field social worker. This rises to £28,300 with experience.
- Salaries rise to £31,000–£35,000 for a senior post team leader. Senior social services managers can earn up to £50,000.

Residential social worker

- There are no national pay scales for residential social workers; you could start at around £17,500 per year depending on the job, qualifications and experience.
- You can progress to £28,000+, depending on qualifications, experience and responsibilities.

Further information

General Social Care Council
Goldings House
2 Hays Lane
London
SE1 2HB
020 7397 5100
www.gscc.org.uk

Northern Ireland Social Care Council
7th Floor, Millennium House
19–25 Great Victoria Street
Belfast
BT2 7AQ
028 9041 7600
www.niscc.info

Scottish Social Services Council
Compass House
11 Riverside Drive
Dundee
DD1 4NY
01382 207101
www.sssc.uk.com

Care Council for Wales/Cygnor Gofal Cymru
6th Floor, West Wing
Southgate House, Wood Street
Cardiff
CF10 1EW
029 2022 6257
www.ccwales.org.uk

Trade Union Official

What the work involves

- You will be negotiating with employers over pay, working conditions, health and safety, dismissal and redundancy.
- Working in regional offices, you will recruit members, train shop stewards, support local officials and negotiate individual cases with employers.
- In head office, you will work on national policies and negotiate at national level.
- At all levels, your role will be to bring about the best deal for the workforce by finding common ground between employers and employees.

The type of person suited to this work

As the work is about obtaining good working conditions for your members, it is important to have a genuine interest in people's welfare and to believe in the aims of your union. You will need to see issues from different view points.

You will spend time dealing with individuals or groups, which requires good speaking, listening and negotiating skills – being able to calm people down at times. You may have to speak in public, which takes confidence.

Union matters involve problem-solving and negotiation which needs a patient, methodical approach and the ability to research and analyse information.

Working conditions

As a local shop steward you will have another job and attend to union business part time.

Paid officials at regional and national level are office-based.

You may travel quite extensively to meetings, tribunals and conferences so a driving licence is useful.

You will make maximum use of ICT and will probably have a lot of phone work – some after normal work hours.

The future outlook

Most people become paid union officials after voluntary experience.

Your prospects depend very much on the size of the union, ie they are greater with the large unions which are never out of the news.

In the case of some unions, there is no fixed pay and promotion structure. Most training is in house. Head-office posts are usually in London. Some people move from union work into politics by becoming councillors or Members of Parliament.

entry level

To both enter and train while working in this career, you will need qualifications at Level 3–8. Please refer to explanation on page vii.

Qualifications and courses

- The two main routes into trade union work are via a branch or regional office, or by joining the staff at head office.
- Head-office staff are usually qualified in the area in which they specialise, for example law or economics. They may have qualified and worked in these areas beforehand or they may be direct entrants with either a relevant degree or the equivalent – such as NVQ/SVQ Levels 3 and 4. Workers at union headquarters may have worked their way up through the organisation from branch or regional office level.
- Branch or regional office staff will have spent several years involved in union work in an unpaid capacity, either as a representative or as a shop steward.
- Training for trade union officials is mainly on the job. The Trade Union Congress (TUC) runs regular short training programmes.
- It may be possible to take NVQs/SVQs in administration or other relevant subjects.

Other related opportunities

- Equal Opportunities / Equalities Officer p17
- Health and Safety Adviser p19
- Human Resources / Personnel Officer p20
- Political Work p346

Advantages/disadvantages

- The work is varied, but you may be working on one theme in preparation for a meeting.
- You will work with a very wide range of people.
- Some people may be aggressive and unpleasant and sometimes you have to support people you do not agree with.
- You may have to work long and unsocial hours.

Earnings guide

- Local shop stewards/union representatives are generally unpaid.
- If you are working as a paid official, expect around £15,000 per year on entry.
- As a policy officer you can expect to start at around £18,000–£25,000.
- As an experienced regional official you could earn £30,000–£50,000.
- A general secretary could get as much as £100,000.

Further information

Trades Union Congress
Congress House
Great Russell Street
London
WC1B 3LS
020 7636 4030
www.tuc.org.uk

Scottish Trades Union Congress
333 Woodlands Road
Glasgow
G3 6DF
0141 337 8100
www.stuc.org.uk

Volunteer Organiser

What the work involves

- Your job will be to organise volunteers to give additional help in hospitals, social service departments and volunteer organisations.
- After interviewing volunteers, you will match them to the kind of work that suits them, such as volunteer driving, hospital visiting or befriending.
- You will deal with administration, budgets, correspondence and report writing.
- Other tasks will be preparing publicity material, attending meetings, training volunteers and liaising with other agencies.

entry level

To both enter and train while working in this career, you will need qualifications at Level 3–8. Please refer to explanation on page vii.

Qualifications and courses

- No formal qualifications are needed to enter this career, but relevant work experience as a volunteer is valuable.
- A degree or professional qualification can be an asset.
- Professional courses vary. The National Association of Voluntary Service Managers offers a certificate for those working in the health and social care service.
- The Directory of Social Change runs short courses.
- The National Centre for Volunteering organises many 1- or 2-day courses which cover key areas of volunteer involvement.
- Learndirect offers an online course entitled Managing Volunteers. This is primarily a distance learning course for those who are already volunteer leaders.

The type of person suited to this work

As volunteers come from many different backgrounds, it is important to be able to get on with all sorts of people and keep them motivated. You will need tact and patience, as not all volunteers are suited to the kind of volunteering they think they want to do.

It is essential to be confident when looking for volunteering opportunities and have good communication skills to sell placements to volunteers and volunteers to placements. You will need to be flexible to fit in with everyone's needs.

The job will demand a good deal of administration and record-keeping, which requires excellent organisational and time-management skills.

Working conditions

You will be based in an office or work from home, depending on the size of the organisation you work for.

You will travel locally to arrange placements and visit volunteers, so a driving licence is useful.

You will make a lot of use of ICT and the phone in your work.

The future outlook

You are unlikely to start this work straight from school. Opportunities are increasing, but there is keen competition for jobs and you may have to move to gain experience.

Promotion prospects are limited and many jobs may be part time. Volunteer organising is a good background for moving into careers such as social work or other management posts in the voluntary sector. You will have opportunities for further training, mainly through short courses.

CRCI:V

CLCI:KEM

Other related opportunities

- Charity Fundraiser p527
- Debt Counsellor / Money Adviser p531
- Social Worker p545
- Welfare Rights Officer / Worker p550
- Youth and Community Worker p551

Advantages/disadvantages

- This work is varied and provides a challenge.
- You will get satisfaction from helping volunteers get placements and from improving the lot of many people in need.
- You may work some evenings and weekends.
- Some people may be unpleasant and difficult to please.

Earnings guide

- Starting salaries arearound £17,000 per year. This rises to £25,000 with experience.
- As a manager you can expect up to £30,000.
- Earnings can be up to £38,000 for those in large organisations, with supervisory or substantial experience.

Further information

Association of Chief Executives of Voluntary Organisations
83 Victoria Street
London
SW1H 0HW
0845 345 8481
www.acevo.org.uk

Directory of Social Change
24 Stephenson Way
London
NW1 2DP
020 7391 4800
www.dsc.org.uk

Warden (Accommodation)

What the work involves

- Wardens look after the welfare of people living in supervised accommodation, including the elderly, people with disabilities, temporary hostel residents and students.
- You will make sure that meals are organised, cooked and served at set times, and that cleaning and maintenance are up to standard.
- It will be your responsibility to make sure health and safety standards are met, insurance is up to date and that security is effective.
- You will also collect rents and fees and organise social events, and sort out any disputes.

The type of person suited to this work

As you could be responsible for the accommodation of many different groups of people, it is important to be able to get on with all sorts of people and to have a friendly, outgoing personality. You will need to be understanding, patient and tolerant.

There are likely to be crises in the job so it is important to be able to cope under pressure and make decisions quickly. Problem solving is useful in these situations.

If you are dealing with rents and fees, being good with figures is helpful. There will be a lot of administration work which needs a well-organised and methodical approach.

Working conditions

Most of your work will be indoors, but you may handle maintenance and repair work, using tools and climbing ladders.

You will be on the go all day and evening so you will need lots of physical stamina.

You will use ICT for administration and record-keeping.

Many accommodation wardens live on-site or in the grounds, but you may travel locally, so a driving licence is useful.

The future outlook

Although there are opportunities throughout the UK, there are few vacancies for wardens. Most jobs are in cities and major towns. The main employers are local authorities, housing associations, private companies, voluntary organisations, universities and colleges.

Promotion is likely to be from assistant warden to warden. You may have to move jobs to progress your career. It is possible to move into other caring jobs such as social work.

entry level

To both enter and train while working in this career, you will need qualifications at Level 2–3. Please refer to explanation on page vii.

Qualifications and courses

- There are no particular qualifications necessary to become a warden. However, it would be an advantage to have previous experience of caring for people, such as nursing or working with the disabled, elderly or homeless.
- The minimum entry age is 20 due to the responsibilities involved.
- It is possible to study for the Chartered Institute of Housing (CIH) National Certificate in Housing as well as NVQ/SVQ Levels 2, 3 and 4 in Housing.
- Qualifications in care, including NVQs/SVQs, are also useful.
- Wardens (managers) with the Youth Hostels Association (YHA, England and Wales) generally either start as seasonal assistants and work their way up, or are mature entrants with relevant work experience, for example as managers. A broad skills set can be useful as duties may include cooking, gardening, maintenance, housekeeping, acting as guide and marketing the youth hostel, as well as office work.

CRCI:V

CLCI:IB

Other related opportunities

- Care Assistant p525
- Caretaker p416
- Home Care Assistant p534
- Hotel Manager p95
- Housekeeper p97

Advantages/disadvantages

- The work is varied and you will need to be able to multi-task.
- You will get great job satisfaction from helping people.
- Some residents may be difficult to deal with.
- You will work long hours, evenings and weekends and may have to live in.

Earnings guide

- Starting salaries are around £11,300–£12,500 per year.
- Wages can rise to £17,000 with experience.
- Earnings can be up to £21,000 with substantial experience, and in some instances, having individual responsibility for a group in supported accommodation.
- Accommodation and food may also be provided.

Further information

Chartered Institute of Housing
Octavia House
Westwood Way
Coventry
CV4 8JP
024 7685 1700
www.cih.org

General Social Care Council
Goldings House
2 Hays Lane
London
SE1 2HB
020 7397 5100
www.gscc.org.uk

Scottish Social Services Council
Compass House
11 Riverside Drive
Dundee
DD1 4NY
01382 207101
www.sssc.uk.com

www.cityandguilds.com/myperfectjob

Welfare Rights Officer / Worker

What the work involves

- You will give people advice and information on benefits, health, safety, housing, disability and consumer rights.
- You may represent people at tribunals or appeals, explaining legal points to them.
- You will research information for people and write reports.
- You will give people advice and information on benefits, health, safety, housing, disability and consumer rights.
- Other tasks include advising people on rules for particular services or benefits and helping them complete claims forms.

entry level

To both enter and train while working in this career, you will need qualifications at Level 2. Please refer to explanation on page vii.

Qualifications and courses

- There are no set entry requirements for this work; relevant knowledge and experience are considered more important than formal qualifications. However, a good standard of education including GCSEs (A–C)/S grades (1–3) in English and maths may be an advantage.
- Prior to becoming a welfare rights officer, most candidates have experience of working in one of the following: a voluntary advice centre, an appropriate local council department or the employment service.
- NVQs/SVQs are available at Levels 2–4 in Advice and Guidance.
- Knowledge of a minority language can be an advantage.
- For graduate entrants, degrees in subjects such as social sciences or law/legal studies can be useful.
- Volunteering can be a route into the profession, in order to gain any requisite training and experience.

The type of person suited to this work

As people from all walks of life consult welfare rights officers, it is important to be able to get on with many different types of people. Good speaking and listening skills are essential, and also writing skills – for reports. Discretion is important because you will be given a lot of confidential information.

It is vital to give correct information, so you will need to enjoy research to make sure the advice you give is completely accurate and up to date.

ICT skills are extremely useful for report writing and record keeping. You will access databases and the internet when seeking information for a client.

Working conditions

You will be based in an advice centre which will be open to the public.

A driving licence could be useful because you may visit people in their own homes and travel around locally.

You will definitely use computers in your work.

Attending meetings, liaising with other agencies and updating your own knowledge could take time.

The future outlook

School-leavers are unlikely to go straight into this work. Jobs are with advice centres, local authorities, health services and voluntary organisations. In fact, most welfare rights workers are found in the voluntary sector. Some contracts will be short term.

Training is mainly in house. Promotion could be to supervisor or manager, or you may specialise in a particular area. It is possible to move into related areas such as money advice, benefits or employment rights.

CRCI:V

CLCI:KEB

Other related opportunities

- Advice Centre / Benefits Adviser p524
- Debt Counsellor / Money Adviser p531
- Education Welfare Officer p532
- Equal Opportunities / Equalities Officer p17
- Social Worker p545
- Solicitor / Notary Public p349

Advantages/disadvantages

- The work is varied and challenging.
- You will get great job satisfaction from helping people.
- The job could involve working some evenings and weekends.
- This can be stressful work and you might feel under pressure at times.

Earnings guide

- Entry salaries are around £18,000–£20,000 per year.
- Wages can rise to £25,000 with experience.
- Salaries up to £29,000 are possible for those in a supervisory or management position.

Further information

www.cityandguilds.com/myperfectjob

Citizens Advice Bureau
Myddelton House
115–123 Pentonville Road
London
N1 9LZ
020 7833 2181
www.citizensadvice.org.uk

Citizens Advice Scotland
2 Powderhall Road
Edinburgh
EH7 4GB
0131 550 1000
www.cas.org.uk

Advice UK
12th Floor, 2 London Bridge House
25 London Bridge Street
London
SE1 9ST
020 7407 4070
www.adviceuk.org.uk

Youth and Community Worker

What the work involves

- You will work with people in their local community, encouraging them to take part in local learning opportunities and community activities.
- You could be in charge of a community centre, arranging activities for people of all ages, such as youth clubs, over-60s lunch clubs and playgroups.
- Youth workers are mainly involved with young people while community workers try to make sure that people of all ages in the local community have access to opportunities.
- The work is usually with groups of people.

The type of person suited to this work

As the work involves contact with all sorts of people, it is important to be able to get on with everyone and earn their trust. You also need to be genuinely interested in the local community and in equal opportunities.

You will spend a lot of time organising and developing projects, which means you will need imagination and initiative to come up with good ideas, and good organisational and administrative skills, plus lots of energy and drive, to carry them out.

Local people have a say in what they want in their area, so you must be a good listener, able to balance local groups' ideas with local and national government policies.

Working conditions

You might be based in a community centre or in an area office.

Depending on your job, you could also be based in a school, FE college or Connexions centre.

You work where young people go, including drop-in centres, cafés and youth clubs; this includes attending evening and weekend sessions.

Some workers travel around their local area, so a driving licence is useful.

The future outlook

Youth and community work is a growth area. As well as roles in youth club and community centre management, there are new strands to the work with developing rock music, drama, art or skateboarding groups. Local lifelong learning adult centres also require youth and community workers.

Local authorities have a defined promotion structure but in some jobs you may have to move around to widen your experience. You could progress to work for voluntary organisations or for a specific young people's services, for example Connexions.

entry level

3–8

To both enter and train while working in this career, you will need qualifications at Level 3–8. Please refer to explanation on page vii.

Qualifications and courses

- Voluntary experience in youth and community work is always valuable. A disclosure check with the Criminal Records Bureau will be made for everyone working in this area.
- People in part-time or voluntary youth work can study for NVQs in Youth Work at Levels 2 and 3.
- Professional training courses will usually require GCSEs/S grades (A–C/1–3) and A levels/H grades or equivalent for candidates under 21. Entry requirements may be waived for mature applicants with relevant experience.
- In England, the National Youth Agency validates DipHE, degree and postgraduate courses, including the DipHE in community and youth work studies, the Foundation degree in Community Studies (Development and youth work), degrees in Youth and Community work and community development and youth work, as well as postgraduate courses in community and youth work. Some postgraduate courses require a first degree in a related subject to enter.
- In Scotland, there are three routes: BA/BA Honours degree, postgraduate certificate/ diploma and a work-based route.
- Additional aptitudes which are needed include caring for people, and high-level skills in communication, managing and organising, and working with others.
- Full-time youth and community workers normally need to do a professional training course.

CRCI:V

CLCI:KEG

Other related opportunities

- Careers Adviser p526
- Education Welfare Officer p532
- Lecturer p178
- Personal Adviser – Connexions p539
- Probation Officer p540
- Social Worker p545
- Teacher p184

Advantages/disadvantages

- This work provides variety and challenge.
- You will have contact with many different people.
- You will play a major part in developing your local community and/or the lives of young people.
- You might have to work evenings, weekends and public holidays.

Earnings guide

- Once qualified you can earn between £18,000 and £25,000 per year.
- Salaries rise to around £27,000 with experience.
- Salaries are £28,500–£30,000 for managers.
- You may be paid an additional amount for working unsocial hours.

Further information

National Youth Agency
17–21 Albion Street
Leicester
LE1 6GD
0116 285 3700
www.nya.org.uk

Community Learning Scotland
Rosebery House
9 Haymarket Terrace
Edinburgh
EH12 5LQ
0131 313 2488
www.communitylearning.org

PAULO
4th Floor, Kimberley House
47 Vaughan Way
Leicester
LE1 4SG
0116 251 7979

Lifelong Learning UK
5th Floor, St Andrew's House
18–20 St Andrew Street
London
EC4A 3AY
0870 757 7890
www.lifelonglearninguk.org

Youth Link Scotland
Rosebery House
9 Haymarket Terrace
Edinburgh
EH12 5EZ
0131 313 2488
www.youthlink.co.uk

Wales Youth Agency
Leslie Court
Lôn y Llyn
Caerphilly
CF83 1BQ
029 2085 5700
www.wya.org.uk

Youth Council for Northern Ireland
Forestview
Purdys Lane
Belfast BT8 7AR
028 9064 3882
www.youthcouncil-ni.org.uk

Skills for Care and Development (Sector Skills Council for social care and working with children and young people)
www.skillsforcareanddevelopment.org.uk

Here's Nicola Martin's story:

Counsellor

Nicola had always been interested in people and what makes them tick and so after doing an Honours degree in Social Science she worked as a locum social worker in a hospital, which is when she became interested in working with cancer patients, especially teenage cancer patients. She then went on to do a postgraduate degree in Social Science (Social Work) and went back to work in the hospital where she had been a locum, training on the job and attending conferences and workshops. Two years ago she moved to work in a hospice that caters specifically for those who are terminally ill with cancer. The patients range from young children to elderly people, but the majority are young adults.

WHAT THE JOB ENTAILS

'I provide counselling and support not only to the patients but also to their families and work on what the impact of a deteriorating illness will mean to them. I work with children prior to their parent's death, and also afterwards giving them bereavement counselling. I also provide support for the other team members at the hospital, but bereavement counselling is my biggest duty – working with art, modelling plaster, painting and colouring as a form of therapy. With the parents who are patients I help them before they die by collecting "memory storage" where we prepare photographs and mementos for their children.'

For Nicola, the best thing about her job is working with the children – especially after a few sessions, when she sees them start to pick up and express themselves through their art. She likes to see them get back on their feet. She also likes working with a close, supportive team. The downside of the job is that there is a lot of sadness attached to it. Because of this, Nicola feels you need to have a good balance between your work life and your private life in order to make this career a success.

WHAT YOU NEED TO SUCCEED

'You need to be able to recognise when you have had a bad day and go and do something about it. That's why it is essential to have a sense of humour to do this job. You also have to have the ability to connect with people, to be patient and a good listener. The best way to see if it is for you or not is to go and do some work in a care environment. Take a summer job in a residential home, do voluntary work with a children's summer camp or work at a youth club or local charity for a week. That will soon let you see if you have got the commitment to do this job or not.'

Intrigued by how air, rail or road travel can help improve our lives? Lots of jobs include transport services or systems, such as:

- **Air Cabin Crew**
- **Driver**
- **Rail Track Worker**
- **Transport Manager**
- **Warehouse Manager**

But what's it like working in this area?
Here's Tony Watts's story:

Importer / Exporter

Tony, 25, originally studied Maths and Computer Sciences in England but is currently working for STALMARK, a steel importer/exporter located in Helsinki, Finland. The job came about because the company is owned by his fiancée's family. The steel is mainly imported from Spain by ship to Helsinki from where it is sold and exported on. Tony uses English, Finnish and Spanish during his working day and has had five years of Finnish lessons (he says his Spanish is not so hot). He is mainly office-bound, dealing with orders, invoices, customer enquiries and payments.

WHAT THE JOB ENTAILS

'We only have two main members of staff here: me and a Sales Agent. Say someone places an order for some steel tubes or for some specially painted steel, I send the order to Spain asking for the price and a delivery date. They then confirm when they can deliver, and when the steel gets on the ship I have to make sure it is forwarded to the right person. Then I send the bills out, and I also make sure the money comes in, which is the good bit!'

Tony is also responsible for all customer services, so if there is a problem such as damaged goods he must discover whether the damage happened in transit or if it is a manufacturing fault and then he must sort the problem out.

WHAT YOU NEED TO DO THIS JOB

'Obviously, languages are very important. English can be used a lot but it is better to use people's own native tongue – in general it is more polite to use a client's own language. You also need social skills because you need to build up relationships with your suppliers and your clients because then you will be on their favoured list and they will be more willing to use you in the future. This business is all about relationships. Finally, you need to have a nose for business and you need to keep an eye on the steel markets because if prices start to go through the roof it can seriously affect your profits.'

Tony has been in Helsinki for 15 months and is getting married there this year. He sees his immediate future working for the family firm in Helsinki, and there is the possibility of eventually taking over the business. Tony could also move sideways into exporting/importing for another company.

WHAT IS GOOD AND BAD ABOUT WHAT HE DOES

'This is a small company and I love the fact I get to see the whole process. I am not just a cog in the machine – I get to see the whole thing from start to end. On the downside, it would be nice to have more people around for social interaction because there are only two of us here, but living and working in Helsinki is nice!'

Air / Ship Broker

What the work involves

- You will act as a go-between, linking the people who need to move cargo or passengers with the businesses who can move them to the right place, at the right time and at the best possible price.

Air broker

- Organising passenger, cargo and emergency transport by air for a range of individuals, businesses and relief agencies will be part of your job. You may also work for an air charter company.

Ship broker

- You will arrange the transport of cargo for a manufacturer who has sold goods overseas. You may also work for shipowners.

The type of person suited to this work

To attract customers you should be able to sell your expertise. You will also need to negotiate and agree the best prices and terms. In a job where you will be dealing with people frequently, communication skills are essential.

You should cope well under pressure and with tight deadlines. For example, in air broking you may need to get emergency supplies and relief workers out to fairly distant places in just a few hours.

Your maths skills will also need to be good as you will be preparing quotes – calculating charges based on weight and volume, discounts, duties and currency conversion. ICT skills are also helpful.

Working conditions

You will mainly work in an office, with a lot of time spent at a workstation using the phone and a computer.

Hours are often long and irregular as goods/ people need to be transported at all times of the day or night, including holidays and weekends.

Working in a competitive business, with frequent short deadlines, means that this can be a stressful job.

The future outlook

Brokers work for specialist broking or chartering companies. Air transport is growing rapidly and sea transport steadily. It's a competitive business.

Ship and air brokers sometimes go on to specialise in the sale and purchase of ships and planes.

Ship broker
Most ship brokers are members of the London Baltic Exchange. The exchange offers support to brokers and keeps a register of those looking for work.

Most jobs are in London and the south-east of England. Because of the limited numbers of companies that employ ship brokers, entry is very competitive.

entry level

3–8

To both enter and train while working in this career, you will need qualifications at Level 3–8. Please refer to explanation on page vii.

Qualifications and courses

- You will need a minimum of 4 GCSEs/S grades, including English, maths and ideally a foreign language. The majority of entrants are graduates. Useful subjects are geography, international business studies, transport/logistics courses and languages (especially French, Russian and Spanish).
- To be eligible for student membership of the Institute of Chartered Shipping Brokers, you will normally need to have a minimum of 2 A levels/3 H grades or equivalent, have gained one year's employment in an organisation which has a bona fide connection with shipping business including serving at sea, or have completed the Institute's Foundation Diploma.
- All Key Skills, but especially communication, ICT and numeracy, would be useful.
- Work experience within airline, export, telesales or transport areas is often an essential requirement for trainee broking jobs.

Air broker

- You would train on the job for 6–12 months taking courses in areas such as airfreight security and transportation of dangerous goods.

Ship broker

- You would usually obtain professional qualifications by distance learning from the Insitute of Chartered Shipbrokers. Courses include Understanding Shipping.
- The Baltic Exchange also offers professional shipbroking courses. Shipping business degrees are also available.

CRCI:WA

CLCI:YAS

Other related opportunities

- Distribution Manager p562
- Freight Forwarder p566
- Importer / Exporter p567
- Purchasing Administrator p577
- Transport Manager (Road) p585

Advantages/disadvantages

- Because the job involves working to short deadlines, it can be very stressful. However, achieving this, and earning commission and/or bonuses for work completed can be really rewarding.
- The job offers a lot of variety as it requires you to deal with a wide range of customers worldwide.
- You may get to travel to different parts of the world.

Earnings guide

- Starting salaries range from £20,000–£28,000 per year, depending on the company.
- With experience, you could earn £28,000–£48,000.
- At senior levels it is possible to earn £65,000+.
- Commission is paid on contracts arranged, which would increase your earnings. You could also earn bonuses for good performance.

Further information

Skills for Logistics
14 Warren Yard
Warren Farm Office Village
Milton Keynes
MK12 5NW
01908 313360
www.skillsforlogistics.org

Institute of Chartered Shipbrokers
85 Gracechurch Street
London
EC3V 0AA
020 7623 1111
www.ics.org.uk

Baltic Exchange
38 St Mary Axe
London
EC3A 8BH
020 7283 9300
www.balticexchange.com

Air Cabin Crew

What the work involves

- Once you have checked the cabin, you will welcome your passengers on board and make sure they are comfortable.
- You will be responsible for safety and security on board – this will include making sure that customers are safely belted up and their bags are put away, and demonstrating safety procedures.
- During the flight you will help to care for any young children and sick passengers, giving First Aid if needed.
- You will also serve food and drinks and sell items such as jewellery, toys and alcohol.
- You will ensure passengers are ready for landing and will see them all safely off the plane.

The type of person suited to this work

As you will be taking care of your passengers and trying to keep them happy and safe you will need to be welcoming, friendly, well groomed, confident and caring, with a clear voice.

You should be happy working in a team with the rest of the crew, but also be able to be on your own as you will spend some nights alone away from home.

As you will serve refreshments and clean up, you will need to be prepared to get your hands dirty.

Your ability to stay calm under pressure will be vital if you need to deal with an emergency, for example giving First Aid or dealing with a serious incident such as restraining a violent passenger.

Working conditions

You will work in a cramped, noisy, warm cabin. In bad weather the cabin may be unstable.

Planes fly 24/7 which means long hours, shifts and regular work at weekends and bank holidays.

There is also a risk of security incidents or accidents and, although low, it can cause stress and delay.

You may have health problems, for example ear pain from cabin pressure or jet lag from long flights.

The future outlook

Vacancies are with airlines; these operate mainly in the south-east of England and at large regional airports.

There is fierce competition for jobs, although there are growing opportunities, with a growth in numbers of smaller airlines and an increase in routes.

With experience, you could progress to working as a purser (looking after a particular cabin such as first class) and then to cabin service director.

You could go on to train new cabin crew.

entry level

To both enter and train while working in this career, you will need qualifications at Level 2–3. Please refer to explanation on page vii.

Qualifications and courses

- Entry requirements depend on the airline, many require 4–5 GCSEs (A–C)/S grades (1–3) or equivalent and fluency in English. You will need to be at least 18 and be physically fit, and there are height and weight restrictions. You will also need a valid passport allowing unrestricted world travel. Most airlines will expect you to be able to swim 25 metres. It is also an advantage if you can speak another language.
- Key Skills in communication and working with others are useful but even more important is having put these skills into practice by having gained work experience with the public within a caring, catering or travel agency type job.
- You could study a related college or university course, for example a BTEC/SQA National Certificate/Diploma or HNC/D in travel and tourism, or a degree in travel and tourism or a modern language.
- Nationally recognised qualifications for air cabin crew include the Edexcel Certificate in Preparation for Air Cabin Crew Service, EMTA Awards Ltd's Intermediate Certificate in Air Cabin Crewing, NCFE Level 2 Certificate in Airline Cabin Crew and Edexcel BTEC Level 3 National Award, Certificate or Diploma in Aviation Operations.
- Once accepted by an airline you will take part in their 4 to 6 week training course followed by an opportunity to take NVQ/SVQ Levels 2 and 3 in Aviation Operations in the Air (Cabin Crew).

CRCI:WA

CLCI:YAB

Other related opportunities

- Airline Customer Service Agent p557
- Catering / Restaurant Manager p85
- Holiday Representative p365
- Pilot p573
- Tour Guide p379
- Tour Manager p381
- Transfer Representative p384
- Travel Agency Sales Consultant p385

Advantages/disadvantages

- You will travel to dream destinations, but on short flights you will not always get off the plane!
- No two working days will be the same.
- Whilst working with people can be very rewarding, you may have to deal with difficult or demanding passengers.
- Increased security can lead to frustrating delays.

Earnings guide

- £12,000–£14,000 per year is usual for starting salaries.
- With experience this rises to £15,000–£21,000.
- £25,000+ is possible for senior crew.
- Allowances are paid for working away from home and unsocial hours.
- You may be offered flight and meal allowances.

Further information

GoSkills (Sector Skills Council for passenger transport)
Concorde House
Trinity Park
Solihull
B37 7UQ
0121 635 5520
www.goskills.org

Edexcel
Customer Service
One90, High Holborn
London
WC1V 7BH
0870 240 9800
www.edexcel.org.uk

EMTA Awards Ltd (EAL)
SEMTA House
14 Upton Road
Watford
Herts WD18 OJT
01923 652 400
www.eal.org.uk

NCFE national awarding body
Citygate
St James' Boulevard
Newcastle upon Tyne
NE1 4JE
0191 239 8000
www.ncfe.org.uk

www.cityandguilds.com/myperfectjob

Air Traffic Controller

What the work involves

- You will be responsible for a specific section of airspace, keeping air traffic flying safely and quickly.
- Using computers, radar, radio equipment and weather reports you will check pilots' flight plans and current positions.
- You will use a radio to give pilots the instructions, advice and information they need to fly safely.
- Any difficult weather, security alerts or emergencies will mean that you would have to make quick but safe decisions.

The type of person suited to this work

The lives of the passengers in your air space will be your responsibility. To avoid disaster you will have to take quick, calm, logical action and stay alert at all times, even at the end of your shift.

You cannot afford to be unclear when you are sending instructions to pilots, so you need to be confident and able to speak clearly.

You should be keen on ICT and maths. When checking your pilot's flight plans you will use lots of new technology and calculate distances and angles.

The technology and software used is regularly upgraded to improve safety, so you will need to be willing to train throughout your working life.

Working conditions

You will work from 37 to 40 hours a week at a flight control centre, or in an airport traffic control tower.

As it's a 24/7 job, shift work is usual and includes nights, weekends and holidays.

You will use computers, radar displays and radio headphones.

The lighting in the control room is kept at the right level to help you read the radar screens.

The future outlook

Most of the 2,500 UK air traffic controllers are employed by the National Air Traffic Services (NATS) and work in one of three main area control centres: Swanwick in Southampton, West Drayton near London and Prestwick in Scotland. Others work at airports.

There are regular trainee vacancies as air traffic continues to increase. There are now more than 2,300 flights from the UK each year – with record new flight levels being recorded each year. However, entry is competitive with about 150 people applying for each vacancy.

With experience, you could manage and train other air traffic controllers.

entry level

3–8

To both enter and train while working in this career, you will need qualifications at Level 3–8. Please refer to explanation on page vii.

Qualifications and courses

- The main route into this work is to apply to National Air Traffic Services (NATS). You will need a minimum of 5 GCSEs (A–C)/S grades (1–3), including English and maths. Post-GCSE qualifications are also usually required, such as 2 A levels, 3 H grades or equivalent. Many entrants are graduates. Applicants should be over 18 years of age.
- You will also need a good standard of health, hearing, colour vision and a clear voice.
- All Key Skills are useful for this job but especially communication, information technology and numeracy skills.
- NATS entrants are trained at the College of Air Traffic Control, next to Bournemouth International Airport. You will start by doing a 9–15 month course, during which an allowance is paid. After graduation trainees go on to an operational unit for validation training. It takes 3–4 years to become fully qualified.
- Some air traffic controllers are employed directly by airport operators. Private employers either recruit people with air traffic control experience or send trainees to the College of Air Traffic Control. Some also take on trainees with 5 GCSEs/S grades (A–C/1–3) including English and maths, or equivalent qualifications.

CRCI:WA

CLCI:YAB

Other related opportunities

- Coastguard p495
- Engineer: Professional p205
- Pilot p573
- Royal Air Force (RAF) p512

Advantages/disadvantages

- No two working days are the same: you will work at different times.
- You will be well paid for the level of responsibility you take on.
- Excellent training is on offer including an exciting 15 hours' flying time, but you will have to pass all your assessments.

Earnings guide

- Trainee air traffic controllers get a training allowance of £10,000 per year at college.
- This can rise to £15,000–£20,000 during the validation period.
- When fully qualified and with experience you can get up to £45,000+.
- Supervisors could expect up to £85,000.
- Shift work payments can increase earnings.

Further information

Civil Aviation Authority
Personnel Department, Room 216
CAA House
45–59 Kingsway
London
WC2B 6TE
020 7453 6040
www.caa.co.uk

National Air Traffic Services Ltd
Fifth Floor
Brettenham House South
London
WC2E 7EN
020 7309 8666
www.nats.co.uk

Royal Aeronautical Society
4 Hamilton Place
London
WCJ 7BQ
020 7670 4326
www.aerosociety.com

GoSkills (Sector Skills Council for passenger transport)
Concorde House
Trinity Park
Solihull
B37 7UQ
0121 635 5520
www.goskills.org

Airline Customer Service Agent

What the work involves

- You will be responsible for making sure that passengers and their baggage board the right aircraft.
- You will greet passengers, provide information, ask security questions and check tickets and passport details.
- Once you have weighed and put luggage on the conveyor belt you will issue boarding passes and prepare paperwork for customs.
- Some passengers might need extra help because of their age or disability.
- You may also work at the flight gate, making announcements and checking boarding cards and passports.

entry level

To both enter and train while working in this career, you will need qualifications at Level 2–3. Please refer to explanation on page vii.

The type of person suited to this work

As the public face of your airline, you will need a pleasant, confident and helpful manner with a well-groomed appearance.

You need to be confident with ICT. You will use a sophisticated computer system to allocate seats, print boarding cards and baggage labels and produce post-flight figures.

It is vital that you like people, as you may be helping people with disabilities and unaccompanied children from check-in, through security and customs and on to their flight. You will also need to be able to deal with difficult situations. Communication skills are essential for working with your colleagues and other airport staff.

Working conditions

You will wear a uniform and work indoors in an airport.

When you are working at the check-in desk you may sit behind a counter for long periods.

If you are escorting passengers or helping with boarding at a gate, you will spend periods of time on your feet, sometimes walking quite long distances.

Hours may include shifts covering evenings, weekends and holidays.

The future outlook

Employers are either airlines or the ground handling companies that work on behalf of airlines. About 70% of passenger handling work takes place at the four main airports – Heathrow, Gatwick, Stansted and Manchester – so there are more opportunities if you live within travelling distance of one of the big four.

There is a lot of competition for jobs, many of which are seasonal.

There may be opportunities for promotion to a supervisory or managerial role. You could go on to train new customer service agents. Some passenger service agents with experience move on to working as air cabin crew.

Qualifications and courses

- Entry requirements vary, but many employers prefer applicants with 3–5 GCSEs (A–C)/S grades (1–3), including English and maths. Minimum age for entry varies from 16 to 20 years of age. There is no upper age for entry. You will need to be physically fit, and there may be height and weight restrictions. It's an advantage to be able to speak another language.
- Key Skills in communication and information technology are useful but even more important is being able to demonstrate having put these skills into practice, by doing some work experience with the public in a caring, catering or travel agency job.
- You could study a related college or university course, for example a BTEC/SQA National Certificate/Diploma or HNC/D in travel and tourism, an Edexcel BTEC Level 3 National Award, Certificate or Diploma in Aviation Operations or a degree in travel and tourism or a modern language.
- Once accepted you will be trained for 4–8 weeks in all aspects of the job.
- NVQs/SVQs in Handling Aircraft Passengers at Levels 2 and 3 may be available.

CRCI:WA

CLCI:YAB

Other related opportunities

Advantages/disadvantages

- Working with people can be very rewarding.
- If there is a delay to their flight, you may have to deal with difficult or demanding passengers.
- If you are keen to work in an air cabin crew job then experience in this work will be a big advantage.

Earnings guide

- Starting salaries are around £11,000–£14,000 per year.
- Experienced customer service agents can earn £15,000–£20,000.
- At supervisory or management level you could earn up to £24,000.
- Shift allowances are usually paid. There may be opportunities to earn overtime pay.

Further information

GoSkills (Sector Skills Council for passenger transport)
Concorde House
Trinity Park
Solihull
B37 7UQ
0121 635 5520
www.goskills.org

Royal Aeronautical Society
4 Hamilton Place
London
WCJ 7BQ
020 7670 4326
www.aerosociety.com

EMTA Awards Ltd (EAL)
SEMTA House
14 Upton Road
Watford
Herts
WD18 OJT
01923 652 400
www.eal.org.uk

Edexcel
Customer Service
One90
High Holborn
London
WC1V 7BH
0870 240 9800
www.edexcel.org.uk

www.cityandguilds.com/myperfectjob

Airport Baggage Handler

What the work involves

- You will be responsible for safely loading, unloading and transporting baggage, cases, and freight around an airport.
- By checking the baggage against flight lists, you will sort items to make sure you get the baggage to the right place on time.
- Once you have loaded up you will drive vehicles between aircraft and terminal.
- You will then lift the baggage onto the ramp or conveyor belt to move it onto the plane or into the baggage hall.
- If you spot any unusual or suspicious baggage, you will use a radio to get security back-up.

entry level

1

To both enter and train while working in this career, you will need qualifications at Level 1. Please refer to explanation on page vii.

The type of person suited to this work

As you will be responsible both for making sure that all baggage goes to the right place by checking labels against flight lists, and for reporting suspicious baggage, you should be alert with an eye for detail. You will be the sort of person who likes to be active and busy as you will be expected to move at speed to get aircraft loaded and unloaded in a short timescale.

Flexibility and a willingness to get your hands dirty are also vital, as you may need to carry out jobs such as helping to clean the aircraft and keep runways free of hazards such as snow and birds. You should enjoy working as part of a team.

Working conditions

You will wear a uniform and work mainly outdoors in all weathers. You may need to work in cramped spaces such as cargo holds.

You will work around 39 hours per week on a shift system.

Working near aircraft can be noisy, but you will have ear protectors.

Your job will involve a lot of bending, lifting and carrying. This can make it an active, but physically tiring job.

The future outlook

Most of the 5000 UK baggage handlers work for large airlines, airports or handling agents at the biggest airports, such as Heathrow, Gatwick, Stansted and Manchester. There are usually vacancies and currently demand outstrips supply. Seasonal work is on offer at busy holiday periods.

Technological changes could make this job safer in the future: for example, the development of mechanised belt loaders is predicted to reduce the risk of injury.

Promotion is possible to a supervisory post or managing ground transport on the runways.

Qualifications and courses

- There are no minimum entry requirements for this job. You will usually need to be at least 18, be physically fit with normal colour vision, pass medical and strict security checks and may need a clean driving licence.
- Key Skills in communication and working with others are useful. You will also need some numeracy skills to identify the correct conveyor belt for each flight.
- Given that you will be working a variety of shifts at various times, day or night, it is advisable to live near the airport and possess personal transport.
- Once accepted you will be trained in all aspects of the job including barcode recognition equipment, lift equipment and operating vehicles safely and effectively.
- NVQs/SVQs in Providing Aviation Operations on the Ground at Levels 2 and 3 may be available. Other qualifications available include BTEC Nationals or C&G at Levels 2 and 3 in Aviation Operations or Aviation Operations on the Ground.
- Baggage handlers generally need to live within easy access of an airport, and have their own transport.

CRCI:WA | CLCI:YAB

Other related opportunities

- Airline Customer Service Agent p557
- Courier p559
- Driver p563
- Hotel Porter p96
- Lift Truck Operator p568
- Loader p569
- Port Operative p575
- Removals Operative p581
- Stores Assistant p584
- Warehouse p586

Advantages/disadvantages

- You will have to move fast to get baggage transported, but this means that you will have a busy working day.
- If you are working for an airline, one of the perks may be subsidised travel opportunities.
- You may have to work outside in poor weather conditions.

Earnings guide

- Starting salary is usually £11,000–£14,500 per year.
- Experienced baggage handlers can earn £16,000+.
- Team leaders can earn up to £21,000.
- Allowances are paid for shift work and this together with overtime pay can increase your earnings.

Further information

www.cityandguilds.com/myperfectjob

GoSkills (Sector Skills Council for passenger transport)
Concorde House
Trinity Park
Solihull
B37 7UQ
0121 635 5520
www.goskills.org

Royal Aeronautical Society
4 Hamilton Place
London
WCJ 7BQ
020 7670 4326
www.aerosociety.com

Courier

What the work involves

- You will collect fragile, valuable or urgent letters and packages and deliver them within an agreed time limit.
- Once you have been allocated your job, you will travel to a collection point for pick-up. You will load up the goods and then take them to the drop-off point where you will obtain a signature for delivery.
- Motorcycle couriers may travel long distances and van couriers carry larger parcels in a town or city.
- You will need to check the lights, brakes and tyres of your motorbike, van or bicycle regularly.
- Some couriers do not use their own vehicle: for example, there are overseas and air couriers who transport documents or goods in person.

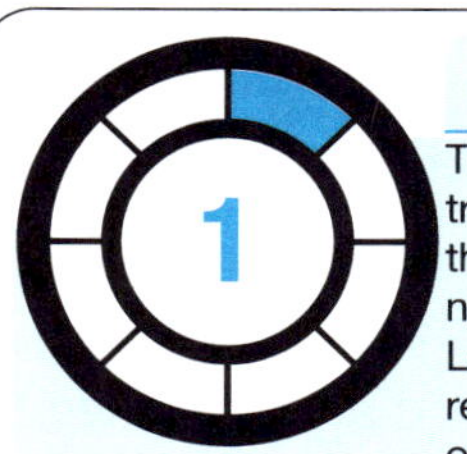

entry level

To both enter and train while working in this career, you will need qualifications at Level 1. Please refer to explanation on page vii.

The type of person suited to this work

Couriers often work in a particular part of the UK or a large town or city, so you will need to know all the short cuts. Map-reading skills are essential. You may only be paid for the number of deliveries you do so you need to be quick and know where you are going.

You will be in constant contact with customers, collecting items, asking for instructions and getting signatures for deliveries, so you need to be good with people. You should also be reliable – you may be dealing with high value or very urgent items. If anything goes wrong the customer will not use your company again.

Working conditions

You will spend a lot of time travelling but with regular stops to make deliveries. Long distance or overseas deliveries may mean time away from home.

Motorcycle and bicycle couriers will be out in the weather at all times.

Courier services operate 24/7 and many couriers work on overnight deliveries.

You may have to provide your own car or van. Motorcycle and bicycle couriers usually use their own bikes.

The future outlook

Couriers are employed by companies who offer a fast delivery service. Cyclists and motorcyclists are often self-employed and own their bikes. The Foreign and Commonwealth Office employs diplomatic couriers to take documents overseas.

Work can be irregular but currently delivery is a growth area with a shortage of couriers especially in the South-East. The continued growth of online shopping and customer online tracking means that the demand for same and next day courier delivery, in particular, is on the increase.

Technology is starting to change this industry. Mobile phones have been the norm for communicating but the internet and email are now also used. ICT skills are therefore likely to be more important in the future.

Promotion generally depends on the size of the courier company – large companies may have sales and management opportunities. It may be possible to become self-employed and start your own courier service. However, high operational costs (fuel, congestion charges, etc) are currently making it difficult for small companies.

Qualifications and courses

- No particular educational qualifications are needed. Most employers will require good health and you will need to be physically fit especially if you are riding a bike. You will also need to be at least 17 – many couriers are over 21 because of high insurance costs for young drivers. School leavers could start as bicycle couriers.
- Employers ask for a full UK driving licence for driver couriers and motorcycle couriers will need the CBT qualification issued by the DVLA. Motorcycle and bicycle couriers usually use their own bikes.
- Couriers driving light trucks will also need to have their C1 Category licence if they passed their driving test after 1 January 1997.
- Key Skills in communication and working with others are useful.
- Training is normally on the job with an experienced courier showing you what to do.
- Apprenticeships/Skillseekers are available for candidates aged 16–24
- You may be able to do an NVQ/SVQ at Level 2 in Carry and Deliver Goods. An NVQ/SVQ Level 2 is also available in Transporting Goods by Road.

CRCI:WE

CLCI:YAT

Other related opportunities

- Airport Baggage Handler p558
- Driver p563
- Motor Vehicle Work p217
- Postal Delivery Person p576
- Rail p578
- Warehouse p586

Advantages/disadvantages

- Pay rates are good but if you are using your own transport you will have running, insurance and maintenance costs.
- Making up to 20 journeys a day and possibly working 50-hour weeks make this a stressful job.
- Most couriers take up the job because they are attracted to the freedom of travel. However most couriers do lots of repeat deliveries in a small, often congested, urban area.

Earnings guide

- Couriers are often paid on a self-employed basis by each delivered item, so earnings vary.
- Employed couriers can earn £10,500–£13,500 per year (£15,000+ in London).
- Experienced couriers can earn up to £23,000 per year (£25,000+ in London).
- Couriers travelling by air may be employed by airlines on a one-off basis and receive a free or reduced cost flight instead of wages.

Further information

Skills for Logistics
14 Warren Yard
Warren Farm Office Village
Milton Keynes
MK12 5NW
01908 313360
www.skillsforlogistics.org

Driving Standards Agency
Stanley House
56 Talbot Street
Nottingham
NG1 5GU
0115 901 2500
www.dsa.gov.uk

Chartered Institute of Logistics and Transport
Logistics and Transport Centre
Earlstree Court, Earlstree Road,
Corby
NN17 4XQ
01536 740104
www.ciltuk.org.uk

www.cityandguilds.com/myperfectjob

Cruise Ship Work

What the work involves

- Cruise liners require lots of different services if the passengers are to be kept safe, happy and healthy. Alongside entertainers, catering, medical and deck crew there are roles which are specific to cruise liners. These are:

Purser

- As a purser you will provide the administrative services that are needed to keep the criuse ship operating and make sure that the passengers have a good holiday whilst they are on board. You might work in the reception area, do secretarial duties or order stock for the food and beverages sections.
- As well as providing passengers services you might also support crew members by paying their salaries or updating and maintaining records.

Steward

- You will be responsible for keeping the public and private areas that passengers use clean and serviced to a very high standard.
- You might do housekeeping duties in cabins, be responsible for laundry or keep restaurants and passenger areas clean and tidy.

The type of person suited to this work

If you do not mind working hard and you want a job that includes travelling to different countries and having your accommodation and sometimes your meals provided, cruise ship work could be for you!

As you will probably have some contact with passengers, you should be happy meeting, talking with and helping people of all types with different backgrounds and nationalities. You should be polite and happy to help, and have good customer service skills.

Although you will work as part of a team, you will also need lots of initiative and be able to work alone. You should also be aware of your own and others' health and safety.

Working conditions

You will be expected to work long shifts, which for some posts can last up to ten hours. Although cruise ships appear to be glamorous, you might work in cramped conditions including in rough weather. However, you will get to see other parts of the world and meet lots of new people.

You might have to share your accommodation with other members of staff.

Short-term, holiday and summer work is available.

The future outlook

In the last seven years the cruise ship industry has become the second fastest growing sector in the UK and USA. The largest super-liners have become mobile holiday resorts and require over a thousand staff if they are to keep up to 3000 passengers happy and safe.

Due to rivalry between the main cruise companies and the targeting of new passenger markets, for example families, there has been a growth in number of new super-liners. The means that the employment situation is expected to remain positive for the forseeable future.

There is a well-recognised progression process in place on cruise ships. This starts at crew or cadet level and rises to officer level via a number of stages. However, in reality not everyone wants to apply for promotion, as earnings can actually be reduced because customers pay fewer tips to more senior staff.

When it is time to return to dry land, the skills gained on board will be useful in many areas of the business sector (purser) or hospitality and catering (steward). As a result your future career opportunities should be wide-ranging and positive.

Other related opportunities

- Administrator p6
- Catering / Restaurant Manager p85
- Hotel / Accommodation Room Attendant p94
- Housekeeper p97
- Waiting Staff p100

Advantages/disadvantages

- You might be away from home for months at a time.
- You will be able visit lots of places around the world.
- Your accommodation could be cramped and you might have to share with other crew members.
- Pay can be better than on shore.

Earnings guide

- Salaries are higher than in comparable on-shore posts. Salaries will depend on the company and liner that you work for, so contact companies for their earnings guide. Starting salaries normally range from £17,000–£20,000, rising to £22,000–£26,000 with experience.
- A chief purser or steward can earn between £45,000 and £55,000.
- Accommodation and food are also normally included. Some employees may also receive tips from passengers.

CRCI:AD/C/WF | CLCI:CAT/IB/YAL

Qualifications and courses

entry level

To both enter and train while working in this career, you will need qualifications at Level 1–8. Please refer to explanation on page vii.

Purser

- A levels/H grades or equivalent are normally required, and many employers prefer a degree in a related subject such as hospitality or travel and tourism. The normal entry requirements for a degree in a travel or hospitality subject are 2 A levels/3 H grades, or equivalent. No specific A level subjects are required. The University of Plymouth offers a degree in Cruise Operations Management.
- Related experience, for example working in a hotel or holiday resort, reception work or administration, is normally required. For senior positions, managerial experience may be required.
- Knowledge of a language other than English is an advantage.

Steward

- There are no formal entry requirements for this work, but relevant experience in the leisure and hospitality industry is normally required.
- Training is provided on the job, and covers subjects such as safety, health, environment, survival and rescue, fire, First Aid, etc, as well as company-specific training.
- It may be possible to gain NVQs/SVQs in areas such as hospitality, catering and housekeeping.

Further information

Caterer website
www.caterer.com
Lists hospitality vacancies.

Passenger Shipping Association
1st Floor,
41–42 Eastcastle St
London
W1W 8DU
020 7436 2449
www.the-psa.co.uk

Here's Melanie Gates's story:

Air Traffic Controller

Flying and airplanes have always been important to 24-year-old Melanie who initially wanted to become a pilot. Because of this she did work experience at Bournemouth Airport both with the Flying Club and in the control tower. She found air traffic really interesting and it became her first career choice. After her A levels she started a Physics degree at Southampton University but she also applied to the National Air Traffic Services (NATS) and was accepted onto their one-year training course at the College of Air Traffic Control, Bournemouth. She gave up her degree to complete this course. Melanie now works at Heathrow and is married to Rob who is also an Air Traffic Controller.

WHAT THE JOB ENTAILS

'My job is all about controlling airplanes. There are four different positions we operate. GMP (Ground Movement Planner) is where we issue aircraft their start-up and push-back clearances; GMC (Ground Movement Controller) is the person responsible for giving aircraft their taxiing instructions. Then we have Departures and Arrivals which obviously control aircraft taking off and landing, and at most airports this role is carried out by one person as there is only one runway for planes to use, but at Heathrow we have two runways and two controllers.'

WHAT'S HOT AND WHAT'S NOT ABOUT THE JOB

'No two days are ever the same. I find the variety both challenging and rewarding and I don't think air traffic is something you could ever get bored with. Also, the wages are good and the people you work with tend to be on the same wavelength. However, the shift pattern can be anti-social, but I think the sacrifice of the odd Saturday night off is well worth it!'

Melanie says you have to be highly professional and determined, with self-belief and a sense of humour, to do what she does. Aptitude for the job is much more important than formal qualifications and grades. The training is very comprehensive and she says if you work hard and listen to people throughout your training you will definitely see the rewards once you are qualified.

WHAT THE FUTURE HOLDS

'At the moment I am happy as a controller and I have recently qualified as an instructor and that is very rewarding, teaching a new student and watching them progress. However, there are many ways for me to progress into supervisory roles or to specialise in training or operations. I could go further into management but I'm actually very interested in a spin-off career such as the investigation of aircraft incidents and accidents. I can't really say which way I will progress but I'm sure whatever direction I take I will continue to enjoy the challenges.'

CRCI:AD/C/WF | CLCI:CAT/IB/YAL

Distribution Manager

What the work involves

- You will be responsible for planning and managing the control and movement of goods or raw materials held in stock.
- Your role will involve ensuring that the right quantity of goods arrives on time and in excellent condition.
- Using ICT, you will manage stock levels and monitor the ordering and storage of goods.
- Your job will include liaising and negotiating with customers and suppliers.
- Distribution managers work for distribution and manufacturing companies, wholesalers and major retail companies such as supermarkets.

The type of person suited to this work

Distribution is a fast-moving industry and ICT is at its centre, so your computer skills will need to be excellent. Like the computer programs you will use, you will need to be systematic and logical but you will also need brilliant communication skills to deal with people at different levels.

It may be that the goods you have to order come from far-flung places. This means that the supply chain you will be managing might be very complex. You will also need to able to deal with the stress of making sure that you get the goods at the best price and supply them in the right condition.

Working conditions

Most of your work will be in an office, working on a computer and using a phone. You will also travel to meetings with suppliers or customers and visit storage depots.

Your hours will be mainly office hours, Monday–Friday, but you may have to do shift work or work weekends and evenings on a rota system.

There may be travel away from home and, for some, travel overseas.

The future outlook

There are more than 83,000 distribution managers working for a wide range of companies, including warehouse and distribution firms but also manufacturers, major retail companies, the Armed Forces and central and local government. It is a growth industry because if it is done well organisations have less waste and bigger profit margins.

You can move on into general management of larger units, or more specialised roles – for example with scope for project management and possibly foreign travel.

entry level

To both enter and train while working in this career, you will need qualifications at Level 4–8. Please refer to explanation on page vii.

Qualifications and courses

- There are no specific entry requirements; however, many employers recruit graduates. It is also possible to work your way up from a junior post by gaining NVQ/SVQ qualifications or professional qualifications.
- Degrees and postgraduate courses are available in areas such as logistics,transport management and supply chain management. The usual minimum entry requirements for a degree course are 5 GCSEs/S grades and 2 A levels/3 H grades or equivalent. For postgraduate courses, a relevant degree or a professional qualification and relevant work experience are required.
- People working in the industry can study for the CILT's professional qualifications at college or by distance learning. The Introductory Certificate is suitable for employees new to the profession. The Certificate is aimed at supervisors and first line managers. The Professional Diploma is intended for middle managers, including recent graduates, and fulfils the requirements for membership of the Institute.
- Senior distribution managers can take the CILT Advanced Diploma or study for a Master's in Logistics. A distance learning MSc is offered by Aston University in partnership with CILT.
- Distribution Managers may find it helpful to take the Certificate of Professional Competence of the Department of Transport (Department of the Environment in Northern Ireland).

CRCI:WB

CLCI:YAS

Other related opportunities

- Air / Ship Broker p554
- Freight Forwarder p566
- Importer / Exporter p567
- Transport Manager (Road) p585
- Warehouse p586

Advantages/disadvantages

- As a key figure in your company, you will have the satisfaction of making sure your supply chain works and that your customers are happy.
- The demands of coordinating vehicles, products and people, and tight deadlines, can make this a stressful role.

Earnings guide

- Salaries start at £19,000–£20,000 per year, increasing to £22,000–£24,000.
- Experienced managers earn around £27,000–£35,000+.
- Senior managers can earn up to £60,000.
- There may be allowances for unsocial hours and a company car.

Further information

Skills for Logistics
14 Warren Yard
Warren Farm Office Village
Milton Keynes
MK12 5NW
01908 313360
www.skillsforlogistics.org

Freight Transport Association
Hermes House
St Johns Road
Tunbridge Wells
TN4 9UZ
01892 526171
www.fta.co.uk

Careers in Logistics
www.careersinlogistics.co.uk

Chartered Institute of Purchasing & Supply
Easton House
Easton on the Hill
Stamford
Lincolnshire
PE9 3NZ
01780 756777
www.cips.org

Driver

What the work involves

Driver

- As a driver you will play an essential part in transporting people and goods by road to locations all over the country and possibly overseas.

Bus driver

- You will drive a bus, taking your passengers on short journeys and collecting fares or checking passenger passes.
- You will be responsible for ensuring the safety of your passengers and also for the security of the bus during your shift.

Coach driver

- You will drive a coach, taking your passengers on trips or long journeys.
- You will issue and check tickets, pack away luggage and give advice to customers about the journey.

Chauffeur

- You will be responsible for driving people and their luggage to wherever they want to go.
- You may drive your employer to work, meetings or social events, take children to school, drive a bride to her wedding, or drive a funeral car.

Large Goods Vehicle driver

- You will drive a vehicle over 7.5 tonnes – this will involve planning a route and collecting, transporting and delivering goods throughout the UK and sometimes to Europe.
- Loading and unloading may be part of the job and you will need to make sure your delivery is secure.

Taxi driver

- You will drive a taxi or minicab to take your customers to where they want to go by the quickest route.
- Using a radio to locate your next job, or looking for people signalling in the street, you will pick up passengers, help them with their bags and collect their fares.

Van Driver

- You willl drive a van or light truck up to 7.5 tonnes, to take goods to and from different places such as shops, offices, factories and household deliveries.
- Loading your van at a collection point and unloading at drop-offs will be regular tasks.

Driver's mate

- You will travel with a driver and help them to load and unload a van, truck or LGV.
- Working as a team with your driver you will help them decide on the best route, reverse safely and deal with customers.

The type of person suited to this work

You must be a calm, unflappable person as you will need to be able to cope with heavy traffic and timetables, as well as other road users! You will be responsible for the people or goods you are transporting, so a good understanding of safety and security is essential.

A pleasant manner is important because you will be dealing with customers or passengers who may be difficult, especially if you are running late. But you will also need to enjoy your own company if you are driving an LGV.

There is nearly always some paperwork involved, for example you may have to record your hours or write reports about vehicle faults or accidents.

Working conditions

You will spend quite long periods of time sitting in a driver's seat or cab, which can be quite cramped, though modern LGVs and coaches can be very comfortable.

You will probably have to work shifts, including early mornings, evenings, weekends and holidays.

You may have to wear a uniform for some roles, which could include a company hat, tie and coat.

As well as dealing with everyday road conditions, there is always a risk of traffic accidents.

You may need to help lift heavy loads and there can be a risk of back problems.

You may be away from home for long periods, in the UK or abroad.

The future outlook

Bus/coach driver

There are over 100,000 drivers working in 6,000 bus and coach companies in the UK. There are currently more vacancies than applicants. Most employers recruit people without PCV licences and train them themselves. Bus and coach operators are introducing measures to help keep drivers safe such as CCTV and exact fare safes.

With experience, you could apply for promotion to supervisor, service controller or driving instructor.

Chauffeur

Chauffeurs can work for specialist car companies or may be employed by a large company or organisation or a private individual. There are very few vacancies. The British Chauffeurs Guild runs an employment agency for their members.

Large goods vehicle driver

Main employers are haulage, transport and distribution and manufacturing companies. There is currently a shortage of experienced LGV drivers, but many people apply for LGV training vacancies. You could buy your own vehicle and become self-employed.

Taxi driver

There are about 450,000 taxi/minicab drivers in the UK and 80% of them are self-employed. It is a growth industry but once you have completed all the necessary checks and knowledge tests there is usually a waiting list to get your licence plate. Some drivers work towards owning their own fleets of taxis or go on to drive specialist vehicles.

Van driver

There are specialist delivery and transport companies but you could find employment with any company that does its own deliveries, for example large manufacturers and retailers. Some drivers go on to take the LGV or PCV test and progress to lorry or bus driving. Others become self-employed and own their own vans. The impact of internet shopping has helped to expand the size of businesses and related warehouse work. Drivers working in this area are required to have good customer care skills as they may have more door-to-door contact with customers.

Driver's mate

Haulage contractors, transport companies and large companies employ drivers' mates mainly for their LGV drivers. Employment as a driver's mate might lead to a job as a driver.

Qualifications and courses

entry level

To both enter and train while working in this career, you will need qualifications at Level 1. Please refer to explanation on page vii.

- Drivers need a full UK driving licence, to be in good health and at least 18 (often 21). PCV and LGV drivers also have to train for a Drivers Certificate of Professional Competence (CPC).

Bus/coach driver

- Most employers prefer GCSEs/S grades (A–C/1–3), particularly in English and maths. In order to obtain the requisite Passenger Carrying Vehicle (PCV) licence, you will need a full UK driving licence and satisfactory medical. You can either gain the PVC licence yourself, prior to entry, from the Driving Standards Agency, or obtain this whilst training on the job.
- Once employed, bus and coach drivers can work towards an NVQ/SVQ in Road Passenger Transport/Transporting Passengers by Road.

Chauffeur

- Experience in a related job such as taxi, police or armed forces driving may be an advantage. Many chauffeurs hold an advanced driving certificate.

Large goods vehicle driver

- You will need an LGV licence. Some employers offer training. For entrants aged between 16 and 21, there is the Young Drivers LGV Training Scheme, which leads to NVQ/SVQ Level 2 in Transporting Goods by Road and the LGV licence. GCSEs/S grades (A–E/1–5) including English and maths may be an advantage.
- NVQs/SVQs are also available in Transporting Goods by Road, Transporting Livestock by Road or Transporting Petroleum by Road.

Taxi driver

- Applicants for a taxi licence must be aged 21 or over and have held a full EU driving licence for at least 12 months. A medical and police check are required. Candidates need to pass a test on their knowledge of local routes.
- Some local authorities run training schemes and might require annual medicals. The Driving Standards Agency (DSA) has recently developed a Hackney Carriage/Private Hire Test Assessment, used by some licensing authorities. You can anticipate high insurance costs, if under 25 years of age.

Van driver

- You will need to gain the C1 Category licence if the weight of the vehicle you plan to drive and its load is between 3.5 and 7.5 tonnes.
- People working as drivers can take NVQ/SVQ Level 2 in Carry and Deliver Goods, or Levels 2 and 3 in Driving Goods Vehicles.

Driver's mate

- No specific qualifications are needed, but English, maths and geography skills can be an advantage. Some employers require a minimum age of 17.

Other related opportunities

- Airport Baggage Handler p558
- Courier p559
- Driving Examiner / Driving Instructor p565
- Lift Truck Operator p568
- Loader p569
- Motor Vehicle Work p217
- Port Operative p575
- Postal Delivery Person p576
- Rail p578
- Removals Operative p581
- Warehouse p586

Advantages/disadvantages

- You will be driving for long periods but there are strict rules about rest periods. Many LGVs have sleeping bunks and fridges and even cookers. Drivers say that they enjoy the feeling of being away from home and on the road.
- This is often a sociable job in which you could meet lots of different people. You may well have regular passengers or customers.
- This job can be hazardous, with the possibility of threats from passengers, but you may be trained in self defence and vehicle security.

Earnings guide

Bus/coach driver

- Trainees working towards their PCV license earn about £11,000. Starting salaries on qualification are about £15,500 per year, increasing to up to £22,000 with experience.
- Shift work and overtime can increase your wages.

Chauffeur

- You may earn from £22,000 and up to £30,000 with experience. Overtime and gratuities can increase your wages.

Large goods vehicle driver

- Starting salaries are £12,500–£14,500. With experience you could earn up to £20,000–£25,000.
- Drivers of specialist vehicles such as fuel or chemical tankers can earn up to £35,000.

Taxi driver

- Your earnings depend on the number of fares and tips you collect, and whether you own or rent your cab.
- Earnings range from £12,000 to £30,000+ in London.

Van driver

- You may earn £12,000 when starting out. This rises to £15,000–£22,500 with experience.

Driver's mate

- Salaries vary widely from £9,300 to £15,500. Drivers' mates with specialist skills in storage or goods handling may earn up to £24,000.

Further information

City & Guilds

www.cityandguilds.com/myperfectjob

Driving Standards Agency
Stanley House
56 Talbot Street
Nottingham
NG1 5GU
0115 901 2500
www.dsa.gov.uk

GoSkills (Sector Skills Council for passenger transport)
Concorde House
Trinity Park
Solihull
B37 7UQ
0121 635 5520
www.goskills.org

Skills for Logistics
14 Warren Yard
Warren Farm Office Village
Milton Keynes
MK12 5NW
01908 313360
www.skillsforlogistics.org

CHAUFFEUR

British Chauffeurs Guild Ltd
13 Stonecot Hill
Sutton
Surrey SM3 9HP
020 8544 9777
www.britishchauffeursguild.co.uk

LGV DRIVER

Freight Transport Association
Hermes House
St Johns Road
Tunbridge Wells
TN4 9UZ
01892 526171
www.fta.co.uk

Road Haulage Association Ltd
Roadway House
35 Monument Hill
Weybridge
Surrey KT13 8RN
01932 841515
www.rha.net

TAXI DRIVER

Licensed Taxi Drivers Association
Taxi House
Woodfield Road
London
W9 2BA
020 7286 1046
www.ltda.co.uk

Licensed Private Hire Car Association (LPHCA)
213 Kenton Road
Harrow
Middlesex HA3 OHD
07956 329 288
www.lphca.co.uk

CRCI:WE

CLCI:YAD

Driving Examiner / Driving Instructor

What the work involves

- You will teach people how to drive safely, and well enough to pass their driving test.
- Sitting next to your trainee driver, you will explain or assess basic motor and road skills as well as safe and courteous driving.
- You will keep written records of lessons, payments and performance. Examiners write short reports.
- At the end of each lesson or test you will provide feedback to the trainee driver on how they have performed.
- You could be a specialist examiner or instructor, for example working with trainee LGV or PCV drivers, or motorbike riders.

The type of person suited to this work

Not only will you need to be a good, safe driver, you will also need teaching or assessing skills. Instructors need to plan lessons to cover individual weaknesses whilst examiners need to assess whether a trainee driver should be given a full driving licence.

Driving instruction or examining is a people business. You will meet lots of different people and your instructions will need to be clear and safe, so your communication skills need to be well developed.

People learning to drive or being examined are often stressed and anxious, so you will need to be calm, steady and patient. A sense of humour can be an asset.

Working conditions

You will be based in a car most of the time, giving lessons or undertaking exams. There is a risk of traffic accidents.

Driving instructor

Instructors can spend more than eight hours a day sitting in the car ready to operate the dual controls to avert problems. Early morning, evening and weekend work is common.

Driving examiner

Driving examiners tend to work mainly 8.30 am–4.30 pm, taking up to seven tests per day.

The future outlook

Driving instructor

Driving instructors may work for driving schools, operate under a franchise, or have their own businesses. Around 80% of instructors are self-employed. There is currently a high demand for driving instructors in some areas of the country. However, there are no restrictions on the numbers of instructors, so in some areas there is strong competiton for pupils.

Driving examiner

Driving examiners are trained and employed by the Driving Standards Agency (DSA). The 1600 driving examiners work from one of the 400 test centres throughout England, Scotland and Wales.

entry level

1

To both enter and train while working in this career, you will need qualifications at Level 1. Please refer to explanation on page vii.

Qualifications and courses

- There are no formal educational requirements for either job.
- Key Skills in communication and working with others are useful.

Driving instructor

- To work as a driving instructor, you must be registered with the Driving Standards Agency as an Approved Driving Instructor (ADI). You will need to be over 21 and have held a full clean driving licence for four out of the last six years, with no criminal or motoring convictions.
- The ADI examination is in three parts: an IT-based theory test and a video-based hazard perceptions test; a practical driving test; and a practical teaching test. Applicants must pass the practical driving test within 3 attempts.
- NVQ/SVQs at Level 3 in Driving Instructor and in Bus/Coach Driving Instructor are available.

Driving examiner

- To work as a driving examiner you should be at least 21, have held a UK or European Union driving licence continuously for four years, and have no more than three current penalty points on your driving licence. You will need to pass an exam, driving test and interview before being selected for training and further assessment by the Driving Standards Agency (DSA).

CRCI:WE

CLCI:YAD

Other related opportunities

- Driver p563
- Work-based Training p188

Advantages/disadvantages

- It can be very rewarding to enable learners to become safe, qualified drivers.
- You may be able to negotiate your own hours and/or work for yourself.
- If you run your own car to give lessons you will have to pay for your fuel, insurance and maintenance costs.
- Examiners can face difficult situations when trainees react badly to being told they have failed. You will be trained on how to deal with upset candidates.

Earnings guide

Driving instructor

- If you are a self-employed driving instructor your earnings will depend on how much you charge for lessons and the number of trainees you teach. Instructors charge £15–£25+ per hour for a driving lesson.
- Full time driving instructors could earn £15,000 as a starting salary. With several years' experience this can rise to around £24,000-£30,000.
- Your income will be reduced by the costs of running and maintaining your vehicle or paying a franchise fee.

Driving examiner

- Full-time driving examiners earn about £20,500 per year, rising to £23,000 with experience. Supervising examiners may earn up to £30,000+.
- Salaries are higher in London.

Further information

Driving Instructors Association
Safety House
Beddington Farm Road
Croydon
CR0 4XZ
0845 345 5151
www.driving.org

Motor Schools Association of Great Britain Ltd
101 Wellington Road North
Stockport
Cheshire
SK4 2LP
0161 429 9669
www.msagb.co.uk

GoSkills (Sector Skills Council for passenger transport)
Concorde House
Trinity Park
Solihull
B37 7UQ
0121 635 5520
www.goskills.org

www.cityandguilds.com/myperfectjob

Freight Forwarder

What the work involves

- You will organise the transport of goods across the world for importers and exporters.
- Your role will involve working out if the freight needs special handling and whether it should go by sea, road or air.
- Arranging the packing, carriage, collection and storage of the goods will be part of your job.
- You will be responsible for dealing with paperwork, applying for customs clearance and calculating insurance, transport and customs costs.

The type of person suited to this work

As you will deal with lots of different customers, some of whom may not speak fluent English, your communication skills must be excellent. You will need to communicate by telephone, fax, letter, email or face to face.

You must be determined and have excellent bargaining skills to get the best prices and terms. You will also be a good problem-solver. For example, you might have to work out how to transport a valuable racehorse from Hong Kong to the UK.

Your basic maths skills will need to be good as you will be asked to calculate exchange rates, or work out if a large piece of cargo will fit into the cargo hold of a small aircraft.

Working conditions

Most of your work will be in an office at a workstation using the telephone, computer and fax.

You will also need to travel to meet customers and contractors – this could mean being away from home.

You may need to work extra hours or shifts to cover urgent deliveries and world time zones.

Working to meet strict deadlines can make this a stressful job.

The future outlook

Freight forwarding agents are specialised companies that collect and deliver goods for importers/exporters. Freight forwarding offices are usually in cities and near airports and ports. Opportunities are growing but it is a competitive industry and it helps if you have related work experience.

As you progress, there are opportunities to specialise in specific countries and industries. You could work within the entertainment industry, shipping film and concert sets around the world, or with medical and pharmaceutical supplies.

entry level

3–8

To both enter and train while working in this career, you will need qualifications at Level 3–8. Please refer to explanation on page vii.

Qualifications and courses

- Qualifications vary from a minimum of 4 GCSEs, including English and maths, to A levels, BTEC National in logistics, or a degree. Language skills are useful.
- You can enter with a degree, HND or Foundation degree in a related subject, for example logistics, supply chain management, international transport or transport management. Some companies have graduate training schemes.
- Key Skills in communications, ICT, problem solving and working with others are useful.
- Training after GCSE/S level or Advanced/Higher levels is usually an NVQ/SVQ in International Trade and Services, Traffic Office, or Distribution, Storage and Warehousing Operations.
- The British International Freight Association provides specialist training and a professional qualification for freight forwarders.
- Certificates and Diplomas in International Trade are also available from the Institute of Export.
- Entry to specialist degree courses in such subjects as international transport, logistics, supply chain management and transport management will require a minimum of 2 A levels/3 H grades and 5 GCSEs/S grades (A–C/1–3) or equivalent. For HNC/HND courses, you will normally need at least 1 A level/2 H grades and 4 GCSEs/S grades (A–C/1–3) or equivalent.

CRCI:WB

CLCI:YAS

Other related opportunities

- Air / Ship Broker p554
- Airline Customer Service Agent p557
- Distribution Manager p562
- Importer / Exporter p567
- Transport Manager (Road) p585
- Warehouse p586

Advantages/disadvantages

- This work varies. You may be specialising in, for example, moving film and TV crews and their equipment or handling perishable goods such as fruit.
- You may get a chance to travel or work overseas.
- You will get a buzz from helping customers meet tight delivery deadlines.

Earnings guide

- Trainees usually earn around £12,000–£15,000 per year.
- With experience you could earn around £17,000–£25,000.
- £30,000–£50,000 is possible for senior freight forwarders, directors and managers.

Further information

Skills for Logistics
14 Warren Yard
Warren Farm Office Village
Milton Keynes
MK12 5NW
01908 313360
www.skillsforlogistics.org

Institute of Export
Export House
Minerva Business Park,
Lynch Wood
Peterborough
PE2 6FT
01733 404400
www.export.org.uk

Chartered Institute of Logistics and Transport
Logistics and Transport Centre
Earlstree Court
Earlstree Road
Corby
NN17 4XQ
01536 740104
www.ciltuk.org.uk

Careers in Logistics
www.careersinlogistics.co.uk

Freight Transport Association
Hermes House
St Johns Road
Tunbridge Wells
TN4 9UZ
01892 526171
www.fta.co.uk

Importer / Exporter

What the work involves

- You will organise all aspects of exporting or importing goods for companies who source or sell them overseas.
- Liaising with shipping and forwarding companies, you will get the best prices, sources, quality and delivery services.
- You will deal with all the necessary financial paperwork, including invoicing and checking, and issuing Letters of Credit so that payment can be made.
- Working out accurate costings, including customs duties, insurance and forwarding charges will also be part of your job.
- You will use ICT to monitor the whole process.

The type of person suited to this work

As you will be making arrangements with a wide range of customers by telephone and email, your communication skills and social confidence needs to be good. Language skills are a real advantage. A well-organised approach is essential for keeping up with all the different tasks the job involves.

Dealing with numbers will be one of your key strengths because you will be responsible for working out currency exchanges and import and export duties. In addition, ICT skills are vital. You must have a flair for negotiation as you will need to bargain with shipping and distribution companies, as well as your customers and suppliers.

Working conditions

Most of your work will be in an office using the telephone, computer and fax.

You may need to work early mornings or late evenings if your customers or suppliers operate in a different time zone.

You may travel to meet suppliers or customers, which at higher levels could involve significant overseas travel.

The future outlook

As more products are bought and sold in a global market, the numbers of companies employing an import/export specialist have increased. Large freight-forwarding companies and import and export agencies also employ importers/ exporters.

Vacancies are competitive and usually require work experience in a related area, for example freight forwarding.

Some import/export specialists move across into overseas sales management as progression can be limited in small export/import departments.

entry level

3–8

To both enter and train while working in this career, you will need qualifications at Level 3–8. Please refer to explanation on page vii.

Qualifications and courses

- You can enter export or import at different levels. It is possible to enter following GCSEs/S grades or A levels/H grades, and work towards an NVQ/SVQ in International Trade and Services or a professional qualification. While there are no set minimum qualifications, most employers will expect: 4 GCSEs/S grades (A–C/1–3) including English and maths.
- Apprenticeships/Skillseekers may be available for candidates aged 16–24.
- You can enter with a degree, HND or Foundation degree in a related subject, for example logistics, supply chain management, international transport, business or languages. Some companies have graduate training schemes.
- The Institute of Export offers professional qualifications for people working in the field of international trade. The Advanced Certificate in International Trade leads to Associate Membership of the Institute, and the Diploma in International Trade leads to Graduate Membership. These qualifications are offered at colleges of further and higher education and by distance learning. Candidates must be at least 18 with 4 GCSEs/S grades at A–C/1–3 and 1 A level/H grade or equivalent, or an NVQ/SVQ Level 2 in International Trade and Services, or an Introductory Certificate of International Trade (Institute of Export), or be 21 years old with three years' practical experience.

Other related opportunities

- Air / Ship Broker p554
- Distribution Manager p562
- Freight Forwarder p566
- Marketing p151

Advantages/disadvantages

- This job allows you to use specialist skills to make the global supply chain work.
- Tight deadlines and budgets mean that stress is very much part of the job.
- If you move into managerial level work you will travel overseas to meet suppliers and customers.

Earnings guide

- Starting salaries at clerk level range from £12,500 to £15,000 per year.
- Experienced staff with more responsibility can earn up to £30,000.
- Import or export managers can earn up to £70,000.

Further information

Skills for Logistics
14 Warren Yard
Warren Farm Office Village
Milton Keynes
MK12 5NW
01908 313360
www.skillsforlogistics.org

Institute of Export
Export House
Minerva Business Park, Lynch Wood
Peterborough
PE2 6FT
01733 404400
www.export.org.uk

Chartered Institute of Logistics and Transport
Logistics and Transport Centre
Earlstree Court
Earlstree Road
Corby
NN17 4XQ
01536 740104
www.ciltuk.org.uk

Freight Transport Association
Hermes House
St Johns Road
Tunbridge Wells
TN4 9UZ
01892 526171
www.fta.co.uk

Lift Truck Operator

What the work involves

- You will use a lift truck, which has a special lifting and carrying platform, to load, unload, move and stack heavy goods.
- Once you have made sure your truck is working safely, you will drive it to collect the items you will be moving.
- You will operate the controls so that your fork or lifting gear is under the load to raise it safely.
- You will then deliver the goods, either to a vehicle for transportation or to a depot or warehouse for stacking.

The type of person suited to this work

An aptitude for driving is vital, because you will be manoeuvring your lift truck in very narrow awkward spots and watching out for hazards at all times. A responsible, mature outlook is required for working to strict safety rules. A good standard of physical fitness is helpful.

The ability to plan your work is also crucial so that when the transport arrives to deliver or collect your goods, you are in the right place at the right time.

You will be operating the truck on your own, but you will also need to be a team player as others will be working alongside you to do the job, for example warehouse operatives and LGV drivers.

Working conditions

Your work will be both inside a warehouse or factory and also outside in loading bays in all weather conditions.

Operating your equipment will mean sitting in a driving seat for long periods. There is also a risk of accidents.

Hours vary depending on your employer. You may work regular hours Monday to Friday, but many jobs include shift work covering evening, nights and weekends.

The future outlook

Lift truck operators work for any employer who uses lift truck equipment to move heavy goods. They can work for the manufacturing, transport, haulage, warehouse or retail industry. There are about 100,000 lift truck operators in the UK.

With experience, you can move on into supervisory or management jobs such as warehousing. You could go on to train new lift truck operators. Some large employers train lift truck operators up to become LGV drivers or Lift Truck Instructors.

entry level

To both enter and train while working in this career, you will need qualifications at Level 1. Please refer to explanation on page vii.

Qualifications and courses

- There are no minimum entry qualifications for this job but basic maths is useful to work out safe loads and weights. You will need to be physically fit and may have to pass a medical. Entrants may have experience of warehouse work, but direct entry is also possible.
- Key Skills in numeracy and working with others are useful.
- You will need to be at least 18 to work without supervision. A driving licence is required if the truck is to be used on public roads.
- You will receive basic training approved by the Health and Safety Commission, either in the workplace or in a training centre. A certificate of basic training is awarded on successful completion of theoretical and practical tests.
- Lift truck operators can work towards the NPTC (National Proficiency Tests Council) Level 2 Certificate of Competence in Fork Lift Truck Operations or NVQ/SVQ Levels 1 and 2 in Specialised Plant and Machinery Operations.
- Apprenticeships/Skillseekers may be available in such areas as Storage and Warehousing, Wholesale and Distribution, leading to NVQs/SVQs Levels 2 and 3.

CRCI:WB

CLCI:YAS

Other related opportunities

- Airport Baggage Handler p558
- Construction Plant Operator p49
- Driver p563
- Loader p569
- Port Operative p575
- Warehouse p586

Advantages/disadvantages

- You may be based outside in poor weather conditions.
- If you are keen on driving, large employers might give you the chance to move on to LGV driver training.
- It can be stressful to get a load out quickly, but there's a buzz when transport leaves on time.

Earnings guide

- Starting wages are about £12,000–£13,000 per year.
- With experience you could earn £14,000–£20,000.
- Some specialist operators can earn up to £28,000.
- There may be shift allowances and the opportunity to do overtime.

Further information

www.cityandguilds.com/myperfectjob

Skills for Logistics
14 Warren Yard
Warren Farm Office Village
Milton Keynes
MK12 5NW
01908 313360
www.skillsforlogistics.org

Association of Industrial Truck Trainers
The Spring Board Centre
Mantle Lane
Coalville
Leicestershire
LE67 3DW
01530 277857
www.aitt.co.uk

United Kingdom Warehousing Association
Walter House
418–422 The Strand
London
WC2R 0PT
020 7836 5522
www.ukwa.org.uk

National Plant Operators Registration Scheme (NPORS)
PO Box 204
Northwich
Cheshire
CW9 7PL
01606 49909
www.npors.com

Loader

What the work involves

- Loaders are operatives who load and unload goods into or out of a container or lorry.
- You will be responsible for moving goods, either by hand or using specialist lifting equipment.
- Vehicles may need to be loaded in delivery order and always carefully to make best use of the valuable space.
- You may be operating a lift truck or a specialist lorry loader (crane) if you are loading or unloading heavy items.
- You may also have additional tasks such as cleaning the loading bay or working as a driver's mate.

entry level

To both enter and train while working in this career, you will need qualifications at Level 1. Please refer to explanation on page vii.

The type of person suited to this work

If you like practical tasks and being outside in all weathers, this job is for you. You will also need to be prepared to learn about and follow safety rules because you will be working in a loading bay alongside a heavy goods operating plant. A good level of physical fitness is essential.

You will need to be good at working with others, for example drivers, and listening to any instructions you may be given to keep yourself and others safe.

You should also be good at working out how items can be fitted tightly into a space, as no employer is happy to pay high transportation costs for fresh air!

Working conditions

Most of your work will be outside in the loading depot. There may be some limited cover.

Hours vary. You may work regular hours, Monday to Friday, but it is often shift work and sometimes permanent night work.

There is a risk of accidents.

You may have to wear safety boots and gloves. Some employers require you to provide your own safety clothing.

The future outlook

A range of firms employ loaders, but usually expect you to do other duties. You could work for a manufacturing company moving goods from the factory floor onto wagons, or for a parcel company sorting and loading in delivery order, or a building materials supplier using a lorry loader to lift bricks onto a wagon.

It is possible to progress from this type of work, after additional training, into delivery, driving or warehouse management.

Qualifications and courses

- There are no minimum entry qualifications for this job. You will need to be physically fit and may have to pass a medical. Some employers prefer you to have a driving licence and be at least 18.
- Key Skills in communication and working with others are useful.
- You may be able to take an NVQ/SVQ Level 2 in Transporting Goods by Road and NVQ/SVQ Level 3 in Road Haulage and Distribution Operations or an NVQ/SVQ Levels 1–3 in Distribution, Warehousing and Storage Operations.
- If your employer expects you to operate a lift truck, they will give you basic training approved by the Health and Safety Commission. You may also be able to work towards NVQ/SVQs Levels 1 and 2 in Specialised Plant and Machinery Operations.
- If your employer expects you to operate a hydraulic lorry loader you will need to take a 2-day Lorry Loader Operating Safety Course. Many employers also expect you to be a category C driver to train as a specialist lorry loader.

Other related opportunities

- Airport Baggage Handler p558
- Driver p563
- Lift Truck Operator p568
- Port Operative p575
- Removals Operative p581
- Warehouse p586

Advantages/disadvantages

- If you are keen on going into LGV driving, your employer may be willing to train you.
- It is stressful working at speed to get a delivery loaded or unloaded.
- This job provides the satisfaction of working as part of a team to get deliveries out on time.

Earnings guide

- Starting salaries are usually £9,300–£11,000 per year.
- Loaders working as specialist lift truck operators can earn up to £20,000.
- Hydraulic lorry loaders who also work as an LGV driver can earn up to £26,000.
- Shift work or permanent nights increase earnings.

Further information

Skills for Logistics
14 Warren Yard
Warren Farm Office Village
Milton Keynes
MK12 5NW
01908 313360
www.skillsforlogistics.org

United Kingdom Warehousing Association
Walter House
418–422 Strand
London
WC2R 0PT
020 7836 5522
www.ukwa.org.uk

Association of Industrial Truck Trainers
The Spring Board Centre
Mantle Lane
Coalville
Leicestershire
LE67 3DW
01530 277857
www.aitt.co.uk

National Plant Operators Registration Scheme (NPORS)
PO Box 204
Northwich
Cheshire
CW9 7PL
01606 49909
www.npors.com

www.cityandguilds.com/myperfectjob

Lock Keeper

What the work involves

- You will look after the locks that change the water level on inland waterways, such as canals and rivers, to allow boats to travel up and down different gradients.
- You will oversee a series of locks and check that boat crews operate them safely.
- Registering boats and collecting fees may be part of your job.
- You will probably undertake some general maintenance work on your 'patch' to ensure it is safe and clear of rubbish.
- Your work could involve liaising with environmental bodies and other lock keepers.

The type of person suited to this work

Locks vary in size and complexity. You will need to be strong to operate some locks, while others are hydraulic and don't require strength, but demand reasonable technical ability.

Working with the public, explaining lock operation and keeping an eye on their safety, means that you will need to be good at dealing with people. You may have to collect fees, so you should be honest and good with money.

Lock keepers are responsible for keeping their stretch of water clean and safe so you will need to be keen on doing practical jobs, such as keeping your areas of water and pathways clear of vegetation and litter.

Working conditions

You will undertake most of your work outdoors in all kinds of weather.

You will be expected to work longer hours, including evenings and weekends at busy times like the summer.

You may live in a house provided by the company. Some of these are based in remote places whilst others are located in more built-up areas.

Your job will include some heavy lifting.

The future outlook

The number of boats on inland waterways has grown, but as locks are modernised, some can be operated very easily by boat crews.

Jobs are mainly with British Waterways and the Environment Agency but have competitive entry. Employers increasingly recruit general waterways operatives, sometimes on a seasonal or temporary basis. They carry out mainly practical maintenance work as well as bridge or lock keeping.

Opportunities for promotion are limited but it is possible to move to a supervisory job.

entry level

1

To both enter and train while working in this career, you will need qualifications at Level 1. Please refer to explanation on page vii.

Qualifications and courses

- There are no minimum qualification entry requirements for this job but it may be useful to have some GCSEs/S grades.
- You will need good general fitness and to be able to swim.
- Employers look for practical skills, for example in DIY or sailing. Most lock keepers have previous waterways experience.
- Key Skills in communication and working with others are useful.
- Training is mainly practical and provided on the job by experienced colleagues.
- You may be able to work towards NVQs/SVQs such as Level 2 in Maintaining and Conserving Coasts, Rivers and Waterways.

Other related opportunities

- Countryside Work p235
- Groundsperson / Greenkeeper p251
- Labourer p60
- Marine Engineering / Marine Industry p213

Advantages/disadvantages

- You may be provided with a house in an attractive area.
- Your employer will expect you to be responsible for the safety of people using your stretch of water and this can involve you in conflict.
- You may have to start work very early in the mornings.

Earnings guide

- Starting pay can be £11,500–£15,000 per year. The higher rates are paid if shift work is involved.
- Experience can increase pay levels up to £20,000.
- Accommodation may be included and some lock keepers supplement their earnings by selling refreshments and gifts to visitors.

CRCI:WF

CLCI:YAG

Further information

www.cityandguilds.com/myperfectjob

British Waterways – For vacancies in Scotland
Scottish Region
Canal House
Applecross Street
Glasgow
G4 9SP
0141 332 6936
www.britishwaterways.co.uk

British Waterways – For vacancies in Northern England
Personnel Department
Fearns Wharf
Neptune Street
Leeds
LS9 8PB
0113 281 6800
www.britishwaterways.co.uk

British Waterways – For vacancies in rest of UK
Personnel Department
Willow Grange
Church Road
Watford
WD17 4QA
01923 201120
www.britishwaterways.co.uk

Environment Agency
08708 506506
www.environment-agency.gov.uk
Check website for details of local offices

Merchant Navy

What the work involves

- You will work on board a ship which is part of the UK Merchant Fleet. The Merchant Navy is a collective term for the UK shipping industry.
- Officers are part of the ship's management team and supervise the work of ratings.

Deck officers

- At sea you will use specialised equipment to help navigate the ship.
- In port you will be responsible for cargo handling and ship stability.

Engineering officers

- A ship is like a small town, and you will be responsible for supervising the maintenance of all the machinery and technical equipment on board.
- At sea you may need to manufacture and install spare parts to repair any damage.

Ratings

- You will work as a deck, engineering or catering rating.
- Jobs vary depending on your rating but you will carry out tasks as part of a team with your ship's officers and other ratings.

The type of person suited to this work

Life at sea is very different from life on shore. You will need strong teamwork skills when you are living and working, possibly for months at a time, with others.

You must be able to remain calm and unflappable in an emergency, and work with the rest of the crew to safeguard your passengers and your ship. A good level of physical fitness is essential for all roles in the Merchant Navy.

Officers

You should have a strong ability and interest in technology. Modern ships use advanced satellite and computer systems. When you are at sea it will be down to you to find solutions to any serious problems that may arise.

Ratings

Ratings need an interest in their job area. It also helps if you are flexible and have excellent practical skills. You will also need a mature and responsible approach to your work.

Working conditions

You will be working on a boat, often out at sea. In bad weather this can be uncomfortable.

Ships operate 24/7. You will work for four hours on watch followed by eight hours off.

Conditions vary but living conditions are usually of a high standard.

Leave entitlement is good: for example, after a voyage lasting four months you will get two months off.

You will be provided with a uniform.

The future outlook

The UK merchant fleet includes ferries, cruise ships, containerships, tankers, bulk carriers and specialised vessels. Ships carry over 90% of world trade and sea-borne trade is forecast to keep growing. Passenger ferries have had a slight decline but the passenger cruise business is expanding. However, jobs on cruise ships are very popular so you will probably need to get experience on another vessel first.

Once qualified you will be able to work for different types of shipping employers: for example, you could work for the Royal Fleet Auxiliary supporting the Royal Navy at sea.

Officers

Around 18,000 qualified deck and engineering officers are employed in the industry. The UK shipping industry recruits on average 600 trainees a year.

Progression can be through the officer ranks to captain or chief engineering officer. Some seafarers move into shore-based posts, such as lecturing, port management, ship broking and marine insurance.

Ratings

The recruitment of trainee UK ratings is fairly limited. Catering ratings are often recruited already trained. Progression for ratings, if they get the right qualifications and experience, can be to chief petty officer or to third officer.

Qualifications and courses

- At all levels you will need to be in excellent health with good eyesight and perfect colour vision, and be able to swim.

Officer Cadet

- A good standard of eyesight (with glasses or contact lenses if needed) is required for prospective deck (navigation) personnel. For Officer Cadet Training you can enter with at least 4 good GCSEs/S grades in English, maths, physics or a combined science; or with A levels/H grades.

Deck officers

- Entry at this level requires sponsorship from either a shipping company or a training organisation; The Merchant Navy Training Board (MNTB) has a list of organisations currently providing sponsorship. Entry requirements are generally an HND, 4 GCSEs/S grades (A–C/1–3) in maths, with either physics or science, or a Scottish Professional Diploma. A degree sponsorship requires 2 A levels/H grades, usually including maths or physics, or equivalent. For a Foundation degree, 120 UCAS points, plus GCSEs/S grades (A–C/1–3) in English and maths (A–B/1–2), physics or science.
- Entrants normally continue their training towards the Maritime Agency's Watch Keeping Navigation Officer's Certificate of Competency.

Engineering officers

- You can train for the Watch Keeping Engineering Officer's Certificate of Competency, an HND or degree in marine engineering and NVQ/SVQ Level 3 in Merchant Vessel Engineering for engineering officers.

Ratings

- There are no minimum entry requirements but it is useful to have at least 3 GCSEs/S grades (A–D/1–4); maths, physics and English are all useful.

entry level

To both enter and train while working in this career, you will need qualifications at Level 1–8. Please refer to explanation on page vii.

- The most useful Key Skill is working with others.
- Ratings are trained through the Marine Traineeship, which takes 12–18 months. This includes six weeks of training at college, followed by 6 –8 months at sea, and then further periods at college and at sea. You will work towards NVQ/SVQ qualifications at Level 2.
- You can progress onto a Marine Apprenticeship, leading to NVQ/SVQ Level 3 in Marine Vessel Operations or Marine Engineering Operations.

Other related opportunities

- Fisherman / Woman p245
- Marine Engineering / Marine Industry p213
- Pilot p573
- Port Operative p575
- Royal Navy p516

Advantages/disadvantages

- British ships operate all over the world so you will travel widely. If you are working on a cruise ship you will travel to dream destinations but opportunities to go ashore can be limited.
- You will be spending a lot of time with the crew and will develop strong friendships.
- Once you are trained and you have got some experience, you will be able to choose the type of ship you work on.
- Your earnings may be tax-free if you are away from the UK on a long voyage.
- Whilst you will have to spend long periods of time at sea, you will be able to take relatively long periods of leave to make up for this.

Earnings guide

- You will have free food and accommodation when you are at sea.

Officers

- Third officers earn about £22,500 per year.
- Second officers can earn up to £28,000.
- Chief officers can earn about £35,000.
- Captains and chief engineers can earn £55,000+.

Ratings

- Starting salaries for trainee ratings are about £14,500.
- On qualification and experience pay can rise to £19,000.
- Senior ratings can earn upwards of £22,500.

Further information

Careers in Shipping
Carthusian Court
12 Carthusian Street
London
EC1M 6EZ
0800 085 0973
www.gotosea.org.uk

Marine Society
202 Lambeth Road
London
SE1 7JW
020 7654 7000
www.marine-society.org

Merchant Navy Training Board
Carthusian Court
12 Carthusian Street
London
EC1M 6EZ
020 7417 2800
www.mntb.org.uk

Maritime & Coastguard Agency- Human resources team
Bay 3/19 Spring Place
105 Commercial Road
Southampton
SO15 1EG
023 8032 9308
www.mcga.gov.uk

Pilot

What the work involves

- You will be responsible for the safety of your passengers, crew and cargo and will need to carry out a range of safety, route and fuel checks before each flight.
- When flying you will keep in radio contact with air traffic controllers, inform and direct the crew, plan your route and use computer systems to control and monitor the aircraft.
- After each flight you will need to write a report and record any problems that took place.

Airline/commercial

- You will be employed to fly planes, with passengers or freight on board, on short- or long-haul flights for pleasure or business.

Helicopter

- You will fly helicopters with passengers or equipment on board, for a wide range of business, leisure and emergency trips.

The type of person suited to this work

You must have a strong sense of responsibility as you will have the lives of lots of people in your hands. You will need to be technical and confident enough to take charge of your aircraft but you will also need to follow the instructions of air traffic control exactly as they are given. Good communication and team-work skills are essential.

Even when you have earned your wings, your health, plus your skills and competencies on aircraft/helicopters, will be regularly assessed, so you must be keen to keep on learning and be committed to keeping fit.

Working conditions

You will wear a uniform and sit for hours in a noisy, fairly cramped flight deck.

Planes fly 24/7 so you will have to work some unsocial hours and holidays. You may get jet lag if you work on long-haul flights.

Bad weather can make flying conditions uncomfortable and even dangerous.

Helicopter pilots involved in rescue work are expected to operate in often dangerous conditions.

The future outlook

Competition for vacancies, particularly sponsored training places, is intense. Competition for pilot training in the forces is also intense and pilots must serve for a minimum of 12 years before they can take up employment with a commercial employer. You could pay for your own training through an approved training school, but this is a very expensive route.

Airline/commercial

There are over 200 companies employing pilots in the UK. As a newly qualified pilot you would begin as a second pilot working with a training captain on short-haul flights, to give you maximum experience of take-offs and landings.

Promotion is from second officer, to first officer and to captain. Promotion to captain usually requires at least 5,000 flying hours, which takes up to ten years. Flights are predicted to increase in number over the next decade.

Helicopter

Main employers are offshore and onshore companies, plus the emergency services. Employment prospects in the UK offshore sector are currently good. Some helicopter pilots take more advanced training as a pilot. There are some limited opportunities for self-employment. There are predictions that helicopters may be used more in the future.

Qualifications and courses

- In all cases you will need to be physically fit with good health, hearing and eyesight as well as normal colour vision.
- All Key Skills are useful but especially numeracy, communication and ICT.
- You will need to get a Commercial Pilot's Licence CPL (A) and at least the taught part of the higher level Airline Transport Pilot's Licence ATPL (A) to be a commercial pilot, or the CPL (H) or ATPL (H) to be a helicopter pilot. There are two main ways to do this:
- You can pay for a full-time 15-month training course or if you have a Private Pilot's Licence (PPL) do a part-time modular course. You should be good at physics and maths. Full-time training courses typically cost between £50,000 and £65,000.
- You may be able to obtain one of the competitive full or partial employer sponsorships. You will usually need at least 5 GCSEs/S grades (A–C/1–3), including English, maths and science, and 2 A levels/3 H grades, preferably in maths and physics. Many employers recruit graduates.

entry level

To both enter and train while working in this career, you will need qualifications at Level 3–8. Please refer to explanation on page vii.

You should be at least 18 and may find it easier to gain sponsorship if you have got a Private Pilot's Licence (PPL).

Other related opportunities

- Air Cabin Crew p555
- Air Traffic Controller p556
- Engineer: Professional p205
- Merchant Navy p571
- Royal Air Force (RAF) p512

Advantages/disadvantages

- This job involves a lot of responsibility which can be stressful but rewarding.
- You will need to raise a lot of money if you can't get sponsorship. Helicopter training is even more expensive.
- It is an exciting job that sometimes involves travelling to exotic locations, but you will need to rest and so may not be able to do much sight-seeing.

Earnings guide

Airline/commercial

- Co-pilots start on around £25,000 per year.
- Experienced pilots earn up to £430,000.
- All salaries increase with experience and a captain can earn up to £85,000.
- Perks can include subsidised travel, plus a subsistence allowance when working away from home.

Helicopter

- Newly qualified commercial helicopter pilots can earn about £25,000+.
- Experienced pilots carrying passengers can earn £45,000–£70,000.

Further information

Air League
Broadway House
Tothill Street
London
SW1H 9NS
020 7222 8463
www.airleague.co.uk

British Airline Pilots Association
81 New Road
Harlington
Hayes
Middlesex
UB3 5BG
020 8476 4000
www.balpa.org.uk

British Helicopter Advisory Board
The Graham Suite, West Entrance
Fairoaks Airport
Chobham
Surrey
GU24 8HX
01276 856100
www.bhab.org

Civil Aviation Authority
Personnel Department,
Room 216
CAA House
45–59 Kingsway
London
WC2B 6TE
020 7453 6040
www.caa.co.uk

GoSkills (Sector Skills Council for passenger transport)
Concorde House
Trinity Park
Solihull
B37 7UQ
0121 635 5520
www.goskills.org

CRCI:WA

CLCI:YAB

Port Operative

What the work involves

- You may work at a commercial or passenger port.
- Most port operatives work as stevedores or in passenger operations.
- If you are a stevedore, you will use vehicles and machinery to load and unload cargo onto ships and move it to and from port loading bays and storage areas.
- If you are working in passenger operations, you will control and guide passengers and sometimes their vehicles as they drive through the port.

The type of person suited to this work

You must be a practical person and be good with machinery. You will use lifting equipment, fork-lift trucks, cranes and elevators to load and unload your cargo into and out of the ship's hold.

Working at speed to load cargo or passengers in a short period of time to get the ship out of port means you need to be a quick worker. At the same time you will need to think about the safety of your passengers and other workers, yourself and the condition of your cargo.

Do not even think about this job if you do not like heights. You will need to climb up and down ladders and may operate cranes. A good level of physical fitness is essential.

Working conditions

Most of your work will be outside in all weathers. You will also work in the ship's hold which can be cramped, stuffy, noisy and hot.

You will work 40 hours per week in shifts of eight hours. Shifts will include nights and, especially in passenger operations, holidays and weekends.

There could be a risk of back or other injury as you will be doing lots of lifting and bending.

The future outlook

Ships carry over 80% of world trade. Opportunities for port operatives are quite stable. Port operatives are employed by a port authority or a private company. Some are employed only on a casual or seasonal basis.

Technological changes could make this job less strenuous in the future with the introduction of more specialised cargo-moving equipment.

It is possible to progress to become a supervisor or into operations or port management.

entry level

1

To both enter and train while working in this career, you will need qualifications at Level 1. Please refer to explanation on page vii.

Qualifications and courses

- There are no formal entry requirements for this work, but if you have not got GCSEs/S grades in English and maths, employers may check your writing and numeracy skills. Many entrants are over 21.
- Physical fitness is required, it helps to be able to swim, and you may need normal colour vision. Candidates usually have to pass a medical.
- Key Skills in communication, working with others and numeracy will be useful.
- A driving licence is usually required. It helps to have experience operating cranes, fork-lift trucks or heavy goods vehicles.
- You will have about two weeks of entry training, covering safety, First Aid, sea survival and understanding of cargo handling. Candidates are then normally trained on the job by a supervisor or experienced worker. You can work towards an NVQ/SVQ Level 2 in Ports Stevedoring, Marine Operations (Ports) or Port Passenger Operations.

Other related opportunities

- Airport Baggage Handler p558
- Driver p563
- Labourer p60
- Lift Truck Operator p568
- Loader p569
- Merchant Navy p571
- Removals Operative p581

Advantages/disadvantages

- If you like using machinery, this job will give you the opportunity to train in operating a wide range of different equipment and vehicles.
- You will work as part of a team and be able to share the satisfaction of turning a ship around in time.

Earnings guide

- Starting salaries are about £12,000 per year.
- You can earn £15,000–£20,000 as you gain experience.
- You can earn more if you operate equipment needing additional skills, for example large cranes.
- Shift work and overtime can bring your wages up to £25,000.

Further information

Skills for Logistics
14 Warren Yard
Warren Farm Office Village
Milton Keynes
MK12 5NW
01908 313360
www.skillsforlogistics.org

Port Skills and Safety Ltd
Room 220
Africa House
64–78 Kingsway
London
WC2B 6AH
020 7242 3538
www.portskillsandsafety.co.uk

GoSkills (Sector Skills Council for passenger transport)
Concorde House
Trinity Park
Solihull
B37 7UQ
0121 635 5520
www.goskills.org

British Ports Association
Africa House
64–78 Kingsway
London
WC2B 6AH
020 7242 1200
www.britishports.org.uk

Postal Delivery Person

What the work involves

- You will have responsibility for the sorting and daily delivery of mail to homes, shops, factories and offices for your patch.
- Your day will start at the sorting office getting your mail ready for delivery, by sorting and packing your bag in the best order for your route.
- You will then deliver your mail by foot or bicycle or, in rural areas, by van.
- You may also be responsible for mail collections from post boxes and places of work.
- You will meet lots of different people whilst on your round.

entry level

To both enter and train while working in this career, you will need qualifications at Level 1. Please refer to explanation on page vii.

The type of person suited to this work

Your round could include several hundred addresses and cover up to eight miles a day so you will need to be fit, especially if you are doing the job on foot or by bicycle. You will also have to like being outdoors as you will be expected to deliver the mail in all weathers.

Honesty and reliability are vital qualities in this job. You will be carrying lots of valuable and urgent mail around and you are responsible for delivering it to the right place.

Do not think of this job if you do not like meeting people, because you will be talking to and advising customers every day when you are out on your round.

Working conditions

Most of your work will be outside in all weathers. A uniform, footwear and protective clothing will be provided.

If on foot, you may have to carry your mail in bags, though there will be arrangements to transport you and your mail out to the start of your route.

Shift work with an early morning (5am) start or late evening (10pm) finish is usual.

You may have to walk up steep hills and deal with minor hazards.

The future outlook

Postal delivery workers mainly work for the Royal Mail. Despite the growth of email and texting, the amount of mail sent continues to grow.

Recruitment tends to be steady and there are opportunities in urban and rural areas throughout the UK. Some workers start out with temporary work over the Christmas period and are retained.

It is possible to move into parcel deliveries, supervisory or managerial work.

Qualifications and courses

- No specific qualifications are required for this job. Candidates should be aged 18 or over, and selection is by an aptitude test, a fitness assesment and interview. You may have to have a medical examination.
- The ability to ride a bicycle and/or a driving licence with no more than six penalty points may be required.
- Key Skills in communication are useful.
- Postmen/women receive induction training. Further training is done on the job.
- Apprenticeships/Skillseekers are available for candidates aged 16–24. However, most candidates need to be at least 18 years of age and are recruited following an aptitude test (to check your ability to read addresses properly), fitness assessment and a competency-based interview.
- Training is chiefly on-the-job, lasting 18 months, and can include the chance to work towards an NVQ/SVQ in Mail Services at Level 2. With a minimum of one year's experience, you can seek advancement to supervisory or managerial levels.

CRCI:WB

CLCI:YAT

Other related opportunities

- Courier p559
- Driver p563
- Meter Reader p447
- Milk Delivery Person p448
- Warehouse p586

Advantages/disadvantages

- With a regular round you will really get to know your customers.
- There may be some hazards on your round; you will soon learn what to avoid. All the walking or cycling will keep you fit.
- Although you will have to start work by 5am if you are on the early shift, you will finish at around lunchtime.

Earnings guide

- The starting rate for staff over 18 is around £16,400 (more in London).
- After one year's experience you would earn about £18,000–£20,000 (more in London).
- There are additional payments for overtime and driving duties.

Further information

www.cityandguilds.com/myperfectjob

Royal Mail Group plc
148 Old Street
London
EC1V 9HQ
www.royalmail.com

Skills for Logistics
14 Warren Yard
Warren Farm Office Village
Milton Keynes
MK12 5NW
01908 313360
www.skillsforlogistics.org

Purchasing Administrator

What the work involves

- You will be responsible for buying the goods or services needed by a business, and providing the best value for money.
- Your first job is to find out what your employer wants to buy and how much the budget is.
- An important aspect will be to find the best suppliers and negotiate with them to get products or services at the right conditions and price.
- You will record your agreement in a formal contract.
- You will then be responsible for quality checks to make sure that the goods or services provided are of the standard agreed.

The type of person suited to this work

The reputation and profitability of your employer would be on the line if you bought poor value goods and services, so you will need to have a flair for identifying good suppliers, negotiation, tact and persuasion to do well in this job. Your communication skills also need to be excellent because you will deal with suppliers, from across the globe, and colleagues every day.

You will also need to be keen on computers, as you will use them both to research and keep in touch with suppliers.

Having a head for figures is essential as you will be dealing with your employer's budget and calculating all the costs involved in procuring your goods or services.

Working conditions

Most of your work will be undertaken in a busy office, using a phone and computer (including software such as spreadsheets and databases).

You may travel to meet suppliers and customers, which can mean time away from home.

You will work mainly office hours Monday to Friday. If your suppliers are in a different time zone to the UK, this can mean early mornings or late nights.

The future outlook

This is a developing area with more employers using a qualified purchaser to obtain the best value goods and services. Purchasing administrator jobs are competitive, but there is a shortage of qualified applicants for purchasing manager jobs.

Some buyers move into specialist areas, for example construction or chemicals. ICT purchasing is a new specialism and is predicted to grow with the expansion of e-business.

Promotion prospects are good, especially in large organisations.

entry level

3–8

To both enter and train while working in this career, you will need qualifications at Level 3–8. Please refer to explanation on page vii.

Qualifications and courses

- Employers usually ask for a degree or HND qualification. It may be possible to enter at a lower level and progress with experience and on-the-job training.
- The Chartered Institute of Purchasing and Supply (CIPS) accredits some degree courses in business (with purchasing options), logistics and supply chain management, and purchasing and supply chain management.
- Typical entry requirements for an HND are 1 A level/2 H grades and 4 GCSEs/S grades (A–C/1–3) or equivalent, and for a degree 2 A levels/3 H grades and 5 GCSEs/S grades (A–C/1–3), including maths and English.
- To progress you will need the CIPS professional qualifications. The Certificate and Advanced Certificate and the Graduate Diploma can be studied full time or part time at college, or by distance learning.
- The Certificate has no formal entry requirements. On completion of the Certificate, you can progress to the Advanced Certificate.
- The Graduate Diploma is made up of the Foundation Stage (exemptions available to accredited graduates) and the Professional Stage. You will need 2 A levels/three H grades and 3 GCSEs/S grades (A–C/1–3), a National Certificate/Diploma or the CIPS Advanced Certificate, or to be over 21 with relevant work experience.
- You can take NVQ/SVQs at Levels 2, 3 and 4 in Supply Chain Manangement as an alternative route.

Other related opportunities

- Air / Ship Broker p554
- Buyer p438
- Marketing p151
- Merchandiser p446

Advantages/disadvantages

- If successful, you can reach high levels of responsibility, and even travel overseas, early in your career.
- There is no doubt that this job is stressful. Businesses spend over half their money on the goods and services they need to buy, so mistakes could be expensive.

Earnings guide

- Starting pay for purchasing administrators is about £17,000 per year.
- For experienced purchasing administrators or new purchasing managers the salary range is £20,000–£29,000.
- £33,000 is usual for senior purchasing managers.
- £60,000+ is possible for purchasing directors.

Further information

Chartered Institute of Purchasing & Supply
Easton House
Easton on the Hill
Stamford
Lincolnshire
PE9 3NZ
01780 756777
www.cips.org

Skills for Logistics
14 Warren Yard
Warren Farm Office Village
Milton Keynes
MK12 5NW
01908 313360
www.skillsforlogistics.org

Skillsmart Retail
40 Duke Street
London
W1A 1AB
0800 093 5001
www.skillsmartretail.com

Rail

What the work involves

- Rail companies require skilled staff in a range of areas to help ensure that train services run efficiently and safely.

Track maintenance worker

- You will check the safety of the railway tracks and repair and maintain them. Making sure that all fastenings on the tracks are secure and laying new and replacement track will also be part of your job.
- You will also report or repair faults and damage on the line including bridges, tunnels and level crossings.

Station assistant

- You will respond to queries, assist some passengers on to and off the train safely, and deal with complaints.
- Your role also involves operating ticket barriers and making announcements.
- You will make sure that train doors are closed and signal to the guard when it's safe to set off.

Signalling technician

- You will be responsible for installing, servicing and repairing the signalling equipment that controls the movement of trains.
- When a fault is reported you will work out how to repair the problem.
- You will use technical drawings and tools to repair or replace faulty parts.

Train driver

- You will be responsible for driving the engines of trains carrying passengers or goods.
- Your job will involve carrying out safety checks, obeying signals and speed limits, and stopping at stations.
- You will need to look out for any problems with equipment in the driver's cab, or on the track, and report any faults or problems using the cab's phone or radio system.

Train conductor

- You will be responsible for safety, ticket checks and passenger comfort on trains.
- You will also make announcements, operate the door-locking mechanism and give signals to the driver to start the train.
- Walking through the carriages, you will be checking, and (if needed) selling, tickets.

The type of person suited to this work

You will be working in a high-profile industry where the safety of passengers is your responsibility, so you will need to have a safety-conscious and mature attitude. In an emergency situation you will need to be confident enough to take control until back-up help arrives.

Passengers will rely on you to get trains out on time so you will need to be reliable and punctual. However, when things go wrong some customers can become impatient and awkward, so you need excellent communication skills and patience to keep them calm and informed.

A good level of physical fitness will help you deal with the everyday demands of these roles.

CRCI:WD

CLCI:YAF

Working conditions

The average working week is 35 hours. All workers do shifts and some evening and weekend work.

You will wear a uniform and protective clothing when needed.

All jobs, except for station assistant, involve travel and possibly nights away from home.

Track maintenance worker

You will normally work outdoors, often at nights and during holiday periods when trains are not running.

Station assistant

This job involves working on station platforms in all weathers.

Signalling technician

You will work mainly outside alongside the tracks.

Train driver

You will spend long periods of time sitting alone in a small cab. This is a responsible job, requiring alertness to react quickly to warning signals inside or outside of the cab.

Train conductor

You will walk up and down the train carrying the ticket machine and a bag of cash.

The future outlook

If you work on trains or in a smaller station you will work for one of the 25 train operating companies. Network Rail employs staff for the larger stations. Britain has the fastest growing railway network in Europe, with journeys up by 42.1% over last 10 years. Train operating companies recruit regularly and there are skills shortages in many areas, particularly technical and engineering roles.

Network Rail is the company with responsibility for all aspects of the railway infrastructure including the track, bridges, viaducts, tunnels, level crossings, stations and signalling systems. Some track and signalling work is done by approved contractors, monitored by Network Rail engineers.

Track maintenance worker

Network rail employs 30,000 track maintenance workers. With an ageing network, and an increasing number of faults reported, work prospects are increasing. You could progress into supervisory roles.

Station assistant

You can progress to become senior station assistant or go on to become a station manager.

You can also apply to train as a conductor or be recommended for driver training.

Signalling technician

The number of technician jobs is increasing with the introduction of more sophisticated technical systems. You may be able to gain promotion from junior to senior technician, and then team leader or manager. Some people move into telecommunications.

Train driver

You may have the chance of moving into specialist jobs such as high speed or Eurostar trains or may gain promotion to driver leader or manager.

Train conductor

A number of trains on short journeys are now driver-only, however these areas have increased the number of revenue protection jobs (travelling on a number of trains checking tickets and passes).You can progress to inspection, supervisory or managerial work or go into driver training.

Qualifications and courses

- You will need to be physically fit and at least 18, with good eyesight and hearing, and you will have to pass a medical examination.

Track maintenance worker

- There are no formal entry requirements for this job, although reading and writing skills are important. Previous experience of manual work is useful.
- Track workers are trained on the job. It is possible to work towards NVQ/SVQ Levels 2 and 3 in Railway Engineering: Permanent Way Maintenance/Renewals.
- Apprenticeships/Skillseekers may be available for those aged 16–24 and include residential training.

Station assistant

- Some employers ask for 4 GCSEs/S grades (A–C/1–3). You may need experience of working with the public.
- You will be trained on the job after an induction course. It is possible to work towards an NVQ/SVQ Level 2 in Rail Transport Operations (Passenger Services) or in Customer Service. Apprenticeships/Skillseekers for those aged 16–24 may be available.

Signalling technician

- Entrants to this job often have experience or qualifications in a related field, for example, electronics.
- School or college-leavers may be recruited on an Apprenticeship/ Skillseekers. The normal entry requirements are 3–5 GCSEs/S grades (A–C/1–3), including English, maths and science, or an equivalent qualification. Apprenticeship/Skillseekers trainees work towards NVQ Levels 2 and 3 in Railway Engineering: Rail Signal Installation/ Testing/Maintenance.

Train driver

- There are no specific entry qualifications for this job, although some train operators look for GCSEs/S grades in English and maths. You will need to be at least 21 and pass aptitude/skills tests and an interview. Applicants must have a full UK driving licence.

entry level

To both enter and train while working in this career, you will need qualifications at Level 1–3. Please refer to explanation on page vii.

- Training includes theoretical sessions, practice with a driving instructor, and route learning with an experienced driver. Trainee drivers may work towards NVQ/SVQ Level 2 in Rail Transport Operations (Driving).

Train conductor

- There are no specific entry qualifications for this job, although cash handing skills are useful. You will need to pass aptitude tests and an interview. Training includes theoretical sessions, and practice on board trains. Trainee guards/conductors/train managers may work towards NVQ/SVQ Level 2 in Rail Transport Operations (Passenger Services).

Other related opportunities

- Airline Customer Service Agent p557
- Courier p559
- Driver p563
- Engineer: Technician p208
- Railway Fitter / Electrician p223

Advantages/disadvantages

- There is a real sense of satisfaction from a job well done, when trains run on time and your passengers or goods arrive at their destination safely.
- Delays will mean pressure – either to get maintenance work done as quickly as possible, or to keep passengers comfortable and informed.
- Most railway workers are not keen on the shift work, but the pay is higher to compensate.
- Working with the public can be stressful, especially when you have to explain delays or accidents.

Earnings guide

Track maintenance worker

- Starting salary is from £12,000 to £15,000 per year. With experience and supervisory responsibility this can rise up to £20,000.
- Some senior track workers, working unsocial hours, can earn up to £30,000.

Station assistant

- Starting salary is around £12,500.
- Experienced assistants earn up to £18,000 and team leaders £21,000.

Signalling technician

- Starting salary is about £15,000 and with experience can be up to £28,000.
- Highly skilled and experienced workers can earn more than £35,000.

Train driver

- While training you can earn from £12,000–£15,000 and after training £25,000–£31,000.
- Experienced drivers can earn over £40,000.

Train conductor

- Starting salary is about £12,000,
- When trained and with experience £18,000–£21,000.
- With overtime it is possible to make up to £25,000.

Further information

GoSkills (Sector Skills Council for passenger transport)
Concorde House
Trinity Park
Solihull
B37 7UQ
0121 635 5520
www.goskills.org

Network Rail
40 Melton Street
London
NW1 2EE
020 7557 8000
www.networkrail.co.uk

Careers in Rail
www.careersinrail.org

Eurotunnel
UK Terminal
PO Box 302
Folkestone
Kent
CT19 4QZ
08457 697397
www.eurotunnel.com

Association of Train Operating Companies
3rd Floor
40 Bernard Street
London
WC1N 1BY
020 7841 8000
www.atoc-comms.org

CRCI:WD

CLCI:YAF

Removals Operative

What the work involves

- You will move furniture and personal belongings from one location to another.
- Fragile items will need to be carefully packed and large items need to be taken apart to fit them into the removals van.
- You will have to pack the van in a planned way to make the most of the space and prevent damage in transit.
- Once you have driven the goods to their destination you will have to unload and unpack.
- You will also need to put large items of furniture back together again and put items where the customer wants them.

entry level

1

To both enter and train while working in this career, you will need qualifications at Level 1. Please refer to explanation on page vii.

The type of person suited to this work

The removals business is a people business. Your customers will be stressed about moving and will need your help. They will also rely on you to keep calm and cheerful. Your careful nature and honesty are also vital as you will be dealing with valuable and fragile items on a regular basis.

As you will be working in a small team you will need to be good at working with others and listening to any instructions you may be given to keep yourself and others safe.

You should be fit and enjoy practical work. You will be lifting and carrying large items and sometimes removing door or window frames to get them out of or into a property.

Working conditions

Most of your work will be either in your van or in customers' homes or workplaces. Some trips can involve time away from home and quite long journeys.

Basic hours are 39–40 per week, but some days will be very long as you will have to work until the job is finished. A lot of moves take place at weekends.

You may be at risk of back injuries as there is a lot of lifting and carrying.

The future outlook

There are removals companies throughout the UK, though most are based in urban areas.There are about 30,000 removal operatives and it is a steady area of work as people and businesses are always on the move. The level of work may be affected by the housing market.

Promotion prospects are limited, but you may be able to progress on to driving, specialist packing, supervisory or managerial work.

Self-employment may be possible by buying or leasing a van and offering a removal service.

Qualifications and courses

- No particular educational qualifications are needed although GCSEs/S grades in English and maths are useful. You will need to be in good health and physically fit. Some firms will accept you at 16, whilst others specify a minimum age of 18, or even 21. A full driving licence is sometimes required.
- Key Skills in communication and working with others are useful.
- Most people are trained on the job by experienced staff. Some firms send staff on short courses run by the British Association of Removers. Courses include removals management and specialist packing.
- You may be able to take an NVQ/SVQ Level 2 in Storage and Warehousing, or Carry and Deliver Goods and NVQs/SVQs Levels 2 and 3 in Driving Goods Vehicles, or other related areas.

CRCI:WG | CLCI:YAT

Other related opportunities

- Airport Baggage Handler p558
- Driver p563
- Loader p569
- Port Operative p575
- Roadie p406
- Warehouse p586

Advantages/disadvantages

- The job may involve early starts and late finishes, especially during house removals when legal processes can cause delays.
- You will get satisfaction from doing a really professional job when you complete the move. Plus, happy customers may give tips.

Earnings guide

- Starting wages are about £12,000–£13,000 per year.
- Experienced removal operatives earn from £15,000–£18,000.
- Supervisory staff may earn up to £24,000.
- Wages can sometimes be increased by overtime pay or shift allowances.

Further information

Skills for Logistics
14 Warren Yard
Warren Farm Office Village
Milton Keynes
MK12 5NW
01908 313360
www.skillsforlogistics.org

British Association of Removers
Tangent House
62 Exchange Road
Watford
Hertfordshire
WD18 0TG
01923 699480
www.bar.co.uk

IoP: The Packaging Society
c/o Institute of Materials, Minerals and Mining
Springfield House
Springfield Business Park
Grantham
Lincolnshire
NG31 7BG
01476 514590
www.iop.co.uk

www.cityandguilds.com/myperfectjob

Road Crossing Assistant (Schools)

What the work involves

- You will help children to cross the road safely on their way to and from school.
- You will be responsible for schools' road patrol signs, switching them on at the start of your duty, and off at the end of your shift.
- You will stand at a regular place, usually close to a school, until a few children need to cross.
- Once you have decided that it is safe, you will stop the traffic with your sign and hand signals and then guide the children across.
- You will also check that children are behaving safely in the area nearby.
- In some areas you may be involved in working in schools, helping children to learn about road safety.

entry level

To both enter and train while working in this career, you will need qualifications at Level 1. Please refer to explanation on page vii.

The type of person suited to this work

Your safety awareness has to be good to do this job. The roads are getting busier and although when you put out your stop sign motorists should stop and let the children cross, some of them may not. You will need to be alert as you will be watching the traffic to identify hazards in order to prevent accidents.

Getting children safely to school also means that you will need to be good at dealing with children. You should be able to get on with them but also tell them off if they are behaving in an unsafe way. A friendly manner and sociable outlook is essential in a job where you will deal with parents and children every day.

Qualifications and courses

- No specific qualifications are required for this job. Many employers expect you to be at least 18. There are no upper age limits but you would need to pass an annual medical check after the age of 65. You would need to have good eyesight, hearing and general health, and pass a criminal record check to make sure you are suitable for work with children.
- Key Skills in communication and working with others are useful.
- Previous experience of working with children is useful.
- It is useful to have a working knowledge of the Highway Code.
- Training is usually on offer. There is a mixture of safety training off the job, as well as on-the-job training working with an experienced person.

Working conditions

Most of your work will be outside in all weathers which can be pleasant in the sunshine, but harder work in the cold and wet.

A uniform is provided including a waterproof, high visibility coat, hat and gloves.

Average hours are 7.5 per week and are worked term time only. Some assistants only work an hour a day.

There is a risk of traffic accidents and aggression from motorists.

The future outlook

Although crossing assistants work in conjunction with schools, they are employed by the local authority (council). There are about 30,000 school road crossing assistants and there is always a demand for new recruits. Some employers are experiencing a serious shortage of applicants.

Many local authorities employ school crossing patrol coordinators to recruit, train and supervise the crossing assistants. The experience of working with children can lead on to a range of related jobs such as school escort or classroom assistant.

CRCI:WE

CLCI:YAD

Other related opportunities

- Childminder p528
- Parking Attendant / Traffic Warden p504
- School Lunchtime Supervisor p181
- Teaching / Classroom Assistant p187

Advantages/disadvantages

- You will be an important part of the school community.
- The job offers only limited hours, but many crossing assistants combine the job with other school support jobs, such as school meals supervisor.
- There is a risk of aggression from motorists.

Earnings guide

- Pay depends both on the hours you work and the local authority you work for.
- For those working 10–15 hours a week, the salary is around £2,500–£4,000 per year.
- To encourage new entrants, some authorities offer combined employment schemes that offer the chance to work additional hours in other school roles, such as catering.

Further information

www.cityandguilds.com/myperfectjob

Employers' Organisation for Local Government
Layden House
76–86 Turnmill Street
London
EC1M 5LG
020 7296 6600
www.lgcareers.com

Local Government Careers
www.lgcareers.com

Local Government Jobs
www.lgjobs.com

Road Safety Officer

What the work involves

- You will be working to reduce the number of motorists, cyclists and pedestrians injured or killed on the roads in your area.
- You will educate the public by giving presentations to groups such as children.
- Your role may involve organising training schemes for cyclists or drivers.
- Promoting national road safety campaigns by distributing leaflets and running exhibitions may also be part of your job.
- You will collect information about traffic accidents and make recommendations about how to prevent them.

entry level

To both enter and train while working in this career, you will need qualifications at Level 3–8. Please refer to explanation on page vii.

The type of person suited to this work

As this job is all to do with marketing and persuading, you will need to be an excellent communicator. You will use these skills to develop publicity materials and encourage people to behave more responsibly on the roads.

Self-confidence is vital to build good working relationships with lots of other professionals, such as safety engineers, police officers and local councillors.

To persuade others, you will need teaching or training skills and to be able to work with all age groups. You could give advice on fitting child car seats outside supermarkets, or teach small groups of young children how to cross the road safely.

Qualifications and courses

- Entrants to this job may have a degree or relevant experience. Experience and personal qualities are as important as academic qualifications. A driving licence is essential.
- Key Skills in communication, working with others and ICT would be useful.
- It is possible to work towards an NVQ/SVQ in Transportation at Levels 3–5 or a BTEC Professional Diploma in Accident and Safety Management.
- The National Staff Training Group offers a training programme for road safety officers. Phase 1 of the programme provides training for newly appointed officers. Phase 2 consists of a residential short course, and Phase 3 involves a series of seminars. Completion of Phase 2 training can lead to Associate Membership of the Institute of Road Safety Officers (IRSO).
- Requirements for becoming a member of IRSO are a relevant degree, a BTEC Professional Development Diploma in Accident and Safety Management, or NVQ/SVQ Levels 3/4 in Transportation.

Working conditions

Most of your work will be office-based, but you will make visits to schools and other locations.

You will usually work 37 hours a week, Monday to Friday. Some evening work is required.

When working on-site with engineers, or investigating accidents, you will wear high visibility clothing.

Your office work will involve using a computer to collect and analyse information.

The future outlook

Road safety officers usually work for local authorities and work towards targets to lower the number of people killed and injured on the roads. Some jobs are temporary as they are paid for by short-term government funding.

Promotion can be to a specialist post, for example publicity, or working with schools, or into management. There are also some jobs coordinating national safety and environmental initiatives, for example the National Walk to School Campaign.

Other related opportunities

- Health and Safety Adviser p19
- Police: Community Support Officer p508
- Police p506
- Public Relations Officer p161
- Teacher p184

Advantages/disadvantages

- You will have the satisfaction of seeing the results of your work in reduced death and injury figures in your area.
- There may be delays or obstacles to putting in place the safety improvement work you have recommended, which can be frustrating.

Earnings guide

- Newly qualified officers earn £18,000–£22,000 per year.
- Experienced officers earn up to £32,000.
- Officers with management responsibility can earn £35,000+.
- Local authorities may offer essential car user allowances.
- Some employers also offer performance related bonus schemes.

Further information

Local Authority Road Safety Officers' Association
www.larsoa.org.uk

Employers' Organisation for Local Government
Layden House
76–86 Turnmill Street
London
EC1M 5LG
020 7296 6600
www.lgcareers.com

Institute of Road Safety Officers
www.irso.org.uk

MOL Enquiry Team D9
Moston Centre
Ashley Lane
Moston
Manchester
M9 4WU
0161 203 2103
www.mol-openlearning.co.uk
For info about Diploma in Accident and Safety Management

Stores Assistant

What the work involves

- You will store machinery components and supply them when needed.
- As new parts arrive or go out to customers or staff, you will check they are the right ones, and then input the details onto your computer.
- You will unpack deliveries and store them in the right location.
- You may deal with customers directly, locating parts they ask for, taking payment and packing their purchases.
- You may assemble orders for dispatch to customers, printing off a dispatch note and packing the order.

entry level

To both enter and train while working in this career, you will need qualifications at Level 1–2. Please refer to explanation on page vii.

The type of person suited to this work

If you are technical but also enjoy contact with people, this job will offer the right mix for you.

All machinery is made up of different components and new models are being introduced all the time, so it is likely that you will have hundreds of different parts to keep up to date with and store and supply. The only way to keep track is to keep records on a computer, so your computer skills need to be excellent.

Your communication skills also need to be good. You will be dealing with either customers, for example if you are selling car parts, or with other workers if you are working in a factory stores.

Working conditions

You will work a 37–40-hour week; this could include shift work or overtime at busy periods. In retail outlets you may work at weekends with time off in the week.

You will work in a store room, sometimes seated at a computer, but also walking around to collect, pack, unpack and store parts. You may work behind a counter.

This is an active job that requires physical fitness.

The future outlook

Stores assistants work for companies who store products, tools or parts. You could work, for example, for a factory that needs parts for maintenance, or for a specialist repair company supplying parts to their service engineers. There are a steady number of vacancies.

Some stores are small and may only employ one assistant. Your prospects of promotion are higher in larger stores, or ones which are part of a larger organisation. With experience, you could manage a stores centre or office.

Qualifications and courses

- There are no minimum entry requirements for this job although GCSEs/S grades (A–C/1–3), including English and maths, and evidence of good computer skills are useful. You need to be physically fit, and if a colour storage system is used you need normal colour vision. Some employers require applicants to have a driving licence and be qualified to drive a fork-lift truck.
- Apprenticeships/Skillseekers may be available for those aged 16–24. A Foundation Apprenticeship has no formal entry requirements, and leads to NVQ/SVQ Level 2 in Distribution, Warehousing and Storage Operations or an NVQ/SVQ Level 2 in Vehicle Parts Distribution and Supply. An Advanced Apprenticeship leads to NVQ/SVQ Level 3 in Distribution, Warehousing and Storage Operations, or an NVQ/SVQ Level 3 in Vehicle Parts Distribution and Supply. Three to four GCSEs/S grades may be required.
- Training is normally in the workplace and there may be opportunities to do block- or day-release and work towards NVQ/SVQs.

CRCI:WG

CLCI:YAT

Other related opportunities

- Airport Baggage Handler p558
- Vehicle Parts Operative p461
- Warehouse p586

Advantages/disadvantages

- This job can be rewarding but stressful, for example when the computer tells you a part is in stock but you cannot find it.
- If you qualify, there are opportunities to progress, especially in stores that are part of a larger company.

Earnings guide

- Trainee stores assistants can earn £11,500–£14,000 per year.
- Experienced assistants can earn up to £17,000+.
- Supervisory stores workers can earn up to £25,000.

Further information

Skills for Logistics
14 Warren Yard
Warren Farm Office Village
Milton Keynes
MK12 5NW
01908 313360
www.skillsforlogistics.org

United Kingdom Warehousing Association
Walter House
418–422 Strand
London
WC2R 0PT
020 7836 5522
www.ukwa.org.uk

Retail Motor Industry Federation
201 Great Portland Street
London
W1W 5AB
020 7580 9122
www.rmif.co.uk

Chartered Institute of Logistics and Transport
Logistics and Transport Centre
Earlstree Court
Earlstree Road
Corby
NN17 4XQ
01536 740104
www.ciltuk.org.uk

Transport Manager (Road)

What the work involves

- You will work for a business that moves goods or passengers, planning the routes and work timetables of your drivers.
- You will oversee the day-to-day movement of your vehicles, checking that they are in the right places at the right times.
- Putting health and safety regulations into place, and monitoring compliance, will be part of your role.
- Your job will include checking costs to make sure that your company makes a profit.
- You may also recruit and train drivers, and deal with customer complaints.

The type of person suited to this work

Planning timetables, journeys and loads means that you will need to be the organised type. You should also be logical and enjoy using computers to manage and develop information.

You will cost up journeys, work out timetables and stick to a strict budget, so you must enjoy working with figures.

Your communication skills will need to be top notch, because you will spend a lot of time talking to drivers, suppliers, general managers and customers.

When you are out there in the depot, the job will be hands on. For example, you may be quality checking a vehicle repair, or chasing up drivers to get your vehicles out on time.

Working conditions

Most of your work will be based in an office. You will also spend time at vehicle depots, and may need to travel to carry out spot checks on your drivers.

Transport is a 24/7 business, so you may need to work shifts and weekends.

Out in the depot, you may have to work in a noisy environment that can be affected by exhaust and fuel spillage fumes.

The future outlook

Transport is on the move and it is a growing industry. You could work for a range of employers such as logistics and distribution companies, road haulage firms, manufacturers, retail chains or coach and bus operators.

It is possible to be promoted to area or general manager. Prospects are better if you are flexible about moving to a larger company or into other modes of transport, for example rail, sea or air.

Transport planning is currently a severe skill shortage area, and it is possible to move into it with management experience in the transport sector.

entry level

3–8

To both enter and train while working in this career, you will need qualifications at Level 3–8. Please refer to explanation on page vii.

Qualifications and courses

- It is possible to enter the transport industry with qualifications ranging from a few GCSEs/S grades (including English and maths) to a degree. Many people start in a lower level job and work their way up to management.
- Apprenticeships/Skillseekers are available. There are also NVQ/SVQ Levels 2 and 3 in Road Passenger Transport (passenger work) and Traffic Office (freight work).
- Some companies recruit graduates to management positions. It is possible to enter with a degree in any subject. There are specialist degrees and postgraduate courses in transport management, transport planning and logistics.
- Once working you can study for the Chartered Institute of Logistics and Transport's professional qualifications part time at college or by distance learning. The Certificate is aimed at supervisors and first line managers. The Professional Diploma is intended for middle managers, including recent graduates, and fulfils the requirements for membership of the Institute. New or aspiring senior transport managers can take the CILT Advanced Diploma or study for an MSc in Logistics or Passenger Transport Management. Master's courses are offered by Aston University in partnership with CILT, and take 3 years by distance learning.
- The essential qualification to become a road transport senior manager is the Certificate of Professional Competence of the Department of Transport (Department of the Environment in Northern Ireland). This course is roughly equivalent to NVQ Level 3.

Other related opportunities

- Air / Ship Broker p554
- Distribution Manager p562
- Freight Forwarder p566
- Warehouse p586

Advantages/disadvantages

- No two days are the same – traffic levels, problems and weather conditions vary from day to day.
- You will have the satisfaction of seeing an instant result when you make decisions. The way you manage a problem can mean happier customers.

Earnings guide

- Starting salaries are usually £22,000–£23,000 per year.
- Experienced managers can earn £25,000–£35,000.
- Senior managers earn up to £50,000. A small number employed by major companies can earn up to £80,000.
- Allowances are usually paid for shift work and unsocial hours.

Further information

Skills for Logistics
14 Warren Yard
Warren Farm Office Village
Milton Keynes
MK12 5NW
01908 313360
www.skillsforlogistics.org

GoSkills (Sector Skills Council for passenger transport)
Concorde House
Trinity Park
Solihull
B37 7UQ
0121 635 5520
www.goskills.org

Chartered Institute of Logistics and Transport
Logistics and Transport Centre
Earlstree Court
Earlstree Road
Corby
NN17 4XQ
01536 740104
www.ciltuk.org.uk

Institute of Transport Administration
www.iota.org.uk

Transport jobs
www.transportationopportunities.org.uk

Warehouse

What the work involves

Manager

- You will be in overall charge of the warehouse, responsible for maintaining stock levels, storing the goods safely and in the right condition, and dispatching them onwards when needed.
- Managing a team of staff, and making sure that essential health and safety training is taking place, will be part of your role.
- You will use a computer to monitor stock levels and orders, and to check the times when deliveries are due in and dispatches due out of your warehouse.

Worker

- You will be responsible for checking a delivery or dispatch to make sure that the goods are in the right condition and quantity.
- Once you have approved the delivery or dispatch, you will input details into a hand-held computer terminal.
- If trained you may drive a lift truck, or if not you may help to move or pack the goods (for example, helping to load lorries to make the best use of space).

The type of person suited to this work

Warehouses often store valuable stock – such as medical supplies or audio-visual equipment – so you will need to be honest and security conscious.

You will also need to be a team player because getting the goods in and out of the warehouse quickly but safely is a team task. Warehouses can be dangerous places, because of the use of machinery to move and stack goods at heights, so you should be able to follow or put in place safety regulations.

You should enjoy working with computers. Deliveries and dispatches are recorded and monitored on the warehouse's computer tracking system – so your working day is likely to be planned by a computer.

Working conditions

Protective clothing may be needed when warehousing some goods.

You will work a 37–40-hour week but this could include shift work or overtime at busy periods.

Manager
You will work both at a computer in an office and out in the warehouse.

Worker
You will spend a lot of time on your feet; you may also need to lift heavy items and climb ladders.

The future outlook

Warehouses are owned and managed by companies who either store large quantities of goods for their own businesses, or charge customers to store goods for them. The biggest employers of warehouse staff are retail and manufacturing companies, logistics and distribution service providers and specialist freight and haulage companies. Opportunities are increasing for warehouse management work.

Some warehouses are small, for example the ones at the rear of supermarkets, and only employ a few warehouse workers. Others can be the size of several football pitches and employ both management and workers.

Warehouses are becoming more computerised and some of the heavier work is being automated. This is likely to change the job in the future. Some warehouses will have fewer operatives and some are already 'lights out' warehouses with no human workers at operative level.

Manager
There are good opportunities for promotion either by moving to a larger warehousing operation or into general management.

Worker
With experience you can become a team leader or supervisor, or with additional qualifications move into warehouse management.

CRCI:WG

CLCI:YAT

Qualifications and courses

entry level

To both enter and train while working in this career, you will need qualifications at Level 1–8. Please refer to explanation on page vii.

Manager

- There are no specific entry qualifications for this job. It is possible to work as a warehouse worker, gain NVQ/SVQ qualifications or the professional qualifications of the Chartered Institute of Logistics and Transport (CILT), and progress to supervisory or management roles. Good management, ITC, literacy and numeracy skills can be an advantage.
- Some employers may require qualifications such as A levels/H grades. Increasingly, companies recruit graduates. Degrees are on offer in related subjects such as logistics and supply chain management. The usual minimum entry requirements for a degree course are 2 A levels/3 H grades or equivalent.
- People working in the industry can study for the CILT's professional qualifications part time at college or by distance learning. The Introductory Certificate in Logistics and Transport is aimed at new entrants and the standard Certificate is aimed at supervisors and first line managers. The Professional Diploma is intended for middle managers, including recent graduates, and fulfils the requirements for membership of the Institute. New or aspiring senior warehouse managers can take the CILT Advanced Diploma or study for an MSc in Logistics. The MSc is offered by Aston University in partnership with CILT, and takes 3 years by distance learning.

Worker

- There are no minimum entry requirements for this job. You will need to be physically fit, and a medical may be required.
- Apprenticeships/Skillseekers may be available for those aged 16–24. This leads to NVQ/SVQ Levels 2 and 3 in Distribution, Storage and Warehousing Operations. Three GCSEs/S grades may be required.
- Most training takes place on the job. The National Proficiency Tests Council's Level 2 Certificate of Competence in Fork Lift Truck Operations may be offered by employers.

Other related opportunities

- Airport Baggage Handler p558
- Distribution Manager p562
- Driver p563
- Freight Forwarder p566
- Lift Truck Operator p568
- Loader p569
- Postal Delivery Person p576
- Removals Operative p581
- Stores Assistant p584
- Transport Manager (Road) p585

Advantages/disadvantages

- Warehouse work can be stressful as goods often need to be shipped out quickly – they may only be stored for a few hours!
- You can get a brilliant feeling of team spirit from working together to get a job done on time.
- The work can peak at certain times of the year such as Christmas, but many workers appreciate overtime pay, especially at that time of year.

Earnings guide

Manager

- Starting pay is £14,500–£17,000 per year. Experienced managers can earn up to £28,000 with experience, and up to £40,000+ with large companies.

Worker

- Starting pay is about £12,000, rising with experience to £17,500.
- Team leaders can earn up to £23,000.
- Some employers offer performance bonus schemes in addition to salaries.

Further information

Skills for Logistics
14 Warren Yard
Warren Farm Office Village
Milton Keynes
MK12 5NW
01908 313360
www.skillsforlogistics.org

Chartered Institute of Logistics and Transport
Logistics and Transport Centre
Earlstree Court
Earlstree Road
Corby
NN17 4XQ
01536 740104
www.ciltuk.org.uk

United Kingdom Warehousing Association
Walter House
418–422 Strand
London
WC2R 0PT
020 7836 5522
www.ukwa.org.uk

Careers in Logistics
www.careersinlogistics.co.uk

Chartered Institute of Purchasing & Supply
Easton House
Easton on the Hill
Stamford
Lincolnshire
PE9 3NZ
01780 756777
www.cips.org

Transport jobs
www.transportationopportunities.org.uk

www.cityandguilds.com/myperfectjob

CRCI:WG

CLCI:YAT

Index of Levels

Level 1

Level 2

Level 3

Level 4–8

Index